MEDICAL PSYCHOLOGY

Contributions to Behavioral Medicine

MEDICAL PSYCHOLOGY
Contributions to Behavioral Medicine

Edited by

CHARLES K. PROKOP

Department of Psychiatry
Texas Tech University Health Sciences Center
School of Medicine
Lubbock, Texas

LAURENCE A. BRADLEY

Department of Psychiatry and Behavioral Medicine
Section on Medical Psychology
Bowman Gray School of Medicine
Winston-Salem, North Carolina

ACADEMIC PRESS 1981
A Subsidiary of Harcourt Brace Jovanovich, Publishers
New York London Toronto Sydney San Francisco

ACADEMIC PRESS, INC.
111 Fifth Avenue, New York, New York 10003

United Kingdom Edition published by
ACADEMIC PRESS, INC. (LONDON) LTD.
24/28 Oval Road, London NW1 7DX

Library of Congress Cataloging in Publication Data
Main entry under title:

Medical psychology.

Includes bibliographies and index.
1. Medicine and psychology. I. Prokop, Charles K.
II. Bradley, Laurence A. [DNLM: 1. Psychology, Clinical.
2. Behavior. WM 105 M486]
R726.5.M43 616'.001'9 80-1676
ISBN 0-12-565960-1

PRINTED IN THE UNITED STATES OF AMERICA

81 82 83 84 9 8 7 6 5 4 3 2 1

Contents

4

Assessment of Hypertension

Iris B. Goldstein

5

Issues and Approaches to the Psychosocial Assessment of the Cancer Patient

Ivan Barofsky

6

A Quantitative and Qualitative Approach to Neuropsychological Evaluation

Thomas J. Boll, Daniel S. O'Leary, and Jeffrey T. Barth

7

Functional Analysis of Alcohol Problems

Mark B. Sobell and Linda C. Sobell

8

Assessment of Chronic Pain

Laurence A. Bradley, Charles K. Prokop, W. Doyle Gentry, Laurie H. Van der Heide, and Edward J. Prieto

9

The Psychosocial Assessment of the Chronically Ill Geriatric Patient

Sandra M. Levy

TREATMENT AND PREVENTION OF MEDICAL DISORDERS

10

Treatment of Cardiovascular Disorders

J. Alan Herd

11

Primary Prevention of Cardiovascular Disease in Children and Adolescents

Thomas J. Coates, Cheryl Perry, Joel Killen, and Lee Ann Slinkard

12

Psychological Preparation for Stressful Medical Procedures

Philip C. Kendall and David Watson

13

Intervention with the Cancer Patient

David K. Wellisch

14

Rehabilitation and Treatment of Central Nervous System Dysfunction: A Behavioral Medicine Perspective

Jeffrey T. Barth and Thomas J. Boll

15

Behavioral Treatment of Alcohol Problems

Ted D. Nirenberg, Seth Ersner-Hershfield, Linda C. Sobell, and Mark B. Sobell

16

Behavioral Approaches to the Treatment of Chronic Pain

Harold A. Ziesat, Jr.

17

Treatment of the Chronically Ill Geriatric Patient

Sandra M. Levy

18

Therapeutic Options in the Management of Obesity

Richard B. Stuart, Christine Mitchell, and Judith A. Jensen

19

Behavioral Treatment of Smoking Behavior

Russell E. Glasgow and Douglas A. Bernstein

20

Behavioral Approaches in the Treatment of Bronchial Asthma

A. Barney Alexander

21

EMG Biofeedback in the Treatment of Stress-Related Disorders

Thomas G. Burish

22

The Use of Biofeedback for Treating Patients with Migraine Headaches, Raynaud's Disease, and Hypertension: A Critical Evaluation

David S. Holmes

SPECIAL TOPICS IN MEDICAL PSYCHOLOGY AND BEHAVIORAL MEDICINE

23

Adherence to Health Care Regimens

Frank T. Masur III

24

Professional Services Evaluation in a Medical Setting

Thomas W. Miller

25

Methodological Issues in Medical Psychology and Behavioral Medicine Research

Charles K. Prokop and Laurence A. Bradley

26

Medical Psychology and Behavioral Medicine: Summary and Future Concerns

Laurence A. Bradley, Charles K. Prokop, and David A. Clayman

List of Contributors

Numbers in parentheses indicate the pages on which the authors' contributions begin.

A. Barney Alexander (373) Psychophysiology Department, National Asthma Center, Denver, Colorado 80204

Ivan Barofsky (55) Health Services Research and Development Center, Johns Hopkins Medical Institutions, Baltimore, Maryland 21205

Jeffrey T. Barth (67, 241) Department of Behavioral Medicine and Psychiatry, University of Virginia Medical School, Charlottesville, Virginia 22908

Douglas A. Bernstein (355) Department of Psychology, University of Illinois, Urbana–Champaign, Champaign, Illinois 61820

Thomas J. Boll (67, 241) Department of Psychology, University of Health Sciences, The Chicago Medical School, North Chicago, Illinois 60064

Laurence A. Bradley (1, 91, 485, 497) Department of Psychiatry and Behavioral Medicine, Section on Medical Psychology, Bowman Gray School of Medicine, Winston-Salem, North Carolina 27103

Thomas G. Burish (395) Department of Psychology, Vanderbilt University, Nashville, Tennessee 37240

Margaret A. Chesney (19) Behavioral Medicine Program, Stanford Research Institute, Menlo Park, California 94025

David A. Clayman (497) Department of Behavioral Medicine and Psychiatry, West Virginia University Medical Center, Charleston, West Virginia 25330

Thomas J. Coates (157) Department of Psychiatry, Division of Pediatric Cardiology and Division of Heart Education, Johns Hopkins Hospital, Baltimore, Maryland 21205

Jean R. Eagleston (19)[1] Center for Research on Stress and Health, Stanford Research Institute, Menlo Park, California 94025

Seth Ersner-Hershfield (267) Center for Mental Health, Newton Memorial Hospital, Newton, New Jersey 07860

W. Doyle Gentry (5, 91) Department of Psychiatry and Behavioral Sciences, University of Texas Medical Branch, Galveston, Texas 77550

[1]Present address: Counseling Psychology Program, Stanford University, Stanford, California 94305.

Russell E. Glasgow (355) Psychology Department, North Dakota State University, Fargo, North Dakota 58105

Iris B. Goldstein (37) Department of Psychiatry, University of California, Los Angeles, Los Angeles, California 90024

J. Alan Herd (141) The Sid W. Richardson Institute for Preventive Medicine, The Methodist Hospital, Houston, Texas 77030

David S. Holmes (423) Psychology Department, University of Kansas, Lawrence, Kansas 66045

Judith A. Jensen (321) Department of Psychology, University of Utah, Salt Lake City, Utah 84132

Philip C. Kendall (197) Department of Psychology, University of Minnesota, Minneapolis, Minnesota, 55455

Joel Killen (157) Department of Counseling Psychology, Stanford University, Stanford, California 94305

Sandra M. Levy (119, 307) National Cancer Institute, Department of Health and Human Services, National Institutes of Health, Bethesda, Maryland 20014

Frank T. Masur III (441) University of Tennessee, Center for the Health Sciences, Department of Family Medicine, Memphis, Tennessee 38105

Joseph D. Matarazzo (5) Department of Medical Psychology, University of Oregon School of Medicine, Portland, Oregon 97201

Thomas W. Miller (471) Department of Psychology, Veterans Administration Medical Center, Buffalo, New York 14215

Christine Mitchell (321) Weight Watchers International, Salt Lake City, Utah 84132

Ted D. Nirenberg (267)[2] Vanderbilt University, Nashville, Tennessee 37240; and Alcohol Programs, Dede Wallace Center, Nashville, Tennessee 37204

Daniel S. O'Leary (67)[3] Department of Neurology, University of Virginia School of Medicine, Charlottesville, Virginia 22901

Cheryl Perry (157) Stanford Heart Disease Prevention Program, Institute for Communications Research, Stanford University School of Medicine, Stanford, California 94305

Edward J. Prieto (91) Department of Psychology, Fordham University, Bronx, New York 10458

Charles K. Prokop (1, 91, 485, 497) Department of Psychiatry, Texas Tech University Health Sciences Center, School of Medicine, Lubbock, Texas 79430

Lee Ann Slinkard (157) Department of Health Psychology, University of California, San Francisco, San Francisco, California 94143

Linda C. Sobell (81, 267) Clinical Institute, Addiction Research Foundation, Toronto, Canada

Mark B. Sobell (81, 267) Clinical Institute, Addiction Research Foundation, Toronto, Canada

Richard B. Stuart (321) Family and Community Medicine, University of Utah, Salt Lake City, Utah 84132

Laurie H. Van der Heide (91) Department of Psychology, Fordham University, Bronx, New York 10458

David Watson (197) Department of Psychology, University of Minnesota, Minneapolis, Minnesota 55455

David K. Wellisch (223) Department of Psychiatry and Behavioral Sciences, UCLA Neuropsychiatric Institute, University of California, Los Angeles, Los Angeles, California 90024

Harold A. Ziesat, Jr. (291) Department of Psychiatry, University of Rochester Medical Center, Rochester, New York 14642

[2]Present address: Sea Pines Behavioral Institute, Hilton Head Island, South Carolina 29928, and Georgia Southern College, Statesboro, Georgia 30458.

[3]Present address: Department of Psychology, University of Health Science, The Chicago Medical School, North Chicago, Illinois 60064.

Preface

The relationship between the medical professions and psychology has undergone a dramatic change within the past 10 years. Many psychologists working in medical settings have expanded their areas of expertise and have begun to participate directly in the assessment, treatment, and prevention of medical problems. Medical professionals, in turn, have come to value many of the applied and research skills displayed by psychologists in medical settings. This new relationship between psychology and medicine is reflected in the establishment of several interdisciplinary training programs in behavioral medicine, the formation of professional associations that emphasize interdisciplinary efforts and behavioral–medical practice and research, and the recent publication of numerous books concerning behavioral medicine and related topics.

One effect of these events has been a proliferation of definitions of the roles of both behavioral medicine and psychology within the medical field. In addition, several of the books concerning behavioral medicine have been limited in focus either because of overly restrictive definitions of behavioral medicine and medical psychology, or because of narrow content areas. This volume offers definitions of medical psychology and behavioral medicine, and discusses the relationship between these complementary disciplines. In addition, the volume presents critical reviews by outstanding clinical investigators regarding the status of diagnostic, treatment, and preventive approaches to a wide variety of medical disorders.

The volume is composed of four major sections. W. Doyle Gentry and Joseph D. Matarazzo first trace the history of the relationship between psychology and medicine and assess the current status of psychology's role within the medical center. The second and third sections deal with approaches to the assessment and treatment–prevention, respectively, of various medical disorders. The third section also examines several special problems within the provinces of medical psychology and behavioral medicine. The fourth section presents reviews of clinical and research topics of particular interest to all medical psychologists and behavioral medicine specialists.

This volume will be of value to research investigators and practitioners within the behavioral sciences and medicine. Critical and comprehensive reviews of the assessment, treatment, and prevention of medical disorders are provided. Thus, the volume will be especially useful for teaching purposes both within medical and university settings and will serve as a source book for scholars and practitioners.

We acknowledge the cooperation and support of Highland Hospital Division of Duke University Medical Center; the Department of Psychiatry, Texas Tech University Health Sciences Center, School of Medicine; the Department of Psychology, Fordham University; the Fordham University Research Council; and the Department of Psychiatry and Behavioral Medicine, Bowman Gray School of Medicine. Invaluable secretarial assistance was provided by Anne Dick, Joyce Davis, Peggy Mackiewicz, Shirley Feldman, and Mary N. White. Special thanks are due to W. Doyle Gentry who introduced us to the fields of medical psychology and behavioral medicine and who supported our efforts throughout the production of this book. Finally, we would like to thank Academic Press and all of our contributors for their expertise and effort.

1

The Relationship between Medical Psychology and Behavioral Medicine

LAURENCE A. BRADLEY
CHARLES K. PROKOP

Definition of Behavioral Medicine

The term "behavioral medicine" was first used by Birk (1973) in the context of defining biofeedback as a learning theory based approach to the treatment of medical disorders. Pomerleau and Brady (1979) have retained and expanded upon Birk's use of the term, and have defined behavioral medicine as

> (*a*) the clinical use of techniques derived from the experimental analysis of behavior—behavior therapy and behavior modification—for the evaluation, prevention, management, or treatment of physical disease or physiological dysfunction; and (*b*) the conduct of research contributing to the functional analysis and understanding of behavior associated with medical disorders and problems in health care [p. xii].

A quite different definition of behavioral medicine has been offered by Asken (1979). He has defined behavioral medicine as "the study of psychological reactions that occur secondarily or as a result of physical illness and its treatment [p. 70]." This definition differs in two important ways from that offered by Pomerleau and Brady. First, the definition implies that the only proper focus of behavioral medicine is the study of the psychological sequelae of physical illness. Thus, prevention of physical illness is ruled out, and treatment is limited to attempts to indirectly influence the course of physical disorders through the modification of psychological factors. Following this definition, the role of practitioners of behavioral medicine is very similar to that of liaison psychiatrists in a medical setting. The second difference between the definition offered by Asken and that offered by Pomerleau and Brady is that Asken's definition does not limit the treatment interventions associated with behavioral medicine to those derived from the experimental analysis of behavior.

A third, and more widely accepted, definition of behavioral medicine is that originally developed at the Yale Conference on Behavioral Medicine and later articulated and amended by Schwartz and Weiss (1977, 1978). This amended definition of behavioral medicine is

> The interdisciplinary field concerned with the development and integration of behavioral and biomed-

Medical Psychology
Contributions to Behavioral Medicine

ISBN 0-12-565960-1

ical science knowledge and techniques relevant to health and illness and the application of this knowledge and these techniques to prevention, diagnosis, treatment, and rehabilitation [1978, p. 250].

A major difference between the Schwartz and Weiss definition and those offered by the others is that Schwartz and Weiss emphasize the interdisciplinary nature of behavioral medicine. Thus, equal emphasis is given to the contributions of the behavioral and biomedical sciences. An example of this emphasis upon interdisciplinary efforts is provided by an examination of the masthead of the *Journal of Behavioral Medicine,* the official journal of the Academy of Behavioral Medicine Research. The editorial board of the journal consists of 37 persons with Ph.D degrees, 17 persons with M.D. degrees, and 5 persons with Ph.D. and M.D. degrees.

The definition of behavioral medicine provided by Schwartz and Weiss also differs from that of Pomerleau and Brady in that treatment interventions are not limited to those derived from learning theory. The Schwartz and Weiss definition, therefore, is consistent with that of Asken on the dimension of the theoretical basis of treatment. Contrary to Asken, however, both Schwartz and Weiss, and Pomerleau and Brady agree that practitioners of behavioral medicine may intervene either at the preventive level or directly upon the disorder itself. The adequacy of the definition of behavioral medicine provided by Schwartz and Weiss will be examined in the section entitled "Medical Psychology's Relationship to Behavioral Medicine."

Definition of Medical Psychology

Current definitions of medical psychology are less precise than those of behavioral medicine. The various definitions differ both in terms of the scope of activities included, and the theoretical orientations of those involved. With regard to the scope of activities within medical psychology, Asken (1979) has provided the broadest definition. He has defined medical psychology as "the study of psychological factors related to any and all aspects of physical health, illness and its treatment at the individual, group, and systems level [p. 67]." Indeed, Asken has noted that medical psychology actually subsumes the area of behavioral medicine. Another broad definition of the scope of activities within medical psychology has been provided by Gentry and Matarazzo in Chapter 2 of this volume. They have defined medical psychology as "the practice of psychology within the medical school establishment. This includes not only clinical services (i.e., practitioner), but also the important role of the medical educator and researcher [p. 12]."

A far more restrictive view has been offered by Pomerleau (1979). Pomerleau's definition limits the activity of the medical psychologist to primarily social and psychological assessment of persons with medical disorders. Pomerleau does note, however, that some medical psychologists do participate in the treatment of medical disorders using behavioral intervention strategies (Pomerleau, 1979).

These definitions also differ from one another with regard to the theoretical orientations attributed to medical psychologists. For example, Asken and Gentry and Matarazzo believe that medical psychologists may adhere to any theoretical orientation. In fact, Gentry and Matarazzo point out that clinical and experimental psychologists of varying schools of thought all may be considered to be medical psychologists as long as they participate in some form of activity in a medical school setting. Pomerleau, however, implies that the assessment activities of medical psychologists may be performed within the context of psychodynamic, trait-oriented, or behavioral paradigms, but he restricts treatment interventions to those derived from learning theory.

Medical Psychology's Relationship to Behavioral Medicine

An examination of these numerous definitions illustrates that there is a lack of consensus regarding the attributes that differentiate behavioral medicine from medical psychology, and those that are shared by the two disciplines. It is essential to clarify the commonalities between behavioral medicine and medical psychology in order to reduce the risk that important contributions from one discipline might be overlooked by the other (cf. Asken, 1979). It is equally important to identify the differences between the disciplines in order to educate (*a*) professionals involved in health care services; (*b*) recipients and evaluators of those services; and (*c*) governmental funding agencies with respect to what particular skills they may expect members of the individual disciplines to possess. In addition, it is important to clarify the differences between medical psychology and behavioral medicine in order to foster the development of distinct theoretical viewpoints and bodies of empirical data that may eventually enrich one another and thereby lead to improved health care.

Stone, Cohen, and Adler (1979) have attempted to explicate the differences and similarities between medical psychology and behavioral medicine. In doing so, they have defined both disciplines as subspecialties of a new area which they have labeled "health psychology." Although their emphasis upon the prevention of disorders and the maintenance of health is desirable, the creation of a new descriptive label may increase the confusion that currently exists among professionals regarding medical psychology and behavioral medicine. Masur (1979) has attempted to clarify the relationship between the two disciplines by conceptualizing medical psychology as the contributions of psychology to behavioral medicine as defined by Schwartz and Weiss (1978). Medical psychology is described as encompassing the development of "intervention strategies and educational systems directed at improving prevention, diagnosis, treatment, management, and rehabilitation of patients with physical diseases [Masur, 1979, p. 259]." Masur has succeeded in adding clarity only to the extent that other professionals accept Schwartz and Weiss' definition of behavioral medicine. It is critical, therefore, to examine the value of the Schwartz and Weiss definition of behavioral medicine before further assessing Masur's position.

The Schwartz and Weiss definition of behavioral medicine possesses a distinct advantage in that it avoids the unduly restrictive quality of the definition offered by Pomerleau and Brady. Limiting behavioral medicine to a single theoretical orientation or professional discipline at this early stage may serve to retard the development of clinical advances. In contrast, the inclusion of a wide variety of professionals and theories within behavioral medicine, as advocated by Schwartz and Weiss, encourages the development of new clinical approaches that may be critically evaluated from a variety of perspectives. In addition, the Schwartz and Weiss definition sufficiently emphasizes the prevention of medical disorders and the maintenance of health as stressed by Stone *et al.* (1979) without additional descriptive terms. Therefore, we accept the current definition of behavioral medicine provided by Schwartz and Weiss and encourage other professionals to concur.

Similar to Schwartz and Weiss' definition of behavioral medicine, Masur's (1979) conception of medical psychology avoids an overly restrictive view of the role of psychology in the medical setting. While Masur has clearly articulated that the problem areas addressed by medical psychology are identical to those addressed by behavioral medicine, he has not specified the unique contributions made by medical psychology to the problems of health maintenance and to prevention, diagnosis, treatment, and rehabilitation of illness. We believe that medical psychology provides three relatively unique contributions to the larger field of behavioral medicine. First, certain approaches to assessment may be best provided by medical psychologists. For example, training in (*a*) the assessment of brain–behavior relationships; (*b*) the construction of psychometric instruments and interpretation of patients' responses to these instruments; and (*c*) the functional analysis of behavior that encompasses measurement of overt and covert controlling stimuli, is rarely provided in settings other than psychology training programs.

Second, there are some approaches to treatment and to rehabilitation that currently are unique to medical psychology. For example, to date, the only published reports of the effectiveness of stress inoculation training for various disorders have been produced by psychologists. In addition, cognitive retraining approaches to the rehabilitation of central nervous system dysfunction are currently being investigated primarily by psychologists. It should be noted that psychologists are frequently involved in the training of other professionals in prevention, treatment, and rehabilitation approaches. Therefore, several disciplines that contribute to behavioral medicine may be expected to adopt these treatment approaches as they have adopted other approaches (e.g., operant conditioning, self-management) developed by psychologists.

Although several psychological treatment approaches may become less identified with medical psychology alone, psychology may be expected to enjoy a third unique role in prevention and treatment activities in the sense that psychologists receive specialized, intensive training in experimental design and statistics. Psychologists, therefore, are particularly well-suited to evaluate a wide variety of diagnostic techniques as well as preventive and treatment interventions.

In summary, medical psychology focuses upon the same problem areas as do other behavioral medicine specialties. The contributions of medical psychology that differentiate it from the larger field of behavioral medicine are its unique assessment approaches and its capability to provide empirical evaluations of diagnostic, preventive, and treatment methods. The results of these evaluations may provide for major advances and improvements in the quality of medical care and health maintenance.

The construction of this volume is consistent with the relationship between medical psychology and behavioral medicine presented in this chapter. Following a discussion of the history and current status of medical psychology, the volume presents comprehensive reviews of the major problem areas of interest to both medical psychologists and behavioral medicine specialists. These include reviews of the assessment and treatment approaches that are relatively unique to medical psychology as well as the preventive and treatment approaches that are shared by those in medical psychology and the other behavioral medicine specialties. The volume concludes with discussions of special topics of relevance to both medical psychology and behavioral medicine. The unique contribution of this volume to behavioral medicine, as in the case of other medical psychology efforts, is its emphasis upon critical evaluations of the current literature. We hope that the calls for methodological refinements expressed in this volume will encourage those involved in medical psychology and behavioral medicine to be cautious in their clinical claims, as well as rigorous and innovative in their research efforts (cf. Miller, 1974).

References

Asken, M. Medical psychology: Toward definition, clarification, and organization. *Professional Psychology,* 1979, *10,* 66–73.

Birk, L. (Ed.). *Biofeedback: Behavioral medicine.* New York: Grune and Stratton, 1973.

Masur, F. T. An update on medical psychology and behavioral medicine. *Professional Psychology,* 1979, *10,* 259–264.

Miller, N. E. Introduction: Current issues and key problems. In N. Miller, T. Barber, L. DiCara, J. Kamiya, D. Shapiro, & J. Stoyva (Eds.), *Biofeedback and self-control, 1973.* Chicago: Aldine, 1974.

Pomerleau, O. F. Behavioral medicine: The contribution of the experimental analysis of behavior to medical care. *American Psychologist,* 1979, *34,* 654–663.

Pomerleau, O. F., & Brady, J. P. Introduction: The scope and promise of behavioral medicine. In O. F. Pomerleau & J. P. Brady (Eds.), *Behavioral medicine: Theory and practice.* Baltimore: Williams and Wilkins, 1979.

Schwartz, G. E., & Weiss, S. M. What is behavioral medicine? *Psychosomatic Medicine,* 1977, *39,* 377–381.

Schwartz, G. E., & Weiss, S. M. Behavioral medicine revisited: An amended definition. *Journal of Behavioral Medicine,* 1978, *1,* 249–251.

Stone, G. C., Cohen, F., & Adler, N. E. (Eds.). *Health psychology: A handbook.* San Francisco: Jossey-Bass, 1979.

2

Medical Psychology: Three Decades of Growth and Development

W. DOYLE GENTRY
JOSEPH D. MATARAZZO

The establishment of a Division of Health Psychology within the American Psychological Association (Matarazzo, Note 1), the publication of texts such as *Health Psychology* (Stone, Cohen, & Adler, 1979) and *Contributions to Medical Psychology* (Rachman, 1977), the special issue on "Psychologists in Health Care Settings" which appeared in the APA journal *Professional Psychology* (Budman & Wertlieb, 1979), and the recent survey of psychologists in schools of medicine (Nathan, Lubin, Matarazzo, & Persely, 1979) all serve as tangible evidence of the emergence of professional psychology as a vital force in modern-day medical care, medical research, and medical education. This chapter will attempt to (*a*) highlight some of the more interesting aspects of the growth and development of psychology within the medical school establishment (i.e., medical psychology); (*b*) discuss the crucial issue of whether or not professional training in psychology is adequately preparing psychologists for faculty positions in medical schools; and (*c*) suggest exactly how this subspecialty of medical psychology fits into the new field of "behavioral medicine," the latter being defined in terms of an integrative and multidisciplinary approach to issues of health and illness (Schwartz & Weiss, 1978a, 1978b).

Actually, what we have witnessed in recent years is the *reemergence,* rather than the *emergence,* of the psychological approach to medical diagnosis and treatment. That is, the relationship between the professions of naturopathic medicine and philosophic psychology is as old as written history. The history of medicine records that civilization's first physicians, in fact, were naturopath–philosopher–priests who performed the dual roles of healer and scholar–teacher. The notion that there is an exquisitely delicate interrelationship between mind (psyche) and body (soma) also was recognized in mankind's very first written documents. Writers who have chronicled the history of thinking about the influences of mind on bodily functioning have been able, from antiquity, to provide examples of this interrelationship. Notable among these recurring examples have been the dry mouth and racing heart associated with an anticipated confrontation with one's enemy; the pain of headache or misery of diarrhea associated with

Medical Psychology
Contributions to Behavioral Medicine

ISBN 0-12-565960-1

emotional stress; and the acute heart attack, epileptic convulsion, asthmatic attack, severe anorexia and weight loss, and related life-threatening physical reactions associated with severe stress. References to these and similar mind–body end products are found in the surviving literary documents from Babylonia, the Greek papyrus, the writings of Homer, Plato, and Aristotle, and in the Old and New Testaments, as well as in the writings of ancient and modern physicians and psychologists dating from Hippocrates through writers of today.

It was only during the past several centuries, especially during the last half of the nineteenth century, that physicians and psychologists could be identified as members of distinct professions, separate from the professions of theology and philosophy that had claimed them during the previous 5000 years. The profession of medicine, as we know it today, is no older than the profession of psychology. Nonetheless, the four-year curriculum leading to the doctor of philosophy degree in psychology which was first introduced in the United States by Johns Hopkins University (and served as the model for all subsequent graduate programs in psychology) antedated by 25 years the similarly required four-year program leading to the doctor of medicine degree which was brought about by Abraham Flexner's (1910) survey of the shocking state of medical education in this country.

Even as Flexner was publishing the recommendation that would introduce the four-year curriculum for modern-day medical students (two years of preclinical sciences followed by two years of clinical studies), efforts were being made by professional psychologists to *reintroduce* the psychological approach to health and illness into the field of clinical medicine. The symposium on "The Relations of Psychology and Medical Education," sponsored by the American Psychological Association, at its 1911 annual meeting is a prime example of such an attempt (Franz, 1912, 1913). The psychologists participating in this symposium, Shepard Ivory Franz and John Broadus Watson, and their physician-colleagues, Adolf Meyer, E. E. Southard, and Morton Prince, agreed (*a*) that medical students enter training with too little knowledge of psychology; (*b*) that such knowledge is essential to proper medical training; (*c*) that in fact courses in psychology should precede courses in psychiatry and neurology; and (*d*) that more hours should be devoted to psychology in the medical curriculum.

Interestingly, as the number of medical schools in the United States decreased significantly between 1910 (116 schools) and 1950 (70 schools), the number of professional psychologists employed in such institutions began to increase. It is impossible to document the growth of medical psychology in precise terms during this period; but it is noteworthy that this was the time during which pioneering medical psychologists such as Starke Hathaway at Minnesota, Carney Landis at Columbia University's College of Physicians and Surgeons, George Yacorzynski at Northwestern, Carlyle Jacobsen at Cornell, Ward Halstead at Chicago, Lee Travis at Iowa, and Walter and Catherine Miles at Yale emerged (Jacobsen, 1950).

It was only after 1950, with the first survey of professional psychologists in medical schools (Page & Passey, 1949), and in the three decades since, that we have been able to understand the full nature and extent of psychology's emergence into modern-day medical schools. This, and the ensuing surveys, will be the basis for the remainder of our comments concerning the role of psychology within medicine.

Growth Trends in Medical Psychology

On the basis of numerous national surveys conducted on psychologists employed in medical schools in this country between 1949 and 1979, it is possible to reach a number of both positive and negative conclusions regarding patterns of growth and development in medical psychology.[1]

Positive Trends

It is quite clear that there has been a phenomenal growth in the number of psychologists employed

[1]Readers interested in a detailed account of the growth and development of psychology in a single medical school (University of North Carolina School of Medicine) should read Routh and Clarke (1976).

in medical schools. As can be seen in Figure 2.1, the number of identified medical psychologists has risen from a total of 255 in 1953 (Mensh, 1953) to 2,336 in 1976 (Lubin, Nathan, & Matarazzo, 1978). This represents an increase of 916% over a period of less than 30 years!

Second, there seems to have been a marked increase in the growth rate of medical psychology in recent years, despite earlier statements to the contrary. Witkin, Mensh, and Cates (1972), for example, had noted that the period of very rapid growth had ended, based on their comparison of the 31% increase in medical psychologists between the years 1964–1968 versus the 187% increase observed from 1955 to 1964. Such comparisons are, however, misleading since one must take into consideration the effect of the increasing size of the total number of medical psychologists on percentage increase data. In short, the addition of only 1 new medical psychologist to a group of 10 represents a 10% increase; whereas, the addition of 10 new psychologists to a group of 1000 represents an increase of only 1%. This point is important in that it suggests a positive rather than a negative growth rate continuing today. As Table 2.1 indicates,

Table 2.1 Average Number of New Psychologists Identified in Medical Schools Each Year

Survey years	Average increases per year
1953–1955	46
1955–1959	59
1959–1964	82
1964–1968	77
1968–1976	130

there were about 130 new medical psychologists identified *each year* for the period from 1968 to 1976, as compared to only 77 newly identified persons from 1964 to 1968, and 46 per year for the period from 1953 to 1955. In fact, the annual growth rate in medical psychology has not slowed down at all; rather it is double what it was a decade ago and triple what it was in the early 1950s!

Third, as can be seen in Figure 2.2, there also has been a linear growth in the average size of the medical psychology faculties within the university medical centers in this country (Nathan, Lubin,

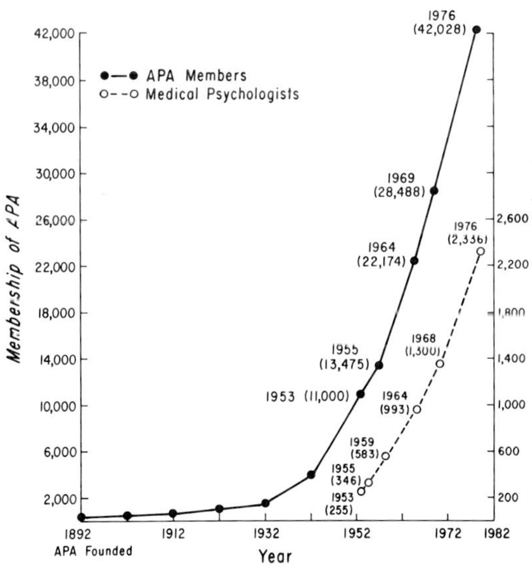

Figure 2.1. Psychologists in APA and on faculties of U.S. medical schools.

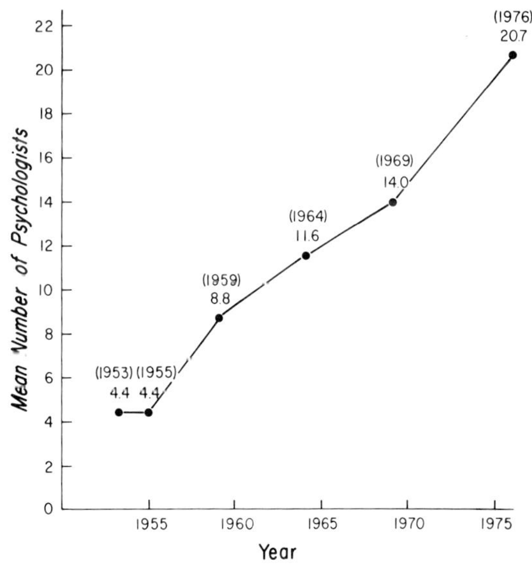

Figure 2.2. Mean number of psychologists in American medical schools from 1953 to 1976. Adapted from Nathan, Lubin, Matarazzo, and Persely, 1979.

Matarazzo, & Persely, 1979). Whereas the number of psychologists employed in a single medical school ranged from 1 to 17 in 1955 and from 1 to 51 in 1964, the most recent survey indicated that the numbers range from 1 to 112 (Lubin *et al.*, 1978). Today, the number of medical psychologists is *small* (1–10 members) in 40% of such medical centers, *moderate* (11–30 members) in another 40%, and *large* (more than 30 members) in the remaining 20%. In at least seven medical schools, there are currently more than 50 psychologists employed on the staff.

Fourth, professional psychologists are employed today in virtually all (98%) medical schools in the United States, as compared to only 73% of such institutions in 1953 (Mensh, 1953). As of the last survey, the only two medical schools not reporting employing at least one psychologist were the University of Massachusetts and the University of South Alabama, the latter being a "provisional" medical school without full accreditation (Lubin *et al.*, 1978).

Fifth, and very important, the ratio of available psychologists in medical schools to the number of medical students has decreased significantly from 1:88 in 1955 to 1:34 in 1964 and, finally, to 1:24 in 1976. In effect, the increase in medical school psychologists in this country has far exceeded the growth of medical students; between 1955 and 1976 there was a 675% increase in the number of medical psychologists as compared to only a 183% rise in the number of medical students. Clearly, medical students should have greater access to professional psychologists than ever before!

Sixth, there seems to be a growing representation by medical school psychologists within the parent professional organization (APA). In 1955 only 2.5% of the APA membership were identified as working in medical schools, as compared to 6.0% in 1976. This represents an increase of 675% in the number of medical psychologists belonging to APA compared to a 292% increase in overall APA membership during those 21 years. This increased number of professional psychologists (both those employed by university medical centers and community hospitals) wanting formal recognition for their activities and interests in the field of medicine is undoubtedly one of the main reasons for the recent establishment of the Division (38) of Health Psychology within APA. Figure 2.1 shows the growth of both APA membership and medical school psychology faculty during the past three decades.

Seventh, there seems to be greater job status and job security among medical psychologists today as compared to earlier times. For example, only 47% of medical psychologists were employed full-time in 1955, whereas 71% were employed full-time in the 1976 survey. Also, the percentage of psychologists employed full-time for 10 or more years has increased from 5% in 1955 to 23% in 1976. This suggests that medical school psychologists have become more *mature* (stayed long enough to develop marketable skills in the medical establishment and gained valuable experience) over the years, and also that they have found stable, permanent employment settings. In effect, turnover rates are very low in medical school settings!

The proportion of medical school psychologists hired at the Ph.D. level also has increased significantly. Whereas 25% of psychologists working in medical schools in 1955 had something less than a doctorate degree, today only 6% have not completed the Ph.D. There has also been a fivefold increase in the percentage of medical psychologists holding the rank of Full Professor, with only 4% at this rank in 1955 and 19% in 1976 (Nathan, Lubin, Matarazzo, & Persely, 1979). Similar increases have been noted for the ranks of Associate and Assistant Professor, reflecting again the tendency of medical psychologists to remain in medical school settings long enough to advance their professional careers.

Eighth, there seems to be much greater balance in recent years regarding the functions of psychologists in medical schools. As Table 2.2 shows, there has been a noticeable shift away from a preeminent research role, which characterized the majority of medical school psychologists in the 1950s and 1960s, to a situation today, where psychologists are involved equally in clinical service, research, teaching, and administrative roles. Interestingly, within the clinical service area, there has been a marked tendency for medical school psychologists to shift their interests from diagnostic pursuits to therapeutic ones, even though the total amount of

Table 2.2 Percentage of Time Spent in Various Activities by Psychologists Employed Full-Time in Medical Schools

	Survey years		
Activities	1955	1964	1977
Clinical service	22	18	19
Diagnostic	17	11	7
Therapy	5	7	12
Teaching	18	24	31
Research	34	45	28
Administrative	11	10	22

Note. Adapted from Nathan, Matarazzo and Persely, 1979. The percentage of time does not total 100% in all cases.

time and energy devoted to clinical pursuits has remained relatively constant over time. Elsewhere it has been pointed out that psychologists have been increasingly utilized in medical center decision-making committees dealing with faculty recruitment, tenure review, promotion considerations, curriculum development (Nathan, Lubin, Matarazzo, & Persely, 1979), research review, and admission policies (Witkin *et al.*, 1972). This diversification of psychologists' activities in university medical centers is extremely important in terms of their ability to survive and prosper in this *new* professional setting, and no doubt accounts for the fact that at least "... 75% think that the current advantages of working in a medical school are accruing faster than the disadvantages ... [Nathan, Millham, & Lubin, 1979, p. 102]."

Negative Trends

Fortunately, the list of negative issues is shorter, albeit extremely crucial to the future development of professional psychology within the medical school establishment. First, and perhaps most important, medical psychology continues to be administered by the profession of psychiatry in all but four of the 115 schools of medicine in the United States. The exceptions known to us are the Departments of Medical Psychology at the University of Oregon Health Sciences Center and at the Uniformed Services University of the Health Sciences in Bethesda, Maryland; the Department of Human Behavior at Hershey, Pennsylvania; and the Department of Psychology and Social Sciences at Rush–Presbyterian–St. Luke's Medical Center in Chicago. In fact, today there are more medical psychologists working within Departments of Psychiatry (79%) in medical schools than was true in 1955 (68%).

Is this bad? From one standpoint it is not. That is, the most recent survey of psychologists working in medical schools showed that there were few if any tangible differences between medical psychologists working within versus those working outside psychiatry in terms of such important issues as the development of training programs, rank, committee appointments, and hospital voting rights (Nathan, Millham, & Lubin, 1979). Similarly, there were no significant differences between these two groups with regard to the types of activities they engaged in (i.e., diagnosis and therapy, research, and teaching–supervision). However, it also has been repeatedly pointed out that medical school psychologists as a group feel that they lack adequate independent recognition as professionals within the medical school establishment, that to some extent they are not fully able to utilize their skills as psychologists, and that they feel like "second-class citizens" as long as they reside administratively under the umbrella of psychiatry (Witkin *et al.*, 1972). The latter feeling is in part the result of obvious inequities in salaries and policies regarding academic promotion (rank) that continue to exist for psychologists and psychiatrists working within the same department (Johnson & Williams, 1979). In effect, psychologists working within a Department of Psychiatry earn 75% as much as psychiatrists of equivalent rank. Table 2.3 illustrates this problem by showing the distribution of psychiatry faculty by discipline and rank.

Finally, it has been suggested that the contribution of psychologists to the medical school curriculum can be seriously affected by their administrative ties with psychiatry (Stone, Gentry, Matarazzo, Carlton, Pattishall, & Wakeley, 1977). That is, some psychologists are uncomfortable with their "forced identification" with *psychiatric* teaching programs and thus may be reluctant to volunteer for medical student teaching, may only

Table 2.3 Distribution of Psychiatry Faculty by Discipline and Rank

	Psychiatrists		Psychologists	
Rank	Number[a]	Percentage	Number[a]	Percentage
Professor	303	22.47	108.5	12.90
Associate Professor	299	21.88	156.5	18.61
Assistant Professor	506.5	37.07	326	38.79
Instructor	242	17.71	185.5	22.07
Other	16	1.17	64	7.61
Total	1366.5	100.3	840.5	99.98

Source. From Johnson and Williams, 1979.
Note. Distribution is based on 42 respondents; χ^2 (4) = 13.62, p less than .01.
[a] Includes part-time faculty members.

do the minimum required in such courses, and/or may engage in poor and ineffective teaching behavior. Similarly, where medical psychologists are confronted by policies that prohibit (or do not actively encourage) them from having knowledge about or influence over matters such as the distribution of funds budgeted for medical education, decisions about the format of teaching and when or where courses will be taught, which textbooks will be used, and so forth, it is unlikely that they will give education a high priority in their hierarchy of professional activities.

A second major problem facing medical psychologists seems to be their reluctance to venture outside the traditional realm of psychiatry with respect to research and clinical service programs. Published articles and books dealing with the actual or potential applications of psychological skills to a wide range of medical disorders (Dembroski, Weiss, Shields, Haynes, & Feinleib, 1978; Fordyce, 1976; Foreyt & Rathjen, 1978; Gentry, 1975; Gentry & Cameron, 1975; Gentry & Williams, 1979; Katz & Zlutnick, 1975; Pomerleau & Brady, 1979, Sternbach, 1974; Stone *et al.*, 1979; Williams & Gentry, 1977), as well as this volume illustrate the *recent* change in direction that medical psychologists in and outside of medical school settings have taken in terms of clinical pursuits. However, it is safe to say that such activities are still the *exception rather than the rule* in most universities and community medical centers in this country. In short, medical psychology continues to be defined more in terms of where the psychologists are working (i.e., in medical schools) rather than by the nature of their interests and activities (e.g., with coronary, cancer, dialysis, or asthmatic patients).

When one examines research done by medical psychologists, the situation looks even less encouraging. By far the majority (80%) of medical school psychologists carry out their research either alone or with another psychologist or psychiatrist, rather than in collaboration with medical specialists operating outside of psychiatry (Nathan, Lubin, Matarazzo, & Persely, 1979). Clearly, while we are seeing an increasing volume of research published by psychologists that deals with some aspect of physical illness or physiological dysfunction, the quality of the research leaves much to be desired. For example, many medical psychologists focus more on issues of statistical significance in proving their case than they do (if at all) on issues of *clinical* significance. They are often insensitive to other (medical) variables that can produce the observed outcome in illness behavior treatment. These variables usually are mistakenly attributed to psychological influences, for example, failing to take into account medication usage or medication change when assessing the therapeutic effectiveness of biofeedback or other behavior therapy techniques on elevated blood pressure in patients with essential hypertension. Also, they may fail to understand simple medical distinctions between issues of *disease* versus *disorder*, for example, making the statement that behavior modification strategies (systematic desensitization or biofeedback) are effective in reducing asthma or coronary heart disease, when in fact they mean that such techniques are to some extent helpful in reducing coughing behavior (disorder) or reducing the patient's chances of experiencing a heart attack (an episodic disorder) over some period of time.

Until medical psychologists become more closely affiliated with their medical colleagues (e.g., in cardiology, internal medicine, orthopedic surgery), it is unlikely that their research findings will impact greatly on the biomedical community. As will be pointed out later, the latter tendency of medical school psychologists to engage in solitary or single-discipline research will no doubt have serious implications for their ultimate role in what is now being called "behavioral medicine."

Training in Medical Psychology

Given the vital role that psychology in medical schools is playing in medical care, medical education, and medical research and the apparent continuing increase in the number of new medical psychology faculty hired each year, a crucial question becomes: To what extent are we preparing and training psychologists for positions in the medical school, or at least exposing them to relevant experiences?

A survey by Cohen, Lubin, and Nathan (1979) provides a partial answer. They sent a questionnaire to the 115 medical schools operating in the United States in 1976, asking about training of psychologists in medical schools. They were particularly interested in programs that offered a doctorate or Master's degree in psychology, but which had their home bases in medical schools as opposed to universities. They found that only nine of the responding 105 medical schools (9%) had an ongoing degree-granting program in psychology (e.g., programs in clinical psychology, biopsychology or neuropsychology, and experimental physiological psychology) and another 13 (12%) were planning such a program (e.g., programs in medical psychology, health care psychology, and psychosocial medicine). This, the investigators suggested, was a *beginning* in the attempt to solve the training needs for psychologists to work in medical settings.

Similarly, Gentry, Street, Masur, and Asken[2] recently have surveyed all APA-approved graduate and internship training programs in clinical psychology to determine the nature and the extent of training in medical psychology. They found that 52% of the responding graduate programs offered specific courses dealing with medical psychology topics, such as biofeedback, psychosomatic medicine, neuropsychology, health psychology, and psychopharmacology. A total of 73% of the programs offered courses that at least dealt partially with relevant subject matter (e.g., biological approaches to clinical psychology, behavior therapy, alcoholism). Most of the programs utilized practicum facilities in which students were exposed to medical patients or psychiatric patients with medical problems (89%); these included veterans administration hospitals, university and other medical centers, and private clinics and hospitals. It was interesting to note, however, that the coursework specifically dealing with medical psychology and the practicum experiences were almost always elective, rather than required, and furthermore that only 8% of the graduate programs were offering a subspecialty in medical psychology to clinical students.

Gentry *et al.*[2] found that most of the clinical psychology internship settings (74%) had formalized clinical experiences in medical psychology (e.g., consultation-liaison services to medical/surgical wards, biofeedback and behavior modification services to medical patients, and activities on pediatric and neuropsychological services). These experiences involved diagnostic as well as therapeutic skills, and they brought the interns into contact with a wide range of patients and problems (e.g., cancer, pain, coronary disease, sexual dysfunction). In 39% of the settings, these experiences with medical psychological problems were required.

[2]Unpublished report. For details, contact: Dr. W. Doyle Gentry, Department of Psychiatry and Behavioral Sciences, University of Texas Medical Branch, Galveston, Texas 77550.

It also was clear that training experiences in medical psychology more recently had been introduced in graduate programs, as compared to internship programs. The former had included an emphasis on medical or health psychology for an average of three years (range of 1 to 12 years), as compared to an average of five years (range of 1 to 20 years) for the latter.

The combined facts that (*a*) at least 63% of the internship sites and 78% of the university programs could identify one or more faculty with interests and/or expertise in the field of medical psychology; (*b*) one-quarter to one-third of the student trainees were interested in such training; and (*c*) between 32% and 42% of the programs were anticipating new or extended training experiences in medical psychology caused the authors of this survey to be encouraged about the current status of such training and more importantly future prospects for same.

Medical Psychology and Related Concepts

It is important to distinguish what is meant by the terms *medical psychology, health psychology, psychosomatic medicine, behavioral medicine,* and *behavioral health* if one is to fully appreciate contemporary developments in this field. Medical psychology, as we have used the term here, is defined as the practice of psychology within the medical school establishment. This includes not only clinical services (i.e., practitioner), but also the important roles of medical educator and researcher. Furthermore, it includes *all* subspecialties of psychology (e.g., clinical, social, developmental, experimental, and physiological). It is an inclusive, rather than exclusive definition of activities. It should be pointed out that others such as Pomerleau and Brady (1979) have taken a more narrow view of medical psychology, defining it as

> a broad field of activity, one in which psychometric assessment, projective testing, and personality theory have played major roles. The emphasis in medical psychology has been on the understanding of medical illness in its psychological and social context rather than on therapy [p. xi].

The latter definition excludes the valuable contributions of medical psychologists in the field of traditional psychotherapy (Olbrisch, 1977) and behavior therapies (Williams & Gentry, 1977) with physically ill persons (referring to such endeavors as behavioral medicine), as well as the contributions to medicine made by such social psychologists, as Irving Janis on decision-making and health (Janis & Rodin, 1979), and other nonclinical psychologists such as Gary Schwartz, Richard Evans, and Richard Lazarus. Our definition is the same as that used by Asken (1979) and Masur (1979), but more inclusive than that of Rachman (1977; Rachman and Philips, 1975) who, like Pomerleau and Brady, place a rather restrictive emphasis on the *application of clinical psychological principles* to medicine.

Psychosomatic medicine, as noted by Schwartz and Weiss (1977), is a field of endeavor which traditionally has focused its attention on issues of etiology and pathogenesis of physical disease. It has primarily involved work carried out by individuals who combined training in psychiatry and medicine (often being referred to as a subspecialty of psychiatry), and it only recently has broadened its scope to include input from different behavioral science disciplines (e.g., psychology, sociology, and epidemiology). The range of health problems dealt with in psychosomatic medicine has been anything but broad (e.g., Weiner, 1977), and there has been too little attention given to issues of intervention or prevention. While medical school psychologists have contributed to the field of psychosomatic medicine, their efforts have not been limited to same.

Behavioral medicine, on the other hand, has been defined[3] as (Schwartz & Weiss, 1978b): "The

[3]Believing the above definition of behavioral medicine to be too broad, Pomerleau and Brady (1979) have adopted a definition emphasizing the primary role of behavioral psychology. They suggest that:

> Behavioral medicine can be defined as (*a*) the clinical use of techniques derived from the experimental analysis of behavior—behavior therapy and behavior modification—for the evaluation, prevention, management, or treatment of physical disease or physiological dysfunction; and (*b*) the conduct of re-

interdisciplinary field concerned with the development and *integration* of behavioral and biomedical science knowledge *and* techniques relevant to health and illness and the application of this knowledge and these techniques to prevention, diagnosis, treatment, and rehabilitation [p. 250]." As such, behavioral medicine does not limit itself to the contributions of any single discipline, any one theoretical or conceptual model, or to an emphasis on diagnostic versus therapeutic concerns. As Masur (1979) correctly points out, medical psychology is but one of many disciplines contributing to the whole of behavioral medicine, along with sociology, epidemiology, nutrition, anthropology, psychiatry, dentistry, and medicine proper.

The other two terms "health psychology" and "behavioral health" have been used less often and to some extent they have not been clearly distinguished from the concepts of "medical psychology" and "behavioral medicine." Stone (Note 2) and Matarazzo (Note 1) both have defined health psychology as if it were synonymous with medical psychology, describing it as the application of educational, scientific, and professional *psychological* principles to issues of health maintenance and illness prevention. Stone, in particular, has stressed the unique role of psychologists as change agents (interventionists), in contrast to other types of behavioral scientists; and, within the framework of health psychology, he has specified different types of intervention (e.g., attitude change, stress management, health education) and different targets of intervention (e.g., patients, families, providers, health care systems). Similarly, Matarazzo (Note 1) has taken the element of "prevention" and has coined the new term *behavioral health* as a complementary discipline to *behavioral medicine*. These concepts appear to add a certain amount of confusion to the still fluid and continually evolving relationship between medical psychology and the larger field of behavioral medicine, but they have merit in that they place an equal emphasis on issues of health, prevention, and the concept of "wellness."

search contributing to the functional analysis and understanding of behavior associated with medical disorders and problems in health care [p. xii].

As Masur (1979) points out, this is the same type of emphasis placed on behavioral medicine by special interest groups closely allied with the Association for the Advancement of Behavior Therapy (AABT).

Future Directions

What may we conclude from this discussion of psychology (and psychologists) in medical education, its growth trends, its relationship to the field of behavioral medicine, and its current "state of the art" with respect to professional training? What developments can we expect in the next decade, given the events of the last three?

First, it seems safe to say that we will see a continuation of the increasing number of psychologists seeking employment on medical school faculties throughout this country. The increase in the numbers of medical school psychologists during the last 30 years has been, in fact, a linear one; and, there are no signs that the growth period is over. As we have seen from the most recent surveys, medical psychologists are finding life in the medical school environment for the most part rewarding, with at least 70% indicating that the advantages far outweigh the disadvantages.

Second, the few data that are available regarding the status of professional training for psychologists for positions in schools of medicine are encouraging in that they suggest that psychologists indeed are being prepared for the positions that may be available to them in years to come. In fact, many psychologists will begin their employment in medical schools already sensitized to critical issues and topics in medical research and education, rather than being forced to learn such things "on the job" as did their counterparts 30 years ago. This will certainly accelerate both the quantity and quality of medical psychologists' (working in medical schools and elsewhere) contributions to health care and the new knowledge related to their contributions.

Third, it seems likely that few new autonomous Departments of Medical Psychology will emerge in medical schools in years to come. Rather, medical psychologists will continue to find themselves administratively housed in Departments of Psychiatry or Departments of Behavioral Science. The fact that 20 years elapsed between the founding of the first Department of Medical Psychology at the University of Oregon Health Sciences Center and the founding of the second such department at the Uniformed Services University of the Health Sciences hardly constitutes "a harbinger of a trend" in this country (Nathan, Millham, & Lubin, 1979, p. 102). On the other hand, it also is clear that many of the inequities that previously affected psychologists in Departments of Psychiatry (lower salaries for comparable academic rank) are disappearing, thus making life for medical psychologists much more satisfying despite their lack of professional autonomy comparable to that enjoyed by most of the other disciplines represented in the same schools of medicine.

Medical psychology also appears to have a vital role in the emerging field of behavioral medicine; in fact, it was medical psychologists who played key roles in the initial development of the field (Schwartz & Weiss, 1978a, 1978b). Medical school psychologists should be a dominant force in the field of behavioral medicine, if only because (*a*) they constitute the largest single group of nonphysician behavioral scientists employed in medical schools (Buck, 1961), far outnumbering sociologists and anthropologists; and (*b*) as licensed health professionals in their respective states they do have, in fact, the unique capacity to intervene in health and illness behavior, as Stone (Note 2) suggested. The only real problems that medical school psychologists may face in the future in this regard have to do with their tendency to work in isolation (e.g., not to engage in collaborative research except with fellow psychologists or psychiatrists) and also the apparent desire of some to define behavioral medicine as the primary, perhaps exclusive, domain of psychology, thereby excluding or deemphasizing important contributions of other disciplines (Pomerleau & Brady, 1979).

To summarize, one may be only comforted by reflecting on the rather dramatic growth and development of medical school psychology over the last 30 years. The emergence of behavioral medicine, behavioral health, health psychology and their variants give promise of a decade which may presage an even fuller emergence of psychology in schools of medicine.

Reference Notes

1. Matarazzo, J. D. *Behavioral health and behavioral medicine: Frontiers for a new health psychology.* Presidential address to Division 38 (Health Psychology), American Psychological Association, New York, September, 1979.
2. Stone, G. C. *Health and behavior.* Paper presented at the Annual Meeting of the American Psychological Association, San Francisco, 1977.

References

Asken, M. J. Medical psychology: Toward definition, clarification, and organization. *Professional Psychology,* 1979, *10,* 66–73.

Buck, R. L. Behavioral scientists in schools of medicine. *Journal of Health and Human Behavior,* 1961, *2,* 59–64.

Budman, S. H., & Wertlieb, D. (Eds.). Psychologists in health care settings. *Professional Psychology,* 1979, *10,* 397–644.

Cohen, L. D., Lubin, B., & Nathan, R. G. Graduate degree training in psychology in medical centers. *Professional Psychology,* 1979, *10,* 110–114.

Dembroski, T. M., Weiss, S. M., Shields, J. L., Haynes, S. G., & Feinlieb, M. (Eds.). *Coronary-prone behavior.* New York: Springer-Verlag, 1978.

Flexner, A. *Medical education in the United States and Canada: A report to the Carnegie Foundation for the Advancement of Teaching* (Bulletin No. 4). New York: Carnegie Foundation, 1910.

Fordyce, W. E. *Behavioral methods for chronic pain and illness.* St. Louis: Mosby, 1976.

Foreyt, J. P., & Rathjen, D. P. *Cognitive behavior therapy.* New York: Plenum, 1978.

Franz, S. I. The present status of psychology in medical education and practice. *Journal of the American Medical Association,* 1912, *58,* 909–921.

Franz, S. I. On psychology and medical education. *Science,* 1913, *38,* 555–566.

Gentry, W. D. Psychological evaluation and coronary heart disease. In J. C. Davis & J. P. Foreyt (Eds.), *Mental examiner's source book.* Springfield, Illinois: Charles C. Thomas, 1975.

Gentry, W. D., & Cameron, R. Psychodiagnostic evaluation of pain and disability. In J. C. Davis & J. P. Foreyt

(Eds.), *Mental examiner's source book.* Springfield, Illinois: Charles C. Thomas, 1975.

Gentry, W. D., & Williams, R. B. (Eds.), *Psychological aspects of myocardial infarction and coronary care* (2nd ed.). St. Louis: Mosby, 1979.

Jacobson, C. Psychology in medical education. In W. Dennis (Ed.), *Current trends in the relation of psychology to medicine.* Pittsburgh: University of Pittsburgh Press, 1950.

Janis, I. L., & Rodin, J. Attribution, control, and decision making: Social psychology and health care. In G. C. Stone, F. Cohen, & N. E. Adler (Eds.), *Health psychology.* San Francisco: Jossey-Bass, 1979.

Johnson, J. H., & Williams, T. A. The psychologist in the department of psychiatry. *Professional Psychology,* 1979, *10,* 318-323.

Katz, R. C., & Zlutnick, S. (Eds.). *Behavior therapy and health care: Principles and applications.* New York: Pergamon, 1975.

Lubin, B., Nathan, R. G., & Matarazzo, J. D. Psychologists in medical education: 1976. *American Psychologist,* 1978, *33,* 339-343.

Masur, F. T. An update on medical psychology and behavioral medicine. *Professional Psychology,* 1979, *10,* 259-264.

Mensh, I. N. Psychology in medical education. *American Psychologist,* 1953, *8,* 83-85.

Nathan, R. G., Lubin, B., Matarazzo, J. D., & Persely, G. W. Psychologists in schools of medicine: 1955, 1964, and 1977. *American Psychologist,* 1979, *34,* 622-627.

Nathan, R. G., Millham, J., & Lubin, B. Organizational structure and roles of psychologists in schools of medicine. *Professional Psychology,* 1979, *10,* 97-103.

Olbrisch, M. E. Psychotherapeutic interventions in physical health: Effectiveness and economic efficiency. *American Psychologist,* 1977, *32,* 761-777.

Page, H. E., & Passey, G. E. The rule of psychology in medical education. *American Psychologist,* 1949, *4,* 405-409.

Pomerleau, O. F., & Brady, J. P. (Eds.). *Behavioral medicine: Theory and practice.* Baltimore: Williams and Wilkins, 1979.

Rachman, S. *Contributions to medical psychology* (Vol. 1). New York: Pergamon, 1977.

Rachman, S. J., & Philips, C. *Psychology and medicine.* London: Temple Smith, 1975.

Routh, D. K., & Clarke, M. Psychology in a small medical school. *Professional Psychology,* 1976, *7,* 94-106.

Schwartz, G. E., & Weiss, S. M. What is behavioral medicine? *Psychosomatic Medicine,* 1977, *39,* 377-381.

Schwartz, G. E., & Weiss, S. M. Yale conference on behavioral medicine: A proposed definition and statement of goals. *Journal of Behavioral Medicine,* 1978, *1,* 3-12. (a)

Schwartz, G. E., & Weiss, S. M. Behavioral medicine revisited: An amended definition. *Journal of Behavioral Medicine,* 1978, *1,* 249-252. (b)

Sternbach, R. A. *Pain patients: Traits and treatment.* New York: Academic Press, 1974.

Stone, G. C., Cohen, F., & Adler, N. E. *Health psychology.* San Francisco: Jossey-Bass, 1979.

Stone, G. C., Gentry, W. D., Matarazzo, J. D., Carlton, P. L., Pattishall, E. G., & Wakeley, J. H. Teaching psychology to medical students. *Teaching Psychology,* 1977, *4,* 111-115.

Weiner, H. *Psychobiology and human disease.* New York: Elsevier, 1977.

Williams, R. B., & Gentry, W. D. (Eds.). *Behavioral approaches to medical treatment.* Cambridge, Mass.: Ballinger, 1977.

Witkin, H. A., Mensh, I. N., & Cates, J. Psychologists in medical schools. *American Psychologist,* 1972, *27,* 434-440.

ASSESSMENT OF MEDICAL DISORDERS

3

Type A Behavior: Assessment and Intervention

MARGARET A. CHESNEY
JEAN R. EAGLESTON
RAY H. ROSENMAN

The occurrence of clinical coronary heart disease (CHD) was rare at the turn of the century. Now, this disease is responsible for one-third of all deaths in western societies. With this increase, CHD has received the attention of the medical and scientific communities and has stimulated research regarding its risk factors and clinical expressions. The parallel between the rise in CHD incidence and rapid industrialization in western societies, for example, has suggested that factors related to twentieth-century patterns of life and work may be related to CHD risk. Pursuing this point of view, Dr. Meyer Friedman and Dr. Ray H. Rosenman have studied a constellation of behaviors that they have labeled the Type A behavior pattern.

According to Friedman and Rosenman (1959), the Type A behavior pattern is "primarily characterized by intense ambition, competitive 'drive', constant preoccupation with occupational 'deadlines' and a sense of time urgency [p. 1295]." Testing the hypothesis that Type A behavior leads to heart disease, Rosenman and Friedman conducted a longitudinal study of 3524 men. At the 8½-year follow-up, those subjects identified as having the Type A behavior pattern at the study's onset had twice the rate of clinical coronary disease, twice the rate of fatal heart attacks and five times the rate of recurring coronary events experienced by subjects lacking the Type A behavior pattern, (i.e., subjects who were identified as Type B) (Rosenman, Brand, Jenkins, Friedman, Straus, & Wurm, 1975). Furthermore, this level of risk, approximately equal to that associated with other CHD risk factors, was also independent of the other risk factors (Brand, Rosenman, Sholtz, & Friedman, 1976; Rosenman, Brand, Sholtz, & Friedman, 1976). Since the initial study, the role of the Type A behavior pattern has been confirmed in autopsy (Friedman, Rosenman, Straus, Wurm, & Kositchek, 1968) and angiographic studies (Blumenthal, Williams, Kong, Schanberg, & Thompson,

Preparation of this chapter was supported in part by the National Institute of Mental Health Grant 31269. Additional information regarding training in the assessment of Type A behavior can be obtained from Ray H. Rosenman, SRI International, 333 Ravenswood Avenue, Menlo Park, California 94025.

ISBN 0-12-565960-1

1978; Frank, Heller, Kornfeld, Sporn, & Weiss, 1978; Matthews & Krantz, Note 1; Zyzanski, Jenkins, Ryan, Flessas, & Everist, 1976).

In response to the growing number of independent studies confirming the risk associated with the Type A behavior pattern, the Coronary-Prone Behavior Review Panel, convened by the National Heart, Lung, and Blood Institute, recognized Type A behavior as a CHD risk factor (Forum on Coronary-Prone Behavior, 1978). Given the high personal and social costs of CHD, interest in the assessment and modification of Type A behavior has increased. In this chapter, both the measurement of Type A behavior and interventions designed to reduce its risk will be reviewed.

Assessment of Type A Behavior

The major Type A assessment procedure is the Structured Interview (SI). The SI evolved during Friedman and Rosenman's early studies of the prevalence of the Type A behavior pattern in men and women (Friedman & Rosenman, 1959; Rosenman & Friedman, 1961). The method of subject selection in these investigations involved a two-stage process. First, the Type A and Type B behavior patterns were described in detail to individuals who then identified associates who most closely fit the Type A description. Second, Rosenman or Friedman interviewed each of these peer-selected subjects to assess the degree of development of the Type A behavior pattern. The content of this interview emphasized health history and status and included questions on smoking, work, exercise, sleep and dietary habits, and parental history of coronary heart disease and illnesses. Friedman and Rosenman's clinical assessment of the behavior pattern was based not only on the content of the subject's responses, but also on the presence or absence of Type A behavior displayed during the course of the interview.

The Structured Interview

In May 1960, the Western Collaborative Group Study (WCGS), a prospective study, was begun to examine the role of the Type A behavior pattern in the pathogenesis of CHD. As part of the experimental design, it was important that the interviews for assessing the behavior pattern of the subjects be rated "blind" by one of the investigators (Rosenman). Accordingly, a standardized interview that could be administered by a trained interviewer was written based on the questions Rosenman and Friedman had asked in their earlier studies. These interview questions covered three themes considered important to the behavior pattern: (*a*) degree of drive and ambition; (*b*) degree of past and present competitive, aggressive, and hostile feelings; and (*c*) degree of time urgency.

The WCGS subject interviews were audiotaped for the subsequent "blind" rating. Because the Type A behavior pattern includes nonverbal as well as verbal or speech behaviors, the interviewers were instructed to note certain subject behaviors (e.g., mental and emotional alertness, speed of motion, gesturing, body restlessness, and facial grimaces). This interview procedure, which has become known as the Structured Interview (SI), served as the basis for the assessment of the Type A or Type B behavior pattern in the landmark WCGS research (e.g., Friedman *et al.*, 1968; Rosenman, Friedman, Jenkins, Straus, Wurm & Kositchek, 1966, 1967; Rosenman, Friedman, Straus, Jenkins, Zyzanski, & Wurm, 1970; Rosenman, Friedman, Straus, Wurm, Kositchek, Hahn, & Werthessen, 1964).

Ratings of the SI are based on the relative presence or absence of specific behaviors characteristic of the Type A and Type B behavior patterns. Table 3.1 summarizes the behaviors that comprise the clinical descriptions of the Type A and Type B behavior patterns. Although the literature commonly refers to Type A and Type B behavior, the assessment of the behavior pattern with the SI was originally made using the following five-point scale.

A-1: Fully developed pattern
A-2: Many Type A characteristics present, but not the complete pattern
X: An even mix of Type A and B characteristics

Table 3.1
Profiles of the Type A and Type B Behavior Patterns

Characteristics	Type A	Type B
Speech		
Rate	Rapid	Slow
Word production	Single-word answers; acceleration at the end of sentences	Measured; frequent pauses or breaks
Volume	Loud	Soft
Quality	Vigorous; terse; harsh	"Walter Mitty"
Intonation/inflection	Abrupt; explosive speech; key word emphasis	Monotone
Response latency	Immediate answers	Pauses before answering
Length of responses	Short and to the point	Long; rambling
Other	Word clipping; word omission; word repetition	
Behaviors		
Sighing	Frequent	Rare
Posture	Tense; on the edge of the chair	Relaxed; comfortable
General demeanor	Alert; intense	Calm; quiet attentiveness
Facial expression	Tense; hostile; grimace	Relaxed; friendly
Smile	Lateral	Broad
Laughter	Harsh	Gentle chuckle
Wrist clenching	Frequent	Rare
Responses to the interview		
Interrupts interviewer	Often, particularly on question 13	Rarely, even on question 13
Returns to previous subject when interrupted	Often	Rarely
Attempts to finish interviewer's questions	Often	Rarely
Uses humor	Rarely	Often
Hurries the interviewer ("yes, yes," "m-m,' head nodding)	Often	Rarely

(continued)

Table 3.1—*Continued*

Characteristics	Type A	Type B
Competes for control of the interview	Wide variety of techniques—interruptions; verbal duets; extraneous comments; lengthy or evasive answers; questioning or correcting the interviewer	Rarely
Hostility	Often demonstrated during the interview through mechanisms such as boredom, condescension, authoritarianism, challenge	None
Typical content		
Satisfied with job	No, wants to move up	Yes
Hard-driving, ambitious	Yes, by own and others' judgements	Not particularly
Feels a sense of time urgency	Yes	No
Impatience	Hates waiting in lines; will not wait at a restaurant; annoyed when caught behind a slow-moving vehicle	Takes delays of all kinds in stride and does not become frustrated or annoyed
Competition	Enjoys competition on the job; plays all games (even with children) to win	Does not thrive on competition and rarely engages in competitive activities
Admits to polyphasic thinking and activities	Often does or thinks two (or more) things at the same time	Rarely does or thinks two things at once
Hostility	In content and stylistics—argumentative responses; excessive qualifications; harsh generalizations; challenges; emotion-laden words; obscenity	Rarely present in any content

B-3: Many Type B characteristics but with some Type A characteristics

B-4: Relative absence of Type A characteristics[1]

It is important to note that the SI originally used in the WCGS was not developed as a standardized assessment procedure to be used beyond the WCGS. The initial purpose of the interview was to present a situation that would elicit the Type A behavior pattern while the subject was being observed and his responses tape-recorded, so that the subject's behavior later could be assessed. Originally, it was thought that the content of the questions, as well as a few interviewing techniques (e.g., stalling on a particular question in order to allow the subject to interrupt), would be the determinants of the interview ratings. As an outgrowth of the interviewers' experiences and the audits of the taped interviews, the concept of creating a challenging situation began to form. The full relationship between such challenge and Type A behavior was not understood, but it was observed that more aspects of the Type A behavior pattern were revealed when the interview was more challenging (Rosenman, Note 2). In 1962, with the second assessment of the WCGS subjects, the interview was shortened and the content was changed slightly. An emphasis was placed on challenging the subjects, and a trend toward standardization of interview style was begun. This revised version of the SI has been used in research subsequent to 1962 and currently is taught by Rosenman to other researchers.

The SI consists of a set of main questions, which are pursued with challenging probes based on the subject's responses. Table 3.2 displays the current version of the SI. It typically takes 10-15 min to administer and is audiotaped or videotaped for later assessment by trained raters.

During the administration of the SI, the interviewer creates a challenge situation and presents a standardized environmental stimulus that will result in Type A behavior from the subject if the pattern is part of the subject's behavioral repertoire. Because the SI is a structured experimental situation, the theory and technique must be mastered before an interviewer can successfully administer the interview. The task is not just one of memorizing and then asking a series of questions; rather, as with other forms of psychological assessment (e.g., WISC-R or Rorschach), the interviewer must be trained to conduct the interview and concurrently assess the behavior sample.

The major emphasis in SI training is placed upon the maintenance of interviewer consistency along a number of dimensions: (*a*) vocal style—including speed of questioning, volume and intonation, and inflection; (*b*) overall length of the interview; (*c*) question content; and (*d*) behavior. It is important that the interviewer's behavior and style of interaction do not vary with each subject. The desirable interviewer style perhaps can be described best as "coldly professional," although "aggressive", "hostile", "businesslike", and "confrontive" have also been used to describe it.

Evaluating the SI and Alternative Assessment Procedures

As noted in the previous section, the SI was the first formal assessment procedure for the Type A behavior pattern. Despite the subjective nature of classifications based on the SI, interrater reliability ranges from .64 to .84 (Caffrey, 1968; E. Friedman, Hellerstein, Eastwood, & Jones, 1968; Jenkins, Rosenman, & Friedman, 1968; Matthews, Glass, Rosenman, & Bortner, 1977). The lower interrater reliabilities (.64) are found with newly trained raters (Caffrey, 1968) or when four categories (A-1, A-2, X, B) are used rather than the dichotomous A-B classification.

The test-retest reliability of the SI has been examined in a number of studies. As would be expected, the reliability of dichotomous Type A-B ratings is greater than that of interview ratings using the four-point scale (Jenkins *et al.*, 1968; Keith, Lown, & Stare, 1965). In the largest stability

[1]Because no differences were found between the power of B-3 and B-4 classifications in predicting clinical atherosclerosis in work since the WCGS, the B-3 and B-4 categories are often combined. Currently, the majority of research on coronary-prone behavior patterns is using this modified scale that consists of only the four points A-1, A-2, X, and B.

Table 3.2
Structured Interview Protocol[a]

I would appreciate it if you would answer the following questions to the best of your ability. Your answers will be kept in the strictest confidence. Most of the questions are concerned with your superficial habits and none of them will embarrass you. (Begin taping now.)

Your code number is ______.

1. May I ask your age?
2. What is your job here at ______?
   (a) How long have you been in this type of work?

+3. Are you SATISFIED with your job level?
   (a) Why? Why not?

+4. Does your job carry HEAVY responsibility?
   (a) Is there any time when you feel particularly RUSHED or under PRESSURE?
   (b) When you are under PRESSURE does it bother you?

+5. Would you describe yourself as a HARD-DRIVING, AMBITIOUS type of person in accomplishing the things you want, OR would you describe yourself as a relatively RELAXED and EASY-GOING person?
   (a) Are you married?
   (b) (If married) How would your WIFE describe you in those terms—as HARD-DRIVING and AMBITIOUS or as relaxed and easy-going?
   (c) Has she ever asked you to slow down in your work? Speed up?
   (d) (If no) NEVER?
   (e) How would SHE put it in HER OWN words?
   (f) Do you like to get things done as QUICKLY as possible?

+6. When you get ANGRY or UPSET, do people around you know about it?
   (a) How do you show it?
   (b) Do you ever pound on your desk? Slam a door? Throw things?

+7. Do you think you drive HARDER to ACCOMPLISH things than most of your associates?

8. Do you take work home with you?
   (a) How often?
   (b) Do you really do it?

9. Do you have children? (If no children—Have you ever played with small children?) With your children, when they were around the ages of 6 and 8, did you EVER play competitive games with them, like cards, checkers, Monopoly?
   (a) Did you ALWAYS allow them to WIN on PURPOSE?
   (b) Why or why not?

10. When you play games with people YOUR OWN age, do you play for the FUN of it, or are you REALLY in there to WIN!
11. Is there any COMPETITION in your job?
   (a) Do you enjoy this?

*12. When you are in your automobile, and there is a car in your lane going FAR TOO SLOWLY for you, what do you do about it?
   (a) Would you MUTTER and COMPLAIN to yourself? Honk your horn? Flash your lights?
   (b) Would anyone riding with you know that you were ANNOYED?

13. Most people who work have to get up fairly early in the morning, in your particular case, uh-what-time-uh-do-you-uh, ordinarily uh-uh-uh-get-up?

*14. If you make a DATE with someone for, oh, two o'clock in the afternoon, would you BE THERE on TIME?
(a) Always? Never?
(b) If you are kept waiting, do you RESENT it?
(c) Would you SAY anything about it?
(d) Why or why not?

15. If you see someone doing a job rather SLOWLY and you KNOW that you could do it faster and better yourself, does it make you RESTLESS to watch him?
(a) Would you be tempted to STEP IN AND DO IT yourself?
(b) Have you ever done that?
(c) What would you do if someone did that to you?

16. Do you OFTEN do two things at THE SAME TIME—like reading while watching TV, shaving while taking a shower, writing or reading while talking on the telephone?
(a) Never? Always?

17. Do you OFTEN find that while you are listening to ONE thing you are also THINKING about something ELSE?
(a) Never? Always?

18. What IRRITATES you most about your work, or the people with whom you work?
(a) Why is that so bad?

19. Do you EAT rapidly? Do you WALK RAPIDLY? After you've FINISHED eating, do you like to sit around the table and chat, or do you like to GET UP AND GET GOING?

*20. When you go out in the evening to a restaurant and you find 8 or 10 people WAITING AHEAD OF YOU for a table, will you wait?
(a) Most of the time, how long will you wait?
(b) What will you do while you are waiting?
(c) Are you impatient while you are waiting?

21. What would you do if you had made a reservation at a restaurant and upon arriving the hostess tells you that there will be a 20-minute wait?
(a) What if after waiting 20 minutes the hostess says that it will be another 20 minutes?

22. Would you EVER ask another person in a restaurant to stop smoking?
(a) What would you say? How would you do it?
(b) (If no) What if your companion asked you to ask the man smoking a cigar to stop: How would you do it?
(c) If no, Why not?

23. How do you feel about WAITING in lines—bank lines, supermarket lines, post office lines?
(a) How long would you wait?
(b) What will you do while you are waiting?
(c) Are you frustrated while waiting?

*24. Do you ALWAYS feel anxious to GET GOING and FINISH whatever you have to do?
(a) Always? Never?

25. Do you have the feeling that TIME is passing too RAPIDLY for you to ACCOMPLISH all the things that you THINK you should GET DONE in one day?
(a) Do you OFTEN feel a sense of TIME URGENCY or TIME PRESSURE?

26. Do you HURRY in doing most things?

That completes the interview. Thank you very much.

Closure: This completes the interview of Subject (give code numbers).

---

[a] + = interruptions, * = challenges.

study to date, 1131 men in the WCGS were interviewed twice over a period of 12 to 20 months. The stability of the behavior pattern's dichotomous rating was found to be .82 (Jenkins *et al.,* 1968).

Despite the stability of the SI over time and rating reliability, paper and pencil self-report questionnaires have been developed in attempts to assess the behavior pattern more objectively and efficiently. The first such scale, the Jenkins Activity Survey (JAS) was developed from an item pool based on the SI questions and clinical experience (Jenkins, Rosenman, & Friedman, 1967). Items were selected for the JAS as a function of their ability to discriminate between individuals classified by the SI as Type A or B. The JAS was further refined to yield a composite Type A scale and three factor-analytically-derived subscales: Speed and Impatience, Job Involvement, and Hard-Driving. In retrospective studies conducted in Europe and in the United States, the JAS Type A scale demonstrated an ability to differentiate between controls and CHD cases. In addition, the JAS was compared to the SI in the WCGS, and the Type A scale showed a 72% agreement with SI classification (Zyzanski & Jenkins, 1970). Although the JAS Type A scale was found to be significantly related to CHD in this prospective study, the power of the relationship between the Type A scale and CHD was significantly weaker than that between the SI and CHD (Brand, Rosenman, Jenkins, Sholtz, & Zyzanski, in press). Unfortunately, none of the three factor-analytically-derived subscales was significantly related to CHD (Jenkins, Rosenman, & Zyzanski, 1974).

Like the SI, the JAS has been examined as a predictor of degree of atherosclerosis in angiographic studies. In one such study, the JAS was found to significantly predict coronary atherosclerosis (Zyzanski *et al.,* 1976). This finding, however, has not been confirmed in two other angiographic studies (Blumenthal *et al.,* 1978; Dimsdale, Hackett, Block, & Hutter, 1978). Indeed, Blumenthal *et al.,* (1978) administered both the JAS and SI to subjects and reported that only the SI correlated significantly with angiographic findings.

Recently, seeking to identify the mechanisms by which the Type A behavior pattern exerts its effects on the coronary vasculature, researchers have examined differences between Type A and Type B subjects in their physiologic reactivity to stressful challenge tasks. In one study, in which both the SI and JAS were used to assess the behavior pattern, the ratings of the SI were significantly related to physiological reactivity while the JAS Scale scores were not (Dembroski, MacDougall, Shields, Petitto, & Lushene, 1978).

At least six other questionnaire scales have been developed to assess Type A behavior. Vickers (Note 3) and Sales (see Caplan, Cobb, French, Harrison, & Pinneau, 1975) designed two such scales for use in the occupational stress research conducted by the Institute for Social Research at the University of Michigan (Caplan *et al.,* 1975). To date there is little evidence to validate these two scales as measures of the Type A behavior pattern as assessed by the SI. They have neither been found to correlate significantly with SI ratings, nor have they been studied in relation to heart disease risk or incidence in either prospective or retrospective research.

Two subscales from standard psychological measures have been examined for their ability to measure the Type A behavior pattern. One of these, a subscale from the Adjective Checklist (Gough & Heilbrun, 1975; ACL) consists of 20 adjectives that have been found to be significantly related to the SI (Rahe, Hervig, & Rosenman, Note 4). This subscale's relationship to the SI has been subsequently cross-validated and found to be significant (r = .31, p < .001) (Chesney, Black, Feuerstein, Rosenman, Calligan, & Chadwick, Note 5). The second subscale that has been used as a Type A measure is the activity subscale from the Thurstone Temperament Schedule (Thurstone, 1949; TTS). The relationship between this subscale and the SI also has been found to be significant (r = .32, p < .001) (Chesney, *et al.,* Note 5). Although this subscale, like the one from the ACL, is significantly related to the SI, the strength of the relationship is only moderate and the scales' power in predicting heart disease has not been explored.

Recently, yet another scale has been studied in the context of Type A behavior assessment. This measure, the Framingham Type A scale

(Haynes, Levine, Scotch, Feinleib, & Kannel, 1978; FTAS), consists of 10 items from the extensive interview questionnaire administered in the Framingham Heart Study. These items, selected because their content appeared relevant to the Type A behavior pattern, have been found to significantly predict both the prevalence and the incidence of CHD in men and women at an 8-year follow-up (Haynes, Feinleib, Levine, Scotch, & Kannel, 1978). However, when the 10-item FTAS was administered independent of the entire Framingham questionnaire, only a moderate relationship ($r = .21$, $p < .01$) was found between the FTAS and the SI (Chesney *et al.*, Note 5). The FTAS, then, may be measuring a different aspect of "coronary-prone" behavior than that assessed by the SI. Further, the FTAS has not yet been studied as a predictor of CHD when administered as a self-contained scale, nor has its predictive strength been cross-validated. Such cross-validation research is in progress (Haynes, Note 6).

Completing this list of Type A questionnaires, is a 14-item scale that was developed by Bortner (1969). Prior to designing this pencil and paper instrument, Bortner and Rosenman developed a test battery consisting of performance measures such as the Rod and Frame Test and time-estimating tasks to measure the Type A behavior pattern (Bortner & Rosenman, 1967). Although this test battery showed a 66% agreement with SI classification, its correlation with the JAS was not significant ($r = .02$). The test battery and the JAS, then, were measuring quite different aspects of the Type A behavior pattern. Nonetheless, emerging from research on the test battery was the 14-item rating scale that utilized a semantic-differential format. Lending support to the scale's validity, subjects rated as either Type A or Type B on the basis of the SI were found to have significantly different scores on the scale (Bortner, 1969). Furthermore, in a case-control study, subjects who had a history of myocardial infarction were found to have significantly higher scores on this scale than controls (Heller, 1979).

In summary, a number of self-report written questionnaires significantly correlate with the SI and show promise as Type A assessment procedures. However, none of these questionnaires has been found to have the *predictive* validity of the global assessment of the Type A behavior pattern that is based on the SI.

Interview Variations and Extensions

The SI has been used most often in population groups composed of middle-aged, middle to upper socioeconomic class, employed, white males. Therefore, revisions have been required for research of Type A behavior in other populations including women (Waldron, 1978) and undergraduate college students (Dembroski *et al.*, 1978; Scherwitz, Berton & Leventhal, 1977). In addition, the SI has been translated into French and Flemish for purposes of studying its cross-cultural validity (Kittel, Kornitzer, Zyzanski, Jenkins, Rustin, & Degre, 1978), and into Czech and German for use in studies in Czechoslovakia and East Germany (Horvath, Note 7).

An interview based upon SI and JAS items has been used with adolescents (Butensky, Faralli, Heebner, & Waldron, 1976). Unlike the SI, however, the rating of this interview relies primarily on the content of responses rather than on the subject's response style. Matthews has investigated development of the Type A behavior pattern in children (Matthews, 1977). Since interviews are not likely to be satisfactory with children, she has developed an instrument—the Matthews Youth Test for Health (MYTH)—that utilizes teachers' behavioral observations of children. Recent studies (Matthews & Angulo, Note 8) have provided positive data regarding the reliability and validity of the MYTH.

In an ongoing intervention study of post-myocardial-infarction patients, Friedman and his colleagues at Mt. Zion Hospital are using another variation of the SI. This revision of the SI consists of a longer set of questions (including items more pertinent to heart-disease patients) and a slightly different interview style. A major purpose of this interview is not to assess Type A behavior, but rather to compile an even larger collection of behavioral observations than that produced by the standard SI. These more extensive and detailed observations of primarily Type A behavior are being used in an effort to refine and quantify the rating system.

Although the SI variations described above suggest wide generalizability of Type A behavior, the reliability and validity of these variations have not been studied systematically. Therefore, it is unclear at this time to what extent these variations accurately assess Type A behavior. Determination of the predictive values for all SI variations awaits prospective studies.

Finally, it should be noted that a few investigators have developed protocols that include the standard SI and add additional questions to the end of the interview. Dembroski, MacDougall, and Lushene (1980) report using a seven question, American history quiz of "allegedly well-known events" which was delivered in an extremely challenging manner that emphasized performance. Electrocardiogram and blood pressure monitoring was done during both the SI and the quiz. Among other findings, they note that Type A subjects showed significantly greater blood pressure elevations than Type B subjects during the quiz.

Another protocol that consists of an elaboration on the original SI is that used by the present authors. Specifically, after conducting the SI in the standard manner, and stating that the interview is completed, subjects are asked to provide feedback on the interview experience. During this "debriefing" session, the interviewer asks very general and open-ended questions (e.g., "What was the interview like for you?" "What reactions do you have to the interview?" "Were there any parts of the interview that were annoying?") and changes the interviewing style (i.e., no longer confrontive and challenging but rather supportive and encouraging). Currently, we are conducting research regarding possible differences in subject behavior during the SI and the debriefing. This research will assist in estimating the generalizability of behavior shown during the SI to that shown under more naturalistic conditions—the conditions that will ultimately test the success of ameliorative interventions.

Modification of Type A Behavior

It has been suggested that attempts to change Type A behavior are premature at this time. Certainly, the design of maximally effective interventions for Type A behavior depends on making needed progress and development in clarifying the behavior pattern, its measurement, and the mechanisms by which it produces its effects. Nevertheless, theoretical understanding of Type A behavior may be promoted by intervention research. Carefully controlled, systematic investigations of alternative intervention strategies could shed light on the behavior pattern and its role in CHD. Such studies, however, will be forced to grapple with several problematic issues that make Type A intervention a unique challenge.

Choosing the Target Behavior

The first issue is identification of the target behavior on which to intervene (Roskies, 1980). The Type A behavior pattern is a constellation of descriptive characteristics, many of which were presented earlier in Table 3.1. There are two major approaches to Type A intervention: (*a*) altering the constellation of characteristics by using a "shotgun" approach directed at changing as many of the characteristics as possible; and (*b*) changing only the characteristic that is responsible for the increased risk.

The first strategy, global change of the Type A lifestyle, has disadvantages. Not all of the Type A characteristics have been shown to be associated with CHD risk. In fact, among those characteristics that have been examined for their predictive power, there appear to be inconsistencies across measures. For example, while the interview rating of impatience is predictive of CHD (Matthews, *et al.,* 1977), the Speed and Impatience subscale of the JAS is not an adequate CHD predictor (Jenkins *et al.,* 1974). Without additional research to identify which characteristics of the behavior pattern are related to CHD, global interventions that attempt to accomplish the very difficult task of changing lifestyle might eliminate many Type A characteristics without altering the individual's CHD risk.

Despite the current lack of information concerning specific coronary-prone target behaviors, one might still advocate global interventions for the Type A behavior pattern as long as the interventions had no suspected negative consequences. However, unlike many of the behavior patterns of neurotic and psychotic individuals, the Type A behavior pattern initially may be adaptive for some individuals. Mettlin's (1976) research, for example, indicates that Type A behavior may be an integral factor in the modern occupational career. It has been suggested previously that Type A behavior is not necessary for professional success, and that many Type B persons are corporate executives (Friedman & Rosenman, 1974); nonetheless, in support of Mettlin's assertion, a number of independent studies have found Type A behavior to be positively correlated with socioeconomic status as defined in terms of education and occupation (cf. Zyzanski, 1978). It should be noted that, to date, there has been no systematic research on the impact of changing various characteristics of Type A behavior on immediate or long-term productivity, professional advancement, or accomplishment. In the absence of such research, it might be considered questionable to embark on global lifestyle changes, particularly with individuals who have no history of CHD, since doing so may interfere with career aspirations and success.

The second approach to intervention calls for a specific key target behavior on which to focus treatment—preferably a specific behavior that is related to the mechanism by which Type A behavior leads to CHD. Unfortunately, such a key target behavior has not yet been identified.

Evaluation

The second major issue that Type A interventions must address is evaluation. Outcome measures are required to determine the effectiveness of any intervention; however, the most important measures for modification of Type A behavior, actual CHD morbidity and mortality, are not practical for intervention studies, particularly those using healthy subjects. The SI and the JAS, while valid and reliable measures of Type A behavior, were not designed to assess the effectiveness of interventions, and thus may not serve well as process or outcome measures. For example, as the Type A behavior pattern becomes better known, it is possible that the interview, and perhaps the JAS, will be recognized by subjects as Type A measures and will become vulnerable to faking. In addition, the JAS contains personal history items that present problems for repeated administrations because they will not change following treatment (e.g., "When you were in high school or college did you play on any athletic teams?")

Research on Type A interventions has utilized assessments of other CHD risk factors (e.g., blood pressure, serum cholesterol, and serum triglyceride levels) as outcome measures. Although these are definite candidates for inclusion in an evaluation battery, they are not the most sensitive measures of Type A behavior change because Type A has been shown to carry the risk of CHD independent of these factors (Brand *et al.,* 1976). Thus, an intervention might be very effective in reducing CHD risk from Type A behavior without modifying other CHD risk factors.

The lack of adequate outcome measures, with the exception of actual CHD status, makes it difficult to evaluate interventions or to interpret their results. This problem is magnified if one is interested in intervening in the Type A behavior of women and children, groups for which the SI and the JAS have not yet been clearly demonstrated to predict CHD.

Target Populations

Another important issue concerns the target populations appropriate for Type A intervention. Individuals who have developed CHD are obviously candidates for interventions. It may also be possible for Type A interventions to play a role in preventing heart disease if such interventions are introduced prior to or early in the disease process. However, according to Friedman (1978), early intervention may prove difficult. Friedman has observed that Type A individuals free of CHD do not tend to demonstrate the strong motivation for change that characterizes the patient who has had a myocardial infarction. The possible benefit to healthy individuals of avoiding heart disease in later years may not outweigh societal rewards of Type A behavior. Strategies to enhance motivation for early, preventive behavior change (e.g., enlisting support from the patient's spouse and family, or providing biofeedback in terms of changes in cardiovascular functioning) need to be explored.

Despite the fact that specific answers to the three issues described in this chapter require research, a number of investigators have studied possible strategies for changing Type A behavior in both postcoronary and healthy subjects. The following represents a review of Type A intervention studies which are available in the published literature or are currently in progress.

In *Type A Behavior and Your Heart,* Friedman and Rosenman (1974) provided suggestions, based on clinical experience, for altering Type A behavior. They recommended instructing or counseling Type A individuals with the goal of changing the coronary-prone behavior pattern and fostering a new philosophical outlook and style of life. In a subsequent paper, Rosenman and Friedman (1977) described their current approach as one that emphasizes (*a*) group counseling; (*b*) self-monitoring of Type A behaviors (such as interrupting and hurrying the speech of others); (*c*) use of self-instructions to respond to situations without Type A behaviors; (*d*) instruction and practice of deceleration of motor activities and deep muscle relaxation; (*e*) development of avocational interests that are not likely to elicit Type A characteristics (such as time urgency and hostility); (*f*) use of behavioral contracts with rewards and punishments contingent upon performing certain target behaviors; and (*g*) self-management of the environment to reduce the potential for environmentally induced Type A behavior (e.g., reduce telephone interruptions at work). In a pilot study of this intervention approach, 12 Type A men met for 18 months in a group led by a psychoanalyst (Rosenman & Friedman, 1977). While the anecdotal reports of this treatment strategy are encouraging, they are not conclusive. There is a need for controlled research using several measures of Type A behavior change and CHD risk.

An ambitious examination of the effectiveness of the type of intervention recommended by Rosenman and Friedman (1977) is currently underway at the Harold Brunn Institute of Mt. Zion Hospital in San Francisco under the direction of Dr. Friedman. In this study, 600 postcoronary Type A and Type B patients are receiving group treatment incorporating a broad spectrum of intervention strategies over a 5-year period. These strategies include self-observation and monitoring to increase awareness of Type A behavior, self-management of the environment, behavioral contracting, deep muscle relaxation, anxiety management training, and cognitive restructuring directed toward modifying Type A behavior. The morbidity and mortality rate of this treatment group will be compared with that of a control group consisting of 300 post-myocardial-infarction patients receiving standard medical treatment and health education. The critical questions addressed by this study are whether there will be differences in morbidity and mortality rates between the groups following treatment and whether the morbidity and mortality rates of Type A postcoronary patients will be reduced with behavior therapy.

Rahe and his colleagues (Rahe, 1975; Rahe, O'Neil, & Arthur, Note 9) also studied the effectiveness of group therapy for postcoronary patients. Although this study did not assess patients on the Type A behavior pattern, it provided evidence of the potential effectiveness of the approach that is currently being used in the Harold Brunn Institute study. From a group of 60 cases, 40 were randomly selected to receive short-term therapy (4–6 sessions) while the remaining 20 served as the control group. Unfortunately, the behavior pattern of these patients was not assessed. The therapy focused on discussion of an educational booklet that contained heart attack treatment and rehabilitation information. At an 18-month follow-up, the patients who had participated in the group therapy program had fewer rehospitalizations than the control group and reported less time urgency and overwork.

While the preceding studies of Type A or postcoronary interventions represent relatively global behavior change strategies, several investigators have studied the effectiveness of teaching Type A individuals specific alternative strategies for managing their stress responses. For example, Roskies and her associates compared a group receiving psychotherapy intervention with a group receiving behavioral intervention (Roskies, Spevack, Surkis, Cohen, & Gilman, 1978). In this study, 29 healthy, male, Type A volunteer subjects between 39 and 57 years of age were randomly assigned to either a psychotherapy or a behavior therapy group. The psychotherapy treatment was conducted by two psychoanalytically oriented therapists and focused on modifying the need of the Type A subjects to master and control their environment. The behavior therapy group focused on teaching the Type A individuals to modify their behavior in response to stress. Specifically, subjects in the behavioral treatment group were taught to relax using a sequence of progressive relaxation procedures followed by abbreviated muscle relaxation and specific neck, shoulder, and breathing exercises. After acquiring these relaxation skills, the subjects were taught cue-related relaxation and "emergency" relaxation procedures (i.e., relaxing while in stressful situations). The subjects in the behavior therapy group were instructed to practice their relaxation skills for two 15-min sessions daily, and to monitor their tension levels. During the monitoring, if subjects noted tension, they were instructed to use their relaxation skills to reduce the tension to a comfortable level.

Following the 14-week course of therapy, Roskies *et al.* (1978) compared the effectiveness of the two treatment approaches on a number of outcome measures. Both groups showed significant pre–post treatment reductions in mean systolic blood pressure, serum cholesterol levels, self-reported time pressure, and number of self-reported psychological symptoms. Significant differences were not found on either mean diastolic blood pressure or serum triglycerides.

There are two difficulties associated with the Roskies *et al.* (1978) investigation. First, in the absence of a control group (waiting list or placebo), it is difficult to interpret the similar effects of the two treatment approaches. Nevertheless, the reductions in serum cholesterol and self-report changes that Roskies *et al.* (1978) observed suggest that Type A behavior and CHD risk may be amenable to change; these findings await replication in a controlled study that is underway at this time (Roskies, Kearney, Spevack, Surkis, Cohen, & Gilman, 1979). The second difficulty with the study is that the numerous outcome measures did not include an appropriate measure for assessing Type A behavior changes. It is possible that although the available outcome measures did not necessarily reflect this improvement, either or both of the treatment strategies was successful in reducing the CHD risk associated with the Type A subjects. Thus, the lack of appropriate Type A behavior change measures makes it difficult to evaluate the effectiveness of the psychoanalytic and behavioral treatment approaches.

An intervention known as Cardiac Stress Management Training (CSMT) was developed by Suinn (1980) to teach coping strategies for stress. This training program is based on two procedures: Anxiety Management Training (AMT) and Visuo-Motor Behavior Rehearsal (VMBR). AMT involves training patients to identify physical cues of arousal to stress and teaching them to use relaxation techniques to reduce their stress response. VMBR is covert rehearsal procedure designed to assist patients in utilizing non-Type A or alternative behaviors in those situations that habitually elicit Type A responses. According to Suinn, the purpose of CSMT is to encourage behavior patterns that retain the patient's productivity without the CHD risks of the previous Type A pattern.

Suinn has performed two controlled studies of CSMT. In the first evaluation study (Suinn, 1975), 10 postcoronary patients participated in CSMT in addition to standard medical management. Another 10 postcoronary patients receiving only the usual rehabilitation served as a control group. Following six sessions of CSMT, the treatment group showed significantly greater reductions in serum cholesterol and triglycerides than did the control group. These results, though encouraging, are difficult to interpret since Type A measures were not used as either an indication of initial status or an indication of behavior change.

In a subsequent study, Suinn and Bloom (1978) evaluated CSMT with a nonclinical population. Unlike the previous studies, the JAS was administered to measure Type A behavior before and following the six treatment sessions. Fourteen Type A subjects (12 males and 2 females) were randomly assigned either to the nontreatment control group or to the treatment group which received six sessions of CSMT. Following treatment, the CSMT group, relative to the control subjects, showed significant reductions on the State and Trait Anxiety scales of the STAI (Spielberger, Gorsuch, & Lushene, 1970) and on the JAS Speed and Impatience and Hard-Driving subscales. The JAS Type A scale was not significantly changed following treatment. It is important to note that only the Type A scale on the JAS has been found to predict CHD—the other subscales have not (Jenkins *et al.*, 1974). Unlike the study by Roskies *et al.* (1978), blood pressure reductions were noted but not significant. In addition, contrary to Suinn's (1975) previous findings with postcoronary patients, changes in serum lipid levels were not significant.

In a recent intervention study, Jenni and Wollersheim (1979) evaluated the effectiveness of two treatments, Stress Management Training and Cognitive Therapy, for reducing stress in 10 subjects classified as Type A by an oral interview (not specified as the SI). Pre- and posttreatment measures of anxiety and self-reported Type A behavior were assessed using the STAI and the Bortner Type A scale (Bortner, 1969), respectively. Significant reductions in both state and trait anxiety were observed under each treatment regimen and significant reductions in Bortner Type A scale scores were observed only for the Cognitive Therapy group. Recognizing that Type A behavior and anxiety are not synonymous, Jenni and Wollersheim found no correlation ($r = .01$) between the Bortner Type A scale and trait anxiety in their data. This finding is consistent with Chesney *et al.* (Note 5) in showing no correlation between Type A behavior ratings based on the SI and measures of anxiety. Since the Bortner Type A scale is not an anxiety measure, the results reported by Jenni and Wollersheim (1979) suggest that the cognitive therapy approach may have changed self-reported Type A behavior as well as anxiety. However, the small treatment-group sizes, the use of identical as opposed to parallel forms of pre- and posttreatment measures, and the lack of evidence regarding the predictive validity of the Bortner scale for heart disease, preclude drawing definitive conclusions concerning CHD risk reduction from this study.

In summary, among the specific intervention studies, the results reported by Roskies *et al.* (1978), Suinn (1975), and Jenni and Wollersheim (1979) are encouraging but difficult to interpret as reflecting CHD risk reduction in the absence of significant changes on predictive measures. The results reported by the above-noted investigators, like those of the other intervention studies reviewed here, suggest that the Type A pattern may be sensitive to treatment. However, in the absence of appropriate outcome measures, the assessment of the effectiveness of CSMT and other Type A interventions can lead only to tentative conclusions.

Future Directions

Today, with heart disease the leading cause of death in the United States, and with the Type A behavior pattern a recognized risk factor for CHD, investigators of Type A behavior have begun to attempt to modify Type A behavior and, in so doing, reduce its CHD risk. The best assessment procedure for Type A is the SI, a procedure that serves well as a diagnostic tool, but is inadequate to meet the needs of current intervention research.

Specifically, the global nature of the SI assessment does not indicate appropriate target behaviors or treatment approaches. In addition, the SI does not currently lend itself to outcome evaluation. The interview ratings do not permit assessment of progress during treatment and may be insensitive to change even after successful intervention. Alternative forms of the SI are necessary since the current interview may be vulnerable to faking on repeated measurements, especially by subjects who have participated in a treatment program that has focused on modifying behaviors incorporated in SI ratings (e.g., speed stylistics, competition). Thus, the functional needs of the SI have changed to include more specific identification of target behaviors, selection of treatment strategies, and evaluation of treatment outcome.

Building upon the foundation laid by the SI, research in Type A behavior assessment must now be directed toward the new functions. With regard to intervention, controlled clinical research is needed that will reflect the new findings emerging from other areas of Type A behavior investigation, such as psychophysiological reactivity (for a review, see

Dembroski, MacDougall, Herd & Shields, Note 10). The following recommendations for this intervention research have been adapted from those made by Gentry and Suinn (1978) at the Forum on Coronary-Prone Behavior:

Selection of Target Behaviors

With reduction of CHD risk as the ultimate goal of Type A interventions, these should be focused on those target behaviors that appear to be significantly related to CHD status.

Operational Definitions of Target Behaviors

As Gentry and Suinn (1978) suggested, it is recommended that the intervention method be directly related to the particular target behavior under study. The constellation of Type A characteristics that is emerging from accumulated research suggests that the Type A behavior pattern is multidimensional with cognitive, behavioral, emotional, and physiological components. As potential target behaviors are proposed, they should be operationally defined in terms of the components, and intervention strategies should be selected that directly relate to them. For example, cognitive restructuring (Meichenbaum, 1977) would be appropriate for changing cognitive behaviors. To modify overt behaviors, behavior change strategies such as modeling or contingency contracting could be applied. If the target is an emotion (e.g., anxiety or fear), strategies developed to change emotional responses such as anxiety management training (Suinn, 1980) would be used. Physiological change strategies such as biofeedback of autonomic arousal or the administration of propranolol would be applicable if the target behaviors were defined in physiological terms.

Individually Tailored Interventions

It is likely that not all the components of coronary-prone behavior operate with equal frequency, intensity and duration in all Type A individuals. By assessing target behaviors that are operationally defined in terms of each component, it may be possible for interventions to be tailored to individual behavior patterns. For example, a Type A person may report little in terms of behavioral, emotional, or cognitive "Type A" responses, but show marked sympathetic nervous system response to uncontrollable stressors. One might then consider using biofeedback to reduce the physiological reaction, while leaving the patient's behavior, thoughts, and feelings unchanged. Further research examining the feasibility and relative effectiveness of such tailored approaches is needed.

Generalization, Adherence, and Maintenance

Type A behavior has been defined as a "style of life," a habitual manner of responding to the environment. The Type A intervention literature suggests that short-term treatments may bring about changes related to Type A behavior (cf. Suinn & Bloom, 1978). These quick gains, as Suinn (1980) pointed out, may be important given the Type A individual's characteristic impatience. However, extrapolating from other behavior-change literature, specifically that on smoking cessation and obesity, it is likely that generalization, long-term adherence, and maintenance of change—all of which may be critical in sustaining reduction of CHD risk—may require innovative or modified treatment strategies. Further research is needed to explore these problems and the effectiveness of their possible solutions such as ambulatory psychophysiological monitoring for biofeedback of response generalization and "booster" sessions to increase compliance and maintenance.

Evaluation Methodology

Operational definitions of target behavior may assist in intervention evaluations. However, while the assessment methodology and actual understanding of Type A behavior continue to evolve, it would be beneficial to collect measures of the multiple components of Type A behavior rather than focusing assessment on only single target behaviors. For example, in the evaluation of CSMT (Suinn, 1980), physiological reactivity data could be collected in addition to the self-report and biochemical assessments. These multiple measures might provide insight into the mechanisms by which Type A behaviors are changed.

Environmental Change

Finally, since the environment may play a role in Type A behavior, both by presenting stressors to Type A individuals and reinforcing their coronary-prone behavior, it is recommended that intervention strategies that are designed to change the environment be studied. First, it would be of interest to evaluate the effects of programs designed to train Type A individuals to modify their physical and social environments in order to reduce the amount of stress, and to change the reinforcement contingencies for their Type A behavior. The second environmental change strategy for Type A intervention goes beyond treating the Type A individual and focuses on modifying home and work environments that could change or prevent Type A behavior and its CHD risks, while maintaining personal and social productivity.

These approaches to environmental change may appear inviting. However, it is important to recall that Type A intervention strategies are in the developmental stage and that the lack of clearly defined target behaviors and assessment procedures has proven to be a serious stumbling block in even the simplest approach to modifying Type A behavior. In summary, we do not have the answers to two key questions: What components of Type A behavior are associated with CHD risk? And, if these behaviors are changed, is CHD risk reduced? These answers will begin to emerge when issues such as those discussed here are addressed and when controlled clinical research trials have been performed.

Reference Notes

1. Matthews, K. A., & Krantz, D. S. *Components of Pattern A associated with interview assessment and coronary artery disease: A case control study.* Unpublished manuscript, Kansas State University, 1978.
2. Rosenman, R. H. Personal communication, March 1978.
3. Vickers, R. *A short measure of the Type A personality.* Unpublished manuscript, Ann Arbor: University of Michigan, Institute for Social Research, 1973.
4. Rahe, R. H., Hervig, L., & Rosenman, R. H. *Heritability of Type A Behavior.* Paper presented at the Annual Meeting of the American Psychosomatic Society, New Orleans, March, 1978.
5. Chesney, M. A., Black, G. W., Feuerstein, M., Rosenman, R. H., Calligan, M. D., & Chadwick, J. H. *Coronary prone behavior: Characteristics and therapeutic implications.* Paper presented at the Annual Meeting of the American Psychological Association, Toronto, Canada, August, 1978.
6. Haynes, S. Personal communication, January 1979.
7. Horvath, M. Personal communication, October 1979.
8. Matthews, K. A., & Angulo, J. *Measurement of the Type A behavior pattern in children: Assessment of children's competitiveness, impatience-anger, and aggression.* Unpublished manuscript, 1979.
9. Rahe, R. H., O'Neil, T., & Arthur, R. J. *Brief group therapy following myocardial infarction: Eighteen-month follow-up of a controlled trial.* Unpublished manuscript. San Diego, Ca: Naval Health Research Center, 1975.
10. Dembroski, T. M., MacDougall, J. M., Herd, J. A., & Shields, J. L. *The Type A coronary-prone behavior pattern: A review.* Unpublished manuscript, Eckerd College, 1979.

References

Blumenthal, J. A., Williams, R., Kong, Y., Schanberg, S. M., & Thompson, L. W. Type A behavior and angiographically documented coronary disease. *Circulation,* 1978, *58,* 634–639.

Bortner, R. W. A short rating scale as a potential measure of Pattern A behavior. *Journal of Chronic Diseases,* 1969, *22,* 87–91.

Bortner, R. W. & Rosenman, R. H. The measurement of Pattern A behavior. *Journal of Chronic Diseases,* 1967, *20,* 525–533.

Brand, R. J., Rosenman, R. H., Jenkins, C. D., Sholtz, R. I., & Zyzanski, S. J. Comparison of coronary heart disease prediction in the Western Collaborative Group Study using the Structured Interview and the Jenkins Activity Survey assessments of the coronary-prone Type A behavior pattern. *Journal of Chronic Diseases,* in press.

Brand, R. J., Rosenman, R. H., Sholtz, R. I., & Friedman, M. Multivariate prediction of coronary heart disease in the Western Collaborative Group Study compared to the findings of the Framingham Study. *Circulation,* 1976, *53,* 938-955.

Butensky, A., Faralli, V., Heebner, D., & Waldron, I. Elements of the coronary-prone behavior pattern in children and teen-agers. *Journal of Psychosomatic Research,* 1976, *20,* 439-444.

Caffrey, B. Behavior patterns and personality characteristics related to prevalence rates of coronary heart disease. *Journal of Chronic Diseases,* 1968, *21,* 191-204.

Caplan, R. D., Cobb, S., French, J. R. P., Harrison, R. V., & Pinneau, S. R. *Job demands and worker health.* (U.S. Department of Health, Education, and Welfare, Publication No. [NIOSH] 75-160). Washington, D.C.: U.S. Government Printing Office, 1975.

Dembroski, T. M., MacDougall, J. M., & Lushene, R. Interpersonal interaction and cardiovascular response in Type A subjects and coronary patients. *Journal of Human Stress,* 1979, *5,* 28-36.

Dembroski, T. M., MacDougall, J. M., Shields, J. L., Petitto, J., & Lushene, R. Components of the Type A coronary-prone behavior pattern and cardiovascular responses to psychomotor performance challenge. *Journal of Behavioral Medicine,* 1978, *1,* 159-176.

Dimsdale, J. E., Hackett, T. P., Block, P. C., & Hutter, A. M. Type A personality and extent of coronary atherosclerosis. *American Journal of Cardiology,* 1978, *42,* 583-586.

Forum on Coronary-Prone Behavior. *Coronary-prone behavior and coronary heart disease: A critical review.* Report of the Coronary-Prone Behavior Review Panel. Submitted to the National Heart, Lung and Blood Institute, National Institutes of Health, 1978.

Frank, K. A., Heller, S. S., Kornfeld, D. S., Sporn, A. A., & Weiss, M. B. Type A behavior pattern and coronary angiographic findings. *Journal of the American Medical Association,* 1978, *240,* 761-763.

Friedman, E., Hellerstein, H., Eastwood, G., & Jones, S. Behavior pattern and serum cholesterol in two groups of normal males. *American Journal of Medical Science,* 1968, *255,* 237-244.

Friedman, M. Modifying "Type A" behavior in heart attack patients. *Primary Cardiology,* 1978, 9-13.

Friedman, M., & Rosenman, R. H. Association of specific overt behavior pattern with blood and cardiovascular findings—blood cholesterol level, blood clotting time, incidence of arcus senilis, and clinical coronary artery disease. *Journal of the American Medical Association,* 1959, *169,* (12) 1286-1296.

Friedman, M., & Rosenman, R. H. *Type A behavior and your heart.* New York: Knopf, 1974.

Friedman, M., Rosenman, R. H., Straus, R., Wurm, M., & Kositchek, R. The relationship of behavior Pattern A to the state of the coronary vasculature: A study of fifty-one autopsy subjects. *American Journal of Medicine,* 1968, *44,* 525-537.

Gentry, W. D., & Suinn, R. M. Behavioral intervention. In Forum on Coronary-Prone Behavior, *Coronary-prone behavior and coronary heart disease: A critical review.* Report of the Coronary-Prone Behavior Review Panel. Submitted to the National Heart, Lung, and Blood Institute, National Institutes of Health, 1978.

Gough, H. H., & Heilbrun, A. B. *The adjective checklist.* Palo Alto: Consulting Psychologists Press, 1975.

Haynes, S. G., Feinleib, M., Levine, S., Scotch, N., & Kannel, W. The relationship of psychosocial factors to coronary heart disease in the Framingham study: II. Prevalence of coronary heart disease. *American Journal of Epidemiology,* 1978, *107,* 384-402.

Haynes, S. G., Levine, S., Scotch, N., Feinleib, M., & Kannell, W. B. The relationship of psychosocial factors to coronary heart disease in the Framingham Study: Methods and risk factors. *American Journal of Epidemiology,* 1978, *107,* 362-383.

Heller, R. F. Type A behavior and coronary heart disease. *British Medical Journal,* 1979, *2,* 368.

Jenkins, C. D., Rosenman, R. H., & Friedman, M. Development of an objective psychological test for the determination of the coronary-prone behavior pattern in employed men. *Journal of Chronic Diseases,* 1967, *20,* 371-379.

Jenkins, C. D., Rosenman, R. H., & Friedman, M. Replicability of rating the coronary-prone behavior pattern. *British Journal of Preventive and Sociological Medicine,* 1968, *22,* 16-22.

Jenkins, C. D., Rosenman, R. H., & Zyzanski, S. J. Prediction of clinical coronary heart disease by a test for the coronary-prone behavior pattern. *New England Journal of Medicine,* 1974, *290,* 1271-1275.

Jenni, M. A., & Wollersheim, J. P. Cognitive therapy, stress management training, the Type A behavior pattern. *Cognitive Therapy and Research,* 1979, *3,* 61-73.

Keith, R., Lown, B., & Stare, F. Coronary heart disease and behavior patterns. *Psychosomatic Medicine,* 1965, *27,* 424-434.

Kittel, F., Kornitzer, M., Zyzanski, S. J., Jenkins, C. D., Rustin, R. M., & Degre, C. Two methods of assessing the Type A coronary-prone behavior pattern in Belgium. *Journal of Chronic Diseases,* 1978, *31,* 147-155.

Matthews, K. A. Caregiver—child interactions and Type A coronary-prone behavior pattern. *Child Development,* 1977, *48,* 1752-1756.

Matthews, K. A., Glass, D. C., Rosenman, R. H., & Bortner, R. W. Competitive drive, Pattern A, and coronary heart disease: A further analysis of some data from the

Western Collaborative Group Study. *Journal of Chronic Diseases*, 1977, *30*, 489–498.

Meichenbaum, D. *Cognitive-behavior modification: An integrative approach.* New York: Plenum, 1977.

Mettlin, C. Occupational careers and the prevention of coronary-prone behavior. *Social Science and Medicine,* 1976, *10,* 367–372.

Rahe, R. H. Liaison psychiatry on a coronary care unit. *Journal of Human Stress,* 1975, *1,* 13–21.

Rosenman, R. H., Brand, R. J., Jenkins, C. D., Friedman, M., Straus, R., & Wurm, M. Coronary heart disease in the Western Collaborative Group Study: Final follow-up experience of 8½ years. *Journal of the American Medical Association,* 1975, *233,* 872–877.

Rosenman, R. H., Brand, R. J., Sholtz, R. I., & Friedman, M. Multivariate prediction of coronary heart disease during 8.5 year follow-up in the Western Collaborative Group Study. *American Journal of Cardiology,* 1976, *37,* 903–910.

Rosenman, R. H., & Friedman, M. Association of specific behavior pattern in women with blood and cardiovascular findings. *Circulation,* 1961, *24,* 1173–1184.

Rosenman, R. H., & Friedman, M. Modifying Type A behavior pattern. *Journal of Psychosomatic Research,* 1977, 21, 323–331.

Rosenman, R. H., Friedman, M., Jenkins, C. D., Straus, R., Wurm, M., & Kositchek, R. The prediction of immunity to coronary heart disease. *Journal of the American Medical Association,* 1966, *198,* 1159–1162.

Rosenman, R. H., Friedman, M., Jenkins, C. D., Straus, R., Wurm, M., & Kositchek, R. Clinically unrecognized myocardial infarction in the Western Collaborative Group Study. *American Journal of Cardiology,* 1967, *19,* 776–782.

Rosenman, R. H., Friedman, M., Straus, R., Jenkins, C. D., Zyzanski, S. J., & Wurm, M. Coronary heart disease in the Western Collaborative Group Study—A follow-up experience of 4½ years. *Journal of Chronic Diseases,* 1970, *23,* 173–190.

Rosenman, R. H., Friedman, M., Straus, R., Wurm, M., Kositchek, R., Hahn, W., & Werthessen, N. T. A predictive study of coronary heart disease—The Western Collaborative Group Study. *Journal of the American Medical Association,* 1964, *189,* 103–110.

Roskies, E. Considerations in developing a treatment program for the coronary-prone (Type A) behavior pattern. In P. O. Davidson & S. M. Davidson (Eds.), *Behavioral medicine: changing health life styles.* New York: Brunner/Mazel, 1980.

Roskies, E., Kearney, H., Spevack, M., Surkis, A., Cohen, C., & Gilman, S. Generalizability and durability of treatment effects in an intervention program for coronary-prone managers. *Journal of Behavioral Medicine,* 1979, *2,* 195–208.

Roskies, E., Spevack, M., Surkis, A., Cohen, C., & Gilman, S. Changing the coronary-prone (Type A) behavior pattern in a non-clinical population. *Journal of Behavioral Medicine,* 1978, *1,* 201–216.

Scherwitz, L., Berton, K., & Leventhal, H. Type A assessment and interaction in the behavior pattern interview. *Psychosomatic Medicine,* 1977, *39,* 229–240.

Spielberger, C. D., Gorsuch, R. L., & Lushene, R. *State-trait anxiety inventory.* Palo Alto: Consulting Psychologists Press, 1970.

Suinn, R. M. Anxiety management training for general anxiety. In R. M. Suinn & R. Weigel (Eds.), *The innovative psychological therapies: Critical and creative contributions.* New York: Harper & Row, 1975.

Suinn, R. M. Pattern A behaviors and heart disease: Intervention approaches. In J. M. Ferguson & C. B. Taylor (Eds.), *The comprehensive book of behavioral medicine* (Vol. 1). Jamaica, N.Y.: Spectrum Publications, 1980.

Suinn, R. M., & Bloom, L. J. Anxiety management training for Pattern A behavior. *Journal of Behavioral Medicine,* 1978, *1,* 25–36.

Thurstone, L. L. *Thurstone temperament schedule.* Chicago: Science Research Associates, 1949.

Waldron, I. The coronary-prone behavior pattern, blood pressure, employment and socioeconomic status in women. *Journal of Psychosomatic Research,* 1978, *22,* 79–87.

Zyzanski, S. J. Associations of the coronary-prone behavior pattern. In T. M. Dembroski, S. M. Weiss, J. L. Shields, S. G. Haynes, & M. Feinleib. (Eds.), *Coronary-prone behavior.* New York: Springer-Verlag, 1978.

Zyzanski, S. J., Jenkins, C. D., Ryan, T. J., Flessas, A., & Everist, M. Psychological correlates of coronary angiographic findings. *Archives of Internal Medicine,* 1976, *136,* 1234–1237.

Zyzanski, S. J., & Jenkins, C. D. Basic dimensions of the coronary-prone behavior pattern. *Journal of Chronic Disease,* 1970, *22,* 781–795.

4

Assessment of Hypertension

IRIS B. GOLDSTEIN

Hypertension is generally defined as a state of chronically elevated blood pressure, usually above a level of 140/95 mmHg. This is subject to variability, however, since it is also defined in terms of a population of a given age. For a small percentage of the cases of hypertension (10%) a cause, such as kidney dysfunction, cerebral disease, coarctation of the aorta, or other physiological malfunctions can be found. For the majority of cases, however, there is no known etiology; these are termed "essential" (Eyer, 1975; Gutmann & Benson, 1971).

Although the exact etiology of essential hypertension is unknown, there is ample evidence to suggest that psychological factors are involved in its development (Cochrane, 1971; Davies, 1971; Glock & Lennard, 1956; Gutmann & Benson, 1971, Henry & Cassel, 1969; McGinn, Harburg, Julius, & McLeod, 1964; P. R. Robbins, 1969; Scotch & Geiger, 1963; D. Shapiro & Goldstein, in press). The precise role of these psychological factors, and how they influence hypertensive individuals, is a subject of considerable controversy. For example, research clearly shows that blood pressure is raised temporarily by emotional states, but there is very little evidence that these states, when prolonged, lead to hypertension. With the growth of interest in and research on the role of behavioral processes in the pathogenesis, treatment, and prevention of hypertension and other physical disorders, more and more attention is being given to the assessment of personality, individual differences, and behavioral patterns associated with such disorders.

The purpose of this chapter is to discuss the psychological techniques that have been used to assess hypertensives and to evaluate the usefulness of such techniques for future endeavors. Basically, the research in this area falls into two major categories. The first of these involves assessing hypertensives' reactions to stress by studying their reactivity to various stimuli. Investigators in such studies have compared the physiological responses of hypertensives to the reactions of normotensives. The underlying theory is that individuals who develop a persistently elevated blood pressure level will also exhibit a tendency to respond to emotionally disturbing events with abnormal increases in blood pressure.

The preparation of this chapter was supported by National Heart, Lung, and Blood Institute Research Grant HL-19568.

Medical Psychology
Contributions to Behavioral Medicine

ISBN 0-12-565960-1

A second group of studies concerns the assessment of the psychological characteristics of hypertensives. Such studies have generally used psychological tests and interviews to assess personality. The assumption underlying most of these studies is that hypertensives possess certain unique personality characteristics setting them apart from normotensives. Whether these characteristics have caused the hypertension or are a result of the disorder is not known.

In reviewing the assessment literature, an attempt will be made to determine if there is evidence to support the underlying assumptions of the research. Answers will be sought to the following two questions: (*a*) Is there anything unique about hypertensives' reactions to stress? and (*b*) Do hypertensives possess any personality characteristics that differentiate them from other individuals?

Before elaborating on assessment techniques in any detail, it is important to point out certain recurring problems in the studies, since they help to explain the lack of uniformity in results. Because of the complexities involved, methodology and experimental design differ greatly from one investigation to the next. A basic problem centers about the definition of hypertension. First of all, the various types of hypertension are not discriminated from one another, and essential hypertensives are often combined with those subjects whose symptoms are of endocrine, renal, or some other origin. Secondly, there is no agreement as to what level of arterial pressure defines hypertensives and differentiates them from normotensives. Smith (1977) believes that none of the arbitrary dividing lines which have been used in the past have any inherent validity. One experimenter may use a pressure as low as 120/80 mmHg as a dividing line, while another may go as high as 180/110 mm Hg (Pickering, 1968). Consequently, an individual who is labeled hypertensive for the purpose of one study may well be called normal in another. Finally, there is a lack of consistency in the utilization of systolic and diastolic pressures. Subjects may be selected on the basis of their systolic blood pressure, their diastolic pressure, or on some combination of the two.

Another basic difference that exists between investigations of hypertension is the number of blood pressure readings taken on a given individual. While there is no agreement on how many blood pressure measurements are necessary to obtain a stable value, the degree of intrasubject variability present (see Sokolow, Werdegar, Perloff, Cowan, & Brenenstuhl, 1970) can mask small differences between groups being compared. Furthermore, a single casual measurement can easily lead to the misclassification of a given individual (Smith, 1977).

Another major problem centers about the selection of subjects for the experimental group. Quite often they are taken from widely varying populations. Some researchers have obtained subjects from blood pressure extremes in so-called normal populations, thereby eliminating some of the problems that are associated with chronically ill individuals. More often, however, subjects are inpatients of medical facilities or are recruited from clinics. Because these people are patients, they are often treated differently and may be under a great deal of stress and anxiety. Having to take prescribed medications may lead to hypochondriacal concerns. Even if patients are off all drugs for purposes of the study, drug effects often persist for some undetermined length of time.

Probably one of the greatest concerns in hypertensive research is the selection of appropriate control groups. Just what constitutes the type of population with which hypertensives should be compared is not completely clear. Saslow, Gressel, Shobe, DuBois, and Schroeder (1950) indicated a need to control for age, sex, race, cultural pattern, education, occupation, and socioeconomic level. Many different types of populations have been utilized as controls, and in some studies there is no control group at all.

Assessing the Hypertensives' Reactions to Stressful Stimuli

A substantial portion of the literature has been concerned with the response of hypertensives to stress and the extent to which these reactions to various stimuli may differ from those of normotensives. The basic assumption of these investigations has been that patients with elevated blood pressure are also hyperreactive in response to a variety of stimuli. Concern here is with the concept of "reactivity" as contrasted with basal blood pressure levels.

The concept of blood pressure hyperreactivity among hypertensives is supported by the early investigations of Lacey (1950, 1956; Lacey, Bateman, & Van Lehn, 1953) and of Malmo (1957). According to Lacey's theory of "response specificity," individuals exhibit idiosyncratic patterns of somatic reactions to stress. The results of Malmo's research on "symptom stereotypy" indicate that under conditions of stress, individuals with psychosomatic complaints respond maximally with disturbances in certain "critical symptom areas." Engel and Bickford (1961) have also reported the existence of autonomic response specificity and the tendency for hypertensives to have overreactive blood pressure responses to environmental stressors.

In order to induce stress in hypertensives under laboratory conditions, a variety of stimuli, known as pressors, have been utilized by investigators. The term "pressor" refers to an externally applied stimulus used to induce a blood pressure response. Beginning with the interview technique, research utilizing various pressors will be described and evaluated in order to determine if the blood pressure reaction of hypertensives differs from that of normotensives.

Interview Data

Stressful Content of Interview Early clinical investigators of hypertensives noted fluctuations in their patients' blood pressures during various interview sessions. As far back as 1920, O'Hare (1920) commented on the blood pressure elevation which patients showed in response to a discussion of life problems. Alexander (1939) also noted that blood pressures among hypertensive patients were markedly elevated during sessions which were particularly stressful or disturbing to them. With a very small number of patients, Schneider and Zangari (1951) revealed that whenever hypertensives became anxious during an interview, their systolic and diastolic blood pressures rose. By introducing conflictive topics, Wolf, Pfeiffer, Ripley, Winter, and Wolff (1948) were able to produce sharp increases in the blood pressure of hypertensives. While moderate blood pressure increases occurred in a group of normotensives, both the intensity and duration of their reactions were markedly lower than the reactions of the hypertensives (see also Wolf, Cardon, Shepard, & Wolff, 1955). In a similar comparison of hypertensives and normotensives during a discussion of life situations, Groen, Hansen, Hermann, Schäfer, Schmidt, Selbmann, Vexküll, and Weckman (1977) concluded that hypertension is merely "a quantitative exaggeration of the same processes which regulate blood pressure in different situations in normotensive individuals [p. 307]."

Arousal of Hostility A consistent theme in the psychiatric literature has been the production of elevated blood pressures in hypertensives during the arousal of hostility (see pp. 42–43). Observing hypertensives during interviews, Van der Valk (1957) noted marked blood pressure increases in response to topics of rejection by others, hostility, or ambivalence towards parents. When patients were discussing material with hostile content, blood pressure was reported by Kaplan, Gottschalk, Macliocco, Rohovit, and Ross (1961) to rise in hypertensives and fall in normotensives. During discussions of disturbing interpersonal problems, Wolff and Wolf (1951) noted that resentment elevated blood pressure, while despair or depression lowered it. This phenomenon was particularly prevalent among hypertensives. Recording the blood pressure of essential hypertensives undergoing psychoanalysis, Moses, Daniels, and Nickerson (1956) found that anxiety raised blood pressure and rage elevated it to even higher levels.

Although Schachter (1957) did not produce emotional changes by means of an interview technique, his results substantiated interview studies by showing that hypertensives responded to both fear (threat of electric shock) and anger (the blundering and badgering of a technician) with significantly greater increases in blood pressure than did normotensives.

Personal Nature of Interview Other investigators have reported that the content of the interview is not the significant factor in producing a rise in blood pressure among hypertensives.

Hardyck, Singer, and Harris (1962) noted that among six hypertensive female patients, the degree of the patient's involvement in communicating information was important in determining her pressor response, regardless of what the information might be. In their observations of four hypertensive patients, Adler, Hermann, Schäfer, Schmidt, Schonecke and Vexküll (1976) found that blood pressure increased during the discussion of topics such as personal failure or loss of status.

Pfeiffer and Wolff (1950) felt that the critical variable during the interview was the emotional conflict that was induced by the discussion of topics of important personal significance. Innes, Miller, and Valentine (1959), in a study of hypertensives, neurotics, and controls, reported that blood pressure rose when there were many self-references and when the rate of speech was rapid. Results from this study and that of Pfeiffer and Wolff indicated that both hypertensives and controls showed a rise in blood pressure during the discussion of personal topics but that the return to baseline occurred more rapidly in the controls than in the hypertensives. Mckegney and Williams (1967) and Williams, Kimball, and Williard (1972) also indicated that the greatest diastolic blood pressure elevation in both hypertensives and normotensives occurred during the personal discussion phase of an interview, but that the effect was most marked among the hypertensives.

The major methodological problem with most of these interview studies is that control groups were often absent and the results were frequently based on very small samples. The studies also tended to lack systematic sampling of blood pressures throughout the interviews. Furthermore, many of the early interviews consisted of gathering life histories. In spite of these problems, there is an amazing amount of consistency in this area: Hypertensive patients usually overreact in their blood pressure responses to interview situations.

The Cold Pressor and Other Stressful Stimuli

Cold Pressor Test The most frequently used technique for assessing blood pressure reactivity has been the cold pressor test. As originally developed by Hines and Brown (1933), the individual immerses his hand (although sometimes a foot is used) in crushed ice water of 4–5°C for approximately 1 min. Although all subjects showed some increase in blood pressure, Hines and Brown (1933, 1936) demonstrated larger increases in patients with essential hypertension. Furthermore, while the blood pressure of normotensives returned to basal level within two minutes after the hand had been removed from the water, hypertensives showed a greater delay in return to baseline (Hines, 1940). The hyperreactivity of hypertensives to cold pressor has been confirmed by Alam and Smirk (1938), Ayman and Goldshine (1938), Smithwick and Robertson (1951), and Thacker (1940). Voudoukis (1978), however, found that the cold pressor response was similar in normals and in hypertensive patients.

Hines (1940) also felt that people who had normal but highly reactive blood pressures in response to the cold pressor test were most likely to develop hypertension later in life. In a follow-up study of 21 originally normotensive hyperreactors, 38% had developed hypertension within 6 years, whereas none of the hyporeactors to the cold pressor test developed hypertension within the same time period. Subsequent attempts to utilize the cold pressor test as a predictor of the development of hypertension in normotensives have proved unsuccessful (Feldt & Wenstrand, 1942). In a 7-year follow-up study of 166 officers in the Army Air Corps (Armstrong & Rafferty, 1950) and a 12- and 18-year follow-up of 201 healthy men selected for flight training (Harlan, 1958) there was no correlation between the response to the cold pressor test and the development of hypertension.

Breath Holding Test A variety of other techniques have been utilized to assess the blood pressure response. In 1939 Ayman and Goldshine developed the breath holding test, a technique which, according to their reports, gave a similar but greater reaction than the cold pressor test (Ayman & Goldshine, 1939). The subject was asked to hold his breath in a quiet expiration, with nose and mouth closed for 20 sec. Assumedly the lack of oxygen or increase of carbon dioxide served as a stressor.

Exercise Alam and Smirk (1938) utilized exercise of an ischaemic limb as a pressor and found that blood pressure rise persisted in both normotensives and hypertensives after the exercise ceased. Exercise on a bicycle ergometer was similarly found to increase blood pressure in normotensives and hypertensives (Groen *et al.*, 1977).

Tilt Sannerstedt, Julius, and Conway (1970) studied young patients with borderline hypertension and a normotensive control group at rest and in tilted position after 10 min of 45° head-up tilt. During the tilt, only the controls showed a significant drop in mean brachial artery pressure. A 70° weight-bearing tilt led to a rise in diastolic blood pressure which was more marked in hypertensive patients than in normotensives (Hull, Wolthuis, Cortese, Longo, & Triebwasser, 1977).

Sorting Steel Balls The sorting of steel ball bearings of different sizes, interrupted by noises and variations in light intensity, was developed by Lorimer, Macfarlane, Provan, Duffy, and Lawrie (1971) as a stressor. Blood pressure rose in hypertensives and normotensives, but the increases were significantly greater in the hypertensives.

Movies and Thematic Apperception Test (TAT) Sapira, Scheib, Moriarity, and A. P. Shapiro (1971) recorded cardiovascular responses in normotensives and hypertensives during the viewing of two contrasting movies: one of a physician being rude to a patient and one in which the physician was quite pleasant. While the hypertensives responsed to both movies with a significantly greater pressor response than the normotensives, there were differences in the perception of the two groups, due to the hypertensives' inability to perceive any differences in the films. Weiner, Singer, and Reiser (1962) reported that hypertensives showed a less reactive pressor response to Thematic Apperception cards than a control group, due to their need "to protect themselves by basic vascular hyperreactivity [p. 494]."

Mental Stressors A fairly common mental stressor, the performance of arithmetic under duress, has led to increases in blood pressure which persisted longer in hypertensives than in a normotensive group (Brod, 1970; Brod, Fenel, Hejl, & Jurka, 1959). Similarly, Baumann, Helgard, Gödicke, Hartrodt, Naumann, and Läuter (1973) reported blood pressure increases in hypertensives which were twice as high as those of a control group and showed a protracted fall at the end of the task.

The blood pressure response to mental arithmetic was studied in adolescents with a genetic risk for hypertension (i.e., individuals who had at least one parent with essential hypertension). Results of this investigation revealed a sustained increase in diastolic blood pressure among labile subjects (i.e., those with widely varying blood pressure) and many of the genetic subjects, and the absence of an early drop in blood pressure as seen in the controls (Falkner, Onesti, Angelakos, Fernandes, & Langman, 1979).

Palmer (1950) recorded blood pressure in 100 hypertensive patients, while each patient leafed through a notebook on heart disease and high blood pressure. Although blood pressure increases were noted, the responses of controls were not studied. Nestel (1969) found the blood pressure response of labile hypertensive patients to the Raven Progressive Matrices (a set of complex visual puzzles) to be greater than that of a control group of normotensives. Moos and Engel (1962) attempted to establish conditioned reactions to meaningful, verbally presented stimuli and to a test for semantic generalization. The hypertensives responded to the stimuli with relatively high, sustained increases in systolic blood pressure.

Multiple Stimuli

Some investigators have used several stimuli in order to determine reactivity levels in hypertensive patients. Jost, Ruilmann, Hill, and Gulo (1952) presented the following sequence of stimuli: (*a*) an intense buzzer and light; (*b*) a series of questions, some of which were emotionally disturbing; (*c*) a digit span test with success and forced failure; and (*d*) a 4-min control run. In general, the blood pressure responses of the hypertensives were of greater intensity and duration than those of a control group.

Engel and Bickford (1961) stimulated normals and hypertensives with a car horn, mental arithmetic, proverb recognition, cold pressor, and exercise. Although several physiological measures were recorded, hypertensives reacted maximally in blood pressure, irrespective of the nature of the stimulus. In another study (A. P. Shapiro, 1961) saline injection, cold pressor, and a frustrating color reading task all produced blood pressure increases which were greater in hypertensives than in normotensives. Furthermore, normotensives with a family history of hypertensive disease showed significantly greater increases than those without such a history.

In contrast to the above studies, Hejl (1957) reported that normals and hypertensives responded to cold pressor and mental arithmetic with the same percent change in blood pressure. With the utilization of a postural test, a breath-holding task, a cold pressor test, and exercise, Remington, Lambarth, Moser, and Hoobler (1960) found no consistent differences among normotensive, labile, and hypertensive groups. They concluded that no single test could identify the hypertensive subject.

Thus it appears that a variety of stimuli, at least to the extent that they are perceived as stressful, produce blood pressure increases in almost all subjects. Although there is some disagreement regarding the precise effect stimuli have on hypertensives, their blood pressure reactions are generally more exaggerated and of longer duration than those of normotensives.

The nature of the stimulus may be an important determinant of the blood pressure response. For example, from his experiments, A. P. Shapiro (1961) concluded that so-called emotional stimuli (such as intravenous injection of saline) bring about greater increases in systolic blood pressure due to increased cardiac output, while purely physical stimuli (such as cold pressor) increase diastolic blood pressure through their effects on peripheral resistance.

A Future Role for Laboratory Stressors

Although there is little research on the utilization of laboratory stressors to evaluate procedures for lowering blood pressure, this appears to be a promising area. In her study, Patel (1977) attempted to determine if the pressor response to stressful stimuli would change as a result of training subjects to relax. When exercise and cold pressor tests were repeated at the beginning and end of the study, the group which had received relaxation training showed a significantly smaller rise in blood pressure than the control group.

In a study now in progress, D. Shapiro and Goldstein (Note 1) are evaluating the effectiveness of drugs and behavioral therapy in lowering the blood pressure of essential hypertensives. Not only have these treatments affected basal blood pressure levels, but they have also altered the pressor reactivity to cold pressor, a white noise, and a digit transformation task. There has been some indication that the blood pressure responses which patients displayed to the stressors is related to the success of the various therapies used.

Psychological Assessment of Hypertensives

In their appraisal of the literature, Glock and Lennard (1956) concluded that psychological factors play some role in the onset or development of hypertension. The exact nature of this role, however, is still debatable. Some specific hypotheses about the psychological makeup of hypertensives will be discussed, and an attempt will be made to see if there is sufficient evidence that hypertensives exhibit personality traits that differentiate them from other individuals. Except for the early case studies, the majority of these investigations share the common feature of having personality assessed by means of psychological tests, from the very subjective projective techniques to more objective self-report inventories.

Early Case Studies of Personality

The earliest investigations of the personality of hypertensives were conducted in clinical settings and were essentially case studies. Foremost among the early theories about hypertension was Franz Alexander's (1939) concept that chronic, inhibited, hostile impulses influence blood pressure changes. He suggested that in hypertensive patients there was a conflict between passive dependent feelings and strong aggressive hostile impulses. Over a period of time the continued inhibition of hostile tendencies led to permanent histological changes and a chronic elevation of blood pressure. Not only did Alexander describe the hypertensives as inhibited and hostile, but neurotic as well.

The concepts of submissiveness, inhibition, and neurotic symptomatology have been reiterated quite frequently in early case studies of hypertensives (Binger, Ackerman, & Cohn, 1945; Dunbar, 1943; Hambling, 1951; Moses *et al.,* 1956; Rennie, 1939; L. L. Robbins, 1948). This material is reviewed in more detail by Buss (1961) and McGinn *et al.* (1964). Because there were no control groups in these studies, there is no substantial evidence that any of the characteristics associated with hypertensive patients are unique to their disorder. Furthermore, because patients in these investigations were seen in private psychoanalytic practices, neurotics from middle class backgrounds tended to be overrepresented in the sample. Finally, much of the psychoanalytic theory in which the studies have been rooted was stated in such a manner as to be untestable.

Studies of Prehypertensives

In an effort to understand the psychological characteristics associated with hypertension, some investigators have studied prehypertensives, individuals who have not yet been labeled "hypertensive" but who appear likely to develop hypertension as they grow older. Very often these studies of prehypertensives have been done on individuals at the higher end of the normal blood pressure continuum. For example, Hamilton (1942) found that high blood pressure in college students was associated with low assertiveness, low dominance, and susceptibility to anger. As compared to students with lower diastolic pressures, those with higher pressures showed some difficulty in adjustment on the Rorschach (Brower, 1947a), and exhibited depression and psychopathic behavior on the Minnesota Multiphasic Personality Inventory (MMPI) (Brower, 1947b). Harris, Sokolow, Carpenter, Freedman, and Hunt (1953) selected one sample of college women whose blood pressures exceeded 140/90 mmHg (prehypertensives) and another with blood pressures under 120/80 mmHg. All of the women role-played a drama that induced anger, and their behavior was rated by judges. The resulting ratings showed that more negative adjectives were used by observers to describe the "prehypertensives" and more positive words were chosen to describe the normals. Similar findings were observed four years later in a follow-up study (Kalis, Harris, Bennett, & Sokolow, 1961), and in a study of hypertensive women (Kalis, Harris, Sokolow, & Carpenter, 1957).

From a large population of college students, Harburg, Julius, McGinn, McLeod, and Hoobler (1964) took a series of blood pressure readings on each student: an initial one at registration; readings in the physician's office; and recordings by the subject at home. Among the various blood pressure measurements, there were significant but small associations between high blood pressure categories and the characterization of subjects as submissive, sensitive, and neurotic by the Sixteen Personality Factor questionnaire (16 PF). In addition, and providing a further indication of submissiveness, those subjects who had single high systolic readings (labiles) on their first entry into the physician's office were more likely to yield in an argument and change their opinions to agree with their partners whose initial systolic readings were low.

In an examination of college records of men who later developed hypertension, Paffenbarger, Thorne and Wing (1968) found that the self-appraised personality trait of being "subject to nervousness" was the only one out of a total of 104 traits that showed a significant correlation with later hypertension. Brunswick and Collette (1977) interviewed and rated a sample of black adolescent boys and girls on 11 indicators of well-being and found that the high blood pressure group scored in a direction indicative of emotional problems. Group differences, however, were not statistically significant.

In a series of studies by Thomas and her colleagues (Bruce & Thomas, 1953; Thomas, 1961, 1967) psychological tests were administered to medical students who were divided into groups according to the presence or absence of a parental history of hypertension and/or coronary disease. The results of the Habits of Nervous Tension Questionnaire (HNT) showed no significant differences between groups for either depression, anxiety, or anger. On the Rorschach, individuals with a positive family history of hypertension exhibited more aggression-hostility, obsessive-compulsive trends, and feelings of inadequacy, but less impulsiveness and total affective reactivity than individuals with negative histories. Most of these results, however, were only suggestive and the authors felt that further substantiation was necessary.

With regard to studies in this area, the label of prehypertension must be used cautiously, since there has been very little substantiation of the fact that these subjects did indeed develop hypertension in later life. Furthermore, the blood pressures of many of the subjects would ordinarily be more representative of the "borderline hypertensive." Finally, one must be cautious about generalizing from a population as specialized as the college students used in the majority of these investigations.

Neuroticism

Results with Eysenck's Inventories Because many hypertensives who participated in early clinical studies showed signs of neurosis, investigators have attempted to determine whether or not they were more neurotic than individuals with normal blood pressure levels. The basic instrument used to assess neuroticism has been a paper and pencil inventory, Eysenck's Maudsley Personality Inventory (Eysenck, 1959; MPI).

Utilizing the MPI, Sainsbury (1960, 1964) concluded that patients with psychosomatic disorders, including hypertension, exhibited higher levels of neuroticism and were less extroverted than nonpsychosomatic controls. In 1962, Robinson found that a large sample of hypertensives scored as high on a Compound Neuroticism score (from the MPI and other tests) as a group of neurotic patients, thereby confirming Sainsbury's results.

In a later study, however, Robinson (1964) concluded that patients who had high blood pressure but had not been previously diagnosed as hypertensive were no more neurotic than a group of randomly selected individuals. He suggested that neurotic hypertensives were more likely to be selected for hospital treatment because of their symptoms or because of selection by their own physicians. Furthermore, he found that hypertensive patients who did not consult with their doctors had fewer psychological symptoms (which positively correlated with neuroticism scores on the MPI) than those patients who saw their doctors (Robinson, 1969). Using the Eysenck Personality Inventory (EPI), a newer version of the MPI, on undiagnosed hypertensives, Cochrane (1973) confirmed Robinson's results and found no relationship between blood pressure and neuroticism.

In a relatively homogeneous group of factory workers, Davies (1970) found that individuals with high blood pressure readings had fewer functional symptoms, lower neuroticism scores on the EPI, and gave less frequent histories of a neurotic childhood. While such results were exactly opposite to early studies linking neurosis with hypertension, Cochrane (1973) claimed that the blood pressures of Davies' subjects were not high enough to characterize them as hypertensive.

Hypertensive patients and healthy men from industry were given the following three questionnaires: EPI, 16 PF, and Cornell Medical Index (CMI). Test differences centered around a syndrome described as neurosis, felt to be due to the hypertensive's reaction to the role of patient. Because the patient group differed markedly from the healthy group, Kidson (1973) investigated the nonpatients and found that these subjects' diastolic pressures were negatively correlated with neuroticism, a finding similar to that of Davies.

Results with Other Instruments Sandberg and Bliding (1976) obtained a single blood pressure reading (a measure of lability) from a sample of Swedish Army trainees. On a 32-item scale of neurosis, they observed no differences between men with higher and with lower blood pressure readings. Furthermore, hypertensive patients were no more likely to display psychiatric symptoms than any other group of patients (Hodes & Rogers, 1976). Mann (1977) also found no correlation between blood pressure and neurotic symptoms assessed during a standard interview. In an investigation of a predominantly black population, Meyer, Derogatis, Miller, and Reading (1978) concluded that fewer patients with hypertension are in need of psychiatric consultation than are patients with other complaints.

Apparently there is no sound evidence to suggest that hypertensives are any more neurotic than their normotensive counterparts. If patients are selected for study before they are aware of their hypertension, they are less likely to exhibit any neurotic symptoms. Results of a study of Kasl and Cobb (1970) indicated that among a sample of men those, whose blood pressures remained high longest, not only reported longer lasting subjective stress but scored lower on Block's Ego Resilience Scale (from the MMPI), indicating poor adjustment. Perhaps the hypertensive is exhibiting anxiety about the possible consequences of the disorder.

Depression and Anxiety

Closely related to the concept of neurosis are the symptoms of anxiety and depression. In an investigation of 25 severely depressed patients, Heine, Sainsbury and Chynoweth (1969) found that ratings of anxiety and agitation, but not those of depression (from the Hamilton Depression Rating Scale) correlated with blood pressure levels when patients were ill. With larger numbers of depressed patients and the addition of a control group, Heine and Sainsbury (1970) reported that "repeated spells of depressive illness, when characterized by anxiety and agitation, lead to a sustained rise in blood pressure [p. 128]." When chronically ill patients were given the Zung Self-Rating Depression Scale, there was no correlation between depression and hypertension. As a matter of fact, anxiety was the only clinical diagnosis to relate significantly with both depression and hypertension. One must bear in mind, however, the fact that these studies of depressed patients were conducted on a very select population, the elderly or chronically ill. With a larger sample of subjects with less chronic disorders, Wheatley, Balter, and Levine (1975) found no significant differences between hypertensive and control groups on self-rating and physicians' ratings of depression, anger-hostility, or anxiety.

Suppressed Hostility

Since Alexander (1939) and his contemporaries, hypertensive patients have been described as being incapable of overtly expressing hostility. Saul, Sheppard, Selby, Lhamon, Sachs, and Master (1954) found that dreams of college students with high blood pressures were significantly more hostile than dreams of students with lower pressures. Hypertensives also yielded a higher proportion of hostile items in verbal samples than a group of controls (Kaplan *et al.,* 1961).

Rosenzweig Picture Frustration Study (PFS) A projective technique designed to assess hostility is the PFS. By eliciting reactions to 24 cartoon-like situations, the PFS purports to reveal patterns of response to everyday situations in terms of direction of aggression (extrapunitive, intropunitive, or impunitive) and type of reaction (obstacle-dominant, ego-defensive, or need-persistive) (Rosenzweig, Fleming, & Clark, 1947).

While Matarazzo (1954) found no differences between hypertensives and their controls on the PFS and the Allport Ascendance-Submission Test, there were significant behavioral differences in overt behavioral aggression, in that a much larger percentage of controls refused to complete a task for which they were severely criticized. Lewinsohn's (1956) and McDonough's (1964) investigations of the PFS also failed to reveal significant differences in overt aggression between hypertensives and normotensives. Neiberg (1957) concluded that the arousal of hostility produces equivalent changes on the PFS in both hypertensives and normotensives, although during prestress conditions, hypertensives do show a greater inhibition of aggression.

The Rorschach Although analysis of hostile content of the Rorschach did not differentiate hypertensives from controls, other projective data did indicate that hypertensives are not necessarily aggressive, but see their environment as hostile and dangerous (Thaler, Weiner, & Reiser, 1957). Ostfeld and Lebovits (1959) revealed no differences in the hostile responses of black essential hypertensives and renal hypertensives on the Rorschach. Ostfeld and Shekelle (1967) defined three patterns of MMPI scores relating to psychological conflicts of hostility and passive-dependent characteristics. The resulting analysis of the data of a large sample of men in an industrial setting revealed no blood pressure differences between groups fitting any of the three MMPI patterns.

Other Measures of Hostility Using the CMI, the Taylor Manifest Anxiety Scale (MAS), and the Rorschach, Ghosh and Bashey (1966) revealed that carcinoma patients had significantly higher anxiety levels than a group of essential hypertensives, but that the hypertensives were much better at expressing anger and hostility. Such a picture of hypertension, however, may be more a function of the diseased condition of the carcinoma patients rather than of any personality characteristics prevalent in hypertensives. Pilowsky, Spalding, Shaw, and Korner (1973) failed to find significant correlations between various measures of cardiovascular functioning and a sentence completion test of aggressive responses.

The Hostility and Direction of Hostility Questionnaire (HDHQ), which provides a measure of total hostility and the degree to which it is directed either inward or outward, failed to differentiate among subjects in a large sample of volunteers with varying blood pressure levels (Cochrane, 1973). Mann (1977) also utilized the HDHQ and found that, in contrast to the hypothesis which claimed that the hypertensive was unable to express hostility, hypertensives were actually more hostile than normotensives. He admitted that the findings were unexpected and warranted further investigation.

In an extensive investigation of urban blacks, Naditch (1974) administered Rotter's Internal–External scale and Cantril's Self-Anchoring Striving scale. From such measures, he revealed a higher rate of hypertension among men who have a combination of high discontent and a perceived external locus of control, "an orientation in which people believe that they are unable to affect what they subjectively believe to be deficiencies in their lives [p. 112]." As Naditch pointed out, the feelings of chronic frustration to which such an orientation can lead certainly suggest that there may have been some underlying hostility present. It is not completely clear, however, that such hostility was necessarily repressed.

Evidence for the Existence of Suppressed Hostility in Hypertensives In a carefully executed study by Harburg, Erfurt, Hauenstein, Chape, Schull, and Schork (1973), blacks and whites in four areas of Detroit were interviewed in their homes and their blood pressures were recorded. A strong relationship was found to exist between suppressed hostility (from a specially developed scale measuring "Anger-In" and "Anger-Out") and high blood pressure, both of which were prevalent among black males in high stress areas. Furthermore, the darker the skin color, the more likely the existence of both suppressed hostility and hypertension.

The Anger-In Anger-Out scale was administered along with the Buss–Durkee Personality Inventory, the Institute for Personality and Ability Testing Anxiety scale (IPAT), and the 16 PF in an investigation of mild essential hypertensives divided into those with relatively elevated levels of plasma renin activity and those with normal renin levels. Unlike the high renin essential hypertensives who were found to be controlled, guilt-prone, and submissive with a high level of unexpressed anger, normal renin patients did not differ from normal control subjects (Esler, Julius, Zweifler, Randall, Harburg, Gardiner, & DeQuattro, 1977).

Due to varying results, no consistent conclusions can be reached regarding the relationship between hypertension and hostility. In general, there appears to be very little support for Alexander's hypothesis of inhibited aggression in hypertensives. The fact that positive findings were obtained with blacks suggests that such a hypothesis may be more valid in certain segments of the population than in others. Furthermore, suppressed hostility may be more prevalent among those individuals with elevated plasma renin activity, as Esler *et al.* (1977) have suggested. Recent evidence by Baer, Collins, Bourianoff, and Ketchel (1979) revealed that hypertensives reported more enhanced and longer lasting hostility than normotensives, a fact which is not consistent with denial or suppression of that emotion.

A General Picture of the Hypertensive

Studies Portraying the Hypertensive as Different from Normals Rather than associating hypertension with a few specific personality traits, some investigators have attempted to show that hypertensives differ psychologically in various ways from individuals without symptoms of high blood pressure. From a personality inventory which he constructed, Ayman (1933) described hypertensives as more sensitive, quick-tempered, and hyperactive than a group of normotensive patients. Results with the Rorschach showed that hypertensives were consciously hostile, hysterical, obsessive-compulsive, and caught in a passive-aggressive conflict (Kemple, 1945). Although there was no evidence concerning how hypertensives differed from normals, Rorschach responses indicated hypertensives were more dependent than arthritics and patients with parkinsonism (Booth, 1946).

Hypertensives depicted themselves on the Draw-a-Person Test (DAP) as inadequate, socially withdrawn, and indecisive in a study by Modell and Potter (1949). When Gressel, Shobe, Saslow, DuBois, and Schroeder (1949) interviewed hypertensives, psychosomatic patients, and patients with serious medical disorders, they characterized the hypertensives on rating scales as being obsessive-compulsive and showing subnormal assertiveness.

In a more recent study (Pilowsky *et al.,* 1973), correlations between blood pressure and scores on the Edwards Personal Preference Scale (EPPS), the IPAT, and the CMI suggested that hypertensives were self-abasive, neurotic, emotionally immature, guilt-prone, tense, and prone to suppressing emotions. Like many of the earlier studies, this investigation was based on a small number of patients and lacked a control group. In addition, the test results could very likely have been a result of the reaction to a stressful catheter implant.

Wennerholm and Zarle (1976) administered the Rotter Internal-External Control scale, the Marlowe-Crowne Social Desirability scale, and the MMPI to patients with essential hypertension and to a control group. Although there were numerous test differences between the groups, they were not carefully matched and many of the hypertensives were anticipating renal transplants or hemodialysis.

Lack of Differentiation between Hypertensives and Normals Many investigators have found that hypertensives exhibit psychological traits which do not differ from those of normotensives. Using the Guilford-Martin Inventory, Storment (1951) found this to be true for hypertensives and a group of normotensive medical patients. The Rorschach, TAT, and a figure drawing test also failed to reveal any personality structure unique to the hypertensive (Weiss, English, Fischer, Kleinbart, & Zatuchni, 1952).

In a study by Lewinsohn (1956), the MMPI failed to differentiate among ulcer patients, essential hypertensives, neurotics, and controls with minor medical disorders. Innes, Miller, & Valentine (1959) also found no MMPI differences among hypertensive pregnant women, normotensive women after delivery, psychoneurotic women, and another group of hypertensive women. Matched groups of essential hypertensives, renal hypertensives, and normotensives did not differ on either the clinical scales of the MMPI or on the patterns of their MMPI profiles (Ostfeld & Lebovits, 1959). Furthermore, an item analysis of the MMPI as a whole revealed no meaningful differences between groups.

When 144 normal volunteers were given the 16 PF, the MPI, the Taylor MAS, and the IPAT, none of the test scales were significantly correlated with blood pressure. There were also no significant differences in neuroticism and anxiety when extremes in blood pressure were investigated (Spelman & Ley, 1966). The Cesarek-Marke Personality Schedule (CMPS) was administered to normotensives and hypertensives of varying degrees of severity. Out of 44 comparisons on the CMPS, only three were statistically significant, a result which could have been expected to occur by chance (Berglund, Ander, Lindström, & Tibblin, 1975). The results of a study in progress (D. Shapiro & Goldstein, Note 1) with 61 essential hypertensives have thus far revealed that the entire patient sample fits well within the normal test ranges for a number of psychological tests (MMPI, Guilford-Zimmerman Temperament Survey, and the Spielberger State-Trait Anxiety Scale). When studies on general personality patterns are viewed together, there appear to be almost no major differences that clearly differentiate hypertensives from normotensives.

Possible New Directions.

There have been some carefully designed studies, although they are few in number, that have isolated characteristics that seem to be unique to at least certain types of hypertensives. These investigations differ from many of the studies in the literature in that they have utilized unique methods of personality assessment or data analysis.

Blood Pressure Lability Ostfeld and Lebovits (1960) examined similar samples of normotensive and hypertensive black outpatients over periods of from 4 to 12 months. Subsequent analyses of the data revealed a significant positive correlation in both groups between systolic and diastolic lability and MMPI characteristics of immaturity, narcissism, impulsivity, and the tendency to complain about physical symptoms. What is of particular interest is the fact that MMPI scores of hypertensives whose blood pressure varied markedly resembled the scores of normal individuals with labile blood pressure more than those of patients with essential hypertension whose arterial pressure was stable. In this case, it was lability, rather than blood pressure level, that was related to certain psychological variables.

Hypertension—A Multidimensional Variable The failure to achieve significant relationships between psychological variables and elevated blood pressure may be due to the way in which the data have been analyzed. As part of a longitudinal study on coronary heart disease, Lebovits, Lichter, and Moses (1975) collected a variety of data on a large sample of men between the ages of 40 and 55. They felt that the use of a multivariate technique would tap more complex behavioral dimensions than the standard *t* tests. Factor analysis revealed different factor patterns among coronary and noncoronary groups; many of the factors contained loadings of diastolic and systolic pressure and MMPI variables in addition to a variety of other measures. It was concluded that hypertension may indeed be a multidimensional variable and that more than one personality pattern may be linked to hypertension.

This conclusion has received independent support from the results of Baer *et al.* (1979) and of Esler *et al.* (1977). Baer *et al.* have produced evidence for the existence of two extreme subgroups of essential hypertensives, each demonstrating a different profile on the 16 PF. Hypertensives with elevated 16 PF profiles were found to be more anxious and tense, less stable and controlled, and less effective in problem solving than those with low profiles.

Type A Research Because elevated blood pressure is a major determinant of coronary heart disease, the research of Friedman and Rosenman (1959) on an overt behavior pattern associated with a high prevalence of coronary heart disease (Type A) is relevant to the study of hypertension. This pattern consists of excessive drive, aggressiveness, competitiveness, pressure for vocational productivity, sense of time urgency, and restless motor mannerisms. Type B, a contrasting pattern, was found among individuals who tended to be more relaxed and easy-going. Classification of individuals as A or B is based on Friedman and Rosenman's standard interview or the Jenkins Activity Survey (JAS), an objective, self-administered questionnaire.

Most studies of Type A individuals have indicated that such persons develop coronary heart disease but do not necessarily have hypertension. In fact, Rosenman (Note 2) has stated that Type A behavior is not necessarily correlated with hypertension because the Type A personality is able to externally discharge feelings of stress, and generally does not build up enough tension to lead to an increase in blood pressure. There is some evidence, however, for a relationship in females between Type A behavior and hypertension. Rosenman and Friedman (1961) reported a three-to sevenfold higher incidence of diastolic hypertension in women exhibiting a Type A pattern (34.8%), as compared to a 4.5% incidence among Type B women. Shekelle, Schoenberger, and Stamler (1976) found that diastolic blood pressure was significantly associated with Type A patterns in older women only (45–64 years of age). In a study of inner-city black women, Smyth, Call, Hansell, Sparacino, and Strodtbeck (1978) reported that Type A women tended to be hypertensive while Type B women were more likely to be normotensive, but the differences failed to reach significance.

Although much of the research in the area of personality has produced negative results, the studies in this section demonstrate the need for further investigation of the concepts of blood pressure lability, multidimensional assessments of hypertension, and Type A patterning in women. Chapter 3 by Margaret Chesney, Jean Eagleston, and Ray Rosenman presents a detailed discussion of the Type A behavior pattern.

Summary and Conclusions

The literature in two major areas of investigation involving the assessment of hypertension has been reviewed. The first of these areas involves assessing hypertensive individuals' reactions to various laboratory stressors. Among the frequently utilized stressors have been interviews, cold pressor tests, and numerous other physical and mental stressors. In spite of the variety of techniques, subjects, and experimental designs used in these studies, there are relatively consistent trends which have continued to exist from the early investigation of O'Hare (1920) to the present. The basic assumption of these studies has been verified, in that there is sufficient evidence that the response to stress shown by hypertensives is indeed unique. Even though almost all individuals, regardless of their basal blood pressure levels, tend to respond to stress with an increase in blood pressure, the blood pressure responses of hypertensives are exaggerated in intensity and take a relatively long time to return to baseline. Having evidence of the hyperactivity to stress shown by hypertensives, we should be in a better position to treat the disorder. In other words, if coping with stress is a significant problem for hypertensive patients, treatment should center around altering their perceptions of and responses to stressful events. Although behavioral techniques are presently being utilized to lower baseline blood pressures, very little, except for the work of Patel (1977), has been done to modify the hypertensive's response to stress.

A possible future role for laboratory stressors lies in their being utilized to assess the effects of various treatments aimed at lowering the blood pressure of hypertensive patients. Because of the growing interest in behavioral, as opposed to drug treatment, Patel (1977) and D. Shapiro and Goldstein (Note 1) have used exercise, cold pressor tests, noise, and digit transformation tasks to assess the blood pressure reactions of patients who have been trained in various ways to lower their blood pressure. While this is a relatively new area, there are indications that patients who have successful outcomes in certain behavioral therapies show greater blood pressure decreases in response to laboratory stressors than other less successful patients.

A second major area of research that has been discussed is the psychological assessment of hypertensives. While the early assessments were based on interviews and were basically clinical in nature, a major portion of the research has been conducted with various kinds of psychological tests. Some of these, like the Rorschach, are rather subjective instruments and have questionable validity. This is not true, however, for all of the tests, since many of the self-report inventories were developed as objective and standardized means of assessing behavior with substantial evidence regarding their reliability and validity.

The primary assumption underlying the use of interviews and test inventories to assess personality traits in hypertensives was that hypertensive patients were somehow psychologically different from individuals with so-called normal blood pressures. While this may be true, there is not enough evidence to confirm such a conclusion. The basic problem is that this area is notable for the lack of consistent results. In fact, if any consistency does exist, it is of a negative nature. This is to say, hypertensive patients exhibit very few psychological traits that differentiate them clearly from normotensives.

In spite of the negative results, there are some possible directions which appear to be worth pursuing. One of these involves different approaches to data analysis than those usually relied on in research investigations. For example, Ostfeld and Lebovits (1960) reported that a widely varying blood pressure (lability), rather than blood pressure level, was more closely related to a particular pattern of traits and behavior. The concept of lability needs to be investigated further to understand those individuals whose blood pressure is normally low but who exhibit abnormal blood pressure reactions in response to certain situations.

Another new and interesting area that should be

explored involves the research on the Type A individual. Although not all Type A people are hypertensive, there is evidence that many of the women who have diastolic hypertension also exhibit a Type A pattern of behavior. In trying to lower the blood pressure of such women, one must bear in mind the complex pattern of their response to the environment which must be altered.

Finally, the basic assumption involved in the investigation of hypertensives' personalities has generally been that the distribution of personality traits and blood pressure are linearly related. Results of investigations by Baer *et al.* (1979) and Lebovits *et al.* (1975) have indicated that this may not be the case. Rather than being a single personality pattern that is representative of hypertensives, hypertension may be a multidimensional variable. That is to say, there may be more than one subgroup of hypertensives, each portraying different behavior patterns. Whether these are related to differing plasma renin levels (Esler *et al.*, 1977), differing racial backgrounds (Harburg *et al.*, 1973; Naditch, 1974), or to a combination of factors is not known. It may well be that one subgroup of hypertensives tends to exhibit behaviors such as submissiveness and the repression of hostility, while another subgroup suffers from high anxiety levels. If this were true, it would be important to classify hypertensives according to their behavior patterns and then to determine the appropriate treatment to reduce their blood pressures. For example, the former group might be taught assertion training, while the latter group might become involved in therapy aimed at desensitizing the anxiety. The role of assessment then becomes one of an adjunct to the treatment of hypertensive disorders. This appears to be the appropriate future role for the psychological assessment of hypertensives.

Reference Notes

1. Shapiro, D., & Goldstein, I. B. Hypertension: Analysis of drug and behavioral therapies. Research in progress.
2. Rosenman, R. H. *Type A and stress.* Paper presented at a psychological colloquim held at Northwestern University, Evanston, Illinois. Spring, 1976.

References

Adler, R., Hermann, J. M., Schäfer, N., Schmidt, T., Schonecke, O. W., & Vexküll, T. V. A context study of psychological conditions prior to shifts in blood pressure. *Psychotherapy and Psychosomatics,* 1976/77, *27,* 198–204.

Alam, N., & Smirk, F. H. Blood pressure raising reflexes in health, essential hypertension, and renal hypertension. *Clinical Science,* 1938, *3,* 259–266.

Alexander, F. Emotional factors in essential hypertension. *Psychosomatic Medicine,* 1939, *1,* 173–179.

Armstrong, H. G., & Rafferty, J. A. Cold pressor test follow-up study for seven years on 166 officers. *American Heart Journal,* 1950, *39,* 484–490.

Ayman, D. On so-called psychogenic influences in hypertension. *American Journal of Medical Science,* 1933, *186,* 213–223.

Ayman, D., & Goldshine, A. D. Cold as a standard stimulus of blood pressure. *New England Journal of Medicine,* 1938, *219,* 650–655.

Ayman, D., & Goldshine, A. D. The breath-holding test: A simple standard stimulus of blood pressure. *Archives of Internal Medicine,* 1939, *63,* 899–906.

Baer, P. E., Collins, F. H., Bourianoff, G. G., & Ketchel, M. F. Assessing personality factors in essential hypertension with a brief self-report instrument. *Psychosomatic Medicine,* 1979, *41,* 321–330.

Baumann, R., Helgard, Z., Gödicke, W., Hartrodt, W., Naumann, E., & Läuter, J. The influence of acute psychic stress situations on biochemical and vegetative parameters of essential hypertensives at the early stage of the disease. *Psychotherapy and Psychosomatics,* 1973, *22,* 131–140.

Berglund, G., Ander, S., Lindström, D., & Tibblin, G. Personality and reporting of symptoms in normotensive and hypertensive 50-year-old males. *Journal of Psychosomatic Research,* 1975, *19,* 139–145.

Binger, C. A. L., Ackerman, N. W., & Cohn, A. E. *Personality in arterial hypertension.* New York: American Society for Research in Psychosomatic Problems, 1945. (Psychosomatic Medicine Mongraph No. 8).

Booth, G. Organ function and form perception: Use of the Rorschach method with cases of chronic arthritis, parkinsonism, and arterial hypertension. *Psychosomatic Medicine,* 1946, *8,* 367–385.

Brod, J. Haemodynamics and emotional stress. In M. Koster, H. Musaph, & P. Visser (Eds.), *Psychosomatics in essential hypertension.* Basel, New York: Karger, 1970. (Biblioteca Psychiatrica No. 144.)

Brod, J., Fenel, V., Hejl, Z., & Jurka, J. Circulatory changes underlying blood pressure elevation during acute emotional stress (mental arithmetic) in normotensive and hypertensive subjects. *Clinical Science,* 1959, *18,* 269-279.

Brower, D. The relation between certain Rorschach factors and cardiovascular activity before and after visuo-motor conflict. *Journal of General Psychology,* 1947, *37,* 93-95. (a)

Brower, D. The relationship between Minnesota Multiphasic Personality Inventory scores and cardiovascular measures before and after experimentally-induced visuo-motor conflict. *Journal of Social Psychology,* 1947, *26,* 55-60. (b)

Bruce, J. M., & Thomas, C. B. A method of rating certain personality factors as determined by the Rorschach test for use in a study of the precursors of hypertension and coronary artery disease. *Psychiatric Quarterly* (Suppl.), 1953, *27,* 207-238.

Brunswick, A. F., & Collette, P. Psychophysical correlates of elevated blood pressure: A study of urban black adolescents. *Journal of Human Stress,* 1977, *3,* 19-31.

Buss, A. *The psychology of aggression.* New York: Wiley & Sons, 1961.

Cochrane, R. High blood pressure as a psychosomatic disorder: A selective review. *British Journal of Social and Clinical Psychology,* 1971, *10,* 61-72.

Cochrane, R. Hostility and neuroticism among unselected essential hypertensives. *Journal of Psychosomatic Research,* 1973, *17,* 215-218.

Davies, M. H. Blood pressure and personality. *Journal of Psychosomatic Research,* 1970, *14,* 89-104.

Davies, M. H. Is high blood pressure a psychosomatic disorder? A critical review of the evidence. *Journal of Chronic Diseases,* 1971, *24,* 239-258.

Dunbar, F. *Psychosomatic diagnosis.* New York: Hoeber, 1943.

Engel, B. T., & Bickford, A. F. Response specificity Stimulus-response and individual-response specificity in essential hypertensives. *Archives of General Psychiatry,* 1961, *5,* 478-489.

Esler, M., Julius, S., Zweifler, A., Randall, O., Harburg, E., Gardiner, H., & DeQuattro, V. Mild high-renin essential hypertension: Neurogenic-human hypertension. *New England Journal of Medicine,* 1977, *296,* 405-411.

Eyer, J. Hypertension as a disease of modern society. *International Journal of Health Services,* 1975, *5,* 539-558.

Eysenck, H. J. *Manual of the Maudsley Personality Inventory.* London: University of London Press, 1959.

Falkner, B., Onesti, G., Angelakos, E. T., Fernandes, M., & Langman, C. Cardiovascular response to mental stress in normal adolescents with hypertensive parents. Hemodynamics and mental stress in adolescents. *Hypertension,* 1979, *1,* 23-30.

Feldt, R. H., & Wenstrand, D. E. W. The cold-pressor test in subjects with normal blood pressure: Report on observations on 350 subjects with special reference to the family history. *American Heart Journal,* 1942, *23,* 766-771.

Friedman, M., & Rosenman, R. H. Association of specific overt behavior pattern with blood and cardiovascular findings. *Journal of the American Medical Association,* 1959, *169,* 1286-1296.

Ghosh, B. N., & Bashey, H. I. An exploratory study of psychological and social factors in essential hypertension among Indian patients: A psychosomatic approach. *Journal of the Indian Medical Association,* 1966, *47,* 267-272.

Glock, C. Y., & Lennard, H. L. Studies in hypertension. V: Psychologic factors in hypertension: An interpretive review. *Journal of Chronic Diseases,* 1956, *5,* 174-185.

Gressel, G. C., Shobe, F. O., Saslow, G., DuBois, P. H., & Schroeder, H. A. Personality factors in arterial hypertension. *Journal of the American Medical Association,* 1949, *140,* 265-272.

Groen, J. J., Hansen, B., Hermann, J. M., Schäfer, N., Schmidt, T. H., Selbmann, K. H., Vexküll, T. V., & Weckman, P. Haemodynamic responses during experimental emotional stress and physical exercise in hypertensive and normotensive patients. *Progress in Brain Research,* 1977, *47,* 301-308.

Gutmann, M. C., & Benson, H. Interaction of environmental factors and systemic arterial blood pressure: A review. *Medicine,* 1971, *50,* 543-551.

Hambling, J. Emotions and symptoms in essential hypertension. *British Journal of Medical Psychology,* 1951, *24,* 242-253.

Hamilton, J. A. Psychophysiology of blood pressure. *Psychosomatic Medicine,* 1942, *4,* 125-133.

Harburg, E., Erfurt, J. C., Hauenstein, L. S., Chape, C., Schull, W. J., & Schork, M. A. Socio-ecological stress, suppressed hostility, skin color, and black-white male blood pressure: Detroit. *Psychosomatic Medicine,* 1973, *35,* 276-295.

Harburg, E., Julius, S., McGinn, N. F., McLeod, J., & Hoobler, S. W. Personality traits and behavioral patterns associated with systolic blood pressure levels in college males. *Journal of Chronic Diseases,* 1964, *17,* 405-414.

Hardyck, C., Singer, M. T., & Harris, R. E. Transient

changes in affect and blood pressure. *Archives of General Psychiatry,* 1962, *7,* 15-20.

Harlan, W. R. Long-term studies of blood pressure: Prognostic reliability of the cold pressor test and observations on blood pressure variation. *Circulation,* 1958, *18,* 733-734.

Harris, R. E., Sokolow, M., Carpenter, L. G., Freedman, M., & Hunt, S. P. Response to psychologic stress in persons who are potentially hypertensive. *Circulation,* 1953, *7,* 874-879.

Heine, B., & Sainsbury, P. Prolonged emotional disturbance and essential hypertension. *Psychotherapy and Psychosomatics,* 1970, *18,* 341-348.

Heine, B. E., Sainsbury, P., & Chynoweth, R. C. Hypertension and emotional disturbance. *Journal of Psychiatric Research,* 1969, *7,* 119-130.

Hejl, Z. Changes in cardiac output and peripheral resistance during simple stimuli influencing blood pressure. *Cardiologia,* 1957, *31,* 375-381.

Henry, J. P., & Cassel, J. C. Psychosocial factors in essential hypertension: Recent epidemiological and animal experimental evidence. *American Journal of Epidemiology,* 1969, *90,* 171-200.

Hines, E. A. The significance of vascular hyperreaction as measured by the cold pressor test. *American Heart Journal,* 1940, *19,* 408-416.

Hines, E. A., & Brown, G. E. A standard test for measuring the variability of blood pressure: Its significance as an index of the prehypertensive state. *Annals of Internal Medicine,* 1933, *7,* 209-217.

Hines, E. A., & Brown, G. E. The cold pressor test for measuring the reactability of the blood pressure: Data concerning 571 normal and hypertensive subjects. *American Heart Journal,* 1936, *11,* 1-9.

Hodes, C., & Rogers, P. High blood pressure and psychiatric disorder in general practice. *Journal of the Royal College of General Practitioners,* 1976, *26,* 178-184.

Hull, D. H., Wolthuis, R. A., Cortese, T., Longo, M. R., & Triebwasser, J. H. Borderline hypertension versus normotension: Differential response to orthostatic stress. *American Heart Journal,* 1977, *94,* 414-420.

Innes, G., Miller, W. M., & Valentine, M. Emotion and blood pressure. *Journal of Medical Sciences,* 1959, *105,* 840-851.

Jost, H., Ruilmann, C. J., Hill, T. S., & Gulo, M. J. Studies in hypertension: II. Central and autonomic nervous system reactions of hypertensive individuals to simple physical and psychologic stress situations. *Journal of Nervous and Mental Diseases,* 1952, *115,* 152-162.

Kalis, B., Harris, R. E., Bennett, L., & Sokolow, M. Personality and life history factors in persons who are potentially hypertensive. *Journal of Nervous and Mental Diseases,* 1961, *132,* 457-468.

Kalis, B. L., Harris, R. E., Sokolow, M., & Carpenter, L. G. Responses to psychologic stress in patients with essential hypertension. *American Heart Journal,* 1957, *53,* 572-578.

Kaplan, S. M., Gottschalk, L. A., Magliocco, E. B., Rohovit, D. D., & Ross, W. D. Hostility in verbal productions and hypnotic dreams of hypertensive patients. *Psychosomatic Medicine,* 1961, *23,* 311-322.

Kasl, S. V., & Cobb, S. Blood pressure changes in men undergoing job loss: A preliminary report. *Psychosomatic Medicine,* 1970, *32,* 19-38.

Kemple, C. Rorschach methods and psychosomatic diagnosis: Personality traits of patients with rheumatic disease, hypertensive cardiovascular disease, coronary occlusion, and fracture. *Psychosomatic Medicine,* 1945, *7,* 85-89.

Kidson, M. A. Personality and hypertension. *Journal of Psychosomatic Research,* 1973, *17,* 35-41.

Lacey, J. I. Individual differences in somatic response patterns. *Journal of Comparative and Physiological Psychology,* 1950, *43,* 338-350.

Lacey, J. I. The evaluation of autonomic responses: Towards a general solution. *Annals of the New York Academy of Science,* 1956, *67,* 125-163.

Lacey, J. I., Bateman, D. E., & Van Lehn, R. Autonomic response specificity: An experimental study. *Psychosomatic Medicine,* 1953, *15,* 8-21.

Lebovits, B., Lichter, E., & Moses, V. K. Personality correlates of coronary heart disease: A re-examination of the MMPI data. *Social Science and Medicine,* 1975, *9,* 207-219.

Lewinsohn, P. M. Personality correlates of duodenal ulcer and other psychosomatic reactions. *Journal of Clinical Psychology,* 1956, *12,* 296-298.

Lorimer, A. R., Macfarlane, G., Provan, G., Duffy, T., & Lawrie, T. D. V. Blood pressure and catecholamine responses to "stress" in normotensive and hypertensive subjects. *Cardiovascular Research,* 1971, *5,* 169-173.

McDonough, L. B. Inhibited aggression in essential hypertension. *Journal of Clinical Psychology,* 1964, *20,* 447.

McGinn, N. F., Harburg, E., Julius, S., & McLeod, J. Psychological correlates of blood pressure. *Psychological Bulletin,* 1964, *61,* 209-219.

Mckegney, F. P., & Williams, R. B. Psychological aspects of hypertension: II. The differential influence of interview variables on blood pressure. *American Journal of Psychiatry,* 1967, *123,* 1539-1549.

Malmo, R. B. Anxiety and behavioral arousal. *Psychological Review,* 1957, *64,* 276-287.

Mann, A. H. Psychiatric morbidity and hostility in hypertension. *Psychological Medicine,* 1977, *7,* 653-659.

Matarazzo, J. D. An experimental study of aggression in

the hypertensive patient. *Journal of Personality,* 1954, *22,* 423-447.

Meyer, E., Derogatis, L. R., Miller, M., & Reading, A. Hypertension and Psychological distress. *Psychosomatics,* 1978, *19,* 160-168.

Modell, A. H., & Potter, H. W. Human figure drawing of patients with arterial hypertension, peptic ulcer, and bronchial asthma. *Psychosomatic Medicine,* 1949, *11,* 282-292.

Moos, R. H., & Engel, B. T. Psychophysiological reactions in hypertensive and arthritic patients. *Journal of Psychosomatic Research,* 1962, *6,* 227-241.

Moses, L., Daniels, G. E., & Nickerson, J. L. Psychogenic factors in essential hypertension. *Psychosomatic Medicine,* 1956, *18,* 471-485.

Naditch, M. P. Locus of control, relative discontent and hypertension. *Social Psychiatry,* 1974, *9,* 111-117.

Neiberg, N. A. *The effects of induced stress on the management of hostility in essential hypertension.* Unpublished doctoral dissertation, Boston University, 1957.

Nestel, P. J. Blood pressure and catecholamine excretion after mental stress in labile hypertension. *Lancet,* 1969, *2,* 692-294.

O'Hare, J. P. Vascular reactions in vascular hypertension. *American Journal of Medical Science,* 1920, *159,* 369-380.

Ostfeld, A. M., & Lebovits, B. Z. Personality factors and pressor mechanisms in renal and essential hypertension. *Archives of Internal Medicine,* 1959, *104,* 43-52.

Ostfeld, A., & Lebovits, B. Blood pressure lability: A correlative study. *Journal of Chronic Diseases,* 1960, *12,* 428-439.

Ostfeld, A., & Shekelle, R. B. Psychological variables and blood pressure. In J. Stamler, R. Stamler, & T. N. Pullman (Eds.), *The epidemiology of hypertension.* New York: Grune & Stratton, 1967.

Paffenbarger, R. S., Thorne, M. D., & Wing, A. L. Chronic diseases in former college students. VIII. Characteristics in youth predisposing to hypertension in later years. *American Journal of Epidemiology,* 1968, *88,* 25-32.

Palmer, R. S. Psyche and blood pressure: One hundred mental stress tests and fifty personality surveys in patients with essential hypertension. *Journal of the American Medical Association,* 1950, *144,* 295-298.

Patel, C. Biofeedback-aided relaxation in the management of hypertension. *Biofeedback and Self-Regulation,* 1977, *2,* 1-41.

Pfeiffer, J. B., & Wolff, H. G. Studies in renal circulation during periods of life stress and accompanying emotional reactions in subjects with and without essential hypertension: Observations of neural activity in regulation of renal blood flow. *Research Publication Association of Nervous Mental Disorders,* 1950, *29,* 929-953.

Pickering, G. *High blood pressure.* London: J. & A. Churchill, Ltd., 1968.

Pilowsky, I., Spalding, D., Shaw, J., & Korner, P. I. Hypertension and personality. *Psychosomatic Medicine,* 1973, *35,* 50-56.

Remington, R. D., Lambarth, B., Moser, M., & Hoobler, S. W. Circulatory reactions of normotensive and hypertensive subjects and the children of normal and hypertensive parents. *American Heart Journal,* 1960, *59,* 58-70.

Rennie, T. A. C. The role of personality in certain hypertensive states. *New England Journal of Medicine,* 1939, *221,* 448-456.

Robbins, L. L. Psychological factors in essential hypertension. *Bulletin Menninger Clinic,* 1948, *12,* 195-202.

Robbins, P. R. Personality and psychosomatic illness: A selective review of research. *Genetic Psychology Monographs,* 1969, *80,* 51-90.

Robinson, J. O. A study of neuroticism and casual arterial blood pressure. *British Journal of Social and Clinical Psychology,* 1962, *2,* 56-64.

Robinson, J. O. A possible effect of selection on the test scores of a group of hypertensives. *Journal of Psychosomatic Research,* 1964, *8,* 239-243.

Robinson, J. O. Symptoms and the discovery of high blood pressure. *Journal of Psychosomatic Research,* 1969, *13,* 157-161.

Rosenman, R. H., & Friedman, M. Association of specific behavior pattern in women with blood and cardiovascular findings. *Circulation,* 1961, *24,* 1173-1184.

Rosenzweig, S., Fleming, E. E., & Clark, H. J. Revised scoring manual for the Rosenzweig Picture Frustration Study. *Journal of Psychology,* 1947, *24,* 164-208.

Sainsbury, P. Psychosomatic disorders and neurosis in outpatients attending a general hospital. *Journal of Psychosomatic Research,* 1960, *4,* 261-273.

Sainsbury, P. Neuroticism and hypertension in an outpatient population. *Journal of Psychosomatic Research,* 1964, *8,* 235-238.

Sandberg, B., & Bliding, A. Problems and symptoms in army basic trainees with stress-induced hypertensive reactions. *Journal of Psychosomatic Research,* 1976, *20,* 51-59.

Sannerstedt, R., Julius, S., & Conway, J. Hemodynamic responses to tilt and beta-adrenergic blockade in young patients with borderline hypertension. *Circulation,* 1970, *42,* 1057-1064.

Sapira, J. D., Scheib, E. T., Moriarity, R., & Shapiro, A. P. Differences in perception between hypertensive and normotensive populations. *Psychosomatic Medicine,* 1971, *33,* 239-250.

Saslow, G., Gressel, G. C., Shobe, F. O., DuBois, P. H., & Schroeder, H. A. The possible etiological relevance of personality factors in essential hypertension. *Research Publications of the Association for Nervous and Mental Diseases,* 1950, *29,* 881-899.

Saul, L., Sheppard, E., Selby, D., Lhamon, W., Sachs, D., & Master, R. The quantification of hostility in dreams with reference to essential hypertension. *Science,* 1954, *119,* 382-383.

Schachter, J. Pain, fear, and anger in hypertensives and normotensives: A psychophysiologic study. *Psychosomatic Medicine,* 1957, *9,* 17-29.

Schneider, R. A., & Zangari, V. M. Variations in clotting time, relative viscosity, and other physiochemical properties of the blood accompanying physical and emotional stress in normotensive and hypertensive subjects. *Psychosomatic Medicine,* 1951, *13,* 289-303.

Scotch, N. A., & Geiger, H. J. The epidemiology of essential hypertension. A review with special attention to psychologic and sociocultural factors. II: Psychologic and sociocultural factors in etiology. *Journal of Chronic Diseases,* 1963, *16,* 1183-1213.

Shapiro, A. P. An experimental study of comparative responses of blood pressure to different noxious stimuli. *Journal of Chronic Diseases,* 1961, *13,* 293-311.

Shapiro, D., & Goldstein, I. B. Behavioral patterns as they relate to hypertension. In J. Rosenthal (Ed.), *Clinical pathophysiology of arterial hypertension.* New York: Springer. (In press)

Shekelle, R. B., Schoenberger, J. A., & Stamler, J. Correlates of the JAS Type A behavior pattern score. *Journal of Chronic Diseases,* 1976, *29,* 381-394.

Smith, W. M. Epidemiology of hypertension. *Medical Clinics of North America,* 1977, *61,* 467-486.

Smithwick, R. H., & Robertson, C. W. The phenomenon of hyperreactivity: Definition and illustrations. *Angiology,* 1951, *2,* 143-156.

Smyth, K., Call, J., Hansell, S., Sparacino, J., & Strodtbeck, F. L. Type A behavior pattern and hypertension among inner-city black women. *Nursing Research,* 1978, *27,* 30-35.

Sokolow, M., Werdegar, D., Perloff, D. B., Cowan, R. M., & Brenenstuhl, H. Preliminary studies relating portably recorded blood pressure to daily life events, in patients with essential hypertension. In M. Koster, H. Musaph, & P. Visser (Eds.), *Psychosomatics in essential hypertension.* Basel, New York: Karger, 1970 (Biblioteca Psychiatrica No. 144.)

Spelman, M. S., & Ley, P. Psychological correlates of blood pressure. *Medical Journal of Australia,* 1966, *2,* 1138-1140.

Storment, C. T. Personality and heart disease. *Psychosomatic Medicine,* 1951, *13,* 304-313.

Thacker, E. A. A comparative study of normal and abnormal blood pressures among university students, including the cold-pressor test. *American Heart Journal,* 1940, *20,* 89-97.

Thaler, M., Weiner, H., & Reiser, M. F. Exploration of the doctor-patient relationship through projective techniques: Their use in psychosomatic illness. *Psychosomatic Medicine,* 1957, *19,* 228-239.

Thomas, C. B. Pathogenetic interrelations in hypertension and coronary artery disease. *Diseases of the Nervous System,* 1961, *22,* 39-45. (Monograph Suppl.)

Thomas, C. B. The psychological dimensions of hypertension. In J. S. Stamler, R. Stamler, & T. N. Pullman (Eds.), *The epidemiology of hypertension.* New York: Grune & Stratton, 1967.

Van der Valk, J. M. Blood-pressure changes under emotional influences, in patients with essential hypertension, and control subjects. *Journal of Psychosomatic Research,* 1957, *2,* 134-146.

Voudoukis, I. J. Cold pressor test and hypertension. *Angiology,* 1978, *29,* 429-439.

Weiner, H., Singer, M. T., & Reiser, M. F. Cardiovascular responses and their psychological correlates. I: A study in healthy young adults and patients with peptic ulcer and hypertension. *Psychosomatic Medicine,* 1962, *24,* 477-498.

Weiss, E., English, O. S., Fischer, H. K., Kleinbart, M., & Zatuchni, J. The emotional problems of high blood pressure. *Annals of Internal Medicine,* 1952, *37,* 677-688.

Wennerholm, M. A., & Zarle, T. H. Internal-external control, defensiveness, and anxiety in hypertensive patients. *Journal of Clinical Psychology,* 1976, *32,* 644-648.

Wheatley, D., Balter, M., & Levine, J. Psychiatric aspects of hypertension. *British Journal of Psychiatry,* 1975, *127,* 327-336.

Williams, R. B., Kimball, C. P., & Williard, H. N. The influence of interpersonal interaction on diastolic blood pressure. *Psychosomatic Medicine,* 1972, *34,* 194-198.

Wolf, S., Cardon, P. V., Shepard, E. M., & Wolff, H. G. *Life stress and essential hypertension.* Baltimore: Williams & Wilkins, 1955.

Wolf, S., Pfeiffer, J. B., Ripley, H. S., Winter, O. S., & Wolff, H. G. Hypertension as a reaction pattern to stress: Summary of experimental data on variations in blood pressure and renal blood flow. *Annals of Internal Medicine,* 1948, *29,* 1056-1076.

Wolff, H. G., & Wolf, S. The management of hypertensive patients. In E. T. Bell (Ed.), *Hypertension.* Minneapolis: University of Minnesota Press, 1951.

5

Issues and Approaches to the Psychosocial Assessment of the Cancer Patient

IVAN BAROFSKY

What role do psychosocial factors play in cancer? Do they contribute to the origin of cancer? Do they increase or impede its progress? Do they facilitate death? A priori answers to these questions have been used to justify the administration of particular psychosocial assessment instruments to cancer patients. The theoretical and empirical justification for these activities, as well as the need for an alternative research strategy are discussed in this chapter. The proposed research strategy encourages a description, in addition to a systematic manipulation, of the variables that determine a cancer patient's psychosocial status prior to deriving the theoretical implications of the available data. These particular variables determine the quality of care and the quality of life of a patient. Only when these have been optimized will it be possible to identify the role of prior psychosocial variables in the etiology and course of cancer. Once this goal is accomplished, or approximated, it will be possible to provide a rational basis for selecting and developing assessment instruments. Until this is done, however, any attempt at a psychosocial assessment of the cancer patient will be confounded by ongoing events.

A cancer originates from a biological accident—an accident that happens to a person who stands no greater chance for physical or psychological deviance than other members of the population as a whole. This accident occurs when some agent or act (usually environmental in origin) succeeds in the very unlikely event of altering the form of a cell while retaining the cell's ability to reproduce. This accident causes a mutation that releases the reproductive control mechanisms of that cell.

It is generally agreed that people differ in their genetic predisposition to suffer such an accident (cf. Fraumeni, 1977). The recent report that all the members of a particular family who had renal cancer also had inherited a chromosomal aberration (A. J. Cohen, Li, Berg, Marchetta, Tsai, Jacobs & Brown, 1979) confirms that there can be a biological basis to this predisposition. It is quite possible that eventually specific biological substrates will be identified for all 100 or so forms of cancer, and that each person will be found to dif-

Medical Psychology
Contributions to Behavioral Medicine

ISBN 0-12-565960-1

fer in the probability that any specific substrate will predispose the individual to develop a particular type of cancer. In general, however, it cannot be stated that cancer is uniquely determined (e.g., by genetic factors), except in very rare instances. Instead, the occurrence of cancer is the product of a very unlikely sequence of events that are most likely environmentally induced (Knudson, 1977; Miller, Note 1).

The consequence of this biological accident, cancer, is the epidemic growth of the affected cell. When these newly formed cells invade a vital organ or disrupt a vital function, then specific interventions are required to protect the person's life. Two basic types of intervention, based on particular conceptions of the biology of cancer, have evolved. In the first approach the visually (e.g., by X ray) evident disease and sometimes tissue and adjacent structures, such as lymph nodes, are removed. In the second approach the patient is treated with agents or procedures that attack cancer cells throughout the body.

In the first and older treatment approach, surgical removal of a tumor was deemed rational since tumors were seldom found beyond the primary site and the lymphatic system was assumed to provide the means of limiting this spread (Halstead, 1894–95). Adjacent structures and tissue were removed to provide a wider disease-free margin. Thus, it was posited that a person could be cured of cancer because cancer cells could be successfully removed. Recurrence was due to poor technique or limited tissue removal.

In the second, more modern view, cancer, when it is clinically identifiable, is viewed as a systemic disease and the lymphatic system plays only a limited role in regulating the spread of the disease (e.g., Fisher & Fisher, 1966; Fisher, 1977). Under this assumption cancer can be cured if the treatment reduces the number of cells to the point where the body's normal mechanism for controlling foreign or aberrant cells, the immunological system, can act effectively. Thus, cancer cells are considered to be normally present in the body and are in excess when the person is "with disease," and are present but "controlled" when the patient is "not with disease." Some investigators have suggested that the immunological system is disrupted when a person has cancer (i.e., immune surveillance) so that cancer cells can continue to increase in number. The evidence for this very popular hypothesis, however, is mixed (Möller & Möller, 1978; Schwartz, 1975).

Currently most cancer patients die from complications produced (*a*) directly by their disease or (*b*) indirectly by treatment-related factors. For example, a chemotherapeutic agent may control a cancer but may also increase the chances that the person will die from a drug-related cardiovascular problem. As a result, an individual whose cancer is controlled is still at risk, but the risk is only indirectly related to their having had cancer.

To label cancer patients as "cured" can be interpreted to mean that the mortality rate for this *group* of persons corresponds to the rate found for the population as a whole. Groups of patients with specific diseases (e.g., Hodgkin's disease, choriocarcinoma) or groups with specific histological classifications of a specific disease (e.g., Level I melanoma, Duke A colorectal cancer) fit this description.

To apply the label "cured" to *individuals,* however, implies that they have attained a new state which has a much clearer social and psychological meaning than biological significance. The social and psychological meaning of the label comes from changes in (*a*) how the individuals think of themselves; (*b*) how they plan for the future; and (*c*) how they reveal their medical history (implying that what was, no longer is). The ambiguity of the biological significance of the label comes, of course, from the absence of a precise means to assess all residual disease and the capacity of patients to combat any residual disease. What the label does permit, however, is a clear statement of how these people will be cared for. Thus, if there is little clinically evident disease requiring treatment and sufficient time has elapsed so that it is possible to estimate that the probability of recurrence is low, then these persons will not have to return for a medical examination. To be "cured," therefore, can be operationally defined for individuals in terms of what is required to care for them and what behavioral and social changes this label permits.

Finally, terminal illness can also be operationally

defined in terms of how individuals are provided care. Here the change is from one pattern and/or frequency of care to another, rather than total removal from care for extended periods of time, as may occur for "cured" patients. Terminally ill patients may not receive the diagnostic tests or therapeutic regimens that patients who have some chance of extended survival would, but they do receive other forms of care.

A cancer patient, therefore is

1. A person whose physical and psychological characteristics are no different than those of the population as a whole, but who has experienced a biological accident
2. A person who is at greater risk to experience recurrence of the original disease or some complication related to it
3. A person who, if labeled as cured or terminally ill, will experience a change in the medical care received.

These statements define the medical care and health systems approach to the psychosocial assessment of the cancer patient. They deny the role of psychosocial factors in the origin but not necessarily in the clinical course of cancer. These are a statement of a model that would justify how certain assessment procedures may be selected.

Other statements justify other assessment procedures. Making these statements explicit, therefore, is required if the significance of any assessment approach is to be appreciated.

Models of Psychosocial Assessment

At least three models of psychosocial assessment can be identified. Each differs in its approach to the relationship between behavior and cancer. One set of assessment procedures begins by examining intrapsychic events, another begins as individuals adapt to changes within themselves and in their environment, while a third assumes that the systems within which individuals find themselves function to determine how and in what way they act. The first model is labeled the *psychogenic model,* since many of its adherents assume that psychological processes are involved in the origin and natural history of the person's disease. The second or *coping model* focuses on person–environment interaction and makes no statement about etiology. The third model, the *health systems model,* assumes a dominant or at least a primary role for cancer patients' unique health care environments in determining their psychosocial status, and makes no statement on etiology or skills.

Any individual assessment may contain elements of each model but each also will have a primary focus. For example, depression in cancer patients, for the health systems model, could be due to psychological responses to the disease and its treatment or to the task of adapting to the illness, but these reasons would be of secondary importance if the presence of depression was related to the fact that the person was not provided with sufficient social support. Social support, which is something that can be determined by how the person's health care environment is structured would, therefore, be the contributing condition for either the presence or absence of depression in cancer patients.

The Psychogenic Model

Proponents of the strong statement of this model (e.g., Bahnson, 1969; Greer, 1979; Kissen, 1963, 1967; Simonton, Matthews-Simonton, & Creighton, 1978) specifically postulate that psychological factors are involved in the origin of cancer. These psychological factors can include unresolved unconscious conflicts, responses to personal traumatic events (e.g., loss of a spouse), personality factors, etc. (Figure 5.1). Such factors are assumed to either directly or indirectly (through their effect on the endocrine system) alter the immune surveillance system. It is usually assumed that suppression of the immune system is the antecedent event required to transform an aberrant cell into the collection of cells called a tumor (see Figure 5.1). Some even have argued that this sequence of events can be reversed and used to combat cancer (e.g., Fiore, 1979; Simonton *et al,* 1978).

The evidence linking stress, psychodynamic conflicts, and personality characteristics to the etiology of cancer has recently been extensively reviewed (e.g., Fox, 1978, 1980; Morrison & Paffen-

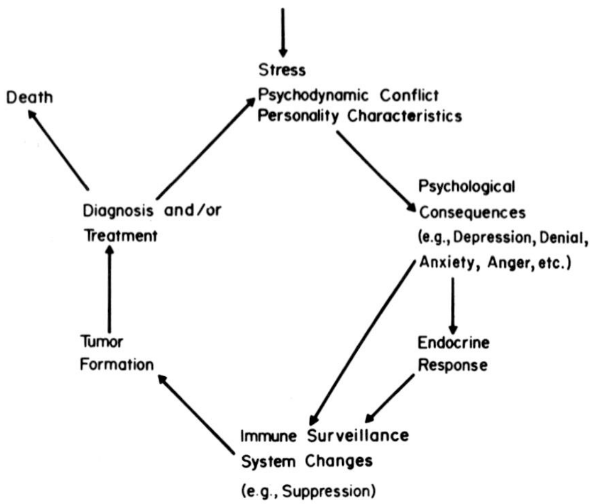

Figure 5.1. How psychosocial factors may contribute to the onset of cancer is depicted in this model.

barger, 1980) and found to be methodologically and empirically deficient. However, as long as methodological deficiencies confound interpretation of the available data, it will not be possible to definitely reject (or accept) the hypothesized involvement of psychological factors in the onset of cancer. There is, however, evidence to suggest that these variables can affect the clinical course of cancer (e.g., Derogatis, Abeloff, & Melisaratis, 1979). Proponents of this weaker or limited application of the psychogenic model (Table 5.1) rely upon evidence demonstrating correlations between various personality and/or psychiatric states (e.g., denial, depression, anxiety) and survival (Derogatis *et al.*, 1979) or disease recurrence (e.g., Rogentine, van Kammen, Fox, Docherty, Rosenblatt, Boyd, & Bunney, 1979) to support a role for psychosocial factors in cancer. In both interpretations of the psychogenic model, however, psychosocial factors modulate the *rate* at which events occur (e.g., length of survival, disease free interval, time from exposure to carcinogens and disease onset, etc.), so that a clear cause and effect relationship is postulated.

Additional correlating evidence demonstrates that psychiatric symptoms increase during the active treatment phase of the disease (e.g., Maguire, Lee, Bevington, Kuchemaun, Crabtree, & Cornell, 1978). These data, however, are strongly dependent on structural factors (e.g., how the patient was cared for), although it may yet be shown that personality patterns account for individual differences in response to cancer treatment.

Table 5.1 Models for the Psychosocial Assessment of the Cancer Patient

	Psychosomatic component
1. Etiology of cancer	
Response to stress	
Psychodynamic conflicts	Strong statement
Personality characteristics	
2. Clinical history of cancer	
Active treatment to disease control	
Recurrence rate	Weak statement
Terminal phase	
3. Reactive psychiatric symptoms	
Active treatment phase	Undetermined

If the stronger interpretation of the psychogenic model is correct, then cancer has a major psychosomatic component comparable to the role of psychosocial factors in cardiovascular diseases (e.g., Henry & Cassel, 1969). A similar statement *cannot* be made for the weaker version of the model, since it is not possible to separate the effect of the disease and its treatment upon the individual from the contributions of the individual to the natural history of the disease. If there is a strong psychosomatic dimension to cancer then it should express itself during each phase of the disease (onset to termination). The weaker model acknowledges that methodological difficulties severely limit the extent of the relationship that can be hypothesized between psychosocial variables and cancer, and proceeds to collect data from this perspective.

The nature of the assumptions made by the various interpretations of the psychogenic model has implications for the selection and application of standardized psychological assessment instruments. The strong form assumes that the same psychological processes that lead to psychopathology can lead to cancer. Thus, psychological tests standardized on normal and psychopathological populations can be administered without concern.

The weak interpretation cannot make such assumptions, and in fact must demonstrate that the effects of the disease and treatment on the cancer patient does not confound the reliability and validity of any assessment instrument. This amounts to reestablishing the validity and reliability of the instrument for the cancer patient population.

Pathogenic or Psychogenic Symptoms One of the critical issues in using standardized psychological tests with cancer patients is that at times responses to the tests may reflect a disease-dependent, as opposed to a psychogenic, disturbance. Consider the example (Fox, 1978) of the measurement of hypochondriasis by use of the Minnesota Multiphasic Personality Inventory (Hathaway & McKinley, 1951; MMPI) in cancer patients. To the extent that symptom reporting was disease-dependent, the high scores on the hypochondriasis scale of the MMPI would not reflect psychopathology. However, very often it is extremely difficult to determine whether there is *no* disease-dependent basis to symptom reports; this reflects the fact that diagnostic tests or procedures can be insensitive. This is as true for studies using the MMPI with persons already diagnosed as having cancer as it is for those studies that are used to predict who will be psychologically predisposed to cancer. It was even true for the original validating studies for the MMPI. The difference between these studies is the extent of the error in the detection of bodily dysfunctions. Clearly, the chances of such an error is many times greater for the cancer patient than for the psychiatrically disturbed patient (e.g., Davies, Quinlan, Mckegney, & Kimball, 1973).

In general then, assessment instruments which include components that could yield false-positive responses (responses to items that may involve disease-dependent bodily dysfunctions) have the potential to be confounded when used to assess the psychiatric, psychological, or social status of the cancer patient. For the MMPI this is clearest for the hypochondriasis scale, but it may also include the depression, masculinity-femininity, and hypomania scales.

Neuropsychological Complications of Cancer Does the presence of disease impair the ability of the cancer patient to answer a questionnaire or respond to an interviewer's questions? It is generally agreed that neuropsychological complications of most types of cancer are minimal until the more terminal phases of the disease or unless the person has a specific type or placement of a brain tumor. Thus, in studies of most types of cancer the psychomotor or intellectual functioning of cancer patients should not impair the validity of standardized assessment instruments.

However, it cannot be assumed that *treatments* for cancer will have no adverse neuropsychological consequences. Brain surgery, systemic chemotherapy, and particularly radiation of the brain can potentially produce neuropsychological complications. Gordon (Note 2), in fact, reports impaired neuropsychological functioning following radiation to the brain despite the absence of gross electroencephalographic changes in brain functioning resulting from this therapy.

Probably the best model to investigate this problem, however, involves study of the cured childhood cancer patient. The available evidence is mixed, ranging from reports of long-term impairment in a minority of cases (Holmes & Holmes, 1975) to no evidence of impairment following short-term assessment (Tull, Sibley, Freeman, Cohen, Duffner, Brecher, Rowland, & Berger, Note 3). This problem clearly deserves continued study, especially in the elderly population which constitutes the majority of cancer patients.

Age Although cancer is a disease of the elderly, the extent to which this is true varies as a function of the type of disease. For example, the incidence of Hodgkin's disease peaks within at least two age ranges: young adults and the elderly. The same pattern can be observed for other types of cancer (e.g., testicular cancer). The diseases among the aged seem more dependent on environmental factors; thus, the role of psychosocial factors in the origin of the disease may be very different depending upon the patient's age. Administration of the same assessment instrument to a sample of patients of different ages with the same disease may, therefore, reflect quite different mediating processes. The stronger psychopathology model would predict that assessment instruments would discriminate between these groups and failure to do so would raise questions about the validity of the instrument used.

Patient age has an additional impact upon assessment since random samples of cancer patients will tend to be older than the age of the original standardization groups. It may be necessary to restandardize the norms and content of any particular test in order to insure its validity and that it is "culture" free.

Summary The psychogenic model postulates that psychosocial factors cause or modulate the natural history of cancer. The stronger version of the model assumes that psychosocial factors are active agents in the origin, clinical course, and terminal phase of the disease, while the weaker version argues from the best available data for a limited role for psychosocial factors during specific portions of the history of the disease. Selection and administration of assessment instruments will vary as a function of the version adopted. The stronger interpretation encourages administration of standardized psychosocial assessment instruments to cancer patients, while the weaker one raises questions about the validity and reliability of these instruments when given to the cancer patient and encourages a demonstration that any particular application of an assessment instrument is not confounded.

The Coping Model

Coping refers to a set of behavioral and psychological skills that individuals acquire in the course of adapting and responding to experiences. Coping with cancer is one such set of experiences and can lead to expanded skills. The ability of individuals to cope in the past is the best predictor of their ability to cope with cancer. The process of coping involves the recognition of the problem, a specific response to the problem, and the outcome of this response. Coping is also a reiterative process in which solutions to problems are evaluated, corrections are made and new approaches are tried.

Various lists of coping strategies have been proposed (e.g., Weisman & Worden, 1976–77) but these can be reduced to three broad categories: (*a*) techniques designed to minimize distress; (*b*) activities that attempt to deal with specific issues; and (*c*) activities that involve others (Mages & Mendelsohn, 1979). Techniques that deal with distress may involve efforts to avoid certain situations or feelings, to control events, and to detach oneself from potentially upsetting situations. Efforts to deal with specific issues may include seeking information, participating in decision making, or learning new skills to compensate for lost functions. Becoming involved with others may include the person's family and friends, or self-help groups (e.g., Reach for Recovery). In general, then, coping involves specific psychological (intrapsychic) processes and specific behaviors, which may vary as a function of the stage of the disease or the age of the patient.

While the question of how coping can be measured is relevant to this discussion, the measurement of coping is critically dependent on its definition. Lazarus and Launier (1978) defined coping as

> efforts, both action-oriented and intrapsychic, to manage (i.e., master, tolerate, reduce, minimize) environmental and internal demands, and conflicts among them, which tax or exceed a person's resources [p. 311].

Clearly, coping has been defined here as a *purposeful* and *intentional* act. Authors differ on the relationship and distinction between "defenses" and "coping" (R. Cohen & Lazarus, 1979; Haan, 1977). Some have viewed defenses as distorting reality, while coping has been seen as adaptive and oriented to reality (Haan, 1977). R. Cohen and Lazarus (1973) preferred not to make this distinction, claiming that it reflects a value judgment on the part of the observer and involves inferences that may not be based on adequate data. In effect, they were objecting to the observer attributing purpose and intention to a person's behavior. However, in rejecting the distinction between defenses and coping, they implicitly assumed that one part of the coping process includes defenses. Thus, their objection to the attribution of purpose and intention in others was not complete. The teleological nature of coping and attributing purpose and intent to behavior is a major conceptual issue in the assessment of coping.

Averill and Opton (1968) pointed out that there are two ways to evaluate coping; either as a *disposition* and/or as a *process*. Coping as a disposition, or trait or style, refers to the relatively stable and consistent character of how people deal with their problems. Coping as a process refers to the observation of a person's behavior as it occurs; the mode of the coping (i.e., its purpose and intent) is inferred from this observation. Available evidence suggests that coping dispositions are weakly or nonsignificantly related to actual observed coping behavior (Austin, 1974; R. Cohen & Lazarus, 1973; Hoffman, 1970), and as R. Cohen and Lazarus (1979) pointed out, this raises serious questions as to what tests of coping actually measure. Coping also may be viewed as a developmental process, consisting of various stages; this also would tend to confound attempts at identifying stable patterns of coping.

The assessment of coping as a naturalistic process requires the development of techniques and/or procedures that permit a description of both what a person is doing and thinking in any encounter. This creates a variety of methodological problems. For example, how a mode of "coping" is to be separated from the complex of interpersonal, intrapersonal, and problem solving behaviors has yet to be solved. In addition, the very method used to obtain information about coping remains the subject of active debate. Currently, both self-reports and observer-reports are used, although the relationship between the two has not been extensively studied. If defense mechanisms are assumed to be unconscious, then their presence can only be inferred by an observer. The particular task given an observer may be just to judge if a behavioral event has occurred or it may be to judge the meaning or significance of a behavior (e.g., was that an adaptive response?). While the reliability of such judgments can be established by the use of explicit criteria, their validity remains a matter of conjecture. For example, knowing that a person is a cancer patient can still lead to reliable ratings by an observer but whether these ratings are valid remains to be determined.

Another methodological issue involves the difficulty of defining what is being studied. R. Cohen and Lazarus (1979) illustrated this in their discussion of the difference between denial and avoidance. The problem with separating these coping processes is that the same outcome may have occurred by more than one method. Thus, a person may not confront a reality by negating its existence (denial) or by not thinking about it (avoidance).

To Lazarus, coping is a transactional process, rather than a series of static dispositions (R. Cohen & Lazarus, 1979). In addition, he has conceptualized coping as a transient phenomenon that requires repeated measures to establish its existence. This conception of coping encompasses both a statement of a research objective as well as an admission of the complexity of the phenomenon.

Probably the most important methodological issue to be addressed involves how coping behavior is determined to be effective or adaptive. This again is, in part, a question of judging the intent or purpose of the behavior in the abstract, but also requires making this judgment between different domains of the individual (psychological, social), over different time periods (in the short or long-run), and as a function of different situations. Hackett and Weisman (1964) illustrated the last point when they found denial psychologically "beneficial" for the myocardial infarction patient but not for the terminal cancer patient.

In general, the methodological issues that beset the study of coping makes one feel that the closer one approaches the phenomenon, the further away it becomes. This is in part due to the complexity of the phenomenon (thus, persistence in studying the phenomenon is scientifically justified), but it is also due to the fact that the core question raised by the study of coping ("Is some behavior or thought adaptive?") may not be completely answerable.

Summary This discussion of coping has taken generous advantage of the ideas and thoughts of Lazarus and his coworkers (R. Cohen & Lazarus, 1979; Lazarus, Averill, & Opton, 1974) and has been limited to the methodological issues they raise relative to doing research in coping. Its relevance to the psychosocial assessment of the cancer patient should be obvious. In contrast to the widespread enthusiasm for research in coping, the current appraisal expresses a fundamental concern that the limitations inherent in the concept of coping will inevitably restrict the value of research efforts. Yet, coping is clinically a very useful concept. Clinicians, as opposed to scientists, have to deal with ever present problems and thus need a framework that helps order their experience with patients. To the extent that coping provides this it will remain a useful part of clinical practice.

The Health Systems Model

Weisman (1979) has used the phrase "safe conduct" to describe what a physician or nurse provides to patients experiencing the maze of events stretching from discovery of their illness, through treatment and recurrence, and possibly to death. It is a phrase that captures the affect and intent implied by the various activities making up the health care process. Weisman, of course, is particularly interested in how patients cope with the tasks involved in this safe conduct, but he also appreciates the provider's role. The health systems model states, in effect, that the success of patients and/or providers in securing "safe conduct" will be a major determinant of the psychosocial status of the cancer patient.

Figure 5.2 illustrates how a person's past history with each of the three sets of psychosocial variables being discussed (psychogenic factors, coping strategies, health care experiences) contributes to their current psychosocial status. The figure also demonstrates that patients' health system experiences reflect their particular coping strategies and psychological character and that psychosocial variables are just one of several determinants of survival in cancer patients. The relationship between these variables can best be discussed within the context of an experimental report.

Derogatis *et al.* (1979) found that metastatic breast cancer patients who survived for more than a year reported more anxiety, alienation, depression and guilt, poorer adjustment to their illness, and poorer attitudes towards their physician than

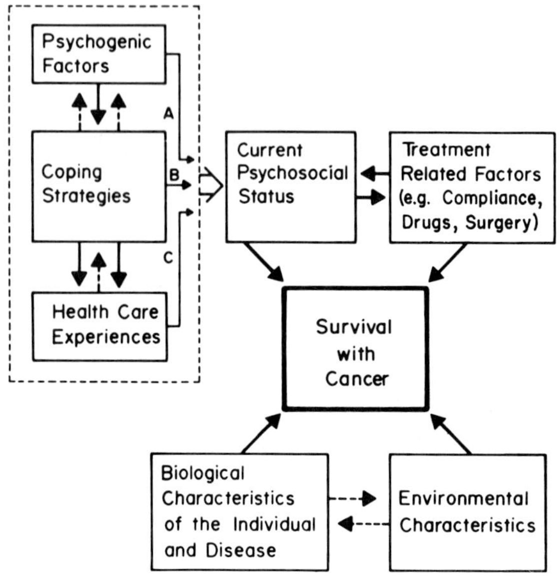

Figure 5.2. The multiple determinants of survival of the patients with cancer are depicted.

patients who survived for shorter periods. Thus, measures of psychopathology (e.g., anxiety, alienation, depression, guilt), coping, (e.g., adjustment to illness) and experiences with the health care system (e.g., attitude towards physician) differed between the long-surviving and short-surviving patients. Derogatis *et al.* (1979) interpreted these data as supporting the proposition that psychological characteristics contribute to the survival of the person, and noted that the biological or disease status of both groups of patients was not statistically different. The data, however, revealed that the short-surviving patients had, on the average, a shorter interval between mastectomy and recurrence (approximately 30%), and a lower physical activity score (Karnofsky scale; approximately 20%). What clearly differentiated the groups was the fact that the short-surviving patients had more than twice as much chemotherapy as the long-surviving patients. The type of chemotherapy given the patients was not described in the paper, nor was the potential contribution of this factor to the differential survival of the patients discussed. Thus, from the perspective of Figure 5.2, their study partialed out biological but not treatment-related, factors that may have contributed to differences in observed survival.

In terms of psychosocial variables, it appeared that each level of analysis contributed to the observed difference in survival of the patients. What was not clear from this report, however, was the relationship between the variables. Thus, whether the depression scores or level of adjustment to illness scores were correlated with the patients' attitude towards their physician was not reported. The model presented in Figure 5.2 suggests that such a relationship between the variables would be expected and, to the extent that the model is correct, it would also be expected to be the strongest determinant of a person's current psychosocial status. Stated differently, past and present experiences with accessing medical care facilities, relationships with providers, styles for coping with the medical care system, and the extent to which personality facilitates successful use of the health care system should be the major determinants of a person's current psychosocial status. Derogatis *et al.* (1979) did not include the environment within which individuals found themselves as one of the factors that contributes to the observed relationship between psychological factors and survival. The power of the environment in determining psychological states was illustrated in a study by Plumb and Holland (1977). They found that cancer patients reported no more depression than their cancer-free relatives. The implications of the study was that when both groups were in a particular environment, such as a medical care setting where a person's survival was at issue, both responded in the same way psychologically. Having cancer was a relevant but secondary issue.

The Derogatis *et al.* (1979) paper illustrates, more than most others in this field, the relationship between the various determinants of survival in cancer patients (Figure 5.2). However, it does not acknowledge the importance of health care variables as determinants of the psychosocial status of the patient. The importance of health care experiences as part of a person's psychosocial status is not only that it confounds the assessment of other variables, but that it may also contribute to these variables (dotted lines in Figure 5.2). Thus, patients' experiences with the health care system may affect how they cope, and may even contribute to their psychopathological status.

A study by Maguire *et al.* (1978) illustrates this point. They found that a nurse practitioner who was trained to recognize psychiatric symptoms could, with appropriate referral, significantly reduce the reports of long-term depression and anxiety in mastectomy patients. The care process was thus organized in such a way that reports of psychopathological symptoms could be acted upon and the process of care was thereby a determinant of the psychosocial status of the patient. Thus, those who postulate a role for psychological factors in survival must determine if these factors are situationally determined (e.g., in response to the person's particular health care environment) or if they are a more permanent feature of the individual (e.g., a personality factor). If a person's psychosocial status is to a large extent situationally determined, then such factors need to be partialed out before the true extent of the contribution of psychological factors to survival can be determined.

Summary

Several issues become clear as a result of this discussion. First, psychologists must be very careful in the application of their art to this new area of the study of the psychology of the medical patient. There are many opportunities to replicate errors made in other fields, including the error of transporting measurement instruments from one situation to another without careful consideration of the differences between the original and new application sites. This seems to have not been heeded by those who use various projective and standardized tests with cancer patients.

Not only must psychologists carefully consider how to use their available measurement instruments, but they also must learn to accept with caution apparent links between psychological and biological measures. A prime example of this is the hypothesized relationship between psychological factors and immune depression. Available evidence (Schwartz, 1975) suggests that both immune suppression *and* stimulation may *or* may not be associated with the etiology of cancer and this will vary as a function of type of cancer. Psychologists who generate models based on a particular piece of attractive data run the risk of having their credibility questioned, especially if these models are to be used to justify a kind of therapy for the patient (e.g., Simonton, *et al.,* 1978).

The most logical course for psychologists interested in the cancer patient is to keep clearly in mind the complex group of variables (Figure 5.2) which can contribute to survival and then to develop experimental models that can be used to estimate the contribution of each of these factors. This more empirical approach is required if, for example, the contribution of psychosomatic factors to cancer prognosis is to be determined. A relatively unexplored area is the role that health care variables play in determining the survival of the cancer patient. If these variables are in fact an important contributor to survival then they also provide a means of impacting survival.

Acknowledgements

The author acknowledges with thanks the review of this chapter by P. German, S. Shapiro, D. Steinwachs, B. Fox, and S. Levy. The final form of the paper, however, is the responsibility of the author.

Reference Notes

1. Miller, D. C. *On the nature of susceptibility to cancer.* Paper presented at the Third Annual Meeting of the American Society of Preventive Oncology, New York. 1979.
2. Gordon, W. Personal communication, April, 1980.
3. Tull, R., Sibley, R., Freeman, A., Cohen, M., Duffner, B., Brecher, M., Rowland, J., & Berger, P. *Complications of central nervous system therapy in childhood acute lymphocytic anemia.* Paper presented at the annual meeting of the American Psychological Association, New York, August 1979.

References

Averill, J. R., & Opton, E. M., Jr. Psychophysiological assessment: Rationale and problems. In P. McReynolds (Ed.), *Advances in psychological assessment* (Vol. 1). Palo Alto: Science and Behavior, 1968.

Austin, S. H. *Coping and psychological stress in pregnancy, labor, and delivery with "natural childbirth" and medicated patients.* Unpublished doctoral dissertation, University of California, Berkeley, 1974.

Bahnson, C. B. Psychophysiological complementarity in malignancies: Past work and future vistas. *Annals of the New York Academy of Sciences,* 1969, *164,* 319–334.

Cohen, A. J., Li, F. P., Berg, S., Marchetta, D. J., Tsai, S., Jacobs, S. C., & Brown, R. S. Hereditary renal-cell carcinoma associated with a chromosomal translocation. *New England Journal of Medicine,* 1979, *301,* 592–595.

Cohen, R., & Lazarus, R. S. Active coping processes, coping dispositions, and recovery from surgery. *Psychosomatic Medicine,* 1973, *35,* 375–389.

Cohen, R., & Lazarus, R. S. Coping with the stresses of illness. In G. C. Stone, F. Cohen, & N. E. Adler (Eds.), *Health psychology: A handbook.* San Francisco: Jossey-Bass, 1979.

Davies, R. K., Quinlan, D. M., Mckegney, F. P., & Kimball, C. P. Organic factors and psychological adjustment in advanced cancer patients. *Psychosomatic Medicine,* 1973, *35,* 464–471.

Derogatis, L. R., Abeloff, M. D., & Melisaratis, N. Psychological coping mechanisms and survival time in metastatic breast cancer. *Journal of the American Medical Association,* 1979, *242,* 1504–1508.

Fiore, N. Fighting cancer: One patient's perspective. *New England Journal of Medicine,* 1979, *300,* 284–289.

Fisher, B. Biological and clinical observations regarding the use of surgery and chemotherapy in the treatment of primary breast cancer. *Cancer,* 1977, *40,* 574–587.

Fisher, B., & Fisher, E. R. Transmigration of lymph nodes by tumor cells. *Science,* 1966, *152,* 1397–1398.

Fox, B. H. Premorbid psychological factors as related to cancer incidence. *Journal of Behavioral Medicine,* 1978, *1,* 45–133.

Fox, B. H. Psychological issues in cancer. In S. M. Weiss, J. A. Herd, & B. H. Fox (Eds.) *Perspectives on behavioral medicine.* New York: Academic Press, 1980.

Fraumeni, J. F., Jr. Clinical patterns of familial cancer. In J. J. Mulvihill, R. W. Miller, & J. F. Fraumeni, Jr. (Eds.), *Genetics of human cancer.* New York: Raven, 1977.

Greer, S. Psychological enquiry: A contribution to cancer research. *Psychological Medicine,* 1979, *9,* 81–89.

Haan, N. *Coping and defending: Processes of self-environment organization.* New York: Academic Press, 1977.

Hackett, T. P., & Weisman, A. D. Reactions to the imminence of death. In G. H. Grosser, H. Wechsler, & M. Greenblatt (Eds.), *The threat of impending death.* Cambridge, Massachusetts: M.I.T. Press, 1964.

Halstead, W. S. The results of operations for the cure of cancer of the breast performed at Johns Hopkins Hospital from June, 1889 to January, 1894. *Johns Hopkins Hospital Reports,* 1894–1895, *4,* 297.

Hathaway, S. R., & McKinley, J. C. *Manual for the Minnesota Multiphasic Personality Inventory.* New York: Psychological Corporation, 1951.

Henry, J. P., & Cassel, J. C. Psychosocial factors in essential hypertension: Recent epidemiologic and animal experimental evidence. *American Journal of Epidemiology,* 1969, *90,* 171-200.

Hoffman, H. E. Use of avoidance and vigilance by repressors and sensitizers. *Journal of Consulting and Clinical Psychology,* 1970, *34,* 91-96.

Holmes, H. A., & Holmes, F. F. After ten years, what are the handicaps and life styles of children treated for cancer? *Clinical Pediatrics,* 1975, *14,* 819-823.

Kissen, D. M. Personality characteristics in males conducive to lung cancer. *British Journal of Medical Psychology,* 1963, *35,* 27-36.

Kissen, D. M. Psychosocial factors, personality and lung cancer in men aged 55-64. *British Journal of Medical Psychology,* 1967, *40,* 29-43.

Knudson, A. G. Genetic and environmental interactions in the origin of human cancer. In J. J. Mulvihill, R. W., Miller, & J. F. Fraumeni, Jr. (Eds.), *Genetics of human cancer.* New York: Raven, 1977.

Lazarus, R. S., Averill, J. R., & Opton, E. M., Jr. The psychology of coping: Issues of research and assessment. In G. V. Coelho, D. A. Hamburg, & J. E. Adams (Eds.), *Coping and adaptation.* New York: Basic Books, 1974.

Lazarus, R. S., & Launier, R. Stress-related transactions between person and environment. In L. A. Pervin & M. Lewis (Eds.), *Perspectives in interactional psychology.* New York: Plenum, 1978.

Mages, N. L., & Mendelsohn, G. A. Effects of cancer on patients' lives: A personological approach. In G. C. Stone, F. Cohen, & N. E. Adler (Eds.), *Health psychology: A handbook.* San Francisco: Jossey-Bass, 1979.

Maguire, G. P., Lee, E. G., Bevington, D. J., Kuchemaun, C. S., Crabtree, R. J., & Cornell, C. E. Psychiatric problems in the first year after mastectomy. *British Medical Journal,* 1978, *1,* 963-965.

Möller, G., & Möller, E. Immunological surveillance against neoplasia. In J. E. Castro (Ed.), *Immunological aspects of cancer.* Baltimore: University Park Press, 1978.

Morrison, F. R., & Paffenbarger, R. S. Epidemiologic aspects of bio-behavior in the etiology of cancer: A critical review. In S. M. Weiss, J. A. Herd, & B. H. Fox (Eds.), *Perspectives on behavioral medicine.* New York: Academic Press, 1980.

Plumb, M. M., & Holland, J. Comparative studies of psychological function in patients with advanced cancer-1. Self-reported depressive symptoms. *Psychosomatic Medicine,* 1977, *39,* 264-276.

Rogentine, G. N., van Kammen, D. P., Fox, B. H., Docherty, J. P., Rosenblatt, J. E., Boyd, S. C., & Bunney, W. E. Psychological factors in the prognosis of malignant melanoma: A prospective study. *Psychosomatic Medicine,* 1979, *41,* 647-655.

Schwartz, R. S. Another look at immunological surveillance. *New England Journal of Medicine,* 1975, *293,* 181-183.

Simonton, O. C., Matthews-Simonton, S. M., & Creighton, J. *Getting well again.* Los Angeles: Tarcher, 1978.

Weisman, A. D. *Coping with cancer.* New York: McGraw-Hill, 1979.

Weisman, A. D., & Worden, J. W. The existential plight in cancer: Significance of the first 100 days. *International Journal of Psychiatry in Medicine,* 1976-77, *7,* 1-15.

6

A Quantitative and Qualitative Approach to Neuropsychological Evaluation

THOMAS J. BOLL
DANIEL S. O'LEARY
JEFFREY T. BARTH

Psychological assessment requires a description or identification of a person's current level of functioning in the psychological realm of life. It is often difficult, however, to delineate the borders of the psychological realm since the human processes that are commonly accepted as psychological are not necessarily synonymous with the processes that should be investigated in a thorough and professional assessment of psychological functioning. As commonly used to describe some aspect of a person, the term *psychological* most frequently suggests an affect or emotion. Someone with a "psychological problem" has a difficulty in the personality-interpersonal-emotional sphere. To characterize someone's difficulties as psychological, be they physical, social, occupational, or academic, is to suggest the absence of an organic, structural (or in lay terms a "real") basis for the problem. Instead it implies that the person is either consciously or unconsciously, purposely or unintentionally, serving as the major source of the difficulty. The term psychological has a second, only slightly less common use. It is often used to describe a manner of thinking as when one utilizes "reverse psychology" to get another to act or think in a certain way. Using psychology implies using strategy and reasoning. This use of the term includes all of the higher level mental processes.

Both of these common uses reflect an accurate, but too restricted, understanding of the human characteristics fairly defined as psychological. Rarely are motor and sensory functions referred to as psychological, and even less frequently are such functions formally included in a complete psychological evaluation, despite the history of psychological measurement which began not with emotions or cognitions, but with primarily "nonmental" procedures. Cattell (1890) utilized tasks of speed, strength, reaction time, and pain sensation in his mental measurements. Galton (1893), who employed auditory discrimination, visual length estimation, and even measurement of body parts to assess the basis of human behaviors, was knighted

Preparation of this chapter and supporting research was funded in part by Contract NO1-NS-7-2329 Perceptual Studies in Epilepsy to Stanley Berent and Contract NO1-NS-5-2329 Bio-Psycho-Social Aspects of Epilepsy to Thomas J. Boll from the National Institute of Neurological and Communicative Disorders and Stroke.

Medical Psychology
Contributions to Behavioral Medicine

ISBN 0-12-565960-1

for his psychological studies in which he used sensorimotor tasks to distinguish between mentally defective and normal persons.

One need not return to the last century to find references to the importance of basic sensorimotor processes. A glance at any modern psychiatry text which discusses the Mental Status Examination will demonstrate the necessity of attention to such issues as coordination, gait, posture, motor ability, and sensory ability. To include this portion of human abilities within the rubric of *ego functions* places them in the mainstream of "things psychological." Assessment of simple sensorimotor functions as well as the more complex emotional and cognitive processes can be seen as an underlying theme running from the origins of formal psychological measurement through past and present mental status examinations to modern clinical neuropsychology. Appreciation of a patient from this widest possible perspective should be part of any attempt to describe and/or identify his current neuropsychological functioning. Assessment requires, at the minimum, procedures likely to measure such a range of functions.

Having argued for the fullest appreciation of things psychological, it is useful to discuss the referent for such "things." The human brain is the organ of human psychological function; it is the organ of the mind. Great advances in our understanding of the integrated responsibilities of the various areas of the brain and an appreciation of the types of psychological consequences produced by damage to those areas have occurred during the past 100 years. It should be noted, however, that brain-behavior relationships are complex when considered alone. One-to-one relationships between focal areas of cerebral impairment and other than simple motor and sensory behavioral deficits, if they exist, are rare and not major interests in clinical neuropsychology. Nevertheless, the correlation between normal and impaired brain functions and human adaptive capacity has progressed to allow examination of some of the more general brain-behavior relationships based on the formal psychological assessment procedures employed in clinical diagnosis and description (Barth & Boll, Chapter 14; Boll, 1978; Golden, 1981; Filskov & Goldstein, 1974; Smith, 1975, 1981).

Given that the brain is the organ of human behavior and psychological function, a list of human abilities or functions referable, at least generally, to overall cerebral geography provides a map of what must be considered in any comprehensive psychological examination. It also provides a minimum list of those brain-behavior relationships which must be recognized if the neurological contribution to human psychological adjustments is to be considered. The most defensible anatomical-functional organization is the division of the cortex into the right and left cerebral hemispheres. Why the two structurally similar cerebral hemispheres contribute differentially to human abilities has not yet been ascertained. Each cerebral hemisphere appears to represent an adequate neural substrate for the entire human behavioral repertoire. The reason why varying degrees of predominance for certain functions accrue to one cerebral hemisphere over the other and the mechanism responsible for this are also unexplained. The minimal anatomical differences that have been discovered, (e.g., enlarged planum temporale of the left cerebral hemisphere) may or may not be part of that explanation. Despite these major areas of neuroscientific uncertainty, there does exist a considerable body of knowledge relevant to the organization of behavior in the brain. This information has been well-described in a series of recent comprehensive publications including both theoretical and data based presentations (Filskov, Grimm, & Lewis, 1981); Hécaen & Albert, 1978; Kinsbourne, 1981; Lezak, 1976; Luria, 1973). For this reason, a complete geographic listing of brain-behavior functions will not be attempted in this chapter. Rather, we shall discuss the range of behavior which should be sampled by a comprehensive neuropsychological assessment and describe a number of tasks that are designed to measure these abilities. Issues relevant to the interpretation of the test battery as a whole as well as to its validity also will be investigated.

The Complexity of Brain–Behavior Relationships

No single behavior, no matter how complex or central to overall human functioning, can be expected to adequately reflect the presence or consequence of changes in brain function. The normal brain is far from a bucket of water whose fullness is equally changed no matter where water is withdrawn. The behavioral correlates of an impaired brain structure depend upon factors such as the location, size, rate of growth, and type of lesion. The adequacy of the neuropsychological description of a patient depends upon the ability of the clinician to appreciate these and other factors.

Even a brief mention of human neuropsychological organization suffices to underline the inadequacy of a single test to determine the brain–behavior relationships which, in the past, was considered an acceptable part of the practice of psychological evaluation. Disorders of language, resulting in most patients from impairment of the left cerebral hemisphere, are quite compatible with perfectly normal visuospatial skills. In fact, it is possible to identify a significantly impaired language disorder in a patient whose Verbal IQ is above average and who seems unimpaired in casual conversation and clinical interview. Visuospatial disorders, on the other hand, are commonly associated with right cerebral hemisphere impairment. These need not be accompanied by language impairment, motor deficits or memory loss. Thus, a single test measuring only language function, or only visuospatial abilities, will necessarily be insensitive to a large percentage of cases of cerebral impairment.

It might seem quite impressive to delineate the intricacies of a language disorder or to recognize that while visuospatial skills are intact, auditory nonverbal processes prevent the comprehension of important environmental sounds. Such discrepancies have little clinical relevance, however, outside of an understanding of the patient's broader behavioral competencies and deficits. An aphasic patient who is also hopelessly spatially disorganized presents a rather different problem of adjustment and rehabilitation than one whose other psychological functions are essentially intact. Tactile and kinesthetic deficits preventing use of complex machinery may have more relevance to a millwright than a memory problem, while for a graduate student quite the opposite would be true. No single ability serves as a linchpin; thus, while no clinical examination can tap the entire behavioral repertoire, the explicit examination of a broad sample of human skills for adequacy as well as for impairment is absolutely necessary for clinical understanding.

Within the clinical neuropsychological examination a wide range of functional human processes must be explored. While human behavior is a complex and subtle phenomenon and any attempt to divide it into separate topic areas will be artificial and thus unsatisfactory, some arbitrary division is necessary if behavior is to be evaluated and discussed. The scheme used here divides human behavior into content and process areas. The content areas include simple sensory and motor functions as well as more complex functions involved in language and perception. The process areas include those systems that operate in such a manner as to allow the demonstration of the content areas on a day-to-day basis. The most notable of these processes are attention and concentration, memory, and problem solving ability.

Content Areas

Motor and Sensory Functions Examination of motor functions requires testing the patient's ability to imitate motor actions and perform them on command. It also includes assessment of coordination, strength, and control (steadiness, skill). The sensory examination attends primarily to the auditory, visual, and tactile modalities. In each of these areas of ability, both sides of the body are tested while working independently and simultaneously, in concert and in competition with one another.

The integrated expression of simple and complex motor skills with sensation and sensory perception is broadly defined as athletic ability. This ability is dependent upon visual and auditory nonverbal perception as well as upon motor skills. It also assumes a well integrated internal awareness of performance by various body parts. Routine motor–tactile–kinesthetic repertoires, such as those required to drive a car, and the less routine ones, such as those required to run, turn, bounce a ball, change speeds and directions and propel an object in one direction while jumping in another, require a degree of internal synchrony just as exemplary of brain–behavior relationships as is complex behavior in the ares of language performance.

Language Language competence is an intricate area, which could easily require many hours to examine. There are many aspects of language that can' be assessed by the standard clinical tests. To these tests can be added few or many other procedures depending upon the context of the examination. The Wechsler Intelligence Scales tap many language-related areas including arithmetic calculation, fund of information, vocabulary, verbal expression, verbal comprehension, verbal abstraction, immediate memory, and mental manipulation of verbal symbols. The Wechsler Memory Scale assesses verbal learning as well as short-term, long-term, and distant memory, and attentional capacity. The addition of a brief screening test such as the Halstead-Wepman Aphasia Screening Battery (Halstead & Wepman, 1949), which uses confrontational examination to provide a scorable, but primarily qualitative assessment of specific language-related areas, is a useful complement to the somewhat more quantitative Wechsler scales. More complete and time demanding examinations provide commensurately greater amounts of information. Qualitatively oriented procedures such as the Boston Diagnostic Aphasia Examination (Goodglass & Kaplan, 1972) and the carefully quantified Porch Index of Communicative Abilities (Porch, 1971) are excellent examples of more complete procedures for language evaluation.

Perception Perception is an area of human functioning which is frequently assessed in a routine clinical examination. However, the reason this examination is frequently performed is not because of the recognition of the need for specific information in this important area of human performance, but rather because of the mistaken and clinically outmoded notion that the perceptual apparatus has a peculiar proclivity for brain damage. What is even worse is that persons holding this quaint idea of brain-behavior relationships reduce perception to its visuospatial mode. While such antiquated concepts no longer represent a credible model for clinical practice, one still occasionally sees "tests for brain damage," many of which tap exclusively visuospatial capacities.

Psychological skills and functions in the general area of perception predominantly involve the auditory, visual, and tactile modalities. The overlap between perception and other areas of psychological functioning is obvious in auditory perception which includes nonverbal tones and environmental sounds as well as the more obvious auditory–verbal sounds of language. Procedures such as the Speech Sounds Perception Test, and tasks from the Seashore Test of Musical Talent (most notably the Rhythm and Tonal Memory Tests) are frequently included in neuropsychological evaluations (Boll, 1981b; Milner, 1958). Common sounds such as a doorbell ringing or keys jingling represent technically simple test stimuli; however, difficulty with the recognition of such sounds gives information regarding both the nature of brain impairment and concomitant environmental behavioral difficulties.

The Wechsler Intelligence and Memory Scales (see p. 73) assess the attention to and the reception, manipulation, reproduction, and recollection of shapes and figures. These abilities are most commonly associated with functions of the right parietal-occipital area of the right cerebral hemisphere. Failure to recognize new and even familiar faces suggests a variety of psychiatric explanations for what is, in fact, a recognizable neuropsychological reaction to bilateral posterior cerebral hemisphere lesions. Recognition of the neurobehavioral nature of this phenomenon obviously influences the interventions one may consider.

Tactile perception, the recognition of common shapes and objects (right cerebral hemisphere function) and awareness of body parts (left cerebral hemisphere function), is a frequently ignored area of investigation except in formal neuropsychological procedures. In brain damaged as well as in normally functioning children, even minor difficulties which occur during the period of cognitive development have been demonstrated to strongly correlate with more general aspects of mental and academic ability (Boll, Berent, & Richards, 1977; Boll, Richards & Berent, 1978).

Process Areas

Attention and Concentration Attention and concentration may be disrupted by many types of neurological impairment occurring in a variety of locations. Psychological tests such as Digit Span, Speech Sounds Perception Test, Rhythm and Tonal Memory Tests, and the Trail Making Tests (cf. Boll, 1981b) tap differing aspects of attention and concentration. When attentional mechanisms are deficient, the adequacy of mental content is rendered irrelevant by virtue of its lack of availability to the patient. Deficits in attention assessed qualitatively at the bedside frequently suggest that more formal neuropsychological evaluation is not appropriate and must await improvement in this second most basic (after consciousness) mental process.

Memory Memory is best judged neuropsychologically across three dimensions.

1. *Time span.* Clinical practitioners have traditionally divided memory into four time spans: immediate memory, 0 to 60 sec; short-term memory, 1 min to 1 hour; long-term memory, over 1 hour; and distant memory, stored events in one's past life.
2. *Modality.* Modality of memory refers to the use of auditory, visual or tactile channels through which information is processed.
3. *Material.* Material of memory refers to the figural, verbal, or numerical nature of that which is to be remembered.

Milner reported that the temporal lobes are responsible for short-term auditory memory of both verbal and nonverbal material. Visual memory, whether for nonverbal patterns or written language, is processed by the parietal lobes. Milner also reported the standard relationship between verbal and figural memory in the left and right cerebral hemispheres, respectively (Milner, 1962, 1967, 1968). Obviously a number of tests tapping various aspects of memory functioning, including the Wechsler Intelligence Scale and Memory Scale (especially with Russell's modification [Russell, 1975]) and the Visual Retention Task (Benton, 1963) are part of routine evaluation for many clinicians not identified as neuropsychologists. The explicit recognition of the complexity of memory and specific attention to each of the three areas of memory is, however, commonly left to a neuropsychological evaluation. Even the traditional neuropsychological examination seems minimal when one begins to realize the complexity and importance of memory. Procedures assessing tactile and incidental memory are imbedded in traditional neuropsychological procedures such as the Halstead Battery. Another procedure of excellent clinical value for adults and children which assesses several aspects of verbal memory is the Selective Reminding Task (Buschke, 1973). More experimental procedures that often employ verbal and nonverbal association lists can also be included when specific questions must be addressed. An excellent review of issues and techniques in the area of memory has been provided by Russell (1981).

Problem Solving Problem solving is an even more amorphous area than that of attention and memory. As used here, problem solving includes the ability to efficiently organize, learn, change sets, sort out relevant from irrelevant cues, test hypotheses, and benefit from reinforcement. Many patients with brain damage appear quite normal in the clinical interview. Their fund of information, vocabulary, and past memory are excellent. They appear attentive, use language well, and have no motor, sensory or perceptual deficits. Yet, when required to exercise judgment, plan their lives, manage their treatment regime, or learn new (particularly unfamiliar) material, they do so slowly and inconsistently. Such patients frequently frustrate both themselves and others as expectations greatly exceed performance. In such cases, lack of motivation has been frequently but incorrectly assumed to account for their failures and, thus, attempts to elicit increased effort have been made. Unfortunately, motivation without ability leads to frustration, loss of self-esteem, and depression. Such emotional reactions are often, in turn, incorrectly assumed to be either purely or primarily psychiatric, rather than secondarily related to the brain impairment itself. Such failure to distinguish the nature of the patient's deficits, both in quantity and in kind, lead to inappropriate efforts directed at improving coping, adaptation, and performance (Barth & Boll, Chapter 14).

Judgment and problem solving abilities are often severely impaired following even surprisingly mild and generalized neurological disorders.

Impairment of judgment and problem solving is also the most difficult type of deficit with which the patient and doctor must deal. The impairment is difficult for the patient because it frequently results in crucial deficits in managing the complex, new and unfamiliar aspects of academic and occupational tasks. Such difficulties, especially in the absence of serious physical or mental damage, produce appearance versus performance discrepancies. Impairment of judgment and problem solving is difficult for the doctor because the reason for the patient's complaints of reduced ability are not found on mental status or even the most common psychological test procedures. Only the most skilled qualitative analysis of routine procedures and the use of more sophisticated neuropsychological procedures will allow proper assessment of this essential element of the patient's behavioral repertoire. Patients at risk following central nervous system impairment have not received complete health care if assessment of judgment and problem solving has not been attended to as vigorously and in as sophisticated a manner as all other aspects of their acute and long-term health care program.

Mental Stamina

A final aspect of human performance which does not qualify as either a content or a process of one's psychological repertoire, but is important to it, is that of mental stamina, resilience, and endurance. In the acute phases of neurological deficit, when impairments are obvious and expectations are reduced to meet the patients' obvious deficits, adjustment problems are frequently minimized even in the face of relatively severe and obviously upsetting disorders. During the recovery phase, when physical and other obvious deficits recede, it is necessary to be sensitive to the possibility that mental stamina may still be at a very low level. At a point when the level of psychological performance returns to normal and even most qualitative indices suggest adequacy of functioning, a continuing deficit may render the patient less capable than was previously the case. The patient may well be able to manage even very complex tasks with a high level of adequacy, but for a short period of time only. Sustained mental effort may result in a rapid decline in higher cognitive performances. The patient may report that in the morning, school and occupational tasks go smoothly, but that shortly before or after noon, difficulties in concentration, attention, and task persistence that are very disruptive arise. Further adding to their difficulties, patients with a heavy work or academic load are frequently frightened by the implications of this. When these difficulties are coupled with the routine irritability, lethargy and upset that follow a variety of neurological illnesses and injuries, it is not difficult to understand why patients with almost minimal content and process impairments will present complaints of reduced ability. It is just as easy to understand why these same complaints are frequently passed off as "functional" in nature and the patient is referred for mental health counseling to help deal with the unreality of the reported situation. Instead of a psychiatric diagnosis and referral, however, what is often necessary is a sophisticated recognition that the patient's situation is not only a very real one, but one that is entirely the result of neurological impairment that may have occurred as much as 12 to 18 months before. Without such sophisticated recognition, those patients (i.e., those with the most subtle deficits but whose life situation requires highest cognitive performance) are likely to be most frequently mismanaged and misunderstood, thereby further exacerbating their frustration and anxiety and the resultant difficulties they experience.

Neurological Assessment

It is important to recognize that no battery of tests may be considered adequate for assessing all of the aspects of human performance relevant to questions of brain-behavior relationships. At the same time, sets of psychological procedures subject to interpretation by trained neuropsychologists through complex inferential systems of *quantitative* and *qualitative* analysis can and do provide sufficient information for the initial understanding and patient description that are critical for treatment planning. Such procedures also provide data to guide further investigation and to suggest areas in need of further inquiry.

The Halstead-Reitan Battery and Allied Procedures (Boll, 1981b) are the most widely employed and discussed set of procedures in clinical practice. They represent one of several examples of acceptable neuropsychological procedures designed to sufficiently appreciate the complexity of brain-behavior relationships in order to address the content and process areas previously referred to in this chapter. This battery includes both standard procedures common to a broad range of clinical psychological practice and procedures considered specific to neuropsychological practice. This distinction between standard clinical and neuropsychological procedures refers more to the context of use than the nature of the tests themselves. The complexity of the examinations, rather than any particular behavior measured, distinguishes the neuropsychological tests from the more traditional clinical psychological batteries. Because these procedures have been recently described in considerable detail (Boll, 1978, 1981b), description here will be limited to the areas they cover, providing the reader with an initial impression of their use.

Wechsler Adult Intelligence Scale (Wechsler, 1955)

This comprehensive measure of psychometric intelligence allows qualitative and quantitative analysis of the data. It also provides an opportunity to use several inferential methods, i.e., pathognomic sign, level and pattern of performance (see pp. 75–76), in conducting the analyses. Beginning with level of performance, the Wechsler scales allow reliance upon an extensive standardized sample to place the person within the overall population of individuals most appropriate for such comparison. The between and within subtest comparisons (pattern of performance) allow both quantitative and qualitative analysis of various patterns of behavioral strength and weakness, providing information about the neuropsychological repertoire of the patient. Evaluation of the patient's method of approach and display of particular difficulties within the Verbal and Performance scales allows for a more qualitative assessment of the presence or absence of pathognomic signs of neuropsychological deficit. The complementary use of several inferential methods and both qualitative and quantitative analysis of the data offers the neuropsychologist many initial hypotheses to be tested through further evaluation. In addition, the Wechsler scales' traditional psychometric familiarity makes communication of these results an important point of reference in the context of the more specialized and less familiar neuropsychological tasks. Furthermore, attempts to assess change in ability which traditionally has looked to such indices as socioeconomic status, occupational status, and educational accomplishment can, at least in some instances, rely upon some aspects of the Wechsler scales to reflect past accomplishments. Relationships within the Wechsler scales may provide the first clues of a discrepancy between past accomplishments and current functional capabilities.

The Wide Range Achievement Test (Jastak & Jastak, 1976)

A brief sample of reading, spelling, and arithmetic computation, this test provides yet another sample of expressive capacity in the language area and information regarding current functional literacy, an important factor in rehabilitation. Furthermore, because many patients in the early stages of a deteriorating mental condition, as well as those who have recently experienced a sudden mental deterioration, perform considerably less adequately on the arithmetic subtest than on reading and spelling, the Wide Range Achievement Test gives further qualitative clues to changes in mental competence and capacity thereby raising a variety of hypotheses to be tested in the context of a total evaluation.

The Wechsler Memory Scale (Wechsler, 1945)

Russell's modification of the Wechsler Memory Scale (Russell, 1975), which repeats the logical memory and visual reproduction portions of the original scale with a $\frac{1}{2}$-hour delay, represents a procedure that uses both verbal and figural materials to tap attention, immediate, short-term, long-term, and distant memory. Quantitative analysis of differential degrees of difficulty within the scale and comparisons between the memory quotient and the intelligence quotient aid in the evaluation of changes in memory capacity. Qualitative interpretations that assess performance on easy versus difficult items within subtests (such as the Verbal Paired Associates Task) are also essential in interpreting the significance of specific scores.

The Selective Reminding Task (Buschke, 1973)

This task, which presents 12 words to be remembered and repeated across 12 trials, allows assessment of memory storage and retrieval, and consistency in the use of verbal material.

Halstead-Wepman Aphasia Screening Test (Halstead & Wepman, 1949)

This test is a brief specific confrontational language examination, which demands patient performance that is quite different from that seen on tasks which are ostensibly more complex in their verbal requirements. It is not clinically unusual to find a patient with a bright normal and even superior Verbal IQ and an entirely adequate Wechsler Memory Scale performance, who on the simple naming, word finding, reading, writing, and spelling tasks in this test, demonstrates a degree of impairment entirely outside of normal limits and pathognomonic for impairment of brain functions. The test relies exclusively upon qualitative evaluation and a pathognomonic sign approach to assess language competence and the presence and type of aphasic disorder.

The Motor and Sensory Examination

The motor and sensory examination traditionally embedded in the Halstead-Reitan Battery and Allied Procedures includes assessments of speed, strength, coordination, and problem solving. It also provides evidence for single and bilateral simultaneous tactile, auditory, and visual integrity. As with so many of the procedures in the Halstead Battery, this set of measurements allows qualitative and quantitative assessments. Scores for the motor and sensory examination provide a direct, reliable, and highly valid quantitative assessment of the patient's performance in these important areas. Comparison of the relative efficiency of the two sides of the body (see p. 76) across simple and complex motor and sensory areas demands a qualitative interpretation in the context of deviations from expected levels of performance and overall level of functioning. The nature of the errors and the context of the person's other cognitive abilities require further qualitative interpretation.

The Halstead Battery

The psychological-behavioral measures that carry the formal label of the Halstead Battery make up approximately 25–30% of the overall Halstead-Reitan Battery and Allied Procedures and include primarily measures of higher level cognitive functioning, attention, concentration, and memory. This aspect of the overall assessment procedure provides excellent coverage of the areas of general problem solving, learning, and mental efficiency that frequently have been demonstrated to be especially sensitive to subtle changes in brain functions in the earliest phases of deterioration of cerebral competence. This set of tasks, like the others in the battery, require interpretation utilizing multiple inferential methods in a complementary fashion and demand both quantitative and qualitative assessment for their understanding. Halstead's tests include

1. The *Category Test* which requires efficient hypothesis testing, switching of mental sets, and the ability to benefit from trial-and-error experience and reinforcement feedback. This task also requires the ability to remember the correct solution and avoid distraction by irrelevant stimuli once that solution has been acquired.
2. The *Memory* and *Localization* components of the *Tactual Performance Test* provide assessment of incidental learning and memory skills. It provides a measure of memory in the tactile modality which complements other procedures assessing visual and auditory memory functions. It should be noted that this test is particularly sensitive to a deficit in the ability to benefit from life experiences to which an individual does not specifically attend; this type

of deficit often occurs following neurological insult, although it frequently is clinically imperceptible.

3. *The Speech Sounds Perception Test* and *Seashore's Test of Rhythm* measure not only verbal and nonverbal auditory perception, but also complex attentional capacity and the ability to develop and maintain independent task performance through internal motivation.

4. The *Trail Making Test, Parts A and B,* require a patient to simultaneously remember more than one aspect of a situation and to alternate, in a sequential fashion, between different requirements in a single task. The increased complexity and linguistic requirements of Part B, relative to Part A, frequently produce a major reflection of disruption in patients suffering significant cognitive deterioration on a neurological basis in advance of the expectations for their age.

The Minnesota Multiphasic Personality Inventory

Personality factors are both a primary and a secondary concern in cases of cerebral impairment. No neuropsychological evaluation can be considered adequate without a serious attempt to appreciate (*a*) the patient's current manner of personality functioning and coping and (*b*) the areas in which the patient is experiencing distress and dysfunction. For the population of patients who cannot complete the Minnesota Multiphasic Personality Inventory because of their educational background or current neurological deficits, projective evaluations are often employed. For the majority of patients who are not severely deteriorated or functionally illiterate, however, the MMPI provides a primarily quantitatively based evaluation of the stresses of neurological deficit and their consequences as well as an assessment of the degree of agitation, depression, and emotional distress frequently produced by nonneurological insult. This quantitatively based procedure is obviously subject to qualitative modification by means of complex inferential interpretive schemes that enhance the richness of the information provided. It should be pointed out that no specific personality profile on this or any other psychological test is associated with or diagnostic of the presence of neurological impairment (Russell, 1976). What the Minnesota Multiphasic Personality Inventory does provide is further descriptive information about the patient's current coping and adaptational capacity, the level of adjustmental comfort or discomfort, and the areas in need of further investigation in the context of a total health care program.

Multiple Inferential Methods to Enhance Qualitative and Quantitative Interpretative Analysis

Evaluation of a patient's performance must rely upon both *quantitative* and *qualitative* aspects of that performance. It is naively simple and simply naive to assert that either approach alone is sufficient. No set of procedures requiring complex human inference can become entirely quantitative. By the same token, no reputable psychologist fails to appreciate the value of rigor, standardized techniques, and numbers as a communication vehicle. While no recognized approach to neuropsychological examination relies exclusively on quantitative or qualitative procedures, some approaches tend to emphasize one over the other. The clinical interpretation of the behavior of patients is always both a qualitative and quantitative process with a degree of emphasis placed upon one or the other, dependent upon the purpose of the examination (the patient's requirements), the nature of the patient's problem, and the training of the clinician. This general rule of clinical practice applies neither more nor less to the ability than to the personality aspects of human functioning.

The complete Halstead–Reitan Battery and Allied Procedures is designed specifically to allow the complementary use of multiple inferential methods and thereby demands both qualitative and quantitative analysis of the data obtained. The four inferential methods primarily associated with this set of evaluation procedures are (*a*) level of performance; (*b*) pattern of performance; (*c*) specific or pathognomonic sign; and (*d*) comparative efficiency of the right versus left side of the body.

Level of Performance

Examination of the level of performance is primarily a quantitative inferential approach. Normative data, cut-off scores, and standard comparison group information provide a robust framework within which to describe the person's current level of psychological-behavioral functioning and competence. Initial predictions can be made about a patient's ability to perform in a variety of academic, occupational and rehabilitation settings. This type of information is at the center of the American psychological measurement tradition and can be obtained from a wide variety of tasks in the neuropsychological battery, many of which are subject to evaluation with other interpretational methods as well.

Pattern of Performance

Pattern analysis represents both a qualitative and quantitative inferential scheme. From a purely quantitative point of view, cut-off scores and the discrepancy between quantitative measures of verbal and visuospatial abilities as well as between higher and lower level psychological functions can point toward important areas of strengths and deficits. Discrepancies between Verbal and Performance IQs have a known statistical frequency. The direction of these differences has a reasonably stable relationship to functions of the right and left cerebral hemispheres in the context of broader neuropsychological evaluation. At the same time, the types of performances contributing to the relatively high and low points in the pattern provide for qualitative assessment of the degree of significance that can be attributed to any quantitative deficit. Qualitative understanding of the demands of the task and the types of performances that went into each aspect of a particular pattern further contribute to the final evaluation of their overall neuropsychological significance.

Specific or Pathognomonic Sign

This inferential method, while not immune to quantification, has been included specifically in the Halstead-Reitan procedures not only because of the richness of the information it provides, but also because it underlines the importance of qualitative as well as quantitative understanding. Certain motor, sensory, and especially linguistic and constructional performances can be viewed as abnormal without reference to quantification. Their significance is sufficiently specific and robust as to provide direct commentary not only on the integrity of brain functions but also on the anterior, posterior and right-left dimensions of the neurological deficit producing the behavioral aberrations.

Comparative Efficiency of the Right versus Left Sides of the Body

The comparative performance of the two sides of the body demands the utilization of motor and sensory tasks not typically included in standard psychological evaluations. It also provides an evaluation of what are commonly referred to as lower level psychological functions not necessarily influenced by factors such as educational level and motivation which are known to affect aspects of higher level cognitive activity. Because it is unlikely that motivational, emotional, or cultural factors will differentially influence performance of the two sides of the body, information regarding the relative efficiency of the right and left body sides is highly important from both a quantitative and a qualitative point of view to aid in the interpretation of other information not independent of motivational, emotional, or cultural variables. From a purely psychological point of view, motor and sensory information pertaining to the integrity of the two sides of the body and the contribution this information makes to an understanding of the functioning of the two cerebral hemispheres is exceptionally important with regard to coping and adaptation, occupational activities, and rehabilitation potential.

Summary

It must be clear that neither the examination procedures nor the inferential methods used for their interpretation can stand alone or bear the weight of the evaluation of overall brain-behavior relationships. It is, in fact, respect for the complexity of these brain-behavior relationships that demands not only a reasonably comprehensive set of psychological-behavioral procedures, but also the interrelated network of interpretational understanding. From a purely practical point of view, this complex interrelationship of inferential methods and qualitative and quantitative analyses across a reasonably broad sample of behavior allows trained technical and professional personnel to continue their efforts to provide an adequate neuropsychological assessment within a clinically practical time limit. Granting that all possible expressions of human deficit and all possible areas of human knowledge and performance cannot be tapped short of a lifetime of individual observation, some sampling procedure is a necessity. The validity of the Halstead-Reitan Battery and Allied Procedures as both a diagnostic and descriptive tool has been found to be extremely high across a broad range of neuropathological entities (Filskov & Goldstein, 1974; Reitan, 1964). It also has been found to be highly useful within the context of developing coping and adaption strategies as well as in evaluating rehabilitational programs (Barth & Boll, Chapter 14). A recent review of validity studies of this entire battery and its component parts may be found in Boll (1978, 1981b).

Issues of Validity

There are two important issues of validity which deserve consideration. The first, and traditionally the only, issue to receive attention in the psychology literature is the ability of the procedures in question to identify the entity or entities under examination. In the field of neuropsychology, the standard search is for differences (statistically significant ones only need apply) between brain-damaged populations and populations without brain damage or other medical, behavioral, or psychiatric difficulties likely to affect performances on behavioral measures. Success is measured by a test's ability to differentiate between these two populations. Clinical utility, however, raises the standard of validity to successful differentiation among individuals according to population membership.

Starting with Halstead's original work (Halstead, 1947), the expanding battery of tests has enjoyed consistent validation within this model. Reitan (1955) and Vega and Parsons (1967) provided the early impressive demonstrations of group separation using the entire battery. Separations between types of pathological processes and between anterior versus posterior or right versus left cerebral hemisphere lesions were also demonstrated (Filskov & Goldstein, 1974; Reitan, 1964). Specific populations, including those with degenerative disease (Boll, Heaton & Reitan, 1974; Reitan & Boll, 1971), pseudoneurologic conditions (Matthews, Shaw & Kløve, 1966), traumatic injuries (Dodrill, 1978; Kløve & Matthews, 1974), questionable brain disorders (Tsushima & Towne, 1977), and minimal brain dysfunction (Reitan & Boll, 1973), were found to behave in reliably different fashions on this battery of tests from non-brain-damaged persons. Efforts to separate persons with disorders characterized by changing diagnostic criteria and increasing suspicion of neurobiological disorder (e.g., schizophrenia) from other patients with definite but mild diffuse neurological disorders met, not surprisingly, with mixed results (Boll, 1974; Klonoff, Fibiger, & Hutton, 1970; Watson, Thomas, Anderson, & Felling, 1968). However, strong associations were found between several criteria used to diagnose brain damage and measures of the behavioral changes due to brain damage. Criteria against which the battery has been assessed include the physical neurological examination (Russell, Neuringer, & Goldstein, 1970), electroencephalogram (Kløve & White, 1963), and pneumoencephalographic status (Matthews & Booker, 1972). That changes in health or integrity of the brain and brain functions have a measurable correlate should be no surprise to anyone who recognizes the brain as the organ of human behavior. It was, of course, necessary to provide, in scientific terms, a demonstration of this type of validity in order to show the usefulness of the Halstead-Reitan Battery and Allied Procedures in clinical practice. Demonstrations of the applicability of neuropsychological procedures to (*a*) the assessment of populations such as substance abusers (Grant & Judd, 1976; Parsons & Farr, 1981) and those with learning disabilities (Rourke, 1981), and (*b*) aid in issues of forensic psychology (Satz & McMahon, 1981) and rehabilitation (Barth & Boll, Chapter 14) indicate the growing clinical utility of neuropsychology and the expanding role of clinical psychology as it emerges from its purely mental health orientation into a broader health care profession.

The second issue of validity is the meaning of data that fail to provide discrimination between groups. These data are frequently described as negative results. In the field of psychology, negative results have bad, or at least less than desirable, connotations. In medicine (from whence, in fact, most patients seen by medical or health care psychologists originate), negative results are far from meaningless. They not only convey important information but typically they convey information viewed with high regard—good news! For example, if an adult begins to have seizures, the cause may be a serious brain disorder such as cerebral neoplasm or abscess. Certain neuroradiological procedures such as brain scan and CAT scan are commonly performed as part of the evaluation of adult seizure disorders. If these studies are negative (normal), much information specific to diagnosis and treatment has been provided. This is true despite the fact that these two procedures "failed" to identify a cause for the seizures. They recorded no evidence of brain damage even when the patient's symptoms made it clear that the brain was not normal. In terms of old-fashioned hit rates, the conclusion would be that the brain scan and CAT scan simply may not be good tests for brain damage. In fact, they are not used merely as tests for brain damage and no test, radiological, psychological, or otherwise, should be. No competent neurologist or neurosurgeon is even interested in such a thing. Neurologists and neurosurgeons are interested in describing, diagnosing, and treating neurological impairment. This requires knowing what is not there and what does not need treatment as well as knowing what is wrong and what is amenable to intervention. Thus, the results of the brain scan and CAT scan were not incorrect. They very accurately described one aspect of the patient's neurological situation. In so doing they removed the need to treat a tumor or abscess and left the cause of the seizures to be determined by other procedures equally correct in their descriptions of the aspects of the brain they are designed to assess.

This same principle may be applied to psychological measurement. Patients with brain damage are not dead or totally destroyed. Many function quite well in life and most retain at least some areas of neuropsychological adequacy. In addition, it should be noted that various patients displaying similar behavioral difficulties may suffer different neuropathological disorders. Thus, understanding brain-behavior relationships demands not only knowledge of what has gone wrong but knowledge of what has not. Negative results on some behavioral measures are necessary for accurate diagnosis and description of a patient's specific neuropathological disorder (e.g., head injury versus tumor) and, thus, are not wrong or invalid. On the contrary, they describe accurately the patient's condition or psychological status. Lauretta Bender has criticized the limiting implications of a purely quantitative approach to the Visual Motor Gestalt Test. She has indicated that there are no "errors" in performing this set of tasks. Rather, any performance correctly reflects current experience, level of maturation, and the effects of any number of environmental, organic, and psychosocial variables on total personal (ego) functioning (Bender, 1967). Interpretation of the data cannot rest on the basis of the test scores alone but must be left to the professional clinician to understand in the fullest context of the total evaluation.

Conclusion

The decade of the 1970s was marked by considerable growth of the use of neuropsychological procedures with patients (*a*) following head injury and cerebral vascular accident, (*b*) as a part of overall care for epilepsy and degenerating disorders of the elderly, and (*c*) as an aid in evaluation of neurological and neurosurgical procedures such as removal of partial cerebral artery obstructions (Boll, 1981a; Goldstein, Kleinknecht, & Gallo, 1970; King, Gideon, Haynes, Dempsey, & Jenkins, 1977). The 1980s and 1990s will be characterized by increased interest in better management of long-term disorders and the recognition of long-term sequelae of a broad range of neurological and general medical disorders.

References

Bender, L. Visual Motor Gestalt function in 6 and 7-year-old normal and schizophrenic children. In J. Zubin & G. Jervis (Eds.), *Psychopathology of mental development.* New York: Grune & Stratton, 1967.

Benton, A. L. *The revised visual retention test: Clinical and experimental applications.* New York: Psychological Corporation, 1963.

Boll, T. J. Psychological differentiation of patients with schizophrenia versus lateralized cerebrovascular, neoplastic, or traumatic brain damage. *Journal of Abnormal Psychology,* 1974, *83,* 456-458.

Boll, T. J. Diagnosing brain impairment. In B. B. Wolman (Ed.), *Clinical diagnosis of mental disorders.* New York: Plenum, 1978.

Boll, T. J. Behavioral assessment of neuropsychological disorders. In D. H. Barlow (Ed.), *Behavioral assessment of adult disorders.* New York: Guilford Press, 1981. (a)

Boll, T. J. The Halstead-Reitan Neuropsychological Battery. In S. B. Filskov & T. J. Boll (Eds.), *Handbook of clinical neuropsychology.* New York: Wiley, 1981. (b)

Boll, T. J., Berent, S., & Richards, H. Tactile-perceptual functioning as a factor in general psychological abilities. *Perceptual and Motor Skills,* 1977, *44,* 535-539.

Boll, T. J., Heaton, R., & Reitan, R. M. Neuropsychological and emotional correlates of Huntington's chorea. *Journal of Nervous and Mental Disease,* 1974, *158,* 61-69.

Boll, T. J., Richards, H., & Berent, S. Tactile-perceptual functioning and academic performance in brain impaired and unimpaired children. *Perceptual and Motor Skills,* 1978, *47,* 491-495.

Buschke, H. Selective reminding for analyses of memory and learning. *Journal of Verbal Learning and Verbal Behavior,* 1973, *12,* 543-550.

Cattell, J. McK. Mental tests and measurements. *Mind,* 1890, *15,* 373-380.

Dodrill, C. B. The hand dynamometer as a neuropsychological measure. *Journal of Consulting and Clinical Psychology,* 1978, *46,* 1432-1435.

Filskov, S. B., & Goldstein, S. G. Diagnostic validity of the Halstead-Reitan Neuropsychological Battery. *Journal of Consulting and Clinical Psychology,* 1974, *42,* 383-388.

Filskov, S. B., Grimm, B. H., & Lewis, J. Brain behavior relationships. In S. B. Filskov & T. J. Boll (Eds.), *Handbook of clinical neuropsychology.* New York: Wiley, 1981.

Galton, F. *Inquiries into human faculty and its development.* London: Macmillan, 1893.

Golden, C. J. A standardized version of Luria's Neuropsychological Tests: A quantitative and qualitative approach to neuropsychological evaluation. In S. B. Filskov & T. J. Boll (Eds.), *Handbook of clinical neuropsychology.* New York: Wiley, 1981.

Goldstein, S. G., Kleinknecht, R. A., & Gallo, A. E. Neuropsychological changes associated with carotid endarterectomy. *Cortex,* 1970, *6,* 308-322.

Goodglass, H., & Kaplan, E. *The assessment of aphasia and related disorders.* Philadelphia: Lea & Fibiger, 1972.

Grant, I., & Judd, L. I. Neuropsychological and EEG disturbances in polydrug users. *American Journal of Psychiatry,* 1976, *133,* 1039-1042.

Halstead, W. C. *Brain and intelligence: A quantitative study of the frontal lobes.* Chicago: University of Chicago Press, 1947.

Halstead, W. C., & Wepman, J. M. The Halstead-Wepman Aphasia Screening Test. *Journal of Speech and Hearing Disorders,* 1949, *14,* 9-13.

Hécaen, H., & Albert, M. L. *Human neuropsychology.* New York: Wiley, 1978.

Jastak, J. F., & Jastak, S. R. *The Wide Range Achievement Test.* Wilmington: Guidance Associates of Delaware, 1976.

King, G. D., Gideon, D. A., Haynes, C. D., Dempsey, R. L., & Jenkins, C. W. Intellectual and personality changes associated with carotid endarterectomy. *Journal of Clinical Psychology,* 1977, *33,* 215-220.

Kinsbourne, M. The development of cerebral dominance. In S. B. Filskov & T. J. Boll (Eds.), *Handbook of clinical neuropsychology.* New York: Wiley, 1981.

Klonoff, H., Fibiger, C. H., & Hutton, G. H. Neuropsychological patterns in chronic schizophrenia. *Journal of Nervous and Mental Disease,* 1970, *150,* 261-300.

Kløve, H., & Matthews, C. G. Neuropsychological studies of patients with epilepsy. In R. M. Reitan & L. Davison (Eds.), *Clinical neuropsychology: Current status and applications.* Washington, D.C.: Winston, 1974.

Kløve, H., & White, P. T. The relationship of degree of electroencephalographic abnormalities to the distribution of Wechsler-Bellevue scores. *Neurology,* 1963, *13,* 423-430.

Lezak, M. D. *Neuropsychological assessment.* New York: Oxford University Press, 1976.

Luria, A. R. Neuropsychological studies in the U.S.S.R., Part 1. *Proceedings of the National Academy of Science,* 1973, *70,* 959.

Matthews, C. G., & Booker, H. E. Pneumoencephalo graphic measurements and neuropsychological test performance in human adults. *Cortex,* 1972, *8,* 69-92.

Matthews, C. G., Shaw, D. J., & Køve, H. Psychological test performances in neurologic and "pseudoneurologic" subjects. *Cortex,* 1966, *2,* 244-253.

Milner, B. Psychological defects produced by temporal lobe excision. *Association for Research in Nervous and Mental Disease, Research Publications,* 1958, *36,* 244-257.

Milner, B. Laterality effects in audition. In V. B. Mountcastle (Ed.), *Interhemispheric relations and cerebral dominance.* Baltimore: Johns Hopkins Press, 1962.

Milner, B. Brain mechanisms suggested by studies of temporal lobes. In F. L. Darley (Ed.), *Brain mechanisms underlying speech and language.* New York: Grune & Stratton, 1967.

Milner, B. Visual retention and recall after right temporal excision in man. *Neuropsychologia,* 1968, *6,* 191-210.

Parsons, O. A., & Farr, S. P. The neuropsychology of alcohol and drug abuse. In S. B. Filskov & T. J. Boll (Eds.), *Handbook of clinical neuropsychology.* New York: Wiley, 1981.

Porch, B. *Porch Index of Communicative Ability.* Palo Alto: Consulting Psychologists, 1971.

Reitan, R. M. An investigation of the validity of Halstead's measures of biological intelligence. *Archives of Neurology and Psychiatry,* 1955, *73,* 28-35.

Reitan, R. M. Psychological deficits resulting from cerebral lesions in man. In J. M. Warren & K. Akert (Eds.), *The frontal granular cortex and behavior.* New York: McGraw Hill, 1964.

Reitan, R. M., & Boll, T. J. Intellectual and cognitive functions in Parkinson's disease. *Journal of Consulting and Clinical Psychology,* 1971, *37,* 364-369.

Reitan, R. M., & Boll, T. J. Neuropsychological correlates of minimal brain dysfunction. *Annals of the New York Academy of Sciences,* 1973, *205,* 65-88.

Rourke, B. Neuropsychological assessment of children with learning disabilities. In S. B. Filskov & T. J. Boll (Eds.), *Handbook of clinical neuropsychology.* New York: Wiley, 1981.

Russell, E. W. A multiple scoring method for assessment of complex memory functions. *Journal of Consulting and Clinical Psychology,* 1975, *43,* 800-809.

Russell, E. W. The Bender-Gestalt and the Halstead-Reitan Battery: A case study. *Journal of Clinical Psychology,* 1976, *32,* 355-361.

Russell, E. W. The pathology and clinical examination of memory. In S. B. Filskov & T. J. Boll (Eds.), *Handbook of clinical neuropsychology.* New York: Wiley, 1981.

Russell, E. W., Neuringer, C., & Goldstein, G. *Assessment of brain damage: A neuropsychological key approach.* New York: Wiley, 1970.

Satz, P., & McMahon, E. A. Clinical neuropsychology: Some forensic applications. In S. B. Filskov & T. J. Boll (Eds.), *Handbook of clinical neuropsychology.* New York: Wiley, 1981.

Smith, A. Neuropsychological testing in neurological disorders. *Advances in Neurology,* 1975, *7,* 49-110.

Smith, A. Principles underlying human brain functions in neuropsychological sequelae of different neuropathological processes. In S. B. Filskov & T. J. Boll (Eds.), *Handbook of clinical neuropsychology.* New York: Wiley, 1981.

Tsushima, W. T., & Towne, W. S. Neuropsychological abilities of young children with questionable brain disorders. *Journal of Consulting and Clinical Psychology,* 1977, *45,* 757-762.

Vega, A., & Parsons, O. A. Cross-validation of the Halstead-Reitan tests for brain damage. *Journal of Consulting Psychology,* 1967, *31,* 619-625.

Watson, C. G., Thomas, R. W., Anderson, D., & Felling, J. Differentiation of organics from schizophrenics at two chronicity levels by use of the Reitan-Halstead organic test battery. *Journal of Consulting and Clinical Psychology,* 1968, *32,* 679-684.

Wechsler, D. A. A standard memory scale for clinical use. *Journal of Psychology,* 1945, *19,* 87-95.

Wechsler, D. A. *Wechsler Adult Intelligence Scale manual.* New York: Psychological Corporation, 1955.

7

Functional Analysis of Alcohol Problems

MARK B. SOBELL
LINDA C. SOBELL

The field of alcohol studies has been changing radically over the past several years. Old ideas, largely predicated on anecdote and conjecture, are being replaced by concepts more consistent with empirical evidence (Pattison, Sobell, & Sobell, 1977). The traditional view of alcohol problems has been found to have serious limitations that compromise its utility. This chapter presents a different theoretical view of alcohol problems, compatible with the emerging concepts.

Several years of research have convincingly demonstrated that alcohol problems are complex, involving biological, physiologic, and sociocultural components, and pervading highly diverse and sometimes unique aspects of an individual's life and environment. These multifarious factors are readily subsumed in a functional analysis approach to alcohol problems.

The functional analysis model described in this chapter is intended to have heuristic value, rather than being a profound statement of theory. While the model incorporates certain basic assumptions, its major values are fourfold:

1. It provides a method for simplifying, classifying and arranging complex clinical data in a meaningful way.
2. It assures a relatively comprehensive assessment of person–environment interactions as they relate to drinking behavior.
3. It provides an opportunity to consider multiple alternatives for treatment intervention, each of which can be evaluated for potential advantages and disadvantages.
4. It suggests additional clinical data that may be needed in a given case.

In these ways, the model is a clinical tool. It provides the clinician with an orientation conducive to developing effective treatment strategies that are individualized and minimally intrusive on the client's life.

The functional analysis model of drinking decisions developed from a broad scope behavioral orientation to drinking problems (Sobell, Sobell, & Sheahan, 1976), which will be evident throughout this chapter. Considerable evidence suggests that it

Medical Psychology
Contributions to Behavioral Medicine

ISBN 0-12-565960-1

is useful to view all drinking, including problem drinking, as a discriminated operant behavior. That is, drinking occurs in some situations and not others (a discriminated behavior), and when it does occur it serves a purpose for the drinker. More specifically, drinking is acquired and maintained as a function of its consequences (an operant behavior). Thus, it is assumed that drinking is usually purposeful, despite the fact that some people may not always be able to articulate their reasons for drinking. Despite this behavioral foundation, however, biological and other factors (e.g., inferred psychological processes) are considered important and compatible with the basic model.

A Functional Analysis Model of Drinking Decisions

Figure 7.1 presents a simplified model for the functional analysis of drinking decisions and will be the focus of this paper. In Figure 7.1, behavioral options are portrayed for a given individual within a given context at a specified point in time. It is important to note that the model describes normal as well as abnormal drinking.

Before proceeding, it is critical to establish a definition for problem drinking. Over the past several years, numerous attempts have been made to define problem drinking or its variants (American Psychiatric Association, 1968, 1978; Bacon, 1976; Jellinek, 1960; Keller, 1960; National Council on Alcoholism, 1972). To date, however, no definition based on absolute criteria has achieved consensual acceptance in the field, largely because one can always find exceptions to the rule. This state of affairs may exist because drinking problems are idiosyncratically defined to some extent. When using a functional analysis model, these labeling difficulties are obviated somewhat, because problem drinking for any individual is defined by the total resultant consequences for the drinker or for society. It is implicitly recognized that what produces adverse consequences for one individual may not do so for another, or for that matter, may not do so for the same drinker in different circumstances.

Structure of the Model

Before examining applications of the functional analysis model, it is necessary to have a clear understanding of the various factors which constitute the model and their interrelationships.

Setting Events In the functional analysis model, the term, setting events, is used to connote a complex of factors which, taken as a whole, set the stage for a possible drinking decision. Some of the component factors are invariant (e.g., genetic endowment, physical limitations), others are relatively stable but subject to modification (e.g., beliefs or expectations about drinking, response tendencies, prevailing mood state), and still others are situation-specific (e.g., physical setting, presence of specific others, ease of access to alcohol). Stress is placed upon delineating a group of factors which, acting in combination, make it likely that an individual might decide to drink. The group of setting events is referred to as a "complex" emphasizing that multiple factors probably contribute to most drinking decisions. This is in contrast to approaches which emphasize a single factor (e.g., the presence of anxiety or tension) to the virtual exclusion of other influences.

The individual may or may not be aware of the various components of the setting events complex. Similarly, it is recognized that many aspects of the setting events complex may be beyond the purview of the clinician. To reiterate, however, the purpose of the model is to serve as a clinical aid. In fact, an inordinate amount of detail may have little practical value. Conversely, an overly simplified exposition may suggest either too few treatment strategies or interventions that could have unanticipated adverse consequences. In using the model as a tool, the key is to reach a pragmatic balance, having compiled enough assessment information to be relatively confident that most of the major setting events have been identified, without spending an undue amount of effort elucidating trivial components. In brief, the clinician should carefully evaluate the wide range of potential setting events before determining which factors are most likely to result in a drinking decision.

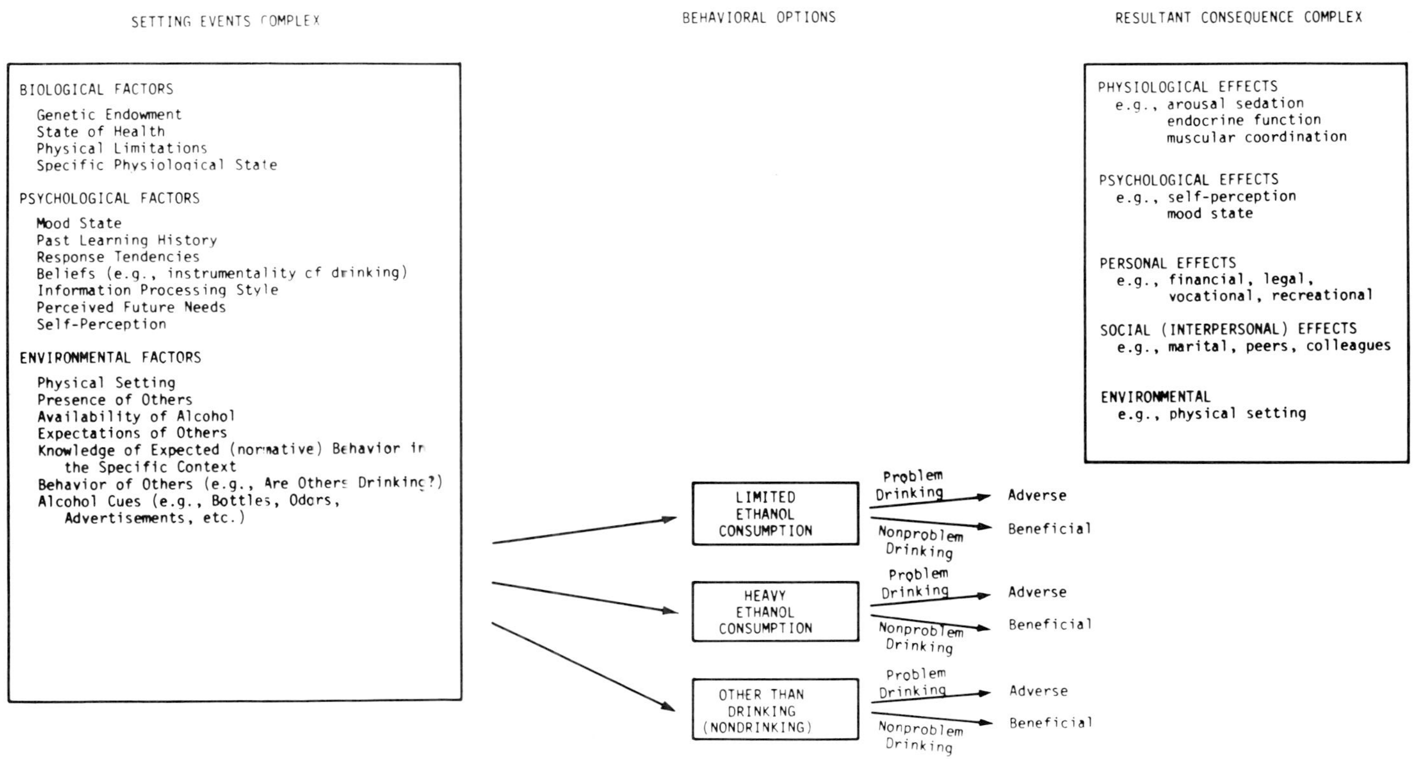

Figure 7.1. A simplified model for the functional analysis of drinking decisions. This model is basically intended as a clinical tool which the clinician can use to assure a comprehensive analysis of an individual's drinking behavior. Although presented as applicable for a specific individual at a particular point in time, that limitation is to facilitate description and explanation. In practice, the model is more appropriately used as a guide to help the therapist develop treatment strategies that save cost, effort, and risks.

Behavioral Options When delineating behavioral options for an individual at a given point in time, three distinctions must be made. First, some options involve drinking and others do not. Second, if someone chooses to drink, their explicit intention might be to drink heavily (for present purposes, heavy drinking is defined as drinking with the avowed intention of becoming clearly intoxicated) or to drink in a limited manner (not with a goal of becoming clearly intoxicated). Third, no matter what particular behavior is enacted, the total resultant outcome can have either a negative or positive valence. (Special cases, such as when outcomes are essentially neutral, are beyond the present consideration.)

As mentioned earlier, use of the term "problem" or a similar referent to describe a behavior reflects a value judgement related to the consequences or risk of consequences associated with that behavior. Thus, in this model it is the response–consequence contingency that defines whether or not a given behavior is a problem. Applying this criterion, the same behavior may be designated as either a problem or nonproblem behavior, depending upon the likely consequences of the behavior in the situation in which it occurs. For example, the consumption of two glasses of wine with dinner might not constitute a problem for the drinker unless the consumption occurred at a dinner for the elders of a fundamentalist, antidrinking religious group. This flexibility is a major strength of the model. The appropriateness of behaviors is evaluated by considering the total possible resultant consequences, thus accounting for behavior–environment interactions.

An important consideration in clinical casework is assessment of the client's behavioral repertoire. For example, some people are relatively unskilled at performing adaptive behaviors, and helping such individuals to establish adequate response repertoires (e.g., assertive skills, interpersonal conversational skills) is requisite to developing effective nondrinking alternatives. Delineation of a person's response capabilities is also important for determining whether a person's behavior can be attributed to response deficits or to other factors, such as insufficient motivation (see the section on pragmatic applications of the model, pp. 85–89).

Consequences Like setting events, consequences of behaviors are usually multifaceted. While the temporal contiguity of various consequences and behaviors is thought to be a particularly important factor in behavioral explanations of drinking, this issue has not been adequately investigated. Nevertheless, it has been hypothesized that drinking usually produces relatively immediate positive consequences (e.g., change in mood state, avoidance of something aversive, social approval), which are then generally followed by primarily negative but delayed consequences (e.g., hangover, having to deal with problems created for oneself while drinking, etc.). The immediate positive consequences are hypothesized to be the most important influences on behavior because of their close temporal contiguity with the drinking. In fact, many of the delayed aversive consequences of drinking may go unnoticed by the drinker. For example, some drinkers may not be aware that other people have started to avoid opportunities to socialize with them in drinking situations. The types of consequences which need to be considered are far reaching, including physiological effects, psychological effects (e.g., one's self-perception, beliefs), personal effects (e.g., legal problems, economic effects), social or interpersonal effects, and environmental effects.

Using the Model

Effective use of the functional analysis model requires certain prerequisite skills and knowledge by clinicians: (*a*) a broad knowledge of alcohol and alcohol problems; (*b*) a generic background in the study of psychopathology; and (*c*) skills in clinical interviewing, and behavioral assessment and evaluation. The importance of these latter skills has been stressed by others (Goldfried & Davison, 1976; Goldstein, 1975; Kanfer & Grimm, 1977; Lazarus, 1971; Miller, 1976; Wolpe, 1969). In essence, the model can be useful only to the extent that clinicians are able to specify its components.

The value of the model can be best demonstrated by considering examples and implications for therapeutic strategies. In a global sense, the model is useful for identifying an individual's major life problems, both immediate and long-term. An assessment of general drinking situations and consequences, as well as the existing behavioral repertoire, allows the clinician to gain an initial perspective on the problem areas which can be addressed in treatment. Although more detailed analysis of specific past and present drinking situations helps to structure the general model, analysis of specific drinking decisions is more useful for identifying potentially effective treatment strategies. It should be noted that clients often are not very proficient at describing either the setting events that precede their drinking or the total consequences and potential consequences of their drinking. Thus, it is usually necessary for clinicians to actively assist clients in identifying and objectively assessing the setting events and consequences. Moreover, clients who actively participate in drinking decision analyses should be better able to understand and modify their drinking behavior. Finally, such analyses are also valuable in training clinicians to construct comprehensive and well reasoned treatment plans.

Pragmatic Applications

Much of the remainder of this chapter focuses on how the functional analysis model can be used in treatment planning. At the outset, it is important to recognize that the model is simply part of a larger conceptual system; a system predicated on behavior occurring over time. There are many links which are relevant when the model is conceptualized as part of a feedback system that reflects ongoing interactions between the individual and the environment. For example, the consequences of a behavior may serve to change the initial setting events complex such that drinking is no longer a high probability response. Thus, an individual who drinks predominantly in response to social cues might decide to have an after dinner drink largely to gain social approval from others (e.g., the host or hostess might ask the person to sample a new type of liqueur). Having sampled the drink, the setting events complex might change such that requesting further alcohol would be inappropriate. Conversely, an individual who chooses to drink in pursuit of a change in feeling state (e.g., from anxious to relaxed) might find that just a few drinks do not achieve the desired effect. In this case, the essential components of the original setting events might remain basically unchanged, leading to the need for further decisions. The options remaining would include further drinking or some response other than drinking. The choice of further drinking in such a situation might be conceptualized as a high risk option, if one hypothesizes that heavy drinking has a greater likelihood of producing negative consequences than does limited drinking. Moreover, if a person continues to drink and achieves the desired mood change, heavier drinking may be more likely to occur in similar future situations. In such cases, nondrinking options (e.g., jogging, going to a movie, meditation) might provide more positive long-term outcomes.

With respect to making drinking decisions, two additional points need to be considered. First, not all nondrinking options (e.g., using bartiturates to feel sedated, robbing a bank) are likely to produce less aversive resultant consequences than continued drinking. Thus, the potential effectiveness of various nondrinking responses should also be considered. Second, the option exercised should help to change the setting events complex in a desired and beneficial manner. For instance, while avoiding a situation might temporarily obviate the necessity of dealing with the setting events (e.g., by physically removing oneself from a particular setting), it is conceivable that the major components of the setting events complex either may not change or may be likely to recur in the future when avoidance may be precluded as an option. Thus, the acquisition or practice of behaviors that are likely to change the setting events complex would be a preferred alternative to a simple avoidance response.

A brief consideration of treatment goals is relevant when discussing pragmatic applications of the model. For years, the primary treatment goal for persons with drinking problems has been abstinence. Abstinence as the sole treatment goal intrinsically suggests that for any individual who has had a drinking problem, any ingestion of alcohol is likely to result in adverse effects or substantial risk of such effects. While this may be the case for many individuals (e.g., certainly for persons who have suffered significant physical damage as a result of their drinking), a considerable body of research, conducted primarily over the last 20 years, indicates that nonproblem drinking outcomes are not uncommon (reviewed in Sobell, 1978). Based largely on correlational data, such outcomes seem most likely to be achieved by persons with less severe drinking histories (e.g., those who have never been physically addicted to alcohol). Although too few rigorous studies have been conducted to determine which individuals can successfully achieve nonabstinent goals and how those goals can best be achieved, it is a fact that such outcomes routinely occur, even when persons have been treated in programs that strongly emphasize abstinence.

The functional analysis model provides a more flexible approach to treatment goals, as it emphasizes the consequences of behavior. Namely, the outcome to be avoided is an aversive consequence of the behavior. Thus, the desired outcome is a *reduction in drinking to a nonproblem level.* Interestingly, such a treatment goal incorporates both abstinent and nonabstinent outcomes. While in most cases total abstinence may be the only way to avoid further drinking problems, this may not be necessary in all cases.

It is readily apparent that the functional analysis model can identify several potentially effective treatment strategies and points of intervention for any given case. Of course, the choice of a particular strategy should be related to the ease with which treatment can be effected and how well the client can comply with the treatment strategy. *Effective* interventions refer to treatment which resolves current problems and has a high probability of avoiding similar problems in the future. Given a variety of potentially effective treatment strategies, however, it must be recognized that the various strategies will involve different costs for both the client and the therapist (or treatment program). The costs may be related to time, effort, modification of lifestyle, or economics, all of which represent demands upon the client and therapist if treatment is to be implemented.

Consistent with clinical ethics, the personal costs which treatment might exact from clients must be considered in treatment planning. For example, hospitalization or residential treatment usually makes greater short-term demands upon clients than outpatient treatment. Strategies involving the establishment of new peer group affiliations (as when a client is advised to join Alcoholics Anonymous) may involve greater demands than those involving only minor changes in the client's social network (e.g., avoiding associating with a single individual). It is suggested that the strategies enacted should be *efficient in terms of requiring the least total change in lifestyle for the client,* as long as they effectively attain treatment goals. For example, an individual who is employed full-time at a new job and supporting a family may be evaluated as potentially benefiting from either inpatient or outpatient treatment. In this case, however, outpatient treatment would be the most efficient strategy because it would not put the family's income or the person's job at risk. In cases where the potential effectiveness of treatments are uncertain, it may be helpful to develop a hierarchy of feasible strategies ordered in terms of efficiency. The most efficient strategies could then be implemented first, with more demanding treatments used only if initial efforts do not produce satisfactory results.

Returning to a more literal application of the model, Figure 7.2 illustrates the numerous and subtle ways in which a set of consequences can impact on various aspects of future behavior. Such considerations are critical for evaluating the potential effectiveness and efficiency of interventions. For example, if an individual tends to become verbally abusive when drinking, others might come to recognize that pattern and avoid future drinking situations involving that individual.

Another example relevant to Figure 7.2 involves the notion that an effective response will often achieve its effect by changing the prevailing setting events. One implication of this consideration is that the use of avoidance strategies as behavioral options should be given careful and critical evaluation with regard to long-term benefits. For example, changing the physical environment may change the momentary setting events such that drinking is no longer a high probability behavior. However, if this is all that happens, the response

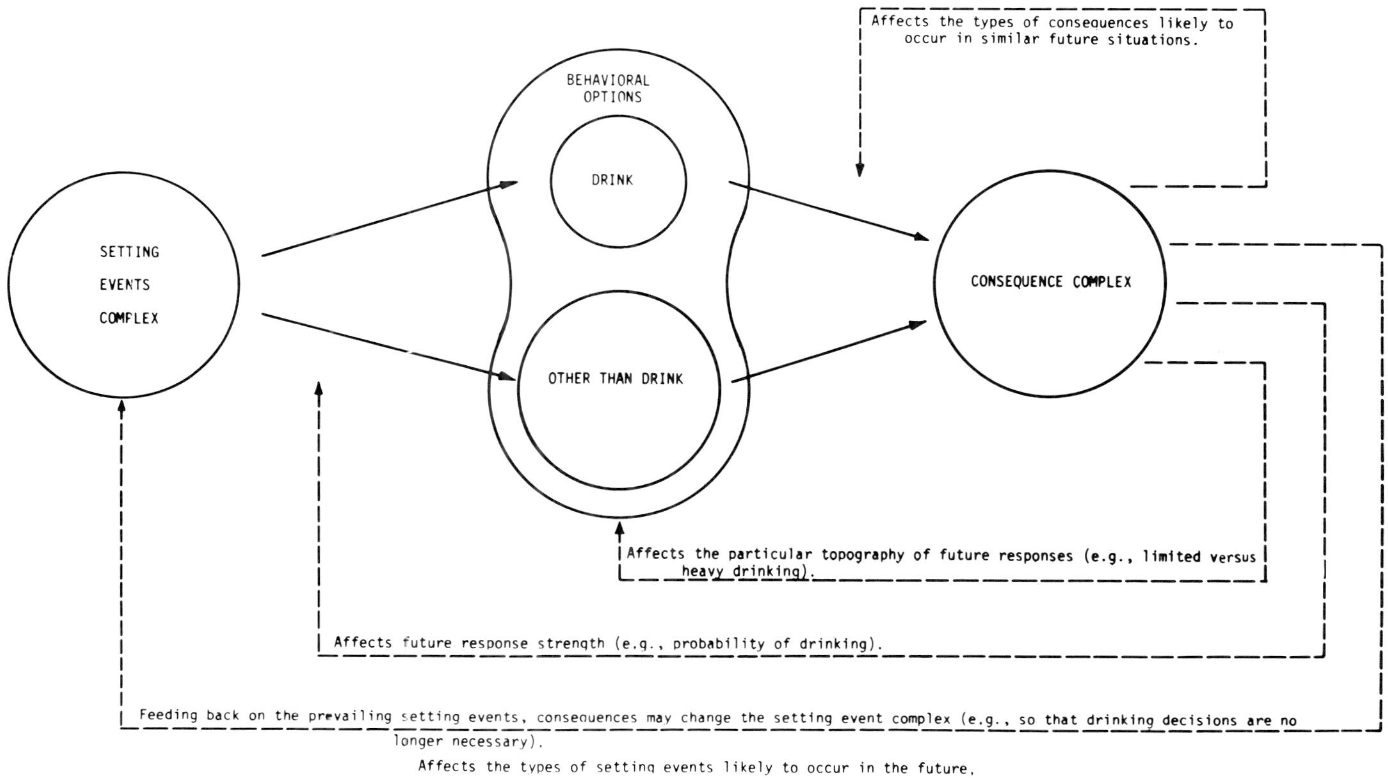

Figure 7.2. The potential impact of consequences on future behavior.

strength of drinking options may be essentially unchanged should the same or similar circumstances occur in the future (i.e., when an avoidance option may not be feasible). The use of Antabuse as the sole treatment intervention also constitutes a simple avoidance strategy. Unless coupled with other interventions aimed at developing alternative nonproblem options, simple avoidance strategies might be evaluated as not very effective in terms of lessening the potential for future problem drinking.

The above examples suggest that attention must also be given to assessing whether the individual has an adequate behavioral repertoire for responding to setting events in a nonproblem manner. Since an extensive literature already exists describing methods of enhancing clients' behavioral repertoires (e.g., relaxation training, assertive training, social skills training), those methods will not be discussed here. We will, however, consider other options which have not yet been adequately investigated. Many of these options may be achieved through cognitive behavior modification methods. They involve modifying a person's self-perceptions, beliefs, and attitudes which, hypothetically, comprise part of the setting events complex.

There are many ways in which cognitive factors might influence drinking decisions and, thus, be components of the functional analysis model. For example, there may be discrepancies between the way setting events are perceived by an individual and how they are perceived by others (i.e., what actually happened). In some cases, the individual may be attending to selective aspects of the environment, and thus, may not recognize that all that is necessary for making adaptive decisions is simply more information. In these cases simply helping individuals perform a behavioral analysis of their drinking might constitute a sufficient intervention.

Cognitive influences can also be quite subtle; thus, an individual might be aware of important environmental factors but have a distorted perception of those factors. For instance, a person may misinterpret a friend's innocuous comment as a personal insult. We frequently make inferences about environmental events: We attribute motives to others, we seek explanations for our own mood states, and we infer the consequences likely to be contingent upon our various behavioral options. When our inferences are incorrect, our perceived behavioral options might be unduly constrained. Suppose, for example, that a person has acquired a pattern of drinking heavily in certain circumstances because at one time that behavior was effective in avoiding certain consequences. Further suppose that these conditions changed, such that the original aversive consequences no longer would occur were the individual not to drink heavily. This situation describes the classic dilemma involved in the extinction of avoidance behavior. As long as the behavior continues to be emitted in what were once avoidance situations, the individual does not have an opportunity to learn that aversive consequences no longer follow nonperformance of the avoidance response.

In essence, lack of awareness of important environmental cues, distortions of perceived environmental cues, and inaccurate inferences are processes which can affect the validity of the identification of setting events, the identification of feasible behavioral options, and the identification of anticipated consequences for various behaviors (the expected effectiveness of behaviors). The model is further complicated by the fact that such cognitive problems can relate to past events (e.g., misinterpretation of past response–consequences relationships), present events, and future events (e.g., incorrect expectations of long-term consequences of behaviors). In cases where a functional analysis identifies cognitive problems that might be related to problem drinking, treatment strategies such as cognitive restructuring (Lazarus, 1971) should be considered.

Although problem solving skills have received some attention in the clinical behavior therapy literature (D'Zurilla & Goldfried, 1971; Goldfried & Davison, 1976; Sobell & Sobell, 1973, 1978), this area of clinical research has yet to be adequately explored. Nevertheless, it is obvious that many treatment strategies are predicated on an assumption that clients do not possess adequate skills to resolve their own problems. The functional analysis model might help clients learn, in a structured manner, how to analyze and respond more adaptively to problems. In this regard, the model can be used as a training vehicle. That is, by providing a framework for organizing observations and selecting interventions, it can be used to train clients to analyze their own behavior and make rational decisions. Similarly, the model might have preventive applications, such as helping adolescents learn how to make decisions which will benefit them in the long run.

Another application of the model derives from delineating expected consequences of behavioral options. Specifically, it may become apparent that in a given situation, there are no options with fully beneficial consequences. There may also be no easy solution. In these instances, the option of choice should clearly be that which promises the least aversive total outcome. When the therapist and client outline the options which exist and recognize that some negative consequences might be unavoidable, such recognition can aid clients in taking actions that they might have otherwise avoided.

The model also stresses the need for treatment to generalize to the extratreatment environment. Thus, acquisition of an expanded behavioral repertoire within therapy may have limited utility in changing real life setting events, unless issues such as the environmental maintenance of the newly acquired behaviors are addressed in treatment.

Another issue for which the model has clinical relevance concerns the vague construct of motivation. This construct is most often used to characterize a client's unwillingness to engage in certain behaviors. In this regard, motivation is often regarded as an explanation rather than a description of behavior. The functional analysis model suggests that a more precise analysis of motivational problems is possible. For example, clients may have inaccurate perceptions of setting events or anticipated consequences, such that they incorrectly perceive the probable effectiveness of a particular behavior. The client also may not be aware of various potentially effective options which exist. At a more subtle level, a client may have performed an unrealistic cost-benefit analysis for the various options identified. Thus, rather than being a vaguely defined internal state that results in inaction, motivation is a problem which is subject to functional analysis and moreover can be meaningfully addressed in treatment.

Application to Chronic Addictive Drinking

This chapter would be incomplete without at least some discussion of how the model relates to chronic addictive drinking. Clearly, the first step toward such a pattern of behavior relates to choice of a heavy drinking option that is frequently reinforced by what are perceived to be generally positive consequences. As drinking becomes more frequent, more generalized, and an individual's acquired tolerance to alcohol increases, the risk of long-term aversive consequences also increases. In reference to Figure 7.2, it may be that the consequences of the actual drinking (e.g., physical dependence evidenced by withdrawal symptoms when drinking ceases) come to form part of the setting events complex that, in turn, sets the occasion for further drinking. This is, in fact, the vicious cycle which has long been speculated to underlie all addictive drug use. It is also reasonable to hypothesize that a person who drinks for subjective consequences (e.g., a drastic change in mood state) would be more at risk of developing an addictive drinking pattern than an individual for whom drinking primarily served a social purpose. The reason for this is that as a person's acquired tolerance to alcohol increases, greater amounts of alcohol must be consumed in order to experience the same subjective effects of alcohol. Thus, the model suggests that an individual who drinks primarily for the purpose of changing internal states would be at greater risk for developing drinking problems than a person who drinks primarily in relation to environmental consequences. This hypothesis is, of course, subject to experimental test.

Conclusion

This chapter has described how a functional analysis model of drinking decisions can serve as a conceptual tool for organizing clinical data and developing individualized treatment plans. While a myriad of possible applications of the model exist, selected examples have been presented to demonstrate the model's use and clinical value. The model also provides a quasi-theoretical structure for helping clinicians understand the development of drinking problems and suggests possible preventive interventions.

References

American Psychiatric Association, *Diagnostic and statistical manual: Mental disorders (DSM II).* Washington, D.C.: American Psychiatric Association, 1968.

American Psychiatric Association, *Diagnostic and statistical manual: Mental Disorders (DSM III).* Washington, D.C.: American Psychiatric Association, 1978. (Draft)

Bacon, S. D. Defining adolescent alcohol use: Implications for a definition of adolescent alcoholism. *Journal of Studies on Alcohol,* 1976, *37,* 1014–1019. (Report of meeting)

D'Zurilla, T. J., & Goldfried, M. R. Problem solving and behavior modification. *Journal of Abnormal Psychology,* 1971, *78,* 107–126.

Goldfried, M. R., & Davison, G. C. *Clinical behavior therapy.* New York: Holt, Rinehart & Winston, 1976.

Goldstein, A. P. Relationship enhancement methods. In F. H. Kanfer & A. P. Goldstein (Eds.), *Helping people change.* New York: Pergamon, 1975.

Jellinek, E. M. *The disease concept of alcoholism.* New Brunswick, N.J.: Hillhouse Press, 1960.

Kanfer, F. H., & Grimm, L. G. Behavioral analysis: Selecting target behaviors in the interview. *Behavior Modification,* 1977, *1,* 7–28.

Keller, M. Definition of alcoholism. *Quarterly Journal of Studies on Alcohol,* 1960, *21,* 125–134.

Lazarus, A. A. *Behavior therapy and beyond.* New York: McGraw-Hill, 1971.

Miller, P. M. *Behavioral treatment of alcoholism.* New York: Pergamon, 1976.

National Council on Alcoholism. Criteria Committee. Criteria for the diagnosis of alcoholism. *Annals of Internal Medicine,* 1972, *77,* 249–258.

Pattison, E. M., Sobell, M. B., & Sobell, L. C. *Emerging concepts of alcohol dependence.* New York: Springer, 1977.

Sobell, M. B. Alternatives to abstinence: Evidence, issues and some proposals. In P. E. Nathan, G. A. Marlatt, & T. Løberg (Eds.), *Alcoholism: New directions in behavioral research and treatment.* New York: Plenum, 1978.

Sobell, M. B., & Sobell, L. C. Individualized behavior therapy for alcoholics. *Behavior Therapy,* 1973, *4,* 49–72.

Sobell, M. B., & Sobell, L. C. *Behavioral treatment of alcohol problems: Individualized therapy and controlled drinking.* New York: Plenum, 1978.

Sobell, M. B., Sobell, L. C., & Sheahan, D. B. Functional analysis of drinking problems as an aid in developing individual treatment strategies. *Addictive Behaviors,* 1976, *1,* 127–132.

Wolpe, J. *The practice of behavior therapy.* New York: Pergamon, 1969.

8

Assessment of Chronic Pain

LAURENCE A. BRADLEY
CHARLES K. PROKOP
W. DOYLE GENTRY
LAURIE H. VAN DER HEIDE
EDWARD J. PRIETO

There have been many attempts to develop a definition of pain that would satisfy professionals across diverse disciplines (cf. Merskey & Spear, 1967; Sternbach, 1968; Weisenberg, 1977). Despite the difficulties involved in defining a construct that may be considered simultaneously to be a subjective experience, a noxious stimulus, or a self-protective behavior (Sternbach, 1974), the International Association for the Study of Pain (IASP) has recently developed a standard taxonomy which defines pain as "an unpleasant sensory and emotional experience associated with actual or potential tissue damage, or described in terms of such damage [IASP Subcommittee on Taxonomy, 1979, p. 250]." Although this definition may not be entirely satisfactory to all investigators and practitioners (cf. Clark & Hunt, 1971; Fordyce, 1978; Weisenberg, 1977), it does convey the multidimensional and subjective nature of pain of various etiologies. In addition, the definition distinguishes the term *pain* from persons' *pain complaints.* Pain complaints are defined as "the tendency to present in the clinical situation with pain as a symptom [Sternbach, 1978b, p. 253]." This distinction is quite important since a number of psychological and social factors may influence the extent to which individuals express their pain experiences (Sternbach, 1978a).

Unlike acute pain which is "of recent onset or short duration [Sternbach, 1978a, p. 243]," chronic pain is defined as "pain of at least several months' duration [Sternbach, 1978a, p. 243]"; the criterion used in the literature is usually a period of six months. The long duration of the pain experience, however, is not what causes chronic pain to be considered "a malefic force that often imposes severe emotional, physical, economic, and sociologic stress on the patient and his family as well as on society [Bonica, 1976, p. xxvii]." Chapman (1977) notes that the pervasive, negative effects of chronic pain are related to the (*a*) medication abuse; (*b*) submission to many ineffective surgical procedures; (*c*) changes in community, family, and peer group status; and (*d*) significant, in-

Support for the preparation of this chapter was provided in part by a grant from the Fordham University Research Council.

Medical Psychology
Contributions to Behavioral Medicine

ISBN 0-12-565960-1

explicable suffering displayed by many chronic pain patients. These negative sequelae to chronic pain are compounded by the slow development of knowledge concerning the complex neural mechanisms of pain (cf. Casey, 1978; Chapman, 1978) and the psychosocial factors which affect pain experience and pain complaints (cf. Sternbach, 1976; Weisenberg, 1977). As a result, the effective treatment of chronic pain, as documented by Ziesat in Chapter 16, has proven to be quite difficult.

Before chronic pain may be effectively treated, the patient must be comprehensively assessed. A comprehensive evaluation includes at the very least the production of a clinically useful personality profile and a determination of the severity of the patient's pain experience (Sternbach, 1976). Psychologists have made important contributions to the assessment and treatment of pain through their systematic efforts to develop measures of the pain experience and the personality attributes that may, in fact, contribute to this experience. The collaboration of psychologists with neurologists, anesthesiologists, pharmacologists, and others in behavioral medicine programs indicates that psychologists will continue to strongly influence the evaluation and treatment of chronic pain in medical settings (cf. Anastasi, 1979). Despite the psychologists' contributions to the specific area of pain assessment, however, there currently does not exist a comprehensive reference source with regard to the strengths and weaknesses of assessment research with chronic pain patients.

The present chapter presents a brief definition of measurement and then critically reviews chronic pain assessment involving the measurement of objects and events and the use of subjective estimations (cf. Chapman, 1976). Most of the investigations examined in this chapter were conducted in clinical settings. Only those laboratory studies that are relevant to the assessment of chronic pain will be discussed; the interested reader may wish to refer to Procacci, Zoppi and Maresca (1979), Sternbach (1978b), and Wolff (1978) for reviews of pain assessment in the laboratory setting.

Readers who are relatively unfamiliar with the voluminous pain literature also may wish to consult one or more introductions to the field of pain research before reading the present chapter. Several excellent introductory reviews exist; these include articles by Liebeskind and Paul (1977) and Weisenberg (1977), a collection of reviews edited by Bonica (1977) and Sternbach's (1978c) edited volume.

Measurement Issues

Measurement is defined as "the assignment of numbers to objects or events to represent quantities of attributes according to rules [Chapman, 1976, p. 346]." Thus, measurement is differentiated from nominal scaling in which persons or events are assigned to various categories. It should be noted, however, that despite the shortcomings of nominal scaling (e.g., questionable reliability of categorization judgments by single raters, questionable validity of observers' judgments of others' pain experiences), the technique is still used to distinguish patients with regard to organic versus functional etiology of pain (e.g., Fordyce, Brena, Holcomb, DeLateur, & Loeser, 1978), intensity of pain or suffering (e.g., Wilson, Blazer, & Nashold, 1976), and response to experimental treatments (e.g., Blume, 1976).

Chapman (1976) states that in pain research objects (persons or animals), events (persons' or animals' responses to noxious stimulation), and subjective estimations (persons' verbal or numerical estimates of subjective pain states) are measured. Assessment of the severity of a patient's pain experience is most often performed using either subjective estimates or measurement of events. Evaluation of a patient's personality attributes that are related to the pain experience, however, is performed using object measurement.

Measurement of Objects

As noted above, the objects studied in pain research are humans or animals. Only human subjects are used, however, in the literature relevant to chronic pain. Measurements are usually made of various personality attributes that may be related to persons' pain experience (e.g., Beals & Hickman, 1972; Elton, Stanley, & Burrows, 1978; Gentry, Shows, & Thomas, 1974; Maruta, Swanson, & Swenson, 1976a, 1976b; Shaffer, Nussbaum, & Little, 1972; Sternbach, Wolf, Murphy, & Akeson, 1973a, 1973b; Woodforde & Merskey, 1972a). These personality studies have been helpful in providing insight concerning the effects of chronic pain upon cognition, affect, and behavior. In summarizing the personality literature, Sternbach (1974, 1976) noted that as pain progresses from an acute to a chronic state, the autonomic nervous system responses to acute pain that are indicative of anxiety (e.g., increased heart rate, blood pressure, and muscle tension) tend to habituate, and the vegetative signs of depression and hypochondriasis (e.g., disturbances of sleep, appetite and sexual drive, irritability, withdrawal of interests, weakening of relationships, and somatic preoccupation) tend to be displayed.

An important shortcoming of the personality studies, however, has been that they usually have presented composite responses of chronic pain patients to various psychometric instruments. These studies, therefore, have tended to foster an "illusion of homogeneity [Fordyce, 1976, p. 141]" regarding the attributes of chronic pain patients. That is, examination of patients' composite responses to various psychometric instruments has tended to foster the idea that all chronic pain patients manifest the same personality attributes. Gentry *et al.* (1974), for example, note that chronic low back pain (LBP) patient samples are almost uniformly characterized in the literature as displaying elevations (T score $\geqslant 70$) on scales *Hs, D* and *Hy* ("neurotic triad") of the Minnesota Multiphasic Personality Inventory (MMPI). Although there exists evidence of differences among the MMPI profiles of LBP patients as a function of (*a*) patient sex (Beals & Hickman, 1972; Gentry *et al.*, 1974; Maruta *et al.*, 1976a, 1976b; Shaffer *et al.*, 1972; Sternbach *et al.*, 1973b); (*b*) pending litigation (Sternbach *et al.*, 1973b); and (*c*) duration of chronic pain (Gentry *et al.*, 1974), only two studies (Bradley, Prokop, Margolis, & Gentry, 1978; Sternbach, 1974) have attempted to define the characteristics of homogeneous MMPI profile subgroups of individuals within LBP patient samples rather than discuss the attributes of the "chronic LBP patient."

Variability of patient response to psychometric instruments has also been demonstrated in several British investigations of relationships between chronic pain and personality dimensions of neuroticism and extraversion as defined by Eysenck (1960). Observing females with advanced carcinoma of the cervix, Bond (1971, 1973, 1976) repeatedly found that the experience of chronic pain is positively associated with scores on the neuroticism scale of the Eysenck Personality Inventory (Eysenck & Eysenck, 1964; EPI). Given that Woodforde and Merskey (1972a) also found a relationship between chronic pain and increased neuroticism on the EPI, it is tempting to posit a consistent relationship between these two variables. The inference of such a relationship, however, must be tempered by the fact that Merskey (1972) failed to establish a relationship between pain and neuroticism when he administered the Maudsley Personality Inventory (Eysenck, 1956; MPI) to a sample of psychiatric patients; this failure to replicate occurred despite the fact that correlations between the EPI and MPI are usually in the range of .70–.80. In addition, Bond (1973) reported that patients with severe pain due to cancer showed no decrease in neuroticism on the EPI following stereotaxic percutaneous cordotomy that left them completely free of pain.

With regard to the dimension of extraversion, Bond (1971, 1973, 1976), also has reported that verbal pain behavior in the form of requests for analgesic medication is positively associated with scores on the extraversion scale of the EPI. Nonetheless, in a study of diurnal variation in the experience of chronic pain among introverts and extraverts, Folkard, Glynn, and Lloyd (1976) found that introverts (as measured by the EPI) reported more pain than did extraverts during the late morning and early afternoon; the two patient groups reported similar amounts of pain during the late afternoon and evening.

In summary, evidence suggests that various disturbances of cognition, affect and behavior may be found in a large number of chronic pain patients. However, the nature of these disturbances appears to be dependent upon many factors such as etiology and chronicity of pain, patient sex, setting in which the patient is evaluated, and type of assessment instrument used in evaluating the patient. As noted by Mechanic (1978), one cannot make generalizations about the attributes of persons with chronic pain or other psychological stressors from isolated groups of patients. Chronic pain patients are indeed a heterogeneous group with regard to their reactions to pain as measured by various psychometric instruments (Chapman, Sola, & Bonica, 1979).

Object Measurement for Diagnostic Purposes

Despite the failure to develop a personality profile of chronic pain patients (Liebeskind & Paul, 1977), psychometric instruments are often used in medical settings to evaluate the attributes of individual pain patients that may have implications for choice of treatment. The instrument most often used for patient evaluation is the MMPI (Fordyce, 1976). The following discussion will review the literature regarding the use of the MMPI for differentiating organic from functional pain and predicting patient response to treatment. The discussion will conclude with suggestions for research on the validity of short forms of the MMPI for use with pain patients and a brief critique of other psychometric instruments that sometimes are used to evaluate pain patients.

Differentiation of Organic and Functional Pain Organic and functional (or "psychogenic") pain are defined as pain of physiologic and psychological origin, respectively (cf. Sternbach, 1974). Although a large number of prominent pain researchers have rejected these terms (e.g., Fordyce, 1976; Merskey, 1978a, 1978b; Sternbach, 1974), many medical and psychological practitioners continue to distinguish between organic and functional pain patients.

The first use of the MMPI to evaluate organic versus functional pain was reported by Hanvik (1951). He noted that the MMPI profiles of functional pain patients were characterized by the "conversion V" configuration or elevations on scales *Hs* and *Hy* and relatively low scores on scale *D*. In addition, Hanvik developed a Low Back Pain (*Lb*) scale composed of 25 items which differentiated between samples of organic and functional pain patients. Dahlstrom (1954) replicated the successful discrimination of organic and functional patients with the *Lb* scale; nonetheless, the reliability of the *Lb* scale has been questioned (Graham, 1977) and little validity data for the scale have been produced since Dahlstrom's (1954) early report.

Since the publication of Hanvik's (1951) work, several studies have produced results that have suggested that differential diagnosis of organic versus functional pain should not be made on the basis of MMPI scores (Carr, Brownsberger, & Rutherford, 1966; Fordyce *et al.*, 1978; Lair & Trapp, 1962; Sternbach *et al.*, 1973b). In contrast, a number of investigations (Calsyn, Louks, & Freeman, 1976; Freeman, Calsyn, & Louks, 1976; Louks, Freeman, & Calsyn, 1978; McCreary, Turner, & Dawson, 1977) have supported the notion that the MMPI may be used to classify chronic pain patients into organic, functional, or "mixed" (i.e., physiological findings are present but cannot sufficiently account for the severity of the pain experience) etiological groups. Nearly all of the studies cited above have used the same experimental paradigm. That is, with the exception of Louks *et al.* (1978), who examined the relationship between MMPI code types and physicians' judgments of pain etiology, all of the investigations have compared the composite MMPI profiles of patients classified on the basis of physicians' judgments as organic, functional, or mixed. Studies that have produced negative evidence have reported either that there are no significant differences between organic and functional patients on the MMPI scales (Fordyce *et al.*, 1978; Sternbach *et al.*, 1973b) or that while there are some significant differences, the large overlap between patient group scores on various scales precludes the use of the MMPI for diagnostic purposes (Carr *et al.*, 1966; Lair & Trapp, 1962). Studies that have produced positive evidence have consistently noted that functional and mixed patients produce significantly higher scores than do organic patients on scales *Hs* and *Hy* (Calsyn *et al.*, 1976; Freeman *et al.*, 1976; McCreary *et al.*, 1977). Louks *et al.* (1978) found a significant tendency for patients with "normal" MMPI profiles to be classified as displaying organic pain. It also has been reported that the *Lb* scale and another functional pain scale developed in France, the *DOR* (Pichot, Perse, Lekeoux, Dureau, Perez, & Rychewaert, 1972), may be used in combination with one another to correctly classify approximately 75% of the patients placed in various etiological groups (Calsyn *et al.,* 1976; Freeman *et al.,* 1976).

The validity of all of the studies cited above, however, has been compromised by two methodological shortcomings. First, the physicians who examined patients could not have determined with great accuracy whether or not physiological factors were insufficient to account for the amount of pain and disability reported by patients given the many social and cultural factors (cf. Weisenberg, 1977) which affect persons' perceptions and reports of pain (Bradley, Prieto, Hopson, & Prokop, 1978). Indeed, only one study (Fordyce *et al.,* 1978) provided a measure of interphysician agreement on patient classification. A high level of agreement, it should be noted, may be regarded as a demonstration of interjudge reliability or internal validation of physicians' judgments (Feinstein, 1977). Fordyce *et al.* (1978) reported that six physicians who used Q-sorts to place 100 pain patients along a continuum from organic to nonorganic pain produced a mean interjudge correlation of only .59. To summarize, then, there is little or no evidence of the validity of physicians' classification of patients into organic, functional, or mixed etiological groups.

A second methodological deficiency associated with all of the MMPI studies is that repeated univariate analyses of data were performed. As noted by Cox and Chapman (1976), repeated application of univariate tests to data produced by one sample of subjects may either lead to significant results due to chance alone or indicate marginal or insignificant results when there are actually interactions among the dependent variables that vary across subject groups.

There are also criticisms that are specific to the studies performed by Freeman, Louks, and Calsyn which have produced the majority of positive findings for the use of the MMPI in differential diagnosis. First, their subject samples were not independent of one another. The 36 patients used in the original investigation (Freeman *et al.,* 1976) represent, then, approximately 50% of the subjects used in the latter studies (Calsyn *et al.,* 1976; Louks *et al.,* 1978). Second, the use of the *Lb* and *DOR* scales to discriminate between patient groups is questionable given the recent criticisms of the validity of the scales (Towne & Tsushima, 1978; Tsushima & Towne, 1979) and the applicability of the *DOR* to American patient samples (Bradley, Prieto *et al.,* 1978). The error rate in patient classification of approximately 25% reported by Freeman *et al.* (1976) and Calsyn *et al.* (1976) and the small amount of variance in *Lb* and *DOR* scores accounted for by MMPI code types (15–24%) reported by Louks *et al.* (1978) suggest that individual patients probably could not be discriminated with great accuracy from one another on the basis of their *Lb* and *DOR* scores. Finally, the Louks *et al.* (1978) investigation is subject to criticism concerning the sorting rules used to produce MMPI code types (Bradley, Prieto *et al.,* 1978).

In a recent attempt to overcome the methodological limitations of previous studies, Cox, Chapman and Black (1978) analyzed the MMPI profiles of patients with (*a*) chronic pain of unknown etiology (functional); (*b*) chronic pain of known surgical etiology (organic); and (*c*) acute pain due to surgery (organic). A multivariate analysis of variance (MANOVA) revealed a significant between-group difference across the MMPI scales; however, this finding was due solely to differences between the acute and the two chronic pain patient groups. A hierarchic clustering procedure was applied to patients' MMPI scores but it failed to produce a substantial cluster composed solely of patients with chronic pain of unknown etiology. It was concluded, therefore, that attempts to differentiate organic and functional pain using the MMPI serve only to oversimplify the complex psychological processes involved in the pain experience.[1]

Another series of multivariate investigations has identified replicable, homogeneous MMPI profile subgroups within the independent samples of LBP (Bradley, Prokop *et al.,* 1978) and multiple pain patients (Prokop, Bradley, Margolis, & Gen-

[1]Some effort has been directed toward developing physiological discriminators between organic and functional pain. Gentry, Newman, Goldner, and von Baeyer (1977), however, presented negative evidence regarding the validity of a graduated spinal block procedure (McCollum & Stephen, 1964). Mooney, Cairns and Robertson use a "pentathol pain study" [1975, p. 187] to identify the source of patients' pain as either peripheral or nonperipheral. The authors present no validation data for this technique.

try, 1980) who failed to respond to traditional medical-surgical treatments and/or presented a questionable physiological basis for their pain. Figures 8.1–8.4 show the replicated profile subgroups for both males and females within the LBP and multiple pain patient samples. Although there were some differences between the LBP and multiple pain patient subgroups, the subgroup profiles characterized by (*a*) elevations on scales *Hs, D* and *Hy;* and (*b*) no elevations on any clinical scales were found among both LBP and multiple pain patients. In addition, the conversion V profile was found only among female LBP and multiple pain patients. These results suggest that LBP and multiple pain patients who are likely to be classified as displaying functional pain complaints clearly cannot be characterized as homogeneous groups in terms of their responses to the MMPI. Indeed, these pain patients produce various pathological and relatively normal profiles that may be associated with unique behavioral attributes and differential response to various treatments. Given these results and those reported by Cox *et al.* (1978), it is recommended that psychologists who use the MMPI to assess pain patients not attempt to classify patients as organic, functional, or mixed and instead redirect their efforts toward delineating replicable MMPI profile subgroups within their respective pain patient populations and the pain-related correlates uniquely associated with each profile subgroup. These correlates may consist of (*a*) demographic or medical attributes (e.g., history of previous surgeries or debilitating diseases, litigation for financial compensation), as well as measures described more fully on pages 103–110 such as (*b*) measures of behavior, and (*c*) measures using subjective estimations. In this manner, psychologists may develop actuarial predictions regarding the relationships between the MMPI profile types displayed by their pain patients and various pain-related behaviors and attributes that may have implications for choice of treatment modality.[2] For the present, however, psychological evaluations of pain patients should be made to determine if there are cognitive, affective or behavioral disturbances that may be related to their pain experiences and that require treatment regardless of the presence or absence of physical findings (cf. Sternbach, 1973).

Prediction of Patient Response to Treatment A major impetus for investigations of the predictive validity of the MMPI was a retrospective study by Wilfling, Klonoff and Kokan (1973). Male veterans who had undergone spinal fusion during the preceding 2–9 years were given orthopedic and neurological examinations and were administered the MMPI and several other psychometric instruments. It was found that veterans who were categorized as having "good" outcomes scored significantly lower on MMPI scale *D* than did subjects with either "poor" or "fair" outcomes; the good outcome veterans also scored significantly lower on *Hy* than those with fair outcomes. In addition, veterans who had required multiple surgical interventions scored significantly higher on scales *Hs* and *Hy* than did those who underwent single operations.

Although the Wilfling *et al.* (1973) study was retrospective and lacked reliability checks on the classifications of treatment outcomes, it has been consistently cited by other investigators (McCreary, Turner, & Dawson, 1979; Waring, Weisz, & Bailey, 1976; Wiltse & Rocchio, 1975) as providing a precedent for predictive validity studies of the MMPI. The results of the predictive validity investigations, however, are generally weak and inconsistent. For example, Waring *et al.* (1976) found that LBP patients' preoperative MMPI clinical scale scores showed no significant associations with surgeons' postoperative outcome ratings. In a similar investigation, nonetheless, Blumetti and Modesti (1976) reported that LBP patients' preoperative scores on scales *Hs* and *Hy* significantly differentiated between those patients

[2]Toomey, Ghia, Mao, and Gregg (1977) provided some independent evidence in support of this suggestion. They noted that several personality and affective factors, as measured by various instruments including the MMPI, and non-pain-related medical illnesses were related to acupuncture treatment response. Similar results were reported by Hossenlopp, Leiber, and Mo (1976).

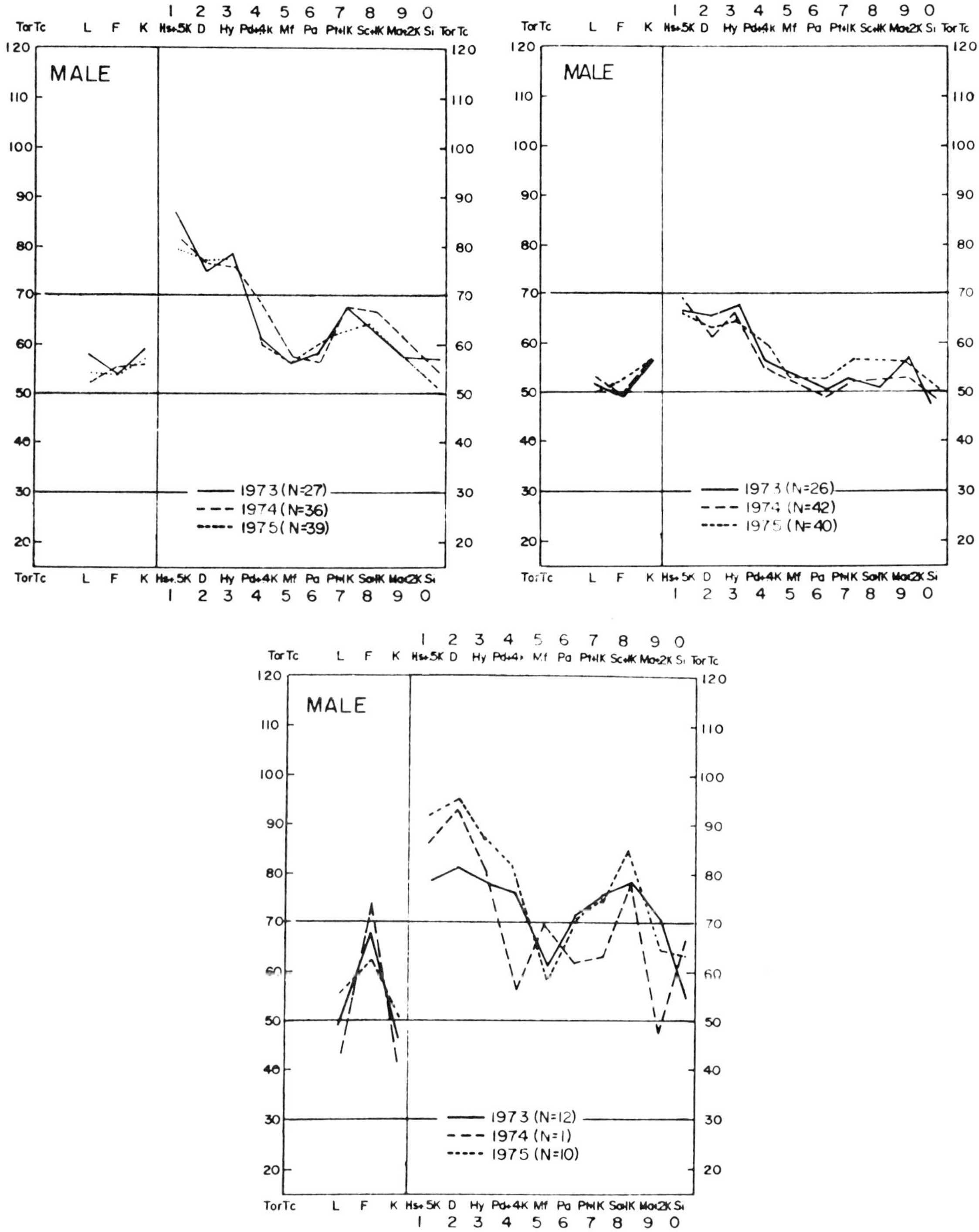

Figure 8.1. Replicated MMPI profile subgroups for male LBP patient samples. (From "Multivariate Analyses of the MMPI Profiles of Low Back Pain Patients" by L. A. Bradley, C. K. Prokop, R. Margolis, and W. D. Gentry, *Journal of Behavioral Medicine,* 1978, *1,* 253-272. Copyright 1978 by Plenum Press. Reprinted by permission.)

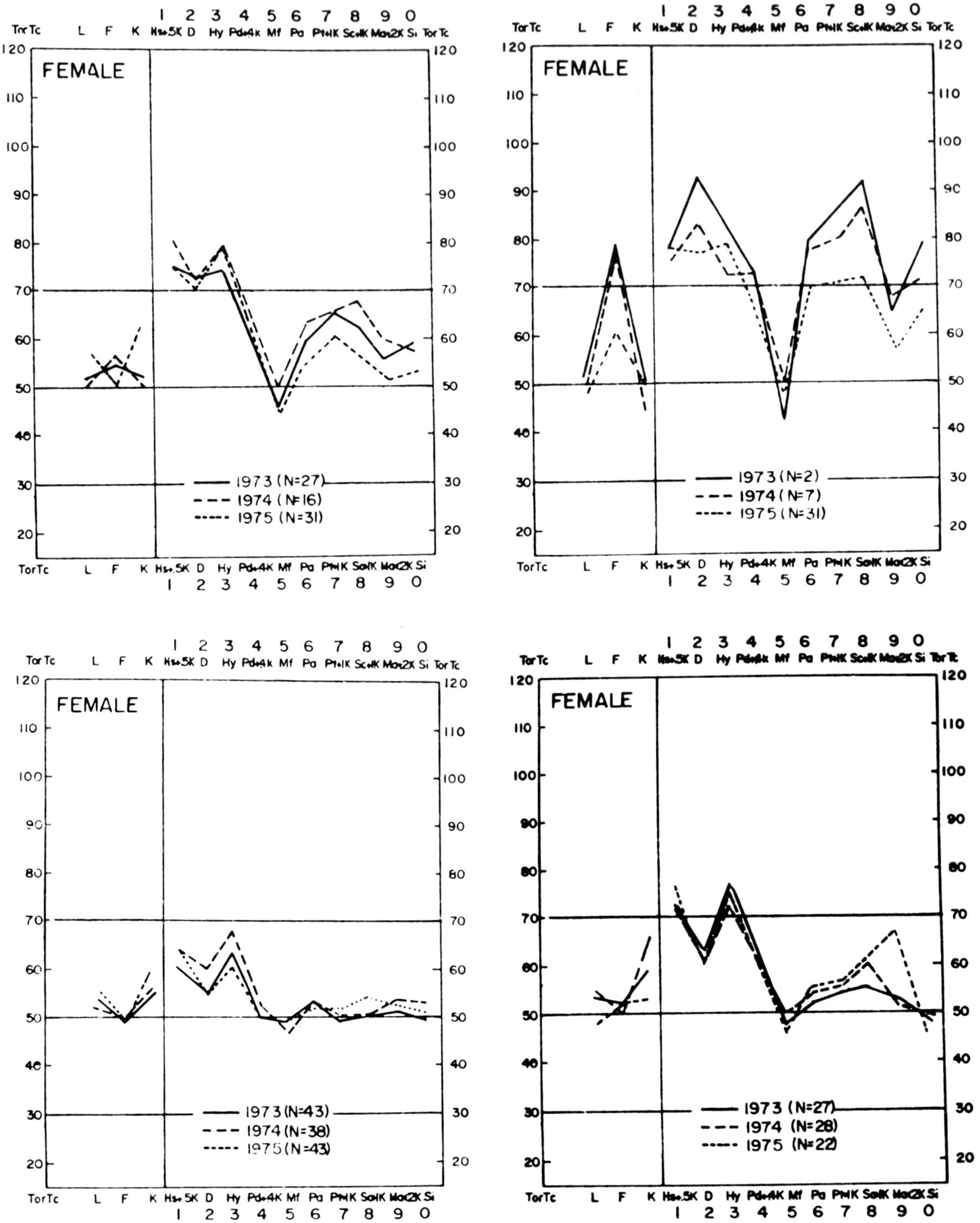

Figure 8.2. Replicated MMPI profile subgroups for female LBP patient samples. (From "Multivariate Analyses of the MMPI Profiles of Low Back Pain Patients" by L. A. Bradley, C. K. Prokop, R. Margolis, and W. D. Gentry, *Journal of Behavioral Medicine,* 1978, *1,* 253–272. Copyright 1978 by Plenum Press. Reprinted by permission.)

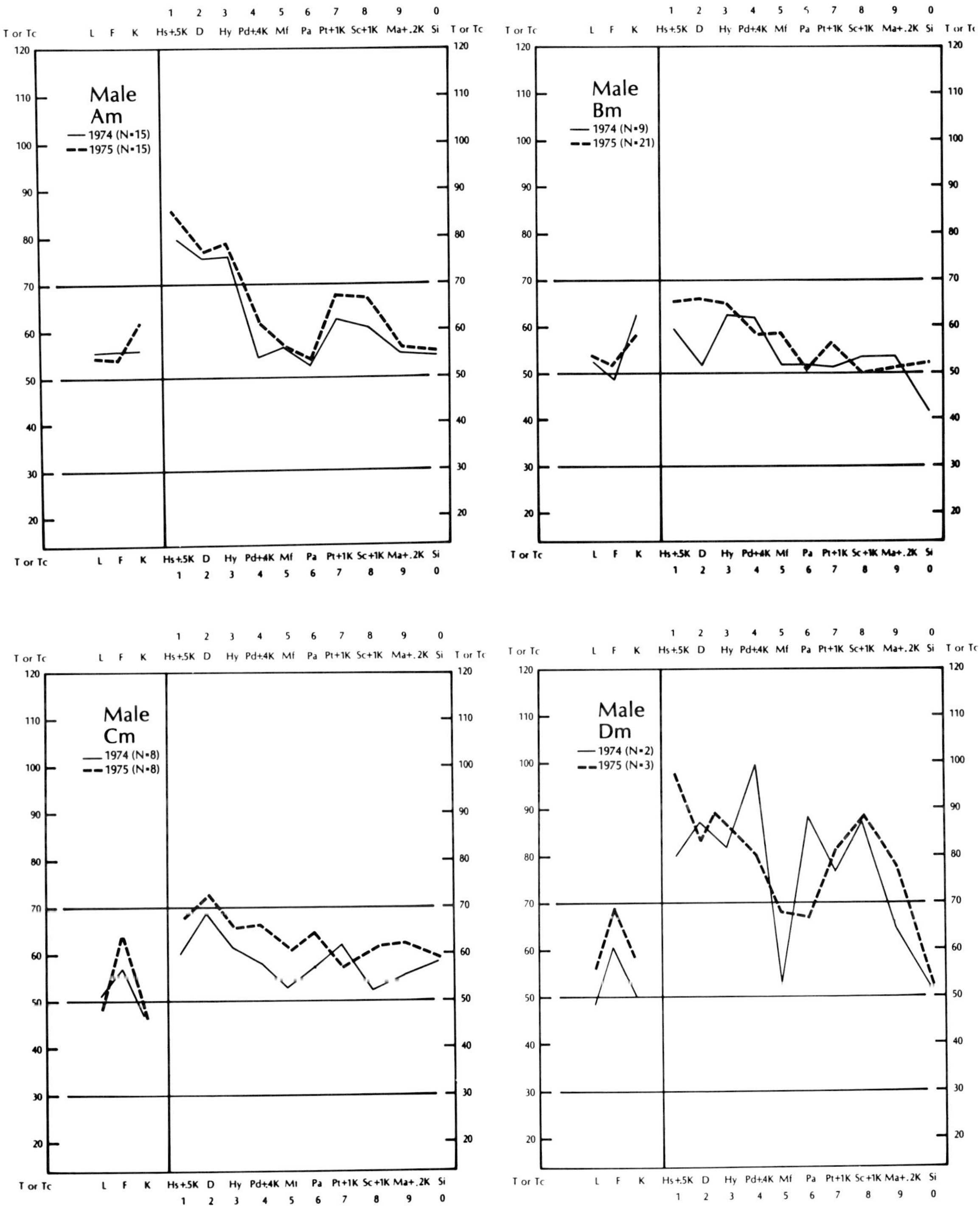

Figure 8.3. Replicated MMPI profile subgroups for male multiple pain patient samples. (From "Multivariate Analyses of the MMPI Profiles of Multiple Pain Patients" by C. K. Prokop, L. A. Bradley, R. Margolis, and W. D. Gentry, *Journal of Personality Assessment*, 1980, *44*, 246-252. Copyright 1980 by the Society for Personality Assessment, Inc. Reprinted by permission.)

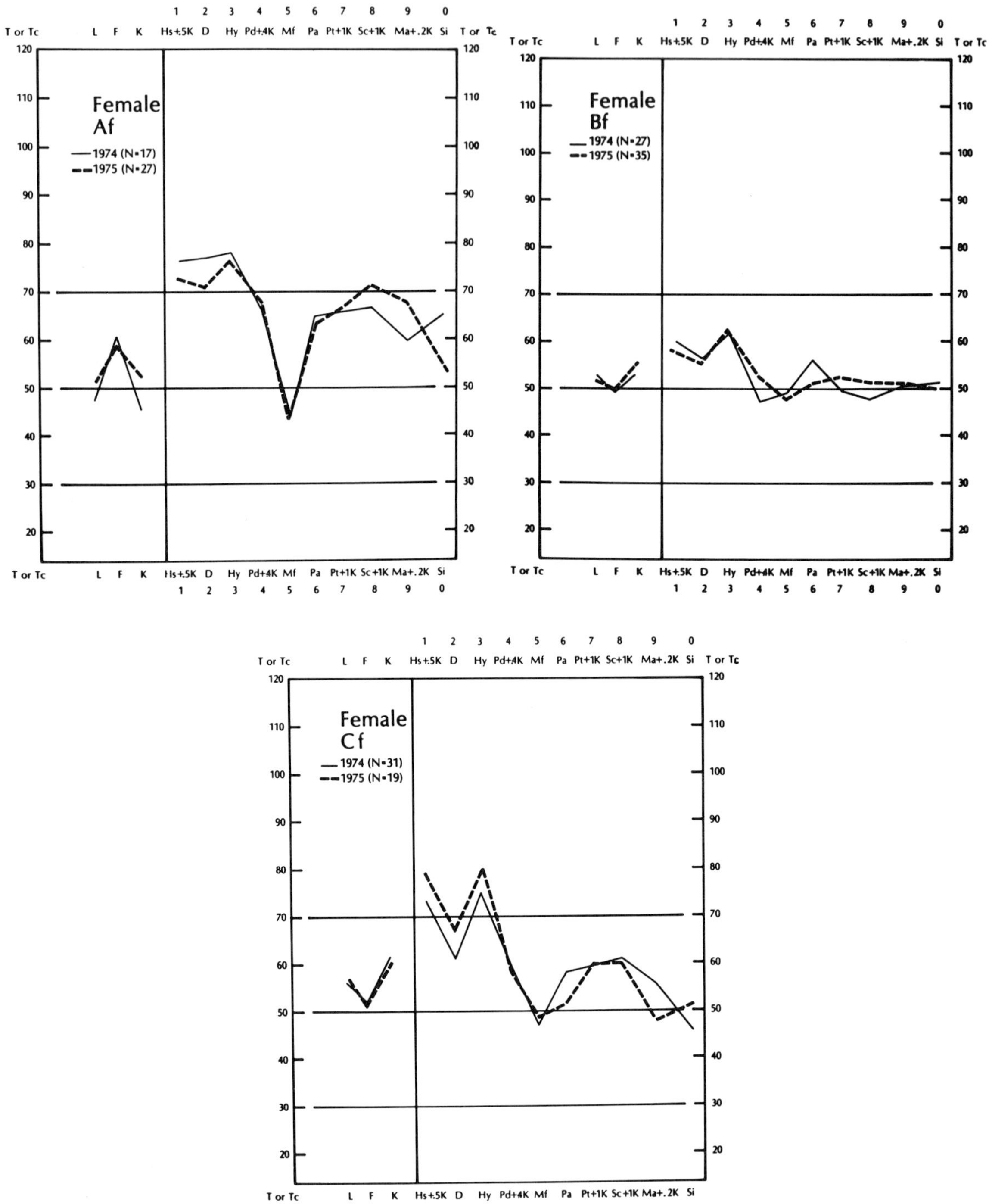

Figure 8.4. Replicated MMPI profile subgroups for female multiple pain patient samples. (From "Multivariate Analyses of the MMPI Profiles of Multiple Pain Patients" by C. K. Prokop, L. A. Bradley, R. Margolis, and W. D. Gentry, *Journal of Personality Assessment,* 1980, *44,* 246–252. Copyright 1980 by the Society for Personality Assessment, Inc. Reprinted by permission.)

judged postoperatively by unspecified raters to be either improved or unimproved. One laboratory has produced different results as a function of the types of patients, treatments, and outcome measures employed. Jamison, Ferrer-Brechner, Brechner, and McCreary (1976) and McCreary *et al.* (1979) both examined heterogeneous samples of chronic pain patients who were administered a variety of treatments. On the one hand, Jamison *et al.* (1976) noted that scores on scale *K* distinguished between inpatients judged by unspecified raters as having either successful or unsuccessful outcomes following various surgical treatments. On the other hand, McCreary *et al.* (1979) used outpatients' self-ratings of (*a*) amount of pain relief; (*b*) ability to return to normal activity; and (*c*) current pain intensity as outcome criteria for a wide range of nonsurgical interventions. It was found that patients who reported relatively successful outcomes on the criteria of pain intensity and return to normal activities produced significantly lower *Hs* scores than did patients with unsuccessful outcomes. However, there was a large overlap between the *Hs* scores of patients with successful and unsuccessful outcomes. Using a cut-off score of 71 on *Hs*, 36% of the successful patients were classified as having poor prognoses and 38% of the unsuccessful patients were labeled as having good prognoses. A large percentage of prognostic errors also was found when poor prognosis was defined by five MMPI scale configurations featuring elevations on scales *Hs*, *D*, *Hy*, or *Sc*.

It should be noted that all of the studies discussed above suffer from various methodological flaws which render their results tentative. These include the use of (*a*) outcome judgments for which there are no reliability checks (Blumetti & Modesti, 1976; Jamison *et al.*, 1976; Waring *et al.*, 1976); (*b*) heterogeneous patient samples (Jamison *et al.*, 1976; McCreary *et al.*, 1979); and (*c*) heterogeneous surgical (Blumetti & Modesti, 1976; Jamison *et al.*, 1976; Waring *et al.*, 1976) and nonsurgical (McCreary *et al.*, 1979) treatments. In contrast, Wiltse and Rocchio (1975) found replicable, positive findings concerning the MMPIs predictive validity in an investigation that used a homogeneous group of inpatients with back pain and sciatica (with no history of previous back operations) who received chemonucleolysis. Although surgeons' postoperative ratings were used as criteria, Wiltse and Rocchio found that patients' preoperative scores on scales *Hs* and *Hy* and surgeons' preoperative ratings of the functional component of patients' symptoms were the best outcome predictors. Eighty-seven percent of patients with *T* scores equal to or less than 64 on *Hs* and *Hy* had good or excellent surgical outcomes; only 25% of patients with *T* scores equal to or greater than 75 had equivalent outcomes. The results were replicated with a sample of patients who underwent a lumbar laminectomy. The positive findings reported by these investigators, therefore, strongly suggest that the MMPI may prove to be a useful predictive instrument in cases where specific treatments for homogeneous patient groups are evaluated.

In summary, the literature regarding the use of the MMPI for diagnostic and predictive purposes is plagued with methodological deficiencies. However, the results of the better designed studies (e.g., Bradley, Prokop, *et al.*, 1978; Cox *et al.*, 1978; Prokop *et al.*, 1980; Wiltse & Rocchio, 1975) lead to the conclusions that psychologists who use the MMPI should attempt to develop actuarial diagnostic procedures for pain patients and then conduct controlled, prospective studies of responses to specific treatments by MMPI profile subgroup members with pain of the same etiology (e.g., LBP due to disc degeneration, pain of the extremities due to causalgia, cervical back pain of unknown etiology). These prospective studies will be discussed in greater detail in the Conclusion.

Short Forms of the MMPI An important issue in MMPI research that has been relatively neglected by medical psychologists concerns the validity of the various short forms of the MMPI used with chronic pain patients. In the medical setting one often finds that patients have difficulty answering either the 566-or 399-item versions of the MMPI (Form R). This is particularly true of patients who experience severe pain and those who lack facility with the English language. Several short forms of the MMPI have been produced (cf. Faschingbauer & Newmark, 1978; Newmark & Faschingbauer, 1978); however, only the Faschingbauer Abbreviated MMPI (Faschingbauer, 1974; FAM) and the Midi-Mult (Dean, 1972) have been compared in the chronic pain literature (Freeman, Calsyn, & O'Leary, 1977; Turner & McCreary, 1978). The experimental evidence regarding the validity of the short MMPI forms used with chronic pain patients is consistent with the evidence derived from validity studies with psychiatric patients (cf. Faschingbauer & Newmark, 1978). That is, relative to their scores on the Midi-Mult, pain patients' FAM scores correlate more highly with their full MMPI scale scores (Turner & McCreary, 1978). However, the concordance rates for 2- and 3-point code types between the FAM and the full MMPI reported by Freeman *et al.* (1977) (35% and 18%, respectively) and Turner and McCreary (1978) (34% and 14%, respectively) are quite low. In addition, there has been no attempt to determine if interpretations derived from pain patients' scores on the FAM or other short MMPI forms are similar to those derived from their full MMPI scores (cf. Newmark, Conger, & Faschingbauer, 1976; Poythress & Blaney, 1978). At the present, then, there is little justification for the use of the FAM or Midi-Mult with chronic pain patients. Practitioners and researchers who wish to use a short MMPI form should continue the practice of administering the first 399 items of Form R as described by Dahlstrom, Welsh, and Dahlstrom (1972).

Other Assessment Instruments A number of alternative instruments to the MMPI have been developed for use with chronic pain patients. These include the Illness Behavior Questionnaire (Pilowsky & Spence, 1975; IBP), the Pain Apperception Test (Petrovich, 1957; PAT) and two brief diagnostic screening instruments (Thomas & Lyttle, 1976; Hendler, Viernstein, Gucer, & Long, 1979). Given the negative evidence concerning the validity of the PAT (Haase, Banks, & Lee, 1975; Ziesat & Gentry, 1978) and the lack of cross-validation studies for the screening tests, only the IBQ will be critically examined.

Pilowsky (1978a, 1978b) adopted Mechanic's (1962) term "illness behavior" and developed the concept of abnormal illness behavior as a unifying label for the various cognitive, affective, and behavioral disturbances associated with chronic pain. Abnormal illness behavior

> refers to syndromes in which the individual's mode of perceiving, evaluating and responding to those aspects of himself which he assesses in terms of illness and health, is maladaptive . . . it persists even though a doctor or other suitably qualified social agent provides a proper assessment of the person's health status and the course to be followed in relation to it [Pilowsky, 1978b, p. 209; reprinted by permission of Raven Press, New York].

Pilowsky and Spence (1975) administered a questionnaire consisting of 52 items with a dichotomous response format and three additional items regarding age, sex, and length of illness to 100 patients with chronic pain of various etiologies. A factor analysis of the patients' questionnaire responses produced seven orthogonal dimensions: (*a*) general hypochondriasis; (*b*) conviction of disease; (*c*) psychological versus somatic focus of disease; (*d*) affect inhibition; (*e*) affect disturbance; (*f*) denial of life problems not related to pain; and (*g*) irritability. The patients' scores on the derived factor scales were then submitted to a clustering procedure which produced three relatively normal patterns of scores and three patterns of scores indicative of abnormal illness behavior (Pilowsky & Spence, 1976a).

The use of factor analysis in the development of the IBQ may be criticized since the 2:1 ratio of respondents to items was well below the ratio of *at least* 5:1 suggested by Gorsuch (1974). The low respondent to item ratio suggests that the correlation matrix entered in the analysis may have been quite unstable. In addition, the use of a dichotomous response format for the majority of items may have introduced spurious extra common factor variance into the matrix and thereby have distorted the factor solution (cf. Comrey, 1978). Furthermore, no data regarding the reliability of the factor scales have been presented by Pilowsky and Spence. A series of studies (Pilowsky & Spence, 1976b, 1976c, 1976d) has been performed that has appeared to produce some evidence for the construct validity of the IBQ. The internal and external validity of the studies, nonetheless, is suspect since it is likely that the responses of the same 100 patients used in the original factor analysis (Pilowsky & Spence, 1975) also were used in the latter construct validity studies.[3]

Recently, Pilowsky, Chapman, and Bonica (1977) reported that the IBQ profiles of patient samples drawn from a university pain clinic and family medicine clinic were significantly different from one another. Relative to the family medicine patients, the pain clinic patients showed higher scores on the disease conviction and denial of life problems scales and produced lower scores on the psychological versus somatic focus of disease scale. Although the Pilowsky *et al.* (1977) investigation provides some evidence for the construct validity of the IBQ, it must be concluded that any evaluation of the utility of the instrument for research or clinical purposes must be reserved until the IBQ scales are cross-validated using large patient samples and more evidence is presented regarding the psychometric characteristics of the scales.

Summary

Presently, the use of object measurement for descriptive, diagnostic, and predictive purposes may be characterized as unsophisticated. Examination of chronic pain patients' scores on various psychometric instruments has tended to foster the illusion that chronic pain patients represent a homogeneous group. This illusion of homogeneity, in turn, may be responsible in part for the large number of attempts to use the MMPI to differentiate between organic, functional, and mixed etiologies of patients' pain and predict diverse patients' responses to a wide variety of treatments. It is suggested that researchers and practitioners who use the MMPI with chronic pain patients administer either the full item set or the first 399 items of Form R. Patients' responses then may be used to devise actuarial diagnostic systems and investigations of the efficacy of specific treatments for homogeneous patient groups.

[3]The same (*a*) male–female ratio; (*b*) mean age and length of pain duration; and (*c*) correlation between age and pain duration were reported for the patient sample in each of the IBQ studies (Pilowsky & Spence, 1975, 1976a, 1976b, 1976c, 1976d).

The IBQ may eventually prove to be useful for diagnostic or predictive purposes. At present, however, the weaknesses associated with its development and most of the examinations of its construct validity suggest that any conclusions based upon work with the IBQ must be regarded as tenuous.

Measurement of Events

The events that are measured in chronic pain research are always behavioral and usually consist of human responses to noxious stimulation (cf. Chapman, 1976). There are, however, two contrary views of behavioral measurement. On the one hand, Chapman (1976) proposes that the validity of behavioral indices of pain is difficult to demonstrate in the absence of concomitant verbal responses. It cannot be verified, for example, that a person's behavior, such as reclining on a sofa, occurs as a function of pain unless the person also states that reclining reduces the experience of pain. On the other hand, Fordyce and his colleagues (Fordyce, Fowler, Lehmann, & DeLateur, 1968) posit that an individual's behavior is as critically important an indicator of pain as the verbal pain report. Indeed, verbal report is considered to be a behavioral index of pain that may not always be consistent with other behavioral pain indices (Fordyce *et al.*, 1978).

If one accepts, as the present authors do, the definition of pain behavior as "all behavior generated by the individual commonly understood to reflect the presence of nociception [Fordyce, 1978, p. 54]," then verbal report of pain, itself, must be considered as one type of pain behavior and not as a criterion for defining a particular response as a valid pain behavior.[4] The following discussion will

[4]An empirical demonstration of the hazards involved in accepting Chapman's view of behavioral measurement is provided in a well-controlled study of the effects of acupuncture and placebo treatments upon shoulder pain due to tendonitis or bursitis (Berk, Moore, & Resnick, 1977). It was found that patients' verbal reports of pain were significantly reduced by acupuncture and placebo treatments; however, measures of patients' range of motion were not affected by either treatment. Similar results were reported by Murphy (1976).

focus primarily upon the assessment of pain behaviors advocated by Fordyce (1976) and will note several unresolved issues meriting further examination.

Pain Behaviors

Pain behaviors are considered by Fordyce and other adherents of his views to be operants that may occur without antecedent stimuli and that may be modified by environmental consequences or events. In a series of influential papers, Fordyce and his colleagues (Fordyce, 1973, 1976; Fordyce *et al.,* 1968; Fordyce, Fowler, DeLateur, Sand, & Trieschmann, 1973) have developed a sophisticated treatment program (described by Ziesat in Chapter 16) for inpatients with chronic pain who display pain behaviors that are not modifiable by medical–surgical treatment and that lead to a cessation or reduction of productive or well behaviors. Since the outcome of the program is assessed in terms of fluctuations in various behavioral units, it is essential that detailed analysis and measurement be performed of the pain and well behaviors that are to be diminished or increased (or learned), respectively.

In a detailed analysis of his measurement procedures, Fordyce (1976) notes that one must be able to count or quantify the various behaviors identified for modification within specifiable time periods. The unit of measurement used for quantification is the "movement cycle [Fordyce, 1976, p. 80]" which begins when the patient starts a particular behavior and ends when the patient is capable of repeating the behavior. The counting of movement cycles within specific time periods provides information concerning the rate of the behavior. For example, verbal references to pain may be quantified such that one movement cycle is equivalent to a single pain statement (e.g., "My back hurts"). One can count the number of verbal movement cycles during several one-hour time periods to produce a measure of the rate of verbal references to pain. As another example, a walking movement cycle for a severely incapacitated patient might be defined as the advance of both feet during a five-minute period. For a more physically able patient, a walking movement cycle may be defined as completion of a walk along a 200 foot track during a period of 30 minutes (Fordyce, 1976, pp. 80–81). In addition to being quantified, it is also necessary for movement cycles to be recorded accurately. Fordyce (1976) provides an excellent discussion of the use of monitoring devices such as diaries, performance records, graphs, and mechanical counters that can be used by patients, their spouses or other family members, and treatment staff (see Ciminero, Nelson, & Lipinski [1977] and Rugh & Schwitzgebel [1977] for additional discussions of recording and storage devices).

Fordyce *et al.* (1973) provide an example of the analysis and measurement of pain and well behaviors in an inpatient treatment program. Thirty-six chronic pain patients received between 4 and 12 weeks of inpatient treatment and an average of 3 weeks of outpatient treatment. The behaviors of interest were walking, weaving, and sit-ups; all of which were quantified as movement cycles within specific time periods. Pain medication intake (quantified as unit potency values based upon the average effective dosage of morphine) and number of hours of uptime recorded each week also were examined. There were (*a*) significant increases across the first to last inpatient trials with regard to movement cycles of walking, weaving and sit-ups; (*b*) significant increases in uptime hours from preadmission baseline levels to the last week of outpatient contact; and (*c*) significant reductions in pain medication intake during inpatient treatment.

The influence of Fordyce's behavioral approach to pain measurement may be found in several recently published investigations (Bourhis, Boudouresque, Pellet, Fondarai, Ponzio, & Spitalier, 1978; Breivik, Helsa, Molnar, & Lind, 1976; Brena & Unikel, 1976; Frost, Hsu, & Sadowsky, 1976). It should be noted, however, that these investigators did not consistently quantify their behavioral measures in terms of movement cycles as recommended by Fordyce. For example, in an investigation of the efficacy of various psychotropic medications upon pain due to advanced cancers, Bourhis *et al.* (1978) instructed nurses to *rate* patients' pain complaints and activity levels on five-category scales rather than quantify and record movement cycles of patients' behaviors. Breivik *et al.* (1976) used the gross measure of patients' return to work or rehabilitation for other work to assess the relative effectiveness of injections of bupivacaine and methylprednisolone versus bupivacaine and saline. Brena and Unikel (1976) and Frost, Hsu, and Sadowsky (1976), however, used behavioral measures that more closely resembled those advocated by Fordyce (1976). Brena and Unikel used patients' displays of walking, performance of household chores, and participation in active sports as outcome measures in a program of contingency management and nerve blocks. Frost *et al.* (1976) evaluated the use of acupuncture for migraine headaches in terms of patients' reports of medication intake and headache incidence.

Perhaps the most sophisticated use of behavioral measurement may be found in a recent comparison of the effects of verbal reinforcement and graphic feedback upon the activity levels of chronic LBP patients (Cairns & Pasino, 1977). Activity levels were measured in terms of movement cycles; these movement cycles were defined as distance walked or ridden on a stationary exercycle (equipped with an odometer) during physical therapy sessions of standard length. In contrast to Fordyce, Fowler *et al.* (1968, 1973), Cairns and Pasino used a multiple baseline reversal design which permitted independent assessment of three reinforcement strategies (verbal reinforcement, visual feedback, or verbal reinforcement combined with visual feedback) and a nonreinforcement control condition on walking and bicycle riding. In addition, the sequences in which reinforcement was delivered for (or withdrawn from) walking and bicycle riding were counter-balanced across patients. It was found that relative to the control group and to their own baseline levels, patients who received either verbal reinforcement alone, or verbal reinforcement with visual feedback, displayed significantly greater walking and bicycle riding distances. The absence of significant within- and between-group effects for visual feedback alone suggested that the provision of verbal reinforcement may have been responsible for the positive effects of the verbal reinforcement–visual feedback strategy.

Summary and Implications for Future Research

The measurement of pain behaviors, as advocated by Fordyce (1976), is a very practical approach to chronic pain assessment in that it provides the diagnostician or therapist with measures of disability displayed by the patient in physical mobility and other activities that are directly related to functioning in vocational, social, and leisure endeavors. The use of behavioral measurement also avoids the pitfalls of relying upon unreliable subjective pain reports obtained in diagnostic interviews (Fordyce, 1978; Sternbach, 1978a) and of attempting to distinguish between organic and functional pain (Fordyce, 1978). Furthermore, the measurement of pain behavior is ideally suited for evaluation purposes in inpatient treatment programs such as those described by Fordyce (1976) and Cairns, Thomas, Mooney, and Pace (1976) in which the treatment goal of pain reduction is secondary to that of returning the patient to satisfying vocational and social endeavors.

It should be noted that reliance upon behavioral measurement for all diagnostic purposes is inadequate for two reasons. First, as stated in the Introduction, a comprehensive pain evaluation should include assessment of personality factors that may contribute to the patient's pain experience and complaints (and other pain behaviors). Fordyce (1976) uses the MMPI for this purpose and suggests that the Halstead–Reitan Battery (see Boll, O'Leary, & Barth, Chapter 6; Reitan & Davison, 1974) also should be used in many cases to determine impairment of cortical functions. The second inadequacy associated with behavioral measurement is that it cannot provide information that may be essential for determining the presence of some underlying pathology such as the locus, temporal quality, and sensory and affective aspects of the pain experience (Sternbach, 1978a).

Finally, there are several unresolved issues in the measurement of pain behaviors that require further investigation. The first issue is the accuracy and reliability of behavioral pain measures. Behaviorally oriented investigators in pain research have tended to assume, as have most other behavioral assessors, that once a decision is reached regarding the behavioral sample to be evaluated, valid measures of that behavior will follow (cf. Goldfried & Linehan, 1977). Both Fordyce (1976) and Sternbach (1974) have stressed the importance of careful training of health professionals (e.g., nurses, occupational and physical therapists) so that accurate and reliable measures of movement cycles will be recorded. Given that these health professionals are usually asked to record a small number of discrete behaviors during relatively brief time periods, it is likely that if they receive adequate training they will provide reliable and accurate data (cf. Goldfried & Linehan, 1977). Nonetheless, pain clinic administrators may wish to perform reliability checks at random intervals so that possible sources of observer unreliability, such as "drift" (Kent & Foster, 1977), may be corrected. If such reliability checks prove to be valuable, their utility should be reported in the literature.

There is a greater probability of inaccurate measurement when patients are asked to self-monitor behaviors such as uptime (e.g., Fordyce *et al.*, 1973). Sternbach (1974) proposes that patients may be expected to keep "fairly accurate [p. 123]" records of activity levels and medication intake because they tend to hope that their data will help the therapist provide effective treatment. Nonetheless, it would be valuable to compare patients' self-recordings with those of their spouses or those of staff members who covertly observe them in inpatient settings (cf. Nelson, 1977). Comparisons between patient self-recordings and those of automated devices, such as mechanical uptime recorders (described by Cairns & Pasino, 1977), also would aid in the evaluation of self-monitored assessments.

A second unresolved issue that is related to reliability and accuracy of pain behavior measures is the extent to which reactivity affects self-monitored assessments. Reactivity refers to the phenomenon in which "behavior change is initiated by the procedure of self-monitoring [Nelson, 1977, p. 218]." Although there is some inconsistency in the behavioral assessment literature, it may be hypothesized that pain patients' self-recordings are affected by (*a*) whether or not the recordings involve pain-related or effective, well behaviors; (*b*) type of feedback (e.g., graphs versus numerical counts) produced; (*c*) number of behaviors monitored; and (*d*) the schedule (continuous versus intermittent) of self-monitoring (cf. Ciminero, Nelson, & Lipinski, 1977; Nelson, 1977). Evaluation of reactivity effects is quite important because no studies in the pain literature have attempted to separate the amount of patients' behavioral change due to specific treatments and that due to self-monitoring alone. Nelson (1977) provides several suggestions for experimental designs which allow for some separation of effects due to self-monitoring from those due to specific treatments.

The final issue in behavioral assessment which deserves investigation is the possibility that behavioral assessment and related treatments may not be appropriate for all chronic pain patients. This point is easily overlooked since in all of the studies reviewed in this chapter, patients who were unable to abide by the established treatment contracts were dropped from the analyses of results. There is only one study (Swanson, Swenson, Maruta & Floreen, 1978) which describes the characteristics of patients whose behavior deteriorated while they remained in a behaviorally oriented pain management program. Additional work is needed to identify patients for whom emphasis upon behavioral assessment and treatment is ill-advised. Conversely, further studies similar to that of Cairns and Pasino (1977) are needed to determine what specific types of feedback are most beneficial to patients to whom behavioral assessment and treatment techniques may be applied with little possibility of adverse consequences.

Subjective Estimations

Many pain assessment procedures are based upon numerical estimations of subjective pain states. The following discussion will critically examine pain assessment techniques that rely solely on subjective judgments and involve quantification of subjective judgments by means of titration procedures.

Subjective Judgments

Numerical or Verbal Scales The procedure developed by Beecher (1959) for human analgesic assays in which subjects rate the intensity of their clinical pain along a numerical or verbal scale is probably the most frequently used method of pain assessment (Chapman, 1976). Apart from the criticism that assignment of numbers to subjective pain states does not constitute measurement (Chapman, 1976), numerical or verbal scales suffer from a lack of sensitivity (Huskisson, 1974; Wolff, 1978). This lack of sensitivity is due to the fact that the scale values or categories must be limited (e.g., 0–6) since human sensory information processing is restricted to effective discrimination of approximately seven categories. In addition, when using numerical or verbal scales, one must use caution in making the assumption that one is dealing with an interval level scale and, thus, the differences between the scale values are equal to one another. This assumption is unwarranted since the differences actually are unknown (Huskisson, 1974).

Visual Analogue Scales Another procedure which uses subjective estimates of pain is the visual analogue scale, in which the subject is asked to indicate his level of pain by marking a 10-cm line labeled "no pain" at one end and "unbearable pain" at the other (cf. Merskey, 1973). As noted by Huskisson (1974), the infinite number of points between the ends of the scale eliminates the problem of limited categories associated with numerical and verbal scales. A visual analogue scale also may be converted into a graphic rating scale which includes descriptive terms placed at intervals along the scale; however, in constructing such a scale one must make the tenuous assumption that there are equal intervals between descriptive terms. A series of investigations has compared visual analogue and graphic rating scales with one another (Scott & Huskisson, 1976), with verbal rating scales using adults (Scott & Huskisson, 1976; Woodforde & Merskey, 1972b), and with verbal rating scales using children (Scott, Ansell, & Huskisson, 1977). Comparisons also have been made between visual analogue scales and pressure algometer and audiometric scaling procedures (Woodforde & Merskey, 1972b). The evidence indicates that responses to visual analogue scales show uniform distributions and are most consistently and highly correlated with responses to verbal rating scales. In addition, given the infinite number of points between the extremes, visual analogue scales appear to be sensitive to small changes in perceived pain intensity following analgesic treatment (Scott & Huskisson, 1976; Twycross, 1976). Finally, the simplicity of the visual analogue scale procedure allows it to be used with children as young as five years with no greater incidence of failure than that associated with adults (Scott *et al.*, 1977). Although visual analogue scales have been used extensively in European investigations, particularly those of Bond and his colleagues (e.g., Bond, 1971, 1973; Bond & Pilowsky, 1966; Pilowsky & Bond, 1969; Spring, Wittek, & Wörz, 1976), they have not been used very often in American studies. However, Scott and Huskisson (1976) provide excellent suggestions to researchers who are interested in constructing their own visual analogue scales for experimental purposes.

Titration Procedures

Modified Submaximum Effort Tourniquet Technique Several investigators have devised operations which may be used to quantify subjective estimations through titration procedures. Sternbach and his colleagues (Sternbach, Murphy, Timmermans, Greenhoot, & Akeson, 1974) developed a modification of the submaximum effort tourniquet technique (Smith, Egbert, Markowitz, Mosteller, & Beecher, 1966; SETT). The procedure yields a subjective pain estimate on a numerical scale (0–100), a matched clinical pain score, a pain tolerance score, and a pain ratio score which is computed by multiplying the ratio of the clinical pain score to the tolerance score by 100. Since patients' pain estimates are consistently higher than their pain ratio scores (Sternbach *et al.*, 1974), the pain ratio score is assumed to provide a measure of the severity of perceived pain which, relative to the subjective estimate, is free of influence due to communicative style. Some support for this notion has been found in a series of studies performed by Timmermans and Sternbach (1974, 1976). It should be noted, however, that P. A. Moore and his colleagues (P. A. Moore, Duncan, Scott, Gregg, & Ghia, 1979) recently reported that pain ratings (expressed on visual analogue scales) are not a linear function of elapsed time during the SETT; thus, the mathematical relationship between the variables of pain rating responses and elapsed time appears to have been responsible for the consistent discrepancy between pain estimates and pain ratio scores reported by Sternbach *et al.* (1974). The suggestion then that pain ratio scores are relatively bias-free measures of perceived pain intensity appears unwarranted.

The validity of the matching procedure involved in the modified SETT has been questioned in two investigations (J. D. Moore, Weissman, Thomas, & Whitman, 1971; von Graffenreid, Adler, Abt, Nüesch, & Spiegel, 1978) that found the procedure to be insensitive to the effects of mild analgesics. Consistent with this evidence, Sternbach and his colleagues reported that none of the three component scores or the pain ratio scores produced by chronic pain patients were sensitive to the differential analgesic effects of morphine, codeine, aspirin, and placebo (Sternbach, Deems, Timmermans, & Huey, 1977). More promising results, however, were found in two studies that involved the administration of chlorimipramine (Sternbach, Janowsky, Huey, & Segal, 1976) and transcutaneous electrical stimulation (Sternbach, Ignelzi, Deems, & Timmermans, 1976; TENS) to chronic pain patients. The inconsistent evidence regarding the validity of the modified SETT procedure seems attributable in part to the low test–retest reliabilities of the clinical pain (.50–.88), pain tolerance (.66–.94) and pain ratio (.28–.59) scores (cf. Sternbach *et al.,* 1974). In addition to the psychometric deficiencies discussed above, subjecting a chronic pain patient to a measurement procedure which induces further pain may be questioned on ethical grounds (Sternbach, 1978a). Given the psychometric and ethical shortcomings of the modified SETT procedure, it appears that at the present time, carefully constructed visual analogue scales are the most useful for assessing perceived intensity of patients' pain.

McGill Pain Questionnaire

It was noted in the Introduction that pain is thought to be a multidimensional experience with both sensory and affective components (cf. Casey, 1978). Therefore, the subjective estimation procedures which only provide assessments of pain intensity cannot be used to fully evaluate patients' pain states. As a result, there has been considerable effort directed toward developing verbal descriptor scales which measure the various dimensions of pain. Melzack and Torgerson (1971), for example, used an interval scaling procedure to produce a pain intensity scale consisting of five verbal descriptors. The descriptors were then used as anchor words for subjects of widely different cultural, socioeconomic, and educational backgrounds in a second scaling procedure that produced category scales of 16 subclasses of verbal descriptors (Melzack & Torgerson, 1971). The verbal descriptor subclasses together comprised the *sensory* (i.e., temporal, spatial, thermal, and other related properties), *affective* (i.e., tension, fear, autonomic, and other related properties), and *evaluative* (i.e., overall subjective intensity) descriptor classes; the descriptor classes were posited to correspond to the three major dimensions of pain.

Melzack (1975) expanded the 16 subclasses to 20 in order to encompass descriptors that were deemed necessary for patients to adequately describe their pain. These 20 subclasses comprise the current McGill Pain Questionnaire (Melzack, 1975; MPQ) that actually provides three types of pain data. These are the (*a*) Present Pain Intensity (PPI) or a numerical estimate along the original interval scale produced by Melzack and Torgerson (1971); (*b*) Number of Words Chosen (NWC) from among the 20 subclasses of pain descriptors; and (*c*) Pain Rating Index (PRI) which may be the sum of the rank values of the descriptors chosen in each major class or in all three classes.

Several investigators have provided positive evidence regarding the reliability (Melzack, 1975), validity (Fox & Melzack, 1976; Melzack & Perry, 1975), and objectivity (Dubuisson & Melzack, 1976) of the MPQ. Nonetheless, some of the assumptions underlying the MPQs development recently have been questioned. For example, Bailey and Davidson (1976) factor analyzed subjects' intensity ratings of 39 verbal pain descriptors in order to determine if intensity actually is the salient dimension along which verbal descriptors vary. Consistent with Melzack and Torgerson's (1971) assumptions, an intensity factor was found that accounted for the largest amount of variance relative to the other five extracted factors.

Agnew and Merskey (1976) provided somewhat more negative evidence regarding the assumptions underlying the MPQ. These investigators classified each of the open-ended verbal pain descriptors used by organic, functional, and mixed chronic pain patients into one of the descriptor subclasses originally established by Melzack and Torgerson (1971). They found that patients with organic diagnoses used sensory–thermal words more frequently than did those patients with functional diagnoses. In addition, female patients characterized as having pain due solely to anxiety used sensory–temporal words more often than did females with other diagnoses. It was concluded that verbal descriptors were not very useful for the purpose of discriminating among patients with pain of various etiologies. However, this conclusion must be regarded as tenuous since Agnew and Merskey (1976) failed to establish the reliability of both the diagnostic decisions concerning patients and the classifications of patients' verbal pain descriptors.

Doubts also have been expressed with regard to the factor structure of the MPQ. Crockett, Prkachin, and Craig (1977) factor analyzed the MPQ responses of college students exposed to shock at either threshold or tolerance levels and back pain patients in a diagnostic clinic setting. Two factors were extracted that were composed solely of affective and sensory descriptors, respectively; three additional factors also were found that were composed of various combinations of sensory, affective, and evaluative descriptors. Leavitt, Garron, Whisler, and Sheinkop (1978) factor analyzed back pain patients' choices of pain descriptors from among 74 MPQ descriptors presented in a randomly ordered sequence. Seven factors were extracted; five were composed entirely of sensory descriptors and the other two factors were defined primarily by sensory and affective descriptors, respectively. The reported findings (Crockett *et al.*, 1977; Leavitt *et al.*, 1978) suggest that Melzack and Torgerson's (1971) three-factor conceptualization of the MPQ may be quite inappropriate. An investigation (Prieto, Hopson, Bradley, Byrne, Geisinger, Midax, & Marchisello, 1980) was recently performed, however, using methodological procedures (e.g., a homogeneous LBP patient sample, a 10:1 patient to item ratio) that, relative to those used in previous studies, minimized distortion of the factor solution. Four factors were found; three were composed solely of sensory, affective, and evaluative subclasses, respectively, while the fourth was defined by both sensory and affective subclasses. Although this investigation requires replication with other patient samples, the results provide relatively strong support for Melzack and Torgerson's (1971) conceptualization of the MPQs underlying structure and for the continued use of the sensory, affective, and evaluative PRIs for scoring purposes.[5] The results also suggest that the use of factor scales derived from the Crockett *et al.* (1977) or Leavitt *et al.* (1978) studies for differentiation of various patient groups (cf. Leavitt, Garron, D'Angelo, & McNeill, 1979) is unwarranted given that the methodological deficiencies of those investigations may have resulted in the production of spurious factors (see Chapter 24 for a more detailed discussion of methodological errors in factor analytic studies).

Finally, it should be noted that an attempt has been made to modify the MPQ in order to reduce the possible confounding of patients' responses due to the presence of an interviewer or the rank-ordered placement of the verbal descriptors within each subclass. Reading and Newton (1978) used samples of women with pain related to dysmenorrhea or IUD contraceptives for the rescaling of the MPQ verbal descriptors; in addition, the investigators produced a self-administered, counterbalanced, card-sort format for the MPQ. Although positive evidence regarding the reliability and validity of the revised MPQ was presented, the instrument's use is currently restricted to patients with gynecological pain. Reading and Newton (1978) suggest that it is possible to empirically define various card-sort descriptor pools for different pain syndromes. It is not clear, however, if the advantages of the card-sort format warrant the

[5]However, the exclusion of 15% of potential subjects from the investigation due to inability to speak or read English suggests that the MPQ may not be tenable for use with patients from low socioeconomic backgrounds or who are unfamiliar with the English language (cf. Wolff, 1978).

cumbersome task of producing numerous, specific, descriptor pools.

In summary, the current evidence suggests that the reliability, validity and objectivity of the MPQ are acceptable. In addition, the MPQ provides, in accordance with our current theories and taxonomy (IASP Subcommittee on Taxonomy, 1979), a unique, multidimensional assessment of the pain experience. The data regarding the factor structure of the MPQ are both scant and mixed. Therefore, while investigators may continue to use the MPQ with some confidence (cf. Prieto *et al.*, 1980), refinements in the structure, scoring, and interpretation of the sensory, affective and evaluative PRIs may well be reported in the future as additional factor analytic and construct validity studies are performed and replicated.

Ratio Scales of Verbal Pain Descriptors As noted in the preceding discussion, the development of the MPQ represents a major advance in the assessment of pain. The scaling procedure used in the MPQs development, however, is rather unsophisticated relative to the psychophysical scaling procedures of magnitude estimation and cross-modality matching that have been used recently to develop bias-free, ratio scales of verbal pain descriptors. For example, Tursky (1976) produced three descriptor scales (i.e., intensity, reaction, and sensation) that were analogous to the PPI and the evaluative and sensory classes developed by Melzack and Torgerson (1971). Although the reliability and validity of the scales were established by Tursky (1976), the scales have not received further investigation in the literature to date.

Gracely, McGrath, and Dubner (1978a, 1978b) also have used magnitude estimation and cross-modality matching to develop bias-free scales of sensory intensity and affect which resembled the PPI and the evaluative descriptor class of the MPQ, respectively. Gracely and his colleagues have presented impressive evidence concerning the reliability, objectivity (Gracely *et al.*, 1978a), and validity (Gracely *et al.*, 1978b; Gracely, Dubner, & McGrath, 1979) of the descriptor scales. In addition, Gracely, Dubner, McGrath and Heft (1978) recently demonstrated that noxious stimulation (i.e., application of ethyl chloride to the exposed dentin of a recently excavated cavity preparation) that resembled clinical pain could be scaled along sensory and affective dimensions as readily as electrocutaneous stimulation of intact teeth. This suggests that the sensory and affective scales may provide valid evaluations of patients' clinical pain experiences. However, further investigations using chronic pain patients are required before the scales may be accepted as clinically useful instruments.

Summary

There have been two very important advances in the use of subjective estimations for pain patient evaluation during the past five years. One advance has been the growing recognition (cf. Chapman, 1976; Sternbach, 1978a; Wolff, 1978) that the use of numerical or verbal scales of subjective estimations of pain intensity are not sufficient to adequately assess a person's pain experience. Although the highly favorable, initial evaluations (cf. Liebeskind & Paul, 1977) of Sternbach's modified SETT procedure (Sternbach *et al.*, 1974) now appear to have been premature, positive evidence has been produced regarding the psychometric characteristics of the MPQ (Melzack, 1975). The MPQ will probably be refined as additional data are accumulated; nonetheless, the current evidence suggests that the MPQ holds great promise as a unique instrument for the multidimensional assessment of the pain experience. Also promising are the sophisticated, but clinically untested, ratio scales of sensory and affective verbal descriptors developed by Gracely and his colleagues (Gracely *et al.*, 1978a, 1978b). It is certain that in the future there will be a large number of investigations of both the MPQ and the ratio scales of verbal descriptors. One important task for these investigations will be to determine if the level of verbal sophistication required by the instruments may make them impractical for use with a significant portion of the chronic pain patient population.

Conclusions

This chapter has presented a critical review of the empirical literature regarding chronic pain assessment involving measurement of objects and events and the use of subjective estimations. There are both unique advantages and shortcomings associated with each of the three major types of evaluation procedures. For example, in the preceding discussion concerning subjective estimations, it was noted that the MPQ (Melzack, 1975) and the ratio scales of verbal descriptors (Gracely *et al.*, 1978a, 1978b) have the unique advantage, relative to other assessment procedures, of providing information concerning multiple dimensions of the pain experience. Both of the instruments, however, rely upon verbal self-report that may be contradicted by other types of pain assessments such as measurement of events (cf. Berk *et al.*, 1977; Murphy, 1976).

With regard to the measurement of events, it was noted that well-trained observers may provide reliable data regarding patients' behavior which are ideally suited for evaluative purposes in inpatient settings similar to those described by Fordyce (1976) and Cairns *et al.* (1976). Data collected by means of patients' self-monitoring also may be quite valuable although the reliability of these data and the possible effects of reactivity upon the data are currently unknown. However, behavioral evaluations cannot provide information about specific aspects of the pain experience such as the various sensory and affective qualities that may be essential for determining the etiology of the perceived pain.

Finally, it was noted that object measurement is essential to any pain patient evaluation since it is always necessary to assess personality attributes that may contribute to patients' pain experiences and behaviors. The MMPI, which is the most frequently used instrument for the personality evaluation of pain patients, appears to be ideally suited for such evaluations given the large number of MMPI investigations involving medical patients reported in the literature (cf. Dahlstrom, Welsh, & Dahlstrom, 1975, pp. 41–59). It is ironic that the major disadvantage of the MMPI is that there is very little documentation of empirically developed relationships among various MMPI profile types and pain-related behaviors and attributes that are important for both evaluative and treatment purposes.

The preceding discussion indicates that it is most beneficial to use all three major assessment procedures to evaluate chronic pain. Both Black and Chapman (1976) and Duncan, Gregg, and Ghia (1978) have expressed similar thoughts concerning the need to systematically assess pain with multiple instruments. Indeed, Duncan *et al.* (1978) have developed a computerized storage and retrieval system for information regarding patients' (*a*) degree of physical disease; (*b*) level of psychosocial impairment (object measurement); and (*c*) severity of pain behavior (subjective estimations and event measurement). Although the computerized assessment system has been used primarily for descriptive and teaching purposes (cf. Duncan *et al.*, 1978), it may prove to be quite valuable for diagnostic purposes. That is, if psychologists are to make judgments regarding diagnosis and treatment on the basis of large amounts of data regarding medical history and numerous pain assessment procedures, the optimal method for combining data to perform those judgments would appear to be statistical prediction (e.g., Dawes, 1979; Meehl, 1954) that can be most economically and quickly performed by computer analysis. It is necessary, then, to return to the suggestions presented on pages 94–101 regarding the pressing need for investigators to empirically develop diagnostic predictions for various groups composed of patients with chronic pain of the same etiology. It is suggested that the familiar MMPI scale scores be used as predictor variables (i.e., the profile subgroups) and that the criteria (i.e., the pain-related correlates) consist of medical and demographic data as well as pain assessments involving measurements of objects and events and subjective estimations. Once the pain-related correlates were established for various MMPI profile subgroups of patients with the same pain etiologies (including "unknown"), it then would be possible to examine the effects of specific treatments upon the various measures of patients' (*a*) personality attributes (e.g., responses to the EPI); (*b*) behavior (e.g., uptime, average daily analgesic intake); (*c*) subjective pain estimates (e.g., responses to visual analogue scales); and (*d*) verbal pain reports (e.g., responses to verbal descriptor scales of various aspects of the pain experience). Put another way, the goal of research concerning the assessment of chronic pain should be to contribute to the understanding of what specific treatments may be applied to what pain patient subgroups to best alter what pain-related experiences, behaviors, and attributes (cf. Bradley, Prokop *et al.*, 1978; Prokop *et al.*, 1980). The task that has been proposed is quite challenging; investigators probably will find differences in their results across treatment settings and perhaps between various ethnic or cultural groups within single settings (cf. Weisenberg, Kreindler, Schachat, & Werboff, 1975). In addition, the assessment (and treatment) decisions made on the basis of statistical relationships will be far from perfect. However, given that statistical models of judgments nearly always are superior to those made on the basis of clinical judgment (Dawes, 1979), the development of actuarial diagnostic systems and subsequent treatment studies may allow psychologists to reduce the large amount of interindividual variability in patients' treatment response currently documented in the literature (cf. Liebeskind & Paul, 1977).

Acknowledgments

The authors wish to thank W. Crawford Clark for his helpful comments concerning an earlier version of this chapter.

References

Agnew, D. C., & Merskey, H. Words of chronic pain. *Pain,* 1976, *2,* 73–81.

Anastasi, A. *Fields of applied psychology* (2nd ed.). New York: McGraw-Hill, 1979.

Bailey, C. A., & Davidson, P. O. The language of pain: Intensity. *Pain,* 1976, *2,* 319–324.

Beals, R. K., & Hickman, N. W. Industrial injuries of the back and extremities. *Journal of Bone and Joint Surgery,* 1972, *54-A,* 1593–1611.

Beecher, H. K. *Measurement of subjective responses.* New York: Oxford University Press, 1959.

Berk, S. N., Moore, M. E., & Resnick, J. H. Psychosocial factors as mediators of acupuncture therapy. *Journal of Consulting and Clinical Psychology,* 1977, *45,* 612–619.

Black, R. G., & Chapman, C. R. The SAD index for clinical assessment of pain. In J. J. Bonica & D. Albe-Fessard (Eds.), *Advances in pain research and therapy* (Vol. 1). New York: Raven Press, 1976.

Blume, H. G. Radiofrequency denaturation in occipital pain: A new approach in 114 cases. In J. J. Bonica & D. Albe-Fessard (Eds.), *Advances in pain research and therapy* (Vol. 1). New York: Raven Press, 1976.

Blumetti, A. E., & Modesti, L. M. Psychological predictors of success or failure of surgical intervention for intractable back pain. In J. J. Bonica & D. Albe-Fessard (Eds.), *Advances in pain research and therapy* (Vol. 1). New York: Raven Press, 1976.

Bond, M. R. The relation of pain to the Eysenck Personality Inventory, Cornell Medical Index, and Whitely Index of Hypochondriasis. *British Journal of Psychiatry,* 1971, *119,* 671–678.

Bond, M. R. Personality studies in patients with pain secondary to organic disease. *Journal of Psychosomatic Research,* 1973, *17,* 257–263.

Bond, M. R. Pain and personality in cancer patients. In J. J. Bonica & D. Albe-Fessard (Eds.), *Advances in pain research and therapy* (Vol. 1). New York: Raven Press, 1976.

Bond, M. R., & Pilowsky, I. Subjective assessment of pain and its relationship to the administration of analgesics in patients with advanced cancer. *Journal of Psychosomatic Research,* 1966, *10,* 203–208.

Bonica, J. J. Introduction to the First World Congress on Pain: Goals of the IASP and the World Congress. In J. J. Bonica & D. Albe-Fessard (Eds.), *Advances in pain research and therapy* (Vol. 1). New York: Raven Press, 1976.

Bonica, J. J. Introduction to symposium on pain. *Archives of Surgery,* 1977, *112,* 749.

Bourhis, A., Boudouresque, G., Pellet, W., Fondarai, J., Ponzio, J., & Spitalier, J. M. Pain infirmity and psychotropic drugs in oncology. *Pain,* 1978, *5,* 263–274.

Bradley, L. A., Prieto, E. J., Hopson, L., & Prokop, C. K. Comment on "Personality organization as an aspect of back pain in a medical setting." *Journal of Personality Assessment,* 1978, *42,* 573–578.

Bradley, L. A., Prokop, C. K., Margolis, R., & Gentry, W. D. Multivariate analyses of the MMPI profiles of low back pain patients. *Journal of Behavioral Medicine,* 1978, *1,* 253–272.

Breivik, H., Hesla, P. E., Molnar, I., & Lind, B. Treatment of chronic low back pain and sciatica: Comparison of caudal epidural injections of bupivacaine and oral methylprednisolone with bupivacaine followed by saline. In J. J. Bonica & D. Albe-Fessard (Eds.), *Advances in pain research and therapy* (Vol. 1). New York: Raven Press, 1976.

Brena, S. F., & Unikel, I. P. Nerve blocks and contingency management in chronic pain states. In J. J. Bonica & D. Albe-Fessard (Eds.), *Advances in pain research and therapy,* (Vol. 1). New York: Raven Press, 1976.

Cairns, D., & Pasino, J. A. Comparison of verbal reinforcement and feedback in the operant treatment of disability due to chronic low back pain. *Behavior Therapy,* 1977, *8,* 621-630.

Cairns, D., Thomas, L., Mooney, V., & Pace, J. B. A comprehensive treatment approach to chronic low back pain. *Pain,* 1976, *2,* 301-308.

Calsyn, D. A., Louks, J., & Freeman, C. W. The use of the MMPI with chronic low back pain patients with a mixed diagnosis. *Journal of Clinical Psychology,* 1976, *32,* 532-536.

Carr, J. E., Brownsberger, C. N., & Rutherford, R. S. Characteristics of symptom-matched psychogenic and "real" pain patients on the MMPI. *Proceedings of the 74th Annual Convention of the American Psycholological Association,* 1966, *1,* 215-216. (Abstract)

Casey, K. L. Neural mechanisms of pain. In E. C. Carterette & M. P. Friedman (Eds.), *Handbook of perception* (Vol. VI B). New York: Academic Press, 1978.

Chapman, C. R. Measurement of pain: Problems and issues. In J. J. Bonica & D. Albe-Fessard (Eds.), *Advances in pain research and therapy* (Vol. 1). New York: Raven Press, 1976.

Chapman, C. R. Psychological aspects of pain patient treatment. *Archives of Surgery,* 1977, *112,* 767-772.

Chapman, C. R. The hurtful world: Pathological pain and its control. In E. C. Carterette & M. P. Friedman (Eds.), *Handbook of perception* (Vol. VI B). New York: Academic Press, 1978.

Chapman, C. R., Sola, A. E., & Bonica, J. J. Illness behavior and depression compared in pain center and private practice patients. *Pain,* 1979, *6,* 1-7.

Ciminero, A. R., Nelson, R. O., & Lipinski, D. P. Self-monitoring procedures. In A. R. Ciminero, K. S. Calhoun, & H. E. Adams (Eds.), *Handbook of behavioral assessment.* New York: Wiley, 1977.

Clark, W. C., & Hunt, H. F. Pain. In J. A. Downey & R. C. Darling (Eds.), *Physiological basis of rehabilitation medicine.* Philadelphia: W. B. Saunders, 1971.

Comrey, A. L. Common methodological problems in factor analytic studies. *Journal of Consulting and Clinical Psychology,* 1978, *46,* 648-659

Cox, G. B., & Chapman, C. R. Multivariate analysis of pain data. In J. J. Bonica & D. Albe-Fessard (Eds.), *Advances in pain research therapy* (Vol. 1). New York: Raven Press, 1976

Cox, G. B., Chapman, C. R., & Black, R. G. The MMPI and chronic pain: The diagnosis of psychogenic pain. *Journal of Behavioral Medicine,* 1978, *1,* 437-443.

Crockett, D. J., Prkachin, K. M., & Craig, K. D. Factors of the language of pain in patient and volunteer groups. *Pain,* 1977, *4,* 175-183.

Dahlstrom, W. G. Prediction of adjustment after neurosurgery. *American Psychologist,* 1954, *9,* 353. (Abstract)

Dahlstrom, W. G., Welsh, G. S., & Dahlstrom, L. E. *An MMPI handbook, Vol. 1: Clinical interpretation.* Minneapolis: University of Minnesota Press, 1972.

Dawes, R. M. The robust beauty of improper linear models in decision making. *American Psychologist,* 1979, *34,* 571-582.

Dean, E. F. A lengthened Mini: The Midi-Mult. *Journal of Clinical Psychology,* 1972, *28,* 68-71.

Dubuisson, D., & Melzack, R. Classification of clinical pain descriptions by multiple group discriminant analysis. *Experimental Neurology,* 1976, *51,* 480-487.

Duncan, G. H., Gregg, J. M., & Ghia, J. N. The pain profile: A computerized system for assessment of chronic pain. *Pain,* 1978, *5,* 275-284.

Elton, D., Stanley, G. V., & Burrows, G. D. Self-esteem and chronic pain. *Journal of Psychosomatic Research,* 1978, *22,* 25-30.

Eysenck, H. J. The questionnaire measurement of neuroticism and extraversion. *Revista di Psicologia,* 1956, *50,* 113-140.

Eysenck, H. J. *The structure of human personality.* London: Methuen, 1960.

Eysenck, H. J., & Eysenck, S. G. B. *Manual of the Eysenck Personality Inventory.* London: University of London Press, 1964.

Faschingbauer, T. R. A 166 item short form of the MMPI: The FAM. *Journal of Consulting and Clinical Psychology,* 1974, *42,* 645-655.

Faschingbauer, T. R., & Newmark, C. S. *Short forms of the MMPI.* Lexington, Mass.: D.C. Heath, 1978.

Feinstein, A. R. A critical overview of diagnosis in psychiatry. In V. M. Rakoff, H. C. Stancer & H. B. Kedward (Eds.), *Psychiatric diagnosis.* New York: Brunner/Mazel, 1977.

Folkard, S., Glynn, C. J., & Lloyd, J. W. Diurnal variation and individual differences in the perception of intractable pain. *Journal of Psychosomatic Research,* 1976, *20,* 289-301.

Fordyce, W. E. An operant conditioning method for managing chronic pain. *Postgraduate Medicine,* 1973, *53,* 123-128.

Fordyce, W. E. *Behavioral methods for chronic pain and illness.* St. Louis: C. V. Mosby, 1976.

Fordyce, W. E. Learning processes in pain. In R. A. Sternbach (Ed.), *The psychology of pain.* New York: Raven Press, 1978.

Fordyce, W. E., Brena, S. F., Holcomb, R. F., DeLateur, B. J. & Loeser, J. D. Relationship of patient semantic pain descriptions to physicians' diagnostic judgements, activity level measures, and MMPI. *Pain,* 1978, *5,* 293-303.

Fordyce, W. E., Fowler, R. S., DeLateur, B. J., Sand, P. L., & Trieschmann, R. B. Operant conditioning in the treatment of chronic pain. *Archives of Physical Medicine and Rehabilitation,* 1973, *54,* 399–408.

Fordyce, W. E., Fowler, R. S., Lehmann, J. F., & DeLateur, B. J. Some implications of learning in problems of chronic pain. *Journal of Chronic Diseases,* 1968, *21,* 179–190.

Fox, E. J., & Melzack, R. Transcutaneous electrical stimulation and acupuncture: Comparison of treatment for low back pain. *Pain,* 1976, *2,* 141–148.

Freeman, C. W., Calsyn, D. A., & Louks, J. L. The use of the Minnesota Multiphasic Personality Inventory with low back pain patients. *Journal of Clinical Psychology,* 1976, *32,* 294–298.

Freeman, C., Calsyn, D. A., & O'Leary, M. Application of Faschingbauer's abbreviated MMPI with medical patients. *Journal of Consulting and Clinical Psychology,* 1977, *45,* 706–707.

Frost, E. A. M., Hsu, C., & Sadowsky, D. Acute and chronic pain: A study of the comparative values of acupuncture therapy. In J. J. Bonica & D. Albe-Fessard (Eds.), *Advances in pain research and therapy* (Vol. 1). New York: Raven Press, 1976.

Gentry, W. D., Newman, M. C., Goldner, L., & von Baeyer, C. Relation between graduated spinal block technique and MMPI in diagnosis and prognosis of chronic low back pain. *Spine,* 1977, *2,* 210–213.

Gentry, W. D., Shows, W. D., & Thomas, M. Chronic low back pain: A psychological profile. *Psychosomatics,* 1974, *15,* 174–177.

Goldfried, M. R., & Linehan, M. M. Basic issues of behavioral assessment. In A. R. Ciminero, K. S. Calhoun, & H. E. Adams (Eds.), *Handbook of behavioral assessment.* New York: Wiley, 1977.

Gorsuch, R. L. *Factor analysis.* Philadelphia: W. B. Saunders, 1974.

Gracely, R. H., Dubner, R., & McGrath, P. Narcotic analgesia: Fentanyl reduces the intensity but not the unpleasantness of painful tooth pulp sensation. *Science,* 1979, *203,* 1261–1263.

Gracely, R. H., Dubner, R., McGrath, P., & Heft, M. New methods of pain measurement and their application to pain control. *International Dental Journal,* 1978, *28,* 52–65

Gracely, R. H., McGrath, P., & Dubner, R. Ratio scales of sensory and affective pain descriptions. *Pain,* 1978, *5,* 5–18. (a)

Gracely, R. H., McGrath, P., & Dubner, R. Validity and sensitivity of ratio scales of sensory and affective verbal pain descriptors: Manipulation of affect by diazepam. *Pain,* 1978, *5,* 19–29. (b)

Graham, J. R. Review of Minnesota Multiphasic Personality Inventory special scales. In P. McReynolds (Ed.), *Advances in psychological assessment* (Vol. 4). San Francisco: Jossey-Bass, 1977.

Haase, R. R., Banks, D. L., & Lee, D. Y. A validity study of the Pain Appreciation Test. *Journal of Clinical Psychology,* 1975, *31,* 747–751.

Hanvik, L. J. MMPI profiles in patients with low back pain. *Journal of Consulting Psychology,*1951, 15, 350–353.

Hendler, N., Viernstein, M., Gucer, P., & Long, D. A preoperative screening test for chronic back pain patients. *Psychosomatics,* 1979, *20,* 801–808.

Hossenlopp, C. M., Leiber, L., & Mo, B. Psychological factors in the effectiveness of acupuncture for chronic pain. In J. J. Bonica & D. Albe-Fessard (Eds.), *Advances in pain research and therapy* (Vol. 1). New York: Raven Press, 1976.

Huskisson, E. C. Measurement of pain. *Lancet,* 1974, *2,* 1127–1131.

IASP Subcommittee on Taxonomy. Pain terms: A list with definitions and notes on usage. *Pain,* 1979, *6,* 249–252.

Jamison, K., Ferrer-Brechner, M. T., Brechner, V. L., & McCreary, C. P. Correlation of personality profile with pain syndrome. In J. J. Bonica & D. Albe-Fessard (Eds.), *Advances in pain research and therapy* (Vol. 1). New York: Raven Press, 1976.

Kent, R. N., & Foster, S. L. Direct observational procedures: Methodological issues in naturalistic settings. In A. R. Ciminero, K. S. Calhoun, & H. E. Adams (Eds.), *Handbook of behavioral assessment.* New York: Wiley, 1977.

Lair, C. V., & Trapp, E. P. The differential diagnostic value of the MMPI with somatically disturbed patients. *Journal of Clinical Psychology,* 1962, *18,* 146–147.

Leavitt, F., Garron, D. C., D'Angelo, C. M., & McNeill, T. W. Low back pain in patients with and without demonstrable organic disease. *Pain,* 1979, *6,* 191–200.

Leavitt, F., Garron, D. C., Whisler, W., & Sheinkop, M. B. Affective and sensory dimensions of back pain. *Pain,* 1978, *4,* 273–281.

Liebeskind, J. C., & Paul, L. A. Psychological and physiological mechanisms of pain. *Annual Review of Psychology,* 1977, *28,* 41–60.

Louks, J. L., Freeman, C. W., & Calsyn, D. A. Personality organization as an aspect of back pain in a medical setting. *Journal of Personality* Assessment, 1978, *42,* 152–158.

McCollum, D. E., & Stephen, C. R. The use of graduated spinal anesthesis in the differential diagnosis of pain of the back and lower extremities. *Southern Medical Journal,* 1964, *57,* 410–416.

McCreary, C., Turner, J., & Dawson, E. Differences between functional versus organic low back pain patients. *Pain,* 1977, *4,* 73–78.

McCreary, C. Turner, J., & Dawson, E. The MMPI as a predictor of response to conservative treatment for low back pain. *Journal of Clinical Psychology,* 1979, *35,* 278-284.

Maruta, T., Swanson, D. W., & Swenson, W. M. Low back pain patients in a psychiatric population. *Mayo Clinic Proceedings,* 1976, *51,* 57-61. (a)

Maruta, T., Swanson, D. W., & Swenson, W. M. Pain as a psychiatric symptom: Comparison between low back pain and depression. *Psychosomatics,* 1976, *17,* 123-127. (b)

Mechanic, D. The concept of illness behavior. *Journal of Chronic Diseases,* 1962, *15,* 189-194.

Mechanic, D. Effects of psychological stress on perceptions of physical health and use of medical and psychiatric facilities. *Journal of Human Stress,* 1978, *4,* 26-32.

Meehl, P. E. *Clinical versus statistical prediction: A theoretical analysis and a review of the evidence.* Minneapolis: University of Minnesota Press, 1954.

Melzack, R. The McGill Pain Questionnaire: Major properties and scoring methods. *Pain,* 1975, *1,* 277-299.

Melzack, R., & Perry, C. Self-regulation of pain: The use of alpha-feedback and hypnotic training for the control of chronic pain. *Experimental Neurology,* 1975, 46, 452-469.

Melzack, R., & Torgerson, W. S. On the language of pain. *Anesthesiology,* 1971, *34,* 50-59.

Merskey, H. Personality traits of psychiatric patients with pain. *Journal of Psychosomatic Research,* 1972, *16,* 163-166.

Merskey, H. The perception and measurement of pain. *Journal of Psychosomatic Research,* 1973, *17,* 251-255.

Merskey, H. Diagnosis of the patient with chronic pain. *Journal of Human Stress,* 1978, *4,* 3-7. (a)

Merskey, H. Pain and personality. In R. A. Sternbach (Ed.), *The psychology of pain.* New York: Raven Press, 1978. (b)

Merskey, H., & Spear, F. G. The concept of pain. *Journal of Psychosomatic Research,* 1967, *11,* 59-67.

Mooney, V., Cairns, D., & Robertson, J. The psychological evaluation and treatment of the chronic back pain patient—A new approach (Part 2). *Journal of the Orthopedic Nurses' Association,* 1975, *2,* 187-189.

Moore, J. D., Weissman, L., Thomas, G., & Whitman, E. N. Response of experimental ischemic pain to analgesics in prison volunteers. *Journal of Clinical Pharmacology,* 1971, *11,* 433-439.

Moore, P. A., Duncan, G. H., Scott, D. S., Gregg, J. M., & Ghia, J. N. The submaximal effort tourniquet test: Its use in evaluating experimental and chronic pain. *Pain,* 1979, *6,* 375-382.

Murphy, T. M. Subjective and objective follow-up assessment of acupuncture therapy without suggestion in 100 chronic pain patients. In J. J. Bonica & D. Albe-Fessard (Eds), *Advances in pain research and therapy* (Vol. 1). New York: Raven Press, 1976.

Nelson, R. O. Methodological issues in assessment via self-monitoring. In J. D. Cone & R. P. Hawkins (Eds.), *Behavioral assessment: New directions in clinical psychology.* New York: Brunner/Mazel, 1977.

Newmark, C. S., Conger, A. J., & Faschingbauer, T. R. The interpretive validity and effective test length functioning of an abbreviated MMPI relative to the standard MMPI. *Journal of Clinical Psychology,* 1976, *32,* 27-32.

Newmark, C. S., & Faschingbauer, T. R. Bibliography of short forms of the MMPI. *Journal of Personality Assessment,* 1978, *42,* 496-502.

Petrovich, D. V. The Pain Apperception Test: A preliminary report. *Journal of Psychology,* 1957, *44,* 339-346.

Pichot, P., Perse, J., Lekeoux, M. O., Dureau, J. L., Perez, C. I., & Rychewaert, A. La Personalité des sujets presentant des douleurs dorsales fonchonnelles valeur de l'Invenlaire Multiphasique de Personnalité du Minnesota. *Revue de Psychologie Applique,* 1972, *22,* 145-172.

Pilowsky, I. Pain as abnormal illness behavior. *Journal of Human Stress,* 1978, *4,* 22-27. (a)

Pilowsky, I. Psychodynamic aspects of the pain experience. In R. A. Sternbach (Ed.), *The psychology of pain.* New York: Raven Press, 1978. (b)

Pilowsky, I., & Bond, M. R. Pain and its management in malignant disease: Elucidation of staff-patient transactions. *Psychosomatic Medicine,* 1969, *31,* 400-404.

Pilowsky, I., Chapman, C. R., & Bonica, J. J. Pain, depression, and illness behavior in a pain clinic population. *Pain,* 1977, *4,* 183-192.

Pilowsky, I., & Spence, N. D. Patterns of illness behavior in patients with intractable pain. *Journal of Psychosomatic Research,* 1975, *19,* 279-287.

Pilowsky, I., & Spence, N. D. Illness behavior syndromes associated with intractable pain. *Pain,* 1976, *2,* 61-71. (a)

Pilowsky, I., & Spence, N. D. Is illness behavior related to chronicity in patients with intractable pain? *Pain,* 1976, *2,* 167-173. (b)

Pilowsky, I., & Spence, N. D. Pain and illness behaviour: A comparative study. *Journal of Psychosomatic Research,* 1976, *20,* 131-134. (c)

Pilowsky, I., & Spence, N. D. Pain, anger, and illness behaviour. *Journal of Psychosomatic Research,* 1976, *20,* 411-416. (d)

Poythress, N. G., & Blaney, P. H. The validity of MMPI

interpretations based on the Mini-Mult and the FAM. *Journal of Personality Assessment,* 1978, *42,* 143-147.

Prieto, E. J., Hopson, L., Bradley, L. A., Byrne, M., Geisinger, K. F., Midax, D., & Marchisello, P. J. The language of low back pain: Factor structure of the McGill Pain Questionnaire. *Pain,* 1980, *8,* 11-19.

Procacci, P., Zoppi, M., & Maresca, M. Experimental pain in man. *Pain,* 1979, *6,* 123-140.

Prokop, C. K., Bradley, L. A., Margolis, R., & Gentry, W. D. Multivariate analyses of the MMPI profiles of multiple pain patients. *Journal of Personality Assessment,* 1980, *44,* 246-252.

Reading, A. E., & Newton, J. R. A card sort method of pain assessment. *Journal of Psychosomatic Research,* 1978, *22,* 503-512.

Reitan, R. M., & Davison L. A. (Eds.), *Clinical neuropsychology: Current status and applications.* Washington, D. C.: Winston, 1974.

Rugh, J. D., & Schwitzgebel, R. L. Instrumentation for behavioral assessment. In A. R. Ciminero, K. S. Calhoun, & H. E. Adams (Eds.), *Handbook of behavioral assessment.* New York: Wiley, 1977.

Scott, P. J., Ansell, B. M., & Huskisson, E. C. Measurement of pain in juvenile chronic polyarthritis. *Annals of the Rheumatic Diseases,* 1977, *36,* 186-187.

Scott, P. J., & Huskisson, E. C. Graphic representation of pain. *Pain,* 1976, *2,* 175-184.

Shaffer, J. W., Nussbaum, K., & Little, J. M. MMPI profiles of disability insurance claimants. *American Journal of Psychiatry,* 1972, *129,* 403-407.

Smith, G. M., Egbert, L. D., Markowitz, R. A., Mosteller, F., & Beecher, H. K. An experimental pain method sensitive to morphine in man: The submaximum effort tourniquet technique. *Journal of Pharmacology and Experimental Therapeutics,* 1966, *154,* 324-332.

Spring, A., Wittek, R., & Wörz., R. Interdependence of low back pain and psychiatric symptomatology. In J. J. Bonica & D. Albe-Fessard (Eds.), *Advances in pain research and therapy* (Vol. 1), New York: Raven Press, 1976.

Sternbach, R. A. *Pain: A psychophysiological analysis.* New York: Academic Press, 1968.

Sternbach, R. A. Psychological aspects of pain and the selection of patients. *Clinical Neurosurgery,* 1973, *21,* 323-333.

Sternbach, R. A. *Pain patients: Traits and treatments.* New York: Academic Press, 1974.

Sternbach, R. A. Psychological factors in pain. In J. J. Bonica & D. Albe-Fessard (Eds.), *Advances in pain research and therapy* (Vol. 1). New York: Raven Press, 1976.

Sternbach, R. A. Clinical aspects of pain. In R. A. Sternbach (Ed.), *The psychology of pain.* New York: Raven Press, 1978. (a)

Sternbach, R. A. Psychological dimensions and perceptual analyses, including pathologies of pain. In E. C. Carterette & M. P. Friedman (Eds.), *Handbook of perception* (Vol. VI B). New York: Academic Press, 1978. (b)

Sternbach, R. A. (Ed.). *The psychology of pain.* New York: Raven Press, 1978. (c)

Sternbach, R. A., Deems, L. M., Timmermans, G., & Huey, L. Y. On the sensitivity of the tourniquet pain test. *Pain,* 1977, *3,* 105-110.

Sternbach, R. A., Ignelzi, R. J., Deems, L. M., & Timmermans, G. Transcutaneous electrical analgesia: A follow-up analysis. *Pain,* 1976, *2,* 35-41.

Sternbach R. A., Janowsky, D. S., Huey, L. Y., & Segal, D. S. Effects of altering brain serotonin activity on human chronic pain. In J. J. Bonica & D. Albe-Fessard (Eds.), *Advances in pain research and therapy* (Vol. 1). New York: Raven Press, 1976.

Sternbach, R. A., Murphy, R. W., Timmermans, G., Greenhoot, J. H., & Akeson, W. H. Measuring the severity of clinical pain. In J. J. Bonica (Ed.), *Advances in neurology* (Vol. 4). New York: Raven Press, 1974.

Sternbach, R. A., Wolf, S. R., Murphy, R. W., & Akeson, W. H. Aspects of chronic low back pain. *Psychosomatics,* 1973, *14,* 52-56. (a)

Sternbach, R. A., Wolf, S. R., Murphy, R. W., & Akeson, W. H. Traits of pain patients: The low-back "loser." *Psychosomatics,* 1973, *14,* 226-229.(b)

Swanson, D. W., Swenson, W. M., Maruta, T., & Floreen, A. C. The dissatisfied patient with chronic pain. *Pain,* 1978, *4,* 367-378.

Thomas, M. R., & Lyttle, D. Development of diagnostic checklist for low back pain patients. *Journal of Clinical Psychology,* 1976, *32,* 125-129.

Timmermans, G., & Sternbach, R. A. Factors of human chronic pain: An analysis of personality and pain reaction variables. *Science,* 1974, *184,* 806-808.

Timmermans, G., & Sternbach, R. A. Human chronic pain and personality: A canonical correlation analysis. In J. J. Bonica & D. Albe-Fessard (Eds.), *Advances in pain research and therapy* (Vol. 1), New York: Raven Press, 1976.

Toomey, T. C., Ghia, J. N., Mao, W., & Gregg, J. M. Acupuncture and chronic pain mechanisms: The moderating efforts of affect, personality and stress on response to treatment. *Pain,* 1977, *3,* 137-145.

Towne, W. S., & Tsushima, W. T. The use of the low back and the dorsal scales in the identification of functional low back pain patients. *Journal of Clinical Psychology,* 1978, *34,* 88-91.

Tsushima, W. T., & Towne, W. S. Clinical limitations of

the low back scale. *Journal of Clinical Psychology,* 1979, *35,* 306–308.

Turner, J., & McCreary, C. Short forms of the MMPI with back pain patients. *Journal of Consulting and Clinical Psychology,* 1978, *46,* 354–355.

Tursky, B. The development of a pain perception profile: A psychophysical approach. In M. Weisenberg & B. Tursky (Eds.), *Pain: New perspectives in therapy and research.* New York: Plenum, 1976.

Twycross, R. G. The measurement of pain in terminal carcinoma. *Journal of International Medical Research,* 1976, *4,* 58–67.

von Graffenreid, B., Adler, R., Abt, K., Nüesch, E., & Spiegel, R. The influence of anxiety and pain sensitivity on experimental pain in man. *Pain,* 1978, *4,* 253–263.

Waring, E. M., Weisz, G. M., & Bailey, S. I. Predictive factors in the treatment of low back pain by surgical intervention. In J. J. Bonica & D. Albe-Fessard (Eds.), *Advances in pain research and therapy* (Vol. 1). New York: Raven Press, 1976.

Weisenberg, M. Pain and pain control. *Psychological Bulletin,* 1977, *84,* 1008–1044.

Weisenberg, M., Kreindler, M. L., Schachat, R., & Werboff, J. Pain: Anxiety and attitudes in black, white and Puerto Rican patients. *Psychosomatic Medicine,* 1975, *37,* 123–135.

Wilfling, F. J., Klonoff, H., & Kokan, P. Psychological, demographic, and orthopedic factors associated with prediction and outcome of spinal fusion. *Clinical Orthopedic and Related Research,* 1973, *90,* 153–160.

Wilson, W. P., Blazer, D. G., & Nashold, B. S. Observations on pain and suffering. *Psychosomatics,* 1976, *17,* 73–76.

Wiltse, L. L., & Rocchio, P. D. Preoperative psychological tests as predictors of success of chemonucleolysis in the treatment of low back syndrome. *Journal of Bone and Joint Surgery,* 1975, *57-A,* 478–483.

Wolff, B. B. Behavioral measurement of human pain. In R. A. Sternbach (Ed.), *The psychology of pain.* New York: Raven Press, 1978.

Woodforde, J. M., & Merskey, H. Personality traits of patients with chronic pain. *Journal of Psychosomatic Research,* 1972, *16,* 167–172. (a)

Woodforde, J. M., & Merskey, H. Some relationships between subjective measures of pain. *Journal of Psychosomatic Research,* 1972, *16,* 173–178. (b)

Ziesat, H. A., & Gentry, W. D. The Pain Apperception Test: An investigation of concurrent validity. *Journal of Clinical Psychology,* 1978, *34,* 786–789.

9 The Psychosocial Assessment of the Chronically Ill Geriatric Patient

SANDRA M. LEVY

The geriatric population has been relatively neglected in clinical psychological research. As a result, this chapter (as well as its companion treatment chapter later in this volume) stands out from the other chapters in this text. Because differentiation of subject matter generally follows greater depth of scientific understanding, it would not seem appropriate to devote a chapter, for example, to the psychosocial assessment of the child as patient; one would expect a more differential treatment based on our understanding of the complexity of the subject matter (the leukemic child and his family, or the overweight adolescent, etc.). Thus, the relative neglect of the older patient by clinical researchers and the general assumption of undifferentiated sameness among geriatric patients, should be understood from the outset. Hopefully, because of the recent upsurge of research in the general area of aging and human development, a sense of the heterogeneity and complexity of this population will emerge from this chapter.

This chapter provides an overarching framework within which to view the assessment process, details special issues related to the assessment of the geriatric patient, and discusses common disorders of the aging patient which have become the targets of assessment. The major portion of the chapter is concerned with issues of diagnosis from a within person perspective (ranging from the differentiation between assessment of organic brain syndrome and reversible, behavioral disorder, to functional assessments of daily activity levels) to a between person and environmental or milieu perspective. The chapter concludes with a discussion of the function of the psychologist in the geriatric health care delivery system.

The Assessment Process

General Issue: The Negotiation of Diagnosis and Observer Variables

While most of this chapter is directed toward examining sources of variance in the aging patient's behavior due to patient variables such as cohort or motivational effects, a brief examination of ob-

Medical Psychology
Contributions to Behavioral Medicine

ISBN 0-12-565960-1

server variables is appropriate at the outset. Historically, the control of observer bias (beliefs, expectancies, etc.) by standardized instruments and procedures has been regarded as essential for valid psychological assessment. Nevertheless, the total clinical evaluation process of the patient occurs within a larger context of many disciplines and institutional policy. How a particular patient is finally viewed—that is, *what* the patient is and *what* can be expected from the patient is often the end result of covert, implicit "negotiations" within a staff team concerned with the patient's performance. Due to the increasing reliance on behavioral assessment techniques, time sampling of behaviors in question, and interjudge objectivity, however, this fact has not received the attention it might have in the past (for example, when psychodynamic considerations of countertransference issues were thought to be an important source of bias in assessing or diagnosing patient functioning). No matter how objective our ratings have become, in the last analysis, patient disposition is a product of team consensus and institutional ideology. While psychologists have not given much thought to these issues, sociologists (especially those taking an ethnomethodological approach to "reality") have continued to call attention to observer variables as they influence the diagnostic process. Gubrium (1975) and Gubrium and Buckholdt (1977) investigated the diagnoses of elderly patients in a nursing home and found them to be a kind of negotiated and constructed reality of each patient, built up between staff by verbal exchange. Utilizing transcribed staff conferences as their base of analysis, the authors traced a developing reality of individual patients that gets built up by "evidence" supplied to flesh out the notion of the patient as a particular "type" suggested by staffing participants. The authors noted that the "type" a patient becomes, sometimes shifts within the same staff conference depending on the persuasiveness of the speaker and the general makeup of the team.

Ultimately, these assessments are not objective. For example, with a patient who is a deteriorated, 86-year-old diabetic male, with hypertension and evidence of arterosclerotic heart disease and suspected chronic brain syndrome, stereotypes concerning typical behavior held unexamined by the staff, across disciplines, may color the outcome in a very negative way.

Specific Issues Related to Assessment of the Geriatric Patient: Patient Variables

Much has been written in recent years concerning the distinction between cohort differences (i.e., differences manifested between generations due to historical change), maturational change (i.e., species-linked change inherent in a developing organism), and time of testing effects (i.e., variance in behavioral output due to situational conditions such as unusual fatigue, external distraction, and level of illumination). Gerontologists have tried to separate out the sources of physiological, cognitive, and personality-behavioral variants among the aged in order to more fully understand the nature of human aging and the parameters of modifiability in the elderly individual's behavior. While controversy exists in the literature (Baltes & Schaie, 1976; Horn & Donaldson, 1977) concerning the methodological validity of the more recent research designs and teasing out the separate routes of change, for the purposes of this chapter it is only necessary to point out that true developmental change does seem to occur in the aging human organism. However, it also appears that behavioral and cognitive performance are more plastic, that is, modifiable as a function of environmental conditions, than had been assumed in the past. (For a thorough discussion of adult developmental changes, see Birren & Schaie, 1977; and Talland, 1968.)

While physiological and neurological decrements associated with aging are discussed later, the decrease in somatic functioning as it relates to essential differences between the young and old organism (or between a middle-aged and elderly patient) and the possible effects of these differences on performance require special attention. Cole (1970) identified eight physical differences between the young and old that presumably could make a difference in behavioral variables of endurance and stress tolerance. For example, the author pointed out that the "power of the heart"—the ratio of work to the duration of systole per beat—shows a decrease in the elderly, therefore diminishing myocardial reserve. In general, decremental changes occur across most body systems from renal and pulmonary to endocrine, and properties of the body, such as body cell mass, diminish over time.

While it is clear that aging and younger organisms are physiologically dissimilar, how this difference translates into behavioral variations is not entirely clear. Furry and Baltes (1973) examined the notion that poor intellectual performance in the aged subject may be less a function of reduced competence than a function of the individual's higher susceptibility to fatigue. When young, middle-aged, and old subjects were tested with and without conditions of pretest fatigue, the older subjects' test performance was found to be significantly suppressed, and to deviate most from that of the younger subjects under conditions of pretest fatigue. Among the younger subjects, however, no effects due to fatigue were found.

Eisdorfer (1977) noted that there is some evidence that the sympathetically controlled, adrenal medullary system that stimulates catecholamine secretion in response to environmental factors, decreases in function with advanced age (between ages 60 and 90). Eisdorfer also noted that there may be a causal link between a decrease in catecholamine secretion in aged individuals and an increased sensitivity to this neurotransmitter. If this is the case, then cautiousness and withdrawal may be observed in elderly individuals under stress as a function of increased sensitivity to autonomic arousal and oversensitivity to internal stress reaction.

An interaction sometimes occurs between physiological or sensory decrements and time of testing conditions, which may contribute to performance deficits. For example, visual defects in the elderly include decreased transparency of the lens, changes in the vitreous humor, and changes in the retina (Fozard, Wolf, Bell, McFarland, & Podolsky, 1977). Discussing the practical implications of these visual decrements, Fozard *et al.* (1977) point out that while the level of illumination required for various tasks by the elderly is greater than for younger individuals, the former's greater susceptibility to the effects of glare makes environmental compensation difficult. In general, it is important to keep in mind that apparent conceptual confusion on projective tests or seeming random response performance on structured instruments may be a function of visual, auditory, or motor decrements, rather than a reflection of a psychological disorder.

In addition to fatigue or hypersensitivity to catecholamine production as a cause of motivational loss and withdrawal from task, others (Oberleder, 1964, 1967; Okun & DiVesta, 1976; Okun & Elias, 1977; Okun, Siegler, & George, 1978) have noted that lack of incentive may be due to cautiousness and fear of failure. Oberleder (1967) suggested that the lack of motivation on the part of elderly patients in a testing situation may represent a need to escape from a condition where the drive level is heightened (by fear response), but the gratification from successful performance is denied. Labouvie, Hoyer, Baltes, and Baltes (1974) also suggested that incentive is low because reinforcement for the elderly may be idiosyncratic and not really apparent. However, while it may be true that the right incentives need to be found to overcome behavioral deficit, performance improvement by reinforcement may be limited. Grant, Storandt, and Botwinick (1978), using psychomotor tasks, found that while monetary incentives did not cause significantly higher performance scores among elderly subjects, practice did.

In addition to motivational and time of testing effects, cohort differences remain pervasive. In fact, changes on the physiological level could be cohort-specific rather than species-linked, due to general health care limits and/or prenatal effects in an older generation. Because the elderly were born and grew up in another era, testing stimuli may not always have the same significance for them as for younger subjects, nor do the elderly always possess the requisite skills to perform up to normative standards. It is a notorious problem for those who attempt to clinically assess the elderly that norms established for a younger population, when applied to older persons, frequently result in a misclassification of functionally healthy old people as grossly impaired. For example, Davies (1968) found that applying Reitan's cut-off points on the Trail-making Test to the performance of

540 normal subjects aged 20–70 years of age, caused 90% of those in the upper age category (age 60–70) to be classified as brain damaged.

Performance deficit has also been thought to occur in the elderly because of the cohort differences in cognitive mediational skills. Meichenbaum (1974) attempted to build in covert problem-solving techniques by modeling overt (vocalized) to covert (silent) self-instructional mediation. While not reporting the success of this approach with elderly subjects, Meichenbaum generalized from his success with other populations (schizophrenics, children, etc.) to support the plausibility of correcting similar mediational deficits in the elderly. Meichenbaum suggested that such deficits may in fact represent gaps in skill learning that are cohort-specific rather than age-related performance deficits.

In summary, while the elderly are not a homogeneous group, they are an essentially different population—somatically, motivationally, and experientially—from the young and most assessment devices are not normed for this group. When norms for the elderly are obtained, the mean age is frequently less than 50 years of age. Great caution, therefore, must be exercised in applying assessment techniques developed for the young, and utilizing them to evaluate the elderly. Some tests that have been developed for aged patients do exist. Most of them are intended to differentiate senile dementia from functional disorders, and most have been developed on institutionalized elderly.

The emphasis in this chapter is on functional diagnosis, rather than nosological classification. That is, emphasis is placed on assessing what the geriatric patient can do in order to determine what can be modified to eliminate excess disabilities. Specific diseases of aging are examined, and current modes of evaluating the extent of these deficits in geriatric patients are discussed.

The Geriatric Patient

Diseases of Aging

As we saw, there are some intrinsic changes that occur with aging. As Freeman (1965) pointed out in his discussion of body composition in the aged, as much as 40% of the cell population may disappear in organs such as the lungs, kidneys, heart, and brain by age 75. Physical decline, in general, tends to be quite remarkably similar cross-culturally (Shanas, 1974), with about 2 to 4% of the elderly over age 75 bedfast at home, and about the same number bedfast in institutions. In the cultures studied by Shanas (Denmark, Britain, United States, Poland, Yugoslavia, and Israel), three-fourths of the elderly are relatively independent and ambulatory. In a community survey by Rosencranz and Philblad (1970), 1700 elderly over 65 years of age were interviewed. Interviewees were asked to rate the state of their own physical health and to report functional capabilities for performing certain activities of daily living. Rosencranz and Philblad found that there was a definite increase in poor health with advancing age among females, and that there were fewer males than females in both the good health and bad health categories. The authors explained their findings by suggesting that males left the geographic area if they were healthy, and went to institutions if they were very ill. In general, the self-perception of overall health related well to the functional index scores. Those who reported themselves in the poorest overall health, even though living independently in the community, could not cut their own toenails, walk up stairs, bathe, or dress themselves. Again, the decline appeared to be more rapid for females than for males.

Although these findings might be criticized as being gained solely from self-reports (although the finding of correspondence between self-report and physician assessment of somatic status has been found across a number of studies [Palmore, 1974; Pfeiffer, 1970]), it is clear from both the aggregate of research literature, as well as from clinical experience, that a large proportion of the elderly population is chronically ill with one or more disease conditions. Two particular diseases of aging are brain disorder due to vascular or neurological change, and depressive disorder.

Brain Disorders in the Elderly: Neural and Vascular Disease It is becoming increasingly recognized that many cognitive and behavioral manifestations of senility in the aged are, in fact (*a*) secondary to acute medical conditions; (*b*) iatrogenically caused by treatments of various kinds, from improper drug prescription to physical restraint; or (*c*) functional in origin, reflecting severe depression (Adams, Fisher, Hakim, Osemann, & Sweet, 1965; Butler & Lewis, 1977; Libow, 1977). In the next section of this chapter, the differential assessment of chronic brain versus functional disorder is discussed. Here, an overview of brain dysfunction in the elderly is provided. (For a detailed discussion of central nervous system disorder in the elderly, see Eisdorfer & Cohen, 1978.)

Controversy exists over whether brain degeneration or senility is a natural biological process, or whether the cognitive manifestation of senility reflects a variety of pathological processes due to disease, malnutrition, injury, and the like. For some time Critchley (1931, 1956, 1965) has suggested that the latter is the case. In 1965, he reported the findings of an analysis of outpatient private consults referred to a practicing neurologist over a 17-year period (from 1946 to 1962). The study revealed that of the 535 patients over 70 years of age who were examined, 206 were diagnosed as having cerebral vascular degeneration, while the bulk of the remaining patients had one form or another of neurological, degenerative disease (Parkinson's disease, motor neuron disease, cerebellar atrophy, etc.), (Critchley, 1965). Although this patient sample was obviously not a random sample, since the patients had been selected out for referral to a neurologist, Libow (1977) estimated that from 5 to 15% of all people over 65 years of age living in the community, and from 25 to 50% of the aged living in institutions show significant signs of senile dementia.

Butler and Lewis (1977) described, in some clinical detail, the distinguishing features of acute brain pathology and chronic brain disorder due to cellular degeneration or vascular change. Briefly, reversible or acute brain syndrome, symptomatically ranging from mild confusion to severe delirium, with loss of recent memory, restlessness, and anxiety, may result from a variety of medical conditions (such as heart failure, infections, malnutrition, toxic substances, head injury, plus a host of other causes). The course of the acute disorder obviously in part depends upon treatment, but both high rate of immediate death and complete recovery following treatment are typical of brain dysfunction secondary to other conditions.

Chronic brain disease, on the other hand, is generally considered irreversible, although as will be discussed in Chapter 17, recently there have been attempts to reverse the effects of chronic brain conditions through hyperbolic oxygenation (Eisner, 1975). Chronic brain syndrome can be further differentiated into chronic disorder due to cellular atrophy, and chronic disorder due to a change in the vascular system that supplies blood to the brain tissue. Clinically, the course of the former is progressive and steadily downward, eventuating in death. The insidious course of the disease process, initially manifested by occasional memory lapses and shifts in personality and emotional makeup, and terminating in inevitable decline into stupor, where the patient does not remember even his or her own name (Fishback, 1977), clinically differentiates brain disease from cerebral vascular disorder in the aged. The latter, due to hardening of the blood vessels (artereosclerosis) or narrowing or closing of the vessels (atherosclerosis) results in deterioration of cerebral tissue over discrete areas. Because of this initial localization of damage, the course of cerebral vascular disease in the elderly is erratic, with gradual or sudden onset of confusion. Impairment of memory tends to be spotty, rather than general as in cerebral degenerative disease, and diversity of symptoms is great, both between patients and within the same patient. Remissions may be possible in some cases, but because of the generally fragile condition of the vascular system, with each new insult, additional, irreparable damage ensues. When death occurs, it is usually the result of artereosclerotic heart disease or cerebral vascular accidents, with accompanying complications (Butler & Lewis, 1977, p. 87).

It is recognized that severe cognitive and mood disturbance in the elderly due to organic brain dysfunction, still referred to as dementia in the medical literature, is actually clinically quite heterogeneous (McDonald, 1969). But because of the differential prognosis of disease course, it becomes rather important to be able diagnostically to differentiate degenerative brain disease from a vascular disorder. Berkett (1972) performed 31 necropsies on the brains of elderly patients who had died during hospitalization in order to look for evidence of vascular infarct and brain disease. Of the 31 cases, 14 had infarcts without positive evidence of senile brain disease, and 10 had senile brain disease without evidence of infarct. Using these results he attempted to post-dict to significant differences in the case histories of the two groups, as well as to the responses recorded on the rating form by interviewers assessing significant symptom areas chosen from a review of the literature. While Berkett recognized the methodological flaws in the data (selected bias of necropsy cases due to inability to gain permission in a sizeable portion of cases, and only a few significant differences occurring between the two groups which could have occurred by chance alone), the differential findings in patient backgrounds were consistent with clinical findings reported in the literature. The results suggested a more acute onset, better preservation of personality and insight, and greater mood fluctuation in the vascular group. Also, neurological features, such as hemiplegia, more accurately predicted brain infarcts than did any cognitive or personality feature.

Depression in the Aged In many cases, the behavioral and cognitive manifestations of depression in the elderly may resemble the clinical deterioration in patients with cerebral disorder. In older age groups the depressed subject may not admit to the symptoms of depression itself, but rather to the accompanying anxiety, or somatic or hypochondriacal symptoms, or to loss of concentration and difficulty in memory. Clearly, symptoms such as these could lend themselves to diagnoses of anxiety states, somatic disorder, or organic brain syndrome. The ability, then, to differentiate depression from organic disorder becomes paramount.

Depression in the aged, although a more frequently occurring problem in this age group than in younger groups (the incidence and prevalence is highest in the age group of 55 to 70), has many clinical similarities with depression occurring earlier in life, including its episodic nature, its tendency to remit, and its potential for favorable outcome (Epstein, 1976). While depression in the aged can be classified as endogenous (with clinical similarity to manic–depressive disorder) or reactive, a common, atypical picture of masked depression is also found in the elderly. The clinical presentation of this type of depression is apathy, withdrawal, somatic complaints, and functional slowness. For example, the reluctance to reply to questions during an interview is sometimes attributed to "just old age," when the lack of communication is really a sign of significant depression.

According to Lipton (1976), psychopharmacological evidence suggests that depression in older age groups is associated with alterations in the synthesis, storage, release, and utilization of chemical neurotransmitters. Enzymes, involved in these mechanisms are both under genetic control and alter with age. At a period of life when psychosocial stresses are generally high, interactions of stress events and these biological changes produce the frequent picture of depression. It is thought that a late life onset of depression, without previous history of the disorder, is indicative of a smaller genetic and greater environmental component (Mendlewicz, 1976), and while the clinically depressed aged respond well to tricyclic drugs, dose levels need to be reduced relative to those administered to younger patients. (This area of psychopharmacological treatment of the elderly will be discussed in Chapter 17.)

While masked depression in the geriatric patient is often expressed through hypochondriacal concern, it is important to be aware that depression can also be the result of infections or other physical disorders. As Epstein (1976) points out, it is frequently hard to determine whether somatic complaints are primarily physical, psychological, or both. Physical illness in the aged often develops in a slow, progressive fashion, and it may be that a somatic disease process underlies the mood state. On the other hand, hypersomatic concern can prompt the report of symptoms resembling cases of angina pectoris, gastrointestinal disease, etc. (Epstein, 1976). Because behavioral manifestations (such as sleep disturbance) and somatic complaints (such as loss of appetite), traditionally thought to reflect depressive mood, are also manifestations of actual physical disorders that frequently plague the elderly, the validity of such depression scales as Beck's (1967) or Zung's (1965), containing items which reflect the importance of physical symptoms in mood states, may not be valid signs of depression in the elderly.

Finally, alcoholism, as well as physical illness, seems to be an important cause of depression in this group. Suicide, a particular risk in older males, is frequently associated with alcohol ingestion and depression (Resnick & Kantor, 1970). In fact, an elderly patient with a history of depression, use of central nervous system depressants, including alcohol, recent life stress, and any earlier attempt at suicide is at high risk for self-destructive behavior.

In sum, as in any other problem with multiple causes, precision in differential diagnosis between neurological and mood disorders is obviously important in determining the prognosis and treatment for depression in the elderly.

Assessment of the Geriatric Patient from an Organismic Perspective

Organic Brain Syndrome versus Functional Disorder: The Notion of Excess Disability

The hospitalized geriatric patient presents a particularly difficult and challenging assessment task for the psychologist. Behavioral and cognitive deficits are typically present, but the source of the regressed or dysfunctional behavior is rarely completely obvious. Whatever the nature of the physical disorder, whether cardiovascular, renal, pulmonary, or neurological, the psychological overlay of symptoms poses problems for both assessing prognosis and planning treatments. For example, in a recent review of hospitalized cancer patient treatments by rehabilitation teams (Levy, in press), the need for a geriatric specialist was frequently pointed out by the staff in the various medical facilities. The geriatric patients, particularly the very old, were frequently confused, disoriented, and unable to communicate, and it was not clear to the staff whether their symptoms were functional due to distress and unfamiliarity of surroundings, or the result of brain metastases or neurological degeneration. The geriatric patient also presents unique problems related to nutrition, exercise, and drug tolerance. While the focus in this chapter is on the assessment of severely regressed geriatric patients, the overall uniqueness of this medical patient group, and the general necessity for sophisticated psychological assessment in any comprehensive treatment endeavor focused on the elderly, needs again to be underscored.

There is some controversy in the literature concerning the effects of hospitalization on the geriatric patient's functioning. Although comparability of study results is lacking due to the variety of facilities, patient populations, and assessment approaches used, the weight of the evidence suggests that hospitalization does cause iatrogenic dysfunction for various reasons and to varying degrees of seriousness. While both Lieberman (1969) and Rodstein, Savitsky, and Starkman (1976) found initial psychological and behavioral deterioration in hospitalized patients, these authors concluded that the gross long-term effects did not seem to result from institutionalization. Lieberman (1969) and Tobin and Lieberman (1976) make the assertion that most psychological decrement occurs prior to hospitalization, and not after. The changes that occurred in their sample of elderly over the course of institutionalization were subtle, and generally represented mood changes toward chronic depression and hopelessness. Rodstein *et al.* (1976), however, found that significant medical changes were likely to develop after hospitalization in those patients with previous poor health who evidenced an "advanced state of confusion" and depressive tendencies. Depression was found to be concomitant to physical deterioration rather than associated with previous physical status; depression was also found to exacerbate patients' reactions to their medical illness, which in turn hastened decline in the level of functioning. Iatrogenic disorders in connection with treatment effects are discussed in Chapter 17.

In a study analyzing the comparative usefulness of sources of information in accurately diagnosing hospitalized geriatric patients, Kellett, Copeland, and Kelleher (1975) found that since multiple pathologies were present on admission, and direct communication with the patient was often difficult because of defects in perception, diagnosis on first interview was generally subject to change. The diagnosis of dementia, however, was the most stable, with only 13% of patients originally diagnosed in this category receiving alternative diagnoses subsequent to admission. The initial diagnoses of neurosis and toxic states were the least stable. The authors concluded that information from relatives and repeated interviews with the patients contributed most to accurate diagnosis in 95% of the cases. They also noted that information gained from psychological tests contributed very little over and above the information gathered at interview.

Brody, Kleban, Lawton, and Silverman (1971) defined *excess disability* as the gap between existing and potential function in those already (presumably, validly) diagnosed as having brain disease. For the purpose of this chapter, however, the term is applied to all dysfunction that is reversible. Therefore, it would seem appropriate to address the concept in the context of differential diagnosis between organic impairment and functional disorder. The question is one of *how much* the visible impairment is a function of organic, neurological pathology, and the answer, depending on the true source of impairment, ranges from none to total.

As mentioned earlier, a multitude of factors lead to potentially reversible dysfunction. For example, some studies (Covert, Rodriques, & Solomon, 1977; Miller, 1975; Snyder & Harris, 1976) have shown that medication errors related to the abuse of PRN orders (drug to be taken as needed) can cause behavioral deficits that can be treated by increasing or altering dosage levels. (Unnecessary drug-induced decrements are covered more fully in Chapter 17.)

Libow (1977) details more generally the causes of potentially reversible "pseudo-senility," including medication errors, metabolic imbalances (e.g., hyperthyroidism, which may present in the elderly as depression), nutritional deficiencies (more than 10% of the elderly have simultaneous deficiencies of at least three or four important vitamins), tumors, hepatic conditions, cardiac conditions, transient vascular conditions, pulmonary conditions, and postsurgical or posttrauma states presenting as dementia. In that same article, Libow describes the Fromaje technique, a test of organic function, that he feels is more inclusive than many tests including the Pfeiffer's Mental Status Questionnaire (1975), which mainly taps memory. Although Libow's test includes aspects that tap reasoning, judgment, emotional state, and overall social functioning, its administration and scoring require a great deal of clinical interpretation. He does not report reliabilities related to test administration, but the content would suggest clinical validity. Again, however, it is unlikely that the instrument could be reliably used by raters with varying amounts of clinical experience.

There are, in fact, a wide variety of scales developed for the purpose of distinguishing organically brain-damaged patients from functionally disabled patients. These can be viewed in two general categories: one category focuses primarily on the mental status of the patient, assessing perceptual-motor and cognitive functioning; the other category is broader in scope, assessing functional behavior in the larger institutional context. We will view the first category as primarily aimed at differentiating types of disorders and the second category as generally more concerned with answering the question—irrespective of the degree to which the deficiencies are organic in origin—what can the patient still do? Both levels of assessment are clearly important.

As Eisdorfer and Cohen (1978), as well as Schaie and Schaie (1977) have observed, the majority of the more than 60 psychometric tests used with the elderly lack both norms and validity data. Obviously their application to impaired geriatric populations can be very misleading. Some traditional, as well as nontraditional tests, have been developed and/or used to assess the presence or absence of organic brain disorder in the aged. Space does not permit an extensive review of the psychometric literature related to tests such as the Rorschach, the Wechsler Adult Intelligence Scale, or forms of the Minnesota Multiphasic Personality Inventory, and the interested reader is referred to the two reviews just indicated for more extensive coverage.

Among the tests that have proved useful in differentiating brain-damaged from non-brain-damaged elderly is the "background interference" technique (Canter, 1966) for increasing the sensitivity of the Bender–Gestalt test for the identification of brain-damaged subjects (Hain, 1964). Utilizing the subject's own performance as a base rate, Bender performance was assessed by standard procedure (utilizing plain paper for test response), and then using paper with a background pattern. The results indicated that brain-damaged patients show decrements in Bender performance under the Background Interference Procedure (BIP) compared to standard conditions, whereas little or no change was shown by other patients. Unfortunately, in that 1966 study, only 14 patients were in the 60 to 69 age group, and only one patient was over age 70 (mean ages of groups were 43, 35, 32, 36, and 30). In a later study (Canter & Straumanis, 1969), however, it was demonstrated that the BIP procedure used in conjunction with the Bender–Gestalt was useful in discriminating between chronic brain syndrome patients and healthy elderly subjects. The conventional use of Bender error scores and the discrepancy between WAIS Vocabulary and Block Design scores (a "hold/don't hold" measure reflecting the relation of abilities that tend to deteriorate in the imparied to those that do not) would have identified at least one-fourth of these healthy aged as having organic brain damage. The use of the BIP permitted a discrimination between normal decline and degree of pathology in the brain syndrome patients.

A number of tests have been devised in recent years to assess brain damage in seriously behaviorally and cognitively dysfunctional geriatric patients (Fishback, 1977; Libow, 1977; Pattie & Gilleard, 1975; Pfeiffer, 1975; Plutchik, Conte, & Lieberman, 1971). Haglund and Schuckit (1976) compared four cognitive tests of impairment in a group of 279 male elderly patients. These tests included the Short Portable Mental Status Questionnaire (Pfeiffer, 1975), Face–Hand Test (Fink, Green, & Bender, 1952), Kahn–Goldfarb Mental Status Exam (Kahn, Goldfarb, Pollack, & Peck, 1960), and Memory For Design test (Graham & Kendall, 1960). They found that the Short Portable Mental Status Questionnaire, or SPMSQ, (a ten item mental status questionnaire, originally standardized and validated on both community and institutional elderly), best predicted to clinical organic syndrome. However, in a multiple regression analysis, the final R^2 was only .39, with the SPMSQ accounting for 16% of the variance in organicity status. While the development of a short test that predicts to clinical diagnosis of organicity may have some value (even though it may add little increased information over that derived from clinical interview), the proportion of variance accounted for is so low that one must question the overall worth of the enterprise.

Pattie and Gilleard (1975) reported the validation of the Clifton Assessment Scale, a new geriatric assessment schedule, against the criteria of clinical diagnosis and discharge from the hospital. Simple mental abilities (counting from 1 to 20, reading the alphabet in 10 seconds with no errors, etc.) were assessed in 100 consecutive admissions of patients over 60 years of age to an acute ward of a psychiatric hospital. In addition to the new scale developed by these authors, the Stockton Geriatric Rating Scale, a rating scale measuring daily activity functioning, was also administered. Although scores on both instruments successfully discriminated between functionally and organically imparied patients (unfortunately, the authors do not specify precisely how that clinical diagnosis was determined), the subtest that seemed to discriminate best was one that measured information items (name the U.S. President, etc.). Further, in 12 of 13 cases that were reclassified subsequent to testing, the information/orientation score correctly predicted the direction of change. Predictive validity of the test was also demonstrated in that scores significantly differentiated between those who returned home, those who remained in the minimal care ward, and those who were moved to a chronic stay ward. The authors concluded that their procedure as a whole was useful in predicting the extent of care a patient was likely to require.

Irving, Robinson, and McAdam (1970) assessed the validity of a battery of cognitive tests which had been constructed to diagnose organic brain impairment in the elderly (Colored Progressive Matrices [Raven, 1960], Mill Hill Vocabulary Scale, Form I Senior [Raven, 1958], Face–Hand Test [Fink, Green, & Bender, 1952], Synonym Learning Test [Kendrick, 1965], and Inglis Paired Associate Learning Test, Form A [Inglis, 1959]). Forty-seven clinically diagnosed organic or functionally disabled aged patients, matched for sex and age, were assessed using these tests, and it was found that all *except* the Mill Hill Vocabulary

Test discriminated between the groups. The authors explained the latter finding by suggesting that vocabulary levels in organically impaired individuals tend to be preserved relative to other abilities, and that these patients were new admissions who were not yet showing signs of severe intellectual deterioration. This was a fairly carefully done study in the sense that cut-off points on the various tests were empirically derived to best differentiate the groups in an initial pilot project, and then the results were cross-validated in a replication study.

In terms of progressive order of cognitive loss, Fishback (1977) described a new "visual counting test" used with severely organically impaired patients. He criticized the other common tests of organicity, such as Kahn, Goldfarb, Pollack, and Peck's (1960) Mental Status Exam, or Pfeiffer's (1975) Short Portable Mental Status Questionnaire for their lack of utility for *severely* regressed patients, for whom it would be unreasonable to assume that they would know the current President's name. (This criticism would also hold true for the Clifton Assessment Scale [Pattie & Gilleard, 1975] described above.) Fishback suggested that patients lose, in the following order, their sense of time, place, person recognition, number, and finally their own name. In addition to a 35-item set of questions tapping information that the patient might know (such as where his room was), Fishback also devised a "visual counting task" that consisted of asking patients to count the number of fingers held up before their face, or the number of fingers placed on the palm of their hand. Although the author claimed a high correlation between the scores on these cognitive tests and the degree of senile dementia, it is unfortunate that no actual correlations were reported. The author did note an order effect, with patients performing better on the 35 information-type items, if they had done well on the counting test initially. There was also a socioeconomic status effect, with patients with more educational attainment performing better on subsequent items than patients with lower educational levels.

The content of all of these tests reflects variations of the traditional Mental Status Exam. There is a certain redundancy of content in all of them, and while the predictive criteria are based on clinical judgments of organic symptoms that are not in every case clearly specified, it would appear that an instrument such as the Clifton Assessment Scale (Pattie & Gilleard, 1975), or the Visual Counting Test in conjunction with the information items that Fishback utilized would be valid adjuncts to clinical impression.

Turning to the question of functional rating in a daily context, irrespective of the source of dysfunction, a number of behavioral rating scales have been developed for use with an elderly patient population. (See Salzman, Korchansky, Shader, & Cronin, 1972, for a list of scales that were developed up until that date for specific use with geriatric patients.) Six scales, the Stockton Geriatric Rating Scale (Meer & Baker, 1966; SGRS), the Physical and Mental Impairment-of-Function Evaluation (Gurel, Linn, & Linn, 1972; PAMIE), the Index of Activities of Daily Living (Katz, Ford, Moskowitz, Jackson, & Jaffe, 1963; ADL), the Geriatric Rating Scale (Plutchik, Conte, Lieberman Baker, Grossman, & Lehrman, 1970; GRS), the Sandoz Clinical Assessment–Geriatric (Shader, Harmatz, & Salzman, 1974; SCAG), and the Older American Resources and Service Functional Assessment Questionnaire (Fillenbaum, 1975; OARS), are the most widely cited in the literature. The first scale, the 33-item SGRS, assesses four stable factors: physical disability, apathy, communication, and socially irritating behavior. In the view of this writer, it is the most carefully validated of the instruments cited above.

Taylor and Bloom (1974) cross-validated the SGRS in a total hospital population where the primary diagnosis for patients was organic brain syndrome. With a sample of 493, ward behavior was independently rated using the SGRS. Results for the ratings indicated that the scale showed both good interrater reliability and concurrent validity with severity of diagnosis made independently. Two interesting findings occurred in this well done study. First, the researchers found a bimodal distribution of impairment scores, and second, females appeared to be significantly more impaired in the upper age group. That is, decline was associated with age for females, but not for males in this sample. Several investigators (e.g., Rosencranz & Philblad, 1970) have also found females to be more impaired than males; however, the results from other studies (e.g., Plutchik *et al.* 1970) show that this is not a universal finding.

With respect to the finding of bimodality of impairment distribution, Taylor and Bloom (1974) concluded that a linear model of decline in intellectual and behavioral performance with age may not be valid. (For example, interpretation of scores on the WAIS for those over the age of 75 is generally arrived at by linear extrapolation.) Here, the failure to observe a linear decline in cognitive performance with age is consistent with the hypothesis offered by others (Gutmann, 1975) that there may in fact be biological and psychological superiority among really old survivors.

While we have not specifically addressed, to any extent, the measurement of mood—particularly depression—in the geriatric patient, mention should be made here of limits in this regard. As briefly mentioned earlier, content of many of the depression scales is inappropriate for this population since a large number of the items supposedly reflecting mood may in fact be a reflection of physical impairment in the elderly. Additionally, elderly patients have been known to refuse to respond to certain items on depression scales because they felt that they were not appropriate (e.g., questions having to do with sexual function). Consequently, these patients' scores on those scales could not validly reflect their true level of depression. In addition, as also mentioned earlier, depression among aged is frequently "masked," expressed through apathy or physical complaint. Therefore, while functional depression (over and above somatic disorder) is prevalent in geriatric patients, the severity of mood disturbance may be more accurately reflected in ratings of daily activity (isolation, apathy, and evidence of excess disability), than by standardized clinical measurements.

Neuropsychological Assessments

Although the focus of this chapter has been on clinically administered cognitive tests that are able to discriminate between functionally and organically impaired aged, as well as behavioral rating scales that measure daily activity function, mention should be made of the techniques to specifically measure the neuropsychological level of higher cognitive function. Until recently, there has been a dearth of norms for geriatric patients on standard neuropsychological tests, such as the Halstead–Reitan Battery (Reitan, Note 1). For example, in a chapter by Kløve (1974) concerned with validation studies and clinical neuropsychology, the mean age for their oldest adult group was 35 years! A general finding that appears to hold across individual neuropsychological studies utilizing elderly subjects is that there is some evidence that the performance of normal elderly resembles that of people with right hemisphere damage, suggesting that there might be a tendency for right hemisphere dysfunction, with a corresponding resistance to left hemisphere (particularly motor region) change (Reitan & Fitzhugh, 1971). In his study concerned with neuropsychological assessment of the elderly, Klisz (1978) concludes that because of the perceptual and motor difficulty experienced by very old patients when administered a lengthy neuropsychological test battery, both new norms should be developed, and alternative forms of tests should be devised.

Preliminary data providing unpublished norms for an elderly population have been developed by Leuthold, Bergs, Matthews, and Harley (Note 2). Utilizing the standard Halstead-Reitan Battery, in addition to other tests such as the WAIS, the authors developed norms for three samples of subjects ($N = 193$) who were Veterans Administration patients, ranging from 55 to 79 years of age. Gross neurological and vascular disorders were screened from their subject pool. Each sample was subdivided into age groups, 55–59, 60–64, 65–69, 70–74, and 75–79. The authors found that the oldest group (75–79) generally performed better than those in the 65–69 age range. (This finding supports the earlier interpretation of Taylor and Bloom's [1974] findings concerning the possibility of bimodal distribution of cognitive function in the aged.) Table 9.1 and Table 9.2 display means, standard deviations, and rank order of group performance for the three samples of patients on the Category and Tactual Performance Test from the Halstead-Reitan Battery. Although generally scores are well within the impaired range for this

Table 9.1 Means, Standard Deviations, and Rank Order of Category Test Error Score by Age Groups

Sample		Age 55–59	60–64	65–69	70–74	75–79
1		64.13	59.78	72.65	85.59	69.60
		28.20	19.46	28.54	35.79	26.21
	Rank	2	1	4	5	3
2		58.30	55.40	64.89	76.33	65.11
		23.91	15.52	19.17	23.34	23.70
	Rank	2	1	3	5	4
3		65.43	63.42	71.64	85.59	69.60
		28.21	18.95	30.46	35.78	26.21
	Rank	2	1	4	5	3

Note. From "Neurological Test Battery Performance in Older Veterans Administration Hospital Population," by C. Leuthold, L. Bergs, C. Mathews, and P. Naries, unpublished. Reprinted by permission.

Table 9.2 Means, Standard Deviations, and Rank Order of Tactual Performance Test Raw Scores by Age Groups

Sample		Age 55–59	60–64	65–69	70–74	75–79
				Memory		
1		4.56	4.36	3.69	3.78	3.22
		2.28	2.15	1.49	2.09	2.04
	Rank	1	2	4	3	5
2		5.07	4.80	4.03	4.12	3.58
		1.84	1.83	1.23	1.95	1.83
	Rank	1	2	4	3	5
3		4.48	4.24	3.61	3.78	3.22
		2.41	1.88	1.57	2.09	2.04
	Rank	1	2	4	3	5
				Location		
1		1.44	1.40	1.13	.73	.78
		1.63	1.48	.94	1.03	1.07
	Rank	1	2	3	5	4
2		1.61	1.58	1.27	.82	.86
		1.65	1.48	.93	1.06	1.11
	Rank	1	2	3	5	4
3		1.41	1.18	1.06	.73	.78
		1.70	1.19	.91	1.03	1.07
	Rank	1	2	3	5	4
				Time per Block		
1		2.21	2.70	2.18	3.55	3.34
		3.28	3.76	1.83	4.18	3.52
	Rank	2	3	1	5	4
2		1.34	1.41	1.53	2.18	2.42
		.89	1.00	.85	1.49	1.23
	Rank	1	2	3	4	5
3		2.40	2.94	1.73	3.55	3.34
		3.54	3.86	1.44	4.18	3.52
	Rank	2	3	1	5	4

Note. From "Neurological Test Battery Performance in an Older Veterans Administration Hospital Population," by C. Leuthold, L. Bergs, C. Matthews, and P. Naries, unpublished. Reprinted by permission.

group using Reitan's norms, it is interesting to note in this display that the oldest age group did indeed function better than many younger subjects on the Category Test, generally thought to be a reflection of overall cognitive reasoning ability. The oldest age group did not perform as well on the Tactual Performance Test with regard to Time for Form Placement and Localization of Forms by Memory; this performance decrement is likely a reflection of right, parietal loss of function. Admittedly, this population is not overly representative of the elderly population at large; Veterans Administration patients generally have a higher incidence of alcoholism, as well as a generally disproportionately lower socioeconomic status. With these limitations in mind, however, this preliminary attempt to develop norms for this group is an important contribution to the available pool of population norms for tests of this nature.

Predicting Mortality in the Aged

A number of studies over the years (Goldfarb, 1969; Jarvik, 1975; Jarvik & Falk, 1963; Lieberman, 1969; Riegel & Angleitner, 1975; Riegel & Riegel, 1972; Riegel, Riegel, & Meyer, 1967) have attempted to isolate variables that would predict death in a geriatric population. For example, in a recent study by Neiditch and White (1976), a number of functional rating scales as well as intellectual tests were administered to a sample of 36 geriatric patients with mixed diagnosis during the first, third, fifth, and eighth weeks after admission to the hospital. Five months later, follow-up on patients was carried out to determine whether they had been discharged, died, or remained hospitalized. A combination of two measures, one reflecting urinary incontinence and the other reflecting orientation (from the Brief Psychiatric Rating Scale [Overall and Gorham, 1962] and the Modified Minimal Social Behavior Scale [Lawton, 1971]), allowed prediction of patient status at five months with 75% accuracy. The results further suggested that geriatric patients who demonstrated improvement in their clinical status and cognitive skills did so within the first few weeks of admission, and were then discharged. Those who remained in the hospital tended either to stabilize or decline. Those who were most disoriented and incontinent on admission or shortly after, tended not to survive.

Palmore and Cleveland (1976) reviewed and criticized the earlier work on predictors of mortality on the basis that most had used very small numbers of subjects or were limited to examination of intellectual functioning. Further, these studies showed inconsistent findings, and failed to distinguish between terminal decline in function (linear relationship to time before death), terminal drop in functioning (curvilinear relationship to time before death), and decline associated with aging, per se. In their reported work, Palmore and Cleveland analyzed the data from a 20-year longitudinal study of individuals over 60 years of age by step-wise multiple regression analysis to test for the presence of decline in function associated with age, as well as the presence of the terminal decline or drop in a variety of functions preceding death. The authors measured daily activity functioning, as well as self-report of health, objective health status, and individual life satisfaction. They found no significant terminal drop effects. All health measures had substantial declines with age, and the physician's physical function rating (and the old person's self-rating), showed additional terminal decline. Intellectual performance had a substantial decline with age and a small terminal decline. Most activities declined with age, but showed no significant terminal decline. The authors concluded that despite declines in health, intelligence, and activity level, there was little decline in overall life satisfaction. The subjects in this study were 178 members of Duke University's longitudinal study panel who had died from natural causes by December, 1974. While this panel is not representative of older people in general (they were all volunteers who were relatively advantaged in terms of education and socioeconomic status), still, the results of this study are valuable in shedding light on the issue of sudden drop in functional performance preceding death, as distinct from gradual and progressive decrements.

It may be true that abrupt change in patient functioning that would allow prediction of death does not occur, but there are some shifts in the environment that appear to predict to death. For example, Rowland (1977), in a review of studies examining environmental events predicting death for the elderly, concluded that environmental relocation within an institution was significantly associated with decline and death in patients who were already severely ill, whose mental functioning was imparied through functional or organic syndrome, or who were severely depressed. She noted that it was not evident whether the depressed and mentally impaired were at risk because of those conditions, or whether it was because they were also in poor physical health.

In sum, indices of very compromised organic status (incontinence,, confusion, and overall progressive decline in functional levels) appear to predict to termination of life in the geriatric patient.

Personality Assessments of the Geriatric Patient

Very little is going to be said here concerning traditional personality assessment in this patient group for several reasons; one, for reasons of professional bias, and two, because of the nature of the population with which we have been concerned.

Issues involved in the assessment of personality in the elderly, including the issues of construct validity and cohort suitability of traditional tests that were addressed earlier in this chapter, are many and complex. However, in the severely compromised geriatric patients, an assessment of behavioral and cognitive function potential is seen to be more imperative. In fact, as Butler and Lewis (1977) point out, a "leveling effect" seems to take place as organic impairment increases, and this is particularly true when the damage is sudden or massive. Indeed, emotional reaction to loss of function is taken as a positive sign of energy reserve over and above organic loss, to allow the patient more than vegetative functioning. Even in the less deteriorated geriatric patient, it still remains true that the functional assessment is practically more crucial than whether the patient is a passive-aggressive personality type. And as we are primarily concerned here with the psychological treatment of medical disorders, no discussion of differential diagnosis of psychiatric disorder is provided.

It is a theoretically interesting issue whether personality changes with age, or whether a form of pathology at one life stage is pathological at another. There is some suggestion that hostility and paranoia, clearly maladaptive in midlife, has survival value in the old (Gutmann, 1975). Again, however, the interested reader is referred to Schaie and Parham (1976), Neugarten (1977), and Gutmann (1977), for more extensive treatment of these issues.

Research Needs

It is clear from a review of the body of geriatric assessment literature that some success has been achieved in the areas of gross screening of organic impairment and the valid and reliable measurement of daily living activities. Further development of measures that differentially discriminate between types of organic impairment against valid criteria other than clinical judgments is needed. The study by Berkett (1972), which utilized postmortem techniques to determine statistically significant, preterminal signs differentiating vascular from neurological disorder is an example of this kind of research. In addition, clearly, norms need to be developed for neuropsychological tests—perhaps of an abbreviated form—that would more finely discriminate between unimpaired and impaired areas of cognitive functioning.

Finally, an examination of environmental parameters of the testing context that support or elicit patient behavior needs to be carried out. For example, under what kinds of testing conditions do severely depressed or organically impaired patients become motivated to perform up to their potential? Although this is not a unique question related to assessment of the elderly, the particular environmental conditions, including reinforcement contingencies, may very well be cohort-specific. Assessment skills need to be developed by the tester that would foster an experimental mentality in uncovering excess disability of function. For example, within a cognitive mediational framework, the skilled geriatric specialist might attempt to incorporate lost (or never learned) cognitive mediational skills to determine if the patient can be trained to solve problems (Meichenbaum, 1974).

Analysis of the Geriatric Patient from an Ecological Perspective

Measurement of the Environment

In recent years, institutional environments of the elderly have been examined, described, and measured from a number of perspectives in order to determine the physical and social sources of behavioral variance in elderly patients. Some perspectives have been rather novel. For example, Senn and Steiner (1978–79), taking an ethological approach to environmental analysis, believe that in many cases, institutional arrangements fail to support innate, phylogenetically programmed classes of behavior. They suggest, for example, that, as in other species, when people are deprived of their own familiar territory, there results a reduction of inclination to behave assertively. The resultant apathy and withdrawal, as discussed earlier in this chapter, are major problems among the institutionalized aged. These authors suggest that eating, dressing, and voiding are all behaviors that are supported by ritualistic observance that includes the presence of environmental "releasers." While human behavior may not be under the automatic control of environmental stimuli to the degree of the behavior of lower species, the suggestion that humans share some innate needs with other species is consistent with the developmental literature (Marks, 1969; White, 1959).

In addition to Senn and Steiner's (1978–1979) ethological method for analyzing environments (naturalistic observation, behavioral classification, and experimental verification), others have attempted to develop measuring devices that reflect both physical and interpersonal environments within institutions. An example of the former is the technique of architectural and behavioral mapping used by Cluff and Campbell (1975). As participant observers, the researchers took up residence in a newly opened nursing home, and using an architectural plan of the facility, moved about recording times, location, and activities within each area. Identities of the actors were coded, and behaviors were recorded using four basic categories: (*a*) isolated inactive; (*b*) isolated active; (*c*) mixed inactive; and (*d*) mixed active. They found that the volume of personal traffic was most dense at the beginning of a long corridor, and that residents tended to gravitate toward the corridor when their rooms were isolated or in low density areas. They also found staff traffic decreased as a function of distance from the nursing station, and that residents' satisfaction decreased as the distance between their rooms and the social areas widened.

In a factor analysis of staff perception of the character of the institutional environment, Pincus (1968) found four factors reflecting environmental dimensions. His findings suggest that the environment could be assessed on the basis of (*a*) public–private dimension (the extent to which the resident was allowed personal territory); (*b*) structured–unstructured (the degree to which order is controlled by rules); (*c*) resource sparse–resource rich (the degree to which the institution provided opportunity for diverse and enriched experience); and (*d*) isolated–integrated (the degree to which the institution and its residents maintained ties with the larger community). Although Pincus did not report any morale or perception ratings by residents, the dimensional factors describing these aspects of the environment appeared to be reliably measured by independent assessment. On the other hand, Moos, Gauvain, Lemke, Max, and Mehren (1979) developed a Sheltered Care Environment Scale (SCES) measuring similar factors—in this case, level of independence and exploration allowed, as well as degree of organized structure and interpersonal cohesion or conflict—and assessed both resident and staff perception. Using this instrument in a variety of settings, they found differential perception patterns of staff and patients. For example, the nursing home staff generally perceived more emphasis on patient independence and rated patient physical comfort lower than the residents did. Overall these results suggest the usefulness of a measuring instrument such as the SCES for tracking perceptual change over time, and monitoring discrepancies in patient–staff expectations.

Person–Environment Fit and Behavioral Dysfunction

Lawton (1971) has suggested that perfect person–environment congruence is represented by a situation where the environmental demands never exceed the individual's capacity to respond competently. In offering what he refers to as an "environmental docility hypothesis," Lawton proposed that individuals are more susceptible to environmental influence as their competency diminishes. Lower competence (for example, as an individual is no longer able to master effectively the social environment) becomes a signal reflecting a need for a more homogeneous, less demanding milieu.

Some controversy exists, however, about the suitability of homogeneity for even the most regressed patients. For example, Lipman and Slater (1977) found that the more confused patients were not able to resist unfair social demands made by the more capable residents and therefore argued for homogeneity of functional level among patients; Kahana and Kahana (1970) reported that the oldest of impaired residents in an age-mixed, heterogeneous psychiatric facility did better in terms of cognitive and motivational functioning than matched elderly patients on a homogeneous ward.

The general issue of person–environment fit is

only beginning to be examined, and it is an area that provides rich opportunity for the investigator to uncover systematically ecological parameters that may make an essential difference in geriatric patient functioning.

In a provocative conclusion to their work, *Last Home for the Aged,* Tobin and Leiberman (1976) discuss the particular environmental press or level of contextual demand in three nursing homes that were included in their study. These particular environments placed a premium on activity and assertive behavior. One clear finding that emerged in their follow-up study of adjustments to those environments was that the residents who entered and remained behaviorally passive tended not to survive. One explanation for the passivity was that those passive newcomers were already on a terminal course (although objectively, there was no significant difference in physical status of survivors versus nonsurvivors on admission), but it is also possible that the effects of behavioral passivity were exacerbated by this particular environmental press for assertive action on the part of the residents. The authors suggest that the character of the institution (along the dimensions outlined by Moos *et al.* [1979], for example) be determined ahead of placement, with the aim of optimal fit between personal tendency and environmental demands and constraints. As Mechanic (1974) asserts, the congruence between the social structure provided and the environmental demands that are made, is a major determinant of individual adaptation; the patient's ability to cope with the environment depends in part on the solutions the environment provides to support the patient's own capabilities. And at the end of life, given the inherent frailty within the person, the necessity for fit between the geriatric patient and the arrangements of the environment becomes crucial.

The Function of the Psychologist in the Geriatric Health Care Delivery System

As the technology of medical science allows the maintenance of life's vegetative processes for long periods of time, the psychologist's ability to assess the cognitive, affective, and behavioral components of functioning in the physically impaired aged becomes paramount. If we do not want to simply maintain the old in geriatric warehouses, then it is the psychologist's responsibility to determine the nature and variety of dysfunctions that can be altered. In a recent work devoted to the area of health psychology (Stone, Cohen, & Adler, 1979), Schofield (1979) had the following to say concerning the place of the psychologist in the general health care delivery system:

> With the recognition that our delivery of health care services, both preventive and therapeutic, lags behind the potential of our medical technology, there is increased desire to design health care systems that will be both comprehensive and integrated. Such a system must provide for adequate appraisal of both the somatic and psychological components that are interactive in the person as a functional unit. The assessment of the psychological status of the patient constitutes the primary area for application of the special skills, techniques, the knowledge of clinical psychology, and a basic element of its role as a health care profession [p. 455].

Keeping in mind the discussion of observer variables at the outset of this chapter, this assessment process applied to the elderly is a particularly demanding task. The personal and environmental setting for this assessment—and the cultural stereotypes concerning the old—all lend themselves to a negotiated diagnosis colored by negative expectancy. As Gubrium (1975) pointed out, since the 86-year-old, partially deaf and blind paralytic, too easily becomes merely a typical case of senility, the ability to differentiate excess disability from organic necessity remains the responsibility of the skilled geriatric psychologist.

Reference Notes

1. Reitan, R. *Manual for administration of neuropsychological test batteries for adults and children.* Privately published by the author, Indianapolis, 1969.
2. Leuthold, C., Bergs, L., Matthews, C., & Harley, S. *Neuropsychological test battery performance in an older Veterans Administration Hospital population.* Unpublished manuscript, 1979.

References

Adams, R., Fisher, C. Hakim, S., Osemann, R., & Sweet, W. Symptomatic occult hydrocephalus with "normal" cerobrospinal fluid pressure: A treatable syndrome. *New England Journal of Medicine,* 1965, *273,* 117-126.

Baltes, P., & Schaie, K. On the plasticity of intelligence in adulthood and old age: Where Horn and Donaldson fail. *American Psychologist,* 1976, *31,* 720-726.

Beck, A. *Depression: Causes and treatment.* Philadelphia: University of Pennsylvania Press, 1967.

Berkett, D. The psychiatric differentiation of senility and arteriosclerosis. *British Journal of Psychiatry,* 1972, *120,* 321-325.

Birren, S., & Schaie, K. (Eds.). *Handbook of the psychology of aging.* New York: Van Nostrand Reinhold, 1977.

Brody, E., Kleban, M., Lawton, M., & Silverman, H. Excess disabilities of mentally impaired aged: Impact of individualized treatment. *The Gerontologist,* 1971, *11,* 124-133.

Butler, R., & Lewis, M. *Aging and mental health.* St. Louis: C. V. Mosby, 1977.

Canter, A. A background interference procedure to increase sensitivity of the Bender-Gestalt test to organic brain disorder. *Journal of Consulting Psychology,* 1966, *30,* 91-97.

Canter, A., & Straumanis, J. Performance of senile and healthy aged persons on the BIP Bender test. *Perceptual Motor Skills,* 1969, *28,* 615-698.

Cluff, P., & Campbell, W. The social corridor: An environmental and behavioral evaluation. *The Gerontologist,* 1975, *15,* 516-523.

Cole, W. Medical differences between the young and the aged. *Journal of the American Gerontological Society,* 1970, *18,* 589-614.

Covert, A., Rodriques, T., & Solomon, K. The use of mechanical and chemical restraints in nursing homes. *Journal of the American Geriatrics Society,* 1977, *25,* 85-89.

Critchley, M. The neurology of old age. *Lancet,* 1931, *1,* 1119.

Critchely, M. Neurological changes in the aged. In Association for Research in Nervous and Mental Disorders, *The Neurological and Psychiatric Aspects of the Disorders of Aging* Baltimore: Williams and Wilkins, 1956.

Critchely, M. Neurological disabilities. In J. Freeman (Ed.), *Clinical features of the older patient.* Springfield, Ill.: Charles C. Thomas, 1965.

Davies, A. The influence of age on Trail Making Test performance. *Journal of Clinical Psychology,* 1968, *24,* 96-98.

Eisdorfer, C. Stress, disease, and cognitive change in the aged. In C. Eisdorfer & R. Freidel (Eds.), *Cognitive and emotional disturbance in the elderly: Clinical issues.* Chicago: Yearbook Medical Publishers, 1977.

Eisdorfer, C., & Cohen, P. The cognitively impaired elderly: Differential diagnosis. In M. Storandt, I. Siegler, & M. Elias (Eds.), *The clinical psychology of aging.* New York: Plenum, 1978.

Eisner, D. Can hyperbaric oxygenation improve cognitive functioning in the organically impaired elderly? A critical review. *Journal of Geriatric Psychiatry.* 1975, *8,* 173-188.

Epstein, L. Symposium on age differentiation in depressive illness. Depression in the elderly. *Journal of Gerontology,* 1976, *31,* 278-282.

Fillenbaum, G. The validity and reliability of the OARS questionnaire. In Duke University Center for the Study of Aging and Human Development, *Multidimensional functional assessment: The OARS methodology: A manual.* Durham, 1975.

Fink, M., Green, M., & Bender, M. The face-hand test as a diagnostic sign of organic mental syndrome. *Neurology,* 1952, *3,* 46-58.

Fishback, D. Mental status questionnaire for organic brain syndrome, with a new visual counting test. *Journal of the American Geriatrics Society,* 1977, *25,* 167-170.

Fozard, J., Wolf, E., Bell, B., McFarland, R., & Podolsky, S. Visual perception and communication. In J. Birren & K. Schaie (Eds.), *Handbook of the psychology of aging.* New York: Van Nostrand Reinhold, 1977.

Freeman, J. Body composition in aging. In J. T. Freeman (Ed.), *Clinical features of the older patient.* Springfield, Ill.: Charles C. Thomas, 1965.

Furry, C., & Baltes, P. The effect of age differences in ability-extraneous performance variables on the assessment of intelligence in children, adults, and elderly. *Journal of Gerontology,* 1973, *28,* 73-80.

Goldfarb, A. Predicting mortality in the institutionalized aged. *Archives of General Psychiatry,* 1969, *21,* 172.

Graham, F., & Kendall, B. Memory for designs test: Revised general manual. *Perceptual Motor Skills,* 1960, *11,* 147-188.

Grant, E., Storandt, M., & Botwinick, J. Incentive and practice in the psychomotor performance of the elderly. *Journal of Gerontology,* 1978, *33,* 413-415.

Gubrium, J. *Living and dying at Murray Manor.* New York: St. Martin's, 1975.

Gubrium, J., & Buckholdt, D. *Toward maturity.* San Francisco: Jossey-Bass, 1977.

Gurel, L., Linn, M., & Linn, B. Physical and mental impairment-of-function evaluation in the aged: The PAMIE scale. *Journal of Gerontology,* 1972, *27,* 83-89.

Gutmann, D. Alternatives to disengagement: The old men of the highland Druze. In D. Levine (Ed.), *Culture and personality: Selected readings.* Chicago: Aldine, 1975.

Gutmann, D. The cross-cultural perspective: Notes toward a comparative psychology of aging. In J. Birren & K. Schaie (Eds.), *Handbook of the psychology of aging.* New York: Van Nostrand Reinhold, 1977.

Haglund, R., & Schuckit, M. A clinical comparison of

tests of organicity in elderly patients. *Journal of Gerontology,* 1976. *31,* 654–659.
Hain, J. The Bender-Gestalt test: A scoring method for identifying brain damage. *Journal of Consulting Psychology,* 1964, *28,* 34–40.
Horn, J., & Donaldson, G. On the myth of intellectual decline in adulthood. *American Psychologist,* 1977, *32,* 369–373.
Inglis, J. A paired-associate learning test for use with elderly psychiatric patients. *Journal of Mental Science,* 1959, *105,* 440–443.
Irving, G., Robinson, R., & McAdam, W. The validity of some cognitive tests in the diagnosis of dementia. *British Journal of Psychiatry,* 1970, *117,* 149–156.
Jarvik, L. Thoughts on the psychobiology of aging. *American Psychologist,* 1975, *30,* 576–584.
Jarvik, L., & Falk, A. Intellectual stability and survival in the aged. *Journal of Gerontology,* 1963, *18,* 173–176.
Kahana, B., & Kahana, E. Changes in mental status of elderly patients in age-integrated and age-segregated hospital milieus. *Journal of Abnormal Psychology,* 1970, 75, 177–181.
Kahn, R., Goldfarb, A., Pollack, M., & Peck, A. A brief objective measure for the determination of mental status in the aged. *American Journal of Psychiatry,* 1960, *117,* 326–334.
Katz, S., Ford, A., Moskowitz, R., Jackson, B., & Jaffe, M. Studies of illness in the aged: The index of ADL, a standardized measure of biological and psychosocial function. *Journal of American Medical Association,* 1963, *185,* 914–919.
Kellett, J., Copeland, J., & Kelleher, M. Information leading to accurate diagnosis in the elderly. *British Journal of Psychiatry,* 1975, *126,* 423–430.
Kendrick, D. A synonym learning test for use with elderly psychiatric subjects: A validation study. *British Journal of Social and Clinical Psychology,* 1965, *4,* 63–71.
Klisz, D. Neuropsychological evaluation in older persons. In M. Storandt, I. Siegler, & M. Elias (Eds.), *The clinical psychology of aging.* New York: Plenum, 1978.
Kløve, H. Validation studies in adult clinical neuropsychology. In R. Reitan & L. Davison (Eds.), *Clinical neuropsychology: Current status and applications.* New York: Wiley, 1974
Labouvie, G., Hoyer, W., Baltes, M., & Baltes, P. Operant analysis of intellectual behavior in old age. *Human Development,* 1974, *17,* 259–272.
Lawton, M. Assessment, integration and environments for older people. *The Journal of Mental Science,* 1959, *105,* 440–443.
Lawton, M. The functional assessment of elderly people. *Journal of the American Geriatrics Society,* 1971, *19,* 465.
Levy, S. *The development and evaluation of cancer rehabilitation programs: The state of the art as reflected in ten demonstration projects.* Washington, D.C.: U.S. Public Health Service, National Institutes of Health, National Cancer Institute, DHEW Publication, in press.
Libow, L. Senile dementia and "pseudosenility": Clinical diagnosis. In C. Eisdorfer & R. Freidel (Eds.), *Cognitive and emotional disturbance in the elderly: Clinical issues.* Chicago: Yearbook Medical Publishers, 1977.
Lieberman, M. Institutionalization of the aged: Effects on behavior. *Journal of Gerontology.* 1969, *24,* 330–340.
Lipman, A., & Slater, R. Status and spatial appropriation in eight homes for old people. *The Gerontologist,* 1977, *17,* 250–255.
Lipton, M. Age differentiation in depression: Biochemical aspects. *Journal of Gerontology,* 1976, *31,* 293–299.
McDonald, C. Clinical heterogeneity in senile dementia. *British Journal of Psychiatry,* 1969, *115,* 267–271.
Marks, I. *Fears and phobias.* London: Academic Press, 1969.
Mechanic, D. Social structure and personal adaptation: Some neglected dimensions. In G. Coelho, D. Hamburg, & J. Adams (Eds.), *Coping and adaptation.* New York: Basic Books, 1974.
Meer, B., & Baker, S. The Stockton geriatric rating scale. *Journal of Gerontology,* 1966, *21,* 392–403.
Meichenbaum, D. Self-instructional strategy training: A cognitive prosthesis for the aged. *Human Development,* 1974, *17,* 273–280.
Mendlewicz, J. The age factor in depressive illness: Some genetic considerations. *Journal of Gerontology,* 1976, *31,* 300–303.
Miller, M. Iatrogenic and neurisgenic effects of prolonged immobilization of the ill aged. *Journal of the American Geriatrics Society,* 1975, *23,* 360–369.
Moos, R., Gauvain, M., Lemke, S., Max, W., & Mehren, B. Assessing the social environments of sheltered care settings. *The Gerontologist,* 1979, *19,* 74–82.
Neiditch, J., & White, L. Prediction of short-term outcome in newly admitted psychogeriatric patients. *Journal of the American Geriatrics Society,* 1976, *24,* 72–78.
Neugarten, B. Personality and aging. In S. Birren & K. Schaie (Eds.), *Handbook of the psychology of aging.* New York: Van Nostrand Reinhold, 1977.
Oberleder, M. Effects of psycho-social factors on test results of the aging. *Psychological Reports,* 1964, *14,* 383–387.
Oberleder, M. Adapting current psychological techniques for use in testing the aged. *The Gerontologist,* 1967, *7,* 3.
Okun, M., & DiVesta, F. Cautiousness in adulthood as a function of age and instructions. *Journal of Gerontology,* 1976, *31,* 571–576.
Okun, M., & Elias, C. Cautiousness in adulthood as a

function of age and payoff structure. *Journal of Gerontology,* 1977, *32,* 451–455.

Okun, M., Siegler, I., & George, L. Cautiousness and verbal learning in adulthood. *Journal of Gerontology,* 1978, *33,* 94–97.

Overall, J., & Gorham, D. The brief psychiatric rating scale. *Psychological Reports,* 1962, *10,* 799.

Palmore, E. (Ed.) *Normal aging II.* Durham: Duke University Press, 1974.

Palmore, E., & Cleveland, W. Aging, terminal decline, and terminal drop. *Journal of Gerontology.* 1976, *31,* 76–81.

Pattie, A., & Gilleard, C. A brief psychogeriatric assessment schedule: Validation against psychiatric diagnosis and discharge from hospital. *British Journal of Psychiatry,* 1975, *127,* 489–493.

Pfeiffer, E. Survival in old age: Physical, psychological and social correlates of longevity. *Journal of American Gerontological Society,* 1970, *18,* 273–285.

Pfeiffer, E. A short portable mental status questionnaire for the assessment of organic brain defect in elderly patients. *Journal of the American Geriatrics Society,* 1975, *23,* 433–441.

Pincus, A. The definition and measurement of the institutional environment in homes for the aged. *The Gerontologist,* 1968, *8,* 207–210.

Plutchik, R., Conte, H., & Lieberman, M. Development of a scale (GIES) for assessment of cognitive and perceptual functioning in geriatric patients. *Journal of the American Geriatrics Society,* 1971, *19,* 615–623.

Plutchik, R., Conte, H., Lieberman, M., Baker, M., Grossman, J., & Lehrman, N. Reliability and validity of a scale for assessing the functioning of geriatric patients. *Journal of the American Geriatrics Society,* 1970, *18,* 491–500.

Raven J. *Guide to using the Mill Hill vocabulary scale and the progressive matrices scale.* London: H. K. Lewis, 1958.

Raven, J. *Guide to using the coloured progressive matrices.* London: H. K. Lewis, 1960.

Reitan, R., & Fitzhugh, K. Behavioral deficits in groups with cerebral vascular lesions. *Journal of Consulting and Clinical Psychology,* 1971, *37,* 215–223.

Resnick, H., & Kantor, S. Suicide and aging. *Journal of the American Geriatric Society,* 1970, *18,* 152–158.

Riegel, K., & Angleitner, A. The pooling of longitudinal studies of aging. *International Journal of Aging and Human Development,* 1975, *1,* 57–66.

Riegel, K., & Riegel, R. Development, drop, and death. *Developmental Psychology,* 1972, *6,* 306–319.

Riegel, K., Riegel, R., & Meyer, G. A Study of dropout rates in longitudinal research in aging and the prediction of death. *Journal of Personality and Social Psychology,* 1967, *4,* 342–348.

Rodstein, M., Savitsky, E., & Starkman, R. Initial adjustment to a long-term care institution: Medical and behavioral aspects. *Journal of the American Geriatrics Society,* 1976, *24,* 65–71.

Rosencranz, H., & Philblad, C. Measuring the health of the elderly. *Journal of Gerontology,* 1970, *25,* 129–133.

Rowland, K. Environmental events predicting death for the elderly. *Psychological Bulletin,* 1977, *84,* 349–372.

Salzman, C., Kochansky, G., Shader, R., & Cronin, D. Rating scales for psychotropic drug research with geriatric patients: II. Mood ratings. *Journal of the American Geriatrics Society,* 1972, *21,* 215–221.

Schaie, K., & Parham, I. Stability of adult personality: Fact or fable? *Journal of Personality and Social Psychology,* 1976, *34,* 146–158.

Schaie, K., & Schaie, S. Clinical assessment and aging. In J. Birren & K. Schaie (Eds.), *Handbook of the psychology of aging.* New York: Van Nostrand Reinhold, 1977.

Schofield, W. Clinical psychologists as health professionals. In G. Stone, F. Cohen, & N. Adler (Eds.), *Health psychology: A handbook.* San Francisco: Jossey-Bass, 1979.

Senn, B., & Steiner, J. Don't tread on me. *International Journal of Aging and Human Development,* 1978–79, *9,* 177–186.

Shader, R., Harmatz, J., & Salzman, C. A new scaie for clinical assessment in geriatric populations: Sandoz Clinical Assessment-Geriatric (SCAG). *Journal of the American Geriatrics Society,* 1974, *107,* 22–30.

Shanas, E. Health status of older people: Cross-national implications. *American Journal of Public Health,* 1974, *64,* 261–264.

Snyder, B., & Harris, S. Treatable aspects of the dementia syndrome. *Journal of the American Geriatrics Society,* 1976, *24,* 179–183.

Stone, G., Cohen, F., & Adler, N. (Eds.), *Health psychology—A handbook.* San Francisco: Jossey-Bass, 1979.

Talland, G. *Human aging and behavior.* New York: Academic Press, 1968.

Taylor, H., & Bloom, L. Cross-validation and methodological extension of the Stockton geriatric rating scale. *Journal of Gerontology,* 1974, *20,* 190–193.

Tobin, S., & Lieberman, M. *Last home for the aged.* San Francisco: Jossey-Bass, 1976.

White, R. Motivation reconsidered: The concept of competence. *Psychological Review,* 1959, *66,* 297–334.

Zung, W. A self-rating depression scale. *Archives of General Psychiatry,* 1965, *12,* 63–70.

TREATMENT AND PREVENTION OF MEDICAL DISORDERS

10 Treatment of Cardiovascular Disorders

J. ALAN HERD

Success in treating cardiovascular disease has improved steadily during the past 10 years. Fewer people suffer heart attacks, die of strokes, and develop valvular heart disease. Surgical correction of congenital heart disease is now more often successful than in the past and surgical replacement of diseased blood vessels usually succeeds in restoring blood flow to normal. These treatment successes are the result of our improved understanding of the causes, mechanisms, and management of common diseases of the heart and blood vessels.

Associated with improvements in treatment is the reduction in death rate from cardiovascular disease. Since 1970, the death rate from cardiovascular disease has fallen more than 16% (National Heart, Lung, and Blood Institute, 1978). The most common cause of death from cardiovascular disease is coronary heart disease; the reduction in death rate from cardiovascular disease parallels the reduction in death rate from coronary heart disease. Even more impressive improvements have been achieved in other types of cardiovascular disease. Deaths from stroke have declined by 22%; deaths from hypertensive disease have declined by 38%; and deaths from rheumatic heart disease have declined by 25%. In contrast, deaths from causes unrelated to cardiovascular disease have only been reduced 8% since 1970. The death rate from cancer actually has increased by approximately 2% and the death rate from chronic lung disease has increased by 10%. Although it is difficult to determine causal relations between our success in treating heart disease and the reduction in death rate from cardiovascular disease, epidemiological evidence suggests that improvements in treatment may have improved longevity.

The consequences of cardiovascular disease, however, remain severe. The total economic cost of illness in 1975 has been estimated at 245 billion dollars (National Heart, Lung, and Blood Institute, 1978). Diseases of the circulatory system were estimated to cost 50 billion dollars or 21% of the total economic cost. Approximately half of the costs are attributed to mortality and approximately half to medical care and disability. It should be noted that the social and psychological implications of morbidity and mortality have not been measured in any quantitative manner. However, it is reason-

Medical Psychology
Contributions to Behavioral Medicine

ISBN 0-12-565960-1

able to suggest that the crippling disability and death of middle-aged adults has a profound effect on the morale, human performance, and behavior of family members in close association with the patient.

Although great improvements have been made in the treatment of most cardiovascular diseases, many victims of these diseases still die suddenly without receiving treatment. Approximately half the people who develop clinical manifestations of coronary heart disease die before they can receive any treatment (Kannel, Doyle, McNamara, Quickenton, & Gordon, 1975; Kuller, Cooper, & Perper, 1972). Those who survive long enough to receive treatment can expect to live at least an additional five years (Frank, Weinblatt, & Shapiro, 1973; Kannel, 1976; Weinberg, 1976). Who survives longest and has the best function depends upon (*a*) the severity of cardiovascular disease; (*b*) the effectiveness of medical and surgical treatment for each type of disease; and (*c*) the ability of the patients to follow the prescribed medical regimen. Thus, further improvements in reducing morbidity and mortality from cardiovascular disease can be achieved if these diseases are detected in their early stages and treatment is started before disastrous complications ensue. Additional benefits also depend upon the ability of patients with manifest cardiovascular disease to make use of the effective treatments. Although medical and surgical procedures still can be improved, success in reducing morbidity and mortality from cardiovascular diseases in the future will occur when the behavioral management of patients with cardiovascular disease is improved.

Assessing Cardiovascular Disease

Successful treatment of cardiovascular disease begins with a quantitative assessment of its physical and behavioral concomitants. The basic disease process must be identified, the clinical manifestations evaluated, and likelihood of progression or reversal of disease determined.

Basic Disease Processes

Blood Vessel Disease The most common cause of blood vessel disease in this country is atherosclerosis. This is a disease that starts early in childhood with lipid deposits in the inner layer of arterial walls (Ross & Glomset, 1976). These deposits are seen first in the aorta and later in the coronary arteries, cerebral arteries, femoral arteries, and renal arteries. The extent and severity of blood vessel disease influences the likelihood for successful treatment. In the past, it was believed that atherosclerosis and its complications were part of the normal aging process. However, many people escape blood vessel disease entirely. Results of studies in experimental animals (Armstrong & Megan, 1972) and clinical studies of patients with blood vessel disease (Barndt, Blankenhorn, Crawford, & Brooks, 1977; Basta, Williams, Kioschos, & Spector, 1976; Blankenhorn, Brooks, Selzer, & Barndt, 1978; Knight, Scheibel, Ampltaz, Varco, & Buchwald, 1972) suggest that atherosclerosis is reversible and that treatment can improve blood flow through affected blood vessels.

Heart Disease Normal function depends upon normal structure, normal contraction of heart muscle, and normal electrical activity. When the heart does not function normally it fails to pump enough blood to meet the needs of other organs for oxygen and metabolic substrates. At rest, enough blood is pumped to meet the metabolic requirements of the brain and other internal organs. During exercise, the increased metabolic requirements of the skeletal muscles are met by a marked increase in the amount of blood pumped by the heart (Rowell, 1974). In well-trained athletes, the heart may pump at an increased rate and pressure to deliver a six times greater volume. Consequently, a heart that functions normally at rest may fail to meet the metabolic requirements of exercise. Therefore, severity of heart disease is judged not only by the basic disease process but also by the ability of the heart to meet the demands of exercise.

Normal contractions of heart muscle depend upon a normal supply of blood through coronary arteries supplying the left ventricle. The most common cause of abnormal heart function is coronary artery disease caused by atherosclerosis. Severity of the disease depends upon the number of affected vessels, the site of the most severe lesions, and the kind of abnormal heart function in the portion of the myocardium supplied by diseased blood vessels. The death rate for patients with disease of one vessel is approximately 15% in five years whereas the death rate is three times as great for patients with severe disease in three major vessels (Bruschke, Proudfit, & Sones, Jr., 1973a, 1973b). In all patients with atherosclerosis of coronary arteries, arterial lesions show a 50% progression rate in two years unless intensive treatment is maintained (Benis, Gorlin, Kemp, & Herman, 1973).

Abnormal contraction of heart muscle may occur with other diseases. Diffuse diseases of heart muscle may follow viral or bacterial infections. They also may occur with chronic alcoholism (Brigden & Robinson, 1964; Spodick, Pigott, & Chirife, 1972). Most patients with myocardial disease have an enlarged heart, abnormal heart rhythms, abnormal electrocardiograms, or an inability of the heart to pump blood sufficient to meet the needs of other organs.

Special problems in cardiac function arise when the pacemaker and conduction system of the heart is involved. The most common cause of lesions to this system is atherosclerosis; abnormalities of heart rate, rhythm, and conduction of impulses through the heart frequently are the first signs of coronary artery disease (Lie, 1975). However, many patients have abnormalities of heart rates and rhythms without coronary artery disease. Some abnormalities of rate, rhythm, and conduction are very common and seldom indicate serious disease (Fisher & Tyroler, 1973; Levitt, Cogin, Somberg, & Kleid, 1976). Patients with disturbances of the conduction system are most likely to have coronary artery disease when the left main branch of the ventricular conduction system is involved. In all patients with abnormalities of rate, rhythm, or conduction, the presence of coronary artery disease is more dangerous than the presence of an abnormality on the electrocardiogram alone (Kotler, Tabatznik, Mower, & Tominaga, 1973).

Renal Disease Diseases of the kidney can cause cardiovascular problems through their effect on blood pressure control mechanisms. Normal kidney function controls the amount of sodium and water excreted and influences the water and electrolyte balance in the body. This balance affects blood volume which, in turn, influences the amount of blood pumped by the heart and the resultant arterial blood pressure (Safar, Weiss, Levenson, Loudon, & Milliez, 1973). While fewer than 5% of all patients with systemic arterial hypertension have high levels of blood pressure caused by kidney disease (Wilhelmsen & Berglund, 1977), surgical correction of some forms of kidney disease can cure systemic arterial hypertension (Shapiro, McDonald, & Scheib, 1976) and these correctable forms of renal disease can be identified with x-ray, chemical, and renal function examinations (Hunt, Strong, Sheps, & Bernatz, 1969).

Endocrine Diseases Endocrine disorders also can cause systemic arterial hypertension. Abnormal amounts of epinephrine and norepinephrine secreted from tumors in the adrenal medulla may cause hypertension by constricting blood vessels, reducing renal function, and enhancing cardiac function (Radtke, Kazmier, Rutherford, & Sheps, 1975). Tumors of the adrenal cortex may release large amounts of salt-retaining hormones that cause the kidney to retain water and electrolytes, and expand blood volume. Although tumors secreting these hormones may cause systemic arterial hypertension, they are rare, being responsible for elevations in blood pressure in fewer than 1% of patients with hypertension (Wilhelmsen & Berglund, 1977).

Essential Hypertension More than 95% of patients with systemic arterial hypertension do not have any known cause for their disorder (Wilhelmsen & Berglund, 1977). The basic disease process is unknown. Research from many laboratories has revealed that numerous genetic, nutritional, environmental, and behavioral factors may contribute to the development of abnormally high levels of arterial blood pressure. It should be noted, however, that essential hypertension can be treated successfully (levels of blood pressure brought to normal) even though the basic disease process usually cannot be cured (see. p. 148).

Clinical Manifestations of Cardiovascular Disease

Evaluating the signs and symptoms of cardiovascular disease is as important to successful treatment as diagnosis of the basic disease process. The severity of clinical manifestations of cardiovascular disease may be used at first to provide an index of the degree to which a patient's daily activities are limited by the disease (i.e., an index of the severity of the disease). However, as treatment progresses, the clinical manifestations of disease and the limitations in daily activity may be used as indices of the success of treatment, and the prospects for improving cardiovascular function in the future.

Some manifestations of cardiovascular disease such as low tolerance for exercise, abnormal heart rhythm, and high blood pressure can be evaluated precisely using standard clinical laboratory techniques. Other signs and symptoms such as pain, fatigue, weakness, depression, and disruption of interpersonal relations are more difficult to evaluate. Although indications for specific medical and surgical treatment usually are based on precise laboratory measures, the success of treatment must be judged by the patient's ability to perform normal daily activities. Therefore, evaluating clinical manifestations of cardiovascular disease must include measures of performance in all normal daily activities as well as measures derived under strict laboratory conditions.

Reduced Tolerance for Physical Activity Assessment of the capacity for physical work comes from the medical history, exercise tolerance testing, and behavioral assessment of patients. Patients with heart disease frequently are aware of the limitations in their daily physical activities and can report how far they can walk without stopping, how many stairs they can climb, and what circumstances cause shortness of breath. The amount of exercise patients can perform is best tested under laboratory conditions by having patients walk or run on a treadmill or pedal a stationary bicycle. Any limitations defined in the laboratory can then be compared to limitations reported by patients during normal daily activities.

Behavioral assessment involves comparing previous patterns of behavior and levels of function with present patterns and levels. This information can be obtained from the patient, from a spouse or close personal friend, and from employers, colleagues, and friends. Current patterns of behavior are best assessed using a diary of activities, problems, and pleasant events (Fordyce, 1976). With all of these techniques of behavioral assessment, the decrements in level of function attributable to cardiovascular disease can be determined. A thorough analysis includes considerations of personal characteristics, situational factors, and influences of cardiovascular disease. While vocational performance has received more attention in the literature than any other measure, normal function must be assessed using a variety of social, psychological, and behavioral measures.

Neurological Deficits The usual cause for neurological deficits in patients with cardiovascular disease is atherosclerosis of carotid arteries (Carter, 1972). Assessment can be made by medical history, physical examination, and behavioral procedures. The effects of a massive cerebral vascular accident may be unmistakable but the effects of transient ischemic attacks may be difficult to detect (Connelly, Dyken, Futty, Poskanzer, Calanchini, Swanson, Price, Haerer, & Gotshall, 1978). Patients with cerebral vascular disease may report disturbances of cognitive function and physical examination may reveal disturbances of memory, problem solving, and speech as well as sensory deficits and motor weakness. Behavioral procedures require information from family and friends, and direct observations of speech, motor activities, and activities of daily living (see Boll, O'Leary, & Barth, Chapter 6; Levy, Chapter 9).

Cardiac Arrhythmias Assessment of cardiac arrhythmias includes taking a medical history, a physical examination, resting electrocardiogram, electrocardiography during normal daily activities, and exercise tolerance testing. The latter two assessment techniques are particularly important since medical history, physical examination, and resting electrocardiograms frequently do not disclose the presence of cardiac arrhythmias.

Techniques for recording electrocardiograms during normal daily activities provide the means for behavioral assessment of cardiac arrhythmias (Taggart, Gibbons, & Somerville, 1969). Portable electrocardiographs usually have some means of recording the occurrence of symptoms, intense physical activity, or emotional upsets. The combination of a diary of daily activities, notations of time in relation to activities and symptoms, and continuous electrocardiograms frequently makes it possible to correlate social, psychological, and behavioral influences with the occurrence of cardiac arrhythmias.

Angina Pectoris The symptom called angina pectoris consists of pain, heaviness, a squeezing sensation, or a crushing sensation usually felt deep inside the chest. These sensations may also be felt in the neck, back, shoulder, or left arm. Usually angina pectoris occurs during physical exertion and has a predictable relation to the amount of physical activity. Occasionally angina pectoris may occur during emotional upsets and is typically relieved within a few minutes after cessation of physical activity. In severe cases of coronary artery disease, however, it may occur at rest (Scheidt, Wolk, & Killip, 1976). It is most ominous when the intensity, frequency and duration of the episodes increase with less physical activity.

Assessment of angina pectoris usually can be made from the medical history, a resting electrocardiogram, and exercise tolerance testing. As with any subjective measure, the severity of pain associated with myocardial ischemia is difficult to evaluate. In addition to obtaining details concerning effects of physical activity, the physician should also determine the relation of chest pain to other normal daily activities. Behavioral assessment includes the details of limitations resulting from chest pains that are reported by the patient and observed by family members, friends, and others. Exercise tolerance testing usually will induce pain that is caused by myocardial ischemia. Frequently, abnormalities of the electrocardiogram during exercise in association with chest pain produce almost certain diagnostic signs for coronary artery disease (Martin & McConahay, 1972). Occasionally, coronary angiography must be performed to determine the cause of severe debilitating chest pain requiring surgical correction (Selzer, 1977).

Myocardial Infarction The symptoms of myocardial infarction usually include severe deep crushing chest pain in the region of the sternum in association with nausea, fatigue, feeling of faintness, sweating, and anxiety. Sometimes these symptoms develop during physical activity, but often they occur at rest. Sometimes the only evidence of myocardial infarction is sudden death. Most patients who ultimately have myocardial infarction, experience ominous symptoms several days or several hours before the myocardial infarction (Lichstein, Alosilla, Chadda, & Gupta, 1977). They may have chest pain which occurs spontaneously and persists for long periods of time; they may feel weak, fatigued, or nauseated; and they may experience chest pain at rest. These premonitory symptoms are usually ignored and patients frequently delay seeking medical help during this early period when the myocardial infarction is developing.

Systemic Arterial Hypertension Symptoms of systemic arterial hypertension do not occur until the disease has advanced to its severe stages and may have caused damage to the heart, brain, eyes, or kidneys. In this country, most patients with hypertension are discovered as part of routine physical examination or community screening programs. The lack of symptoms may be one reason for the poor results of treatment. Approximately one-half of all patients found to have hypertension fail to achieve good control of their blood pressure levels and do not adhere to the prescribed medical regimens (Sackett & Haynes, 1976).

Diagnosis of systemic hypertension depends upon finding elevated levels of blood pressure on repeated measurements under resting conditions at home as well as in a physician's office or medical clinic. Many patients with elevated blood pressure on one examination will have normal levels on repeat examination. Since weight reduction, regular physical exercise, and restriction of sodium in the diet may reduce blood pressure to safe levels in patients with mild hypertension, evaluation of diet and normal physical activities are important parts of the assessment procedure.

Risk Factors for Cardiovascular Disease

Clinical manifestations of cardiovascular disease usually occur as the result of some basic disease process that has taken a long time to develop and progress to a serious stage. Our knowledge of mechanisms underlying basic disease processes in human subjects comes from studies of many patients with cardiovascular disease and populations of normal subjects without clinical manifestations of cardiovascular disease. Those characteristics that occur with relatively greater frequency among patients who develop cardiovascular disease have been labeled risk factors. Although epidemiological studies do not prove that any single risk factor is a cause of cardiovascular disease, they provide insight into possible mechanisms of disease.

Modification of some risk factors also can be used to judge the success of treatment of cardiovascular disease. Some therapeutic interventions have been shown to reduce morbidity and mortality from cardiovascular disease and reduce the severity of some risk factors (see pp. 149–151).

Coronary Artery Disease All of the risk factors known to be associated with coronary artery disease can be used to predict approximately 50% of the occurrence of clinical manifestations. As a result, approximately one-half of the patients who develop clinical manifestations of coronary artery disease do not have abnormal risk factors and approximately one-half of all individuals with abnormal risk factors will not develop clinical manifestations of coronary artery disease. However, approximately 80% of all patients with clinical manifestations of coronary artery disease are in the upper 10% of risk according to severity of risk factors.

UNAVOIDABLE RISK FACTORS Some risk factors such as age, sex, and family history of coronary artery disease are immutable. Consequently, they receive little attention in discussions of risk factors.

MAJOR RISK FACTORS Elevated levels of serum cholesterol, arterial hypertension, and cigarette smoking are associated with increased risk for developing clinical manifestations of coronary artery disease. A large number of epidemiological studies have demonstrated the importance of these risk factors in predicting death and disability from coronary artery disease. Furthermore, combinations of these three risk factors predict a greater likelihood of disease than simple addition of risk from each characteristic separately. Thus, men with all three major risk factors have more than 10 times the risk for disease than men who have none of these risk factors (Kannel, McGee, & Gordon, 1976).

MINOR RISK FACTORS The realization that the three major risk factors are elevated in only one-half of the patients with clinical manifestations of coronary artery disease has led to a search for other risk factors. Several groups of investigators have demonstrated that obesity is associated with higher serum levels of cholesterol and higher levels of systemic arterial blood pressure (see Coates, Perry, Killen & Slinkard, Chapter 11). Thus, obesity may be a risk factor for coronary artery disease. It also has been shown that regular exercise and physical fitness are associated with a lower risk for coronary artery disease (Doyle, Kannel, McNamara, Quickenton, & Gordon, 1976). Thus, sedentary living may be a risk factor. The Western Collaborative Group Study revealed that Type A behavior pattern was associated with higher levels of serum cholesterol, higher levels of systemic arterial blood pressure, and greater numbers of cigarettes consumed. In addition, there was an independent effect of Type A behavior pattern on the risk for developing clinical manifestations of coronary artery disease (see Chesney, Eagleston, & Rosenman, Chapter 3). Consideration of these minor risk factors improves ability to predict death and disability from coronary artery disease. A substantial number of patients with clinical manifestations of coronary artery disease, however, have neither major nor minor risk factors.

SPECIAL RISK FACTORS There are several risk factors that may occur in a small proportion of individuals at high risk for coronary artery disease. These are diabetes mellitus, genetic factors, and abnormal exercise tolerance tests. Patients with diabetes mellitus have approximately twice the risk for developing coronary artery disease as those who do not (Garcia, McNamara, Gordon, & Kannel, 1974). Individuals with parents or siblings who have early onset of death or disability from coronary heart disease have a greater risk of also being affected (Rowley, 1978). Approximately 20% of patients with coronary artery disease under the age of 60 years have increased levels of serum lipids that also occur in other members of their families (Goldstein & Brown, 1975) whereas less than 1% of the general population have familial patterns of elevated serum lipid values. Abnormal electrocardiographic responses to exercise are associated with a five- to ten-fold increase in the likelihood of developing clinical manifestations of coronary artery disease relative to those who have normal electrocardiographic responses (Stuart & Ellestad, 1976). How these special risk factors influence the development of coronary artery disease is unknown.

Cerebral Vascular Disease

MAJOR AND MINOR RISK FACTORS Epidemiological studies have shown that cerebral vascular disease is associated with the same risk factors as coronary artery disease. However, the relative risk of each of the major risk factors differs. Elevated levels of systemic arterial blood pressure, in particular, bring a greater risk for cerebral vascular disease than for coronary artery disease. Minor factors have approximately the same relative risk for the two conditions.

SPECIAL RISK FACTORS A small proportion of patients with cerebral vascular disease have diabetes mellitus, histories of transient ischemic attacks, and physical findings characteristic of obstructions to blood flow through one or both carotid arteries. Success in treating these special risk factors reduces the likelihood of death and disability from cerebral vascular disease.

Peripheral Vascular Disease

MAJOR AND MINOR RISK FACTORS Peripheral vascular disease caused by obstructions to blood flow through iliac, femoral, popliteal, and tibial arteries is associated with the same risk factors as other diseases caused by atherosclerosis. Cigarette smoking, however, has a greater association with peripheral vascular disease than with other clinical diseases caused by atherosclerosis. Consequently, abstinence from cigarette smoking is an important part of the treatment for peripheral vascular disease.

SPECIAL RISK FACTORS The incidence of peripheral vascular disease is greatly increased in patients with diabetes mellitus. Arterial insufficiency in the leg is partly the result of disease of small arteries and arterioles and partly the result of atherosclerosis of large arteries.

Aortic Disease A major complication of aortic atherosclerosis is an aneurysm of the abdominal aorta. This complication is associated with major and minor risk factors related to atherosclerosis in the other major arteries. Although aortic aneurysms can be repaired surgically, the long-range prospects for survival usually are limited by subsequent development of coronary artery disease or cerebral vascular disease.

Sudden Death Approximately half of the people who die suddenly without evidence of accidental injury, poisoning, or suicide are apparently in good health at the time of their deaths and have no evidence of cardiovascular disease (Kannel *et al.*, 1975). However, a large majority of adults who die suddenly have severe narrowing of at least one coronary artery. The risk profiles for sudden death and myocardial infarction are similar and patients with high risk for coronary artery disease also have a high risk of sudden death.

MAJOR RISK FACTORS The risk factors for sudden death are arterial hypertension, obesity, heavy cigarette smoking, and sendentary living (Doyle *et al.*, 1976; Julian, 1976). These are the same risk factors that are associated with coronary artery disease but the strengths of their associations with coronary artery disease and sudden death differ slightly.

SPECIAL RISK FACTORS Patients most likely to die suddenly are those with a previous history of sudden death who have been successfully resuscitated, patients with a previous history of coronary artery disease, patients with cardiac rhythm disturbances in association with coronary artery disease, and patients with chronic obstructive pulmonary artery disease with coronary artery disease. Patients who are known to have coronary artery disease are particularly liable to sudden death.

Cardiomyopathy The cause of cardiomyopathy in most patients is not known. However, diffuse disease of heart muscle frequently occurs in chronic alcoholics (Burch & Walsh, 1960). Successful treatment of cardiomyopathy includes complete abstinence from intake of ethanol (Demakis, Proskey, Rahimtoola, Jamil, Sutton, Rosen, Gunnary, & Tobin, 1974).

Valvular Heart Disease Patients with the greatest risk for developing valvular heart disease are those who have had rheumatic fever, a history of viral heart disease, or bacterial infections of heart valves. The greatest risks for complications of valvular heart disease occur in patients with recurrence of rheumatic fever, viral valvulitis, or severe bacterial infections with bacterial endocarditis. However, a common cause of symptoms in patients with valvular heart disease is progression of coronary artery disease. Consequently, successful treatment of patients with valvular heart disease includes control of major and minor risk factors that might promote atherosclerosis and impair coronary blood flow.

Treatment of Cardiovascular Disease

Essential Hypertension

Severity and Treatment The therapeutic approach to essential hypertension should be governed by the level of arterial blood pressure under resting conditions. Those patients with levels of diastolic blood pressure greater than 115 mmHg should be treated immediately and intensively with antihypertensive medication. Patients with diastolic levels of blood pressure between 105 and 115 mmHg also should be treated with antihypertensive medication, particularly if they have clinical manifestations of coronary artery disease or cerebral vascular disease. Patients with diastolic levels of blood pressure between 95 and 105 mmHg may receive a trial of nonpharmacologic treatment although many clinicians advocate treatment with mild antihypertensive medication for this group of patients.

Antihypertensive Medication Several drugs are used for the treatment of essential hypertension. Oral diuretic drugs may be used to reduce plasma volume and reduce peripheral vascular resistance (Frohlich, 1975; Mroczek, Davidov, & Finnerty, 1974). The administration of propanolol serves to reduce the effects of sympathetic nervous system stimulation on the kidney and to reduce renal secretion of renin (Drayer, Keim, Weber, Case, & Laragh, 1976). Other drugs include hydralazine, methyldopa, clonidine, minoxidil diazoxide, and guanethidine. All these agents have slightly different modes of action and are added in various combinations as necessary to control the level of blood pressure.

Nonpharmacologic Treatment Reductions of arterial blood pressure to safe levels frequently can be accomplished without the use of antihypertensive medication in patients with diastolic blood pressures lower than 105 mmHg. These nonpharmacologic treatments are also useful adjuncts to the administration of antihypertensive medication in patients with higher levels of diastolic blood pressure.

DIET Weight reduction and sodium restriction may substantially lower blood pressure (Reisin, Abel, Modan, Silverberg, Ellahou, & Modan, 1978). However, body weight must be reduced to values well below average weight for height and sodium intake must be restricted to less than 70 meq/day. Severe weight reduction and sodium restriction diets are difficult to follow and blood pressure control using dietary regimens frequently is inadequate (Mroczek, Moir, Davidov, & Finnerty, 1977).

EXERCISE A regular program of endurance exercise sufficient to produce a physiological conditioning effect may reduce elevated levels of arterial blood pressure to safe values (Tobian, 1978). The combination of weight reduction and exercise conditioning may be more effective than either diet or exercise alone.

BEHAVIORAL METHODS Applications of behavioral methods to the treatment of essential hypertension include blood pressure and muscle tension biofeedback and relaxation techniques, psychotherapy, environmental modification, and suggestion (Holmes, Chapter 22; Shapiro, Schwartz, Ferguson, Redmond, & Weiss, 1977). Evaluations of these methods have involved small numbers of subjects in short-term situations. Reports of these studies indicate small reductions in blood pressure in some patients, particularly those with mild hypertension.

Adherence to Therapeutic Regimens Although antihypertensive treatment can lower arterial blood pressure to safe levels in nearly all patients, satisfactory blood pressure control is achieved in fewer than half (Sackett & Haynes, 1976). Physicians frequently fail to convince patients of the necessity for continuing treatment and fail to provide effective follow-up to maintain satisfactory effects of treatment. Patients frequently fail to take medication as prescribed or follow nonpharmacologic treatment regimens. The occurrence of side effects of drugs, the cost of antihypertensive medication, the inconvenience of nonpharmacologic treatment, and a reluctance to follow any kind of treatment for long periods of time all combine to reduce the effectiveness of therapeutic regimens (see Masur, Chapter 23).

Summary When properly prescribed and faithfully followed, antihypertensive regimens will reduce elevated levels of arterial blood pressure to safe values. Successful treatment is possible both in patients with essential hypertension and patients with hypertension caused by renal disease.

Coronary Artery Disease

Risk Factor Reduction

TARGET POPULATION An effective program to reduce the risk factors is the best method of lowering the morbidity and mortality from coronary artery disease. For greatest effectiveness, this should begin before the atherosclerotic lesions become irreversible and the clinical manifestations of coronary artery disease become evident. While theoretically everyone should follow risk factor reduction programs, from a practical point of view, not all individuals are likely to follow ideal programs and attention must be focused on the individuals most likely to benefit from them. This includes patients with clinical manifestations of coronary artery disease, children and siblings of patients with coronary artery disease, (Blumenthal, Jesse, Hennekens, Klein, Ferrer, & Courley, 1975) and subjects with two or three major risk factors identified in routine physical examination or community screening programs.

Methods of Risk Factor Reduction

CIGARETTE SMOKING Results of smoking cessation programs are difficult to evaluate. Usually it is impossible to differentiate the effects of a smoking cessation program and the spontaneous efforts of subjects to stop smoking on their own. Indeed, urging smokers to quit through their own personal initiative may be as effective as elaborate smoking cessation techniques (Marston & McFall, 1971). In all programs, the majority of smokers who wish to quit smoking manage to do so temporarily. However, smoking relapses occur in the majority of those who attempt to quit (Glasgow & Bernstein, Chapter 19; Scherchuck, 1976).

DIET One objective of risk factor reduction is to lower serum levels of cholesterol to values below 200 mg/dl. For some patients a moderate reduction in total caloric intake and the proportion of calories provided in animal fat will lower the levels of serum cholesterol to safe values (Glueck, Mattson, & Bierman, 1978). Other patients must adhere to more stringent diets. Caloric intake for sedentary adults (in kilocalories) should be approximately 20 times the desirable body weight (in kilograms) and up to twice as much for individuals engaged in prolonged strenuous daily physical activity (National Academy of Sciences/National Research Council, 1974). Overweight adults should restrict their caloric intake to less than 1200 calories a day. Daily protein intake should be no more than 0.8 grams per kilogram of desirable body weight or approximately 15% of total calorie consumed. Daily intake of fat and oil should comprise no more than 20% of the total calories for adults and less than half of this amount should be animal fat. The remainder of calories, 60–70% of the total, should be provided in complex carbohydrates supplied in the form of vegetables, legumes, tubers, whole grain, and raw fruit rather than as refined simple sugars. Cholesterol intake should be reduced below 100 mg a day. In general, each of the three major meals should contain 20 to 40%

of the total calories and the remainder eaten in snacks.

Procedures to be followed in establishing the use of a high carbohydrate low fat diet include specific menus for each day, instructions for purchasing of food, and the use of food diaries. Despite the best intentions of patients, implementation of an ideal diet is difficult (Stuart, Mitchell, & Jensen, Chapter 18; West, 1973). Attention must be given to social and cultural patterns of eating, and patients must be educated to alter the way their eating habits affect their life patterns and social interactions.

Exercise The objective of an exercise program is to undertake physical activities involving rhythmic use of large muscle groups for 20 to 30 minutes three or four times each week. The intensity of exercise should be enough to increase oxygen uptake at least three times greater than at rest. While many patients can tolerate increases in oxygen uptake that are ten times greater, the intensity of physical activity must be individualized according to objective measures of each patient's capacity for physical work.

Systemic Arterial Hypertension Elevated levels of arterial blood pressure should be treated vigorously using antihypertensive medication and nonpharmacologic procedures as necessary to reduce severity of this risk factor.

Medication Satisfactory reductions in serum cholesterol and levels of arterial blood pressure may not occur without hypocholesterolemic or antihypertensive medication. In addition, adherence to prescribed diets may not reduce serum cholesterol below 200 mg/dl unless agents such as clofibrate, cholestyramine, or nicotinic acid are administered. These agents may have serious side effects and their use must be supervised by a physician.

Ileal Bypass Surgery An extreme form of treatment for severe obesity is partial ileal bypass. In this surgical procedure, portions of the small intestine are short-circuited by direct connection of proximal portions of the ileum to the colon. This procedure reduces the area of small intestine available for absorbing digested food and excludes the portion of small intestine in which cholesterol secreted in bile is reabsorbed (see Stuart, Mitchell, & Jensen, Chapter 18, for a critical discussion of this procedure).

Behavioral Management Those patients who are strongly committed to reasonable goals according to a realistic timetable with enthusiastic support of their spouses or close personal friends are most likely to achieve success in reducing cardiovascular risk factors by means of behavioral management. Management of a risk factor reduction program involves contingency contracting, methods for recording progress, periodic evaluation, and continual revision in the program according to problems that arise and progress made. Contingency contracting should be negotiated with the patient and the spouse or a close personal friend. It involves assessing the patient's (*a*) medical and psychological condition; (*b*) personal goals and expectations for achieving those goals; (*c*) liabilities to participation and evidence of personal commitment; and (*d*) establishing schedules of extrinsic reinforcement for desired behaviors and withdrawal of reinforcement for maladaptive behaviors. It should be noted that the schedules and forms of reinforcement and reinforcement withdrawal must be agreed upon by the therapist, patient, and spouse or friend (who often is reponsible for delivering or withholding reinforcement) and documented in writing.

Evaluation of progress in a behavioral management program should be based upon specific, prospectively chosen indicators. Only three or four indicators should be selected and they should be chosen according to improvements in cardiovascular risk factors. For example, reduction in body weight and reductions in serum levels of cholesterol are more likely to indicate success in following prescribed diets than self-reports of eating habits in food diaries. A gradual increase in capacity for physical work is more likely to indicate adherence to an exercise program than records of attendance in an exercise class. When progress is apparent, the program should continue although it may require some modification. When progress does not occur, the program should be revised. In either case, continual evaluation of the patient's progress is essential (see Coates, Perry, Killen, & Slinkard, Chapter 11 for examples of treatment programs using contingency contracting).

Summary Many etiological factors are responsible for atherosclerosis; thus, reducing disability and death from coronary artery disease may depend upon modifying many other factors besides the major risk factors. Results of clinical studies with humans indicate that major and minor risk factors can be reduced and the results of studies with experimental animals indicate that atherosclerotic lesions can regress. In addition, quantitative angiographic studies of femoral arteries and coronary arteries suggest that atherosclerosis in human arteries does regress in asociation with severe reduction in risk factors. On the other hand, clinical studies with equivocal outcomes concerning morbidity and mortality from coronary artery disease have been associated with small changes in cardiovascular risk factors. If substantial benefits from risk factor reduction are to occur, it is necessary to achieve complete cessation of cigarette smoking, reduction of systemic arterial blood pressure to average levels, and reduction of serum cholesterol levels to values below 200 mg/dl.

Angina Pectoris

Medication Most patients with angina pectoris use medication to prevent the occurrence of chest pain or to treat the pain when it does occur. The drug most commonly prescribed to patients with angina pectoris is trinitroglycerine. Absorbed through the mucosa of the mouth, this drug dilates blood vessels, reduces the work of the heart, and restores myocardial oxygen supply. Another drug commonly used is propranolol (Warren, Brewer, & Orgain, 1976). This drug blocks the beta-adrenergic effects of sympathetic nervous system activity on the heart. Consequently, it reduces heart rate and the force of cardiac contraction, decreasing myocardial requirements for oxygen with little effect on the capability of the heart to pump blood in response to metabolic demands for blood from other organs. Proper use of these drugs is an essential part of successful treatment for coronary artery disease.

Exercise Conditioning An exercise training program involving prescribed levels of physical activity (usually three to four sessions per week, each lasting 20-30 minutes) serves to increase the amount of physical work that a patient may perform without experiencing chest pain. Some improvement occurs because of an increased ability of the heart to pump blood that is attributable to reduced heart rate and blood pressure responses to exercise. Another effect of exercise training is the conditioning of skeletal muscle to extract greater amounts of oxygen and metabolic substrates from blood during activity.

Risk Factor Reduction Frequency and severity of angina pectoris can be reduced markedly by reduction in body weight, control of systemic arterial blood pressure, and substantial decreases in levels of cholesterol and triglycerides. Cessation of cigarette smoking is absolutely essential to reduce the frequency and severity of angina pectoris and to reduce the likelihood of sudden death or myocardial infarction.

Surgery Indications for surgery in patients with angina pectoris depend upon the severity of angina, the extent and severity of coronary arterial disease, and ventricular function. Results of controlled clinical trials have indicated that intensive medical therapy should be used to control angina pectoris, particularly when patterns of chest pain are unstable (National Cooperative Study Group, 1978). Patients with severe angina pectoris who should be treated surgically include those with left main coronary artery obstruction (Kouchoukos, Oberman, Russell, & Jones, 1975; Sung, Mallon, Richter, Ghahramani, Sommer, Kaider, & Myerburg, 1975) and patients with angina pectoris that is unresponsive to medical management (Aronow & Stemmer, 1975). It has not been demonstrated that coronary bypass surgery improves survival in angina patients with other patterns of coronary artery disease (Aronow & Stemmer, 1974). However, bypass surgery does frequently relieve angina pectoris.

Medical management of patients with successful coronary bypass surgery is even more of a problem than managing patients who do not have surgery. The dramatic reduction in angina pectoris that often follows successful surgery (Mathur, Guinn, Anastassiades, Chahine, Korompai, Montero, & Luchi, 1975) diverts attention from the inevitable progression of coronary atherosclerosis that occurs if no changes are made in risk factors (Pasternak, Cohn, Selzer, & Langston, 1975). Instead of changing their patterns of improper diet, inactivity, high blood pressure, and cigarette smoking, patients with successful bypass surgery may continue their former style of living.

Behavioral Management Intensive medical treatment of patients with angina pectoris includes precise management of daily physical activity, severe restriction of diet, careful control of arterial blood pressure, and complete cessation of cigarette smoking. While these principles of medical treatment can be readily imposed on patients in hospitals, they are difficult to impose upon outpatients. Specific instructions must be established and progress must be continually evaluated. There is little likelihood that success in treatment of angina pectoris or any other manifestation of cardiovascular disease will occur under a program based on intuitive day-by-day management. Eventually, faithful adherence to the medical regimen will increase physical working capacity, reduce angina pectoris, and improve overall quality of life. Successful medical treatment also will obviate the indications for coronary bypass surgery as well as reduce the likelihood of myocardial infarction and sudden death. These physiological and psychological benefits must be presented to patients in behavioral terms to exploit their full motivational potential.

Myocardial Infarction

Acute Myocardial Infarction The diagnosis of acute myocardial infarction is an indication for treatment under specialized conditions of coronary care unit facilities. Patients who do not have any further complications of acute myocardial infarction are maintained at bed rest for 4 days followed by progressive mobilization over the next 5–10 days. The total hospitalization for patients with uneventful recovery from acute myocardial infarction usually is 9–14 days.

Rehabilitation The objectives of post-myocardial-infarction rehabilitation programs are to reduce death and disability from cardiovascular disease, to improve the response to medical treatment, and to reduce the costs of that treatment (Naismith, Robinson, Shaw, & MacIntyre, 1979; Schiller & Baker, 1976). Components of rehabilitation programs are designed to encourage patients to exercise regularly, lose weight, alter their diet, take the prescribed medications, and stop smoking. Behavioral techniques are necessary to increase adherence to these prescribed programs, to detect and treat depression, and to improve personal and social adjustments following cardiovascular disease.

Factors known to influence adherence to cardiac post-myocardial rehabilitation programs are previous history of myocardial infarction, cigarette smoking, Type A behavior pattern, previous patterns of behavior and levels of function, involvement of spouse, depression, and commitment to the program (Oldridge, Wicks, Hanley, Sutton, & Jones, 1978; Stern, Pascale, & Ackerman, 1977). A practical approach to post-myocardial rehabilitation includes determining previous patterns of behavior and levels of function, obtaining baseline measures, prescribing treatment, assessing progress using physiological measures, and evaluating improvements in personal and social adjustments using objective criteria and quantitative scales.

It should be noted that determining the success of a treatment program requires more than subjective reports from the patient. Even behavioral assessments by impartial trained observers may not reveal the true worth of treatment outcomes. Some effort must be made to ascertain the clinical and social significance of the patient's progress. Demonstrating a statistically significant improvement may have no practical impact on personal and social adjustment (Kazdin, 1977; Prokop & Bradley, Chapter 25). The patient may report feeling better and functioning more effectively but if these reports cannot be confirmed by independent evidence, meaningful progress may not have occurred.

Risk Factor Reduction The occurrence of acute myocardial infarction is a serious risk factor for sudden death or further disability. Improving prospects for survival involves reduction of all major and minor risk factors according to the methods already described.

Medication In addition to drugs such as oral diuretics (for control of arterial blood pressure levels) and propranolol (for control of angina pectoris and cardiac arrhythmias), other pharmacological agents are frequently prescribed. Drugs such as acetylsalicylic acid and sulfinpyrazone frequently are prescribed to reduce platelet aggregation and prevent thrombosis. Hypocholesterolemic agents such as clofibrate, cholestyramine, and nicotinic acid may be prescribed in an effort to reduce serum levels of cholesterol.

Cardiac Arrhythmias

Most patients with serious disturbances of cardiac rhythm can be treated using antiarrhythmic agents. The success of treatment, however, depends upon patient adherence to the prescribed medical regimen. Patients with defects in conduction of impulses through the heart may require surgical treatment. Insertion of an electronic pacemaker can prevent some forms of serious rhythm disturbances and severe, life-threatening reductions in heart rate.

Cardiomyopathy

Patients with enlarged hearts and reduced left ventricular function may be improved by administration of drugs such as digoxin. Development of heart failure with retention of sodium and water may require additional treatment with diuretic agents. In general, these patients do not benefit from exercise conditioning programs. In fact, prolonged bed rest frequently is an important part of treatment.

Successful treatment of cardiomyopathy also includes attention to the primary causes of the disorder. Frequently, the etiologic agents and pathogenic mechanisms are unknown. However, chronic ingestion of ethanol can be a cause of cardiomyopathy and, thus, treatment includes abstinence from ethanol (Demakis *et al.*, 1974).

Valvular Heart Disease

Surgical replacement of diseased valves should be considered for patients whose cardiac function is inadequate to supply blood flow in proportion to the metabolic requirements of other organs. Other indications for surgery are severe cardiac arrhythmias and angina pectoris.

Cerebral Vascular Disease

Successful treatment of cerebral vascular disease requires control of major and minor cardiovascular risk factors, intensive treatment of acute cerebral vascular accidents (Marston & McFall, 1971), surgical repair of diseased carotid arteries in their extracranial course (Easton & Sherman, 1977), and administration of agents that reduce aggregation of platelets and thrombosis (Fields, Lemak, Frankowski, & Hardy, 1977, 1978). All these components of treatment for cerebral vascular disease are similar to the components of treatment for coronary artery disease. Patients with cerebral vascular disease usually are older than patients with coronary artery disease and their physical, social, and behavioral function must be evaluated according to criteria appropriate to their age.

Peripheral Vascular Disease

Surgical repair or replacement of diseased iliac, femoral, popliteal, and tibial arteries can frequently restore normal function to leg muscles. However, surgical treatment must be followed by intensive medical treatment to reduce the severity of major and minor risk factors.

Conclusions

The treatment of all of the cardiovascular diseases discussed require some form of medical intervention such as medication, hospitalization, or surgery. However, several psychological approaches discussed by other contributors to this volume also play an important role in the management of patients with cardiovascular disorders. They are an inherent part of encouraging patients to exercise regularly, reduce weight, alter diet, take medication, and stop smoking. Psychological approaches are used to improve personal and social adjustments following cardiovascular disease and to evaluate individual treatments according to objective signs of progress.

Evaluating the benefits of treatment for cardiovascular disorders is hampered by the large numbers of subjects and long periods of time required to demonstrate reductions in death and disability. However, improvements in physical working capacity, reductions in symptoms of cardiovascular disease, and improvements in cardiovascular risk factors can be observed in fewer subjects in shorter periods of time. The results of investigations regarding the treatment of cardiovascular disorders have increased our understanding of the physiological, biochemical, and psychological mechanisms associated with improvements in clinical condition of patients with cardiovascular disease.

References

Armstrong, M. L., & Megan, M. B. Lipid depletion in atheromatous coronary arteries in rhesus monkeys after regression diets. *Circulation Research,* 1972, *30,* 675-680.

Aronow, W. S., & Stemmer, E. A. Bypass graft surgery versus medical therapy of angina pectoris. *American Journal of Cardiology,* 1974, *33,* 415-420.

Aronow, W. S., & Stemmer, E. A. Two-year follow-up of angina pectoris: Medical or surgical therapy. *Annals of Internal Medicine,* 1975, *82,* 208-212.

Barndt, R., Jr., Blankenhorn, D. H., Crawford, D. W., & Brooks, S. H. Regression and progression of early femoral atherosclerosis in treated hyperlipoproteinemic patients. *Annals of Internal Medicine,* 1977, *86,* 139-146.

Basta, L. L., Williams, C., Kioschos, J. M., & Spector, A. A. Regression of atherosclerotic stenosing lesions of the renal arteries and spontaneous cure of systemic hypertension through control of hyperlipidemia. *American Journal of Medicine,* 1976, *61,* 420-423.

Benis, C. E., Gorlin, R., Kemp, H. G., & Herman, M. V. Progression of coronary artery disease: A clinical arteriographic study. *Circulation,* 1973, *47,* 455-464.

Blankenhorn, D. H., Brooks, S. H., Selzer, R. H., & Barndt, R., Jr. The rate of atherosclerosis change during treatment of hyperlipoproteinemia. *Circulation,* 1978, *57,* 355-361.

Blumenthal, S., Jesse, M. J., Hennekens, C. H., Klein, B. E., Ferrer, P. L., & Courley, J. E. Risk factors for coronary artery disease in children of affected families. *Journal of Pediatrics,* 1975, *87,* 1187-1192.

Brigden, W., & Robinson, J. Alcoholic heart disease. *British Medical Journal,* 1964, *2,* 1283-1289.

Bruschke, A. V. G., Proudfit, W. L., & Sones, F. M., Jr. Progress study of 590 consecutive nonsurgical cases of coronary disease followed 5-9 years. I. Arteriographic correlations. *Circulation,* 1973, *47,* 1147-1153. (a)

Bruschke, A. V. G., Proudfit, W. L., & Sones, F. M., Jr. Progress study of 590 consecutive nonsurgical cases of coronary disease followed 5-9 years. II. Ventriculographic and other correlations. *Circulation,* 1973, *47,* 1154-1163. (b)

Burch, G. E., & Walsh, J. J. Cardiac insufficiency in chronic alcoholism. *American Journal of Cardiology,* 1960, *6,* 864-874.

Carter, A. B. Clinical aspects of cerebral infarction. In J. P. Vinken & G. S. Bruyn (Eds.), *Handbook of clinical neurology: Vascular disease of the nervous system* (Vol. 2). New York: North Holland & American Elsevier, 1972.

Conneally, P. M., Dyken, M. L., Futty, D. E., Poskanzer, D. C., Calanchini, P. R., Swanson, P. D., Price, T. R., Haerer, A. E., & Gotshall, R. A. Cooperative study of hospital frequency and character of transient ischemic attacks: VIII. Risk factors. *Journal of the American Medical Association,* 1978, *240,* 742-746.

Demakis, J. G., Proskey, A., Rahimtoola, S. H., Jamil, M., Sutton, G. C., Rosen, K. M., Gunnary, R. M., & Tobin, J. R. The natural course of alcoholic cardiomyopathy. *Annals of Internal Medicine,* 1974, *80,* 293-297.

Doyle, J. T., Kannel, W. B., McNamara, P. M., Quickenton, P., & Gordon, T. Factors related to suddenness of death from coronary disease: Combined Albany-Framingham studies. *American Journal of Cardiology,* 1976, *37,* 1073-1078.

Drayer, J. I. M., Keim, H. J., Weber, M. A., Case, D. B., & Laragh, J. H. Unexpected pressor responses to propranolol in essential hypertension: An interaction between renin, aldosterone, and sympathetic activity. *American Journal of Medicine,* 1976, *60,* 897-903.

Easton, J. D., & Sherman, D. G. Stroke and mortality rate in carotid endarterectomy: 228 consecutive operations. *Stroke,* 1977, *8,* 565-568.

Fisher, F. D., & Tyroler, H. A. Relationship between ventricular premature contractions on routine electrocardiography and subsequent sudden death from coronary heart disease. *Circulation,* 1973, *47,* 712-719.

Fields, W. S., Lemak, N. A., Frankowski, R. F., & Hardy, R. J. Controlled trial of aspirin in cerebral ischemia. *Stroke,* 1977, *8,* 301-314.

Fields, W. S., Lemak, N. A., Frankowski, R. F., & Hardy, R. J. Controlled trial of aspirin in cerebral ischemia: Part II. Surgical group. *Stroke,* 1978, *9,* 309-319.

Fordyce, W. E. Behavioral concepts in chronic pain and illness. In P. O. Davidson (Ed.), *Behavioral management of anxiety, depression, and pain.* New York: Brunner/Mazel, 1976.

Frank, C. W., Weinblatt, E., & Shapiro, S. Angina pectoris in men: Prognostic significance of selected medical factors. *Circulation,* 1973, *47,* 509-517.

Frohlich, E. D. Use and abuse of diuretics. *American Heart Journal,* 1975, *89,* 1-3. (Editorial)

Garcia, M., McNamara, P. M., Gordon, T., & Kannel, W. B. Morbidity and mortality in diabetics in the Framingham population: 16 year follow-up study. *Diabetes,* 1974, *23,* 105-111.

Glueck, C. J., Mattson, F., & Bierman, E. L. Diet and coronary heart disease: Another view. *New England Journal of Medicine,* 1978, *298,* 1471-1473.

Goldstein, J. L., & Brown, M. S. Hyperlipidemia in coronary heart disease: A biochemical genetic approach. *Journal of Laboratory and Clinical Medicine,* 1975, *85,* 15-25.

Hunt, J. C., Strong, C. G., Sheps, S. G., & Bernatz, P. E. Diagnosis and management of renovascular hypertension. *American Journal of Cardiology,* 1969, *23,* 434-445. (Review)

Julian, D. G. Toward preventing coronary death from ventricular fibrillation. *Circulation,* 1976, *54,* 360-364.

Kannel, W. B. Some lessons in cardiovascular epidemiology from Framingham. *American Journal of Cardiology,* 1976, *37,* 269-282.

Kannel, W. B., Doyle, J. T., McNamara, P. M., Quickenton, P., & Gordon, T. Precursors of sudden coronary death: Factors related to the incidence of sudden death. *Circulation,* 1975, *51,* 606-613.

Kannel, W. B., McGee, D., & Gordon, T. A general cardiovascular risk profile: The Framingham study. *American Journal of Cardiology,* 1976, *38,* 46-51.

Kazdin, A. E. Assessing the clinical or applied importance of behavior change through social validation. *Behavior Modification,* 1977, *1,* 427-451.

Knight, L., Scheibel, R., Amplatz, K., Varco, R. L., & Buchwald, H. Radiographic appraisal of the Minnesota partial ileal bypass study. *Surgical Forum,* 1972, *23,* 141-142.

Kotler, M. N., Tabatznik, B., Mower, M. M., & Tominaga, S. Prognostic significance of ventricular ectopic beats with respect to sudden death in the late postinfarction period. *Circulation,* 1973, *47,* 959-966.

Kouchoukos, N. T., Oberman, A., Russell, R. O., Jr., & Jones, W. B. Surgical versus medical treatment of occlusive disease confined to the left anterior descending coronary artery. *American Journal of Cardiology,* 1975, *35,* 836-842.

Kuller, L., Cooper, M., & Perper, J. Epidemiology of sudden death. *Archives of Internal Medicine,* 1972, *129,* 714-719.

Levitt, B., Cagin, N. A., Somberg, J. C., & Kleid, J. J. Ventricular rhythm disorders and sudden cardiac death. *American Journal of Medicine,* 1976, *61,* 449-451. (Editorial)

Lichstein, E., Alosilla, C., Chadda, K. D., & Gupta, P. K. Significance and treatment of nocturnal angina preceding myocardial infarction. *American Heart Journal,* 1977, *93,* 723-726.

Lie, J. T. Histopathology of the conduction system in sudden death from coronary heart disease. *Circulation,* 1975, *51,* 446-452.

Marston, A. R., & McFall, R. M. A comparison of behavior modification approaches to smoking reduction. *Journal of Consulting and Clinical Psychology,* 1971, *36,* 153-162.

Martin, C. M., & McConahay, D. R. Maximal treadmill exercise electrocardiography: Correlations with coronary arteriography and cardiac hemodynamics. *Circulation,* 1972, *46,* 956-962.

Mathur, V. S., Guinn, G. A., Anastassiades, L. C., Chahine, R. A., Korompai, F. L., Montero, A. C., & Luchi, R. J. Surgical treatment for stable angina pectoris: Prospective randomized study. *New England Journal of Medicine,* 1975, *292,* 709-713.

Mroczek, W. J., Davidov, M. E., & Finnerty, F. A. Large dose furosemide therapy for hypertension: Long-term use in 22 patients. *American Journal of Cardiology, 1974, 33,* 546-549.

Mroczek, W. J., Moir, D., Davidov, M. E., & Finnerty, F. A. Sodium intake and furosemide administration in hypertension patients with renal insufficiency. *American Journal of Cardiology,* 1977, *39,* 808-812.

Naismith, L. D., Robinson, J. F., Shaw, G. B., & MacIntyre, M. M. J. Psychological rehabilitation after myocardial infarction. *British Medical Journal,* 1979, *1,* 439-442.

National Academy of Sciences/National Research Council. *Recommended dietary allowances* (8th ed.). Washington, D.C.: National Academy of Sciences, 1974.

National Cooperative Study Group. Unstable angina pectoris: National cooperative study group to compare surgical and medical therapy. II. In-hospital experience and initial follow-up results in patients with one, two, and three vessel disease. *American Journal of Cardiology,* 1978, *12,* 839-848.

National Heart, Lung, and Blood Institute. *National Heart, Lung, and Blood Institute's fact book for fiscal year 1978.* DHEW Publication No. (NIH) 79-1656. Washington, D.C.: National Institutes of Health, 1978.

Oldridge, N. B., Wicks, J. R., Hanley, C., Sutton, J. R., & Jones, N. L. Noncompliance in an exercise rehabilitation program for men who have suffered a myocardial infarction. *Canadian Medical Association Journal,* 1978, *118,* 361-364.

Pasternak, R., Cohn, K., Selzer, A., & Langston, M. F., Jr. Enhanced rate of progression of coronary artery disease following aortacoronary saphenous vein bypass surgery. *American Journal of Medicine*, 1975, *58*, 166–170.

Radtke, W. E., Kazmier, F. J., Rutherford, B. D., & Sheps, S. G. Cardiovascular complications of pheochromocytoma crisis. *American Journal of Cardiology*, 1975, *35*, 701–705.

Reisin, E., Abel, R., Modan, M., Silverberg, D. S., Ellahou, H. E., & Modan, B. Effect of weight loss without salt restriction on the reduction of blood pressure in overweight hypertensive patients. *New England Journal of Medicine*, 1978, *298*, 1–6.

Ross, R., & Glomset, J. A. The pathogenesis of atherosclerosis. *New England Journal of Medicine*, 1976, *295*, 369–377; 420–425.

Rowell, L. B. Human cardiovascular adjustments to exercise and thermal stress. *Physiological Reviews*, 1974, *54*, 75–159.

Rowley, P. T. Genetics for the cardiologist: Part II. Chromosomal and polygenic inheritance and genetic counseling. *Modern Concepts of Cardiovascular Disease*, 1978, *47*, 67–70.

Sackett, D. L., & Haynes, R. B. *Compliance with therapeutic regimens*. Baltimore: Johns Hopkins University Press, 1976.

Safar, M. E., Weiss, Y. A., Levenson, J. A., Loudon, G. M., & Milliez, P. L. Hemodynamic study of 85 patients with borderline hypertension. *American Journal of Cardiology*, 1973, *31*, 315–319.

Scheidt, S., Wolk, M., & Killip, T. Unstable angina pectoris: Natural history, hemodynamics, uncertainties of treatment, and the ethics of clinical study. *American Journal of Medicine*, 1976, *60*, 409–417.

Scherchuck, L. A. Problems of high-risk populations and high-risk nonresponders: Smoking behavior. In J. W. Cullen, B. H. Box, & R. N. Ison (Eds.), *Cancer: The behavioral dimensions*. New York: Raven Press, 1976.

Schiller, E., & Baker, J. Return to work after a myocardial infarction: Evaluation of planned rehabilitation and of a predictive rating scale. *Medical Journal of Australia*, 1976, *1*, 859–862.

Selzer, A. Cardiac ischemic pain in patients with normal coronary arteriograms. *American Journal of Medicine*, 1977, *63*, 661–665.

Shapiro, A. P., McDonald, R. H., Jr., & Scheib, E. Renal arterial stenosis and hypertension: II. Current criteria for surgery. *American Journal of Cardiology*, 1976, *37*, 1065–1068.

Shapiro, A. P., Schwartz, G. E., Ferguson, D. C. E., Redmond, D. P., & Weiss, S. M. Behavioral methods in the treatment of hypertension. *Annals of Internal Medicine*, 1977, *86*, 626–636.

Spodick, D. H., Pigott, V. M., & Chirife, R. Preclinical cardiac malfunction in chronic alcoholism: Comparison with matched normal controls and with alcoholic cardiomyopathy. *New England Journal of Medicine*, 1972, *287*, 677–680.

Stern, M. J., Pascale, L., & Ackerman, A. Life adjustment postmyocardial infarction: Determining predictive variables. *Archives of Internal Medicine*, 1977, *137*, 1680–1685.

Stuart, R. J., Jr., & Ellestad, M. H. Upsloping S-T segments in exercise stress testing: Six-year follow-up study of 438 patients and correlation with 248 angiograms. *American Journal of Cardiology*, 1976, *37*, 19–22.

Sung, R. J., Mallon, S. M., Richter, S. E., Ghahramani, A. E., Sommer, L. S., Kaider, G. A., & Myerburg, R. J. Left main coronary artery obstruction: Follow-up of thirty patients with and without surgery. *Circulation*, 1975, *52*, 112–118.

Taggart, P., Gibbons, D., & Somerville, W. Some effects of motor-car driving on the normal and abnormal heart. *British Medical Journal, 1969*, *4*, 130–134.

Tobian, L. Hypertension and obesity. *New England Journal of Medicine*, 1978, *298*, 46–47.

Warren, S. G., Brewer, D. L., & Orgain, E. S. Long-term propranolol therapy for angina pectoris. *American Journal of Cardiology*, 1976, *37*, 420–426.

Weinberg, S. L. Natural history six years after acute myocardial infarction: Is there a low-risk group? *Chest*, 1976, *69*, 23–28.

West, K. M. Diet therapy of diabetes: An analysis of failure. *Annals of Internal Medicine*, 1973, *79*, 425–434.

Wilhelmsen, L., & Berglund, G. Prevalence of primary and secondary hypertension. *American Heart Journal*, 1977, *94*, 543–546. (Editorial)

11

Primary Prevention of Cardiovascular Disease in Children and Adolescents

THOMAS J. COATES
CHERYL PERRY
JOEL KILLEN
LEE ANN SLINKARD

Joan is a junior high school student. She is outgoing and popular, but she is not especially interested in school. Her mother smokes, and one of her best friends has recently encouraged her to start. Chances are 1 in 4 that Joan will become a regular smoker.

Richard is a 16-year-old junior in high school who is 20% above ideal weight. His only square meal is dinner. The rest of his food comes from fast foods and snacks. He will probably be overweight when he grows up.

Melissa is an attractive sophomore. She is like other persons her age: She spends about 2% of her time in moderate physical activity and only about 0.5% of her time in strenuous physical activity.

Mark is in the fourth grade. He probably spends 60 to 70% of his time during recess standing around talking to friends.

Fred and Mary are typical sixth-grade students. Their calories are distributed among the food groups in the following way: 42% fat, 12% protein, 46% carbohydrate (24% sugar).

Joan, Richard, Melissa, Mark, Fred, and Mary are typical children and adolescents in American society. This means that they are at greater risk than their peers in many other countries for developing cardiovascular disease, suffering from heart attack, or dying prematurely from a cardiovascular disorder.

Cardiovascular Disease May be Preventable

Cardiovascular disease is the leading cause of death and premature death in the United States. In 1975, 52.5% of all deaths in the United States were attributed to diseases of the heart and blood vessels; 994,513 individuals died because of heart

Preparation of this chapter was supported in part by Young Investigator Award Grant No. 1.R23.HL24297, from the National Heart, Lung, and Blood Institute to Thomas J. Coates, by Grant No. NIH HL21906-01A1, from the National Heart, Lung, and Blood Institute to the Stanford Heart Disease Prevention Program, and by a Grant from the National Interagency Council on Smoking and Health to Cheryl Perry.

ISBN 0-12-565960-1

disease (American Heart Association, 1976). Like many chronic illnesses, a number of environmental factors and behavior patterns are believed to be related to cardiovascular disease. Cigarette smoking, elevated blood pressure, elevated levels of serum cholesterol (especially LDL: low density lipoproteins), and diabetes increase risk for premature cardiovascular disease (Blackburn, 1974; Kannel & McGee, 1979; Kuller, 1976; Pooling Project Research Group, 1978). Type A behavior (coronary-prone behavior pattern) and elevated levels of serum triglyceride share a less certain relationship with cardiovascular disease than the other factors listed but they also are considered to be potentially important. (Blackburn, 1974, 1978). On the other hand, it has been shown that high levels of HDL (high density lipoproteins) decrease the risk of cardiovascular disease (N. E. Miller, 1979).

Specific behavior patterns may be associated with increases or decreases in risk factors. Blood pressure, for example, is possibly influenced by overweight, lack of physical activity, and excessive dietary salt intake (Task Force on Blood Pressure Control, 1977). Possible relationships between transient or chronic stress, Type A behavior, and blood pressure also have been suggested (Shapiro & Surwit, 1976). Increased LDL is presumably related to excess cholesterol and saturated fat, lack of physical activity and fiber in the diet, and overweight. Increased HDL (which is negatively related to cardiovascular disease) presumably is influenced by increases in physical activity and dietary fiber, reductions in dietary saturated fat, and decreases in weight (Blackburn, 1974, 1978).

If cardiovascular risk factors are related to specific behavior patterns, then cardiovascular disease theoretically can be prevented if persons can be helped to (*a*) refrain from smoking; (*b*) maintain ideal weight; (*c*) increase consumption of dietary fiber; (*d*) decrease consumption of dietary cholesterol, saturated fat, salt, and sugar; (*e*) increase aerobic physical activity; (*f*) reduce stress; and (*g*) modify specific coronary-prone behaviors (e.g., time urgency, hostility).

While relationships between cardiovascular disease and the major risk factors (i.e., elevated blood pressure, elevated blood cholesterol, smoking) are well-established, the links between specific behavioral and dietary patterns and these risk factors remain controversial. More at question is the proposition that cardiovascular disease can be reduced by helping persons change their behavior patterns. Several national clinical trials have been designed to test the hypothesis that changes in behavior will lead to modification of the risk factors and reduce morbidity and mortality from cardiovascular disease. These include the Multiple Risk Factor Intervention Trial (1976; MRFIT) and the Stanford Multifactor Risk Reduction Program (Farquhar, 1978).

The degree to which children and adolescents should be encouraged to change common life style patterns remains quite controversial. Some investigators assert that all American youth are at risk and should be helped to change eating, exercise, smoking, and stress-related habits; they view cardiovascular disease as a societal epidemic that can be lessened only through large-scale community intervention programs (Farquhar, Maccoby, Wood, Alexander, Breitrose, Brown, Haskell, McAlister, Meyer, Nash, & Stern, 1977; Maccoby, Farquhar, Wood, & Alexander, 1977). The behavior and risk factor patterns of American youth may be used as evidence for the previous proposition. For example, Huenemann, Hampton, Behnke, Schapiro, and Mitchell (1974), in their studies of high school students in Berkeley, California, reported that males spent 37% of their time asleep, 56% in light and very light activity, 6% in moderate activity, and 1.5% (about 20 minutes per day) in strenuous activity. Girls spent .5% of their time in strenuous activity. Coates, Jeffery, and Slinkard (in press) reported that elementary students spent 60 to 70% of their recess time either sitting or standing. The students were perfectly still most of the time.

The diets of children and adolescents share the same deficits and excesses characteristic of the entire population. Over 40% of the calories eaten are from fat; saturated fat accounts for 15 to 18% of the calories eaten, and dietary cholesterol is well in excess of 300 mg per day (Frank, Voors, Schilling, & Berenson, 1977; Fryer, Lamkin, & Vivian,

1971). In a series of epidemiological studies, a sizeable number of children and adolescents have shown elevations in blood cholesterol (Frerichs, Srinivasan, Webber, & Berenson, 1976; Lauer, Connor, Leaverton, Reiter, & Clarke, 1975).

On the other hand, a large number of investigators and advisory panels have taken a "wait and see" position regarding heart disease prevention efforts among children and adolescents. The Task Force on Blood Pressure Control (1977), for example, followed a traditional "risk factor" approach in recommending screenings and treatment for children showing persistently elevated blood pressures and blood lipids.

Both of the perspectives just described suggest the need to study patterns of risk factors, physiology, and behavior in young persons so that (*a*) etiologies and natural histories can be documented to suggest optimal times for interventions; (*b*) early interventions can be designed to promote knowledge, behaviors, and attitudes that might be maintained throughout life; and (*c*) treatment resources can be utilized effectively.

Prevalence and Natural History of Cardiovascular Risk Factors in Youth

Elevated Blood Pressure

Prevalence Estimates of the prevalence of hypertension vary widely among studies. Rates ranging from 0.9% (National Center for Health Statistics, 1973) to 36% (Kotchen, Kotchen, Schwertman, & Kuller, 1974) have been reported (cf. Kilcoyne, 1975). Important methodological problems need to be addressed in these epidemiological studies. Reported prevalence rates can be affected by many factors: The size of the sample employed (smaller samples might increase estimates of prevalence), the representativeness of the sample (e.g., patient population versus samples drawn at random), the criterion used to define elevated blood pressure (e.g., an absolute or percentile criterion), and the methods used for measuring blood pressure (e.g., location, position, and size of pressure cuff, and which of the Korotkoff sounds are used to define diastolic blood pressure). The number of times blood pressure is assessed, the interval between measurements, and the ages of the sample members can also influence prevalence estimates (Kilcoyne, 1975; Task Force on Blood Pressure Control, 1977). Table 11.1 compares data from the Bogalusa Heart Study (Voors, Foster, Frerichs, Webber, & Berenson, 1976), the Muscatine, Iowa Study (Lauer *et al.,* 1975), the Task Force on Blood Pressure Control (1977), the National Center for Health Statistics (1973, 1977), and the Chicago Study (Miller & Shekelle, 1976). In the Bogalusa Study, blood pressures were recorded at the end of a 90- to 120-min screening examination. Children were escorted to a quiet screened-off corner of the room and blood pressures were taken independently by three different observers using two types of instruments. The standards reported in the Task Force Report rely on data from three separate studies (Muscatine, Rochester, and Miami). All persons were measured once using a Mercury sphygmomanometer with standard cuff. In the Chicago Study, participants lay quietly on a cot for 5 to 10 minutes after which a single blood pressure was obtained using a standard sphygmomanometer.

Differences in Table 11.1 might be attributable to location, sampling variation, racial or socioeconomic class characteristics, or measurement procedures. There is obviously a need to standardize the measurement of blood pressures so that studies are comparable and practitioners have close guidelines on how to determine relative risk.

Establishing precise prevalence rates of hypertension among young persons is less important than documenting the range and extent to which their blood pressures might be elevated. The prevalence data cited provides a conservative estimate of the number of young persons needing assistance in managing blood pressure. Treatment should be focused not only on those with persistent extreme elevations but on all young persons in the upper ranges of blood pressure. There is not a critical threshold or dividing line of blood pressure than can be used to predict morbidity and mortality. People are not at risk on one side of a

Table 11.1
Reported Blood Pressures from Different Studies

		Age					
		5		10		15	
		Systolic	Diastolic	Systolic	Diastolic	Systolic	Diastolic
Bogalusa (Voors *et al.* 1976)	M	97.6	62.8	98.6	61.3	108.8	67.6
Muscatine	M	94.4	63.1	109.3	72.8	122.3	78.4
(Lauer *et al.* 1975)	F	91.8	61.3	108.6	72.3	116.3	78.3
Miami	M	99.8	63.9	—	—	—	—
(Task Force Report, 1977)	F	97.3	64.8	—	—	—	—
Mayo	M	—	—	113.5	72.0	125.4	72.3
(Task Force Report, 1977)	F	—	—	114.3	71.8	121.3	72.3
Chicago[a]	M	—	—	—	—	126.1	68.1
(Miller & Shekelle 1976)	F	—	—	—	—	119.7	68.1
National Health[b] Survey	M	105.5[c]	65.0	110.9	66.8	133.8	75.8
(1973, 1977)	F	105.7	65.3	113.3	68.3	127.9	75.3

[a] Data given for white males and females only; subjects include 15- and 16-year-old students.
[b] White subjects only.
[c] 6-year-olds.

specific point and free from risk on the other side (Borhani, 1975; Kannel, Castelli, McNamara, & Sorlie, 1969). Blood pressure is a continuous variable when it is considered as a risk of morbidity and mortality for cardiovascular disease.

Natural History Persons who are hypertensive in college tend to remain hypertensive (Diehl & Hesdorffer, 1933; Perera, 1950). In studying chronic disease in former college students, Paffenbarger, Thoren, and Wing (1968) studied precursors to hypertension in 671 (8.7%) of 7,685 men who attended the University of Pennsylvania. The men averaged 19 years of age when the college data were taken. The average age of doctor-diagnosed hypertension was 36 years, and the average age of the men at questionnaire response was 46 years. Six factors at college age predicted hypertension in later life (listed in order of strength of relationship): (*a*) higher blood pressure; (*b*) faster pulse rate; (*c*) greater ponderosity; (*d*) history of parental hypertension; (*e*) firstborn status, and (*f*) less participation in sports. Incidence of elevated blood pressure (greater than 130/80) in college was 2.5 times greater for hypertensive adults than for the rest of the sample. Combinations of factors, of course, increased relative risk.

Elevation of blood pressure (regardless of whether or not a person is classified as hypertensive) in late adolescence increases relative risk of sustained hypertension later in life and the complications that follow. At what age do blood pressures become predictive? At what point might it be possible to identify those potentially at risk and teach them strategies for controlling their blood pressures?

Clinical studies suggest that adolescents identified as hypertensive tend to remain hypertensive and are at greater risk for health problems than their normotensive peers. Heyden, Bartel, Hanes, and McDonough (1969) first identified 47 adolescents (15–25 years old, greater than 140 and/or 90 mmHG) from a total screening sample of 435 persons. Thirty were followed seven years later: 2 died from cerebral hemorrhage, 1 suffered from hypertensive vascular disease, 15 suffered from sustained hypertension, and 12 were normotensive. Increase in weight over the seven years was the only decisive factor in determining who was to become hypertensive. Londe, Bourgoigne, Robson, and Goldring (1971) first identified 74 hypertensive children (systolic and/or diastolic greater than the ninetieth percentile) 4–18 years of age. Sixty-five percent ($N = 46$) remained hypertensive when followed at intervals of 3 to 8 years.

There have been fewer large-scale longitudinal studies; the evidence remains supportive of the proposition that "tracking" occurs (cf. Task Force on Blood Pressure Control, 1977). Clarke, Schrott, Leaverton, Connor, and Lauer (1978) followed 820 subjects in the Muscatine Study for 6 years. Six-year correlations for systolic and diastolic blood pressure were .30 and .18, respectively.

Blood pressure readings among young persons are more labile than blood pressures among adults. It has been reported that children and adolescents identified as hypertensive at one reading are quite likely to fall into the arbitrary normotensive range at a second reading (Kilcoyne, 1975; Miller & Shekelle, 1976). Valkenburg, Groustra, Klein, VanLaar, and Werdmuller (1977) first screened subjects, selected those in various risk categories, performed a rescreening, and then followed the subjects one year later. The data are presented in Table 11.2. Regression toward the mean occurred from screening to rescreening within the group described by the authors as "pathological"; the borderline group, however, tended to retain their high status. The three-way classification appeared remarkably stable from rescreening to evaluations one year later among all groups.

Evidence of tracking will be found only when extraneous sources of variability are well controlled and subjects are well adapted to blood pressure recording. Insel and Chadwick (in press) estimated coefficients of *intra*subject variability (percent of variance in a single blood pressure accounted for by variation within persons). In a study of 7,840 school children, the coefficients averaged 70% for diastolic blood pressure and 50% for systolic blood pressure. It may be necessary to obtain multiple and repeated measures in adolescents before asserting that average blood pressure has been estimated accurately. A stable index is necessary to provide accurate predictions of later blood pressure. It may be that accurate determinations for this population can be made only with 24-hour continuous monitoring.

The Bogalusa study provides an excellent example of the control of extraneous sources of variability upon blood pressure recording. Voors, Webber, and Berenson (1979) reexamined 1101 of their cohort after 1 year. Observations from a group of 35 fifth-graders examined monthly for 8 months were used to estimate intrasubject variability. This estimate was used to reduce to zero in a statistical adjustment the regression toward the mean of the blood pressure of the examined children. In a multiple regression analysis, the previous year's blood pressure contributed partial correlation coefficients of .60 to .70. This indicates a high degree of tracking when the sources of variability are controlled.

Smoking

Prevalence Some encouraging, but also discouraging, shifts in smoking rates have occurred among young persons in recent years. Table 11.3 presents data on smoking prevalence from nationwide surveys performed for the National Clearing House for Smoking and Health and the National Institute of Education. The percentage of regular smokers (11.7%) in 1979 compared favorably with the 15.6% prevalence reported in 1974. In every age category, reported smoking among males declined (4.2 to 3.2 in the 12–14 age group; 18.1 to 13.5 in the 15–16 age group; 31.0 to 19.3 in the 17–18 age group). Females, however, did not show similar declines in the 12–14 and 17–18 age ranges.

Natural History The natural history of smoking is not well-documented, and results obtained in earlier surveys may not generalize because of changes in public attitudes and smoking rates among adults. Smoking rates among teenagers escalate sharply beginning in junior high school and continue to rise until early adulthood. The National Survey on Drug Abuse (Abelson, Fishburne, & Cisin, 1977) reported the following percentages of current regular smokers in 1977: 12–13 years,

Table 11.2
Percent of Males in Each Classification Group Whose Systolic Blood Pressure Increased, Decreased or Stayed the Same from Screening to Rescreening and to One-Year Follow-Up

Initial classification		Screening-rescreening (percent)	Screening-1 year (percent)	Rescreening-1 year (percent)
Pathological[a]	Decrease	53	67	29
N=41	Same	46	33	59
	Increase	2	0	12
Borderline[b]	Decrease	34	32	11
N=77	Same	64	66	80
	Increase	2	2	9
Control	Decrease	19	23	5
N=71	Same	79	73	84
	Increase	2	5	11

Note. Adapted from "Natural History of Blood Pressure and Cholesterol in Children 5-19 Years of Age, Selected for these Risk Factors on a Statistical Basis from an Open Population Sample" by H.A. Valkenburg, F.N. Groustra, F. Klein, A. Van Larr, and S.I. Werdmuller, *Atherosclerosis and the Child,* edited by J.G.A.V. Hautvast and H.A. Valkenburg. Rotterdam: Erasmus University, 1972.
[a] $\geqslant$ 140/90.
[b] 5-9 yr S $\geqslant$ 125; D $\geqslant$ 80.
10-14 yr S $\geqslant$ 130; D $\geqslant$ 80.
15-19 yr S $\geqslant$ 140; D $\geqslant$ 85.

10%; 14-15 years, 22%; 16-17 years, 35%; 18-25 years, 44%; 26-34 years, 45%; 35+ years, 36%.

Many adolescents experiment with smoking and do not become habitual smokers, and many become habitual smokers only to drop the habit later. Unfortunately, definitive prospective studies charting the progress of smoking and critical associated variables have not been performed. The few longitudinal studies completed do provide some insight into several factors associated with continued or terminated smoking in adolescents.

I. M. Newman (1970, 1971) conducted longitudinal studies over a two-year period and determined that smoking status was related to peer group membership and the degree to which young persons felt they were meeting parents' and schools' expectations. Changes in smoking status across the two years of the study appeared related to changes in the peer group or to school achievement. Two prospective studies, Laoye, Creswell, and Stone, (1972) and Silber (1968), reported that the best predictor of future smoking was whether or not persons said they would continue to smoke. Downey and O'Rourke (1978) found, in a group of seventh graders who were followed until ninth grade, that never-smokers who remained never-smokers initially exhibited more unfavorable attitudes and beliefs toward smoking than persons who became smokers. In summary, determinants of the natural history of smoking appear to be initial attitudes, peer group membership, and predictions about personal behavior. Undoubtedly, these variables interact in complex ways. Needed are definitive studies to chart the progress of individuals' smoking behavior and the factors related to their progress throughout long periods of time.

Blood Lipids

Prevalence Numerous early reports documented serum cholesterol and triglyceride levels in newborns, infants, and children (Dyerberg & Hjorne, 1973; Fallot, Tsang, & Glueck, 1974; Frederickson & Breslow, 1973; Hames & Greenberg, 1961; Stark, 1971). The marked differences in observed lipid levels reported in the different studies, were attributed partly to methodological differences among analyses. The Lipid Research Centers, in collaboration with the Center for Disease Control, have standardized the techniques and laid the foundation for definitive epidemiological studies. Valuable information on the distribution of serum

Table 11.3
Estimated Prevalence of Current Regular Cigarette Smoking: Ages 12–18, United States, 1968–1979

Age group	Sex	*1968* Percent	*1974* Percent	*1979* Percent
12–14	Male	2.9	4.2	3.2
	Female	0.6	4.9	4.3
15–16	Male	17.0	18.1	13.5
	Female	9.6	20.2	11.8
17–18	Male	30.2	31.0	19.3
	Female	18.6	25.9	26.2
12–18	Male	14.7	15.8	10.7[a]
	Female	8.4	15.3	12.7[a]
	Both Sexes	11.5	15.6	11.7

Source. Nationwide teenage smoking surveys performed for National Clearinghouse for Smoking and Health (1968, 1974) and National Institute of Education (1979). (Adapted from Green, 1980.)
Note. Current regular smokers include those who smoke at least weekly. In 1979, approximately 90% of current regular smokers used cigarettes on a daily basis.
[a] This reports a total estimated prevalence of 1.6 million males and 1.7 million females or a total of 3.3 million persons.

lipid and lipoprotein levels in children is now being provided by pediatric populations in Bogalusa, Louisiana (Frerichs *et al.*, 1976), Muscatine, Iowa (Lauer *et al.*, 1975), and Rochester, Minnesota (Task Force on Blood Pressure Control, 1977).

Table 11.4 presents some data fom the Bogalusa investigation demonstrating the range of average values for children in the study. Several trends are noteworthy. First, there is a dramatic increase in serum lipid and lipoprotein levels during the first years of life. Both genetic and environmental factors probably are influential, and the relative contributions of each need to be examined. It may be that early intervention will be quite influential in preventing later elevated levels of serum cholesterol.

The Bogalusa study showed a relatively small number of children exceeding the normal range of cholesterol and therefore considered at risk according to conventional definition. Only 0.5% of black and white children exceeded the upper LDL cholesterol limit of 170 mg/100 ml. Only 1.7% of black and 4.7% of white children showed elevated

Table 11.4
Serum Lipid and Lipoprotein Cholesterol Levels In Children 0–14 Years in the Bogalusa Study[a]

	Total cholesterol	Triglycerides	LDL	VLDL	HDL
	mean (P5 to P95)[b]	mean (P5 to P95)	mean (P5 to P95)	mean (P5 to P95)	mean (P5 to P95)[c]
Newborns	[a]	—	—	—	—
(cord blood)	68 (42–103)	34 (14–84)	29 (17–50)	2 (1–2)	35 (13–60)
Infants					
6 mo.	132 (89–185)	89 (45–169)	73 (40–111)	9 (1–25)	51 (23–88)
12 mo.	145 (99–193)	73 (42–158)	81 (49–121)	7 (2–25)	51 (22–81)
Children					
2–14 yr.	162 (122–213)	60 (57–130)	87 (57–130)	6 (1–21)	67 (32–202)

[a] Data from Srinivasan, Frerichs, and Berenson (1978).

VLDL cholesterol (> 25 mg/100 ml). Combined hyperproteinemia was seen in only .1% of black and .1% of white children.

In the Muscatine Study (Lauer *et al.*, 1975), conciderably greater numbers of school children fell into the "risk" ranges. Of 4829 school children examined, 24% had levels of total serum cholesterol greater than or equal to 200 mg/dl; 9% were greater than or equal to 220 mg/dl; 3% were greater than 240 mg/dl; and 1% were greater than 260 mg/dl.

Examining children at the upper range of the distribution ignores the possibility that the total population may be at risk because *average* levels are high. Golubjatnikov, Paskey, and Inhorn (1972) studied total serum cholesterol levels in a random sample of 200 Mexican and 328 Wisconsin school children. The mean serum cholesterol level of the 5 to 14-year-old Mexicans was 99.9 mg/100 ml. By contrast, the mean cholesterol level of Wisconsin pupils was almost twice as high (186.5 mg/100 ml). Savage, Hammon, Bartha, Dippe, Miller, and Bennet (1976) compared serum cholesterol levels in American caucasian and Indian (Pima) children and adolescents. Cholesterol levels at birth were similar for both groups, but levels in Pimas from 5 to 16 years of age (M = 148 mg/100 ml) were 15–30 mg/100 ml lower than those among the white populations. Cholesterol levels in adult Pimas (190 mg/100 ml) were up to 50–60 mg/100 ml lower than those in American whites.

Natural History In four cross-sectional screens, 8,090 school children have been studied in the Muscatine Study. Of these, 320 have been followed for a 6-year period. A 6-year correlation of .61 was found for cholesterol and a 4-year correlation for fasting triglyceride was .40 (Clarke *et al.*, 1978). A significant population of children with initially high values demonstrated consistently high values throughout the study period. Elevated levels of cholesterol tended to persist despite fluctuations with age; thus, early elevations appear to place a person at risk for elevations later in childhood and adolescence. Clearly, prospective studies are needed to determine the degree to which early elevations persist into adulthood and place persons at increased risk for cardiovascular disease later in life.

Srinivasan, Frerichs, Webber, and Berenson (1976) described the progression of age of various lipoprotein fractions using cross-sectional data. Girls tended to have higher VLDL and LDL concentrations than boys. VLDL showed a progressive increase with age, LDL decreased with age, and HDL remained relatively unchanged. Barclay (1972) and Nichols (1969), however, showed that adult males have higher levels of LDL and VLDL and lower levels of HDL than females; the increase in VLDL with age was more pronounced in males than in females.

Lee (1967) observed distinct patterns of change in observing individual children longitudinally. The total serum cholesterol of 35 boys and 20 girls was determined at six-month intervals over a period of 10 years. Noteworthy was a finding that dramatic increases in total cholesterol were correlated with the period of rapid adolescent growth among males.

These findings suggest that biochemical changes occur during adolescence and early adulthood which may increase or decrease persons' risk of cardiovascular disease. Some of the changes are sex-linked and may not be true of all persons in the population. However, clear-cut patterns of age- and sex-dependent changes in serum lipoprotein concentrations might not be apparent in cross-sectional studies because of wide individual differences in degree and rate of sexual development. It may be critical to conduct longitudinal studies to determine patterns of change and behavioral factors associated with those patterns. That information may be central in determining where, when, and how to intervene in risk-enhancing trends.

Variables Associated with Major Risk Factors in Children[1]

In this section, we attempt to document current knowledge about environmental and psychosocial variables associated with increases or decreases in

[1]There is a genetic contribution to each of the risk factors, but heredity of course, does not account for all of the variance. In addition to determining genetic and environmental contribution for most risk factors in children, studies are also needed to determine the environments necessary to

major risk factors for children. We seek to specify targets for change that might be used in risk reduction programs based on behavior change.

Obesity

The status of obesity as a risk factor for cardiovascular disease remains controversial (cf. Mann, 1977). The investigators in the Framingham study concluded that overweight made an important and independent contribution to risk of coronary heart disease (Gordon & Kannel, 1973). On the basis of the Seven Countries' study, Keys (1970) concluded that overweight was a modest contributor to coronary heart disease, principally because of its association with blood pressure and serum cholesterol. Weight reduction, however, can be effective in reducing blood pressure, glucose intolerance, and serum lipids.

Obesity contributes to increases in the risk factors among children and adolescents. Decreases in obesity are correlated with reductions in risk factors.

Blood Pressure The prevalence of overweight and obesity is higher among children and adolescents classified as hypertensive than those classified as normotensive. Londe *et al.* (1971) studied 74 hypertensive children aged 4–18 years from a general practice. The prevalence of obesity was higher in hypertensive (53%) than in normotensive controls (14%). Heyden *et al.* (1969) first identified 47 adolescents (15–25 years old, systolic and/or diastolic blood pressure greater than 140 and/or 90 mmHg, respectively) from a total screening sample of 435 persons. Thirty were followed 7 years later; 2 had died from cerebral hemorrhage, 1 suffered from hypertensive vascular disease, 15 suffered from sustained hypertension, and 12 were normotensive. Increased weight was the only decisive factor in determining who was susceptible for the development of sustained hypertension. Those who developed sustained hypertension at the 7-year follow-up had gained weight while those who became normotensive had not. Lauer, Clarke, and Rames (1978) reported data on 1953 children whose blood pressures were measured on three occasions in a large epidemiological survey. They later reexamined 13% of the students with pressures above 140/90 mmHg. One percent of the total sample retested above this level. Of this group, 50% were extremely obese. Among the six hypertensives who were lean, 50% were found to have hypertension secondary to kidney disorders or use of birth control pills.

Blood pressures are higher among samples of obese children and adolescents than among samples of normal weight children and adolescents. In an investigation of 320 male high school students, de Castro, Biesbroeck, Erickson, Farrell, Leong, Murphy, and Green (1976) found that the obese (at least 20 pounds above mean weight for height) had average blood pressures of 124/80 mmHg while the nonobese had average blood pressures of 116/73 mmHg. Court, Hill, Dunlop, and Boulton (1974) studied 109 obese persons (1.1–17.8 years of age) who ranged from 3 to 113% overweight. The correlation between measures of subscapular skinfold and blood pressures were robust (systolic: males = .88, females = .78; diastolic: males = .80, females: = .70). Coates, Jeffery, Slinkard, Killen, and Danaher (in press) reported significant relationships between systolic blood pressure and weight ($r = .58$) and percent overweight ($r = .50$) in 36 overweight adolescents (13–17 years of age; 15–100% overweight for sex, age, and height). These same relationships were found before and after the students participated in a weight loss program.

These correlations between blood pressure and weight hold in black and white children and across the entire range of blood pressure and age groups (Dube, Kapoor, Rotner, & Tunick, 1975; Holland & Beresford, 1975; Miller & Shekelle, 1976; Stine, Hepner, & Greenstreet, 1975; Voors *et al.*, 1979). Lauer *et al.* (1975) reported that triceps skinfold correlated significantly with systolic (r

potentiate genetic capabilities in specific individuals. We document here only the relationships between known variables and risk factors. In most cases, relatively small proportions of the variance of risk factors are accounted for by the variables that have been studied. There is especially a need to examine relationships between ongoing behavioral and cognitive variables such as stress and anger and other risk factors. We also suggest that typical epidemiological methods where large groups of persons are studied at one or few points in time may not be sensitive to these processes. Alternatives such as time-series analyses may be required.

= .39) and diastolic blood pressure (r = .36). Students in the upper decile of relative weight were overrepresented in the upper end of the blood pressure distribution: 28.6% had systolic blood pressures greater than the ninetieth percentile. Voors *et al.* (1979) reported that bivariate Pearson correlation coefficients between body weight and systolic/diastolic blood pressures were .54/.48, in 3,524 children 5–14 years of age in Bogalusa, Louisiana. Ponderosity index consistently entered in a stepwise multiple regression equation in predicting to systolic and diastolic blood pressure among all age groups.

Blood Lipids The correlations between weight, relative weight, or measures of body fat with serum cholesterol and triglyceride concentration are weaker among children and adolescents relative to those usually found among adults. Clarke *et al.* (1978) studied 885 children 12–18 years old. Among females, weight was negatively correlated with total cholesterol (r = −.318) and triceps skinfold was negatively correlated with triglyceride concentrations (r = −.308) among 16-year-olds only. A greater number of significant relationships were found among males. Among 17-year-olds, weight was correlated with cholesterol (r = .249) and triglycerides (r = .281). Triceps skinfolds and cholesterol were correlated among 13-year-olds (r = .347) and 17-year-olds (r = .381). Correlations among triceps skinfold and triglycerides were .407 among 15-year-olds and .324 among 17-year-olds. Lauer *et al.* (1975) reported significant but modest correlations between triceps skinfolds and cholesterol (r = .17) and triceps skinfold and triglycerides (r = .25). Florey, Uppal, and Lowy (1976) found no relationship between weight and cholesterol in 2,388 school children 9–12 years old.

These data do not support the hypothesis that relative weight is related strongly in a linear function to total serum cholesterol concentration. However, the obese do tend to be overrepresented in the upper part of the distribution of cholesterol values. In the Muscatine study, Lauer *et al.* (1975) reported that 17.8% of those whose skinfold thicknesses exceeded the ninetieth percentile were at or above the ninetieth percentile for triglyceride. Clarke *et al.* (1978) reported that 20% of the obese students had cholesterol concentrations greater than 200 mg/100 ml as compared to 11% and 10% of medium and lean students respectively.

Coates *et al.* (in press) measured relationships between weight and percent overweight and total serum cholesterol, LDL cholesterol, HDL cholesterol, and serum triglycerides in 36 adolescents who were 9 to 100% overweight. Correlations between weight and total cholesterol (r = .29) and triglycerides (r = .29) were modest. By contrast, correlations between weight and HDL cholesterol were robust (r = −.58). It may be that strong relationships between weight and cholesterol exist only for the overweight adolescent. On the other hand, overweight may be marginally related to total cholesterol but may exert its influence in risk for cardiovascular disease by decreasing concentrations of HDL cholesterol. These relationships among overweight and lipoprotein fractions deserve study in larger epidemiological studies using children across the full range of relative weight.

The Efficacy of Weight Loss Weight loss can promote positive reductions in cardiovascular risk factors among children and adolescents. Coates *et al.* (Note 1) reported significant correlations between pounds lost and changes in (*a*) systolic blood pressure (r = .31); (*b*) HDL cholesterol (r = .36); and (*c*) triglycerides (r = −.70). Correlations between pounds lost and changes in LDL cholesterol and diastolic blood pressure were not significant. These data suggest that weight loss may be a critical objective in attempts to modify important cardiovascular risk factors.

Family

Blood Pressure Risk factors and risk factor behaviors are correlated among family members; both genetic and behavioral influences are probably operative. Holland and Beresford (1975) studied 501 families selected at random but stratified by family size and social class. The major determinants of blood pressures in children 5–8 years of age were parental weight and blood pressure. Children's blood pressures also were highly correlated with those of their siblings. Kass, Zinner,

Margolius, Yhu, Rosner, and Donner (1975) extended these findings downward to a sample ranging from 2 to 14 years of age. They also studied the sample 4 years later and found familial aggregations that again were significant. Langford and Watson (1973) reported similar correlations for diastolic blood pressure among full sibs aged 14–20 (r = .379) and among half sibs (r = .354). This sample, however, was composed entirely of black females.

Feinleib, Garrison, Borhani, Rosenman, and Christian (1975) estimated that as much as 60% of variance in blood pressure may be due to genetic factors. Correlations among monozygous twins' (N = 249) blood pressures (.55/.58) were higher than the correlations found among dizygous twins (N = 264; .25/.27). Using data from other studies to show the generally lower correlation among siblings, Feinleib *et al.* (1975) estimated relative genetic and environmental contributions to blood pressure using a simple additive model.

Feinleib *et al.*'s data must be interpreted cautiously because, as the investigators pointed out, their results were derived from studying persons in a relatively homogeneous environment. Genetic variance might have been inflated because environmental variance had been suppressed. Second, concordance among spouses has been reported. Sackett (1975) reviewed several studies and concluded that while spouse concordance does exist, the process of concordance remains to be elucidated. He cautiously suggested that selection, rather than a shared environment, is more adequate in explaining this phenomenon. Once again, however, the data concerning spouse concordance are far from clear.

Weinberg, Shear, Avet, Frerichs, and Fox (1979) used path analysis to separate familial aggregation into genetic and environmental influences. Their data was produced by full siblings and half siblings, aged 2–18 years, from the Bogalusa study. The statistically significant aggregations they found could be explained equally well by either genetic or environmental influences except in two cases: systolic blood pressure in the total (black and white) sample which required heritability and diastolic blood pressure in the white sample, which required an environmental influence.

In summary, there is strong evidence that children of hypertensive parents are at increased risk for elevated blood pressures. The genetic contribution to risk appears important but the influence of the shared familial macroenvironment and microenvironment has yet to be elucidated fully. Nonetheless, the aggregations suggest that family intervention is warranted regardless of whether the contribution is primarily genetic or environmental. Salutary behaviors may assist the entire family if the entire family adheres to their use (see pp. 186–188).

Tobacco Smoking is clearly a familial phenomenon. In study after study, both parent and sibling smoking are correlates of adolescent smoking (Bewley & Bland, 1977; Creswell, Hoffman, & Stone, 1970; Horn, Courts, Taylor, & Solomon, 1959; Kelson, Pullella, & Otterland, 1975; U.S. Department of Health, Education, and Welfare, 1972, 1976). These data will be discussed in more detail on page 169.

Overweight Garn and Clarke (1975) analyzed data from the Ten-State Nutrition Survey to explore intrafamilial correlations of obesity. Parent–child fatness correlations approximated .25. A second analysis was completed by dividing parents and children into three categories: lean (triceps skinfold below P_{15}), medium (triceps skinfold between P_{16} and P_{84}), and obese (triceps skinfold above P_{85}). Children of the obese were significantly fatter at all ages than children of the lean. Interestingly, children of lean parents did not show the normal increases in fatness during adolescence. Among males, in fact, there was a decline in relative fat in the children of the lean.

Siblings also were quite similar. Nearly 30,000 sibling pairs were surveyed in the Ten-State Project. The correlations between siblings was .37 for triceps skinfold and .35 for subscapular skinfold. Coates, Jefferey, and Wing (1978) replicated these familial weight relationships in their nonclinical community sample. The correlation between mothers' and fathers' weights (r = .17) and percent overweight (r = .22) were not significant but were smaller in magnitude than those reported by Garn, Cole, and Bailey (1976). Children's percent overweight did not correlate significantly with parents' percent overweight, but the first siblings' percent overweight was positively correlated (r = .63) with that of the parents.

Although a genetic explanation seems an obvious hypothesis, two analyses suggest that environmental factors are quite important. First, spouses tend to be similar in triceps (r = .25) and subscapular fatfold (r = .21). When husbands are divided into the three fatness categories, their wives progress in fatness according to the fatness levels of their husbands. A similar relationship holds for husbands of lean, medium, and obese wives. These relationships could be due, of course, to spouse selection. Second, adopted children also resemble their foster parents in relative fatness. Garn, Cole, and Bailey (1976) analyzed data from 147 pairings of adopted children and parents from the Tecumseh project. The adopted children of lean parents were lean and the adopted children of obese parents were obese. The fatness progression among children was nearly stepwise as various parental fatness combinations (lean-lean, lean-medium, etc.) were examined. Moreover, fat pet owners tend to have fat dogs (Mason, 1970). Again, selection rather than other variables could be operative. Longitudinal research is needed to separate the alternative explanations.

Other Factors

Blood Pressure Sex, race, and socioeconomic class are related to increases in blood pressures among young persons. Differences between sexes in average blood pressures presumably emerge in late adolescence. The Task Force on Blood Pressure Control (1977) reported no blood pressure differences between males and females from 2 to 14 years of age. After the age of 14, however, average blood pressures and the prevalence of hypertension among males increased above the levels reported for females. Voors *et al.* (1976) also found quite similar pressures among males and females aged 1-15 years. Other studies with older adolescents have reported characteristic sexual differences both among blacks (Dube *et al.*, 1975; Kilcoyne, 1975) and whites (Kotchen *et al.*, 1974; Miller & Shekelle, 1976).

Average blood pressure readings for black males and black females exceed those found in white males and females; the prevalence of hypertension in black males is reportedly twice that in white males and is associated with higher morbidity and mortality (Stamler, Stamler, Riedlinger, Algera, & Roberts, 1976). Voors *et al.* (1976) found that black children had significantly higher blood pressures than white children. This difference became obvious beginning at age 10. The National Health Examination Survey (National Center for Health Statistics, 1973, 1977) also reported small but consistent differences in mean diastolic pressures between black and white children aged 5-11 years.

Lower socioeconomic class may be associated with elevated blood pressure. Langford, Watson, and Douglas (1968), in a study of 5,000 black students and 5,500 white students, reported higher blood pressures in rural than in city students, and an inverse relationship between socioeconomic status and blood pressure among urban students. The usual black-white blood pressure differences were abolished when black upper income girls were compared with rural whites, and significantly reversed in males when the same comparison was made. Kotchen *et al.* (1974) replicated these results among black students. Inner city blacks had higher blood pressures than blacks attending a racially integrated school in a middle class residential area. Among blacks, higher blood pressures were found in children whose parents worked as laborers than in children of parents in professional occupations.

Studies of the salt-hypertension hypothesis among children and adolescents have been sparse. Langford and Watson (1973) selected 100 black female sibling pairs for study. Diastolic blood pressures were taken three times per day over 8 days in the subjects' homes. Each of the girls also collected a 24-hour urine specimen for 6 consecutive days. The Na/Ca ratio was lower (M = 20.4) among those with lower pressures (less than 105 mmHg systolic) than among those with higher pressures (M = 34.4, greater than 125 mmHg systolic). However, blood pressures were not correlated with sodium excretion or Na/Ca ratio. Salt may contribute to blood pressure but not according to a direct linear function. Langford and Watson (1975) studied 108 black girls 19-21 years of age using blood pressures collected over 8 days and urine samples over 6 days. One significant correlation emerged; the correlation between diastolic blood pressure and Na/K ratio was .372. The authors concluded that in the salt sensitive portion of the population, blood pressure may be a direct function of salt intake and an indirect function of potassium and perhaps calcium intake.

While the role of salt in the genesis and maintenance of elevated blood pressure among children and adolescents remains to be elucidated, clinical studies with adults support the utility of reducing and controlling mild hypertension by restricting sodium intake (Corcoran, Taylor, & Page, 1951; Dole, Dahl, Cotzias, Eder, & Krebs, 1950). The relative efficacy of many antihypertensive medications parallels the potency of these drugs in promoting sustained sodium depletion. Several recent clinical studies have supported the utility of reducing mild hypertension by restricting sodium intake (Morgan, Adam, Gillies, Wilson, Morgan & Carney, 1978). This proposition has not been tested with young persons; if the proposition eventually is confirmed, salt restriction might provide a useful and convenient treatment for children and adolescents.

While the hypotensive efficacy of relaxation therapies seem promising (Agras & Jacob, 1979), the role of environmental or psychological stress in the genesis and maintenance of hypertension among young persons remains controversial. The hypothesis that stress contributes to hypertension deserves study, however, because of the need to provide a more complete account of elevated blood pressure. Voors *et al.* (1976) were able to account for 32 to 40% of the variance in blood pressure among young persons using the combinations of variables studied typically in epidemiologic surveys (height, ponderosity, maturation, hemoglobin, sex, race, and age). Clearly there is a need to study and define other factors related to and responsible for the maintenance and treatment of elevated blood pressures among young persons.

Tobacco Use Five large-scale studies have yielded fairly consistent data about the factors that differentiate adolescents who report smoking from those who report that they do not smoke. The results are summarized in Table 11.5. Smoking is strongly associated with (*a*) parent smoking; (*b*) peer smoking; (*c*) social precocity; (*d*) scholastic achievement; (*e*) educational aspirations; and (*f*) extracurricular pursuits.

Two recent studies have identified additional factors related to adolescent smoking. The National Cancer Institute and the American Cancer Society (1977) interviewed 260 teenage females and 246 teenage males in their homes using a detailed and lengthy questionnaire. This study confirmed previous research and suggested that the presence of school smoking areas, use of alcohol and other drugs, rebellious behavior, and lack of self-confidence also were positively related to smoking.

All of the studies described above presented correlational data on factors related to smoking; these studies did not prospectively identify early factors that might be related to later smoking. Banks, Bewley, Bland, Dean, and Pollard (1978), however, reported the first year results of a 5-year longitudinal study of 6,330 adolescents 11–16 years of age. Boys were more likely to smoke if their fathers smoked and girls were more likely to smoke if their mothers smoked. Irrespective of parental smoking, persons were quite likely to smoke if siblings smoked. Other factors related to smoking were social precociousness, having a part-time job or more money to spend, socializing with friends in the evening, and truancy from school.

Additional theory-based longitudinal studies are needed to parcel out predictors of later smoking. These kinds of data are essential both for understanding the phenomenon and also for making wise judgment about the most economical allocation of resources for developing effective remedies.

Blood Lipids Black children have greater total serum cholesterol and lower triglyceride levels than do white children (Frerichs *et al.*, 1976). Between the ages of 5 and 14 years, black children, relative to whites, have 5% greater levels of total cholesterol, 14% greater levels of HDL cholesterol, approximately equal levels of LDL cholesterol, and 18% lower levels of VLDL cholesterol (Srinivasan *et al.*, 1976). The greater HDL cholesterol level in blacks accounts for the racial difference observed in total cholesterol. Thus, if HDL is indeed protective, blacks may have a metabolic protective edge for risk of cardiovascular disease as early as 4–5 years of age.

There is general agreement that the diet of American children is high in fat and cholesterol compared to levels in other population groups that have less coronary artery disease later in life (Fryer, Lamkin, & Vivian, 1971). However, relations between cholesterol and diet have not been found in studies of adults (Keys, 1970). The Bogalusa group (Frank, Berenson, & Webber, 1978) studied 185 children from their sample using a 24-hour dietary recall method. The mean caloric intake was 2,141 calories, with 13% derived from protein, 49% from carbohydrates, and 38% from fats. Interestingly, 34% of total calories came from snacks, and sucrose constituted 18% of total calories. About 20% of dietary cholesterol also came from snacks. The correlation between dietary and blood cholesterol was .17; diet explained only 3% of the variance of total cholesterol. However, when children were classified according to serum cholesterol level (below the twenty-fifth percentile, between the twenty-fifth and seventy-fifth

Table 11.5
Summary of Findings From Studies of Correlates of Smoking Among Youth

	Study					
Variables	Horn *et al.* (1959)	Creswell *et al.* (1970)	Kelson *et al.* (1975)	USDHEW (1972)	USDHEW (1976)	Other studies showing same relationships
1. Urban		+			+	
2. School system	+				+	
3. Parent smoking	+	+	+	+	+	Bewley, Bland, & Harris (1974); Cartwright & Thompson (1969); McKennel (1969); Merki, Creswell, Stone, Huffman, & Newman (1968); Palmer (1970); Windsor (1972); Wohlford (1970)
4. Sibling smoking				+		Bewley *et al.* (1974); Bewley & Bland (1977); Kahn & Edwards (1970); Mausner & Mischler (1967); Silber (1968); Windsor (1972)
5. Peer smoking				+	+	Bewley *et al.* (1974); Bewley & Bland (1977); Kahn & Edwards (1970); Mausner & Mischler (1967); Palmer (1970)
6. Age within grade	+	+				
7. Participation in sports	−	−				
8. Participation in extra curricular activities	−	−				

percentiles, at or above the seventy-fifth percentile), those in the lowest group consumed significantly less fat than those in the middle or highest groups.

Connor, Cerqueira, Connor, Wallace, Malinow, and Casdorph (1978) surveyed the Tarahumara Indians of Mexico for plasma lipids and dietary intake. These Indians are notable because of their remarkable physical endurance and diets low in fat from animal sources. Lipoprotein cholesterol concentrations were lower than those of persons living in the United States: LDL—87 mg/dl; VLDL—21 mg/dl; HDL—25 mg/dl. Their diet was also low in cholesterol (71 mg/day), fat (12% of calories), and saturated fat (2% of calories). Carbohydrates (75% of calories) and fiber (19 mg/day) were high. Most important, total plasma cholesterol correlated positively with dietary cholesterol intake ($r = .874$). It should be noted that direct observation and dietary records were used to estimate nutrient intake, a strategy that might be used in other populations to study diet-lipid-blood pressure-weight relationships. Others have observed that definitive studies of the diet–cholesterol hypothesis may require cross-population investigations to increase variability in eating patterns (Keys, 1970).

Table 11.5—*Continued*

Variables	Study Horn *et al.* (1959)	Creswell *et al.* (1970)	Kelson *et al.* (1975)	USDHEW (1972)	USDHEW (1976)	Other studies showing same relationships
9. Participation in community activities		–				
10. Educational aspirations	–	–		–		Windsor (1972)
11. Parent education level	–	–	–	–		Windsor (1972)
12. Parent approval of smoking			+			Cartwright & Thompson (1969); McKennel (1969)
13. Number of parents in home				–		
14. Student work outside of the home				+		
15. Scholastic performance	–	–				Veldman & Brown (1969); Bewley & Bland (1977); Fodor, Glass, & Weiner (1968); McKennel (1969); Newman (1970); Pumroy (1967); Rogers & Reese (1964); Windsor (1972)
16. Social precocity				+	+	Veldman & Brown (1969); Lieberman Research (1969); Newman (1970)

Note. + = positive relationship to smoking. – = inverse relationship to smoking.

The Coronary-Prone Behavior Pattern

The Type A or coronary-prone behavior pattern is associated with increased risk of cardiovascular disease. The cornerstone of the assertion stems from the findings of the Western Collaborative Group Study (Rosenman, Brand, Sholtz, & Friedman, 1976). In this prospective study of 3,154 men aged 39–59, Type A subjects exhibited 2.37 times the rate of new coronary heart disease observed in their Type B counterparts. After adjustment for the four traditional risk factors (age, cholesterol, systolic blood pressure, and smoking), the approximate relative risk was 1.97. Jenkins, Zyzanski, and Rosenman (1976) reported that Type A Behavior was associated with increased risk of reinfarction among persons already having clinical coronary disease. The Type A behavior pattern also has been associated with increased severity of atherosclerosis in three separate studies as confirmed by coronary angiography (Blumenthal, Williams, Kong, Schonberg, & Thompson, in press; Williams, 1978; Zyzanski, Jenkins, Ryan, Flessas, & Everist, 1976).

Matthews (Note 1) has been especially prominent in investigationg developmental antecedents of Type A behavior in children and adolescents. The enterprise is not without difficulty. First, the coronary-prone behavior pattern is comprised of many discrete behavior patterns: speech stylistics, motor behavior (e.g., rapid body movements, tense facial and body musculature, hands and teeth clenching, and excessive gesturing), self-reported attitudes (time urgency), and excessive physiologic response (Friedman, Byers, Diament, & Rosenman, 1975). Which of these discrete behavior patterns are predictive of coronary heart disease remains a matter for empirical inquiry (Tasto, Chesney, & Chadwick, 1978).

Second, it remains questionable empirically and conceptually whether the coronary-prone behavior pattern is manifested the same way in children as it is in adults. Finally, studies need to be conducted to determine the contributions of environment and genetics to the overall coronary-prone behavior pattern.

Matthews (Note 1) provided four criteria for the assessment of Type A in children: The measure should (*a*) include ratings of three major behavioral indicators of Pattern A (competitive achievement-striving, aggressiveness, and a sense of time urgency); (*b*) provide for individual differences and not only dichotomous classification; (*c*) be completed by an external observer; (*d*) be reliable and valid.

The Matthews Youth Test for Health (Matthews, 1976; MYTH) contains 17 five-point rating scales of children's competitiveness, impatience, and aggression as rated by classroom teachers. The test is reliable (interrater reliability = .83; Cronbach's alpha = .90), and data on validity are currently being collected and assessed. Matthews and Angulo (Note 2), for example, tested the construct validity of the MYTH in a subsample of children who were challenged to win a car race against an experimenter. Type As won the race against a female but not a male experimenter by a wider margin than Type Bs. Type As also aggressed against a Barbie doll earlier in the experimental session and were more impatient than Type Bs throughout the session. Matthews and Krantz (1976) reported that the "hard-driving" and "competitiveness" components of the Type A pattern has a modest genetic component. With regard to the environmental component of Type A behavior, Matthews, Glass, and Richins (1977) found that mothers gave fewer positive evaluations of task performance to Type A children than to Type B children, and that Type A children were pushed to try harder more often than Type B children. In addition, Matthews (1977) found that Type A children, relative to Type B children, elicited more positive evaluations and positive pushes (e.g., "You did so well. Why not try for five?") from Type B care-givers. Other studies have reported modest similarities between parents and children (Bortner, Rosenman, & Friedman, 1970), suggesting a modeling effect. In summary, the data indicate a reciprocal effect may exist between the environmental and genetic components of children's Type A behavior. Children become more competitive when urged to behave this way and when reinforced for competitiveness. At the same time, competitive and impatient children elicit a greater frequency of positive evaluations and urges to perform better than the less competitive children. Matthews (Note 1) also summarized from the literature on achievement motivation, aggression, and time urgency how these behavioral clusters could be transmitted through modeling and reinforcement.

It is critical for research to begin to regard the specific behavioral or physiological patterns correlated with the coronary-prone behavior pattern that place a person at increased risk of heart disease. It is also necessary to chart the natural history of those patterns. It may soon become tempting to begin to design programs that modify specific behavior patterns in the belief that they are harmful. Without further evidence, we may be doing persons a disservice in changing behavior patterns such as competitiveness or achievement striving which are, in fact, quite functional (and not necessarily related to disease) for coping in contemporary society (see Chesney, Eagleston, & Rosenman, Chapter 3).

Promising Trends for the Prevention of Cardiovascular Disease

We are living in an exciting age. We have mastered many of the infectious agents that formerly plagued society and now recognize the central pathogenic role of lifestyle. Many sectors in society, together with responsible agencies in government, are committing resources toward (*a*) deepening our understanding of those pathogenic factors; (*b*) learning more about processes involved in the initiation and maintenance of behavior change; and (*c*) disseminating programs and policies that have been shown to have beneficial behavior change implications.

We know that each of the behaviors related to cardiovascular risk—smoking, physical activity, obesity, nutrition, stress, and Type A behavior—are not easy to change. We know of programs that are disseminated with enthusiasm but are bereft of data. We also can point to numerous programs that demonstrate interesting knowledge and attitude change but which cannot demonstrate the effects of these on behavior. Needed are well-documented programs of research demonstrating effective methods for changing behaviors, knowledge, and attitudes in young persons.

It is sometimes believed that it will be easier to induce change among adolescents than among adults. This proposition is not necessarily true. While helping adolescents to live different lifestyles may hold great promise for promoting health, building effective programs may be more challenging with young persons than with adults. Children and adolescents may have no immediate health hazard to prompt consideration of change. In addition, it cannot be assumed that healthy lifestyles will persist once they have begun to be practiced.

The challenge is twofold. It is necessary to translate the principles of behavior change into programs that meet the needs of adolescents and which can be implemented in settings where adolescents congregate. Second is the need to design programs that will lead adolescents to maintain healthful lifestyles. While it would exceed the data to assert that the technology (or even the theory) is available for accomplishing that task, it can be asserted that there are pockets of hope. In each risk factor area, progress has been made in understanding the nature of the conditions maintaining the pattern, and beginnings have been made in specifying processes and procedures needed to produce clinically efficacious behavior change. The final section of this chapter describes some of those promising trends and charts important areas for research and development.

Smoking Prevention and Cessation

Many programs dealing with adolescent smoking have been initiated in the past few years. The direct link between smoking and lung cancer and heart disease, coupled with the apparent ineffectiveness of ongoing smoking education programs, triggered nationwide concern. Federal funding resulted in the National Interagency Council on Smoking and Health, the American Cancer Society, the American Heart Association, and several government agencies sponsoring innovative projects. In reviewing the results of these projects the research literature uniformly paints the same picture. Many programs are successful in changing knowledge and attitudes of adolescents, but are not sufficient to modify behavior (Thompson, 1978; Wynder & Hoffman, 1979).

Ellis (1980) provided a compendium of smoking

prevention and cessation programs that represents the current state of the art in this field. Approaches to the adolescent smoking problem are categorized as (*a*) youth-coordinated; (*b*) illustrations of the immediate effects of smoking; (*c*) youth-to-youth teaching programs; (*d*) lifestyle education; (*e*) health hazard appraisal; (*f*) health education curricula with smoking components; and (*g*) smoking cessation programs. The majority of the programs presented in the compendium offer relatively weak evaluation strategies, with only a few using control groups or physiological monitoring to validate self-reports. Still, the usefulness of these programs should not be underestimated. Progress in this field may require testing novel approaches so that others can capitalize on reported strengths and then systematically develop more effective programs.

Several sociopsychological factors related to the onset and maintenance of smoking appear particularly important in designing prevention and cessation programs. The combined effects of peer pressure, adult modeling, cigarette advertising, and other social factors create an environment that reinforces smoking by providing attractive models and potent social cues. These social factors have been the explicit focus of several ongoing programs, with results that call for cautious optimism. A review of the most successful of these programs will now be presented.

The University of Houston Project One of the most influential approaches to the prevention of smoking is that of Evans (1976). The approach is based upon McGuire's (1964) concept of psychological inoculation which is analogous to inoculation in medical terminology. That is, if we expect the individual to encounter the cultural analogue of germs (i.e., social pressures toward adoption of a behavior detrimental to health), then we can prevent "infection" if we expose the person to a weak dose of those "germs" in a way that facilitates the development of "antibodies" (i.e., skills for resisting pressure to smoke).

Evans and his colleagues (Evans, Rozelle, Mittlemark, Hansen, Bane, & Havis, 1978) developed a procedure for translating these concepts into a worthwhile classroom strategy. The package used in their study involved specific information on the social pressures to smoke, focused discussions, feedback, and monitoring.

The information portion of the study consisted of four sessions in seventh-grade students' physical education classes. A short videotape was presented during each session that carried messages concerning social pressures to smoke. Four themes were presented in the first session: (*a*) information about the dangers of smoking; (*b*) the advantages of not smoking, (*c*) the effects of smoking on other people; and (*d*) a description and illustration of peer pressure and its effects on smoking behavior. The remaining sessions focused on the effects of adult models and mass media on smoking adoption.

Following the videotapes, students were involved in writing responses to questions dealing with the messages presented. Small group discussion followed in which methods of coping with these pressures were explored. Some of the classes also were given feedback of their smoking behavior in one, five, and ten-week intervals following the program pretest. The experimenters posted a chart comparing the degree of smoking or nonsmoking in a particular class to the other classes. Finally, posters reinforcing basic contents of the program were displayed in the feedback classes.

A total of 750 seventh-grade students participated in the program. Students receiving all components of the program, those given the feedback portion alone, and those who were monitored for smoking but not given feedback, initiated smoking at significantly lower rates than those students in the control group. That is, over 18% of the control group but only 10% of the treatment groups had begun smoking. The powerful effect of monitoring, and the relatively short intervention phase, (10 weeks) should be noted.

Project CLASP (Counseling Leadership About Smoking Pressures) McAlister, Perry, and Maccoby (1979) expanded Evans' work by employing older students as peer leaders to deliver the intervention. Active involvement in identifying and resisting pressures to smoke through role-playing, contests, and small group discussions enhanced learning the pressure resistance skills. Peer leaders taught these social skills in teams during a seven-session program with an entire seventh-grade class ($N = 336$) in San Jose, California.

Three intensive sessions at the beginning of the school year were devoted to strengthening the students' commitment not to become dependent on tobacco and demonstrating the subtle social influences that favor smoking. During the second session, verbal or cognitive responses appropriate to various pressures were demonstrated and the students were encouraged to develop and present their own ideas on how to handle situations. During the third session, students created skits in which they role-played verbal responses to various inducements to smoke. Four subsequent sessions, spread throughout the year, were boosters in which specific themes from the previous sessions were expanded and additional coping strategies taught.

In the first reported results of this intervention (McAlister *et al.,* 1979) one school served as a treatment school while two others served as controls. A baseline and two follow-up surveys of self-reported smoking were supplemented with random samplings of exhaled breath conducted in a manner that was similar to Evans' (1976) procedure for increasing accuracy of self-report. About 2% of the students in the treatment and control schools reported "smoking during the past week" at the beginning of the school year. By the end of the school year, 9.9% of the students in the control schools, but only 5.6% of the students in the treatment school, reported smoking during the past week.

During the second year of the intervention, the treatment group received two follow-ups, both focusing on the immediate physiological effects of smoking. When surveyed the following June, 7.1% of the treatment subjects, 18.8% of students in one control school, and 21.0% of the students in the second control school reported smoking in the past week, with the largest increase in onset occurring during Spring. Obviously, smoking prevention requires continual skills training and reinforcement to maintain treatment effects, particularly during the years in which persons are most vulnerable to take up the tobacco habit.

The program was replicated during the second year with the incoming group of seventh-grade students in the same treatment and control schools. Boosters were held once a month in an effort to stave off the risk of smoking during Spring. Additional attention was given to training peer leaders, with particular emphasis on appropriate reinforcement techniques, prior to the booster sessions. By the end of the school year, 2.2% of the treatment group, 18.2% of the students in the first control school, and 14.0% of the students in the second control school reported smoking in the past week. Smoking in the treatment group was significantly lower than in the control group and also less than half the rate of the previous seventh-grade treatment group at the end of one year of treatment. Follow-up surveys with both treatment groups are currently underway. The use of attractive, slightly older models, active participation in social skills training, and a systems approach to school interventions appear to be particularly potent components in preventing the onset of smoking.

Robbinsdale Antismoking Project The same principles that were explored by Evans and McAlister were expanded further in the projects at the University of Minnesota (Murray, Johnson, Luepker, Pechacek, Jacobs, & Hurd, Note 3). Four schools, representing an entire school district, received a variety of treatments and five monitoring sessions during the intervention year (1977–1978) and follow-up year (1978–1979). Seventh-grade students in one school were monitored for smoking but received no instruction. The students in a second school were shown films similar to those designed by Evans' group. The films were followed by small group discussions on pressure situations and role-playing of resistive techniques. In the third school, same age peers (opinion leaders) were trained to direct intervention sessions similar to those in the second school.

The Minnesota group used self-reports and saliva thiocyanate measures to assess the amount of smoking in each seventh-grade group. Smokers were broken down as regular (at least once per month), experimental (trying once or twice), or nonsmokers (never having smoked). Students in the monitoring-only school were much more likely than students in the other two schools with interventions to begin smoking; extra components appeared to enhance the efficiency of the total program.

Biofeedback Helping students become aware of the effects of tobacco appears to be a useful, attractive approach to smoking prevention with high school students. The New Hampshire Lung Association (see Ellis, 1980) developed a biofeedback program that compared smokers with themselves (before and after smoking a cigarette) and with nonsmokers on a variety of physiological measures: carbon monoxide in the breath, pulse rate, skin temperature, and manual control. The program was implemented in schools in New Hampshire using high school students as classroom facilitators. Students learned about the scientific methods underlying the tests and then monitored their reactions in a week-long program. A preliminary analysis, using self-report only, indicated that 2 months after the completion of the project, 25% of the smokers had quit, 36% had reduced the amount smoked, and 18.8% switched to lower tar and nicotine cigarettes. Apparently, confronting students with the dangers of smoking within a meaningful time-frame had an effect on their smoking behavior.

The Life Skills Training Program The Life Skills Training Program, one component of the Know Your Body Program (Botvin, Eng, & Williams, Note 4; Williams, Arnold, & Wynder, 1977), attempted to focus on both psychological and social factors related to smoking. The ten-session program was administered to eighth-, ninth-, and tenth-grade classes in the metropolitan New York area. The program used a combination of group discussion, modeling, and behavioral rehearsal to teach students basic life skills that might enable them to resist direct social pressure to smoke, decrease social anxiety that may occur in social situations, and promote greater autonomy and self-confidence. The program included sessions on self-image, decision making, media, social skills, assertiveness, and methods for coping with anxiety. Preliminary results were encouraging, showing a 67% decrease in the number of new experimental smokers.

The program was expanded during the second year to include peer leaders as facilitators and increase the number of sessions to twelve (Botvin & Eng, Note 5). Additional emphasis was placed on the immediate effects of smoking and skills for dealing with social anxiety. Two seventh-grade classes in two New York City suburban schools received the treatment ($N = 426$). At posttest, 8% of the students in the treatment program indicated they had begun smoking, whereas 19% of the control group were new smokers ($p < .02$). Of particular note were the sex differences in treatment effects. The girls in the treatment group were smoking significantly less than those in the control groups (8% versus 37%), whereas virtually no differences appeared for the males (8% versus 9%). The focus on social anxiety and social skills appears more effective with females, although this finding may be confounded with current increases in female smoking in general.

Stanford Heart Disease Prevention Program Perry, Killen, Telch, Slinkard, and Danaher (1980) combined biofeedback and peer teaching to encourage prevention and cessation among high school students. The program was designed to encourage students to participate in Project CLASP as peer leaders as well as to provide a method for dealing with the increases in smoking that occur throughout the high school years.

The program had five major objectives. The program (*a*) taught students to identify pressures to smoke in their environment; (*b*) described methods and required practice of behaviors to deal with these pressures; (*c*) identified the immediate health hazards of smoking; (*d*) described an effective approach to quit smoking; and (*e*) identified ways in which high school students can take an active role in reducing the incidence of smoking in general. Finally, the students made commitments to reduce their consumption of tobacco, quit smoking, or not start smoking. Health teachers and Stanford graduate students served as facilitators for this predominantly student-centered curriculum.

The program was conducted over 1 week in five separate class sessions. It began with small group discussions on the pressures to smoke tobacco. Each group was responsible for answering specific questions regarding social pressures and ways to cope with those pressures. A slide show reinforced the discussion.

The next day was spent on cigarette advertising. Students viewed ads and then identified ways in which advertisements pressured young people to smoke. The movie *Too Tough To Care* summarized this discussion. Biofeedback was the topic of the third day. Stanford graduate students administered tests of carbon monoxide, blood pressure, skin temperature, lung capacity, and pulse rate to all of the students. Smokers and nonsmokers were compared on these measures. A chart displaying these comparisons was hung in the classroom as a visual reminder to the students.

In the final 2 days, self-management strategies were taught to the students: goal-setting, imagery rehearsal, and self-reinforcement. The program ended with small group brainstorming sessions centering on what a high school student can do to help adults, friends, and younger students to not begin or quit smoking.

The program was evaluated using self-reports of smoking and carbon monoxide breath tests taken at the beginning and end of the school semester in three treatment and two control schools. When asked "Have you smoked in the past month?" 29.2% of the treatment and 26.3% of the control students responded "yes" prior to the program. Following the program, the percentages shifted to 23.6% for the treatment students and 30.4% for the control students ($p < .05$). In a posttest only evaluation of the carbon monoxide breath tests, 5.2% of the treatment students and 13.3% of the control students showed readings greater than 10 ppm ($p < .001$). The treatment students also showed, relative to the control students, significantly more knowledge of the pressures to smoke, the immediate health hazards of smoking, and the ways in which they could reduce the incidence of smoking in their community and their school.

The results of these projects paint an optimistic picture for research in smoking prevention. Teaching social skills to cope with the pressures to smoke, presenting the environmental factors that influence onset, providing viable models that promote nonsmoking behavior, and introducing evidence of the immediate harmful effects of smoking, all appear to be components of programs that are particularly convincing to adolescents. Changing the environment in which the adolescent resides by reinforcing nonsmoking and alternative "adult" behavior appears far more important than changing the psychological make-up of individuals at risk. The adolescent "society" can be viewed as "at risk" because it reflects the anticipations of an adult world that reinforces smoking. The task of future research in smoking prevention is to capitalize on and extend the successes of these programs within the context of the developmental processes of adolescence, by providing alternative channels for adolescents to symbolize adulthood and by giving them skills to cope with the social pressures to smoke.

Reducing Overweight

Obesity in children and adolescents predicts overweight later in life; it also is quite intractable and remarkably difficult to treat (Coates & Thoresen, 1978). Coates and Thoresen (1978) made three recommendations for the treatment of obesity, based on theoretical understandings of change processes and advances documented in promising experimental studies.

1. The distinction between learning, practice, and performance in the natural environment often is neglected. Bandura (1977b) has repeatedly emphasized the difference between learning and performance; programs typically attend to the former without recognizing the central importance of the latter. In Bandura's reciprocal interaction model (Bandura 1977a, 1978), modeling and performance are influential in teaching new skills. The external environment, as filtered through the person's belief systems, is central in influencing current behavior. The environment both cues and provides consequences for behavior performed by the person.

   When translated into weight loss programs, this theoretical position implies not only that effective teaching strategies (e.g., vicarious and participant modeling) be used, but also that natural environments be constructed to promote and support ongoing weight loss. We cannot expect to teach persons about weight loss in a classroom setting and expect them to apply those concepts and skills to lose weight (Jeffery & Coates, 1978).

2. Coates and Thoresen (1978) noted that weight loss was facilitated by highly structured programs. These kinds of programs may provide the supports necessary for achieving and maintaining behavior change.
3. Coates and Thoresen (1978) recommended that programs place emphasis on and reward weight loss instead of habit change. There is no magical set of weight loss strategies applicable to or needed by everyone (Coates & Thoresen, 1980). Persons can lose weight in a variety of ways. People need to be successful in their weight loss endeavors, identify strategies that work for them, and to be encouraged to continue practicing those strategies for maintenance of weight loss.

Other recommendations can be gleaned from promising empirical studies in the behavioral treatment of obesity.

Weight loss early in a program might be especially important. Jeffery, Wing, and Stunkard (1979) found that weight losses in weeks 1 through 5 were correlated with weight losses between weeks 6 and 20 ($r = .44$). Those who lost no weight in weeks 1 through 5 lost only 1.4 pounds during the next 15 weeks. Those who lost 10 pounds or more in weeks 1 through 5 lost 15.2 pounds during the next 15 weeks.

The same patterns may be true for adolescents. Gross, Wheeler, and Hess (1976) treated 10 obese adolescent girls in 10 weekly sessions which included self-monitoring, rearranging the physical and social environment, nutritional information, and individual problem solving. At the end of 10 weeks, four subjects had gained or maintained weight, three subjects had lost from 2 to 8 pounds, and three had lost more than 15 pounds. At a 27-week follow-up the following results were documented: (*a*) of those who had maintained or gained weight immediately following treatment, three continued to gain while one lost 10 pounds; (*b*) the losses of those who had lost 2–8 pounds during treatment ranged from 6 to 14½ pounds; and (*c*) of those who had lost 15 or more pounds, losses at follow-up ranged from 21 to 40 pounds. In general, continued success could be predicted from weight losses during the program.

Wing and Jeffery (1979) noted in their comparison of treatments that studies using *intensive motivational procedures* achieved the best weight losses. For example, subjects coming in daily to receive human chorionic gonadatropin (HCG) injections lost an average of 17.6 pounds over 5 to 6 weeks. Placebo controls (daily contact plus injection with saline solution) lost an average of 14.4 pounds. Daily contact, by itself, may greatly enhance clients' motivation to begin and continue losses.

Intensive treatments may be similarly effective with children and adolescents. Heyden, DeMaria, Barbee, and Morris (1973) placed eight adolescents (11 to 17 years of age, 145 to 259 pounds) on a 700-calorie diet that included fasting for 1 or 2 days per week, sodium restriction and vitamin and protein supplements. Mothers and children saw the physicians frequently for encouragement and direction. These subjects lost an average of 40.2 pounds in seven months. Losses ranged from 10 pounds (in the subject originally weighing 145 pounds) to 74 pounds. Only one subject was unsuccessful. She lost 25 pounds in 3 months but then regained it at 6 months. These impressive outcomes were replicated later with seven other adolescents.

Attempts to achieve the same results with treatments, administered in a group format led by the adolescents who were originally treated individually, were not nearly as successful. Weight losses at 1 to 7 months (subjects continued until they terminated) ranged from 0 to 69 pounds but averaged 11.8 pounds. Most subjects discontinued the program after 1 to 2 months.

How might intensive treatment be offered in a cost-effective way? Jeffery and Wing (1979) reported a feasible method for maintaining frequent contact with subjects. Thirty-four overweight adults were assigned to (*a*) no personal contact (group meeting once per week for 6 weeks to receive instructions in self-monitoring, exercise, stimulus control, rate of eating, preplanning and social support); (*b*) personal contact (group meeting plus two personal contacts per week with undergraduate research assistants; or (*c*) phone contact (group meeting plus two telephone contacts per week with research assistants) treatments. In the two additional contacts per week, both the personal and the phone contact subjects reported weight that morning and calories eaten that day to the assistants. All subjects also deposited $20 at the first treatment session, to be refunded at the end of treatment contingent on 100% adherence to the attendance requirements of their various groups. Increasing the frequency of contact produced average results that were greater than those usually reported in behavioral weight-loss studies. Mean weight losses over 5 weeks were 5.33 pounds ($SD = 3.87$) for no contact subjects, 8.73 pounds ($SD = 4.84$) for personal contact subjects, and 10.05 pounds ($SD = 6.75$) for phone contact subjects.

Meaningful monetary deposits might also increase the cost-effectiveness of intensive treatment. Jeffery, Thompson, and Wing (1978) required 31 severely obese subjects to deposit $200.00 prior to treatment. Contracts based on attendance, weight maintained, or caloric intake were made between the patients and the researchers. Subjects in the attendance contract condition received $20 back each week for attending. Subjects in the calorie contract condition received $20 back each week that their mean daily caloric intake was equal to or less than the amount needed to produce a weight loss of 2 pounds each week. Subjects in the weight contract condition received a $20 refund if they maintained an overall rate of weight loss of two pounds each week or were two pounds below their lowest previous weight. Attendance contract subjects lost an average of 8.6 pounds. Subjects in the calorie contract group lost an average of 19.4 pounds while subjects in the weight contract group lost 21.0 pounds.

Coates, Jeffery, Slinkard, Killen, and Danaher (in press) combined frequent contact and contingency contracts in a weight loss program for adolescents. Thirty-six adolescents (13–17 years old, 9 to 100% overweight) were taught basic weight loss skills in ten 1-hour sessions using videotape, modeling, role-playing, group discussion, and reading. Overweight students were taught problem-solving skills to analyze their individual eating patterns; they then devised and tried out possible solutions for identified eating problems.

All subjects were required to deposit the equivalent of 15 weeks of their allowance or 50% of their estimated earnings from part-time employment. Reward contingencies (for weight loss or habit change) and frequency of contact (daily or weekly) were crossed in a factorial design. Subjects in the weight loss reward groups received deposit refunds for achieving weight loss goals of at least 1 pound per week. In the habit change groups, subjects received refunds for keeping caloric intake below an individually established goal level. Subjects in the daily contact groups came in each morning or afternoon to receive refunds for meeting weight loss or habit change goals. Weekly contact subjects visited once a week for refunds earned. Outcome data are summarized in Figure 11.1. A repeated measured analysis of the variance of percent above ideal weight revealed a significant trials effect ($p < .05$). Using contrast analysis, the daily contact-weight loss group (Group 1) was the only group to show significant weight changes from baseline to weight at posttreatment, and from baseline to weight at follow-up. The same

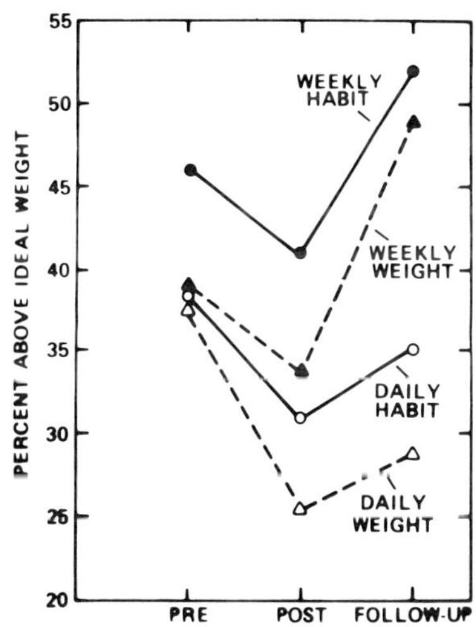

Figure 11.1. Weight loss as a function of reward contingency and frequency of contact. (From Coates, Jeffery, Slinkard, Killen, and Danaher [in press], used with permission.)

pattern was observed in an analysis of pounds above ideal weight.

Botvin, Cantlon, Carter, and Williams (1979) reported the results of a school-based weight-reduction program conducted as part of the Know Your Body Program. After participating in a schoolwide health profile screening, students in the experimental condition were invited to participate in a 10-session weight reduction program that included behavior modification, nutrition education, and exercise management. Controls received pre-and posttreatment assessment only. Of the 37 experimental subjects, 70% showed decreases in triceps skinfold while 30% showed an increase or no change. Of the 68 control subjects, 43% showed decreases and 57% showed increases or no change in this measure ($p < .01$). Prior to treatment, 30% of the experimental subjects were equal to or greater than 130% of ideal weight; this was reduced to 17% after treatment. Of the control subjects, 39% before treatment and 35% following treatment were equal to or greater than 130% of ideal weight.

While all of the results described above are promising, their clinical significance is moderate. Additional laboratory work and field studies clearly are needed. Especially needed are programs of research that deviate from the models currently being used so that we can improve upon the modest treatment effects documented in this section.

Nutrition-Behavior Change

Nutrition educators are aware of the need to motivate behavior change in students, disseminate knowledge, and to evaluate behavioral outcomes so that progress is possible (Whitehead, 1957). But while the importance of documented behavior change is acknowledged, the principles of behavior change often are not employed systematically and evaluations frequently are weak.

Go (1976) completed a content analysis of 90 curriculum guides designed for grades K–12. The major conclusions of the analysis pointed to the inadequacies of the guides: (*a*) concepts were frequently underdeveloped and often were not related to lesson objectives and learning activities; (*b*) cognitive and affective learning objectives were stressed while behavioral objectives were not; (*c*) practice was downplayed, so that students were not given appropriate opportunities to practice critical skills; (*d*) the programs were strongly teacher-dominated rather than being oriented toward students' activity and involvement; and (*e*) most of the guides provided no guidelines for evaluation and none of the guides were accompanied by data attesting to their efficacy or to their shortcomings.

Podell, Keller, and Mulvihill (1978) reported findings that are typical for many nutrition education studies. High school biology students participated in a cardiovascular nutrition education program. A "Heart Disease Awareness Week" was promoted by publicity in school newspapers and demonstrations of low cholesterol diets in Home Economics classes. Five hours of cardiovascular education took place in biology classes. There were significant improvements in knowledge of cardiovascular nutrition and attitude toward a low cholesterol pattern of eating. There also was significant improvement in reported eating patterns. However, students receiving the program showed increases in serum cholesterol comparable to those shown by students in control schools. It is difficult to know, from these self-report data, whether actual changes occurred in food choices or if failure to observe changes in serum cholesterol reflect failure of students to significantly change dietary habits.

Only with careful and objective evaluation will it be possible to determine what approaches are promising and those which should be disseminated. Rappenthal (1977), for example, documented the efficacy of a simple nutrition program change, namely having lunch after rather than before recess. Plate waste studies showed a 25% decrease in vegetables, 36% decrease in salads, 54% decrease in fruits, and 86% decrease in milk in the trash. Madsen, Madsen, and Thompson (1974) demonstrated that simple reinforcement could be used to encourage impoverished Head Start children to consume unfamiliar but nutritious foods. However, the choice of reinforcers was unfortunate. Teachers provided sugar-coated cereal, small candies, and praise contingent upon eating behavior; they also rewarded children who finished an entire meal with additional treats and praise. Hopefully, nutritious reinforcers can be identified for future programs.

Direct observation also has been found useful in studies of food substitutes. Herbert-Jackson and Risley (1977) found that protein intake of young persons could be increased by textured vegetable protein. Similarly, Herbert-Jackson, Cross, and Risley (1977) found that toddlers and preschoolers' consumption of milk was not affected by its butterfat content.

Epstein, Masek, and Marshall (1978) modified time of activity (before or after the meal) and used a token reward system to improve food intake in six black children of low socioeconomic backgrounds. The activity program led to decreased caloric intake, while the eating regulation program led to improved food choices. Decreases in percentage overweight were observed in all children.

These studies document the importance of explicit use of behavior change principles and careful evaluation in nutrition programs. The investigation described below examined procedures by which behavior change principles and evaluation procedures may be incorporated within programs that can be used as part of classroom curricula on a widespread basis.

Coates, Jeffery, and Slinkard (in press) attempted to develop a cardiovascular nutrition and activity program using principles of behavior change and to evaluate the program by measuring direct observations of eating and physical activity at school. The program was developed to teach change using twelve 45-min class sessions (six nutrition classes followed by six exercise classes) over a 4-week period. Three elements of this program seemed most critical: behavioral commitment, feedback and incentives, and family involvement. Students at this (or any) age often have difficulty translating general principles into specific behavior changes. Daily goal sheets, on which students made a written commitment to substitute specific "heart-healthy" foods for foods normally in their lunches and to engage in "heart-healthy" playground activities, seemed essential in promoting behavior change. Students knew precisely what had to be done to meet program goals and to earn available social rewards.

The feedback system, which provided students with objective information regarding their progress, appeared essential in motivating improvement. Students typically expressed amazement at how far they had progressed and also at how far they had to go to eat and exercise in heart-healthy ways. An unplanned bonus was achieved when we presented data separately for boys and girls. The competition between the sexes was keen.

Finally, the token incentive system proved to be enormously popular. We used stickers, buttons, and a rubber stamp—all containing a heart (the logo of the Stanford Heart Disease Prevention Program). Intermittently, the instructors circulated on the playground dispensing hearts to students whose lunches contained a specified number of heart-healthy food items or who were engaging in heart-healthy activities. Students who earned heart stickers plastered them all over their lunch pails and notebooks. Students also insisted on pasting the heart stamps on their books, papers, hands, and foreheads. These token incentives were important both in motivating and in cueing performance of desired actions; they were especially effective when instructors circulated unpredictably on the playground during lunch periods dispensing hearts and stamping hands and foreheads.

Because sending handouts home is a relatively weak method for involving families, we employed two more powerful strategies to encourage behavior change in the home. First, the token reward system reinforced, at school, behavior that had to occur at home. Heart-healthy lunches, made by parents or students, required students to negotiate that specific food items at least be available. In addition, PTA members were encouraged to call friends and inform them of the program.

The program was implemented first in two elementary schools adjacent to Stanford University in two successive years. In each year, three fourth-grade classes in one school and three fifth-grade classes in a second school were involved. A time series multiple baseline design was employed: Lessons in the fifth grade were lagged behind lessons in the fourth grade.

To evaluate the program, direct observation, paper-and-pencil measures, and phone interviews with parents were used. While the students were eating lunch, observers approached each student individually and wrote down the contents of that lunch. Following lunch, individual students were observed for a one-minute period. At each 5-sec interval, the observer made a judgment regarding the student's activity level (sitting, standing, walking, climbing, running, standing still but moving upper trunk) according to preestablished operational definitions. Observer agreement, checked once weekly, was consistently high (mean percent agreement = .97, *SD* = .02). Following lunch, the observers inspected the trash and tabulated the items found. Paper-and-pencil questionnaires were administered before and after the classes to assess changes in knowledge, food, and activity preferences and eating at home.

Foods in lunches were classified as "heart-healthy" (target food items in the lessons) or non-heart-healthy. Figure 11.2 presents the nutrition behavior changes for the first year study. At both schools, the average daily number of heart-healthy foods in students' lunches increased during the program, remained high following the program, and maintained above baseline levels when follow-up data were collected. The postprogram data were collected at the end of the Spring term, while the follow-up data were collected in the Fall following summer vacation. Students also increased in knowledge and in reported preference for heart-healthy foods and activities, respectively, after the program. These results also were maintained at follow-up. In addition, parents reported in phone interviews that they were eating more heart-healthy foods at home both immediately following the program and at follow-up. Equally important was the fact that students and parents both reacted favorably to the program.

Increasing Physical Activity

The federal government has devoted substantial expenditures to investigate methods for increasing physical activity (President's Council on Youth Fitness, 1961). It generally has been recommended that public information be disseminated and more exercise opportunities be provided since young persons are sedentary (Coates *et al.*, in press; Huenemann *et al.*, 1974) and their fitness levels are below those observed among children in other countries (Cureton, 1964). There remains, how-

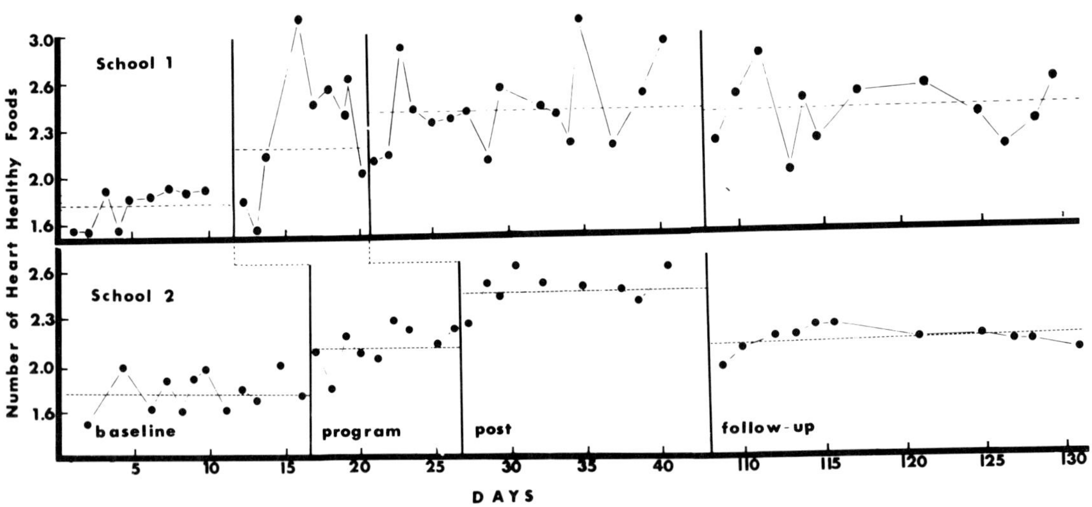

Figure 11.2. Nutrition behavior change during the first year of a cardiovascular nutrition and activity program. (From Coates, Jeffery, Slinkard, Killen, and Danaher [in press], used with permission.)

ever, a clear need to find ways to motivate young people to use the information and the increased number of facilities.

Gilliam (1979) reported the effects of a 6-week strenuous physical activity program on blood lipids in 14 girls 8–10 years of age. The physical activity program was conducted for 40 min each day for 5 days a week. The program was designed to elevate heart rate to 180 beats per minute for 10–15 minutes daily, and to at least 140 beats per minute for the remaining 25–30 min. Significant increases in HDL cholesterol and significant decreases in triglycerides were observed. Once the program terminated, however, lipid levels returned to baseline. The problem is the same as in other behavioral areas: how may healthful behaviors be maintained once they are initiated?

Programs emphasizing changes in activity have produced some positive results with children while they were in effect. Moody, Wilmore, Girandola, and Royce (1972) engaged 28 obese girls in a 29-week daily exercise program of walking, jogging, and running within the context of a high school physical exercise program. Neither the obese girls nor the 40 normal weight controls lost much weight (2.2 versus 1.2 pounds, respectively). The obese girls did show an average triceps skinfold reduction of 52.5 mm while the normal-weight girls showed a reduction of 23.9 mm. Apparently the program was somewhat beneficial for both groups. Seltzer and Mayer (1970) evaluated the efficacy of a 10-month program that combined nutrition education, physical education, and psychological support with 350 obese elementary and secondary students. Overall, subjects showed no changes in weight or triceps skinfold measures at the end of the program. Obese treatment subjects tended to show slower growth rates in triceps skinfold and body weight, but these differences were statistically significant only in male elementary students. Mayer (1975) recently reported follow-up data regarding the program reported by Seltzer and Mayer (1970). Results were maintained only as long as subjects were engaged in the program. Funding cutbacks forced its cessation, and any effects due to the program were eliminated when groups were compared 3 years following its termination. Evidence for both continued weight loss and maintenance in exercise regimens would appear necessary if such programs are to have significant and lasting impact.

Several recent studies with adults have demonstrated the efficacy of contingency management in encouraging physical activity such as encouraging geriatric patients to use a stationary bicycle (Libb & Clements, 1969) and encouraging high school and college students to increase swimming (McKenzie & Rushall, 1974), football (Komaki & Barrett, 1977) and baseball (Heward, 1978). Wysocki, Harl, Iwata, and Riordan (1979) demonstrated that contingency contracting was effective immediately and at 12 months in helping college students improve and maintain capacity to earn aerobic points. Subjects deposited valuable objects with the experimenters, and then earned them back for meeting weekly point objectives. Without question, we need at present to combine these technologies with aerobic training to promote independent and maintained levels of physical exercise that will be health-enhancing.

General Health Education

The assumptions that behavior is more easily changed in children than adults and that healthy behavior will persist has led many to emphasize the importance of health education for young persons. Based on this belief, many school systems have compulsory health education curricula.

Reeder (1978, 1979) completed a comparative study of five comprehensive and widely used health education programs: Feelin' Good (Kunzelman YMCA program), Health Activities Project (Berkeley Hall of Science), Primary Prevention (Title IV–C, Chenowith, Oregon), Primary Grade Curriculum Project, and The School Health Curriculum Project. These programs were considered exemplary because they contained elements thought to enhance health education: (*a*) participatory teaching techniques; (*b*) a wide variety of teaching methods and resources; (*c*) parent involvement, clear objectives, practice in achieving specific goals; and (*d*) decision making by participants.

However, all of these projects fell short when they were evaluated. All of the projects reviewed used only in-class measures that usually emphasized knowledge and attitude change. The School Health Curriculum Project is an important example of how these programs are developed and the kind of evaluation typically employed. The program is organized so that different body systems are emphasized at successive grades: Grade 2—ears; Grade 3—eyes; Grade 4—digestive system; Grade 5—lungs and respiratory system; Grade 6—heart and circulatory system; Grade 7—brain and nervous system. Each unit includes an introduction to the importance of the body system, the structure and function of the system, diseases to which the system is subject, prevention of disease, and a variety of creative activities in which students can demonstrate what they have learned. The program is currently used in over 400 school districts in 34 states. Evaluations have shown positive relations between enrollment in the program and knowledge, attitudes, and smoking behavior. Since all of the outcomes, however, are based on self-report, the possibility for bias is present.

Ellis (1980) summarized three other projects currently underway, including (*a*) The Sunflower Project, designed to teach children in grades K–6 to develop an appreciation for lifestyles that minimize the risk of heart disease; (*b*) The Chicago Heart Health Curriculum Project, which includes components in the cardiovascular system, food, exercise, and smoking; and (*c*) The Primary Grades Health Curriculum (the Seattle Project), designed to teach good health practices to young elementary school children through an understanding of and appreciation for body systems and functions. Each project has demonstrated beneficial effects on knowledge and attitude; improvements in behavior, documented with sensitive and objective procedures, have not been shown.

The Know Your Body Program (Williams *et al.*, 1977; KYB) is an attempt to use physiological measures to estimate efficacy. Know Your Body is now active in several schools in the New York area, involving 4600 children between the ages of 11 and 14 in a prospective trial of risk factor identification and intervention. An initial health screening (height, weight, blood pressure, plasma cholesterol, glucose, hematocrit, fitness, health knowledge, and a survey of cigarette and alcohol consumption) is followed by feedback of results to participants in a "Health Passport" and is reinforced by a multidimensional health education program. The program seeks to capitalize on students' personal knowledge of their own risk factors and to build upon this cornerstone for appropriate health behavior change. Parent, teacher, and student activities are combined to create a psychological and social environment that supports initiative and maintenance of behavior change.

The program is being evaluated in terms of behavior change recognizable through reduction in the number of risk factors on repeated annual screening examinations. In the preliminary screen, (Williams *et al.*, 1977) 43% of the students were designated as abnormally high in cholesterol (>160 mg%), about 10% of the students reported smoking currently, about 12% of the students were greater than 120% ideal weight, and 2% of the students showed elevated systolic (>140 mmHg) or diastolic (>90 mmHg) blood pressure.

Data on the effectiveness of the program are still preliminary, but do suggest that KYB curriculum alone is not sufficient to modify students' health behavior (Ellis, 1980). Interestingly, it has been reported that the program will be disseminated to several other sites, despite the lack of initial positive outcomes.

A prevailing ethos may be hindering advances in health education research with young persons. Program descriptions often emphasize the uniqueness of the activities to which the students will be exposed and how many states or school districts are using the materials (e.g., School Health Curriculum Project). True advance in our ability to prevent disease may come from failures as well as successes. If failures are hidden through sales promotion or insensitive evaluation, it may not be possible to identify features of programs that should be retained, discarded, or refined.

Beginning Early and Maximizing Prevention

Obesity among infants is common (Hutchinson-Smith, 1970; Taitz, 1971). Shukla, Forsyth, Anderson, and Morwah (1972) reported that 16.7% of the infants studied were obese, and 27.7% were between 10 and 20% above standard weight. These data suggest that, since prevention may be the best treatment, focusing effort on preventing obesity during infancy and other high risk periods may be especially useful.

Weight gain during the first part of life may be associated with feeding practices. Trowell (1975) attributed obesity in infancy to the prevalent use of bottle feeding combined with the fear of undernutrition. That is, previously high infant mortality rates and the effects of malnutrition has caused our culture to reinforce overfeeding and rapid weight gain. With regard to the prevalence of bottle feeding, it should be noted that the amount of formula fed to an infant can vary according to the size of the container and the mother's impressions regarding the amount she should be feeding her infant. Not recognized, however, is the fact that infants differ widely in caloric needs. This may be related to the finding that breast-fed infants gain weight at a rate slower than that of bottle-fed infants (Hooper, 1965; Hutchinson-Smith, 1970; Stewart & Westropp, 1953; Taitz, 1971). In addition, solid and semisolid foods currently appear earlier than they did previously in infants' diets. This trend also may contribute to excess calories and excess weight gain among infants.

Piscano, Lichter, Ritter, and Siegel (1978) placed 80 infants born in 1970 on the Prudent Diet at 3 months of age (or when they reached 13 pounds if they did not weigh that much at 3 months). The diet emphasized low saturated fats, low salt, low sugar, and low cholesterol. Typical items included fresh fruit cooked without sugar, fresh vegetables, meats (white/red ratio of 2/1), skimmed milk and cheeses, plain yogurt, and natural gelatin. The comparison group was 50 newborns, born between 1964 and 1970, fed conventional diets. At 3 months of age (before the diet had started), 37.5% of control females and 35% of control males were overweight (weight percentiles exceeded height percentiles by more than one standard deviation) as compared to 29.4% of diet females and 21% of diet males. By age 3 the findings were dramatic: 16.7% of control females and 34.8% of control males were overweight as compared to 0% of diet females and 2.56% of diet males.

Primary prevention also may be effective in promoting low levels of serum cholesterol and in increasing levels of physical activity. Friedman and Goldberg (1976) placed infants on a low saturated fat and low cholesterol diet from birth. When compared to a matched control group at 3 years, no significant differences between the groups were found in percentile height, weight, head circumference, skinfold thickness, total serum protein, hemoglobin, number of sick visits, and number of failures on the Denver Developmental Screening Test. Total serum cholesterol levels between the two groups were significantly different (145.1 ± 1.4 versus 130.1 ± 2.1, $p < .05$) for the low and regular diet subjects, respectively.

Rose and Mayer (1968) studied activity and caloric intake in relation to relative weight in thirty-one 4-to-6-month-old infants living under normal home conditions. Neither infant size nor weight gained were related to caloric intake. However, activity level and total calories were correlated positively ($r = .47$) and triceps skinfold was negatively correlated with activity ($r = -.53$) and with calories eaten per kilogram of body weight ($r = -.71$). Thus, as the infants became more overweight, they consumed less and also were less active. It should be noted that data on caloric intake were from dietary records and thus may have suffered possible reporting biases. Replications would be useful together with more sensitive measures of caloric intake.

These data have important implications for the prevention of obesity and the encouragement of physical activity in very young persons. If the potential exists for identifying young persons at risk for becoming inactive, then it might be possible to design strategies to encourage increases in physical activity at a very early age before behavioral habits are well established.

Intervening with infants is clearly controversial. On the one hand, the report from the Committee on Nutrition of the American Academy of Pediatrics (1972) took the position that diet changes should not be recommended for the entire population but only for those at risk because of family history or other factors. On the other hand, Kannel and Dawber (1972), Blackburn (1974), and the Inter-society Commission for Heart Disease Resources (1970) recommended early and widespread preventive intervention. Blackburn (1974) summarized the argument against prevention by stating that "the prudent diet is fine for kids and others having bad family histories . . . but not for most American kids who should, rather, be encouraged to eat their way through the meat-and-dairy-fat-rock-candy mountain [p. 32]."

Treating the Family

All of the cardiovascular risk factors show intrafamilial correlations. Both genetic and environmental factors are usually implicated. These facts, together with the proposition that maintenance of behavior change should be enhanced if change is supported by the family system, suggest that the family may be an important target for health behavior intervention. While the proposition cannot be faulted, methods for effectively involving all family members await development.

Witschi, Singer, Wu-Lee, and Stare (1978) demonstrated the short-term efficacy of family involvement in nutrition behavior change. Forty-six families kept diet records for 2 weeks. A nutritionist assigned to the family then studied the records and made recommendations for dietary change. During the study period, a polyunsaturated vegetable oil and margarine were supplied to the family. Average reductions in serum cholesterol were promising: adult women—10.7%; adolescent females—10.4%; adolescent males—10.0%; and adult men—9.1%. The results were impressive but no details were provided concerning the specific intervention components; thus, meaningful replication was precluded.

Brownell, Heckerman, Westlake, Hayes, and Monti (1978) assigned obese men and women to one of three treatment conditions: Group 1—cooperative spouse, couples training; Group 2—cooperative spouse but no couples training (spouses agreed to participate but were told that it would not be possible to participate due to exessive numbers of subjects); Group 3—noncooperative spouse (spouses of subjects refused to participate). Subjects and spouses in Group 1 were trained together to (*a*) model appropriate behaviors; (*b*) be supportive in noticing habit change; (*c*) assist with stimulus control procedures; (*d*) engage in alternative activities during tempting times; and (*e*) monitor their partner's behavior as well as their own. Unlike other subjects, those in Group 1 actually continued to lose weight following treatment, and generally maintained their 30.2 (SD = 15.1) pound average weight loss at 6 months.

Family-based treatments with children and adolescents have been moderately successful. Rivinus, Drummond, & Combrinck-Graham (Note 7) obtained modest results with a difficult population, but no comparisons were made with alternative treatments. Coates and Thoresen (in press) obtained significant short-term losses and Wheeler and Hess (1976) obtained modest short-term losses. Neither, however, specifically examined the impact of family involvement. Kingsley and Shapiro (1977) showed that weight losses in children were equal (and modest) when mothers and children were treated in pairs or separately.

Stanley, Glaser, Levin, Adsner, and Coley (1970) treated 11 adolescents (12–15 years of age, 149–264 pounds) using a combination of inpatient and family-oriented outpatient procedures. The 6-week inhospital program had several components: 1200-calorie diet, dietary education, exercise and activity, recreation, and individual and group counseling. Parents met with a pediatrician or psychiatric social worker once a week. Weight changes during the period ranged from a loss of 66 pounds to a gain of 49 pounds. Two subjects were regarded as successes, four others held their weight to preadmission levels, while the last five subjects gained from 14 to 49 pounds.

The results of these investigations suggest that merely involving the parents or other family members is not sufficient to produce major treatment gains. Training and specific motivational aids may be required to obtain clinically significant results. Aragona, Casady, and Drabman (1975) enhanced the efficacy of parent training using contingency contracts to promote weight loss among 5–11-year-old girls. Two variations of an experimental treatment were employed. Parents in Group 1 (response cost + reinforcement, N = 4) contracted to complete graphs and charts of their children's weight and calorie intake, encourage their children to exercise, and use stimulus control procedures along with social and activity reinforcement. Parents in Group 2 (response cost only, N = 3) contracted to do all of the same, but were not instructed to use reinforcement techniques. Parents in Group 3 (control, $N = 5$) received no treatment. All parents deposited an amount of money according to a sliding scale. Refunds were made over the next 12 weeks for attendance (25% of refund), for completing charts and graphs (25%), and if their child lost a predetermined amount of weight (50%).

Weight losses were strikingly uniform in Group 1 (X −13.33, −11.66, −9.00, −11.33; $M = 11.3$). Group 2 showed greater variability (X −13.66, −12.66, −2.33; M = 9.5). The five control subjects gained an average of 0.9 pounds (range = −4.50 to + 4.50). The weight losses in the treatment groups were clinically and statistically significant, given the 12-week duration of the study. It should be noted that the range of money deposited was not given. This might be a critical variable, as Coates *et al.* (Note 1) found that the amount of deposit and weight loss were correlated ($r = -.29$). While Groups 1 and 2 did not differ significantly in average weight losses, it would be interesting to know if reinforcement training enhanced the quality of parent–child interactions. It is possible that Group 1 parents could have used positive procedures, while the untrained Group 2 parents may have employed aversive procedures to achieve the same objective. Direct observations of parent–child interactions might enhance our knowledge considerably.

Follow-up data from the Aragona *et al.* (1975) study were promising. Edwards (1978) analyzed these data using a Weight Index of actual weight (pounds)/actual height (inches)−normal weight/normal height. Perfect adherence to norms would yield WI = 0, while a child who is underweight according to height and age norms would receive a negative WI. Norms used were the ninety-fifth percentile weight-height ratios of same aged children derived from national norms (Guthrie, 1975). Treatment effects were assessed by subtracting the mean weight index score from the weight index at the ninety-fifth percentile at pretreatment, posttreatment, and follow-up. While the control group showed relatively stable WI scores, the two treatment groups showed similar treatment effects. Most important, these appear maintained at follow-up using the WI index. However, the apparent increase in the response-cost only group should be interpreted cautiously as one subject accounted for most of the weight gains.

Coates *et al.* (in press) reported promising nutrition change results in school children and their families immediately following a school-based program and at follow-up after summer vacation. The family was probably the key to maintenance, but the difficulty lay in finding ways to involve the family actively. Two strategies were used. Short and practical nutrition messages (instead of complicated exchange diets or recipes) were sent home and children were reinforced at school for changes that had to occur at home. They received a red "heart-healthy stamp" for bringing the required number of heart-healthy foods in their lunches. Obviously, this required negotiation with parents and parental cooperation in securing and making target foods available.

Finally, Coates, Slinkard, and Killen (Note 7) examined the efficacy of parental involvement in a weight loss program with adolescent students. Thirty-one adolescents (mean percent above ideal weight = 30.6%, range = 7.2 to 72.5%) were assigned to one of two treatment groups: parental involvement versus no parental involvement. All students attended weekly classes to learn weight loss skills and problem solving skills via videotape, role play, and group discussion. They also were charged a $35 nonrefundable fee for service and were required to deposit $130 with us at the beginning of the program. The students were reinforced for weight losses of 1 pound per week. For the first 15 weeks of the program, they were refunded $1 each day that their weight was 1 pound below that recorded 7 days previously and their lowest preceding weight. For the remaining 5 weeks of the program, they were given refunds of $5 per week for maintaining their weight at posttreatment levels. The remainder will be refunded for attending follow-up evaluations.

Parents of students assigned to the parental involvement group were required to deposit an additional $95 with us. This was returned at the rate of $5 per week for 13 weeks for completion of behavioral homework assignments. These parents also met in separate group meetings to learn skills for helping their children lose weight. Significant differences between the two groups were found in changes of percent overweight. Results are presented in Table 11.6 ($p < .001$).

Weight losses, although statistically significant, were less than expected. We hypothesized that weight losses in the treatment groups would equal those achieved by the daily contact-reinforcement for weight loss group in the Coates *et al.* (in press) study. One major change in procedure, however, could explain the differences in obtained results between the two studies. The contingencies were much more stringent in the Coates *et al.* (Note 7) investigation. The parent involvement subjects were required to be one pound below their weight of the previous week, *and their lowest previous weight.* This stringent requirement discouraged some subjects who experienced lapses or setbacks in weight loss efforts. If maintenance data are promising, future studies might focus on optimal contingency and parent involvement procedures to maximize initial and long-term weight loss.

Treating the Community

Many programs of primary prevention place major emphasis on teaching skills to the individual in the belief that knowledge of behaviors that promote health will follow. The late John H. Knowles, an eloquent spokesman for preventive services, placed primary responsibility on the individual. He wrote

> Prevention of disease means forsaking the bad habits which many people enjoy—overeating, too much drinking, taking pills, staying up at night, engaging in promiscuous sex, driving too fast, and smoking cigarettes—or to put it another way, it means doing those things which require special effort—exercising regularly, going to the dentist, practicing contraception, ensuring harmonious family life, submitting to screening examinations [1977, p. 5].

Knowles went from this proposition to the position that individual health was, therefore, the major responsibility of the individual person.

> I believe the ideas of a "right" to health should be replaced by the idea of an individual moral obligation to preserve one's health. . . . More and more the artificer of the possible is society and not the individual; he thereby becomes more dependent in things external and less in his own internal resources [1977, p. 5].

It does not follow because an individual's behavior leads to illness, that it is only the individual's responsibility to use internal resources to modify behaviors leading to illness and wellness. The position is naive psychologically since it ignores the powerful and ongoing influence of the external environment in regulating behavior.

If the cardiovascular risk factors are so prevalent (see pp. 159–164), perhaps effort should be directed at treating environments encouraging cardiovascular risk (as well as individuals at risk). By analogy, it makes little sense to spray pesticides all about to kill mosquitoes without draining the swamps which incubate the larvae.

Clinical attention needs to be directed to the person's micro- and macroenvironment as well as to the individual. The reciprocal interaction model of behavior change places comparable emphasis on internal (self-control) and external environmental factors (Bandura, 1978; Coates & Thoresen, 1979). The interactive system includes the person, the person's physical and social micro- and macroenvironments, and the person's behaviors. The model provides a framework for analyzing the ways in which a variety of environmental factors (e.g., media, peers, family, home) influences the individual's cognitive processes (e.g., knowledge, beliefs, and emotional reactions) and be-

Table 11.6
Changes in Percent Overweight and Weight: Study 2

	Pre	Post	Difference
Percent overweight			
Parent involvement	32.12	23.82	−8.30
	(16.13)	(14.20)	(5.30)
No parent involvement	29.10	26.10	−3.00
	(13.64)	(13.32)	(12.68)
Weight			
Parent involvement	171.84	161.78	−10.06
	(21.82)	(19.03)	
No parent involvement	174.06	168.16	−5.90
	(33.28)	(19.79)	

haviors (e.g., eating, physical exercise, and social conversation). At the same time, the influence of the individual's cognitive processes and behaviors on the external environment can be analyzed. Influences, then, are multidirectional. An obese adolescent male, for example, may have learned specific weight-loss skills, such as declining food offers from insisting grandparents. These skills may not be used, however, unless environmental conditions support their use. Once the person actually performs the difficult action with support from the environment he may begin to evaluate his abilities and actions differently. His behavior toward his grandparents may also influence them to behave differently in the future.

Clinical strategies need to pay attention to all three of the sources of influence noted. An individual's behaviors and beliefs must be modified, and the micro- and macroenvironment should be designed to support the new behaviors and beliefs. In treating a widespread problem such as obesity (as well as nutrition and activity patterns), the environment *and* the individual require clinical attention for efficacious and maintained change.

The Stanford Three Community study provides an example of the efficacy of a combined approach (cf. Farquhar *et al.*, 1977; Maccoby *et al.*, 1977). A multimedia campaign was conducted for 2 years in two California communities. An intensive instruction program with high-risk subjects also was used in one of the communities, while a third community was used as a control. The campaigns were designed to increase the participants' knowledge of risk factors for cardiovascular diseases and to change risk-producing behaviors (cigarette smoking, exercise, daily caloric intake, sugar, salt, saturated fat, and dietary cholesterol). The media campaign alone resulted in knowledge and behavior changes. Adding the intensive instruction program increased the efficacy of the program for those participants initially evaluated to be at high risk.

The Stanford Five City Multifactor Risk Reduction Program is currently underway in five (two treatment and three control) California communities. The objectives and scope of the research have been broadened. Community organization, health professionals education, direct adult instruction, and programs in the schools will be added to a mass media campaign. Knowledge and behavior changes are expected to lead to changes in cardiovascular risk factors, which in turn are expected to lead to reduction in morbidity and mortality due to cardiovascular disease.

The North Karelia Study provides another example of community intervention (Blackburn, 1978; Puska, Tuomilehto, Salinen, Viztrano, & Mustaniemi, Note 8). The study grew out of the findings of the Seven Countries Study (Keys, 1970) which identified Finland as having the highest measured rate of atherosclerotic disease in the world. The report mobilized the efforts of community leaders who engaged the support of the Heart Association, health experts, and the Finnish government. The change tactics involved small and large media, town meetings, heart education, population screening for high risk persons, upgrading of hypertension clinics, face-to-face interventions, and direct environmental modification in the areas of smoking and sources of foods containing fat. Significant changes in health behavior and disease have been noted.

Puska, Koshela, McAlister, Paelonen, Vartiainen, and Homan (1979) reported on one component of the total effort. They designed a comprehensive smoking cessation course which was broadcast over Finnish television in 1978. The course consisted of seven sessions, each lasting 45 min, broadcast over a period of 1 month. Early data on the efficacy of the program were collected from national sample surveys. About half of the population of Finland saw at least part of the program. Approximately 7% of the adults (about 250,000 persons) followed at least four sessions. National surveys revealed a noticeable decrease in smoking only among women, where the proportion smoking decreased from 20.7 to 18.5% in the 2 months following the time that the program was conducted. Although the magnitude may appear small, these kinds of programs are cost-effective and can create a climate to encourage others to quit as well.

Conclusion

Cardiovascular disease is complex. The factors that influence its development and course are many and are well practiced by our society. Should we hope? Should we despair? Should we bother? On the one hand, the problems are so massive as to defy reasonable intervention. On the other hand, the siren of small successes lures us onward.

Probably the most alluring aspect of studying precursors to cardiovascular disease in childhood lies in the unknown. Even if ultimately certain risk factors or the disease itself prove resistant to modification, research and treatment with children must continue because the gulf between what is known and what can be known is especially wide with this age group. Major questions remain about the natural history of biological and psychosocial variables, and the ultimate utility of changing them in terms of reduced morbidity and mortality from cardiovascular disease. Perhaps more compelling is the gulf separating us from what we need to change and the current techniques for doing so. Technical and theoretical advances are needed to help us understand even better how to help young persons make and sustain important lifestyle changes.

Reference Notes

1. Matthews, K. *Progress in the study of developmental antecedents of Pattern A.* Paper presented at the meeting of the American Psychological Association, New York, September, 1979.
2. Matthews, K., & Angulo, J. *Measurement of the Type A behavior pattern in children: Assessment of children's competitiveness, impatience-anger, and aggression.* Unpublished manuscript, University of Pittsburgh, 1978.
3. Murray, D., Johnson, C. A., Luepker, R., Pechacek, T., Jacobs, D., & Hurd, P. *Social factors in the prevention of smoking in seventh grade students: A follow-up experience of one year.* Paper presented at the meeting of the American Psychological Association, New York, September, 1979.
4. Botvin, G. J., Eng, A., & Williams, C. L. *Life skills training: A psychosocial approach to the prevention of cigarette smoking.* Paper presented at the meeting of the American Public Health Association, Los Angeles, September, 1978.
5. Botvin, G., & Eng, A. *A comprehensive approach for the prevention of cigarette smoking.* Paper presented at the National Interagency Council on Smoking and Health Youth Conference, Atlanta, August, 1979.
6. Rivinus, T. M., Drummond, T., & Combrinck-Graham, L. *A group behavior treatment program for overweight children: The results of a pilot study.* Unpublished manuscript, University of Pennsylvania, 1973.
7. Coates, T. J., Slinkard, L. A., & Killen, J. *Weight loss with adolescents: Efficacy of parent involvement, frequent contact, and reinforcement for weight loss.* Paper presented at the meeting of the Association for the Advancement of Behavior Therapy, San Francisco, November, 1979.
8. Puska, P., Tuomilehto, J., Salinen, J., Viztrano, J., & Mustaniemi, H. *Community control of acute myocardial infarction in North Karelia.* Paper presented at the meeting of the International Cardiovascular Congress, Arizona, 1977.

References

Abelson, H. I., Fishburne, P. M., & Cisin, I. *National survey on drug abuse: 1977* (DHEW Publication (ADM) 78-618). Washington, D. C.: U.S. Government Printing Office, 1977.

Agras, S., & Jacob, R. Hypertension. In O. V. Pomerleau & J. P. Brady (Eds.), *Behavioral medicine: Theory and practice.* Baltimore: Williams & Wilkins, 1979.

American Heart Association. *Heart facts.* Dallas: AHA, 1976.

Aragona, J., Casady, J., & Drabman, R. S. Treating overweight children through parental training and contingency contracting. *Journal of Applied Behavior Analysis,* 1975, *8,* 269.

Bandura, A. Self-efficacy: Toward a unifying theory of behavior change. *Psychological Review,* 1977, *84,* 191–215. (a)

Bandura, A. *Social learning theory.* Englewood Cliffs: Prentice-Hall, 1977. (b)

Bandura, A. The self-system in reciprocal determinism. *American Psychologist,* 1978, *33,* 344–358.

Banks, M. H., Bewley, B. R., Bland, J. M., Dean, J. R., & Pollard, V. Long-term study of smoking by secondary school children. *Archives of Diseases of Childhood,* 1978, 53, 12–19.

Barclay, M. Lipoprotein class distribution in normal and diseased states. In G. J. Nelson (Ed.), *Blood lipids and lipoprotein.* New York: Wiley, 1972.

Bewley, B. R., & Bland, J. M. Academic performance and social class factors related to cigarette smoking by school children. *British Journal of Preventive and Social Medicine,* 1977, *31,* 18–24.

Bewley, B. R., Bland, J. M., & Harris, R. Factors associated with the starting of cigarette smoking by primary school children. *British Journal of Preventive and Social Medicine,* 1974, *28,* 37–44.

Blackburn, H. Progress in the epidemiology and prevention of coronary heart disease. In P. Yu & J. F. Goodwin (Eds.), *Progress in cardiology.* New York: Lea & Feibiger, 1974.

Blackburn, H. Physical activity and cardiovascular health: The epidemiological evidence. In G. Landry & P. Urban (Eds.), *Physical activity and human well-being.* Miami: Symposia Specialists, 1978.

Blumenthal, J. A., Williams, R. B., Kong, D., Shonberg, S. M., & Thompson, L. W. Coronary-prone behavior and angiographically documented coronary disease, *Circulation,* in press.

Borhani, N. O. Implementation and evaluation of community hypertension programs. In O. Paul (Ed.), *Epidemiology and control of hypertension.* New York: Grune & Stratton, 1975.

Bortner, R. W., Rosenman, R. H., & Friedman, M. Familial similarity in pattern A behavior. *Journal of Chronic Diseases,* 1970, *23,* 39-43.

Botvin, G., Cantlon, A., Carter, B. J., & Williams, C. L. Reducing adolescent obesity through a school-health program. *Journal of Pediatrics,* 1979, *95,* 1060-1062.

Botvin, G., & Eng, A, Health promotion in the schools. In T. J. Coates (Ed.), *Behavioral medicine: A practical handbook.* Campaign, Ill.: Research Press, in press.

Brownell, K. D., Heckerman, C. L., Westlake, R. J., Hayes, S. C., & Monti, P. M. The effect of couples training and partner cooperativeness in the behavioral treatment of obesity. *Behaviour Research and Therapy,* 1978, *16,* 323-333.

Cartwright, A., & Thompson, J. G. Young smokers: An attitude study among school children touching also on parental influence. *British Journal of Preventive and Social Medicine,* 1969, *14,* 28-34.

Clarke, W. R., Schrott, H., Leaverton, P. E., Connor, W. E., & Lauer, R. L. Tracking of blood lipids and blood pressures in school age children: The Muscatine study. *Circulation,* 1978, *58,* 626-634.

Coates, T. J., & Thoresen, C. E. Obesity in children and adolescents. A review. *American Journal of Public Health,* 1978, *68,* 143-151.

Coates, T. J., & Thoresen, C. E. Obesity in children and adolescents: The problem belongs to everyone. In B. Lahey & A. Kazdin (Eds.), *Advances in clinical child psychology.* New York: Plenum, 1979.

Coates, T. J., & Thoresen, C. E. Treating obesity in children and adolescents: Is there any hope? In J. M. Ferguson & C. B. Taylor (Eds.), *The comprehensive handbook of behavioral medicine* (Vol. 2). Jamaica, N.Y.: Spectrum, 1980.

Coates, T. J., & Thoresen, C. E. Behavior and weight change in three obese adolescents. *Behavior Therapy,* in press.

Coates, T. J., Jeffery, R. W., & Slinkard, L. A. The heart health program: Introducing and maintaining nutrition behavior change in children. *American Journal of Public Health,* in press.

Coates, T. J., Jeffery, R. W., Slinkard, L. A., Killen, J. D., & Danaher, B. G. Frequency of contact and contingent reinforcement in weight loss, lipid change, and blood pressure reduction in adolescents. *Behavior Therapy,* in press.

Coates, T. J., Jeffery, R. W., & Wing, R. R. The relationship between persons' relative body weights and the quality and quantity of food stored in their homes. *Addictive Behavior,* 1978, *3,* 178-184.

Committee on Nutrition of the American Academy of Pediatrics. Childhood diet and coronary health disease. *Pediatrics,* 1972, *49,* 305-307.

Connor, W. E., Cerqueira, M. T., Connor, R. W., Wallace, R. B., Malinow, R., & Casdorph, H. R. The plasma lipids, lipoproteins, and diet of the Tarahumara Indians of Mexico. *American Journal of Clinical Nutrition,* 1978, *31,* 1131-1142.

Corcoran, A. C., Taylor, R. D., & Page, I. H. Controlled observations on the effect of low sodium diet therapy in essential hypertension. *Circulation,* 1951, *3,* 1-16.

Court, J. M., Hill, G. J., Dunlop, M., & Boulton, T. J. C. Hypertension in childhood obesity. *Australian Pediatric Journal,* 1974, *10,* 296-300.

Creswell, W. H., Hoffman, W. J., & Stone, D. B. *Youth smoking behavior: Characteristics and their educational implications.* Champaign-Urbana, Ill.: University of Illinois Anti-Smoking Education Study, 1970.

Cureton, I. K. Improving the physical fitness of youth. *Monograph of the Society for Research in Child Development,* 1964, *29,* 1-221.

de Castro, F. J., Biesbroeck, R., Erickson, C., Farrell, P., Leong, W., Murphy, D., & Green, R. Hypertension in adolescents. *Clinical Pediatrics,* 1976, *15,* 24-26.

Diehl, H. S., & Hesdorffer, M. D. Changes in blood pressure of young men over a seven year period. *Archives of Internal Medicine,* 1933, *52,* 948-953.

Dole, V. P., Dahl, L. K., Cotzias, G. C., Eder, H. A., & Krebs, M. E. Dietary treatment of hypertension: Clinical and metabolic studies of patients on the rice-fruit diet. *Journal of Clinical Investigation,* 1950, *29,* 1189-1206.

Downey, A. M., & O'Rourke, T. W. The utilization of attitudes and beliefs as indicators of future smoking behavior. *Journal of Drug Education,* 1978, *6,* 283-295.

Dube, S. K., Kapoor, S., Ratner, H., & Tunick, F. L. Blood pressure studies in black children. *American Journal of Diseases in Children,* 1975, *129,* 1177-1180.

Dyerberg, J., & Hjorne, N. Plasma lipid and lipoprotein levels in childhood and adolescence. *Scandinavian*

Journal of Clinical Laboratory Investigations, 1973, *31,* 473–479.

Edwards, K. A. An index for assessing weight change in children: Weight/height ratios. *Journal of Applied Behavior Analysis,* 1978, *11,* 421–430.

Ellis, B. H. *Smoking programs for youth.* National Cancer Institute. Washington, D. C.: U.S. Government Printing Office, 1980.

Epstein, L. H., Masek, B., & Marshall, W. Pre-lunch exercise and lunchtime calorie intake. *Behavior Therapist,* 1978, *1,* 15.

Evans, R. I. Smoking in children: Developing a social psychological strategy of deterrence. *Preventive Medicine,* 1976, *5,* 122–127.

Evans, R. I., Rozelle, R. M., Mittlemark, M. B., Hansen, W. B., Bane, A. L., & Havis, J. Deterring the onset of smoking in children: Knowledge of immediate physiological effects and coping with peer pressure, media pressure, and parent modeling. *Journal of Applied Social Psychology,* 1978, *7,* 126–135.

Fallot, R. W., Tsang, R. C., & Glueck, C. J. Hypercholesteremia and hypertriglyceridemia in children. *Preventive Medicine,* 1974, *3,* 390–405.

Farquhar, J. W. The community-based model of life-style intersection trials. *American Journal of Epidemiology,* 1978, *108,* 103–11.

Farquhar, J. W., Maccoby, N., Wood, P. D., Alexander, J. K., Breitrose, H., Brown, B. W., Haskell, W. L., McAlister, A. L., Meyer, A. J., Nash, J. D., & Stern, M. P. Community education for cardiovascular health. *Lancet,* 1977, *1,* 1192–1195.

Feinleib, M., Garrison, R., Borhani, N., Rosenman, R., & Christian, J. Studies of hypertension in twins. In O. Paul (Ed.), *Epidemiology and control of hypertension.* New York: Grune & Stratton, 1975.

Florey, C. du V., Uppal, S. L., & Lowy, C. Relation between blood pressure, weight, and plasma sugar and serum insulin levels in school children aged 9–12 years in Westland, Holland. *British Medical Journal,* 1976, *1,* 1368–1371.

Fodor, J. T., Glass, L. N., & Weiner, J. M. Smoking behavior, cognitive skills, and educational implications. *Journal of School Health,* 1968, *38,* 94–98.

Frank, G. C., Berenson, G. S., & Webber, L. S. Dietary studies and the relationship of diet to cardiovascular disease risk factor variables in ten-year old children: The Bogalusa Heart Study. *American Journal of Clinical Nutrition,* 1978, *31,* 328–340.

Frank, G. C., Voors, A. W., Schilling, P. E., & Berenson, G. S. Dietary studies of rural school children in a cardiovascular survey. *Journal of the American Dietetic Association,* 1977, *71,* 31–35.

Frederickson, D. S., & Breslow, J. L. Primary hyperlipoproteinemia in infants. *Annual Review of Medicine,* 1973, *24,* 315–324.

Frerichs, R. R., Srinivasan, S. R., Webber, L. S., & Berenson, G. S. Serum cholesterol and triglycerides in 3446 children from a biracial community: The Bogalusa Heart Study. *Circulation,* 1976, *54,* 302–309.

Friedman, E., & Goldberg, S. J. An evaluation of the safety of a low saturated fat, low-cholesterol diet beginning in infancy. *Pediatrics,* 1976, *58,* 655–657.

Friedman, M., Byers, S.O., Diamant, J., & Rosenman, R. H. Plasma catecholamine response of coronary-prone subjects (Type A) to specific challenge. *Metabolism,* 1975, *24,* 205–210.

Fryer, B. A., Lamkin, G. H., & Vivian, V. M. Diets of preschool children in the North American region. *Journal of the American Dietetic Association,* 1971, *59,* 228–232.

Garn, S. M., & Clark, D. C. Nutrition, growth, development, and maturation: Findings from the Ten-State Nutrition Survey of 1968–1970. *Pediatrics,* 1975, *56,* 306–319.

Garn, S. M., & Clark, D. C. Trends in fatness and the origins of obesity. *Pediatrics,* 1976, *57,* 443–456.

Garn, S. M., Cole, P. E., & Bailey, S. M. Effect of parental fatness levels on the fatness of biological and adoptive children. *Ecology of Food and Nutrition,* 1976, *6,* 1–3.

Gilliam, T. Coronary heart disease prevention begins with children. *The Main Artery,* 1979, *1,* 1–4.

Go, C. *An analysis of selected curriculum guides used for nutrition education in grades K-12.* Berkeley: Society for Nutrition Education, 1976.

Golubjatnikov, R., Paskey, T., & Inhorn, S. L. Serum cholesterol levels of Mexican and Wisconsin school children. *American Journal of Epidemiology,* 1972, *96,* 36–39.

Gordon, T., & Kannel, W. B. The effects of overweight on cardiovascular diseases. *Geriatrics,* 1973, *28,* 80–88.

Green, D. W., *Teenage smoking: Immediate and long-term patterns.* Washington, D.C.: National Institute of Education, 1980.

Gross, M. A., Wheeler, M., & Hess, K. The treatment of obesity in adolescents using behavioral self-control. *Clinical Pediatrics,* 1976, *15,* 920–924.

Guthrie, H. *Introductory nutrition.* St. Louis: C. V. Mosby, 1975.

Hames, C. G., & Greenberg, B. G. A comparative study of serum cholesterol levels in school children. *American Journal of Public Health,* 1961, *51,* 374–385.

Herbert-Jackson, E., Cross, M. Z., & Risley, T. R. Milktypes and temperature: What will young children drink? *Journal of Nutrition Education,* 1977, *9,* 76–79.

Herbert-Jackson, E., & Risley, T. R. Behavioral nutrition: Consumption of foods of the future by toddlers. *Journal of Applied Behavior Analysis,* 1977, *10,* 407–413.

Heward, W. L. Operant conditioning of a .300 hitter? The effects of reinforcement on the offensive efficiency of a barn-storming baseball team. *Behavior Modification,* 1978, *2,* 25–40.

Heyden, S., Bartel, A. G., Hanes, C. G., & McDonough, J. R. Elevated blood pressure levels in adolescents, Evans County, Georgia. *Journal of the American Medical Association,* 1969, *11,* 1683–1689.

Heyden, S., deMaria, W., Barbee, S., & Morris, M. Weight reduction in adolescents. *Nutrition and Metabolism,* 1973, *15,* 295–304.

Holland, W. W., & Beresford, S. A. A. Factors influencing blood pressure in children. In O. Paul (Ed.), *Epidemiology and control of hypertension.* New York: Grune & Stratton, 1975.

Hooper, P. D. Infant feeding and its relationship to weight gain and illness. *Practitioner,* 1965, *194,* 391–402.

Horn, D., Courts, F. A., Taylor, R. M., & Solomon, E. Cigarette smoking among high school students. *American Journal of Public Health,* 1959, *49,* 1497–1511.

Huenemann, R. L., Hampton, M. C., Behnke, A. R., Schapiro, L. R., & Mitchell, B. W. *Teen-age nutrition and physique.* Springfield, Ill.: Charles C. Thomas, 1974.

Hutchinson-Smith, B. The relationship between the weight of an infant and lower respiratory infection. *Medical Officer,* 1970, *123,* 257.

Insel, P., & Chadwick, J. Conceptual barriers to the treatment of chronic disease: Using pediatric hypertension as an example. In T. J. Coates, A. C. Peterson, & C. Perry (Eds.). *Adolescent health: Crossing the barriers.* New York: Academic Press, in press.

Intersociety Commission for Heart Disease Resources. Primary prevention of the atherosclerotic diseases. *Circulation,* 1970, *42,* 1155–1170.

Jeffery, R. W., & Coates, T. J. Why aren't they losing weight? *Behavior Therapy,* 1978, *9,* 856–860.

Jeffery, R. W., Thompson, P. D., & Wing, R. R. Effects on weight reduction of strong monetary contracts for caloric restriction for weight loss. *Behaviour Research and Therapy,* 1978, *16,* 363–369.

Jeffery, R. W., & Wing, R. R. Frequency of therapist contact in the treatment of obesity. *Behavior Therapy,* 1979, *10,* 186–192.

Jeffery, R. W., Wing, R. R., & Stunkard, A. J. Behavioral management of obesity: The state of the art, 1976. *Behavior Therapy,* 1979, *9,* 189–199.

Jenkins, C. D., Zyzanski, S. J., & Rosenman, R. H. Risk of new myocardial infarction in middle-aged men with manifest coronary heart disease. *Circulation,* 1976, *53,* 342–347.

Kahn, E. B., & Edwards, C. N. Smoking and youth: Contributions to the study of smoking behavior in high school students. *Journal of School Health,* 1970, *40,* 561–562.

Kannel, W. B., Castelli, W. P., McNamara, P. M., & Sorlie P. Some factors affecting morbidity and mortality in hypertension. *Millbank Memorial Fund Quarterly,* 1969, *47,* 116–142.

Kannel, W. B., & Dawber, T. R. Atherosclerosis as a pediatric problem. *Journal of Pediatrics,* 1972, *80,* 544–554.

Kannel, W. B., & McGee, D. C. Diabetes and cardiovascular risk factors: The Framingham study. *Circulation,* 1979, *59,* 8–12.

Kass, E. H., Zinner, S. H., Margolius, H. S., Yhu, L., Rosner, B., & Donner, A. Familial aggregation of blood pressure and urinary Kallikrein in early childhood. In O. Paul (Ed.), *Epidemiology and control of hypertension.* New York: Grune & Stratton, 1975.

Kelson, S. R., Pullella, J. L., & Otterland, A. The growing epidemic: A survey of smoking habits and attitudes toward smoking among students in grades 7 through 12 in Toledo and Lucas County (Ohio) public schools, 1964 and 1971. *American Journal of Public Health,* 1975, *55,* 923–928.

Keys, A. (Ed.). Coronary heart disease in seven countries. *Circulation,* 1970, *41,* I1–I211.

Kilcoyne, M. M. Adolescent hypertension. *American Journal of Medicine,* 1975, *58,* 735–739.

Kingsley, R. J., & Shapiro, J. A comparison of three behavioral programs for control of obesity in children. *Behavior Therapy,* 1977, *8,* 30–36.

Knowles, J. H. *Doing better and feeling worse.* New York: Norton, 1977.

Komaki, J., & Barrett, F. T. A behavioral approach to coaching football: Improving the play execution of the offensive backfield in a youth football team. *Journal of Applied Behavior Analysis,* 1977, *10,* 657–664.

Kotchen, J. M., Kotchen, T. A., Schwertman, N. L., & Kuller, L. H. Blood pressure distributions of urban adolescents. *American Journal of Epidemiology,* 1974, *99,* 315–324.

Kuller, L. H. Epidemiology of cardiovascular diseases: Current perspectives. *American Journal of Epidemiology,* 1976, *104,* 425–456.

Laoye, J., Creswell, W. H., & Stone, D. B. A cohort study of 1205 secondary school smokers. *Journal of School Health,* 1972, *44,* 47–52.

Langford, H. G., & Watson, R. L. Electrolytes, environment, and blood pressure. *Clinical Science and Molecular Medicine,* 1973, *45,* 111s–113s.

Langford, H. G., & Watson, R. L. Electrolytes and hypertension. In O. Paul (Ed.), *Epidemiology and control of hypertension.* New York: Grune & Stratton, 1975.

Langford, H. G., Watson, R. L., & Douglas, B. H. Factors affecting blood pressure in population groups. *Transactions of the Association of American Physicians,* 1968, *81,* 135-146.

Lauer, R. M., Connor, W. E., Leaverton, P. E., Reiter, M. A., & Clarke, W. R. Coronary heart disease risk factors in school-children: The Muscatine study. *Journal of Pediatrics,* 1975, *86,* 697-706.

Lauer, R. M., Clarke, W. R., & Rames, L. K. Blood pressure and its significance in childhood. *Postgraduate Medical Journal,* 1978, *54,* 206-210.

Lee, V. A. Individual trends in the total serum cholesterol of children and adolescents over a ten-year period. *American Journal of Clinical Nutrition,* 1967, *20,* 5-12.

Libb, J. W., & Clements, C. B. Token reinforcement in an exercise program for hospitalized geriatric patients. *Perceptual and Motor Skills,* 1969, *28,* 957-958.

Lieberman Research. *The teenager looks at cigarette smoking.* Study conducted for the American Cancer Society, 1969.

Londe, S., Bourgoigne, J. J., Robson, A. M., & Goldring, D. Hypertension in apparently normal children. *Journal of Pediatrics,* 1971, *78,* 569-577.

McAlister, A. L., Perry, C., & Maccoby, N. Adolescent smoking: Onset and prevention. *Pediatrics,* 1979, *63,* 650-657.

Maccoby, N., Farquhar, J. W., Wood, P. D., & Alexander, J. K. Reducing the risk of cardiovascular disease. *Journal of Community Health,* 1977, *3,* 100-114.

McGuire, W. Inducing resistance to persuasion: Some contemporary approaches. In L. Berkowitz (Ed.), *Advances in experimental social psychology* (Vol. 1). New York: Academic Press, 1964.

McKennel, A. L. Implications for health of social influences on smoking. *American Journal of Public Health,* 1969, *59,* 1998-2004.

McKenzie, T. L., & Rushall, B. S. Effects of self-recording on attendance and performance in a competitive swimming training environment. *Journal of Applied Behavior Analysis,* 1974, 7, 199-206.

Madsen, C. H., Madsen, C. K., & Thompson, F. Increasing a rural head start children's consumption of middle class meals. *Journal of Applied Behavior Analysis,* 1974, 7, 257-262.

Mann, G. V. The influence of obesity in health. *New England Journal of Medicine.* 1974, *291,* 178-185.

Mann, G. V. Diet-heart: End of an era. *New England Journal of Medicine,* 1977, *297,* 644-650.

Mason, E. Obesity in pet dogs. *The Veterinary Record,* 1970, *86,* 612-616.

Matthews, K. *Mother-child interaction and determinants of Type A behavior.* Unpublished doctoral dissertation, University of Texas at Austin, 1976.

Matthews, K. Caregiver-child interactions and the Type A coronary-prone behavior pattern. *Child Development,* 1977, *48,* 1752-1756.

Matthews, K., Glass, D. C., & Richins, M. The mother-son observation study. In D. C. Glass (Ed.), *Behavior patterns, stress, and coronary disease.* Hillsdale, N.J.: Erlbaum, 1977.

Matthews, K. A., & Krantz, D. S. Resemblances of twins and their parents in pattern A behavior. *Psychosomatic Medicine,* 1976, *28,* 140-144.

Mausner, B., & Mischler, J. B. Cigarette smoking among junior high school students. *Journal of Special Education,* 1967, *1,* 61-66.

Mayer, J. Obesity during childhood. In M. Winik (Ed.), *Childhood obesity.* New York: Wiley, 1975.

Merki, D. J., Creswell, W. H., Stone, D. B., Huffman, W., & Newman, I. The effects of two educational methods and message themes in rural youth smoking behavior. *Journal of School Health,* 1968, *38,* 448-454.

Miller, N. E. The evidence for antiatherogenicity of high density lipoproteins in men. *Lipids,* 1979, *13,* 914-919.

Miller, R. A., & Shekelle, R. B. Blood pressure in tenth grade students. *Circulation,* 1976, *54,* 993-1000.

Moody, D. L., Wilmore, J. H., Girandola, R. N., & Royce, J. P. The effects of a jogging program on the body composition of normal and obese high school girls. *Medicine and Behavior in Sports,* 1972, *2,* 210-213.

Morgan, T., Adam, W., Gillies, A., Wilson, M., Morgan, G., & Carney, S. Hypertension treated by salt restriction. *Lancet,* 1978, *1,* 227-230.

Multiple Risk Factor Intervention Trial. A national study of primary prevention of coronary heart disease. *Journal of the American Medical Association,* 1976, *235,* 825-827.

National Cancer Institute. *Cigarette smoking among teenagers and young women* (U.S. Department of Health Education and Welfare, DHEW Publication No. (NIH) 77-2203). Washington, D.C.: U.S. Government Printing Office, 1977.

National Center for Health Statistics. *Blood pressure levels of children 6-11 years* (Publication (HRA) 74-1617, Vital and Health Statistics Series 11, No. 135.). Washington, D. C.: U.S. Government Printing Office, 1973.

National Center for Health Statistics. *Blood pressure levels of youths 12-17 years* (Publication (HRA) 77-1645, Vital and Health Statistics Series 11, No. 163.). Washington, D. C.: U. S. Government Printing Office, 1977.

Nichols, A. V. Functions and interrelationships of different classes of plasma lipoproteins. *Proceedings of the National Academy of Science,* 1969, *64,* 1128-1137.

Paffenbarger, R. S., Thoren, M. C., & Wing, A. L.

Chronic diseases in former college students. VIII. Characteristics of youths predisposing to hypertension in later years. *American Journal of Epidemiology,* 1968, *88,* 25-32.

Palmer, A. B. Some variables contributing to the onset of cigarette smoking among junior high school students. *Social Science and Medicine,* 1970, *4,* 359-366.

Perera, G. A. The course of primary hypertension in the young. *Annals of Internal Medicine,* 1950, *49,* 1348-1350.

Perry, C. P., Killen, J., Telch, M., Slinkard, L. A., & Danaher, B. G. Modifying smoking behavior of teenagers. A school-based intervention. *American Journal of Public Health,* 1980, *70,* 722-724.

Piscano, J. C., Lichter, H., Ritter, J., & Siegal, A. P. An attempt at the prevention of obesity. *Pediatrics,* 1978, *61,* 360-364.

Podell, R. N., Keller, K., & Mulvihill, M. N. Evaluation of the effectiveness of a high school course in cardiovascular nutrition. *American Journal of Public Health,* 1978. *68,* 573-576.

The Pooling Project Research Group. *Relationship of blood pressure, serum cholesterol, smoking habit, relative weight, and ECG abnormalities to incidence of major coronary events.* Dallas, Texas: American Heart Association Monograph, 1978.

President's Council on Youth Fitness. *Youth physical fitness: Suggested elements of a school-centered program.* Washington, D. C.: U.S. Government Printing Office, 1961.

Pumroy, D. K. Cigarette smoking and academic achievement. *Journal of Genetic Psychology,* 1967, *77,* 31-34.

Puska, P., Koshela, K., McAlister, A., Paelonen, V., Vartiainen, E., & Homan, K. A comprehensive television smoking cessation programme in Finland. *International Journal of Health Education,* 1979, *22,* 1-28. (Supplement.)

Rappenthal, B., La Tercera nutrition education project for elementary pupils. *Journal of the American Dietetic Association,* 1977, *71,* 53-54.

Reeder, J. P. *An exploratory study in health education for preschool and elementary children.* Columbia, Mo.: Stephens College, 1978.

Reeder, J. P. *An addendum to an exploratory study in health education for preschool and elementary children.* Columbia, Mo.: Stephens College, 1979.

Rogers, K. D., & Reese, G. Smoking and high school performance. *American Journal of Diseases of Children,* 1964, *108,* 117-121.

Rose, H. E., & Mayer, J. Activity, caloric intake and the energy balance of infants. *Pediatrics,* 1968, *41,* 18-29.

Rosenman, R. H., Brand, R. J., Sholtz, R. I., & Friedman, M. Multivariate predictions of coronary heart disease during 8.5 year follow-up in the Western Collaborative Group Study. *American Journal of Cardiology,* 1976, *37,* 902-910.

Sackett, D. L. Studies of blood pressures in spouses. In O. Paul (Ed.), *Epidemiology and control of hypertension.* New York: Grune & Stratton, 1975.

Savage, P. J., Hammon, R. F., Bartha, G., Dippe, S. E., Miller, M., & Bennett, P. H. Serum cholesterol levels in American (Pima) Indian children and adolescents. *Pediatrics,* 1976, *58,* 274-282.

Seltzer, C. C., & Mayer, J. An effective weight control program in a public school system. *American Journal of Public Health,* 1970, *60,* 679-689.

Shapiro, D., & Surwit, R. S. Learned control of physiological function and disease. In H. Leitenberg (Ed.), *Handbook of behavior modification and behavior therapy.* Englewood Cliffs: Prentice-Hall, 1976.

Shukla, A., Forsyth, H. A., Anderson, C. M., & Marwah, S. M. Infantile overnutrition in the first years of life: A field study in Dudley, Worcestershire. *British Medical Journal,* 1972, *4,* 507-515.

Silber, E. J. Smoking among teenagers. *Bulletin of the New York Academy of Medicine,* 1968, *44,* 1521-1525.

Srinivasan, S. R., Frerichs, R. R., Webber, L. S., & Berenson, G. S. Serum lipoprotein profile in children from a biracial community: The Bogalusa Heart Study, *Circulation,* 1976, *54,* 309-315.

Srinivasan, S. R., Frerichs, R. R., & Berenson, G. S. Serum lipids and lipoproteins in children. In M. D. Strong (Ed.), *Atherosclerosis: Its pediatric aspects.* New York: Grune & Stratton, 1978.

Stamler, J., Stamler, R., Riedlinger, W. F., Algera, G., & Roberts, R. H. Hypertension screening of one million Americans. *Journal of American Medical Association,* 1976, *235,* 2299-2306.

Stanley, E. J., Glaser, H. H., Levin, D. G., Adsner, P. A., & Coley, B. A. Overcoming obesity in adolescents. *Clinical Pediatrics.* 1970, *9,* 29-36.

Stark, P. Hypercholesteremia in school children: A preliminary report. *American Journal of Clinical Pathology,* 1971. *56,* 515-522.

Stewart, A., & Westropp, C. Breast feeding in the Oxford Child Health Survey. *British Medical Journal,* 1953, *2,* 305-308.

Stine, O. C., Hepner, R., & Greenstreet, R. Correlation of blood pressure with skinfold thickness and protein levels. *American Journal of Diseases of Children,* 1975, *129,* 905-911.

Taitz, L. S. Infantile overnutrition among artificially fed infants in the Sheffield region. *British Medical Journal,* 1971, *1,* 315-316.

Task Force on Blood Pressure Control. *Pediatrics,* 1977, *59,* 797-820.

Tasto, D. L., Chesney, M. A., & Chadwick, J. H. Multidimensional analysis of coronary-prone behavior. In T. M. Dembroski, S. M. Weiss, J. L. Shields, S. G. Haynes, & M. Feinleib (Eds.), *Coronary-prone behavior.* New York: Springer, 1978.

Thompson, E. L. Smoking education programs: 1960–1976. *American Journal of Public Health,* 1978, *68,* 250–257.

Trowell, H. Pathological growth and maturation in infants associated with modern methods of feeding. *Journal of Tropical Medicine and Environmental Child Health,* 1975, *21,* 192–198.

U. S. Department of Health, Education and Welfare. *Teenage smoking: National patterns of cigarette smoking, ages 12 through 18 in 1968 and 1970* (DHEW Publication No. (NIH) 76-931). Washington, D.C.: U.S. Government Printing Office, 1972.

U. S. Department of Health, Education and Welfare. *Teenage smoking: National patterns of cigarette smoking, ages 12 through 18, in 1972 and 1974* (DHEW Publication No. (NIH) 76-931). Washington, D.C.: U.S. Government Printing Office, 1976.

Valkenburg, H. A., Groustra, F. N., Klein, F., Van Laar, A., & Werdmuller, S. I. Natural history of blood pressure and cholesterol in children 5-19 years of age, selected for these risk factors on a statistical basis from an open population sample. In J. G. A. V. Hautvast & H. A. Valkenburg (Eds.), *Atherosclerosis and the child.* Rotterdam: Erasmus University, 1977.

Veldman, D. J., & Brown, O. M. Personality and performance characteristics associated with cigarette smoking among college freshmen. *Journal of Consulting and Clinical Psychology,* 1969, *33,* 109–119.

Voors, A. W., Foster, T. A., Frerichs, R. R., Webber, L. S., & Berenson, G. S. Studies of blood pressure in children ages 5–14 in a total biracial community—The Bogalusa Heart Study. *Circulation,* 1976, *54,* 319–327.

Voors, A. W., Webber, L. S., & Berenson, G. S. Time course studies of blood pressure in children: The Bogalusa Heart Study. *American Journal of Epidemiology,* 1979, *109,* 320–324.

Weinberg, R., Schear, C. L., Avet, L. M., Frerichs, R. R., & Fox, M. Path analysis of environmental and genetic influences on blood pressure. *American Journal of Epidemiology,* 1979, *109,* 588–596.

Wheeler, M. E., & Hess, K. W. Treatment of juvenile obesity by successive approximation control of eating. *Journal of Behavior Therapy and Experimental Psychiatry,* 1976, *7,* 235–241.

Whitehead, F. E. Nutrition education for children in the U.S. since 1900: Part II. *Journal of the American Dietetic Association,* 1957, *33,* 885–880.

Williams, C. L., Arnold, C., & Wynder, E. L. Primary prevention of chronic disease beginning in childhood. *Preventive Medicine,* 1977, *6,* 344–357.

Williams, R. B. Psychophysiological processes, the coronary-prone behavior pattern, and coronary heart disease. In T. M. Dembroski, S. M. Weiss, J. L. Shields, S. G. Haynes, & M. Feinleib (Eds.), *Coronary-prone behavior.* New York: Springer, 1978.

Windsor, R. A. Smoking habits and attitudes of 414 youth in Illinois, ages 9 to 12. *Journal of School Health, 1972, 42,* 558–560.

Wing, R. R., & Jeffery, R. W. Outpatient treatments of obesity: A comparison of methodology and clinical results. *International Journal of Obesity,* 1979, *3,* 261–279.

Witschi, J. C., Singer, M., Wu-Lee, M., & Stare, F. J. Family cooperation and effectiveness in a cholesterol-lowering diet. *Journal of the American Dietetic Association,* 1978, *72,* 384–388.

Wohlford, P. Initiation of cigarette smoking: Is it related to smoking behavior? *Journal of Consulting and Clinical Psychology,* 1970, *34,* 148–151.

Wynder, E. L., & Hoffman, D. Tobacco and health: A societal challenge. *New England Journal of Medicine,* 1979, *300,* 894–903.

Wysocki, T., Harl, G., Iwata, B., & Riordan, M. Behavioral management of exercise: Contracting for aerobic points. *Journal of Applied Behavioral Analysis,* 1979, *12,* 55–64.

Zyzanski, S. J., Jenkins, C. D., Ryan, T. J., Flessas, A., & Everist, M. Psychological correlates of coronary and angiographic findings. *Archives of Internal Medicine,* 1976, *136,* 1234–1237.

12

Psychological Preparation for Stressful Medical Procedures

PHILIP C. KENDALL
DAVID WATSON

Picture yourself on a typical hospital ward. Imagine the ward in your mind and think about how you feel. You've just spoken briefly with your temporary roommates and have decided to retire for the evening. Health concerns occupy your thoughts and you are worried about the medical procedures that will be undertaken. In this hypothetical example you are scheduled to undergo endoscopic procedures to examine your gastrointestinal track.

Your endoscopic study begins with the application of a local anesthetic to the throat by swabbing and is followed by the insertion of a flexible tube (12 mm in diameter, 9 cm in length) through your mouth and into your gastrointestinal track. The tube is held down for 15–30 minutes so that portions of your inner track may be transmitted as an image that can be seen by the physician or photographed with a camera. Finally, the tube is removed.

You probably have received some sedative medication prior to the endoscopic study; however, the procedure cannot be accomplished safely unless you are sufficiently aware to follow directions and breathe correctly. Breathing is especially important since failure to breathe through the mouth is likely to cause you to gag or to swallow the tube.

As a reader, you may be able to divorce yourself from such a potential experience. After all, you haven't been having any difficulties with your gastrointestinal track! Nevertheless, consider the following example.

You have been informed by your physician that it is probable that you have coronary artery disease. The cardiologists, therefore, have decided that it would be worthwhile to undertake coronary catheterization and angiographic procedures to help determine the most appropriate medical treatment. Will you be scheduled for open heart surgery? How many arteries show disease? How serious is the heart disease? Would a bypass be desirable? Should you be maintained on medications? Should the physician recommend no treatment at this time?

Dressed in a white hospital robe, you are es-

Medical Psychology
Contributions to Behavioral Medicine

ISBN 0-12-565960-1

corted to the catheterization laboratory on a gurney by a nurse technician. You enter the lab and are told to assume a supine position on a platform; the technician straps you in. At this point you notice that the room is lined with scientific equipment and that several cardiologists and nurse technicians are simultaneously involved in a variety of independent tasks.

You've received only a slight tranquilizer because it will be necessary for you to follow directions throughout the 1-3 hour procedure. An incision is made into your femoral artery at the groin and into this artery the cardiologist inserts the catheter. The catheter is moved within the artery until it reaches the desired portion of the heart chamber. A dye is injected through the catheter into the heart. A camera, suspended above your chest, projects the event on a TV screen and photographs each dye injection. The dye highlights the diseased tissue providing the physician with data on the severity of the disease that may be used to help determinate the best method to treat your disorder. Because you must not keep the dye in your heart for long, the physician repeatedly tells you to "cough" to help flush the dye from your system. Similarly, for useful photographs of your heart to be taken, the physician tells you to take deep breaths to move the lungs away from the area to be photographed. The TV screen may be visible to you and you may watch your heart on the screen as numerous professionals scurry about monitoring the equipment, checking your physical signs, coaching you on following instructions, and commenting on the quality of the pictures that the procedure is producing.

While people's reactions to the stressful nature of the invasive quality of medical procedures such as endoscopy and catheterization differ, it appears that some degree of discomfort, worry, tension, and anxiety are almost universal. The necessity of the medical procedures for the patient's physical health typically supplant any choice on the patient's part and often there is little the patient can do to either make the time pass more quickly or reduce the seriousness of potential danger that exists. It seems reasonable to conceptualize these invasive medical procedures as "crises" (e.g., Auerbach & Kilmann, 1977) and to consider certain crisis intervention strategies (e.g., Butcher & Maudal, 1976; Butcher & Koss, 1978) as ways to intervene. Psychological preparations, provided by professionals with interests in areas such as medical psychology, can make an extremely valuable contribution to an undisturbed hospital experience. Such preparations can help to prevent patients' untoward emotional disturbances and facilitate emotional well-being, as well as improve their adjustment during the actual medical procedures.

Recognition of the importance of psychological interventions with medical patients has been a comparatively recent development (Frank, 1979). Nevertheless, a diverse range of intervention techniques have been employed in an effort to relieve the distress of invasive medical procedures. The methods employed have varied in terms of the type of help provided, the broadness versus specificity of the techniques used, and the extent to which the techniques are tailored to take into account individual differences among the needs and resources of different patients. Not surprisingly, there is also a diverse range of stressful medical procedures for which interventions have been designed and studied. This chapter considers the various intervention strategies within several broad categories: (*a*) psychological support; (*b*) information provision; (*c*) skills training; (*d*) hypnosis; (*e*) relaxation training; (*f*) filmed modeling; and (*g*) cognitive-behavioral interventions. Some studies could fit into more than one category and the categories themselves are not entirely independent. An attempt is made, however, to impose some order by considering each category separately.

Psychological Support

Historically, the development of intervention methods for hospitalized patients has seen a move to more rigorous evaluation of more specific therapeutic techniques. Since the strategy we have termed "psychological support" was perhaps the earliest of the major categories to develop (indeed, it could be argued that this intervention strategy has been used—if informally and unsystematically — since the first time a doctor attempted to reassure a patient), it is not surprising that it is rather nondescript and includes a number of diverse approaches. Included among the psychological support methods used are brief individual psychotherapy, group discussions to allow patients to voice their fears and anxieties, and puppet and play therapy (with children). What unifies these approaches is the common attempt to provide patients with reassurance and support to facilitate their adjustment to hospitalization.

One of the better studies employing psychological support was conducted by Gruen (1975), who examined the effectiveness of brief individual psychotherapy in alleviating the distress among myocardial infarction patients. Patients in the experimental group received an average of one-half hour of therapy 5–6 days a week during their stay in the hospital. The therapeutic intervention emphasized the development of a good patient–therapist relationship, reflection of the patient's feelings, reassurance to the patient that his or her fears and anxieties were normal and appropriate, reinforcement of the patient's coping mechanisms and ability to cope successfully with the current stressful situation, and encouragement of the patient to take a more active part in the medical situation. The control group consisted of patients who were matched on such variables as age, sex, religion, and severity of illness but who did not receive any form of therapeutic intervention.

The results of the Gruen's (1975) study showed that the patients who received psychological support spent significantly fewer days in intensive care, and significantly fewer days "on the monitor" (i.e., under intensive observation). There was also a trend for the treated patients to spend fewer days in the hospital, a trend which reached significance when the best adjusted patients (those who presumably would be *least* affected by any therapeutic intervention) were removed from both groups. Several measures of the patients' current, transient mood states were also used but the results showed no significant differences on either the Taylor Manifest Anxiety Scale (Taylor, 1953; TMAS), the State–Trait Anxiety Inventory (Spielberger, Gorsuch, & Lushene, 1970; STAI) State Anxiety (A-State) scale, the Multiple Affect Adjective Check List (Zuckerman & Lubin, 1965; MAACL) Anxiety scale, or the Nowlis Adjective Check List (Nowlis & Green, Note 1; NACL) Anxiety scale. These data indicate that the experimental patients were not less anxious than the controls. However, the treated patients described themselves (on the NACL) as higher on the Urgency scale (more "carefree," "playful," and "witty") and Affection scale ("affectionate," "kindly," "sociable," and "warmhearted") than did controls. Finally, a four-month follow-up indicated that the treated patients were significantly less fearful of another heart attack and had resumed normal activities to a greater extent than had the controls.

Taken together, the results indicate that Gruen's intervention was an effective aid, and that its effectiveness extended beyond the hospital stay itself. This positive evaluation of the study, however, must be tempered by three cautions which illustrate three important methodological principles pertinent to psychological intervention with medical patients. First, it is unclear as to what aspect of the intervention produced the positive results. Any aspect or combination of aspects of therapy could have been responsible for the significant gain. On the other hand, since the controls were not given commensurate attention by a staff member, the results could have been due merely to the increased attention built into the therapeutic intervention. That this might be the case is supported by the results of a study conducted by Lucas (1975). Lucas used a four-group design to investigate the effectiveness of various preoperative interventions in heart surgery patients. The groups consisted of (*a*) patients who received a preoperative intervention involving active focusing on plans for recovery and future life; (*b*) patients who were asked to merely think about recovery and future plans; (*c*) patients who were only given attention commensurate with that provided to those in groups (*a*) and (*b*), but who received no treatment; and (*d*) a nontreatment control group. The results indicated that the first three groups recovered significantly better than did the no-treatment controls, but that they did not differ significantly among themselves. These results suggest that attention can lead to significant improvement in postsurgery recovery and illustrate our first methodological point; studies of the efficacy of psychological preparation should control for the effects of differential attention. It should be emphasized, however, that this point is mainly relevant for research purposes. Failure to control for differential attention means only that the reason *why* the intervention worked remains ambiguous; it *does not* indicate that the intervention may not have been successful.

The second caution regarding the Gruen (1975) study is that the intervention differentially affected the dependent variables that were used. That is, the psychological support was effective in getting the patients out of the hospital more quickly and allowing them to return more completely to their normal life, but it did not reduce the patient's level of anxiety. Since invasive medical procedures typically induce a high level of stress in patients, it would seem highly desirable for interventions to also be effective at reducing the patient's anxiety. These findings illustrate a second methodological issue. Since a given intervention may affect only *some* of the dependent variables, the most satisfactory studies are those which employ a wide array of dependent variables.

The third caution, as Gruen points out, is that the intervention was not needed by all of the patients. This is illustrated by the fact that the differences between the groups became much more striking when the best adjusted patients were removed from each group. The third methodological issue, then, is that psychological interventions should take into account individual differences among patients.

The Gruen (1975) study thus serves as an example of the effectiveness of psychological support as an intervention strategy. We have closely examined this study to illustrate three methodological issues relevant to research in the area of psychological preparation for medical procedures. We will return to these later in a specific discussion of methodological issues.

Another study of psychological support was conducted by Schmitt and Wooldridge (1973), in conjunction with information provision and a behavioral intervention. Their experimental patients attended a one-hour group discussion (consisting of 2–5 patients) the evening before surgery. Patients discussed their feelings about the upcoming procedure, reassured each other that their feelings and fears were normal, and exchanged information about the procedure. The group leader provided additional procedural information and behavioral information (such as proper breathing and coughing techniques, leg exercises, and ways to turn and get out of bed). Additionally, most of the treated patients received a one-to-one intervention (lasting from 15 minutes to one hour) on the morning of the surgery. This session focused on the patient's immediate feelings and needs. The patients were encouraged to verbalize any anxiety that they might be feeling, and the therapist provided support, reassurance and some additional information. The control patients received "routine hospital care," which generally included some behavioral information about coughing and breathing deeply, how to turn, etc. Schmitt and Wooldridge found that their treated patients slept better than the controls, had less difficulty in voiding and urinary retention, took less medication on the second and third postoperative days, resumed an oral diet sooner, and spent fewer days in the hospital. In addition, while there were no group differences in state anxiety on the evening before surgery, the treated patients reported less anxiety on the morning of surgery.

Lindemann and Stetzer (1973) employed a psychological support intervention that encouraged patients to talk about their fears and anxieties and thereby, hopefully, reduce them. Patients in the treatment group were visited preoperatively by a nurse who answered questions and encouraged them to talk about their feelings and fears concerning the upcoming surgery. In addition, all patients, both treatment and control, were trained in deep breathing, coughing, and bed exercises. The results provided only slight support for the efficacy of the program. There were no group differences in the number of days hospitalized, the number of analgesics administered, or the physiological problems subsequent to surgery. The Palmar Sweat Index (PSI), an index of anxiety, showed a greater increase among the controls when administered postoperatively. Further analysis indicated that this effect was found only among patients who underwent minor surgery, while patients in the moderate and severe surgery groups showed no such difference.

Another study employing psychological support for adult patients was conducted by Surman, Hackett, Silverberg, and Behrendt (1974). The subjects in their study were patients undergoing cardiac surgery. All patients (both experimental and control) underwent a standard educational program on heart surgery given by the nursing staff. The experimental group received an additional 60–90 minute interview, the goals of which were to (*a*) reinforce the preoperative teaching of the nursing staff; (*b*) provide psychological support and a means through which the patients could voice their concerns about the forthcoming surgery; and (*c*) hypnotize patients and teach them self-hypnosis for their own use in the postoperative period. The results provided no support for the efficacy of the intervention. The two groups showed no differences in postoperative delirium, pain, anxiety, depression, or use of medication. The authors interpreted their findings as an indication that a single preoperative visit does not constitute an effective psychotherapeutic intervention. Though this interpretation is feasible, it is also possible that the interview itself was an inadequate intervention.

The studies reviewed thus far provide no unequivocal evidence supporting the efficacy of psychological support interventions for adult medical patients. The Gruen (1975) study provides perhaps the most compelling evidence, but even here it seems that the therapy provided help for only some of the patients. This is not to say that psychological support is completely counterindicated for all patients. For those patients who seem to be having trouble adjusting to the hospital environment, a system of psychological support combined with methods to be discussed subsequently that appear to be more effective in reducing the stress and anxiety associated with invasive medical procedure is certainly warranted.

Psychological Support with Children

Cassell (1965) studied the effects of a brief "puppet therapy" on children (ages 3–11) undergoing cardiac catheterization. Children in the treatment group were given two sessions of puppet therapy, one pre- and the other postsurgery. During the therapy session, as many aspects of the catheterization procedure as possible were explained through the use of puppets. In addition, through the puppets the children were shown that the staff recognized the frightening nature of the catheterization. The children were also encouraged to use the puppets to act out their fears and feelings regarding the medical procedure.

Cassell found that the treated group exhibited less emotional disturbance, as measured by observer ratings of their behavior, during the catheterization procedure itself, and that the treated children expressed more willingness to return to the hospital in the future for further treatment. On the other hand, the two groups did not differ in their level of emotional disturbance in the hospitalization period following catheterization. The results thus provide some support for the effectiveness of the puppet therapy, but, as in the study with adults, the failure to control for the increased attention given to the treatment group remains problematic.

Coleman (1975) used two treatment groups in a study of the effectiveness of play therapy and parent education in reducing the anxiety of pediatric surgery patients (ages 8–11). One treatment group consisted of children who participated in play therapy and an orientation program following hospitalization. This procedure included simulation of anxiety-producing stimuli in a play situation, and the provision of procedural information (through visits to the x-ray, operating, and recovery rooms). A second treatment group consisted of children who received the previously described treatment, in addition to which their parents went through an orientation program of their own. The control group received no treatment. Children in all groups were given the Children's Manifest Anxiety Scale (Castaneda, McCandless, & Palermo, 1956; CMAS) both prior to and on the evening of hospital admission, and again seven days following discharge from the hospital. Although both parents and children seemed to respond positively to the treatment programs, analysis showed no significant group differences on the CMAS. Thus, the play therapy orientation treatment was not successful in producing significant changes in children's anxiety. It should be noted that the CMAS is more a measure of trait anxiety than state anxiety and may not be sensitive to relatively transient emotional states. Further, there are problems associated with the self-report assessment of anxiety in children (Finch & Kendall, 1979) that may also be involved.

A study by Lehman (1975) analyzed the effect of having mothers room-in with their children (aged 3–5 years) who were hospitalized for tonsillectomies and/or adenoidectomies. Children with rooming-in mothers had fewer major postoperative complications (such as hemorrhaging or vomiting) than did the children whose mothers did not room-in, and there was also a trend for these children to exhibit fewer behavioral disturbances on a postsurgery follow-up questionnaire. On the other hand, the rooming-in children showed a tendency to display more aggressive behavior in the hospital, and to receive more analgesics.

As was the case with adult interventions, psychological support studies with children have produced some evidence of effectiveness but these findings are equivocal. Again, the sorts of interventions described are probably best used in conjunction with other methods of established efficacy in the reduction of hospitalization-related stress. Nevertheless, these studies have called attention to the psychological needs of children undergoing invasive medical procedures.

Information Provision

Research on the effects of providing patients with information about their impending medical procedures was stimulated by Marmor (1958) and Janis (1958). For example, Marmor (1958) proposed that when patients are moderately fearful due to a situational stress they engage in the "work of worry" which helps them to prepare for and adjust to the stress. Janis (1958) has reported on the results of interviews of surgery patients that supported the importance of moderate fear levels. Janis' patients fell along a curvilinear path with the best adjustment associated with moderate amounts of fear. Subsequently, it was hypothesized that providing patients with preoperative information would increase emotional drive, energize the "work of worry", and cause a reduction in untoward emotional responses.

More recent research has indicated that the type of information that is provided to patients can be described as *procedural,* that is, information about the nature of the medical procedure itself, where and when it will take place, what the mortality rate is, etc., and *sensory,* or information regarding the sensations that the patients should expect to feel during the medical procedure.

The information types can be separated conceptually, but it has been difficult for researchers to isolate the two types of information provision for the purposes of research. It has also been the case that both types of information provision have been included in studies that were designed to assess the effects of other types of interventions. For example, we have already discussed studies by Schmitt and Wooldridge (1973) and Surman *et al.* (1974) which included procedural information in their psychological support interventions. Though many studies have provided information as a part of a multicomponent intervention that has precluded examination of its specific effects, some investigations have addressed directly the utility of different types of information provision.

Procedural Information

Vernon and Bigelow (1974) examined the effectiveness of preoperative procedural information in reducing the anxiety of male patients hospitalized for the repair of inguinal hernias. The treatment patients received extra detailed information about the upcoming procedure 2 days prior to surgery, while the control patients did not receive this extra information. Half of the treated patients were seen again on the evening before surgery, and their anxiety (on the MAACL), adjustment, and amount of information were measured at that time; the other half of the treated patients were similarly assessed on the fourth or fifth postoperative day.

A manipulation check revealed that the treated patients did indeed have more information concerning the hernia repair procedure. An analysis of the data, however, showed only a few marginally significant differences between the treated and the control patients. These results would seem to cast some initial doubt on the utility of providing extra *procedural* information; however, the authors report that the failure to find group differences most likely stemed from the fact that the patients did not seem to find the surgery particularly stressful. Indeed, examination of the mean MAACL mood scores indicated that all subjects were well within the resting or nonstress range. The absence of a strong stressor would certainly have limited the effectiveness of any intervention.

Sensory Information

Egbert, Battit, Welch, and Bartlett (1964) investigated the utility of establishing physician-patient rapport and provided patients with sensory information as a component of this intervention. The patients in this study were undergoing intraabdominal operations. All patients were visited the night before surgery by the anesthetist, at which time they were given brief (procedural) information concerning their operation (e.g., the preparation for anesthesia, the time and approximate duration of the operation, etc.). In addition, the treated patients were given specific sensory information about the pain that they would feel postoperatively. They were informed about the location of the pain, its severity, and its duration. Additionally, the treated patients were trained in some behavioral skills designed to relieve most of the pain—that is, by muscle relaxation, proper turning, etc. An anesthetist also visited the treated patients one to two times a day postoperatively to reinforce the information and training provided.

The Egbert *et al.* (1964) results indicated that although the two groups did not differ in their use of narcotics for pain on the day of operation itself, the treatment group had a significantly lower level of narcotic use on each of the succeeding five days. In addition, the treated patients were released from the hospital significantly sooner (2.7 days) and were rated by a second anesthetist (blind to condition) as being in less pain. Although the evidence supporting the efficacy of this intervention is considerable, it is unclear how much of the effect was due solely to the provision of sensory information, how much was due to the behavioral skills training, and how much was due to the greater time and attention given to the special care patients.

A more careful design was used by Johnson and Leventhal (1974), who compared the effectiveness of different interventions in reducing the distress of patients undergoing an endoscopy examination. All patients were provided with procedural information (e.g., where they would receive premedications, where the exam would take place, what equipment would be used) but only some of the patients were provided with sensory information. These patients were told what specific sensations they would expect to see, feel, taste, and hear. The second intervention group was given behavioral training information, including specific instructions for rapid mouth breathing and panting to reduce gagging during the throat painting, and behaviors to be performed during the tube insertion. The third treatment group received both the sensory and the behavioral training types of information. A fourth group was not given any information beyond the procedural information.

The data were analyzed separately for patients of two age groups (i.e., those younger than 50 years and those older). No group differences were found in tension-related arm movements during the procedure, and an analysis of heart rate increase showed only a marginal difference between the three treatment groups and controls among the under 50-year-olds. Only the group that received sensory information took significantly less medication than the controls (among the under 50-year-olds). Both the combined information and sensory-only groups gagged less than controls for both age groups. However, the tube passage procedure took longer for the combined information group than it did for controls of all ages. Taken as a whole, the data indicate some support for the usefulness of sensory information, but little or no support for the usefulness of the behavioral training information. It should also be noted that although the study's design allowed for the specific evaluation of certain components of the intervention, the results did not clearly indicate the relative superiority of the different informational intervention procedures.

In a study by Mohros (1976), patients undergoing gastrointestinal endoscopy were divided into four groups: (*a*) reassuring sensory information (i.e., reassuring information concerning the pain and discomfort that could be expected during the examination), combined with general sensory information (e.g., subjects were told that swallowing the tube would feel like swallowing a lump in the throat); (*b*) reassuring procedural information (i.e., reassuring information concerning the safety of the equipment and endoscopy procedure) plus general sensory information; (*c*) general sensory information only; and (*d*) no information controls. Dependent measures used were the dosage of tranquilizer required during the endoscopy, heart rate changes, number of avoidance movements during the examination, and a self-report measure of distress. No significant group differences were found on either the tranquilizer dosage or avoidance movement measures. The reassuring sensory plus general sensory information group had only marginally lower distress scores, but showed a significant decrease in heart rate. Overall, the data indicated only mild support for the effectiveness of any of the information provision interventions.

Another study examining procedural and sensory information was reported by Johnson, Morrissey and Leventhal (1973). The patients (scheduled for a gastrointestinal endoscopy examination) were divided into three groups: (*a*) a sensory information group that heard a message describing sensations that patients typically experience at various points in the examination; (*b*) a procedural information group that heard a message that included descriptions of the endoscopy clinic, the endoscopy procedure, the tubing and other materials involved, and the skill and experience of the examination team; and (*c*) a no-message control group. Additionally, all patients received an explanation of the examination procedure (i.e., all subjects received procedural information). There were no group differences in gagging, heart rate, or restlessness variables. Both of the information groups exhibited fewer tension-related hand and arm movements than did either of the other two groups. Again, these data provide some support for the efficacy of sensory information.

The literature on the utility of providing information for the reduction of patient distress and the improvement of patient adjustment provides only equivocal evidence. However, the results of the studies reviewed can be said to provide more support for the efficacy of sensory information over simple procedural information in achieving the desired goals. Indeed, the failure of the procedural preparatory communications led Johnson (1975) to speculate about the importance of the quality of the information that is provided. Johnson's (1975) suggestion that sensory information also be included appears to have received some support. Nevertheless, attempts to separate the effects of procedural information from sensory information are hampered by the fact that, as Turk and Genest (1979) noted, "it is difficult to prevent the provision of some form of procedural information in medical settings as this is considered to be an important component of good medical practice [p. 292]."

Information Provision: Interactions with Individual Differences

One potential shortcoming of the studies that provided information to patients was their assumption of the "patient uniformity myth [Kiesler, 1966]." Essentially, this myth involves the erroneous assumption that all patients will respond to a psychological intervention in a uniform manner. Or, stated differently, assumption of the myth can be said to result in the search for the one best way for all patients. Recognition of this myth suggests that we investigate the most pertinent differences among people that would help isolate subgroups of patients for which specific treatments would be optimally effective. The amount of information that a patient desires, for example, may be important. Indeed, Sime (1976) found wide individual variation in the amount of information that patients desired preoperatively.

An example of how information provision and personality variables may interact is provided by Andrew (1970). The subjects in this study were hospitalized for hernia or other minor surgery. Half of the subjects heard an eight-minute tape discussing the origins of hernias, the dangers of delaying surgery, and the surgery process itself, while the others were given no such informational treatment. Additionally, the subjects were classified into one of three coping-style groups based upon their answers to a sentence-completion task: (*a*) sensitizers (patients who readily acknowledge negative emotions such as fear and anxiety); (*b*) avoiders (patients who deny or distance themselves from such negative feelings); and (*c*) neutrals (those in between). Dependent variables employed were the length of postsurgery stay in the hospital and the amount of medication needed. A portion of the results are presented in Table 12.1. Among the "sensitizers," there were no differences on either dependent variable between those who had heard the tape and those who had not (i.e., prepared, unprepared). Among the "neutrals," on the other hand, those who had heard the tape spent significantly fewer days in the hospital and required less medication. Among the "avoiders," however, those who had heard the tape required more medication than those who had not. Thus, the information provided appeared to help one group, not affect a second, and hinder a third. These results suggest the importance of taking into account individual differences in information-seeking when considering an information provision intervention.

Table 12.1 Mean Recovery Measures for the Prepared and Unprepared Subjects

Subjects	Days	Medications
Prepared		
Avoiders	9.00	12.75
Neutrals	5.54	4.69
Sensitizers	6.20	5.60
Unprepared		
Avoiders	6.50	5.00
Neutrals	8.33	10.83
Sensitizers	5.50	4.83

Note. Adapted from "Recovery from Surgery, With and Without Preparatory Instruction for Three Coping Styles," by J. Andrew, *Journal of Personality and Social Psychology, 1970, 15,* 212–217. Copyright © 1970 by the Journal of Personality and Social Psychology. Reprinted by permission.

A very similar conclusion can be drawn from the results of a study conducted by DeLong (1970), who examined the reactions of patients (undergoing major abdominal surgery) to various types of information. Half of the patients were given specific information, that is, information specifically pertaining to the upcoming medical procedure. The other patients were provided with general information, that is, information not directly relevant to the upcoming operation. The patients' characteristic coping styles were measured using a sentence completion test. On the basis of this test, the patients were divided into those preferring an active, vigilant defense against stress (copers), those preferring a repressive, avoidant defense (avoiders), and those falling in the middle (neutrals).

The overall results indicated that patients who were provided with specific information were discharged from the hospital earlier and had less complicated recoveries than those who were given the general information. Coping style, however, interacted with the type of information provided. Neutrals tended to show good recoveries, and were not affected by the type of information given them. Among the copers, however, the specific information patients fared significantly better than those who received the general information. Avoiders, on the other hand, tended to have slow and complicated recoveries regardless of the type of information; however, avoiders in the specific information group made more complaints postoperatively than those in the general information group. It would again seem that procedural information is beneficial to one group of patients (copers), has little effect on another group (neutrals), and is troublesome to a third (avoiders).

A study by Auerbach, Kendall, Cuttler, and Levitt (1976) illustrates another personality variable that can affect how patients react to differing types of information. These authors investigated how locus of control (Rotter, 1966) interacted with the specificity versus generality of the information provided. The patients in their study were undergoing dental surgery. One group of patients viewed a general information videotape that disseminated information about the dental clinic and about the usual dental procedures followed in the clinic. Another group viewed a specific information videotape which described the procedures and sensations that they would expect to face during their upcoming surgery. The subjects were also administered the Rotter (1966) Internal-External Locus of Control scale and divided into "internals" and "externals" on the basis of their test responses. Internals are characterized as perceiving themselves as having personal control over the reinforcement they obtain. Externals are said to perceive their reinforcement as being determined by factors outside of their personal control.

On the basis of the dentists' ratings of the subjects' adjustment during the procedure, there were no main effects for either type of information or locus of control. However, within the locus of control groups, internals who viewed the specific information tape fared better than those who viewed the general information tape. The converse was true of the externals, who responded more favorably to the general information tape. This interaction is depicted in Figure 12.1. We again see the importance of tailoring information provision strategies to the individual needs of each patient.

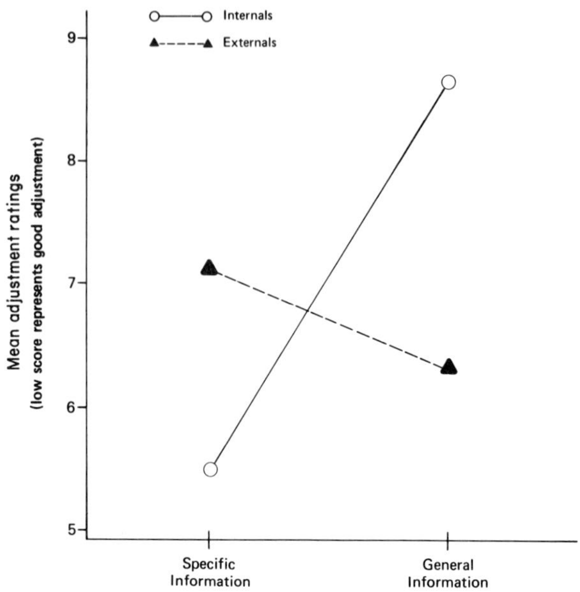

Figure 12.1 Mean adjustment ratings for internal and external subjects differing in type of information received prior to dental surgery (general versus specific). (Adapted from "Anxiety, Locus of Control, Type of Preparatory Information, and Adjustment to Dental Surgery" by S. M. Auerbach, P. C. Kendall, H. F. Cuttler, and N. R. Levitt, *Journal of Consulting and Clinical Psychology,* 1976, *44,* 809–818. Copyright 1976 by the Journal of Consulting and Clinical Psychology. Reprinted by permission.

Information Provision with Children

We have already discussed two studies with children that used some information provision together with psychological support (Cassell, 1965; Coleman, 1975). The Cassell study yielded positive results, although the combination of support with information together with the failure to control for the increased attention given to the treatment group makes an interpretation of the effects of the information difficult.

Two other studies with children deserve brief mention. Both used information provision in conjunction with some other form of intervention. Melamed and Siegel (1975), discussed later in more detail, showed their treated children a modeling film which also included procedural information. The procedural information included an explanation of various hospital procedures and scenes depicting the operating and recovery rooms. Control patients saw a 12-min film depicting a nature trip. Analysis of the PSI showed that the controls were significantly more anxious both pre- and postoperatively. In addition, a behavioral problems checklist indicated a significant pre- to postsurgery increase in problems among the control children, but no such increase among the treated patients. Thus, the coping plus information intervention led to significant improvement in both affect and behavior.

Wolfer and Visintainer (1975) used an intervention that combined procedural and sensory information provision with behavioral training and psychological support. Patients were seen at six different times during the hospitalization; mothers of the treatment patients were also given information, including some training in how to help their children. The control patients received the regular nursing care. At each of four postintervention events (a blood test, preoperative medication, transport to surgery, waiting in the operating suite) the treated children were rated as being less upset and more cooperative (these ratings, however, may have been biased by observer knowledge of the experimental condition). The experimental patients also were rated as having easier fluid intake and shorter time to first voiding. Furthermore, the parents of the treated children rated the posthospitalization adjustment of their children as being better, said that they were more satisfied with the care, and reported their own anxiety as being lower (again, however, the parents were not blind as to experimental condition). Though the intervention was effective, the interpretation of the Wolfer and Visintainer results is hampered by the possible bias in the ratings of observers and parents, in the multifaceted nature of their intervention, and in their failure to control for the differential attention paid to the treated children.

In short, three of the four investigations of the efficacy of information provision with children (Cassell, 1965; Melamed & Siegel, 1975; Wolfer & Visintainer, 1975) have produced positive results. Due to methodological limitations such as combining of information provision with other treatments, however, it must be concluded that no unequivocally supportive evidence has been found for the effectiveness of information provision with children.

Summary

The effects of providing information for adults and children are not clearcut. Sensory information appears to be a more important aspect of preparatory communication than procedural information but information provision is sometimes found to interact with patients' individual styles. The evidence underscores the need for the development of differential forms of psychological preparation for different subgroups of patients.

Skills Training

The intervention technique of skills training teaches patients specific behaviors that will facilitate their adjustment. Common procedures include training in how to breathe deeply and cough, how to turn properly in bed, and leg exercises. The actual skills that are taught are designed specifically for the type of medical procedure the patient is undergoing.

We have already discussed some studies that, in conjunction with other approaches, utilized skills training. It will be recalled that Schmitt and Wooldridge (1973), for example, gave their treated patients training in deep breathing, coughing, leg exercises, and easier ways of turning and getting out of bed. This training was provided in conjunction with additional procedural information and a group discussion which allowed patients to exchange information and provide psychological support for each other. The controls were provided "routine nursing care." While the results provided considerable support for the efficacy of this multifaceted intervention, the effects of the skills training, per se, were not isolated.

Johnson and Leventhal (1974), however, used a design that allowed an examination of the efficacy of skills training and found no support for the effectiveness of the skills training approach. Training did not lessen gagging, tension-related arm movements, time required for tube passage, medications needed, or heart rate increase.

Two studies have examined skills training exclusively. Lindeman and Van Aernam (1971) contrasted what they called "structured" and "unstructured" patient teaching. The structured patients were taught diaphragmatic breathing, leg and foot exercises, and special techniques for coughing and turning. The unstructured patients received the normal preoperative teaching provided by the nursing staff. Nurses could teach how much and whatever they wanted, but usually included a few general statements about the need to deep breathe, cough, and turn postoperatively. A check indicated that the structured group increased their ability to cough and breathe deeply to a significantly greater extent than did the unstructured patients.

Lindeman and Van Aernam reported that while the two groups did not differ in the number of analgesics they needed postoperatively, the structured group spent significantly fewer days in the hospital (6.5 versus 8.4). The results indicated that more intensive behavioral skills training was better than standard nursing practice in terms of one measure—length of stay in the hospital.

Lindeman (1972) later compared the effectiveness of the same structured training method in different external circumstances. Patients in the study were undergoing various types of surgery. All patients were given training in deep breathing, coughing, and movement in bed. Half of the patients were given this teaching individually, while the other half were given the training in small groups (2–10 patients at a time). Within each treatment condition, patients were further classified into three categories according to site of incision: (*a*) major chest, neck, and upper abdominal; (*b*) lower abdominal; and (*c*) other sites. An analysis of the data showed no group differences in the number of analgesics needed postoperatively; the patients given the group teaching, however, spent significantly fewer days in the hospital (6.67 versus 8.68). Lindeman also reported a significant teaching group by site of incision interaction; a closer analysis of the data revealed that the overall group difference was almost entirely due to patients in the other site incision category. Mean hospital stay was virtually identical for the two training groups within each of the first two incision categories, but differed significantly within the other site category. The results are difficult to interpret, but suggest that (at least for patients who are undergoing certain types of operations) patients gain more from a skills training session when other patients are also present.

Behavioral skills training, when it has been effective, seems to work best at aiding patient recovery, reducing the distress of pain, and getting the patient back on a normal schedule and out of the hospital more quickly. On the other hand, it does not seem to be particularly effective in reducing patients' anxiety and subjective distress. Other intervention techniques may be more suited for alleviating these latter problems.

Hypnosis

Medical use of hypnosis dates back to the modern origin of "animal magnetism" in the work of the Viennese physician Franz Anton Mesmer (1734–1815). Early use of hypnosis (examplified in the work of such researchers as Braid and Esquiral) emphasized its possibilites as an analgesic. For example, James Esdaile, an English surgeon practicing in India, reported using hypnosis as an analgesic in approximately 1,000 operations (300 involving major surgery) during the years of 1845–1851.

Recently hypnotic induction has been used to reduce the anxiety and distress of hospitalized patients. Field (1974), for example, used an hypnotically induced relaxation intervention with orthopedic surgery patients. The treatment patients heard a 20-min tape that included a simplified description of the surgical procedure in addition to "hypnotic preparation" that included suggestions of relaxation, comfort, sleep, eye closure, quick recovery and confidence, and freedom from pain both during and after surgery. The control patients heard a 15-min tape that described the facilities available in the hospital.

Field found no significant group differences in either the surgeon's rating of the patient's nervousness or on speed of recovery. Although the overall group differences were not significant, the extent to which the treatment patients *actually relaxed* after hearing the tape correlated −.49 with nervousness and .46 with speed of recovery. Although Field does not report any data concerning hypnotic susceptibility (the trait that reflects a person's general ability to be hypnotized), it is possible that this dimension was highly related to the extent to which patients were able to relax. While these results do not support the usefulness of a hypnotic induction tape, they can be said to suggest that a hypnotic intervention might be appropriate for a subset of the patient population—that is for those patients high in hypnotic susceptibility. It should also be noted that a more appropriate test of the efficacy of hypnosis would involve individual inductions with an actual hypnotist present.

McAmmond, Davidson, and Kovitz (1971) compared the effectiveness of hypnosis and systematic relaxation training in reducing the anxiety of highly stressed dental patients. Each of their treatment groups met twice a week for a total of seven sessions. The relaxation group heard a 16-minute relaxation training tape based on the systematic relaxation techniques of Wolpe and Lazarus (1966). The patients were encouraged to practice the techniques between sessions. Hypnotic training centered around an induction technique that utilized eye fixation, visual imagery, and progressive relaxation. Hypnotic patients were repeatedly given suggestions that they would no longer be afraid to have their dental work done and that they would feel no discomfort in the dental situation. Control patients received no treatment until the test day when they came to the dentist's office. At this time they received brief pain relief and relaxation instructions immediately before the dental treatment. Similarly, the relaxation patients heard the relaxation tape—and the hypnosis group was put into an hypnotic trance—immediately before treatment commenced.

No group differences were found on a pain tolerance measure or on the STAI-A-State, the latter result indicating that patients' self-report of anxiety did not differ across groups. The hypnosis group rated their participation in the study as having been more successful than the relaxation patients, who in turn rated their experience in the study more highly than the controls. In skin conductance, both of the treatment groups exhibited less anxiety than the controls, but did not differ from each other. Perhaps the most interesting finding came from the follow-up conducted five months after treatment. Only one of nine relaxation patients had seen a dentist in the intervening period, while five of ten controls and all eight of the hypnosis group had consulted a dentist during that time; this difference between relaxation and hypnosis groups is significant.

Hypnotic inductions appear to be only somewhat helpful in facilitating patient recovery and reducing patient anxiety (Field, 1974; McAmmond *et al.*, 1971; Surmon *et al.*, 1974). However, these data are weak and the studies few. More research needs to be done in order to demonstrate the effectiveness of this strategy by employing more optimal interventions (e.g., individual inductions with the hypnotist present) in order to provide a more compelling test of the usefulness of hypnosis. In addition, future research and future use of hypnosis by health care personnel should be more sensitive to the influence of hypnotic susceptibility. Future researchers should include a standard hypnotic-susceptibility scale (Tellegen, 1979), such as the 34-item absorption scale (Tellegen & Atkinson, 1974). Health care personnel wishing to use hypnosis as an intervention technique are advised to screen patients with such a scale in order to determine which patients might benefit most from this technique.

Relaxation Training

Training patients in relaxation skills often follows the procedure described by Jacobson (1929). Jacobson's progressive relaxation training procedure was designed to train patients to use their own intitiative to learn "to localize tensions when they occur during nervous irritability and excitement and to relax them away [p. 40]." Relaxation training is also an important facet of Wolpe's (1958) systematic desensitization.

Within the areas of psychological preparations for medical procedures, relaxation training is often used as one aspect of a multicomponent intervention procedure (e.g., Egbert *et al.*, 1964). It is included to insure that patients know how to relax so as to ease any discomfort during their postprocedure adjustment. In the previously discussed study by Egbert *et al.* (1964), for example, surgical patients in the treatment group were given training in the achievement of relaxation through deep breathing exercises as well as sensory and procedural information.

Miller (1976) reported the results of a study examining the effectiveness of electromyographic (EMG) feedback and progressive relaxation training in reducing the stress reactions of patients with histories of negative reactions to dental treatment. Miller divided her dental patients into three groups: (*a*) EMG feedback; (*b*) progressive relaxation; and (*c*) a self relaxation control group.

The results of her study supported the efficacy of both intervention strategies. EMG levels decreased significantly from pre- to posttreatment for both treatment groups, but not for the self-relaxation controls. The two treatment groups did not differ from each other on this measure. All three patient groups exhibited significant decreases on both the Dental Anxiety Scale (Corah,

1969) and the STAI-A-State, with the treatment groups showing comparable decreases that were greater than those of the controls on both variables. On the A-Trait portion of the STAI, however, only the EMG feedback group showed a significant decline. In general, the results strongly support the efficacy of both interventions in a dental situation.

Wilson (1977) compared the effectiveness of information provision (both sensory and procedural) with a form of behavioral training in aiding the recovery of cholecystectomy and abdominal hysterectomy patients. One group of patients was given information regarding sensations and procedures to be expected during hospitalization. Another group was given behavioral training in systematic muscle relaxation. The results indicated that both information provision and relaxation training significantly reduced length of hospital stay. In addition, the relaxation training was also able to reduce reported distress of pain and the number of days that injections for pain were required.

The effects of relaxation training with a more stressful, more catastrophic medical procedure (heart surgery) are less clearcut (Aiken & Henrichs, 1971; Pearson, 1976). Pearson's (1976) treatment patients heard a 30-min relaxation tape at each of three training sessions (spaced one day apart during the week prior to surgery). A no-treatment control group was matched for such factors as age, education, type and duration of surgery, and marital status. Analysis of the STAI-A-State, systolic blood pressure, respiration rate, heart rate, length of stay in intensive care, and postoperative behavior showed no significant group differences; only on postoperative drug use did the treated patients show better recovery. Pearson suggested that these results might reflect the fact that the patients did not learn the relaxation training sufficiently well for it to be effective. However, another possibility is that relaxation training may not be sufficient with potentially catastrophic medical procedures. Additional attention to other factors may be required in such cases.

Aiken and Henrichs (1971) taught open heart surgery patients a method of systematic relaxation that was a modification of the basic systematic desensitization procedure described by Wolpe and Lazarus (1966). In addition to an initial training session, treatment patients had a daily 15-min to 1-hour session with a nurse specialist, who supervised the relaxation exercises and talked with each patient regarding their fears and concerns. The patients also practiced the relaxation exercises on their own at least four times a day for an average of 3.5 days. The results showed a nonsignificant difference between the treated patients and the controls in incidence of postoperative psychiatric reactions (defined as an experience of impairment of consciousness with motor restlessness, disordered thinking, sensory disturbances, visual and/or auditory illusions or hallucinations, and paranoid ideations), but the treated patient's surgery involved significantly less time, fewer units of blood, and a lesser degree of hypothermia.

The findings indicate that relaxation training can be quite effective in facilitating a patient's recovery. In addition, Miller (1976) reported results indicating that relaxation was effective in reducing a patient's self-reported state anxiety. Relaxation skills thus seem to be an important component of a patient's overall adjustment during hospitalization.

Filmed Modeling

Vicarious learning, observational learning, or modeling are terms that are often used interchangeably to refer to the effects of the observation of another person's behavior. The therapeutic effects of modeling have been outlined (e.g., Bandura, 1971) and numerous studies have demonstrated the ability of modeling to, for example, both induce anxiety (Kendall, Finch, & Montgomery, 1978) and reduce fear and avoidance (Bandura & Menlove, 1968).

The use of a videotaped presentation of a patient undergoing gastrointestinal endoscopy was investigated by Shipley, Butt, Howitz, and Farbry (1978). Shipley *et al.* divided their patients into three groups: (*a*) a treatment group that saw the treatment videotape three times; (*b*) a group that saw the same treatment tape only once; and (*c*) a control group that saw a 26-min videotape unrelated to their hospitalization. The patient in the 18-min treatment videotape showed a normal amount of distress and displayed characteristic difficulties (e.g., gagging) during the procedure. Additionally, the authors attempted to control the effects of having accurate procedural-sensory information by providing all patients with extensive information about the endoscopy.

Analysis of heart rate at (*a*) initial baseline; (*b*) the minute prior to the insertion of the endoscope; and (*c*) 6–10 min subsequent to insertion showed no group differences. However, the treatment group who had seen the film three times had a lower heart rate during the first 5 min following insertion of the scope than either of the other two groups. Additionally, physicians and nurses rated the treatment group who had seen the film three times as having less anxiety than the controls prior to the examination, and both treatment groups as less anxious than controls during the examination. No postexamination group differences were found. On the STAI-A-State, the groups rated themselves as being equally anxious during the preexamination period, while both of the treatment groups had lower A-State scores than controls following the endoscopy. Finally diazepam (which was given only to those patients judged by the physician to be quite anxious) was required by a significantly lower proportion of the three-viewings treatment patients (20%) than either the one-viewing treatment group (45%) or the control group (50%). These data indicated that seeing a patient actually go through (and survive) an endoscopy can lead to a reduction in anxiety before, during, and after the procedure.

A series of studies on the effects of filmed models was conducted by Melamed and her colleagues. In one such study, Melamed and Siegel (1975) attempted to reduce the distress of child surgical patients. The children were scheduled to undergo surgery for hernias, tonsillectomies, or urinary genital tract difficulties. The treatment group in this study saw a 16-min film in which a "coping model" underwent surgery ("coping model" refers to a model who is initially anxious and fearful but who eventually overcomes the anxiety). Coping models have been found to be more effective than models who exhibit only mastery behavior (e.g., Kazdin, 1974; Meichenbaum, 1971). The treatment film also included explanations given by members of the hospital staff of various hospital procedures and it included scenes depicting the operating and recovery rooms. The control group saw a 12-min film that depicted a nature trip.

The authors reported findings that offer rather strong support for the effectiveness of their intervention. The results for the PSI are shown in Figure 12.2. Analysis of the between-groups differences indicated that the treatment group was significantly less aroused both preoperatively and at follow-up. Within-group analysis further explicated the nature of the group differences. The treatment group exhibited a significant increase in arousal from pre- to postfilm, indicating that the initial effect of the film was to make the children more aroused. However, the treated children then

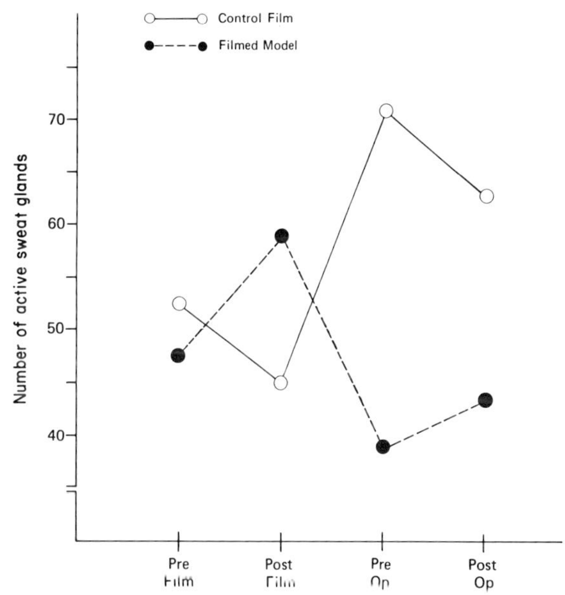

Figure 12.2. Number of active sweat glands for the experimental and control groups across the four measurement periods. (Adapted from "Reduction of Anxiety in Children facing Hospitalization and Surgery by Use of Filmed Modeling" by B. G. Melamed and L. S. Siegel, *Journal of Consulting and Clinical Psychology* 1975, *43,* 511-521. Copyright 1975 by the Journal of Consulting and Clinical Psychology. Reprinted by permission.)

showed a significant decline in arousal from the postfilm level to both the preoperative and follow-up assessments. This result suggests that the treatment film, after initially increasing arousal, was subsequently able to reduce it. The control patients, on the other hand, had significantly higher arousal levels preoperatively and at follow-up than they did during the pre- and postfilm periods.

Analysis of a Hospital Fears Rating Scale (HFRS) also revealed support for the film intervention. Since the control group scored significantly higher on this measure at the prefilm assessment, a covariance analysis was performed in order to statistically control the initial group differences. The results indicated that the control patients scored significantly higher than the treatment patients both preoperatively and at follow-up. Similar results were also found for observer ratings of anxiety. Again, the treated children had a lower mean score than the controls both preoperatively and at follow-up. Finally, the control children showed a significant increase in behavior problems (as measured on a Behavior Problems Checklist) from prefilm to follow-up, while the treatment children exhibited no change on this measure.

Two aspects of the data collected by Melamed and Siegel make their findings particularly noteworthy: (*a*) many different types of evidence (physiological, self-report, and observers' ratings) converge to indicate that the intervention was effective in reducing the anxiety of children undergoing surgery; and (*b*) they provide evidence to show that the group differences they found do not only exist preoperatively, but also persist for at least three to four weeks subsequent to discharge from the hospital. The efficacy of their coping model and procedural information intervention appears quite strong.

Melamed and her colleagues have conducted two studies investigating the effect of filmed models on children's behavior in a dental situation. In the first, (Melamed, Hawes, Heiby, & Glick, 1975) the children (ages 5–11) came into a dental clinic for at least two treatment sessions. During the first session their teeth were cleaned and examined, while during the second at least one tooth restoration was performed for each child. During the second session (but prior to the tooth restoration) each of the patients saw a videotape. The treatment children saw a tape in which an initially fearful 4-year-old went through a typical dental procedure with a "sensitive and friendly dentist." The child was shown coping with his anxiety and in the course of the tape he discovered that there was nothing to fear in the procedure. The child model was verbally reinforced for his cooperation, and was given a toy at the end of the dental procedure. The control group children saw a film of comparable length in which a similar child was involved in activities unrelated to dentistry. No group differences were found on the PSI, which was measured both before and after the children saw the film, and again after the tooth restoration. A Children's Fear Survey Schedule (CFSS), a self-report measure of anxiety, also failed to show significant differences. A behavior profile rating, however, indicated that the control children made significantly more disruptive behaviors during the restoration procedure than did the treatment patients (i.e., 9.30 versus 2.68). In addition, both observers and dentists rated the control children as more fearful during the tooth restoration. The second study (Melamed, Weinstein, Hawes, & Katin-Borland, 1975) used an identical videotape intervention, again with children (ages 5–9) undergoing a tooth restoration. The control children did not see a videotape, but were asked to draw pictures in the videotape room. Again, the behavior profile ratings indicated that the control children made significantly more disruptive behaviors than the treatment children during the tooth restoration. In addition, the observers and the dentists rated the treated children as significantly less anxious, and the observers rated them as more cooperative during the procedure. The CFSS again failed to show significant group differences.

The somewhat mixed results from these two studies offer some support for the efficacy of the coping model intervention. While the videotape did not affect self-reported anxiety, it was effective in reducing observer ratings of anxiety and in decreasing uncooperative behavior. Machen and Johnson (1974) conducted a study which also examined the ability of filmed modeling to aid young children, 3–6 years old, undergoing tooth restoration. Machen and Johnson divided their dental patients into three groups. Those in the model learning group saw an 11-min videotape of a child undergoing dental treatment. The child displayed desirable behavior throughout ("mastery model") and was rewarded by the dentist with praise (the dentist and assistant used in the tape also provided the actual dental treatment). Children in the desensitization group received a 20-min therapy session that consisted of the introduction and description of dental instruments and equipment. The instructions and equipment were presented in order of increasing anxiety-arousal. Additionally, the children in this group were invited to handle the instruments and become familiar with the dental routine. Patients in the control group received no extra intervention.

All of the children were seen three times at the dental clinic. During the first visit, their teeth were cleaned and examined. During each of the two succeeding visits a tooth restoration was performed. During the dental treatment, each child's behavior was rated by two observers stationed behind a one-way mirror. At each rating point, the observers rated the child's behavior on a scale from 1 ("definitely negative" which would include such behavior as refusal of treatment, overt resistance and hostility, or extreme fear and crying) to 4 ("definitely positive," which would include good rapport with the dentist, no fear, etc.) Ratings were made at six points during the treatment, so that the total score for each child could range from 4 to 24. Analysis of these ratings indicated that both interventions led to substantial improvement in the behavior of the children. During the second and third treatment sessions (those during which the tooth restorations were performed) both of the treatment groups had higher mean behavior ratings than the controls. At neither time did the two treatment groups significantly differ from one another. The results indicated that in a stressful dental situation both a model learning and a desensitization intervention can lead to substantial improvements in the behavior of child dental patients.

Our review of the literature indicates strong support for the usefulness of filmed modeling interventions. While the results concerning the other reviewed intervention strategies have been either generally negative or mixed, the findings for the coping modeling techniques have been extremely favorable. Several different types of evidence (physiological, observers' and physicians' ratings, self-report, medication use, etc.) converge to indicate the efficacy of the coping intervention strategy. It should be pointed out, however, that the studies employing this strategy have generally tested them on patients facing less severe medical interventions (e.g., dental treatment, endoscopy, minor surgery); thus, it could be that this intervention strategy might be less effective with more catastrophic medical procedures (e.g., open heart surgery). Certainly, however, the strategy has proven quite successful with those types of patients on whom it has been tried.

Cognitive-Behavioral Interventions

Albeit apparent in the title, cognitive-behavioral interventions (Kendall & Hollon, 1979a; Mahoney, 1977; Meichenbaum, 1977) are strategies that seek to affect patients' cognitive functioning (e.g., what they say to themselves) and behavioral adjustment by addressing patients at both the cognitive and behavioral levels. Correspondingly, treatment evaluation is examined through changes in both behavior and cognition (Kendall & Hollon, 1979b).

Before examining some of the recent work using cognitive-behavioral procedures, it will be valuable to first describe a study that employed a cognitive intervention (Langer, Janis, & Wolfer, 1975). One important component of the cognitive-behavioral approach to intervention is the modification of the patients' self statements. The Langer *et al.* (1975) study, therefore, is important because it illustrates an intervention that utilized reappraisals as a coping strategy.

The cognitive intervention consisted of emphasizing to the patients the extent to which stress can be elevated or reduced via selective attention and cognition. In conjunction with this, patients were taught to direct their attention to the more favorable aspects of the surgical situation whenever they were experiencing discomfort. Within the Langer *et al.* study, four conditions were compared: (*a*) cognitive reappraisal ("coping") only; (*b*) information provision; (*c*) coping plus information provision; and (*d*) control. Importantly, the interventions for all three of the treatment groups (and an interview conducted with the control patients) all lasted approximately the same amount of time (about 20 minutes).

The data showed a clear superiority of the coping intervention over that of information provision. Nurses' ratings of patients' preoperative anxiety and ability to cope both showed significant group differences. The two coping groups (coping alone and coping plus information) were rated the lowest in anxiety, and highest in ability to cope; the information-only group was rated as highest in anxiety and lowest in ability to cope, and the control group was intermediate on both ratings. The coping strategy groups also fared significantly better in postoperative requests for pain relievers and sedatives. In addition, although nonsignificant, there was a trend for patients in the coping groups to have a shorter overall stay in the hospital. In general, the evidence does not indicate that the information-provision intervention alone was beneficial to the patients. This finding should not be alarming, given that the patients received *procedural* information. However, the data do show that the coping strategy both with and without information provision, was effective in reducing patients' pain and anxiety.

Stress-inoculation training (Meichenbaum, 1976; Meichenbaum & Turk, 1976) is a cognitive-behavioral approach applicable to the preparation of patients for stressful medical procedures. Stress-inoculation training provides the person with a set of skills that are useful to deal with upcoming stressful situations. Like medical inoculations, "a person's resistance is enhanced by exposure to a stimulus strong enough to arouse defenses without being so powerful that it overcomes them [Meichenbaum & Turk, 1976, p. 3]."

The actual stress-inoculation training involves three stages: (*a*) discussion of the nature of coping and stress; (*b*) rehearsing the coping skills; and (*c*) testing the application of the coping skills under stress conditions. Laboratory research on stress-inoculation training indicates that it is an effective procedure for anxiety management (Meichenbaum & Cameron, Note 2), the control of anger provocation (Novaco, 1974, 1979), pain (Meichenbaum & Turk, 1976), and analogue stress (Girodo & Stein, 1978).

A recent study reported by Kendall, Williams, Pechacek, Graham, Shisslak, and Herzoff (1979) compared the effectiveness of two types of interventions in reducing the stress of patients undergoing cardiac catheterization. The first intervention procedure was a cognitive-behavioral treatment similar to stress inoculation, and the second was patient-education, similar to information provision approaches. Patients in the cognitive behavioral treatment group received individual training in the identification of those aspects of the hospitalization procedure that aroused anxiety in them and in the application of their own idiosyncratic coping strategies to lessen that anxiety. This training was provided in stages. The therapist first explained to the patients that stress is a response that everyone experiences and copes with in some way. The therapist then confided some source of stress in his or her own life and discussed the strategy that he or she had used to reduce it. Thus, the patients were initially exposed to a coping model who was at first anxious, but who worked adaptively to overcome the anxiety. The therapist then had the patients discuss sources of stress in their own lives and the means they had used to overcome them. The therapist next modeled ways in which the strategies that the patients had in their own repertoire could be used against the current sources of stress—namely, those in the hospital situation. Finally, the therapist helped the patients to rehearse the process of identifying anxiety-producing stimulus cues and using the patients' own preferred coping strategies to deal effectively with the stress (see Kendall, in press, for a more detailed description).

Patients in the information provision treatment group received individual teaching related to heart disease and the catheterization procedures that they were to be exposed to on the following day. The catheterization procedure was explained to the patients using two sample catheters and a model of the heart. In addition, patients in this group were given a four-page pamphlet that contained additional information concerning the heart and the catheterization procedure. The patients were allowed time to ask questions about any of the material presented. The educational material provided in the patient education group, both verbal and written, included procedural and sensory information. Both of the treatment interventions lasted about 45 min. To control the effects of the increased attention given to the treated patients, an attention-placebo control group was employed. Patients in this group received a nondirective visit from the therapist who listened to the patient and accurately reflected the feelings expressed by the patient. The discussion tended to focus on the patient's job, family, etc., but the patient was allowed to steer the conversation toward any area that was not directly related to either of the interventions. A fourth group of patients were not given any sort of treatment intervention but, rather, received the typical conditions that all patients would have received had the interventions not been provided. These subjects were the current hospital conditions controls.

The results of the Kendall *et al.* (1979) study offer support for both of the interventions, and provide particularly strong support for the cognitive–behavioral method. First, in regard to the patients' self-reported anxiety (STAI-A-State), the results showed no preintervention group differences. Subsequent to the intervention, however, both the treatment groups and the attention-placebo control group had a significantly lower level of anxiety than did the no-intervention controls. The fact that the attention-placebo controls scored lower than the current-conditions controls subsequent to their interview indicates the effect that increased attention alone can have on a patient's state of mind. However, analysis of the anxiety levels during catheterization indicated that this placebo effect did not persist. At that time, both of the treatment groups had significantly lower mean A-State scores than the controls. No differences between the two groups were found on the A-State.

Physicians (those cardiologists performing the catheterization) and technicians (those assisting in the actual procedure) rated each patient's behavior during catheterization. These ratings reflected (separately) the physician's and the technician's estimate of the extent to which the patient appeared to be tense, anxious, uncooperative, and maladjusting during the catheterization. The physicians rated the cognitive–behavioral group as being the best adjusted. The information provision treatment group fared significantly less well than the cognitive–behavioral patients, and in turn was rated as significantly better than the two control groups. The results for the technicians' ratings were identical—the cognitive–behavioral treatment group was rated significantly better adjusted than the information treatment group, which in turn received better ratings than either of the controls. The cognitive–behavioral procedures were effective in reducing anxiety and increasing behavioral adjustment, and these positive effects were significantly better than attention-placebo or current hospital conditions controls.

However, the finding that the cognitive–behavioral strategy produced greater benefits than information provision must be tempered by the fact that some of the patients in the Kendall *et al.* (1979) study had undergone catheterization once before. Patients who had already gone through the cardiac catheterization procedure would presumably already know a good deal about it and for these patients the information provision strategy might not be expected to produce additional benefits.

Whatever the effectiveness of information provision, the cognitive–behavioral therapeutic intervention produced substantial improvements in both patient self-reports and in observers' ratings. We suggest that the cognitive–behavioral approach employed by Kendall *et al.* (1979) is a particularly promising method for alleviating the distress of medical patients since:

1. One feature of the cognitive–behavioral approach is its utilization of the patient's *own preferred coping strategies*. Our review of the literature has repeatedly suggested how individual patient differences can significantly interact with a given intervention to produce

different effects in different patients. The cognitive-behavioral technique allows for a greater appreciation of individual patient differences. Rather than *providing* all of the patients with a given technique, the cognitive-behavioral intervention facilitates, rehearses, and reinforces those preferred strategies already being utilized by the patient.
2. The cognitive-behavioral approach does not *preclude* the use of other intervention techniques. Sensory and procedural information provision, skills training, and relaxation could be incorporated into the intervention for a particular patient.
3. The procedure was quick and efficient. The total time required for the intervention was only about 45 minutes (not counting other bedside visits), a figure that is below many of the others reported in the literature.

Kendall *et al.* (1979) also developed an instrument to assess patients' self-statements during the catheterization procedures. The self-statement inventory (SSI) consisted of 20 thoughts that people have in hospital stress situations. Ten of the items were positive self-statements (e.g., "I was thinking about the wonders of medical science and how lucky I was that they could do this for me") and ten were negative self-statements (e.g., "I kept expecting that the procedure would damage my body"). Subjects retrospectively completed the SSI just after the cardiac catheterization procedure was complete. Results of a correlational analysis indicated that the physicians' and technicians' ratings of adjustment were significantly and negatively related to the patients' negative self-statements ($r = -.34$ and $-.37$, respectively). These findings support the relationship between undesirable, maladjusted behaviors and negative self-statements.

The research on the effectiveness of cognitive-behavioral procedures in the area of invasive medical procedures is just beginning. However, the utility of the stress-inoculation method and the effectiveness of the cognitive-behavioral procedures employed in the Kendall *et al.* (1979) study are strong indications of their potential efficacy in the future.

Psychological Preparation: Suggestions for Research and Clinical Practice

Research Suggestions

The reader will recall that following a description of the first study covered in this chapter we mentioned three methodological points: (*a*) the need for appropriate control groups, such as attention controls (*b*) the desirability of multiple dependent measures; and (*c*) the merit of taking into account individual differences among patients. Future researchers in this area should consider each of these points.

In several studies, treatment groups were compared with control groups that received only marginal contact. The failure to adequately control attention and expectancy makes it impossible to determine if the group differences in patient comfort and adjustment are due to the treatment procedures per se. Attention controls, as in the Kendall *et al.* (1979) study, allow for a more precise determination of the effectiveness of the psychological preparations and should be employed whenever possible.

Three types of dependent measures are taken in this area of research: (*a*) patients' emotional responses; (*b*) observers' ratings of adjustment; and (*c*) hospital stay data. Some intervention procedures affect certain response modes whereas other interventions may produce changes on other measures. As a result, patient emotionality (e.g., anxiety, discomfort, pain), adjustment ratings (e.g., cooperation during the medical procedure, absence of psychological distress), and hospital stay data (e.g., length of stay, amount of medications requested) should be gathered in future studies of psychological preparations.

Lastly, the importance of individual differences among patients must not go unrecognized. Patients' desires for specific information, types of coping style, and locus of control are just a few examples of the types of individual differences that should be considered. Alternately, preparatory interventions can refrain from imposing any one strategy and facilitate the patients' own coping styles. As in all of the intervention research, the question should be what type of treatment, presented how, when, and by whom, will produce what effects for what types of patients (Kiesler, 1966).

The psychological preparation of patients for medical procedures is an area that is ripe for additional research. Indeed, this is perhaps one of the most important new perspectives within medical psychology.

Suggestions for Clinical Practice

The following suggestions for clinical practice are not independent of those pertinent to research. Rather, they are purposefully related in order to encourage the scientist-practitioner role of the psychologist in the medical setting. Provision of service is important, but it should be combined with carefully designed research evaluation.

Our clinical suggestions are best considered in light of the background of current practice. Therefore, we have provided a time-line illustration of the typical events, interventions, and assessments that are a part of preparatory interventions. As shown in Figure 12.3, there are several major events that divide the patient's travel through the period relevant to the medical procedures. Typically, the psychological preparation takes place after the patient's arrival at the hospital but before the stressful procedures are undertaken. Assessments of the patient's emotionality (E) are typically gathered before and after the medical procedure, adjustment data (A) during the procedure, and hospital stay data (H) after the hospital visit is complete.

Our specific suggestions correspond to the time-line as indicated by the numbered arrows within Figure 12.3. These suggestions are not to replace the current practice, but are recommended as additional efforts that should prove worthwhile. For instance, the first suggestion concerns the patient's first being informed of the necessity of the medical procedure. At point 1, an attempt should be made to ascertain the patient's history regarding reactions to stressful medical procedures—Is the person "at risk?" Much of this type of information can be gathered by phone or from a brief questionnaire. Also, this is the time to request that the patient complete certain psychological (individual difference) measures

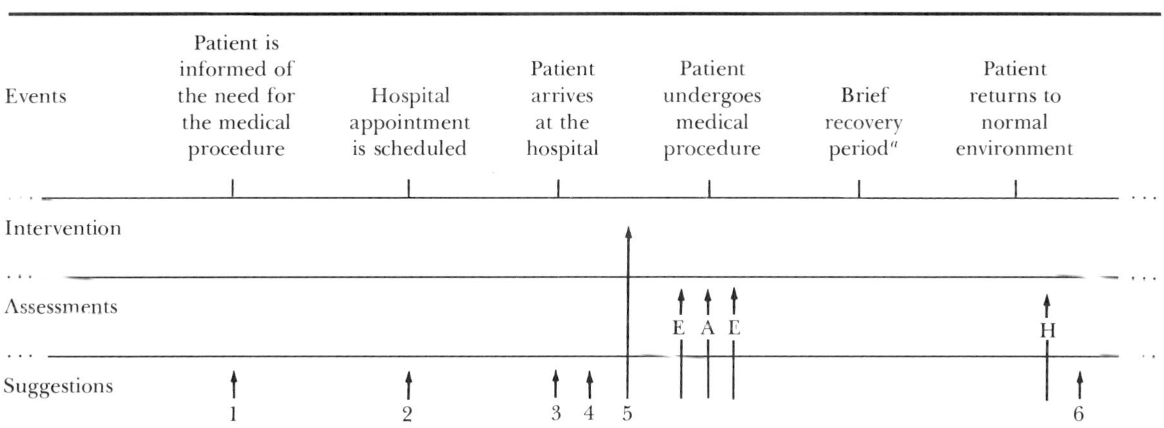

[a] Only in cases of actual hospitalization.
Note. E = emotionality data; A = Adjustment data; H = Hospital stay data.

Figure 12.3. A time-line illustration of the typical events, time of intervention, and schedule of assessments in research on the psychological preparation for stressful medical procedures. Suggestions are indicated by numbered arrows (see text).

such that the clinician can determine what types of information and preparatory intervention would be most appropriate.[1]

At point 2, one can again check to see if the patient will potentially be severely upset ("at risk") by the medical procedures. For example, dramatic changes in self-reported anxiety or plans concerning the procedure may indicate a need for caution.

Based on the results of the individual differences measures given at Point 1, the patient can now be given (if appropriate) sensory and procedural information. Most patients are not all that knowledgeable about medical practice and some, especially those who should be provided with the information, will go to a book or to a friend to find out a little about what will happen to them. The prepared sensory and procedural information should be provided at this time in order to prevent the patient from being either frustrated when self-gathered information is different from the information that is provided, annoyed by an absence of information, or inordinately fearful on the day of the procedure when outside information turns out to be different from what will actually happen in the hospital. Moreover, a patient who wants information and has it presented will be able to discuss the data with friends prior to coming to the hospital and benefit from such potentially positive preparation. Last, though not least important, the patient who wants additional information and is given it in advance will be a more satisfied patient.

Point 3, just after the patient has arrived at the hospital, is when the psychologist should make a brief bedside visit for an introduction and a brief conversation. No data is to be collected during this visit; a second visit should be scheduled for this purpose. Point 4 would be the second brief visit and any data that needed to be collected (e.g., self-reported anxiety levels, personality inventories, ratings of preprocedural adjustment) could be gathered at this time.

The intervention is provided at Point 5. By now, the patient knows the psychologist and a relationship has been developing. The brief visits made earlier serve to establish the psychologist as reliable, trustworthy, and genuinely interested in the patient's well-being. In certain instances it would be desirable at Point 5 to again evaluate the patient's emotionality and adjustment. These data will allow for an examination of any changes due to the intervention that was just provided.

Point 6, following the typical assessments and some time after the medical procedures have been conducted, is an opportunity to interview the patient. The patient's retrospective analysis can be valuable to identify aspects of the medical procedures that were especially stressful and aspects of the intervention that were particularly helpful. This information could then be used for further study or for modification of subsequent interventions.

[1]Informed consent for purposes of research should be collected at this time (see Kendall and Pechacek, Note 3).

Reference Notes

1. Nowlis, V., & Green, R. F. *Factor-analytic studies of the Mood Adjective Checklist.* (Tech. Rep. 11. Rochester: University of Rochester, Research Program on Mood and Attitude Change), 1965.
2. Meichenbaum, D., & Cameron, R. *Stress inoculation: A skills training approach to anxiety management.* Unpublished manuscript. University of Waterloo, 1973.
3. Kendall, P. C., & Pechacek, T. F. *Guidelines for constructing consent forms in behavioral medicine research.* Unpublished manuscript, University of Minnesota, 1979.

References

Aiken, L. H., & Henrichs, T. F. Systematic relaxation as a nursing intervention technique with open heart surgery patients. *Nursing Research,* 1971, *20,* 212–217.

Andrew, J. Recovery from surgery, with and without preparatory instruction, for three coping styles. *Journal of Personality and Social Psychology,* 1970, *15,* 223–226.

Auerbach, S. M., Kendall, P. C., Cuttler, H. F., & Levitt, N. R. Anxiety, locus of control, type of preparatory information, and adjustment to dental surgery. *Journal of Consulting and Clinical Psychology,* 1976, *44,* 809–818.

Auerbach, S. M., & Kilmann, P. R. Crisis intervention: A review of outcome research. *Psychological Bulletin,* 1977, *84,* 1189–1217.

Bandura, A. Psychotherapy based upon modeling procedures. In A. Bergin & S. Garfield (Eds.), *Handbook of psychotherapy and behavior change.* New York: Wiley, 1971.

Bandura, A., & Menlove, F. L. Factors determining vicarious extinction of avoidance behavior through symbolic modeling. *Journal of Personality and Social Psychology,* 1968, *8,* 99-108.

Butcher, J. N., & Koss, M. P. Research on brief and crisis-oriented therapies. In S. L. Garfield & A. E. Bergin (Eds.), *Handbook of psychotherapy and behavior change* (2nd ed.). New York: Wiley, 1978.

Butcher, J. N., & Maudal, G. R. Crisis intervention. In I. B. Weiner (Ed.), *Clinical methods in psychology.* New York: Wiley, 1976.

Cassell, S. Effect of brief puppet therapy upon the emotional responses of children undergoing cardiac catheterization. *Journal of Consulting Psychology,* 1965, *29,* 1-8.

Castaneda, A., McCandless, B. R., & Palermo, D. S. The children's form of the Manifest Anxiety Scale. *Child Development,* 1956, *27,* 317-326.

Coleman, K. P. Preventing and reducing anxiety in pediatric surgical patients. (Doctoral dissertation, Kent State University, 1975). *Dissertation Abstracts International,* 1976, *36,* 5819A.

Corah, N. L. Development of a dental anxiety scale. *Journal of Dental Research,* 1969, *48,* 396.

DeLong, R. D. Individual differences in patterns of anxiety arousal, stress-relevant information, and recovery from surgery (Doctoral dissertion, University of California, Los Angeles, 1970). *Dissertation Abstracts International,* 1971, *32,* 554B.

Egbert, L. D., Battit, G. W., Welch, C. E., & Bartlett, M. K. Reduction of post-operative pain by encouragement and instruction of patients. *New England Journal of Medicine,* 1964, *270,* 825-827.

Field, P. B. Effects of tape-recorded hypnotic preparation for surgery. *International Journal of Clinical and Experimental Hypnosis,* 1974, *22,* 54-61.

Finch, A. J., & Kendall, P. C. The measurement of anxiety in children: Research findings and methodological problems. In A. J. Finch & P. C. Kendall (Eds.), *Clinical treatment and research in child psychopathology.* New York: Spectrum, 1979.

Frank, J. D. Psychotherapy of bodily disease: An overview. In C. A. Garfield (Ed.), *Stress and survival: The emotional realities of life threatening illness.* St. Louis: C. V. Mosby, 1979.

Girodo, M., & Stein, S. J. Self-talk and the work of worrying in confronting a stressor. *Cognitive Therapy and Research,* 1978, *2,* 305-307.

Gruen, W. Effects of brief psychotherapy during the hospitalization period on the recovery process in heart attacks. *Journal of Consulting and Clinical Psychology,* 1975, *43,* 223-232.

Jacobson, E. *Progressive relaxation.* Chicago: University of Chicago Press, 1929.

Janis, I. L. *Psychological stress.* New York: Wiley, 1958.

Johnson, J. E. Stress reduction through sensation information. In I. G. Sarason & C. D. Spielberger (Eds.), *Stress and anxiety* (Vol. 2.). New York: Wiley, 1975.

Johnson, J. E., & Leventhal, H. Effects of accurate expectations and behavioral instructions on reactions during a noxious medical examination. *Journal of Personality and Social Psychology,* 1974, *29,* 710-718.

Johnson, J. E., Morrisey, J. F., & Leventhal, H. Psychological preparation for an endoscopic examination. *Gastrointestinal Endoscopy,* 1973, *19,* 180-182.

Kazdin, A. E. Covert modeling, model similarity, and reduction of avoidance behavior. *Behavior Therapy,* 1974, *5,* 325-340.

Kendall, P. C. Stressful medical procedures: Cognitive-behavioral strategies for stress management and preparation. In D. Meichenbaum & M. Jaremko (Eds.), *Stress prevention and management: A cognitive-behavioral approach.* New York: Plenum, in press.

Kendall, P. C., Finch, A. J., & Montgomery, L. E. Vicarious anxiety: A systematic evaluation of a vicarious threat to self-esteem. *Journal of Consulting and Clinical Psychology,* 1978, *46,* 997-1008.

Kendall, P. C., & Hollon, S. D. (Eds.). *Cognitive-behavioral interventions: Theory, research, and procedures.* New York: Academic Press, 1979.(a)

Kendall, P. C., & Hollon, S. D. Cognitive-behavioral interventions: Overview and current status. In P. C. Kendall & S. D. Hollon (Eds.), *Cognitive-behavioral interventions: Theory, research, and procedures.* New York: Academic Press, 1979. (b)

Kendall, P. C., Williams, L., Pechacek, T. F., Graham, L. E., Shisslak, C., & Herzoff, N. Cognitive-behavioral and patient education interventions in cardiac catheterization procedures: The Palo Alto medical psychology project. *Journal of Consulting and Clinical Psychology,* 1979, *47,* 49-58.

Kiesler, D. J. Some myths of psychotherapy research and the search for a paradigm. *Psychological Bulletin,* 1966, *65,* 110-136.

Langer, E. J., Janis, I. L., & Wolfer, J. A. Reduction of psychological stress in surgical patients. *Journal of Experimental Social Psychology,* 1975, *11,* 155-165.

Lehman, E. J. The effects of rooming-in and anxiety on the behavior of pre-school children during hospitalization and followup. (Doctoral dissertation, Cornell University, 1975). *Dissertation Abstracts International,* 1976, *36,* 3052B.

Lindeman, C. A. Nursing intervention with the presurgical patient: Effectiveness and efficiency of group and individual pre-operative teaching—phase two. *Nursing Research,* 1972, *21,* 196-209.

Lindeman, C. A., & Stetzer, S. L. Effects of preoperative visits by operating room nurses. *Nursing Research,* 1973, *22,* 4-16.

Lindeman, C. A., & Van Aernam, B. Nursing intervention with the presurgical patient—the effects of structured and unstructured preoperative teaching. *Nursing Research,* 1971, *20,* 319-331.

Lucas, R. H. The affective and medical effects of different preoperative interventions with heart surgery patients. (Doctoral dissertation, University of Houston, 1975). *Dissertation Abstracts International,* 1976, *36,* 5763B.

McAmmond, D. M., Davidson, P. O., & Kovitz, D. M. A comparison of the effects of hypnosis and relaxation training on stress reactions in a dental situation. *American Journal of Clinical Hypnosis,* 1971, *13,* 233-242.

Machen, J. B., & Johnson, R. Desensitization, model learning, and the dental behavior of children. *Journal of Dental Research,* 1974, *53,* 83-87.

Mahoney, M. J. Reflections on the cognitive-learning trend in psychotherapy. *American Psychologist,* 1977, *32,* 5-13.

Marmor, J. The psychodynamics of realistic worry. *Psychoanalysis and Social Science,* 1958, *5,* 155-163.

Meichenbaum, D. Examination of model characteristics in reducing avoidance behavior. *Journal of Personality and Social Psychology,* 1971, *17,* 298-307.

Meichenbaum, D. A self-instructional approach to stress management: A proposal for stress inoculation training. In C. D. Spielberger & I. G. Sarason (Eds.), *Stress and anxiety in modern life.* New York: Winston, 1976.

Meichenbaum, D. *Cognitive-behavior modification: An integrative approach.* New York: Plenum, 1977.

Meichenbaum, D., & Turk, D. The cognitive-behavioral management of anxiety, anger, and pain. In P. O. Davidson (Ed.) *The behavioral management of anxiety, depression, and pain.* New York: Brunner/Mazel, 1976.

Melamed, B. G., Hawes, R. R., Heiby, E., & Glick, J. Use of filmed modeling to reduce uncooperative behavior of children during dental treatment. *Journal of Dental Research,* 1975, *54,* 797-801.

Melamed, B. G., & Siegel, L. J. Reduction of anxiety in children facing hospitalization and surgery by use of filmed modeling. *Journal of Consulting and Clinical Psychology,* 1975, *43,* 511-521.

Melamed, B. G., Weinstein, D., Hawes, R. R., & Katin-Borland, M. Reduction of fear-related dental management problems with use of filmed modeling. *Journal of the American Dental Association,* 1975, *90,* 822-826.

Miller, M. P. The effects of electromyographic feedback and progressive relaxation training on stress reactions in dental patients. (Doctoral dissertation, University of Oklahoma, 1976). *Dissertation Abstracts International,* 1977, *37,* 6340B.

Mohros, K. L. L. Effects of reassuring information and sensory information on emotional response during a threatening medical examination. (Doctoral dissertation, University of Minnesota, 1976). *Dissertation Abstracts International,* 1977, *38,* 1304-1305A.

Novaco, R. A treatment program for the management of anger through cognitive and relaxation controls. Unpublished doctoral dissertation, Indiana University, 1974.

Novaco, R. The cognitive regulation of anger and stress. In P. C. Kendall & S. D. Hollon (Eds.). *Cognitive-behavioral interventions: Theory, research, and procedures.* New York: Academic Press, 1979.

Pearson, S. C., Jr. Preoperative systematic relaxation training for anxiety reduction in open heart surgery (Doctoral dissertation, Washington State University, 1976). *Dissertation Abstracts International,* 1976, *37,* 1932B.

Rotter, J. B. Generalized expectancies for internal versus external control of reinforcement. *Psychological Monographs: General and Applied,* 1966, *80* (609), 1.

Schmitt, F. E., & Wooldridge, P. J. Psychological preparation of surgical patients. *Nursing Research,* 1973, *22,* 108-115.

Shipley, R. H., Butt, J. H., Horwitz, B., & Farbry, J. E. Preparation for a stressful medical procedure: Effect of amount of stimulus preexposure and coping style. *Journal of Consulting and Clinical Psychology,* 1978, *46,* 499-507.

Sime, A. M. Relationship of preoperative fear, type of coping, and information received about surgery to recovery from surgery. *Journal of Personality and Social Psychology,* 1976, *34,* 716-724.

Spielberger, C. D., Gorsuch, R. L., & Lushene, R. L. *STAI: Manual for the State-Trait Anxiety Inventory.* Palo Alto: Consulting Psychologist's Press, 1970.

Surman, O. S., Hackett, T. P., Silverberg, E. L., & Behrendt, D. M. Usefulness of psychiatric intervention in patients undergoing cardiac surgery. *Archives of General Psychiatry,* 1974, *30,* 830-835.

Taylor, J. A. A personality scale of manifest anxiety. *Journal of Abnormal and Social Psychology,* 1953, *48,* 285-290.

Tellegen, A. On measures and conceptions of hypnosis. *American Journal of Clinical Hypnosis,* 1979, *21,* 219-237.

Tellegen, A., & Atkinson, G. Openness to absorbing and self-altering experiences ("absorption"), a trait related to hypnotic susceptibility. *Journal of Abnormal Psychology,* 1974, *83,* 268–277.

Turk, D. C., & Genest, M. Regulation of pain: The application of cognitive and behavioral techniques for prevention and remediation. In P. C. Kendall & S. D. Hollon (Eds.), *Cognitve-behavioral interventions: Theory, research, and procedures.* New York: Academic Press, 1979.

Vernon, D. T. A., & Bigelow, D. A. Effect of information about a potentially stressful situation on responses to stress impact. *Journal of Personality and Social Psychology,* 1974, *29,* 50–59.

Wilson, J. F. Determinants of recovery from surgery: Preoperative instruction, relaxation training and defensive structure. (Doctoral dissertation, University of Michigan, 1977). *Dissertation Abstracts International,* 1977, *38,* 1476–1477B.

Wolfer, J. A., & Visintainer, M. A. Pediatric surgical patients' and parents' stress responses and adjustment as a function of psychologic preparation and stress-point nursing care. *Nursing Research,* 1975, *24,* 244–255.

Wolpe, J. *Psychotherapy by reciprocal inhibition.* Stanford: Stanford University Press, 1958.

Wolpe, J., & Lazarus, A. A. *Behavior therapy techniques.* London: Pergamon Press, 1966.

Zuckerman, M., & Lubin, B. *Manual for the Multiple Affect Adjective Check List.* San Diego: Educational and Industrial Testing Service, 1965.

13

Intervention with the Cancer Patient

DAVID K. WELLISCH

Cancer confronts both the patient and the patient's family with a myriad of previously unexperienced problems, and thus may be viewed as a life crisis that impacts upon the entire family unit. This chapter will take a systems approach to these problems, with the assumption that cancer is an emotional crisis for the patient's family system, and that this system must interact with the health care delivery system for the duration and clinical course of the disease.

One out of four Americans can expect a diagnosis of cancer during their lifetime, and two out of three American families will have to cope with cancer in a family member. Cancer can no longer be conceptualized as a death sentence; one-third of all people with a cancer diagnosis will live at least five years beyond diagnosis (American Cancer Society, 1978). Psychologically, this is a mixed blessing because increased longevity while bearing cancer can be a highly problematic lifestyle.

Cancer is a collection of more than 100 diseases. There are wide variations in the implications, stresses, and psychological adjustments called for by these different entities. This chapter will attempt, when possible, to address issues and interventions specific to some forms of cancer which may be irrelevant for other cancers.

Regardless of the form of cancer, however, the patient's emotional response to cancer may best be characterized by what has been termed "death images" (Lifton, 1978). Cancer, perhaps more than any other disease, presents images of primordial suffering and terror that make it a uniquely devastating entity, both psychologically and physically. It is not as though no other disease kills, but this disease (or collection of diseases) has long been associated with man's most unspoken and primitive fears, those of boundless suffering. As Pattison (1974) succinctly stated: "People will not suffer long, but they will endure pain [p. 693]." Such images have been responsible in part for the plethora of clinical effort and writing to be reviewed and enlarged upon in this chapter.

These images, which integrate and express cultural perceptions of cancer, are powerful statements of the types of fears and attitudes that the disease evokes. One example of such a fear was the Ingmar Bergman film *Cries and Whispers,* which

Medical Psychology
Contributions to Behavioral Medicine

ISBN 0-12-565960-1

portrayed a group of sisters caring for a dying sister. The dying sister regressed to a state of infantile emotional and physical dependency which stimulated pathological regressions in the other family members. Susan Sontag (1978), herself a cancer patient, wrote of the metaphors of warfare which are expressions of our cultural associations to this disease. She stated

> Cancer cells do not simply multiply; they are 'invasive'. . . . However 'radical' the surgical intervention, however many 'scans' are taken of the body landscape, most remissions are temporary; the prospects are that 'tumor invasion' will continue, or that rogue cells will eventually regroup and mount a new assault on the organism [pp. 64–65].

It is little wonder, given this type of culturally affixed imagery, that cancer has an emotional impact beyond most other diseases of man.

Age is a significant variable in approaching intervention with the cancer patient. While the developmental phase in the life cycle is a significant factor by itself, in regard to adjusting to the life crisis of cancer, it becomes an unavoidable issue. In this regard, this chapter will pay special attention to the life cycle and devote separate sections to psychotherapeutic intervention with the adult, adolescent, and child cancer patient. Even this breakdown is inexact given the very different life issues faced by people, such as a terminally ill, 32-year-old adult mother of two young children versus a dying, 64-year-old widowed adult man with grown children.

This chapter is divided into six sections. All six of these will directly focus on psychotherapy or consultation modalities, including: (*a*) individual therapy with the adult cancer patient; (*b*) individual therapy with the child and adolescent cancer patient; (*c*) group therapy with cancer patients; (*d*) interventions with staff; (*e*) family therapy; and (*f*) less conventional interventions.

Individual Therapy Intervention with the Adult Cancer Patient

This writer's conception of psychotherapeutic intervention with the adult cancer patient starts with a definition of what it is not and then moves toward definitions of what it is. It is not thanatology or purely a psychotherapeutic interaction involving only issues of death and dying. It has been the author's clinical experience that issues of death and dying do occupy an important part of psychotherapy with cancer patients, but only a part. In discussing this issue, Shneidman (1978) noted "The important point to be noted is that when these topics do come up (death and dying) . . . as they almost invariably do . . . the thanatologist does not run from them, or from the patient [p. 13]." The cancer patient is a *living* person facing new and bewildering life stresses; the psychotherapist may help to unravel or clarify these stresses, or may help by simply being available and willing to listen in a supportive or enhancing fashion. With this in mind, psychotherapy is directed toward maximal life enhancement with the understanding that even death and the dying process are developmental stages of life adjustment. If the psychotherapist formally defines himself or herself as a thanatologist, the following question must be asked: Will this restrict and delimit the field of psychotherapeutic interaction to a sector, albeit a very important sector, of the issues at hand?

As in individual psychotherapy with other patients, individual psychotherapy with the adult cancer patient must closely adhere to the patient's defense mechanisms. However, the management of, and therapeutic interaction around, the cancer patient's defenses must be approached with caution. It must be understood, at the outset, that the crisis of cancer generates "primitive and primordial" fears as described by Pattison (1974). No one could live without psychological and/or psychophysiological decompensation in the face of such fears without powerful defense mechanisms to keep such threatening emotional fantasies in check. The psychotherapist with the noncancer patient often may interpret the patient's defenses in order to reach deeper, more conflicting material. In psychotherapy with the cancer patient, however, the therapist does not want to interpret, and thereby diminish or sidestep, the patient's defenses. The defenses are present for the purpose of the patient's emotional survival, and this must be respected and understood as a *sine qua non* of this type of therapy. Wahl (1972), in his writing on brief psychotherapy with hospitalized medical patients, stated

> A well-known classic rubric of conventional psychotherapy is: "First interpret resistance and defense and only then content." The purpose of this is to reduce barriers to the development of a strongly positive transference. In the patients I describe (medically ill inpatients), however, very little resistance material of a classic sort seems to present itself [p. 75].

These defenses, therefore, are psychological features of the situation that are necessary, but rarely obstructionistic, either to the development of the relationship or to the flow of material once the relationship has been formed. To this end, Shneidman (Note 1) told an illustrative story of the psychotherapeutic relationship with a hospitalized cancer patient in her 60s.

> I would see her one day and she would want to talk frankly of her death. The next day I would see this dying woman and she would want to talk of a vacation she would take to the Caribbean after she was well again. The next day she would be back to a confrontation with her thoughts of death and so on.

This brief vignette very well portrays the waxing and waning of the cancer patient's defenses, and the fact that no one can easily tolerate discussing the reality of oncoming nonexistence on a daily basis without the utilization of mechanisms such as denial.

The primary issues to be confronted in psychotherapy with the cancer patient are dependent upon the phase of the patient's treatment or disease. Kubler-Ross (1969) proposed five phases of adjustment to the knowledge of death which have become widely cited and utilized. Although clinicians argue over the sequence, appropriateness, and completeness of her model, few argue that cancer itself presents a clinical course which elicits a sequence of different emotional responses from the patient. Psychotherapeutic intervention varies depending on the patient's place in the clinical course of the disease, as well as on the time when the patient and therapist come together. For example, it would be inappropriate to do in-depth work focusing on death and dying issues with a patient in the early treatment phase who must learn to live with chemotherapy and radiation. It would be equally inappropriate to focus rigidly on marital issues or major marital adjustment or change in the dying patient with days or weeks to live.

The phase of the patient's illness dictates the intervention issues and style. An important paper on psychological adjustment in the first 100 days after diagnosis indicated patients who were (*a*) pessimistic by nature; (*b*) had marital problems; (*c*) came from a multiproblem family; and (*d*) had many regrets about the past, had the most severe adjustment problems, and probably needed psychotherapy most (Weisman & Worden, 1977). These authors termed this first 100 days "the existential plight," which other writers (Pattison, 1974) have described as a recurring psychological dilemma organized around questions such as "What will become of me?" and "Why me?" Different phases in the disease's clinical course generate major, and potentially predictable, emotional responses. For example, the patient suffering recurrence of the disease will be likely to feel extreme panic, and possibly frustrated rage, while the patient undergoing lengthy chemotherapy might be likely to feel depression as a more primary emotional issue.

Regardless of the phase of treatment or illness, the patient will bring his or her usual personality style into the cancer situation. This style stands out in bold relief during the strenuous process of living with cancer, and is important to focus on in psychotherapy. The patient's personality style, if abrasive or passive-dependent, can erode the much needed alliances and social supports of the patient. The patient must be given the dignity of being treated like a person, even if this involves confrontation. Cancer does not eliminate personality or relationship problems; rather, it tends to magnify them in the ill patient.

Pattison (1974) suggested eight major fears that confront the patient with a terminal illness. These include

1. Fear of the unknown—which represents not so much the unknown death but the unknown of annihilation of self.

2. Fear of loneliness—which follows from the mutual withdrawal of the patient and others, and eventuates in a sense of deprivation akin to anaclitic depression loss of necessary human nurturance).
3. Fear of loss of family and friends—this loss for patients is as if family and friends were dying, and calls for "anticipatory grief work," as described by Rosner (1962).
4. Fear of loss of the body—where the patient may view himself as disfigured and unlovely, hence unlovable.
5. Fear of loss of self-control—which follows as an inevitable consequence of this debilitating disease process.
6. Fear of pain—which is a multifaceted and multidetermined phenomenon in cancer, involving both physical perception as well as emotional attitude.
7. Fear of loss of identity—with cancer presenting an overall sense of dissolution in regard to one's body, social and intimate relationships, and total consciousness, which is antithetical to integrity of cohesive identity.
8. Fear of regression—with cancer producing the ultimate regression of the self into selflessness.

Pattison carefully points out that this is his sequence of concepts, and may not exactly correspond to that of the patient at hand. However, in the author's clinical experience, these eight themes can form an important grid for psychotherapeutic interaction with the cancer patient, or at least aid the therapist in identifying likely major conflicts.

Senescu (1963) listed six major areas of patient response to the disease which closely parallel those of Pattison (1974), primarily noting that cancer, in its regressive pull, reawakens old conflicts around dependency needs, and that reconciling the dependence-independence issues in cancer is a major emotional task. In a companion paper, Senescu (1966) suggested four sensible general goals in establishing psychotherapeutic communication with the cancer patient: (*a*) encouraging the patient to maintain maximal functioning (vocational, social and family); (*b*) working with the patient to deal with denial so that it does not interfere with well-being or acceptance of necessary care (but is still respected with regard to its necessity to the patient); (*c*) convincing the patient not to give up usual sources of pleasure; and (*d*) helping the patient not to create more pain and distress than is already inherent in the condition and situation.

Given its magnitude, the cancer population includes a proportion of chronically or acutely emotionally unstable patients. This group of patients will often be referred early and will need maximal psychosocial intervention. An important adjunct to the psychotherapeutic interaction with this population can be psychopharmacological medications. Holland (1973) outlined the adjunctive use of minor tranquilizers, antidepressants, and major tranquilizers with cancer patients. She carefully pointed out that psychological disturbances potentially helped by these drugs cannot be aided if physical pain is obtrusively present. Caution must be exercised with these drugs, given that the underlying etiologies for severe psychological symptoms in the cancer patient may often be organic, and the drugs may only mask these problems. This writer has observed maximal benefit from a program including effective psychotherapy plus judicious use of psychopharmacological medications when indicated. This has been most true with cancer patients having previous histories of depressive episodes, and who are now struggling with severe reactive depressions. Psychotherapy alone, in this instance, will usually not be effective. The indications for utilization of antianxiety or antidepressant medications are generally the same as with cancer-free patients. For example, a persistent sleep disorder characterized by early morning awakenings which was not responding to psychotherapy would call for a trial of antidepressant medication. The cancer patient who suffers from anxiety at a level exhausting to the patient, the family, and medical care givers deserves a trial of a minor tranquilizer, especially if the patient cannot settle down enough to make use of psychotherapy. The trap here, as always, lies in viewing the utilization of medication as the therapy itself, especially when the cancer patient inspires counter-transferential helplessness in the therapist (Renneker, 1957). Drugs never substitute for human intervention in this area.

Individual Therapy Intervention with the Child and Adolescent Cancer Patient

The Child

The diagnosis of cancer in a child represents the epitome of tragedy and stress for the child and the family. The implications of such a diagnosis threaten to break the biologic imperative of survival of the young, and render null and impotent the most basic protective function of the parental role.

The status of the child with cancer has changed dramatically in the last decade. It has been estimated that, in the best cancer treatment centers, it is possible to eradicate the disease in 50% of the patients (Wilbur, 1975). Childhood cancer must be viewed, therefore, as a chronic illness with an uncertain outcome and treatment extending over several years. The course is rocky, because although remissions frequently occur, so do recurrences. This becomes, for all concerned, a state of living on an emotional roller-coaster.

The majority of literature on childhood cancer is largely family focused, with the minority of the literature being focused on the child alone. Apparently, the predominant assumption is that family treatment is adequate to meet the child's needs. In addition, intervention into other areas of the child cancer patient's social matrix is often discussed, such as work with the health care deliverers (Van Eys, 1976) or school personnel (Katz, Kellerman, Rigler, Williams, & Siegel, 1977). One wonders if the child's needs are truly completely met by such a systems-based approach, or if this represents counter transferential phobic avoidance on the part of caregivers.

Three general issues seem most crucial. First and foremost, it is vital to remember that the presenting difficulties will be primarily reactive in nature. Koocher and Sallen (1978) articulated this particularly well in stating

> Basically sound families are confronting an inordinate amount of stress, which they are powerless to control. In such circumstances even the most well-adjusted families will be unable to escape reactive emotional difficulties linked to powerful reality events [p. 28].

Such well-integrated families and patients do not enter the cancer arena with psychological deficits; this predicts coping rather than decompensation.

A second vital issue is that of the child's developmental level. The developmental level must be carefully attended to in terms of the child's conceptual grasp of what is happening. There is much disagreement in the literature concerning when ill children begin to grasp issues of life, death, and mourning in an intellectual and emotional sense. Rothenberg (1979), Director of The Pediatric Liaison Service at the University of Washington, believes that children between the ages of two and seven have a sense of death as temporary, while those above seven see it as more permanent. In this author's experience, this is idiosyncratic and highly dependent on the individual child. Additionally, regression in the face of such stress may lead to the loss of some previously grasped concepts, such as death.

A third important concept is the understanding of the child's defense mechanisms and coping styles. In a wide ranging review of children's reactions to loss from a developmental perspective, Nagera (1970) pointed out that the child's ego approximates that of the adult, but a child cannot easily contain the grief or engage in the process of mourning of which the adult ego is capable. This could be understood to include grief for the self in regard to one's own losses. Conversely, Deutsch (1937) observed that it may be narcissistic self-protection, rather than an inability to grasp the concepts, that leads the child to evidence an absence of grief.

Fantasies can be important coping mechanisms in chronically ill children. While some of these can be positive, others can be negative, such as the fantasy that "I (because of having been a bad child) caused my own cancer." A primary and crucial intervention with children is to deal with this notion as straightforwardly as possible.

Several points regarding intervention and the consideration of clinical management demand attention in regard to children with cancer. Perhaps the most basic theme is the child's need for predictable routines, and the disruption of all usual routines caused by the diagnosis and treatment of cancer. The most basic structure to bind anxiety for the child is the cohesive family unit, and this may be fragmented by the need to stay in the hospital. A major countermeasure to this is to have one parent stay with the child in the hospital whenever possible (Wilbur, 1975). This may reduce separation anxiety, and also reduce phobic reactions secondary to such high anxiety states. As the child adjusts to the hospital environment, the need for parental presence will be reduced.

A major antidote to depression in the child can be normalization of activities. The child should not be allowed, if avoidable, to languish in bedclothes all day long. Normalization of routine can be a major intervention, in itself, for pediatric cancer patients. This may include such activities as school work, recreation, and social interaction. Naturally, the child will have intense feelings about hospitalization and treatment, but may not be able to easily discuss such feelings. This is a situation which calls for play therapy where the child's feelings might best be expressed symbolically and interpreted. Although family therapy is obviously vitally important, the child cancer patient deserves individual attention in working toward articulating the inevitable feelings of anger, anxiety, and hostility. Some hospitals have utilized play groups and doctor play using dolls to promote emotional working through of the emotional conflicts which illness induces.

The making of home visits after hospital discharge can be a helpful intervention to the family, and can also make the child more secure. This increases the sense of continuity between home and hospital, and reduces the sense of responsibility for this "newly conceived person", the child now diagnosed with cancer (Evans, 1975).

During the treatment phase, a frequent problem for children undergoing chemotherapy is classically conditioned vomiting, which begins to generalize and be responsive to cues in the environment or to thoughts about the treatment environment. A regimen of relaxation training and hypnosis has been suggested by Gardiner (1976) as a successful intervention procedure to deal with this problem. In this author's clinical experience, these can be supplemented by low doses of antianxiety agents, such as Valium, to initiate the relaxation response desired.

In the remission stage, it is often difficult for parents to treat a child with cancer normally. Three problems often occur in parental management: (*a*) overprotectiveness; (*b*) overpermissiveness; and (*c*) overindulgence (Lansky, Lowman, Gyulay, & Briscoe, 1975). These are not comforting responses for the child as they are unfamiliar. In addition, Lansky *et al.* (1975) suggested that these responses carry with them the covert message, "Only people who are not expected to live get this type of attention [p. 15]."

It has been advocated that the child with cancer return to the normal school envirnment as soon as possible, given that neither the hospital nor homebound school foster optimal development (Komp & Crockett, Note 2). In an extensive discussion of the problems of reintegration of the child cancer patient into the school setting, Katz *et al.* (1977) noted that hair loss due to treatment is a high priority problem for the child in the school setting. This can be dealt with by using wigs, but remains a visible reminder of the disease and consequent difference of the child with cancer. Katz *et al.* emphasized the need for careful school liaison, but cautioned against the school also becoming overprotective of the child. The fact that the child may have missed large blocks of school while in the hospital for treatment strengthens the need for an effective interface between school and hospital.

The Adolescent

Many of the issues cited in regard to intervening with the pediatric cancer patient are also true for the adolescent cancer patient. However, given the developmental issues of adolescence, which differ markedly from those of preadolescence, cancer becomes a special crisis with unique features for the adolescent.

Three major adolescent developmental issues which intersect with cancer diagnosis and treatment are discussed by Kellerman and Katz (1977). These include (*a*) establishment of autonomy, including development of emotional and economic independence from parents; (*b*) psychosocial–psychosexual development, involving acceptance of new sexual roles, new peer relationships, and acquiring socially responsible behavior patterns; and (*c*) developing a future orientation, including preparing for an occupation, marriage, and family life. Needless to say, all of these central developmental imperatives of adolescence are powerfully affected and controlled by cancer, and all deserve attention and intervention whenever possible. In describing loss of autonomy, Kellerman and Katz (1977) state

> Prolonged medical treatment, particularly during periods of hospitalization, contributes toward a shift in control from the adolescent to the institution and its staff. The process of reinforced dependence and regression is inherent in medically ordained periods of compliance and inactivity during which the adolescent is passive and has things done to him [p. 128].

This writer has observed that power struggles may occur in such settings between the oncology staff and adolescent patients. It becomes imperative, therefore, for the psychological consultant to intervene both with the staff and the adolescent patient. With the staff, educational discussions focused around development of ways to grant meaningful autonomy to the adolescent must occur. The problem must also be discussed with the adolescent, so the adolescent becomes an active *partner* in the treatment, rather than feeling like, or being, a passive object.

The assault of treatment on the psychosexual identity of the adolescent must be taken with the utmost seriousness. This point was beautifully made in the recent movie *Promises in the Dark,* which concerned the treatment of a 17-year-old girl with osteosarcoma. One important and telling scene involved her homecoming from the hospital, at which time she assertively banished all friends and family from her room, only then to remove her scarf, thus revealing partial baldness secondary to chemotherapy. Not only would adolescent cancer patients rather be alone than be seen without hair, but they frequently state "I'd rather be dead than lose my hair to chemotherapy." This might seem illogical or even disordered thinking to a medical staff, but is utterly serious to the adolescent. The consultant must impress this upon both staff and parents, so that informed empathy, rather than ridicule or struggle, becomes the interactional dynamic. In addition, discussions of sexuality between mental health personnel and adolescent cancer patients can be helpful. This writer, in talking with a bright 18-year-old Hodgkin's disease patient, discovered massive anxiety and real misconceptions surrounding resumption of sexual identity. Kellerman and Katz (1977) caution in this regard

> Shame and embarrassment related to physical change can lead to the adolescent refusing to return to school and to withdrawal from premorbid social experiences. The abandonment of normal activities, during periods when these activities are not medically restricted can lead to prolonged periods of depression [p. 128].

In terms of future preparation, adolescents require and deserve extended and honest interactions with their treatment providers. In the movie *Promises in the Dark,* this is exemplified when the 17-year-old patient confronts her doctor with the point blank question "Where did they take my leg after it was removed in the operation?" The adolescent, unlike the child, must be an equal partner and decision maker in the treatment process. It can be expected that questions will be raised regarding education, careers, marriage, and especially children, in light of the issue of treatment-related sterility. Sterility is not always predictable, but sometimes negative reproductive consequences can occur from earlier chemotherapeutic interventions (Siris, Leventhal, & Vaitukaitis, 1976).

Group Therapy with Cancer Patients

Group therapy with cancer patients has been used in a multiplicity of circumstances, settings, and styles. There are a large number of questions to consider in terms of setting up such a group, and the literature is generally in agreement on certain issues. For example, several writers agree that a group size of five to seven patients is optimal (Corder & Anders, 1974; Kelly & Ashby, 1979; Yalom & Greaves, 1977).

There is also some agreement regarding the issue of prescreening members, with the weight of sentiment being that those who are utilizing massive denial should not be treated in the group context (Kelly & Ashby, 1979; Yalom & Greaves, 1977). Although denial is readily evident and appropriate in these groups, profound denial can halt the process entirely. Patients who need denial to such an extent probably would not benefit from revealing their inner feelings in such groups.

The issue of group leadership is a central issue which is often dealt with by relying upon a multidisciplinary approach. For example, in a military setting (Corder & Anders, 1974), a chaplain was the group leader, while in a hospital outpatient setting, a nurse-social worker team became coleaders (Kelly, & Ashby, 1979). In this author's clinical experience, a team approach utilizing medical and mental health professionals provides a good balance.

The setting for the group is important; some groups are held in an inpatient oncology setting, others in outpatient oncology settings, and others in environments completely divorced from the oncologic setting, such as a Department of Psychiatry or community agency. One team of researchers argued that the inpatient setting was not a responsive environment for group therapy, given that the patients were too busy with medical matters and already had adequate support (Kelly & Ashby, 1979). However, another group (Ferlic, Goldman, & Kennedy, 1979) demonstrated, via a controlled study, the utility of group therapy in an inpatient oncology ward setting.

It appears that a key ingredient for success in group therapy with cancer patients is preparation. With adequate preparation it seems that the setting becomes inconsequential, and not an impediment to effective group organization or group interaction. A fine example of this is the group support sessions described by Schwartz (1977). This was a program lasting several weeks; each session was a 2-hour block containing films and videotapes followed by discussion groups. Apparently such an approach lowers the potential threat of the group, since most all of the attendees did utilize the group discussion portion. The Ferlic *et al.* (1979) paper also described a combined lecture plus discussion group format that was well utilized in an inpatient setting.

It is possible to conduct group therapy with cancer patients in a lower structure mode directed toward discussion alone, but this route seems laden with difficulties. It may be that where discussion is limited or highly structured, patients can utilize this to a greater degree with less fear or denial. In a very descriptive paper about clinical issues and resistance in a classic "death and dying" group, Whitman, Gustafson, and Coleman (1979) observed the reliance on the rigid use of containment to bind high levels of anxiety. They also noted that where patients with cancer in differing stages of progression in groups are together, patterns of defenses and patterns of ability to communicate may be vastly different. Yalom and Greaves (1977) solved this problem by deliberately structuring their group to include only end-stage cancer patients. The Yalom and Greaves paper also demonstrated that resistance can be effectively managed if the leaders are very skilled and experienced and have a solid grasp of countertransference issues. They observed the therapist to have the potential to project inability to cope onto the group members, with this demanding careful observation lest it block the process.

The issue of groups based around a particular diagnosis versus those with a potpourri of types of cancer is discussed in the literature. Schwartz (1977) and Winick and Robbins (1977) described groups limited to mastectomy patients in the hospital and in the community. Both papers reported high rates of utilization, with the Winick paper indicating 1700 women having been served over several years. The unitary diagnosis group appears to go into less depth, but to be useful and bearable to more patients.

Perhaps, given the almost overwhelming resistances described in unstructured group settings with very sick cancer patients, group therapy should only be employed with very ill or advanced patients by very senior therapists. For less ill patients, group therapy combined with educational formats seems a highly viable approach. Such groups seem to work especially well if interfaced with the usual flow of a program such as described by Winick and Robbins (1977).

A final issue involves whether or not to include treating physicians in the group. Corder and Anders (1974) made it clear that although the groups were enlightening to the physicians, their presence might block discussions of the doctor–patient relationship, as members might be inhibited by the presence of treating physicians. In addition, if the discussions center primarily on medical treatment, this might reduce the potential for psychological themes to emerge or develop.

Intervention with Staff

One of the most helpful and decisive approaches to intervention with cancer patients involves consultation with the staff treating the patients. The oncology ward or outpatient clinic is a system which can often be isolated or closed, and it is often shunned or avoided just as the cancer patient is avoided. In a teaching hospital, such as the University of California, Los Angeles, the house staff frequently do not look forward to a rotation on the oncology service, and they are often anxious to leave. Janes and Weisz (1970) similarly described the experience of house staff on the Stanford oncology service

> The resident's commitment is finite, i.e., he can count the days remaining until his responsibility ends. Second, no matter how grim the patient's situation becomes, the doctor can take refuge in the intellectual research aspects of the case [p. 337].

The emotional "culture" fostered by the staff of the cancer center is transmitted to the patients and their families in the fashion described by Stanton and Schwartz (1949) in their famous paper examining the emotional conflicts of staff as they are acted out and incorporated by the patients. Thus a stressed or depressed staff may quickly cause patients to feel distress or depression beyond expected levels.

As with all other approaches to interventions with cancer patients, intervention through the staff is an involved process, and a multiplicity of approaches has been attempted. As with other intervention modalities, a general model for intervention with staff has emerged, involving a central theme with minor variations.

The consultant providing intervention with the staff must first understand how the cancer ward or clinic operates, both in terms of its overt structure and covert conflicts or operations. For example, the structure of a university teaching hospital, with attending physicians, residents, interns, and nurses, is very different from a private or public nonteaching hospital which has only attending physicians and nurses. Understanding the power hierarchy of each setting is crucial.

Another primary matter for the psychological consultant to attend to is the operational task(s) of the oncology service. There can be wide variations in what is done in various services. Perhaps the most important difference between services is whether they are involved in both research and treatment or in treatment alone. Research services, such as those described by Janes and Weisz (1970), tend to include very ill patients who are placed on drug protocols. The physicians who run these services have a commitment to good patient care as well as a primary commitment to research and its outcome over lengthy periods of time. This tends to split the physicians and nurses, given that the nurses on such units do not usually have the research perspective, do not glean rewards from the research, and as described by Janes and Weisz "feel that things are being done *to* the patient rather than *for* the patient [p. 338]." This type of conflict has repeatedly been observed by this writer in the course of consulting to a research oncology unit where bone marrow transplantations on end-stage leukemic patients are performed (Fawzy, Wellisch, & Yager, 1977). Units which are not engaged in research are not free from staff conflicts, but the types of conflicts may differ. The consultant must know enough of the technical work of the unit in order to understand the conflict within the staff culture.

Intervention with Nurses

Intervention with the staff may be conducted by approaching staff according to their professional discipline. It would perhaps be easier if the same interventions could be employed with all professional groups in the unit or clinic, but, in reality, this is usually not possible. Devising an intervention program for oncology nurses is the easiest for several reasons. First, oncology nurses are most in danger of psychological "burn-out" (Maslach,

1976), as they experience the most intensive and continual exposure to the patient population. Patients and nurses alike suffer from the results of burn-outs. Patients suffer because the nursing staff forms an impenetrable emotional wall and ceases to care for their needs, while staff are prone to develop a variety of psychophysiological problems, including migraine headaches and ulcers. Behavioral dysfunctions such as alcohol/drug abuse, marital discord, and emotional breakdown may also appear (Maslach, 1976).

A key issue for the consultant to face with the nursing staff concerns the degree to which relating to cancer patients and their families is helpful, as excessive emotional involvement may lead to burn-out. The trend toward overinvolvement with too many patients is a chronic problem with oncology nurses. They may easily become involved in an ongoing cycle of losses, each of which comes to mean too much to the nurses. No human being can emotionally survive such a cycle without establishing an appropriate distance, and the consultant may be of great help in this regard due to his/her ability to be more objective than the nurse.

Klagsbrun (1970) detailed a process of changing an oncology ward by becoming a consultant to a nurse group. He found the nurses receptive, and initially largely unaware of the importance of their role in influencing the patients' experience of their illness. Helping the nurses to recognize their importance became the first step in the intervention process. The consultant's initial focus was on patient problems, but the group process quickly shifted to the problems within the nurse group. Finally, the nurses' perceptions of their problems in relation to the physicians was examined. Klagsbrun felt two major shifts were achieved improving the ward emotional culture, and subsequently the patients' emotional adjustment to their disease: (*a*) the nurses were better able to understand and recognize the physicians' needs for distance from the patients, especially when things were deteriorating; and (*b*) instead of resenting the physicians' attitudes and waiting for the physicians to intervene, the nurses were able to recognize their own responsibility for dealing with the patients' emotional conflicts. This writer's experience with such nurse groups has paralleled that of Klagsbrun; nurses appear able and motivated to look at such conflicts, and easily move from patient focused material to personal issues and processes independent of the patients. Physicians, however, frequently react differently; this is particularly true of housestaff in training. The reasons for this and alternative interventions will be discussed in the next section.

Three issues with consulting to oncology nurses are very important to consider. First, the consultant must avoid becoming identified as the nurses' consultant; the ease of consulting to the nurses may lead the consultant to take the path of least resistance and avoid the physicians. If this occurs, the consultant's ultimate effectiveness in helping the patients will be severely hampered, as the physicians exert a tremendous influence on the psychological experience of the patients on the service. Given this reality, physicians must become a part of the consultation process. Second, the consultant must not become an advocate for the nurses to the hospital nursing administration. The study of Maslach (1976) suggested many job variations (i.e., shorter shift hours, lower patient–staff ratio, varied assignments, sanctioned time outs) which might reduce risk of burn-out, but even if these are valid interventions, it is not the consultant's role to argue for them with nursing administration. The consultant can offer suggestions to the system, but it is not the consultant's responsibility to find avenues to implement such changes. If the consultant assumes the go-between role, he or she may soon be embroiled in conflicts between administration and staff, conflicts which are far beyond the scope of the consultant's role. The staff, however, may covertly or overtly push for the consultant to assume such an inappropriate role, or the consultant, through misguided omnipotent needs, may seek such a role. Third, the consultant must avoid becoming a direct psychotherapist to member(s) of the oncology nursing staff. This writer has learned that this complicates and confuses the consultant's role, as the consultant may be viewed as the advocate of the nurse being treated, rather than as an impartial, objective consultant. The best policy is to refer the nurse to someone outside of the hospital system and thus allow everyone to interact without special constraints.

Intervention with Physicians

Consultation to the physicians of a cancer unit can be very meaningful, but is also very different from consultation to oncology nurses. The socialization for the physician's role is very different than for the nurse's role; such socialization starts at the beginning of medical training, if not long before medical school. Underlying psychological dynamics may lead the individual to choose a medical career; a need to deny or control death is perhaps the primary unconscious motivation. An adequate discussion of these important processes, both internal and external, is beyond the scope of this section, but they are masterfully discussed by Coombs and Powers (1977). By the time physicians are working on an oncology service, these attitudes and emotional defense mechanisms are deeply ingrained, and must be understood rather than resisted or fought by the consultant. Struggling against such attitudes may lead to a stiffening of resistance toward psychological intervention for the patients, as well as a worsening of the physician–nurse conflicts on the service, and the consultant may be viewed only as a hostile ally of the nurses. The consultant in such a position then becomes a part of the problem rather than a part of the solution.

Several authors (Janes & Weisz, 1970; Richards & Schmale, 1974; Schwab, 1968) have suggested a consultation–teaching conference organized around one patient each week as a means of intervening with physicians in oncologic settings. The treating physician presents the case to the consultant, and provides information on the patient's medical and psychosocial course and complications. The consultant then leads the conference toward a consensus as to the previously unrecognized psychological aspects of the patient's problem, and an intervention plan is developed. Such conferences can include both an interview of the patient by the consultant plus staff presentation, or staff presentation alone. By participating in this process, physicians may begin to see themselves as a part of the process that influences patients' adjustment (or lack of adjustment) to cancer's course. Participation in the conference may be followed by individual attention (Richards & Schmale, 1974).

The intervention process with physicians, in contrast to the process with nurses, is less likely to move, in a group context, away from patient-centered material toward the physicians' personal concerns. As Richards and Schmale have suggested, individual supervision has the potential of bringing some of these personal aspects to light. In this writer's experience, as the consultant becomes a known entity on the service, numerous hallway consultations between the physician and the consultant occur. It is in these informal, time-limited interactions that the physicians' true feelings and perceptions regarding the cancer patients are offered. If the consultant can only meet in groups with the physicians, and is never otherwise available, the likelihood of these interactions is lessened or obviated. Thus, the physicians can respond as do the nurses, but in different circumstances, over longer periods of time, and perhaps in more subtle ways.

Richards and Schmale listed five psychological areas of paramount interest to physician trainees. These include (*a*) patients' delay in seeking or accepting treatment offered; (*b*) patients' reactions to diagnosis, treatment, and stage of disease; (*c*) trainees' reactions to patients that may lead to too much, too little, or delayed treatment; (*d*) family strengths or weaknesses that may interfere with or help the patients' abilities to cope with their disease; and (*e*) patients' somatic symptoms that may be intensified or minimized as a result of beliefs, experiences, and personality structure. These issues may provide initial topics with which the consultant may begin to penetrate physician disinterest or resistance toward psychological consultation on an oncology service.

Intervention with the Family

Cancer is a major threat on many levels to the integrity of the family unit. Cancer cannot be conceptualized as only an individual facing a crisis; instead, the impact of cancer on the family unit must be acknowledged. As one very articulate elderly wife of a cancer patient stated: "Cancer is like another member of my family, it moved in, took over, and moved me out."

This perception is vivid, appropriate, and suggests the major intervention tasks necessary to help the family of a cancer patient. The family must be helped to adjust to this new presence in their midst, as they attempt to strike a balance between maintaining a semblance of normal family life and making the necessary concessions to the disease and treatment. These concessions may be economic, situational, sexual, social, and interpersonal. Family therapy, therefore, becomes a highly important focus of intervention for the cancer patient.

As with the individual, developmental issues are critical. The family of a child cancer patient, the family of an adult cancer patient with multiple young dependents, and the elderly couple where one spouse has cancer, have vastly different problems. Part of family therapy with cancer as an issue is always directed toward the social and economic realities that affect the family. These can differ widely, and require more or less attention depending upon the life cycle phase of the family.

In the child focused literature, two general styles of family communication emerge. One is a protective approach toward the child by the family, while the other is an open approach. In a review of these styles, Shore (1972) concluded that the open approach is generally desired by the child, and the protective approach may contribute to a passive, more troubled, and more withdrawn child.

A common problem when families must deal with a member's cancer is the tendency to project their own fears onto the patient, a process referred to by Bowen (1978) as "family projection." In this process, the family members protect their own feelings by locating their personal fragility or distress in the cancer patient. In the course of family therapy with cancer patients, the therapist will often need to intervene into such a process. Shore (1972) noted that this need for intervention may eventuate in limited or negative adjustment on the patient's part. Kaplan, Smith, Grobstein and Fischman (1973) observed 50 families with leukemic children, and concluded that reality denying patients can prevent adaptive coping, but rarely prevent appropriate medical treatment. There is also an enormously high frequency of marital conflicts and marital dissolutions in this population. This may be a reaction to the unremitting stresses and frustrations generated by leukemia in a child; these stresses can lead to separation and cause an unsympathetic perspective on the illness to develop. Marital therapy to facilitate appropriate focusing of frustrations, and to encourage similar perspectives on the problems at hand, is necessary in these cases.

Several papers have described group efforts to help parents of pediatric cancer patients (Gilder, Buschman, Sitarz, & Wolff, 1978; Heller, & Schneider, 1977). In such multiple family therapy efforts, it seems that the self-help model whereby families are trained to help each other is useful only to a limited extent. Families with problems of this magnitude appear to need help from objective professionals. This is not to say that groups such as Candlelighters, composed of parents with terminally ill children, cannot serve a role, but the extent of the role must be carefully considered. Spinetta, Kard, & Sheposh (Note 3), in a follow-up study of parents following the death of a child from leukemia, elicited three factors which predicted adaptive coping: (*a*) a consistent philosophy of life which the family held prior to diagnosis, and which could support the family after the death by providing them with a philosophical meaning of life; (*b*) the availability of a viable and ongoing support system; and (*c*) functional communication ability which had allowed the family to effectively communicate with the child prior to death.

For adults, cancer being introduced into the family system offers concerns similar to those of the family with the pediatric patient, but offers some different concerns as well. Sheldon, Ryser, and Krant (1970) noted that the major concerns of adult cancer patients regarding their families involved concerns for the effect of their illness on the family's emotional and financial security.

Several papers on adult focused family therapy with cancer patients have emphasized similar points, which include (*a*) concerns for problematic role reversals, whereby parents become children and children become parents (Sheldon *et al.*, 1970; Wellisch, 1979); (*b*) the need for a close alliance and coordination with the treating physicians (oncologists, hematologists, or others) where joint interventions are frequent, a process which can be very different from conventional family therapy (Wellisch, Mosher, & Van-Scoy, 1978; Cohen & Wellish, 1978); and (*c*) in the case of body image changes in one partner, such as mastectomy in the woman, the male partner may strongly identify with the loss, and need to jointly mourn the loss in order that effective working through of the experience on a marital–family level may occur (Grandstaff, 1976; Wellisch, Jamison, & Pasnau, 1978).

Clinical interventions with families of cancer patients can be different from conventional family therapy interventions. For example, conventional family therapy generally starts with a defined problem, with the therapist and family contracting to work in an uninterrupted fashion to solve the problem. Usually this involves symptom remission (Minuchin, 1974; Minuchin, Rosman, & Baker, 1978). In cancer oriented family therapy, the family usually utilizes family therapy as a series of discrete crisis interventions correlating with the course of the disease. This might mean that a family would seek several sessions of family therapy to cope with the diagnosis of cancer in a family member, and not return for more family therapy for several months or even years, possibly when the patient has suffered a recurrence of disease and the family is once again in crisis. As stated previously, in conventional family therapy the therapist often does not interact with outside physicians or health care teams, while in cancer focused family work, this is a *sine qua non* and cannot be effectively avoided. The site of the family therapy in conventional work is usually the therapist's office, while in working with cancer patients and their families, the therapist must often be flexible enough to work in the patient's home, in the patient's hospital room, or in the treating physician's office. This is due to the frequent inability of the patient to come to the therapist's office due to the extent of the disease.

Four general areas are central in family oriented therapy with cancer patients. First, it is important to work on an "educational" basis teaching the family how to communicate with the patient. This process may involve teaching the family about the patient's needs, the patient's utilization of defense mechanisms, and providing role modeling for the family for talking with the patient. Second, issues of management and attention to affirmative intimacy and emotional boundary keeping are critical. In an important paper on the subject, Napier (1978) pointed out

> Realization of this ideal (affirmative intimacy) is complicated, however, for the emotional distance which affirms one member may violate another and leave a third feeling relatively unaffected . . . because nurturance and intimacy are matters of singular importance to the human organism, unsuccessful movements toward these targets generate crisis situations [p. 6].

Cancer almost always exerts a strong push toward increased family togetherness in both physical–temporal and emotional ways. This can radically alter the precancer emotional distance and boundary keeping needs of family members, and create the crisis to which Napier alludes. This may be especially true for adolescents with an ill parent, who need the psychological separateness and distance from the family that can be reversed by cancer in a parent. The family therapist can be very helpful in attending to and helping to restore these important emotional boundaries to a semblance of their precancer states. Family members may feel powerfully obligated to be close to the patient and to each other when cancer exists, but may not be able to emotionally cope with such closeness.

Third, attention must be paid to the effect of cancer on the dependence–independence axis of the family and/or marital relationship. Cancer, in its clinical course, will always lead to increased dependence of the patient upon the family, which can manifest itself both physically and emotionally. This becomes a complicated interactional issue between family and patient. This writer has repeatedly observed families to elicit overdependence in family members with cancer, and in selected instances to counter or block appropriate dependency needs in ill members. This problem most often manifests itself in a style which reinforces excessive dependence, and can feel like an overwhelming burden to the family should such an interactional style be established between patient and family.

Finally, the therapist should pay close attention to the management of family frustration regarding the burdens and limitations of the illness. Without intervention, such frustration often leads to displacement onto targets such as physicians and nurses or other family members. It is easy for the family to lose sight of what they are really frustrated and angry about, and hard for them to resurrect relationships, such as with physicians, that are damaged by displaced explosions of anger.

The therapist doing family work of this type should consider several clinical pitfalls involving counter-transference problems. Primary among these is overidentification with the family. This is a ubiquitous problem in family therapy, but never more so than in family therapy with cancer as a central issue. Here, the family therapist may be trying to unconsciously reexperience or work through incompletely resolved personal losses. Another problem is that of pushing the family for more change than is possible. This can stem more from the therapist's needs than from those of the family itself. A third therapist-induced problem involves validating the family projective process in which it is believed that the patient cannot deal with the cancer, and therefore must be "protected." This again is a common problem of conventional family therapy which achieves powerful intensity when cancer is a focal problem. A final counter-transferential error involves the therapist allying with the family against the primary physician. Sometimes the physician may have missed something or been insensitive to the patient or family. However, just as often the patient and family place the physician in an untenable bind which they resist acknowledging. The family therapist, in blindly allying with the family against the physician, may be seeking a form of omnipotent control over the situation. This may be due to latent, but destructive, needs for competition with the physician for "control" of the patient and family. Even if the physician is glaringly wrong on a point, the family therapist must carefully inspect such competitive needs.

Less Conventional Interventions

Visualization Therapy

The subject of visualization techniques combined with relaxation exercises as a form of psychological intervention with cancer patients is becoming more widely discussed. These intervention modalities have probably best been articulated in, and are most frequently associated with, the recent work of Carl and Stephanie Simonton (Simonton & Simonton, 1975). In their work, the Simontons have delineated a holistic conception of etiology and intervention for cancer patients, and view a form of visualization-relaxation therapy as an essential adjunct to conventional medical treatment. They are primarily concerned with the belief systems of patients, their families, and the treating physicians and the effect of these belief systems on the patients' diseases. In regard to the patients' belief systems they have stated that "His beliefs about his disease, his treatment and himself are very big factors, having a significant role in the course his body takes during and after treatment [p. 31]." The core of their psychotherapeutic process consists of the acceptance by patients of the belief that they must be a participant in combating the disease process, and must similarly accept responsibility for the disease. They have cautioned that responsibility is not blame, stating (1975):

> For some reason we have a conception of responsibility being the same as blame. This is one reason for our inability as a society to deal with the emotional aspects of our diseases. We feel that if we accept responsibility we are to blame, should feel guilty, or have done something wrong [1975, p. 39].

The Simontons' approach has received much attention and has polarized the field of psychological intervention with cancer patients. They represent that group of professionals who believe that psychological intervention may be helpful not only in the emotional resolution of the problems cancer mobilizes, but who further believe that such intervention may in fact be life prolonging and/or life saving.

Perhaps the major tenet that underlies the thinking of the Simontons and those whom they represent is the concept of the cancer prone personality. This concept has gained momentum in the past two decades, but the issue of the cancer prone personality is far from closed. The lack of consensus on this issue must be considered by mental health or medical practitioners when dealing with cancer patients and their families. The most thoughtful and comprehensive review of this very complicated concept was conducted by Fox (1978). In his landmark article, Fox reviewed the bulk of the studies which propose to link what he termed psychological factors and/or stress to incidence of cancers of humans. He concluded that these studies have a multitude of problems, including flaws in methodology, control of independent variables, sample sizes, definitions of terms, instrumentation, and time perspective. Thus, it may not be concluded, at the present time, that cancer is either a "psychosomatic illness" or the result of personality or stress factors. For the mental health professional working with cancer patients, *both* the Simontons' writings *and* Fox's review are mandatory in order to properly deal with the questions patients will ask about these issues (see Barofsky, Chapter 5).

Given these very real limitations, the most that can be said to patients is that the notion of the cancer prone personality is an interesting speculation which is unproven at the present time. This writer has seen some cancer patients embrace and be motivated by the notion of their responsibility for cancer, while others are both irritated and appalled by such a notion. The mental health professional has an obligation not to attempt to convince the patient of the truth of this concept, as it is an unproven theory.

Hypnosis

Hypnosis can serve as an important tool for psychological intervention with the cancer patient within certain defined limitations. In a series of papers, hypnosis has been described as useful in helping the cancer patient more effectively cope with the psychological, as well as pain related, aspects of cancer (Sacerdote, 1966, 1968, 1970). Hypnosis has been thought to be useful with severely ill medical patients by providing a means of anxiety reduction, thereby reducing the spasm-pain-spasm cycle associated with severe anxiety. It has also been suggested that hypnosis facilitates an outpouring of endorphins which reduce pain from within the body. Hypnosis can be an invaluable aid to help the cancer patient relax, and thereby reduce that portion of nausea associated with chemotherapy that may have been a conditioned response.

This writer has seen two instances where hypnosis has led to iatrogenic problems or been counterproductive with cancer patients. The first was with a 26-year-old leukemic patient undergoing bone marrow transplantation. The patient had previously experienced two brief psychiatric hospitalizations, and had been diagnosed as a borderline personality. Hypnosis was attempted to facilitate anxiety reduction and perceptual changes related to the patient's severe itching that occurred secondary to the heavy doses of radiation which is part of the bone marrow transplantation induction protocol. While in a mild hypnotic state, this patient reexperienced a repressed memory of a sibling's death, which was affectively linked to panic, confusion, and guilt. The patient displayed signs of a severe anxiety attack and was psychotic and paranoid for several days after the hypnotic episode. This case strongly suggests that caution must be exercised if hypnosis is considered as a part of the treatment program for unstable cancer patients.

In a second case, hypnosis was attempted with a 52-year-old patient with metastatic breast cancer. She was an obsessively anxious and highly dependent woman who experienced constant tension and sleep problems, and refused medication for these symptoms. During the attempted hypnotic induction, she became increasingly anxious, fought relaxation, and the induction was discontinued. She reflected the previously described notion that the cancer patient needs to be in control of his or her defenses, and can relax these only at infrequent times. Sacerdote (1978) also cautions that hypnosis is not a panacea where chronic pain is a major symptom, and indicates that one out of five patients have an innate capacity to benefit from this approach.

Psychedelic Drugs

Finally, a radical experimental approach to psychotherapy with cancer patients was described by Grof (1972). In his experimental study he administered LSD to terminal cancer patients in an attempt to alter depressed cancer patients' attitudes about their illness. To quote Grof:

> Many of the subjects who have experienced the death-rebirth phenomenon (via the LSD/psychotherapy experiment) reported that their concept of death and attitude toward dying underwent a dramatic change; their fear of death was considerably diminished and the process of dying appeared as a fantastic cosmic adventure in consciousness rather than in biological disaster [p. 66].

These LSD sessions were held after rapport had been established between therapist and patient. The sessions were held in the patient's hospital room, and sessions lasted from 8 to 10 hours. Of the 31 patients in the study, 28 received LSD only once, while the remaining three had as many as six sessions. Pre- and postpsychological testing and structured interviewing was conducted, and post-LSD sessions were also conducted so the therapists might help the patients integrate their experiences. According to project outcome data, 29% of the patients showed dramatic improvement in mood (post-LSD therapy), while 42% were moderately improved, and 29% were unchanged. The fact that none of the patients were viewed as worsened or decompensated after the LSD experience contradicts this writer's clinical experience with the diminishing of cancer patients' defense mechanisms. Not only were some of these patients reported to be less depressed, but they also were more able to cope with pain after LSD therapy. The project thesis was that the acceptance and surrender to loss of control experienced through LSD may parallel, and thus ease, the apprehension regarding such loss of control to death.

This study was highly experimental, and would never become a routine procedure. However, it does make a powerful statement regarding emotions and death. It is evidently the perception of the experience, and its symbolic imagery, which shapes the emotional attitudes associated with death. These attitudes may be modifiable, whether through a short term intervention using LSD, or with longer term intervention through psychotherapy. The perception is the experience, and for cancer patients this perception appears more modifiable than might otherwise be expected.

Conclusions

This chapter has reviewed a variety of approaches to intervention with the cancer patient. It may be seen from the forgoing material that many issues (e.g., age, disease stage, family structure) are important in such interventions, and that the professional must attend to all of these if an intervention is to be effective. Additionally, the staff involved in treating cancer patients has particular needs which may be helped in a through consultation, as they deal directly with emotionally charged issues daily.

Most of the literature that was reviewed in this chapter has been largely descriptive and lacked rigorous methodology or follow-up measures. As cancer becomes more treatable, and more patients survive for longer periods of time after the initial diagnosis, more rigorous research examining intervention strategies directed toward the psychological needs of cancer patients and their families and health care providers will become possible. Additionally, the prevention of cancer through modification of behaviors discussed elsewhere in this volume (i.e., smoking) also offers rich research opportunities, as do longitudinal investigations examining issues related to the concept of the cancer prone personality. By participating in such efforts, medical psychology and behavioral medicine specialists may make significant contributions to treatment, prevention, and rehabilitation efforts involving cancer.

Reference Notes

1. Shneidman, E. Personal communication, 1974.
2. Komp, D. M., & Crockett, J. *Educational needs of the child with cancer.* Paper presented at Second National

Conference on Human Values and Cancer of the American Cancer Society, Chicago, September 1977.

3. Spinetta, J., Kard, T., & Sheposh, J. P. *Effective parental coping following the death of a child from cancer.* Paper presented at the meeting of The Western Psychological Association, San Francisco, 1978.

References

American Cancer Society, Inc. *1978 Cancer facts and figures.* New York: American Cancer Society, 1978.

Bowen, M. Family therapy and family group therapy. In M. Bowen (Ed.), *Family therapy in clinical practice.* New York: Jason Aronson, 1978.

Cohen, M. M., & Wellisch, D. K. Living in limbo: Psychosocial intervention in families with a cancer patient. *American Journal of Psychotherapy,* 1978, *32,* 560-571.

Coombs, R. H., & Powers, P. S. *Socialization for death: The physician's role.* Beverly Hills: Sage Publications, 1977. (Monograph)

Corder, M. P., & Anders, R. L. Death and dying—a discussion group. *Journal of Psychiatric Nursing and Mental Health Services,* 1974, July-August, 10-14.

Deutsch, H. Absence of grief. *Psychoanalytic Quarterly,* 1937, *6,* 12-22.

Evans, A. E. Practical care in childhood cancer. *Cancer,* 1975, *35,* 871-875.

Fawzy, F., Wellisch, D. K., & Yager, J. Psychiatric liaison to the bone marrow transplantation project. In C. Hollingsworth & R. O. Pasnau (Eds.), *The family in mourning.* New York: Grune and Stratton, 1977.

Ferlic, M., Goldman, A., & Kennedy, B. J. Group counseling in adult patients with advanced cancer. *Cancer,* 1979, *43,* 760-766.

Fox, B. H. Premorbid psychological factors as related to cancer incidence. *Journal of Behavioral Medicine,* 1978, *1,* 45-122.

Gardiner, G. G. Childhood, death and human dignity: Hypnotherapy for David. *International Journal of Clinical and Experimental Hypnosis,* 1976, *24,* 122-139.

Gilder, R., Buschman, P. R., Sitarz, A. L., & Wolff, J. A. Group therapy with parents of children with leukemia. *American Journal of Psychotherapy,* 1978, *32*(1), 276-286.

Grandstaff, N. W. The impact of breast cancer on the family. *Frontiers of Radiation Therapy and Oncology,* 1976, *11,* 145-156.

Grof, S. LSD and the human encounter with death. *Voices,* 1972, Winter, 64-76.

Heller, D. B., & Schneider, C. D. Interpersonal methods for coping with stress: Helping families of dying children. *Omega,* 1977, *8,* 319-331.

Holland, J. Psychological aspects of cancer. In J. F. Holland & E. Frei III (Eds.), *Cancer medicine.* Philadelphia: Lea and Febiger, 1973.

Janes, R. G., & Weisz, A. E. Psychiatric liaison with a cancer research center. *Comprehensive Psychiatry,* 1970, *11,* 336-345.

Kaplan, D. M., Smith, A., Grobstein, R., & Fishmann, S. E. Family mediation of stress. *Social Work,* 1973, *18,* 60-69.

Katz, E. R., Kellerman, J., Rigler, D., Williams, K. O., & Siegel, S. E. School intervention with pediatric cancer patients. *Journal of Pediatric Psychology,* 1977, *2,* 72-76.

Kellerman, J., & Katz, E. R. The adolescent with cancer: Theoretical, clinical and research issues. *Journal of Pediatric Psychology,* 1977, *2,* 127-131.

Kelly, P. P., & Ashby, G. C. Group approaches for cancer patients: Establishing a group. *American Journal of Nursing,* 1979, *79,* 914-915.

Klagsbrun, S. C. Cancer, emotion and nurses. *American Journal of Psychiatry,* 1970, *126,* 1237-1244.

Koocher, G. P., & Sallen, S. E. Pediatric oncology. In P. R. Mograb (Ed.), *Psychological management of pediatric problems.* Baltimore: University Park Press, 1978.

Kubler-Ross, E. *On death and dying.* New York: Macmillan, 1969.

Lansky, S. B., Lowman, J. T., Gyulay, J., & Briscoe, K. *A team approach to coping with cancer.* Lawrence, Kan.: University of Kansas Medical Center, 1975.

Lifton, R. J. *The broken connection.* New York: Simon and Schuster, 1978.

Maslach, C. Burned out. *Human Behavior,* 1976, *5,* 17-22.

Minuchin, S. *Families and family therapy.* Cambridge: Harvard Press, 1974.

Minuchin, S., Rosman, B. L., & Baker, L. *Psychosomatic families.* Cambridge: Harvard University Press, 1978.

Nagera, H. Children's reactions to the death of an important object. *Psychoanalytic Study of the Child,* 1970, *26,* 360-400.

Napier, A. The rejection-intrusion pattern: A central family dynamic. *Journal of Marriage and Family Counseling,* 1978, *4,* 5-12.

Pattison, E. M. Help in the dying process. In S. Arieti (Ed.), *American handbook of psychiatry* (Vol. 1.). New York: Basic Books, 1974.

Renneker, R. E. Countertransference reactions to cancer. *Psychosomatic Medicine,* 1957, *19,* 405-418.

Richards, A. I., & Schmale, A. H. Psychosocial conferences in medical oncology. *Annals of Internal Medicine,* 1974, *80,* 541-545.

Rosner, A. A. Mourning before the fact. *Journal of American Psychoanalytic Association,* 1962, *10,* 564-570.

Rothenberg, M. B. The dying child. In J. D. Noshpitz

(Ed.), *Basic handbook of child psychiatry,* (Vol. 1.). New York: Basic Books, 1979.

Sacerdote, P. The uses of hypnosis in cancer patients. *Annals of New York Academy of Science,* 1966, *125,* 1011-1019.

Sacerdote, P. Involvement and communication with the terminally ill patient. *American Journal of Clinical Hypnosis,* 1968, *10,* 244-248.

Sacerdote, P. Theory and practice of pain control in malignancy. *International Journal of Clinical Hypnosis,* 1970, *18,* 160-180.

Sacerdote, P. Teaching self-hypnosis to patients with chronic pain. *Journal of Human Stress,* 1978, *4,* 18-21.

Schwab, J. J. *Handbook of psychiatric consultation.* New York: Appleton-Century-Crofts, 1968.

Schwartz, M. D. An information and discussion program for women after a mastectomy. *Archives of Surgery,* 1977, *112,* 276-281.

Senescu, R. A. The development of emotional complications in the patient with cancer. *Journal of Chronic Disease,* 1963, *16,* 813-832.

Senescu, R. A. The problem of establishing communication with the seriously ill patient. *Annals of the New York Academy of Science,* 1966, *125,* 696-702.

Sheldon, A., Ryser, C. P., & Krant, M. D. An integrated family oriented cancer care program: The report of a pilot project in the socioemotional management of chronic disease. *Journal of Chronic Diseases,* 1970, *22,* 743-755.

Shneidman, E. Some aspects of psychotherapy with dying persons. In C. A. Garfield (Ed.), *Psychosocial aspects of terminal patient care.* New York: McGraw-Hill, 1978.

Shore, L. Family communication in the crisis of a child's fatal illness: A literature review and analysis. *Omega,* 1972, *3,* 187-201.

Simonton, O. C., & Simonton, S. S. Belief systems and management of emotional aspects of malignancy. *Journal of Transpersonal Psychology,* 1975, *7,* 29-47.

Siris, E. S., Leventhal, B. C., & Vaitukaitis, J. L. Effects of childhood leukemia and chemotherapy on puberty and reproductive function in girls. *New England Journal of Medicine,* 1976, *294,* 1143-1148.

Sontag, S. *Illness as metaphor.* New York: Farrar, Straus, & Giroux, 1978.

Stanton, A. H., & Schwartz, M. S. The management of a type of institutional participation in mental illness. *Psychiatry,* 1949, *12,* 13-23.

Van Eys, J. Supportive care for the child with cancer. *Pediatric Clinics of North America,* 1976, *23,* 215-223.

Wahl, C. W. The technique of brief psychotherapy with hospitalized psychosomatic patients. *International Journal of Psychoanalysis and Psychotherapy,* 1972, *1,* 69-82.

Weisman, A. D., & Worden, J. W. The existential plight in cancer: Significance of the first 100 days. *International Journal of Psychiatry in Medicine,* 1977, *7,* 1-15.

Wellisch, D. K. Adolescent acting out when a parent has cancer. *International Journal of Family Therapy,* 1979, *1,* 230-241.

Wellisch, D. K., Jamison, K., & Pasnau, R. O. Psychosocial aspects of mastectomy II: The man's perspective. *American Journal of Psychiatry,* 1978, *135,* 543-546.

Wellisch, D. K., Mosher, M., & Van-Scoy, C. Management of family emotional stress: Family group therapy in a private oncology practice. *International Journal of Group Psychotherapy,* 1978, *28,* 225-231.

Whitman, H. H., Gustafson, J. P., & Coleman, F. W. Group approaches for cancer patients. *American Journal of Nursing,* 1979, *79,* 910-913.

Wilbur, J. R. Rehabilitation of children with cancer. *Cancer,* 1975, *36,* 809-812. (Supplement.)

Winick, L., & Robbins, G. F. Physical and psychologic adjustment after mastectomy. *Cancer,* 1977, *39,* 478-486.

Yalom, I. D., & Greaves, C. Group therapy with the terminally ill. *American Journal of Psychiatry,* 1977, *134,* 396-400.

14

Rehabilitation and Treatment of Central Nervous System Dysfunction: A Behavioral Medicine Perspective

JEFFREY T. BARTH
THOMAS J. BOLL

There is too much vitality and individualism out there for conformity to conquer. [Scrimgeour, 1975, p. 17]

There is a tremendous volume of literature that purports to address the issue of the treatment and rehabilitation of brain damage and central nervous system (CNS) dysfunction. The content of much of this literature is reminiscent of whistling in the dark when one is afraid, or perhaps similar to the situation where a highly stressed patient binds anxiety by talking incessantly without really saying anything of relevance. Articles with titles such as "Rehabilitation of the Brain Injured Adult" or "A Comprehensive Treatment Program for Stroke Victims" seldom live up to their advance billing. These articles generally emphasize diagnostic criteria and measurements, since our assessment skills far surpass our knowledge of effective treatment methods. Occasionally, ancient treatment modalities with questionable outcomes are discussed, yet little scientific rigor is applied to facilitate analysis and answer pertinent questions regarding efficacy of rehabilitation techniques. In their discussion of treatment methods with cerebral palsy children, Taft, Delagi, Wilkie, and Abramson (1962) state that "experimental evidence is scanty, superimposed theory abundant, treatment empiric, and results impressionistic [p. 238]." Much of this difficulty is due to the fact that the development of CNS treatment methodology is still in its infancy and many health care professionals are ill prepared for dealing with the uncertainties associated with untested methods. Unfortunately, some scientists are trained to be gods but none are taught the necessary treatment miracles to live up to that reputation (Flora, 1976). This in turn creates discouragement which is reflected in a paucity of meaningful research and a pessimism regarding our treatment efforts.

Given that the darkest hour is just before dawn, it is important to realize that the picture may not be quite as bleak as we are painting it. In reviewing the rehabilitation literature, several names have surfaced which have made extremely valuable contributions to the area of treatment of CNS dysfunction. This chapter will selectively explore several aspects of the treatment and rehabilitation of CNS dysfunction in order to examine the state of

Medical Psychology
Contributions to Behavioral Medicine

ISBN 0-12-565960-1

the art as it applies to the medical psychologist, the clinical psychologist, and the clinical neuropsychologist, as behavioral scientists. Our hope is to provide a brief practical guide to the types of effective therapy available for patients who suffer from CNS dysfunction and to promote understanding, increase appropriate referrals, and encourage cross-fertilization of theoretical and practical approaches to treatment by acquainting the reader with the work of several health care disciplines.

Before we enter the murky waters of treatment, however, it is necessary to address some issues regarding terminology, neuroanatomy, neuropathologic conditions, brain–behavior relationships, neurological and neuropsychological assessment, and factors affecting the spontaneous or natural recovery process.

Terminology

Asken (1979) and Masur (1979) recently have attempted to define medical psychology and the role of the psychologist in the health care setting. Masur's definition has refocused Asken's formulations and has given medical psychology the objective of the development of "intervention strategies and educational systems directed at improving prevention, diagnosis, treatment, management, and rehabilitation of patients with physical diseases [Masur, 1979, p. 259]." (See Chapter 1 for a detailed discussion of this issue.) The clinical psychologist utilizes the same diagnostic, management, and treatment framework, but concentrates almost exclusively on mentally ill patients. The clinical neuropsychologist assesses brain–behavior relationships in neurologically compromised adults and children and recently has begun to explore issues in management and rehabilitation. It is important to conceptualize rehabilitation and treatment of CNS dysfunction from an interdisciplinary approach that includes the subspecialities of psychology as well as other health service fields such as physical medicine; biomedical engineering; occupational, physical and recreational therapies; speech assessment and therapy; and vocational rehabilitation. This inter-disciplinary approach to health care problems, often including fields that are not traditionally considered as part of the health care network such as anthropology and epidemiology, has been termed "behavioral medicine." Behavioral medicine has gained widespread acceptance throughout this country and is likely to revolutionize health care by uniting the health delivery services and offering appropriate, individualized, and comprehensive behavioral as well as medical treatment (Stroebel, 1979).

Most professionals agree that the terms brain damage, cerebral dysfunction or impairment, and organicity cause great confusion, stimulate intense emotion, and convey little meaning (Logue, 1975). In an attempt to clarify these terms the following definitions are offered:

1. *Brain damage* refers to structural lesion(s) of the cerebral hemispheres and/or brain stem.
2. *Cerebral dysfunction (impairment)* is an inability of the brain to function normally due to structural lesion(s) or other interferences such as metabolic disorders or chemical imbalances, regardless of their etiology, including emotional excesses and stimulus deprivation.
3. *Organicity* "is utilized as a description of certain behavioral patterns which are commonly found in individuals with brain damage [Diller, Buxbaum, & Chiotelis, 1972, p. 254]."

For the purposes of clarity and consistency, this chapter will incorporate the terms brain damage and cerebral dysfunction or impairment with particular reference to structural lesions of the brain and brain stem. The term CNS dysfunction will also be used in this fashion when referring to lesions of the brain, brain stem, and spinal cord. The term organicity, long overdue for an unmarked burial, will not be seen again in this chapter.

If we accept the previously noted definition of brain damage, we still must ask ourselves if this term is valid and useful when applied for diagnostic purposes. The term brain damage is much too nondescript and general to be used as a diagnostic label; it also has the added liability of perpetuating the myth of a unitary concept of brain damage which has reinforced the continuation of a search for a single test for neurologic impairment. This is true despite frequent, strongly worded, and well-documented appeals opposing such practice (Boll,

1978; Hartlage, 1966; Herbert, 1964; Lishman, 1978; McFie, 1960; Reitan, 1962; Reitan & Davison, 1974; Yates, 1966). Fortunately, it is generally accepted that brain damage must be viewed as a multidimensional phenomenon because it represents many different structural pathological entities and related behavioral disturbances. Factors such as size of lesion, location of lesion, pathological process, age and level of premorbid psychological and cognitive functioning of the patient, and condition of the patient at the time of assessment, can greatly influence what are determined to be the behavioral sequelae of the brain impairment (Smith, 1975, 1980). For this reason it is extremely important to describe brain damage in terms of its structural and functional components.

If one is to fully understand brain damage with the hope of initiating effective treatment, it is imperative that one have a basic knowledge of the intricacies of cerebral impairment as reflected in neuroanatomy, neuropathology, brain-behavior relationships, assessment procedures, and the natural recovery of function from brain insult. These are precisely the requirements for advanced study in clinical neuropsychology and neurologically oriented health care psychology and clinical psychology described by Boll (1976) and Matthews (1976).

Neuroanatomy

Although it generally is accepted that structural lesions are not always directly related to behavioral pathology, it is not advisable to ignore neuroanatomy altogether. In fact, many of the leading neuropsychologists of our time such as Reitan (1962), Luria (1963), Matthews (1976), and Meier (1980) advocate a solid background and understanding of neuroanatomy as one of the foundations in the study of the neurosciences. Just as one expects the cardiologist to have spent some time acquainting himself with the structural layout of the heart and circulatory system, one also expects health care psychologists, clinical psychologists, and clinical neuropsychologists to study the organ of behavior—the brain (Jarvis & Barth, 1979). While it is true that psychologists deal with behavior and do not treat (in a medical sense) the structural aspects of brain damage, it is difficult to produce accurate and lasting changes in patient behavior if one doesn't fully understand the nature of the underlying problem. Luria (1966) described the cerebral cortex as being divided into three functional systems or areas (primary, secondary, and tertiary) that interact to create behavior. This behavior, however, may be adversely affected by a lesion in any one or combination of the three functional areas. There are numerous examples that illustrate this principle, but one which is close to all of our hearts is the automobile that won't start. In this situation, unfortunately, our lack of understanding of the inner workings of a car engine lead us to think strictly in terms of behavior; that is, the car will not start! To our chagrin, we know that when this happens, the trouble often is not as straightforward as a defective starter; thus, we must take the car to the mechanic whose background ensures proper assessment and treatment of the engine. That is, although it is apparent that the car won't start, without understanding the engine and how it works, any treatment intervention would be no better than hit or miss. This is due to the obvious fact that automobiles are complex machines in which any number of disorders in one or more systems may account for the failure to start. Is it any less obvious that one should gain a certain amount of expertise in the area of human brain functioning before initiating assessment and treatment procedures?

Since it is not the purpose of this chapter to review basic functional neuroanatomy, it is suggested that the reader consult a neuroanatomy text (e.g., Chusid, 1976). For the novice, a simple introductory neuroanatomy chapter or article (Boll, 1978; Golden, 1978; Lezak, 1976; Walsh, 1978) will offer a sufficient foundation for understanding the location and function of the major brain structures and systems.

Neuropathology

In addition to understanding neuroanatomy, psychologists must be familiar with neuropathological conditions. This is particularly important since rehabilitation and treatment of CNS dysfunction must focus on specific behavioral deficits and are dependent upon clear communication with members of various health care disciplines. In the past, brain pathology could be summed up in one word, "prenitis," which loosely translates to "brain fever." The word is intriguing and perhaps it should be revived, although we already have another universal term that reflects brain damage and the generalized psychiatric effects of brain impairment—organic brain syndrome (OBS) (cf. Benson & Blumer, 1975; Freedman, Kaplan, & Sadock, 1975). Since almost all neuropathological conditions may be identified by this term, without additional descriptors, it has become as useless as the labels brain damage and prenitis. Fortunately, more specific and meaningful terms are used to describe the pathologic entities responsible for impaired cerebral processes (and injuries to the brain stem and spinal cord). Most of the terms may be grouped within six general categories: (*a*) infectious processes; (*b*) neoplastic diseases; (*c*) cerebrovascular disorders; (*d*) head trauma; (*e*) degenerative diseases; and (*f*) toxic disorders. Some pathologic conditions such as cerebral palsy, epilepsy, and minimal brain dysfunction (MBD) do not easily fit into a single category and there are other conditions such as schizophrenia that defy consistent neurodiagnosis. Transorbital and prefrontal lobotomies performed prior to 1955 may be considered to be neuropathological disorders, yet they also may be classified as forms of psychosurgery. The reader may refer to Boll (1978), Golden (1978), Lezak (1976), Lishman (1978), Logue (1975),and Wright, Schoefer, and Solomons (1979) for brief descriptions of neuropathology, and to Chusid (1976), Merritt (1973), and Samuels (1978) for more detailed approaches to this subject. The issues of MBD, schizophrenia, and pre-1955 lobotomies (psychosurgery) are addressed by Boll (1978), Golden (1978), Goldstein (Note 1), Logue (1975), Rutter (1977), Sargant and Slater (1972), Valenstein (1973), and Wolfik (1973).

Brain-Behavior Relationships

The third prerequisite for effective treatment of CNS dysfunction is knowledge of the effects of CNS impairment on brain-behavior relationships (the behavioral sequelae of CNS dysfunction). Virtually every behavior that is mediated by the cerebral hemispheres, brain stem, and spinal cord is subject to compromise following insult to the central nervous system. Thus, it is not sufficient merely to be acquainted with neuroanatomy and pathology. There also must be a *functional* component to this knowledge; that is, one must be familiar with brain-behavior relationships if one is to attain a comprehensive understanding of CNS dysfunction and its treatment. Golden's (1978) chapter entitled "Functional Localization in the Brain," and Lezak's (1976) chapter "The Behavioral Geography of the Brain," in addition to the Luria (1973) volume, present much of the pertinent literature regarding localized brain functions and the consequences of discrete cerebral lesions. Included in these reviews are studies that differentiate right and left cerebral hemisphere functions (visuospatial versus verbal), and those that concentrate on the roles of the frontal, parietal, temporal, and occipital lobes and other cerebral structures and systems. Additional sources of information regarding functioning of the central nervous system include Butter (1968), Carlson (1977), Kolb (1973), and Thompson (1967).

The sequelae of impairment to the central nervous system may be grouped within three general classifications: (*a*) sensory-motor or physical; (*b*) cognitive-intellectual; and (*c*) social-behavioral. A representative list of the physical sequelae would include motor impersistence (Fogel & Rosillo, 1971b), sexual dysfunction and its resultant psychological distress (Kaplan, 1974; Smith & Bullough, 1975), sensory and perceptual disorders (Barth, 1979; Boll & Reitan, 1972; Logue, 1975), physical illnessess such as infections, circulatory insufficiencies and pain (Krupp & Chatton, 1975), and aphasia and communication disorders (Fields, 1975; Hécaen & Albert, 1978; Travis, 1971; Johnson, Note 2). Cognitive-intellectual sequelae include symptoms such as hyperactivity, dissociation, perseveration, reading and academic difficulties, figure-ground reversals, visuoperceptual-motor disorders, poor concept formation, and memory and attentional difficulties. It should be noted that these symptoms also have been associated with minimal brain dysfunction (MBD) and learning disabilities, however, a direct relationship between CNS dysfunction and MBD or learning disabilities has been seriously questioned (Cruickshank, 1967; Reitan, 1976; Wright *et al.,* 1979). Finally, the social-behavioral sequelae include a large number of symptoms such as limitations in judgment and abstract reasoning, concrete thinking and mental inflexibility, difficulty in organizing, impaired learning and inability to profit from new experiences, anxiety, withdrawal, depression, low frustration tolerance and irritability, suspiciousness, hostility, poor self-concept, reduced social and vocational skills, euphoria, emotional lability, impulsiveness, regression, thought disorders, attention seeking and manipulation, denial and lack of awareness, and lack of motivation (Cook, 1976; Diller *et al.,* 1972; Fields, 1975; Fitts, 1972; Fogel & Rosillo, 1969; Jarvis & Barth, 1979; Lezak, 1978; Lishman, 1973; Pincus & Tucker, 1974; Reiser, 1975; Reitan, 1976; Sahakian, 1970; Siris, Werner & Pipenger, 1977; Wright *et al.,* 1979; Goldstein, Note 1). These symptoms (sometimes referred to as characterological changes) may constitute exacerbations of previously established coping behaviors and defense mechanisms (Jarvis & Barth, 1979). However, due to the fact that pretrauma data are limited in most cases, it is difficult to determine which of the symptoms are directly caused by CNS dysfunction (i.e., a structural lesion causing aberrant behavior or behavioral pathology developing as a new coping mechanism) and which are actually exacerbations of previously existing behavior patterns. In any case, these behaviors may be very disruptive to the patient's family and those initiating the rehabilitation procedures.

To emphasize the psychiatric component of brain damage, Rutter (1977) reported a unique set of children's data gathered from epidemiological studies of the entire population of the Isle of Wight. In these investigations it was determined that while the base rate of psychiatric disorders in the general population of children was 6.6%, 34.3% of all brain-injured children demonstrated psychiatric disturbances (in addition to other disorders). These data provide dramatic evidence that social-behavioral disorders and cognitive-intellectual deficits are significantly more likely to occur (or be noticed) in individuals who incur brain damage.

Assessment

The fourth component of effective treatment of CNS dysfunction is accurate assessment of pathological conditions, their anatomical substrates, and the resultant behavioral manifestations (changes from previous levels of functioning). If one were interested only in neuropathology and its anatomical basis, physical medicine undoubtedly could provide most of the data for assessment purposes through traditional (e.g., physical neurological examination and laboratory studies) and advanced neurodiagnostic techniques (e.g., variations of the computerized axial tomography or CAT Scan) (Forster, 1973; Golden, 1978; Krupp & Chatton, 1975). Without delineating and understanding the behavioral manifestations of CNS impairment, however, one would be at a distinct disadvantage in planning a rehabilitation program for the brain-injured patient. Neuropsychological evaluations, in particular, aid in defining the relationship between CNS dysfunction and behavior (rather than merely describing the structural lesions), and thus affords the opportunity to evaluate treatment by monitoring objective behavior changes (Boll, 1977; Golden, 1976a, 1976b, 1978; Herbert, 1964; McFie, 1960; Reitan & Davison, 1974; Suchett-Kaye, Sarkar, Elkan, & Waring, 1971).

Several traditional psychological and intellectual assessment tools have been modified and used to evaluate brain damage and other severe disabilities (Botterbusch, 1976; Hartlage, 1966; Herbert, 1964). Some of the assessment techniques have also been combined with other diagnostic tools to form multiple test batteries such as the Halstead Reitan Neuropsychological Test Battery and Allied Procedures (Boll, 1978, 1980; Reitan & Davison, 1974), and the Luria-Nebraska Neuropsychological Test Battery (Hammeke, Golden, & Purisch, 1978) from Christensen's *Luria's Neuropsychological Investigation* (1975). The rationale for utilizing batteries rather than a single test, and the descriptions and validational processes associated with neurologic and behavioral interpretation of test results are found in Chapter 6 of this volume and in Boll (1978, 1980); Boll and Barth (1980); Golden (1978); Lezak (1976); Lishman (1978); Reitan (1962, 1975); Reitan and Davison (1974); Russell, Neuringer, and Goldstein (1970); Smith (1975); Swiercinsky (1978); and Walsh (1978). It is important to keep in mind that multiple test procedures and inferential methods are necessary to fully and accurately assess the multidimensional aspect of CNS dysfunction and its behavioral consequences. Furthermore, only an accurate assessment and understanding of brain-behavior relationships will suggest effective intervention strategies. It also should be stressed that taking time to carry out behavioral observations, gather accurate histories, and review medical and psychological patient charts will reap many diagnostic and treatment rewards.

Recovery

The final prerequisite for effective treatment of CNS dysfunction is knowledge of the natural recovery process and the factors that affect recovery. Two volumes produced by Porter and Fitzsimons (1975) and Stein, Rosen, and Butters (1974) are particularly useful in reviewing the cumulative literature on recovery from CNS trauma. Although there is continual controversy regarding the mechanism of recovery (i.e., reinnervation [regeneration] versus assumption of functional control by another cerebral system [plasticity] versus recovery of impaired but not destroyed tissue surrounding the area of damage), most professionals agree that natural recovery follows a declining curve which is most rapid for the first three to six months. Indeed, 80-95% of recovery is expected within 12 to 18 months following CNS trauma (Bond & Brooks, 1976; Hurwitz & Adams, 1972; Logue, 1975; Porter & Fitzsimons, 1975; Stein *et al.*, 1974). Contrary to these data, however, Lezak (1979) recently has reported a "secondary regression" of intellectual functioning in several cases 18 months post trauma.

Prognosis for recovery depends on several variables, among which are:

1. Length of coma and post traumatic amnesia (PTA): longer coma and PTA yields increasingly poor prognosis (Carlsson, Von Essen, & Lofgren, 1968; Jennett, 1972; Smith, 1961)
2. Visual field deficits: presence of deficits yields poor prognosis for recovery and survival (Haerer, 1973)
3. Premorbid cognitive abilities and emotional stability: lower emotional stability and premorbid cognitive abilities increasingly limit improvements on these same dimensions (Lishman, 1973; Porter & Fitzsimons, 1975)
4. Age at onset: evidence is mixed although recent findings suggest that both early (before age 5) and late (over age 55) onset of injury increase the possibility of poor recovery (Carlsson *et al.*, 1968; Gogstad & Kjellman, 1976; Isaacson, 1975; Overgaard, Hvid-Hansen, Land, Pedersen, Christensen, Haase, Hein, & Tweed, 1973; Boll, Note 3)
5. Size (severity) and location of lesion: location is critical in determining extent and type of impairment and recovery, while size often is positively correlated with amount of dysfunction and negatively correlated with recovery (Bond & Brooks, 1976; Fields, 1975; Lezak, 1979; Teuber, 1974; Wisniewska-Roszkowska, Jedynecki, & Ziolkowski, 1975).

Recovery from CNS trauma also is a function of many other variables such as motivation, the uniqueness of the particular individual, and the criteria used to measure recovery. Two poignant examples of problems associated with criterion measures are cited by Jennett (1972) and Fuld and Fisher (1977). Jennett describes physicians' assessments of "excellent" outcome from severe head injuries as sometimes including "hemiplegia, dysphasia, or field deficits and the 'good' recoveries include(ing) those who require assistance to walk [p. 200]." Similarly, Fuld and Fisher suggest that family members and physicians often overlook intellectual changes (documented by psychometric testing) in head injured patients. It is the authors' own experience that many mild head injuries cause cognitive and psychological impairment which goes undetected in traditional neurological examinations. Such deficits are frequently unnoticed and/or denied by family members. The manifestation of the impairments may later cause great stress for the patient and the family. The denial on the part of family members may be due, in part, to a tendency to assume that someone who seems able must be failing to perform various domestic or vocational tasks due to emotional or motivational problems. These are less acceptable reasons for failure than are "real" physical deficits. Realization that an actual reduction in ability has occurred typically facilitates increased support and diminishes anger associated with incorrect assumptions of the patient's lack of effort.

Treatment and Rehabilitation Techniques

The prerequisite knowledge of neuroanatomy, neuropathology, brain-behavior relationships, assessment procedures, and natural recovery processes was reviewed to demonstrate their vital relationship with CNS dysfunction and its treatment. One must understand each prerequisite for treatment if the outcome of that treatment is to be positive. The remainder of the chapter presents some general intervention techniques for treatment of CNS dysfunction. These techniques are classified within four categories: (*a*) psychological treatment; (*b*) biofeedback and neuromuscular reeducation; (*c*) cognitive retraining; and (*d*) the Luria Rehabilitation Model.

As already mentioned, there has been a fast growing trend toward implementing behavioral medicine or interdisciplinary approaches to health care problems and rehabilitation. These approaches involve treatment teams that often include physicians; psychologists; social workers; physical, recreational, and occupational therapists; vocational rehabilitation specialists; biomedical engineers; educational consultants; and speech pathologists (Borhani, 1974; Chatel & Dunning, 1976; Feigenson, Gitlow, & Greenberg, 1979; Maruszewski, 1969; Sterling, 1967). Although treatment teams have been particularly visible on comprehensive stroke units, they are gaining popularity in most treatment specialties. These treatment teams are not limited to specialists and professionals already mentioned; indeed, it is becoming increasingly apparent that paraprofessionals and informal treatment networks, including family members and friends of the injured individual, can be of great value in the rehabilitation process (Gersten, Foppe, Gersten, Maxwell, Mirrett, Gipson, Houston, & Grueter, 1975).

The neuropsychologist, as well as other psychologists in many health care settings, is an essential member of the treatment team. The neuropsychologist's role is to provide assessment data for confirmation of pathology and description of behavioral sequelae, and to help develop and coordinate the treatment effort by offering a comprehensive view of the individual's brain functioning and delineating specific needs for reintegration of brain functions (Brinkman, 1979; Golden, 1976a, 1976b, 1978; Maruszewski, 1969).

Once treatment methods are developed and agreed upon by the team for a particular case, two questions need to be answered: (*a*) When should treatment-rehabilitation be initiated, and (*b*) when should treatment-rehabilitation be terminated? Although evidence is scanty and intuition is plentiful, several studies suggest that treatment initiated immediately following recovery from the acute medical stages of CNS insult is more successful than treatment begun at later intervals (Fields, 1975; Stern, McDowell, Miller, & Robinson, 1971; Suchett-Kaye *et al.*, 1971; Teuber, 1974). This is not to say that treatment is useless if a significant amount of time has elapsed since cerebral trauma, but there is a higher probability of success if treatment is begun at the earliest possible moment (Maruszewski, 1969).

There is no convincing evidence regarding an optimum time for terminating treatment programs, although it is frequently postulated that there is a point of diminishing returns for professional intervention. Termination is, in all likelihood, an individual matter which must be considered in terms of the unique set of variables associated with a particular case. One should keep in mind, however, that hundreds or even thousands of repetitions of a rehabilitation task may be necessary before patients can integrate a particular behavior or cognition into their repertoire, just as a naive child may require many trials to learn certain behaviors and concepts.

Finally, the question always arises, "Is treatment helpful or is improvement actually a function of the spontaneous recovery process?" Again, we are dealing with variables that are unique to each specific case. Several animal and human studies, however, have suggested that treatment may be helpful in promoting recovery and that in some instances rehabilitation efforts are essential to recovery (Lehmann, Delateur, Fowler, Warren, Arnhold, Schertzer, Hurka, Whitmore, Masock, & Chambers, 1975a; Rosner, 1970; Weinberg, Diller, Gordon, Gerstman, Lieberman, Lakin, Hodges, & Ezrachi, 1977; Yu, 1976). Unfortunately, as in most of the literature in this area, because few studies have used adequate control procedures, the conclusion that treatment has an independent effect upon recovery currently may not be accepted with great confidence. The following review of intervention techniques for CNS dysfunction must be considered with this caution in mind.

Psychological Treatment

Factors Affecting Treatment Outcome When discussing the psychological treatment and rehabilitation of the individual with CNS dysfunction, it is important to consider some of the factors affecting recovery and effective remediation. Although numerous variables may affect outcome, some specific factors have recently been identified. It should be noted that the variables to be discussed have been examined in the context of traditional psychotherapeutic interventions for persons with CNS dysfunction. Some of these variables, nonetheless, may also affect the outcomes produced by other treatments discussed in the remaining sections of this chapter.

Fogel and Rosillo (1971a) evaluated the psychological attributes of 110 physically handicapped patients who were in rehabilitation programs and determined that progress in therapy was related to

> (1) ability to recognize and evaluate the extent of life problems (including rehabilitation); (2) ability to make correct decisions concerning solution of these problems; (3) ability to handle stress; (4) frequency of use of rationalization; and (5) characteristic role status in interpersonal relationships according to a scale of dominance-submission [p. 15].

Although these patients were not necessarily brain impaired, their physical disabilities presented them with some of the same difficulties experienced by brain-injured patients undergoing rehabilitation.

Lehmann *et al.* (1975b), in a study of 114 stroke victims, provided evidence that recovery is related to severity of lesion, general health, perceptual deficits, and age. They also found, as did Smolkin and Cohen (1974), that education and socioeconomic status were positively correlated with successful outcome (i.e., return home). In addition, Lehmann *et al.* (1975b) reported that the amount of family involvement in treatment, support, and aftercare was positively associated with the success of therapy.

Patient motivation is another important factor in rehabilitation of the brain injured (Christmas, Humphrey, Richardson & Smith, 1974; Fogel & Rosillo, 1969; Hyman, 1972; Lublin, 1979). Other factors such as patient attitude toward the treatment program, independence, level of self-concept, and flexibility of patient goals also may affect outcome (Fogel & Rosillo, 1969; Hyman, 1972). Some of these variables may be influenced by psychotherapeutic intervention, emotional support, and small-step behavioral reinforcement of goal attainment. There also is some evidence that hypnotic suggestion may be successfully used to modify patient motivational levels and attitudes (Crasilneck & Hall, 1970).

Some attention has been directed toward factors that negatively affect treatment outcome. Ford (1977) described the factors that contribute to failure in rehabilitation as being

> unrealistic and over optimistic assessment of objectives . . . ; failure to consult the family in the formulation of these objectives; (and) failure to identify the less gross psychological and social aspects of the patient's problem [pp. 98–99].

A final factor that may affect treatment outcome is the degree to which the therapist understands that the behavior displayed by persons with CNS dysfunction in therapy may not be regarded as equivalent to the same behavior shown by neurologically intact individuals in the context of the psychotherapeutic situation. Reviewing the literature on psychological reactions to spinal cord injury, Cook (1976) suggests that although denial is a primary problem in such disorders, it may have different therapeutic implications than the types of denial usually encountered by the clinical psychologist. Cook cites Dinardo's (1971) doctoral dissertation in which it was reported that contrary to what usual therapeutic models would predict, denial was positively correlated with good adjustment. This suggests that denial need not be confronted for positive results to be obtained. In some cases of cerebral dysfunction, denial also may take on a different meaning which includes a true lack of awareness of various physical difficulties due to impaired mental processes. Denial, therefore, may be productive since it is sometimes better to know little about one's present condition in relation to previous level of functioning.

Goldstein (Note 1) and Small (1973) view many of the psychological reactions to brain damage as "protective" mechanisms as opposed to traditional "defense" mechanisms. Both are employed to deal with anxiety; protective mechanisms, however, are developed as a method of dealing with impaired abilities and the resultant anxiety, whereas defense mechanisms may be caused by anxiety over conflicts, etc. In treating individuals with CNS dysfunction it is important to understand and respect their protective, coping mechanisms and help them to achieve success and avoid failures. Directly confronting the coping mechanisms, as may be suggested by traditional psychotherapeutic models, might have a demoralizing effect on the individual. Small (1973) also warns psychologists of other possible difficulties and errors that may occur in the rehabilitation effort such as: (*a*) interpreting impaired memory functions as repression; (*b*) becoming angry over the patient's rationalizations and outbursts of rage when they are actually coping mechanisms to protect a delicate self-concept; (*c*) having to redefine resistance as the patient's attempt to hold on to success experiences rather than to chance failure; and (*d*) the fact that the therapist must be unusually active in directing the individual and offering reinforcement in very great quantitites and in novel ways.

Treatment Approaches The factors previously discussed are but a few of the variables that may affect rehabilitation efforts with any given individual. Thus, it is necessary to adhere to a systematic, comprehensive, and individualized approach to treatment. Lishman (1978) states that it is necessary to develop a

> systematic evaluation of residual disabilities and assessment of the causes operating in the individual case. In general it is less important to place the patient in a firm diagnostic category than to aim at a comprehensive understanding of his individual problems, personality, and environment. Treatment will often need to follow a many-sided approach . . . [p. 255].

Psychological therapies with brain-impaired individuals are often multifaceted and involve interaction with other professional, paraprofessional, and nonprofessional groups and individuals. The following discussion examines some of the traditional psychological approaches available to the psychologist as part of the treatment team's rehabilitation efforts.

BEHAVIOR MODIFICATION Standard behavior modification techniques such as those outlined by Leitenberg (1976) and Wolpe (1969) are accepted as standard psychotherapeutic methods for treating individuals suffering from cerebral dysfunction. A fine overview of behavioral treatment in rehabilitation medicine is offered by Ince (1976). Some specific studies and techniques deserve a brief review.

A particularly interesting case study by Foxx and Azrin (1972) involved the use of "restitution" (overcorrection) with one brain-damaged and two retarded individuals. Restitution therapy was composed of defining the aberrant behavior and the psychological and social consequences of that behavior, and stopping the individual during the inappropriate act and forcing him, through guided training (use of time out procedures) to overcorrect all of the effects of the act. Foxx and Azrin reported successful extinction of inappropriate behaviors such as outbursts of physical rage, aggression, and screaming by means of restitution therapy.

Martin (1976) suggested that traditional behavior modification techniques may be used in conjunction with biofeedback (i.e., neuromuscular training-EMG feedback [see pp. 252–254], and reinforcement of appropriate posturing and muscle control), to provide optimal treatment benefits to patients with cerebral palsy. Indeed, Martin noted that the psychologist is in the unique position of being able to offer these techniques to the treatment team.

Finally, a more traditional group of case studies examined the use of positive reinforcement of appropriate behavior in conjunction with inattention toward disruptive behavior (Hollon, 1973). The key to the success of this program and that of Foxx and Azrin (1972), as would be the case in any behavior modification procedure, was consistency in methods and goals applied to the patient by *all* of the individuals who interacted with that person. It may be, then, that regardless of the behavioral technique used to reduce inappropriate behavior and foster positive behavior, if the reinforcements are appropriate and the training is consistent, the patient's behavior will change and the patient will become more amenable to other forms of therapy and rehabilitation. Nevertheless, future work should be directed toward the examination of what behavioral regimens may be applied to particular patient populations in order to optimally modify various appropriate and inappropriate behaviors.

INTERVENTIONS FOR MEMORY AND DISORIENTATION PROBLEMS Much has been written regarding mnemonic aids for remediation of memory impairments in brain-damaged individuals. Three particularly interesting strategies are (*a*) the use of visual imagery in conjunction with tasks such as paired associate learning (Lewinsohn, Danaher & Kikel, 1977); (*b*) the Airplane List method (Crovitz, 1979; Higbee, 1977); and (*c*) the PQRST approach to remembering stories or paragraphs (Glasgow, Zeiss, Barrera, & Lewinsohn, 1977). The visual imagery method involves the presentation of two words and having the patient describe ridiculous images which link the two. These images then become the cues to memory. The Airplane List represents a whimsical variation of the visual imagery method. The patient must remember the first word (airplane) in a list and then link each word to the next by making up a ludicrous story. If the first three words to be remembered are, airplane, giraffe, and bologna, as in Crovitz's (1979) example, the following passage would be read: "The first word is airplane. Remember that however you like. The next word is giraffe, because the airplane is filled with giraffes sitting in the seats. The next word is bologna, because each of the giraffes is holding a bologna and takes bites out of it [p. 121]." The PQRST method of remembering printed material includes the components of Previewing the materials, developing Questions regarding the text, Reading the text, Stating the facts in the text, and Testing oneself regarding the previously formulated questions. It is quite obvious that while these three mnemonic devices are valuable in cueing memory functions, these techniques must be applied to the individual's everyday existence if they are to be useful.

Since brain-damaged individuals often lack sufficient awareness of their surroundings and are easily confused, Folstein and McHugh (1976) suggested that an important facet of treatment is making the patients' environment static, routine, and as homelike and familiar as possible by surrounding them with many personal belongings. Some of the patient's confusion may be due to memory impairment for which the intervention techniques previously discussed may be useful. Fowler and Fordyce (1972) reviewed some of the more traditional memory aids such as having the individual carry a pocket-size notebook for daily routine reminders; placing signs on walls in strategic locations in the house or hospital; keeping messages as simple as possible (using familiar associations); and implementing constant reminders. Other prosthetic memory aids such as portable hour timers have been used with some success to help train individuals to remember and adhere to daily schedules (Fowler, Hart,& Sheehan, 1972). Behavior modification also may be employed to aid in the memory process as demonstrated by

Dolan and Norton (1977) who used contingent reinforcement to facilitate acquisition and retention by brain-damaged individuals.

TREATMENTS FOR SEXUAL DYSFUNCTION A specific problem which many brain-injured patients face is sexual dysfunction. This can take a variety of forms such as impotence or fears concerning ability to successfully perform sexual acts. Steinbock and Zeiss (1977), in their discussion of sexual dysfunction among cerebral palsy patients, suggest that these problems should be addressed directly by an interdisciplinary team made up of sexual counselors, gynecologists, orthopedists, geneticists, and other appropriate professionals. An initial difficulty may be that patients will hesitate to discuss their dysfunction and related fears; it is therefore imperative that the team recognize the sensitivity of the issue and help patients feel sufficiently comfortable to voice their concerns. Following this initial step, residual sexual capacity should be assessed through detailed medical-neurological examinations, exposing patients to reassuring and stimulating sexual materials (in a private setting), and patient self-reports (Kaplan, 1974). Finally, further sexual counseling may be helpful in exploring sexual techniques and relationship-building methods that utilize the individual's intact sexual abilities and emotional capacities (cf. Heslinga, Schellen, & Verkuyl, 1974).

INFORMATION PROVISION AND GROUP THERAPY FOR FAMILIES OF PATIENTS Comprehensive treatment of patients demonstrating CNS dysfunction includes dealing with the needs of family members (and significant others) since they undoubtedly will influence the ultimate rehabilitation potential of the patient. Several authors (Dzau & Boehme, 1978; Golden, 1976a, Lezak, 1978; Wise, 1975; Wright *et al.*, 1979) have suggested that it is necessary to educate the family regarding the progression and treatment of the pathology and inform them of the team approach to assessment and therapy. Much of this is done in order to relieve anxiety and integrate the family into the rehabilitation team. Lezak (1978) and Wright *et al.* (1979) also have noted that the family must be encouraged to gain realistic expectations, learn appropriate management and therapy techniques, and deal with their own emotional distress.

With particular regard to the emotional distress experienced by family members, it should be noted that many behaviors (e.g., suspiciousness, withdrawal) associated with brain damage are extremely disconcerting to the involved families and are difficult to change, short of strict behavior modification programs. It, therefore, is important to inform family members that these inappropriate behaviors are a function of patients' attempts to cope with an environment in which they suddenly find themselves inadequately prepared to function due to impaired abilities and cognitions. That is, the individuals usually are not being obstinate or "hateful," but are dealing with the environment in the best possible manner given their impairment. This knowledge often helps the family members to deal with their own guilt, anxiety, depression and anger toward the patient, and turn their energies toward understanding, empathy, and better decision making.

Six helping statements are offered to families in Lezak's (1978) excellent paper regarding living with brain-damaged patients:

(1) Anger, frustration, and sorrow are natural emotions for close relatives of brain injured patients.
(2) Caretaking persons must take care of themselves first if they are going to be able to continue giving the patient good care.
(3) The caretaker must ultimately rely on his own conscience and judgment in conflicts with the patient or other family members.
(4) The role changes that inevitably take place when an adult becomes dependent or irresponsible can be emotionally distressing for all concerned.
(5) The family member can probably do little to change the patient and thus need not feel guilty or wanting when their care does not result in improvement.
(6) When it appears that the welfare of dependent children may be at stake, family members must explore the issue of divided loyalties and weigh their responsibilities [pp. 12-13].

When providing information is not enough to aid the families of persons with CNS dysfunction, various forms of group therapy may be helpful. Group therapy for persons with cerebral impairment and their families has been attempted in many settings and may offer a means of dealing with misinformation and a variety of emotional and rehabilitation issues (Blyth, 1969; Edwards, 1967; Roessler, Milligan, & Onlson, 1976; Tumbarello & McDonald, Note 4). Through contact with individuals with similar problems, these group sessions also may provide support and hope for those who are discouraged by the prospects of a future of impairment, dependence, and frustration. Tumbarello and McDonald (Note 4) in reviewing group methods discussed by Salhoot (1974), have described some of the advantages of employing group therapy with disabled individuals:

1. It gives patients a chance to "give" which they do not often have an opportunity to do—this may lead to improved self-esteem and independence.
2. It affords patients a protected environment in which to express feelings and engage in new relationships.
3. It is a less intense situation than that found in individual therapy.

Tumbarello and McDonald (Note 4) also have described their use of group Rational Emotive Therapy (RET) with brain-injured patients to facilitate the educative goals of Maxmen (1978) which included patients' (*a*) acceptance of help from other patients; (*b*) understanding that their problems are not unique; (*c*) realization that they can help other patients; and (*d*) definition and discussion of their inappropriate behavior. Understanding, accepting, and coping with the disabilities produced by CNS dysfunction also have been taught using RET, behavior modification techniques and assertiveness training, with the initial descriptive reports indicating "success" in dealing with many important emotional and behavioral issues (Tumbarello & McDonald, Note 4).

Many other pathological conditions, symptoms, and intervention strategies have received some attention in the literature, however, there has been little programmatic investigation of these variables. It may be concluded, then, that psychological treatment of CNS dysfunction is still in its infancy. Those who provide psychological treatment to patients or their families should not restrict themselves to those techniques discussed in this section; instead they should utilize and examine the effectiveness of every technique at their disposal.

Biofeedback and Neuromuscular Reeducation

The neuropathological conditions discussed in the section on neuropathology may cause permanent nerve injury resulting in death, total or partial paralysis, mild to severe sensory-perceptual-motor deficiencies, or any combination of impairments. Medical professionals and physical therapists traditionally have attempted to deal with these sensorimotor disabilities. Recently, however, psychologists skilled in biofeedback procedures have added "a real-time physiological mirror [Stroebel, 1979, p. 13]" to the treatment of these disorders and others (i.e., stress reactions) using the techniques of neuromuscular reeducation (Brown, 1977). Neuromuscular reeducation involves the use of bioelectrical technology (biofeedback devices with supracutaneous transducers), usually in the form of electromyography (EMG), to locate and monitor active motor and sensory neurons or units within impaired muscles. This information is then relayed, via an auditory and/or visual feedback loop, to the patient since these active motor and sensory units may be too weak to be noticed without such scanning and amplification (Gaarder & Montgomery, 1977). The purpose of this procedure is to make patients aware of their internal physiological processes and the extent of the intact sensorimotor pathways so that they may strengthen these pathways through initiating voluntary control over previously involuntary muscular systems (Inglis, Campbell, & Donald, 1976). For example, compromised movement often is a result of deficient sensory inputs and/or motor neuron transmission insufficiencies (Barth, 1979). In these cases, neuromuscular reeducation using biofeedback training may augment the sensory system and thereby increase awareness and motor control (Gaarder & Montgomery,

1977). Training may be particularly effective if it is conducted in conjunction with strengthening the adjacent muscle areas (Owen, Toomin, & Taylor, 1975). Specific reviews of biofeedback methodologies, techniques, and procedures employed in neuromuscular reeducation are not offered in this chapter, but may be found in Gavin (1978) and Owen *et al.* (1975).

Blanchard and Young (1974) note that neuromuscular reeducation has been a part of the biofeedback literature since 1960 when Marinacci and Horande (1960) reported several successes in neuromuscular retraining with hemiplegics and individuals with peripheral nervous system disorders. This study, as well as most of the outcome literature in the area to date, is characterized by flawed methodology, most notably an alarming lack of control procedures. Nonetheless, the biofeedback and neuromuscular reeducation outcome literature is briefly reviewed.

A particularly interesting area of rehabilitation in which biofeedback procedures have been used is that of intervention for various types of motor dysfunction (hemiplegia, flacidity, spasticity, and foot drop) that occur secondary to cerebrovascular accidents (CVAs). Several case studies (e.g., Amato, Hermsmeyer, & Kleinman, 1973) and multisubject investigations have reported significant improvement in neuromuscular control for patients provided with EMG feedback (Andrews, 1964; Baker, Regenos, Wolfe, & Basmajian, 1977; Basmajian, Kukulka, Narayan, & Takebe, 1975; Basmajian, Regenos, & Baker, 1977; Brudny, Korein, Grynbaum, Friedmann, Weinstein, Sachs-Frankel, & Belandres, 1976; Brudny, Korein, Grynbaum, & Sachs-Frankel, 1977; Brudny, Korein, Levidow, Grynbaum, Lieberman, & Friedmann, 1974; Epstein, Malone & Cunningham, 1978; Flom, Quast, Boller, Berner, & Goldberg, 1976; Johnson & Garton, 1973; Kleinman, Reggin, Keister, Goldman, & Korol, 1977; Mroczek, Halpern, & McHugh, 1978).

There have also been a number of studies on the effectiveness of neuromuscular reeducation and control training for treating speech and motor functions in cerebral palsy patients (Finley, Niman, Standley, & Ender, 1976; Harris, Spelman, & Hymer, 1974; Harrison & Connolly, 1971; Wooldridge & Russell, 1976), spasmodic torticollis (Brierley, 1967; Brudny, Grynbaum, & Korein, 1974; Brudny *et al.*, 1976; Cleeland, 1973), and tardive dyskinesia (Albanese & Gaarder, 1977). The results of these investigations suggest the provision of biofeedback training in conjunction with additional operant techniques (reinforcers) immediately post trauma may successfully relieve various neuromuscular symptoms.

Contrary to the investigations just described, two studies have examined the use of neuromuscular reeducation with patients suffering CVAs and other CNS dysfunction up to 10 years post cerebral insult (Baker *et al.*, 1977; Basmajian *et al.*, 1977). The positive results reported in these studies must be considered tentative, but they offer new optimism for the rehabilitation of CNS disorders that previously may have been considered untreatable.

Finally, the effectiveness of neuromuscular reeducation involving EMG feedback in treating urinary and fecal incontinence and retention secondary to CNS trauma has been examined in a case study (Pearne, Zigelbaum, & Peyser, 1977). The results suggested that relaxation exercises coupled with biofeedback regarding control of external sphincter muscles may be an effective intervention for both retention and incontinence disorders. Another special technique which may help remediate fecal incontinence involves the use of an inflatable balloon and a pressure sensitive transducer placed in the rectum. The balloon is inflated to trigger and train reflex sphincter contraction. Successful retraining and control has been reported using this technique (Engel, Nekovmanesh, & Schuster, 1974).

Aside from its use in neuromuscular reeducation, biofeedback training has been experimentally applied to control seizure disorders. The evidence to date is scanty, but the use of electroencephalographic (EEG) feedback may help individuals to control bioelectrical brain wave activity (cf. Basmajian, 1979) and thus reduce their rates of seizure activity and abnormal EEG patterns (Lubar & Babler, 1976; Sterman & Friar, 1972; Wyler, Lockard, Ward, & Finch, 1976). This treatment requires patients to learn to produce alpha rhythms (8–14 Hz) during EEG monitoring in order to reduce fast spike activity indicative of seizure disorders.

As mentioned earlier, these research efforts generally lack rigorous experimental methodologies and control procedures. Biofeedback applications with patients demonstrating CNS dysfunction are encouraging, however, and may offer psychologists an alternative method of intervention for patients whose difficulties are not readily modified by standard physiotherapy techniques.

Cognitive Retraining

The most innovative work in the literature on rehabilitation of CNS dysfunction has been that performed in Israel and at New York University Medical Center Institute of Rehabilitation Medicine by Ben-Yishay and Diller (1973); Ben-Yishay, Diller, Gertsman, and Gordon (1970); Ben-Yishay, Diller, Mandleberg, Gordon, and Gertsman (1971); and Ben-Yishay, Diller, Mandleberg, Gordon, and Gerstman (1974). They propose that effective rehabilitation encompasses three elements: (*a*) diagnosis or assessment of the dysfunction and the patient's view of the disorder; (*b*) development of tasks that reflect the deficits associated with the dysfunction; and (*c*) establishment of a treatment program which utilizes these and related tasks. Ben-Yishay *et al.* (Note 5) suggest that the three elements of rehabilitation may be approached from three different but related viewpoints. The first is that of the psychometrist who conceptualizes CNS dysfunction as composed of elements or behavioral-neuropsychological deficits that must be specifically, and individually, identified and remediated. The second viewpoint is that of the biologist who regards CNS dysfunction as a group of disorders or a pattern of aberrant behaviors that must be treated as a whole by bringing the behaviors to the attention of the patient. The third approach is that of the engineer who defines CNS dysfunction in terms of stimulus-response chains and operants and contingencies related to the individual's environment. The engineer attempts remediation by manipulating environmental stimuli and reinforcers. Each of these theoretical approaches may promote effective rehabilitation efforts and have been successfully employed with traumatic head injuries and CVAs.

Ben-Yishay and his colleagues have found that it is impossible to retrain higher level cognitive abilities and skills if attention and concentration are diminished as a result of the cerebral insult. They have developed several tasks that require varying degrees of attention to time, visual and auditory tracking and scanning, judgment and anticipation, motor coordination, internal sequencing, and mental imagery. These tasks, although too numerous to describe in detail here, require the individual to estimate and/or anticipate the passage of certain time intervals and stop a counting device (through movements mediated by eye-hand coordination) at the appropriate point. Additional tasks involve a rapid motor response to a visual cue which is recorded in terms of reaction time; reproduction of numeric and alphabetic visual stimuli presented in both the right and left visual fields; and the integration of visual, auditory, and motor stimuli to form behavioral patterns that are internalized through repetition and then independently reproduced upon request.

Ben-Yishay *et al.* (1978) also have espoused a modular approach to the remediation of cerebral dysfunction which includes treatment of disorders associated with poor eye-hand coordination. They have incorporated a stepwise retraining program, presently being used with CVA patients, which utilizes an electronic adaption of the Purdue Peg Board. This task involves tapping a pressure sensitive switch on the peg board, first with the index finger of the nonimpaired hand, and then with that of the impaired hand. The difficulty of this task is slowly increased to include movement from one pressure switch to another; tapping and moving from one recessed pressure switch to another; and similar procedures using pressure sensitive posts that the patient must grasp between the index finger and the thumb and then release.

Other skill retraining programs using a modular approach designed by Ben-Yishay and his colleagues require practice and relearning of (*a*) variations of the Block Design subtest of the Wechsler Adult Intelligence Scale (WAIS) in a stepwise "saturation cueing" fashion (Ben-Yishay *et al.*, 1978; Ben-Yishay *et al.*, 1979; Diller *et al.*, 1974); (*b*) cognitive-perceptual integration of constructional skills (Ben-Yishay *et al.*, 1970; Ben-Yishay *et al.*, 1971, 1974); (*c*) variations of the Similarities subtest of the WAIS; (*d*) reading and summarizing paragraphs of varying complexitites; and (*e*) reformulating telegrams to retrain verbal abstraction abilities. Remediation of spatial neglect is attempted by means of visual scanning tasks that require the patient to scan a table to pick up all of the money that has been placed on it and then to view the neglected areas pointed out by the therapist, and cancellation tasks involving the marking of a single stimulus on a paper filled with multiple stimuli (example, put a line through all of the As in the following: A C M B A S Q A T N . . .). Other spatial neglect tasks require the patient to (*a*) read and/or copy a short paragraph or address using an anchoring procedure in which the patient must always scan to a red line drawn to the left margin of the stimulus material before reading or writing the next line; (*b*) visually scan a moving object or lights which span from the far left to the far right; and (*c*) receive tactile stimulation in a certain location on the back from the therapist and then point to the corresponding spot on a mannequin's back (with appropriate feedback and reinforcement) (Diller, 1976; Diller & Weinberg, 1977; Weinberg & Diller, 1968; Weinberg *et al.*, 1977). Spouses are encouraged to learn behavior modification techniques (reinforcement of appropriate verbal responses) to help remediate aphasic disorders, and group therapy sessions are provided for brain-injured patients so that they can become resocialized, gain support systems, build positive self-esteem, offer help to others, and create and attain appropriate treatment goals.

These treatment methods have been useful in remediating specific cognitive, perceptual, and motor deficits that are secondary to neurological insult. The patient selection criteria, however, for the studies of these therapies are stringent and published outcome data are limited. The selection criteria often include age restrictions (18–55 years), ability to participate in a strenuous four-hour-a-day program, independent self-care living skills, a minimum IQ of 80 on either verbal or performance aspects of the WAIS, and motivation to participate in the program. In addition, the cognitive retraining methods examined in the outcome studies are assessed in terms of patient functioning on measurement devices which closely resemble the training tasks. This leaves unanswered the question of whether the retraining generalizes to more abstract cognitive processes. We are hopeful that future studies using less restricted patient populations and more appropriate outcome measures will be forthcoming.

In summary, Ben-Yishay and Diller have made significant contributions to the field of assessment and rehabilitation of neurologically impaired individuals. Of these contributions, three deserve special mention. First, they have offered new hope to patients who are one year or more post cerebral trauma, since their remediation methods have been reported to be effective in training specific attentional, perceptual, and cognitive skills (as measured by psychometric tasks) with this population. Their work also has generated new research and enthusiasm in professionals who are faced with the long-term care of individuals with CNS dysfunction. And finally, Ben-Yishay and Diller have provided some evidence for their contention (and our intuition) that *cognitive* retraining is possible with patience, stepwise cueing, reinforcement methods, and massive amounts of task repetition.

Rehabilitation Procedures Derived from the Theory of A. R. Luria

Golden (1978), Gudeman, Golden, and Craine (Note 6), and Marmo (1974) favor therapeutic approaches that not only treat obvious behavioral symptomatology, but primarily focus on underlying integrative systems. Their rehabilitation philosophies are most congruent with those of A. R. Luria who developed a very complex theoretical approach to brain–behavior relationships and rehabilitation.

Although little objective data exists to support his hypotheses, Luria (1963) suggested that remediation of CNS dysfunction must be aimed at restoring or reformulating the functional neurological systems that control behavior through processes such as deinhibition of the temporarily damaged cerebral systems, assumption of functional control by intact brain areas for acts that have been interrupted following insult, or complete reorganization of destroyed activities through different brain structures. Golden (1978), in a review of Luria's theory, argues that rehabilitation must be based on a firm knowledge of neurological systems since

> formation of an effective new functional system depends on the integrity of the area which must form the new functional system . . . (thus the rehabilitation specialist) must be interested not only in what deficits are present but what strengths are present as well . . . (the professional must) provide training that enables the patient to efficiently form the most workable alternative functional system (Golden, 1978, p. 190].

Many aspects of the Luria model of rehabilitation are similar to the methods of Ben-Yishay and Diller. Golden (1978) suggests that one should first assess the deficits and determine which are most relevant to the *patient* from a psychological point of view. Then a task should be constructed which (*a*) involves the dysfunctional behavior but utilizes many other intact systems and abilities; (*b*) can be varied in difficulty from simple to complex; (*c*) can be objectively quantified; (*d*) lends itself to immediate patient feedback; and (*e*) can control the number of patient errors. Golden (1978) offers the following 14 methods for varying the difficulty of the rehabilitation task:

> (1) Speed of presentation of items; (2) numbers of items presented at a time; (3) sensory modality in which the problem is presented; (4) number of spatial dimensions (one versus two versus three); (5) concreteness; (6) size; (7) color; (8) familiarity; (9) complexity; (10) speed of response required; (11) duration of effort required; (12) amount of information from alternate sensory modalities; (13) requirements for the correct answer, slowly raising the criterion; and (14) the amount of extra information given the subject [p. 196].

The Luria-based treatment approach, as does the Ben-Yishay-Diller method, encourages rehabilitation specialists to develop their own retraining strategies and offers some specific remediation procedures. The gross and fine motor control methods developed by Luria and expanded upon by Golden (1978) incorporate traditional limb movements used by physical therapists, peg board tasks, industrial-vocational techniques such as twisting screws with a screwdriver, and relatively complex movements such as those used in playing musical instruments. The complexity of these tasks may be varied by using Golden's 14 variables (Golden, 1978).

Rehabilitation techniques commonly employed by speech therapists for individuals suffering aphasia also are incorporated in the Luria-based system. An example of such treatment is that of encouraging the patient to say the first letter of a word by presenting it in printed form along with a pictorial and verbal representation of the word. The therapist also may have the patient view the therapist's lips while mouthing the word or sound and then have the patient attempt to mimic this vocalization while looking in a mirror. It is quite obvious that a speech therapist's special skills are required and should be enlisted in this situation.

Luria (1963) and Golden (1978) describe other cognitive retraining techniques that attempt to remediate higher level mental functions such as abstract reasoning, judgment, concept formation, and sequencing. They note that the ability to categorize figures, objects, and words is critical to everyday functioning and can be retrained if one first helps the patient practice such exercises using only two categories with simple and clear-cut ideas and cues. Gradually the number of categories, as well as the complexity and abstractness of the items, can be increased as the patient reaches higher success criterion levels. This same orientation is employed in teaching sequencing with variations of the WAIS Picture Arrangement subtest. In both categorization and sequencing training, it is necessary for the patient first to identify and describe the stimulus materials and then speculate as to their relationship. If difficulties are encountered in even the most simple presentations, some amount of cueing may be necessary.

It is speculated that impairment in visuospatial problem solving can be remediated using tasks that are pertinent to everyday situations such as map reading (Golden, 1978) by requesting the patient to either trace a route from one location to another or describe the process by which one would get from the bedroom to the bathroom or from one's house to a friend's residence. Other less relevant visuospatial and orientation practice techniques include drawing geometric figures such as the Bender-Gestalt designs, completing figure-ground tasks such as those found in the Frostig Developmental Test of Visual Perception, and attempting maze games.

Luria (1963) offers many more rehabilitation strategies based on specific theoretical approaches to brain-behavior relationships that only recently have begun to attract attention in the United States. His methods, as we have found in most of our inquiries into the treatment literature, have neither been refined, nor adequately assessed in controlled studies; nonetheless, Luria's treatment approach, unlike many other approaches, has evolved from a theory of brain functioning rather than the reverse. It should be noted, however, that this theory of brain functioning and resultant treatment techniques are not tied to objective neurological and behavioral data which have been subjected to rigorous analysis, but rather are based on intense observation and informed speculation by one of the outstanding neuroscientists of our time. Caveat emptor!

Other Rehabilitation Approaches

As noted in the section on terminology, psychologists are not the only rehabilitation specialists who offer their skills in the remediation of cerebral impairment. In fact, the psychologist is "the new kid on the block" compared to physicians and other medical personnel, speech therapists, special education professionals, physical, occupational, and recreational therapists, vocational rehabilitationists, and biomedical engineers.

Medical specialists traditionally are the first professionals to attempt to rehabilitate the brain-impaired individual. This rehabilitation at first usually involves acute medical care and treatment of life threatening events associated with CNS trauma. Thus, the quality of life is a secondary concern to the overall issue of survival. Many physicians, nurses, and other medical personnel, however, later become involved in the nonacute aspects of rehabilitation, such as medical and nursing maintenance and referral to other health care professionals, neurosurgery, and psychosurgery (Valenstein, 1973), chemotherapy (Bassuk & Schoonover, 1977; Krupp & Chatton, 1975; Merritt, 1973), hyperbaric oxygenation therapy (Ben-Yishay & Diller, 1973) and electrical stimulation (cerebellar and spinal cord stimulation) procedures (Bensman & Szagho, 1978; Jacques, Shelden, & Rogers, 1979; Vincente, Kerkhoff, & Yashon, 1979).

Speech therapists often apply their skills to the treatment of aphasia and dysphasic disorders secondary to cerebral trauma. They are trained to diagnose the many specific types of aphasia and initiate specialized treatment for speech disorders (Brookshire, 1973; Darley, Aronson, & Brown, 1975; Sarno, 1972; Travis, 1971). Specific and unique therapies such as melodic intonation (Hécaen & Albert, 1978; Sparks, Helm, & Albert, 1974), delayed auditory feedback and metronome therapy (Eisenson, 1975), nondominant cerebral hemisphere therapy (Johnson, Note 2), group therapy (Redinger, Forster, Dolphin, Godduhn, & Weisinger, 1971), and relaxation training and behavior modification techniques (Bollinger & Stout, 1976; Goodkin, 1969; Marshall & Watts, 1976) are presently being evaluated to determine their usefulness with various communication disorders. Although data are far from conclusive regarding the utility of speech therapy for aiding the recovery of communication functions, we have a responsibility to refer patients for these services. At the very least, the speech therapist attempts to motivate the patient to engage existing residual potentials and exercise the cerebral system which has incurred the insult. Speech therapy provides the structure and stimulation that best represents our knowledge of the factors which may facilitate the most advantageous recovery cycle.

Various approaches to the treatment of handicapped children have been developed by workers in the field of special education such as Barsch (1967), Cruickshank, Bentzen, Ratzeburg, and Taunhauser (1961), Doman-Delacato (cf. Freeman, 1967), Fernald (1943), Frostig (1966), Getman (1965), Gillingham and Stillmen (1960), Kephart (1960), McGinnis (1963), and Strauss and Lehtinen (1947). These educational specialists have developed theories of learning disabilities and minimal brain dysfunction (i.e., developmental and perceptual delays and dysfunction) that suggest specific remediational processes involving mastery of certain tasks. The value of some of these treatment methods, particularly Doman and Delacato's patterning (neuromuscular reflex) therapy has been questioned by Abbie (1974), Freeman (1967), and Robbins (1962); and several professional associations (e.g., American Academy for Cerebral Palsy, American Academy of Neurology, American Academy of Pediatrics, American Academy for Physical Medicine and Rehabilitation, American Congress of Rehabilitation Medicine, American Academy of Orthopedics) also have gone on record as strongly opposing the Doman-Delacato approach to therapy ("The Doman-Delacato treatment," 1968). Criticisms include (*a*) lack of verifiable data to substantiate claims of successful treatment; (*b*) lack of valid assessment procedures; (*c*) inflexibility in treatment schedule which may result in neglect of other family members' needs; and (*d*) use of guilt induction in the therapy. It should be noted that the other treatment methods for handicapped children have not met with such staunch opposition despite the paucity of controlled studies of their effectiveness.

Physical, occupational, and recreational therapists all utilize their special talents to help return brain-injured patients to their families, communities, and jobs. To aid in the remediation of disorders related to CVAs and cerebral palsy, physical and occupational therapists use passive and active movement of the limbs and torso to inhibit spasticity and to facilitate normal motor activity as advocated by the popular neurodevelopmental theory of Bobath (cf. Gillette, 1969; Hurwitz & Adams, 1972; Licht, 1958; Taft *et al.*, 1962; Willard & Spackman, 1971). Proprioceptive Neuromuscular Facilitation (PNF), developed by Kabat and expanded by Knott and Voss, is used to treat neurological as well as orthopedic problems by generalization of patterns of movement and sensation in entire muscle groups from intact to impaired areas (cf. Eklund & Steen, 1969; Herman & Mecomber, 1971; Licht, 1958; Taft *et al.*, 1962; Willard & Spackman, 1971). Rood's sensory stimulation therapy which employs ice and light brushing movements over affected muscular systems to facilitate motor control is also widely accepted and used by physical, occupational, and recreational therapists (Licht, 1958; Willard & Spackman, 1971). These health care providers often combine their efforts with those of other specialists, such as speech therapists, to form one integrated treatment modality aimed at treating the whole individual (Levitt & Miller, 1973). To date, there is little empirical data to support the utility of these rehabilitation techniques; however, single case reports are encouraging and suggest success in specific instances.

Vocational training and physical aids for independently coping with disabilities are offered by vocational rehabilitation specialists and biomedical engineers. Vocational assessment and use of guides such as the *Dictionary of Occupational Titles* are designed to delineate vocational aptitude and interest, and facilitate "job fit" (Mallik & Sablowsky, 1975). Vocational aids, such as specially designed chairs that allow disabled individuals to sit at "standing level" for machinery operation, and pressure sensitive switches for individuals with motor control problems, also enable brain-injured individuals to participate in meaningful employment (Mallik & Mueller, Note 7). *The Disability and Rehabilitation Handbook* (Goldenson, 1978) is an excellent source of rehabilitation services that currently are available for handicapped individuals.

Concluding Remarks

Since research in the field of rehabilitation can be difficult due to clinical and ethical constraints, Parsons and Prigatano (1978) suggest that a revival of single case and descriptive studies may be useful. There is a place for such methodology since it affords the clinician valuable information that might be discarded or withheld due to difficulties such as small sample size and inadequate control procedures. As noted throughout this chapter, however, the conclusions drawn from case and descriptive studies must be critically examined by well-controlled, experimental procedures.

An important aspect of treatment and rehabilitation of CNS dysfunction that has received little attention is follow-up. We have almost no information regarding patient functioning several years post trauma and intervention with the treatment techniques discussed in this chapter. We also are unaware of the "psychological implications (which) may show up long after the individual has been discharged from the hospital [Brodwin, 1976, p. 609]." Good follow-up procedures and constant long-term contact with patients is mandatory if we are to refine our current intervention strategies.

A treatment issue which has not been directly addressed in this chapter is that of remediation of disorders versus patient coping and adaptation. Some disorders simply cannot be remediated given our present knowledge, and some patients cannot participate in strenuous rehabilitation processes. Nonetheless, the behavioral and psychological sequelae of compromised brain functions often can be treated and adaption to impairment can be facilitated. The present chapter has reviewed several useful methods for teaching patients to cope with the difficulties associated with CNS dysfunction and making patients and their families more comfortable with these disabilities (e.g., mnemonic aids, group therapy, information provision). Thus, a two-pronged attack appears to be necessary in the treatment of CNS dysfunction. The first aspect of treatment should be to make use of and refine our present coping and adaptation methods since they represent the current state of the art. This is not to say that we should not attempt remediation efforts but rather that we should make use of and improve our coping strategies while we provide treatment strategies. The second aspect should be to mount specific, coordinated research programs to develop treatment methods and test their effectiveness with various types of neuropathological conditions. We have the appropriate experimental methodology, assessment techniques, data analysis capabilities, professional personnel, and patients to conduct this research and make the gains necessary to begin to offer consistent and effective treatment for CNS dysfunction. The establishment of a national rehabilitation research institute could do much to facilitate and coordinate such projects.

Acknowledgments

The authors wish to thank Lillie Jordan and Susan Boll for their assistance in preparing this manuscript, and Michael Seidenberg, David Leen, Glenn Mills and Neal Johnson for their critical reviews.

Reference Notes

1. Goldstein, K. *The effect of brain damage on the personality.* Paper presented at the Annual Meeting of the American Psychoanalytic Association, Atlantic City, May 1952.
2. Johnson, N. B. *Language rehabilitation of non-dominant hemisphere impairment.* Paper presented at the Second Annual Postgraduate Course on The Rehabilitation of the Traumatic Brain Injured Adult, Richmond, Virginia, June 1978.
3. Boll, T. J. *Influence of age-at-onset of brain damage on intellectual, perceptual, memory and motor performance of young children.* Paper presented at the meeting of the American Psychological Association, Montreal, Canada, 1973.
4. Tumbarello, R. J., & McDonald, L. *Group therapy for head trauma rehabilitation clients.* Unpublished manuscript, 1979. (Available from St. Francis Hospital, Psychology Department, North Rd., Poughkeepsie, N.Y. 12601.)
5. This information was gathered at the Seventh Annual Workshop for Rehabilitation Professionals, NYU Medical Center, N.Y., May, 1979. Workshop monographs include: Ben-Yishay, Ben-Nachum, Cohen, Gerstman, Gordon, Gross, Hofien, Piasetsky, and Rattok (1978); Ben-Yishay, Diller, Rattok, Ross, Schaier, and Scherger (1979); and Diller, Ben-Yishay, Gerstman, Gordon, Weinberg, Mandleberg, Schulman, and Shah (1974). Also consult Diller (1980) for further information.
6. Gudeman, H., Golden, C., & Craine, J. The role of neuropsychological evaluation in the rehabilitation of the brain-injured patient: A program in neurotraining. *Clinical Psychology,* 1977, MS. 1693, 44.
7. Mallik, K., & Mueller, J. *Vocational aids and enhanced productivity of the severely disabled.* Paper presented at the Devices and Systems for the Disabled Conference sponsored by Krusen Center for Research and Engineering, Philadelphia, 1975.

References

Abbie, M. Treatment of minimal brain dysfunction. *Physiotherapy,* 1974, *60,* 203-207.

Albanese, H., & Gaarder, K. Biofeedback treatment of tardive dyskinesia: Two case reports. *American Journal of Psychiatry,* 1977, *134,* 1149-1150.

Amato, A., Hermsmeyer, C. A., & Kleinman, K. M. Use of electromyographic feedback to increase inhibitory control of spastic muscles. *Physical Therapy,* 1973, *53,* 1063-1066.

Andrews, J. M. Neuromuscular re-education of the hemiplegic with the aid of the electromyograph. *Ar-*

chives of Physical Medicine and Rehabilitation, 1964, *45,* 530-532.

Asken, M. Medical psychology: Toward a definition, clarification and organization. *Professional Psychology,* 1979, *10,* 66-73.

Baker, M., Regenos, E., Wolfe, S. L., & Basmajian, J. V. Developing strategies for biofeedback-applications in neurologically handicapped patients. *Physical Therapy,* 1977, *57,* 402-408.

Barsch, R. H. *Achieving perceptual-motor efficiency.* Seattle: Special Child Publications, 1967.

Barth, J. T. A review of neuromuscular re-education: A neurological-biofeedback perspective. *American Journal of Clinical Biofeedback,* 1979, *2,* 32-33.

Basmajian, J. V. *Biofeedback: Principles and practice for clinicians.* Baltimore: Williams & Wilkins, 1979.

Basmajian, J. V., Kukulka, C. G., Narayan, M. G., & Takebe, K. Biofeedback treatment of foot-drop after stroke compared with standard rehabilitation technique: Effects on voluntary control and strength. *Archives of Physical Medicine and Rehabilitation,* 1975, *56,* 231-236.

Basmajian, J. V., Regenos, E. M., & Baker, M. P. Rehabilitating stroke patients with biofeedback. *Geriatrics,* 1977, *32,* 85-88.

Bassuk, E. L., & Schoonover, S. C. *The practitioner's guide to psychoactive drugs.* New York: Plenum, 1977.

Bensman, A. S., & Szagho, M. R. Cerebellar electrical stimulation: A critique. *Archives of Physical Medicine and Rehabilitation,* 1978, *59,* 485-487.

Benson, D. F., & Blumer, D. *Psychiatric aspects of neurologic disease.* New York: Grune & Stratton, 1975.

Ben-Yishay, Y., Ben-Nachum, Z., Cohen, A., Gerstman, L., Gordon, W., Gross, Y., Hofien, D., Piasetsky, E., & Rattok, J. *Working approaches to remediation of cognitive deficits in brain damaged.* Supplement to the sixth annual workshop for rehabilitation professionals, New York, June 1978.

Ben-Yishay, Y., & Diller, L. Changing of atmospheric environment to improve mental and behavioral function: Application in treatment of senescence. *New York State Journal of Medicine,* 1973, *73,* 2877-2880.

Ben-Yishay, Y., Diller, L., Gerstman, L., & Gordon, W. Relationship between initial competence and ability to profit from cues in brain-damaged individuals. *Journal of Abnormal Psychology,* 1970, *75,* 248-259.

Ben-Yishay, Y., Diller, L., Mandleberg, I., Gordon, W., & Gerstman, L. J. Similarities and differences in block design performance between older normal and brain-injured persons: A task analysis. *Journal of Abnormal Psychology,* 1971, *78,* 17-25.

Ben-Yishay, Y., Diller, L., Mandleberg, I., Gordon, W., & Gerstman, L. J. Differences in matching persistence behavior during block design performance between older normal and brain-damaged persons: A process analysis. *Cortex,* 1974, *10,* 121-132.

Ben-Yishay, Y., Diller, L., Rattok, J., Ross, B., Schaier, A., & Scherger, P. *Working approaches to remediation of cognitive deficits in brain damaged.* Supplement to the seventh annual workshop for rehabilitation professionals, New York, May 1979.

Blanchard, E. B., & Young, L. D. Clinical applications of biofeedback training: A review of evidence. *Archives of General Psychiatry,* 1974, *30,* 573-589.

Blyth, Z. Group treatment for handicapped children. *Journal of Psychiatric Nursing and Mental Health Services,* 1969, *7,* 172-173.

Boll, T. J. The three legged base of clinical neuropsychology. *Journal of Pediatric Psychology,* 1976, *1,* 63-66.

Boll, T. J. A rationale for neuropsychological evaluation. *Professional Psychology,* 1977, *8,* 64-71.

Boll, T. J. Diagnosing brain impairment. In B. Wolman (Ed.), *Diagnosis of mental disorders: A handbook.* New York: Plenum, 1978.

Boll, T. J. The Halstead-Reitan Neuropsychological Battery. In S. B. Filskov & T. J. Boll (Eds.), *Handbook of clinical neuropsychology.* New York: Wiley, 1980.

Boll, T. J., & Barth, J. T. Neuropsychology of brain damage in children. In S. B. Filskov & T. J. Boll (Eds.), *Handbook of clinical neuropsychology.* New York: Wiley, 1980.

Boll, T. J., & Reitan, R. M. Motor and tactile-perceptual deficits in brain damaged children. *Perceptual and Motor Skills,* 1972, *34,* 343-350.

Bollinger, R. L., & Stout, C. E. Response-contingent small-step treatment: Performance based communication intervention. *Journal of Speech and Hearing Disorders,* 1976, *41,* 40-51.

Bond, M. R., & Brooks, D. N. Understanding the process of recovery as a basis for the investigation of rehabilitation for the brain injured. *Scandinavian Journal of Rehabilitation Medicine,* 1976, *8,* 127-133.

Borhani, N. O. Stroke surveillance: The concept of stroke team in diagnosis, treatment and prevention. *Stroke,* 1974, *5,* 78-80.

Botterbusch, K. F. *The use of psychological tests with individuals who are severely disabled.* Madison: University of Wisconsin Materials Development Center, 1976.

Brierley, H. The treatment of hysterical spasmodic torticollis by behavior therapy. *Behavior Research and Therapy,* 1967, *5,* 139-142.

Brinkman, S. D. Rehabilitation of the neurologically impaired patient: The contribution of the neuropsychologist. *Clinical Neuropsychology,* 1979, *1,* 39-44.

Brodwin, M. G. Follow-up of disabled patients discharged from a rehabilitation center. *Rehabilitation Counseling Bulletin,* 1976, *19,* 607–609.

Brookshire, R. H. *An introduction to aphasia.* Minneapolis: BRK Publishers, 1973.

Brown, B. B. *Stress and the art of biofeedback.* New York: Harper and Row, 1977.

Brudny, J., Grynbaum, B. B., & Korein, J. Spasmodic torticollis: Treatment by feedback display of the EMG. *Archives of Physical Medicine and Rehabilitation,* 1974, *55,* 403–408.

Brudny, J., Korein, J., Grynbaum, B. B., Friedmann, L. W., Weinstein, S., Sachs-Frankel, G., & Belandres, P. V. EMG feedback therapy: Review of treatment of 114 patients. *Archives of Physical Medicine and Rehabilitation,* 1976, *57,* 55–61.

Brudny, J., Korein, J., Grynbaum, B. B., & Sachs-Frankel, G. Sensory feedback therapy in patients with brain insult. *Scandinavian Journal of Rehabilitation Medicine,* 1977, *9,* 155–163.

Brudney, J., Korein, J., Levidow, L., Grynbaum, B. B., Lieberman, A., & Friedmann, L. W. Sensory feedback therapy as a modality of treatment in central nervous system disorders of voluntary movement. *Neurology,* 1974, *24,* 925–932.

Butter, C. M. *Neuropsychology: The study of brain and behavior.* Belmot, Cal.: Brooks/Cole, 1968.

Carlson, N. R. *Physiology of behavior.* Boston: Allyn & Bacon, 1977.

Carlsson, C. A., Von Essen, C., & Lofgren, J. Factors affecting the clinical course of patients with severe head injuries. *Journal of Neurosurgery,* 1968, *29,* 242–251.

Chatel, D. A., & Dunning, D. Maximizing rehabilitation following cerebral vascular accident: The concept of a unified comprehensive stroke team. *Rhode Island Medical Journal,* 1976, *59,* 271–280.

Christensen, A. *Luria's neuropsychological investigation.* New York: Halstead Press, 1975.

Christmas, F. M., Humphrey, M. E., Richardson, A. E., & Smith, E. M. The response of brain damaged patients to a rehabilitation regime. *Rheumatology and Rehabilitation,* 1974, *13,* 92–97.

Chusid, J. G. *Correlative neuroanatomy and functional neurology.* Los Altos, Ca.: Lange, 1976.

Cleeland, C. S. Behavioral techniques in modification of spasmodic torticollis. *Neurology,* 1973, *23,* 1241–1247.

Cook, D. W. Psychological aspects of spinal cord injury. *Rehabilitation Counseling Bulletin,* 1976, *19,* 535–543.

Crasilneck, H. B., & Hall, J. A. The use of hypnosis in the rehabilitation of complicated vascular & post-traumatic neurological patients. *The International Journal of Clinical and Experimental Hypnosis,* 1970, *18,* 145–159.

Crovitz, H. F. Memory training in brain damaged patients: The airplane list. *Cortex,* 1979, *15,* 131–134.

Cruickshank, W. A. *The brain-injured child in home, school and community.* New York: Syracuse University Press, 1967.

Cruickshank, W. A., Bentzen, F. A., Ratzeburg, F. H., & Taunhauser, M. T. *A teaching method for brain-injured and hyperactive children.* New York: Syracuse University Press, 1961.

Darley, F. L., Aronson, A. E., & Brown, J. R. *Motor speech disorders.* Philadelphia: W. B. Saunders, 1975.

Diller, L. A model for cognitive retraining in rehabilitation. *The Clinical Psychologist,* 1976, *29,* 13–15.

Diller, L. Rehabilitation and clinical neuropsychology. In S. Filskov & T. Boll (Eds.), *Handbook of clinical neuropsychology.* New York: Wiley, 1980.

Diller, L., Ben-Yishay, Y., Gerstman, L. J., Gordon, W., Weinberg, J., Mandleberg, I., Schulman, P., & Shah, N. Studies in cognition and rehabilitation in hemiplegia. Institute of Rehabilitation Medicine, NYU Medical Center, *50,* 1974. (Monograph)

Diller, L., Buxbaum, J., & Chiotelis, S. Relearning motor skills in hemiplegia: Error analysis. *Genetic Psychology Monographs,* 1972, *85,* 249–286.

Diller, L. V., & Weinberg, J. Hemiinattention in rehabilitation: The evolution of a rational remediation program. *Advances in Neurology,* 1977, *18,* 63–82.

Dinardo, Q. E. Psychological adjustment to spinal cord injury (Doctoral dissertation, University of Houston, 1971). *Dissertation Abstracts International,* 1971, *36,* 4206–4207B (University Microfilms No. 71-72, 248).

Dolan, M. P., & Norton, J. C. A programmed training technique that uses reinforcement to facilitate acquisition and retention in brain-damaged patients. *Journal of Clinical Psychology,* 1977, *33,* 496–501.

Dzau, R. E., & Boehme, A. R. Stroke rehabilitation: A family-team education program. *Archives of Physical Medicine and Rehabilitation,* 1978, *59,* 236–239.

Edwards, S. L. Group work with brain-damaged patients. *Hospital and Community Psychiatry,* 1967, *18,* 267–270.

Eisenson, J. *Stuttering: A symposium.* New York: Harper & Row, 1975.

Eklund, G., & Steen, M. Muscle vibration therapy in children with cerebral palsy. *Scandinavian Journal of Rehabilitation Medicine,* 1969, *1,* 35–37.

Engel, B. T., Nekovmanesh, P., & Schuster, M. M. Operant conditioning of rectrosphinteric response in the treatment of fecal incontinence. *New England Journal of Medicine,* 1974, *290,* 646–649.

Epstein, L. H., Malone, D. R., & Cunningham, J. Feedback influenced EMG changes in stroke patients. *Behavior Modification,* 1978, *2,* 387–401.

Feigenson, J. S., Gitlow, H. S., & Greenberg, S. D. The disability oriented rehabilitation unit—a major factor influencing stroke outcome. *Stroke,* 1979, *10,* 5-8.

Fernald, G. M. *Remedial techniques in basic school subjects.* New York: McGraw-Hill, 1943.

Fields, W. S. Cerebrovascular disease: Rehabilitation. In W. S. Fields (Ed.), *Neurological and sensory disorders in the elderly.* New York: Grune & Stratton, 1975.

Finley, W. W., Niman, C., Standley, J., & Ender, P. Frontal EMG-biofeedback training of athetoid cerebral palsy patients. *Biofeedback and Self-Regulation,* 1976, *1,* 169-181.

Fitts, W. H. The self concept and psychopathology. *Studies on the self-concept and rehabilitation.* (Monograph IV) Nashville: Dede Wallace Center, 1972.

Flom, R. P., Quast, J. E., Boller, J. D., Berner, M., & Goldberg, J. Biofeedback training to overcome post-stroke foot-drop. *Geriatrics,* 1976, *31,* 47-51.

Flora, G. C. Treatment of patients with (neurological) disease. *South Dakota Journal of Medicine,* 1976, *29,* 17-18.

Fogel, M. L., & Rosillo, R. H. Correlation of psychological variables and progress in physical rehabilitation. *Diseases of the Nervous System,* 1969, *30,* 593-601.

Fogel, M. L., & Rosillo, R. H. Correlation of psychologic variables and progress in physical rehabilitation: III. Ego functions and defensive and adaptive mechanisms. *Archives of Physical Medicine and Rehabilitation,* 1971, *52,* 15-21. (a)

Fogel, M. L., & Rosillo, R. H. Motor impersistence in physical rehabilitation. *Confinia Neurologica,* 1971, *33,* 309-322. (b)

Folstein, M. F., & McHugh, P. R. Phenomenological approach to the treatment of "organic" psychiatric syndromes. In B. B. Wolman (Ed.), *The therapist's handbook: Treatment methods of mental disorders.* New York: Van Nostrand Reinhold, 1976.

Ford, B. Rehabilitation of the brain-damaged patient. *The Medical Journal of Australia,* 1977, *2,* 97-99.

Forster, F. M. *Clinical neurology* (3rd ed.). St. Louis: C. V. Mosby, 1973.

Fowler, R. S., & Fordyce, W. Adapting care for the brain-damaged patient. *American Journal of Nursing,* 1972, *72,* 2056-2059.

Fowler, R. S., Hart, J., & Sheehan, M. A prosthetic memory: An application of the prosthetic environment concept. *Rehabilitation Counseling Bulletin,* 1972, *16,* 80-85.

Foxx, R. M., & Azrin, N. H. Restitution: A method of eliminating aggressive-disruptive behavior of retarded and brain damaged patients. *Behavior Research and Therapy,* 1972, *10,* 15-27.

Freedman, A. M., Kaplan, H. I., & Sadock, B. J. (Eds.). *Comprehensive textbook of psychiatry/II.* (Vol. 1) (*2nd ed.*). Baltimore: Williams & Wilkins, 1975.

Freeman, R. D. Controversy over "patterning" as a treatment for brain damage in children. *Journal of the American Medical Association,* 1967, *202,* 385-388.

Frostig, M. *Developmental test of visual perception.* Palo Alto, Ca.: Consulting Psychologists Press, 1966.

Fuld, P. A., & Fisher, P. Recovery of intellectual ability after closed head-injury. *Developmental Medicine and Child Neurology,* 1977, *19,* 495-502.

Gaarder, K. R., & Montgomery, P. S. *Clinical biofeedback: A procedural manual.* Baltimore: Williams & Wilkins, 1977.

Gavin, J. Techniques and strategies for neuromuscular re-education. *American Journal of Clinical Biofeedback,* 1978, *1,* 24-27.

Gersten, J. W., Foppe, K. B., Gersten, R., Maxwell, S., Mirrett, P., Gipson, M., Houston, H., & Grueter, B. Effectiveness of aides in a perceptual motor training program for children with learning disabilities. *Archives of Physical Medicine and Rehabilitation,* 1975, *56,* 104-110.

Getman, G. N. The visuomotor complex in the acquisition of learning skills. In J. Hellmuth (Ed.), *Learning disorders* (Vol. 1). Seattle: Special Child Publications, 1965.

Gillette, H. E. *Systems of therapy in cerebral palsy.* Springfield, Ill.: Charles C. Thomas, 1969.

Gillingham, A., & Stillman, B. *Remedial training for children with specific disability in reading, spelling and penmanship.* New York: Lithographing Corp., 1960.

Glasgow, R. E., Zeiss, R. A., Barrera, M., & Lewinsohn, P. M. Case studies on remediating memory deficits in brain-damaged individuals. *Journal of Clinical Psychology,* 1977, *33,* 1049-1054.

Gogstad, A. C., & Kjellman, A. M. Rehabilitation prognosis related to clinical and social factors in brain injured or different etiology. *Social Sciences and Medicine,* 1976, *10,* 283-288.

Golden, C. J. The role of the psychologist in the training of the neurologically impaired. *Professional Psychology,* 1976, *1,* 579-584. (a)

Golden, C. J. The value of neuropsychological testing to the physician. *South Dakota Journal of Medicine,* 1976, *29,* 29-31. (b)

Golden, C. J. *Diagnosis and rehabilitation in clinical neuropsychology.* Springfield, Ill.: Charles C. Thomas, 1978.

Goldenson, R. M. (Ed.). *Disability and rehabilitation handbook.* New York: McGraw-Hill, 1978.

Goodkin, R. Changes in word production, sentence production and relevance in an aphasic through verbal conditioning. *Behavior Research and Therapy,* 1969, *7,* 93-99.

Haerer, A. F. Visual field defects and the prognosis of stroke. *Stroke,* 1973, *4,* 163-168.

Hammeke, T. A., Golden, C. J., & Purisch, A. D. A standardized, short, and comprehensive neuropsychological test battery based on the Luria-neuropsychological evaluation. *International Journal of Neuroscience,* 1978, *8,* 135-141.

Harris, F. A., Spelman, F. A., & Hymer, J. W. Electronic sensory aids as a treatment for cerebral palsied children: Inapproprioception, Part II. *Physical Therapy,* 1974, *54,* 354-365.

Harrison, A., & Connolly, K. The conscious control of fine levels of neuromuscular firing in spastic and normal subjects. *Developmental Medicine and Child Neurology,* 1971, *13,* 762-771.

Hartlage, L. Common psychological tests applied to the assessment of brain damage. *Journal of Projective Techniques and Personality Assessment,* 1966, *30,* 319-338.

Hécaen, H., & Albert, M. L. *Human neuropsychology.* New York: Wiley, 1978.

Herbert, M. The concept and testing of brain-damage in children: A review. *Journal of Child Psychology and Psychiatry,* 1964, *5,* 197-216.

Herman, R., & Mecomber, S. A. Vibration-elicited reflexes in normal and spastic muscle in man. *American Journal of Physical Medicine,* 1971, *50,* 169-183.

Heslinga, K., Schellen, A. M. C. M., & Verkuyl, A. *Not made of stone: The sexual problems of handicapped people.* Springfield, Ill.: Charles C. Thomas, 1974.

Higbee, K. *Your memory: How it works and how to improve it.* Englewood Cliffs: Prentice-Hall, 1977.

Hollon, T. H. Behavior modification in a community hospital rehabilitation unit. *Archives of Physical Medicine and Rehabilitation,* 1973, *54,* 65-68.

Hurwitz, L. J., & Adams, G. F. Rehabiliation of hemiplegia: Indices of assessment and prognosis. *British Medical Journal,* 1972, *1,* 94-98.

Hyman, M. D. Social psychological determinants of patients' performance in stroke rehabilitation. *Archives of Physical Medicine and Rehabilitation,* 1972, *53,* 217-226.

Ince L. P. *Behavior modification in rehabilitation medicine.* Springfield, Ill.: Charles C. Thomas, 1976.

Inglis, J., Campbell, D., & Donald, M. W. Electromyographic biofeedback and neuromuscular rehabilitation. *Canadian Journal of Behavioral Science,* 1976, *8,* 229-323.

Isaacson, R. L. The myth of recovery from early brain damage. In N. R. Ellis (Ed.), *Aberrant development in infancy: Human and animal studies.* New York: Halstead Press, 1975.

Jacques, S., Shelden, C. H., & Rogers, D. T. Spinal cord stimulation in the treatment of multiple sclerosis: Preliminary report. *Clinical Neuropsychology,* 1979, *1,* 45-47.

Jarvis, P. E., & Barth, J. T. The neglect of physical-neurological factors in community mental health practice: A proposal for a better balance. *Clinical Neuropsychology,* 1979, *1,* 20-23.

Jennett, B. Prognosis after severe head injury. *Clinical Neurosurgery,* 1972, *19,* 200-207.

Johnson, H. E., & Garton, W. H. Muscle re-education in hemiplegia by use of electromyographic device. *Archives of Physical Medicine and Rehabilitation,* 1973, *54,* 320-325.

Kaplan, H. S. *The new sex therapy.* New York: Brunner/Mazel, 1974.

Kephart, N. C. *The slow learner in the classroom.* Columbus, Ohio: Charles E. Merrill, 1960.

Kleinman, K., Reggin, C., Keister, M., Goldman, H., & Korol, B. Use of EMG feedback to inhibit flexor spasticity and increase active extension in stroke patients. *Biofeedback and Self Regulation,* 1977, *1,* 327.

Kolb, L. C. *Modern clinical psychiatry* (8th ed.). Philadelphia: W. B. Saunders, 1973.

Krupp, M. A., & Chatton, M. J. *Medical diagnosis and treatment.* Los Altos, Ca.: Lange, 1975.

Lehmann, J. F., DeLateur, B. J., Fowler, R. S., Warren, C. G., Arnhold, R., Schertzer, G., Hurka, R., Whitmore, J. J., Masock, A. J. & Chambers, K. H. Stroke: Does rehabilitation affect outcome? *Archives of Physical Medicine and Rehabilitation,* 1975, *56,* 375-382. (a)

Lehmann, J. F., DeLateur, B. J., Fowler, R. S., Warren, C. G., Arnhold, R., Schertzer, G., Hurka, R., Whitmore, J. J., Masock, A. J., & Chambers, K. H. Stroke rehabilitation: Outcome and prediction. *Archives of Physical Medicine and Rehabilitation,* 1975, *56,* 383-389. (b)

Leitenberg, H. *Handbook of behavior modification and behavior therapy.* Englewood Cliffs, N.J.: Prentice-Hall, 1976.

Levitt, S., & Miller, C. The inter-relationship of speech therapy and physiotherapy in children with neurodevelopmental disorders. *Developmental Medicine and Child Neurology,* 1973, *15,* 188-193.

Lewinsohn, P. M., Danaher, B. G., & Kikel, S. Visual imagery as a mnemonic aid for brain-injured persons. *Journal of Consulting and Clinical Psychology,* 1977, *45,* 717-723.

Lezak, M. D. *Neuropsychological assessment.* New York: Oxford University, 1976.

Lezak, M. D. Living with the characterologically altered brain injured patient. *Journal of Clinical Psychiatry,* 1978, *39,* 592-598.

Lezak, M. D. Recovery of memory and learning

functions following traumatic brain injury. *Cortex,* 1979, *15,* 63-72.

Licht, S. (Ed.). *Therapeutic exercise.* Baltimore: Waverly Press, 1958.

Lishman, W. A. The psychiatric sequelae of head injury: A review. *Psychological Medicine,* 1973, *3,* 304-318.

Lishman, W. A. *Organic psychiatry.* Oxford: Blackwell Scientific Publications, 1978.

Logue, P. E. *Understanding and living with brain damage.* Springfield, Ill.: Charles C. Thomas, 1975.

Lubar, J. R., & Babler, W. W. Behavioral management of epileptic seizures following EEG biofeedback training of the sensorimotor rhythm. *Biofeedback and Self-Regulation,* 1976, *1,* 77-104.

Lublin, J. S. Solid gains are shown in preventing strokes in treating victims: Deaths, new cases decline; CAT Scans, biofeedback aid work with afflicted: Brain bypass has promise. *The Wall Street Journal,* July 1979, pp. 1; 37.

Luria, A. R. *Restoration of function after brain injury.* New York: Macmillan, 1963.

Luria, A. R. *Higher cortical functions in man.* New York: Basic Books, 1966.

Luria, A. R. *The working brain.* New York: Basic Books, 1973.

McFie, J. Psychological testing in clinical neurology. *Journal of Nervous and Mental Disease,* 1960, *131,* 383-393.

McGinnis, M. A. *Aphasic children: Identification and evaluation by the association method.* Washington, D.C.: Alexander Graham Bell Association for the Deaf, 1963.

Mallik, K., & Sablowsky, R. Model for placement—Job laboratory approach. *Journal of Rehabilitation,* 1975, *41,* 14-20.

Marinacci, A. A., & Horande, M. Electromyogram in neuromuscular re-education. *Bulletin of the Los Angeles Neurological Society,* 1960, *25,* 57-71.

Marmo, N. A. A new look at the brain-damaged adult. *The American Journal of Occupational Therapy,* 1974, *28,* 199-206.

Marshall, R. C., & Watts, M. T. Relaxation training: Effects on the communicative ability of aphasic adults. *Archives of Physical Medicine and Rehabilitation,* 1976, *57,* 464-467.

Martin, J. A. Behavior modification and cerebral palsy. *Journal of Pediatric Psychology,* 1976, *1,* 48-50.

Maruszewski, M. Neuropsychology in neurological rehabilitation. *International Journal of Psychology,* 1969, *4,* 73-75.

Masur, F. T. III. An update on medical psychology and behavioral medicine. *Professional Psychology,* 1979, *10,* 259-264.

Matthews, C. G. Problems in the training of neuropsychologists. *The Clinical Psychologist,* 1976, *29,* 11-13.

Maxmen, J. An educative model for inpatient group therapy. *International Journal of Group Psychotherapy,* 1978, *28,* 321-338.

Meier, M. Education for competency assurance in human neuropsychology: Antecedents, models and directions. In S. B. Filskov & T. J. Boll (Eds.), *Handbook of clinical neuropsychology.* New York: Wiley, 1980.

Merritt, H. H. *A textbook of neurology* (5th ed.). Philadelphia: Lea & Febiger, 1973.

Mroczek, N., Halpern, D., & McHugh, R. Electromyographic feedback and physical therapy for neuromuscular retraining in hemiplegia. *Archives of Physical Medicine and Rehabilitation,* 1978, *59,* 258-267.

Overgaard, J., Hvid-Hansen, O., Land, M., Pedersen, K. K., Christensen, S., Haase, J., Hein, O., & Tweed, W. A. Prognosis after head injury based on early clinical examination. *Lancet,* 1973, *2,* 631-635.

Owen, S., Toomin, H., & Taylor, L. P. *Biofeedback in neuromuscular re-education.* Los Angeles: Biofeedback Research Institute, 1975.

Parsons, O. A., & Prigatano, G. P. Methodological considerations in clinical neuropsychological research. *Journal of Consulting and Clinical Psychology,* 1978, *46,* 608-619.

Pearne, D., Zigelbaum, S., & Peyser, W. Biofeedback-assisted EMG relaxation for urinary retention and incontinence: A case report. *Biofeedback and Self-Regulation,* 1977, *2,* 213-217.

Pincus, J. H., & Tucker, G. J. *Behavioral neurology.* New York: Oxford University Press, 1974.

Porter, R., & Fitzsimmons, D. W. *Outcome of severe damage to the central nervous system.* New York: American Elsevier, 1975.

Redinger, R. A., Forster, S., Dolphin, M. K., Godduhn, J., & Weisinger, J. Group therapy in the rehabilitation of the severely aphasic and hemiplegic in the late stages. *Scandinavian Journal of Rehabilitation Medicine,* 1971, *3,* 89-91.

Reiser, M. F. *American handbook of psychiatry* (2nd ed.). New York: Basic Books, 1975.

Reitan, R. M. Psychological deficit. *Annual Review of Psychology,* 1962, *13,* 415-444.

Reitan, R. M. Assessment of brain-behavior relationships. *Advances in Psychological Assessment,* 1975, *3,* 186-207.

Reitan, R. M. Neurological and physiological bases of psychopathology. *Annual Review of Psychology,* 1976, *27,* 189-216.

Reitan, R. M., & Davison, L. A. *Clinical neuropsychology: Current status and applications.* New York: Wiley, 1974.

Robbins, M. A study of the validity of Delacato's theory of neurological organization. *Exceptional Children,* 1962, *32,* 517-523.

Roessler, R., Milligan, T., & Onlson, A. Personal adjustment training for the spinal cord injured. *Rehabilitation Counseling Bulletin,* 1976, *19,* 544-550.

Rosner, B. S. Brain functions. *Annual Review of Psychology,* 1970, *11,* 555-594.

Russell, E. W., Neuringer, C., & Goldstein, G. *Assessment of brain damage: A neuropsychological key approach.* New York: Wiley, 1970.

Rutter, M. Brain damage syndrome in childhood: Concepts and findings. *Journal of Child Psychology and Psychiatry,* 1977, *18,* 1-21.

Sahakian, W. S. *Psychopathology today: Experimentation, theory, and research.* Itasca, Ill.: F. E. Peacock, 1970.

Salhoot, T. T. The use of two group methods with severely disabled persons. In R. Hardy & J. Cull (Eds.), *Group counseling and group psychotherapy techniques in special settings,* Springfield, Ill.: Charles C. Thomas, 1974.

Samuels, M. A. (Ed.). *Manual of neurologic therapeutics: With essentials of diagnosis.* Boston: Little, Brown, 1978.

Sargant, W., & Slater, E. *An introduction to physical methods of treatment in psychiatry* (5th ed.). New York: Science House, 1972.

Sarno, M. T. *Aphasia: Selected readings.* Englewood Cliffs, N.J.: Prentice-Hall, 1972.

Scrimgeour, G. J. Has ASAP failed? *Traffic Safety,* 1975, *75,* 17-36.

Siris, J. H., Werner, W. L., & Pipenger, C. E. Epilepsy associated with mental illness. *New York State Journal of Medicine,* 1977, *77,* 1906-1908.

Small, L. *Neuropsychodiagnosis in psychotherapy.* New York: Brunner/Mazel, 1973.

Smith, A. Duration of impaired consciousness as an index of severity in closed head injuries: A review. *Diseases of the Nervous System,* 1961, *22,* 69-74.

Smith, A. Neuropsychological testing in neurological disorders. In W. J. Friedlander (Ed.), *Advances in neurology* (Vol. 7). New York: Raven Press, 1975.

Smith, A. Principles underlying human brain functions reflected in neuropsychological sequelae of different neuropsychological processes. In S. B. Filskov & T. J. Boll (Eds.), *Handbook of clinical neuropsychology.* New York: Wiley, 1980.

Smith, J., & Bullough, B. Sexuality and the severely disabled person. *American Journal of Nursing,* 1975, *75,* 2194-2197.

Smolkin, C., & Cohen, S. Socioeconomic factors affecting the vocational success of stroke patients. *Archives of Physical Medicine and Rehabilitation,* 1974, *55,* 269-271.

Sparks, R., Helm, N., & Albert, M. Aphasia rehabilitation resulting from melodic intonation therapy. *Cortex,* 1974, *10,* 303-316.

Stein, D. G., Rosen, J. J., & Butters, N. *Plasticity and recovery of function in the central nervous system.* New York: Academic Press, 1974.

Steinbock, E. A., & Zeiss, A. M. Sexual counseling for cerebral palsied adults: Case report and further suggestions. *Archives of Sexual Behavior,* 1977, *6,* 77-83.

Sterling, H. M. Pediatric rehabilitation. *Archives of Physical Medicine and Rehabilitation,* 1967, *48,* 474-479.

Sterman, M. B., & Friar, L. Suppression of seizure in an epileptic following sensorimotor EEG feedback training. *Electroencephalography and Clinical Neurophysiology,* 1972, *33,* 89-95.

Stern, P. H., McDowell, F., Miller, J. M., & Robinson, M. Factors influencing stroke rehabilitation. *Stroke,* 1971, *2,* 213-218.

Strauss, A. A., & Lehtinen, L. E. *Psychopathology and education of the brain-injured child.* New York: Grune & Stratton, 1947.

Stroebel, C. F. The application of biofeedback techniques in psychiatry and behavioral medicine. *Psychiatric Opinion,* 1979, *16,* 13-17.

Suchett-Kaye, A. I., Sarkar, U., Elkan, G., & Waring, M. Physical, mental and social assessment of elderly patients suffering from cerebrovascular accident with special reference to rehabilitation. *Gerontologia Clinica,* 1971, *13,* 192-206.

Swiercinsky, D. *Manual for the adult neuropsychological evaluation.* Springfield, Ill.: Charles C. Thomas, 1978.

Taft, L. T., Delagi, E. F., Wilkie, O. L., & Abramson, A. S. Critique of rehabilitative techniques in treatment of cerebral palsy. *Archives of Physical Medicine and Rehabilitation,* 1962, *43,* 238-243.

Teuber, H. L. Recovery of function after lesions of the central nervous system: History and prospects. *Neurosciences Research Program Bulletin,* 1974, *12,* 197-211.

The Doman-Delacato treatment of neurologically handicapped children. *Neurology,* 1968, *18,* 1214-1216.

Thompson, R. E. *Foundations of physiological psychology.* New York: Harper & Row, 1967.

Travis, L. E. *Handbook of speech pathology and audiology.* New York: Meredith, 1971.

Valenstein, E. S. *Brain control.* New York: Wiley, 1973.

Vincente, P. J., Kerkhoff, T. R., & Yashon, D. Cognitive and emotional changes before and during long-term chronic cerebellar-stimulation: A longitudinal case report. *Clinical Neuropsychology,* 1979, *1,* 6-8.

Walsh, K. W. *Neuropsychology: A clinical approach.* New York: Churchill Livingstone, 1978.

Weinberg, J., & Diller, L. On reading newspapers by hemiplegics: Denial of visual disability. *Proceedings of the 76th Annual Convention of the American Psychological Association,* 1968, *3,* 655-656. (Summary)

Weinberg, J., Diller, L., Gordon, W. A., Gerstman, L. J., Lieberman, A., Lakin, P., Hodges, G., & Ezrachi, O. Visual scanning training effect on reading-related tasks in acquired right brain damage. *Archives of Physical Medicine and Rehabilitation,* 1977, *58,* 479-486.

Willard, H. S., & Spackman, C. S. *Occupational therapy.* Philadelphia: J. B. Lippincott, 1971.

Wise, T. N. Psychiatric involvement in Huntington's chorea. *Psychosomatics,* 1975, *16,* 135–137.

Wisniewska-Roszkowska, K., Jedynecki, A., & Ziolkowski, W. 10 years observation and rehabilitation of stroke disability. *Gerontologia Clinica,* 1975, *17,* 67–71.

Wolfik, D. Minimal brain dysfunction: An approach to treatment. *Medical Journal of Australia,* 1973, *2,* 601–605.

Wolpe, J. *The practice of behavior therapy.* New York: Pergamon, 1969.

Wooldridge, C. P., & Russell, G. Head position training with the cerebral palsied child: An application of biofeedback techniques. *Archives of Physical Medicine and Rehabilitation,* 1976, *57,* 407–414.

Wright, L., Schoefer, A. B., & Solomons, G. *Encyclopedia of pediatric psychology.* Baltimore: University Park Press, 1979.

Wyler, A. R., Lockard, J. S., Ward, A. A., & Finch, C. A. Conditioned EEG desynchronization and seizure occurrence in patients. *Electroencephalography and Clinical Neurophysiology,* 1976, *41,* 501–512.

Yates, A. J. Psychological deficit. *Annual Review of Psychology,* 1966, *17,* 111–144.

Yu, J. Functional recovery with and without training following brain damage in experimental animals: A review. *Archives of Physical Medicine and Rehabilitation,* 1976, *57,* 38–41.

15

Behavioral Treatment of Alcohol Problems

TED D. NIRENBERG
SETH ERSNER-HERSHFIELD
LINDA C. SOBELL
MARK B. SOBELL

During the past decade, interest in the behavioral treatment of alcohol problems has proliferated. Factors accounting for this trend include (*a*) increasing public health and economic concerns regarding alcohol abuse; (*b*) the relatively poor showing of traditional alcohol treatment approaches; (*c*) increasing government support for alcohol research; and (*d*) increasing success and acceptance of behavioral therapy.

In light of accumulating empirical evidence, the traditional concepts of alcoholism (Pattison, Sobell, & Sobell, 1977) have been questioned. The belief that alcoholism represents a unitary phenomenon has been replaced by the realization that alcohol abuse is a complex multidimensional set of behaviors. The assumption that alcohol is governed by an irreversible disease entity has been challenged by empirical evidence demonstrating that drinking behavior is basically governed by general principles of behavior (i.e., the influence of antecedents and consequences).

Like the old adage "no two people are exactly alike," it has become apparent that no two alcohol abusers are alike. Therefore, a detailed assessment of the variables that maintain problem drinking is essential to enable the therapist to choose the most appropriate treatment procedure(s). This chapter reviews the efficacy of behavioral treatment for alcohol problems. For convenience, six major categories of treatment are described: (*a*) skills training of various types, including interpersonal, problem solving, vocational, nonproblem drinking, and alcohol education; (*b*) aversive conditioning; (*c*) contingency management; (*d*) relaxation and biofeedback techniques; (*e*) marital therapy; and (*f*) self-management. The issues of treatment utilization and application are also addressed in this chapter.

Treatment Approaches

Skills Training

Several behavioral techniques have been used to teach alcohol abusers adaptive behaviors as alternatives to abusive drinking. Skills training methods are designed to modify behaviors antecedent to

Medical Psychology
Contributions to Behavioral Medicine

ISBN 0-12-565960-1

problem drinking, develop alternative adaptive behaviors, and modify the actual drinking response.

Interpersonal Skills A thorough review of the interpersonal skills training literature is beyond the scope of this chapter. However, limited evidence suggests that many alcohol abusers (*a*) have insufficient interpersonal skills, and consequently, may not receive appropriate social reinforcement (P. M. Miller & Eisler, 1977; O'Leary, O'Leary, & Donovan, 1976); (*b*) drink in response to interpersonal situations with which they cannot adequately cope (Higgins & Marlatt, 1975; P. M. Miller, Hersen, Eisler, & Hilsman, 1974); and (*c*) change their interpersonal behavior either as a result of consuming alcohol or believing that they have consumed alcohol (Marlatt & Rosenhow, 1980).

Most interpersonal skills training with alcohol abusers has focused on assertiveness training. Such training is designed to teach people to express their views so as to derive maximum reinforcement (cf. Lange & Jakubowski, 1976; P. M. Miller, 1976; Rimm & Masters, 1974). Treatment typically encompasses role playing, modeling, videotape feedback, and therapeutic instruction. While preliminary data suggest that assertiveness training enhances alcohol abusers' assertive skills, its actual effect on subsequent alcohol consumption is not well-documented. For example, in one case study (Eisler, Hersen, & Miller, 1974; P. M. Miller, 1978) with a male alcoholic who drank heavily in response to stressful interpersonal work situations, it was found that he had difficulty (*a*) speaking with subordinates in regard to their poor work performance; (*b*) confronting his employer about unreasonable work requests; (*c*) refusing unnecessary purchases from salespersons; and (*d*) effectively handling unreasonable complaints from patrons. Videotapes of the client role playing these situations revealed that he had poor eye contact as well as changes in affect and general compliance with unreasonable requests. His training included role playing with instructions and feedback regarding appropriate assertive responses. After several treatment sessions, a general within-session improvement of assertive skills was apparent, but the effect of the training on his drinking behavior was unknown because he dropped out of treatment prematurely.

Hirsch, von Rosenberg, Phelan, and Dudley (1978) used assertiveness training with inpatient alcoholics. Using several pre- and posttests for assertiveness (Rathus Assertiveness Scale, Behavioral Assertiveness Test, and Assertive Behavior Index), they compared subjects exposed to either (*a*) assertiveness training; (*b*) an open-ended discussion group focusing on why group members behaved unassertively and how to discriminate between assertive and unassertive behavior; or (*c*) a control group whose members were allowed to participate in all unit activities except those involving assertiveness training. The assertiveness training group subjects' posttest scores were significantly superior to other subjects' scores on all assertiveness scales. Once again, however, the influence of training on posttreatment alcohol consumption was not addressed.

Foy, Miller, Eisler, and O'Toole (1976) used assertiveness training to teach drink refusal skills to two chronic alcoholics who reported difficulty refusing alcoholic drinks which were offered to them. Training consisted of videotaped modeling, role playing, behavioral rehearsal, verbal instructions, and feedback. Assessment at the end of treatment and after three months of follow-up revealed improvement on all ratings of effective drink refusal. The subjects also reported that they had better control over their drinking after treatment. Since the ability to refuse drinks appears to be a significant concern for problem and nonproblem drinkers, this issue might be further addressed in prevention, as well as treatment, programs.

In a controlled outcome study, Chaney, O'Leary, and Marlatt (1978) evaluated the effectiveness of social skills training with 40 inpatient alcoholics. The subjects were randomly assigned to one of three treatment groups: (*a*) skills-training; (*b*) discussion; or (*c*) control. The skills-training group received instructions in assertiveness and problem solving skills. Training consisted of eight semiweekly 90-minute sessions with three to five participants. After a basic introduction to problem solving, the subjects were presented with problem situations that had been rated by independent observers as creating (*a*) frustration and anger; (*b*) interpersonal temptation; (*c*) a negative emotional state; and (*d*) intrapersonal temptation. Through the use of instruction, modeling, coaching, and behavioral rehearsal, the subjects learned to effectively cope with each of these situations. In the discussion group, the therapist presented the same problem situations that were used in the skills group, but encouraged the participants, in a nondirective manner, to discuss their feelings regarding the situations. The control group was exposed to regular treatment program activities.

The subjects were interviewed one year after treatment. The content of the interview was verified by at least one collateral. Eight outcome measures were collected: Days of controlled drinking; days drunk; total number of drinks; average length of drinking episodes; days hospitalized; days abstinent; days employed; and number of weekly aftercare meetings attended. While no significant differences were found between the discussion and control group, the skills training group reported fewer days drunk, fewer overall drinks consumed, and a shorter average drinking period than the other two groups.

Problem Solving Skills Since people are frequently confronted with problem situations, their ability to effectively handle these situations is related to current and future attainment of reinforcement. Based on the assumption that some people lack adequate skills to deal with problems, several investigators have incorporated problem solving into treatment approaches. The basic problem solving program, as outlined by D'Zurilla and Goldfried (1971), consists of five steps: (*a*) a general orientation; (*b*) problem definition and formulation; (*c*) generation of alternatives; (*d*) decision making; and (*e*) verification. For a detailed description of problem solving training, the reader is referred to Goldfried and Goldfried (1975) and Goldfried and Davison (1976).

M. B. Sobell and L. C. Sobell (1973, 1978) incorporated problem solving training into their broad-spectrum behavioral treatment for inpatient alcoholics. Since problem solving was one of several treatment components in this study, the specific influence of such training cannot be ascertained. As noted earlier, Chaney *et al.* (1978) also used problem solving in combination with other treatment components.

Vocational Skills While considerable attention has been given to employees with drinking problems, the relationship between work behavior and alcohol abuse has received only cursory attention. In one study where subjects were assumed to have the necessary job skills, the effectiveness of assertiveness training on specific job problems was examined (Foy, Massey, Dyer, Ross, & Wooten, 1979). The subjects were three males whose alcohol abuse appeared to be related to interpersonal problems regarding their employment. Although the authors reported general improvement on assertiveness ratings at posttreatment and follow-up, no data were reported in regard to subjects' drinking behavior.

P. M. Miller, Stanford, and Hemphill (1974) incorporated vocational counseling into a broad-spectrum treatment for alcoholics. The eight-week inpatient program, followed by one year of outpatient sessions, included contingency management; functional analysis of alcohol-related behavior; covert sensitization; and training in self-management skills, social skills, relaxation and recreational activities. Vocational counseling was also included and consisted of training in preparing a job resume, job interviewing, and the social skills necessary to handle difficult interactions with an employer or coworker. Further, a contract between the client and his employer was negotiated regarding the client's use of Antabuse. In reviewing this study, P. M. Miller (1976) noted that 62% of the patients who had completed the program were abstinent or drinking in a more controlled manner 8-24 months after follow-up.

Nonproblem Drinking Skills The use of a nonproblem drinking treatment goal produced considerable interest in the development of techniques to train clients how to drink appropriately. Early investigations concentrated on specifying the actual drinking behaviors of subjects (Kessler & Gomberg, 1974; Saunders & Richard, 1978; Schaefer, Sobell, & Mills, 1971; M. B. Sobell, Schaefer, & Mills, 1972; Williams & Brown, 1974). Later investigations examined the influence of setting variables on alcohol consumption. In one study, Rosenbluth, Nathan, and Lawson (1978) observed male and female patrons (ages 18–22) of a university-sponsored beer parlor and found that (*a*) males drank more and faster (least number of sips) than females; (*b*) subjects in groups drank more than those in pairs; (*c*) couples drank faster than same sex pairs; and (*d*) the time when drinking began (prior to or after 9:30 P.M.) was not correlated with either the amount consumed or the speed of drinking.

Caudill and Marlatt (1975) investigated the influence of high or low rate of drinking models on subjects' total beverage consumption in a wine-tasting task. Subjects exposed to high drinking rate models drank significantly more wine and took more sips than subjects in the low model or the no model control group. Hendricks, Sobell, and Cooper (1978) replicated Caudill and Marlatt's (1975) findings, but found that the manipulation was only effective in a coaction situation (when the subject and model drank simultaneously). Cooper, Waterhouse, and Sobell (1979) later reported that the coaction effect also extends to female subjects. Garlington and Dericco (1977) found that subjects who drank in a simulated bar changed their drinking rates in the direction of either a high or a low drinking model.

Although knowledge of the topography of drinking responses and the influence of setting variables is far from complete, a few studies have examined the clinical efficacy of modifying drinking behavior. Mills, Sobell, and Schaefer (1971) shaped the drinking behavior of 13 inpatient chronic alcoholics. Target behaviors included (*a*) changing drinking preference from straight drinks to mixed drinks, wine, or beer; (*b*) decreasing the tendency to gulp drinks; and (*c*) decreasing the number of drinks consumed. During training sessions, subjects were allowed to order a total of five standard drinks (approximately one-half ounce ethanol content each). As a consequence of proscribed drinking behaviors, the subjects received painful but harmless electric shocks. Strong shocks were delivered when the subjects ordered and then gulped a straight drink, ordered more than three drinks, or consumed any more than three drinks. Mild shocks were delivered if subjects ordered and sipped a straight drink or ordered and gulped a mixed drink. Ordering and sipping three or less mixed drinks or ordering nonalcoholic drinks were not punished. The nine subjects who completed all 14 sessions exhibited shaping over sessions; they reduced their consumption to three or less drinks per session, ordered mixed rather than straight drinks, and decreased their frequency of gulping.

P. M. Miller, Becker, Foy, and Wooten (1976) used a multiple baseline design to evaluate the influence of verbal instructions on the drinking behavior of three chronic alcoholic males. In a laboratory setting, two subjects were sequentially instructed to take smaller sips, increase their intersip interval, and mix weaker drinks. In order to equate baseline drinking between subjects, the third subject was instructed to reduce the potency of his drinks prior to the experimental manipulations. Instructional control proved effective in changing the targeted components of the drinking response. Frequently, however, modification of one component of the drinking response led to nondesirable changes in other components (larger sips, smaller intersip interval, or mix stronger drinks). These findings suggest that unless all components of the drinking response are simultaneously modified, overall alcohol consumption may not change.

Blood alcohol level (BAL) discrimination training is another method that has been used to modify drinking behavior. Basically, the subjects are given an alcoholic beverage (the actual strength of which may be known or unknown to the subjects) and then asked to estimate their BAL. During this time, they also receive feedback regarding the accuracy of their BAL estimations (for procedural details see Briddel & Nathan, 1975 and Caddy, 1978). Often, subjects are given guidelines for computing their BAL based on amount of ethanol consumed and temporal duration of consumption. With practice, both problem and nonproblem drinkers are able to quite accurately estimate their BAL (Lovibond & Caddy, 1970; Silverstein, Nathan, & Taylor, 1974).

Several recent investigations have attempted to delineate the critical components of BAL discrimination training. The role of interoceptive (i.e., physical sensations) and exteroceptive (i.e., instructions, verbal feedback, reinforcement) cues has received primary attention (e.g., Lansky, Nathan, & Lawson, 1978; Maisto & Adesso, 1977; Nathan, 1978). Overall, it appears that neither alcoholics nor non-problem drinkers are able to accurately and consistently estimate their BAL if they only received interoceptive cue training. This finding, however, may have limited clinical relevance, since exteroceptive cue training tends to be effective. In a treatment situation, it makes little difference whether clients estimate their BALs based on knowledge of how much ethanol they have consumed over a specified period of time as opposed to their recognizing the physical manifestations of BAL (e.g., facial flushing, numbness).

Several investigators (Caddy & Lovibond, 1976; Lovibond & Caddy, 1970; Vogler, Weissbach, Compton, & Martin, 1977) have included training in a discriminated conditioned aversion to high BALs with BAL discrimination training. After reaching a specified BAL, subjects received painful electric shocks if they consumed additional drinks. Varieties of BAL discrimination training have occasionally been used as a component of multifaceted behavioral treatment programs (Strickler, Bigelow, Lawrence, & Liebson, 1976; Wilson & Rosen, 1975), but the specific contribution of BAL discrimination training in these studies has not been evaluated. Furthermore, the therapeutic efficacy of BAL discrimination training used alone has not yet been established.

Alcohol Education Alcohol education has been included in a number of comprehensive behavioral alcohol treatment programs (M. B. Sobell & L. C. Sobell, 1973; Uecker & Boutilier, 1976; Vogler, Compton, & Weissbach, 1975). Although it is assumed that clients who are informed about the physiologic effects of alcohol and common antecedents to problem drinking would be better able to avoid alcohol abuse, little empirical support is available to evaluate this supposition.

Uecker and Boutilier (1976) found that while alcoholic inpatients' attitudes toward treatment improved following an educational program, the attitudinal improvements were not necessarily related to post-hospitalization abstinence. Stalonas, Keane, and Foy (1979) compared live, videotaped, and written presentations of an alcohol education curriculum to two groups of inpatient alcoholics who were either receiving medical treatment for detoxification or were participating in a multicomponent treatment program. The education program covered topics related to the concepts and methods of alcoholism treatment, the functional analysis of problem drinking, and the use of Antabuse as a treatment aid. All of the subjects who received the videotaped presentation scored highest on a multiple choice test of the material. Unfortunately, while all groups of subjects increased their scores from pre- to posttest, their scores dropped to near baseline at the one-month follow-up. Since the use of alcohol education in treatment and prevention programs has been prolific, its efficacy obviously needs further systematic evaluation.

Aversive Conditioning

Half a century has passed since the first reported use of aversive conditioning as a treatment for alcoholism (Kantorovich, 1929). Although early reports suggested that aversive conditioning was effective, recent studies have noted several critical scientific and ethical limitations of these methods (Hallam, Rachman, & Falkowski, 1972; Rachman & Teasdale, 1969; Wilson, 1978).

Aversive conditioning involves the pairing of a noxious stimulus (e.g., electric shock, nausea producing compound) with one or several characteristics of an alcoholic beverage or related behavior (e.g., taste, smell, and sight of a drink). Theoretically, through Pavlovian conditioning, alcohol or a drinking-related behavior, after repeated association with the aversive stimulus, comes to elicit an aversive reaction similar to that elicited by the noxious stimulus. Consequently, alcohol consumption or the targeted drinking related behavior is extinguished. For a more detailed description of specific procedures, the reader is referred to P. M. Miller (1976) and Nathan (1976).

The literature concerning aversive conditioning can be categorized by the type of noxious stimulus delivered—electrical, chemical, or covert. Electrical aversion, the most frequently used method, pairs faradic shock with a component of alcohol consumption. Although several procedural variations have been employed, recent reviews have concluded that electrical aversive conditioning is relatively ineffective as a therapeutic technique with alcoholics (Nathan & Briddell, 1977; Wilson, 1978). In particular, P. M. Miller, Hersen, Eisler, and Hemphill (1973) and Hallam *et al.* (1972) have presented convincing evidence that whatever efficacy the method might have bears little relationship to a conditioned aversive response.

Chemical aversive conditioning pairs an unpleasant physiological response induced by a drug (e.g., emetine which elicits nausea or anectine which elicits muscular and respiratory paralysis) with a component of alcohol consumption. Although the data base is quite limited, the evidence for the efficacy of chemical aversion has been somewhat more encouraging than electrical aversion. Lemere and Voegtlin (1950) and Voegtlin and Broz (1949) provided an intensive evaluation of chemical aversion. At a one-year follow-up, 60% of the subjects who received emetine conditioning reported continued abstinence. However, the authors' reliance on self-report data in addition to their including several additional treatment procedures (e.g., family counseling, vocational rehabilitation and Antabuse) makes it difficult to delineate the actual therapeutic effects of the aversion treatment. Moreover, no control group was used and subjects were probably highly motivated since they were referred for treatment by their employers. More recently, Wiens, Montague, Manaugh, and English (1976) combined individual therapy sessions with emetine conditioning and found that over 63% of their subjects reported continued abstinence at a 12-month follow-up.

Several investigators have suggested that the relative success of chemical aversion procedures in contrast to the failure of electrical aversion procedures may reflect the biological appropriateness of the two aversive stimuli (Revusky, 1973; Wilson & Davison, 1969). Experimental findings with animals have indicated that taste aversions are more easily conditioned when the noxious unconditioned stimulus is sickness (elicited by x-rays or a poison) rather than electrical shock (e.g., Garcia & Koelling, 1966). It has also been argued that for human subjects, using nausea as the unconditioned stimulus rather than electric shock should more successfully produce taste aversion to alcohol.

Imaginal aversive stimuli have also been used in aversive conditioning. In covert sensitization (Cautela, 1966), subjects close their eyes and then are verbally guided in detailed imagery by the therapist; the imagery typically depicts a situation where the subject drinks alcohol. When subjects indicate that the image is clear and that they are about to drink alcohol, they are instructed to immediately imagine intense feelings of nausea and general malaise. Repeated imagined associations of illness and the act of drinking alcohol are hypothesized to establish a conditioned aversion to alcohol; however, the effectiveness of covert sensitization has not been well-documented. Despite moderate success reported in early studies, inadequate follow-up and/or the use of additional treatment procedures makes it difficult to interpret those results (e.g., Anant, 1967; Ashem & Donner, 1968; Cautela, 1966; Little & Curran, 1978).

In a variation of covert sensitization, Smith and Gregory (1976) reported a case study utilizing anxiety caused by the noxious stimulus of imagining being responsible for a fatal automobile accident while driving under the influence of alcohol. At a 6-month follow-up, the client and significant others reported continued abstinence. Further investigation of novel noxious stimuli which are more personally relevant to the individual could have value since, theoretically, emotional reactions conditioned to such imagery may be less likely to extinguish if the individual does drink.

Contingency Management

Operant Methods Studies investigating contingency management with alcoholics have attempted to systematically apply rewards and punishment for appropriate and inappropriate drinking-related behaviors. A substantial amount of basic research supports the potential efficacy of such methods.

Using single-subject designs, investigators at the Baltimore City Hospital found that inpatient alcoholics moderated their drinking when reward contingencies such as money or access to an enriched environment were in effect. However, during noncontingent periods, the subjects' drinking reverted to baseline levels (Cohen, Liebson, & Faillace, 1971; Cohen, Liebson, Faillace, & Speers, 1971). P. M. Miller, Hersen, Eisler, and Watts (1974) reported a case study in which an outpatient chronic alcoholic manifested many positive BALs during baseline and noncontingent reinforcement periods of the study. However, when the subject was told that he would receive monetary rewards for having a BAL of zero, in randomly scheduled breath tests administered at his home or place of work, almost all his BALs were zero.

Liebson, Tommasello, and Bigelow (1978) randomly assigned 25 male methadone patients who abused alcohol to one of two 6-month treatment groups (*a*) reinforced disulfiram—subjects were given methadone contingent upon ingestion of 250 mg of disulfiram; and (*b*) control—subjects were advised to take disulfiram but given methadone regardless of whether they took disulfiram. During the treatment period, control groups subjects drank 21% of the days, whereas reinforced disulfiram subjects drank only 2% of those days. This difference was statistically significant. Further, the reinforced disulfiram subjects spent less time using illicit drugs, spent more time employed, and had fewer arrests than the control group.

A more comprehensive contingency system affecting clients' functioning in the community was introduced by Hunt and Azrin (1973). This study was based on the premise that if alcoholic subjects could substantially increase the amount of positive reinforcers in their daily living (the continuation of which would be threatened should they resume drinking), they would be motivated to maintain abstinence. Sixteen inpatient alcoholics were randomly assigned to either a community reinforcement or a control condition. The community reinforcement program included (*a*) vocational counseling; (*b*) marital and family counseling; (*c*) the creation of "synthetic" families composed of relatives, or friends or clergy for subjects without a spouse or parents; (*d*) social counseling through participation in a social club specifically designed to provide a setting for nondrinking activities; and (*e*) reinforcer-access counseling, in which the counselor helped clients obtain items (e.g., telephone, newspaper) which would facilitate their access to jobs and friends. Participation in "synthetic family" gatherings, and other activities associated with the community reinforcement program was contingent upon sobriety. Subjects in the control condition received 25 one-hour didactic sessions concerning the social and biologic effects of alcohol and the nature of Alcoholics Anonymous. Six-month follow-up data revealed that the community reinforcement subjects spent significantly less time unemployed, away from home, drinking, and institutionalized than the control subjects.

In a further study of the community reinforcement method, Azrin (1976) embellished the treatment by including (*a*) the use of Antabuse (disulfiram) to forestall impulsive drinking; (*b*) a buddy system whereby a nonprofessional counselor in the community provided advice to the subject on routine practical problems after therapy with the counselor had ended; (*c*) an "early warning system" for problems which might precipitate drinking wherein the client mailed a happiness scale to the counselor each day; and (*d*) group treatment in order to reduce the amount of therapy time per client. Twenty inpatient alcoholics were randomly assigned to either a community reinforcement or control condition. At a 2-year follow-up, the subjects in the community reinforcement group had spent significantly less time drinking, unemployed, out of their home, and institutionalized than their control group counterparts.

The methodology of Azrin's second community reinforcement study (1976) has been criticized on the grounds that the experimental group had more, as well as different elements, than the control group (Nathan, 1976). In an earlier study, however, P. M. Miller (1975) tested the influence of contingency reinforcement by having two groups of subjects receive identical services, but the services were made contingent upon sobriety for one group and noncontingent on sobriety for the other. In that study, Miller randomly assigned 20 chronic Skid Row alcoholics to either an experimental or control group. Community agencies (e.g., Missions, Salvation Army) agreed to make reinforcers (e.g., shelter, clothing, work) available to experimental subjects only when subjects had a BAL of ≤.10%. Whenever subjects were observed to be grossly intoxicated or found to register a BAL >.10%, goods and services were suspended for 5 days. Control subjects received goods and services irrespective of their sobriety. Assessments conducted 2 months before and 2 months after the program started found that experimental subjects, as compared to controls, had decreased intoxication, had fewer arrests for public drunkenness, and had a greater number of hours employed. Unfortunately, although apprised of the efficacy of the program, the community agencies did not continue providing sobriety contingent services.

Involving subjects in the dispersement of reinforcers to themselves and others is an area which has not been adequately investigated. In one such study, however, Fredericksen and Miller (1976) gave 13 male alcoholics in a behaviorally oriented treatment program, points (exchangeable for goods) contingent on the number of comments they made in group therapy. During one phase of the study, the number of points awarded to each subject was determined by the other group members. During an alternate phase, each subject determined the number of points awarded to himself. Each phase was repeated, and separated from the other by noncontingent phases where subjects received a specified number of points regardless of their behavior. The contingency procedures did not affect verbal output. While subjects initially underrewarded themselves in the self-reinforcement phase and overrewarded each other in the peer-reinforcement phase, their reinforcement became more accurate during the second round of each phase. These results suggest that further investigations are needed to determine the value of self- and other-administered reward systems, especially, for outpatient alcoholics.

Contingency Contracting Contingency contracting involves formulating a written agreement which specifies treatment goals and the consequences of achieving or not achieving those goals. Using a laboratory analogue procedure to investigate controlled drinking with inpatient alcoholics, P. M. Miller, Hersen, and Eisler (1974) compared (*a*) verbal instructions limiting drinking to a specified goal; (*b*) written instructions (signed by the subject); (*c*) verbal instructions plus a verbal presentation of reinforcement contingencies (points exchangeable for goods) related to attaining the goal; and (*d*) a mutually signed contract containing written instructions and a written presentation of the reinforcement contingencies. The authors found that the reinforcement contingency groups were significantly more successful in achieving the controlled drinking objectives than the nonreinforcement groups. Thus, for modifying this relatively circumscribed behavior, reinforcement contingencies exerted more influence than a written agreement.

Vannicelli (1979) evaluated the relative efficacy of different contract conditions with 100 inpatient alcoholics: (*a*) no contract; (*b*) staff-authored contracts; (*c*) patient-authored contracts; and (*d*) staff-patient mutually authored contracts. Requiring the signature of the patient and therapist, all contracts specified treatment goals, treatment procedures, and consequences of noncompliance with the contract. Of 14 total treatment outcome measures, only change in job status and time employed differed among the groups, with subjects in the staff-authored contract group faring worse than subjects in the other three groups. Overall, use of contracts produced no added benefits.

Ersner-Hershfield and Sobell (Note 1) evaluated the effectiveness of four different written and verbal behavioral contracts in reducing the number of absences from scheduled outpatient treatment sessions for court-referred alcohol abusers. Fifty subjects were randomly assigned to one of five groups (*a*) verbal contract–verbal agreement; (*b*) verbal contract–written agreement; (*c*) written contract–verbal agreement; (*d*) written contract–written agreement; and (*e*) no contract. Identical attendance requirements and the conditions under which subjects would be referred back to court for noncompliance were specified in all of the contracts. Guidelines for attendance and grounds for termination were constructed on an individual basis for subjects in the no contract group. Subjects under the contract conditions were less likely than subjects in the no contract group to be referred back to court for noncompliance with attendance requirements. Contracts were also found to be most effective in reducing unexcused absences when the method of presentation and agreement were identical (written or verbal).

Refundable Deposits Refundable deposits have been used as an incentive for consistent participation in outpatient treatment programs. In a study by Bigelow, Strickler, Liebson, and Griffiths (1976), 20 male outpatient alcohol abusers posted a monetary deposit which could be refunded contingent upon their taking Antabuse daily for 3 months. The terms of the program were described in a contract signed by the subject and a program representative. If subjects failed to take their Antabuse as scheduled, only partial refunds were given. Subjects reported longer abstinence periods after this program was imposed than during the preceding 3 years. However, since no control group was used, the improvements cannot be clearly attributed to the use of a refundable deposit.

Relaxation and Biofeedback Techniques

Alcohol is well known to be a quick-acting relaxant. While the excessive use of alcohol has often been attributed to its tension-reducing properties (Conger, 1956), the validity of the tension reduction hypothesis (that people drink to relieve stress) is still being debated (cf. Cappell & Herman, 1972; Hodgson, Stockwell, & Rankin, 1979). Whether alcohol actually serves to reduce tension may be irrelevant. If alcohol abusers expect alcohol to relieve stress, drinking may be negatively reinforced, and consequently, a difficult behavior to extinguish. Consistent with this rationale, several investigators have examined whether teaching alternative methods to achieve relaxation can reduce alcohol consumption by alcohol abusers.

Relaxation and Meditation Marlatt and Marques (1977) investigated the effectiveness of relaxation and meditation by comparing four treatment methods; (*a*) meditation based on Benson's (1975) procedure which involves subvocal repetition of the word "one," passive attitude, and relaxed muscles ($N = 10$); (*b*) progressive muscle relaxation, based on Jacobson's (1938) procedure ($N = 8$); (*c*) attention-placebo control, in which subjects were instructed to read enjoyable, relaxing materials ($N = 9$); and (*d*) no treatment ($N = 14$). The subjects were male undergraduates who were blocked on the basis of baseline self-report measures of alcohol intake and then randomly assigned to one of the four groups.

During the 6-week treatment phase, subjects in the meditation, relaxation, and attention-placebo groups were asked to practice their techniques twice daily, to record the amount of time spent in relaxation sessions, and to indicate the subjective level of relaxation experienced after each session. During a seven-week follow-up, practice of the techniques was optional. Daily self-reported drinking data revealed that the meditation, relaxation, and attention-placebo groups all had similar reductions in their daily alcohol consumption, and that the posttreatment means in these three groups were significantly less than that of the no treatment group. Furthermore, the no treatment group significantly increased alcohol consumption from pretreatment to posttreatment on a taste-rating task, whereas the other three groups showed no change. The meditation, relaxation, and attention-placebo groups also showed a posttreatment shift toward a more internal locus of control on the Rotter Locus of Control Scale. Finally, during the follow-up period more subjects in the meditation group practiced their techniques than subjects in the other two treatment groups.

In a similar study, Parker, Gilbert, and Thoreson (1978) randomly assigned 30 inpatient alcoholics to progressive relaxation training, meditation training, or an attention-placebo control group (quiet relaxation). Training was conducted for three weeks and subjects' state anxiety, blood pressure, heart rate, and skin conductance were assessed weekly. Reductions in state anxiety were noted for all groups. Differences were found, however, on the blood pressure measure. Across the three weeks of training, both the progressive relaxation and meditation groups showed stable systolic blood pressures as well as decreased diastolic levels, whereas the attention-placebo group had increased systolic and diastolic readings. The authors suggested that subjects' imminent discharge from the hospital and return to the community posed a stressful situation with which the experimental group, but not the control group, had learned to cope.

Two experiments by Strickler and her colleagues (Strickler, Bigelow, Wells, & Liebson, 1977; Strickler, Tomaszewski, Maxwell, & Suib, 1979) examined the effects of relaxation training on alcoholics' response to stress and drinking in the presence of stress. Strickler *et al.* (1977) gathered frontal electromyographic (EMG) recordings of alcoholics in a laboratory setting during baseline and two subsequent phases. Fourteen subjects first listened to taped presentations of either relaxation exercise instructions or neutral material (the history of an island in Chesapeake Bay). Both groups then listened to a tape of a problem drinker discussing his gradual capitulation to his desire to resume drinking after a period of abstinence. The tape was designed to evoke the kind of stress alcoholics might feel when confronted with drinking-related stimuli. Subjects in the relaxation group had significantly lower EMG levels during both the training phase and the drinking stimuli phase. Control subjects, however, showed increased EMG levels from the baseline phase to the drinking stimuli phase. Thus, the relaxation instructions appeared to reduce alcoholics' EMG levels and attenuate their reaction to drinking-related stimuli.

In the second study, Strickler *et al.* (1979) first had college students participate in an ad lib drinking baseline session. Subjects were then told that they were about to perform a public speaking task (future stressor). Then they listened to either a relaxation instructions tape, a neutral tape (identical to that used by Strickler *et al.*, 1977), or a sensitization tape in which a person with public speaking anxiety described aversive public speaking experiences. During this session, GSR (galvanic skin response) recordings were taken. Subjects in the relaxation condition had lower GSR recordings than subjects in either the neutral or sensitization conditions. A posttreatment assessment of subjects' ad lib drinking revealed that the sip rate of subjects in relaxation groups was significantly lower than that of subjects in the sensitization group. In fact, subjects in the sensitization group had increased their sip rate over baseline, an increase representing a more abusive drinking style. Furthermore, subjects in the relaxation group drank significantly less than subjects in the sensitization and neutral groups. Although relaxation and meditation training appear useful as alternative coping strategies to drinking, generalization of this influence with alcohol abusers has not been adequately explored.

Alpha Biofeedback Alpha biofeedback training has received particular attention because of its etiologic significance. Alpha waves of 8–13 Hz have been linked to subjective reports of relaxation. Early investigations (e.g., Davis, Gibbs, Davis, Jetter, & Trowbridge, 1941) indicated that alcoholics produce lower proportions of alpha waves than nonalcoholics. This finding led to the notion that alcoholics may have an abnormally high level of arousal which they attempt to lessen through alcohol consumption. In this regard, Jones and Holmes (1976) attempted to train subjects to increase their alpha production over baseline. However, neither the alcoholics nor their matched controls changed their alpha output during a three session training period. From these results, the authors concluded that the apparent success of biofeedback with young, bright, and motivated subjects (e.g., college students) may not necessarily generalize to older alcohol abusers. Glaros (1977) has suggested, however, that the absence of alpha activity changes in the Jones and Holmes study may not have been related to the subject population, but rather to the fact that these subjects were trained under conditions that were so conducive to alpha production that there was no opportunity for alpha conditioning since alpha conditioning requires allowing subjects to decrease alpha output.

In a more applied study, Watson, Herder, and Passini (1978) randomly assigned 50 inpatient alcoholics to either an alpha training condition or an attention control condition. Experimental subjects received 10 alpha training sessions which included instruction in deep muscle relaxation and a report of subjects' total alpha output after each session. Control subjects did not receive relaxation training or verbal feedback on their alpha production. The experimental subjects, as compared to the control subjects produced more alpha activity and showed a reduction in state-trait anxiety scores over training. At an 18-month follow-up, the groups still differed in terms of state-trait anxiety, but on 13 drinking disposition measures, the only difference between the groups was that the experimental group reported a longer period of time without drinking.

Electromyographic (EMG) Biofeedback In a study by Steffen (1975) four chronic alcoholics participated in eight 60-min biofeedback training sessions during which they learned to reduce tension in the frontalis muscle. Using a Latin-square design, subjects were also exposed to a placebo condition in which they were provided with irrelevant feedback while asked to reflect on their drinking lives. Compared to pretraining measures, subjects showed greater reductions in muscle tension and self-reported subjective disturbance levels during ad lib drinking periods after EMG training than during ad lib drinking periods following placebo sessions. However, the number of drinks ordered during the ad lib drinking sessions following EMG biofeedback training and placebo sessions did not differ significantly. The author suggested that the EMG training may have helped subjects to reduce tension such that they no longer aimed for rapid intoxication (producing a high BAL), but rather drank at a slower rate more characteristic of social drinkers.

Limited experimental evidence suggests that tension-reduction techniques may be effective alternatives to drinking. While relaxation, meditation, alpha biofeedback, and EMG biofeedback training all lowered subjective ratings of anxiety, only preliminary data is available regarding their subsequent influence on alcoholics' drinking patterns. Also, the generalizability of these laboratory findings to the individual's extratreatment environment has not been investigated. Because most of these techniques require several training and practice sessions and since the pharmacologic effects of alcohol occur quite rapidly, future research should investigate ways of changing the alcoholic's preference for alcohol's rapid effect.

Marital Therapy

While the percentage of alcoholic men who marry is comparable to that of the general population, the separation and divorce rate among this group is 6–10 times that of the general population (Towle, 1974).

One of the first behavioral marital therapy interventions for alcoholics was reported by Cheek, Franks, Laucius, and Burtle (1971). The guiding assumption for that program was that the wives' anger over their husbands' alcohol-related behavior contributed to destructive interaction patterns. Therefore, it was hoped that teaching wives to positively and systematically apply reinforcement would alleviate further marital distress. Twenty-four wives participated in group sessions which included desensitization to stressful situations, relaxation training, and training in reinforcing desirable behavior. Only three participants completed more than five of the 10 scheduled sessions. Wives reported that while the program helped ease tensions at home, the reinforcement training did not modify their husband's drinking. The authors speculated that the wives viewed the reinforcement procedures as entailing a position of control over their husbands which might consequently have diminished the husbands' self-esteem.

Subsequent studies have involved both spouses in treatment. Conjoint therapy affords the opportunity to help the couple activate solutions requiring mutual participation. Hedberg and Campbell (1974) compared behavioral family counseling ($N = 15$), systematic desensitization ($N = 15$), covert sensitization ($N = 15$), and electric shock aversive conditioning ($N = 12$). Behavioral family counseling consisted of assertive training, behavioral rehearsal, contracting, education in the principles of reinforcement and punishment, and the use of the Signal System for the Assessment and Modification of Behavior (Thomas, Carter, & Gambriell, 1969). Subjects were male outpatients who chose treatment goals of abstinence or controlled drinking. Within each treatment group, the techniques were the same for the abstinence goal and the controlled drinking goal. Results were expressed as the percentage of subjects in each group who had attained their declared drinking goal at a 6-month follow-up. Behavioral family counseling subjects reported the highest goal attainment rates (74%), followed by the systematic desensitization group (67%). While the covert sensitization group indicated much lower rates of goal attainment (40%), the electric shock group, which retained only four subjects after eight dropped out, showed only negligible changes (0%). Although this study contained methodological problems, (including nonrandom assignment of subjects to groups and global impressions of change as outcome measures) viewed as a demonstration program, it provides preliminary evidence for the viability of behavioral marital techniques for outpatient alcohol abusers.

P. M. Miller and Hersen (1976) reported an exemplary case study of multicomponent treatment for a couple where the husband's drinking had resulted in arrests, car accidents, and marital problems. Comprehensive assessment and treatment for the marital problems was begun while the husband was in an inpatient alcohol treatment program. The assessment included conjointly interviewing the couple, videotaping a discussion of problem and nonproblem areas in the marriage, and audiotaping two mealtime discussions at home. Through modeling, coaching, videotape feedback, and assertion training, the couple learned to compromise, recognize and verbally reinforce desired behaviors, and increase nonverbal behaviors such as eye contact and smiling. The couple also devised weekly contracts to extend changes to their extratreatment environment. At the end of treatment, the couple reported that the husband abstained from alcohol, that both spouses enjoyed changes in many aspects of their relationship, and that the couple was able to use the skills acquired through therapy to cope with new disagreements. Corroborative data was obtained through a videotaped interaction in the hospital before discharge and a report from the couple's children at a 9-month follow-up contact. Two other case studies have reported successful results using a similar behavioral treatment package with couples where one spouse had a drinking problem (P. M. Miller, 1972; Wilson & Rosen, 1975).

An innovative alcohol treatment approach for couples was reported by McCrady, Paolino, Longabaugh, and Rossi (1978). This study compared group treatment for alcoholic husbands, group treatment for couples (including both husband and wife), and group treatment for couples plus joint admission of the couple to an inpatient alcohol treatment unit. Thirty-three couples were initially blocked on a number of indices of marital adjustment and alcohol use and then randomly assigned to the three conditions. Results at the end of the six-week program and at a 6-month follow-up indicated that the alcohol consumption of the alcoholics involved in couples groups (with or without joint admission of the couple) decreased more than for subjects in individual treatment. No differences were found, however, between the groups on self-report measures of marital problems, depression, anxiety, hostility or psychopathology.

In a review of behavioral marital therapy for male alcoholics and their wives, O'Farrell and Cutter (Note 2) proposed a number of areas for further investigation: (*a*) the unique contribution that behavioral marital therapy makes to alcohol treatment; (*b*) the relative efficacy of behavioral marital therapy and other marital treatments for alcoholics and their spouses; (*c*) the essential components of behavioral marital therapy; and (*d*) the optimal arrangement of behavioral marital therapy components (e.g., whether marital therapy is most effective in couples' group therapy or in individual couples' therapy).

When considering behavioral treatment with alcohol abusers and their spouses, one also needs to consider the value of individual versus couple therapy. In some cases, problem drinking may be maintained by poor marital interactions, but in other cases, the maintaining factors may be independent of the marriage.

Self-Management

The role of individuals as mediators of their own treatment has recently become a salient focus of behavior therapy (Kanfer, 1977). Although the efficacy of self-management techniques has yet to be clearly established, current empirical evidence is quite promising. Investigations have examined the effectiveness of self-control programs, the use of self-help manuals, and self-administered reinforcement and punishment.

Self-control programs with alcohol abusers generally include three sequential steps; (*a*) self-monitoring; (*b*) functional analysis of drinking behavior; and (*c*) manipulation of antecedent and consequential determinants of problem drinking. Self-monitoring simply refers to the process by which clients maintain a record of their daily drinking behavior. L. C. Sobell and M. B. Sobell (1973) described one such log, the Alcohol Intake Sheet, on which the client records information regarding each drinking episode including the amount and type of beverage, the time of drinking, and the circumstances surrounding the drinking situation. Self-monitoring serves two primary purposes by providing the client and therapist with an accurate assessment of the amount of alcohol consumed each day, and providing critical information regarding antecedents and consequences of drinking. After the determinants of drinking are delineated, the client can be assisted in altering them to reduce future abusive drinking.

W. R. Miller (1978) compared the effectiveness of three training packages: (*a*) self-control training; (*b*) self-control training plus BAL discrimination training including discriminated aversive counterconditioning and an avoidance conditioning procedure; and (*c*) aversive counterconditioning. Thirty-two male and 14 female problem drinkers (29 self-referred and 17 court-referred), evaluated as appropriate for a controlled drinking treatment goal, were randomly assigned to treatment groups. Subjects receiving self-control training began self-monitoring their drinking after the first of ten 30-min sessions. At each subsequent session, the information recorded during the week prior to the session was reviewed and determinants of drinking were discussed by the subject and therapist. Self-control strategies to avoid abusive drinking were then suggested (described in detail by W. R. Miller & Munoz, 1976). Outcome measures included client self-reports during assessment interviews, client daily recording cards, and reports of significant others. At the end of treatment, all treatment groups showed a significant reduction in drinking, although the aversive counterconditioning group showed the least improvement. Unfortunately, the influence of self-monitoring could not be determined since all of the subjects were required to self-monitor throughout their treatment.

Three-month follow-up data reported by W. R. Miller (1978) revealed results similar to those reported at treatment termination, and 12-month follow-up data continued to indicate equal improvement for all groups. These findings may be confounded, however, because a self-help manual (W. R. Miller & Munoz, 1975) was given to a random sample of subjects at the end of treatment and to all subjects following their 3-month follow-up interview. As the authors noted, the continued improvement of the aversive counterconditioning group at the 12-month follow-up may have reflected their use of the manual, which included discussion of self-control information and strategies.

W. R. Miller (1977) also reported two studies which examined the utility of a self-help manual. In the first study (W. R. Miller, Gribskov, & Mortell, 1976), problem drinkers received either a self-help manual and self-monitoring cards or the manual and cards plus 10 weekly meetings wherein methods of self-control were discussed with a therapist. The manual presented and discussed self-monitoring procedures, self-control strategies, and alternatives to the use of alcohol (W. R. Miller & Munoz, 1975). Three-month follow-up data from self-reports, reports of significant collaterals, and self-monitoring data revealed that both treatment groups showed a significant reduction in alcohol consumption. The addition of meetings with a therapist did not have any significant effect on subjects' functioning.

In the second study (W. R. Miller, Pechacek, & Hamburg, 1976), the efficacy of incorporating a self-control manual with weekly group therapy meetings was examined. A revised version of the manual (W. R. Miller & Munoz, 1976) covered the following material in the weekly sessions:

> (1) overview of the course and goal setting; (2) rate control training; (3) training in self-reinforcement; (4) introduction to stimulus and control principles; (5) functional analysis of drinking; (6) individual consul-

tation regarding present self-control; (7) introduction to alternatives to drinking; (8) alternatives—progressive relaxation training; (9) alternatives—assertiveness and communication; (10) final assessment and course evaluation [W. R. Miller, 1977, p. 168].

Although a no treatment control group was not included, the authors reported that self-report data and reports of significant others revealed a general improvement among subjects at a three-month follow-up.

While self-administered reinforcement and punishment are essential components of self-management (e.g., Kanfer, 1977), they have received little attention in the alcohol treatment literature. Wilson, Leaf, and Nathan (1975) investigated the influence of experimenter- and self-administered punishment procedures on eight chronic alcoholics in a laboratory setting. Using a single-subject reversal design, electric shock (10 mA applied to the subject's finger tips) was administered to subjects (by the experimenter) after they had consumed alcohol. As might be expected, when the shock contingency was in effect, the subjects' alcohol consumption reduced significantly. A self-administered contingency was also introduced where subjects were asked but not required to self-administer an electric shock when they consumed alcohol. Interestingly, self-administered shock appeared to be as effective as experimenter-administered shock.

Murray and Hobbs (1977) used a multiple baseline design involving three drinking behaviors to investigate the effectiveness of a self-imposed timeout procedure with two subjects (husband and wife). During all phases of treatment, the subjects were instructed to record specific information about their daily alcohol consumption. Then, in sequence, the subjects were asked to administer a self-imposed timeout contingent upon: (*a*) mixing an alcoholic beverage with more than one ounce of alcohol; (*b*) consuming more than four drinks per day; or (*c*) consuming any drink in less than 30 minutes. Self-report data indicated that when a timeout was imposed on a target behavior, a decrease in the particular target behavior occurred. Additionally, the total amount of self-reported alcohol consumption was less during all phases of treatment and at a two-week follow-up than at baseline.

Utilization and Application Issues

Multimodal Treatment Approaches

Over the past decade, research on behavioral approaches to alcohol problems has generated a host of therapeutic techniques. Although some of these techniques have evolved from intensive experimentation, others have received inadequate investigation. In this regard, there is a clear need for further evaluation of the efficacy of specific techniques. The clinical use of these techniques, however, is somewhat more complex, since many clinical programs employ several procedures concurrently in so-called multimodal, broad spectrum, or comprehensive treatment programs (Lazarus, 1965; P. M. Miller, 1976; M. B. Sobell & L. C. Sobell, 1972; Vogler, Compton, & Weissbach, 1975).

M. B. Sobell and L. C. Sobell (1973), for example, evaluated the effectiveness of Individualized Behavior Therapy (IBT) with inpatient chronic alcoholics. The IBT program included: (*a*) individually tailored sessions designed to assess subjects' situational determinants of drinking and generate possible alternative responses to reduce the probability of abusive drinking; (*b*) problem solving training; (*c*) videotape self-confrontation of drunken behavior; (*d*) assertiveness training including methods to resist social pressure to drink; (*e*) aversive contingencies for inappropriate drinking behavior; and (*f*) for some subjects, practice in nonproblem drinking. Four treatment groups were compared using an extensive battery of follow-up measures and frequent follow-up contacts. Forty patients preselected for a controlled drinking treatment goal were randomly assigned to either the IBT program with a goal of controlled drinking or to conventional abstinence-oriented treatment. Thirty patients preselected for an abstinence (nondrinker) treatment goal were randomly assigned to either the IBT program with a goal of abstinence or to a conventional abstinence-oriented treatment. One-year follow-up outcome data, including subject self-reports, corroborative information (family, employer), and official records (driver, arrest, and hospital records), revealed that overall both IBT groups functioned significantly better than their respective conventional treatment control groups (M. B. Sobell & L. C. Sobell, 1973). At a 2-year follow-up, while the IBT controlled drinker subjects continued to function significantly better than their respective control subjects, the difference between the nondrinker groups did not reach statistical significance. The IBT nondrinker group, however, tended to function better than the conventional treatment group (M. B. Sobell & L. C. Sobell, 1976). A unique feature of this study was that independent investigators collected a third year of follow-up data (Caddy, Addington, & Perkins, 1978). Significant group differences present at the second year of follow-up remained significant at the end of the third year.

Pomerleau, Pertschuk, Adkins, and Brady (1978) compared the effectiveness of a multifaceted behavioral treatment program (N = 18) with a traditional group psychotherapy program (N = 14). Subjects were middle-income problem drinkers. Therapy was conducted in a group setting during 12 weekly sessions and 5 follow-up sessions, with treatment extending over 1 year. Behavioral treatment included (*a*) functional analysis of drinking via daily drinking records; (*b*) contingency management aimed at shaping a reduction of drinking; (*c*) identifying situational determinants of drinking; (*d*) strengthening nondrinking activities; (*e*) behavior therapy specific to problems associated with drinking (e.g., tension, lack of assertiveness or depression); and (*f*) maintaining improvement. Traditional treatment included confrontation regarding denial of drinking problems, social support for nondrinking, and psychotherapy regarding tension, nonassertiveness, and depression. While abstinence was the treatment goal for subjects in the traditional program, the behavioral program emphasized moderate drinking (defined as 3 ounces of absolute alcohol on no more than three drinking days and less than 10 ounces per week—a 3-3-10 rule) unless abstinence was medically indicated.

In addition to the regular session fees, subjects in the behavioral group were required to deposit $300.[1] Refund of the deposit was contingent on attendance, record keeping, involvement in nondrinking activities, and having a zero BAL at sessions. Follow-up data revealed that fewer subjects in the behavioral group prematurely dropped out of treatment. Sixteen of 18 subjects assigned to the behavioral treatment and 8 of 14 subjects assigned to the traditional treatment completed treatment. Pomerleau and Adkins (1980) have speculated that behavioral groups had a significantly lower dropout rate than the traditional group as a result of either the positive contingency regarding the refundable deposit or the negative consequences related to the confrontation phase of the traditional treatment program. The majority of dropouts in the traditional treatment group left therapy immediately after the subjects participated in the intense interpersonal confrontation phase of treatment.

Twelve-month follow-up data based on self-report measures revealed that 72% of the behavioral treatment subjects were either abstinent (6%) or had reduced their drinking below pretreatment levels (66%), whereas 50% of the traditional treatment subjects were either abstinent (14%) or had reduced their alcohol consumption (36%). An examination of the relationship between subjects' self-reports and gamma glutamyl transpeptidase levels (elevated enzyme levels are suggestive of acute liver dysfunction) revealed a significant positive correlation (i.e., the greater the self-reported consumption, the higher the enzyme level).

Although multifaceted behavioral treatment programs have proven superior to conventional treatment programs, it is not possible to determine which treatment components were useful and should be included in future studies. Component analysis is essential for determining the most effective treatment procedures and the most cost-effective treatment. In one such study, W. R. Miller (1978) compared clients who received self-control training with clients who received self-

[1]Subjects in the traditional treatment group were not required to pay the $300 refundable deposit; however, all subjects randomly selected for the behavioral group paid their refundable fee (Pomerleau, Note 3).

control training plus BAL discrimination training followed by discriminated aversive counterconditioning and an avoidance conditioning procedure. Both treatments were found to be equally effective. It is also possible that combining treatment components may reduce potential treatment gains. For example, while assertive skills training and contingency management have each been shown to be effective techniques for reducing abusive drinking, the effects of combining these techniques may be quite different. Hypothetically, increasing assertive skills may increase the clients' perceived personal control over life events, while contingency management may increase their perceived environmental control. Thus, the combination of these treatment techniques may prove to be less effective than using either technique alone.

Despite the research need for component analysis, at present, the use of multifaceted alcohol treatment programs appears essential for many clients, since their problems are frequently complex and warrant comprehensive assessment and individualized treatment planning. As our knowledge of specific techniques increases, such findings can be utilized to formulate more cost-effective and minimally restrictive treatment strategies.

Use of Physiological Techniques

A behavioral approach to alcohol abuse entails many of the same components as behavioral approaches to other disorders. However, certain procedures, primarily medically based, are unique to the treatment of alcohol problems. Familiarity with these procedures is essential to conducting effective behavior therapy with alcohol abusers. While the nature and scope of this chapter prohibits an extensive review of this subject, medical procedures and issues considered to be especially pertinent to nonmedical practitioners are discussed.

Antabuse Antabuse (disulfiram) was introduced in the late 1940s as a chemical deterrent to drinking. When an individual takes Antabuse, ingestion of even a small amount of alcohol produces an Antabuse–ethanol reaction characterized by nausea, flushing, increased skin temperature, and hypotension (Kwentus & Major, 1979). Although the efficacy of Antabuse is commonly predicated upon a fear model, such an orientation has an inherent disadvantage since the client typically attributes abstinence to the power of the drug. An alternative approach is to offer a rationale for the use of Antabuse that stresses self-attribution of behavior change.

We favor a rationale that presents Antabuse as a time out from the pressures of making decisions about drinking. During this time out, the client acquires new skills to substitute for drinking. Furthermore, the use of Antabuse is presented as representing the client's daily commitment to treatment (i.e., a self-control paradigm). Conditions under which the use of Antabuse will no longer be necessary are specified in advance. Thus, when the client reaches a predetermined behavioral criterion, Antabuse may be interrupted to allow testing the strength of new skills. The outcome of this trial period determines the advisability of reinstating or discontinuing Antabuse.

Physiological Assessment Familiarity with physiological tests to assess alcohol use is important for several reasons. First, an intoxicated client is not always recognized by the clinician; the phenomenon of acquired tolerance permits some people to appear sober even when they have high BALS (Maisto, Henry, Sobell, & Sobell, 1978; M. B. Sobell, L. C. Sobell, & VanderSpek, 1979). Further, clients themselves may be unaware that they have significantly high BALs when they arrive for a therapy session. Since it is usually not advisable to conduct therapy when clients are drinking (e.g., their memory may be impaired), whenever there is a question of intoxication, the BAL should be assessed. Moreover, it is quite common to encounter clients who are hesitant to divulge their alcohol intake. In these cases, direct assessment of the clients' BAL can often obviate much debate or denial. Measurement of BAL can be accomplished simply and easily by means of gas chromatographs, which analyze breath samples, or by portable breath testers (M. B. Sobell & L. C. Sobell, 1975). Use of these devices can be easily learned.

Portable breath testers also enable clients to obtain reasonably accurate estimates of their own

BAL. This can provide valuable information for clients who do not want to exceed a certain BAL when drinking. Therefore, portable breath testers may be especially appropriate for clients seeking a nonproblem drinking outcome. In view of the unreliability of estimating BAL through internal cues or arithmetic formulae, the relative accuracy and convenience of portable breath testers make them a good therapeutic adjunct.

Another physiological source of information about clients' alcohol consumption is blood tests of liver enzyme activity. Specifically, serum glutamyl oxaloacetic transaminase (SGOT) and gamma glutamyl transpeptidase (γ-GTP) have been found to be related to recent and frequent continued, excessive consumption of alcohol (Luchi, Cortis, & Bucarelli, 1978; Reyes, Miller, Taylor, & Spaulding, 1978). Responsibility for the proper interpretation of these tests lies with physicians, but nonmedical clinicians can certainly refer to the interpretations in planning clients' treatment. Conveying the interpretations to the client can also be helpful. For instance, learning that their alcohol consumption is producing acute liver damage can sometimes mobilize clients to abstain from drinking.

Treatment Goals The traditional treatment goal for alcohol abusers has been abstinence. Given the substantial and growing evidence of successful nonabstinent treatment outcomes (M. B. Sobell, 1978), it has become apparent that clinicians need to determine the most appropriate drinking treatment goal for each client. Although little experimental evidence is currently available, correlational findings suggest that individuals most likely to attain nonproblem drinking outcomes are those who exhibit less pretreatment alcohol consumption, less pretreatment alcohol withdrawal symptomatology and organic complications, and a shorter self-reported history of drinking problems (reviewed in Sobell, 1978). In lieu of adequate empirical evidence, W. R. Miller and Caddy (1977) have also suggested several criteria that may be useful in making treatment goal decisions.

When considering treatment goals, the therapist and client should not feel that they are locked into a decision once an initial choice has been made. For instance, if a therapist finds that a client is unable to maintain moderate drinking even after considerable treatment, this information is crucial and may indicate that abstinence is more appropriate for that client. Furthermore, abstinence and nonproblem drinking goals may also be used at different times with the same client. A good example of such a case comes from a client recently treated by one of the authors (T.N.). The client, a 21-year-old male college student, reported a 3-year problem drinking history, including frequent alcohol-related blackouts, four drunk driving convictions, and multiple public drunk arrests. Assessment indicated that his alcohol problems were related to deficits in his heterosexual interpersonal skills as well as to inadequate assertive skills. The client also requested training in nonproblem drinking. To reach this goal, the client agreed to a three-phase treatment schedule: (*a*) complete abstinence for 2 months, during which time the client self-administered disulfiram; (*b*) complete abstinence for 1 month without disulfiram; and finally; (*c*) nonproblem drinking. The initial goal of 2 months of abstinence was included to give the therapist an opportunity to conduct social skills training and to give the client the opportunity to practice those skills without the interference of drinking. The second goal of 1 month of abstinence without disulfiram was included to allow the client to realize that he could abstain on his own. Self-report at 1-year follow-up revealed that the client was functioning well and engaging in occasional nonproblem drinking. The role of nonproblem drinking in an abstinence-oriented program may also be appropriate. For example, even though a therapist and client may agree that abstinence should be the ultimate goal of treatment, the client initially may be unable to stop all alcohol consumption abruptly. In such cases, abstinence may be more readily attained by reinforcing the client for reducing alcohol consumption in a gradual (shaping) fashion.

Maintaining Treatment Effects An issue of continuing concern is the long-term maintenance of treatment gains. Irrespective of the treatment goal, only a very small percentage of clients maintain complete and successful abstinence or nonproblem drinking from the onset of treatment (Polich, Armor, & Braiker, 1980). Thus, increasing attention is being given to the process of relapse and factors contributing to the maintenance of changes.

Marlatt (Note 4) and Chaney, O'Leary, and Marlatt (1978) investigated the kinds of situations which preceded a relapse to drinking for two populations of male alcoholics. Over half the situations were found to involve interpersonal encounters, in which the person was angered by criticism or unable to resist social pressure to drink. Almost one-third of the situations pertained to intrapersonal factors, temptations, and negative emotional states including anger, depression, anxiety, and boredom.

The number of high risk situations may also play a significant role in precipitating relapse. Litman, Eiser, Rawson, and Oppenheim (1979) asked 120 alcoholics about (*a*) situations perceived as dangerous in evoking relapse; (*b*) types of coping skills; (*c*) perceived effectiveness of the skills; and (*d*) alcohol dependence. The subjects who consumed alcohol within 2 weeks prior to the interview ("relapsers") viewed more situations as potentially dangerous for relapse than did subjects who remained abstinent for 6 months or more ("survivors"). These authors also found that survivors not only used coping behaviors more often, but also reported using more types of effective coping behaviors than did relapsers. This finding is consistent with Lazarus' (1971) observation that the chances of maintaining improvements increases with the number of coping skills in one's behavioral repertoire.

If clients striving for abstinence slip and take a drink, their reaction to this event may strongly influence subsequent alcohol consumption. A common result of a slip is that excessive drinking resumes. Marlatt (1978) has postulated the abstinence violation effect (AVE) to account for this pattern. The AVE occurs when clients commit themselves to an extended period of abstinence and then consume alcohol. The degree of commitment and effort expended to maintain abstinence influences the intensity of the AVE.

The AVE is hypothesized to result from two major cognitive responses: a cognitive dissonance effect and a personal attribution effect. The cognitive dissonance is created by the action of consuming the first drink in the face of a strong commitment to abstinence. Further drinking may relieve the conflict through the tranquilizing properties of alcohol and by provoking alcohol abusers to perceive themselves as persons who have succumbed to the disease of alcohol. Through a personal attribution effect, the individual who has amassed feelings of self-control during the period of abstinence may interpret consumption of the first drink as a reflection of personal weakness and lack of willpower. The self-attribution of failure significantly decreases the likelihood that the person will implement self-control measures to resist further drinking.

The anticipation of high risk situations and the availability of nondrinking strategies to cope with those situations appear essential to avoiding relapse. Chaney (1976) and Chaney *et al.* (1978) trained inpatient alcoholics in a variety of social skills designed to cope with a broad range of high risk situations. Training included modeling and coaching by the therapist, group feedback, and behavior rehearsal. Compared to a discussion group in which subjects disclosed personal feelings about high risk situations and to a group receiving standard inpatient hospital procedures, the skills training group reported shorter and less severe relapse episodes at a 1-year follow-up.

Countermeasures to the AVE may be taken by planning reactions to a drinking episode, should it occur. Such actions might include a reinterpretation of the episode as a learning experience for identifying areas for further work, rather than as a failure experience. The client also can be assured that feelings of guilt or strong desires to drink are natural, and will pass (Marlatt, 1978). Marlatt (1978) has suggested use of a "programmed relapse," in which the client, under the therapist's supervision, experiences the effects of a single drink. Allowing the client to undergo a behavioral rehearsal of skills to counteract the AVE could reinforce the client's sense of self-control. Similar interventions can be used with clients pursuing a goal of nonproblem drinking.

Another method to reinforce or support the gains made in treatment has been to conduct booster sessions which involve a review of therapy procedures. Booster sessions usually occur at intervals of 1 to 3 months following treatment. While the effects of booster sessions on the treatment of obesity and smoking have been examined (cf. Franks & Wilson, 1978), few studies have used such sessions with alcohol abusers. In one reported study, however, Vogler, Weissbach, Compton, and Martin (1977) found that booster sessions did not affect drinking or relapse rates, but the comparison of a booster group with a nonbooster group was confounded by differences in the number of treatment components included in the comparison groups.

Recently, the treatment maintenance effects of follow-up interviews have been investigated. Rather than occurring intermittently, as do booster sessions, frequent and continuing follow-up interviews have been hypothesized to serve an aftercare function for clients (L. C. Sobell & M. B. Sobell, in press). In a study with outpatient alcohol abusers, Ersner-Hershfield, Sobell, Sobell, and Maisto (Note 5) compared follow-up interviews designed to only collect data with interviews which additionally inquired about subjects' welfare and offered supportive comments. Preliminary evidence indicated that subjects exposed to follow-up plus aftercare had superior outcomes, but the differences generally failed to reach conventional levels of significance.

Integrating the client's improvements into community-based activities is another strategy for maintaining gains. The community reinforcement program described by Hunt and Azrin (1973) and Azrin (1976) is an excellent example of such interventions (see the section on contingency management). Involving the client's spouse, family, and friends in reinforcing appropriate behavior is obviously important. Further research will reveal whether generalization and maintenance of treatment gains are enhanced by the participation of significant others in the client's treatment.

Treatment Outcome Evaluation

Alcohol treatment program evaluation has improved dramatically in recent years. However, significant methodological problems still exist (L. C. Sobell & M. B. Sobell, Note 6). Areas where change is still needed include: (*a*) greater standardization of outcome assessment procedures and measures; (*b*) the use of operationally defined, quantifiable, reliable, and valid measures; (*c*) closer analysis of within-subject treatment gains; (*d*) use of planned versus retrospective assessments; (*e*) use of multiple outcome measures to assess convergent validity; (*f*) detailed specification of the population of alcohol abusers under study; (*g*) collection of pretreatment data; (*h*) specification of treatment components; and (*i*) more frequent assessments over longer follow-up intervals. Changes in these areas may clarify many seemingly contradictory and confusing outcome findings.

Prevention

Finally, it seems apparent that basic and applied behavioral research is relevant to the difficult task of preventing alcohol problems. Recent behavioral investigations examining specific situational determinants of drinking behavior may prove useful in identifying precipitating components of alcohol problems. When identified, these potential causal factors may be subject to modification, thereby minimizing the likelihood of future alcohol problems. Regrettably, though, little has been published on this topic. Hopefully, recent federal initiatives in the area of prevention will stimulate such research.

Reference Notes

1. Ersner-Hershfield, S. M., & Sobell, L. C. *Behavioral contracts with clients court-referred for alcohol treatment.* Paper presented at the annual meeting of the Association for the Advancement of Behavior Therapy, San Francisco, December, 1979.
2. O'Farrell, T. J., & Cutter, H. S. G. *Behavioral marital therapy for alcoholics and wives: Review of literature and a proposed research program.* Paper presented at the NATO International Conference on Experimental and Behavioral Approaches to Alcoholism, Bergen, Norway, August 29, 1977.
3. Pomerleau, O. F. Personal communication, January, 1980.
4. Marlatt, G. A. *A comparison of aversive conditioning procedures in the treatment of alcoholics.* Paper presented at

the meeting of the Western Psychological Association, Anaheim, California, 1973.

5. Ersner-Hershfield, S. M., Sobell, L. C., Sobell, M. B., & Maisto, S. A. *The therapeutic value of follow-up interviews for alcohol abusers: An empirical evaluation.* Paper presented at the annual meeting of the American Psychological Association, New York, September, 1979.
6. Sobell, L. C., & Sobell, M. B. *Outcome criteria and the assessment of alcohol treatment efficacy.* Paper presented at the conference on Evaluation of the Alcoholic: Implications for Research, Theory and Treatment, Hartford, Connecticut, October, 1979.

References

Anant, S. S. A note on the treatment of alcoholics by a verbal aversion technique. *Canadian Journal of Psychology,* 1967, *8,* 19-22.

Ashem, B., & Donner, L. Covert sensitization with alcoholics: A controlled replication. *Behaviour Research and Therapy,* 1968, *6,* 7-12.

Azrin, N. H. Improvements in the community-reinforcement approach to alcoholism. *Behaviour Research and Therapy,* 1976, *14,* 339-348.

Benson, H. *The relaxation response.* New York: William Morrow & Co., 1975.

Bigelow, G., Strickler, D., Liebson, I., & Griffiths, R. Maintaining disulfiram ingestion among outpatient alcoholics: A security-deposit contingency contracting procedure. *Behaviour Research and Therapy,* 1976, *14,* 378-381.

Briddell, D. W., & Nathan, P. E. Behavior assessment and modification with alcoholics: Current status and future trends. In M. Hersen, R. Eisler, & P. M. Miller (Eds.), *Progress in behavior modification* (Vol. 2). New York: Academic Press, 1975.

Caddy, G. R. Blood alcohol concentration discrimination training: Development and current status. In G. A. Marlatt & P. E. Nathan (Eds.), *Behavioral assessment and treatment of alcoholism.* New Brunswick, N.J.: Rutgers Center for Alcohol Studies, 1978.

Caddy, G. R., Addington, H. J., & Perkins, D. Individualized behavior therapy for alcoholics. A third year independent double-blind follow-up. *Behaviour Research and Therapy,* 1978, *16,* 345-362.

Caddy, G. R., & Lovibond, S. H. Self-regulation and discriminated aversive conditioning in the modification of alcoholics' drinking behavior. *Behavior Therapy,* 1976, *7,* 223-230.

Cappell, H., & Herman, C. P. Alcohol and tension reduction: A review. *Quarterly Journal of Studies on Alcohol,* 1972, *33,* 33-64.

Caudill, B. D., & Marlatt, G. A. Modeling influences in social drinking: An experimental analogue. *Journal of Consulting and Clinical Psychology,* 1975, *43,* 405-415.

Cautela, J. R. Treatment of compulsive behavior by covert sensitization. *Psychological Record,* 1966, *16,* 33-41.

Chaney, E. F. *Skill training with alcoholics.* Unpublished doctoral dissertation, University of Washington, 1976.

Chaney, E. F., O'Leary, M. R., & Marlatt, G. A. Skill training with alcoholics. *Journal of Consulting and Clinical Psychology,* 1978, *46,* 1092-1104.

Cheek, F. E., Franks, C. M., Laucius, J., & Burtle, V. Behavior modification training for wives of alcoholics. *Quarterly Journal of Studies on Alcohol,* 1971, *32,* 456-461.

Cohen, M., Liebson, I., & Faillace, L. A. The role of reinforcement contingencies in chronic alcoholism: An experimental analysis of one case. *Behaviour Research and Therapy,* 1971, *9,* 375-379.

Cohen, M., Liebson, I., Faillace, L. A., & Speers, W. Alcoholism: Controlled drinking and incentive for abstinence. *Psychological Reports,* 1971, *28,* 575-580.

Conger, J. J. Alcoholism: Theory, problem and challenge. II. Reinforcement theory and the dynamics of alcoholism. *Quarterly Journal of Studies on Alcohol,* 1956, *17,* 296-305.

Cooper, A. M., Waterhouse, G. J., & Sobell, M. B. Influence of gender on drinking in a modeling situation. *Journal of Studies on Alcohol,* 1979, *40,* 562-570.

Davis, P., Gibbs, F., Davis, H., Jetter, W., & Trowbridge, L. The effects of alcohol upon the electrocephalogram (brain waves). *Quarterly Journal of Studies on Alcohol,* 1941, *1,* 626-637.

D'Zurilla, T. J., & Goldfried, M. R. Problem solving and behavior modification. *Journal of Abnormal Psychology,* 1971, *78,* 107-126.

Eisler, R. M., Hersen, M., & Miller, P. M. Shaping components of assertive behavior with instructions and feedback. *American Journal of Psychiatry,* 1974, *30,* 643-649.

Foy, D. W., Massey, F. H., Dyer, J. D., Ross, J. M., & Wooten, L. S. Social skills training to improve alcoholics' vocational interpersonal competency. *Journal of Counseling Psychology,* 1979, *26,* 128-132.

Foy, D. W., Miller, P. M., Eisler, R. M., & O'Toole, D. H. Social skills training to teach alcoholics to refuse drinks effectively. *Journal of Studies on Alcohol,* 1976, *37,* 1340-1345.

Franks, C. M., & Wilson, G. T. *Annual review of behavior*

therapy theory and practice. New York: Brunner/Mazel, 1978.

Fredericksen, L. W., & Miller, P. M. Peer-determined and self-determined reinforcement in group therapy with alcoholics. *Behavior Research and Therapy,* 1976, *14,* 385-388.

Garcia, J., & Koelling, R. A. Relation of cue to consequence in avoidance learning. *Psychonomic Science,* 1966, *4,* 123-124.

Garlington, W. K., & Dericco, D. A. The effect of modeling on drinking rate. *Journal of Applied Behavior Analysis,* 1977, *10,* 207-212.

Glaros, A. G. Comment on "Alcoholism, alpha production, and biofeedback." *Journal of Consulting and Clinical Psychology,* 1977, *45,* 698-699.

Goldfried, M. R., & Davison, G. C. *Clinical behavior therapy.* New York: Holt, Rinehart & Winston, 1976.

Goldfried, M. R., & Goldfried, A. P. Cognitive change methods. In F. H. Kanfer & A. P. Goldstein (Eds.), *Helping people change.* New York: Pergamon Press, 1975.

Hallam, R., Rachman, S., & Falkowski, W. Subjective, attitudinal, and physiological effects of electrical aversion therapy. *Behaviour Research and Therapy,* 1972, *10,* 1-13.

Hedberg, A. G., & Campbell, L. A comparison of four behavioral treatments of alcoholism. *Journal of Behavior Therapy and Experimental Psychiatry,* 1974, *5,* 251-256.

Hendricks, R. D., Sobell, M. B., & Cooper, A. M. Social influences on human ethanol consumption in an analogue situation. *Addictive Behaviors,* 1978, *3,* 253-259.

Higgins, R. L., & Marlatt, G. A. Fear of interpersonal evaluation as a determinant of alcohol consumption in male social drinkers. *Journal of Abnormal Psychology,* 1975, *84,* 644-651.

Hirsch, S. M., von Rosenberg, R., Phelan, C., & Dudley, H. K. Effectiveness of assertiveness training with alcoholics. *Journal of Studies on Alcohol,* 1978, *39,* 89-97.

Hodgson, R. J., Stockwell, T. R., & Rankin, H. J. Can alcohol reduce tension? *Behaviour Research and Therapy,* 1979, *17,* 459-466.

Hunt, G. M., & Azrin, N. H. A community-reinforcement approach to alcoholism. *Behaviour Research and Therapy,* 1973, *11,* 91-104.

Jacobson, E. *Progressive relaxation.* Chicago: University of Chicago Press, 1938.

Jones, F. W., & Holmes, D. S. Alcoholism, alpha production, and biofeedback. *Journal of Consulting and Clinical Psychology,* 1976, *44,* 224-228.

Kanfer, F. H. The many faces of self-control, or behavior modification changes its focus. In R. B. Stuart (Ed.), *Behavioral self-management: Strategies, techniques and outcome.* New York: Brunner/Mazel, 1977.

Kantorovich, N. V. An attempt at associative reflex therapy in alcoholism. *Nov. Refleksol. Fizl. Nervous Sist.,* 1929, *3,* 436-447.

Kessler, M., & Gomberg, C. Observations of barroom drinking: Methodology and preliminary results. *Quarterly Journal of Studies on Alcohol,* 1974, *35,* 1392-1396.

Kwentus, J., & Major, L. F. Disulfiram in the treatment of alcoholism. *Journal of Studies on Alcohol,* 1979, *40,* 428-446.

Lange, A. J., & Jakubowski, P. *Responsible assertive behavior: Cognitive/behavioral procedures for trainers.* Champaign, Ill.: Research Press, 1976.

Lansky, D., Nathan, P. E., & Lawson, P. Blood alcohol level discrimination by alcoholics: The role of internal and external cues. *Journal of Consulting and Clinical Psychology,* 1978, *46,* 953-960.

Lazarus, A. A. Towards the understanding and effective treatment of alcoholism. *South Africa Medical Journal,* 1965, *39,* 736-741.

Lazarus, A. A. *Behavior therapy and beyond.* New York: McGraw-Hill, 1971.

Lemere, F., & Voegtlin, W. L. An evaluation of the aversion treatment of alcoholism. *Quarterly Journal of Studies on Alcohol,* 1950, *11,* 199-204.

Liebson, I. A., Tommasello, A., & Bigelow, G. E. A behavioral treatment of alcohol methadone patients. *Annals of Internal Medicine,* 1978, *89,* 342-344.

Little, L. M., & Curran, J. P. Covert sensitization: A clinical procedure in need of some explanations. *Psychological Bulletin,* 1978, *85,* 513-531.

Litman, G. K., Eiser, J. R., Rawson, N. S., & Oppenheim, A. N. Differences in relapse precipitants and coping behavior between alcohol relapsers and survivors. *Behaviour Research and Therapy,* 1979, *17,* 89-94.

Lovibond, S. H., & Caddy, G. R. Discriminated aversive control in the moderation of alcoholics' drinking behavior. *Behavior Therapy,* 1970, *1,* 437-444.

Luchi, P., Cortis, G., & Bucarelli, A. Forensic considerations on the comparison of serum γ-glutamyl transpeptidase ("γ-GT") activity in experimental acute alcoholic intoxication and in alcoholic car drivers who caused road accidents. *Forensic Science,* 1978, *11,* 33-39.

McCrady, B. S., Paolino, T. J., Longabaugh, R. L., & Rossi, J. Effects on treatment outcome of joint admission and spouse involvement in treatment of hospitalized alcoholics. Unpublished manuscript. Cited in

T. J. Paolino & B. S. McCrady, *The alcoholic marriage.* New York: Grune & Stratton, 1978.

Maisto, S. A., & Adesso, V. J. The effect of instructions and feedback on BAL discrimination training in nonalcoholic social drinkers. *Journal of Consulting and Clinical Psychology,* 1977, *45,* 625-636.

Maisto, S. A., Henry, R. R., Sobell, M. B., & Sobell, L. C. Implications of acquired changes in tolerance for the treatment of alcohol problems. *Addictive Behaviors,* 1978, *3,* 51-55.

Marlatt, G. A. Craving for alcohol, loss of control, and relapse: A cognitive-behavioral analysis. In P. E. Nathan, G. A. Marlatt, & T. Løberg (Eds.), *Alcoholism: New directions in behavioral research and treatment.* New York, Plenum Press, 1978.

Marlatt, G. A., & Marques, J. K. Meditation, self-control and alcohol use. In R. B. Stuart (Ed.), *Behavioral self-management: Strategies, techniques and outcome.* New York: Brunner/Mazel, 1977.

Marlatt, G. A., & Rosenhow, D. J. Cognitive processes in alcohol use: Expectancy and the balanced placebo design. In N. K. Mello (Ed.), *Advances in substance abuse: Behavioral and biological research.* Greenwich, Ct.: JAI Press, 1980.

Miller, P. M. The use of behavioral contracting in the treatment of alcoholism: A case report. *Behavior Therapy,* 1972, *3,* 593-596.

Miller, P. M. A behavioral intervention program for chronic public drunkenness offenders. *Archives of General Psychiatry,* 1975, *32,* 915-922.

Miller, P. M. *Behavioral treatment of alcoholism.* New York: Pergamon Press, 1976.

Miller, P. M. Alternative skills training in alcoholism treatment. In P. E. Nathan, G. A. Marlatt, & T. Løberg (Eds.), *Alcoholism: New directions in behavioral research and treatment.* New York: Plenum Press, 1978.

Miller, P. M., Becker, J. V., Foy, D. W., & Wooten, L. S. Instructional control of the components of alcoholic drinking behavior. *Behavior Therapy,* 1976, *7,* 472-480.

Miller, P. M., & Eisler, R. M. Assertive behavior of alcoholics: A descriptive analysis. *Behavior Therapy,* 1977, *8,* 146-149.

Miller, P. M., & Hersen, M. Modification of marital interaction patterns between an alcoholic and his wife. In J. D. Krumboltz & C. E. Thoreson (Eds.), *Counseling methods.* New York: Holt, Rinehart & Winston, 1976.

Miller, P. M., Hersen, M., & Eisler, R. M. Relative effectiveness of instructions, agreements, and reinforcement in behavioral contracts with alcoholics. *Journal of Abnormal Psychology,* 1974, *83,* 548-553.

Miller, P. M., Hersen, M., Eisler, R. M., & Hemphill, D. P. Electrical aversion therapy with alcoholics: An analogue study. *Behaviour Research and Therapy,* 1973, *11,* 491-497.

Miller, P. M., Hersen, M., Eisler, R. M., & Hilsman, G. Effects of social stress on operant drinking of alcoholics and social drinkers. *Behaviour Research and Therapy,* 1974, *12,* 67-72.

Miller, P. M., Hersen, M., Eisler, R. M., & Watts, J. G. Contingent reinforcement of lowered blood/alcohol levels in an outpatient chronic alcoholic. *Behaviour Research and Therapy,* 1974, *12,* 261-263.

Miller, P. M., Stanford, A. G., & Hemphill, D. P. A social-learning approach to alcoholism treatment. *Social Casework,* 1974, *55,* 279-284.

Miller, W. R. Behavioral self-control training in the treatment of problem drinkers. In R. B. Stuart (Ed.), *Behavioral self-management: Strategies, techniques and outcome.* New York: Brunner/Mazel, 1977.

Miller, W. R. Behavioral treatment of problem drinkers? A comparative outcome study of three controlled drinking therapies. *Journal of Consulting and Clinical Psychology,* 1978, *46,* 74-86.

Miller, W. R., & Caddy, G. R. Abstinence and controlled drinking in the treatment of problem drinkers. *Journal of Studies on Alcoholism,* 1977, *38,* 986-1003.

Miller, W. R., Gribskov, C., & Mortell, R. The effectiveness of a self-control manual for problem drinkers with and without therapist contact. Unpublished manuscript, University of Oregon, 1976. Cited in Miller, W. R. Behavioral self-control training in the treatment of problem drinkers. In R. B. Stuart (Ed.), *Behavioral self-management: Strategies, techniques and outcome.* New York: Brunner/Mazel, 1977.

Miller, W. R., & Munoz, R. F. Control over drinking: A self-help manual. Unpublished manuscript, University of Oregon, 1975. Cited in Miller, W. R. Behavioral self-control training in the treatment of problem drinkers. In R. B. Stuart (Ed.), *Behavioral self-management: Strategies, techniques and outcome.* New York: Brunner/Mazel, 1977.

Miller, W. R., & Munoz, R. F. *How to control your drinking.* Englewood Cliffs, N.J.: Prentice-Hall, 1976.

Miller, W. R., Pechacek, T. F., & Hamburg, S. A minimal therapist contact behavioral treatment for problem drinking. Unpublished manuscript, Palo Alto, Ca.: Veterans Administration Hospital, 1976. Cited in Miller, W. R. Behavioral self-control training in the treatment of problem drinkers. In R. B. Stuart (Ed.), *Behavioral self-management: Strategies, techniques and outcome.* New York: Brunner/Mazel, 1977.

Mills, K. C., Sobell, M. B., & Schaefer, H. H. Training social drinking as an alternative to abstinence for alcoholics. *Behavior Therapy,* 1971, *2,* 18-27.

Murray, R. G., & Hobbs, S. A. The use of a self-imposed timeout procedure in the modification of excessive alcohol consumption. *Journal of Behavior Therapy and Experimental Psychiatry,* 1977, *8,* 377-380.

Nathan, P. E. Alcoholism. In H. Leitenberg (Ed.), *Handbook of behavior modification.* New York: Appleton-Century-Crofts, 1976.

Nathan, P. E. Studies in blood alcohol level discrimination. In P. E. Nathan, G. A. Marlatt, & T. Løberg (Eds.), *Alcoholism: New directions in behavioral research and treatment.* New York: Plenum Press, 1978.

Nathan, P. E., & Briddell, D. W. Behavioral assessment and treatment of alcoholism. In B. Kissin & H. Begleiter (Eds.), *The biology of alcoholism* (Vol. 5, Treatment and rehabilitation of the chronic alcoholic). New York: Plenum Press, 1977.

O'Leary, D. E., O'Leary, M. R., & Donovan, D. M. Social skill acquisition and psychosocial development of alcoholics: A review. *Addictive Behaviors,* 1976, *1,* 111-120.

Parker, J. C., Gilbert, G. S., & Thoreson, R. Anxiety management in alcoholics: A study of generalized effects of relaxation techniques. *Addictive Behaviors,* 1978, *3,* 123-127.

Pattison, E. M., Sobell, M. B., & Sobell, L. C. *Emerging concepts of alcohol dependence.* New York: Springer, 1977.

Polich, J. M., Armor, D. J., & Braiker, H. B. *The course of alcoholism: Four years after treatment.* Santa Monica: Rand Corporation, 1980.

Pomerleau, O. F., & Adkins, D. Evaluating behavioral and traditional treatment for problem drinkers. In L. C. Sobell, M. B. Sobell, & E. Ward (Eds.), *Evaluating alcohol and drug abuse treatment effectiveness: Recent advances.* New York: Pergamon Press, 1980.

Pomerleau, O. F., Pertschuk, M., Adkins, D., & Brady, J. P. A comparison of behavioral and traditional treatment for middle-income problem drinkers. *Journal of Behavioral Medicine,* 1978, *1,* 187-200.

Rachman, S., & Teasdale, J. *Aversion therapy and behavior disorders: An analysis.* London: Routledge & Kegan Paul, 1969.

Revusky, S. H. Some laboratory paradigms for chemical aversion treatment of alcoholism. *Journal of Behavior Therapy and Experimental Psychiatry,* 1973, *4,* 15-17.

Reyes, E., Miller, W. R., Taylor, C. A., & Spaulding, C. T. The activity of γ-glutamyl transpeptidase in the serum of problem drinkers. *Proceedings of the Western Pharmacology Society,* 1978, *21,* 289-297.

Rimm, D., & Masters, J. *Behavioral therapy: Techniques and empirical findings.* New York: Academic Press, 1974.

Rosenbluth, J., Nathan, P. E., & Lawson, D. M. Environmental influences on drinking by college students in a college pub: Behavioral observation in the natural environment. *Addictive Behaviors,* 1978, *3,* 117-121.

Saunders, B., & Richard, G. "In vivo veritas:" An observational study of alcoholics' and normal drinkers' patterns of consumption. *British Journal of Addiction,* 1978, *73,* 375-380.

Schaefer, H. H., Sobell, M. B., & Mills, K. C. Baseline drinking behavior in alcoholics and social drinkers: Kind of drinks and sip magnitude. *Behaviour Research and Therapy,* 1971, *9,* 23-27.

Silverstein, S. J., Nathan, P. E., & Taylor, H. A. Blood alcohol level estimation and controlled drinking by chronic alcoholics. *Behavior Therapy,* 1974, *5,* 1-15.

Smith, R. E., & Gregory, P. B. Covert sensitization by induced anxiety in the treatment of an alcoholic. *Journal of Behavior Therapy and Experimental Psychiatry,* 1976, *7,* 31-33.

Sobell, L. C., & Sobell, M. B. A self-feedback technique to monitor drinking behavior in alcoholics. *Behaviour Research and Therapy,* 1973, *11,* 237-238.

Sobell, L. C., & Sobell, M. B. Frequent follow-up as data gathering and continued care with alcoholics. *International Journal of the Addictions,* in press.

Sobell, M. B. Alternatives to abstinence: Evidence issues and some proposals. In P. E. Nathan, G. A. Marlatt, & T. Løberg (Eds.), *Alcoholism: New directions in behavioral research and treatment.* New York: Plenum Press, 1978.

Sobell, M. B., Schaefer, H. H., & Mills, K. C. Differences in baseline drinking behavior between alcoholics and normal drinkers. *Behaviour Research and Therapy,* 1972, *10,* 257-267.

Sobell, M. B., & Sobell, L. C. Individualized behavior therapy for alcoholics: Rationale, procedures, preliminary results and appendix. *California Mental Health Research Monographs* (No. 13). Sacramento, Ca.: California Department of Mental Hygiene, 1972.

Sobell, M. B., & Sobell, L. C. Individualized behavior therapy for alcoholics. *Behavior Therapy,* 1973, *4,* 49-72.

Sobell, M. B., & Sobell, L. C. A brief technical report on the Mobat: An inexpensive portable test for determining blood alcohol concentration. *Journal of Applied Behavior Analysis,* 1975, *8,* 117 120.

Sobell, M. B., & Sobell, L. C. Second year treatment outcome of alcoholics treated by individualized behavior therapy: Results. *Behaviour Research and Therapy,* 1976, *14,* 195-215.

Sobell, M. B., & Sobell, L. C. *Behavioral treatment of alcohol problems: Individualized therapy and controlled drinking.* New York: Plenum Press, 1978.

Sobell, M. B., Sobell, L. C., & VanderSpek, R. Relationship between clinical judgment, self-report and breath analysis measures of intoxication in alcoholics. *Journal of Consulting and Clinical Psychology,* 1979, *47,* 204-206.

Stalonas, P. M., Keane, T. M., & Foy, D. W. Alcohol education for inpatient alcoholics: A comparison of live, videotape and written presentation modalities. *Addictive Behaviors,* 1979, *4,* 223-229.

Steffen, J. J. Electromyographically induced relaxation in the treatment of chronic alcohol abuse. *Journal of Consulting and Clinical Psychology,* 1975, *43,* 275.

Strickler, D. P., Bigelow, G., Lawrence, C., & Liebson, I. Moderate drinking as an alternative to alcohol abuse: A nonaversive procedure. *Behaviour Research and Therapy,* 1976, *14,* 279-288.

Strickler, D. P., Bigelow, G., Wells, D., & Liebson, I. Effects of relaxation instructions on the electromyographic responses of abstinent alcoholics to drinking-related stimuli. *Behaviour Research and Therapy,* 1977, *15,* 500-502.

Strickler, D. P., Tomaszewski, R., Maxwell, W. A., & Suib, M. The effects of relaxation instructions on drinking behavior in the presence of stress. *Behaviour Research and Therapy,* 1979, *17,* 45-51.

Thomas, E. J., Carter, R. D., & Gambriell, E. D. Some possibilities of behavioral modification with marital problems using "SAM" (Signal System for the Assessment of Modification of Behavior). In R. D. Rubin, H. Fensterheim, A. Lazarus, & C. Franks (Eds.), *Advances in behavior therapy.* New York: Academic Press, 1969.

Towle, L. H. Alcoholism treatment outcome in different populations. *Proceedings from the Fourth Annual Alcohol Conference of the National Institute on Alcohol Abuse and Alcoholism,* 1974.

Uecker, A., & Boutilier, L. Alcohol education for alcoholics: Relation to attitude changes and posttreatment abstinence. *Journal of Studies on Alcohol,* 1976, *37,* 965-975.

Vannicelli, M. Treatment contracts in an inpatient alcoholism treatment setting. *Journal of Studies on Alcohol,* 1979, *40,* 457-471.

Voegtlin, W. L., & Broz, W. R. The conditioned reflex treatment of chronic alcoholism: X. An analysis of 3,125 admissions over a period of ten and a half years. *Annals of Internal Medicine,* 1949, *30,* 580-597.

Vogler, R. E., Compton, J. V., & Weissbach, T. A. Integrated behavior change techniques for alcoholics. *Journal of Consulting and Clinical Psychology,* 1975, *43,* 233-243.

Vogler, R. E., Weissbach, T. A., Compton, J. B., & Martin, G. T. Integrated behavior change techniques for problem drinkers in the community. *Journal of Consulting and Clinical Psychology,* 1977, *45,* 267-279.

Watson, C. G., Herder, J., & Passini, F. T. Alpha biofeedback therapy in alcoholics: An 18 month follow-up. *Journal of Consulting and Clinical Psychology,* 1978, *34,* 765-769.

Wiens, A. N., Montague, J. R., Manaugh, T. S., & English, C. J. Pharmacological aversive counterconditioning to alcohol in a private hospital: One year follow-up. *Journal of Studies on Alcohol,* 1976, *37,* 1320-1324.

Williams, R. J., & Brown, R. A. Differences in baseline drinking behavior between New Zealand alcoholics and normal drinkers. *Behaviour Research and Therapy,* 1974, *12,* 287-294.

Wilson, G. T. Alcoholism and aversion therapy: Issues, ethics, and evidence. In G. A. Marlatt & P. E. Nathan (Eds.), *Behavioral approaches to alcoholism.* New Brunswick, N.J.: Rutgers Center of Alcohol Studies, 1978.

Wilson, G. T., & Davison, G. C. Aversion techniques in behavior therapy: Some theoretical and metatheoretical considerations. *Journal of Consulting and Clinical Psychology,* 1969, *33,* 327-329.

Wilson, G. T., Leaf, R. C., & Nathan, P. E. The aversive control of excessive alcohol consumption by chronic alcoholics in the laboratory setting. *Journal of Applied Behavior Analysis,* 1975, *8,* 13-26.

Wilson, G. T., & Rosen, R. Training controlled drinking in an alcoholic through a multi-faceted behavioral treatment program: A case study. In J. D. Krumboltz & C. E. Thoresen (Eds.), *Counseling methods.* New York: Holt, Rinehart, & Winston, 1975.

16

Behavioral Approaches to the Treatment of Chronic Pain

HAROLD A. ZIESAT, JR.

This chapter covers the behavioral treatment of chronic, benign pain. Chronic, as opposed to acute pain, refers to pain that persists for longer than 6 months. The distinction between chronic and acute pain is important, because the two phenomena are different disorders. Acute pain serves the purpose of alerting the person that damage has been done to the body and, therefore, requires treatment. After the person has been alerted to the bodily damage, the pain serves no further constructive function; this is the point at which chronic pain begins. That is, rather than being just a symptom of a disease, chronic pain becomes a disorder in and of itself.

The term benign does not refer to a lack of severity; benign pain may or may not be severe. Nor does the term benign pain refer to pain that is psychogenic as opposed to somatogenic; benign pain may involve varying degrees of organic disease. Rather, the term benign refers to pain which is not the result of a malignant disease process, such as cancer. Accordingly, this chapter does not examine the problems of acute or malignant pain which usually require treatment procedures quite different from those which are about to be described (cf. Meichenbaum & Turk, 1976; Turk & Genest, 1979).

While a distinction is frequently made between psychogenic and somatogenic pain, this distinction is usually not helpful for patients suffering from chronic pain, because most chronic pain is both psychological and physical. That is, no matter what the origin of the pain, the pain experience is felt in the mind. Thus, all pain is psychological. Likewise, whether or not the pain has an organic cause, there are usually physical results from the pain (e.g., muscular tension) which typically, in turn, serve to exacerbate the pain. It is often helpful to point out to a patient how common these vicious cycles are (e.g., pain leading to muscular tension, leading to increased pain, leading to increased muscular tension, etc.). A chronic pain problem necessarily involves behavior and as such is subject to environmental influences and learning principles. As Sternbach (1968) noted, "It is necessary for the patient to do something . . . in order for us to determine that he is experiencing pain [p. 8]." Fordyce (1976) adds that "clinically, pain cannot

Medical Psychology
Contributions to Behavioral Medicine

ISBN 0-12-565960-1

become a problem until someone communicates that pain is being experienced . . . If and when private experience begins to influence other things the person is doing and is thereby directly or indirectly communicated to others, there begins a pain problem [p. 153]." The basic thesis of the present chapter is that, just as pain behavior may develop in response to operant and classical conditioning processes, it can also be modified via the therapeutic application of instrumental and respondent learning paradigms. The chapter reviews each of the major therapeutic modalities used in treating chronic pain behavior, including biofeedback and inpatient contigency management, and then presents a clinical model for the treatment of chronic pain, providing suggestions for future clinical research.

Therapeutic Modalities

Biofeedback Training

In the early 1970s, clinical research in behavior therapy began to examine the efficacy of "behavioral self-control." Although there is no universally accepted definition of self-control (Mahoney & Arnkoff, 1979) all self-control procedures involve imparting knowledge about behavior modification techniques to clients in order to teach them how to be their own behavior therapists. The interest in self-control was in part a response to the controversy regarding the external control of individual behavior, as well as to the growing volume of outcome data (e.g., Mahoney & Thoresen, 1974) indicating that individuals could regulate their own behavior and that such an approach could contribute to improved follow-up care and generalization of therapeutic change to the natural environment (cf. Kanfer, 1979).

One example of behavioral self-control procedures involves various forms of biofeedback (cf. Burish, Chapter 21; Holmes, Chapter 22). The term biofeedback refers to any procedure that provides individuals with immediate information regarding physiological processes of which they are ordinarily unaware. In response to such feedback, the individuals can learn to modify their physiological behavior (sometimes very subtly), in order to achieve therapeutic change. As discussed below, biofeedback training can be a helpful adjunct to a total behavioral treatment program for certain types of chronic pain.

Two different types of biofeedback that have been used in the treatment of chronic pain are reviewed below. These are EMG and EEG biofeedback. Of the two, more experimental work in the treatment of chronic benign pain has involved EMG biofeedback. Accordingly, the major portion of this section is devoted to studies of EMG biofeedback interventions.

EMG Biofeedback In order to use EMG biofeedback in the treatment of chronic pain, the pain must include a muscular tension component. Relevant disorders include psychophysiological musculoskeletal pain of the back (e.g., chronic low back pain), muscular tension pain in the shoulders and neck, temporomandibular joint (jaw) pain secondary to bruxism, and chronic tension headache (e.g., originating in the frontalis or trapezius muscle). The reader may refer to Burish's discussion (Chapter 21) of the rationale and outcome data regarding EMG treatment of tension headache. Most of what follows is a review of the application of EMG biofeedback to other chronic pain states.

Budzynski and Stoyva (1973) investigated the use of EMG biofeedback in treating temporomandibular joint pain and myofacial jaw pain. They found that subjects who received biofeedback training were able to reduce their masseter EMG activity more than subjects who did not receive biofeedback. However, all of the subjects were normal; that is, they were not actually patients experiencing pain. Thus, while these results were promising, it was questionable whether the results could be generalized to actual patient populations.

Peck and Kraft (1977) studied 18 patients with tension headache, 8 patients with back and shoulder pain, and 6 patients with temporomandibular joint pain. While no inferential statistics were reported, descriptive statistics suggested that the shoulder and back pain patients appeared to show no change in pain level in response to treatment and actually seemed to experience somewhat greater pain at follow-up when compared to baseline. Their EMG levels did show some reduction, but these were small relative to those of the tension headache and the temporomandibular joint pain patients. EMG levels did appear to decline over time for the headache patients, but the lack of inferential statistics made it impossible to know whether this change was statistically significant. In addition, the frequency and duration of their headaches remained essentially unchanged following treatment. Similarly, the temporomandibular joint pain patients displayed somewhat decreased EMG levels over time. However, neither their reported levels of pain nor duration of pain showed any clear improvement. It should be noted that correlations were computed between EMG levels and pain index data for the tension headache and neck pain patients ($R = .57$) and for the shoulder and back pain patients ($R = .53$). The low magnitude of these correlations raises questions concerning the degree of correspondence between EMG levels and subjective pain experience. Thus, patient control of EMG levels may not produce changes in perceived pain.

Philips (1977b) studied the effects of EMG biofeedback on tension headaches and mixed tension-migraine headaches. Three dependent measures (muscle tension levels, intensity-frequency of headache, and medication frequency) were assessed in view of the evidence (Philips, 1977a) that there is some degree of inconsistency between these three components of tension headache. Subjects were given either accurate biofeedback or pseudofeedback. The results indicated that across treatment sessions, patients receiving accurate biofeedback eventually produced resting EMG levels across sessions. In addition, the accurate biofeedback group showed greater reduction in headache intensity and medication frequency than did the pseudofeedback group. Nonetheless, neither the accurate biofeedback nor the pseudofeedback groups showed significant reduction in headache frequency, although both groups were able to decrease their EMG levels within treatment sessions. Finally, among the patients with tension headaches, the reduction in EMG levels were significantly correlated with reduction in headache intensity. Philips concluded that, with tension headache patients, biofeedback is only helpful in lowering the resting EMG level but is not effective in training patients to effectively deal with abruptly increased muscular tension due to acute environmental-emotional stress. Stoyva and Budzynski (1974) demonstrated that EMG biofeedback could be very effective in treating headache patients with high resting levels of muscular tension. Philips suggested therefore that patients with low resting EMG levels and high headache intensity scores might be considered "overreactors [Philips, 1977b, p. 128]," and might be best treated with a procedure other than EMG biofeedback.

EMG biofeedback has also been used in the treatment of other forms of psychophysiologic musculoskeletal pain (e.g., chronic low back pain), although there are few studies evaluating the use of EMG biofeedback in treating such disorders. Hendler, Derogatis, Avella, and Long (1977) studied the effects of EMG biofeedback on 13 patients who suffered from low back and leg pain, or neck, shoulder, and arm pain following disc surgery. While only descriptive, rather than inferential, statistics were reported, 6 of the 13 patients noted subjective sensations of decreased pain on at least four out of the five days after EMG biofeedback treatment. Unfortunately, due to the lack of a placebo control group, the possibility of placebo effects could not be assessed. The authors also found that at 1-month follow-up, all six of the improved patients, who had purchased individual biofeedback machines for home use, had continued using their machines and felt that they were getting some relief. However, it is unclear whether this result reflects a specific treatment effect, or whether the purchase of the machine exerted strong placebo and demand effects.

Khatami and Rush (1978) applied three different treatment approaches, in series, to six outpatients with chronic pain. The three treatment modalities consisted of (*a*) relaxation training; (*b*) cognitive-behavioral treatment of patients' evaluations of and responses to pain; and (*c*) social system intervention designed to instruct family members in the operant control of patients' pain behaviors. It was found that each of the three treatment procedures resulted in a partial reduction in patients' subjective pain estimates. There are, however, several qualifications regarding this study. First, only some of the patients in the relaxation training condition received EMG biofeedback, and the rest received another form of relaxation training such as autohypnosis. The authors did not report how many subjects actually were given EMG biofeedback training. Second, one subject prematurely discontinued therapy after the first session. Therefore, the results are based on only five subjects, and it is possible that the drop-out subject would not have been a treatment success if he had remained in the study. Finally, as the authors themselves pointed out, there was neither a placebo control group nor a waiting list (no treatment) control group. Thus, it is unclear to what extent the reported treatment effects were due to placebo factors.

Patients who suffer from chronic low back pain experience relatively unique pain-related problems. That is, conservative medical treatments such as bedrest, crutches, or braces immobilize patients and may produce further pain. External treatment modalities, such as massage, traction, or ultrasound may provide some pain relief. All of these treatment procedures, however, cast patients in the role of passive recipients of medical treatment, and thus patients do not learn self-control procedures for reducing pain or muscular tension. In an attempt to circumvent these problems, Hockersmith (Note 1) applied EMG biofeedback to chronic back pain patients. He found at 1-month follow-up that a series of twice-daily EMG training sessions produced significant decreases in patients' resting EMG levels from admission to discharge.

Hockersmith commented that an advantage of biofeedback compared to traditional medical treatment, is that it offers the patient an active part in his own treatment and the opportunity to develop more of an internal locus of control regarding his pain. However, the data presented in Hockersmith's study consisted solely of EMG levels; thus, it is unclear whether subjective pain levels actually declined as well. Moreover, the study involved placement of biofeedback electrodes on the *forearms* rather than the back. Apparently, it was hoped that the relaxation response would generalize to the rest of the body, including the back muscles, but it is unclear whether this assumption was tenable (Burish, Chapter 21; Peck & Kraft, 1977). Indeed, Schwartz (1975) pointed out that it may be helpful to program patterns of low arousal responses, rather than teaching patients to relax single muscle groups (cf. Stoyva & Budzynski, 1974).

The relationship between EMG level and chronic low back pain is somewhat problematic. Mooney and Cairns (1978) cited a study by Hufft (1975) in which patients in traction and complaining of severe back pain and spasm were examined using EMG electrode placement directly on the low-back musculature; abnormally high EMG levels were not found. However, Grabel (1973) compared the low back EMG levels of 30 patients with chronic low back pain and 30 patients without a history of low back pain and found the resting EMG levels of the patients with low back pain to be significantly higher.

Furthermore, Nouwen and Solinger (1979) provided low back EMG training to patients with chronic low back pain. The patients receiving the biofeedback training showed a significant decrease in EMG levels and subjective pain estimates, while controls, who were introduced to the EMG apparatus only for measurement of tension levels and then placed on a waiting list, showed no significant changes on either measure. Pain decrement and EMG decreases, however, appeared to be independent, and the patients who had received EMG training had relapsed to their pretreatment tension level on a 3-month follow-up assessment, even though they had maintained their decreases in subjective pain estimates. Follow-up data for the control subjects were not reported. The authors attributed this independence of EMG level and pain estimate to the feeling of self-control which the patients who had received biofeedback training had gained. That is, the patients learned that muscle tension levels, and thus pain, could be controlled and this pain control continued even in the absence of continued muscle tension control.

In summary, the outcome data regarding the use of EMG biofeedback in the treatment of chronic muscular tension pain are largely equivocal. It appears possible to use such treatment in cases of tension headache and temporomandibular pain, although the reductions in muscular tension levels are not always accompanied by a corresponding reduction in subjectively experienced pain. Moreover, muscular pain disorders other than headache and temporomandibular pain (e.g., chronic low back pain, shoulder-hand syndrome) have not been researched adequately regarding the potential application of EMG biofeedback. The results of the research that has been done on these other disorders raises questions regarding the relationship between EMG levels and pain. It could be that EMG biofeedback may be useful in a limited number of disorders (e.g., tension headache in an individual who has a high resting EMG level), or as one adjunctive treatment modality within a comprehensive behavioral pain control program.

EEG Biofeedback There have been few attempts to systematically examine the application of EEG biofeedback to the control of chronic pain. The research that has been done using this modality has involved case study formats, rather than controlled studies with large numbers of subjects. The few studies performed to date are reviewed.

Gannon and Sternbach (1971) trained a patient with postconcussion headaches to produce alpha electrical cortical activity. The authors reported that the patient was eventually able to use the alpha induction to avoid headaches but was unable to use this procedure to terminate headaches which had already begun.

Sternbach (1974) reported using alpha training with a number of chronic pain patients. The author stated that all of these patients displayed "good reduction in pain levels [p. 116]." He concluded that EMG biofeedback is "much more effective [p. 116]" than EEG biofeedback in controlling chronic pain, although he cited no data to support this conclusion.

Pelletier and Peper (1977) studied three subjects who were already accomplished in the art of meditation. Pain was introduced in each case by inserting steel needles into various parts of the body. As this occurred, physiological measures were taken, including EEG, EMG, galvanic skin response, electrocardiogram, and respiration rates. It was found that two of the three subjects increased their alpha EEG activity while they meditated during the pain experience. A multivariate analysis of variance revealed that the increase in alpha production from baseline was significant. The authors concluded that the alpha production may have allowed the subjects to tolerate the pain. However, as the authors also pointed out, the alpha state may have been unrelated to the pain-control; thus, the alpha production may have been simply an epiphenomenon of some aspect of the situation.

Melzack and Perry (1975) compared alpha biofeedback, hypnosis, and a combination of the two, in the treatment of various types of chronic pain. Both hypnotic training and the combined treatment package resulted in decreases in pain, whereas alpha training alone did not. However, change scores derived from the McGill Pain Questionnaire (Melzack, 1975; MPQ) were used to evaluate the results of treatment. Cautions regarding this method of outcome evaluation may be found in Chapter 25.

In summary, too few research studies have been done on EEG biofeedback in the control of pain to warrant a conclusion regarding its effectiveness. Moreover, the studies that have been done neither have been systematic nor have they employed enough subjects to warrant generalization to the overall population of chronic pain patients. Thus far, it is unclear whether this procedure is very promising for the treatment of chronic pain.

Inpatient Contingency Management

According to Sternbach (Note 2), the behavioral treatment of chronic pain, at least in its initial stages, usually is best handled on an inpatient basis. Inappropriate pain behavior may be maintained by a number of environmental contingencies (e.g., reinforcers in family, social, or work situations). It is best, therefore, to initially transfer patients from their natural environment to a system in which more healthy contingencies operate. As their behavior becomes more appropriate and adaptive, the patients gradually can be reintroduced into the home situation. At the same time, the people in the patients' usual environment are instructed in how they can alter their own behavior in order to support the therapeutic change.

Inpatient pain treatment is ordinarily multimodal. Unlike biofeedback training which focuses only on symptom reduction, inpatient treatment involves attempts to change several pain-related behaviors (i.e., to reverse contingencies that tend to maintain a broad spectrum of maladaptive coping responses). On an inpatient pain ward, attention is paid to all aspects of the interaction between the patient's pain and the social environment in order to reduce the possibility of symptom substitution and increase the likelihood that the patient will maintain therapeutic gains following discharge.

The most salient feature of inpatient pain treatment is operant conditioning performed by the entire staff of the unit. It is explained to the patient upon admission that the staff will not provide attention and social support for inappropriate pain behavior. The staff will respond, however, to more positive, adaptive responses such as increases in activity and exercise. Hence, social nonresponsiveness is used to extinguish inappropriate pain behavior and positive reinforcement (e.g., praise, compliments, social attention) is used to shape healthy, constructive behaviors. With this introduction, let us now turn to the specific procedures which various investigators have used in implementing this approach.

Selection of Patients Fordyce (1976, pp. 141–145) has enumerated the major criteria that he uses to identify patients who would be appropriate for operant pain control. First, the patient's pain must include an operant component. That is, the patient must have a history of reinforcement for displaying pain behavior. Second, the target behaviors must be identifiable (i.e., it must be possible to specify which pain behaviors are to be reduced and which healthy behaviors are to be increased). Third, it must be possible to identify reinforcers that would be effective for the particular patient. Finally, it is necessary to consider whether the components of the healthy target behaviors would be within the patient's behavioral repertoire; if not, the treatment program would only lead to failure and frustration. Fordyce maintains that all of the foregoing criteria are necessary in patient selection. Another criterion which is important, but not always absolutely necessary, is the availability of the spouse and/or the family for participation in the patient's treatment. The latter criterion becomes unnecessary only if it has been established that the patient has no significant family structure or that the family members have not contributed to the development and maintenance of the patient's operant pain symptoms. Additional criteria used by Fordyce in patient selection may be found in Sternbach (1974, pp. 92–93).

Fordyce and Steger (1979) have listed three variables that serve as contraindications for inpatient pain treatment. These are

(1) a spouse who will not participate in the treatment program
(2) a patient whose analgesic intake suggests addiction or habituation but who will not attempt to reduce medication use
(3) the provision of pain or illness related compensation payments such that the patient is ensured a "reasonably comfortable existence" for indefinite periods of time [p. 144].

It should be noted that Sternbach (Note 2) will not accept patients for treatment who are actively psychotic or who show no physical findings upon medical examination. These latter contraindications, however, are not accepted by all inpatient pain programs.

Patient Evaluation For any given patient, an inpatient treatment program begins with parallel psychological and neurological evaluations. The psychological evaluations may include, in addition to behavioral analysis of the patient's pain (Fordyce, 1976; Fordyce & Steger, 1979), the administration of several psychological tests in order to better understand the patient's pain problem. The Minnesota Multiphasic Personality Inventory (MMPI) has been extensively used in the assessment of chronic pain (Blumetti & Modesti, 1976; Sternbach, 1974; Sternbach, Wolf, Murphy, & Akeson, 1973a, 1973b; Timmermans & Sternbach, 1974; Wiltse & Rocchio, 1975). The use of both the MMPI code type and an interview regarding the critical items of the MMPI allows for increased understanding of which areas of therapeutic focus would most profitably be included in the patient's treatment program.

Another psychological test that is sometimes administered to pain patients is the Tourniquet-Ischemia Pain Ratio (Smith, Egbert, Markowitz, Mosteller, & Beecher, 1966; Sternbach, Murphy, Timmermans, Greenhoot, & Akeson, 1974; Ziesat, 1978). This is a method of measuring the severity of clinical pain using a magnitude-matching psychophysical procedure. One problem with the Tourniquet Ischemia Pain Ratio, however, is that, in addition to measuring pain, it may also reflect the patient's hypochondriacal tendencies (Ziesat, 1978). Therefore, it is helpful to obtain some measure of hypochondriasis in the initial evaluation. For the latter purpose, Sternbach uses the Whiteley Index (Pilowsky, 1967). Ziesat (1978) has suggested that the Tourniquet Test and the Whiteley Index may be used together. That is, if the Whiteley Index scores are very low, suggesting no significant hypochondriacal tendencies, the clinician can be fairly certain that the Tourniquet Pain Ratio has accurately reflected the patient's clinical pain. If, on the other hand, the Whiteley Index indicates a high degree of hypochondriasis, the Tourniquet Pain Ratio will have to be interpreted with a great deal more circumspection. It should be noted, however, that a study by Sternbach, Deems, Timmermans, and Huey (1977) has raised questions concerning the overall validity of the Tourniquet Pain Ratio (for additional discussion of the Tourniquet Pain Ratio, see Chapter 8).

Finally, the Health Index (Sternbach *et al.*, 1973a), which is a composite of several other tests, may be administered. It is designed to assess manifest depression, chronic invalidism, the impact of pain on daily activities, and the tendency to play pain games with medical personnel.

All of these tests are helpful in assessing both pretreatment emotional functioning and pain behavior. In addition, the tests may be used to provide measures of treatment response. A thorough, critical review of all of the assessment procedures used in evaluating chronic pain would be beyond the scope of this chapter. Instead, the reader is referred to Chapter 8 which deals with assessment issues. Suffice it to say that careful assessment of the pain patient is very important before treatment can begin.

Treatment Outcomes Fordyce, Fowler, Lehmann, DeLateur, Sand, and Trieschmann (1973) studied the effects of behavioral contingency management on 36 chronic pain patients. The treatment program, which varied in length between 4 and 12 weeks across patients, included efforts to help patients return to those activities that had appeared to be reinforcing prior to the onset of the pain problem, such as employment, socialization, and recreation. Outcome measures were taken during the first inpatient week, during the last inpatient week, and in the context of a follow-up questionnaire administered at an average of 22 months after the last outpatient treatment session. These measures included activity level and analgesic intake, subjective pain estimates, and subjective estimates of the degree of interference in activities due to pain. The results indicated improvement on all measures and maintenance of therapeutic change upon follow-up. This was, however, an uncontrolled study. It is therefore unclear whether the treatment was crucial in effecting the therapeutic changes. Furthermore, given that patients received various interventions, such as physical therapy and occupational therapy in addition to operant behavior therapy, it cannot be determined what, if any, aspect of the treatment program produced the reported therapeutic changes. Nevertheless, this early study was important in demonstrating that operant conditioning could be integrated into a treatment program for chronic pain, and in generating further research regarding this approach.

Ignelzi, Sternbach, and Timmermans (1977) have reported the outcome and two and three-year follow-up data for chronic pain patients admitted to Sternbach's inpatient program. They found that, in an approximately linear fashion, activity levels increased while pain estimates and analgesic intake decreased during treatment. Moreover, these therapeutic changes were maintained throughout both follow-up periods. Additionally, surgical patients were more likely to be readmitted for their pain problem than the nonsurgical patients.

Gottlieb, Hockersmith, Koller, and Strite (Note 3) reported on a program for the treatment of chronic back pain involving 37 patients. An assessment of program effectiveness was conducted one month after discharge. Patients were rated on a seven point scale with respect to their degree of rehabilitation. It was reported that 63% of the males and 22% of the females indeed had successful outcomes. Also, 22% of all successful patients were found to be gainfully employed for at least 30 continuous days from the date of discharge. As descriptive, rather than inferential, statistics were presented, it is difficult to accurately evaluate these results. (The authors did, however, indicate that more systematic, inferential statistics regarding these results would soon be available.) The multimodal approach of the program (e.g., EMG and GSR (galvanic skin response) biofeedback training, psychotherapeutic techniques, assertiveness training, family and sex counseling in addition to operant conditioning) further complicates evaluation of the program. Although the authors reported a marked reduction in the elevation of MMPI scales 1 (hypochondriasis), 2 (depression), 3 (hysteria), 8 (schizophrenia), and LB (low back pain), it is unclear what was meant by marked reduction.

Gottlieb, Strite, Koller, Madorksy, Hockersmith, Kleeman, and Wagner (1977) later expanded their study to include 72 patients with chronic back pain. Outcome data regarding ratings of functioning improvement (FI), clinical assessment (CA), and vocational restoration (VR) were reported. The authors found significant improvement between admission and discharge on all 10 FI and CA scales and added that the significant improvements were retained at one-month follow-up on nine of the FI and CA scales. However, these results are difficult to evaluate, because success was defined rather arbitrarily as "an average rating of 3.0 on the ten FI and CA scales, with an increase of at least one on each of these four-point scales [p. 105]." It was also found that 95% of the patients had maintained successful levels of vocational restoration at one-month follow-up and that 82% were either employed or in training after six months following discharge. However, the lack of data makes it impossible to confidently attribute the reported results to the treatment program. The relatively short follow-up period of one month also precludes determination of the long-term stability of the patients' changes.

Cairns, Thomas, Mooney, and Pace (1976) reported on a two-phase treatment program for chronic low back pain patients. During the first phase, each patient underwent (*a*) a complete orthopedic evaluation; (*b*) assessment by a family practice physician; (*c*) a shift in pain medication to a by-the-clock schedule; (*d*) a psychotropic medication regimen, if necessary; (*e*) a psychological evaluation; (*f*) evaluation for and treatment by an occupational therapist; and (*g*) the initiation of a recreational therapy program for hobby development. At the end of Phase 1, the patient's status was reevaluated. If the pain and low functional level persisted, the patient was transferred to Phase 2: operant conditioning.

In Phase 2, specific treatment goals were negotiated with the patient regarding desired activity to be engaged in following discharge; these may have involved vocational, homemaking, or recreational activities. Group therapy also was provided to modify the ways in which the patients used their pain behavior as a tool in their interpersonal relationships. In order to promote generalization of therapeutic change to the natural environment, all family members were encouraged to attend conferences with the staff. The dependent measure was response to a questionnaire mailed to 100 patients at an average of 10 months following discharge. It was found that 70% of the 90 patients who responded reported that treatment significantly reduced their pain level or increased their activity level, with this improvement remaining at the end of the follow-up period. All patients had been switched from narcotics to nonnarcotic analgesics during inpatient treatment, and at the time of the follow-up assessment, 58% of the patients reported that they needed less pain medication than they had prior to hospitalization. Additionally, 74% of the patients had decided not to pursue further medical treatment. Finally, 75% of those patients selected for vocational training were either employed or receiving vocational training at the time of the follow-up assessment. Once again, however, this study's lack of inferential statistics and control groups complicates rigorous evaluation of its effectiveness.

Seres and Newman (1976) evaluated 100 patients with low back pain admitted to a multidisciplinary, multimodal treatment program that included operant conditioning, systematic drug withdrawal, active physical therapy, body-mechanics classes, biofeedback, relaxation training, and educational classes. The average length of the inpatient stay was 21 days with the range being 15-25 days. A follow-up assessment was conducted three months following discharge. Upon admission, 87% of the patients had been taking prescribed pain medications; this figure dropped to 5% by the time of discharge and 22% at three-month follow-up. Furthermore, the average patient showed an improved range of motion and physical tolerance on several exercise and mobility measures. For example, on admission the average patient could raise the knees to about a 72° angle; this figure increased to 115.5° and 120.2° at discharge and follow-up, respectively. Finally, 80% of those patients interviewed at follow-up stated that they had decided not to seek any further medical treatment. It should be noted, however, that positive evaluation of this study must be tempered by the fact that no control groups or inferential statistics were employed and that the multimodal treatment approach precludes attribution of patient change to specific interventions.

Newman, Seres, Yospe, and Garlington (1978) reported on a long-term follow-up study of 36 of the patients who had been treated in the program previously described. This report makes it clear that the treatment program included contingency management techniques with only "some patients [p. 285]." It is also stated that one factor that probably contributed to follow-up results was the fact that a group of former patients had formed an "alumni association" which met regularly for peer reinforcement of therapeutic progress. The follow-up evaluations, which were analyzed by inferential statistics, were conducted 80 weeks after discharge. It was found that statistically significant gains were maintained in the reduction of pain medications and on four measures of physical functioning: (*a*) long-sitting-to-toe; (*b*) straight-leg raise; (*c*) knee-to-chest; and (*d*) overall exercise performance. When the patients were asked to compare their pain intensity with what it had been upon admission, most reported that their pain was the same or slightly worse than it had been upon admission; however, most also stated that they were better able to cope with the pain. These data are in contrast to those of Fordyce *et al.* (1973) who found decreases in subjective estimates of pain per se. This difference may be related to the fact that the Fordyce program focused intensively on operant conditioning for each patient whereas the Newman *et al.* (1978) program did not always do so.

Cairns and Pasino (1977) conducted the first controlled study examining the efficacy of operant techniques in the treatment of chronic pain. Moreover, as with the study by Newman *et al.*, (1978), inferential statistics were used. The subjects were nine patients hospitalized for the treatment of chronic organic and nonorganic low back pain. The dependent measures were uptime and distance pedaled on a stationary exercycle. In the first treatment condition, the physical therapists gave the patients positive verbal reinforcement for increases in activity level. In the second treatment condition, the patients received not only verbal reinforcement from the physical therapists but were also given a graph of their progress, placed above their beds. In the control condition, physical therapists received no specific instructions regarding how they were to respond to the patients during physical therapy sessions. There were significant increases in activity level between baseline and the end of treatment (after approximately 10 therapy sessions) as a function of both treatment conditions. The performance of patients in both treatment conditions also was significantly better than that of patients in the control condition. It may also be noted that the patients in the second treatment condition were initially exposed only to the graph as a form of reinforcement; it was only later that contingent verbal reinforcement was added. In the initial, graph-only condition, there was no increase from baseline in terms of activity level. Therefore, it appears that verbal reinforcement was very important in effecting the therapeutic change in activity level, and that the combination of verbal reinforcement and pictorial reinforcement in the form of a graph could be a powerful treatment for low back pain patients. Moreover, the authors suggested that an even more powerful effect might have been obtained if the verbal reinforcement had been delivered with direct reference to the improvements represented on the graph (e.g., "your graph is moving up; that's good").

Anderson, Cole, Gullickson, Hudgens, and Roberts (1977) presented a study on the behavioral treatment of chronic pain at a university-affiliated rehabilitation setting. A particular strength of the treatment program was that "the family including the hospitalized person was the 'total' patient treated by the program [p. 97]." This approach was followed in order to maximize the chances of generalizing therapeutic change to the home environment. A novel, positive aspect of the program was that goals for the various therapeutic activities (e.g., occupational therapy, physical therapy) were staggered, so that the patient was repeatedly reinforced for reaching goals throughout an extended period of time. However, no control group was employed and only descriptive statistics were presented. The authors stated that of those 34 patients who completed the program, 25 were found to be "leading normal lives," defined as "continuing increased level of activity, total cessation in the use of prescription pain medication, and decreased use of the health care system [p. 99]." Given the methodological deficiencies already noted and the fact that the outcome measures were rather vaguely defined, no definitive conclusions regarding the efficacy of the treatment program may be drawn.

Swanson, Maruta, and Swenson (1979) reported on an inpatient program which included several intervention strategies such as operant conditioning, physical rehabilitation, medication management, group discussion, and education. Dependent measures consisted of modification of patient attitude, reduction in medication use, and improvement in physical functioning. While all of the latter criteria are important, the definition of patient change was largely based on the subjective clinical judgment of staff members. In addition, no control groups were employed. Two strengths of the study, however, were the use of inferential, as well as descriptive, statistics and long-term follow-up (three months and one year). The results suggested a reasonably successful program, with adequate retention of progress over time.

In summary, the research regarding inpatient contingency management of chronic pain has shown some promise. However, methodological weaknesses in the studies makes it difficult to make a more definitive statement regarding treatment efficacy at this time. One major problem has been the lack of experimental controls. As a result, it usually has not been possible to assume that the treatment programs were the active agents responsible for patient change. In addition, many of the outcome studies have involved a shotgun approach, including not only inpatient contingency management but also such treatment modalities as psychotropic medication, transcutaneous electrical analgesia, and surgery. These approaches have prevented most investigators from determining what aspects of their treatment programs actually effected patient changes and what aspects were ineffective. Another methodological problem has been that a large number of the studies have included only descriptive, rather than inferential, statistics. This has forced investigators to rely upon categorizations of patients as improved or unimproved. Nevertheless, most of the reported operant conditioning programs for chronic pain are based upon well-validated principles of behavior modification. The component procedures of such programs (e.g., extinction, modeling, shaping) already have been successfully tested on other behavioral disorders. The task now remains for clinicians to refine research techniques in applying such behavioral procedures to populations of chronic pain patients.

Experimental and Clinical Suggestions

At this time, treatment of chronic pain demands further investigation. There are several reasons for this. First, chronic pain is not only a source of personal anguish for the individual involved, but it is also an expensive drain on society. For example,

Nagi, Riley, and Newby (1973) reported data that suggested that 18% of the general population are bothered by some persistent pain; further, patients with discogenic back pain have been reported to rank 11th among 194 diagnostic groups, in terms of number of days spent in hospitals in the United States (Chaffin, 1974). Bonica (1974) cited data to indicate that low back pain cost the State of California $200 million in 1971. He also suggested that the total cost of low back pain to our society may be as much as $100,000 per patient.

Another reason for the current need for research on pain is the growing trend toward "behavioral medicine" in comprehensive medical treatment programs. More and more, physicians and federal agencies are recognizing that behaviorally trained clinical psychologists have a significant contribution to make in direct collaboration with primary care physicians such as surgeons, internists, and pediatricians. The behavioral treatment of chronic pain is one endeavor which falls under the general rubric of behavioral medicine.

It should again be emphasized that, as documented in the present chapter, much of the previous research in this area has been limited by methodological weaknesses. Future studies should include appropriate control groups so that patient changes may be attributed to the treatment program and investigators eventually may identify the crucial variables involved in effecting the behavioral change. For example, a possible study would be to separate out the individual effects of inpatient contingency management, EMG biofeedback training, tricyclic antidepressant medication, and transcutaneous electrical analgesia, in the treatment of chronic psychophysiological musculoskeletal back pain. This could be done using a standard factorial design, including a reasonably large number of subjects per experimental cell. Many of the previous studies have suffered from an inadequately low *N*. This need not always be the case, given that orthopedic, neurologic, and neurosurgical clinics often treat very large numbers of chronic pain patients. Again, appropriate consultation-liaison relationships between clinical psychologists and primary care physicians could provide very fruitful research possibilities in such settings as university medical centers, Veterans Administration hospitals, and community clinics.

Another major experimental weakness has been the lack of inferential statistics. Many of the investigations described in this chapter reported only descriptive statistics, such as percentages of patients who reported improvement. Such percentages are difficult to interpret without some procedure to determine the probability that such results could not have been due to chance or extraneous factors alone. Future studies would do well to use such procedures as analysis of variance, appropriate posthoc testing, and multivariate analysis of variance (see Chapter 25).

A related methodological topic is that of measurement of change. Many studies thus far have involved loosely conceptualized operational definitions of improvement. It would be well to focus on quantifiable outcome measures involving discrete units of behavior such as the amount of uptime, the distance pedaled on a stationary bicycle, and psychophysical measures. For good reason, the editors of the major journals have begun to favor studies that include *several* types of outcome measures (i.e., behavioral, physiological, and self-report). So far, very little research regarding the treatment of chronic pain has utilized multiple dependent measures. Moreover, further research needs to be done on refining the validity and reliability of outcome measures in this area.

Another potential area of inquiry would be an investigation of the efficacy of an outpatient operant treatment program for chronic pain. Thus far, no researchers have applied the pain unit concept to outpatient practice. Such research would have important practical implications, since outpatient therapy is typically much less expensive than inpatient treatment. A useful future study might compare the effectiveness of multiple-family group therapy with chronic pain patients and their families, compared to that of inpatient contingency management.

In addition to therapeutic techniques involving overt behavioral events, procedures involving covert processes, (i.e., cognitive behavior modification [Meichenbaum, 1977]) may hold some promise in the treatment of chronic pain. Although there is a growing literature on cognitive techniques in treating *acute* pain, very little research has been done on helping *chronic* pain patients modify their self-statements and internal dialogues. However, Holroyd, Andrasik, and Westbrook (1977) taught chronic tension headache patients to alter maladaptive cognitive responses. This included changing the cognitive cues which could trigger anxiety and tension and the cognitions immediately following such an episode. Compared to a biofeedback group and a control group, only the cognitive therapy group significantly improved in headache frequency, duration, and intensity and showed significant reductions in EMG activity. Further clinical research is needed to determine whether cognitive stress-management procedures could be used successfully as an adjunct to a comprehensive inpatient behavioral treatment program or as a major component of an outpatient treatment program for some types of chronic benign pain.

Finally, an important shortcoming of previous research has been the paucity of long-term follow-up data. Many of the studies have reported encouraging data for a short period of time, such as a four-week treatment period. However, it would be desirable to measure outcome several months and several years following the termination of the treatment program. Operant pain is typically a problem which has developed over a long period of time; it is probably correct to assume that it would take a long time to fully resolve such a problem. Moreover, clinical experience indicates that some types of chronic pain patients (e.g., conversion hysterics) respond strongly to placebo interventions. Such patients may initially respond very positively to *any* new treatment such as an electrical neurostimulator, but the pain usually returns. In order to rule out the placebo hypothesis, it is very important to observe the patient over a long period of time.

Thus, there is considerable room for further research. However, until more definitive studies are performed, the clinician may consider the following suggestions, based on both clinical experience and the research that has been completed to date. Moreover, as these techniques are attempted in clinical situations, it is incumbent upon the practitioner to collect outcome data.

First, a thorough behavioral and psychological assessment should be made of any given pain patient. If the clinician is experienced in MMPI interpretation, the instrument may be used to accurately describe the patient and designate particular psychological difficulties that may have important implications for treatment choice. In addition, a careful interview of both the patient and relevant family members should be performed to better determine the nature of the patient's pain. That is, is the pain primarily operant or respondent? Does the pain contain a muscular-tension component?

At this point, it appears that inpatient contingency management should be the treatment of choice for cases of operant pain, at least in the initial stages of treatment. A unit set up along the lines of Fordyce (1976) would be appropriate in this regard. The treatment should include an initial behavioral contract between the patient and the psychologist, contingency management performed by all the staff, a multiple-family group program on a daily basis, and time-contingent management of medications. For those operant pain patients who also have a muscular-tension component to their problem, EMG biofeedback training may be indicated.

Early in the patient's hospitalization, planning must begin for postdischarge life. This would be one focus of family therapy. Such intervention would be necessary in order to change the family's reinforcement of excessive invalid behavior. Several studies have examined family therapy approaches to chronic pain and general psychosomatic disorders. For example, Liebman, Honig, and Berger (1976) have presented a program combining behavior modification and family therapy in the treatment of chronic abdominal pain. The authors noted the importance of working with the family physician, given that a system consisting of the patient, the family, and the physician will sometimes unwittingly reinforce psychosomatic symptoms. The authors also emphasized the importance of behavioral monitoring of the symptoms, both as a part of the treatment process and as an outcome measure.

At least two studies have investigated marital therapy in the treatment of chronic pain. Sharpe and Meyer (1973) reported a case study in which both marital partners where involved in systematic desensitization for treating "cognitive sexual pain" on the part of one of the marital partners. Scheiderer and Bernstein (1976) suggested a procedure, based on a case study, for marital treatment of chronic back pain when one spouse refuses to engage directly in marital therapy. In such a case, unilateral marriage counseling may be used to teach the motivated client to become a "behavioral engineer" in dealing with an unmotivated spouse. In the case reported by Scheiderer and Bernstein, the wife suffered from chronic back pain and was willing to engage in treatment. Therapeutic techniques included progressive relaxation, cognitive restructuring, behavioral monitoring (including a functional behavioral analysis of the antecedent events, overt and covert behaviors, and consequences), positive "self-evaluative–assertion" statements, a behavioral weight-reduction program, operant techniques for improving communication and interaction with the husband, and strategies designed to increase the social activities of the patient and the couple. In learning how to deal with her husband, the patient was taught the behavioral techniques of differential reinforcement, shaping, and extinction.

In short, family therapy should be an important part of any pain treatment program. There are several ways of approaching such therapy, all of which deserve increased clinical and experimental focus. An inpatient or outpatient contingency-management program which only focuses on the identified patient is most likely doomed to failure in the long-run. Additionally, long-term, outpatient follow-up (e.g., eventually moving to infrequent booster sessions) is crucial for maintaining therapeutic change. Behavior therapy should extend to the family and the social environment in which the pain symptoms originally developed.

Reference Notes

1. Hockersmith, V. W. *A successful treatment program for chronic back pain patients.* Paper presented at the meeting of the American Psychological Association, Chicago, 1975.
2. Sternbach, R. A. Personal communication, 1975.
3. Gottlieb, H. J., Hockersmith, V. W., Koller, R., & Strite, L. C. *A successful treatment program for chronic back pain patients.* Paper presented at the meeting of the American Psychological Association, Chicago, 1975.

References

Anderson, T. P., Cole, T. M., Gullickson, G., Hudgens, A., & Roberts, A. H. Behavior modification of chronic pain: A treatment program by a multidisciplinary team. *Clinical Orthopaedics and Related Research,* 1977, *129,* 96–100.

Blumetti, R. E., & Modesti, L. M. Psychological predictors of success or failure of surgical intervention for intractable back pain. In J. J. Bonica & D. Albe-Fessard (Eds.), *Advances in pain research and therapy* (Vol. 1). New York: Raven Press, 1976.

Bonica, J. J. (Ed.). *Advances in neurology* (Vol. 4). New York: Raven Press, 1974.

Budzynski, T. H., & Stoyva, J. M. A biofeedback technique for teaching voluntary relaxation of the masseter. *Journal of Dental Research,* 1973, *52,* 116–119.

Cairns, D., & Pasino, J. A. Comparison of verbal reinforcement and feedback in the operant treatment of disability due to chronic low back pain. *Behavior Therapy,* 1977, *8,* 621–630.

Cairns, D., Thomas, L., Mooney, V., & Pace, J. B. A comprehensive treatment approach to chronic low back pain. *Pain,* 1976, *2,* 301–308.

Chaffin, D. G. Human strength capability and low back pain. *Journal of Occupational Medicine,* 1974, *16,* 248.

Fordyce, W. E. *Behavioral methods for chronic pain and illness.* St. Louis: C.V. Mosby, 1976.

Fordyce, W. E., Fowler, R. S., Lehmann, J. F., DeLateur, B., Sand, P. L., & Trieschmann, R. Operant conditioning in the treatment of chronic pain. *Archives of Physical Medicine and Rehabilitation,* 1973, *54,* 399–408.

Fordyce, W. E., & Steger, J. C. Chronic pain. In O. F. Pomerleau & J. P. Brady (Eds.), *Behavioral medicine: Theory and practice.* Baltimore: Williams & Wilkins, 1979.

Gannon, L., & Sternbach, R. A. Alpha enhancement as a treatment for pain: A case study. *Journal of Behavior Therapy and Experimental Psychiatry,* 1971, *2,* 209–213.

Gottlieb, H. J., Strite, L. C., Koller, R., Madorsky, A., Hockersmith, V. W., Kleeman, M., & Wagner, J. Comprehensive rehabilitation of patients having chronic low back pain. *Archives of Physical Medicine and Rehabilitation,* 1977, *58,* 101–108.

Grabel, J. A. Electromyographic study of low back muscle tension in subjects with and without chronic low back pain (Doctoral dissertation, United States International University, 1974). *Dissertation Abstracts Interna-*

tional, 1973, *34,* 2929B-2930B. (University Microfilms No. 73-29, 991).
Hendler, N., Derogatis, L., Avella, J., & Long, D. EMG biofeedback in patients with chronic pain. *Diseases of the Nervous System,* 1977, *38,* 505-509.
Holroyd, K. A., Andrasik, F., & Westbrook, T. Cognitive control of tension headache. *Cognitive Therapy and Research,* 1977, *1,* 121-134.
Hufft, R. EMG and x-ray evaluation of pelvic traction. *Orthopaedic Seminars.* Downey, Ca.: Rancho Los Amigos Hospital, 1975, 7.
Ignelzi, R. J., Sternbach, R. A., & Timmermans, G. The pain ward follow-up analyses. *Pain,* 1977, *3,* 277-280.
Kanfer, F. H. Self-management: Strategies and tactics. In A. P. Goldstein & F. H. Kanfer (Eds.), *Maximizing treatment gains: Transfer enhancement in psychotherapy.* New York: Academic Press, 1979.
Khatami, M., & Rush, J. A. A pilot study of the treatment of outpatients with chronic pain: Symptom control, stimulus control, and social system intervention. *Pain,* 1978, *5,* 163-172.
Liebman, R., Honig, P., & Berger, H. An integrated treatment program for psychogenic pain. *Family Process,* 1976, *15,* 397-405.
Mahoney, M. J., & Arnkoff, D. B. Self-management. In O. F. Pomerleau & J. P. Brady (Eds.), *Behavioral medicine: Theory and practice.* Baltimore: Williams & Wilkins, 1979.
Mahoney, M. J., & Thoresen, C. E. *Self-control: Power to the person.* Monterey, Ca.: Brooks Cole, 1974.
Meichenbaum, D. *Cognition and behavior modification: An integrative approach.* New York: Plenum, 1977.
Meichenbaum, D., & Turk, D. C. The cognitive-behavioral management of anxiety, anger, and pain. In P. O. Davidson (Ed.), *The behavioral management of anxiety, depression, and pain.* New York: Brunner Mazel, 1976.
Melzack, R. The McGill Pain Questionnaire: Major properties and scoring methods. *Pain,* 1975, *1,* 277-299.
Melzack, R., & Perry, C. Self-regulation of pain: The use of alpha-feedback and hypnotic training for the control of chronic pain. *Experimental Neurology,* 1975, *46,* 452-464.
Mooney, V., & Cairns, D. Management in the patient with chronic low back pain. *Orthopedic Clinics of North America.* 1978, *9,* 543-557.
Nagi, S. Z., Riley, L. E., & Newby, L. G. A social epidemiology of back pain in a general population. *Journal of Chronic Diseases,* 1973, *26,* 769-779.
Newman, R. I., Seres, J. L., Yospe, L. P., & Garlington, B. Multidisciplinary treatment of chronic pain: Long-term follow-up of low-back pain patients. *Pain,* 1978, *4,* 283-292.
Nouwen, A., & Solinger, J. W. The effectiveness of EMG biofeedback training in low back pain. *Biofeedback and Self-Regulation,* 1979, *4,* 103-111.
Peck, C. L., & Kraft, G. H. Electromyographic biofeedback for pain related to muscle tension. *Archives of Surgery,* 1977, *112,* 889-895.
Pelletier, K. R., & Peper, E. Developing a biofeedback model: Alpha EEG feedback as a means for pain control. *The International Journal of Clinical and Experimental Hypnosis,* 1977, *25,* 361-371.
Philips, C. A psychological analysis of tension headache. In S. Rachman (Ed.), *Advances in medical psychology.* Oxford: Pergamon Press, 1977. (a)
Philips, C. The modification of tension headache pain using E.M.G. biofeedback. *Behaviour Research and Therapy,* 1977, *15,* 119-129. (b)
Pilowsky, I. Dimensions of hypochondriasis. *British Journal of Psychiatry,* 1967, *113,* 89-93.
Scheiderer, E. G., & Bernstein, D. A. A case of chronic back pain and the "unilateral" treatment of marital problems. *Journal of Behavior Therapy and Experimental Psychiatry,* 1976, *7,* 47-50.
Schwartz, G. E. Biofeedback self-regulation and the patterning of physiological responses. *American Scientist,* 1975, *63,* 314-324.
Segal, J. Biofeedback as a medical treatment. *Journal of the American Medical Association,* 1975, *232,* 179-180.
Seres, J. L., & Newman, R. I. Results of treatment of chronic low-back pain at the Portland Pain Center. *Journal of Neurosurgery,* 1976, *45,* 32-36.
Sharpe, R., & Meyer, V. Modification of "cognitive sexual pain" by the spouse under supervision. *Behavior Therapy,* 1973, *4,* 285-287.
Smith, G. M., Egbert, L. D., Markowitz, R. A., Mosteller, F., & Beecher, H. K. An experimental pain method sensitive to morphine in man: The submaximum effort tourniquet technique. *Journal of Pharmacology and Experimental Therapeutics,* 1966, *154,* 324-332.
Sternbach, R. A. *Pain: A psychophysiological analysis.* New York: Academic Press, 1968.
Sternbach, R. A. *Pain patients: Traits and treatment.* New York: Academic Press, 1974.
Sternbach, R. A., Deems, L. M., Timmermans, G., & Huey, L. Y. On the sensitivity of the tourniquet pain test. *Pain,* 1977, *3,* 105-110.
Sternbach, R. A., Murphy, R. W., Timmermans, G., Greenhoot, J. H., & Akeson, W. H. Measuring the severity of clinical pain. In J. J. Bonica (Ed.), *Advances in neurology* (Vol. 4). New York: Raven Press, 1974.
Sternbach, R. A., Wolf, S. R., Murphy, R. W., & Akeson, W. H. Aspects of chronic low back pain. *Psychosomatics,* 1973, *14* 52-56. (a)
Sternbach, R. A., Wolf, S. R., Murphy, R. W., & Akeson,

W. H. Traits of pain patients: The low-back "loser." *Psychosomatics,* 1973, *14,* 226–229. (b)

Stoyva, J. M., & Budzynski, T. H. Cultivated low arousal —an anti-stress response? In L. V. DiCara (Ed.), *Recent advances in limbic and autonomic nervous system research.* New York: Plenum, 1974.

Swanson, D. W., Maruta, T., & Swenson, W. M. Results of behavior modification in the treatment of chronic pain. *Psychosomatic Medicine,* 1979, *41,* 55-61.

Timmermans, G., & Sternbach, R. A. Factors of human chronic pain: An analysis of personality and pain reaction variables. *Science,* 1974, *184,* 806-808.

Turk, D. C., & Genest, M. Regulation of pain: The application of cognitive and behavioral techniques for prevention and remediation. In P. Kendall & S. Hollon (Eds.), *Cognitive-behavioral interventions: Theory, research, and procedures.* New York: Academic Press, 1979.

Wiltse, L. L., & Rocchio, P. D. Preoperative psychological tests as predictors of success of chemonucleolysis in the treatment of low-back syndrome. *The Journal of Bone and Joint Surgery,* 1975, *57,* 478-483.

Ziesat, H. A. Correlates of the tourniquet ischemia pain ratio. *Perceptual and Motor Skills,* 1978, *47,* 147-150.

17

Treatment of the Chronically Ill Geriatric Patient

SANDRA M. LEVY

It would be very easy to assume a zealous and missionary tone when addressing the issue of psychosocial treatment of the geriatric patient. An undertone of righteous indignation over the neglect of the elderly runs through much of the literature on this topic in recent years. Smith (1976) points out that the elderly are portrayed as "... aimless, apathetic, debilitated, disruptive, hypochondriacal, insecure, ... out of control, sluggish, seclusive, and temperamental [p. 333]." Smith's article was a review of the content of prescription drug advertisements in medical journals, and indeed somatic therapies generally have been the treatment of choice for cognitive and mood disorders in the elderly (Kral, 1976). Recently, the neglect of this population as a target group for psychological intervention has received much attention (Knight, 1978–1979; Storandt, Siegler, & Elias, 1978), and will not be reviewed in this chapter. (For a general discussion of current modes of intervention with the elderly, see Eisdorfer & Stotsky, 1977.)

Although the focus of this chapter will be on the treatment of chronically ill, institutionalized geriatric patients, it has been estimated (Bennett, 1973) that at least one-third of the elderly living in the community are socially isolated, showing poor social adjustment, maladaptive behavior patterns, and inadequate cognitive functioning. Ernst, Beran, Safford, and Klienhauz (1978) reviewed both the animal studies, as well as literature on human functioning, related to the effects of social isolation. These authors suggested a circularity of decrements leading to cognitive dysfunction and signs of brain dysfunction. They traced the possible relationship between decrease in sensitivity of the sensory receptors leading to a decrement in amount of stimuli reaching the brain, which in turn might lead to cellular atrophy of cortical tissue. The latter is manifested in memory and general ability failure, eliciting signs of disorientation, anxiety, and numerous specific fears. The results of these feelings of vulnerability and an inability to cope lead the elderly further into depression, apathy, and withdrawal, heightening the isolation and general decrement of sensory stimulation, and continuing the downward spiral of dysfunction. However speculative the relationships in this cycle

Medical Psychology
Contributions to Behavioral Medicine

ISBN 0-12-565960-1

might be (and clearly, the connections are complex, and undoubtedly bidirectional in nature), the problem of the effects of isolation for both the elderly in the community and institutions is very great. And while we will not be focusing on the population of elderly living in the community, mention should be made of a variety of innovative, community-based programs involving network building for the old (Bennett, 1973; Garrison & Howe, 1976; Pattison, 1973).

Recent attempts have been made to maintain the chronically ill and handicapped old within the community, and facilities such as day care centers for the elderly (Weissert, 1976) and community-based foster home care for minimally impaired geriatric patients (Bradshaw, Vonderhaan, Keeney, Tyler, & Harris, 1976) have been developed. Although writers such as Tobin and Lieberman (1976), in their longitudinal follow-up study of nursing home residents, argue strongly against "premature institutionalization" and propose the development of alternative community placements, very little systematic research has been performed examining the outcomes of such community placements.

Despite these new efforts, the primary location for treatment of the elderly is the institution. There is widespread belief among gerontologists that only 4-5% of the old actually live in institutions. However, Kastenbaum and Candy (1973), as well as others (Ingram & Barry, 1977; Lesnoff-Caravaglia, 1978-1979), have demonstrated that 20-30% of the elderly in this country die in institutions, and have argued that if the geriatric patients die there, they must also have lived there. While this point might be disputed, it is clear from the figures that if an elderly person lives long enough, the probability is rather high that that person will end up in a long-term care facility.

As indicated earlier, the primary choice of "treatment" for the institutionalized geriatric patient has been pharmacological intervention. Newer treatment approaches, however, are emerging. After first outlining a general framework within which to view the person and the treatment context, a critical review of these newer techniques, as well as the traditional approaches, will be discussed in this chapter, focusing on issues related to care of the dying. A final section will be devoted to research issues related to the measurement of process and outcome in the treatment of geriatric patients.

Framework for Viewing the Geriatric Patient in a Context: A Dialectical Perspective

A Holistic View of the Person

When studying human behavior, geriatric or otherwise, it is important to draw a framework within which to understand the varieties of functioning. While space constraints do not permit elaboration in this regard, an attempt will be made to draw a picture of holistic functioning within a defining context.

In an article concerned with the definition of the field of behavioral medicine, Schwartz and Weiss (1978) emphasized a shift from a dualistic conception of psychosomatic functioning, to a conception of biobehavioral holism—the view of the healthy or ill human as an integrated *gestalt,* with the "whole being greater than the sum of the parts [p. 4]." Because a dualistic conception of human functioning is so engrained in Western thinking, it is very difficult to reconceptualize along holistic lines. For example, recently, while Gentry (1978) distinguished between psychosomatic and somatopsychic disorders manifested in the elderly, he still drew a clear distinction between psychological and physical factors and their relationship. There is a view of human structure which undercuts this dualism, however, that Schwartz and Weiss attempted to grasp. (Gendlin, 1962; Merleau-Ponty, 1962, 1963). Within this view, the lines between *psyche* and *soma* are fundamentally blurred, and even reflexive functioning is integrated and transformed by human intention. While in the grossest form of pathology (such as in brain damage) this integration breaks down, Merleau-Ponty argues that the total dissolution of human structure does not occur until death [Merleau-Ponty, 1963, p. 203].

The observer variable of typifying patient behavior, colored by the nature of the assessment context, was discussed in Chapter 9. The construction of reality (literally what is perceived) was portrayed as a bidirectional process. Berger and Luckmann (1966) described the dialectic process involved in defining the environment and in turn, being defined by the context that is constructed. That basic distinction also holds in terms of the assessment and treatment of patients. The construction of a reality is imposed, shaping the expectancy and intervention strategies of the psychologist.

The view of the human organism as an integrated, holistic structure or system within a larger context, that in turn shapes expectancies and defines possibilities for both patient and caretaker, serves as the framework for our discussion of the treatment targets of geriatric medicine—the geriatric patient and the institutional milieu.

Treatment Targets: Coping Self and Its Context

As was discussed in Chapter 9, certain biological shifts (such as sensory and hormonal decrements) and the eventual waning of energy are apparently essential aspects of human aging. The major therapeutic goals for the psychologist treating the geriatric patients are, therefore, to remediate excess disability (dysfunction over and above physiological necessity) and facilitate coping within the environmental context. Taking an environmental perspective, Lawton (1972) defined adaptation as the balance between environmental demand and organismic possibility. Optimally, a person–environment fit should be sought which will support the functioning of the increasingly frail geriatric patient. As Mechanic (1974) pointed out, the relationship between social structure and personal adaptation has until recently been somewhat neglected. Because decrement is inevitable for the geriatric patient, a major concern in this chapter is with the context as a potentially prophylactic milieu. After a brief review of pathologies within the geriatric population, strategies to alter these dysfunctions are critically reviewed.

Treatment of the Geriatric Patient: Excess Disabilities and Reversible Dementia

The Foci of Treatment

The basic emphasis in this chapter is on ameliorating excess disabilities in the geriatric patient from a behavioral contextual point of view. Therefore, an extended discussion of diseases of aging is not attempted. (For a complete discussion of functional and organic disorders in the elderly, see Cole, 1970; Epstein, 1976; Freeman, 1965; Lipton, 1976; Mendlewicz, 1976; and related chapters in Birren & Schaie, 1977. The reader is also referred to Chapter 9 of this volume for a review of brain and mood disorders in the geriatric patient.) Intrinsic changes that occur with aging can also lead to dysfunctional behaviors in the elderly and contribute to the diagnosis of a disease process. For example, Stare (1977) described physiological changes in digestion with age, including the production of less saliva, reduction in sensitivity of the taste and olfactory receptor cells, and reduction of the quantity of digestive enzymes. Because of these physiological changes, as well as social factors such as isolation, and frequent depression and apathy, many elderly are severely malnourished. This malnutrition can, in turn, produce behavioral and mood changes, such as irritability, depression, confusion, and an inability to make decisions (Sherwood, 1973). These manifestations of semistarvation are either tolerated as typical of old age, or earn the geriatric patient the diagnosis of chronic brain syndrome.

A number of the disorders treated in other chapters of this book, such as cancer, hypertension, and cardiovascular disease, are also diseases of aging, but most of the treatment research related to these disease entities does not deal with patients over 70 years of age. For example, in a study of postinfarction behavior of cardiac patients reported by Garrity (1973), the average age of the patients was 54; and in a study concerned with the relinquishing of the sick role after heart surgery, Brown and Rawlinson (1975) reported ages ranging from 25 to 64 years. While this state of affairs is not always the case, these examples are typical.

Therefore, because of the general dearth of valid studies concentrating on patients over 70, as well as because of the major interest in this chapter on facilitation of coping behavior through social and environmental manipulation, no further discussion of physical disorders associated with the geriatric population is provided. The disorders of most concern remain those discussed in the geriatric assessment chapter of this text: Brain disease due to degenerative process or vascular change and depression. The balance of this chapter focuses on behavioral changes in the geriatric patient through negative intervention (removing noxious stimuli creating iatrogenic disorders), interpersonal stimulation (e.g., providing remotivation treatment), and alteration of the environment into a prophylactic, supportive milieu.

Psychopharmacology and the Elderly Patient

In a community study of drug-taking behavior (including alcohol consumption) of the elderly, Gutmann (1977) listed the four most frequently prescribed categories of drugs given to the elderly: cardiovascular preparations, tranquilizers, diuretics, and sedatives-hypnotics. He also reported a finding of relatively heavy consumption of alcohol and over-the-counter preparations. Gutmann concluded that while it is frequently presumed that the elderly "receive their drugs through friends and relatives [p. 48]," it appeared that that was not the case. In his study population, at least, those elderly received their drugs from their physicians. Only .4% reported taking prescription medication more frequently than they were advised to by their physicians, and almost all users of psychotropic drugs (98.7%) reported that they obtained their sedatives and antidepressants from their family doctors, and took them as prescribed. Gutmann pointed out that while the large majority of elderly used drugs legally and appropriately, the real danger centers on the ingestion of drugs in combination. Further, less than 5% of the elderly were abstainers from any drugs, and roughly half of these community elderly used drugs in combination with over-the-counter medications as well as with alcohol. The major point here, though, is that the physicians prescribed the drugs, and that the elderly ran the real risk of potentially damaging overmedication.

While this danger seems to be quite real among community elderly, institutionalized geriatric patients apparently are also at risk for side effects of overprescription—perhaps more so because of their frail condition.

Much has been written in recent years about the effects of prescription drugs among the elderly, and the differential nature of drug metabolism in this group (Eisdorfer & Fann, 1976; Fann, Wheless, & Richman, 1976; Hall, 1975; Kline & Angst, 1975; Krupka & Vener, 1979). In a chapter concerned with the effects of psychotherapeutic chemical agents on aged patients, Friedel (1977) discussed alterations of typical pharmacological action in geriatric patients. Generally, the blood level of a chemical agent is directly proportional to the amount of drug absorbed and the time it takes to eliminate the drug from the body, while the blood level is inversely related to the volume in which the drug is distributed and to the time lapse between doses of identical quantity. Absorption, distribution, metabolism, and excretion of chemicals, however, alter with age. For example, most psychotherapeutic agents are lipid soluble, meaning that they have an affinity for fat tissue. With age, the adipose tissue-lean tissue ratio increases, and therefore the volume of distribution of lipid soluable drugs increases. This fact, coupled with decreases in excretory capacity, due to age-related decreases in renal function, strongly suggest the need for altered, smaller dosages in geriatric patients. (See Fann, 1976, and Kapnick, 1978, for a thorough discussion of related issues.)

It is not overly surprising that drug-related iatrogenic disorders frequently occur in institutionalized geriatric patients. Recent studies (Covert, Rodrigues, & Solomon, 1977; Howard, Strong, & Strong, 1977; Miller, 1975) have examined medication procedures in chronic care institutions, and have found negative and rather widespread effects of chemical, as well as mechanical restraints of patients. For example, Howard *et al.* (1977) studied the medication of 98 patients in a proprietary nursing home and found that a total of 536 drugs had been prescribed for the 98 patients, the average number of drugs totalling 5.5 per patient. The average number of PRN (*pro re nata,* or as needed) drug orders left by physicians was 3.2 per patient. Twenty-two patients in this facility were receiving eight or more drugs, and one patient was receiving a total of 16 different drugs! These authors pointed out that the physicians left PRN orders for cathartic, analgesic, psychotropic, cardiovascular, and hypnotic medications. Some drugs were inappropriately ordered PRN with essentially no medical follow-up.

Covert *et al.* (1977) also discussed the side effects of mechanical restraints in geriatric patients (for example, patients strapped tightly into their wheelchairs), including impaired circulation, compressed nerves, skin abrasions, and agitation. Miller (1975) reviewed the biochemical, physiological, and behavioral effects of immobilization including lethargy, polydypsia and polyuria, and kineseopathologic sequellae such as inability to coordinate extremities in order to stand, etc. Covert *et al.* suggested alternatives to chemical and physical immobilization (frequently administered because of management problems), such as attempts at reality orientation, sensory stimulation, exercise, and remotivation therapy. Some of these alternative treatments are reviewed in the following. The major point to be made is that, as Gutmann (1977) pointed out in his community study, the pharmaceutical industry, mass media, physicians, and the patient's family have become locked into a medication cycle in which the problems of the human condition are increasingly medicalized. While this is true throughout our society, for the hospitalized, deteriorated geriatric patient, the dangers of overmedicalizing rather than behaviorally intervening, or even expecting change through psychological intervention, is very real.

Psychological Treatments

Review of the Evidence for the Efficacy of a Host of New Approaches In the last 10 to 15 years, a variety of psychological, as opposed to medical, approaches have emerged as forms of treatment for the clinically ill elderly. Examples of some of the more exotic forms include pet therapy (Levinson, 1970), music therapy (Shapiro, 1969), and wine therapy (Kastenbaum & Slater, 1964). The author of a recent review article (Sparacino, 1978–1979) concerned with individual psychotherapy for the aged, concluded that while widespread pessimism on the part of mental health workers has decreased in recent years, the state of the outcome research concerned with the efficacy of various forms of individual treatment has remained poor. For example, the results from a recent study of the effects of brief psychotherapy in the treatment of emotional disorders in physically ill geriatric patients (Godbole & Verinis, 1974) suggested that patients receiving some form of psychotherapy showed more improvement than patients receiving no psychotherapy. Unfortunately, the nontreatment group received no attention placebo and the ratings of impairment were not done blindly. In general, many reports of outcome studies are anecdotal, "how to" expositions, providing clinical case findings, but reporting no controlled comparison of the effectiveness of differential approaches.

Goldfarb (1953, 1955, 1969), one of the earlier writers in the area of psychotherapeutic intervention and group process with the elderly, emphasized capitalizing on the geriatric patient's heightened dependency needs. Goldfarb suggested that therapists present themselves as omnipotent, providing emotional gratification and side-stepping the defensive rigidity in the institutionalized old. Although Goldfarb reported success of his dynamically oriented, group treatment for institutionalized elderly, the exact change mechanisms remained unspecified, and carefully controlled studies, again have not been reported.

An opposite point of view with respect to passive dependency in geriatric patients is held by Schulz (1976). In four separate treatment conditions, patient control over therapeutic visits was manipulated: In group 1, the patients controlled when the visits occurred; in Group 2, the patients were able to predict the visits; in Group 3 the patients received visits randomly; and in Group 4 the patients received no visits. Schulz found that Groups 1, 2, and 3 all improved in functioning compared to Group 4, but Groups 1 and 2 also showed improvement in mood and physical health states. He concluded that perhaps *any* therapy if controlled by the geriatric patient *or* offered at predictable intervals would be potentially effective.[1] Obviously, the current state of the research does not clarify the issue of dependency versus control needs among elderly patients, and further work needs to be done in this area.

Brody, Kleban, Lawton, and Silverman (1971) reported short-term success in reducing "excess disabilities" by tailoring highly individualized treatments for a group of hospitalized geriatric patients. Their individualized treatments included psychosocial, medical, and behavioral forms of intervention, but the authors did not clearly specify what actually was done in their experimental group. Although the authors reported a reduction in excess disabilities (but not medical impairments) in comparison with a control group, these gains were not maintained at a 9-month follow-up (Brody, Kleban, Lawton, & Moss, 1974). While there were many methodological problems with this study (such as biased ward ratings, with these ratings given to outside, independent raters to judge), their conclusion that the reduction of excess disabilities in daily functional activities cannot be maintained without sustained effort is consistent with other findings discussed.

Currently, Reality Orientation Therapy (ROT) for geriatric patients (Barnes, 1974; Browne & Ritter, 1972; Citrin & Dixon, 1977; Drummond, Kirchhoff, & Scarbrough, 1978; Folsom, 1968; Taulbee & Folsom, 1966) and Remotivation Therapy (Mueller & Atlas, 1972; Thralow & Watson, 1974; Toepfer, Bicknell, & Shaw, 1974) have received a great deal of attention by researchers and clinicians. Unfortunately, again the rationale is sound for these approaches, but the evidence is weak for long-term effectiveness. ROT, a blend of individual and milieu approaches, involves a classroom, didactic approach, aimed at bringing the regressed geriatric patient back into the everyday temporal and spatial world. The technique includes homely means such as maps and calendars and a "reality orientation board" upon which the name of the facility, picture of the U.S. President, etc., is hung. While Barnes (1974) reported no significant improvement after the sessions ended, and Citrin and Dixon (1977) reported a limited change (information retained improved but there was no behavioral change), Browne and Ritter (1972) reported "marked improvement" in 16 geriatric patients. (Unfortunately, no quantified data were reported in the latter case.) A study by Brook, Degun, and Mather (1975) manipulated the presence or absence of therapists in two groups of reality orientation patients, both of which were provided the same reality materials. The patients were rated every two weeks by nurses blind to their treatment condition, and the authors reported continued improvement only in the group which continued to interact with the therapist over the 16-week course of treatment. It may be that at least some patients benefit from intensive reality orientation, but the state of the evidence does not now support a wholesale application of this small group approach to institutionalized geriatric patients.

Although admittedly, most of the patients involved in these efforts were severely regressed in terms of cognition and behavior and despite methodological flaws in the various studies, the massive effort on the part of the staff (frequently involving twice daily meetings, seven days a week) did not seem to have paid off in terms of long-range change in the patients.

Remotivation Therapy, a similar kind of group approach, is designed to stimulate geriatric patients' interest in the world around them by having patients share a poem or story and relate the content to their past life and to the present, outside world. Remotivation Therapy has actually been practiced in chronic care institutions since the

[1] In a follow-up study (Schulz & Hanusa, 1978), the authors reported no positive long-term effects attributable to the interventions. In fact, those who had initially benefited from the control and predictability enhancing manipulations of the original study showed clear decline in physical health and morale, while those in the control groups who had shown no original benefit in functioning remained stable at follow-up. The authors pointed out the need to take into account long-term impact when experimenting in field settings, and discussed the ethical issues involved in that method of study. Here, the latter included the potentially destructive effect of negating a sense of self-efficacy by supplying no controllable substitute after the experiment ended.

1950s, but only recently has it been utilized with nursing home patients. Although the evidence is also weak that this group approach is effective with geriatric patients, Toepfer *et al.* (1974) suggested reviewing the technique in behavioral terms, and translating some aspects of remotivation therapy into an operant technique. For example, an integral part of the remotivation sessions is termed "Sharing The World We Live In." Toepfer *et al.* suggested that the leader positively reinforce appropriate verbal responses, while extinguishing inappropriate ones. Although the suggestion seems obvious, and their writing has heuristic value in terms of stimulating operationally defined interventions and more carefully controlled outcome measures, to the best of this writer's knowledge, operant techniques have not been applied within this intervention framework. Thralow and Watson (1974) reported the use of elementary school children as remotivaters paired with 36 experimental geriatric patients, comparing outcome with 36 control patients. The program lasted for 20 weeks, and while there were some significant differences between the two groups at an 11-week follow-up (on three of nine nurses' ratings concerned with ward behavior), at 20 weeks the significant differences had disappeared. In general, the aggregate of research to date concerned with the long-term effects of remotivation on patients' behavior is not encouraging, and more carefully controlled research needs to be done in order to determine what types of patients might benefit most from this relatively inexpensive (lay-administered) form of intervention.

Wine therapy appears to be one of the more promising forms of intervention with geriatric patients (Chien, Stotsky, & Cole, 1973; Mishara, Kastenbaum, Baker & Patterson, 1975). Kastenbaum and Slater (1964) found that while both wine and juice provided at a social hour enhanced group participation, patients in the wine group showed significantly greater group involvement. As these authors pointed out, wine has social meaning for many, and may have considerably less deleterious physical effects than other chemical sedatives and tranquilizers. Chien *et al.* (1973) also found similar results with 64 nursing home patients receiving measured doses of beer or wine. It would seem at the least that this form of intervention should be carefully examined as a facilitator of more appropriate social behavior.

Milieu Therapy and the Effects of Altering the Ecology of the Institution: Behavioral Prosthetics to Operant Shaping of Behavior The alteration of the total milieu obviously requires effort, money, and staff participation. Gottesman (1973) reported that chronically institutionalized elderly patients began to work, have money, become more socially aware, and were less "symptomatic" in an adequately funded institute with a supportive staff. As was discussed at some length in Chapter 9, patient behavior appears to be a function, at least in part, of the architectural facility (Cluff & Campbell, 1975; Ostrander, 1973), and that even the arrangement of furniture can either facilitate or impede social interaction (Lipman & Slater, 1977). An example of an environmental manipulation involving geriatric patients was reported by Cornbleth (1977). Wandering and nonwandering patients were assigned to protected (locked) or nonprotected wards. The wandering patients improved on a physical measure (range of motion) on only the protected ward; on the other hand, while the nonwanderers decreased in function on that physical measure on the protected ward, they improved functionally in the less protected environment. Generally, wanderers showed less improvement overall, and the author concluded that wandering, itself, may be a negative prognostic indicator. At any rate, there was differential patient response to environmental manipulation depending on pretreatment behavioral status. Mishara (1978) also found a differential response to either a token economy manipulation or a total milieu, supportive arrangement. In the token economy condition, patients who were characterized as less institutionalized, in better physical condition, and motivated to engage in target behaviors improved. In the milieu condition, geriatric patients who originally did not respond in an interview, and who were generally passive, showed more improvement.

Interestingly, in that study reported by Mishara,

there was no improvement in verbal behavior in either condition. Generally, the patients did not talk to one another. Lubinski (1978–1979) pointed out in a review of recent research on verbal communication among the elderly, that there is not only a paucity of communication among institutionalized, chronically ill elderly, but also generally little staff interest in whether or not patients talk. Barton (Note 1) reported lack of reinforcement contingencies for social behavior among nursing home patients (as opposed to staff reinforcement for nondisruptive behavior), and in a report of the results of an attempt to use an operant technique to condition the verbal behavior of geriatric patients, Hoyer, Kafer, Simpson, and Hoyer (1974) discussed the low priority among staff to change the social behavior in aged residents.

During the past several years, in fact, a great deal of work has been done with geriatric patients within an operant conditioning framework (Cautela, 1966; Hoyer, 1973; Hoyer, Mishara, & Riedel, 1975; Mishara, Robertson, & Kastenbaum, 1973). (See Cautela & Mansfield, 1977.) In a seminal chapter on "behavioral prosthetics" and the elderly, Lindsley (1964) suggested the use of a free operant conditioning laboratory for diagnostic purposes among geriatric patients. Testing the functional parameters of environmental stimuli in a highly controlled setting would allow the psychologist to describe behavioral possibilities, predict change, implement stimulus contingencies, and evaluate patient behavior. Prosthetic environments are those which supply artificial devices in order to optimize and extend potential functioning. For example, response devices that amplify force, such as automatic doors, or that provide amplification of response topography, such as widely spaced telephone buttons, could be provided to enhance the geriatric patient's range of potential functioning.

Returning once more to the notion of staff expectancy, and the negotiation of behavioral possibilities, Goldstein (1971) described a "tacit agreement" between patients and staff. While the patients in his study tended to present themselves as ill and passive in order to be taken care of, staff tended to push for independence of functioning. There was a tacit agreement, however, between staff and patients that as long as the patients were "good," the staff would not be "mean," "send them away," or otherwise deprive them of basic sustenance. Strauss (1978), in an excellent chapter concerned with the "silent bargains" that occur on geriatric wards, amplifies Goldstein's clinical observations. Due to lack of funding and sparsity of staff, patients tend to be managed on a tight schedule. These elderly patients are frequently in pain and are also socially isolated. The silent bargain to which Strauss refers involves the willingness to tolerate pain at intervals, and to fit their needs into a staff routine, in return for small favors and social contact. Strauss describes this mutual negotiation process between staff and patients in some detail. Certainly, this social process would be important to examine, both as a one-way behavioral shaping process, as well as a two-way social interaction.

Humanizing Dying: The Hospice Movement and Palliative Care

There is very little to say with scientific certainty about dying. Perhaps, as Kastenbaum (1975) has suggested, it is an inherently mysterious topic, finally impenetrable by scientific probing. While that is probably true, there would seem to be some empirically based questions that could be raised—such as disease, demographic, and environmental sources of variance on levels of stress for the dying patient and family—that are not being examined. Kalish (1978) pointed out that while the literature was filled with advice on how to die and how to work with the dying, there is a dearth of careful analyses based on systematically defined qualitative and quantitative data. And while it is true that dying is not unique to the elderly, it is a clinical issue most appropriately dealt with in relation to patients at this end of the life spectrum. Yet, in a recent, definitive handbook on the psychology of aging (Birren & Schaie, 1977), and in an excellent text on the clinical psychology of aging (Storandt *et al.*, 1978), not a word can be found about care of the dying. (In the chapter on assessments in Birren and Schaie's edited handbook, there is a small section on predicting mortality, and that literature was reviewed in this text in Chapter 9.) Therefore, this section raises questions rather than provides answers.

In a perusal of relevant medical journals, it is clear that medical attitudes and practice related to the dying are changing (Agate, 1973; Cassell, 1973; Committee on Medicine in Society, 1973; Noyes, Jochimson, & Travis, 1977). Communication with dying patients is becoming more open and there is increasing support among physicians for the omission of life-prolonging treatments.

One particular ethical issue with clinical implications tends to be repeatedly addressed: Should the patient be told if his or her illness is terminal (Weir, 1977). Kalish (1978) reported data from interview research that suggested that while only roughly half of the respondents would tell another that the other was dying, more than 70% wished that they themselves would be told the truth. While the validity of all interview-derived data must be viewed with some skepticism, this was, at least, a first attempt to uncover differential response tendencies based on ethnic and other demographic characteristics. (Only 60% of Mexican-Americans, for example, wished to be told if their own disease was fatal.)

The many researchable issues in the area of psychological treatments (and palliative or supportive care) for the dying geriatric patient include the following:

1. Environmental parameters that make a difference in the dying process for at least some types of patients. For example, the hospice movement (Saunders, 1973; Woodson, 1978), modeled on the St. Christopher's Hospice in England, has received much attention in this country in the last few years. But the actual effects of a small facility housing only terminally ill patients, in contrast to home care for the dying, for example, has not been systematically studied to date.

2. Differential effects of palliative treatment (for example, the effectiveness of Brompton's mixture (containing a variable amount of morphine, 10 mg of cocaine, 2.5 ml of ethyl alcohol, 5 ml of syrup, and a variable amount of chloroform water) in terminal cancer patients differing by disease site, personality configuration, mood states, as well as environmental support).

3. The use of support groups, such as the Shanti Volunteers (Garfield & Clark, 1978), as potentially effective care providers for some who are dying.

This list does not contain all of the potential research issues. Clearly, the extant research does not reflect the importance of this area. If, indeed, nearly 20 to 30% of the population dies within institutions (Kastenbaum & Candy, 1973), and 70 to 80% dies somewhere else, the exploration of the social and environmental parameters that make a difference in terms of psychological support in human treatment of the dying remains an important area for future exploration.

Major Research Controversies: What to Measure and How

It should be clear from the discussion in this chapter, as well as issues that were discussed in Chapter 9, that in many respects the aged in general, and the geriatric patient in particular, are distinct from the chronologically younger, and later cohorts. Issues of measurement—both what to measure and how to measure it—remain unanswered.

For example, with respect to the nature of pathology in the geriatric patient, is what is pathological at one stage of life necessarily pathological at another? Is there a survival value for some forms of pathology in the old? There are some findings, including cross-cultural ones, that suggest that hostility, aggression—even paranoia—have survival value among the very old (Gutmann, 1975; Tobin & Lieberman, 1976). While certainly paranoid tendencies are maladaptive in early and midlife, it may be that suspicion and hostility facilitate self-definition and foster survival in those who are physically frail. In addition, anger may help counteract the effects of "institutionalism," or the apathy and complete dependence upon institutional support that frequently develops in those who live in chronic care facilities. At any rate, the whole general issue of continuity of personality, as well as pathology across the life cycle, is currently unresolved.

Further, is there any unique pathology associated with aging, per se? Does the inevitable experience of bereavement and loss at the end of life create unique forms of pathology in the elderly patient in terms of content and symptoms? Is "masked" depression in the geriatric patient unique to that category? If there is unique pathology, then the training of psychologists as diagnosticians and caregivers is currently incomplete in most training settings.

Aside from research issues related to the content of pathology, and in addition to the cohort- and age-specific issues related to the assessment of pathology discussed earlier in Chapter 9, the nature of the process of treating the elderly may in fact be essentially different than the process involved in treating later cohorts or younger persons. With respect to intergenerational effects related to treatment, are there unique process variables that need to be monitored, and if so, what are the parameters that define the uniqueness? Are there special kinds of relationship issues between an inevitably younger therapist and a geriatric patient (special "transference- countertransference" issues) that need to be assessed as interfering or facilitating factors in the change process? Some of these issues, such as the nature of behavioral pathology and the continuity of personality, *may* be less important as the geriatric patient deteriorates into a more vegetative existence (Butler & Lewis, 1977).

As was discussed earlier in Chapter 9, given the cohort, aging, and time of testing differences in response to standard measuring instruments, and given the possibility of unique processes occurring within behavioral and cognitive intervention among the very old (such as Butler's [1963] notion of reminiscence), then it follows that special measuring instruments need to be devised in order to monitor shifts in the therapeutic relationship over time and the outcome of differential intervention strategies.

Finally, in addition to the nature of pathology, and the assessment of therapeutic process, considerations of study design with the elderly patient need to be addressed. What should not be surprising at this point is that the issues of cohort and age differences that have been discussed here are rarely dealt with in the general psychological literature. For example, Frank (1979), in a review of the state of outcome research, did not mention these issues at all. In a recent symposium, Hoyer (Note 2) suggested the use of small-*N* or single subject designs as being most appropriate with the elderly patient. Because there is a wide range of intraindividual and interindividual variability found in older patients (Hoyer, 1974), the common practice of large-*N*, between groups designs, with the averaging of group behavior, frequently masks significant individual change when it occurs. While certainly this suggestion is not unique to the geriatric area, too often possibilities for creative assessment of change in the institutional setting are overlooked.

While the aged (like the poor) will always be with us (and more so with the aid of developing medical technology), we are only just beginning to understand the unique differences within the geriatric population and to develop age- and cohort-appropriate treatment approaches for this population.

Before closing this chapter, a comment needs to be made about its brevity. Although an additional number of studies could have been detailed, and thus, the body as a whole could have been lengthened, the substantive contribution would not have been the greater. The thinness of these pages is probably the best indicator of how little good work has been done, and how much needs to be done, on the problems of psychological treatment of the elderly in general and the ill geriatric patient in particular.

Ronald Blythe (1979), in a remarkable article about growing old in modern society, contrasts the process with that in earlier periods of history. Then, life's span was very brief and the common fate of a brief span created a sense of urgency, anxiety, swift-moving ambition, or piety—depending on one's character. But now, the old live on, beyond usefulness and beyond the value of those around them.

> So altered are we that it sometimes seems we are reaching the stage when we may have to announce

ourselves to death, and may find its avoidance of us hurtful and neglectful. In hospitals up and down the land lie the finished lives that have been cut down [p. 36].

We began this chapter by eschewing righteous indignation—and so, we will end it that way. But it would seem clear that much in the way of sound research on the management of cognitive and behavioral dysfunction in the elderly needs to be carried out, and training within the area of geriatric medical psychology needs to lay the foundation for both the research and treatment of this population. It is hoped that in the next edition of this text, this chapter will be twice as long as the present one.

Reference Notes

1. Barton, E. *Apparent staff reinforcement contingencies for nursing home resident behavior.* Paper presented at the 86th Annual Meeting of the American Psychological Association, Toronto, Ontario, Canada, 1978.
2. Hoyer, W. *Design considerations in the assessment of psychotherapy with the elderly.* Paper presented at the Gerontological Society Meeting, Dallas, Texas, November, 1978.

References

Agate, J. Care of the dying in geriatric departments. *Lancet,* 1973, *1,* 364-366.

Barnes, J. Effects of reality orientation classroom on memory loss, confusion, and disorientation in geriatric patients. *The Gerontologist,* 1974, *14,* 138-142.

Bennett, R. Social isolation and isolation-reducing programs. *Bulletin of the New York Academy of Medicine,* 1973, *49,* 1143.

Berger, P., & Luckmann, T. *The social construction of reality.* New York: Doubleday, 1966.

Birren, J., & Schaie, K. *Handbook of the psychology of aging.* New York: Van Nostrand Reinhold, 1977.

Blythe, R. Living to be old. *Harpers,* 1979, *259,* 35-55.

Bradshaw, B., Vonderhaan, W., Keeney, V., Tyler, L., & Harris, S. Community-based residential care for the minimally impaired elderly: A survey analysis. *Journal of the American Geriatrics Society,* 1976, *24,* 423-429.

Brody, E., Kleban, M., Lawton, M., & Moss, J. A longitudinal look at excess disabilities in the mentally impaired aged. *Journal of Gerontology,* 1974, *29,* 79-84.

Brody, E., Kleban, M., Lawton, M., & Silverman, H. Excess disabilities of mentally impaired aged: Impact of individualized treatment. *The Gerontologist,* 1971, *11,* 124-133.

Brook, P., Degun, G., & Mather, M. Reality orientation, a therapy for psychogeriatric patients: A controlled study. *British Journal of Psychiatry,* 1975, *127,* 42-45.

Brown, J., & Rawlinson, M. Relinquishing the sick role following open-heart surgery. *Journal of Health and Social Behavior,* 1975, *16,* 12-26.

Browne, L., & Ritter, J. Reality therapy for the geriatric psychiatric patient. *Perspectives in Psychiatric Care,* 1972, *10,* 135-139.

Butler, R. The life-review: An interpretation of reminiscence in the aged. *Psychiatry,* 1963, *26,* 65-76.

Butler, R., & Lewis, M. *Aging and mental health.* St. Louis: C. V. Mosby, 1977.

Cassell, E. Learning to die. *Bulletin of the New York Academy of Medicine,* 1973, *49,* 1110.

Cautela, J. Behavior therapy and geriatrics. *Journal of Genetic Psychology,* 1966, *108,* 9-17.

Cautela, J., & Mansfield, L. A behavioral approach to geriatrics. In W. Gentry (Ed.), *Geropsychology: A model of training and clinical service.* Cambridge: Ballinger, 1977.

Chien, C., Stotsky, B., & Cole, J. Psychiatric treatment for nursing home patients: Drug, alcohol, and milieu. *American Journal of Psychiatry,* 1973, *130,* 543-548.

Citrin, R., & Dixon, D. Reality orientation: A milieu therapy in an institution for the aged. *The Gerontologist,* 1977, *17,* 39-43.

Cluff, P., & Campbell, W. The social corridor: An environmental and behavioral evaluation. *The Gerontologist,* 1975, *15,* 516-523.

Cole, W. Medical differences between the young and the aged. *Journal of the American Geriatrics Society,* 1970, *18,* 589-614.

Committee on Medicine in Society. Statement on measures to prolong life. *Bulletin of the New York Academy of Medicine,* 1973, *49,* 349-351.

Cornbleth, T. Effects of a protected hospital ward area on wandering and nonwandering geriatric patients. *Journal of Gerontology,* 1977, *32,* 573-577.

Covert, A., Rodrigues, T., & Solomon, K. The use of mechanical and chemical restraints in nursing home. *Journal of the American Geriatrics Society,* 1977, *25,* 85-89.

Drummond, L., Kirchhoff, L., & Scarbrough, D. A practical guide to reality orientation: A treatment approach for confusion and disorientation. *The Gerontologist,* 1978, *18,* 568-573.

Eisdorfer, C., & Fann, W. (Eds.). *Psychopharmacology and aging.* New York: Plenum Press, 1976.

Eisdorfer, C., & Stotsky, B. Intervention, treatment, and rehabilitation of psychiatric disorders. In J. Birren &

K. Schaie (Eds.), *Handbook of aging and human development.* New York: Van Nostrand Reinhold, 1977.

Epstein, L. Symposium on age differentiation in depressive illness. Depression in the elderly. *Journal of Gerontology,* 1976, *31,* 278–282.

Ernst, P., Beran, B., Safford, F., & Kleinhauz, M. Isolation and the symptoms of chronic brain syndrome. *The Gerontologist,* 1978, *18,* 468–474.

Fann, W. *Psychopharmacology and aging.* New York: Plenum Press, 1976.

Fann, W., Wheless, J., & Richman, B. Treating the aged with psychotropic drugs. *The Gerontologist,* 1976, *16,* 322–328.

Folsom, J. Reality orientation for the elderly mental patient. *Journal of Geriatric Psychiatry,* 1968, *1,* 291–307.

Frank, J. D. The present status of outcome studies. *Journal of Consulting and Clinical Psychology,* 1979, *47,* 310–316.

Freeman, J. (Ed.). *Clinical features of the older patient.* Springfield, Ill.: Charles C. Thomas, 1965.

Friedel, R. Pharmacokinetics of psychotherapeutic agents on aged patients. In C. Eisdorfer & R. Friedel (Eds.), *Cognitive and emotional disturbance in the elderly.* Chicago: Yearbook Medical Publishers, 1977.

Garfield, C., & Clark, R. A community model of psychosocial support for patients and families facing life-threatening illness: The Shanti Project. In C. Garfield (Ed.), *Psychosocial care of the dying patient.* New York: McGraw-Hill, 1978.

Garrison, J., & Howe, J. Community intervention with the elderly: A social network approach. *Journal of the American Geriatrics Society,* 1976, *24,* 329–333.

Garrity, T. Vocational adjustment after first myocardial infarction: Comparative assessment of several variables suggested in the literature. *Social Science and Medicine,* 1973, *7,* 705–717.

Gendlin, E. *Experiencing and the creation of meaning.* Ontario: Collier-Macmillan Canada, Ltd., 1962.

Gentry, W. D. Psychosomatic issues in assessment. In M. Storandt, I. Siegler, & M. Elias (Eds.), *The clinical psychology of aging.* New York: Plenum Press, 1978.

Godbole, A., & Verinis, S. Brief psychotherapy in the treatment of emotional disorders in physically ill geriatric patients. *The Gerontologist,* 1974, *14,* 143–148.

Goldfarb, A. Recommendations for psychiatric care in a home for the aged. *Journal of Gerontology,* 1953, *8,* 343–347.

Goldfarb, A. Psychotherapy for aged persons. IV. One aspect of the psychodynamics of the therapeutic situation with aged patients. *Psychoanalytic Review,* 1955, *42,* 180–187.

Goldfarb, A. Institutional care of the aged. In E. Busse & E. Pfeiffer (Eds.), *Behavior and adaptation in late life.* Boston: Little Brown, 1969.

Goldstein, S. A critical appraisal of milieu therapy in a geriatric day hospital. *Journal of the American Geriatrics Society,* 1971, *8,* 693–699.

Gottesman, L. Milieu treatments of the aged in institutions. *The Gerontologist,* 1973, *13,* 23–26.

Gutmann, D. Alternatives to disengagement: The old men of the Highland Druze. In D. Levine (Ed.), *Culture and personality.* Chicago: Aldine, 1975.

Gutmann, D. *A survey of drug-taking behavior of the elderly.* National Institute on Drug Abuse Services Research Administrative Report, 1977.

Hall, M. Use of drugs in elderly patient. *New York State Journal of Medicine,* 1975, *1,* 67–71.

Howard, J., Strong, K. E., Jr., Strong, K. E., Sr., Medication procedures in a nursing home: Abuse of PRN orders. *Journal of the American Geriatric Society,* 1977, *25,* 83–84.

Hoyer, W. Application of operant teaching to the modification of elderly behavior. *The Gerontologist,* 1973, *13,* 18–22.

Hoyer, W. Aging as intraindividual change. *Developmental Psychology,* 1974, *10,* 821–826.

Hoyer, W., Kafer, R., Simpson, S., & Hoyer, F. Reinstatement of verbal behavior in elderly mental patients using operant procedures. *The Gerontologist,* 1974, *14,* 149–152.

Hoyer, W., Mishara, B., & Riedel, R. Problem behavior as operants: Applications with elderly individuals. *The Gerontologist,* 1975, *16,* 452–456.

Ingram, D., & Barry, J. National statistics on deaths in nursing homes. *The Gerontologist,* 1977, *17,* 303–308.

Kalish, R. A little myth is a dangerous thing: Research in the service of the dying. In C. Garfield (Ed.), *Psychosocial care of the dying patient.* New York: McGraw-Hill, 1978.

Kapnick, P. Organic treatment of the elderly. In M. Storandt, I. Siegler, & M. Elias (Eds.), *The clinical psychology of aging.* New York: Plenum Press, 1978.

Kastenbaum, R. Is death a life crisis? On the confrontation with death in theory and practice. In N. Datan & L. Ginsberg (Eds.), *Life-span developmental psychology.* New York: Academic Press, 1975.

Kastenbaum, R., & Candy, S. The four percent fallacy: A methodological and empirical critique of extended care facility population statistics. *International Journal of Aging and Human Development,* 1973, *4,* 15–21.

Kastenbaum, R., & Slater, P. Effects of wine on the interpersonal behavior of geriatric patients: An exploratory subject. In R. Kastenbaum (Ed.), *New thoughts on old age.* New York: Springer, 1964.

Kline, N., & Angst, J. Side effects of psychotropic drugs. *Psychiatric Annals,* 1975, *5,* 441-458.

Knight, R. Psychotherapy and behavior change with the noninstitutionalized aged. *International Journal of Aging and Human Development,* 1978-1979, *9,* 221-236.

Kral, V. Somatic therapies in older depressed patients. *Journal of Gerontology,* 1976, *31,* 311-313.

Krupka, L., & Vener, A. Hazards of drug use among the elderly. *The Gerontologist,* 1979, *19,* 90-95.

Lawton, M. Assessing the competence of older people. In D. Kent, R. Kastenbaum, & S. Sherwood (Eds.), *Research planning and action for the elderly.* New York: Behavioral Publications, 1972.

Lesnoff-Caravaglia, G. The 5 percent fallacy. *International Journal of Aging and Human Development,* 1978-1979, *9,* 187-192.

Levinson, B. The pet in the nursing home: A psychological adventure for the patient. *Silver Threads,* 1970, 3-7.

Lindsley, O. Geriatric behavioral prosthetics. In R. Kastenbaum (Ed.), *New thoughts on old age.* New York: Springer, 1964.

Lipman, A., & Slater, R. Homes for old people: Toward a positive environment. *The Gerontologist,* 1977, *17,* 146-156.

Lipton, M. Age differentiation in depression: Biochemical aspects. *Journal of Gerontology,* 1976, *31,* 293-299.

Lubinski, R. Why so little interest in whether or not old people talk: A review of recent research on verbal communication among the elderly. *International Journal of Aging and Human Development,* 1978-1979, *9,* 237-245.

Mechanic, D. Social structure and personal adaptation: Some neglected dimensions. In G. Coelo, D. Hamburg, & J. Adams (Eds.), *Coping and adaptation.* New York: Basic Books, 1974.

Mendlewicz, J. The age factor in depressive illness: Some genetic considerations. *Journal of Gerontology,* 1976, *31,* 300-303.

Merleau-Ponty, M. *Phenomenology of perception.* London: Routledge and Kegan Paul, 1962.

Merleau-Ponty, M. *The structure of behavior.* Boston: Beacon Press, 1963.

Miller, M. Iatrogenic and neurisgenic effects of prolonged immobilization of the ill aged. *Journal of the American Geriatrics Society,* 1975, *23,* 360-369.

Mishara, B. Geriatric patients in token economy and milieu treatments. *Journal of Consulting and Clinical Psychology,* 1978, *46,* 1340-1348.

Mishara, B., Kastenbaum, R., Baker, F., & Patterson, R. Alcohol effects in old age: An experimental investigation. *Society for Scientific Medicine,* 1975, *19,* 535-547.

Mishara, B., Robertson, B., & Kastenbaum, R. Self-injurious behavior in the elderly. *The Gerontologist,* 1973, *13,* 311-314.

Mueller, D., & Atlas, L. Resocialization of regressed elderly residents: A behavioral management approach. *Journal of Gerontology,* 1972, *3,* 390-392.

Noyes, R., Jochimsen, P., & Travis, T. The changing attitudes of physicians toward prolonging life. *Journal of the American Geriatrics Society,* 1977, *25,* 470-474.

Ostrander, E. Research based nursing home design: An approach for planning environments for the aging. *International Journal of Aging and Human Development,* 1973, *4,* 307-317.

Pattison, E. Social system psychotherapy. *American Journal of Psychotherapy,* 1973, *27,* 396-409.

Saunders, C. The need for in-patient care for the patient with terminal cancer. *Middlesex Hospital Journal,* 1973, *72,* 1-6.

Schulz, R. The effects of control and predictability on the physical and psychological well-being of the institutionalized aged. *Journal of Personality and Social Psychology,* 1976, *33,* 563-573.

Schulz, R., & Hanusa, B. Long-term effects of control and predictability-enhancing interventions: Findings and ethical issues. *Journal of Personality and Social Psychology,* 1978, *36,* 1194-1201.

Schwartz, G. E., & Weiss, S. M. Behavioral medicine revisited: An amended definition. *Journal of Behavioral Medicine,* 1978, *1,* 249-251.

Shapiro, A. A pilot program in music therapy with residents of a home for the aged. *The Gerontologist,* 1969, *9,* 128-133.

Sherwood, S. Sociology of food and eating: Implications for action for the elderly. *American Journal of Clinical Nutrition,* 1973, *26,* 1108-1110.

Smith, M. Portrayal of the elderly in prescription drug advertising. *The Gerontologist,* 1976, *16,* 329-334.

Sparacino, J. Individual psychotherapy with the aged: A selective review. *International Journal of Aging and Human Development,* 1978-1979, *9,* 197-220.

Starc, F. Three score and ten plus more. *Journal of the American Geriatrics Society,* 1977, *25,* 529-533.

Storandt, M., Siegler, I., & Elias, M. (Eds.), *The clinical psychology of aging.* New York: Plenum Press, 1978.

Strauss, A. *Negotiations: Varieties, contexts, processes, and social order.* San Francisco: Jossey-Bass, 1978.

Taulbee, L., & Folsom, J. Reality orientation for geriatric patients. *Hospital and Community Psychiatry,* 1966, *17,* 133-135.

Thralow, J., & Watson, C. Remotivation for geriatric patients using elementary school students. *American Journal of Occupational Therapy,* 1974, *28,* 469-473.

Tobin, S., & Lieberman, M. *Last home for the aged.* San Francisco: Jossey-Bass, 1976.

Toepfer, C., Bicknell, A., & Shaw, D. Remotivation as behavior therapy. *The Gerontologist,* 1974, *14,* 451–453.

Weir, R. (Ed.). *Ethical issues in death and dying.* New York: Columbia University Press, 1977.

Weissert, W. Two models of geriatric day care: Findings from a comparative study. *The Gerontologist,* 1976, *16,* 420–428.

Woodson, R. Hospice care in terminal illness. In C. Garfield (Ed.), *Psychosocial care of the dying patient.* New York: McGraw-Hill, 1978.

18

Therapeutic Options in the Management of Obesity

RICHARD B. STUART
CHRISTINE MITCHELL
JUDITH A. JENSEN

It is generally accepted that weight is gained when a positive energy balance is maintained over time, and that weight is lost through the creation of a negative energy balance. However, the prediction of who will gain, who will lose, and who will maintain weight remains a mystery. Most of the currently available interventions are little more than attempts to control the effects of psychosocial and biochemical phenomena without a comprehensive understanding of their origins.

Obesity is not a unitary condition, but actually an array of disorders of varied origin that are maintained by a complex of factors that are at best poorly understood. Therefore, clinicians who attempt to treat these disorders without careful study of the fascinating underlying factors (e.g., Bray, 1976; Stunkard, 1978) are likely to design weak programs leading to marginal if not negative results.

As tens of thousands of obese individuals seek help to lose weight each year, clinicians cannot await definitive answers to the questions posed by basic research. Therefore, clinicans must strive to make sense out of the often confusing basic and applied research to plan treatment programs in the most professionally responsible manner possible. This paper is one attempt to synthesize the results of an explosive number of studies by evaluating the seven most frequently researched methods in the 1970s. It begins with a thorough review of the characteristics of the treatment methods and the subjects with whom they are used, going on to an assessment of the results achieved by each therapeutic method in light of both its benefits and costs. The final section of the paper presents recommendations for intervention based upon the conclusions reached in the foregoing reviews.

Selection of Studies

We have attempted to review all of the published or presented studies of the effects of varied treatments of obesity which have been presented in English between January 1972 and June 1979. Out of the over 700 reports initially reviewed, we selected 357, based on the adequacy of data on subject

Medical Psychology
Contributions to Behavioral Medicine

ISBN 0-12-565960-1

characteristics, treatment methods, and outcome. While not an exhaustive evaluation (because some published studies were unavailable to us and because we may simply have overlooked others), it is believed that this review offers a reasonably accurate picture of the current status of research on the management of obesity. Because even the selected studies are too numerous to include in a printed bibliography, interested readers are encouraged to write to the senior author for a complete listing.

These studies are divided into seven general categories: (*a*) intestinal bypass surgery; (*b*) gastric surgery; (*c*) fasting; (*d*) drug therapy; (*e*) diet therapy; (*f*) exercise therapy; and (*g*) behavior modification. Some of the methods used in these studies overlap, as caloric restriction and some suggestions or training in behavior change are included in most responsible clinical efforts. Research was assigned to one of the seven major categories on the basis of the author's belief that the chosen method was the focal active element in the treatment, but no clear evidence exists that this is indeed the case. Therefore, not only is the selection of studies for inclusion somewhat arbitrary, but so, too, is their assignment to the specified categories of analysis.

Review of Results

Subject Description

The average age, initial weight, percent overweight, and sex of subjects included in each of the seven types of treatment were recorded when reported. Unfortunately, few published studies report all of this minimal data, so the values reported for each dimension in Table 18.1 may not be generalized to all of the reviewed studies without qualification.

The distribution of males and females in these treatments varies widely. Chi square tests (in which the two types of surgery were combined) show that behavior modification studies have a significantly smaller proportion of males than all of the other types of studies. Drug and diet studies, which do not differ, have a significantly lower proportion of males than the fasting and surgery studies; however, the comparison of diet to exercise did not reach significance, probably because of the small N in the exercise studies ($N = 67$). It should be noted that the number of males treated may be underestimated by these average values. Studies including both sexes often report treating both males and females, but do not report the exact numbers of each. This fact was not included in our calculations. Studies involving only a single sex are almost always conducted using females rather than males. The values from the women-only studies were included in the means presented here, so the number of women may be overestimated.

The mean ages of the subjects in the different treatments vary from a low of 30.85 years in the exercise studies to a high of 41.5 years in the diet studies. Chi square tests on the age distribution of treatment type revealed that all of these distributions were significantly different from each other, except those of the fasting and exercise studies. The diet and behavior modification studies both had a larger proportion of subjects over, as opposed to under, 40 years. Only the exercise studies had a large number of under 30-year-olds. The surgery subjects generally were 31 to 40 years of age because many of the surgeons selected only subjects under 40 for these operations.

When the initial weights of the subjects are compared they fall into three obvious groups: the two types of surgery treatments have subjects who average 300 pounds initially; exercise and fasting studies have subjects who average about 250 pounds; the behavior modification, diet, and drug studies have subjects who average under 200 pounds. To compare these values statistically, the initial weight means from each of the studies were categorized. All the chi square tests on the distributions of initial weights yielded significant values. The two types of surgery were combined in this analysis. The mean initial weight values for the exercise and fasting studies are very similar; however, the distributions of values are quite different, with the larger percentage of exercise subjects having weight means between 350 and 400 pounds.

In summary, it is clear that the seven types of studies draw upon two rather independent pools of subjects. The surgery, fasting, and exercise studies draw upon heavier subjects (averaging

Table 18.1 Characteristics of Subject Participants

	Sex (%) M	Sex (%) F	Age (years)	Initial weight (pounds)	Initial percentage overweight
Behavior modification	5.4	94.6	39.13 (N = 4770)	176.79 (N = 4145)	35.3 (N = 2832)
Dieting	17.1	82.9	41.50 (N = 1866)	194.07 (N = 2455)	56.7 (N = 336)
Drugs	14.3	85.7	34.90 (N = 2103)	187.74 (N = 1734)	43.9 (N = 1835)
Exercise	32.6	67.4	30.85 (N = 84)	251.86 (N = 96)	—
Fasting	35.3	64.7	40.17 (N = 1077)	256.20 (N = 1075)	78.7 (N = 91)
Gastric surgery	17.8	82.2	34.02 (N = 710)	300.62 (N = 637)	—
Intestinal surgery	29.7	70.3	34.25 (N = 2149)	304.12 (N = 1773)	72.4 (N = 697)

287.71 pounds), while the dieting, drug, and behavior modification studies include lighter subjects (averaging 184.16 pounds). While most subjects are in their thirties, surgical and exercise research seems to attract slightly younger participants than do the other methods. Finally, intestinal surgery, exercise, and fasting studies appear to attract a higher proportion of males than the treatment programs which consist primarily of females. In general, these findings are consistent with the trend noted elsewhere (Stuart & Jacobson, 1979) that the management of problems of mild to moderate overweight appears to be essentially a female concern despite the fact that the mortality tables reveal these weight excesses to be much more of a problem for males. Among the massively overweight who are active in some form of weight-control therapy, women still outnumber men, in part because more women than men survive the biological stress of carrying these many extra pounds.

Treatment Characteristics

Therapies for obesity differ on a number of dimensions independent of the focal treatment procedures themselves. These dimensions may represent very important factors that can affect treatment outcomes. Table 18.2 presents a summary of those characteristics of the studies reviewed which were reported by their authors. Unfortunately, all too often not one but several of these critically important dimensions were not communicated in published reports, making it impossible to contrast findings of different studies without considerable qualification or to replicate precisely the methods used. Therefore, as an absolute minimum, it is hoped that all researchers will include the data summarized in Table 18.2 in their reports, and that all journal editors will insist upon the inclusion of these data as a precondition to publishing the research reports.

As regards treatment length, it is clear from Table 18.2 that the average study fell far short of continuing treatment through to the point at which subjects reached goal weight. Even the lightest group of subjects (those receiving behavior modification treatment and initially averaging 176.79 pounds as reported in Table 18.1) were some 30 to 40 pounds overweight and would need approximately as many weeks to reach ideal weight. To offer these subjects the average of 11.8 to 19.2 weeks of treatment described in Table 18.2

Table 18.2 Characteristics of Treatment

	Length of treatment (weeks)	Diet (cal)	Hospitalization	Therapist	Length of follow-up (weeks)	Studies without follow-up (%)
Behavior modification	13.05 (99 studies)	1200	never	variable (MD, RN, SW, Ph.D., nutritionist)	33.5 (53 studies)	33.0 (29/99)
Dieting	18.6 (13 studies)	900	seldom	variable (MD, RN, SW, Ph.D., nutritionist)	133.95 (8 studies)	75.8 (25/33)
Drugs	11.8 (80 studies)	1000	only in HCG studies	MD	12.7 (8 studies)	88.4 (61/69)
Exercise	19.22 (7 studies)	?	2 studies	variable (MD, physical therapist)	8.5 (1 study)	88.9 (9/9)
Fasting	16.65 (15 studies)	0	all but 1 study	MD	216.2 (4 studies)	76.5 (13/17)
Gastric surgery	—	no	always	MD	93.6	—
Intestinal surgery	—	no	always	MD	96.3	—

is to give them a chance to no more than begin their weight-loss efforts. It can be assumed that the larger weight losses associated with the early stages of treatment may be more reinforcing than the asymptotic pattern found as treatment progressed (Stuart, Jensen, & Guire, 1979). Therefore, weight losses during the early stages may have little association with weight losses achieved over a longer term. All studies should thus be required to report the length of client contact, and these contacts should be extended through the point at which clients achieve ideal weight.

Many of the studies make dietary recommendations, and yet few report the caloric value or content of these diets. As will be shown shortly, caloric values have a significant impact upon both the rate of weight loss and the ability to maintain the results.

It is important for researchers to report whether their subjects were hospitalized. Obviously, those who fast in hospitlals are more likely (but by no means certain) to in fact have either zero or very modest caloric consumption. Hospitalization is obviously very costly and disruptive of the subjects' normal lives, and it can be argued that behaviors changed in the synthetic hospital environment may not generalize to and be maintained in the subjects' natural environment. For these reasons, if the delivery of a specific service depends upon hospitalization, this necessity must be considered in the decision to accept or reject that particular method.

The characteristics of therapists who render the treatment may have a significant bearing upon the outcome and cost of services. Clearly, some of the programs reviewed here are offered by physicians. It is likely that other intervention methods will be offered by people under- or overqualified to provide the services. For example, while individual behavior modification intervention uses a vocabulary that is in general use, professional supervision is often a minimum essential for the effective adaptation of the methods to the idiographic characteristics of specific clients. On the other hand, group delivery of behavior modification service may be enhanced if services are delivered by professionally guided lay people (Stuart & Mitchell, 1978). In any event, compliance may be enhanced or diminished by virtue of the professional status and interpersonal skills of service providers, and these must be accounted for if the results are to be interpreted and/or generalized.

Finally, the length of treatment follow-up must be summarized in responsible research reporting. As is seen in Table 18.2, over three-fourths of all of the nonsurgical interventions failed to report follow-up data outside of the behavior modification area, in which some one-third of the studies lacked this important information. While it is necessary to produce weight reduction, the ability to maintain the therapeutically mediated changes is perhaps the essential clinical and research issue in all obesity research. The average duration of the few follow-up evaluations in the fasting and dieting studies appears to be quite acceptable. However, as always, the means conceal a multitude of individual differences, and these averages are artificially inflated by rather long follow-up intervals in a small number of studies. Surgeons followed their patients for an acceptable minimum period, but these long-term evaluations must be sufficient to permit detection of slowly occurring postoperative side effects of the procedures. The drug and exercise studies have woefully inadequate follow-up durations, and even the behavior modification average of 33.5 weeks is insufficient. As a general rule, follow-up intervals should either be at least twice as long as the time between initial client contact and treatment termination or one year, whichever is longer. The logic of this rule of thumb is that clients begin to mobilize themselves for weight losses as soon as they make the decision to begin treatment, and it can be expected that the natural process of weight regain will be a bit more casual than the therapist-aided process of weight loss. Therefore, doubling contact time for follow-up would give a reasonable index of trends in weight maintenance; to adequately control for the effects of seasonal differences (Stuart *et al.*, 1979), 1 year would be minimum follow-up time, with this year beginning at the end of treatment rather than at its start.

In summary, it is as important to describe the conditions of service delivery as it is essential to describe in detail the methods used and the populations involved. It is regrettable that these requirements are all too often overlooked and that the analyses reported here are hampered by these reporting inadequacies.

Weight Changes

Short Term Table 18.3 summarizes the total average weight change and average weekly weight change of subjects undergoing the various types of treatments. As mentioned in the previous section, reporting irregularities and inconsistencies in the design of interventions such as varied treatment durations contribute to important uncertainties in interpreting these results. In statistically evaluating the differences between outcomes, it is important to use nonparametric methods such as the chi square rather than using parametric t tests or analyses of variance, because standard deviations are not reported in most of the papers reviewed.

Omitting consideration of the surgery studies, which obviously do not report weight changes during treatment, chi square analysis of the differences in weight losses across studies reveals that the subjects in the fasting studies lost the most weight, followed, in order, by the subjects in diet, exercise, drug, and behavior modification studies. Each of these comparisons between successive treatment methods is statistically significant. Statistically significant differences also were obtained for comparisons of all of the average weekly rates of weight loss. As reflected in the chi square analysis, while subjects in the behavior modification, dieting, and drug studies appeared to lose weight at roughly the same average weekly rate (.91, .92, and 1.29 pounds/week, respectively), their distributions varied significantly. For example, while only 7.6% of the behavior modification subjects reported an average week-to-week weight gain, 15.6% of the dieters and 20.2% of the drug takers reported such an increase.

Not all of the methods are used in pure culture. For example, three studies report comparisons of behavioral and pharmacological treatments. Ost and Gotestam (1976) compared a behavior modification program and a drug program to a control group over a 16-week treatment period. The behavioral groups lost 20.68 pounds, which is significantly more than the 12.54 pounds lost by

Table 18.3 Summary of Weight Change Information by Treatment Type

	During treatment period					During follow-up period				
		Treatment condition		Control condition			Treatment condition		Control condition	
Treatment type	Length of treatment (weeks)	Total change (pounds)	Change/ week (pounds)	Total change (pounds)	Change/ week (pounds)	Length of follow-up (weeks)	Total change (pounds)	Change/ week (pounds)	Total change (pounds)	Change/ week (pounds)
Behavior modification	13.3 (95 studies)	−8.99 (N = 3890)	−.91 (N = 3985)	−2.53 (N = 681)	−.29 (N = 603)	33.5 (53 studies)	−.20 (N = 1858)	−.04 (N = 1934)	+.37 (N = 446)	.00 (N = 532)
Dieting	23.8 (9 studies)	−25.50 (N = 2212)	−.92 (N = 1797)	−.30 (N = 26)	−.00 (N = 26)	39.4 (5 studies)	−2.21 (N = 32)	+.02 (N = 47)		
Drugs	11.6 (75 studies)	−11.85 (N = 3048)	−1.29 (N = 2918)	−5.93 (N = 1853)	−.76 (N = 1899)	40.0 (5 studies)	+9.53 (N = 94)	+.84 (N = 94)	+5.34 (N = 90)	+.45 (N = 105)
Exercise	19.2 (7 studies)	−16.16 (N = 76)	−1.82 (N = 75)	−22.80 (N = 29)	−3.04 (N = 29)					
Fasting	16.7 (15 studies)	−75.01 (N = 1159)	−5.03 (N = 1071)			104.0 (2 studies)	+13.08 (N = 168)	+.22 (N = 53)		
Gastric surgery						56.3	−83.32 (N = 620)	−1.67 (N = 657)		
Intestinal surgery						96.3	−113.38 (N = 789)	−2.43 (N = 726)		

the drug group. The control group lost 7.78 pounds, which is significantly less than both the other groups. At a 12-month follow-up, the behavioral subjects showed a total loss of 10.12 pounds, the drug subjects, 1.76 pounds, and the control group, 5.28 pounds. Craighead, O'Brien, and Stunkard (Note 1) compared drug, behavior modification, drug plus psychotherapy, and drug plus behavior modification conditions to a control group during a 6-month treatment period. The drug-only group lost significantly less than the behavior modification-only group—15 and 23 pounds, respectively. The drug plus psychotherapy group lost 30 pounds, and drug plus behavior modification, 32 pounds—not a significant difference. Finally, Walker, Ballard, and Gold (1977) conducted a clinical practice test of an anorectic drug at four different obesity clinics, only one of which used behavior modification. The drug groups at the four centers averaged a loss of 7.3 pounds, which was significantly greater than the 1.7 pounds lost by subjects given only a placebo. When the behavior modification plus drug center was studied alone, subjects given the placebo lost 6 pounds, while the drug subjects lost 8.4 pounds. However, this difference was not significant. In this study it appears that drugs improved loss over placebos only when behavior modification was not used—a finding that is difficult to interpret.

Considering the results reported in Table 18.3, two important questions arise: Are the results attributable to differences in the focal methods or can they be better ascribed to differences in subject populations or intervention details such as the length of treatment? In support of the specific effects of treatment, a close analysis of the outcomes achieved in the behavior modification studies is instructive. Among these studies, 66 relied entirely on positive influence techniques, 18 drew primarily upon aversion techniques, and 4 combined the two. The positive influence techniques using stimulus control methods, often coupled with a social reinforcement system, have enjoyed wide popularity (Stuart, 1978; Stuart & Davis, 1978). Aversive techniques ranged from covert sensitization (imagining stomach upset in association with visions of preferred junk foods) to the use of electric shock for deconditioning appetitive responses. The 3396 subjects in the positive programs lost an average total of 14.3 pounds and an average of .926 pounds per week during treatment, in contrast to (*a*) the 163 subjects in the combined approaches whose average total loss was 8.5 pounds and whose average weekly loss was .867 pounds; and (*b*) the aversion programs whose 453 subjects lost an average of 8.3 total pounds and .787 pounds weekly. In light of these findings, different methods may indeed have an impact upon the immediate treatment results.

Shedding further light on the possible active ingredients in effective treatment are data reported by Stuart in 1977. He found in an evaluation of weight-loss results achieved by 4767 members of Weight Watchers classes that those receiving a diet with social support for adherence lost an average of only .92 pounds weekly over 12 weeks, in contrast to those who received the same program to which behavior modification training was added whose average weekly weight loss was 1.34 pounds during the same period. When these results are compared with the findings reported in Table 18.3, it can be seen that the rendering of professionally conceived and directed services (i.e., behavior modification training) in the self-help context of Weight Watchers can enhance the outcome of the same type of service when offered in the rubric of a professionally delivered program, underscoring the significance of the setting as well as the treatment characteristics.

It is also possible, however, that subject and treatment differences can have important explanatory power. For example, Stuart *et al.* (1979) found the rate of weight loss to be predicted by the level of initial weight. In the studies reviewed here, weight loss and initial weights correlated at the level of .33, while correlations between sex, age, and weight loss failed to reach the level of statistical significance. The fact that the subjects in exercise and fasting programs were dramatically heavier than those in the other nonsurgical interventions (see Table 18.1) would lead to the prediction that these subjects would lose weight more quickly than their counterparts regardless of the methods employed.

A second explanation of the weight-loss differences may be found in the caloric levels allowed subjects in each condition. While it is not clear that subjects adhere closely to the dietary instructions they receive, their food intake must be associated with these instructions. Thus, it was found that zero-calorie fasting programs offered the most rapid weight losses, followed by diets of 600 calories per day which netted an average loss of 2.67 pounds per week; diets of 600 to 1000 calories per day which caused an average loss of 2.52 pounds per week; and diets of over 1000 calories per day which yielded an average weekly weight losses of 1.75 pounds. Moreover, in those studies that did not stipulate prescribed daily caloric intake, weight losses were inferior to those obtained in programs that at least did attempt to provide food restriction guidelines. Thus, caloric restriction, independent of the focal technology, may have explained much of the variance in the range of results that has been found.

Finally, based upon prior research reviewed by Stuart *et al.* (1979), it had been expected that average weekly weight losses would be greater in shorter programs because of fluid losses associated with the onset of carbohydrate intake restriction. Inspection of Table 18.3 reveals, however, that this is not the case, implying that the intervention methods may be sufficiently powerful to cancel out this expected natural phenomenon. Therefore, it can be concluded that with regard to weight-loss results at treatment termination, subject differences may contribute to differential outcomes, but the varied treatment methods themselves also appear to make a major contribution to the results.

Long Term These conclusions hold equally well to assessment of longer term maintenance of treatment results, although the pattern of superiority shifts dramatically. Unfortunately, while the maintenance of weight loss is of pivotal concern in obesity control research, many of the reported studies offer *no* follow-up information. Specifically, 89% of the exercise and drug studies lack follow-up data, as do 76% of the fasting and diet studies, in contrast to only 33% of the behavior modification reports. It is also regrettable that many of the studies which did report follow-up data, treated them anecdotally rather than stating them with the same precision that characterized the immediate posttreatment results. Table 18.3 presents the findings of these follow-up evaluations. Here it will be seen that the surgically treated subjects achieved huge total and average weekly weight losses throughout the follow-up period. Drug and fasting subjects regained more of the total weight they had lost, while the diet and behavior modification subjects appeared to maintain their total losses best. These same conclusions hold when average weekly weight losses throughout the maintenance period are considered.

Two additional characteristics of treatment may have a bearing on the power of that method to generate maintainable results. The first is the role of the treatment in facilitating subjects' attribution of increased power to themselves. It can be assumed that when subjects believe that positive outcomes were achieved through their own efforts, these efforts will be continued. On the other hand, attribution of the power to induce change to an outside source can be expected to diminish posttherapeutic reliance upon the intervention methods (see Davison, Tsujimoto, & Glaros, 1973; Valins & Nisbett, 1972). Therefore, it can be predicted that participants in drug studies would be more likely to regain their losses because they ascribe to the drug the capacity to induce change, while subjects in behavior modification programs would be more likely to maintain their losses because of enhanced faith in their own capabilities. Something akin to this phenomenon has been seen in smoking-control studies (e.g., Nentwig, 1978). Figure 18.1 graphically portrays this association. In interpreting this figure, it is important to recognize that it represents mean values obtained from 5 drug studies and 53 behavior modification studies. Of the 80 drug and 99 behavior modification studies, these were the only reports that included all 4 of the following types of data: length of treatment; length of follow-up; weight loss during active treatment; and weight change during follow-up. Unfortunately, these studies were not uniform as to duration of treatment and follow-up, and their reports were based on end-term rather than including a series of week-by-week data points. Regarding the first point, length of follow-up and rate of weight gain correlated at only +.03 for the subjects in programs not involv-

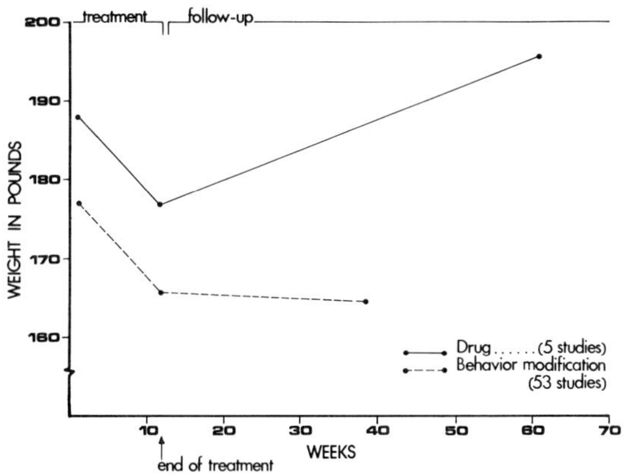

Figure 18.1. Mean long-term weight loss reported in drug and behavior modification studies.

ing surgery, so that differences in follow-up length did not necessarily account for differential results. Regarding the second point, all subjects in the reported drug studies regained weight regardless of the length of follow-up. For example, subjects followed up for only 2 weeks in two studies gained an average of 1.1 (Smith, Innes, & Munro, 1975) and .2 (Wise, 1975) pounds per week, while subjects in a 4-week follow-up gained an average of .6 pounds per week (Langlois, Forbes, Bell, & Grant, 1974); subjects followed for 52 weeks gained an average of .25 pounds per week (Ost & Gotestam, 1976), and subjects followed for 138 weeks (Vernace, 1974) gained an average of .11 pounds per week. Indeed, the seemingly best studies (Vernace, 1974) actually showed that early in the follow-up period subjects regained all or even more weight than was lost, with longer follow-up times simply showing the maintenance of the original pretreatment weight. Thus, it is fairly safe to conclude that while method and reporting inconsistencies qualify the conclusion, there is evidence that drug-aided studies lead to weight changes that are not likely to be maintained, with attribution problems being one possible explanation of this effect.

Also relevant to this conclusion are data reported by Stuart and Guire (1979) (e.g., that 15 months after reaching goal weight, 24.6% of 721 female members of Weight Watchers classes were at or below goal weight; 28.9% were within 5% of goal; and 17.5% were 5 to 10% above goal) which show that in some instances weight lost in a self-help context may be more maintainable than weight lost under professional auspices. Here, again, the explanation may be found in enhanced self-attribution of the power to manage one's own behavior (Stuart & Mitchell, 1978). Therefore, the operation of an attribution effect is one plausible explanation of the results achieved through reliance upon the different approaches.

The outcomes also may differ because of the superiority of one set of programs over the others in teaching maintainable skill changes. While fasting subjects lost weight most quickly, they regained their losses more rapidly (e.g., Johnson & Drenick, 1977) because they learned the least about how to eat under natural social conditions. The same can be said for subjects in studies that mandated severe caloric restriction. For example, two studies (Schteingart, Foss, Lampman, Short, East, Buntman, Michael, & McGowland, 1975; Sohar & Sneh, 1973) used diets of 550 to 600 calories per day and produced rapid weight losses followed by subjects' regaining an average of 1.3 pounds per week during follow-up. In contrast, when participants were allowed to eat 1225 calories per day (e.g., McEwen, Jacobson, Battrum, Crealock, Mitchell, & McLaren, 1972) their weight losses were slower during active treatment, but they continued to lose an average of .31 pounds per week during the first 13 weeks of follow-up.

Turning now to subject characteristics, Stuart (1977) found that some of these did predict outcome and maintenance in various studies, but that few factors sustained their predictive power across studies. Stuart and Guire (1979) reported a strong association between initial weight and the rate of regaining therapeutically lost weight. The analysis of findings in studies with suitable data here revealed a +.25 correlation between initial weight and rate of regain. Older subjects also tended to regain their weight more rapidly than did younger subjects, yielding a correlation of +.25. Because fasting subjects tended to be both heavier and older, at least some portion of the responsibility for their less-than-expected outcome can be attributed to their initial characteristics.

Taken together, when subjects are offered

treatments that enhance their self-attribution of the power to change their behavior, and when the recommended changes are themselves sustainable for long periods of time, the chances of lasting therapeutic benefits can be greatly increased. However, before drawing any firm conclusions about the most effective programs, it is necessary to assess the rates of attrition from each program and their relative costs and benefits. These are discussed in the next sections.

Attrition

The number of subjects who complete an obesity treatment program is an important measure of the success of that treatment. Dropout rates frequently are not reported in treatment studies. In surgical treatment dropout rates have little meaning, since the subjects generally only drop out through death or by having their surgery reversed. The lowest dropout rate in the nonsurgery treatments is found in fasting studies, which show a 19.3% rate in six studies. This is probably a reflection of the fact that many fasting subjects are hospitalized during treatment, and hospitalization constitutes a major financial and time commitment. The exercise and diet studies rarely report dropout rates. Three exercise studies show a high dropout rate of 31.3%, perhaps because of the difficulty of the programs involved. Only 13 of 33 diet studies report dropouts, averaging 28%. The drug and behavior modification studies are more consistent in reporting the rate of dropouts: Fifty-three drug studies averaged a dropout rate of 27.8%, while the 64 behavior modification studies averaged a dropout rate of 24%. Behavior modification treatments appear to produce the best compliance in treatments not involving hospitalization. These rates vary widely within treatment types, probably depending on the length of treatment, the subject population, and the cost of treatment. Behavioral programs may have lower dropout rates for two reasons: First, behavior modification involves procedures with virtually no physical side effects; thus, subjects do not drop out because the treatment is affecting their health. Second, behavioral programs train subjects in lifestyle changes, which are more easily incorporated into daily life than other procedures.

Attrition rates may affect reports of treatment outcomes. Inferences can be mistakenly made if the success of a treatment is assessed solely in terms of those subjects who actually complete treatment. There are several problems involved in such a method of data collection (Jeffrey, 1975). First, differential rates of attrition from treatment and control groups may produce systematic effects in observed weight losses. Second, it is likely that the subjects who remain in a control group despite the weakness of control procedures in producing weight losses are on the average more motivated than those who are encouraged to remain in a treatment condition by substantial early weight losses. Such tendencies, when ignored in data analysis, would tend to attenuate differences between groups and the possibility of identifying the effects of treatment. On the other hand, self-selection of this sort could increase the apparent effectiveness of treatment by removing subjects who do not respond well to treatment. Individuals who do not lose weight are more likely to drop out than those who lose weight easily.

The importance of the threats to the validity of inferences based on data which exclude dropouts is underlined by observations that including these data can decrease reports of successful clinical treatment for smoking (McFall & Hammen, 1971) or reverse inferences about superior and inferior therapies in weight control (Harris & Bruner, 1971). Since attrition may result in systematic effects on treatment assessment, it is necessary to collect data from dropouts and to include them in analyses and evaluations.

Treatment Costs

The obesity treatments reviewed in this chapter vary widely in their effectiveness and in their costs.

Surgery Surgical studies produce greater weight losses than other types of treatment, but at higher costs. These treatments are very expensive, requiring hospitalization and continued treatment by a doctor. Surgical treatments also frequently involve long absences from work because of the necessity for hospitalization and recuperation. The most serious physical hazard from surgery is the risk of postoperative death. Mortality rates range from 2% (Fikri & Cassella, 1974; Kish, Parker, & Joseph, 1975; Telmos & Bodzin, 1977) to 19% (Printen & Mason, 1977) for causes relating to the surgery. Gastric surgery alone shows a mortality rate of 2% (Knecht, 1978) to 19% (Printen & Mason, 1977), with other rates of mortality falling somewhere between (Hornberger, 1976; Mason, Printen & Boyd, 1975). Intestinal surgery shows similar rates from 2% (Fikri & Cassella, 1974) to 11% (DeWind & Payne, 1976).

Other serious complications occur frequently, some at rates close to 100% for subjects of jejunoileal bypass. Life-threatening complications have been reported in 21 to 58% of these operated patients (Bray, Barry, Benfield, Castelnuovo-Tedesco, Drenick, & Passaro, 1976; Dean, Scott, Shull & Gluck, 1977; Halverson, Wise, Wasna, & Ballinger, 1978; King, 1978). Almost every patient suffers from severe diarrhea following surgery, which sometimes continues for many years (Bray, 1977). The diarrhea destroys electrolyte balances and thus requires continual remedial care. Other frequent complications come from liver damage. Griffen, Young, and Stevenson (1977) found that 75% of patients treated with jejunoileal bypass had liver biopsies indicating gross pathology 1 year after surgery. Less frequent complications include renal and urinary stones, wound infections, pulmonary emboli, pneumatosis, cystoides, and arthritis. All reports of bypass surgery reveal serious side effects.

A few studies have compared side effects in gastric and jejunoileal bypasses. Buchwalter (1977) found that gastric bypasses produced greater weight losses with less liver damage and other types of morbidity than jejunoileal bypass. However, the overall picture of gastric and jejunoileal bypass surgery does not suggest important differences in side effects.

Many surgical patients require reoperation to reverse or revise their surgery because of the complications, and often this measure does not prevent their death. Mersheimer, Kazarian, and Dursi (1977) report that their 51 patients had a total of 150 readmissions to the hospital, some for reversal. Halverson *et al.* (1978) concluded from their review of surgery cases that the physical risks of surgery far outweigh the health benefits, even with the grossly overweight. Similarly, Benfield, Greenway, Bray, Barry, Lechago, Mena, and Schedewie, (1976) report that only 43% of their surgery patients had good results without serious complications.

The suggestion has been made in several surgery studies that at least some of the weight loss resulting from surgery is due to a decrease in caloric intake after the operation (Brewer, White, & Baddeley, 1974; Condon, Janes, Wise, & Alpers, 1978; Mills & Stunkard, 1976). Presumably, this decrease is part of an attempt by patients to control the diarrhea and nausea which accompany eating after a bypass operation. The same result might be obtained by the administration of daily emetics over a period of years and would avoid the pain and expense of an operation. Furthermore, after 5 years some subjects show a tendency to begin to regain the weight they had lost, possibly because the bypassed organs begin to resume their original shape (Fikri & Cassella, 1974). Thus, bypass surgery involves both major monetary and major physical costs, and may be more dangerous than gross obesity.

Patients have been asked how the surgery changed their lives. Solow, Silberfarb, and Swift (1974) claim their surgical patients report improved mood and self-esteem and increases in activity levels. On the other hand, Neill, Marshall, and Yale (1978) found that surgical patients had marital discord and sexual problems after their surgery, suggesting that some of the social side effects of rapid weight loss may be problematic. Nonetheless, when 00 patients who had bypass operations were asked 3 years later if they would have the operation again if necessary, 80% said they would (Mreiden, Danowski, Bahl, Sunder, & Clare, 1978), indicating that surviving patients are generally satisfied with the results of their surgery.

Fasting Fasting is second to surgery both in the amount of weight lost and in the cost of treatment. Total fasts are generally carried out in hospital settings where such factors as electrolyte balance are carefully monitored. Even so, cardiac problems have been shown to be a correlate of total fasts on at least some occasions (e.g., Brown, Yetter, Spicer, & Jones, 1978; Singh, Gaarder, Kanegae, Goldstein, Montgomerie, & Mills, 1978; Vertes, Genuth, & Hazelton, 1977). These fasts are expensive in time and money, and, as has been pointed out earlier, are associated with relatively short-term weight losses. It is speculated that regaining the weight lost, with all of the attention showered on those on zero-calorie regimens, may bring about an unusual level of discouragement regarding future efforts.

Drug Therapy Next in both the rate of initial weight loss and in cost are the drug therapy approaches. While the varied pharmacologic agents used in the management of obesity have different properties and therefore somewhat different effects (Blundell & Rogers, 1978; Bray, 1976), the commonly used drugs do tend to share certain general outcomes. Among the noted side effects of drug treatments are the development of drug dependence (i.e., only with amphetamines, no longer used), dizziness (e.g., Scott & Nelson, 1975), dry mouth (e.g., Enzi, Baritussio, Marchior, & Crepaldi, 1976), and mood disturbances (Goldrick, Nestel, & Havenstein, 1974). Drugs cannot be used without the supervision of a physician, but their most formidable cost may be the discouragement that often accompanies the almost certain weight regain.

Exercise Compared to the other methods, exercise produces the most variable weight loss pattern. Bjorntorp (Note 2) has found that increasing the activity level of the massively obese (e.g., 330 pounds and over) may lead to a weight gain because of alterations in insulin receptors at the adipocytes. Most exercise prescriptions call for low-intensity, long-duration activities which can generally be performed independently and with little more than very minimal medical monitoring once it has been established that exercise is safe for the patient and the patient's tolerance level has been established. Because exercise is contrary to the lifestyle of many obese individuals, it is a difficult, if inexpensive, change to make. Therefore, it is sometimes necessary to provide professional or lay supervision of exercise sessions merely to promote adherence. In addition, the weight loss contribution of exercise is relatively small, making it an impractical sole technique.

Behavior Modification The initial weight losses associated with behavior modification are the slightest of those observed here, but they are the most maintainable and are achieved at the least cost. No physical side effects have been reported, although it is possible that interventions relying on electric shock might have attendant risks. Because some of the more convincing applications of behavior modification techniques have been in group settings with lay leaders, the cost of their administration tends to be modest. Fees for these services range from nothing, through a modest weekly charge, to the deposit of funds that are returned as an inducement for attendance. Finally, because the techniques taught during most sophisticated behavior modification programs aim at changes in lifestyle, these procedures are selected in part on the basis of the likelihood that they will be sustained during the months and years following termination of treatment.

Conclusion

Twenty years ago Stunkard and McLaren-Hume (1959) published what must surely be the most often quoted review of the probability of success of obesity treatments. They found only 8 studies that met the stringent criteria set for inclusion in their review, in contrast to more than 300 studies included in this review. Because of their small sample of studies, these earlier reviewers lumped diet and drug treatments together. To compare the results of contemporary studies with those published years ago, all of the treatments other than surgery were grouped to produce an average expectancy. In the earlier review, 72% of the subjects were found to have lost less than 20 pounds, in contrast to 74% in this review. Climbing further up the ladder of success, 20% of the earlier subjects versus 10% of those in this review lost 10 to 20 pounds, while 8% of those in the earlier research, in contrast to 16% of those in the current review, lost over 40 pounds. This latter difference disappears when the fasting studies are deleted. Therefore, the gross picture 2 decades after the Stunkard and McLaren-Hume (1959) shows little change.

One can wonder whether this is a true reflection of a dismal failure to produce better outcomes or whether it can be better explained by other factors. Certainly, in the 20 years since Stunkard and McLaren-Hume's (1959) article, some studies have been published that have posted results which outshine those found in the earlier review (e.g., Stuart, 1967, 1971; and Musante, 1976, in behavior modification; Young, Scanlan, Lutwak, & Im, 1971, in diet therapy; and Gwinup, 1974, in a broad-spectrum approach using drugs). Why, then, are these results not more uniformly achieved? The answer may be due in part to the contingencies under which many of the studies reported here have been undertaken. Elsewhere (e.g., Stuart, 1979) it has been suggested that many of the published studies may have been generated more to produce graduate degrees or publications for their authors than to advance our understanding of effective treatments of obesity. They are offered for short periods of time, oversimplify the treatment process by concentrating on a single dimension, and generally lack any explicit theory of the nature of obesity or its management. These inadequacies in conception and execution can well explain the failure of research reports to match the optimistic expectations of both the researchers and participants in their studies. While it may be an assumption better explained by optimism than by a careful review of the data, it seems that considerable progress has been made in developing tools that can be used in effective weight-control programs. Therefore, the lack of positive findings may be better explained by deficiencies in the application of the component tools than to any weakness inherent in these elements. The following sections offer suggestions for the design and evaluation of comprehensive programs based upon the results of the foregoing review in the hope that the decade of the 1980s will produce outcomes that do surpass the dismal 2-decade-old findings of Stunkard and McLaren-Hume (1959).

Treatment Recommendations

The following recommendations are made with full respect for the role of biological factors in the creation and alteration of body weight. For the time being at least, etiological factors appear to be beyond our control, and weight regulating forces are highly resistant to control. The intervenor is therefore left to face the challenge of manipulating those dimensions of the complex that can be changed, hoping they will have the power to overcome those that are beyond their influence. Rene Dubos (1957) offered a generalized comment on applied science which well characterizes the charge to the obesity therapist. He wrote:

> Everything I have done in the laboratory and everything I have written has been conditioned by the belief that even though man is constrained by his heredity, he has nevertheless a great deal of freedom in shaping his destiny because he can choose and manipulate his surroundings [p. 8].

The therapist thus has the task of changing those aspects of the patient's life and environment that can be changed, recognizing that perhaps only the tip of the iceberg is being treated.

As a first consideration, one must evaluate the health and psychosocial value of weight loss in order to determine the tolerable level of risk and other costs that can and should be incurred in planning and carrying out treatment programs. Unfortunately, there is considerable mystery about the exact association between excess weight and various causes of mortality and morbidity, on the one hand, and the association between weight reduction and changes in these life-threatening forces on the other. Two models of the relationship between weight and disease have been suggested (Rimm, Werner, Bernstein, & van Yserloo, 1972). In one model, genetic and environmental factors are believed to be determinants of several potential causes of coronary heart disease (CHD) such as diabetes, hyperlipidemia, hypertension, and obesity. This minimizes obesity as a primary cause of CHD. In the other model, genetic and environmental factors are believed to predispose individuals to obesity, which in turn is seen as causal of such risk factors for CHD as diabetes, hyperlipidemia, and hypertension. Obesity is identified as a salient cause of CHD in the second model in contrast to its more equivocal role in the first.

For obvious reasons, an experiment to test one model over the other cannot and never will be designed. Therefore, the choice between these two models must be based upon analysis of correlational data with all of the limitations inherent in these data. At this time there is some justification for embracing both models. Keys and his associates (Keys, Aravanis, Blackburn, van Buchem, Buzina, Djordevic, Fidanza, Karvonen, Menotti, Puddu, & Taylor, 1972) may be among the staunchest advocates of the first model. They undertook a multivariate analysis of a number of factors believed to play an important role in the development of CHD, finding that obesity was no more powerful in predicting heart disease than smoking, cholesterol, systolic blood pressure, and age. While height-weight insurance company tables have been strongly criticized (Keys, 1975), researchers like Donald (1973) have concluded that these data support the view that the degree of overweight is closely associated with excessive mortality. Morris (1976), among others, has shown that this association is more true for younger rather than older adults; for those willing to accept naturally occurring associations among parameters measured in special populations (in this instance insurance policy buyers), these insurance company data do offer encouragement for acceptance of the second model advanced by Rimm *et al.* (1972). Similar support stems from research showing that obesity is a prime etiological factor for diabetes (Baird, 1973; Medalie, Papier, Herman, Goldbourt, Tamir, Neufield, & Riss, 1974; West & Kalbfleisch, 1971), but the literature on hypertension and obesity leads to a contrary conclusion. For example, Chiang, Perlman, and Epstein (1969) concluded a major review of the literature on this subject, with the observation that when obesity and blood pressure were studied, with body build held constant, the two were found to be very modestly related.

In light of these findings, the British Medical Research Council recognized obesity as a potential contributor to CHD and other morbid conditions (1974), while later noting that: "The contribution which obesity alone makes to the etiology of coronary heart disease is controversial [British Medical Research Council, 1976, p. 22]." In summary, obesity stands condemned, but it is not yet convicted as a killer disease in its own right.

Given the doubts that remain from this kind of review of the literature, one must wonder how much benefit weight reduction contributes to overcoming excess mortality and morbidity. Just as experimentation with weight gain and mortality and morbidity is impossible, so, too, is a controlled study of the opposite. Sims' (1974) research on the experimental fattening and reducing of normal-weight volunteers is as close as we can come to such a test. He found metabolic changes occurring in overfed men, which were eliminated when weight returned to normal; but it is not certain that the same would hold for individuals whose weight gain is spontaneous and long-term. Working with actuarial data, Dublin (1953) found from a review of the files of 2300 insurance policy holders that excess mortality could be reversed when weight was lost. However, other than reducing the probability of diabetes (Baird, 1973), which has been well documented, it is not clear how weight loss contributes to reduced mortality. For example, Chiang *et al.* (1969) suggested that reductions in hypertension associated with weight loss are well predicted by the small initial losses and may be best explained by the consumption of lower levels of sodium chloride, which is part and parcel of cuts in food consumption rather than by weight loss per se. Specification of the amount of weight loss necessary to lower risk is as elusive as identification of the factors that explain the improved health resulting from weight reduction. The British Medical Research Council (1974) summarized two somewhat opposing attitudes toward the energy with which weight loss should be pursued:

> One attitude would be that any degree of excess fat above that found in healthy young people carries an increased risk of morbidity and mortality, however produced, and should therefore be eliminated. On the other hand, it might be held that, particularly for

> women, the risk associated with mild or moderate degrees of obesity is small and does not justify imposing a way of life which may cause pratical difficulties, anxiety and feelings of guilt [p. 26].

When physiological factors alone are considered, there would appear to be more justification for the second point of view than for the first. For example, Keys (1975) showed that when body mass was considered with other risk factors, the probability of occurrence of CHD rose from 78 to 111 in the highest risk groups; but when body mass was not considered the occurrence rose from 78 to 110, strongly suggesting that weight reduction would be less important in minimizing CHD risk than reductions in blood pressure, smoking, and serum cholesterol. In the same vein, while the general pattern of association between weight elevation and the probability of developing diabetes has been well established (Berger, Muller, & Renold, 1977), for many years it has been found that only about half of the overweight do become diabetic (e.g., Knowles, 1968; Paullin & Sauls, 1922), leaving in doubt the existence of any direct causal linkages. Moreover, one very careful recent study (Berchtold, Berger, Greiser, Dohse, Irmscher, Gries, & Zimmermann, 1977) found a correlation of only .17 between body mass and insulin. From a biological point of view it can be concluded that weight reduction may significantly improve the chances for a long and healthy life, but the beneficial effects may be attributable to factors associated with weight reduction rather than weight loss per se, and the present state of our knowledge does not permit us to predict exactly what health benefits accrue to those moving down the ladder from morbid obesity to normal weight. The fact that the overweight often suffer considerable psychological stress (Stuart, 1977, 1978), which can be relieved by weight loss coupled with the potential benefits of weight reduction, leads to the conclusion that weight-control methods having mild to moderate cost and few if any negative side effects may be universally justified for use among those seeking help in controlling their weight. On the other hand, when the methods are costly and bring with them a high potential for fairly serious side effects, their use, even with those who volunteer to undergo treatment, may be questioned unless immediate weight loss is mandated by existing medical problems.

With these background considerations, some suggestions concerning the potential contribution of each of the weight-control techniques reviewed can be offered.

Behavior Modification

It is clear that the goal of all treatments of obesity is the long-term control of the balance between food intake and energy utilization. It is equally clear that change in the energy balance cannot be achieved or maintained without the individual's active participation. To achieve and to direct this participation constructively, some form of modification of the patient's behavior must be accomplished in every successful treatment program.

While some earlier reviews of the outcomes of treatments in which behavior modification was the primary active agent have indicated that the results obtained are suboptimal (e.g., Stuart, 1975a; Stunkard, 1978; Stunkard & Mahoney, 1976), other reviewers who shared essentially the same methodology have reached more optimistic conclusions. As in the present review, Wilson (1979) and Wing and Jeffery (1979) found that while behavior modification did not produce the most rapid or greatest weight loss during active treatment, participants in its programs were more likely to maintain or even to improve upon the losses they achieved during treatment. Therefore, behavior modification techniques, which are low in cost and have no adverse side effects, should be included in every weight-control effort.

The results of behavioral interventions can be greatly improved if the usual format of their delivery is improved in several important ways. First, an effort to alter the forces that contribute to the patient's urge to eat should be undertaken before eating itself is addressed. Stuart (1979) has termed this as the use of "indirect intervention methods," which are a means of increasing the probable success of the use of "direct methods." This sequence is premised on the assumption that patients' overeating is the best response available to them for meeting their personal objectives at the moment the eating occurs. By helping to change the inner thoughts and feelings that predispose eating, and by modifying such environmental forces as understimulation, encouragement by others to engage in problem eating, and the overavailability of food, the impulse to overeat can be curbed. Techniques to manage eating itself can be expected to be effective only after the stimulants to overeat have been suppressed or eliminated.

Second, because the sources of the urge to eat and the form that overeating takes are as individual as each person's fingerprints, some effort should be made to individualize behavioral instigations (Wilson, 1979). Stuart and Davis (1978) have offered a means of doing this by listing techniques that clients might find helpful and asking them to select those they would like to incorporate into their repertoire, beginning with the steps that they believe they can take with greatest ease. This self-selection and self-pacing format helps to make certain that the intervention program offered is adapted to the patient's goals and skills rather than to the therapist's notion of how the patient should behave. It should be pointed out, however, that individualization of treatment methods does not require private therapy, but can very well be accomplished in group settings in which the support of others is used to motivate individuals to achieve individually selected goals. Indeed, Wilson (1979) has shown that when group and individual methods are contrasted, the former are superior to the latter. This finding is supported by that of Stuart and Mitchell (1978), which indicates that social monitoring and peer help were regarded by participants in one major weight-control program as the most valuable of the nine elements of that program subjected to analysis. Therefore, as a third step it is strongly recommended that behavior change services be offered in individualized ways in a group context.

As a fourth step, treatment programs should be extended through the time that patients achieve their goal weights. While greater weight losses early in the program tend to give shorter programs a rate-of-loss advantage, longer programs are shown to be significantly more productive of weight reductions. Wing and Jeffery (1979), for example, found a correlation of .75 between the length of behavior modification programs and the amount of weight lost, and a similar correlation of .68 for studies using anorectic drugs. As the pattern of weight loss changes over time (Stuart *et al.*, 1979), it would surely be a good idea to modify the content of treatment consistently with changes in patients' concerns as they gradually move closer to their goal weights.

As another step, patients should be offered booster sessions following the achievement of their goal weights. While several studies have shown that the contribution of booster sessions to weight maintenance is not at all certain (e.g., Ashby & Wilson, 1977; Hall, Hall, Borden, & Hanson, 1975; Kingsley & Wilson, 1977), the study with the largest sample size and the longest follow-up program (Stuart & Guire, 1979) did support the usefulness of booster sessions. In this study of members of Weight Watchers classes who did reach goal weight, Stuart and Guire (1979) found that those who continued to follow the recommendations learned during active class participation were more likely to maintain their weight, and those who participated in booster sessions were those most likely to sustain important behavior changes. Specifically, the 32.6% of the members who attended monthly booster sessions averaged 3.1 pounds above their goal weight some 15 months after reaching goal, in contrast to the 13.4-pound gains registered by the 43.2% of the members who did not make use of this option. To make these booster sessions maximally useful, however, they should offer technology different than that applied during weight loss, because the skills required for maintenance are significantly different than those applied during the process of losing weight. For example, as discussed elsewhere (Stuart, 1979), maintainers must learn to continue behavioral self-management techniques without the reinforcement of seeing their weight decline, and often must develop new life goals to replace the now irrelevant goal of making a sufficient lifestyle change to accomplish significant weight reductions.

Finally, it was suggested some time ago (Stuart & Davis, 1972) that comprehensive weight management programs should include significant first-order relatives of the target patient in order to obtain their support in creating physical and social environments conductive to the lifestyle change needed to produce weight loss. Consistent with this recommendation, Brownell (1977) and Wilson and Brownell (1978) did include spouses in some of their treatment offerings, and found that the spousal participation did contribute to improved outcome. However, it should be pointed out that weight losers have listed "family support" as the least highly regarded of nine factors that may contribute to their weight losses. In addition, Stuart and Guire (1979) have found that one partner's weight-control efforts are often the object of contention by the other. Therefore, when spouses are included in treatment, a two-step program should be utilized. First, the partners should be helped to develop a cooperative relationship independent of weight loss. Only when such a relationship is achieved and integrated, should the couple then be asked to move on to collaboration on lifestyle change aimed at better weight control.

In summary, behavior modification techniques may be used independently with reasonable probability of achieving at least modest weight losses that are maintainable over time. These techniques should be included in every other approach to weight control because they alone can produce the lifestyle changes needed for durable weight management. To improve the efficacy of the behavioral technique packages now in use, several changes are recommended: (*a*) the use of indirect techniques to prepare patients for focal eating behavior changes; (*b*) individualization of technique packages; (*c*) the use of group settings for service delivery; (*d*) extension of treatment contacts through the attainment of goal weight; (*e*) provision of booster sessions offering a technology adapted to weight maintenance as opposed to extension of weight-loss recommendations; and (*f*) the inclusion of significant others in treatment programs after cooperative interactions have been established between them and the weight-losing patient.

Diet

Better management of food intake is obviously one of the major expected outcomes of obesity treatment. Literally scores of diets are touted as new weight management breakthroughs every year. Most of these are essentially old ideas dressed up in new packaging, as is the case with the Atkins (1972) reintroduction of the low carbohydrate diet originally credited to Harvey (1872) and later revived by Pennington (1954). Ketogenic diets like this one are associated with some significant negative side effects such as the loss of lean body mass from vital organs rather than the loss of fat, and they should be avoided on that score. They should also be avoided because they require eating eccentricities that patients neither will be willing nor able to follow for their remaining years. As such they are eating regimens that are undertaken for short periods of time, as if to do penance for excessive eating that has led to weight gain, with the promise that once weight is lost eating can return to its normal fat-producing pattern.

Recognizing the risks inherent in imbalanced eating plans and the negative long-range implications of advocating food-use patterns that are not sustainable, the Fogarty International Conference on Obesity (Bray, 1975) recommended against crash diets and advocated a "diet which provides a conventional distribution of its major nutritients . . . one which can be divided into three or more meals per day [p. 2]."

Young (1975) has offered several other guidelines for dietary planning. After recognizing that the diet should satisfy "all nutrient needs except calories [p. 363]," she suggested the diet should (*a*) be adapted as closely as possible to the individual's dietary habits; (*b*) help to guard the weight loser against between-meal hunger; (*c*) be as consistent as possible with the eating habits of the individual's family and friends; and (*d*) be maintainable over the remainder of the individual's life.

Unfortunately, there is no universally acceptable

and effective dietary regimen. The caloric level of the diet must be individually determined, in most cases via trial and error. The basal caloric needs are slightly higher for men than women, but average around 30 kcal/kg (Weisner, Butterworth, & Sahm, 1977) or 1000 calories/m^2 of surface area per day (Gwinup, 1974). Hence, it is estimated that a 150-pound man who is 70 inches tall has approximately 1.7 m^2 of surface area, and therefore would have a basal metabolic requirement of some 1700 calories per day. To this should be added the calories needed to sustain his physical activity. Youths under 20 are estimated to burn about 60 percent more than their basal caloric requirement for this purpose, while the figure falls to 40% for persons 60 and over. Therefore, caloric levels needed to sustain weight will vary as a function of body size and activity level. Variations in the basic rate of metabolism also should be factored into the equation. As a consequence, estimates of optimal caloric levels must be evaluated on a weekly basis to determine whether they produce the expected rate of loss. In ideal circumstances, working with mildly to moderately overweight individuals who are not forced to lose weight rapidly in response to a medical emergency, prescribed diets should lead to an average of 1 to 2 pounds of weight lost per week. In this regard it is important to remember a finding reported earlier—that weight lost rapidly through severe caloric restriction was much more quickly regained than weight lost more slowly through a modest reduction in caloric level. Therefore, while patients may clamor for quick results, responsible professionals will resist this pressure and offer services that are likely to lead to the most lasting results.

The Food and Nutrition Board (1974) has laid down its *Recommended Dietary Allowances,* and these are the relatively universally accepted standards of an adequate diet. Working from these and other sources, the Select Committee on Nutrition and Human Needs (1977) of the United States Senate recommended the following goals for the composition of the average adult's daily diet: 10% saturated and 20% poly- and monounsaturated fats; 12% protein; 40 to 45% complex carbohydrate; and 15% sugar. It is generally agreed that for most weight losers this distribution of calories at a level that permits gradual progress is an optimal standard, with unbalanced diets being reserved for individuals with unusual problems being treated under the supervision of both a physician and a nutritionist or dietitian.

There are numerous sources of acceptable diets, most of which are patterned after the food-exchange lists originated by the American Diabetes Foundation. Stuart and Davis (1972) offer a range of diets that are presented in a format that allows weight losers to plan not only which foods of equivalent caloric value they will select, but also allows them to select convenient times at which these foods can be consumed. Whichever diet is followed, it should be one that has (*a*) very specific and easy to follow instructions so that little about choice, portion, or preparation of foods is left to doubt; and (*b*) flexible enough so that it can be adapted to individual choice. Forcing meat and potatoes on a vegetarian will be about as effective a weight-control program as offering bicycles to fish.

Drugs

Experts participating in the Fogarty International Center Conference on Obesity (Bray, 1975) have offered a number of recommendations concerning the use of varied pharmacological preparations in the management of weight problems. Among the more important recommendations concerning amphetamines and appetite suppressants generally are the following:

> An appetite suppressant drug should only be used as part of treatment and never as the sole therapy and only with adequate efforts to modify diet and exercise.
>
> Since the available data do not indicate that one drug is more effective than another, those drugs with less potential for addiction or abuse would appear to be the preferrable agents.
>
> There are no presently available criteria (except history) by which one can detect patients who may become psychologically or physically dependent upon these drugs. Therapy should be prolonged if weight loss cannot be achieved or continued.

> An appetite suppressant should never be prescribed or dispensed without a careful explanation of the potential side effects. [p. 3]

These experts recommended the use of thyroid hormones only for those patients who show a "significant reduction in metabolic rate . . . during treatment with a markedly hypocaloric diet (often less than 500 calories) [p. 4]." They also dismissed the use of human chorionic gonadotropin (HCG) because they found "no convincing evidence [p. 4]" that it contributed to weight loss beyond the effects of the 500-calorie diet with which it is commonly prescribed.

Given our finding that drug-induced weight changes tend not to be maintained over time (see Figure 18.1), one may question the wisdom of including drugs in obesity therapy as a routine course. It is possible that while the drug may increase the initial rate of weight loss, the attribution effect may undermine not only drug-related treatment effects but also those aspects of behavior self-management learned by participants in more complex treatment packages that include drugs. While it may be argued that drugs may be useful in helping clients to realize that they can lose weight despite their belief that they cannot, the negative attribution effects of these prescriptions probably render them useless over time.

A fine-grained analysis of the effects of the drugs studied in the reports reviewed here is summarized in Table 18.4, which presents the results for different agents. Unfortunately, while the average subject taking these drugs ranged between 185 and 190 pounds, and while 85% of the subjects were women, the varied caloric allowances and treatment lengths makes direct comparison of these outcomes difficult. As noted earlier, the losses associated with use of HCG are probably due to the hypocaloric diet with which the drug is prescribed. The other two best-performing drugs are Mazindol and Phentermine, both anorectic agents. Bray (1976) notes that the most common side effects of the first compound are mild central nervous system stimulation, insomnia, dizziness, and dry mouth, with some potential for stimulation of the cardiovascular system. Bray's (1976) review of the literature on the second drug indicates some tendency to increase blood pressure and produce tachycardia, some insomnia, and some oral dryness. Even the best of these compounds thus are not without possibly significant side effects.

Greater hesitation in the use of drugs also stems from some weaknesses that are inherent in the experiments used to validate their effectiveness. In the typical model, patients are told that they will be randomly assigned to either an active drug condition or one in which they receive a placebo. Giving this information is an ethical imperative. Once the program is begun, patients either do or do not experience the side effects that they know, through word of mouth or from past experience, to be associated with the taking of a drug. As in the research of Johnson and Hughes (1979), those who

Table 18.4 Comparative Effects of Varied Obesity Drugs

				Weight loss per week during treatment	
Drug	*N*	Calories prescribed	Treatment length (weeks)	Drug	Controls
HCG	356	500	10	2.88	2.60
Mazindol	2,642	1000	11.7	1.34	0.68
Fenfluramine	1,857	1100	15.3	0.85	0.31
Diethylpropion	673	1200	10.4	0.94	0.49
Phenylpropanolamine	147	1200	3.0	0.93	0.41
Amphetamine	373	1200	9.0	0.98	0.55
Phentermine	506	1400	12.9	1.31	0.78

received Mazindol did experience the dizziness, nervousness, and insomnia associated with the drug, while those in the control group had no such experiences. Accordingly, at least some of the positive effects ascribed to the drug are better explained by expectancy. Thus, it can be concluded that not only are the weight losses achieved through drug therapies not generally maintained, but there is reason to be suspicious of the factors that produce these changes in the first place.

Exercise

For some time it has been recognized that prescription of increased energy expenditure should be a dimension of all broad-spectrum weight-control programs (e.g. Stuart, 1971). As noted earlier, an increase in the level of exercise does produce weight loss during treatment, although the maintenance of these losses is essentially untested. Interestingly, Bjorntorp (1975) has noted that the massively obese person actually may *gain* weight through exercise (plasma insulin concentration decreased, but peripheral sensitivity to insulin increased to a greater degree), so that exercise is not an unmixed blessing for the weight loser. But advocates of the addition of an exercise component (e.g. Horton, 1975; Stuart & Davis, 1972) have observed that expenditure of as few as 100 kcal extra per day can lead to an annual loss of 10 pounds of body fat. Therefore, at the very least, inclusion of an exercise component can allow the weight loser to soften the level of caloric restriction that would be needed for fat loss, while at best it could add to the benefits of changed eating habits. Fortunately, addition of exercise to the regimen has other advantages as well.

First, Mayer, Roy, and Mitra (1956) showed many years ago that men in the most sedentary occupations ate more than those whose occupations demanded a moderate level of activity. Later, Johnson, Matrapaolo, and Wharton (1972) found that food consumption diminished as subjects completed a 10-week physical conditioning program, a finding that has been replicated in animal research (Katch, Martin, & Martin, 1979). In contrast to the belief that we work up our appetites through physical activity, quite the reverse may well be true for most people, so that adherence to a food plan may be expedited by increased physical activity. In addition, there is laboratory evidence in support of the notion that increased activity leads to the selective loss of fat and the conservation of lean body mass (e.g., Buskirk, Thompson, Lutwak, & Whedon, 1963; Kenrick, Ball, & Canary, 1972; Oscai, Mole, Krusack, & Holloszy, 1973). Therefore, increased activity may help to temper the ill effects and augment the beneficial effects of caloric restriction. Thirdly, increased activity has been shown to contribute to improved cardiovascular functioning (Buskirk, 1973; Fox, Naughton, & Haskell, 1971; Hanson & Nedde, 1970; Rose, 1970). These benefits include reduced pulse rate during exercise and while at rest, increased stroke volume, and decreased peripheral vascular resistence. In addition, exercise has such metabolic benefits as a decrease in fasting and postglucose plasma test insulin concentrations (Bjorntorp, deJounge, Sjorstrom, & Sullivan, 1970). Each of these is a major physiological benefit to which can be added a number of psychological benefits. Stuart (1975b) has elsewhere summarized evidence showing that increased activity has been associated with decreased tension and stress levels, better sleep, increased optimism, better ability to concentrate, greater interest in health-related activities in general, and improved self-confidence. Stuart (1975b) also identified such social advantages from exercise as the opportunity that it provides for an overt self-improvement effort that is much more readily reinforced than the covert decision not to eat a choice morsel, and the added chance to share participation in a health-enhancing effort with another person.

Just as all diets are not alike, neither are all exercise programs equally desirable. It has been found that long-duration, mild-intensity programs are best adapted to the needs of overweight individuals (Stuart, 1975b), so that a walking, stair-climbing, or walk-jog program requiring at least 30 min of effort at least 5 days per week is optimal. In addition, weight losers should be helped to accomplish a lifestyle analysis in which they identify ways they can increase the energy expended while performing routine tasks in their daily lives. For example, standing instead of sitting, pacing instead of standing still, walking short distances instead of driving, and using stairs instead of elevators can all add to the number of calories burned each day.

There are, of course, contraindications for exercise. Factors such as severe stenosis of the three main coronary arteries, progressive angina, impending infarction, certain arrhythmias, valvular diseases, uncontrolled hypertension or diabetes, acute myocarditis, severe electrolyte imbalance, severe varicose veins, anemia, and advanced bone or joint disease are all risk factors that can be exaggerated by increased activity (Fox, Naughton, & Gorman, 1972; Fox, Naughton, & Haskell, 1971; Naughton & Hellerstein, 1973). When patients are fit for exercise, however, and when therapists do take the time to provide the needed motivation for them to do so (Stuart, 1975b; Stuart & Davis, 1978), the long-term effects of any type of weight-management program can be enhanced (e.g., Johnson, Stalonas, Christ, & Pock, 1979). Therefore, like behavior modification and nutritional control, exercise should be a dimension of services offered to every patient for whom it does not pose a health hazard.

Fasting

The results recently reported by Drenick and Johnson (1978) are representative of those found in the fasting literature. Of 207 patients who had been hospitalized for fasting, half regained their original weight 2 to 3 years after treatment, and fewer than 10% maintained weights at less than their original level after 9 years. Reviewing their own data, the authors conclude that: "Fasting as a means to permanent weight regulation offers no advantages over other weight-reduction regimens [p. 131]." Given the potential risks and high cost of fasting (Howard, 1975), which must generally be undertaken in an expensive medical environment, it would seem to have no place in general weight-management programs and must be reserved for use only when very rapid weight loss is essential as a measure in the management of some other related malady.

Surgery

Weight is lost through gastric and bypass surgery at a very heavy cost in direct mortality and indirect morbidity. Commenting on these operations, Bray (1978) noted that for patients who are sufficiently overweight, who have failed at all other means of weight control, and who are sufficiently healthy to withstand the stress of the surgery, this intervention may be justified in an experimental climate. O'Leary (1978) also believes that bypass surgery may be the only method available to massively obese patients whose survival is questioned because of complications of their obesity. One of the most successful surgery groups is that at the University of Iowa (Mason, Printen, Blommers & Scott, 1978). Their average patients lose from 33 to 55% of their excess weight within one year of their operations, although the rather large standard deviations in this sample suggest very wide individual differences. It is not clear whether reducing a 300-pound woman by say 100 pounds (i.e., about half of her hypothetical excess weight) will improve her life expectancy and health enough to justify the threats to both that are inherent in the bypass procedures. It is also not clear that patients learn modified eating habits in this treatment, unless they are inhibited from their habitual patterns by very unpleasant physical effects of food consumption; as a result, reoperation may be necessary after the passage of time to correct stretching of the relevant portion of the alimentary canal. Therefore, it seems clear that until these techniques have been much more thoroughly evaluated, along with assessing alternative procedures such as gastric stapling, the use of surgery should be regarded as experimental and should be restricted only to high-risk patients willing to give their well-informed consent (Stuart, 1978, 1980) to participate in such programs.

Conclusions

We have reviewed a vast literature on attempts at the management of obesity through the methods used most frequently during the decade of the 1970s. In general, we have found that it is as true today as it was 20 years ago that mildly obese people can have a reasonable expectation of maintainable weight loss, while moderately to severely obese individuals are unlikely either to lose or to maintain the loss of significant amounts of weight. We have noted a great array of conceptual and methodological weaknesses in the literature of the 1970s. Because of these problems it is not clear whether needed technologies have yet to be developed or whether those which are available have yet to be applied with adequate care.

Based upon our reading of the studies reviewed here, we believe that an effective weight-control program should combine behavior modification, nutrition management, and exercise control in an individualized but group-administered format, with technologies adapted to the stages of weight change experienced by the participants. We would recommend that such a program be offered to all patients regardless of weight or other characteristics on the assumption that even the massively obese may benefit significantly from such services and must have the opportunity to achieve their goals through the least invasive treatments available to them (Stuart, 1980). We suggest avoidance of the use of drugs at this time because the literature does not support the belief that they contribute lasting benefits, and they may, in fact, undermine the advantages accruing to other dimensions of the service rendered. Fasting and surgical interventions are justified only in unusual circumstances, if at all, in light of their direct and indirect costs. It is clear from a careful reading of the current literature that when surgery is undertaken its side effects may seriously outweigh its advantages, and that surgeries should be restricted to experimental settings, with the informed consent of the patient being scrupulously protected.

Owing to repeated methodological and reporting lapses, we have been prohibited from drawing as much from this review as the effort should have permitted. Because readers of this chapter are also likely to make major contributions to the literature on the management of obesity, we would like to conclude our effort by offering some general recommendations for the planning and reporting of research on the control of obesity.

Recommendations for the Design and Reporting of Obesity Treatment Research

Comparison of the results of varied intervention methods depends upon the availability of research reports that present certain standard information in generally accepted formats. First, if readers are to know to which populations the results can be generalized, it is necessary to report data at least on the sex, age, initial weight, and initial percent overweight of all subjects. These data, among others (Stuart, 1977), have shown that variables such as chronicity, employment status, health, and other characteristics have a bearing on treatment outcome. Second, it is necessary to report treatment methods in detail. These accounts should at least include the following information (*a*) total number of subjects in each treatment condition; (*b*) means of subject recruitment and assignment to each condition; (*c*) details of each intervention condition, including number of sessions, any dietary and behavioral recommendations included with focal methods, treatment format (i.e., group or individual contact), and other information needed by would-be replicators; (*d*) characteristics of therapists and other means of service delivery; and (*e*) means and timing of contacting subjects for follow-up evaluations.

Our third general recommendation would seem to be superfluous, but quite a few published studies failed to report actual weight changes following treatment; therefore, in the Appendix to this paper are a number of measurement considerations. At this point, however, it is important to stress that no report in this area is complete without specifications of weight losses in pounds and/or kilograms. These data must present averages for each group as well as report ranges. When fewer than 30 subjects are included in an investigation, individual weight changes should be reported even if analyses are completed on a group basis only. Reports should also make note of the number of subjects gaining weight, failing to lose, or regaining all or some of the weight lost.

Weight-control studies must also include an evaluation of the long-term effectiveness of treatment. This is an ideal which few studies achieve.

Follow-ups are rare except in behavior modification and surgery studies, and the length of follow-ups in behavior modification are generally too short to be meaningful. A substantial proportion of the studies which do include follow-up, however short, have found that the losses attained by the end of treatment are transient even over these short time periods (e.g., Hall & Hall, 1974). Clearly, comparisons of weight before and after treatment cannot be used alone to assess the efficacy of treatment procedures. As the maintenance of losses over time is required for clinical success, follow-up assessments must be included in treatment evaluations. Stuart (1975a) has proposed that all studies include a follow-up and that as a minimal criterion, each follow-up last at least twice the length of the treatment or one year, whichever is longer.

Follow-ups should be planned with regard to seasonal effect on eating and activity levels (Stuart, 1975a). Ideally, pretreatment, posttreatment, and follow-up data should be collected at approximately the same time of year. As this would require studies to extend over a two-year time span, it is unlikely that such a goal would be frequently attained. Continuing data collection on control groups throughout the follow-up period would allow the effects of seasonal variations in weight to be controlled.

Inferences can also be mistakenly made if the success of a treatment is assessed solely in terms of those subjects who actually complete treatment. Jeffrey (1975) has noted several potential problems involved in such a method of data selection. First, differential rates of attrition from treatment and control groups may produce systematic effects in observed weight losses. Second, it is likely that the subjects who remain in a control group despite the weakness of control procedures in producing weight losses are on the average more motivated than those who are encouraged to remain in a treatment condition by substantial early weight losses. Such tendencies, when ignored in data analysis, would tend to attenuate differences between groups and the possibility of identifying treatment effects. On the other hand, self-selection could increase the apparent effectiveness of treatment by removing subjects from a treatment group who do not respond well. Individuals who do not lose weight in a treatment are more likely to drop out than those who lose weight easily.

The importance of threats to the validity of inferences based on data that exclude dropouts is underlined by observations that including these data can decrease reports of successful clinical treatment in addictive behavior (McFall & Hammen, 1971) or reverse inferences about superior and inferior therapies in weight loss (Harris & Bruner, 1971). Since attrition may result in systematic effects on treatment assessment, it is necessary either to collect data from dropouts and to include them in analysis and evaluation or to exclude incomplete data from calculations.

Another general problem in obesity research lies in the lack of adequate statistical analyses conducted on the data from the studies. Very often studies on weight control include no statistics at all. The values of weight losses in a group of subjects undergoing the same treatment will commonly be highly variable (Penick, Filion, Fox, & Stunkard, 1971); thus average weight losses will be fairly meaningless. To discover if these means represent real weight losses or weight losses superior to other treatments or controls, statistical comparisons are necessary. One difficulty in the use of traditional statistical analyses with weight-loss data is that weight loss is generally a function of original weight, so that those who weigh more originally, lose more weight. If the original weight distributions of groups compared statistically are not identical, then the results of the statistical analysis may be biased toward the group with greater original weight. The use of analysis of covariance with original weight as the covariate can circumvent this problem.

A type of variable which might confound the outcome of a treatment study are those factors which occur as simple concomitants of the treatment process (Frank, 1961), such as therapist attention, reinforcement-punishment, client expectations, or social pressures. While such variables are inherent in the clinical setting and thus nonspecific to treatment, they can distort comparisons between treated and untreated groups. Similarly, the reinforcing effects of therapist attention and the motivation provided by subject expectations in treatment could contribute to differences observed between treated and untreated groups. Therefore, adequate experimental design requires the use of pseudotreatment or attention-placebo control groups to separate the nonspecific effects of the treatment process from those of the actual treatment. To be useful, the procedure employed in placebo control groups should be as equal as possible to the testing and subject-therapist interactions in the treatment conditions. In their review of therapeutic interventions, Kazdin and Wilson (1978) observed that credibility of treatment and control conditions can vary and thus generate differential effects on client expectations. It is important, therefore, to ensure the equivalence of treatment and placebo groups with respect to these nonspecific factors.

As a final requirement, it would be very helpful if research reports included a summary of the theory of obesity that guided the selection of the treatment techniques and an assessment of the results, good or bad, in light of this guiding theory. This would help to reduce the number of reports of mechanistic and naive interventions that appear in print, and it would add interpretive meaning to the findings of those studies that are worthy of dissemination. Were this and the foregoing recommendations heeded in the literature reviewed here, readers would have had the benefit of much more firm conclusions than are now possible.

Appendix: Criteria of Obesity and Weight Change

Before the effectiveness of the many treatments for obesity can be compared, a standard criterion for assessing the results of the treatment must be established. Presently there is no agreement about which of the possible criteria to use (Stuart, 1975a). Finding an adequate criterion has proved to be difficult. A number of criteria have been suggested which are based on weight, height, overweight, body fat, body density, ideal weights, or some combination of these. All have both advantages and disadvantages as criteria that will be discussed as we present them. However, several concerns apply to all of the criteria. The tendency in a number of treatment studies is to present only average data regardless of the criterion used. This may not give an accurate reflection of individual success in treatment. Individual responses to the same treatment are seldom uniform. Thus, one person may lose 35 pounds and another only 5 pounds on the same diet. Claiming that an average of 20 pounds was lost by these two subjects is very misleading, since one lost much more and one much less. Another concern is that the criterion used to assess treatment success also should reflect the importance of the result to the subject. Researchers may be very happy with an average weight loss of 10 pounds, which may, however, be of little significance to a very obese individual.

Amount of weight lost is the most obvious and common criterion for success in treating obesity. Since weight loss is the aim of most of the participants in obesity treatment, it has the advantage of being the measure of importance to the subject. However, its many disadvantages for the researcher seem to outweigh this one advantage. The first disadvantage is that simple weight loss does not include information about the original weight of the subject (Bellack & Rozensky, 1975; Feinstein, 1959) or about the goal weight (Bellack & Rozensky 1975). A weight loss of 20 pounds by an individual with an original weight of 130 pounds and a goal of 110 pounds is assigned the same significance as a weight loss of 20 pounds by a 250-pound person with the same goal. Obviously, the loss of 20 pounds is more important to the person who had only 20 pounds to lose, while it probably would have little effect on the health or personal satisfaction of the heavier individual. Further, an obese person weighing 250 pounds will generally lose weight more quickly than a 130-pound person. More energy is required for the heavier person to move than for the lighter person; so while consuming the same number of calories, a heavier person will probably have a larger energy deficit than a lighter person (Bellack & Rozensky, 1975). Thus, studies using more obese subjects will show larger weight losses than studies using lighter subjects, even with identical treatment methods. A way to avoid this problem is to group subjects into initial weight categories to present weight-loss data so that subjects of similar starting weights may be compared across several studies.

Simple weight loss information also ignores individual weight goals. Two individuals may be of identical initial weights but have different proportions of body fat. Since the goal of obesity treatments presumably is to reduce the amount of body fat—not just body weight—people with less fat will desire to lose less weight. A 150-pound woman with a height of 5 ft 10 in has less weight to lose than a 150-pound woman with a height of 5 ft. Simply grouping these two women by their starting weights and reporting their weight losses as an average value obscures important differences in what they wanted to lose, in the value of the same amount of weight loss to each of them, and in the ease of weight loss for each of them.

A second type of weight loss criterion which has been proposed is the rate of weight loss per day or week. This rate measure suffers from the same disadvantages as the simple weight-loss criterion, plus the problem that the rate of weight loss during the first few weeks is extremely rapid because of the loss of body water, but then slows after the water is lost (Feinstein, 1959). Thus, the rate of weight loss for individuals in short treatment programs will be greater than that for persons in a treatment program covering a longer time (Feinstein, 1959). Rate of weight loss should only be used to compare treatment programs lasting the same number of weeks.

A third type of weight-loss measure is the percentage of body weight lost. This criterion has the advantage of including original body weight in its calculation. Thus, our 130-pound person who loses 20 pounds has lost approximately 15% of body weight, while the 250-pound one who loses 20 pounds has lost only 8% of his or her weight, reflecting in some way the relative importance of this 20-pound loss to the two different people. However, the percentage of weight lost ignores treatment goals. As mentioned above, individuals of the same initial weight may need to lose different amounts of weight depending on their relative proportion of body fat. Such differences in weight-loss goals are not reflected in the criterion of the percentage of body weight lost. This criterion also has been criticized because it gives more value to each pound lost by a lighter person than those lost by a heavier person (Bellack & Rozensky, 1975). Weight loss was criticized above for failure to do just this. The pounds lost by the lighter person are more difficult to lose and of more real significance in their lives than those lost by the heavier person; therefore, placing more value on their loss seems reasonable. The problem then becomes one of assigning a numerical value to this difference. Percent of body weight lost may stress the weight loss of the lighter individual too much or even too little.

A fourth criterion which is based on weight loss is the percent of overweight lost. This criterion has the advantage of including information about both the initial and the goal weights and is calculated by first determining an ideal weight for a subject and then comparing it to the weight lost. An individual who initially weighs 200 pounds, with a goal of 120 pounds, and who loses 40 pounds would have lost 50% of his or her overweight, while another 200-pound individual who loses 40 pounds, but whose goal is 140 pounds, would have lost 67% of his or her overweight. The disadvantages of this criterion mainly involve the methods of determining a goal weight so that pounds overweight can be calculated. Such methods need to be standardized to allow adequate comparison of treatment studies. Using percent overweight as a treatment criterion, the goal weight is generally obtained from the Metropolitan Life Insurance tables that give ideal weights by sex, age, height, and small, medium, and large frame size. No standard method exists for determining frame size, which in practice is usually done by simple visual estimation (Bellack & Rozensky, 1975; Feinstein, 1959; Garn, 1962). The tables themselves may not be accurate (Feinstein, 1959) and should be updated every generation because of increases in average heights and weights. A final problem is that the ideal weights are given as rather large ranges of weights. No agreement has been reached on which point in the range of weights to choose. Thus, when a woman who weighs 130 pounds with an ideal weight of 110 to 115 pounds loses 15 pounds, she can be said to have lost 75 to 100% of her excess weight, depending on which point in the range is chosen. The choice of ideal weight within the range given in the table can make very large differences in the reported success of the treatment. A researcher using the upper limit of the ideal weight range would have much better reported results than one using the lower limit. A reasonable compromise seems to be to choose the middle point of the ideal weight range as the goal weight. Any treatment study using percentage of overweight lost should specify carefully the methods by which goal weights were determined.

Other criteria based on weight losses have been suggested but are rarely used. A criterion similar to the percentage of overweight lost is the performance index suggested by Jolliffe and Alpert (1951) which compared the rate of weight loss to the expected weight loss. Users of this criterion face problems in determining the expected rate of weight loss and the problems of rapid weight loss from water weight described earlier. Also, because of these changes in rates of weight loss, the performance index can only be used on subjects who complete the treatment program (Feinstein, 1959). Feinstein (1959) recommended the use of a reduction index which attempts to integrate initial weight, weight-loss goals, and amount of weight lost in one measure. The reduction index = weight lost/overweight × initial weight/goal weight × 100. An individual with an initial weight of 130 pounds, a goal of 110, and a loss of 20 pounds has an index of 118, while one with an original weight of 250 pounds, a goal of 110 pounds, and a loss of 20 pounds has an index of 3. This index thus greatly exaggerates the problem of giving more value to the pounds lost by the lighter individual by making the 20 pounds lost by the 130-pound person worth 118 while the same 20 pounds in the 250-pound person is worth only 3. Further, this criterion is difficult to interpret and would mean little or nothing to participants in the weight-loss program.

Alternative criteria for measuring treatment success that avoid some problems of the weight-based criteria are those that directly measure body fat. These have several advantages. Presumably, the actual goal of obesity treatments is the loss of fat, not necessarily the loss of weight. Obesity is more correctly defined as overfatness rather than overweight (Brozek & Kinzey, 1960). Using measurements of fat allows initial weight and goal weight to be combined, although such problems as easier fat loss by individuals with more fat and the greater real significance of fat loss by those with less fat to lose are not necessarily avoided by these measurements.

There are a number of ways of directly measuring the amount of body fat such as hydrostatic weighing, radioactive potassium tracing, X rays, and ultrasonic techniques. While these methods are accurate in estimating the amount of body fat, they are not practical outside the laboratory for use in clinical practice. The suggestion has been made that fat can be accurately estimated by measurements of fatfolds at various sites on the body (e.g., Franzini & Grimes, 1976; Garn, 1962), and that progress in obesity treatment can be assessed by successive skinfold measurements (Sloan & Koeslag, 1973). These measurements are made by lifting up the layer of fat, separating it from the muscle, and measuring its width with spring-loaded calipers. These measurements can be made quickly and easily, although they probably increase the embarrassment of the subject.

Unfortunately, skinfold estimates of body fat involve even more problems than the weight criteria. Skinfold measures themselves involve many sources of inaccuracy. First, several researchers have shown that the various caliper designs produce varying results, with some being more accurate than others (Bray, Greenway, Molitch, Dahms, Atkinson, & Hamilton, 1978; Edwards, Hammond, Healy, Tanner, & Whitehouse, 1954). Sanchez and Jacobson (1978) found that the calipers slide during measurements, while Edwards *et al.* (1954) found that the calipers' springs vary in tautness, making the measurements of the same type of calipers vary. Second, the calipers and measurement techniques were designed for and validated on normal weight rather than overweight subjects (Durnin & Rahaman, 1971; Pollock, Laughridge, Coleman, Lennerud, & Jackson, 1975; Womersley & Durnin, 1973; Zwiren, Skinner, & Burskirk, 1973). The calipers cannot reach around the fatfolds of very obese individuals (Bray *et al.*, 1978), and the fat is more difficult to separate from the muscle in more obese subjects (Garn, 1962; Sanchez & Jacobson, 1978; Steel, 1977). Body fat is significantly underestimated by skinfolds in more obese subjects, but is closer to accuracy in lean subjects (Franklin, Buskirk, & Mendez, 1978). The validity of the use of skinfolds to estimate fat with obese subjects is questionable. Third, the reliability of skinfold measurements does not appear to be very high, as measurements have shown a high variability, particularly in more obese individuals (Bray *et al.*, 1978; Burkinshaw, Jones, & Krupowicz, 1973; Johnson & Stalonas, 1977; Kandel, 1969; Pollock *et al.*, 1975; Ruiz, Calley, & Hamilton, 1977; Steel, 1977; Wilmore, Girandola, & Moody, 1970). The variability of skinfold measurements is higher than the variability of weight-loss measurements on the same subjects (Steel, 1977; Pollock *et al.*, 1975). Further, the variability of skinfold measurements of obese subjects at a constant weight taken from week to week were shown to be very high (Bray *et al.*, 1978). Steel (1977) concluded that the individual variability of week-to-week measurements of skinfolds are so large as to be of no use in evaluating a treatment program. Fourth, different observers frequently arrive at different results, especially when the observers are inexperienced (Burkinshaw *et al.*, 1973). And fifth, no agreement has been reached regarding which site on the body should be used to measure the skinfolds. The sites most frequently used are the triceps and subscapular skinfolds, although others have also been measured. Garn, Rosen, and McCann (1971) and Womersley and Durnin (1973) claim that the subscapular region gives a better estimate of fat, while Franzini and Grimes (1976), Johnson and Stalonas (1977), Seltzer and Mayer (1967), Sloan and Koeslag (1973), and Bray *et al.* (1978) favor the triceps. Other researchers have recommended using combinations of sites for the best estimate of body fat (Franzini & Grimes, 1976; Johnson & Stalonas, 1977). Sloan, Burt, and Blyth (1962) showed that the best predictors of body fat in normal weight young women were the iliac and triceps skinfolds, while the best in young men was the thigh measurement. There is also evidence that the location of fat is different in obese subjects than in normal weight subjects (Allen, Peng, Chen, Huang, Chang, & Fang, 1956). As weight changes, the best location for skinfold measurements may change.

Part of the validation procedures for skinfolds as estimators of body fat was the development of equations to predict body fat from various skinfold measurements. These equations have proved to be ungeneralizable across samples (Durnin & Rahaman, 1967; Franklin *et al.*, 1978; Wilmore & Behnke, 1969; Wilmore *et al.*, 1970). Skinfold values and prediction equations are affected by the sex, age, race, and SES of the individual (Brozek & Keys, 1951; Garn, 1962; Sanchez & Jacobson, 1978). In addition, skinfold measures at various body sites are differentially affected by age. Thus, the skinfold site chosen and the measurement methods used should change as the above-noted subject variables change; absolute values of skinfolds cannot be compared across samples and, hence, across treatment studies.

A final consideration in the decision of whether to use skinfolds to measure success in the treatment of obesity is that skinfolds are highly correlated with weights (Bray *et al.*, 1978; Cowgill, 1957; Fuchs, Theis, & Lancaster, 1978; Garn, 1962; Garn *et al.*, 1971; Seltzer, Goldman & Mayer, 1965; Wakat, Johnson, Krzywichi, & Gerber, 1971; Young, Martin, Tensuan, & Blondin, 1962). Bray *et al.* (1978) obtained a correlation of .94 between skinfolds and weight at a particular height. Such high correlations suggest that if skinfold is a good predictor of body fat, then so, too, is weight. Why use skinfold measurements, which are highly unreliable and fraught with technical problems, when weight can be used as effectively in predicting body fat? Further, weight without height has been shown to be directly correlated with body fat (Newens & Goldstein, 1972; Pollock *et al.*, 1975; Wakat, Johnson, Krzywichi, and Gerber, 1971). Also, weight may possibly be an even more accurate measure of obesity then skinfolds. Johnson and Stalonas (1977) found that skinfold estimation of fat led to identifying only 8% of a group of visibly overweight individuals as being obese. Their average weight was 40% over the ideal on the insurance norms. In this case, weight gave a better indication of obesity than skinfolds. Bray *et al.* (1976), on the other hand, found that using a weight/height criterion, 95% of subjects were overweight. A similar number were identified as overweight by triceps skinfold criteria.

An even better argument against the use of skinfolds as a treatment success criterion is that Johnson and Stalonas (1977) found that over a 10-week treatment period their subjects had a significant weight loss, but their skinfold measurements showed an increase in fat. Pollock *et al.* (1975) similarly concluded that skinfold measurements over a period of weeks are useless as an indicator of treatment success.

In conclusion, the best criterion appears to be percentage overweight lost, using the midpoint of the ideal weight range to determine amount overweight. Such a criterion should be supplemented by including information on the actual number of pounds lost, broken down by categories of initial weight. A further measure of interest would be the number of subjects actually reaching their goal weight. Skinfold measurements do not seem to be accurate enough to justify their use alone, nor do they appear to contribute much information not given by weight data. Standardization of methods of reporting the results of obesity treatments along these lines are necessary to make comparisons of treatment effectiveness.

Reference Notes

1. Craighead, L., O'Brien, R., & Stunkard, A. J. *Behavioral and pharmacological treatment of obesity.* Unpublished manuscript, Pennsylvania State University, 1978.
2. Bjorntorp, P. Personal communication, 1978.

References

Allen, T. H., Peng, M. T., Chen, K. P., Huang, T. F., Chang, C., & Fang, H. S. Prediction of total adiposity from skinfolds and the curvilinear relationship between external and internal adiposity. *Metabolism,* 1956, *5,* 346-353.

Ashby, W. A., & Wilson, G. T. Behavior therapy for obesity: Booster sessions and long-term maintenance of weight loss. *Behaviour Research and Therapy*, 1977, *15*, 451-463.

Atkins, D. *The diet revolution.* New York: Bantam Books, 1972.

Baird, J. D. Diabetes mellitus and obesity. *Progress in Nutritional Science*, 1973, *32*, 199-204.

Bellack, A. S., & Rozensky, R. H. The selection of dependent variables for weight reduction studies. *Journal of Behavior Therapy and Experimental Psychiatry,* 1975, *6,* 83-84.

Benfield, J. R., Greenway, F. L., Bray, G. A., Barry, R. E., Lechago, J., Mena, I., & Schedewie, H. Experience with jejunoileal bypass for obesity. *Surgery, Gynecology, and Obstetrics,* 1976, *143,* 401-410.

Berchtold, P., Berger, M., Greiser, E., Dohse, M., Irmscher, K., Gries, F. A., & Zimmerman, H. Cardiovascular risk factors in gross obesity. *International Journal of Obesity,* 1977, *1,* 219-229.

Berger, M., Muller, W. A., & Renold, A. E. Relationship of obesity to diabetes: Some facts, many questions. In H. M. Katzen & R. J. Mahler (Eds.), *Diabetes, obesity, and vascular disease* (Vol. 2). New York: Wiley, 1977.

Bjorntorp, P. Effects of physical conditioning in obesity. In G. A. Bray (Ed.), *Obesity in perspective* (Vol. 2). Washington, D.C.: U.S. Government Printing Office, 1975.

Bjorntorp, P., deJounge, K., Sjorstrom, L., & Sullivan, L. The effect of physical training on insulin production in obesity. *Metabolism,* 1970, *19,* 631-638.

Blundell, J. E., & Rogers, P. J. Pharmacologic approaches to the understanding of obesity. *Psychiatric Clinics of North America,* 1978, *1,* 629-660.

Bray, G. A. *Obesity in perspective* (Vol. 1). Washington, D.C.: U.S. Government Printing Office, 1975.

Bray, G. A. *The obese patient.* Philadelphia: W. B. Saunders, 1976.

Bray, G. A. Current status of intestinal bypass surgery in the treatment of obesity, *Diabetes,* 1977, *26,* 1072-1079.

Bray, G. A. Intestinal bypass surgery for obese patients. *Psychiatric Clinics of North America,* 1978, *1,* 673-690.

Bray, G. A., Barry, R. E., Benfield, J. R., Castelnuovo-Tedesco, P., Drenick, E. J., & Passaro, E. Intestinal bypass operation as a treatment for obesity. *Annals of Internal Medicine,* 1976, *85,* 97-109.

Bray, G. A., Greenway, F. L., Molitch, M. E., Dahms, W. J., Atkinson, R. L., & Hamilton, K. Use of anthropomorphic measures to assess weight loss. *American Journal of Clinical Nutrition,* 1978, *31,* 769-773.

Brewer, C., White, H., & Baddeley, M. Beneficial effects of jejunoileostomy on compulsive eating and associated psychiatric symptoms. *British Medical Journal,* 1974, *4,* 314-316.

British Medical Research Council. *Diet and coronary heart disease.* London: Her Majesty's Stationery Office, 1974.

British Medical Research Council. *Diet and coronary heart disease.* London: Her Majesty's Stationery Office, 1976.

Brown, J. M., Yetter, J. F., Spicer, M. J., & Jones, J. D. Cardiac complications of protein-sparing modified fasting. *Journal of the American Medical Association,* 1978, *240,* 120-122.

Brownell, K. D. *The effect of spouse training and partner cooperativeness in the behavioral treatment of obesity.* Unpublished doctoral dissertation, Rutgers, The State University, 1977.

Brozek, J., & Keys, A. The evaluation of leanness-fatness in man: Norms and interrelationships. *British Journal of Nutrition,* 1951, *5,* 194-206.

Brozek, J., & Kinzey, W. Age changes in skinfold compressibility. *Journal of Gerontology,* 1960, *15,* 45-51.

Buchwalter, J. A. A prospective comparison of the jejunoileal and gastric bypass operations for morbid obesity. *World Journal of Surgery,* 1977, *1,* 757-768.

Burkinshaw, S., Jones, P. R. M., & Krupowicz, D. W. Observer error in skinfold thickness measurements. *Human Biology,* 1973, *45,* 273-279.

Buskirk, E. R. Cardiovascular adaptation to physical effort in healthy men. In J. R. Naughton & H. R. Hellerstein (Eds.), *Exercise testing and training in coronary heart disease.* New York: Academic Press, 1973.

Buskirk, E. R., Thompson, R. H., Lutwak, L., & Whedon, G. R. Energy balance of obese patients during weight reduction: Influence of diet restriction and exercise. *Annals of the New York Academy of Science,* 1963, *110,* 918-940.

Chiang, B. N., Perlman, L. V., & Epstein, F. H. Overweight and hypertension. *Circulation,* 1969, *39,* 403-421.

Condon, S. C., Janes, N. J., Wise, L., & Alpers, D. H. Role of caloric intake in the weight loss after jejunoileal bypass for obesity. *Gastroenterology,* 1978, *74,* 34-37.

Cowgill, G. R. A formula for estimating the specific gravity of the human body with a consideration of its possible uses. *American Journal of Clinical Nutrition,* 1957, *5,* 601-611.

Davison, G. C., Tsujimoto, R. N., & Glaros, A. G. Attribution and maintenance of behavior change in falling asleep. *Journal of Abnormal Psychology,* 1973, *82,* 124-133.

Dean, R. H., Scott, H. W., Jr., Shull, H. J., & Gluck, S. W. Morbid obesity: Problems associated with operational management. *American Journal of Clinical Nutrition,* 1977, *30,* 90-97.

DeWind, L. T., & Payne, J. H. Intestinal bypass surgery for morbid obesity. *Journal of the American Medical Association,* 1976, *236,* 2298-2301.

Donald, D. W. A. Mortality rates among the overweight. In R. F. Robertson (Ed.), *Anorexia and obesity.* Edinburgh: Royal College of Physicians, 1973.

Drenick, E. J., & Johnson, D. Weight reduction by fasting and semistarvation in morbid obesity: Long-term follow-up. *International Journal of Obesity,* 1978, *2,* 123-132.

Dubos, R. J. The evolution of microbial disease. In G. Gabbiani (Ed.), *Reflections on biologic research.* St. Louis: Warren H. Green, 1957.

Dublin, L. I. Relation of obesity to longevity. *New England Journal of Medicine,* 1953, *248,* 971-974.

Durnin, J. V. G. A., & Rahaman, M. M. The assessment of the amount of fat in the human body from measurement of skinfold thickness. *British Journal of Nutrition,* 1967, *21,* 681-689.

Edwards, D. A. W., Hammond, W. H., Healy, M. J. R., Tanner, J. M., & Whitehouse, R. H. Design and accuracy of calipers for measuring subcutaneous tissue thickness. *Nutrition,* 1954, *9,* 133-143.

Enzi, G., Baritussio, A., Marchior, E., & Crepaldi, G. Short-term and long-term clinical evaluation of a non-amphetaminic anorexiant (Mazindol) in the treatment of obesity. *Journal of International Medical Research,* 1976, *4,* 305-318.

Feinstein, A. R. The measurement of success in weight reduction: An analysis of methods and a new index. *Journal of Chronic Diseases,* 1959, *10,* 439-456.

Fikri, E., & Cassella, R. R. Jejunoileal bypass for massive obesity. *Annals of Surgery,* 1974, *179,* 460-464.

Food and Nutrition Board. *Recommended dietary allowances.* Washington, D.C.: National Academy of Sciences, 1974.

Fox, S. M., Naughton, J. P., & Gorman, P. A. Physical activity and cardiovascular health: III. The exercise prescription. *Modern Concepts of Cardiovascular Disease,* 1972, *41,* 25-49.

Fox, S. M., Naughton, J. P., & Haskell, W. L. Physical activity and the prevention of coronary heart disease. *Annals of Clinical Research,* 1971, *3,* 404-419.

Frank, J. D. *Persuasion and healing.* Baltimore: Johns Hopkins Press, 1961.

Franklin, B. A., Buskirk, E. R., & Mendez, J. Validity of skinfold predictive equations on lean and obese subjects. *American Journal of Clinical Nutrition,* 1978, *31,* 563-565.

Franzini, L. R., & Grimes, W. B. Skinfold measures as the criterion of change in weight control studies. *Behavior Therapy,* 1976, *7,* 256-260.

Fuchs, R. J., Theis, C. L., & Lancaster, M. C. A nomogram to predict lean body mass in men. *American Journal of Clinical Nutrition,* 1978, *31,* 673-678.

Garn, S. M. Anthropometry in clinical appraisal of nutritional status. *American Journal of Clinical Nutrition,* 1962, *11,* 418-432.

Garn, S. M., Rosen, N. N., & McCann, M. B. Relative values of different fat folds in a nutritional survey. *American Journal of Clinical Nutrition,* 1971, *24,* 1380-1381.

Goldrick, R. B., Nestel, P. J., & Havenstein, N. Comparison of a new anorexic agent AN 448 with Fenfluramine in the treatment of refractory obesity. *Medical Journal of Australia,* 1974, *1,* 882.

Griffen, W. O., Jr., Young, V. L., & Stevenson, C. C. A prospective comparison of gastric and jejunoileal bypass procedures for morbid obesity. *Annals of Surgery,* 1977, *186,* 500-507.

Gwinup, G. Effect of diet and exercise in the treatment of obesity. In G. A. Bray & J. E. Bethune (Eds.), *Treatment and management of obesity,* New York: Harper & Row, 1974.

Hall, S. M., & Hall, R. G. Outcome and methodological considerations in behavioral treatment of obesity. *Behavior Therapy,* 1974, *5,* 352-364.

Hall, S. R., Hall, R. G., Borden, B. L., & Hanson, R. W. Follow-up strategies in the behavioral treatment of overweight. *Behaviour Research and Therapy,* 1975, *13,* 167-172.

Halverson, J. D., Wise, L., Wazna, M. F., & Ballinger, W. F. Jejunoileal bypass for morbid obesity: A critical appraisal. *American Journal of Medicine,* 1978, *64,* 461-475.

Hanson, J. S., & Nedde, W. H. Preliminary observations on physical training for hypertensive males. *Circulation Research Supplements,* 1970, *1,* 26-27; 49-53.

Harris, M. B., & Bruner, C. G. A comparison of self-control and a contract procedure for weight control. *Behaviour Research and Therapy,* 1971, *9,* 347-354.

Harvey, W. *On corpulence in relation to disease.* London: H. Renshaw, 1872.

Hornberger, H. R. Gastric bypass. *American Journal of Surgery,* 1976, *131,* 415-418.

Horton, E. S., The role of exercise in the prevention and treatment of obesity. In G. A. Bray (Ed.), *Obesity in perspective* (Vol. 1). Washington, D.C.: U.S. Government Printing Office, 1975.

Howard, A. N. Dietary treatment of obesity. In T. Silverstone (Ed.), *Obesity: Its pathogenesis and management.* Acton, Mass.: Publishing Science Group, 1975.

Jeffrey, D. B. Treatment evaluation issues in research of addictive behaviors. *Addictive Behaviors,* 1975, *1,* 23-36.

Johnson, D., & Drenick, E. J. Therapeutic fasting in morbid obesity: Long-term follow-up. *Archives of Internal Medicine,* 1977, *137,* 1381-1382.

Johnson, R. E., Matrapaolo, J. A., & Wharton, M. A. Exercise, dietary intake, and body composition. *Journal of the American Dietetic Association,* 1972, *61,* 399-403.

Johnson, W. G., & Hughes, J. R. Mazindol: Its efficacy and mode of action in generating weight loss. *Addictive Behaviors,* 1979, *4,* 237-244.

Johnson, W. G., & Stalonas, P. Measuring skinfold thickness: A note. *Addictive Behaviors,* 1977, *2,* 105-107.

Johnson, W. G., Stalonas, P. M., Christ, M. A., & Pock, S. R. The development and evaluation of a behavioral weight-reduction program. *International Journal of Obesity,* 1979, *3,* 229-238.

Jolliffe, N., & Alpert, E. The "performance index" as a method for estimating effectiveness of reducing regimens. *Postgraduate Medicine,* 1951, *9.* 106-115.

Kandel, G. E. Evaluating body composition. *Aerospace Medicine.* 1969, *40,* 486-490.

Katch, V. L., Martin, R., & Martin, J. Effects of exercise intensity on food consumption in the male rat. *American Journal of Clinical Nutrition,* 1979, *32,* 1401-1407.

Kazdin, A. E., & Wilson, G. T. *Evaluation of behavior therapy: Issues, evidence, and research strategies.* Ballinger: Cambridge, Mass., 1978.

Kenrick, M. M., Ball, M. F., & Canary, J. J. Exercise and weight reduction in obesity. *Archives of Physical Medicine and Rehabilitation,* 1972, *53,* 323-327.

Keys, A. Overweight and the risk of heart attack and sudden death. In G. A. Bray (Ed.), *Obesity in prespective* (Vol. 2). Washington D.C.: U.S. Government Printing Office, 1975.

Keys, A., Aravanis, C., Blackburn, H., van Buchem, F. S. P., Buzina, R., Djordjevic, B. X., Fidanza, F., Karvonen, M. J., Menotti, A., Puddu, V., & Taylor, H. L. Probability of middle-aged men developing coronary heart disease in five years. *Circulation,* 1972, *45,* 815-828.

King, L. T., Jr. Complications of jejunoileal bypass. *American Surgeon,* 1978, *44,* 505-509.

Kingsley, R. G., & Wilson, G. T. Behavior therapy for obesity: A comparative investigation of long-term efficacy. *Journal of Consulting and Clinical Psychology,* 1977, *45,* 288-298.

Kish, G. F., Parker, F. W., & Joseph, W. L. Intestinal bypass in morbid obesity: Long-term metabolic sequelae. *American Surgeon,* 1975, *41,* 786-792.

Knecht, B. H. Experience with gastric bypass for massive obesity. *American Surgeon,* 1978, *44,* 496-504.

Knowles, H. C. Prevalence and development of diabetes. *Federation Proceedings,* 1968, *27,* 945-947.

Langlois, K. K., Forbes, J. A., Bell, B. W., & Grant, G. F., Jr. A double-blind clinical evaluation of the safety and efficacy of Phentermine Hydrochloride (Fastin) in the treatment of exogenous obesity. *Current Therapeutic Research,* 1974, *16,* 289-296.

McEwen, H., Jacobson, H., Battrum, E. C., Crealock, R. J., Mitchell, M. N., McLaren, B. A. Experience with a hospital-based weight reduction program. *Canadian Medical Association Journal,* 1972, *107,* 43-45.

McFall, R. M., & Hammen, C. L. Motivation, structure, and self-monitoring: The role of non-specific factors in smoking reduction. *Journal of Consulting and Clinical Psychology*, 1971, *37*, 80-86.

Mason, E. E., Printen, K. J., Blommers, T. J., & Scott, D. H. Gastric bypass for obesity after ten years experience. *International Journal of Obesity*, 1978, *2*, 197-206.

Mason, E. E., Printen, K. J., & Boyd, W. C. Optimizing results of gastric bypass. *Annals of Surgery*, 1975, *82*, 405-414.

Mayer, J., Roy, P., & Mitra, K. P. Relation between caloric intake, body weight, and physical work: Studies in an industrial male population in West Bengal. *American Journal of Clinical Nutrition*, 1956, *4*, 169-175.

Medalie, J. H., Papier, C., Herman, J. B., Goldbourt, U., Tamir, S., Neufield, H. N., & Riss, E. Diabetes mellitus among 10,000 adult men. *Israel Journal of Medical Sciences*, 1974, *10*, 681-697.

Mersheimer, W. L., Kazarian, K. K., & Dursi, J. F. A critical analysis of 51 patients with jejunoileal bypass. *Surgery, Gynecology, and Obstetrics*, 1977, *145*, 845-852.

Mills, M. J., & Stunkard, A. J. Behavioral changes following surgery for obesity. *American Journal of Psychiatry*, 1976, *133*, 527-531.

Morris, J. N. *The uses of epidemiology*. London: Churchill, Livingston, 1976.

Mreiden, T., Danowski, T. S., Bahl, V. K., Sunder, J. K., & Clare, D. W. Jejunoileal bypass in retrospect: The views of 90 patients. *Obesity and Bariatric Medicine*, 1978, *7*, 224-228.

Musante, C. J. The dietary rehabilitation clinic: Evaluative report of a behavioral and dietary treatment of obesity. *Behavior Therapy*, 1976, *7*, 198-204.

Naughton, J., & Hellerstein, H. K. (Eds.). *Exercise testing and exercise training in coronary heart disease*. New York: Academic Press, 1973.

Neill, J. R., Marshall, J. R., & Yale, C. E. Mental changes after intestinal bypass surgery. *Journal of the American Medical Association*, 1978, *240*, 447-450.

Nentwig, C. G. Attribution of cause and long-term effects of the modification of smoking behavior. *Behavior Analysis and Modification*, 1978, *2*, 285-295.

Newens, E. M., & Goldstein, H. Height, weight, and the assessment of obesity in children. *British Journal of Preventive and Social Medicine*, 1972, *26*, 33-39.

O'Leary, J. P. Jejunoileal bypass in the treatment of morbid obesity. *International Journal of Obesity*, 1978, *2*, 191-196.

Oscai, L. B., Mole, P. A., Krusack, L. M., & Holloszy, J. O. Detailed body composition analysis on female rats subjected to a program of swimming. *Journal of Nutrition*, 1973, *103*, 412-418.

Ost, L. E., & Gotestam, K. G. Behavioral and pharmacological treatment for obesity: An experimental comparison. *Addictive Behavior*, 1976, *1*, 331-338.

Paullin, J. E., & Sauls, H. C. A study of the glucose tolerance test in the obese. *Southern Medical Journal*, 1922, *15*, 249-253.

Penick, S. B., Filion, R., Fox, S., & Stunkard, A. J. Behavior modification in the treatment of obesity. *Psychosomatic Medicine*, 1971, *33*, 49-55.

Pennington, A. W. Treatment of obesity: Developments of the past 150 years. *American Journal of Digestive Disorders*, 1954, *21*, 65-73.

Pollock, M. L., Laughridge, E. E., Coleman, B., Lennerud, A. C., & Jackson, A. Prediction of body density in young and middle-aged women. *Journal of Applied Physiology*, 1975, *38*, 745-749.

Printen, K. J., & Mason, E. E. Gastric bypass for morbid obesity in patients more than 50 years of age. *Surgery, Gynecology, and Obstetrics*, 1977, *144*, 192-194.

Rimm, A. A., Werner, L. H., Bernstein, R., & van Yserloo, B. Disease and obesity in 73,532 women. *Obesity and Bariatric Medicine*, 1972, *1*, 77-84.

Rose, G. Current developments in Europe. In R. J. Jones (Ed.), *Atherosclerosis: Proceedings of the second international symposium*. New York: Springer-Verlag, 1970.

Ruiz, L., Calley, J. R. T., & Hamilton, P. J. S. Measurements of triceps skinfold thickness: An investigation of sources of variation. *British Journal of Preventive and Social Medicine*. 1977, *25*, 165-167.

Sanchez, C. L., & Jacobson, H. Anthropometry measurements: A new type. *American Journal of Clinical Nutrition*, 1978, *111*, 1116-1117.

Schteingart, D. R., Foss, M. L., Lampman, R. M., Short, M., East, R., Buntman, H., Michael, R. J., & McGowland, J. Obesity: A multidisciplinary approach to management. In A. Howard (Ed.), *Recent advances in obesity research* (Vol. 1). London: Newman, 1975.

Scott, M. E., & Nelson, P. G. Fenfluramine in the treatment of hypertensive patients with refractory obesity. *Ulster Medical Journal*, 1975, *44*, 56-61.

Select Committee on Nutrition and Human Needs. *Dietary goals for the United States*. Washington, D.C.: U.S. Government Printing Office, 1977.

Seltzer, C. C., Goldman, R. F., & Mayer, J. The triceps skinfold as a predictive measure of body density and body fat in obese adolescent girls. *Pediatrics*, 1965, *36*, 212-218.

Seltzer, C. C., & Mayer, J. Greater reliability of the triceps fold over the subscapular skinfold as an index of obesity. *American Journal of Clinical Nutrition*, 1967, *20*, 950-953.

Sims, E. A. H. Studies in human hyperphagia. In G. A. Bray & J. E. Bethune (Eds.), *Treatment and management of obesity*. New York: Harper & Row, 1974.

Singh, B. N., Gaarder, T. D., Kanegae, T., Goldstein, M., Montgomerie, J. F., & Mills, H. Liquid protein diets and Torsade de Points. *Journal of the American Medical Association,* 1978, *240,* 115-119.

Sloan, A. W., Burt, J. J., & Blyth, C. S. Estimation of body fat in young women. *Journal of Applied Physiology,* 1962, *17,* 967-970.

Sloan, A. W., & Koeslag, J. H. A trial of the Ponderax skinfold caliper. *South African Medical Journal,* 1973, *47,* 125-127.

Smith, R. G., Innes, J. A., & Munro, J. F. Double-blind evaluation of Mazindol in refractory obesity. *British Medical Journal,* 1975, *3,* 284.

Sohar, E., & Sneh, E. Follow-up of obese patients: 14 years after a successful reducing diet. *American Journal of Clinical Nutrition,* 1973, *26,* 845-848.

Solow, C., Silberfarb, P. M., & Swift, K. Psychosocial effects of intestinal bypass surgery for severe obesity. *New England Journal of Medicine,* 1974, *290,* 300-304.

Steel, J. J. Measurement of tricep skinfold thickness during the treatment of obesity. *Obesity and Bariatric Medicine,* 1977, *6,* 20-22.

Stuart, R. B. Behavioral control of overeating. *Behaviour Research and Therapy,* 1967, *5,* 357-365.

Stuart, R. B. A three-dimensional program for the treatment of obesity. *Behaviour Research and Therapy,* 1971, *9,* 177-186.

Stuart, R. B. Behavioral control of overeating: A status report. In G. A. Bray (Ed.), *Obesity in perspective* (Vol. 1). Washington, D.C.: U.S. Government Printing Office, 1975. (a)

Stuart, R. B. Exercise prescription in weight management: Advantages, techniques, obstacles. *Obesity and Bariatric Medicine,* 1975, *40,* 16-24. (b)

Stuart, R. B. Self-help in self-management: The case of obesity. In R. B. Stuart (Ed.), *Behavioral self-management,* New York: Brunner/Mazel, 1977.

Stuart, R. B. *Act thin, stay thin.* New York: W. W. Norton, 1978.

Stuart, R. B. The chances of keeping it off after taking it off: The maintenance of weight loss. In P. O. Davidson & S. M. Davidson (Eds.), *Behavioral medicine: Changing health lifestyles.* New York: Brunner/Mazel, 1979.

Stuart, R. B. Ethical practice in behavior therapy. In S. Turner, K. Calhoun, & H. Adams (Eds.), *Handbook of clinical behavior therapy.* New York: Wiley, 1980.

Stuart, R. B., & Davis, B. *Slim chance in a fat world.* Champaign, Ill.: Research Press, 1972.

Stuart, R. B., & Davis, B. *Slim chance in a fat world* (Rev. ed.). Champaign, Ill.: Research Press, 1978.

Stuart, R. B., & Guire, K. Some correlates of the maintenance of weight lost through behavior modification. *International Journal of Obesity,* 1979, *3,* 87-96.

Stuart, R. B., & Jacobson, B. Sex differences in obesity and weight loss. In E. Gombert & V. Franks (Eds.), *Gender differences in psychopathology,* New York: Brunner/Mazel, 1979.

Stuart, R. B., Jensen, J., & Guire, K. Weight loss over time: Concomitants and consequences of a decreasing rate. *Journal of the American Dietetic Association,* 1979, *75,* 258-261.

Stuart, R. B., & Mitchell, C. Peer as opposed to professional programming for weight control: Peers hold the edge. *Psychiatric Clinics of North America,* 1978, *1,* 697-712.

Stunkard, A. J. (Ed.). Obesity: Basic mechanisms and treatment. *Psychiatric Clinics of North America,* 1978, *1,* 459-724.

Stunkard, A. J., & Mahoney, M. J. Behavioral treatment of the eating disorders. In H. Leitenberg (Ed.), *Handbook of behavior modification and behavior therapy.* Englewood Cliffs: Prentice-Hall, 1976.

Stunkard, A., & McLaren-Hume, M. The result of treatment for obesity. *Archives of Internal Medicine,* 1959, *103,* 79-85.

Telmos, A. J., & Bodzin, J. The surgical treatment of morbid obesity: A report of 190 cases. *Obesity and Bariatric Medicine,* 1977, *6,* 50-52.

Valins, S., & Nisbett, R. E. Attribution processes in the development of emotional disorders. In E. E. Jones, D. E. Kanouse, H. H. Kelley, R. E. Nisbett, S. Valins, & B. Weiner (Eds.), *Attribution: Perceiving the causes of behavior,* New York: General Learning Press, 1972.

Vernace, B. J. Controlled comparative investigation of Mazindol, D-Amphetamine, and placebo. *Obesity and Bariatric Medicine,* 1974, *3,* 124-129.

Vertes, V., Genuth, S. M., & Hazelton, I. M. Precautions with supplemented fasting. *Journal of the American Medical Association,* 1977, *238,* 21-26.

Wakat, D. K., Johnson, R. E., Krzywichi, H. J., & Gerber, L. J. Correlation between body volume and body mass in man. *American Journal of Clinical Nutrition,* 1971, *24,* 1308-1312.

Walker, B. R., Ballard, I. M., & Gold, J. A. A multicentre study comparing Mazindol and placebo in obese patients. *Journal of International Medical Research,* 1977, *5,* 85-90.

Weisner, R. L., Butterworth, C. E., & Sahm, D. N. *Handbook of clinical nutrition.* Birmingham: University of Alabama, 1977.

West, K. M., & Kalbfleisch, J. M. Influence of nutritional factors on prevalence of diabetes. *Diabetes,* 1971, *20,* 99-108.

Wilmore, J. H., & Behnke, A. R. An anthropometric estimation of body density and lean body weight in young men. *Journal of Applied Physiology,* 1969, *27,* 25-31.

Wilmore, J. H., Girandola, R. N., & Moody, D. L. Validity

of skinfold and girth assessment for predicting alterations in body composition. *Journal of Applied Physiology,* 1970, *29,* 313-317.

Wilson, G. T. Behavioral treatment of obesity: Maintenance strategies and long-term efficacy. In P. Sjoden, S. Bates, & W. S. Dockens (Eds.), *Trends in behavior therapy.* New York: Academic Press, 1979.

Wilson, G. T., & Brownell, K. D. Behavior therapy for obesity: Including family members in the treatment process. *Behavior Therapy,* 1978, *9,* 943-945.

Wing, R. R., & Jeffery, R. W. Outpatient treatments of obesity: A comparison of methodology and clinical results. *International Journal of Obesity,* 1979, *3,* 261-280.

Wise, P. J. Clinical experience with a new dosage form of phentermine hydrochloride. *Obesity and Bariatric Medicine,* 1975, *4,* 102-105.

Womersley, J., & Durnin, J. V. G. A. An experimental study of variability of measurements of skinfold thickness in young adults. *Human Biology,* 1973, *45,* 281-292.

Young, C. M. Dietary treatment of obesity. In G. A. Bray (Ed.), *Obesity in perspective* (Vol. 2), Washington, D. C.: U.S. Government Printing Office, 1975.

Young, C. M., Martin, M., Tensuan, R., & Blondin, J. Predicting specific gravity and body fatness in young women. *Journal of American Dietetic Association,* 1962, *40,* 102-107.

Young, C. M., Scanlan, S. S., Lutwak, L., & Im, H. S. Effect on body composition and other parameters in obese men of carbohydrate level of reduction diet. *American Journal of Clinical Nutrition,* 1971, *24,* 290-296.

Zwiren, L., Skinner, J. S., & Buskirk, E. R. Use of body density and various skinfold equations for estimating small reductions in body fatness. *Journal of Sports Medicine and Physical Fitness,* 1973, *13,* 213.

19

Behavioral Treatment of Smoking Behavior

RUSSELL E. GLASGOW
DOUGLAS A. BERNSTEIN

It is clearly established that cigarette smoking is hazardous to health. The evidence for this statement is documented in the more than 30,000 articles published on the deleterious effects of tobacco consumption. Furthermore, the recently released Surgeon General's report on smoking and health (1979) strengthens earlier conclusions regarding the relationship between smoking and disease. In the Preface to that massive document, the Surgeon General states that cigarette smoking is the single most important preventable environmental factor contributing to illness, disability, and death in the United States (Richmond, 1979).

Despite widespread acceptance of these facts, a large proportion of the American population continues to smoke. While smoking among adults, particularly among males, has decreased somewhat during the past 20 years, approximately one-third of all adults still regularly smoke cigarettes (Harris, 1979). In addition, in recent years there has been an increase in the percentage of teenage females who regularly smoke cigarettes (Green, 1979). Health care professionals are justifiably concerned about these figures. Their concern is reflected in the fact that smoking cessation programs represent one of the largest preventive health efforts in our country today.

The purpose of this chapter is to summarize the literature concerning behavioral approaches to the modification of cigarette smoking behavior. Rather than reiterating material already available in recent evaluative reviews (Bernstein & Glasgow, 1979; Lichenstein & Danaher, 1976; Pechacek, 1979; Schwartz & Rider, 1978), what we see as the most important conceptual and methodological issues in the field will be emphasized. In the initial section we will consider what is known about various stages of smoking behavior. A second section will consider outcome research on smoking cessation by focusing on key studies which represent each of several different treatment approaches. A somewhat more detailed examination of recent treatment studies will precede a final section which describes what we see as future directions in smoking modification.

Smoking Behavior

At first glance, it might seem that cigarette smoking is a relatively simple habit that should be easily

Medical Psychology
Contributions to Behavioral Medicine

ISBN 0-12-565960-1

amenable to modification by straightforward applications of behavioral principles. Unfortunately, the smoking modification literature of the last 20 years clearly shows that this is not the case. One of the major factors underlying the rather disappointing results of most behavioral (and other) antismoking interventions is the often unrecognized formidability of the phenomenon being attacked. Smoking is a complex behavior that is determined by the (often idiosyncratic) interaction of a variety of cognitive, social environmental, and physiological variables. In order to appreciate the complexities involved, it is helpful to view smoking behavior as consisting of a series of stages involving (*a*) initiation; (*b*) maintenance of habitual smoking; (*c*) cessation; and (*d*) recidivism or continued abstinence (Leventhal & Cleary, 1977; Pomerleau, 1979). This is important because the variables of primary importance in determining smoking behavior do not remain constant across stages. Further, much more is known about some stages than about others.

Stage 1: Initiation of Smoking

In recent years there has been increasing interest in exploring the factors associated with the initiation of cigarette smoking. Most of the research in this area, which has consisted almost entirely of questionnaire surveys of adolescents, has consistently found that the number of smokers in a child's environment is one of the best predictors of whether that child will become a smoker. Teenage smokers are much more likely to have friends who smoke than are nonsmokers; children from homes where both parents and older siblings smoke are four times as likely to become smokers than are children from nonsmoking families (DHEW, 1976). A number of studies have also reported that smoking prevalence in children is inversely related to academic performance. While physiological factors have not been adequately investigated and cannot be ruled out, genetic predisposition does not seem to be a significant determinant of teenage smoking.

Rather, the important factors associated with smoking at this first stage appear to be social. As a result, recent programs for preventing the onset of smoking have focused most heavily on issues such as peer pressure (see Chapter 11 by Coates, Perry, Killen, & Slinkard; also Evans, 1979). One of the current gaps in our knowledge regarding initiation concerns the factors which determine why some children move from experimentation to regular smoking while others do not. The National Institute of Child Health and Human Development is currently sponsoring a number of research projects to answer this question.

Stage 2: Habitual Smoking

After a period of time, usually around 2 years, most "experimental" smokers have become "regular" smokers. Because an understanding of the variables which support habitual smoking is so fundamental to the design of effective intervention strategies, the maintenance stage has received more theoretical attention than any other. We will first discuss two models which stress the regulatory function of habitual cigarette smoking and then turn to models which focus on environmental and cognitive factors.

Management of Affect One of the earliest models of smoking behavior focused on the regulation of internal emotional states (Tomkins, 1966, 1968). Tomkins' model served as the basis for the construction of the Smokers Self-Testing Kit (Ikard, Green, & Horn, 1969), the most widely used paper-and-pencil device for assessing the functions served by an individual's smoking behavior. In this model, self-reported reasons for smoking are classified as reflecting a number of factors including the production of or association with positive emotional states (positive affect smoking) and the reduction of negative emotional states (negative affect smoking). Several studies have found that factor analyses of questionnaire data reliably reproduce similar factors (e.g., McKennell, 1973), but recent work has raised doubts about whether the affect management model accurately predicts smoking behavior (Adesso & Glad, 1978; Briddell, Rimm, Caddy, & Dunn, 1979; Leventhal & Avis, 1976).

Nicotine Regulation There has been an increasing amount of interest during the past decade in the role of nicotine in maintaining cigarette smoking. For several years, at least two laboratories have been producing experimental evidence which indicates that nicotine is an extremely addictive substance (Russell, 1976) and that some smokers will titrate their smoking depending on nicotine levels in the body and the cigarette (Jarvick, 1973). However, it has been the recent work of Schachter and his colleagues (Schachter, Silverstein, Kozlowski, Perlick, Herman, & Liebling, 1977) that has sparked widespread interest in biological factors. This work suggests that the urinary pH level may control smoking behavior (in heavy smokers) by influencing the rate of nicotine excretion. Further, it has been clearly established that nicotine plays an important role in determining the smoking behavior of at least some individuals (Jarvick, 1979; Russell, 1979). Future smoking studies will likely devote more attention to this factor.

Learning-Conditioning It is also clear that learning factors play a role in the smoking process. Through its high frequency of occurrence, smoking inevitably becomes associated with a wide variety of situations and activities. Recent research (Miller, Frederiksen, & Hosford, 1979) as well as everyday experience indicates that many smokers alter their smoking patterns in different social situations. Best and Hakstian (1978) have proposed a situation-specific model of smoking behavior that takes such variations into account. Other research indicates that modeling as well as operant and respondent conditioning may also influence smoking behavior (Glad & Adesso, 1976).

The opponent process theory of habitual smoking (Solomon, 1977; Solomon & Corbit, 1973) attempts to incorporate affective, pharmacological, and conditioning factors. In this complex model, early smoking behavior is reinforced by the pleasant consequences of smoking (the A state). An inevitable consequence of the elicitation of the A state, however, is the subsequent arousal of an opponent process (the unpleasant B state), which counteracts the A state. As smoking becomes habitual, the B process becomes greatly strengthened and the behavior is eventually maintained by escape from or avoidance of the unpleasant B state (withdrawal). Escape or avoidance of withdrawal is produced by smoking a cigarette, which in turn strengthens the B state even more. Thus, an addictive cycle is established. The implications of opponent process theory for smoking modification efforts are not entirely apparent, but several researchers are pursuing the application of this model (Leventhal & Cleary, 1977; Ternes, 1977).

Cognitive Factors Several authors have focused on cognitive factors that may be important in maintaining smoking behavior (Green, 1977; Pechacek & Danaher, 1979). For example, smokers may not exhibit a personal level of belief in the dangers of smoking (Becker & Maiman, 1975); they may view themselves as permanently addicted and incapable of change (Eiser, Sutton, & Wober, 1978); or they may feel that they have no control over their health (Wallston & Wallston, 1978) or their world in general (Kozlowski, 1979). Finally, as suggested by Horn (1979), smokers may conduct a cost-benefit analysis and conclude that the benefits obtained from smoking outweigh the costs.

For smoking as well as other complex behaviors, it is apparent that conceptual models will need to incorporate physiological, cognitive, and environmental factors in order to adequately explain, predict, and control the phenomenon of interest. We shall return to this topic in the section on future directions.

Stage 3: Cessation

While the bulk of theorizing and model-building has focused on the habitual smoking stage, most of the empirical research has concentrated on the modification of smoking behavior. The models just reviewed have, of course, played a clear role in guiding cessation activities. For example, the affect management model suggests utilization of procedures such as relaxation, systematic desensitization, or the development of alternative behaviors that would perform the same functional role as smoking. The nicotine regulation hypothesis leads most directly to the exploration of nicotine chewing gum, alteration of urinary pH, or possibly a nicotine fading detoxification procedure (Foxx & Brown, 1979). Proponents of a conditioning model have developed stimulus control, reinforcement for nonsmoking, and aversive conditioning procedures for smoking cessation. Finally, cognitive theorists emphasize creation of positive expectations for improvement (Blittner, Goldberg, & Merbaum, 1978), attempt to modify clients' locus of control, and stress awareness of the benefits of smoking cessation. The remaining sections of this chapter are devoted to reviewing the status of these various treatment approaches. As will be seen in the later sections, most smoking control programs employ a combination of these strategies. In fact, the relative success of multicomponent programs has provided the impetus toward more comprehensive models of smoking behavior.

There has also been increased interest in smokers' experiences during cessation. Shiffman (1979) has reviewed the literature on tobacco withdrawal symptoms and concluded that an identifiable, albeit variable, withdrawal syndrome does exist. Retrospective studies have found that the severity of initial withdrawal symptoms is a good predictor of success at cessation; this leads to our next topic—recidivism–continued abstinence.

Stage 4: Recidivism or Continued Abstinence

There has been less research on this aspect of smoking behavior than on any other, despite the well-known fact that the great majority of smokers who quit will return to smoking. A fairly consistent time course for recidivism has been established, with the vast majority of relapses occurring within three months after cessation. The relapse curve then gradually flattens out and approaches asymptote somewhere between 3 and 6 months post-cessation (Hunt & Bespalec, 1974).[1]

There have been a number of retrospective analyses which have focused on global individual differences as predictors of continued abstinence. However, the prognostic value of the identified variables (e.g., age, sex, socioeconomic level, smoking pattern, introversion–extroversion) has been relatively limited (Best & Bloch, 1979). Unfortunately, there have been only a few attempts to investigate behavioral factors related to relapse (Pomerleau, Adkins, & Pertschuk, 1978; Best, Note 1; Lichtenstein & Brown, Note 2). These studies indicate that social occasions as well as crises or tension-producing situations are frequent precipitants of relapse and that the factors important in producing long-term abstinence may be different from those involved in initial cessation.

Additional research is clearly needed in this area and future investigators would do well to incorporate knowledge about recidivism in other habit change areas (e.g., drug abuse—Barbarin, 1979; obesity—Hall, 1979; and alcoholism—Marlatt & Gordon, 1978) given the similarity in relapse patterns across these various targets (Hunt, Barnett, & Branch, 1971). General models of maintenance of therapeutic change (e.g., Goldstein & Kanfer, 1979; Hall & Hall, 1979) should also prove useful in designing strategies to prevent relapse.

Outcome Research on Smoking

Early behavioral research on the modification of smoking behavior produced generally disappointing results. The most common finding was that short-term reduction to approximately 30–40% of baseline levels was followed by return to near baseline levels of smoking. Long-term (6 month–1 year) results seldom exceeded 15–20% abstinence (McFall, 1978). McFall and Hammen's (1971) classic study provides a benchmark against which to compare the efficacy of smoking interventions. Their minimal treatment group (consisting of the nonspecific factors of self-monitoring, participating in a structured program, and attending regular meetings) did as well as any of the more specific treatments and produced results almost identical to those described above (see also Bernstein, 1970).

The remainder of this section will describe pre-1977 research on the effects of behavioral smoking control strategies. The various treatment approaches to be reviewed will be evaluated both rel-

[1]However, a recent study has indicated that some smokers may relapse after a period as long as 5 to 6 years (Lichtenstein & Penner, 1977).

ative to (*a*) comparison groups in the same study and (*b*) the "standard" pattern of success described earlier. The general findings regarding each approach will, where possible, be related to our previous discussion of models of smoking.

Tension Reduction Strategies

Many individuals are characterized as "negative affect" smokers because they report using cigarettes to cope with stress and unpleasant emotional states. In the hope of either reducing or providing smokers with alternative ways of coping with these conditions, several investigators have employed relaxation or systematic desensitization. Controlled investigations have either failed to find these interventions superior to other approaches (e.g., Levenberg & Wagner, 1976) or produced unimpressive levels of abstinence (e.g., Sutherland, Amit, Golden, & Roseberger, 1975). Thus, at least one of the major treatment strategies stemming from the affect management model has not proven clinically useful.

Cognitive Control

Most attempts to alter smoking related cognitions have focused on cravings or urges to smoke. The most frequently studied approaches emanate either from Homme's (1965) "coverant control" technique which seeks to increase the frequency of thoughts (covert operants or "coverants") incompatible with smoking or Cautela's (1967) covert sensitization procedure. This latter approach requires the subject to vividly imagine unpleasant consequences (such as nausea) occurring in conjunction with smoking. Despite the intuitive appeal of these cognitive interventions, outcome research has failed to provide evidence of their long-term effectiveness or superiority to placebo procedures (e.g., Sipich, Russell, & Tobias, 1974). This casts doubt upon the utility of cognitive theories of smoking as the sole basis for generating effective treatments.

Stimulus Control

Learning theory formulations of smoking behavior are based primarily on the assumption that smoking is associated with (and ultimately prompted by) environmental cues. Stimulus control strategies involve the gradual reduction of smoking through gradual narrowing of stimuli or cues that are associated with it. A wide variety of stimulus control approaches have been investigated (e.g., Azrin & Powell, 1968; Levinson, Shapiro, Schwartz, & Tursky, 1971). The results of these studies, unfortunately, are quite consistent in indicating that the stimulus control approach does not produce results which are superior to those of control conditions. One interesting finding coming from these studies is that subjects generally do well until they reach the level of approximately 10–12 cigarettes per day. Most subjects have a great deal of difficulty reducing consumption below this level, possibly because each remaining cigarette becomes more reinforcing and difficult to give up (Flaxman, 1978).

Reinforcement of Nonsmoking

Another implication of an operant conditioning view of smoking is that smoking behavior may be reduced by reinforcing alternative behaviors. This has most frequently taken the form of financial rewards, usually part of an initial deposit by the subject, for specified periods of nonsmoking. While there has not been a great deal of controlled research on this approach, available reports are encouraging and have produced clinically meaningful levels of abstinence (e.g., Tighe & Elliot, 1968; Winett, 1973).

Aversion Strategies

A final approach emanating from the social learning theory framework has involved pairing aversive stimuli with actual or imagined smoking. Aversion strategies have generated far more research than any other single approach to the control of smoking. The bulk of the work in this area can be conveniently divided into studies that use either electric shock or cigarette smoke as the aversive stimulus.

Electrical Aversion Overall, the findings regarding electrical aversion have not been encouraging. While there have been uncontrolled reports of success rates as high as 70% abstinence at one year follow-up (Pope & Mount, 1975), controlled investigations have generally not found electrical stimulation to be superior to control conditions or to produce long-term success rates exceeding those discussed for nonspecific treatments. In what was probably the most sophisticated and comprehensive study in this area, Russell, Armstrong, and Patel (1976) failed to find differential effects among contingent shock and a variety of control groups.

Despite this generally negative pattern of findings, two studies employing innovative procedures have reported high success rates. Dericco, Brigham, and Garlington (1977) utilized a multiple baseline component analysis design to demonstrate the effectiveness of an electrical aversion procedure that employed many daily sessions and rather intense levels of shock. A 6-month follow-up revealed that 80% of subjects were still reporting abstinence. Berecz (1976) has argued that investigations of electrical aversion have failed because they have not focused upon early components in the chain of behaviors leading to cigarette smoking. He described an interesting multiple case study which suggests that shocking imagined *urges* to smoke may be more effective than shocking actual or imagined smoking behavior.

Criticisms of the electrical aversion approach have stressed that generalization of treatment effects is unlikely because humans can readily discriminate when shock is and is not imminent. It has also been argued that, relative to the artificial and irrelevant stimulus of electric shock, aversive stimuli more intrinsic to the act of smoking should produce better results (Wilson & Davison, 1969).

Cigarette Smoke In response to the criticisms of the use of electrical aversion, researchers have searched for more naturally occurring and biologically relevant sources of aversive stimulation. After some false starts, this search resulted in what many believe to be a major breakthrough in the modification of smoking behavior: rapid smoking. Before attempting to summarize the voluminous literature on rapid smoking, it is important to differentiate this procedure from related techniques with which it is commonly confused.

Rapid smoking involves smoking at the rate of one inhalation every 6 sec while focusing on the negative sensations produced. This continues until one chooses to stop or until a specified time limit (5–10 min) has elapsed. Thus, rapid smoking is an intense, relatively brief aversive procedure and is to be distinguished from satiation, which involves smoking two to three times the number of cigarettes one would normally consume throughout the course of a day. The outcome literature on satiation is inconclusive but most studies have failed to demonstrate its effectiveness (e.g., Lando & Davison, 1975; Marston & McFall, 1971). The same is true of a procedure in which a machine blows warm smoky air at subjects as they smoke (Franks, Fried, & Ashem, 1966; Wilde, 1964). While initially part of the rapid smoking procedure, this latter technique did not seem to enhance effectiveness and has subsequently been abandoned (Lichtenstein, Harris, Birchler, Wahl, & Schmahl, 1973).

The first impressive reports of success with rapid smoking came from Lichtenstein and colleagues (Lichtenstein *et al.*, 1973; Schmahl, Lichtenstein, & Harris, 1972). These studies reported near 100% abstinence immediately after treatment, and approximately 60% of treated subjects were still reporting to be nonsmokers at 6-month follow-up. Other studies conducted in Lichtenstein's laboratory replicated these promising findings, but also indicated that the technique is more complex than it initially appeared. Factors such as the therapist–client relationship (Harris & Lichtenstein, Note 3) and the criteria for treatment termination (Weinrobe & Lichtenstein, Note 4) were both found to affect outcome. A long-term follow-up on a number of these early rapid smoking studies has indicated that 36–47% of rapid smoking subjects reported abstinence 2 to 6 years after treatment (Lichtenstein & Penner, 1977).

Current Trends in Smoking Research

After a lull of several years, increased interest in smoking and health has recently produced a marked acceleration in the pace of research on smoking and smoking modification. Most of this work has focused either on rapid smoking or on multicomponent programs which incorporate various self-control and long-term maintenance strategies, usually along with some type of aversion component. This section will survey these recent developments.

Rapid Smoking

Early reports from Lichtenstein's laboratory prompted many researchers to replicate and expand knowledge about rapid smoking. Danaher (1977a) has considered these studies in a review to which the interested reader is referred for a detailed coverage. The general picture that emerges is that rapid smoking is probably an effective smoking cessation procedure, but that it will not produce clinically meaningful results if employed in a mechanical, standardized manner. Rapid smoking studies that have closely approximated Lichtenstein's original format have produced results similar to those reported by Lichtenstein *et al.* (1973), while studies that have deviated from that format have produced substantially lower abstinence rates. Factors important to success appear to include warm, supportive therapists and individualized treatment which allows for a flexible number of sessions and trials per session. Thus, while the effectiveness of the rapid smoking procedure has been replicated, the pattern of results casts doubt upon a straightforward punishment or aversive conditioning interpretation of the data.

It has also become apparent that the rapid smoking procedure produces a moderate amount of cardiopulmonary stress and thus may be inappropriate for some smokers. Investigators who have explored the physiological effects of rapid smoking have drawn somewhat conflicting conclusions regarding the medical risks involved. Lichtenstein and Glasgow (1977) reviewed studies conducted prior to 1977 and concluded that rapid smoking is a safe technique *if* procedural safeguards are employed. Recommended safeguards involve (*a*) excluding high risk subjects (i.e., those suffering from pulmonary or cardiovascular disease and individuals over 55); (*b*) requiring physician approval for participation; and (*c*) limiting the duration of exposure to rapid smoking. The results of a recent, comprehensive investigation of the safety of rapid smoking are consistent with these recommendations (Sachs, Hall, & Hall, 1978); however, Russell, Raw, Taylor, Feyerabend, and Saloojee (1978) have proposed somewhat more stringent safeguards based on their own findings.

The potential risks and somewhat limited applicability of rapid smoking have stimulated development of less physiologically stressful smoke aversion interventions. For example, an interesting pattern of findings has emerged from several rapid smoking studies that have employed "normal paced" aversive smoking as a placebo control. The normal paced condition generally produces initial abstinence rates equal to those of rapid smoking. The long-term results of this technique are inferior to those of rapid smoking, but still superior to the 15–20% abstinence figure we have used as a benchmark. A number of investigators are currently exploring the utility of variations on this normal paced focused smoking—particularly in combination with other treatment and maintenance strategies. Initial reports have been encouraging (Hackett & Horan, 1978, 1979; Tori, 1978), but more controlled evaluations are needed.

Nicotine Gum

Because of the apparent role played by nicotine in the maintenance of cigarette smoking, some investigators have sought to develop pharmacological approaches to smoking cessation. Early research focused on the development of nicotine substitutes, primarily lobeline sulfate. These agents were found to produce only weak, temporary effects on smoking that were primarily a function of the nonspecific effects associated with receiving medication (Davison & Rosen, 1972).

More recently, investigators have assessed the utility of nicotine itself as a cessation aid. This research has been spurred by the development of a palatable chewing gum that releases appropriate levels of nicotine (see Russell & Feyerabend, 1978).

The literature on the effectiveness of nicotine chewing gum is inconclusive. A case study of three heavy smokers has reported impressive results (Schneider, Popek, Jarvick, & Gritz, 1977) and an early double blind trial has found nicotine gum superior to a placebo gum, especially among heavier smokers (Brantmark, Ohlin, & Westling, 1973). On the other hand, two double blind studies have failed to find the nicotine gum superior to placebo gum at long-term follow-up (Puska, Bjorkqvist, & Koskela, 1979; Russell, Wilson, Feyerabend, & Cole, 1976). Both of these studies, however, did find some initial superiority for the nicotine gum. It may be that more careful attention to the withdrawal schedule of the gum itself or incorporation of self-control maintenance procedures would enhance long-term effects. This is an area in which there is likely to be a great deal of interest in the near future.

Multicomponent Programs

The most obvious trend in smoking cessation research over the past few years has been the movement toward multicomponent treatment programs. This approach makes eminent sense given its success in other areas (Agras, Kazdin, & Wilson, 1979) and the multidetermined nature of smoking behavior. Typical multicomponent smoking programs have combined several self-control techniques (e.g., stimulus control, relaxation training) and an aversion strategy (usually rapid smoking or satiation).

A number of controlled studies have produced extremely encouraging results from such multicomponent programs, sometimes approaching 60–70% abstinence at 6-month follow-up (e.g., Delahunt & Curran, 1976; Lando, 1977). Recent examples of successful multicomponent programs have addressed various combinations of factors discussed in the first section of this chapter such as: (*a*) stimulus control with a manipulation to increase subjects' expectations and feelings of internal control (Blittner, *et al.*, 1978); (*b*) rapid smoking with covert sensitization (Severson, O'Neal, & Hynd, Note 5); (*c*) nictoine fading with self monitoring/feedback (Foxx & Brown, 1979); and (*d*) a very complex program that included eight different components (Elliot & Denney, 1978).

The results, however, are not uniformly positive. Many studies have employed a "throw in everything but the kitchen sink" philosophy and have demonstrated that more is not necessarily better. Other studies have found that even relatively uncomplicated and seemingly reasonable multicomponent treatments which combine rapid smoking with self-control procedures (Danaher, 1977b) or covert sensitization (Barbarin, 1978) may produce less effective results than the component procedures by themselves. A study by Flaxman (1978) suggests some of the complexities involved in designing successful multicomponent programs. Nevertheless, more work of this nature is clearly indicated since, if carefully developed, multicomponent social learning treatment approaches appear to contain the greatest potential for producing improved treatment outcomes. Recent reviews by Bernstein & Glasgow (1979) and Pechacek (1979) offer more detailed discussion of multicomponent studies.

Minimal Treatment Approaches

Given the magnitude of the smoking problem in our country and the fact that the majority of smokers who want to quit are more interested in do-it-yourself approaches than in formal clinics (Gallup Opinion Index, 1974), there has been an increasing interest in smoking modification programs that require minimal professional involvement. The majority of such programs have consisted of self-help books or manuals. These behavioral bibliotherapy programs have been reviewed by Glasgow and Rosen (1979) who concluded that, while there have been some promising results, the great majority of studies have found only relatively small amounts of behavior change. Still, these programs may be worth developing given their low cost and potentially high cost-effectiveness ratio. Recent self-help manuals by Danaher and Lichtenstein (1978) and Pomerleau and Pomerleau (1977) seem particularly worthy of investigation. Both of these programs are based on multicomponent procedures that have been developed and successfully validated in therapist directed clinics, but have not been evaluated in a controlled fashion under self-administered conditions.

Investigators have also begun to explore the utility of televised cessation programs. While the success rates produced by these programs have typically not been very high (e.g., Dubren, 1977a; Best, Note 1), some encouraging results have been reported both with regard to abstinence rates (McAlister, 1977) and maintenance of treatment effects (Best, Note 1). Given their ability to reach large numbers of smokers who would not otherwise attempt cessation, mass media programs seem to offer great promise.

One major problem facing all minimal treatment approaches is that of compliance or adherence to therapeutic recommendations (Best & Bloch, 1979). It is possible that increased knowledge about the procedures utilized by the large number of smokers who quit on their own (e.g., Perri, Richards, & Schultheis, 1977) and information concerning the credibility, attractiveness, and perceived cost of different smoking modification stragegies will be helpful in addressing this problem. Attention to compliance literature in general is also warranted (e.g., Goldstein & Kanfer, 1979).

Improving Maintenance

Researchers almost universally have agreed that greater attention needs to be devoted to the maintenance of nonsmoking following initial cessation. As in the case of constructing multicomponent programs, however, the best strategy for accomplishing the much needed goal of increased maintenance is not yet clear. There have been some reports of maintenance enhancement effects, largely from uncontrolled studies or pilot investigations, but the overwhelming majority of controlled studies have not identified successful long-term maintenance strategies. The most straightforward approach, that of simply extending client contact or adding booster sessions after the end of treatment, does not appear to improve long-term success rates (Bernstein & Glasgow, 1979; Pechacek, 1979). The results of other studies since those reviews went to press are consistent with this conclusion (Colletti & Kopel, 1979; Elliot & Denney, 1978; Gordon, 1978). Preliminary reports of a tape-recorded telephone encouragement service (Dubren, 1977b) and a problem-solving strategy (Karol & Richards, Note 6) provide interesting leads for further investigation. We feel that a better understanding of the factors underlying continued abstinence and responsible for producing relapse (see p. 358; Marlatt & Gordon, 1978) should aid in the development of appropriate maintenance strategies.

Future Directions

Our brief review of outcome research and current trends in smoking research was designed to provide an overview of where the field has been and where it is today. To complete the picture, we shall now describe a few of the developments which appear likely to characterize and guide future research. These developments include (*a*) increased methodological sophistication in the assessment of smoking behavior; (*b*) interest in finding predictors of treatment outcome and constructing models which suggest how to individualize treatment programs; and (*c*) work with populations other than the usual volunteers who attend smoking cessation clinics.

Methodological Issues

There has been definite improvement in the methodology of social learning based approaches to the modification of smoking in recent years. Unfortunately, many studies are still plagued by such deficiencies as the failure to adequately describe and account for subjects, the lack of certain basic controls, and the absence of long-term follow-up. These issues have been discussed in every review of the area as well as in two guides for the design of smoking cessation studies (McFall, 1978; National Interagency Council on Smoking and Health, 1974). Rather than reiterate these concerns, we have chosen to focus on two positive methodological developments: biological measures of smoking and attention to topographical aspects of smoking behavior.

Physiological Correlates of Smoking For many years global self-reports or self-monitoring records of the number of cigarettes smoked per day have been *the* dependent measure in smoking modification research. Dissatisfaction with and suspicions about the validity of such data (even when corroborated by reports of others) as the sole index of treatment effectiveness has led to the development of a variety of objective, physiological measures of smoking exposure. The most widely used physiological measures involve assessment of the concentration of (*a*) carbon monoxide (CO) in expired breath (e.g., Frederiksen & Martin, 1979; Hughes, Frederiksen & Frazier, 1978) and (*b*) thiocyanate in the blood or saliva (e.g., Brockway, 1978).

The major advantages of carbon monoxide assessment are that it is relatively inexpensive, noninvasive, capable of providing immediate feedback, and indicative of one of the primary pathological processes through which smoking leads to cardiovascular disease. The major disadvantage of CO as a dependent measure is its relatively short half-life (4–6 hours) and, thus, the extent to which it is influenced by the time since one's last cigarette.[2] Thiocyanate, in contrast apparently has a half-life of approximately 14 days and thus may be a superior measure of long-term abstinence. Vogt, Selvin, Widdowsen, and Hulley (1977) have recommended the combination of CO and thiocyanate tests in order to obtain a maximally powerful index.

Recent work with these physiological measures has indeed confirmed earlier suspicions about the validity of self-reports of smoking. Confronting subjects claiming abstinence with discrepant chemical findings has led to higher rates of reported smoking and admissions of duplicity (e.g., Brockway, Kleinman, Edleson, & Gruenwald, 1977; Ohlin, Lundh, & Westling, 1976). While CO and thiocyanate assessment procedures, as well as other recent biological assays, certainly represent a major advance in smoking assessment procedures, they should not be viewed as a panacea or an absolutely valid test of smoking exposure. Both measures are affected by variables other than smoking and neither correlates extremely well with even carefully validated records of the *number* of cigarettes smoked (some of the reasons for this phenomenon are discussed in the next section). Still, these physiological indices are sufficiently well validated to be included in many future outcome studies. Indeed, it may become increasingly difficult to publish studies that rely solely on self-reports of smoking.

Smoking Topography Increased awareness of the complexities and multidetermined nature of smoking behavior has been accompanied by a realization that there are a number of important parameters of smoking behavior in addition to number of cigarettes consumed per day. There is now evidence that differential risks are associated with different types of cigarettes and that inhalation patterns may be related to the amount and type of cigarettes smoked (Jarvick, 1979). It is apparent that smokers who puff lightly and infrequently at 20 Carletons per day are not placing themselves at the same risk as smokers who deeply inhale every puff of a pack of unfiltered Camels. Such findings may at least partially account for the fact that only moderate correlations are usually found between physiological measures and the number of cigarettes smoked per day.

Frederiksen and his colleagues (e.g., Frederiksen & Simon, 1978) have addressed what they term the topographical aspects of smoking behavior and have concluded that a thorough description of a person's smoking behavior should include not only brand and number consumed per day, but also depth of inhalation, puff frequency and duration, and how much of the cigarette is smoked. These components can be reliably measured and manipulated (e.g., Frederiksen, Miller, & Peterson, 1977) and it seems that a composite topographical measure such as the inhalation index proposed by Miller, Frederiksen, & Hosford (1979) would be a use-

[2] From a therapeutic viewpoint, the short half-life of CO may be an advantage. Thus, smokers can see improvement in an obviously health related measure relatively soon after altering their smoking behavior.

ful dependent variable to include in future smoking research.

Discussion of smoking topography also brings up the issue of controlled smoking. For many years it has been assumed (and occasionally demonstrated empirically) that if individuals attempting to modify their smoking do not become completely abstinent, they will soon return to their baseline levels. Frederiksen's work suggests, however, that this need not be the case (Frederiksen & Petersen, 1976). It may be that nonabstinent smokers return to baseline because no one taught them to smoke in a controlled manner and that they, as well as their therapists, have an "all-or-none" cognitive set which precludes the possibility of smoking at reduced levels indefinitely (Marlatt & Gordon, 1978). There appear to be a number of people who, despite anyone's best efforts, either cannot or will not quit smoking and it can be argued that if these individuals are going to continue to smoke, it would be better that they do so in a way that minimizes the attendant risks. The parallel to controlled drinking (see Chapter 15) is apparent and there is no reason to expect that controlled smoking will be any less controversial. The previously mentioned difficulty which smokers in gradual reduction (i.e., stimulus control) programs have in reaching a level of less than 10 cigarettes per day may cause some to wonder if moderation training is a feasible goal. We do not know, but would argue that it is an empirical question. Long-term work with larger numbers of subjects and replications in other laboratories are certainly needed. Still, Frederiksen's pioneering work in this area is encouraging and it may well be that controlled smoking is a reasonable goal for some smokers, especially until abstinence technology advances further.

Prediction of Success and Tailoring of Treatments

One of the most consistent findings in the smoking modification literature, and one that is at least partially responsible for the commonly observed pattern of nonsignificant differences among various intervention approaches, is that of enormous within-group variability in outcome. This suggests the need for learning much more about what treatment or combination of treatments or components of treatments will be most effective for particular smokers.

Unfortunately, most of the available data concerning individual differences as predictors of outcome are not particularly helpful. The literature has tended to focus on broad demographic and personality variables (Kozlowski, 1979). The magnitude of correlations between such variables and cessation, while sometimes statistically significant, is not impressive and almost all studies have focused on success in general rather than in relation to specific intervention programs. Similarly, most current models of smoking behavior are not helpful in designing optimal intervention programs. Most models focus on only one factor affecting smoking and those that attempt to incorporate two or more factors, such as opponent–process theory (e.g., Leventhal & Cleary, 1977; Solomon, 1977; Solomon & Corbit, 1973; Ternes, 1977), fail to attend to variability among smokers. Models that include physiological, cognitive, and environmental dimensions (e.g., Glad, Tyre, & Adesso, 1976) and that attend to individual differences (e.g., Russell, Peto, & Patel, 1974) would seem to offer greater promise for both predicting success and developing truly effective interventions.

Beyond Traditional Cessation Clinics

Almost all past research on the modification of smoking behavior has been conducted in the context of face-to-face meetings with adult volunteers in smoking clinics sponsored by universities or health organizations. As mentioned earlier in this chapter, this approach probably is not the most efficient way to provide smoking reduction services and fails to reach many individuals in need of help. Recently, however, a much needed expansion in the range and modes of delivery of smoking interventions has occurred. One of the most dramatic events has been the involvement of social learning researchers in the design and evaluation of smoking prevention programs. While school and health organizations have provided education about the dangers of smoking for many years, attention is now being directed toward modifying or countering the sociobehavioral factors involved in the initiation process (Evans, 1979; McAlister, Perry, & Maccoby, 1979). These important developments are discussed by Coates *et al.* in Chapter 11.

Another trend has been to approach smokers rather than waiting for them to ask for help. A number of organizations have realized that it is good business, given the documented costs in work days missed by smokers (Smoking and Health, 1979), to sponsor smoking modification programs in work settings. One such program that relied primarily on financial incentives provided by the employer has been described by Rosen and Lichtenstein (1977).

A third innovation has been to focus on individuals who are at particularly high risk for developing one or more of the health consequences of smoking. For example, behaviorally oriented smoking modification programs have been developed for pregnant women (Danaher, Shisslak, Thompson, & Ford, 1978) and chest patients (Russell, 1976). By far the greatest activity in this area has occurred in the context of large scale multiple risk factor reduction trials for the prevention of heart disease (e.g., Maccoby, Farquhar, Wood, & Alexander, 1977; Multiple Risk Factor Intervention Trial, 1979). While it is too early to evaluate the long-term effects of such efforts, the initial results regarding smoking cessation are clearly of interest.

Conclusion

Much progress has been made in the modification of smoking behavior in recent years. We pointed out directions for future research throughout this chapter, but it seems worthwhile to briefly summarize what we see as the most promising and needed developments. We look forward to increasingly sophisticated evaluations and refinements of what appear to be the most effective treatment techniques (rapid smoking and related procedures, reinforcement of nonsmoking and multicomponent treatments). The development of models of smoking that take into account the multidetermined nature of the behavior, that suggest how to optimally combine treatment components, and that provide guidelines for tailoring treatments to individuals would greatly facilitate this process. At the same time, evaluations of more cost-effective and innovative ways of reaching smokers and maintaining abstinence should have high priority.

Acknowledgments

Appreciation is expressed to H. Katherine O'Neill and Kevin D. McCaul for their helpful comments on an earlier version of this manuscript. This work was supported in part by Grants NIHHD 13335 and NIMH DA 02457.

Reference Notes

1. Best, J. A. *Effectiveness of a television/print clinic for smoking cessation.* Paper presented at the annual meeting of the Association for Advancement of Behavior Therapy, Chicago, November 1978.
2. Lichtenstein, E., & Brown, R. A. *Why people smoke: A social learning account.* Paper presented at the annual meeting of the Association for Advancement of Behavior Therapy, Chicago, November 1978.
3. Harris, D. E., & Lichtenstein, E. *The contribution of nonspecific social variables to a successful behavioral treatment of smoking.* Unpublished manuscript, University of Oregon, 1974.
4. Weinrobe, P. A., & Lichtenstein, E. *The use of urges as termination criterion in a rapid smoking treatment program for habitual smokers.* Paper presented at the annual meeting of the Western Psychological Association, Sacramento, California, April 1975.
5. Severson, H. H., O'Neal, M., & Hynd, G. W. *Cognitive coping strategies and aversive counterconditioning in the modification of smoking behavior.* Unpublished manuscript, University of Oregon, 1978.
6. Karol, R. L., & Richards, C. S. *Making treatment effects last: An investigation of maintenance strategies for smoking reduction.* Paper presented at the meeting of the Association for Advancement of Behavior Therapy, Chicago, November 1978.

References

Adesso, V. J., & Glad, W. R. A behavioral test of a smoking typology. *Addictive Behaviors,* 1978, *3,* 35–38.

Agras, W. S., Kazdin, A. E., & Wilson, G. T. *Behavior therapy: Toward an applied clinical science.* San Francisco: W. H. Freeman and Company, 1979.

Azrin, N. H., & Powell, J. Behavioral engineering: The reduction of smoking behavior by a conditioning apparatus and procedure. *Journal of Applied Behavior Analysis*, 1968, *1*, 193-200.

Barbarin, O. A. Comparison of symbolic and overt aversion in the self-control of smoking. *Journal of Consulting and Clinical Psychology*, 1978, *46*, 1569-1571.

Barbarin, O. A. Recidivism in drug addiction: A behavioral analysis. *Addictive Behaviors*, 1979, *4*, 121-132.

Becker, M. H., & Maiman, L. A. Sociobehavioral determinants of compliance with health and medical care recommendations. *Medical Care*, 1975, *13*, 10-24.

Berecz, J. Treatment of smoking with cognitive conditioning therapy: A self-administered aversion technique. *Behavior Therapy*, 1976, *7*, 641-648.

Bernstein, D. A. The modification of smoking behavior: A search for effective variables. *Behaviour Research and Therapy*, 1970, *8*, 133-146.

Berstein, D. A., & Glasgow, R. E. The modification of smoking behavior. In O. F. Pomerleau & J. P. Brady (Eds.), *Behavioral medicine: Theory and practice.* Baltimore: Williams & Wilkins, 1979.

Best, J. A., & Bloch, M. On improving compliance: Cigarette smoking. In R. B. Haynes & D. L. Sackett (Eds.), *Compliance in health care.* Baltimore: Johns Hopkins University Press, 1979.

Best, J. A., & Hakstian, A. R. A situation-specific model for smoking behavior. *Addictive Behaviors*, 1978, *3*, 79-92.

Blittner, M., Goldberg, J., & Merbaum, M. Cognitive self-control factors in the reduction of smoking behavior. *Behavior Therapy*, 1978, *9*, 553-561.

Brantmark, B., Ohlin, P., & Westling, H. Nicotine containing chewing gum as an anti-smoking aid. *Psychopharmacologia*, 1973, *31*, 181-200.

Briddell, D. W., Rimm, D. C., Caddy, G. R., & Dunn, N. J. Analogue assessment, affective arousal, and the smoking taste test. *Addictive Behaviors*, 1979, *4*, 287-296.

Brockway, B. S. Chemical validation of self-reported smoking rates. *Behavior Therapy*, 1978, *9*, 685-686.

Brockway, B. S., Kleinman, G., Edleson, J., & Gruenwald, K. Non-aversive procedures and their effect on cigarette smoking: A clinical group study. *Addictive Behaviors*, 1977, *2*, 121-128.

Cautela, J. R. Covert sensitization. *Psychological Reports*, 1967, *20*, 459-468.

Colletti, G., & Kopel, S. A. Maintaining behavior change: An investigation of three maintenance strategies and the relationship of self-attribution to the long-term reduction of cigarette smoking. *Journal of Consulting and Clinical Psychology*, 1979, *47*, 614-617.

Danaher, B. G. Research on rapid smoking: Interim summary and recommendations. *Addictive Behaviors*, 1977, *2*, 151-166. (a)

Danaher, B. G. Rapid smoking and self-control in the modification of smoking behavior. *Journal of Consulting and Clinical Psychology*, 1977, *45*, 1068-1075. (b)

Danaher, B. G., & Lichtenstein, E. *Become an ex-smoker.* Englewood Cliffs, N.J.: Prentice Hall, 1978.

Danaher, B. G., Shisslak, C. M., Thompson, C. B., & Ford, J. D. A smoking cessation program for pregnant women: An exploratory study. *American Journal of Public Health*, 1978, *68*, 896-898.

Davison, G. C., & Rosen, R. C. Lobeline and reduction of cigarette smoking. *Psychological Reports*, 1972, *31*, 443-456.

Delahunt, J., & Curran, J. P. The effectiveness of negative practice and self-control techniques in the reduction of smoking behavior. *Journal of Consulting and Clinical Psychology*, 1976, *44*, 1002-1007.

Department of Health, Education and Welfare. *Teenage smoking—National patterns of cigarette smoking ages 12 through 18, in 1972 and 1974* (DHEW Publication No. NIH 76-931). Washington, D.C.: U.S. Government Printing Office, 1976.

Dericco, D. A., Brigham, T. A., & Garlington, W. K. Development and evaluation of treatment paradigms for the suppression of smoking behavior. *Journal of Applied Behavior Analysis*, 1977, *10*, 173-181.

Dubren, R. Evaluation of a televised stop-smoking clinic. *Public Health Reports*, 1977, *92*, 358-360. (a)

Dubren, R. Self-reinforcement by recorded telephone messages to maintain non-smoking behavior. *Journal of Consulting and Clinical Psychology*, 1977, *45*, 358-360. (b)

Eiser, J. R., Sutton, S. R., & Wober, M. "Consonant" and "dissonant" smokers and the self-attribution of addiction. *Addictive Behaviors*, 1978, *3*, 99-106.

Elliot, C. H., & Denney, D. R. A multiple-component treatment approach to smoking reduction. *Journal of Consulting and Clinical Psychology*, 1978, *46*, 1330-1339.

Evans, R. I. Smoking in children and adolescents: Psychosocial determinants and prevention strategies. In *Smoking and health: A report of the Surgeon General* (DHEW Publication No. (PHS) 79-50066). Washington, D.C.: U.S. Government Printing Office, 1979.

Flaxman, J. Quitting smoking now or later: Gradual, abrupt, immediate, and delayed quitting. *Behavior Therapy*, 1978, *9*, 260-270.

Foxx, R. M., & Brown, R. A. A nicotine fading and self-monitoring program to produce cigarette abstinence or controlled smoking. *Journal of Applied Behavior Analysis*, 1979, *12*, 111-125.

Franks, C. M., Fried, R., & Ashem, B. An improved apparatus for the aversive conditioning of cigarette smokers. *Behaviour Research and Therapy*, 1966, *4*, 301-308.

Frederiksen, L. W., & Martin, J. E. Carbon monoxide and smoking behavior. *Addictive Behaviors,* 1979, *4,* 21-30.

Frederiksen, L. W., Miller, P. M., & Peterson, G. L. Topographical components of smoking behavior. *Addictive Behaviors,* 1977, *2,* 55-61.

Frederiksen, L. W., & Peterson, G. L. Controlled smoking: Development and maintenance. *Addictive Behaviors,* 1976, *1,* 193-196.

Frederiksen, L. W., & Simon, S. J. Modifying how people smoke: Instructional control and generalization. *Journal of Applied Behavior Analysis,* 1978, *11,* 431-432.

Gallup Opinion Index. Public puffs on after ten years of warnings. In *Gallup Opinion Index* (Report No. 108), 1974.

Glad, W., & Adesso, V. J. The relative importance of socially induced tension and behavioral contagion for smoking behavior. *Journal of Abnormal Psychology,* 1976, *85,* 119-121.

Glad, W. R., Tyre, T. E., & Adesso, V. J. A multidimensional model of cigarette smoking. *The American Journal of Clinical Hypnosis,* 1976, *19,* 82-89.

Glasgow, R. E., & Rosen, G. M. Self-help behavior therapy manuals: Recent developments and clinical usage. *Clinical Behavior Therapy Review,* 1979, *1,* 1-20.

Goldstein, S. P., & Kanfer, F. H. (Eds.). *Maximizing treatment gains: Transfer enhancement in psychotherapy.* New York: Academic Press, 1979.

Gordon, J. R. *The use of rapid smoking and group support to induce and maintain abstinence from cigarette smoking.* Unpublished doctoral dissertation, University of Washington, 1978.

Green, D. E. Psychological factors in smoking. In *Research on smoking behavior* (NIDA Research Monograph No. 17, DHEW Publication No. (ADM) 78-581) Washington, D.C.: U.S. Government Printing Office, 1977.

Green, D. E. Youth Education. In *Smoking and health: A report of the Surgeon General* (DHEW Publication No. (PHS) 79-50066). Washington, D.C.: U.S. Government Printing Office, 1979.

Hackett, G., & Horan, J. J. Focused Smoking: An unequivocably safe alternative to rapid smoking. *Journal of Drug Education,* 1978, *8,* 261-266.

Hackett, G., & Horan, J. J. Partial component analysis of a comprehensive smoking program. *Addictive Behaviors,* 1979, *4,* 259-262.

Hall, S. M. The abstinence phobia. In N. Krasnegor (Ed.), *Behavioral approaches to analysis and treatment of substance abuse* (DHEW Publication No. ADM 79-839). Washington, D.C.: U.S. Government Printing Office, 1979.

Hall, S. M., & Hall, R. G. Maintaining change. In J. Fergusen & C. B. Taylor (Eds.), *Advances in behavioral medicine.* New York: Spectrum, 1979.

Harris, J. E. Cigarette smoking in the United States, 1950-1978. In *Smoking and health: A report of the Surgeon General* (DHEW Publication No. (PHS) 79-50066). Washington, D.C.: U.S. Government Printing Office, 1979.

Homme, L. E. Control of coverants, the operants of the mind. *Psychological Reports,* 1965, *15,* 501-511.

Horn, D. Psychological analysis of establishment and maintenance of the smoking habit. In *Cigarette smoking as a dependence process* (NIDA Research Monograph No. 23, DHEW Publication No. ADM 79-800). Washington, D.C.: U.S. Government Printing Office, 1979.

Hughes, J. R., Frederiksen, L. W., & Frazier, M. A carbon monoxide analyzer for measurement of smoking behavior. *Behavior Therapy,* 1978, *9,* 293-296.

Hunt, W. A., Barnett, L. W., & Branch, L. G. Relapse rates in addiction programs. *Journal of Clinical Psychology,* 1971, *27,* 455-456.

Hunt, W. A., & Bespalec, D. A. An evaluation of current methods of modifying smoking behavior. *Journal of Clinical Psychology,* 1974, *30,* 431-438.

Ikard, F. F., Green, D. E., & Horn, D. A scale to differentiate between types of smoking as related to the management of affect. *International Journal of the Addictions,* 1969, *4,* 649-659.

Jarvick, M. E. Further observations on nicotine as the reinforcing agent in smoking. In W. L. Dunn, Jr. (Ed.), *Smoking behavior: Motives and incentives.* Washington, D.C.: Winston, 1973.

Jarvick, M. E. Biological influences on cigarette smoking. In *Smoking and health: A report of the Surgeon General* (DHEW Publication No. (PHS) 79-50066). Washington, D.C.: U.S. Government Printing Office, 1979.

Kozlowski, L. T. Psychosocial influences on cigarette smoking. In *Smoking and health: A report of the Surgeon General* (DHEW Publication No. (PHS) 79-50066). Washington, D.C.: U.S. Government Printing Office, 1979.

Lando, H. A. Successful treatment of smokers with a broad-spectrum behavioral approach. *Journal of Consulting and Clinical Psychology,* 1977, *45,* 361-366.

Lando, H. A., & Davison, G. C. Cognitive dissonance as a modifier of chronic smoking behavior: A serendipitous finding. *Journal of Consulting and Clinical Psychology,* 1975, *43,* 750.

Levenberg, S. B., & Wagner, M. K. Smoking cessation: Long-term irrelevance of mode of treatment. *Journal of Behavior Therapy and Experimental Psychiatry,* 1976, *7,* 93-95.

Leventhal, H., & Avis, N. Pleasure, addiction, and habit:

Factors in verbal report on factors in smoking behavior. *Journal of Abnormal Psychology,* 1976, *85,* 478-488.

Leventhal, H., & Cleary, P. D. *The smoking problem: A review of the research, theory, and research policies in behavioral risk modification* (Research and Analytic Report Series). Madison: University of Wisconsin, 1977.

Levinson, B. L., Shapiro, D., Schwartz, G. E., & Tursky, B. Smoking elimination by gradual reduction. *Behavior Therapy,* 1971, *2,* 477-487.

Lichtenstein, E., & Danaher, B. G. Modification of smoking behavior: A critical analysis of theory, research, and practice. In M. Hersen, R. M. Eisler & P. M. Miller (Eds.), *Progress in behavior modification,* (Vol. 3). New York: Academic Press, 1976.

Lichtenstein, E., & Glasgow, R. E. Rapid smoking: Side effects and safeguards. *Journal of Consulting and Clinical Psychology,* 1977, *45,* 815-821.

Lichtenstein, E., Harris, D. E., Birchler, G. R., Wahl, J. M., & Schmahl, D. P. Comparison of rapid smoking, warm smoky air, and attention placebo in the modification of smoking behavior. *Journal of Consulting and Clinical Psychology,* 1973, *40,* 92-98.

Lichtenstein, E., & Penner, M. P. Long-term effects of rapid smoking treatment for dependent cigarette smokers. *Addictive Behaviors,* 1977, *2,* 109-112.

McAlister, A. L. Toward the mass communication of behavioral counseling: A preliminary study of a televised program to assist in smoking cessation (Doctoral dissertation, Stanford University, 1976). *Dissertation Abstracts International,* 1977, *37,* 5330B. (University Microfilms No. 77-7128.)

McAlister, A. L., Perry, C., & Maccoby, N. Adolescent smoking: Onset and prevention. *Pediatrics,* 1979, *63,* 650-658.

Maccoby, N., Farquhar, J. W., Wood, P. D., & Alexander, J. Reducing the risk of cardiovascular disease: Effects of a community-based campaign on knowledge and behavior. *Journal of Community Health,* 1977, *3,* 100-114.

McFall, R. M. Smoking cessation research. *Journal of Consulting and Clinical Psychology,* 1978, *46,* 703-712.

McFall, R. M., & Hammen, C. L. Motivation, structure, and self-monitoring: Role of nonspecific factors in smoking reduction. *Journal of Consulting and Clinical Psychology,* 1971, *37,* 80-86.

McKennell, A. C. *A comparison of two smoking typologies* (Research Paper 12). London: Tobacco Research Council, 1973.

Marlatt, G. A., & Gordon, J. R. Determinants of relapse: Implications for maintaining behavior change. *Alcoholism and Drug Abuse Technical Report,* 1978, (No. 78-07).

Marston, A. R., & McFall, R. M. Comparison of behavior modification approaches to smoking reduction. *Journal of Consulting and Clinical Psychology,* 1971, *36,* 153-162.

Miller, P. M., Frederiksen, L. W., & Hosford, R. L. Social interaction and smoking topography in heavy and light smokers. *Addictive Behaviors,* 1979, *4,* 147-153.

Multiple Risk Factor Intervention Trial. Smoking cessation procedures and cessation and recidivism patterns for a large cohort of MRFIT participants. In J. L. Schwartz (Ed.), *Progress in Smoking Cessation: Proceedings of the International Conference on Smoking Cessation, 1978.* New York: American Cancer Society, 1979.

National Interagency Council on Smoking and Health. *Guidelines for research on the effectiveness of smoking cessation programs: A committee report.* New York: National Interagency Council on Smoking and Health, October 1974.

Ohlin, P., Lundh, B., & Westling, H. Carbon monoxide blood levels and reported cessation of smoking. *Psychopharmacology,* 1976, *49,* 263-265.

Pechacek, T. F. Modification of smoking behavior. In *Smoking and health: A report of the Surgeon General* (DHEW Publication No. (PHS) 79-50066). Washington, D.C.: U.S. Government Printing Office, 1979.

Pechacek, T. F., & Danaher, B. G. How and why people quit smoking: Cognitive-behavioral implications. In P. C. Kendall & S. D. Hollon (Eds.), *Cognitive-behavioral interventions: Theory, research, and procedures.* New York: Academic Press, 1979.

Perri, M. G., Richards, C. S., & Schultheis, K. R. Behavioral self-control and smoking reduction: A study of self-initiated attempts to reduce smoking. *Behavior Therapy,* 1977, *8,* 360-365.

Pomerleau, O. F. Behavioral factors in the establishment, maintenance, and cessation of smoking. In *Smoking and health: A report of the Surgeon General* (DHEW Publication No. (PHS) 79-50066). Washington, D.C.: U.S. Government Printing Office, 1979.

Pomerleau, O. F., Adkins, D., & Pertschuk, M. Predictors of outcome and recidivism in smoking cessation treatment. *Addictive Behaviors,* 1978, *3,* 65-70.

Pomerleau, O. F., & Pomerleau, C. S. *Break the smoking habit: A behavioral program for giving up cigarettes.* Champaign, Ill.: Research Press, 1977.

Pope, J. W., & Mount, G. R. The control of cigarette smoking through the application of a portable electronic device designed to dispense an aversive stimulus in relation to subjects' smoking frequency. *Behavioral Engineering,* 1975, *2,* 52-56.

Puska, P., Bjorkqvist, S., & Koskela, K. Nicotine-containing chewing gum in smoking cessation: A double blind trial with half-year follow-up. *Addictive Behaviors,* 1979, *4,* 141-146.

Richmond, J. B. In *Smoking and health: A report of the Surgeon General* (DHEW Publication No. (PHS) 79-50066). Washington, D.C.: U.S. Government Printing Office, 1979.

Rosen, G. M., & Lichtenstein, E. An employee incentive program to reduce cigarette smoking. *Journal of Consulting and Clinical Psychology,* 1977, *45,* 957.

Russell, M. A. H. Tobacco smoking and nicotine dependence. In R. J. Gibbins (Ed.), *Research advances in alcohol and drug problems* (Vol. 3). New York: Wiley, 1976.

Russell, M. A. H. Tobacco dependence: Is nicotine rewarding or aversive? In *Cigarette smoking as a dependence process* (NIDA Research Monograph No. 23, DHEW Publication No. ADM 79-800). Washington, D.C.: U.S. Government Printing Office, 1979.

Russell, M. A. H., Armstrong, E., & Patel, V. A. Temporal contiguity in electric aversion therapy for cigarette smoking. *Behaviour Research and Therapy,* 1976, *14,* 103-123.

Russell, M. A. H., & Feyerabend, C. Cigarette smoking: A dependence on high nicotine boli. *Drug Metabolism Reviews,* 1978, *8,* 29-57.

Russell, M. A. H., Peto, J., & Patel, U. A. The classification of smoking by factorial structure of motives. *The Journal of the Royal Statistical Society,* (Series A) 1974, *137,* 313-333.

Russell, M. A. H., Raw, M., Taylor, C., Feyerabend, C., & Saloojee, Y. Blood nicotine and carboxyhemoglobin levels after rapid-smoking aversion therapy. *Journal of Consulting and Clinical Psychology,* 1978, *46,* 1423-1431.

Russell, M. A. H., Wilson, C., Feyerabend, C., & Cole, P. V. Effect of nicotine chewing gum on smoking behavior and as an aid to cigarette withdrawal. *British Medical Journal,* 1976, *2,* 391-393.

Sachs, D. P. L., Hall, R. G., & Hall, S. M. Effects of rapid smoking. Physiologic evaluation of a smoking-cessation therapy. *Annals of Internal Medicine,* 1978, *88,* 639-641.

Schachter, S., Silverstein, B., Kozlowski, L. T., Perlick, D., Herman, C. P., & Liebling, B. Studies of the interaction of psychosocial and pharmacological determinants of smoking. *Journal of Experimental Psychology: General,* 1977, *106,* 3-40.

Schmahl, D. P., Lichtenstein, E., & Harris, D. E. Successful treatment of habitual smokers with warm, smoky air, and rapid smoking. *Journal of Consulting and Clinical Psychology,* 1972, *38,* 105-111.

Schneider, N. G., Popek, P., Jarvik, M. E., & Gritz, E. R. The use of nicotine gum during cessation of smoking. *American Journal of Psychiatry,* 1977, *134,* 439-440.

Schwartz, J. L., & Rider, G. *Review and evaluation of smoking control methods: 1976 update* (U.S. Public Health Service Publication). Washington, D.C.: National Clearinghouse for Smoking and Health, 1978.

Shiffman, S. M. The tobacco withdrawal syndrome. In *Cigarette smoking as a dependence process* (NIDA Research Monograph No. 23, DHEW Publication No. ADM 79-800). Washington, D.C.: U.S. Government Printing Office, 1979.

Sipich, J. F., Russell, R. K., & Tobias, L. A comparison of covert sensitization and "nonspecific" treatment in the modification of smoking behavior. *Journal of Behavior Therapy and Experimental Psychiatry,* 1974, *5,* 201-203.

Smoking and health: A report of the Surgeon General (DHEW Publication No. (PHS) 79-50066). Washington, D.C.: U.S. Government Printing Office, 1979.

Solomon, R. L. An opponent-process theory of acquired motivation: IV. The affective dynamics of addiction. In J. Maser & M. Seligman (Eds.), *Psychopathology: Experimental models.* San Francisco, W. H. Freeman, 1977.

Solomon, R. L., & Corbit, J. An opponent-process theory of motivation: II. Cigarette addiction. *Journal of Abnormal Psychology,* 1973, *81,* 158-171.

Sutherland, A., Amit, Z., Golden, M., & Roseberger, Z. Comparison of three behavioral techniques in the modification of smoking behavior. *Journal of Consulting and Clinical Psychology,* 1975, *43,* 443-447.

Ternes, J. W. An opponent process theory of habitual behavior with special reference to smoking. In *Research on smoking behavior* (NIDA Research Monograph No. 17, DHEW Publication No. ADM 78-581). Washington, D.C.: U.S. Government Printing Office, 1977.

Tighe, T. J., & Elliot, R. Breaking the cigarette habit: Effects of a technique involving threatened loss of money. *Psychological Record,* 1968, *18,* 503-513.

Tomkins, S. S. Psychological model for smoking behavior. *American Journal of Public Health,* 1966, *56,* 17-20.

Tomkins, S. S. A modified model of smoking behavior. In E. Borgatta & R. Evans (Ed.), *Smoking, health and behavior.* Chicago: Aldine, 1968.

Tori, C. D. A smoking satiation procedure with reduced medical risk. *Journal of Clinical Psychology,* 1978, *34,* 574-577.

Vogt, T. M., Selvin, S., Widdowsen, G., & Hulley, S. B. Expired air carbon monoxide and serum thiocyanate as objective measures of cigarette exposure. *American Journal of Public Health,* 1977, *67,* 545-549.

Wallston, B. S., & Wallston, K. A. Locus of control and

health: A review of the literature. *Health Education Monographs,* 1978, *6,* 107–117.
Wilde, G. J. S. Behavior therapy for addicted cigarette smokers. *Behaviour Research and Therapy*, 1964, *2*, 107–110.
Wilson, G. T., & Davison, G. C. Aversion techniques in behavior therapy: Some theoretical and metatheoretical considerations. *Journal of Consulting and Clinical Psychology,* 1969, *33,* 327–329.
Winett, R. A. Parameters of deposit contracts in the modification of smoking. *Psychological Record,* 1973, *23,* 49–60.

20 Behavioral Approaches in the Treatment of Bronchial Asthma

A. BARNEY ALEXANDER

The past decade has seen significant advances both in our understanding of the role of psychosocial variables in asthma and the development of behavioral approaches to its treatment. This chapter critically reviews the available literature on behavioral treatment methods to provide the reader with a scientific and a practical understanding of the state of the art.

A concise but thorough overview of the nature of bronchial asthma, in both its medical and psychological aspects, is necessary for a working understanding of the approaches to therapy with the asthmatic patient.

The Nature of Bronchial Asthma

The Medical Aspects of Asthma[1]

Description Bronchial asthma is a syndrome characterized by episodes of obstruction to an adequate exchange of air in the lungs. Its clinical manifestations include wheezing respirations, dyspnea, cough, and excessive mucus production. The changes in the bronchi and bronchioles which cause these conditions are mucosal edema, hypersecretion of thick mucus, and contraction of bronchial smooth muscle, all of which result in a reduction in the lumen of the bronchial tubes. An important characteristic of asthma, as opposed to other conditions which may impair the ability of the body to transport air, is that the symptoms are reversible, either through adequate and appropriate pharmacological means or by virtue of normal remission between attacks. This leads to a situation in which asthma sufferers may have completely normal pulmonary function in the periods between episodes of asthma. These periods may be as long as several months or even years.

Preparation of this chapter was supported in part by the following grants to the author: HL 07026 from the National Heart, Lung and Blood Institute and MH 30099 from the National Institute of Mental Health.

[1]For more detailed information on both clinical and scientific medical aspects of asthma the interested reader is encouraged to consult either or both of two excellent volumes: Middleton, E., Reed, C. E., & Ellis, E. F. (Eds.), *Allergy: Principles and Practice.* St. Louis: C. V. Mosby, 1978; and Weis, E. B. and Segal, M. S. (Eds.), Bronchial Asthma: *Its Nature and Management.* Boston: Little, Brown & Co., 1976.

Medical Psychology
Contributions to Behavioral Medicine

ISBN 0-12-565960-1

Asthma is considered to be either extrinsic (due to allergic reaction), intrinsic (nonallergic, infectious, etc.), or mixed. Most patients fall into the latter category, and for most victims, the majority of asthmatic symptoms are related to allergens. Common asthmogenic allergens include tree, grass, and weed pollens; molds and fungi; animal danders and feathers; house and occupational dusts; some foods; insects (but not stings); and some chemicals (but not in their role as irritants).

Nonallergic asthmogenic stimuli include aspirin, exercise, airway irritants, and infections. Exercise is such an ubiquitous asthmogen that exercise-induced bronchospasm has been suggested as a defining characteristic of asthma. Usually, exercise-induced asthma reverses nonproblematically with rest and/or appropriate medication. Common airway irritants include certain chemical gases, aerosal propellants, cold air, and cough. In many patients, certain situations (e.g., some weather conditions and weather changes) can precipitate asthma idiosyncratically by as yet unknown means. Respiratory infections represent one of the most common asthma precipitants and are the cause of some of the most severe and prolonged episodes of asthma, often requiring hospitalization and life-saving therapy. While it is highly uncertain whether bacterial infections can provoke asthma, it is now known that viral infections (e.g., colds and influenza) are very common asthma precipitants.

Incidence The incidence of asthma has been variously estimated to be anywhere from 2 to 20% with the most realistic figure being somewhere around 5% (Davis, 1972). Of these, roughly 60% are less than 17 years of age. Among children, males are affected nearly twice as often as females; however, this proportion equalizes in puberty. Asthma can appear at any age but onset is most likely to occur within the first 5 years of life. While the mortality data (approximately 2 per 100,000) rank asthma among the 60 leading causes of death in the United States, it is the morbidity data that are the most striking. Among chronic diseases, asthma is one of the leading causes of loss of productive time. Asthma is also the third most common reason for visits to physicians due to chronic illness.

Prognosis Precise prognostic data are difficult to obtain. As many as 40% of all asthmatics may show substantial or complete remission of symptoms as they grow older, especially during the early teenage years. The natural course and ultimate outcome of the disorder seem related to many factors, including the severity after onset and sex differences. Not only are girls less likely to be afflicted than boys, but the latter are slightly less likely to experience a remission of symptoms as they grow older. In terms of age of onset, poorer prognosis is associated with the appearance of asthma before the age of two or in adulthood, and allergic individuals manifest a greater incidence of more severe and persistent symptoms. Nevertheless, the expectation of an ultimate favorable outcome for many sufferers cannot be used to support highly conservative therapy in the presence of symptoms. Formerly symptomatic asthma victims typically manifest lingering evidence of lung hypersensitivity, but lung damage does not seem to be significantly associated with asthma, whatever its severity or duration.

Pathogenesis While the etiology of asthma is only incompletely understood, a good deal has been learned regarding the pathogenesis of asthma symptoms in some instances. Although a substantial proportion of asthma symptoms can be attributed to the antigen–antibody reaction, it is clear that immunologic mechanisms can by no means account for all incidences of asthma. Of the three most important nonimmunologic pathogenic factors (hyperirritability to the airways, exercise, and infection), the former has been shown to be due to a vagally mediated bronchoconstrictive irritant reflex. Exercise induced asthma is less well understood, but may involve either or both the release of chemical mediators (e.g., histamine, SRS-A and some prostaglandins, etc.) or the previously mentioned irritant reflex though stimulation by insufficiently warmed air during exertion. The mechanisms involved in infection-induced asthma are still quite speculative. The most comprehensive overall etiologic theory to date is the so-called beta-adrenergic blockade (Szentivanyi, 1968), which posits that asthmatics manifest a reduced responsivity of the bronchodilatory beta-adrenergic receptors in the lung, leaving the lung relatively unprotected from both vagal and humoral constricting factors. Nevertheless, as appealing as this theory may be, the supporting evidence remains somewhat equivocal (Miklich, 1977).

The best genetic data available suggests that familial factors may play a substantially less prominent role than had been previously assumed. Concordance rates in monozygotic twins have been found to be only 19% for asthma, and 25% for all allergic disorders, figures which are only marginally higher than the corresponding figures for dizygotic twins (Edfors-Lubs, 1971).

Diagnosis The clinical diagnosis of asthma is based upon history, certain laboratory tests and, to a lesser extent, characteristic physical findings. A careful history typically reveals episodic dyspnea, chest tightness, wheezing and/or cough, and whether or not the asthma manifests a substantial allergic (extrinsic) component or is largely intrinsic. Complete information regarding the physical environment is essential for both diagnosis and subsequent treatment planning. Findings during a physical examination depend greatly upon the condition of the patient at the time; that is, the presence of an active asthma episode during the examination. While laboratory findings are certainly important in establishing a firm diagnosis of asthma, they are particularly salient in differential diagnosis and precise specification of the nature of the disorder in each individual case. Laboratory procedures, particularly for differential diagnosis, include complete blood counts; nasal secretion and sputum analysis (in particular for eosinophilia indicative of allergy); chest X ray (primarily to exclude other conditions); skin tests; direct challenges of the lungs; exercise challenges; and pulmonary function tests.

Skin tests can be a very useful way of defining those substances to which a person *might* be lung sensitive. False-negatives are very rare; that is, allergic sensitivity of the bronchial tree appears to be invariably associated with skin reactivity. The reverse, however, is not the case: The skin and other organs may exhibit allergic reactivity to an antigen which produces no effect when delivered directly to the lung. For these instances, bronchial challenges of the lung are employed. Unlike skin tests, which may be safely carried out in an office setting, bronchial challenges involve a significant medical risk and are usually done under more carefully controlled conditions to avoid the possibility of severe and/or delayed asthmatic reactions which may require vigorous treatment. Two kinds of challenges can be used. The first involves antigen (pollen, molds, house dust, etc.) prepared in an aerosol for inhalation. The second involves similar direct inhaled challenges of the lung with histamine or methacholine, both of which cause bronchoconstrictive responses in asthmatics from 100 to 1000 times greater than those exhibited by nonasthmatics. For all practical purposes, methacholine challenge results can be taken as definitive when the test is negative, precluding the diagnosis of asthma with a very high degree of certainty. Controlled exercise testing can substantially aid treatment decisions and serve as a guide for recommending activities to patients.

Pulmonary Function Testing Assessment of pulmonary function must be considered essential in the overall evaluation of the asthmatic for purposes of differential diagnosis, precise specification of pathology, establishment of clinical severity, and evaluation of the effectiveness of provocation tests and treatment. These tests include the measurement of lung volumes, pulmonary mechanics, ventilation, regional gas distribution, and arterial blood gas tensions. While many severe, chronic asthmatics manifest residual abnormalities even when asymptomatic, testing is more revealing during periods of acute exacerbations or at differing severity levels of the chronic condition. The most useful of these measures on an ordinary basis are tests of ventilation based upon a forced vital capacity into a spirometer, a device which measures expired volume over time. This procedure involves having the patient exhale as much air as possible into the device at maximum force following a full inhalation. From this record a number of measures can be obtained, the most important of which are the forced expiratory volume in one second (FEV_1), the peak expiratory flow rate (PEFR), and the maximum midexpiratory flow rate (MMEF, the maximum flow rate obtained between 25% and 75% to the total expired volume). FEV_1 and PEFR are highly dependent upon patient effort (i.e., whether the patient "blows" as hard as possible into the device) and are sensitive primarily to large airway obstruction. Because the site of obstruction in asthma may be in either the large or the small airways or both, measures which are differentially sensitive to the central (large) and peripheral (small) airways are necessary. The MMEF is both relatively effort-independent and quite sensitive to small airway pathology. An effort-independent, large airway measurement is more complicated than flow measures: namely, airway resistance or its reciprocal, airway conductance. This measure can be derived in several ways but is most commonly obtained from a whole body plethysmograph. From this large and expensive instrument are also obtained the most useful lung volume measures (e.g., the functional residual capacity and residual volume), primarily measures of small airways. While these measurements provide excellent information, if and when the equipment is available, the most generally useful device is the *Wright,* a portable PEFR meter. Because of its favorable size, cost, and ease of use, it cannot only be employed effectively in the office, but also at home by the patient. Furthermore, it allows for very frequent measurement of lung function, and, in most cases, will provide all of the pulmonary function information that is ever necessary for most aspects of clinical diagnosis and treatment evaluation. As the sole measure for research purposes, however, the effort-dependent nature and exclusive sensitivity to large airways of the PEFR may present problems. In most research contexts, other measures must be employed.

Treatment Treatment of asthma always has one goal: a therapeutic approach that controls the symptoms as much as possible with as little therapy (mainly drugs) as necessary so that both the disease and its treatment minimally interfere with a productive and rewarding lifestyle. With few exceptions the drugs used to treat asthma possess varying degrees of disturbing, and in some cases dangerous, side effects. As will become evident from the succeeding discussion, the hope that behavioral (i.e., nonpharmachological) intervention might significantly reduce, or in some cases even eliminate, the need for drugs in the treatment of asthma has as yet largely failed to materialize to any clinically significant extent. While it will also become evident that the behavioral specialist still has a vital role to play in the treatment of asthma, behavioral strategies will rarely, if ever, represent the primary therapeutic modality. The behaviorist will invariably be working with secondary, albeit often highly important, problems *associated* with the disorder and its medical treatment.

Asthma may be manifested clinically by a few mild attacks in a lifetime to severe, life-threatening, chronic asthma which responds only to the most vigorous therapy, with powerful drugs, on a virtually continual basis. The symptom patterns of most asthmatics are intermediate between these extremes. The drugs available to the physician fall into three categories (*a*) bronchodilators; (*b*) corticosteroids (whose mechanism of action is to date essentially unknown); and (*c*) others (mainly cromolyn sodium, whose precise mechanism of action is also largely a matter of speculation). Also available therapeutically are methods such as immunotherapy.

For therapeutic purposes five classes of clinical manifestation can be distinguished (*a*) mild, sporadic episodes; (*b*) moderate, chronic asthma; (*c*) severe, chronic asthma; (*d*) acute, serious attacks (or breakthroughs from the standpoint of chronic management); and (*e*) status asthmaticus. The last represents a life-threatening medical crisis and is not considered here since successful asthma management is designed to avoid this situation.[2]

The infrequent episode of mild to moderate asthma tends to respond well to symptomatic doses of oral or inhaled sympathomimetics and theophylline compounds. The latter are bronchodilating drugs in the same general class as caf-

[2]No additional drugs are available for its treatment, but appropriate steps must often be taken to stave off, or in the worst instances, to deal with consequences such as respiratory failure and cardiac arrest.

feine (i.e., xanthine). With this type of use, the drugs are usually well tolerated with few significant side effects. Moderate chronic asthma or extended seasonal exacerbations usually require continuous therapy. Typically this will involve round-the-clock (e.g. every 6, 8, or 12 hours) daily therapy with oral theophylline and, if necessary, oral sympathomimetics. In this case, side effects are more important. These include nausea, vomiting, headache, and central nervous system overstimulation. Chronic severe asthma almost always requires regular treatment with corticosteroids (usually prednisone) in addition to the regimens already described.

The major problem in steroid therapy is to avoid suppression of normal hypothalamic-pituitary-adrenal axis function as much as possible. Hence, prednisone therapy every other day (to allow adrenal function recovery on the off-medication day) is preferred if symptom control can be obtained. Serious acute attacks, or breakthroughs in management, usually require parenteral therapy. Typically this involves, in order of priority, subcutaneous epinephrine, intravenous aminophylline (theophylline), and I.V. steroids. Additionally, extended exacerbations in nonsteroid dependent cases may require short bursts of steriod therapy (e.g., for 1 or 2 weeks) until the symptoms are brought under control. Less severe, acute attacks in chronic asthmatics may only require spot treatment with an inhaled sympathomimetic in addition to the regular medication. Other management strategies include pretreatment prior to expected precipitant exposure (e.g., cold air or exercise), and prophylactic therapy with cromolyn sodium. In certain individuals the latter can provide protection against exercise induced asthma, clinical benefit in allergen induced asthma, and steroid sparing effects.

Immunotherapy (the familiar "allergy shots") can sometimes be of benefit to the asthmatic but its true effectiveness in asthma is still controversial. The use of environmental control strategies, such as elimination diets, change of geographical location, elimination of pets, etc., are obvious in selected cases where a clear link between stimulus and response can be demonstrated. However, it must be pointed out that careless recommendations in this regard can sometimes do more harm than good. Examples are almost too numerous to mention, but they include giving up a beloved pet, changing of many or all household articles, relocation (with family or job upheaval), expensive and unusual diets, air purification devices, etc., without any convincing rationale or promise of success prior to the recommendation.

The Psychological Aspects of Asthma

Historical Perspective While the mainstream of medicine continued to view asthma as basically an immunological disorder, within psychosomatic medicine the psychoanalytic formulations of French and Alexander (1941) held sway. They promulgated the hypothesis that the *origin* of asthma was the suppression of an intense emotion, specifically, a suppressed cry for the mother. Although this influential formulation has led to a great deal of unproductive theorizing and futile investigation, until very recently the dominant theme among psychosomatic researchers has been that, in some way, psychological variables play an etiological role in asthma.

A comparison here with peptic ulcer is instructive. It is fairly well accepted that certain forms of psychological stress and conflict can lead more or less directly to increased gastric secretion in normal individuals. For persons who are on the high end of the gastric reactivity continuum, prolonged exposure to the appropriate forms of psychological stress may ultimately lead to ulceration of the stomach or duodenum. This analysis assigns a prominent role to psychological factors in the actual etiology of the lesion. While there surely exists a complex interaction between tissue suceptibility, normal gastric acid levels, secretory reactivity and many evironmental and psychological factors in the development of ulcer in any particular case, this formulation provides for the possibility that a lesion would not appear in the absence of sufficient psychological stress even if all of the other factors were favorable to ulcer development. As such, peptic ulcer would seem to be an excellent example of a truly psychosomatic disease. In contrast, for asthma there is simply no convincing evidence that the pathophysiological characteristics of asthma must, or even can, result in any way from psychological influences (Creer, 1978). The more current view is exactly the opposite; namely, that psychological disturbance can *result from* the continued battle with asthma, or indeed any chronic illness, and that, in some affected individuals, psychological influences such as emotional stress *may* contribute to the frequency and severity of specific episodes of bronchospasm. Hence, many authors (e.g., Creer, 1978), are now taking the position that asthma should not be considered a psychosomatic disorder in any sense. There is good reason to be very sympathetic towards this view, as the concept of psychosomatic usually includes notions regarding an etiologic role for psychological events. Sustained belief that psychological variables contribute in any manner to the *cause* of asthma will only continue to divert attention away from the more fruitful study of the role that psychological influences do play in the lives of affected individuals. Equally as pertinent, the traditional psychosomatic view only furthers the destructive notion, held by most laymen and too many professionals, that asthma is all in the head. Such a belief is monstrously unfair and often psychologically damaging to asthma sufferers and their families. It can also lead to a very dangerous clinical approach to therapy for persons who are sometimes severely ill for no fault of their own.

Family Stress Influence During the past three decades, a good deal has been learned regarding psychological influences in asthma, and in the ensuing paragraphs an attempt is made to describe briefly the extent of our knowledge. Psychological factors in the family constellation appear to play a role in the manifestation of the disorder in some cases, though undoubtedly not in its etiology. For years clinicians have noticed that some childhood asthmatics obtained symptom reduction or remission when separated from their families for one reason or another. In the late 1950s Peshkin even spoke of "parentectomy" as a treatment for asthma in some children (Peshkin, 1960). Evidence for the effectiveness of separation was seen in the significant number of children whose symptoms remitted abruptly when they were sent to residential treatment centers such as the National Asthma Center in Denver. However, it remained highly likely that the benefits of leaving home for a time were due to alterations of the physical, rather than the emotional, environment. In a landmark study, Purcell and his colleagues (Purcell, Brady, Chai, Muser, Molk, Gordon, & Means, 1969), controlled for physical environment effects by removing the families of asthmatic children to a hotel for several weeks while the child remained at home under the care of an adult child-care worker. They found that this experimental separation produced small but statistically significant changes in a number of asthma measures in some children. While these results implicated general family stress in the manifestation of the disorder, more specific attempts to verify that rejecting of engulfing mothers cause asthma have met with the expected lack of success (McLean & Ching, 1973), and attempts to dichotomize asthmatics along an emotional–organic continuum have not proved fruitful (Mattsson, 1975). Hence, a safe conclusion is that such emotional factors may account for a *modest* amount of pulmonary variance in only a minority of asthmatics.

Personality Factors The search for a specific personality pattern associated with asthma has been carried out even more energetically and with less success. As Creer (1978) points out, asthma sufferers have been claimed at one time or another to be overdependent, hypersensitive, overly aggressive, and overly passive. They have been found to be more neurotic than normals and to describe themselves in a less favorable light. In general, when comparisons have been made with those who suffer from other chronic illnesses differences disappear (Neuhaus, 1958). It is now generally conceded that the frequently obtained personality differences between asthmatics and normals are a result of the disease itself and are probably only manifestations of the presence of chronic illness. No evidence suggests that unique personality factors contribute to the development of asthma. All of the investigations in this area have been experimentally flawed and entail the conceptual risk for the field of deemphasizing the importance of the biological processes which underlie asthma (Purcell & Weiss, 1970).

Psychophysiological Aspects Psychophysiological studies have produced more encouraging results. It is a common clinical observation, often supported by patient report, that attacks sometimes appear during, or seem to result from, emotional stress. Certainly, emotional arousal such as anxiety, frequently accompanies asthma episodes. accordingly, a number of attempts have been made to precipitate asthma employing emotional stressors such as disturbing films (Weiss, Lynees, Molk, & Riley, 1976), recordings of the voice of a patient's mother (Hill, 1975), and discussion or hypnotic suggestions of stressful life situations (Clarke, 1970). Generally such stimuli have proved capable at times of producing changes in respiratory patterns and/or slight decreases in pulmonary flow rates, but not of producing frank asthma. The effects have been very modest, though usually statistically significant, and appear only in some individuals. These results, however, present a paradox. Since the cornerstone of therapeutics in asthma has been the well-established bronchodilating effects of beta-adrenergic substances, the question arises as to why such episodes, accompanied as they are by sympathetic arousal, should result in bronchospasm at all. A possible answer has been proposed by Mathé and Knapp (1971) as a consequence of experiments which suggested that some sort of adrenergic defect may be involved. They found that some asthmatics appear to produce less than normal amounts of epinephrine as indicated by decreased urinary epinephrine excretion as a result of emotional stress. These results, however, have not been replicated.

On the cholinergic side, psychophysiological attempts to demonstrate that asthma might represent a vagotonic disorder, or one characterized by a relative parasympathetic dominance, have met with little success (Knapp, Mathé, & Vachon, 1976). Nevertheless, work by Gold and his colleagues (Gold, Kessler, & Yu, 1972) has forced renewed interest in the vagus. They have shown that significant bronchospasm can result from mechanical stimulation of vagally mediated epithelial irritant receptors. Such reflex bronchospasm is presently held to be a likely cause of mechanically induced bronchospasm in humans, such as that which results from coughing, some airborne irritants, cold air, etc. It is a distinct possibility that many examples of so-called emotionally triggered asthma may be due to this mechanism. Gasping as a result of surprise, yelling during anger, and crying or laughing accompanying acute emotional states may represent emotional asthma only very indirectly.

Undoubtedly the most compelling line of research assigning psychological variables a role in the control of airways tone is the work on suggestion, relaxation and placebo effects. A number of reports in the literature (e.g., Luparello, Lyons, Bleecker, & McFadden, 1968) have demonstrated that inhaled aerosolized saline can result in bronchoconstriction when the subject is led to believe that the substance is one to which the patient is known to be sensitive, and that the resultant increase in airway resistance can be reversed by another inhalation of saline believed by the subject to be a standard bronchodilator. The only failures to replicate these effects have employed insensitive measurement methods, a situation confirmed by the above investigators, again underscoring that such effects are probably real but modest indeed. In a series of experiments in our own laboratory (Alexander, 1972; Alexander, Cropp, & Chai, 1979; Alexander, Miklich, & Hershkoff, 1972), we have shown that psychological relaxation can result in both significant decreases in airway resistance and retarding of the natural increase in resistance which occurs when maintenance oral bronchodilators are withheld. Again, these effects, though replicated by other investigators are modest (see pp. 383–386). Finally, Godfrey and Silverman (1973) have noted that premedication with placebo can lead to a significant reduction in the degree of exercise-induced bronchospasm.

Conditioning and Learning Beginning almost a century ago, the possibility that learning or conditioning may influence bronchomotor tone has also received attention. MacKinzie (1886) anecdotally described a woman who was said to develop wheezing from the sight of a paper rose under glass. Nevertheless, during the ensuing nine decades, no convincing laboratory demonstrations of conditioned asthma have been done although several writers have discussed the likelihood of conditioned bronchospasm (e.g., Turnbull, 1962). It remains only an intriguing possiblity that the circumstances under which naturally occurring antigen-induced bronchospasm or sympathomimetically provided relief represent a standard classical conditioning paradigm. Pavlov's dogs, for example, were caused to have a conditioned connection between a bell and salivation by means of a bell being sounded shortly before food powder was blown into their mouths. After many such pairings of the bell and the food powder, the bell alone was capable of producing the reflexive salivation. Illustratively, for the asthmatic the bell might be the visual and olfacotry sensations associated with weeds while pollen would be the food powder. The bronchospasm in this case represents the "reflexive" allergic reaction to pollen just like salivation to food. After enough pairings between weeds and pollen, simply seeing weeds should be capable of causing some conditional bronchospasm. Similarly, the stimuli immediately preceding the inhalation of a pharmachological bronchodilator would soon elicit some conditioned relaxation of bronchial smooth muscle.

While the foregoing analysis is theoretically compelling, there are some problems. In general, these kinds of classically conditioned responses have proved to be unstable and/or hard to develop. With the exception of conditional responses which are highly adaptive for the organism, (e.g., taste aversions to toxins, fear reactions, etc.) classically conditioned connections tend to dissipate or extinguish very rapidly if the conditioned stimulus is not continually paired with the stimulus producing the reflexive reaction (Kling & Riggs, 1971). For our example this means that on every occasion in which grass stimuli (even artificial ones) are not actually associated with either the presence or a sufficient quantity of pollen, an extinction or deconditioning trial will occur. Further, the actual model for the example is technically called *long delay* or *trace* conditioning, an even more unfavorable set of circumstances for the development and maintenance of classically conditioned responses. While the suggestion and placebo effects can certainly be interpreted as due, at least in part, to historical conditioning trials, it is not surprising that both these effects and examples of conditioned asthma have been so elusive. Careful analysis suggests that conditioned bronchoconstriction or dilation would tend to develop only infrequently, and almost never to any great degree in any particular case. As we have seen, natural conditioning trials, which must be numerous and occur under optimal circumstances for conditioned reactions to develop at all, would in most instances be continually defused by natural extinction trials.

More recently, the possibility of biofeedback-assisted learning or volitional control in the lung has been investigated. This work requires the use of elaborate and very expensive instrumentation to provide almost breath-by-breath analysis and feedback information of airway resistance. Furthermore, the validity of the technique employed, forced pressure oscillation, has been severely criticized. These difficulties notwithstanding, and while recognizing the problems, both Vachon and Rich (1976) and Feldman (1976) have reported what appear to be reliable but very small "learned" drops in respiratory resistance in a few subjects. It is becoming increasingly clear in general in biofeedback research that very elaborate experimental control procedures are required before any obtained visceral changes can be confidently ascribed to learned voluntary control (Miller, 1978). As yet, such controls have not been employed in this work.

Overview Despite much enthusiastic and dedicated effort on the part of investigators with a psychosomatic orientation, no really persuasive evidence has been produced to support the enduring notion that psychological variables play *any* role in the *etiology* of asthma. Nevertheless, it can be acknowledged that psychosocial variables may, to some degree, be capable of affecting pulmonary reactions in some individuals and, for a minority of patients, may possibly affect the clinical course of asthma as well. Pessimistic as this assessment may be, a dispassionate appraisal indicates that psychosocial factors exert at best only a comparatively minor influence on pulmonary physiology, and as such, are of little practical, clinical consequence to the majority of asthmatics. Nor are only certain well-defined subgroups of asthma patients, or asthmatic persons as opposed to other individuals, exclusively susceptible to the *pulmonary* effects of psychological stimuli (Mattsson, 1975). To be sure, the lungs of asthmatics are hypersensitive (i.e., more reactive) when they encounter various levels of physical bronchoconstricting influences, but the respiratory tracts of other persons will also react, albeit less dramatically, to similar chemical or mechanical insults. Lung hypersensitivity presents an interesting and instructive model. When subjected to a chemical insult, the pulmonary response of a person *who will experience symptomatic bronchospasm* (that is, an "asthmatic") is potentiated. In other words, asthmatics exhibit a pulmonary reaction much greater than the response of an individual who will never experience symptoms (i.e., a nonasthmatic). It follows that respiratory sensitivity probably lies on a continuum from normal to extremely marked reactivity (e.g., asthmatic hypersensitivity). The practice of distinguishing between asthmatics and nonasthmatics possesses, to be sure, distinct clinical and nosological utility. Treating asthma as a *disease* entity, however, probably masks the fact that the asthma syndrome may well represent a pathological exaggeration of any one of a number of normal control processes of respiration. The apparent discontinuity between asthmatics and nonasthmatics is likely due in large part to the fact that pulmonary function must in most cases decrease on the order of 20% from normal values before *any* loss of function is detectable by either the patient or a physician without special measuring instruments. Likewise, to the extent that any apparent variation is real, it is quite probable that the degree of pulmonary sensitivity to emotional stressors will be found to vary continuously rather than discretely among individuals, and that trans-situational variance in susceptibility will be evident for any given individual as well.

Considering the complex interaction among exogenous environmental, psychosocial, and normal and pathological physiological variables, our understanding of bronchial asthma must become much more sophisticated before we are capable of more than guesswork concerning which specific psychological stimulus will influence the clinical course of asthma in any individual case at any given time. The nature of this problem is at once evident when we realize that past research has failed to generate any substantial evidence of either consistent similarities or differences among asthmatics vis-a-vis psychological variables. Likewise, a point which may be less clear from the preceding review, but one which is unavoidably apparent when the investigations are placed in chronological sequence, is the following: The more recent the vintage of the study, the more persuasively negative is the evidence favoring any link between psychological variables and either the development or the symptomatic manifestations of bronchial asthma. Why this should be the case has to do primarily, it would seem (but not surprisingly so) with the matters of assessment and the rigors of experimental design. Happily, experience usually leads to regular increments in the quality of both.

Assessment in Applied Asthma Research

The problem in asthma is the varying obstruction of proper gas exchange in the lung. If one intends to effect a therapeutic impact on the basic problem in asthma itself, it is *impossible to overemphasize* the necessity of carefully and adequately measuring lung function in the evaluation of intervention outcome. Particularly for controlled experimental purposes, reliance on patient self-report or wheezing assessment (e.g., by stethoscope) is not sufficient, and all manner of misleading or frankly incorrect conclusions can be reached regarding the stimuli and/or treatment procedures relating to changes in asthma symptoms.

There are four basic kinds of outcome assessment data: (*a*) pulmonary function measurements; (*b*) medication requirements; (*c*) asthma attack characteristics; and (*d*) general care requirements. In pulmonary function assessment several important matters must be considered. Because of the constantly fluctuating nature of asthma, long-term measurement should be done on a daily basis (usually morning and evening), dictating the use of inexpensive and portable instruments such as a hand-held peak flow meter, supplemented every one to four weeks by more complete functional assessment including measures sensitive to the two major sites of obstruction—namely, large (central) and small (peripheral) airways. Effort *independent* measures of each site should be collected (e.g., small—MMEF; large—airways resistance or its more desirable variants such as specific airways conductance) in addition to the more usual effort *dependent* measures of large airway function (PEFR, FEV, etc.). It must always be remembered that asthma is characterized by an episodic rhythm, producing symptom remission during which pulmonary function may be completely or in part quite normal.

Medication requirements represent the second most valuable outcome assessment tactic, especially for individuals requiring maintenance drugs on a daily basis. Although drug requirement measures are to one degree or another dependent upon a complex interaction between difficult to specify patient and physician behaviors and judgments, *as needed* (i.e. prn) medications constitute much softer data because their use is largely up to the discretion of the patient. Since the amount and kind of medication can substantially influence lung function and its symptomatic manifestations (i.e., wheezing), the interpretation of drug data is always made *in relation to* other measures (e.g., daily pulmonary function scores, asthma attack counts, etc). A decrease in medication requirements will in most cases represent a beneficial outcome only if lung function and asthma frequency have remained relatively unchanged. Similarly, otherwise noteworthy increases in lung function and/or decreases in symptom frequency may be indicative of success only when drugs have not been increased. These reciprocal relationships between lung physiology, asthma symptomatology, and medications must always be understood and appreciated. Finally, it is best to require that the *type* of medication be held as constant as possible throughout an investigational period because of the great difficulties in establishing action and potency equivalents among different kinds of drugs.

Characteristics of asthma attacks include frequency counts, attack severity, and severity estimates. Measurements of these characteristics rely almost exclusively on patient report using essentially subjective criteria of characteristics which are very difficult to define. At the National Asthma Center we have, on occasion, used telemetered chest sounds, very high frequency clinical examinations or lung function assessments, observer report of audible wheezing, etc., with only modest success.

The final category, general care requirements, includes such things as emergency room visits, hospitalizations, physician office visits, phone calls to physicians, and medical cost and time lost estimates. These are all useful when the time windows over which assessment is being made are quite long (e.g., several months or years) because these events occur relatively infrequently.

Description of the Asthmatic

The early-onset asthma patient and family face some very severe hardships. These youngsters tend to grow up watching the other children play from the livingroom side of the front window. Most have poor self-concepts. Often both academic and social development suffer greatly due to the amount of time lost from school and from the restricted and specialized contacts with age-mates. These children encounter peers and adults who are variously overindulgent or lack understanding of their difficulties. Often these children react with shame and embarrassment or are overly demanding. At home their asthma may become the sole focus around which all family activities and concerns come to revolve. Their parents sometimes may feel guilty, responsible, and helpless; at other times they may be resentful and angry. Certainly an asthma sufferer can learn to manipulate others with the disorder or use it to excuse poor performance. It is often very difficult for patients to clearly sort out what they can really do from what is accomplished in the face of asthma. Many maladaptive and inappropriate behavior patterns can develop as the patient and family struggle with the ravages of this disorder. Such patterns can severely cripple family life and retard the social and psychological development of the child. Often the undesirable behavior patterns substantially affect the course of the disorder.

Asthma is, of course, potentially life-threatening, and many patients have experienced bouts of *status asthmaticus* which on occasion may have brought them close to death. Such experiences often generate enduring anxiety responses that can manifest themselves in fears of death, hospitals, and treatment. Some patients develop conditioned fear responses which can begin at even the first signs of wheezing. The frantic, worried behavior of parents and those treating the patient can exacerbate the young patient's fear. Moods vary with the severity of symptoms and also in relation to medications taken, from the widespread adrenergic effects of the sympathomimetics to the undesirable side effects of the corticosteroids.

The late-onset asthma sufferer faces a somewhat different set of problems because the asthma usually disrupts a lifestyle which has become more or less fixed. Adjusting to asthma late in life can be very difficult for the patient and family, often requiring substantial changes in activities and an adjustment to taking care of a chronic disorder. Like the youthful sufferer, the late-onset asthmatic may become frightened of the symptoms and often very scared by and concerned over the side effects of medications. For the families of both young and old, the financial burdens encountered in continually fighting asthma are almost always oppressive.

Behavioral Methods in Asthma Treatment

To deal effectively with the ravages of asthma often requires the talents of both medical and behavioral specialists. Behavioral intervention methods have been employed in the therapeutic management of asthma in three fairly distinct ways: (*a*) to alter the abonormal pulmonary functioning more or less directly; (*b*) to alter maladaptive emotional concomitants; and (*c*) to alter maladaptive asthma-related behaviors and family patterns. The research and clinical reports available in each of these categories are reviewed in the following sections.

The Alteration of Pulmonary Physiology

The methods which are intended to alter lung function in asthma include relaxation training, biofeedback, direct operant conditioning, and systematic desensitization. Of these, relaxation training has received by far the most attention.

Relaxation Methods The first experiment on the effects of relaxation in asthma was reported by Alexander, Miklich, and Hershkoff (1972). In this study, 20 children were offered 6 sessions of brief progressive relaxation training while another group of 16 children (matched with the first group on age, sex, and as closely as possible on the severity of asthma) received an equivalent number of sessions during which they simply sat quietly. Immediately before and after each session, pulmonary function was measured with a peak expiratory flow rate meter. Because the aim of this study was to investigate the *immediate* effects of relaxation on pulmonary functioning, no attempt was made to assess the potential long-term benefits of the regular practice of relaxation. Results indicated a statistically significant average increase of 21.63 liters per minute for the relaxation subjects, representing about an 11% improvement in pulmonary function, compared to a nonsignificant mean decrease of 6.14 liters per minute for the children in the resting condition. These results were replicated by Alexander (1972) with a new group of children comparable to those participating in the first experiment, employing subjects as their own controls rather than using a control group design. A unique feature of this study was an attempt to discover if there were any ways of predicting which child would be most likely to respond beneficially to relaxation; for example, if relaxation is considered to be a simple extension of resting or inactivity, then the response to resting might predict the response to deliberate relaxation. The results were very similar to the initial study. The average amount of PEFR change during relaxation was 23.5 liters per minute, while during resting there was a nonsignificant increase of 1.52 liters per minute. However, no significant relationship was found between the response to sitting quietly or resting and the response to relaxation, a result suggesting that purposeful relaxation could not be considered simply as an extension of resting. Finally, no other predictor variables were found though many possible candidates were investigated.

A third experiment (Alexander, Cropp, & Chai, 1979) was undertaken to address crucial issues that were not examined in the previous two studies: (*a*) the effect of relaxation on effort-independent measures of both large and small airway function as opposed to simple PEFR measurement; (*b*) follow-up for 1.5 hours after relaxation as opposed to immediately afterwards; and (*c*) the detection of a clinically significant effect (i.e., greater than 25% functional change as opposed to just 11% referred to baseline). The subjects were 14 children, each of whom served in 11 laboratory sessions divided into three distinct phases: resting (phase 1), relaxation training (phase 2), and unaided, self relaxation (phase 3). Each session consisted of a pretest pulmonary function assessment followed by four posttests of pulmonary function, extending the period of careful observation to approximately 1.5 hours postrelaxation. Each pulmonary function test involved measurement with the whole body plethysmograph, followed by a slow vital capacity and two forced vital capacity efforts.

It was found that during rest there was persistent tendency for pulmonary function to manifest a consistent and in most cases, monotonic decline from the pretesting occasion to the fourth posttest. This was due to the fact that testing on each occasion was initiated at a point 6 hours subsequent to the last administration of maintenance bronchodilator; hence, pulmonary function was declining due to the absence of medication. In contrast, the average relaxation response was a statistically significant shift toward maintenance of functions at the pretesting level. Nevertheless, the effect was small and again failed to approach *clinical* significance.

Since the work on relaxation in asthmatic children began, several other studies investigating relaxation effects have appeared in the literature. Tal and Miklich (1976) reported small but statistically significant pre- to postsession increases FEV_1 following each of three sessions of very brief quasihypnotic tape recorded relaxation instruction in 60 asthmatic youngsters. In addition to short-term effects, the long-term effects of relaxation have also been studied. Erskine and Schonell (1979) studied both short (immediate) and long-term effects in a 13-week study of 10 moderate to severe adult asthmatics divided into two matched groups: one received four sessions of progressive relaxation training while the other received four sessions of similar training supplemented by mental (autogenic) relaxation suggestions. FEV_1 and subjective symptom scores were measured both before and after each treatment session and once a week during the 3 pretreatment and 6 posttreatment weeks. No differences were found on any of the measures over time or between groups following treatment or before and after relaxation sessions. Davis, Saunders, Creer, and Chai (1973) also investigated both the short-term and long-term effects in 24 asthmatic children, divided into three equal groups: progressive relaxation training; relaxation training plus forehead EMG biofeedback; and self-relaxation (control). No information regarding how biofeedback was combined with the muscular relaxation procedures was provided. The study was divided into three phases: baseline for 8 days, five treatment sessions, and a post-treatment assessment period of 8 days. Before and after each treatment session, and additionally three times a day throughout the duration of the study, peak expiratory flow rate measures were obtained. No overall differences between groups were found either in terms of immediate changes over sessions, or between baseline and postassessment phases.

Scherr, Crawford, Sergent, and Scherr (1975) reported a similar study. During an 8-week treatment program, 22 children received one-half hour sessions of relaxation training three times weekly between the second and seventh weeks of camp, while a control group of 22 children received no attention whatsoever. As in the Davis *et al.* study, training consisted of progressive relaxation supplemented by forehead EMG biofeedback. Again, no specification was provided regarding the procedure used in combining the two methods. Peak expiratory flow rates were routinely obtained on all children three times daily, but not before and after each session. Children receiving the experimental relaxation program manifested statistically greater improvement in terms of average PEFR from the first to the eighth week of the study, as well as greater reductions in the number of infirmary visits, number of asthma attacks, and steroid usage. Still, the authors very prudently suggested caution in interpreting these findings since no attempt had been made to control for the special attention given the experimental subjects and the medical staff had independently rated members of the control group as having more severe asthma than the subjects in the experimental group.

The two studies just reviewed both used a combination of muscular relaxation and EMG biofeedback. Kotses, Glaus, Crawford, Edwards, and Scherr (1976) attempted to investigate the distinct contribution of EMG biofeedback training. They divided 36 asthmatic children into three equal groups: contingent feedback; noncontingent feedback; and no treatment. For experimental purposes, each noncontingent subject was permanently yoked throughout the duration of the study (nine sessions over 3 weeks) to a randomly selected contingent feedback subject, and children in both groups were told to try to lower the feedback tone. Measures of PEFR were obtained three times daily on all children but not immediately before and after each session. The results indicated that the children in the contingent feedback group manifested a statistically significant increase in weekly mean PEFR compared to the children in the noncontingent and no treatment groups, who did not differ from each other. EMG data indicated decreased frontalis muscle tension in the noncontingent group. There are two major difficulties with this study. First, as in the Scherr *et al.* (1975) experiment, the no treatment group did not constitute control for the attention given to experimental subjects. Although it may appear that the noncontingent yoked control group did provide control for this variable as well as for the presence of the contingent feedback stimulus, more careful scrutiny reveals that this probably was not the case. Because the subjects in both groups were told to try to lower feedback tone (that is, to control forehead muscle activity), the noncontingent subjects were, in reality, presented with an impossible task. Whereas this instruction is fine for subjects receiving true contingent feedback, noncontingent subjects can easily discover that the feedback stimulus bears no relationship whatever to muscle tension, or indeed, to anything about their behavior, and thus can realize that the task is hopeless relative to the instructions presented to them. As discussed by Alexander, White, and Wallace (1977), this can result in a counter-motivated situation in which frustration and even anger are prominent features, and performance suffers accordingly. It is therefore hardly surprising that subjects in the noncontingent group manifested an increase in forehead muscle tension during sessions and experienced no relaxing effect as measured by PEFR changes.

The Davis *et al.* (1973), Scherr *et al.* (1975), Kotses *et al.* (1976), and Erskine and Schonell (1979) investigations addressed a question rather different from that focused upon in the studies by Alexander and his colleagues; namely, the effect of regular relaxation practice extending over periods of several weeks on frequent measures of pulmonary function obtained at times other than before and after the relaxation sessions. However, Davis and her colleagues, and Erskine and Schonell studied *both* immediate and long-term effects of relaxation, finding no evidence for long-range effectiveness, whereas the other two studies found small but statistically significant increases in average peak expiratory flow rates over several weeks of training. While it is tempting to interpret the latter results as suggesting that the regular practice of relaxation may have long-range benefits, the lack of attention placebo control, and the other methodological problems in these studies preclude the drawing of this conclusion. When attention-placebo control was included by Davis *et al.* (1973), long-term benefits failed to materialize and Erskine and Schonell (1979) simply found no effects of relaxation at all. Analogously, it is impossible to conclude that either biofeedback alone or relaxation in conjunction with, or supplemented by, frontalis EMG biofeedback is an effective relaxation technique with which to bring about changes in pulmonary function for asthmatic children. Other research, albeit on nonasthamatic adults (Alexander, 1975; Alexander, White, & Wallace, 1977), indicates rather clearly that EMG biofeedback procedures should not be considered an effective relaxation training method (Alexander, & Smith, 1979). Thus, overall, it must now be accepted that the evidence points *securely* toward the conclusion that no relaxation method of any kind has a *clinically* significant effect on pulmonary physiology in either childhood or adult asthmatics.

Biofeedback Methods The reports by Vachon and Rich (1976) and Feldman (1976) on the use of airway resistance biofeedback in asthmatics have already been mentioned. Because of the elaborate and expensive equipment requirements and the marginal results obtained, biofeedback methods seem not to have received further attention—a lack of enthusiasm which is entirely justifiable in relation not only to the uninspiring results with asthmatics, but with regard to the rather discouraging state of affairs in biofeedback research in general, especially with autonomically mediated responses. The only other attempt to use a biofeedback treatment model with asthmatic individuals was reported by Tiep (Note 1) who cited clinical experience with feeding back to the patient the output of an electronic stethoscope as it monitored wheezing chest sounds. This method, however, has not generated any controlled laboratory research.

Systematic Desensitization This germinal behavior therapy technique inspired some of the first behavioral treatment research in asthma. From the behavioral point of view, psychosomatic symptoms were considered to represent persistent anxiety responses whose effects became manifest, at least in part, as a hyperreaction in some biologically vulnerable target organ. Though we now know that this rationale is inaccurate in asthma, it was argued that if the asthma were being mediated by anxiety, systematic desensitization could be used therapeutically to reduce the anxiety response, and hence, the wheezing.

The initial clinical investigation of desensitization with asthma was published by Walton (1960), who reported the case of a 30-year-old male suffering from asthmatic episodes that were apparently precipitated by anger and resentment, as well as by anxiety. The patient was administered systematic desensitization supplemented by assertiveness training. On the basis of self-ratings only, the patient's asthma reportedly improved commensurately with improvements in the patient's social relationships. The next report was provided by Cooper (1964), who treated a 24-year-old woman with intrinsic asthma. Cooper initially hypothesized that this patient's asthma was psychosomatic in origin (i.e., represented a conditioned anxiety response), but since specific anxiety inducing stimuli could not be detected, Cooper subsequently hypothesized that stimulus generalization was responsible. A variant of systematic desensitization was used consisting of deep muscle relaxation (the anxiety inhibitor) in conjunction with deliberate evocation of anger and excitement by appropriate direct verbal suggestion. As with Walton's (1960) case, the only measure of asthma was patient self-report, but Cooper (1964) reported that treatment was successful, noting that "training the patient to relax in traumatic situations has effectively raised her 'stress threshold' and rendered her relatively immune to asthmatic attacks precipitated by anxiety [p. 355]."

While these two case studies represent pioneering clinical efforts, their value is rather limited for several reasons. First, both reports failed to provide a firm medical diagnosis of asthma. Second, the outcome index consisted only of patient self-reports in each case. Third, the rationale underlying therapy was that the asthmatic episodes were mediated by anxiety, an assumption that is as yet unsupported by persuasive evidence and whose validity is *highly* unlikely.

Moore (1965) conducted the first controlled clinical investigation of the efficacy of systematic desensitization in asthma treatment, comparing systematic desensitization, relaxation alone, and relaxation training supplemented by suggestions of symptom remission. Although differences among the three groups on subjective measures of symptomatology were not found, Moore did report a small yet statistically significant mean improvement in respiratory function in the group treated with systematic desensitization. This study is noteworthy in that it was the first report of any kind to include pulmonary function assessment in addition to some measure of experimental control. While Moore is certainly to be commended, there is, nevertheless, a major problem; namely, measurement of respiratory function on only a weekly basis. Because of the highly intermittent nature of asthma, such a relatively infrequent measurement of peak expiratory flow rate does not permit any reliable conclusions to be drawn concerning either the immediate clinical benefits or the long-term advantages of treatment (Chai, Purcell, Brady, & Falliers, 1968).

The most recent and most definitive test of systematic desensitization was conducted at the National Asthma Center in Denver. Miklich, Renne, Creer, Alexander, Chai, Davis, Hoffman, and Danker-Brown (1977) examined the effects of systematic desensitization, relative to a no treatment control group, in a large scale, long-term investigation in which the criterion index of clinical improvement was FEV_1 measurements collected twice daily throughout the investigation. The study consisted of five phases: (*a*) a baseline of 16 weeks; (*b*) 10 weeks of treatment; (*c*) a 9-week posttreatment period; (*d*) an interim period of 11 weeks during which no data were collected; and (*e*) a follow-up assessment phase of 6 weeks. Twenty-six severely asthmatic children were assigned to either systematic desensitization or no-treatment control. Pulmonary measurements were supplemented by data on frequency and type of medications taken, frequency of hospital admissions, and severity of daily symptoms. Results indicated an extremely small but statistically significant difference between groups on morning FEV_1 only; however, this difference was attributable to attentuated rates of flow in control subjects rather than significant respiratory improvement (i.e., increased FEV_1) in those patients receiving treatment. Thus, systematic desensitization failed to provide lasting therapeutic effects on pulmonary physiology.

Operant Conditioning Finally, three attempts to operantly condition increased flow rates by positive reinforcement have been reported. Khan, Staerk, and Bonk (1973) gave a group of 10 asthmatic children 5 sessions of so-called "linking training," during each of which a continuous series of forced vital capacity efforts was undertaken and individual efforts were reinforced by praise and a red light whenever a particular blow on the spirometer was greater than the immediately preceding one. Following this phase, the children received 10 similar training sessions after mild bronchospasm had been induced experimentally by a variety of means differing from child to child. No data were provided regarding the success these children had in successively increasing flow rates, but comparison of baseline data with measurements 10 months after completion of the training sessions indicated that the children thus trained were significantly different from 10 other asthmatic children (who had received no treatment or attention of any kind) on amount of medication required, the number of emergency room visits, and the number of self-reported asthma attacks. The authors conceptualized their procedures as "conditioning," which is rather presumptuous given the fact that no real specification of conditioning procedures was delineated, no data were provided regarding whether or not conditioning even occurred, and none of the necessary controls for a learning experiment were in fact present. The results obtained were themselves uncontrolled in relation to nonspecific, attention–placebo effects. In a similar but considerably more carefully designed and executed study, Danker, Miklich, Pratt, and Creer (1975) found neither immediate nor long-term increases in flow rates as a result of contingent reinforcement for successively higher forced expirations. They also failed to find any overall improvement in a variety of other indices of asthma. More recently Khan (1977) reported the results of another experiment procedurally similar to his previous effort. In this investigation, the experimental and control groups were each divided into predicted reactors and nonreactors on the basis of pulmonary response to placebo suggestion as employed by Luparello *et al.* (1968). Once again, conditioning was claimed to have transpired, but was not demonstrated, and as before, there were inadequate controls for the confounding effects of attention, length of contact, expectation, and suggestion. No differences were found between predicted experimental reactors and nonreacotrs. Curiously, the author interpreted the results as demonstrating success for his rather peculiar treatment package even though the control reactor group manifested as much change on all measures as the group exposed to treatment. As was previously the case (Khan *et al.*, 1973), no pulmonary function measures were employed in outcome assessment.

The Alteration of Emotional Concomitants

Unlike the methods just discussed, the second category of behavioral interventions includes those designed to effect changes in the emotional concomitants of asthma, the major example of which is anxiety or fear associated with asthma. When properly conceptualized, no assumption is made that emotional reactions can lead, in a causal sense, to either the development of asthma or even to the precipitation of attacks in already affected individuals. These emotional responses are considered to be maladaptive reactions which have become classically conditioned to asthma relevant stimuli (e.g., tightness or wheezing). Such conditioned emotional responses can develop as the direct consequence of extremely frightening, life-threatening episodes, where fear may result from severe dyspnea and hypoxia, the anxious and fearful reactions of family members, physicians, nurses and other medical personnel during acute attacks, and the pain associated with treatment (e.g., venous and arterial punctures), among other salient aspects of a medical crisis. While there is no evidence that the emotional state ever directly worsens lung function, many indirect manifestations exist to the detriment of the asthmatic condition considered as a whole. For example, they can make treating the patient difficult and can thus exacerbate and prolong the attack itself, and of course, lead to increased psychological and physical discomfort for the patient both immediately and over extended periods of time.

It is now quite generally agreed that any of the deconditioning behavior therapies (for example, systematic desensitization or implosion) represent the treatments of choice for clinical phobias (conditioned emotional reactions) in both adults and children. Hence, fear associated with asthma (called "asthma panic") should be eminently treatable by these behavior therapies. In fact, this seems to be the case. At the National Asthma Center numerous cases of asthma panic in youngsters and adults have been successfully treated over the past 10 years with systematic desensitization and its variants (e.g., in vivo desensitization and emotive imagery), and implosion (flooding). In no case was there the intention of altering lung function. Furthermore, treatment success consisted strictly of reduced anxiety and was judged solely on clinical criteria such as subjective reports of improvement by the patient, or observations by nurses, physicians, and others involved in the care of the individuals treated.

Despite the clear clinical effectiveness of the technique, attempts to perform controlled outcome research on the behavioral treatment of asthma fears have been frustrated. The reasons are numerous and relate to the fact that asthma panic does not yield to measurement and study in a straightforward, uncomplicated fashion. First, the behavioral avoidance tests so frequently employed in experimental studies of small animal phobias are inappropriate here. Second, reliable subjective assessments by the patient are quite impossible when a patient may be struggling for life itself. Third, objective observational assessment (for example, by means of the commonly used fear behavior checklists) is also difficult to employ due to the wide range of behaviors through which asthma panic is manifested. During asthma attacks the behavior of highly fearful patients may range from postural rigidity to extreme agitation, crying, screaming, and flailing of limbs, as well as by active attempts to interfere with and even avoid, because of fear, necessary but often painful treatment procedures (e.g., arterial punctures). Fourth, it is often only during periods of naturally occurring, severe asthma attacks that panic becomes a clinical problem requiring treatment, an occasion poorly suited to controlled investigative efforts. Nevertheless, it can be confidently concluded, on the basis of extensive clinical experience, that the deconditioning behavior therapies are the treatments of choice for asthma panic. This recommendation is inferentially supported by convincing experimental and controlled case report data from the successful application of these same techniques to a variety of non-asthma-related clinical fears and anxieties.

The Alteration of Asthma Related Behaviors

The third category of behaviorally based treatment strategies are those intended to alter or control behavioral excesses and/or deficits (i.e., inappropriate asthma related behaviors). These problems are only coincidentally associated with asthma *per se*; that is, these behavior patterns (e.g., malingering or poor social development) can occur in conjunction with any chronic disorder, or even in the normal course of growing up, and are not at all specific to asthma. Needless to say, a chronic disorder in a child can significantly increase the probability of developmental behavior difficulties, although such problems are neither insured by, nor are they exclusive to, the presence of the chronic physical disease or handicap.

The fact that human behavior is to a great extent controlled by its consequences forms the basis of most behavioral approaches to mental health problems. On the one hand, if a behavior is followed by a reward or desirable consequence or by the removal of an ongoing aversive or undesirable condition, the probability of that behavior occurring under similar circumstances in the future is increased. On the other hand, if a behavior is followed by an aversive consequence or the removal or enforced unavailability of a rewarding circumstance, the probabilty of that behavior being repeated is reduced. Techniques based upon the deliberate application of such maintenance contingencies have been used to good effect in the rehabilitation and management of asthma patients, particularly children.

Positive Reinforcement Positive reinforcement refers to the strategy of making a reward contingent upon the occurrence of a desirable behavior. Renne and Creer (1976) used this procedure to teach a young child to use properly an intermittent positive pressure breathing device. They rewarded successively more correct responses (eye fixation, facial posturing, and diaphragmatic breathing) until the child had learned to use the device in its intended manner. They found also that significantly less follow-up medication was required as the child became more proficient in using this therapeutic apparatus.

Satiation Satiation occurs when a reinforcer is available in such large quantities over an extended period that it tends to lose its effect. Creer (1978) reported the case of a young boy who was inappropriately requesting hospitalization for very mild asthma as a way of avoiding school-related stress. A dramatic drop in the number of inappropriate hospitalizations was affected by hospitalizing this boy without delay for three continuous days (satiation) each time he requested an unnecessary admission. That this decrement was functionally related to the specific intervention rather than a spontaneous reduction in asthma severity was attested to by evidence revealing that other clinical indices of asthma (e.g., need for maintenance medications and pulmonary function measures) remained unchanged.

Extinction Extinction occurs when a previously rewarded behavior is no longer reinforced. This procedure, along with the systematic rewarding (positive reinforcement) of desirable behavior, is used widely in clinical behavioral interventions in all manner of problem behavior areas. Neisworth and Moore (1972) used extinction to produce a dramatic reduction in the number of asthmatic coughing episodes, which were well out of line with regard to the severity of a young boy's asthma, by instructing the parents to withhold the sympathy and attention which the coughing had been eliciting, especially at bedtime.

Time Out Time out from positive reinforcement is a procedure which involves removal of positive reinforcement for a specified period of time contingent upon the occurrence of a specified inappropriate behavior. Two examples of the use of this procedure on malingering behavior in asthmatic youngsters have been reported (Creer, 1970; Creer, Weinberg, & Molk, 1974). Each time these boys requested unnecessary admission to the hospital unit at the National Asthma Center, usually to avoid social stress, the ordinarily pleasant surroundings in the hospital (comic books, games, TV, etc.) were removed, and they had to spend their time simply recuperating in bed. A dramatic drop in the frequency and duration of hospitalizations resulted. As we have come to expect, all indices of asthma remained unchanged, attesting to the functional specificity of treatment.

Response Cost Response cost is similar to time out except that it involves the contingent withdrawal of a specified amount of reinforcement rather than withdrawal of reinforcement over a specified period of time. Creer and Yoches (1971) used this procedure to increase the amount of time spent attending to classroom materials in two asthmatic children who had failed to develop academic skills due to the amount of time lost from school because of illness. At the beginning of each classroom session the children were given 40 points, from which one point was subtracted (upon a signal from an observer) for each 30-sec period spent not attending to classroom materials. Consistent with expectations, the children learned to retain the points, which could be exchanged for inexpensive gifts, and hence, to increase appropriate attending behavior. As might be hoped, this generalized to the natural classroom environment and academic performance improved commensurately.

Punishment and Negative Reinforcement *Punishment* is defined as the presentation of an aversive stimulus event contingent upon the occurrence of an undesirable or inappropriate target behavior causing a decrement in response probability. In contrast, *negative reinforcement* occurs when an aversive stimulus event is terminated or removed contingent upon the emission of a desirable or appropriate behavior leading to an increase in the probability of the target response. Both, however, involve aversive control of behavior. Although aversive behavior control enjoys widespread use in our society, both overtly and covertly, ethical considerations demand that, in a therapeutic situation, aversive behavioral control procedures should be applied only after careful and cautious analysis of the probability that treatment will achieve the desired consequences and that aversive techniques be implemented only after all other attempts at clinical intervention have been tried and deemed unsuccessful. As such, they often constitute treatments of last resort. Infrequently, however, the peculiarities of individual cases may dictate their being instituted from the outset as the treatments of choice, a clinical consideration illustrated by the following case reports.

Alexander, Chai, Creer, Miklich, Renne, & Cardoso (1973) incorporated both negative reinforcement and punishment procedures as part of a response suppression shaping program designed to suppress the chronic coughing episodes of a mildly asthmatic boy who had suffered for more than a year with a severe, persistent cough for which no organic etiology could be established despite comprehensive medical testing and ineffective therapy. The procedure required the boy to refrain from coughing for systematically longer periods following a controlled presentation of a precipitating stimulus in order to avoid a brief, but aversive, electric shock to the forearm. He was able to reduce his tendency to cough in a very orderly fashion to each of the four identified precipitants of his coughing. A prominent feature of this case was that the coughing had been maintained by contingent attention being paid to it by the boy's family. Indeed, much of the family's life had come to revolve about the problem. For example, three of the precipitants, the odors of cooking grease, hair spray, and hand soap had required considerable accomodations in the eating and toilet habits of the family, and hence, were a source of constant stress. Other behavioral interventions at the family level were required to alter reinforcement patterns such that the coughing was not reestablished by attention and sympathy once it had been eliminated by the suppression procedure.

Creer, Chai, and Hoffman (1977) used punishment alone in the treatment of another asthmatic boy suffering from a virtually continuous chronic cough. Similar to the previous case, this patient exhibited no organic etiology, and medical treatments had been to no avail. The boy's continual hacking was so upsetting in school that it became necessary to suspend him from classes until his symptoms could be brought under control. The procedure consisted of delivering an electric shock to the boy's forearm contingent upon the occurrence of every cough during the treatment session. The effects of therapy were quite remarkable: a single punishment trial (one cough) was both necessary and sufficient to occasion complete suppression of coughing!

These experimental and clinical reports convincingly underscore the effectiveness of a variety of behavior modification techniques in the rehabilitative treatment and management of a wide range of asthma related maladaptive behaviors. Although the reports available in the literature have been exclusively concerned with childhood or adolescent asthmatics, there is no reason to suspect that the clinical application of these and similar behavioral procedures would be any less effective in the rehabilitation of adult asthmatics.

All of the studies described focused on rehabilitative efforts designed to ameliorate asthma-related behavioral pathology. None either predicted or detected *any* physiological impact on the asthma process, per se. In fact, Creer and his coinvestigators interpreted the failure to detect such changes in indices of either asthma symptomatology or pulmonary physiology as convincing evidence of the functional specificity of their behavioral intervention strategies. Thus, these sorts of behavioral interventions should not be expected to have any significant influence on either the pathophysiological substrates of bronchial asthma or even their daily symptomatic manifestations in respiration.

Conclusions

Historically, asthma was considered to be a premier example of a psychosomatic disease in which psychological variables were thought to play a crucial role in both the etiology and symptomatic manifestations of the disorder. Four decades of increasingly careful and sophisticated research, however, have begun to change these beliefs considerably. Currently, the prevailing opinion is that psychological factors play no part whatsoever in the etiology of asthma and may even be relatively unimportant in the triggering of attacks in most, if not all, afflicted individuals. Precipitation of actual asthma episodes by psychological stress variables in the laboratory has remained an elusive goal. To date, some investigators have been able on occasion to demonstrate small changes in lung dynamics as a result of the application of psychological stimuli (e.g., Godfrey, & Silverman, 1973) and although these changes have sometimes been statistically reliable, they have never been coaxed into the range where they could be considered clinically significant. Conditioning and other psychological theories of asthma have fared very poorly indeed. Most asthma specialists now feel that psychological difficulties can, and regularly do, *result from* having asthma but that there is virtually no persuasive evidence for an influence in the other direction. Nevertheless, the sort of psychological development and adjustment problems caused by struggling with asthma are not substantially different from those which result from having any other chronic disorder.

The role of mental health specialists in the treatment of asthma has pursued a similar course. Psychological therapies have proved ineffective as a cure for asthma. Likewise, attempts to beneficially influence lung function directly in asthmatics through psychological means have met with frustration. Airways biofeedback, systematic desensitization, relaxation, and other methods have been unable to produce therapeutically significant changes in *pulmonary dynamics* in those who suffer from asthma. It must be remembered that *any* positive claim of benefit to an asthmatic from *any* therapy, including psychological ones, *must* be substantiated by reliable pulmonary function measurement. Years of research have shown that assessment on any other basis (e.g., auscultation, clinical examination, patient subjective report, frequency of patient and/or even physician-defined asthma attacks, medication usage when not defined by rigid criteria, etc.) can be, and has been, most deceiving in the hands of clinicians and researchers not specifically familiar and experienced with the disorder.

Given this situation, is there a role for behavioral medicine specialists in the treatment of asthma? The answer is most definitely affirmative. Problems of adjustment to living with asthma, adjustment within families, compliance with treatment regimen, and anxieties and fears associated with asthma attacks themselves do, as expected, abound. Hence, behavioral specialists now find themselves dealing with the consequences of asthma, rather than its cause. For example, deconditioning therapies (e.g., systematic desensitization) have proved remarkably effective in treating asthma-related fears, but not in altering lung function. Similarly, behavior modification techniques in all their variety have been employed with great success in the management of an impressive array of asthma-related difficulties. The treatment of asthma requires knowledge, sympathetic and sophisticated medical therapy, and for many victims, behavioral treatment of commensurate quality and impact.

On the one hand, we are now in a position to state with considerable confidence that continued attempts to significantly alter lung function through psychological means will result in little success. On the other hand, the contribution of behaviorists to the overall treatment effort with asthmatics should continue to be developed with all vigor. The fundamental rationale of behavioral intervention in asthma should be rehabilitation. The research reviewed here, and much clinical experience, points securely in this direction. For some time to come, however, the most crucial step for behaviorists will continue to be the shedding of the misconception that psychological factors contribute to the appearance of asthma symptoms. Once free of this burdensome notion, the behavioral clinician will happily discover that demonstrably effective technologies are currently available for the treatment of the asthmatic. In the many areas where developments are still necessary, there is no longer any need to be shackled by shopworn psychosomatic theories whose major contributions have been the light shed by their own demise. In retrospect this may not have been an ignoble fate. Much has been learned, and more remains to be discovered.

Reference Notes

1. Tiep, B. *Biofeedback approaches specific to the treatment of patients with bronchial asthma.* Paper presented at the Third Annual UCLA Seminar on New Approaches with Biofeedback, Yosemite, California, 1976.
2. Hill, E. *Bronchial reactions to selected psychological stimuli and concomitant autonomic activity and asthmatic children.* Unpublished doctoral dissertation, State University of New York at Buffalo, September 1975.

References

Alexander, A. B. Systematic relaxation and flow rates in asthmatic children: Relationship to emotional precipitants and anxiety. *Journal of Psychosomatic Research,* 1972, *16,* 405–410.

Alexander, A. B. An experimental test of assumptions relating to the use of electromyographic biofeedback as a general relaxation training technique. *Psychophysiology,* 1975, *12,* 656–662.

Alexander, A. B., Chai, H., Creer, T. L., Miklich, D. R., Renne, C. M., & Cardoso, R., The elimination of psychosomatic cough by response supression shaping with electric shock. *Journal of Behavior Therapy and Experimental Psychiatry,* 1973, *4,* 75–80.

Alexander, A. B., Cropp, G. J. A., & Chai, H. The effects of relaxation training on pulmonary mechanics in children with asthma. *Journal of Applied Behavior Analysis,* 1979, *12,* 27–35.

Alexander, A. B., Miklich, D. R., & Hershkoff, H. The immediate effects of systematic relaxation training on peak expiratory flow rates in asthmatic children. *Psychosomatic Medicine,* 1972, *34,* 388–394.

Alexander, A. B., & Smith, D. D. Clinical applications of EMG biofeedback. In R. J. Gatchel & K. P. Price (Eds.), *Clinical applications of biofeedback: Appraisal and status,* New York: Pergamon, 1979.

Alexander, A. B., White, P. D., & Wallace, H. M. Training and transfer of training effects in EMG biofeedback assisted muscular relaxation. *Psychophysiology,* 1977, *14,* 551–559.

Chai, H., Purcell, K., Brady, L., & Falliers, C. J. Therapeutic and investigational evaluation of asthmatic children, *Journal of Allergy,* 1968, *41,* 23–35.

Clarke, P. S. Effects of emotion and cough on airways obstructions in asthma, *Medical Journal of Australia,* 1970, *1,* 535–549.

Cooper, A. M. A case of bronchial asthma treated by behavior therapy. *Behaviour Research and Therapy,* 1964, *1,* 351–356.

Creer, T. L. The use of time-out from positive reinforcement procedure with asthmatic children. *Journal of Psychosomatic Research,* 1970, *14,* 117–120.

Creer, T. L. Asthma: Psychological aspects and management. In E. Middleton, C. Reed, & E. Ellis (Eds.), *Allergy: Principles and practice.* St. Louis: C. V. Mosby, 1978.

Creer, T. L., Chai, H., & Hoffman, A. The application of punishment to eliminate cough: A case of one-trial learning. *Journal of Behavior Therapy and Experimental Psychiatry,* 1977, *8,* 107–109.

Creer, T. L., Weinberg, E., & Molk, L. Managing a hospital behavior problem: Malingering. *Journal of Behavior Therapy and Experimental Psychiatry,* 1974, *5,* 259–262.

Creer, T. L., & Yoches, C. The modification of an inappropriate behavioral pattern in asthmatic children. *Journal of Chronic Diseases,* 1971, *24,* 507-516.

Danker, P. S., Miklich, D. R., Pratt, C., & Creer, T. L. An unsuccessful attempt to instrumentally condition peak expiratory flow rates in asthmatic children. *Journal of Psychosomatic Research,* 1975, *19,* 209.

Davis, D. J. NIAID initiatives in allergy research, *Journal of Allergy and Clinical Immunology,* 1972, *49,* 323-328.

Davis, M. H., Saunders, D. R., Creer, T. L., & Chai, H. Relaxation training facilitated by biofeedback apparatus as a supplemental treatment in bronchial asthma. *Journal of Psychosomatic Research,* 1973, *17,* 121-218.

Edfors-Lubs, M. L. Allergy in 7000 twin pairs. *Acta Allergologica,* 1971, *56,* 249-285.

Erskine, J., & Schonell, M. Relaxation therapy in bronchial asthma. *Journal of Psychosomatic Research,* 1979, *23,* 131-139.

Feldman, G. M. The effect of biofeedback training on respiratory resistance of asthmatic children. *Psychosomatic Medicine,* 1976, *38,* 27-34.

French, T. M., & Alexander, F. Psychogenic factors in bronchial asthma. *Psychosomatic Medicine Monograph,* 1941, *14,* 2-94.

Godfrey, S., & Silverman, M. Demonstration of placebo response in asthma by means of exercise testing. *Journal of Psychosomatic Research,* 1973, *17,* 293-316.

Gold, W. M., Kessler, G. R., & Yu, D. Y. C. Role of vagus nerves in experimental asthma in allergic dogs. *Journal of Applied Physiology,* 1972, *33,* 719-725.

Khan, A. U. Effectiveness of biofeedback and counterconditioning in the treatment of bronchial asthma. *Journal of Psychosomatic Research,* 1977, *21,* 97-104.

Khan, A. U., Staerk, M., & Bonk, C. Role of counterconditioning in the treatment of asthma. *Journal of Psychosomatic Research,* 1973, *17,* 389-392.

Kling, J. W., & Riggs, L. A. (Eds.). *Woodworth and Scholsberg's Experimental psychology* (3rd ed.). New York: Holt, Rinehart, and Winston, 1971.

Knapp, P. H., Mathé, A. A., & Vachon, L. Psychosomatic aspects of bronchial asthma. In E. B. Weis & M. S. Segal, (Eds.), *Bronchial asthma: Its nature and management,* Boston: Little, Brown, 1976.

Kotses, H., Glaus, K. D., Crawford, P. L., Edwards, J. E., & Scherr, M. S. Operant reduction of frontalis EMG activity in the treatment of asthma in children. *Journal of Psychosomatic Research,* 1976, *20,* 453-459.

Luparello, T., Lyons, H. A., Bleecker, E. R., & McFadden, E. R., Jr. Influences of suggestion on airways reactivity in asthmatic subjects. *Psychosomatic Medicine,* 1968, *30,* 819-825.

MacKinzie, J. N. The production of the so-called "rose-cold" by means of an artificial rose, with remarks and historical notes. *American Journal of Medical Science,* 1886, *91,* 45-47.

McLean, J. A., & Ching, A. Y. T. Follow-up study of relationships between family situation and bronchial asthma in children. *The Journal of the American Academy of Child Psychiatry,* 1973, *12,* 142-161.

Mathé, A. A., & Knapp, P. H. Emotional and adrenal reactions to stress in bronchial asthma. *Psychosomatic Medicine,* 1971, *33,* 323-338.

Mattsson, A. Psychologic aspects of childhood asthma. *Pediatric Clincs of North America,* 1975, *22,* 77-88.

Miklich, D. R. Chronic homeostatic vagal efferent activity turndown: A theory of Asthma. *Medical Hypotheses,* 1977, *3,* 226-234.

Miklich, D. R., Renne, C. M., Creer, T. L., Alexander, A. B., Chai, H., Davis, M. H., Hoffman, A., & Danker-Brown, P. The clinical utility of behavior therapy as an adjunctive treatment for asthma. *Journal of Allergy and Clinical Immunology,* 1977, *5,* 285-294.

Miller, N. E. Biofeedback and visceral learning. In M. R. Rosenweig & L. W. Porter (Eds.), *Annual review of psychology* (Vol. 29). Palo Alto: Annual Reviews, 1978.

Moore, N. Behavior therapy in bronchial asthma: A controlled study. *Journal of Psychosomatic Research,* 1965, *9,* 257-276.

Neisworth, J. T., & Moore, F. Operant treatment of asthmatic responding with the patient as therapist. *Behavior Therapy,* 1972, *3,* 95-101.

Neuhaus, E. C. A personality study of asthmatic and cardiac children. *Psychosomatic Medicine,* 1958, *20,* 181-194.

Peshkin, M. M. Management of the institutionalized child with intractible asthma. *Annals of Allergy,* 1960, *18,* 75-79.

Purcell, K., Brady, K., Chai, H., Muser, J., Molk, L., Gordon, N., & Means, J. The effect of asthma in children of experimental separation from family. *Psychosomatic Medicine,* 1969, *31,* 144-164.

Purcell, K., & Weiss, J. H. Asthma. In C. G. Costello (Ed.), *Symptoms of psychopathology.* New York: Wiley, 1970.

Renne, C., & Creer, T. L. The effects of training on the use of inhalation therapy equipment by children with asthma. *Journal of Applied Behavior Analysis,* 1976, *9,* 1-11.

Scherr, M. S., Crawford, P. L., Sergent, C. B., & Scherr, C. A. Effect of biofeedback techniques on chronic asthma in summer camp environment. *Annals of Allergy,* 1975, *35,* 289-295.

Szentivanyi, A. The beta adrenergic theory of the atopic abnormality in bronchial asthma. *Journal of Allergy,* 1968, *42,* 203-244.

Tal, A., & Miklich, D. R. Emotionally induced decreases in pulmonary flow rates in asthmatic children. *Psychosomatic Medicine,* 1976, *38,* 190-200.
Turnbull, J. W. Asthma as a learned response. *Journal of Psychosomatic Research,* 1962, *6,* 59-70.
Vachon, L., & Rich, E. S. Visceral learning in asthma. *Psychosomatic Medicine*, 1976, *38*, 122-130.
Walton, D. The application of learning theory to the treatment of a case of bronchial asthma. In H. J. Eysenck (Ed.), *Behavior therapy and the neuroses.* New York: Macmillan, 1960.
Weiss, J. H., Lyness, J., Molk, L., & Riley, J. Induced respiratory change in asthmatic children. *Journal of Psychosomatic Research*, 1976, *20*, 115-123.

21

EMG Biofeedback in the Treatment of Stress-Related Disorders

THOMAS G. BURISH

The use of EMG biofeedback to treat people with stress-related disorders has become a standard procedure in many hospitals and clinics across the country. Many therapists consider EMG biofeedback to be the most useful of all types of biofeedback (see, for example, Fuller, 1978) and have employed it to treat a wide variety of disorders ranging from chronic anxiety (e.g., Canter, Kondo, & Knott, 1975) to diabetes (Fowler, Budzynski, & VandenBergh, 1976). Although a variety of other procedures are available for reducing stress, including progressive relaxation training (Jacobson, 1938), systematic desensitization (Wolpe, 1958), and various forms of meditation (e.g., transcendental meditation, Goleman & Schwartz, 1976), it frequently has been claimed that EMG biofeedback is either more efficient or more effective than these other procedures (e.g., Canter *et al.*, 1975; Haynes, Moseley, & McGowan, 1975; Reinking & Kohl, 1975). The purpose of this chapter is to critically evaluate the effectiveness of EMG biofeedback as a procedure for helping people to cope with stress and stress-related disorders. Initially, however, a brief summary of issues involved in the definition and measurement of stress and coping is presented.

The writing of this paper was supported in part by Grant CA 25516 from the National Cancer Institute.

Definition and Measurement of Stress and Coping

Before one can evaluate whether EMG biofeedback training enables people to cope more effectively with stress, it is necessary to define the terms *stress* and *coping.* Although most individuals have a subjective understanding of what stress is and attribute various behaviors and disorders to it, there is no universally agreed upon definition. Though they are frequently very colorful, single, all-inclusive definitions of stress generally have been too broad or vague to be meaningful. For example, McQuade and Aikman (1974) stated that "the basic cause of much twentieth century disease is a shadow which has slowly darkened our lives, like the smog that has darkened our cities. This

Medical Psychology
Contributions to Behavioral Medicine

ISBN 0-12-565960-1

shadow is stress [p. 4]." In an attempt to avoid the vagueness of such universal definitions, other authors have preferred more narrow definitions focusing on a specific type or attribute of stress. Perhaps the most well-known such definition is Hans Selye's (1976) definition of biological stress as "the nonspecific response of the body to any demand [p. 55]." Though more useful than general definitions, narrow definitions such as Selye's also pose problems, especially when one tries to integrate the findings from one line of investigation with those from another, each of which purports to be studying stress (see, for example, the controversy between Selye, Lazarus, and Mason described in Lazarus, 1977, and Mason, 1971, 1975). In his historical review of the concept of stress, Mason (1975) sums up these definitional problems by stating that "Perhaps the single most remarkable historical fact concerning the term 'stress' is its persistent, widespread usage . . . in spite of almost chaotic disagreement over its definition [p. 6]."

Because of the difficulties associated with defining stress, many scholars have focused instead on specifying how stress can be measured. Such an approach is generally referred to as providing an operational definition of stress; that is, a definition of the operations or procedures used to measure stress. It is generally agreed upon that responses to stress can involve four different systems: (*a*) the somatic-motor system, in which stress is associated with increased activity as measured by electromyography (EMG levels) or changes in overt behaviors (e.g., trembling and fidgeting); (*b*) the autonomic nervous system, in which stress is associated with increased activation as measured by a variety of physiological responses, for example elevations in heart rate and blood pressure and decreases in skin temperature; (*c*) self-report of affect, in which stress is associated with an increase in the report of negative affects such as anxiety and tension; and (*d*) self-report of cognitive activity, in which stress is associated with an increase in the report of negative activities including worry, confusion, and feelings of loss of control. Although changes in each of these four areas can be measured by relatively precise techniques, frequently changes in one response system will not be paralleled by changes in another response system (Lazarus, 1966, 1977). That is, there is no unidimensional response to stress; it may be reflected by multidimensional changes in any or all of the four response systems. Thus, for example, a person may report feeling anxious and have a rapidly accelerating heart rate yet show a very low EMG level. This lack of correlation between response systems suggests that any comprehensive assessment of stress should include the measurement of all four systems.

Coping with stress basically refers to a self-regulatory process by which a person reduces or prevents those responses which normally occur under stress. Lazarus (1975, 1977) has described two basic types of coping processes. One type, referred to as *direct action,* "concerns efforts by the person to deal with the problem generating the stress emotion in the first place [Lazarus, 1977, p. 81]." That is, the person takes some type of direct action aimed at dealing with the source or cause of the stress responses. For example, a student faced with an important examination may directly cope with the situation by studying for the exam or trying to obtain a copy of the questions; an attorney who is under pressure to prepare a brief may write the brief or assign it to a junior associate; a hiker confronted by a poisonous snake may run away from the snake or try to scare it away. In each of these situations a person takes direct action against the source of the distress. To the extent that the action is successful, the person should feel less anxious, be less worried, show a decrease in physiological arousal, etc.

The other type of coping strategy, referred to as *palliation,* is "primarily oriented to making the person feel better rather than to solving the adaptational problem per se [Lazarus, 1977, p. 81]." The goal of palliation is to deal with one's responses to a stressful situation rather than with the stressful situation itself. Instead of preparing for the examination, for example, the student may take a drink, swallow a tranquilizer, or try to divert attention onto something more pleasant.

EMG biofeedback is generally used to help people cope in a palliative fashion; that is, it is aimed at helping people feel better rather than at altering the environmental situation that is producing the stress. The fact that EMG biofeedback is a palliative procedure rather than a direct action procedure has two implications. First, it implies that EMG biofeedback alone will not enable people to cope effectively in situations in which direct action coping is needed in addition to or instead of palliative coping. For example, it is unlikely that biofeedback alone will be effective in producing long lasting reductions in the frequency or intensity of tension headaches if the headaches are produced by chronic overwork under constant pressure. In such a situation, a direct action strategy which enables a person to change one's lifestyle may be needed. Second, the fact that EMG biofeedback training is generally used to alter a person's stress responses rather than their cause suggests that the appropriate procedure for evaluating its effectiveness is to assess the changes it produces in each of the four stress response systems. The effectiveness of EMG biofeedback, like other palliative procedures, would be limited if it produced a reduction in only one type of stress response, for example, EMG reductions.

Assumptions in the Use of EMG Biofeedback for Coping with Stress

More than any other type of biofeedback training, EMG biofeedback training has been touted as an effective and efficient method for helping people cope with stress and stress-related disorders, primarily because of its alleged ability to enable people to achieve a deep state of relaxation (for example, Gaarder & Montgomery, 1977; Stoyva, 1977). With few exceptions, EMG biofeedback training consists of single site feedback reflecting muscle activity from the frontal region (often referred to as "frontalis" EMG biofeedback, a misnomer since surface electrodes placed above the frontales muscles are sensitive to the activity of a variety of other muscles as well; see Basmajian, 1976). It is assumed that such single site feedback enables the trainee not only to control the muscle tension at the feedback site, but also to accomplish a number of other goals important for general stress-reduction. Budzynski (1977), for example, has stated that

> Through the continuous feedback of the surface EMG . . . the trainee develops first an awareness of, and then control over, the level of that muscle tension (Budzynski, 1973). Eventually, he is able to generalize that control to the other skeletal muscles and thereby affect, indirectly, autonomic and cortical functioning as well. Finally he is trained to transfer that control to everyday life situations outside the clinic or laboratory [p. 437].

Because of a growing number of well-controlled laboratory experiments, it is now possible to critically evaluate the assumptions made by Budzynski and others about the stress-reducing effectiveness of EMG biofeedback training. In this section these assumptions are delineated and the literature relevant to each reviewed. Many of the points presented are in close accord with the valuable comments and interpretations made by Alexander and Smith (1979).

Reduction in EMG

The most basic assumption made about EMG biofeedback is that it will lead to a reduction in muscle tension. This assumption has two correlates: (*a*) muscle tension will be reduced in the target area (i.e., the area from which the feedback emanates); and (*b*) muscle tension reductions in the target area will generalize to nontarget areas.

A large number of studies have assessed whether EMG biofeedback reduces muscle tension in the target area, usually the frontal region, and overall, have strongly upheld this assumption. Research has indicated that EMG biofeedback training results in significant reductions in the target area whether the subject's eyes are open (e.g., DeGood & Chisholm, 1977) or closed (e.g., Haynes, Moseley, & McGowan, 1975), the subject is sitting quietly (e.g., Budzynski & Stoyva, 1969) or solving arithmetic problems (e.g., Solomon & Brehony, 1979), the subject is offered a monetary reward for EMG reduction (e.g., Reinking & Kohl, 1975) or is not offered a monetary reward (e.g., Coursey, 1975), and the feedback is given in the analogue (e.g., Gatchel, Korman, Weis, Smith, & Clarke, 1978) or binary (e.g., Beiman, Israel, & Johnson, 1978) mode. As will be discussed later, EMG biofeedback training consists of a number of components of which the feedback itself is only one, and it may be that not all of these components are necessary for reducing EMG levels. Nonetheless, as a composite package, EMG biofeedback training is clearly effective in reducing muscle tension levels in the target area below those of subjects not given any other type of relaxation training or instructions.

The second corollary to the tension reduction assumption is that EMG biofeedback training reduces muscle tension not only in the target area but also in nontarget areas of the body. This is an important assumption from a therapeutic perspective since EMG biofeedback would have limited value as a general stress-reducing procedure if EMG reductions in the target area did not generalize to other areas of the body. In fact, one of the primary reasons for using the frontal region as a target area is because several years ago Budzynski and Stoyva (1969) asserted that reductions in frontal EMG would generalize to other skeletal muscles.

Since Budzynski and Stoyva's assertion was published in 1969, four experiments have assessed whether EMG biofeedback-produced changes in a target area generalize to other muscles. Alexander (1975) assigned subjects to either a frontal EMG biofeedback group or to a control group which received only instructions to reduce their muscle tension. EMG levels were recorded from the frontal area, forearm (extensor muscles of the hand), and lower leg (extensor muscles of the feet) during three training and two nontraining sessions. Results indicated that the biofeedback training was effective in reducing frontal EMG levels, but that these reductions were *not* accompanied by reductions in either forearm or lower leg EMG levels; in fact, there was a significant *increase* in forearm EMG levels. A separate analysis was then conducted on the forearm EMG data for those subjects who demonstrated the strongest biofeedback training effect (i.e., the greatest decrease in frontal EMG levels), revealing that even subjects who displayed large changes in frontal EMG levels did not show a reduction in forearm EMG level. A similar analysis was not carried out on the leg EMG data since all subjects showed very low leg EMG levels, suggesting a floor effect which would have made further reductions virtually impossible.

Shedivy and Kleinman (1977) conducted a study which differed from Alexander's (1975) in two important ways. First, in addition to the frontal area, EMG levels were recorded from two neck muscles (the sternomastoid and semispinalis/splenius) that are in close proximity to the frontal area and therefore should readily demonstrate a generalization effect. These muscles are also thought to be frequently involved in stress-related disorders such as tension headaches, which makes generalization to these muscles clinically important. Finally, subjects were trained to both increase and decrease frontal EMG levels, thereby allowing the evaluation of generalization in both directions. Results indicated that biofeedback training was effective in increasing and decreasing frontal EMG levels during the appropriate training periods, but that these changes were not accompanied by corresponding changes in the two neck muscles. In fact, semispinalis-splenius EMG levels significantly *increased* during the decrease frontal EMG training periods.

Freedman and Glaros (1979) simultaneously recorded EMG levels from the frontal, masseter, neck (sternomastoid), and forearm extensor muscles, and either did or did not give subjects frontal EMG biofeedback training during six separate training sessions. Results indicated that the biofeedback training was successful in reducing frontal EMG levels, and that these reductions were consistently accompanied by reductions in masseter EMG but not by reductions in neck or forearm EMG. As the authors pointed out, however, the positive relationship between frontal and masseter EMG levels was probably due to the fact that surface electrodes over either area picked up electrical activity from both muscle groups, and thus did not accurately reflect the degree of association between them.

The fourth investigation in this area (Schandler & Grings, 1976) involved two experiments which together included five different groups: (*a*) abbreviated progressive relaxation training; (*b*) visual EMG feedback, (*c*) auditory EMG feedback; (*d*) tactile EMG feedback; and (*e*) no-treatment control. In contrast to the previous studies, the EMG feedback was given from the forearm extensor muscles and generalization was assessed at the frontal EMG site. Results indicated that subjects in the four experimental conditions showed a significant reduction in forearm EMG levels, and this reduction was accompanied by a reduction in frontal EMG for subjects in the tactile feedback and progressive relaxation conditions, but not for subjects in the visual biofeedback or auditory biofeedback conditions.

While not directly assessing biofeedback training, Suarez, Kohlenberg, and Pagano (1979) reported data which relates to the generalization issue and therefore should be mentioned. In an archival study of patients seen at a Biofeedback and Stress Management Clinic, the authors located 150 patients who underwent a standardized baseline session consisting of an initial relaxation phase, a cognitive stressor phase involving serial subtraction of 7s, and a final relaxation phase. EMG levels were recorded from the frontal region and from one or more of seven other regions (masseter, neck, bilateral trapezius, unilateral trapezius, temporal, forearm, and jaw) throughout the baseline session. Correlational analyses revealed that frontal EMG levels were significantly correlated with only one (the unilateral trapezius) of the other seven areas, and that even in this case the correlation was small ($r = .28$) There were no significant positive correlations among any of the other muscle groups, suggesting that none of them provided a better index of general muscle relaxation.

From these data it must be concluded that there is little support for the assumption that reducing EMG levels in the frontal region will reduce EMG levels in other muscle sites, and very limited evidence (one study) that reducing EMG levels in any other muscle site will reduce frontal EMG levels. This conclusion has been reached in other recent reviews (Alexander & Smith, 1979; Surwit & Keefe, 1978) and raises a serious question about the clinical usefulness of frontal EMG biofeedback training as a general muscle relaxation procedure. As a number of investigators have noted (e.g., Alexander, 1975; Schwartz, 1976; Surwit & Keefe, 1978), it may have been physiologically naive in the first place to expect that EMG reductions in the frontal region would generalize to other muscle groups, since feedback from a specific muscle site is by design aimed at *discriminative* training and not at *generalization* training. If general muscle relaxation is to be achieved through biofeedback procedures, it is likely that subjects will have to be given feedback from multiple muscle regions so that some type of general muscle relaxation response is learned.

Importance of the Feedback Component in the EMG Biofeedback Training Procedure

Implicit in the use of EMG biofeedback training is the assumption that the feedback signal itself is an important component of the training procedure. EMG biofeedback training is essentially a training package that has at least three basic components: (*a*) adaptation to the training situation; (*b*) instructions to relax and reduce muscle tension; and (*c*) the feedback signal. Clearly, if for no other reason than expense, it must be demonstrated that the entire treatment package is more effective than the adaptation and/or instructions components alone.[1] Recently, several experiments have investigated this issue.

In order to assess the contribution of the adaptation component of the biofeedback training package, it is necessary to employ a control group of subjects who simply sit quietly and adapt to the laboratory environment for a length of time equal to that spent in the same environment by the biofeedback subjects. Two studies have included such a control condition (Burish & Schwartz, 1980; Haynes, Moseley, & McGowan, 1975), and both have found that subjects receiving biofeedback training produced significantly lower frontal EMG levels than subjects given the adaptation procedures alone.

[1]From a practical point of view, it is virtually impossible to provide the instructions or feedback component without also providing the adaptation component. Hence, all discussion of the instruction or feedback component alone presumes that the adaptation component is also part of the procedure.

Apparently, adaptation alone cannot produce EMG reductions comparable to those achieved with the entire biofeedback training procedure.

Regarding the instructional component, four experiments have been conducted to determine whether simple instructions to relax and reduce muscle tension are as effective as the entire biofeedback training procedure in reducing frontal EMG levels.[2] In the first study, Coursey (1975) gave one group of subjects frontal EMG biofeedback plus instructions to "lower the [feedback] tone you hear as much as possible by relaxing [p. 826]," while two other groups received only a constant tone and either simple instructions to relax as much as possible or more elaborate instructions emphasizing techniques useful in reducing frontal EMG; for example, closing the eyes, letting the jaw drop, and letting the face feel heavy. Comparisons among the conditions indicated that after the first three training sessions, subjects who received either biofeedback or elaborate relaxation instructions produced frontal EMG levels that were similar to each other but considerably lower than subjects who received the simple relaxation instructions. By the end of the sixth and final training session, and during the one follow-up session, however, subjects in the biofeedback condition had significantly lower EMG levels than subjects in either of the instructions conditions. In the next experiment in this area, Stern and Berrenberg (1977) gave subjects either frontal EMG biofeedback training, false feedback training, or only instructions to "relax as deeply as they could [p. 175]." The authors reported that across all three training sessions, subjects who received biofeedback training had significantly lower EMG levels than subjects in either the false feedback or instructions only condition. In the third experiment, Alexander, White, and Wallace (1977) gave one group of subjects three sessions of instructions to relax followed by three sessions of frontal EMG biofeedback training, while a second group of subjects received six sessions of biofeedback training.[3] The investigators emphasized to subjects who received only instructions during the first three sessions that "their earnest and purposeful attempt to relax the relevant muscles *just as much as they possibly could* was absolutely crucial [p. 554, original italics]" in enabling them and the experimenters to evaluate whether subsequent biofeedback training would help them relax even further. The results indicated that at the end of the first three training sessions, both groups of subjects showed significant but equal decreases in frontal EMG. Alexander *et al.* suggested that the reason that their instructions only subjects were so successful in reducing their EMG levels was because the instructions highly motivated them to continually work at reducing their muscle tension throughout all three sessions. Unfortunately, however, no attempt was made to provide any index of level of motivation. In the most recent experiment in the area, Ohno, Tanaka, Takeya, Matsubara, Kuriya, and Komemushi (1978) assigned subjects to either a frontal EMG biofeedback condition or to a condition that was "just told to relax the forehead [p. 63]." The results indicated that after the five training sessions subjects in the biofeedback condition had significantly lower frontal EMG levels than subjects in the instructions only condition. A graphic presentation of the data (Ohno *et al.*, 1978, Figure 1) indicated that the biofeedback subjects had considerably lower EMG levels during each of the five training sessions, though separate analyses were not reported on each session's data.

Overall, the research conducted on the question of whether instructions alone are as effective as the total biofeedback training package in reducing frontal EMG suggests that the answer depends on

[2]A fifth study in the area was conducted by Freedman and Glaros (1979). Unfortunately, however, this study was published in abstract form and presents neither the actual instructions given to subjects nor the mean frontal EMG levels attained by subjects during any of the six training periods they were given. Hence, it is impossible to draw conclusions about the nature or strength of the instructions component from this study.

[3]Actually, two other groups were included who received either three sessions of instructions to relax followed by three sessions of forearm EMG biofeedback training, or six sessions of forearm EMG biofeedback training. However, the data generated from these conditions were rather inconclusive in that there was no significant decrease in EMG level for either group over the first three training sessions.

the nature of the instructions given. When the instructions are rather brief and noninformative, (for example, when they simply tell subjects to relax as much as possible), they do not appear to be effective in reducing muscle tension to a level that can be achieved with biofeedback training. On the other hand, when the instructions are highly motivating and involving, as they seemed to be in the Alexander *et al.* (1977) study, then they appear to be just as effective alone as in combination with the feedback signal, at least over a limited number of sessions. It should be noted, however, that to date no investigator has either systematically measured or demonstrated the importance of the motivating effect of various instructional manipulations, or demonstrated whether instructions of any type can produce large-scale EMG reductions beyond three training sessions. Clearly, additional research is needed to determine the nature and strength of the instructional component of the biofeedback training package.

Increase in Awareness of Tension Level

It has been assumed that the success of EMG biofeedback in reducing muscle tension is dependent on its effectiveness in making otherwise poorly perceived proprioceptive and interoceptive sensations indicative of muscle tension levels available to (and thereby controllable by) the trainee (see, for example, Budzynski, 1977, 1978). Three studies have investigated the validity of this assumption. The first two studies (Kinsman, O'Banion, Robinson, & Staudenmayer, 1975; Staudenmayer & Kinsman, 1976) were similar in deisgn and involved having subjects guess whether their frontal EMG levels at the end of one trial were greater or less than their frontal EMG levels at the end of the previous trial. During the trials subjects either did or did not receive continuous auditory EMG feedback from the frontal area. After a trial was completed, the subjects made their guesses, and then either did or did not receive verbal feedback about the accuracy of their guesses. The results indicated that although subjects in each condition successfully guessed whether their EMG level had increased or decreased at a level above chance, the subjects who received EMG biofeedback guessed significantly better than the subjects in the other conditions *if* their EMG level during a given trial was considerably different (as determined by the number of feedback clicks given) than their EMG level during the preceding trial. Unfortunately, these results as well as the design of the study suggest that the guessing accuracy of the biofeedback subjects was based largely on their perception of the number of feedback clicks given during the trials, not on information provided by any type of internal cues. Sime and DeGood (1977) corrected this problem by withholding feedback during a trial if after that trial the subjects were to estimate whether their EMG level was higher or lower than during the previous trial. Subjects received either EMG biofeedback training, progressive muscle relaxation training, or a placebo-control procedure involving listening to music as an alleged guide for relaxation. For purposes of analysis, subjects were also categorized as having a low, medium, or high level of frontal EMG muscle tension before the start of training. Results indicated that biofeedback training subjects who had low, medium, and high levels of pretraining EMG showed significant improvement in awareness, but that progressive relaxation training subjects showed improvement only at the medium and high levels and placebo-control subjects showed improvement only at the medium level.

Overall, the results of investigations of the awareness assumption suggest that EMG biofeedback training leads to a significant increase in subjects' ability to discriminate changes in their frontal EMG levels. Although encouraging, this finding only lays the groundwork for three equally important questions: Is awareness necessary or even helpful in learning to control EMG levels or to produce general muscle relaxation? Because biofeedback trained subjects show an improvement in estimating changes in frontal EMG level does not necessarily mean that such an awareness is an important component of successful specific or general muscle relaxation. Exactly what are subjects aware of? Have biofeedback trained subjects become aware of some type of proprioceptive or interoceptive sensation that is directly related to muscular relaxation, or have they simply become aware that eye movements, swallowing, and other facial activities are associated with frontal EMG levels? Until these questions are answered, it is impossible to determine the nature or the importance of the type of awareness developed by EMG biofeedback subjects.

Reduction in Autonomic Arousal

It generally has been assumed that high levels of muscle tension are associated with high levels of general autonomic arousal, and therefore that by learning to decrease EMG levels persons could learn to decrease their arousal (e.g., Stoyva & Budzynski, 1974). Several experiments have tested this assumption. Alexander *et al.* (1977) recorded heart rate, respiration rate, skin conductance, and skin temperature from subjects who did and did not receive EMG biofeedback training. Results indicated that there were no differences between the biofeedback and no biofeedback conditions on any of these measures. Schandler and Grings (1976), in an experiment previously described, found that tactile and visual forearm extensor EMG biofeedback training were effective in significantly reducing forearm EMG levels below those of the no treatment control condition; however, these reductions were not consistently accompanied by corresponding differences in autonomic arousal. Specifically, subjects in the visual biofeedback condition showed reductions in heart rate but did not show changes in skin conductance, respiration rate, or systolic blood pressure. Subjects in the tactile biofeedback condition showed reductions only in heart rate and skin conductance. Carlson (1977) and Pegram, Rugh, and Linn (1979) failed to find any differences in the skin temperature levels of subjects who did and did not receive EMG biofeedback training, although in each study the biofeedback condition showed lower frontal EMG levels than the no biofeedback condition. Gatchel *et al.* (1978) divided subjects into an accurate EMG biofeedback group and a false EMG biofeedback group, and after multiple training sessions exposed all subjects to a stressful generalization period. The authors reported that EMG biofeedback training was effective in reducing frontal EMG levels during both training and generalization periods, but that EMG reductions were not consistently accompanied by reductions in the indices of autonomic arousal. Specifically, during the training periods, subjects in the accurate EMG biofeedback condition showed lower heart rates and respiration rates but higher skin conductance levels (indicating greater arousal) than subjects in the false feedback condition, and during the generalization period there were no differences between the groups on any autonomic index. Fee and Girdano (1978) measured the heart rate, respiration rate, skin temperature, and skin potential levels of subjects who received EMG biofeedback training, progressive muscle relaxation training, meditation training, placebo, or no-treatment control procedures. Subjects in the biofeedback group showed significant reductions in frontal EMG but did not show significant changes in any of the autonomic indices. Ohno *et al.* (1978) either did or did not give subjects frontal EMG biofeedback training, and measured respiration rate and heart rate during each of five training sessions. Results indicated that the frontal EMG level of the biofeedback group dropped significantly below that of the no biofeedback group but that there were no differences between groups in respiration rate or heart rate. Further, the correlations between frontal EMG and heart rate (r = .09) and respiration rate (r = .23) were very small, although the latter correlation did reach significance. Finally, during the first phase of a two phase study, Burish and Schwartz (1980) either did or did not give subjects EMG biofeedback training, and either did or did not expose them to stressful conditions during the biofeedback training. During the second phase, all subjects were exposed to a stressful generalization period. Results indicated that although biofeedback was effective in reducing EMG levels during both the training and generalization periods, the EMG changes were not accompanied by corresponding changes in skin temperature, pulse rate, or finger pulse volume.

In contrast to the studies reviewed thus far, one investigation (DeGood & Chisholm, 1977, Experiment II) reported relatively positive results. In this study one group of subjects underwent four types of biofeedback training both with their eyes open and with their eyes closed: (*a*) increase alpha; (*b*) decrease alpha; (*c*) increase frontal EMG; and (*d*) decrease frontal EMG. Regarding the EMG data, the results indicated that relative to their base-level values, subjects significantly increased and decreased their EMG levels during the appropriate biofeedback training period in both the eyes open and eyes closed conditions. During the eyes closed training period, decreased EMG levels were associated with decreased heart rates and respiration rates, reflecting a decrease in autonomic arousal, and decreased finger pulse volumes, reflecting an increase in autonomic arousal. During the eyes closed training period, increased EMG levels were associated with decreased finger pulse volumes and increased respiration rates; heart rates did not change. Data collected during the eyes open training period were similar to those collected during the eyes closed training period except that there was no change in finger pulse volume during the EMG decrease trials. Though somewhat mixed, these results generally show a correspondence between change in frontal EMG and change in autonomic arousal. Certain weaknesses in the study, however, must be considered. First, a no treatment control group was not included, and thus it is impossible to determine which changes were related to biofeedback and which were due to some other nonspecific factor. Second, although not aware of the purpose of this particular experiment, all subjects had previously served as research assistants in other biofeedback projects, and thus may have been aware of the assumed relationship between changes in EMG level and changes in general arousal. It is likely, therefore, that these subjects tried to change their overall level of arousal as an aid to controlling the feedback signal.

In addition to altering EMG levels through biofeedback training and then assessing changes in autonomic indices, several studies have produced changes in autonomic indices and then assessed the effect on EMG levels. Petry and Desiderato (1978) exposed subjects to a threat of shock situation and found that although the threat situation produced increases in heart rate, it had no effect on forearm EMG. Burish and Horn (1979) exposed subjects to either a threat of shock (Experiment I) or to an evaluative threat (poor performance on an IQ test, Experiment II). In addition to frontal EMG, skin temperature was recorded in the first experiment and skin temperature, pulse rate, and finger pulse volume were recorded in the second experiment. The autonomic responses of the threatened subjects increased significantly above those of the nonthreatened subjects in both experiments, while in neither experiment were there any differences between groups in frontal EMG level. Finally, during the first part of a two-part experiment, Naliboff and Johnson (1978) gave subjects biofeedback training to increase and decrease their finger pulse volume while simultaneously monitoring frontal and forearm EMG levels. Although feedback was effective in changing finger pulse volume in the appropriate direction, no differences were found in either frontal or forearm EMG.

Overall, the results of the studies reviewed strongly suggest that changes in EMG levels are seldom accompanied by corresponding changes in indices of autonomic arousal, and thus that EMG biofeedback training is not an effective procedure for producing a general decrease in autonomic arousal.

Reduction in Subjective Arousal

It has generally been assumed that reductions in muscle tension are accompanied by reductions in subjective arousal or increases in subjective relaxation. Alexander and Smith (1979) reviewed five EMG biofeedback studies in which indices of subjective arousal were collected (Alexander, 1975; Coursey, 1975; Reinking & Kohl, 1975; Shedivy & Kleinman, 1977; Sime & DeGood, 1977) and reported that "all subjects, trained and untrained alike, were found to report significant increases in subjective feelings of relaxation during sessions, but such groups were never found to differ from each other [p. 20]." Thus, in these studies biofeedback appeared to provide no additional experience of relaxation beyond that resulting from quietly sitting in the comfortable laboratory environment. Since Alexander and Smith's review was written, a number of additional EMG biofeedback studies have been conducted in which measures of subjective arousal were obtained (e.g., Alexander *et al.*, 1977; Beiman *et al.*, 1978; Carlson, 1977; Gatchel *et al.*, 1978; Burish & Schwartz, 1980). In most of these studies both the subjects who did and did not receive biofeedback training reported less arousal (or more relaxation) over time, but in none of the studies did the biofeedback group report significantly less arousal than all of the various no biofeedback comparison groups. In fact, in one study (Carlson, 1977) subjects who received biofeedback training reported feeling significantly *more* anxious than subjects who received false feedback. These results clearly and consistently indicate that EMG biofeedback training is no more effective in decreasing subjective arousal than are a variety of more simple procedures such as asking a person to sit quietly and relax. It is likely that this finding is due to the fact that in most if not all of the previously cited studies, subjects were asked to indicate their *general* level of relaxation and not the specific level of relaxation of their forehead muscles (or of the specific muscles in any other target area). Since EMG biofeedback apparently decreases muscle tension *only* in the target area, it is therefore not surprising that subjects do not report feeling any deeper level of general relaxation than do subjects who are simply sitting quietly and relaxing on their own.

Reduction in Cognitive Distress

Although several authors (e.g., Lazarus, 1977; Meichenbaum, 1976) have suggested that biofeedback training may help subjects to cognitively cope with stress, little research has been done on this issue. The few studies which have been conducted fall into one of two areas. The first area involves the notion that biofeedback training conducted under stressful conditions may divert subjects' attention from a stressful stimulus to a neutral stimulus (e.g., the feedback tone) and thus may help subjects to avoid thinking about (and hence worrying about) the stressful situation. Only one study in the EMG area has evaluated this possibility (Burish & Schwartz, 1980). In this study subjects either were given frontal EMG biofeedback training or were asked to sit quietly and relax. Half of the subjects (early threat condition) were told before the biofeedback training-relaxation period began that they would receive an electric shock later in the experiment, while the remaining subjects (late threat condition) were not told about the shock until immediately before it was delivered. After receiving the shock, subjects were asked to rate how much they worried about the shock. It was expected that subjects in the late threat conditions would report less worry than subjects in the early threat conditions since they had little time to dwell on (and hence worry about) the shock. It was also predicted that subjects in the biofeedback-early threat condition would report worrying less about the shock than subjects in the no biofeedback-early threat condition. As expected, the results indicated that subjects in the biofeedback-early threat, biofeedback/late threat, and no biofeedback-late threat conditions reported worrying significantly less about the shock than subjects in the no biofeedback/early threat condition. This finding suggests that EMG biofeedback training given during a stressful situation may help people to avoid worrying about the situation, probably because it tends to channel their attention away from the aversive event and onto the biofeedback training task.

The second line of research that has investigated the cognitive consequences of biofeedback training involves assessing changes in feelings of helplessness or personal control that result from biofeedback training. Miller and Dworkin (1977) have stated the assumption as follows:

> One of the significant features of biofeedback training is that it gives the patient the opportunity—indeed, demands of him—to do something for himself . . . learning to perform a coping response, if it is simple and effective enough, will be expected to reduce the patient's feelings of helplessness [p. 145].

Four experiments have investigated EMG biofeedback produced changes in feelings of control and helplessness. Cox, Freundlich, and Meyer (1975) recruited subjects suffering from tension headaches and assigned them to a frontal EMG biofeedback training, progressive relaxation training, or placebo pill condition. Subjects' scores on a version of the Nowicki and Strickland (1973) Locus of Control Scale (which was apparently modified for adult use) were collected during the pretraining and posttraining phases of the study. Results indicated that subjects in the two treatment conditions showed significantly greater reductions in EMG level and significantly greater improvements on several measures of headache distress than subjects in the placebo condition, but that subjects in each condition showed equally significant changes in locus of control in the direction of increased internality. Stern and Berrenberg (1977) assigned both internal and external control subjects, as determined by their score on the personal control subscale (see Mirels, 1970) of Rotter's (1966) Internal-External Locus of Control Scale, to an EMG biofeedback, false feedback, or no feedback condition. Compared to subjects in the false feedback and no feedback conditions, subjects in the EMG biofeedback condition (*a*) had significantly lower frontal EMG levels during each of the three training sessions; (*b*) reported a significantly greater increase in feelings of internal control; and (*c*) attributed their EMG reductions to their own personal effort to a significantly greater extent. The results also indicated that the degree to which subjects changed their locus of control orientation in an internal direction was positively and significantly related ($r = .42$) to the extent to which they reduced their EMG level. Carlson (1977) assigned both internal and external control subjects, as determined by their score on a version of the Nowicki and Strickland (1973) scale modified for use with adults, to an EMG biofeedback condition or to a tone only control condition. Results indicated that compared to subjects in the tone only condition, subjects in the biofeedback condition had significantly lower frontal EMG levels. Within the biofeedback condition, however, only externally oriented subjects showed a significant change in the internal direction. The fact that only external biofeedback subjects changed their locus of control was probably due to the fact that Carlson's subjects fell at the extreme ends of the scale range (M for internals = 3.2, M for externals = 16.1), and thus a floor effect may have prevented the internal subjects from changing in an internal direction. Neither internal nor external subjects in the tone only condition showed a significant change in locus of control. The final study (Carlson & Feld, 1978) investigated the effects of EMG biofeedback training and monetary incentive in reducing frontal EMG, using a 2 (feedback, no feedback) × 2 (incentive, no incentive) factorial design. Half of the subjects in each condition had an internal locus of control orientation, while the other half had an external locus of control orientation, as determined by a modified version of the Nowicki and Strickland (1973) scale. Although the EMG biofeedback subjects in both the incentive and no incentive conditions obtained significantly lower EMG levels than the no biofeedback subjects, there was no relation between biofeedback training and shift in locus of control, nor was degree of EMG reduction related to degree of change in control orientation.

Overall the findings reviewed suggest that EMG biofeedback training may help to reduce how much persons worry about aversive events, and in some situations may increase feelings of personal control. Nonetheless, at least four additional points should be noted.

1. The cognitive stress-reducing effects of biofeedback are not specific to EMG biofeedback training and have been reported as a result of other types of biofeedback training as well (e.g., heart rate; Gatchel, 1975).

2. It should be recalled that EMG biofeedback training had little success in reducing muscle tension in nontarget areas or in reducing autonomic or subjective arousal. Thus, the overall effectiveness of EMG biofeedback training appears to be limited in nature. Specifically, it may help people to reduce cognitive distress or enhance feelings of personal control, but probably does little to reduce the physiological and subjective arousal that generally accompanics cognitive responses to stress.

3. Even if EMG biofeedback is effective in reducing cognitive responses to stress, its practical utility depends on its being demonstrated to be more effective or efficient than other less expensive strategies that have been developed for dealing with cognitive responses to stress (for example, see Meichenbaum, 1977).

4. While successful biofeedback training may lead to reductions in cognitive distress, it is also possible that unsuccessful biofeedback training

may produce increased feelings of helplessness and cognitive discomfort. Lynn and Freedman (1979), for example, report a case of a tension headache patient who felt "depressed and agitated" after failing to control his frontal EMG level during the first training session, and as such avoided looking at the feedback display during the next several training sessions. Just as a feedback signal can convince individuals that they have control over a certain response, it can also convince them that they do not have control.

Transfer to Nontraining Situations

From a clinical perspective, one of the most important assumptions about EMG biofeedback training is that it will enable individuals to gain *self-control* over their muscle tension levels, and thus to produce EMG reductions outside of training as well as during training (e.g., Budzynski, 1977; Lynn & Freedman, 1979). It is also assumed that as with EMG reductions produced during training, EMG reductions produced outside of training will be accompanied by reductions in muscle tension in nontarget areas, lowered physiological and subjective arousal, and decreased cognitive responses to stress. A number of well-controlled experiments have investigated the generalization issue, and have rather consistently indicated that EMG reductions produced in the target muscles during training sessions will generalize to nontraining sessions conducted either in the same setting in which the training was given (Alexander, 1975; Burish & Schwartz, 1980; Carlson & Feld, 1978; Gatchel *et al.*, 1978; Kappes & Michaud, 1978) or in a different setting (Pegram *et al.*, 1979), and under relaxed conditions (Alexander, 1975; Carlson & Feld, 1978; Kappes & Michaud, 1978) or under stressful conditions (Burish & Schwartz, 1980; Gatchel *et al.*, 1978; Pegram *et al.*, 1979). On the other hand, just as reductions in autonomic and subjective arousal are seldom found during EMG biofeedback sessions, they are also seldom found during nonfeedback sessions (Burish & Schwartz, 1980; Gatchel *et al.*, 1978; Pegram *et al.*, 1979). Unfortunately, no research has investigated whether reductions in cognitive distress or increases in feelings of control which sometimes accompany EMG biofeedback training generalize beyond the training environment. Overall, research on the transfer of EMG biofeedback training effects beyond the training situation suggests that subjects carry away from training only what they learned during training, namely, the ability to reduce their EMG levels in a target area.

Comparison to Alternative Techniques

In addition to being an effective stress-reducing procedure in its own right, it is assumed that EMG biofeedback training compares favorably to other techniques used for stress-reduction (e.g., Budzynski, 1977). Five laboratory studies employing normal subjects have compared EMG biofeedback training to some other type of relaxation procedure. Haynes, Moseley, and McGowan (1975), in a one-session study, compared frontal EMG biofeedback training to passive relaxation training (involving training subjects to attend to their muscles and passively allow them to become relaxed), active relaxation training (involving tensing as well as relaxing the muscles), false feedback, and no treatment control procedures. Results indicated that the biofeedback and passive relaxation training groups had significantly lower levels of frontal EMG than did any of the other groups. Reinking and Kohl (1975) compared five different groups: (*a*) frontal EMG biofeedback; (*b*) a passive type of relaxation training in which subjects were instructed to especially focus on relaxing the facial muscles; (*c*) biofeedback plus relaxation training; (*d*) biofeedback plus monetary reward for good performance; and (*e*) a no treatment control. After 12 training sessions all the treatment groups showed significant decreases in frontal EMG, but the groups that received biofeedback training showed significantly greater improvement than the relaxation training group. Combining relaxation training or monetary reward with the biofeedback procedure had no appreciable advantage over providing the biofeedback training alone. Schandler and Grings (1976) gave their subjects either visual or tactile biofeedback training from the forearm extensor muscle, progressive relaxation training, or no treatment. After one session all three treatment conditions showed significantly lower forearm and frontal

EMG levels than the control condition. There were no differences among the treatment conditions on forearm EMG level, but the relaxation training and tactile biofeedback groups had significantly lower frontal EMG levels than the visual feedback group. Sime and DeGood (1977) compared frontal biofeedback training, progressive relaxation training focusing on the forehead muscles, and a control group listening to music as an alleged guide for relaxation. The biofeedback and relaxation training groups were equally effective and produced significantly lower EMG levels than the control condition. Finally, Fee and Girdano (1978) compared five groups: (*a*) frontal EMG biofeedback; (*b*) meditation; (*c*) progressive relaxation; (*d*) a placebo (listening to tapes containing information on emotions); and (*e*) a no treatment control. After 10 sessions of training only the biofeedback and meditation groups showed a significant decrease in frontal EMG. No group showed a consistent reduction in the autonomic indices which were collected.

With the exception of the experiment by Reinking and Kohl (1975), each of the studies reviewed found that EMG biofeedback training was no more effective than some alternate form of relaxation training in reducing the EMG level in specific muscles. These findings suggest that even in the one area in which EMG biofeedback appears to reliably produce an effect, namely reducing the EMG level of target muscles, alternate forms of relaxation can produce an equally reliable effect in an equal amount of time with much less expensive and sophisticated procedures. Moreover, since nonbiofeedback relaxation procedures generally focus on a variety of muscles and not just on those in a specific area (e.g., the forehead), it is possible that they are even more effective than EMG biofeedback in producing a *general* reduction in muscle tension.

Additional Assumptions

Two additional assumptions have been made about the effectiveness of EMG biofeedback training and have received some research attention. First, it has been suggested that teaching people to control their physiological responses to stress, such as increased muscle tension, will reduce performance decrements observed in many task situations carried out under stressful conditions (Lawrence, 1976). Three controlled experiments and one case study have been reported on this topic. In the first experiment (Stoyva & Budzynski, 1974, described in Lawrence & Johnson, 1977) subjects either were or were not given EMG biofeedback training, and then were asked to perform intelligence test items while being bombarded with loud noises and stressful slides of automobile accidents. Results indicated that there were no difference in the performance of the subjects who did and did not receive biofeedback training. In the second experiment (Smith, 1975, described in Lawrence & Johnson, 1977) subjects were assigned either to an EMG biofeedback training, a "simulated self-regulation training," an instructions only, or a no treatment control condition. All subjects were then exposed to stressful hyperbaric situations (being in an environment with greater than normal atmospheric pressure) and asked to relax as much as possible. Performance measures taken during the stressful situations included two cognitive tasks measuring general reasoning ability. Results indicated no differences in performance in the two conditions. The final experiment (Tebbs, Eggleston, Prather, Simondi, & Jarboe, 1974, described in Lawrence & Johnson, 1977) involved either giving or not giving United States Air Force cadets EMG biofeedback training, and then measuring flight performance during real and simulated conditions. Results indicated that there were no differences between the groups during the simulated conditions, but that the cadets who received biofeedback training performed significantly better during actual flight checks. Unfortunately, however, Lawrence and Johnson reported that the cadets were not instructed to use their relaxation training during flight tests, and no equipment was available for monitoring EMG levels. Hence, it was impossible to determine whether the performance differences between groups during flight were due to the biofeedback training.

The case study was reported by Solomon and Brehony (1979) and involved assessing the performance of one subject (the senior author) on mental arithmetic tasks first during 6 baseline sessions and then during 10 biofeedback sessions. Although the subject's performance tended to improve over time, it was impossible to determine whether this change was a practice effect or was a result of the feedback. The only conclusion the authors could reach from their data was that the EMG biofeedback training appeared to "not interfere with the ability to solve multiplication problems [p. 85]." Overall, therefore, there is no evidence that EMG biofeedback training improves performance under stress. Such a conclusion is not surprising, since EMG biofeedback training does not reduce physiological or subjective arousal levels, effects upon which the performance hypothesis presumably is based. Indeed, as Lawrence and Johnson (1977) have pointed out, it may be naive to expect that EMG biofeedback will reduce muscle tension or autonomic arousal under all or even most types of stressful performance situations since in many such situations it is adaptive to be physiologically prepared to make sudden or vigorous physical responses.

A final assumption that has been suggested about EMG biofeedback training is that once individuals are trained to reduce the EMG level of one muscle, it should be easier to teach them to reduce the EMG level of another muscle (see Alexander & Smith, 1979). This assumption represents a more conservative variation of the notion that EMG reductions in a target muscle will automatically (that is, without additional training) generalize to other muscles. In the only study testing this assumption, Alexander *et al.* (1977) gave one group of subjects forearm feedback followed by frontal feedback, while a second group of subjects received their training in the reverse order. Two control groups were also included and were asked to relax on their own during the first part of the study. During the second part of the study they were given either forearm or frontal feedback. The results indicated that training either the forearm or the frontal muscles to relax had no positive effect on subsequently training the other muscle group to relax. These data clearly suggest that biofeedback training carried out on one muscle group does not facilitate the subsequent training of a different muscle group.

Conclusions

Laboratory research on the effectiveness of EMG biofeedback training as a stress-reducing procedure yields three main conclusions.

1. Contrary to what is generally assumed, the data suggest that EMG biofeedback training has very limited success in reducing stress. Specifically, EMG biofeedback has not been shown to have any effect on two of the four components of the stress response: It does not produce changes in autonomic or self-report indices of arousal, and it is only partially effective with a third component; it reduces EMG levels in target muscles but does not reduce EMG levels in nontarget muscles. On the other hand, there is some evidence that EMG biofeedback training may be effective in dealing with the fourth component of the stress response: In some situations it may increase feelings of personal control and, if administered while the person is in a stressful situation, decrease worry.
2. Except for EMG reductions in the target muscles, there is no evidence that EMG biofeedback training produces any effect which generalizes outside of the training situation. Thus, the assumption that EMG biofeedback training enables people to learn a technique which they can use to reduce their anxiety and general arousal in everyday stress situations has no support.
3. It appears that even the most reliably demonstrated effect of EMG biofeedback training, namely an EMG reduction in target muscles, can be accomplished equally well simply by instructing and motivating subjects to relax the target muscles as much as they possibly can.

On the basis of laboratory research with normal populations, the utility of EMG biofeedback training as a general stress-reducing procedure thus appears to be minimal at best.

Clinical Research

In the previous section the laboratory research on EMG biofeedback training was reviewed and the assumptions made about its use as a stress-reducing technique were evaluated. In general, this research offered little optimism about the likelihood that EMG biofeedback would be an effective and efficient procedure for reducing stress and treating people with stress-related disorders, except perhaps for those individuals whose symptoms are due primarily to increased muscle tension in specific muscle groups. However, the fact that EMG biofeedback training had relatively little success in the laboratory with normal populations does not necessarily mean that it will have an equal record in the clinic with patient populations. On the contrary, common sense suggests that people suffering from a stress-related disorder may profit more from a stress-reducing technique than will people not experiencing high levels of stress or not suffering from a stress-related disorder. The following section reviews the empirical evidence on the clinical effectiveness of EMG biofeedback in treating people with specific stress-related disorders. Before these data are reviewed, however, some of the issues which must be considered in evaluating the clinical effectiveness of a treatment procedure in general and EMG biofeedback in particular are discussed. Because these issues have been discussed more thoroughly elsewhere in this volume (see Chapter 25 by Prokop & Bradley), they are only briefly discussed here.

Methodological and Evaluative Considerations in Clinical Research

Spontaneous Recovery A person often naturally or spontaneously recovers from disorders or diseases with no help or treatment from others. Such spontaneous recovery is especially frequent in the case of stress-related disorders such as tension headaches and acute anxiety. Therefore, in order to attribute the cessation of any symptoms to specific treatment, including EMG biofeedback training, the improvement rate in the treatment group must be compared with the (spontaneous) improvement rate of a similar group of patients receiving no active treatment.

Follow-up From a clinical point of view, a successful treatment intervention does not only produce a measurable improvement by the end of the study, but also leads to long-term effects which persist well after the treatment has ended. In fact, in most therapy situations the production and maintenance of long-term gains is as important, if not more important, than the documentation of short-term effects. Therefore, an adequate clinical study should include several follow-up assessments of each outcome variable.

Placebo Factors Biofeedback has been referred to by some researchers as the "ultimate placebo" (Stroebel & Glueck, 1973). That is, the effectiveness of biofeedback training may be due largely to such nonspecific factors as expectancy, demand characteristics, and therapist enthusiasm rather than to any specific factors directly attributable to the biofeedback training. This is not to say that placebo effects are always to be avoided; indeed, many investigators (e.g., Shapiro, 1960) have convincingly argued that clinicians should pay more attention to placebo effects and in some situations employ them appropriately. Nonetheless, in many situations the unknowing use of a placebo may deceive a therapist into delaying or not giving a more effective treatment, and may involve a considerable waste of time and money. Even in situations where a placebo may be useful, it would make little sense to use expensive, time-consuming procedures like biofeedback if a sugar pill or an expectancy manipulation can achieve similar results (Miller & Dworkin, 1977; Tursky, 1979).

Four basic procedures can be recommended to control for placebo effects. These procedures represent ideal controls, and will not be possible to achieve in every situation. First, since placebo effects are often short-lived (Miller, 1978), the inclusion of follow-up procedures capable of demonstrating the long-term effectiveness of the treatment are needed. Second, a control group which receives a treatment known to have no specific therapeutic value but which has the same face validity and attractiveness as the treatment procedure is needed. Third, both the subject and the experimenter should be blind as to which procedure is the known placebo and which is the presumed active treatment. Finally, measures of expectancy should be collected from the subject and the experimenter, and should be found to be equal in the placebo and treatment conditions.

While it is easy to recommend that placebo effects be evaluated and to suggest procedures that should be followed in making the evaluation, it is difficult to design an adequate placebo procedure for biofeedback studies. One rather straightforward placebo treatment which can be used in a variety of biofeedback studies involves giving subjects biofeedback training to control a response theoretically unrelated to the disorder in question. For example, when assessing the effectiveness of EMG biofeedback training in treating tension headaches one could include a control condition in which subjects received alpha (or even beta) biofeedback training. This procedure not only maximizes the likelihood that the placebo treatment will closely resemble the active treatment, but in many situations will also make it possible to keep the subjects and experimenter blind as to which treatment is the placebo. Other suggestions about designing effective placebo controls for biofeedback studies can be found in an excellent article by Katkin and Goldband (1979).

Comparison to Alternative Techniques From a practical point of view, it is important not only that biofeedback be effective in reducing stress and treating people with stress-related disorders, but also that it compare favorably with the best available alternative treatment (Miller, 1978; Miller & Dworkin, 1977). In fact, in many situations it is not the absolute level of effectiveness but rather the *comparative* level of effectiveness that leads a clinician to choose one treatment procedure over another. Moreover, issues of efficiency, cost, and convenience are also important when choosing alternative treatments. Since biofeedback training is a relatively expensive procedure requiring access to specialized equipment, it is important to assess whether its effectiveness and efficiency vis-à-vis other relaxation procedures justifies its use. When comparing the effectiveness of various treatments, it is important to insure that each is administered with an equal degree of technical expertise and therapist enthusiasm. In the sections that follow, special attention is given to those studies in which EMG biofeedback training is appropriately compared to an alternate procedure for treating various stress-related disorders.

Specific Disorders

EMG biofeedback training has been used to treat a host of clinical disorders which are presumed to be stress-related. While this chapter does not critically address the question of whether the specific disorders which have been treated with EMG biofeedback are in fact stress-related, two points should be made in this regard. First, it clearly should be noted that saying that a disorder or symptom is stress-related is not the same as saying that it is caused by stress. In the same way, just as the successful treatment of a headache by aspirin does not mean that the headache was caused by a lack of aspirin, the successful treatment of a disorder by a stress-reduction technique does not necessarily mean that the disorder was caused by stress. Unfortunately, this logical error, sometimes referred to as affirming the consequent, has been made much too often in the stress-reduction area. Second, finding that EMG biofeedback is successful in treating a so-called stress-related disorder does not necessarily mean that EMG biofeedback is successful in reducing stress. As in laboratory research, such a conclusion can only be reached if stress is carefully operationalized and measured, and EMG biofeedback is found to reliably affect these measures.

Since the use of EMG biofeedback training to treat hypertension and asthma has been discussed elsewhere in this volume (see Chapter 10 by Herd and Chapter 20 by Alexander), these areas are not reviewed in this section. It might be noted, however, that the outcome of EMG biofeedback research in these areas resembles the outcome of EMG biofeedback research with other stress-related disorders and therefore provides additional support for the conclusions reached in this chapter.

Tension Headache It is generally assumed that tension or muscle contraction headaches are caused by increased muscle tension in the head and neck areas, and therefore that decreasing the muscle tension in these areas will decrease headache activity (Blanchard & Epstein, 1978). On the basis of this assumption, several researchers have treated tension headache patients with frontal EMG biofeedback training. Research in this area can be divided into three categories: (*a*) case studies; (*b*) studies comparing EMG biofeedback to some type of placebo or no treatment procedure; and (*c*) studies comparing EMG biofeedback to some other type of relaxation procedure.

The earliest research in the area involved case studies and was uniformly positive in its outcome. Budzynski, Stoyva, and Adler (1970), for example, gave frontal EMG biofeedback training to five patients. After 4 to 8 weeks of training each subject showed a significant reduction in both frontal EMG level and headache activity. Similar results have been reported in case studies or single group experiments by Epstein, Hersen, and Hemphill (1974), Epstein and Abel (1977), Reeves (1976), and Wickramasekera (1972).

The encouraging results of the case studies have been buttressed by three investigations comparing EMG biofeedback to some type of control procedure. In the first study, Budzynski, Stoyva, Adler, and Mullaney (1973) assigned 18 tension headache patients to a biofeedback condition, a pseudofeedback condition in which subjects were instructed to listen to a tone to help them relax, or a no treatment control condition. Results indicated that only the biofeedback subjects showed a significant reduction in EMG levels in the laboratory, and that this reduction was maintained at the three-month follow-up. Biofeedback was also successful in significantly reducing headache activity while the other procedures were not. Kondo and Canter (1977) assigned subjects to either a biofeedback or a false feedback condition, and gave all subjects 10 treatment sessions. Biofeedback was found to be significantly more effective than false feedback in reducing both frontal EMG levels and the frequency of headaches. Eighty percent of the biofeedback subjects contacted at the 12-month follow-up reported decreases in headache frequency compared with 40% of the false feedback subjects. Finally, Philips (1977) compared the effectiveness of EMG biofeedback and pseudofeedback in treating 30 tension headache patients. Patients in the biofeedback condition received 12 sessions of either frontal or trapezius EMG biofeedback, depending on what muscle was found to be most tense during a pretreatment recording session. Patients in the pseudofeedback condition listened to noncontingent auditory clicks as an alleged aid to relaxation. The author reported that subjects who received biofeedback training showed significantly lower and less variant EMG levels, significantly decreased headache intensity during training and the 6- to 8-week follow-up period, and took significantly less medication during the follow-up period than did subjects in the pseudofeedback condition. The results of these controlled studies consistently indicate that EMG biofeedback training is an effective procedure for reducing EMG levels and headache activity in people suffering from tension headaches.

The final and perhaps most important group of studies compared the effectiveness of EMG biofeedback training to some other stress-reduction procedure in the treatment of tension headaches. In the first study, Haynes, Griffin, Mooney, and Parise (1975) assigned 24 subjects to either a biofeedback, relaxation training, or no treatment control condition. Subjects in the biofeedback and relaxation training groups were given six treatment sessions during a 3-week period. Both biofeedback and relaxation training were equally effective in significantly reducing headache frequency and overall headache activity below the no treatment control condition, although no significant differences among groups were found for headache intensity or duration. Unfortunately, EMG levels were not reported. In a similar study, Cox *et al.* (1975) assigned subjects to one of three conditions: EMG biofeedback plus cue-controlled relaxation, relaxation training plus cue-controlled relaxation, or a placebo control in which subjects were given a pill that they were told was a "peripheral-acting time-release muscle relaxant known to be effective [p. 893]." The authors reported that EMG biofeedback and relaxation training were equally superior to the placebo in reducing headache activity, frontal EMG levels, and medication intake during training, and that these reductions were maintained at the 4-month follow-up. Chesney and Shelton (1976) measured headache frequency, duration, and severity in a 2 (biofeedback, no biofeedback) × 2 (relaxation training, no relaxation training) factorial design. Subjects in the relaxation training condition received two training sessions with the experimenter and were asked to listen to a relaxation tape at home eight times during a 2-week period, whereas subjects in the biofeedback condition were given eight individual feedback sessions. Subjects who received both biofeedback training and relaxation training apparently received the two group relaxation sessions, eight individual biofeedback sessions, and the homework tapes. By the end of the two-week period subjects in the relaxation training and combined relaxation training plus biofeedback conditions reported lower levels of headache frequency, duration, and severity than subjects in the biofeedback and no treatment control conditions, although the differences were not significant in every comparison. In no case were there significant differences between the biofeedback only and control conditions. Unfortunately, neither EMG levels nor follow-up data were reported. Finally, Hutchings and Reinking (1976) compared a biofeedback condition, relaxation training condition, and combined biofeedback plus relaxation training condition (unfortunately, a no treatment control condition was not included). In contrast to the results of Chesney and Shelton (1976), the authors found that biofeedback and biofeedback plus relaxation training were significantly more effective than relaxation alone in reducing EMG levels and headache activity. However, the authors later reported (Reinking & Hutchings, Note 1) that by the 6 and 12 month follow-up sessions there were no longer any differences among the three conditions.

The results of the EMG biofeedback studies conducted with tension headache patients generate two main findings. First, on the positive side, EMG biofeedback is an effective procedure for reducing frontal EMG levels and self-reports of headache pain in people suffering from tension headaches. Second, on the negative side, EMG biofeedback is generally no more effective in this regard than are more simple and less expensive relaxation training procedures. Overall, therefore, there appears to be no advantage, and some disadvantage in terms of cost, to using EMG biofeedback training to treat tension headaches.

Finally, it should be noted that few biofeedback researchers working in tension headache area (see Budynski *et al.,* 1973; Epstein & Abel, 1977; and Philips, 1977, for exceptions) have screened their subject populations to insure that their headache activity was associated with an increase in frontal EMG levels. Although such a relationship was once assumed, research (Epstein & Abel, 1977; Hart & Cichanski, Note 2; see also a review by Scott, 1979) has clearly shown that this relationship does not exist for all or even most tension headache sufferers. Moreover, research (e.g., Philips, 1977) has also shown that many so-called tension headache patients also have a vascular component to their headaches, and that muscle relaxation procedures such as EMG biofeedback are more successful with pure tension headache patients than they are with people suffering from mixed muscular-vascular headaches. These findings suggest that future research should take additional care in screening and characterizing tension headache patients if intragroup variance is to be reduced and effective individual treatment programs are to be designed.

Chronic Anxiety It is generally assumed that high levels of frontal EMG are related to high levels of anxiety, and therefore that by learning to reduce frontal EMG, persons will be able to reduce anxiety (Burish & Horn, 1979). Two single group studies and four comparison group studies have been conducted on patient populations in order to test this assumption. In the first single group experiment, Raskin, Johnson, and Rondestvedt (1973) gave 10 chronic anxiety patients frontal EMG biofeedback training over a 2 to 12-week period. After the patient reached a criterion EMG level, no biofeedback sessions were interspersed with the biofeedback sessions in order to facilitate generalization of the biofeedback effect to non-training situations. Patients also were told to practice relaxation at home at least once daily. Results indicated that by the end of the treatment program only one patient showed a marked reduction, and 3 a moderate reduction, in anxiety symptoms. Six of the 10 patients showed no improvement. In a more recent study, Acosta, Yamamoto, and Wilcox (1978) gave 6 neurotic patients 10 sessions of frontal EMG biofeedback training. The authors reported that the subjects showed a significant decrease in EMG level over time and that this effect was not related to intelligence, education, social class, motivation, or final disposition of the patient. However, since no measures of anxiety or symptom improvement were reported, it is impossible to determine whether the EMG reductions were associated with the only important clinical outcome. Overall, then, the results of the single group experiments provide little support for the clinical use of EMG biofeedback for treating elevated anxiety.

In the first comparison group study in the area, Canter *et al.* (1975) assigned 28 psychiatric patients with anxiety neurosis to either a frontal EMG biofeedback training or a progressive muscle relaxation training condition. All patients had previously received tranquilizing medication without success. After 10 to 25 training sessions, patients in both conditions showed significant reductions in EMG levels, with the biofeedback group showing greater reductions than the progressive relaxation group. The authors also reported that biofeedback trained subjects showed a greater reduction in anxiety symptoms than the progressive relaxation subjects, though no statistical analyses were conducted on these data. In the next study, Townsend, House, and Addario (1975) compared the effectiveness of frontal EMG biofeedback and group psychotherapy in reducing the symptoms of 18 inpatients in whose disorders "anxiety was a significant factor [p. 598]." Patients in the biofeedback condition received 9 biofeedback training sessions over a 2-week period and were asked to practice relaxing daily at home for 4 weeks. In order to help them practice at home, subjects were given a relaxation tape for the first two weeks of home training. Patients in the group therapy condition received 16 one-hour structured therapy sessions focusing specifically on anxiety. Results indicated that subjects in the biofeedback condition showed significant reductions over time in frontal EMG, mood disturbance as measured by the Profile of Mood States, and state and trait anxiety, while subjects in the group therapy condition did not. However, in general there were no significant differences between the two groups on any of these measures.

Unfortunately, neither the Canter *et al.* (1975) nor Townsend *et al.* (1975) studies included a no treatment or placebo control condition, nor did they carry out any follow-up assessments. Each of these problems was corrected in a study by Lavallée, Lamontagne, Pinard, Annable, and Tétreault (1977). Forty outpatients suffering from chronic anxiety were assigned to one of the four conditions resulting in a 2 (frontal EMG biofeedback, no biofeedback) × 2 (diazepam, no diazepam) factorial design. Patients who received neither biofeedback nor diazepam were given diazepam placebo pills and treated exactly like patients in the diazepam only condition. Patients were treated over a four-week period, and follow-up data were collected 1, 3, and 6 months after the termination of treatment. During treatment each of the three treatment groups showed significantly lower EMG levels and reported feeling significantly less anxious than subjects in the placebo control condition. There were no differences among the treatment groups on either measure. By the one-month follow-up assessment only biofeedback trained patients continued to show a significant reduction in EMG and subjective anxiety levels, but by the 6-month follow-up even this group of patients failed to show any lasting effects.

The final study in the area (Beiman *et al.*, 1978) resembles the first two in that it also suffers from the lack of a no treatment and/or placebo control condition and does not include follow-up assessment. Twenty individuals who indicated that tension was a serious problem were recruited by newspaper ads and were given either frontal EMG biofeedback training or self-relaxation instructions incorporating principles from Benson's (1975) relaxation response training.[4] Subjects in each condition were given five training sessions followed by one posttraining session in which they were asked to relax without further biofeedback or specific in-

[4]Actually, 20 additional subjects were also assigned to groups receiving taped progressive relaxation or live progressive relaxation. Because of procedural differences, however, the authors did not compare these groups to the biofeedback or self-relaxation groups.

structions. All subjects were also asked to practice relaxation daily at home. Results indicated that subjects in both conditions showed significantly lower EMG, heart rate, galvanic skin response (GSR), and self-report of anxiety levels at the end of training compared to their levels at the beginning of training. Between-group comparisons indicated that except for the heart rate measure, on which subjects in the self-relaxation group showed significantly lower levels than subjects in the biofeedback condition, there were no significant differences between groups.

In sum, investigations of the effectiveness of EMG biofeedback in treating people with chronic anxiety are plagued by methodological weaknesses and have produced results that are weak, inconsistent, and short-lived. Specifically, of the six studies conducted in the area, five reported no systematic follow-up data, two were of the case-study variety, and three others failed to include no treatment or placebo control groups. Only one study found biofeedback to be more effective than simpler and less expensive alternate relaxation procedures, and even in this study the effect disappeared within six months after treatment. At present therefore, there is little support for the clinical use of EMG biofeedback training to produce a reduction in chronic anxiety.

Circumscribed Anxiety Six studies have investigated the use of EMG biofeedback training for treating individuals suffering from circumscribed or situationally specific anxiety. Reeves and Mealiea (1975) gave three flight phobics nine training sessions in which low frontal EMG levels, as indicated by a biofeedback tone, were paired with the cue word "relax." After these biofeedback-assisted, cue-controlled relaxation sessions were completed, subjects received four sessions of systematic desensitization. Although all three subjects subsequently were able to enjoy plane flights with little discomfort, it is obviously impossible to determine whether EMG biofeedback played an important role in this treatment.

Three studies have assessed the effectiveness of EMG biofeedback in treating test anxiety. The first investigation was a case study (Wickramasekera, 1972) in which a person suffering from examination phobia was successfully treated with a combination of EMG biofeedback plus systematic desensitization. Several years later Romano and Cabianca (1978) conducted the first controlled study in the area. Forty test anxious students were assigned to one of four conditions: (*a*) EMG biofeedback training; (*b*) automated systematic desensitization; (*c*) EMG biofeedback plus systematic desensitization; or (*d*) no treatment control. Subjects in the three treatment conditions received nine training sessions over a 5-week period. Results indicated that each of the treatment conditions was significantly more effective in reducing self-reports of test anxiety than the no treatment control condition, but that there were no significant differences among the treatment groups. Finally, Counts, Hollandsworth, and Alcorn (1978) compared the effectiveness of (*a*) EMG biofeedback-assisted, cue-controlled relaxation; (*b*) cue-controlled relaxation alone; (*c*) a placebo condition (a music and irrelevant imagery procedure described as anxiety-reducing); and (*d*) a no treatment control condition. Subjects in the treatment and placebo conditions received six training sessions over a 2-week period. The authors reported that both treatment procedures were significantly more effective than the no treatment control procedure in reducing test anxiety and state anxiety, and were significantly more effective than both the no treatment control and the placebo conditions in improving performance on a mental abilities test. Overall, the results of the three studies conducted with test anxious patients suggest that although EMG biofeedback training does not weaken the effectiveness of other relaxation procedures when it is used in combination with them, similar effects can be achieved with the relaxation training procedures alone.

The final study in the area (Miller, Murphy, & Miller, 1978) investigated the effectiveness of EMG biofeedback training, progressive muscle relaxation training, and simple relaxation instructions in the treatment of patients suffering from dental anxiety. Patients' frontal EMG levels and self-reports of dental anxiety, state anxiety, and trait anxiety were measured at pretraining and posttraining dental appointments. Between these appointments subjects in the treatment conditions received 10 sessions of biofeedback or relaxation training. Results indicated that subjects in both treatment groups showed significantly greater reductions in frontal EMG, dental anxiety, and state anxiety than subjects in the instructions only control condition, but that there were no differences between the treatment conditions on any of these measures. These results strengthen and broaden the conclusion that at best EMG biofeedback training is an alternate, not a superior, method of treating people suffering from various types of anxiety disorders.

Insomnia Since elevations in anxiety, sympathetic arousal, and muscle tension are frequently assumed to be important features of insomnia (Freedman & Papsdorf, 1976; Montgomery, Perkin, & Wise, 1975), it has been hypothesized that EMG biofeedback training may be an effective procedure for treating insomnia. Of the three studies reported in this area, the first two are of the uncontrolled single-group variety. Raskin *et al.* (1973) gave EMG biofeedback training to 10 chronic anxiety patients (see pp. 412–414), and found that 6 of 10 patients also suffered from insomnia. By the end of the 2 to 12 week training period, one of the insomnia patients showed marked improvement, four showed moderate improvement, and one showed no improvement. Unfortunately, neither quantitative outcome data nor statistical analyses were reported. Budzynski (1973) reported the treatment of 11 patients with sleep-onset insomnia with a two-phase treatment procedure. Patients were first given frontal EMG biofeedback training to reduce their muscle tension levels, and then given EEG biofeedback training to increase their production of theta brain waves (4–7 Hz). Six of the 11 patients were reported to have improved, 3 dramatically. Again, however, neither quantitative outcome data nor statistical analyses were reported.

In the only controlled study in the area, Freedman and Papsdorf (1976) gave 18 subjects suffering from sleep-onset insomnia either frontal EMG biofeedback training, progressive muscle relaxation training, or a placebo procedure involving physical exercises allegedly aimed at increasing relaxation. Two nights preceding and two nights following the six training sessions, subjects slept in the laboratory and had various EEG, EMG, and sympathetic nervous system responses recorded. The results revealed three important findings.

1. Subjects in both the biofeedback and progressive muscle relaxation training conditions showed comparable and significant decreases in sleep onset time, frontal, masseter, and forearm EMG levels, and heart rate, while subjects in the placebo condition did not show significant decreases on any of these measures. However, the fact that it took subjects in the biofeedback and relaxation training conditions at least 20 min of daily practice to achieve an average decrease in sleep-onset time of 30 and 23 min, respectively, raises questions about the clinical utility of these methods.
2. The reductions in sleep-onset time that were achieved disappeared by the two-month follow-up.
3. The results revealed that the initial measures of frontal, masseter, and forearm EMG were *not* significantly related to sleep onset times. This finding corroborates previous research (Good, 1975) and suggests that elevated muscle tension does not play a major role in sleep onset insomnia, and therefore that procedures aimed primarily at reducing muscle tension will not result in a major improvement in this condition.

Overall, then, there is little evidence that EMG biofeedback is a practical and useful treatment for insomnia, and little reason to suspect that future research will be more encouraging.

Drug Use Two studies have assessed the effect of EMG biofeedback training on alcohol and drug use. Lamontagne, Hand, Annable, and Gagnon (1975) assigned light, moderate, and heavy cannabis users to either an EMG biofeedback, EEG alpha biofeedback, or false feedback condition. Subjects were given four consecutive days of feedback training and were then asked to practice relaxing daily at home during the six-month follow-up period. Results indicated that although all three groups reported a reduction in cannabis use during the follow-up period, there were no significant differences among the conditions. Steffen (1975) assessed the effect of EMG biofeedback assisted relaxation training on the alcohol consumption of four chronic alcoholics. Two subjects received relaxation training followed by attention placebo training while two other subjects received the reverse order. After each training phase subjects were exposed to a four-day unlimited access drinking period. Results indicated that although subjects showed significantly lower blood alcohol levels and reported feeling less disturbed following relaxation training than following the attention-placebo training, they took the same number of drinks after each of the training procedures. Since neither of these studies provides either convincing evidence that EMG biofeedback is effective in treating drug users or a rationale for why it should be effective, it must be concluded that this does not presently appear to be a promising area for further research.

Hyperactivity Two studies have used frontal EMG biofeedback training with hyperactive children. Braud, Lupin, and Braud (1975) gave a 6 ½-year-old hyperactive boy 11 sessions of frontal EMG biofeedback training and encouraged his mother and teacher to ask him to practice relaxation at home and school, especially when he became upset or overactive. The authors reported that the child showed large decreases in EMG level both within and between sessions, and that this EMG control was maintained at the 7-month follow-up. Ratings by the experimenter, parents, and teacher also showed a decrease in hyperactive behavior which was closely associated with whether or not the child practiced relaxing at home and at school. Hampstead (1979) treated six hyperactive children with EMG biofeedback using a design which rotated blocks of three baseline sessions and three treatment sessions in an A-B-A-B-A format. Follow-up data were also obtained and a no treatment comparison group was available for some of the psychological test measures. Results indicated that all six children learned to decrease their EMG levels across training sessions and that these decreases were maintained during the baseline sessions. Five of the six children also showed significant behavioral improvements at home, and one of the four subjects for whom teacher ratings were collected showed significant behavioral improvements at school. Although generally positive in nature, the failure to control for placebo and attention factors and the lack of comparisons with alternative relaxation procedures render it impossible to draw conclusions from these data.

Other Applications Three other studies have been reported in which clinical gains were attributed to the stress-reducing properties of EMG biofeedback training. Haynes (1976) treated a woman suffering from chronic dysphagia spastica (difficulty swallowing because of contractions of the throat muscles) with a combination of frontal EMG biofeedback and home relaxation practice. The patient reported less difficulty swallowing both during treatment and at the six-month follow-up. The authors suggested that the improvement may have been due primarily to an increase in general relaxation as a result of the feedback training.

Finley, Niman, Standley, and Ender (1976) treated six athetoid cerebral palsy patients with frontal EMG biofeedback. All subjects were able to reduce their EMG levels during the 12 training sessions. After training all subjects showed gains in various motor functions, and the mild and moderate cases showed improvement in their speech. The authors suggested that the improvement may have been due to a general relaxation effect which in turn led to improved sensory awareness.

Finally, Fowler *et al.* (1976) taught a diabetic patient to relax at home using a portable EMG biofeedback trainer in combination with relaxation tapes. The patient showed a reduction in daily insulin usage during training and maintained this decrease during the 6-week follow-up. The authors suggested that the biofeedback training helped produce general relaxation, and that general relaxation was responsible for the insulin reduction.

While interesting, these three studies do not allow one to draw any conclusions about the treatment of chronic dysphagia, cerebral palsy, or diabetes with EMG biofeedback. Each study lacked appropriate controls and failed to demonstrate that the general relaxation effect which was hypothesized to be responsible for the clinical gains in fact did occur. This last point is especially relevant to the Haynes (1976) and Finley *et al.* (1976) studies, since their patients suffered from problems specifically related to abnormal muscle tension or control. Thus, even if the clinical improvement demonstrated with such patients could be empirically linked to EMG biofeedback training, it is possible that the primary mechanism responsible for the improvement may be an increase in the patients' control over target muscles, an effect reliably produced by EMG biofeedback, and not a more global reduction in stress or increase in general relaxation, effects seldom produced by EMG biofeedback.

Conclusions and Implications

The most important and consistent conclusion of this review is that there is little research evidence to support the assumption that single-site EMG biofeedback training is an effective method of reducing multidimensional stress responses. Specifically, laboratory research has shown that EMG biofeedback training has little effect on muscle tension in nonfeedback areas, autonomic arousal, self-report of negative affect, or performance under stress. The results of controlled clinical research further suggests that even when EMG biofeedback training is effective in treating various stress-related disorders, it is generally no more effective in this regard than other forms of relaxation training.

The data reviewed also suggest that two qualifications should be made regarding this generally negative conclusion. First, it should be noted that EMG biofeedback training is effective in reducing EMG levels in target muscles, and that this effect will generalize beyond the training situation. Hence, EMG biofeedback training may be an effective procedure for treating disorders in which elevated muscle tension in specific areas forms a significant component of the symptomology. In some cases such muscle tension may simply be one of several symptoms present, but more frequently it will probably be the primary symptom involved in the disorder, as for example, in dysphagia spastica (Haynes, 1976), chronic blepharospasms (spasmodic winking, Peck, 1977), and subvocalization during reading (Hardyck & Petrinovich, 1969). It is important to note that in treating such disorders, EMG biofeedback would be used not as a broad-based stress-reducing procedure but instead as a specific muscle relaxation technique.

The second qualification of the generally negative conclusion about the use of EMG biofeedback as a stress-reducing procedure is that research to date has not assessed the role that individual differences may play in treatment outcome. Most researchers simply give the same treatment to a large number of patients who are similar in some respect and then report the average response of the group. It may be, however, that certain characteristics of persons or their symptomology make it much more probable that biofeedback training will be an effective and appropriate treatment for them, and thus that the identification of such characteristics may enable the clinician to be more successful in developing individually oriented treatment programs. Specifically, it is possible that in the area in which EMG biofeedback has been shown to have a consistent effect, namely, in the reduction of EMG levels in target muscles, individual differences may play an important role in treatment outcome. The greater the extent to which a given individual's problem is due to specific muscle tension, the more likely that EMG biofeedback training will be an effective treatment or adjunct treatment procedure.

In addition to the specific conclusion that EMG biofeedback is of limited utility in helping people cope with stress or overcome stress-related disorders, the data reviewed also suggest a more global conclusion. It will be recalled that several controlled clinical studies were described in which both biofeedback and some other form of relaxation training were employed to treat a stress-related disorder. In many of these studies, neither treatment approach had much success in producing lasting changes. While it is possible that some other relaxation strategy may have been more effective, it is more likely that long lasting changes would have been accomplished only if some direct action coping strategy was introduced to change the relationship between the individual and the environmental factors which were maintaining the symptoms. It may be naive to think not only that a biofeedback procedure aimed at changing the

EMG level of a specific muscle group will produce a general (i.e., multisystem) relaxation effect, but also that any type of relaxation strategy will *by itself* produce and maintain a permanent change in stress-related symptoms if the nature and intensity of the stressor is not modified. In this sense, the best available alternative technique to which biofeedback should be compared will often be a direct action coping strategy and not another relaxation procedure. Clearly, then, there are both theoretical and empirical reasons to question whether EMG biofeedback training is the treatment of choice for many if not all stress-related disorders.

In conclusion, it is clear that at the present time there is little experimental support for the assumptions generally made about EMG biofeedback training, and little clinical data to suggest that it is any more effective in treating stress-related disorders than a variety of more simple and less expensive procedures such as progressive muscle relaxation training. These findings indicate in a clear and unavoidable fashion that unless or until new data demonstrate the usefulness of single site EMG biofeedback training in reducing multiple-system increases in stress, there is little justification for prescribing it for the reduction of stress or for the treatment of stress-related disorders.

Acknowledgments

The author thanks B. Kent Houston, Randy O. Frost, and A. Barney Alexander for their helpful comments on an earlier draft of the manuscript.

Reference Notes

1. Reinking, R. H., & Hutchings, D. *Follow up and extension of "Tension headaches—What method is most effective?"* Paper presented at the meeting of the Biofeedback Research Society, Colorado Springs, Colorado, 1976.
2. Hart, J. D., & Cichanski, K. A. *Biofeedback as a treatment for headache: Conceptual and methodological issues.* Paper presented at the meeting of the Association for the Advancement of Behavior Therapy, San Francisco, 1975.

References

Acosta, F. X., Yamamoto, J., & Wilcox, S. A. Application of electromyographic biofeedback to the relaxation training of schizophrenic, neurotic, and tension headache patients. *Journal of Consulting and Clinical Psychology,* 1978, *46,* 383-384.

Alexander, A. B. An experimental test of assumptions relating to the use of electromyographic biofeedback as a general relaxation training technique. *Psychophysiology,* 1975, *12,* 656-662.

Alexander, A. B., & Smith, D. D. Clinical applications of EMG biofeedback. In R. J. Gatchel & K. P. Price (Eds.), *Clinical applications of biofeedback: Appraisal and status.* New York: Pergamon, 1979.

Alexander, A. B., White, P. D., & Wallace, H. M. Training and transfer of training effects in EMG biofeedback assisted muscular relaxation. *Psychophysiology,* 1977, *14,* 551-559.

Basmajian, J. V. Facts vs. myths in EMG biofeedback. *Biofeedback and Self-Regulation,* 1976, *1,* 369-371.

Beiman, I., Israel, E., & Johnson, S. A. During training and posttraining effects of live and taped extended progressive relaxation, self-relaxation, and electromyogram biofeedback. *Journal of Consulting and Clinical Psychology,* 1978, *46,* 314-321.

Benson, H. *The relaxation response.* New York: Avon, 1975.

Blanchard, E. B., & Epstein, L. H. *A biofeedback primer.* Boston: Addison-Wesley, 1978.

Braud, L. W., Lupin, M. N., & Braud, W. G. The use of electromyographic biofeedback in the control of hyperactivity. *Journal of Learning Disabilities,* 1975, *8,* 21-26.

Budzynski, T. H. Biofeedback procedures in the clinic. *Seminars in Psychiatry,* 1973, *5,* 537-548.

Budzynski, T. H. Clinical implications of electromyographic training. In G. Schwartz & J. Beatty (Eds.), *Biofeedback: Theory and research.* New York: Academic Press, 1977.

Budzynski, T. H. Biofeedback applications to stress-related disorders. *International Review of Applied Psychology,* 1978, *27,* 73-79.

Budzynski, T. H., & Stoyva, J. M. An instrument for producing deep muscle relaxation by means of analog information feedback. *Journal of Applied Behavior Analysis,* 1969, *4,* 231-237.

Budzynski, T., Stoyva, J., & Adler, C. Feedback-induced muscle relaxation: Application to tension headache. *Journal of Behavior Therapy and Experimental Psychiatry,* 1970, *1,* 205-211.

Budzynski, T. H., Stoyva, J. M., Adler, C. S., & Mullaney, D. J. EMG biofeedback and tension headache: A controlled outcome study. *Psychosomatic Medicine,* 1973, *35,* 484–496.

Burish, T. G., & Horn, P. W. An evaluation of frontal EMG as an index of general arousal. *Behavior Therapy,* 1979, *10,* 137–147.

Burish, T. G., & Schwartz, D. P. EMG biofeedback training, transfer of training, and coping with stress. *Journal of Psychosomatic Research,* 1980, *24,* 85–96.

Canter, A., Kondo, C. Y., & Knott, J. R. A comparison of EMG feedback and progressive muscle relaxation training in anxiety neurosis. *British Journal of Psychiatry,* 1975, *127,* 470–477.

Carlson, J. G. Locus of control and frontal electromyographic response training. *Biofeedback and Self-Regulation,* 1977, *2,* 259–271.

Carlson, J. G., & Feld, J. L. Role of incentives in the training of the frontal EMG relaxation response. *Journal of Behavioral Medicine,* 1978, *4,* 427–436.

Chesney, M. A., & Shelton, J. L. A comparison of muscle relaxation and electromyogram biofeedback treatments for muscle contraction headache. *Journal of Behavior Therapy and Experimental Psychiatry,* 1976, *7,* 221–225.

Counts, D. K., Hollandsworth, J. G., & Alcorn, J. D. Use of electromyographic biofeedback and cue-controlled relaxation in the treatment of test anxiety. *Journal of Consulting and Clinical Psychology,* 1978, *46,* 990–996.

Coursey, R. D. Electromyograph feedback as a relaxation technique. *Journal of Consulting and Clinical Psychology,* 1975, *43,* 825–834.

Cox, D. J., Freundlich, A., & Meyer, R. G. Differential effectiveness of electromyographic feedback, verbal relaxation instructions, and medication placebo with tension headaches. *Journal of Consulting and Clinical Psychology,* 1975, *43,* 892–898.

DeGood, D. E., & Chisholm, R. C. Multiple response comparison of parietal EEG and frontalis EMG biofeedback. *Psychophysiology,* 1977, *14,* 258–265.

Epstein, L. H., & Abel, G. G. An analysis of biofeedback training effects for tension headache patients. *Behavior Therapy,* 1977, *8,* 37–47.

Epstein, L. H., Hersen, M., Hemphill, D. P. Music feedback in the treatment of tension headache: An experimental case study. *Journal of Behavior Therapy and Experimental Psychiatry,* 1974, *5,* 59–63.

Fee, R. A., & Girdano, D. A. The relative effectiveness of three techniques to induce the trophotropic response. *Biofeedback and Self-Regulation,* 1978, *3,* 145–157.

Finley, W. W., Niman, C., Standley, J., & Ender, P. Frontal EMG-biofeedback training of athetoid cerebral palsy patients. *Biofeedback and Self-Regulation,* 1976, *1,* 169–182.

Fowler, J. E., Budzynski, T. H., & VandenBergh, R. L. Effects of an EMG biofeedback relaxation program on the control of diabetes. *Biofeedback and Self-Regulation,* 1976, *1,* 105–112.

Freedman, R., & Glaros, A. A generalization gradient in frontal EMG training. *Proceedings of the Tenth Annual Meeting of the Biofeedback Society of America,* 1979, 167–169. (Abstract)

Freedman, R., & Papsdorf, J. D. Biofeedback and progressive relaxation treatment of sleep-onset insomnia: A controlled, all-night investigation. *Biofeedback and Self-Regulation,* 1976, *1,* 253–271.

Fuller, G. D. Current status of biofeedback in clinical practice. *American Psychologist,* 1978, *33,* 39–48.

Gaarder, K. R., & Montgomery, P. S. *Clinical biofeedback: A procedural manual.* Baltimore: Williams & Wilkins, 1977.

Gatchel, R. J. Changeover training sessions of relationship between locus of control and voluntary heart-rate control. *Perceptual and Motor Skills,* 1975, *40,* 424–426.

Gatchel, R. J., Korman, M., Weis, C. B., Smith, D., & Clarke, L. A multiple-response evaluation of EMG biofeedback performance during training and stress-induced conditions. *Psychophysiology,* 1978, *15,* 253–258.

Goleman, D. J., & Schwartz, G. E. Meditation as an intervention in stress reactivity. *Journal of Consulting and Clinical Psychology,* 1976, *44,* 456–466.

Good, R. Frontalis muscle tension and sleep latency. *Psychophysiology,* 1975, *12,* 465–467.

Hampstead, W. J. The effects of EMG-assisted relaxation training with hyperkinetic children: A behavioral alternative. *Biofeedback and Self-Regulation,* 1979, *4,* 113–125.

Hardyck, C. D., & Petrinovich, L. F. Treatment of subvocal speech during reading. *Journal of Reading,* 1969, *1,* 1–11.

Haynes, S. N. Electromyographic biofeedback treatment of a woman with chronic dysphagia. *Biofeedback and Self Regulation,* 1976, *1,* 121–126.

Haynes, S. N., Griffin, P., Mooney, D., & Parise, M. Electromyographic biofeedback and relaxation instructions in the treatment of muscle contraction headaches. *Behavior Therapy,* 1975, *6,* 672–678.

Haynes, S. N., Moseley, D., & McGowan, W. T. Relaxation training and biofeedback in the reduction of frontalis muscle tension. *Psychophysiology,* 1975, *12,* 547–552.

Hutchings, D. F., & Reinking, R. H. Tension headaches—What form of therapy is most effective? *Biofeedback and Self-Regulation,* 1976, *1,* 183–190.

Jacobson, E. *Progressive relaxation.* Chicago: University of Chicago Press, 1938.

Kappes, B., & Michaud, J. Contingent *vs.* noncontingent EMG feedback and hand temperature in relation to anxiety and locus of control. *Biofeedback and Self-Regulation,* 1978, *3,* 51-60.

Katkin, E. S., & Goldband, S. The placebo effect and biofeedback. In R. J. Gatchel & K. P. Price (Eds.), *Clinical applications of biofeedback: Appraisal and status.* New York: Pergamon, 1979.

Kinsman, R. A., O'Banion, K., Robinson, S., & Staudenmayer, H. Continuous biofeedback and discrete posttrial verbal feedback in *frontalis* muscle relaxation training. *Psychophysiology,* 1975, *12,* 30-35.

Kondo, C., & Canter, A. True and false electromyographic feedback: Effect on tension headache. *Journal of Abnormal Psychology,* 1977, *86,* 93-95.

Lamontagne, Y., Hand, I., Annable, L., & Gagnon, M. A. Physiological and psychological effects of alpha and EMG feedback training with college drug users. *Canadian Psychiatry Association Journal,* 1975, *20,* 339-349.

Lavallée, Y. J., Lamontagne, Y., Pinard, G., Annable, L., & Tétreault, L. Effects of EMG feedback, diazepam, and their combination on chronic anxiety. *Journal of Psychosomatic Research,* 1977, *21,* 65-71.

Lawrence, G. H. Use of biofeedback for performance enhancement in stress environments. In I. G. Sarason & C. D. Spielberger (Eds.), *Stress and anxiety* (Vol. 3). Washington, D.C.: Hemisphere Publishing, 1976.

Lawrence, G. H., & Johnson, L. C. Biofeedback and performance. In G. Schwartz & J. Beatty (Eds.), *Biofeedback: Theory and research.* New York: Academic Press, 1977.

Lazarus, R. S. *Psychological stress and the coping process.* New York: McGraw-Hill, 1966.

Lazarus, R. S. A cognitively oriented psychologist looks at biofeedback. *American Psychologist,* 1975, *30,* 553-561.

Lazarus, R. S. A cognitive analysis of biofeedback control. In G. Schwartz & J. Beatty (Eds.), *Biofeedback: Theory and resesearch.* New York: Academic Press, 1977.

Lynn, S. J., & Freedman, R. R. Transfer and evaluation of biofeedback treatment. In A. Goldstein & F. Kanfer (Eds.), *Maximizing treatment gains: Transfer-enhancement in psychotherapy.* New York: Academic Press, 1979.

McQuade, W., & Aikman, A. *Stress,* New York: E. P. Dutton, 1974.

Mason, J. W. A re-evaluation of the concept of "nonspecificity" in stress theory. *Journal of Psychiatric Research,* 1971, *8,* 323-333.

Mason, J. W. A historical view of the stress field. *Journal of Human Stress,* 1975, *1,* 6-12.

Meichenbaum, D. Cognitive factors in biofeedback therapy. *Biofeedback and Self-Regulation,* 1976, *1,* 201-216.

Meichenbaum, D. *Cognitive behavior modification: An integrative approach.* New York: Plenum, 1977.

Miller, M. P., Murphy, P. J., & Miller, T. P. Comparison of electromyographic feedback and progressive relaxation training in treating circumscribed anxiety stress reactions. *Journal of Consulting and Clinical Psychology,* 1978, *46,* 1291-1298.

Miller, N. E. Biofeedback and visceral learning. *Annual Review of Psychology,* 1978, *29,* 373-404.

Miller, N. E., & Dworkin, B. R. Clinical issues in therapeutic applications of biofeedback. In G. Schwartz & J. Beatty (Eds.), *Biofeedback: Theory and research.* New York: Academic Press, 1977.

Mirels, H. L. Dimensions of internal versus external control. *Journal of Consulting and Clinical Psychology,* 1970, *34,* 226-228.

Montgomery, I., Perkin, G., & Wise, D. A review of behavior treatments for insomnia. *Journal of Behavior Therapy and Experimental Psychiatry,* 1975, *6,* 93-100.

Naliboff, B. D., & Johnson, H. J. Finger pulse amplitude and frontalis EMG biofeedback effects of single- and two-system training. *Biofeedback and Self-Regulation,* 1978, *3,* 133-143.

Nowicki, S., & Strickland, B. A locus of control scale for children. *Journal of Consulting and Clinical Psychology,* 1973, *40,* 148-154.

Ohno, Y., Tanaka, Y., Takeya, T., Matsubara, H., Kuriya, N., & Komemushi, S. Biofeedback modification of frontal EMG in normal subjects. *Biofeedback and Self-Regulation,* 1978, *3,* 61-68.

Peck, D. F. The use of EMG feedback in the treatment of a severe case of blepharospasm. *Biofeedback and Self-Regulation,* 1977, *2,* 273-277.

Pegram, G. R., Rugh, J. D., & Linn, E. L. Transfer of training from the natural environment to the laboratory. *Proceedings of the Tenth Annual Meeting of Biofeedback Society of America,* 1979, 198-199. (Abstract)

Petry, H. M., & Desiderato, O. Changes in heart rate, muscle activity, and anxiety level following shock threat. *Psychophysiology,* 1978, *15,* 398-402.

Philips, C. The modification of tension headache pain using EMG biofeedback. *Behaviour Research and Therapy,* 1977, *15,* 119-129.

Raskin, M., Johnson, G., & Rondestvedt, J. W. Chronic anxiety treated by feedback-induced muscle relaxation: A pilot study. *Archives of General Psychiatry,* 1973, *28,* 263-266.

Reeves, J. L. EMG-biofeedback reduction of tension headache: A cognitive skills-training approach. *Biofeedback and Self-Regulation,* 1976, *1,* 217-225.

Reeves, J. L., & Mealiea, W. L. Biofeedback-assisted cue-controlled relaxation for the treatment of flight phobias. *Journal of Behavior Therapy and Experimental Psychiatry,* 1975, *6,* 105-109.

Reinking, R. H., & Kohl, M. L. Effects of various forms of relaxation training on physiological and self-report measures of relaxation. *Journal of Consulting and Clinical Psychology,* 1975, *43,* 595-600.

Romano, J. L., & Cabianca, W. A. EMG biofeedback training versus systematic desensitization for test anxiety reduction. *Journal of Consulting Psychology,* 1978, *25,* 8-13.

Rotter, J. B. Generalized expectancies for internal versus external control of reinforcement. *Psychological Monographs,* 1966, *80* (Whole No. 609).

Schandler, S. L., & Grings, W. W. An examination of methods for producing relaxation during short-term laboratory sessions. *Behaviour Research and Therapy,* 1976, *14,* 419-426.

Schwartz, G. E. Self-regulation of response patterning: Implications for psychophysiological research and theory. *Biofeedback and Self-Regulation,* 1976, *1,* 7-30.

Scott, D. S. A comprehensive treatment strategy for muscle contraction headaches. *Journal of Behavior Therapy and Experimental Psychiatry,* 1979, *10,* 35-40.

Selye, H. *The stress of life* (Rev. ed.). New York: McGraw-Hill, 1976.

Shapiro, A. K. Contribution to a history of the placebo effect. *Behavior Science,* 1960, *5,* 109-135.

Shedivy, D. I., & Kleinman, K. M. Lack of correlation between frontalis EMG and either neck EMG or verbal ratings of tension. *Psychophysiology,* 1977, *14,* 182-186.

Sime, W. E., & DeGood, D. E. Effect of EMG biofeedback and progressive muscle relaxation training on awareness of frontalis muscle tension. *Psychophysiology,* 1977, *14,* 522-530.

Smith, R. W. *Self-regulation as an aid to human effectiveness* (N00014-70-C-0350). San Diego State University Foundation, Coral Gables, Fl.: Applied Science Associates, 1975.

Solomon, L. J., & Brehony, K. A. The effects of EMG feedback training during problem solving. *Biofeedback and Self-Regulation,* 1979, *4,* 81-86.

Staudenmayer, H., & Kinsman, R. A. Awareness during electromyographic biofeedback: Of signal or process? *Biofeedback and Self-Regulation* 1976, *1,* 191-199.

Steffen, J. J. Electromyographically induced relaxation in the treatment of chronic alcohol abuse. *Journal of Consulting and Clinical Psychology,* 1975, *43,* 275.

Stern, G. S., & Berrenberg, J. L. Biofeedback training in frontalis muscle relaxation and enhancement of belief in personal control. *Biofeedback and Self-Regulation,* 1977, *2,* 173-182.

Stoyva, J. Why should muscular relaxation be clinically useful? Some data and 2½ models. In J. Beatty & H. Legewie (Eds.), *Biofeedback and behavior.* New York: Plenum, 1977.

Stoyva, J., & Budzynski, T. H. Cultivated low arousal—An anti-stress response? In L. V. DiCara (Ed.), *Recent advances in limbic and autonomic nervous system research.* New York: Plenum, 1974.

Stroebel, C. F., & Glueck, B. C. Biofeedback treatment in medicine and psychiatry: An ultimate placebo? *Seminars in Psychiatry,* 1973, *5,* 378-393.

Suarez, A., Kohlenberg, R. J., & Pagano, R. R. Is EMG activity from the frontalis site a good measure of general bodily tension in clinical populations? Proceedings of the Tenth Annual Meeting of the Biofeedback Society of America, 1979, 227-229. (Abstract)

Surwit, R. S., & Keefe, F. J. Frontalis EMG feedback training: An electronic panacea? *Behavior Therapy,* 1978, *9,* 779-792.

Tebbs, R., Eggleston, R., Prather, D., Simondi, T., & Jarbo, T. *Stress management through scientific muscle relaxation training and its relation to simulated and actual flying training* (2409). Defense Advanced Research Projects Agency, 1974.

Townsend, R. E., House, J. F., & Addario, D. A comparison of biofeedback-mediated relaxation and group therapy in the treatment of chronic anxiety. *American Journal of Psychiatry,* 1975, *136,* 598-601.

Tursky, B. Biofeedback research methodology: Need for an effective change. In R. J. Gatchel & K. P. Price (Eds.), *Clinical applications of biofeedback: Appraisal and status.* New York: Pergamon, 1979.

Wickramasekera, I. Instructions and EMG biofeedback in systematic desensitization: A case report. *Behavior Therapy,* 1972, *3,* 460-465.

Wolpe, J. *Psychotherapy by reciprocal inhibition.* Stanford, Ca.: Stanford University Press, 1958.

22 The Use of Biofeedback for Treating Patients with Migraine Headaches, Raynaud's Disease, and Hypertension: A Critical Evaluation

DAVID S. HOLMES

The use of biofeedback has probably attracted more professional and public attention than any other topic within the area of medical psychology. The effectiveness of this technique for treating a wide variety of disorders has been widely accepted; however, there is reason for using caution in concluding that biofeedback is effective. The present chapter was written to provide an evaluative review of the existing data concerning *vasomotor biofeedback* and *blood pressure biofeedback* so that the reader will be in a better position to judge the state of our knowledge concerning the effectiveness of these techniques. Attention is focused on these two types of biofeedback because they are used to treat important and frequently occurring disorders and because they have received a good deal of public attention.

This review of the literature is limited to investigations of persons with diagnosed problems. The large body of research based on normal persons is ignored because, although it is interesting and often methodologically superior to the research on patients, conclusions concerning the utility of biofeedback for treating patients that are based on research with nonpatients often requires questionable extrapolations. Indeed, the promises of clinically important effects that were generated by research on normals have often gone unfulfilled when tested on patients, and therefore it was deemed more appropriate to focus on the effects of the treatment on the target populations.

The review is divided into five major sections. In the first section, attention is given to some methodological issues that are relevant to the research on biofeedback but which have been ignored by many investigators. With that material as background, in the next three sections attention focuses on vasomotor biofeedback for treating patients with migraine headaches, vasomotor biofeedback for treating patients with Raynaud's disease, and blood pressure biofeedback for treating patients with hypertension. Finally, in the fifth section, some overall conclusions are drawn and the implications of the material that was reviewed are pointed out.

Some Initial Comments on Methodology

The most important issue to recognize when examining the research on the effectiveness of biofeed-

Medical Psychology
Contributions to Behavioral Medicine

ISBN 0-12-565960-1

back is that the biofeedback training package consists of a number of components; thus, effects that are associated with the training package could be due to any of the components and are not necessarily due to the biofeedback. Specifically, in addition to the biofeedback, the training package contains (*a*) instructions to change the response in question; (*b*) adaptation to the situation; (*c*) attention to the biofeedback; and (*d*) placebo effects. Interestingly, many investigators simply have assumed that biofeedback was the active ingredient in the training package and have ignored the possibility that one of the other components of the training package may have been responsible for the effects. It is very important, however, to determine which component is responsible for the effects. It is theoretically important for understanding the underlying process and it is practically important for maximizing the effects of our treatment to know where efforts should be directed.

Effects of Instructions

The effect of simply instructing subjects to change the response in question has been largely ignored in research on biofeedback because it was assumed that the responses in question were not under direct voluntary control. While it is probably true that they are not under direct voluntarily control, there is no doubt that many of the responses can be voluntarily controlled through indirect means such as thinking arousing or relaxing thoughts, changing breathing patterns, etc. Because of this, when testing the effects of biofeedback, it is essential to compare the responses of subjects who receive instructions plus biofeedback (i.e., biofeedback training) to the responses of subjects in a control condition who receive only instructions to change the response in question. It should be noted that some investigations involved an initial period in which subjects were instructed to change the response in question but were not given biofeedback, and then in a subsequent period were given instructions and biofeedback. If the subjects did better in the second period than in the first, it was concluded that biofeedback had added to the effect that could be achieved with instructions alone. Unfortunately, the comparison of the two periods is confounded with such factors as time and experience, and thus no conclusions can be drawn from such a comparison.

Effects of Adaptation

Given that simply sitting quietly in the laboratory and becoming accustomed to the situation will generally cause a decrease in subjects' arousal (i.e., decreased heart rate and blood pressure, dilation of peripheral blood vessels), it is important that changes in arousal due to adaptation not be attributed to the effects of biofeedback. Therefore, it is necessary to compare the responses of subjects in a biofeedback training condition to the responses of subjects in a no treatment condition who simply sit quietly for a comparable length of time. It might be noted that in attempts to overcome the problem of adaptation, a few investigators have provided their subjects with 2 or 3 adaptation sessions before training was begun. Unfortunately, this is not a completely satisfactory procedure because it has been demonstrated that with some responses it can take as many as 15 sessions before the effects of adaptation are eliminated (cf. Benson, Shapiro, Tursky, & Schwartz, 1971).

Effects of Attention

The act of attending to stimuli (e.g., the flashing lights, moving dials, changing tones, etc. that are used to provide biofeedback) can influence persons' arousal levels independent of the information provided by the stimuli. Therefore, it is often of interest to have an *attention control* condition in which persons attend to a biofeedback (or comparable) display but do not attempt to alter their physiological responses. This control, however, is probably the least important of the controls discussed here.

Placebo Effects

The placebo effect has played an important role in the history of medical practice (Shapiro, 1960). It is crucial, therefore, that in our present research on biofeedback we do not erroneously attribute to the biofeedback effects that are in fact due to the patients' expectancies for cures. Given the widespread publicity biofeedback has received and the space-age electronic wizardry associated with it, biofeedback treatment would appear to be a prime source of placebo effects. It has been argued, however, that "there is nothing wrong with placebo effects . . . In the final analysis, the value of any procedure in medicine depends on how effective and for how long it can bring the symptom and the illness under control [Shapiro, Mainardi, & Surwit, 1977, p. 321]." That is true, but as scientist-clinicians it is important that we do not delude ourselves as well as our clients concerning our treatment procedures; it is only through understanding our treatment procedures that we can improve upon them.

Biofeedback and the Treatment of Migraine Headaches

Migraine headaches involve severe, unilateral, throbbing pain and are frequently accompanied by other symptoms such as nausea, vomiting, dizziness, and sensitivity to light. The common form of migraine headache is the product of extreme dilation of the cranial arteries which has the effect of distending the surrounding pain sensitive fibers. The throbbing nature of the headache is due to hydraulic pulsations of blood through the dilated arteries. As the attack continues, the arteries may become inflamed and rigid, and thus the pain will become constant rather than throbbing. It might be noted that in the classical migraine headache, the early phase may involve intense vasoconstriction. This initial vasoconstriction gives way to the excessive dilation and the related symptoms already mentioned. Migraine headaches are generally treated with substances that produce vasoconstriction (e.g., ergotamine tartrate, Pituitrin,® ephedrine, Benzedrine,® ephinephrine, caffeine), but to be effective these must be taken before the arteries become rigid. (For additional information on migraine headaches, see Dalessio, 1972.)

Because migraine headaches are due to problems with blood flow, and because research with normal subjects suggested that biofeedback training might be effective for teaching persons to control blood flow, biofeedback training appeared to be a particularly appropriate technique for treating patients suffering from migraine headaches. Two approaches have been taken with regard to the biofeedback. In the first and most popular, patients were provided with biofeedback concerning their finger temperature, a measure which reflects the amount of blood in the area, whereas in the second approach patients were provided with biofeedback concerning pulse amplitude in the temporal artery, a measure of extracranial blood flow.

Finger Temperature Biofeedback

Skin temperature is an indirect measure of peripheral blood volume; higher temperature indicates more blood. Biofeedback training to increase finger temperature was thought to be of value for treating patients with migraine headaches for two reasons. First, because increased peripheral blood flow (i.e., peripheral vasodilation) is associated with decreased sympathetic tone and increased relaxation, it is possible that learning to increase that blood flow would aid patients in learning to relax. Second and more specific to the cause of the migraine headache, it was assumed that by increasing blood flow to the periphery, blood flow to the extracranial vasculature would be decreased and thus the pain-causing pressure would be decreased.

The first two reports involving finger temperature biofeedback came from the Menninger Foundation Clinic and attracted widespread national publicity. In the first of these investigations (Sargent, Green, & Walters, 1972), patients with migraine headaches practiced relaxation with the aid of autogenic phrases and received biofeedback that reflected the difference in temperature between hand and head. Although the training was continued for a minimum of a year, the biofeedback was usually withdrawn after the first month, and after that the patients relied exclusively on the autogenic phrases.[1] Two psychologists rated the

[1] It might be noted that in autogenic training as developed by Schultz and Luthe (1969) it is assumed that "the desired

daily self-reports concerning headache activity and analgesic use that were made by the 33 patients for whom pre- and posttraining data were available; one rated 26 (80%) and the other rated 22 (68%) as improved. Global clinical judgments of an internist suggested that 29 (90%) of the patients had improved. From these ratings, it was concluded that the treatment had been effective. Three things should be noted concerning these findings, however: (*a*) no data were presented concerning changes in hand temperature, and thus there is no evidence concerning whether or how much the training actually influenced hand temperature or whether changes in temperature were related to changes in headache activity; (*b*) although judgments concerning improvement were made, no data were reported concerning the magnitude of the improvements, and therefore it cannot be determined whether improvement reflected a 1% or a 100% reduction in symptomatology. (Given the low interjudge reliability of rated improvement reported by the investigators, it appears that changes were difficult to judge and thus were probably small.); and (*c*) it is particularly noteworthy that, regardless of the magnitude of the changes in hand temperature and headache symptomology, the changes cannot necessarily be attributed to the biofeedback because the patients were given both biofeedback training and autogenic training. The possibility that the effects were due to the autogenic training rather than the biofeedback training gains support from the fact that there are other data indicating that autogenic training alone is effective for reducing headache activity (Schultz & Luthe, 1969). It is also unlikely that the effects were due to the biofeedback because, whereas many of the patients were evaluated 3 years after treatment had been terminated, the biofeedback component of the treatment had been terminated after the first month of treatment. Overall, then, this report provided little or no meaningful data and did not provide any evidence that biofeedback was effective for treating patients with migraine headaches.

The following year, the same group of investigators published their second report on the use of autogenic feedback training (Sargent, Green, & Walters, 1972, 1973). Nineteen patients with confirmed migraines, 6 patients with tension headaches and 2 patients with unconfirmed migraine headaches participated in between 1 and 22 months of treatment ($M = 7.7$). Throughout the treatment period, the patients employed the autogenic technique on a daily basis; they received biofeedback training during only the early phase of the treatment and then it was withdrawn. There was agreement across three judges that 12 (63%) of the 19 patients with migraine headaches had improved and that 2 (33%) of the 6 patients with tension headaches had improved. From this brief summary, it should be clear that this investigation suffered from all of the problems that plagued the first report (e.g., absence of objective data concerning changes in hand temperature and headache symptomology, confounding of biofeedback and autogenic training) and thus no conclusions concerning the utility of biofeedback can be drawn from this report either.

Before going on to consider the case studies that have been reported, it might be noted that three other groups have reported investigations that were similar in design to those conducted at the Menninger Foundation. These projects involved 22 (Adler & Adler, 1976), 20 (Mitch, McGrady, & Iannone, 1976) and 388 (Diamond, Medina, Diamond-Falk, & DeVeno, 1979) patients and produced results that are comparable to those of the earlier projects (e.g., 60 or 70% of the patients improved). Again, however, because of the confounding of biofeedback with autogenic training or psychotherapy, the absence of controls and the lack of data, conclusions concerning the utility of biofeedback cannot be drawn from these investigations. With regard to the confounding of various treatments in this group of investigations, it is in-

somatic responses are brought about by passive concentration upon phrases or preselected words" and that in this investigation attention was focused on "heaviness in the limbs, control of heart rate, a sense of warmth in the limbs and abdomen, and cooling of the forehead [Sargent *et al.*, 1972, p. 120]." The phrases used included the following: I feel quite relaxed; my arms and hands are heavy and warm; I feel quiet; my whole body is relaxed and my hands are warm, relaxed and warm.

teresting and instructive to note that when patients who had participated in the research at the Menninger Foundation were followed up 2–6 years after treatment and asked to identify the most helpful part of the treatment, 33% indicated the relaxation exercises (autogenic training), 27% indicated the staff interest and support, and only 13% mentioned the biofeedback mechanism as being helpful (Solbach & Sargent, 1977).

There are three reports of individual cases in which finger temperature biofeedback was used to treat persons suffering from migraine headaches. Although the number of patients involved is very small, in each case an attempt was made to introduce some control. Thus, these case studies merit some attention. The two patients who were discussed in the first report had both been treated unsuccessfully for migraines with EMG biofeedback, and it was suggested that because the previous biofeedback treatment had not been effective, placebo effects could be ruled out as an explanation (Wickramasekera, 1973). Although that is an interesting possibility, it seems unlikely that expectancy effects would not be associated with the new biofeedback treatment; if positive effects were not to be expected, why was the treatment being administered and why was the patient participating? Furthermore, given the widespread publicity concerning temperature biofeedback, it is likely that migraine sufferers would be aware of the fact that hand temperature and not EMG biofeedback was the treatment of choice. The biofeedback treatment was like that described earlier (Sargent *et al.*, 1972, 1973) but autogenic phrases were not used and hence that factor did not confound the treatment. The patients showed increases in hand temperature of about 5°F and 6.5°F, respectively, over the 13 and 14 treatment sessions and the mean hours of reported pain per week dropped from 5.5 and 12.5 to 0.

The second report was based on a patient who was given 12 treatment sessions to decrease finger temperature and then 12 treatment sessions to increase finger temperature (Johnson & Turin, 1975). Because only the treatment to increase finger temperature would be expected to be effective for controlling migraines, the treatment to decrease temperature served as a control. During the treatment to decrease temperature, the patient averaged decreases in temperature of about only 0.5°F and showed increases in the number of headaches reported. During the treatment to increase temperature, the patient averaged increases of about 2°F; although the authors concluded that headache activity decreased, inspection of the data indicates that when the latter half of the baseline period is used as the basis for comparison as is most appropriate to do, there was no decrease in headache activity (see their Table 2, p. 396).

The final report in this group involved four patients and their treatment had three phases (Drury, DeRisi, & Liberman, 1979). The phases consisted of (*a*) a no treatment baseline; (*b*) an introduction to the concept of biofeedback (they read an article concerning the effectiveness of skin temperature biofeedback for treating migraines) and two sessions of training in the use of relaxation techniques and autogenic phrases (but not biofeedback); and (*c*) a few weeks of biofeedback training. It should be noted that during the biofeedback phase, the patients were given social reinforcement and encouragement for good performance. The results indicated that the patients were more effective in increasing skin temperature and reported fewer headaches and a lower medication intake during the period in which they received biofeedback than during the period in which they did not. These effects cannot necessarily be attributed to the biofeedback, however; it is equally plausible that the effects were due to the social reinforcement and encouragement the patients were given or to the strong placebo effect that the investigators introduced by having the patients read the article that extolled the value of biofeedback. Like the previous reports then, this report indicates that patients can increase their finger temperature and that headache activity can be reduced, but it does not provide information concerning how those changes are achieved.

Apart from these case studies, there are three investigations that involved some sort of systematic control procedure or condition; these investigations then may provide a firmer basis for drawing conclusions. In the first of these, three migraine patients first received biofeedback treatment to decrease finger temperature (which would not be expected to decrease migraines) on a twice-weekly basis for 6 weeks (Turin & Johnson, 1976). Following that, those patients plus four other patients received biofeedback treatment to increase finger temperature (which would be expected to decrease migraines) on a twice-weekly basis for about 9 weeks. Concerning headache activity, it was reported that none of the subjects trained to decrease temperature showed clinical improvement but no data were presented on that point. On the other hand, when trained to increase temperature, the seven patients showed a reliable decrease in the number of headaches reported per week (M = .89), number of pills taken per week (M = 2.59) and number of hours of pain reported per week (M = 6.71). These results would appear to provide some support for the use of biofeedback, but one must be somewhat cautious in drawing any conclusions from them because the responses of patients in the increase and decrease phases of the investigation were never actually compared.

The second investigation involved a comparison of headache activity in patients who received training in self-hypnosis, alpha biofeedback or temperature biofeedback once a week for 10 weeks (Andreychuk & Skriver, 1975). Interestingly, the patients in every condition evidenced reliable decreases in headache activity, and there were no differences among the three conditions in terms of the degree to which headaches were reduced. These findings suggest that temperature biofeedback was no more effective than other less specific treatments. It is probably most accurate to conclude therefore that the reduction in headache activity was due to general relaxation or placebo effects and that the biofeedback made no unique contribution.

In the last investigation, six patients in a true feedback group received accurate biofeedback concerning their finger temperature, whereas five patients in an altered feedback group received feedback that was controlled by the experimenter and did not reflect the patients' skin temperature (Mullinix, Norton, Hack, & Fishman, 1978). The patients participated in 6, 30-min training sessions over a 2- to 3-week period and then in additional sessions 1, 2, and 6 weeks later. There were two important findings: First, the patients in the true feedback condition evidenced reliably greater temperature increases than did patients in the altered feedback condition, thus indicating that biofeedback helped in learning temperature control. Second and more clinically important, patients in the two conditions did not differ in the degree to which they reported improvements in headache activity or medication usage, and there was no reliable correlation between improvement in headache activity and the degree to which temperature could be changed. In view of these findings, it was concluded that insofar as biofeedback was effective for influencing headache activity, it did so through a placebo effect.

Before attempting to draw any conclusions, it is important to review the results of an experiment that was conducted to determine whether changes in finger temperature were related to changes in cerebral blood flow (Largen, Mathew, Dobbins, Meyer, & Claghorn, 1978). Since cerebral blood flow is the crucial factor in the migraine headache, the question of whether it can be influenced by altering finger temperature is basic to the biofeedback treatment. In this experiment, 12 female subjects were first trained to either increase or decrease finger temperature with biofeedback. At the end of the training, there was a reliable difference in temperature between subjects who were trained to increase (+3.13°F) or decrease (−1.22°F) temperature, thus indicating that the biofeedback training was effective. On the other hand, however, no relationships were found between those changes and changes in cerebral blood flow. This, of course, has very serious implications for the possible effectiveness of finger temperature biofeedback for treating migraines.

The results concerning the utility of finger temperature biofeedback for treating patients suffering from migraine headaches are discouraging at best.

1. No confidence can be placed in the results produced in the uncontrolled early investigations and case studies.
2. Only one of the three controlled investigations provided positive results, and the results of that one investigation were incompletely reported.

3. There is now evidence that changes in finger temperature are not related to changes in cerebral blood flow, a finding that undermines the basis of the treatment.
4. It appears then that there is little or no evidence that finger temperature biofeedback is (or could be) effective for treating patients with migraines beyond its possible effect as a placebo.

Temporal Artery Pulse Biofeedback

Biofeedback concerning pulse amplitude in the temporal artery, or what is often referred to as cephalic vasomotor response (CVMR) feedback, may be more effective than finger temperature biofeedback for treating patients suffering from migraine headaches because it is more specific to the site of the blood flow problem. In addition to reducing the tonic pain associated with excessively high basal blood volume, the reduction of pulse amplitude would reduce the throbbing pain associated with the phasic increases in volume due to the pulse. One case study and two experiments have been reported concerning the utility of pulse amplitude biofeedback.

The patient on whom the case study was based was a 67-year-old woman who suffered from combined migraine muscle contraction type headaches (Feuerstein, Adams, & Beiman, 1976). Her treatment program was as follows: a five-week pretreatment baseline, six sessions of frontalis EMG biofeedback over 6 weeks, withdrawal of treatment for 8 weeks, six sessions of temporal artery pulse amplitude biofeedback over 7 weeks, and an 8-week follow-up period with no treatment. During all of these phases, the patient recorded her subjective judgments of headache frequency, intensity, and duration. The results of the treatment can be best described as mixed. The EMG biofeedback was not effective for helping the patient control frontalis muscle activity, but was associated first with an increase and then a decrease in vasospasms per minute. During the period of the EMG treatment, the patient reported a reduction of headache frequency and duration. Similarly, the pulse amplitude biofeedback did not enable the patient to reliably reduce pulse amplitude but was associated with first an increase and then a decrease in vasospasms; during the treatment period the patient again reported a reduction of headache frequency and duration. Generally, the authors attributed reductions in headache activity to the changes in vasospasms, but in view of the patterning of those changes (increases as well as decreases), a placebo effect on the self-report measures is a very viable alternative explanation. Given these results, if support is to be found for the utility of pulse amplitude biofeedback for treating patients with migraine headaches, it will have to come from the two experiments that have been reported.

In the first experiment on temporal artery pulse amplitude biofeedback, the patients in the experimental condition received biofeedback for pulse amplitude in the temporal artery, whereas subjects in the control condition received biofeedback for pulse amplitude in the hand (Friar & Beatty, 1976). (It is interesting to note that feedback concerning blood flow in the hand which was considered crucial in past research was considered to be a nonspecific control treatment in this research.) Nineteen patients participated in eight training sessions and one follow-up no training session. Unfortunately, no data were presented for the training sessions. The data from the follow-up session indicated that, when compared to their pretreatment levels, patients in the control condition showed a reduction in pulse amplitude in the hand but not in the head, whereas patients in the experimental condition showed a reduction in pulse amplitude in both the head and the hand. However, a comparison of the reductions in pulse amplitudes in the head indicated that patients in the experimental condition only tended ($p < .10$) to show greater reductions than did the patients in the control condition. With regard to headache activity, it was reported that when compared to their pretreatment levels, patients in the experimental condition showed trends in the direction of fewer major attacks ($p < .10$) and fewer total number of episodes ($p < .20$), whereas the trends were less strong for patients in the control condition. Unfortunately, the investigators did not report comparisons of the experimental and control conditions in terms of changes in headache activity, but from the data that were presented it is clear that there would not have been a reliable difference between the conditions. That is, although patients in the experimental condition tended to show declines in headache activity from their initial levels, those declines were not greater than the declines shown by patients in the control condition. It should also be noted that the slightly greater declines in headache activity reported by experimental patients may have been due to regression to the mean because those patients started with higher levels of headache activity than did the control patients. Finally, the investigators reported that there were no differences between the patients in the experimental and control conditions in their use of analgesics and vasoconstrictors. Overall, the results of this investigation provide no support for the utility of the biofeedback and, as noted by the authors, the limited results that were obtained may have been due to a placebo effect (i.e., the forehead training may have been more convincing than the hand training).

The most recent investigation to employ feedback concerning cephalic vasomotor activity involved four patients, two with migraine headaches and two with tension headaches (Feuerstein & Adams, 1977). To control for placebo effects, one of each type of patient was first treated with vasomotor biofeedback and then with EMG biofeedback whereas the reverse was true for the other two patients. If the treatments are in fact effective beyond placebo effects, the patients with migraine headaches should respond to the vasomotor biofeedback and not to the EMG biofeedback, whereas the patients with tension headaches should respond to the EMG biofeedback and not to the vasomotor biofeedback. The results concerning the physiological changes with the two treatments are mixed. While receiving vasomotor biofeedback, one migraine patient showed a change in blood volume and no change in EMG, whereas the other migraine patient showed no change in blood volume but a change in EMG. Patients with tension headaches showed the same inconsistency in responses when they were exposed to vasomotor biofeedback. From these results it is clear that the vasomotor biofeedback did not have response-specific effects. Turning to the self-reports concerning headache activity, it was found that one migraine patient reported somewhat fewer and shorter but more intense headaches while treated with vasomotor biofeedback rather than EMG biofeedback, whereas the other migraine patient reported essentially no differences in headache activity during the vasomotor and EMG treatment periods. Although the data from both migraine patients suggested declines in headache activity from the baseline period, both the physiological and self-report data clearly indicate that the effects were not specific to the vasomotor biofeedback and thus this investigation does not provide evidence for the specific utility of cephalic vasomotor biofeedback for treating migraine headache patients.

From the results reviewed in the preceding paragraphs, it should be clear that at the present time there is no reliable evidence that biofeedback treatment is effective for treating patients suffering from migraine headaches. In many cases the patients undergoing the biofeedback treatment did report declines in headache activity; however, those declines were not greater than the declines reported by patients in control conditions, thus suggesting that the effects that have been found with the biofeedback treatment have been due primarily to placebo effects. In view of these results, the use of biofeedback as anything more than a placebo treatment for migraine headaches does not seem justified at this time.

Biofeedback and the Treatment of Raynaud's Disease

Raynaud's disease is a functional disorder of the cardiovascular system in which the small arteries or arterioles of the patient's extremities (usually the hands or feet) constrict and thereby limit the flow of blood to those areas. Because of the lack of blood, the patient experiences painful sensations of cold in the afflicted area. In extreme cases, the lack of blood flow to the area results in gangrene and amputation of the digits is necessary. Although the disease is not well-known to the general public, it has been estimated that in its mildest forms it effects approximately 20% of young people, particularly women in whom it is five times more prevalent than in men. At the present time, the etiology of Raynaud's disease is not clear, but it is known that episodes of the disorder can be induced by emotional stress and/or exposure to cold. Because of the involvement of the sympathetic component of the central nervous system, extreme cases are sometimes treated with sympathectomies. (For additional information on Raynaud's disease, see Lewis, 1949; Spittell, 1972.)

When investigators began reporting that blood flow could be influenced with biofeedback training, attention was quickly focused on the possible use of biofeedback for treating patients with Raynaud's disease. Despite the fact that biofeedback would appear to be particularly suited for the treatment of Raynaud's disease, the research on its effectiveness is limited to six case studies and one experiment. It is important that this research be considered and evaluated very carefully because the nature of Raynaud's disease "makes it a model cardiovascular disorder on which to test the efficacy of a behavioral intervention [Surwit, Pilon, & Fenton, 1978, p. 324]," and this body of research is often cited as evidence for the clinical utility of biofeedback.

The first patient on whom we have a case study report was a well-educated upper-class male in his 60s who was suffering from very cold feet (Schwartz, 1973; Shapiro & Schwartz, 1972). Blood volume was recorded from the big toe of each foot, and biofeedback concerning the response in one of the two toes was given after each pulse beat. After a given number of correct responses, the patient was shown a slide as a reward. It was reported that "over 10 sessions he began to show large increases in blood volume [Schwartz, 1973, p. 671]" and that increases were specific to the foot from which feedback was being obtained, but no data were offered in support of those observations and hence they should be accepted cautiously. The patient reported that he achieved his successes both inside and outside of the laboratory by free-associating hot thoughts (e.g., sun, warmth, beaches), and gave no indication that the biofeedback was used or was useful. Although the treatment was reported to be initially successful, after a year the patient indicated that the symptoms had returned. The same approach to treatment was employed with a woman from a lower-middle-class background, but did not result in meaningful increases in blood volume; the authors attributed the ineffectiveness to the severity of her disease and personality-motivational factors (Schwartz, 1973; Shapiro & Schwartz, 1972).

A third case involved a 21-year-old woman who was first given intensive instruction in relaxation and autogenic imagery and then a year of skin temperature biofeedback training supplemented by counseling and assertive training. With the treatment, the patient increased

> her basal skin temperature (both hands) from an average of 23°C to 26°C. She was able to go outdoors in the Montreal winter without elaborate protective garments and had markedly decreased the number of Raynaud's attacks she experienced. . . . However, the patient still complained of pain in her hands even when her skin temperature was normal [Surwit, 1973, p. 486].

As the end of therapy approached and the biofeedback was phased out, the patient lost the ability to control temperature and could not regain it when the biofeedback was reintroduced. The fact that the biofeedback was ineffective when it was reintroduced in the absence of the other therapeutic strategies (i.e., relaxation techniques, autogenic imagery, counseling, assertion training) suggests that the earlier success was probably due to the other therapies, although the author reported that the patient attributed the failure to the fact that she was bored.

The fourth case study involved a 50-year-old woman who was first instructed in the use of relaxation and autogenic techniques and then was given biofeedback concerning the net difference in temperature between her temporal forehead and a finger of one hand (Peper, 1973). After using the biofeedback for 10 min twice a day over a period of 1 month, the patient's basal skin temperature on the finger tip increased from 75°F to 85°F and she reported that for the first time in 30 years she could hold on to the cold steering wheel of her car without gloves.

The fifth case study reported involved a 31-year-old male who was given three sessions of hypnotic training and then four sessions involving autohypnosis and skin temperature biofeedback (Jacobson, Hackett, Surman, & Silverberg, 1973). The biofeedback reflected the temperature difference between the patient's finger and forehead, and the task was to increase the finger temperature. Although there were no changes in finger temperature in the first biofeedback session, within each of the next four sessions the patient evidenced increases of approximately 4°C in finger temperature. There was no reported change in basal skin temperature, but the patient reported that, "for the first time in years, he was able to touch cold objects without producing painful spasm" and that "he could experience anxiety symptoms without concomitant finger pain [Jacobson *et al.,* p. 740]." The investigators reported, however, that "since the subjective reports of clinical improvement predated the objective evidence for this control, it is difficult to identify the factor responsible for it [Jacobson *et al.,* 1973, p. 740]." It was suggested that factors such as the patient's hope for improvement and his positive regard for the procedure (i.e., a placebo effect) may have played a role in the symptom reduction.

In the most recent case study, an interesting attempt was made to achieve some experimental control and to obtain some systematic follow-up data (Blanchard & Haynes, 1975). The subject was a 28-year-old female who complained of cold hands and feet and who was diagnosed as suffering from moderately severe Raynaud's disease that was not serious enough to warrant a medication trial. After four baseline sessions in which she simply sat quietly, the subject participated in six self-control sessions in which she attempted to warm her hand without the aid of biofeedback. Following that, there were six feedback-training sessions in which she attempted to warm her hands and was given biofeedback reflecting the temperature difference between her hand and forehead. Following the biofeedback sessions, there were another six self-control sessions without biofeedback and then there were another six biofeedback training sessions. At 2, 4, and 7 months after the completion of the training, the patient was given additional self-control and biofeedback ("booster") training sessions. The data were scored in terms of the difference between the temperature recorded at the finger and forehead. Inspection of the data indicates that the results from session to session were quite variable, but the reported mean maximum changes in the training phase were as follows: first self-control phase, 1.1°F; first biofeedback training phase, 3.4°F; second self-control phase, 1.4°F; and second biofeedback training phase, 3.7°F. That is, the subject was consistently more effective in increasing temperature when biofeedback was present. During the follow-up sessions, the subject was again more successful in increasing temperature when biofeedback was provided, but the effect was less pronounced. Mean increases were not reported for the follow-up self-control sessions, but for the follow-up biofeedback training sessions the subject showed mean increases of 2.0°, 1.6°, and 2.2°F after four, four, and five "booster" follow-up training sessions, respectively. Finally, the patient reported subjective improvement in her symptomatology and it was found that there was an increase in her baseline hand temperature from 79.0°F to 88.3°F. This investigation more closely ties changes in temperature to biofeedback relative to the other case studies, but it does not rule out the potential placebo effect. Furthermore, in considering these results, it is interesting to note that even if it is concluded that the changes in temperature were due to the biofeedback, the results raise a very serious problem for biofeedback therapy. Specifically, the fact that the effects appeared and disappeared with the presence and absence of biofeedback suggests that the biofeedback had no carry over effect and thus would be of little or no utility outside of the training situation.

Overall, the case studies provide at best only inconsistent and weak support for the utility of biofeedback for treating persons with Raynaud's disease. In view of this, the results of the one controlled experiment on the problem take on increased importance. In that project, 32 female patients were randomly assigned to either an immediate or a delayed treatment condition (Surwit, Pilon, & Fenton, 1978). Therefore, patients in the delayed treatment condition initially served as no treatment controls but later provided treatment data. In terms of treatment, patients were assigned either to a condition in which they only received autogenic training, or to a condition in which they received both autogenic training and finger temperature biofeedback; thus, it was possible to separate the effects due to the autogenic phrases and the biofeedback. The subjects in those conditions were further subdivided into those who received their training in the laboratory and those who received the training at home through the use of audio cassettes and a finger temperature thermometer. The procedures were as follows: All subjects were initially exposed to a cold stress test during which they were instructed to keep their hands as warm as possible. Following this, subjects in the immediate treatment conditions (laboratory and home) began treatment whereas subjects in the delayed treatment condition were not given any treatment. After 4 weeks of treatment or waiting, all subjects were again exposed to the cold stress test. Following that test, the subjects in the delayed treatment condition began 4 weeks of treatment (laboratory and home) and then were once again exposed to the cold stress test.

The results of this experiment are very interesting and, in light of the various controls, very informative. First, it was found that subjects in both the autogenic-only and the autogenic-plus-biofeedback conditions were able to maintain reliably higher finger tempratures during the cold stress test than subjects who had not been treated (delayed treatment condition). Second, and very important, the results indicated that subjects in the autogenic-plus-biofeedback condition and subjects in the autogenic-only condition were *equally* effective in increasing hand temperature, thus indicating that biofeedback did not add to the effect that could be achieved with the autogenic phrases. Third, the home training was found to be as effective for hand warming as the more elaborate laboratory training. And finally, although there was evidence that the introduction of treatment decreased the reported frequency of Raynaud's attacks, "there was no evidence to indicate that the presence of biofeedback enhances clinical improvement produced by autogenic training [Surwit, Pilon, & Fenton, 1978, p. 333]." That is, the autogenic-plus-biofeedback treatment was not more effective than the autogenic-only treatment. Obviously, this controlled demonstration that biofeedback is not more effective than simple autogenic suggestions for helping patients control temperature or reduce the symptoms of Raynaud's disease is devastating in terms of the clinical use of biofeedback. These findings, in combination with the very weak evidence produced by the uncontrolled case studies, provide no justification for the clinical use of biofeedback for the treatment of Raynaud's disease, a disease which has been labeled as a model disorder on which to test the effectiveness of biofeedback treatment (Surwit, Pilon, & Fenton, 1978).

Biofeedback and the Treatment of Hypertension

Hypertension (i.e., high blood pressure) is one of the most pervasive and serious health problems in the United States today. Specifically, it has been estimated that between 15 and 20% of the adult population suffers from hypertension, and the disorder is associated with greatly increased risk of myocardial infarction, congestive heart failure, stroke, dissecting aneurysm, and renal failure.

The nature and results of the research on the effects of blood pressure biofeedback treatment with hypertensive patients are summarized in Table 22.1. The table lists the various biofeedback treatment conditions employed below each experiment (e.g., increase or decrease, massed or spaced schedules). In addition, for each experiment, Table 22.1 indicates (*a*) the number of patients in the biofeedback condition; (*b*) the number of training sessions involved; (*c*) the degree to which patients receiving biofeedback changed in pressure relative to patients in a no treatment control condition, an instructions-only control condition, and/or an attention control condition; and (*d*) the degree to which the patients receiving biofeedback changed in pressure from the beginning-of-training to the end-of-training if there were no controls against which to compare their performance. If biofeedback was provided for diastolic as opposed to systolic blood pressure, a "(D)" follows the condition label and if diastolic as opposed to systolic blood pressure is reported, a "(D)" follows the number indicating pressure change. For one experiment (Shoemaker and Tasto, 1975), the

Table 22.1
Results of Research with Hypertensive Subjects in Multiple Training Sessions

Experiment	N	Sessions	No treatment	Instruction	Attention	Begin/End
Benson, Shapiro, Tursky, & Schwartz (1971)						
Decrease	7	8-34				−16.50
Schwartz & Shapiro (1973)						
Decrease (D)	7	5				0.00 (D)
Blanchard, Young, & Haynes (1975)						
Decrease	4	5-9				−26.45
Elder & Eustis (1975)						
Decrease (mass; D)	4	10				−13.30 (D)
Decrease (space; D)	18	8				− 4.89 (D)
Kristt & Engel (1975)						
Increase	5	14				+15.20
Decrease		14				−12.00
Richter-Heinrich, Knust, Muller, Schmidt, & Sprung (1975)						
Decrease	10	4				−22.00
Kleinman, Goldman, & Snow (1976)						
Decrease	8	9				− 6.00 − 8.00 (D)
Kleinman, Goldman, Snow, & Korol (1977)						
Decrease	8	9				−11.00 − 7.00 (D)
Goldman, Kleinman, Snow, Bidus, & Korol (1975)						
Decrease	7	9				− 6.30 −14.70 (D)
Surwit, Shapiro, & Good (1978)						
Decrease	8	8				− 4.00
Hager & Surwit (1977)						
Decrease	7	56				0.00
Shoemaker & Tasto (1975)						
Decrease (S & D)	5	6	+1.00 −2.40 (D)			
Elder, Ruiz, Deabler, & Dillenkoffer (1973)						
Decrease (D)	6	7		−10.24 (D) − 5.75 −29.77 (D)		
Decrease (praise; D)	6	7		−28.25		
Frankel, Patel, Horwitz, Friedewald, & Gaarder (1978)						
Decrease (D)	7	20	0.00 (D) −2.00			
Blanchard & Epstein (1978)						
Decrease	10	12	−0.80			

table shows that both systolic and diastolic blood pressure biofeedback was provided to patients.

In general, the first 11 investigations summarized in Table 22.1 require little comment because they did not involve conditions to control for the effects of any of the other components of the biofeedback training package. Thus, in those 11 investigations it is not possible to determine the degree to which the reported effects were actually due to the biofeedback. There are a number of points concerning these projects that are worth noting, however. First, in the project reported by Benson *et al.* (1971) the patients participated in a series of no treatment sessions until their pressure stabilized over 5 sessions, and only then were they given biofeedback. This procedure reduced the possibility that the decrease in pressure that was observed during treatment was due to adaptation, although it did not rule out other factors such as a placebo effect. Second, although of considerable magnitude, when tested by the present author, the decrease in pressure reported by Blanchard, Young, and Haynes (1975) was not found to be statistically reliable, $F(1,3) = 0.49$. Third, the investigation reported by Goldman, Kleinman, Snow, Bidus, and Korol (1975) did involve a no treatment condition, but the no treatment condition involved only one-third as many sessions as the treatment condition and had no attrition while there was a 50% attrition rate in the treatment condition (did the patients who did not benefit drop out?). The patients in the treatment condition, furthermore, started out with pressures that were 9.8 mmHg higher than those of patients in the control condition, thus raising the question of differential regression to the mean. For those reasons, it did not seem justifiable to compare the treatment and no treatment conditions here. Fourth, it is interesting to note that in the project reported by Surwit, Shapiro, & Good (1978), the investigators compared the effects of the blood pressure biofeedback training package to the effects of EMG biofeedback and meditation. There were no reliable differences among the performances of the patients in the three conditions. In view of the fact that the changes within the various conditions were minimal (i.e., −4, +1, and −4 mmHg), it appears that the three treatments were equally ineffective.

When attention is turned to the four investigations that employed controls for the other components of the biofeedback training package, the results are distinctly discouraging. Of the four experiments, only the one reported by Elder, Ruiz, Deabler, and Dillenkoffer (1973) revealed substantial differences between the treatment and control conditions, and there are reasons to be cautious about those findings. Specifically, the differences for systolic blood pressure were not statistically reliable and, although that experiment was reported 7 years ago, to date no one (including Elder & Eustis, 1975) has produced comparable results; thus, one might question the overall reliability of the findings. Finally, it is important to note that Frankel, Patel, Horwitz, Friedewald, and Gaarder (1978) compared the changes in blood pressure achieved by patients in a biofeedback condition to those achieved by patients in a placebo condition who received "sham or noncontingent blood pressure feedback arranged to convey a sense of success [p. 281]." The patients in the two conditions showed comparable changes in pressure over the treatment period. Overall then, there does not appear to be any reliable evidence to support the clinical use of blood pressure biofeedback for the treatment of hypertension.

Conclusions

From the research that has been reviewed in this chapter, it should be clear that at the present time there is no consistent scientific support for the effectiveness of biofeedback for treating patients with migraine headaches, Raynaud's disease, or hypertension. Admittedly, there were some case studies that yielded promising results, but those results were not verified by subsequent controlled investigations. With regard to these findings and conclusions, it is interesting to note that recently investigators have been unable to replicate the results of the early work on animals that provided one of the cornerstones of support for biofeedback (Brener, Eissenberg & Middaugh, 1974; Miller & Dworkin, 1974).

The theory underlying the use of biofeedback remains sound, and it is possible that with additional research we will discover techniques by which biofeedback can be used effectively with clinical problems, but at the present time its use does not appear justified for the treatment of patients with migraines, Raynaud's disease, or hypertension. Writing some years ago, Neal Miller recommended that in the area of biofeedback, "investigators should be bold in what they try but *cautious in what they claim* [emphasis added; Miller, 1974, p. xviii]." In view of the existing data, this early admonition takes on additional meaning and importance. Clearly, if medical psychologists are to practice ethically, they must be very cautious in their claims concerning the utility of biofeedback.

References

Adler, C. S., & Adler, S. M. Biofeedback psychotherapy for the treatment of headache: A five-year follow-up. *Headache,* 1976, *16,* 189-191.

Andreychuk, T., & Skriver, C. Hypnosis and biofeedback in the treatment of migraine headache. *International Journal of Clinical and Experimental Hypnosis,* 1975, *23,* 172-183.

Benson, H., Shapiro, D., Tursky, B., & Schwartz, G. Decreased systolic blood pressure through operant conditioning techniques in patients with essential hypertension. *Science,* 1971, *173,* 740-742.

Blanchard, E., & Epstein, L. *A biofeedback primer.* Boston: Addison-Wesley, 1978.

Blanchard, E. B., & Haynes, M. R. Biofeedback treatment of a case of Raynaud's disease. *Journal of Behavior Therapy and Experimental Psychiatry,* 1975, *6,* 230-234.

Blanchard, E. B., Young, L. D., & Haynes, M. R. A simple biofeedback system for the treatment of elevated blood pressure. *Behavior Therapy,* 1975, *6,* 241-245.

Brener, J., Eissenberg, E., & Middaugh, S. Respiratory and somatomotor factors associated with operant conditioning of cardiovascular responses in curarized rats. In P. Obrist, A. Black, J. Brener, & L. DiCara (Eds.), *Cardiovascular psychophysiology.* Chicago: Aldine, 1974.

Dalessio, D. J. *Wolff's headache and other pain.* New York: Oxford University Press, 1972.

Diamond, S., Medina, J., Diamond-Falk, J., & DeVeno, T. The value of biofeedback in the treatment of chronic headache: A five-year retrospective study. *Headache,* 1979, *19,* 90-96.

Drury, R. L., DeRisi, W. J., & Liberman, R. P. Temperature biofeedback treatment for migraine headache: A controlled multiple baseline study. *Headache,* 1979, *19,* 278-284.

Elder, S., & Eustis, N. Instrumental blood pressure conditioning in outpatient hypertensives. *Behaviour Research and Therapy,* 1975, *13,* 185-188.

Elder, S., Ruiz, Z., Deabler, H., & Dillenkoffer, R. Decreased systolic blood pressure through operant conditioning techniques in patients with essential hypertension. *Journal of Applied Behavior Analysis,* 1973, *6,* 377-382.

Feuerstein, M., & Adams, H. E. Cephalic vasomotor feedback in the modification of migraine headache. *Biofeedback and Self-Regulation,* 1977, *2,* 241-254.

Feuerstein, M., Adams, H. E., & Beiman, I. Cephalic vasomotor and electromyographic feedback in the treatment of combined muscle contraction and migraine headaches in a geriatric case. *Headache,* 1976, *16,* 232-237.

Frankel, B. L., Patel, D. J., Horwitz, D., Friedewald, W. T., & Gaarder, K. R. Treatment of hypertension with biofeedback and relaxation techniques. *Psychosomatic Medicine,* 1978, *40,* 276-293.

Friar, L. R., & Beatty, J. Migraine: management by a trained control of vasoconstriction. *Journal of Consulting and Clinical Psychology,* 1976, *44,* 46-53.

Goldman, H., Kleinman, K., Snow, M., Bidus, D., & Korol, B. Relationship between essential hypertension and cognitive functioning: Effects of biofeedback. *Psychophysiology,* 1975, *12,* 569-573.

Hager, J., & Surwit, R. Hypertension and self-control with a portable feedback unit or relaxation. *Psychophysiology,* 1977, *14,* 97-98.

Jacobson, A. M., Hacket, T. P., Surman, O. S., & Silverberg, E. L. Raynaud's phenomenon: Treatment with hypnotic and operant technique. *Journal of the American Medical Association,* 1973, *225,* 739-740.

Johnson, W. G., & Turin, A. Biofeedback treatment of migraine headaches: a systematic case study. *Behavior Therapy,* 1975, *6,* 394-397.

Kleinman, K., Goldman, H., Snow, M., & Korol, B. Relationship between essential hypertension and cognitive functioning II: Effects of biofeedback training generalize to non-laboratory environment. *Psychophysiology,* 1977, *14,* 192-197.

Kleinman, K. M., Goldman, H., & Snow, M. Y. Effects of stress and motivation on effectiveness of biofeedback training in essential hypertensives. *Psychophysiology,* 1976, *13,* 187. (Abstract)

Kristt, D. A., & Engel, B. T. Learned control of blood pressure in patients with high blood pressure. *Circulation,* 1975, *51,* 370-378.

Largen, J. W., Mathew, R. J., Dobbins, K., Meyer, J. S., & Claghorn, J. L. Skin temperature self-regulation and non-invasive regional cerebral blood flow. *Headache,* 1978, 203-210.

Lewis, T. *Vascular disorders of the limbs: Described for practitioners and students.* London: Macmillan, 1949.

Miller, N. E. Introduction: Current issues and key problems. In N. Miller, T. Barber, L. Di Cara, J. Kamiya, D. Shapiro, & J. Stoyva (Eds.), *Biofeedback and self-control, 1973.* Chicago: Aldine, 1974.

Miller, N. E., & Dworkin, B. R. Visceral learning: Recent difficulties with curarized rats and significant problems for human research. In P. Obrist, A. Black, J. Brener, & L. DiCara (Eds.), *Cardiovascular psychophysiology.* Chicago: Aldine, 1974.

Mitch, P. S., McGrady, A., & Iannone, A. Autogenic feedback training in migraine: A treatment report. *Headache,* 1976, *15,* 267-270.

Mullinix, J. M., Norton, B. J., Hack, S., & Fishman, M. Skin temperature biofeedback and migraine. *Headache,* 1978, *17,* 242-244.

Peper, E. Frontiers of clinical biofeedback. *Seminars in Psychiatry,* 1973, *5,* 415-428.

Richter-Heinrich, E., Knust, U., Muller, W., Schmidt, K., & Sprung, H. Psychophysiological investigations in essential hypertensives. *Journal of Psychosomatic Research,* 1975, *19,* 251-258.

Sargent, J. D., Green, E. E., & Walters, E. D. The use of autogenic feedback training in a pilot study of migraine and tension headaches. *Headache,* 1972, *12,* 120-125.

Sargent, J. D., Green, E. E., & Walters, E. D. Preliminary report on the use of autogenic feedback training in the treatment of migraine and tension headaches. *Psychosomatic Medicine,* 1973, *35,* 129-135.

Schwartz, G. E. Biofeedback as therapy: Some theoretical and practical issues. *American Psychologist,* 1973, *28,* 666-673.

Schwartz, G. E., & Shapiro, D. Biofeedback and essential hypertension: Current findings and theoretical concerns. *Seminars in Psychiatry,* 1973, *5,* 493-503.

Schultz, J. H., & Luthe, W. *Autogenic therapy* (Vol. 1). New York: Grune & Stratton, 1969.

Shapiro, A. Contribution to a history of the placebo effect. *Behavior Science,* 1960, *5,* 105-135.

Shapiro, D., Mainardi, A., & Surwit, R. Biofeedback and self-regulation in essential hypertension. In G. E. Schwartz & J. Beatty (Eds.), *Biofeedback: Theory and research,* New York: Academic Press, 1977.

Shapiro, D., & Schwartz, G. E. Biofeedback and visceral learning: Clinical applications. *Seminars in Psychiatry,* 1972, *4,* 171-184.

Shoemaker, J., & Tasto, D. The effects of muscle relaxation on blood pressure of essential hypertensives. *Behavior Research & Therapy,* 1975, *13,* 29-43.

Solbach, P., & Sargent, J. D. A follow-up evaluation of the Menninger pilot migraine study using thermal training. *Headache,* 1977, *17,* 198-202.

Spittel, J. A. Chapter 19. In J. F. Fairbairn, J. L. Juergens, & J. A. Spittel (Eds.), *Peripheral vascular diseases* (4th ed.). Philadelphia: W. B. Saunders, 1972.

Surwit, R. S. Biofeedback: A possible treatment for Raynaud's disease. *Seminars in Psychiatry,* 1973, *5,* 483-489.

Surwit, R. S., Pilon, R. N., & Fenton, C. H. Behavioral treatment of Raynaud's disease. *Journal of Behavioral Medicine,* 1978, *1,* 323-335.

Surwit, R., Shapiro, D., & Good, M. Comparison of cardiovascular biofeedback, neuromuscular biofeedback, and meditation in the treatment of borderline essential hypertension. *Journal of Consulting and Clinical Psychology,* 1978, *46,* 252-263.

Turin, A., & Johnson, W. G. Biofeedback therapy for migraine headaches. *Archives of General Psychiatry,* 1976, *33,* 517-519.

Wickramasekera, I. Temperature feedback for the control of migraine. *Journal of Behavior Therapy and Experimental Psychiatry,* 1973, *4,* 343-345.

SPECIAL TOPICS IN MEDICAL PSYCHOLOGY AND BEHAVIORAL MEDICINE

23 Adherence to Health Care Regimens

FRANK T. MASUR, III

Case 1. A worried young mother complains to her pediatrician that her child is quite ill. The child is extremely irritable, cries incessantly, is refusing food, and presents with a rectal temperature of 102.8°F. Two weeks earlier an emergency room physician had diagnosed the child as having otitis media (an inflammation of the middle ear) and had prescribed appropriate antibiotic therapy. The mother reports that her child briefly improved but that treatment effects were only short-lived and the child has apparently "become sick again."

Case 2. A 25-year-old black male is being followed by his regular family physician for essential hypertension. The diagnosis was initially made when a hypertension screening program at work discovered that the patient consistently ran significantly elevated diastolic blood pressures. The preliminary consultation of the family physician resulted in the initiation of diuretic therapy and instructions to the patient to restrict his sodium intake. Eight weeks after the start of therapy the patient's diastolic pressure was still well above normal and his physician is now considering an alteration in the patient's medical regimen with the addition of more powerful antihypertensive agents.

Case 3. A 65-year-old widow has been followed by her general internist for borderline diabetes, hypertension, and coronary artery disease. Following her first myocardial infarction nearly 3 years ago her medication regimens have become increasingly more complex. She is presently taking two different antihypertensives, one antiarrhythmic and an oral hypoglycemic. She is on a low salt diet, uses potassium supplements, and takes multivitamins. She has become increasingly distressed by more frequent bouts of arthritis in her hands which has prompted her physician to prescribe an antiarthritic agent. After three weeks her condition remains unimproved and she is bitterly complaining that her arthritis has severely restricted her needlepoint and crochet—the only pastimes she really enjoys. Her displeasure is obvious and she tells her internist that she has been considering consulting a chiropractor for her condition.

Although it may not be readily apparent, each of the aforementioned cases shares a common element. In addition to the fact that each case represents a continued need for health care interventions to correct various physical conditions the astute reader also may have noted that in each instance the patient's incomplete adherence to the prescribed treatment might well account for the poor therapeutic response. A plethora of terms

Medical Psychology
Contributions to Behavioral Medicine

ISBN 0-12-565960-1

have been offered to represent the degree or extent to which patient behaviors (e.g., taking medications, restricting activities, following diets, performing exercises) coincide with the clinical prescription of health care providers. Compliance, adherence, therapeutic alliance, and patient cooperation are only a few of many terms that have been used, each with their own denotative and connotative meanings. The present chapter will use the terms compliance and adherence interchangeably. Compliance, although the more popular term, tends to connote an authoritarian provider–patient interaction whereas adherence tends to suggest a more egalitarian interactive system.

This chapter explores the reasons why the mother in Case 1 prematurely terminated antibiotic therapy which resulted in an incomplete clinical trial and the subsequent reinfection of her child. Had the family physician in Case 2 been sufficiently cognizant of the high rate of noncompliance with long-term asymptomatic diseases he or she might not have inadvertently complicated the treatment protocol by unnecessarily prescribing additional medications. Similarly, the internist in Case 3 might well have been shocked and even embarrassed to learn that the real reason for the therapeutic ineffectiveness of the prescribed antiarthritic was not due to any pharmacologic inadequancy, but rather because the patient was not able to manipulate the small, difficult to open child-proof container in which the medicine was dispensed. The patient was unwilling to say anything out of fear of embarrassment while the internist had never considered that unintentional nonadherence was the primary cause of this drug trial failure.

This chapter addresses four major issues with respect to compliance. First, the magnitude of noncompliance as a health care problem is defined. Whether one is a practicing clinician concerned about the clinical effectiveness of a specific treatment (prescriptive and/or proscriptive), or a researcher conducting clinical trials comparing the relative efficiency of various preventive, ameliorative, or rehabilitative efforts, the question of patient–subject compliance demands careful consideration.

Second, a brief review of how compliance is operationally defined comparing the relative merits of diverse definitional approaches and methods of measurement is presented. The third and largest section of this chapter provides a review of the various parameters that have been thought to affect compliance. Finally, various strategies to improve compliance in direct patient care are analyzed.

Nonadherence: The Extent of the Problem

Compliance, over the past decade, has aroused an extraordinary amount of attention and concern among health care providers and researchers from a wide range of disciplines. It would be impossible to provide a totally comprehensive review of the vast compliance literature. A number of general reviews and annotated bibliographies are presently available (Becker & Maiman, 1975; Blackwell, 1973; Christensen, 1978; Davis, 1966; Dunbar & Stunkard, 1979; Haynes, Taylor, & Sackett, 1979; Marston, 1970; Matthews & Hingson, 1977; Mitchell, 1974; Sackett & Haynes, 1976), and the interested reader, particularly the potential researcher, would do well to become acquainted with these.

It has been argued that patient noncompliance has perhaps become one of our best documented but least understood health related behaviors (Becker & Maiman, 1975). Though our understanding of this problem may be limited, its pervasiveness is not. Depending upon the study under review, the proportion of patients who fail to adhere to physicians' orders ranges from 15 to 94% (Davis, 1966). The magnitude of the problem is perhaps made clearer when one considers that at least one-third of the patients in most studies fail to comply and that, in one review, complete failure to take medication occurred in between one-quarter and over one-half of all outpatients (Blackwell, 1972). Boyd, Covington, Stanaszek, and Coussons (1974) found that 18% of 134 outpatients treated through a hospital clinic never even filled their prescriptions. Although it is misleading to directly compare compliance rates from various studies due to the often extreme differences between investigators in operationally defining compliance

(Blackwell, 1973; Davis, 1968a; Stimson, 1974), it is clear that the problem of noncompliance remains a substantial one.

It has been argued that nonadherence produces substantial adverse effects on the quality of health care both directly, by disrupting or negating the preventive or curative value of the specific regimen, or indirectly, by disrupting the patient-provider interaction (Becker & Maiman, 1975).

Although hard data are difficult to offer, most authorities have argued that noncompliance severely compromises the full benefit of the treatment protocol, and as such it frequently results in an inefficient utilization of our entire health care system. There is a good deal of speculation (but little available documentation) that a substantial proportion of present day health care costs could be significantly reduced by substantially improving patient compliance. Repeat outpatient visits, unnecessary hospitilizations to investigate unsuccessful treatment efforts, and the failure of prophylactic programs to prevent unwanted illness (e.g., cerebral vascular accidents secondary to longstanding uncontrolled hypertension) all contribute to increased health care expenditures.

Weinstein and Stason (1976) have offered a quite convincing argument, based upon a costs-benefits analysis of hypertension control, that funds allocated for improving adherence to antihypertensive regimens will produce a greater impact on reducing disability and/or death than will the same expenditures used for the detection and treatment of new cases. While most health care providers dislike defining patient care in monetary terms, Dunbar and Stunkard (1979) have pointed out that as cost-effectiveness analyses begin to be applied to more health care problems, the subject of adherence will become the focus of much attention.

Implied in what has been stated is the common error made by practicing clinicians that the originally offered treatment is somehow ineffective when in fact it could have been quite adequate had only the patient adhered to it. Clinicians either redouble their efforts by offering more (or newer) treatments (with their attendant costs) or the patient is subjected to additional investigative procedures with the hope of determining why the original treatment was ineffective. If the presenting problem persists, it is not uncommon for both patient and practitioner to become frustrated with each other with a subsequent termination of their association and a reinvestigation of the problem by a different clinician (Gillum & Barsky, 1974).

Finally, and most importantly for the clinical researcher, an inadequate appreciation of the importance of compliance can easily lead to gross misinterpretations of research results by which the effectiveness of various treatments are compared and contrasted. Feinstein (1976) cogently argues that compliance is a critical but often overlooked variable in clinical outcome studies. Researchers who ignore compliance, and thereby fail to control for it, significantly reduce the validity of their experimental results. A commonly cited example is where two drugs, A and B, are being compared in their effectiveness for treating a specific condition. If it so happens that the experimental group receiving drug A is less compliant (e.g., due to the drug's unappealing taste, more complex prescription schedule), then, even after controlling for spontaneous remissions, the results might suggest that drug A is actually less effective than drug B. One might erroneously conclude that this differential effectiveness was due to drug B's pharmacological superiority when in fact the difference was due to differing rates of compliance.

Similarly, if one ignores those subjects who fail to complete a research protocol (by definition noncompliers), then one may be seriously biasing subsequent results. In the same way, if, in studying a long-standing clinical condition (e.g., epilepsy), a prospective researcher uses only those patients who are continuing to seek health care services (a form of continued compliance) then the subject pool has been biased since noncompliant patients may well have already dropped out of treatment. A more detailed analysis of these and similar problems is offered by Feinstein (1976) and Goldsmith (1976).

Thus, it is apparent that noncompliance is a pervasive problem which often results in an inefficient utilization of health care services and an unnecessary increase in health care expenditures. The practicing clinician and the clinical researcher alike may erroneously conclude that therapeutic trials are ineffective when they fail to recognize, identify, and control for compliance.

Adherence: Definitions and Measurements

As with any problem that has been extensively researched, the operational definitions of compliance vary considerably across investigations. These definitional differences usually reflect the varied prescriptive and proscriptive behaviors under study (e.g., taking medication, dieting, exercising). In evaluating the degree to which patients keep follow-up appointments subsequent to episodic emergency room care, an investigator might simply count the proportion of office visits kept. On the other hand pounds-lost-to-date and skin caliper measures may be the best compliance criteria for a weight control program involving diet and physical exercise. Since a good deal of the present compliance literature involves the appropriate taking of medications, the various measures of medication compliance are critically examined.

This section addresses the myriad ways that compliance has been clinically and/or experimentally assessed. The use of provider predictions, patient self-report, medication measurements, clinical outcome, direct chemical analysis, and medication monitors are all examined. Each assessment technique will be seen to have individual strengths and limitations.

Provider Prediction

When asked what proportion of their patients complied with their medical directives, 42% of the responding physicians in one study claimed that almost all of their patients adhered. Another 47% said that three-fourths of their patients were cooperative (Davis, 1966). When these figures are contrasted with the high rates of noncompliance cited earlier (Marston, 1970), it is not surprising to learn that physicians and other health care providers are poor predictors of who among their patients will comply. A number of studies have suggested that providers generally underestimate rate of noncompliance in their practice and, even more importantly, that they are inaccurate in their attempts to identify noncompliers (Caron & Roth, 1968; Charney, 1972; Davis, 1966; Kasl, 1975; Moulding, Onstad, & Sbarbaro, 1970).

Mushlin and Appel (1977) sought to test the clinical ability of medical interns and residents to predict patient compliance. Return for follow-up appointments and taking prescribed medications were the two sets of patient behaviors under investigation. Chart reviews and pill counts were the objective criteria against which physician predictions were compared. Although they were able to predict visit compliance better than chance, the physicians were able to accurately predict only 35% of the noncompliers. In predicting medication compliance they fared even worse with three-fourths of their predictions of noncompliance being inaccurate. That health care professionals are generally inaccurate in their predictions and/or assessments of compliance has been demonstrated elsewhere (McClellan & Cowan, 1970; Paulson, Krause, & Iber, 1977).

Patient Self-Report

Because it is simple, fast, and inexpensive the clinician may be apt to use the patient's self-report as one method of assessing compliance. A number of studies evaluating medication compliance have attempted to document the accuracy of interview data by comparing it against more objective data (e.g., pill counts, urine samples, blood tests). The results of these studies are varied, with some demonstrating a good correspondence between self-report and more objective measure (Feinstein, Wood, Epstein, Taranta, Simpson, & Tursky, 1959; Francis, Korsch, & Morris, 1969). Other reports suggest fairly large discrepancies between self-reported compliance and compliance measured by more objective means (Park & Lipman, 1964; Paulson *et al.* 1977; Preston & Miller, 1964; Sheiner, Rosenberg, Marathe, & Peck, 1974). Gordis (1976) has suggested that it is unusual for complying patients to misrepresent themselves as noncompliers and those patients who report themselves as noncompliant are most likely being truthful. The problem is one of correctly identifying the noncompliant patient who claims to have complied. For that degree of identifying accuracy the researcher and/or clinician must employ one or all of the following methods.

Dunbar & Stunkard (1979) have noted that a large number of patients will accurately predict their own noncompliance. Thus, while self-report may be an unreliable index of earlier adherence, clinicians might do well to directly ask their patients to predict their expected compliance in order to identify high risk nonadherers.

Medication Measurements

A simple, inexpensive, and relatively fast way to assess compliance is to measure the remaining amounts of the prescribed medication. Directly counting pills or tablets, measuring and/or weighing liquid solutions, counting empty medication bottles, and checking refill prescription practices have all been employed to inferentially measure adherence. This has involved the inference that absent medication was in fact taken as prescribed. If not enough medication has been used, then direct medication measurements will accurately identify that subgroup of noncompliers who have refused or forgotten to take their medicine. If, however, an appropriate amount of medication is absent, one still does not know whether it was appropriately used or simply discarded. Even if one simply assumes that the medication has been used (Christensen, 1978), it must still be established that it was used correctly (i.e., accurate dosages, proper intervals, or specifically following instruction, e.g., "one tablet to be taken ½ hour before meals"). Roth and Berger (1960) measured the amount of antacid used by hospitalized ulcer patients by regularly collecting the unused medication. The 75 ulcer patients who had been instructed to medicate themselves daily with bedside antacids took less than half of the medicine prescribed.

In a two-year follow-up study of 105 peptic ulcer patients, Roth, Caron, and Bartholomew (1970) evaluated the adequacy of a similar measurement technique by comparing bottle counts with blood bromide levels (sodium bromide had been added to the liquid antacid as a tracer). Using rigorous controls, the results of this study demonstrated a moderately high degree of correspondence between bottle count and drug tracer measures ($r = .80$). For 10 patients the absence of appropriate elevations in blood bromide strongly suggested that they were not taking as much medication as their bottle counts had indicated. For this group, nearly 10% of the population sampled, bottle counts were completely misleading.

Multiple counts have occasionally been employed in assessing compliance. In one 18-month study of arthritic patients, repeat medication counts showed that one-quarter of the evaluated patients were in error by more than 25% of their recommended dosage for more than half of the observation periods (Nugent, Ward, MacDiarmid, McCall, Baukol, & Tyler, 1965).

Gordis (1976) has concluded that the comparative data on the validity of pill counts suggest that directly measuring remaining medication usually results in an overestimation of compliance. This situation is most likely worsened when the prescribed medication is of a type that might be used by other family members (e.g., analgesics, minor tranquilizers, or common antibiotics).

Although pill counts present serious drawbacks for the methodologically conscientious researcher, the practicing clinician may still want to employ this simple assessment strategy while keeping in mind its obvious limitations. It goes without saying that proscriptive treatments are usually not amenable to this approach.

Clinical Outcome

It is obviously tempting to view the patient's improved clinical condition as a clear indication of compliance. A closer analysis, however, may reveal the common logical fallacy of *post hoc ergo propter hoc,* or the fallacy of false cause (Copi, 1961). Clinical improvement, or successful prevention, may in fact be due to extraneous variables and the spontaneous remission of an acute illness that would have run its course despite any therapeutic intervention must always be considered. Patients are frequently encouraged to try multiple treatments (by both professional and nonprofessional "healers") so that it is often difficult to accurately determine which, if any, of the treatment protocols was responsible for the observed improvement (Gordis, 1976).

Even in what might seem to be the obvious case of antihypertensive therapy, the patient's lowered blood pressure might easily be due to changes in work, dietary alterations, decreased interpersonal discord, learning deep muscle relaxation, or any combination of these. Finally, Gordis (1976) has argued that, even if a direct relationship between compliance and outcome were determined, the nature of that relationship would still require clarification and elaboration. Is the relationship linear, bimodal, curvilinear, or exponential?

Perhaps even more importantly, Sackett (1976) notes that we cannot assume that faithful compliance guarantees achievement of the treatment goals (curative and/or preventive). For, in addition to variations in physiology patients may be the unwitting victims of clinical timidity or diagnostic inaccuracy.

Except perhaps for those behavioral interventions in which treatment effects can be manipulated through ABA reversal designs, clinical outcome may not be a valid or reliable index of patient compliance.

Direct Chemical Analysis

In evaluating medication compliance direct measures might include determining the blood levels of the prescribed drug (or its metabolite) or measuring urinary excretion of either the medication or a metabolic byproduct. Where neither the medication nor its byproducts can be easily detected, a marker or tracer substance can be added to the medication. Markowitz & Gordis (1968), for example, were able to detect penicillin which had been prescribed for the maintenance of prophylaxis in rheumatic fever patients by applying urine dipped filter paper to an agar plate freshly streaked with an organism that is extremely sensitive to penicillin (*Sacrina lutea*). Compliant patients could easily be identified since they would have penicillin in their urine which when introducted on to the agar plate via the filter paper would inhibit the growth of the organism.

Using drug excretion tests, noncompliance rates have ranged from 4% for a group of tuberculosis outpatients (Fox, 1958) to 92% for children being treated for streptoccocal infections with oral penicillin (Bergman & Werner, 1963). Of critical importance in devising and utilizing such assessment techniques is the excretion pattern of the drug, metabolite, or tracer being detected (Gordis, 1976). A negative test may simply indicate that the drug has been rapidly excreted and therefore can no longer be detected, whereas a positive test only guarantees that the medication was ingested within the excretion time range saying nothing about before or after this interval. A number of strategies have been employed to deal with this problem. Theoretically, repeated measures for a drug, metabolite, or marker ought to provide a more reliable and valid assessment of patient compliance (Marston, 1970). While this may be true, it often further complicates the interpretation of the results since repeated testings may actually have a reactive effect on the compliance behavior under study. This is especially true where the use of a urine tracer alters the urine in such a way so as to be obvious to the patient (Gordis, 1976).

Although chemical analysis might appear to be the most objective measure of compliance (at least in terms of drug ingestion), it is still difficult to accurately compare compliance rates between studies. In large part, this is due to the varying definitions of compliance that have been proposed. When only a single test is used, the tendency may be for the investigator to classify the patient on a dichotomous scale (i.e., complier versus noncomplier) without any gradations (Weintraub, Au, & Lasagna, 1973). When multiple test points are used, one can define various levels of compliance which, some studies have shown, may wax and wane throughout the course of treatment (Gordis & Markowitz, 1971). The setting in which the compliance test is conducted may also be of importance. However, at least one compliance study has demonstrated that urine samples collected at home did not significantly differ from samples collected within the hospital setting (Maddock, 1967).

Where continuous treatment is considered essential and where the clinician is suspicious of the patient's reliability, direct chemical analysis is still indicated. For example, by developing a breath test for carbon disulfide (a major excretion product of disulfiram) Paulson *et al.* (1977) were able to demonstrate that 35% of those alcoholics who had continued to attend an outpatient treatment program had not taken their medication in the previous 24 hours even though on interview they had insisted that they had.

Biochemical assessments of dietary adherence have also been utilized. For example, with antihyperlipidemic diets biochemical measurements are frequently employed to assess fatty acid changes in triglycerides, adipose tissue, red blood cells, and/or cholesterol esters (Bierenbaum, Fleischman, Raichelson, Hayton, & Watson, 1973; Bierenbaum, Green, Florin, Fleischman, & Caldwell, 1967; Miettenen, Turpeinen, Karvonen, Elosuo, & Paavilainen, 1972; Turpeinen, Miettenen, Karvonen, Roine, Pekkarinen, Lehtosuo, & Alivirta, 1968).

Smoking cessation protocols that previously were dependent upon self-report measures of therapeutic effectiveness are now able to use biochemical assays (e.g., carbon monoxide concentrations, thiocyanate analysis, urinary nicotine levels) as dependent measures of adherence (Paxton & Bernacca, 1979).

Similarly, the clinical assessment of whether the diabetic patient has *consistently* adhered to treatment can be made through an analysis of glycosylated hemoglobin. This assessment technique can provide the clinician with a retrospective measure of blood glucose levels for the previous 60–120 days (Sannella, 1978). Its use is particularly relevant in managing the noncompliant juvenile type diabetic who might only adhere to treatment just prior to medical evaluation.

Finally, in view of the previously noted difficulties associated with using treatment outcome as an index of compliance, chemical analyses have been compared with therapeutic effectiveness (Colcher & Bass, 1972). Three hundred children with streptococcal pharyngitis were randomly assigned to one of three treatment groups. Urine specimens provided a measure of compliance and were correlated with treatment results as defined by repeat throat cultures taken at 9 days, as well as 3 and 6 weeks after initial treatment. One group received an intramuscular injection of penicillin G procaine and penicillin G benzathine; a second group was given a 10-day course of oral penicillin phenoxymethyl (parents of these children received no specific instructions); a third group was prescribed the same oral penicillin as Group 2, but the parents were also provided specific counseling emphasizing the importance of taking the medication. Urine test results demonstrated that there was a statistically significant difference between Group 2 (oral penicillin without instructions) and the other two groups. Although throat cultures were not significantly different between the three groups, it is noteworthy that in terms of relapse rates, Group 2 was significantly more prone to develop reinfection. Thus, urine samples, alone or combined with repeat throat cultures, did not completely demonstrate the differential effectiveness of the treatment strategies studied.

In summary, direct biologic tests of compliance are often considered the most objective measures available, however, there are a number of methodological problems inherent in their use.

Medication Monitors

A most ingenious strategy for assessing medication compliance has been developed for those researchers who want to more objectively determine pill taking practices. Devices often referred to as medication monitors have been designed for this purpose. One particularly interesting medication monitor suitable for any long-term pill regimen (e.g., oral contraceptives) consists of a specially prepared dispenser which can hold the individually wrapped and date-labeled tablets in a stacked sequence (Moulding, 1971, 1979). A thin strip of paper-wrapped photographic film is placed inside the back of the dispenser. Within the dispenser, on top of the stacked medications, is a small uranium source and a spring to drive the source downward when each tablet is removed from the dispenser. As each tablet is removed the radioactive source moves downward creating a record of exposure dots on the film strip. When the dispenser is returned, the researcher can remove the strip and read the pattern of dots that has been produced. Removing the pills at steady regular intervals will produce a consistent pattern of equally dark spots.

Forgetting to remove the pills from the dispenser will cause an excessively dark spot to appear where the radioactive source was left to stand. The complete absence of spots on sections of the photographic strip suggests that multiple dosages were removed from the dispenser simultaneously. As with pill counts, the medication monitor cannot guarantee that the absent pills have been properly consumed. Used in one empirical study, the device was able to demonstrate that 31% of 122 tuberculosis patients took less than 70% of their medication for 1 month or more (Moulding *et al.*, 1970). More will be said about the medication monitor as a means of improving patient compliance later in this chapter.

Summarizing this section it is apparent that a number of approaches have been employed to define and measure compliance. The predictions and/or estimations of compliance by health care providers are usually inadequate. Patient self-report may be of limited value since overestimation of compliance is a frequent result of this approach. Like self-reports, measuring medication tends to overestimate compliance; however, it can be of value in identifying some subgroups of noncompliers. Frequent medication checks may have a reactive effect, thereby improving compliance, a problem more discomforting to the researcher than to the practicing clinician. Treatment outcome measures must be used with special caution in assessing compliance, for many extraneous variables may have accounted for the patient's improved condition. Direct observation is an ideal but often impractical strategy, while medication monitors have gained some recognition as an adjunctive compliance assessment tool.

Variables Influencing Compliance

Nearly all of the compliance research has been conducted with the expressed purpose of identifying those parameters which have a direct or indirect influence on compliance. As one might expect, variables being investigated usually reflect the theoretical orientation (or specific discipline) of the individual researcher. This section reviews the relevant factors that have been studied with the largest section being devoted to those psychosocial or sociobehavioral variables that are of particular importance to the medical psychologist. This section is arbitrarily subdivided into reviews of demographic characteristics, features of the treatment regimen, side effects, duration of treatment, cost, and psychosocial variables influencing compliance.

Demographic Characteristics

In a comprehensive analysis of dozens of studies that examined a variety of demographic variables (age, sex, education, socioeconomic status, occupational status, marital status, race, religion, and income) Haynes (1976a) found that very few studies supported any association between these demographic characteristics and compliance. For example, only 7 out of 36 studies reviewed suggested any relationship between age and compliance. Similarly, only 6 out of 31 studies found any association between sex and adherence. Haynes is quick to note, however, that most of these are clinic based, descriptive studies which by definition are following only those patients who have successfully entered the health care system and continue attendance. As was mentioned earlier, this may have introduced a sample bias which community based prospective studies must address. While most reviewers are usually quick to disregard demographic factors as significantly influencing compliance (Blackwell, 1973; Gillum & Barsky, 1974; Marston, 1970; Matthews & Hingson, 1977; Stone, 1979), Haynes (1976a) has sounded a cautionary note worthy of careful consideration. Since most of the English compliance research has been conducted in the United States one must remain cognizant of the unique, and often inequitable, health care delivery system in this country. Utilization patterns vary substantially with respect to differing medical care systems, (e.g., accessibility, reimbursement). It may well be that demographic factors may exert a greater influence upon *access* to health services than upon compliance with therapy among patients who are already in the system. For example, education, income, and occupational status have been positively associated with preventive dental visits (Kriesberg & Treiman, 1960).

Demographic variables, when viewed within the context of a specific disease, may also prove helpful in predicting those patients who are more likely to be noncompliant. As an example, Gordis, Markowitz, and Lilienfeld (1969), in a study of 136 children on long-term antistreptococcal prophylaxis, were able to identify a specific constellation of factors related to noncompliance. When the patient was an adolescent female with a large sibship, had never been hospitalized for an acute attack of rheumatic fever, had suffered no restriction of daily activities, and had come to clinic visits unaccompanied by either parent, there was a substantially greater chance for noncompliance. When 4 or more risk factors were present, the probability of noncompliance was .90. Similarly, in an evaluation of compliance to immunosuppressive treatment following renal transplantation, Korsch, Fine, and Negrete (1978), using a stepwise discriminant analysis, were able to identify 13 of 14 noncompliant patients. Noncompliant patient families had lower income, were more often fatherless, and had communication difficulties within the family and with the medical establishment. Delay and noncompliance in cancer detection has also been found to be influenced by at least one social background variable, occupational status (Greenwald, Becker, & Nevitt, 1978). Using regression equations it was determined that occupational status combined with three items relating to contact in the health care system (listing a regular physician, having recently visited a physician, and being referred for follow-up by a health care provider) accounted for much of the variance in delay.

It may well be that demographic variables when viewed in isolation have very little if any descriptive or predictive value in understanding compliance. However, when these demographic characteristics are combined with other parameters they may prove helpful in delineating specific high risk patient profiles for specific diseases, specific screening programs, and specific treatment modalities. In this sense, demographic characteristics become part of a large interactionistic view of compliance and health care interventions in general (Ekehammar, 1974; Endler & Magnusson, 1976).

Features of the Treatment Regimen

The type, cost, complexity, side effects, and degree of behavioral change required of various therapeutic regimens are but a few of the features that have been studied in terms of adherence (Davis, 1967; Donabedian & Rosenfeld, 1964; Feinstein, Spagnuolo, Jonas, Levitt, & Tursky, 1966; Jenkins, 1954).

Complexity Haynes (1976a) has noted that the literature to date is fairly consistent in the finding that there is an inverse relationship between the amount of behavioral change required by a therapeutic regimen and measured patient adherence to the regimen. As therapies demand greater degrees of behavioral change compliance drops off precipitously. Treatments which require the termination of old and familiar habits require a degree of behavioral change that substantially reduces compliance (e.g., dieting, cessation of smoking, altering Type A behavior patterns). Treatments requiring the development of new behavioral patterns (e.g., regular exercising) also demand extensive alterations in lifestyle and therefore are generally complied with less than those treatments which, although new, are not as disruptive of the patient's everyday habits. Finally, short courses of therapy are usually considered easier to comply with, although, as noted earlier, even these treatments have alarmingly low compliance rates.

Many authors (and, as a result, many pharmaceutical companies) have extrapolated these general results to the specific question of whether single-dose medication regimens generate better compliance rates than do multiple-dose regimens. An a priori analysis would certainly lead one to deduce that taking one pill a day is easier than taking three or four pills a day. Unfortunately, no clinical studies have examined this question in an experimental fashion. In an excellent review of this issue, Haynes and his associates have concluded that the strategy of reducing the frequency of dosing merits formal empirical testing with proper consideration being given to the various factors that are already known to influence compliance rates (Haynes, Sackett, Taylor, Roberts, &

Johnson, 1977). In a similar vein, the authors caution clinicians against uncritically accepting and endorsing manufacturers' promotions stating that combination products (multiple medication in a single tablet) automatically improve compliance. While this may be true the ultimate question awaits verification through experimentation.

Side Effects Another logical assumption made by clinicians and reflected in pharmaceutical advertising is that drug side effects are a primary, or at least common, cause of nonadherence. Surprisingly, several studies which have attempted to assess patients' reasons for dropping out of treatment and/or other forms of noncompliance have demonstrated that side effects ranked low on lists of stated reasons (Bergman & Werner, 1963; Charney, Bynum, Eldredge, Frank, MacWhinney, McNabb, Scheiner, Sumpter, & Iker, 1967; Hogarty & Goldberg, 1973; Ireland, 1960; McKenny, Slining, Henderson, Devins, & Barr, 1973). Even more noteworthy is the finding of the Veterans' Administration Cooperative Study on Antihypertensive Agents (1972) that there was no difference in reported side effect frequency between the actively treated group and the placebo group. Side effects in both groups were reported at an incidence of only 7% with virtually identical distribution between active treatment and placebo. These results and others have prompted Haynes *et al.* (1977) to conclude that medication side effects are not that prominent and that even when side effects do occur patients do not rate them as major reasons for noncompliance.

Duration of Treatment Haynes (1976a), in a review of 11 studies which compared compliance with varying durations of treatment, concluded that generally speaking, adherence decreases as therapy continues. This conclusion must be tempered somewhat by the observation that many, if not most long-term treatments, are for asymptomatic diseases (e.g., hypertension) or are prophylactic in nature (e.g., rheumatic fever, epilepsy, tuberculosis). One might argue that it is this feature of the disease and not simply the extended course of treatment that contributes to nonadherence.

Cost Finally, surprisingly few studies have investigated the cost of therapy as it relates to compliance. Two studies have found a negative correlation between cost and adherence (Alpert, 1964; Donabedian & Rosenfeld, 1964) whereas a third found no significant relationship (Maddock, 1967).

In summary, it may be concluded that treatment regimens that require extensive alterations of the patient's lifestyle pose serious compliance problems. While it may seem reasonable to expect that less frequent dosages of medication ought to improve compliance, this has yet to be established experimentally. Long-term treatments are generally associated with poorer compliance although this may be partially due to the asymptomatic nature of the disease or the prophylactic orientation of the regimen. Side effects may have little to do with compliance, whereas the relationship between cost of treatment and compliance remains open to investigation.

Psychosocial Variables Influencing Compliance

The general rubric of psychosocial variables is subdivided into four sections, each of which represents a general category of research variables that have been studied in relation to compliance. Although the four parts that compose this section are dealt with individually, in the real world of both clinical practice and research, no such artifical divisions are practical or warranted. The reader is encouraged to view these separate categories simply as a means by which a literature review is facilitated. The four sections include the patient–provider interaction, information–education, behavioral and environmental factors, and finally, the Health Belief Model.

The Patient–Provider Interaction In a recent review Stone (1979) has argued that the interaction between the patient and the health care provider is extremely important with respect to subsequent compliance. It is certainly noteworthy that the issue of the *Journal of Social Issues* in which his article appears is devoted to and entitled "Interpersonal Relations in Health Care" (DiMatteo & Friedman, 1979). A social-psychological analysis of the patient-provider interaction (DiMatteo, 1979), the social power of health care providers as change agents (Rodin & Janis, 1979), and the nonverbal communications between patients and medical practitioners (Friedman, 1979) have all become pertinent behavioral science topics. Unlike the demographic variables considered earlier, the patient-provider interaction system is not an immutable given and as such might well represent the most reasonable and promising intervention point in attempts to improve compliance. Two basic aspects of the patient-provider interaction are important. First, the accuracy with which the patient can recall the provider's directives certainly is a necessary, but not sufficient, element for compliance. This is sometimes referred to as the effectiveness of the patient-provider communication system (Stone, 1979). Secondly, the emotional tone or impact of the interaction may dramatically influence the patient's willingness to adhere to the treatment proposed.

Ley has offered a comprehensive review of the psychological aspects of the patient-physician interaction particularly as this interpersonal system requires the sharing of technical information (Ley, 1977). Ley and Spelman (1967), in a study of three series of medical outpatients, found that within 10 to 80 min of seeing their physicians, the patients could not recall approximately 40% of what they were told. Boyd *et al.* (1974) found that over 60% of patients in their study misunderstood their physician's directives concerning prescribed medications. Even when patients are sincere in their desire to adhere to a regimen, they may vary their medication usage beyond that directed by the physician. For example, the written instruction "Take with meals" can easily be interpreted to be taken before, during, or after one has eaten (Mazzulo, Lasagna, & Griner, 1974). Depending upon the purpose for which the medication has been prescribed (e.g., as an aid in food absorption, as an antacid, as an appetite stimulant or suppressant), variations in medication ingestion might adversely affect the therapeutic effectiveness of the clinical trial.

In another study, Ley, Bradshaw, Eaves, and Walker (1973) showed that general practice patients had forgotten 50% of the statements made to them within less than 5 min of seeing their physician. To make matters worse, a patient analogue study (Ley, 1972) has suggested that individuals are more likely to forget instructions and advice whereas statements regarding diagnosis are remembered best. The differential forgetting of instructions and advice may well have been due to the fact that physicians often place these at the end of their consultation with the patient, for previously published reports have shown that there is a strong primacy effect for the retention of medical information (Ley, 1972). Additionally, and somewhat surprisingly, one study has suggested that laymen are prone to consider instructions and advice to be less important than other medical information (Ley, 1969) which may further diminish recall. At least one empirical test has established improved recall when the practitioner deliberately introduced medical instructions by stressing their importance (Ley, 1966). Other studies have demonstrated that specific instructions are more readily remembered than general rules and that phrasing the instructions in easy to understand nontechnical language facilitates recall (Bradshaw, Ley, Kincey, & Bradshaw, 1975). For a more detailed analysis of these and similar results the interested reader is referred to Ley's comprehensive review (Ley, 1977).

To summarize, the clinician should emphasize the importance of instructions and advice, and should speak in easy to understand language. Lastly, it would be helpful to determine if the patient has clearly received the intended communication by having the patient briefly reiterate the provider's directives. Svarstad (1976) found that patients who had a completely accurate recollection of the physician's expectations conformed to them three times as frequently as those who made one or more errors in recollection.

While the patient's ability to recall relevant facts presented by the provider may influence compliance, the affective elements of the patient-provider interaction may also exert a powerful influence on patient adherence. Within the past decade a tremendous interest in the patient-provider interaction system has generated a number of empirical studies relating this dyadic system to the problem of patient compliance (Davis, 1968a; Francis *et al.*, 1969; Freeman, Negrete, Davis, & Korsch, 1971; Korsch, Gozzi, & Francis, 1968; Korsch & Negrete, 1972; Stimson, 1974; Vincent, 1971). Davis (1968a) employing the Bales (1951) Interaction Process Analysis Categories coded over 200 patient-physician interactions. Although Davis could find no relationship between the specific interactive process of the first patient encounter and later compliance, he did find that the patient was less likely to comply when later interactions were characterized by a negative social-emotional tone. This was frequently manifested by the patient displaying antagonism toward the physician, who simultaneously appeared to withdraw from the interaction. As with all correlational studies, it may be somewhat presumptuous to infer causality from these data. Nevertheless, findings such as these are for the most part supported by other studies as well.

Francis *et al.* (1969), for example, conducted a study involving 800 pediatric outpatient visits to determine what, if any, relationship might exist between the patient-physician verbal interaction and subsequent patient satisfaction and follow-through on medical advice received. Open-ended interviewing revealed that 24% of the mothers were grossly dissatisfied with the care their children had received. Mothers were most dissatisfied when their expectations about the medical visit remained unmet, when they perceived a lack of warmth in their interaction with the physician, and when they failed to receive an explanation of the diagnosis and cause of their child's illness. Thirty-eight percent of the patients were judged to be compliant (primarily determined by interview) and 11% noncompliant (42% were rated as highly compliant and 8% received no treatment regimen). Most importantly in terms of the present discussion, there was a significant positive correlation between patient satisfaction and compliance. Hippocrates, writing in the fourth century, B.C., apparently reached the same conclusion when he wrote "the patient, though conscious that his condition is perilous may recover his health simply through his contentment with the goodness of the physician [1923, Jones trans.]."

DiMatteo (1979) has cogently argued that adequate empirical evidence has been accumulating in the behavioral sciences which, if properly synthesized and adapted, could be scientifically applied to the training of health care professionals to develop and nuture more effective socioemotional relationships with their patients. Detecting the affective components of verbal and nonverbal communication and being able to adequately communicate genuine caring and concern are essential skills for the health care provider (DiMatteo, 1979; Friedman, 1979; Friedman & DiMatteo, 1979; Rodin & Janis, 1979). Although a number of training programs are presently being utilized with the aim of helping providers culture and develop better interpersonal communication skills (DiMatteo, 1979; Kagan, 1974; McGuire, 1976; Werner & Schneider, 1974), the present reviewer is unaware of any prospective study which has demonstrated the longitudinal effectiveness of improved patient-provider communication on patient compliance.

Haynes (1976a) has suggested that the patient's attitude toward health professionals *in general* and the health care system *as a whole* do not appear to be correlated with compliance. Thus, what appears to be important is the patient's affective response to the individual health provider, not toward health professionals as a group.

Finally, it would seem reasonable to assume that patients would comply better with advice received from providers who have given them regular care. Although a number of authors have suggested that clinician continuity fosters improved patient compliance (Alpert, 1964; Becker, Drachman, & Kirscht, 1972; Becker & Maiman, 1975; Caldwell, Cobb, Dowling & deJongh, 1970), most of these observations do not have the advantage of well controlled methodologies. Surprisingly, one of the only prospective studies evaluating the importance of continuity of care failed to demonstrate any significant difference in patient compliance between traditional clinic care and comprehensive continuous care (Gordis & Markowitz, 1971).

In conclusion, there is a fairly consistent finding that patients' stated degree of satisfaction with their interaction with the health professional correlates with subsequent compliance. Health professionals would be wise to develop those interpersonal skills necessary to detect, acknowledge, reflect, and interpret the affective content of the patient's verbal and nonverbal communications. The fact that nearly all of the studies reviewed here are correlational investigations makes it difficult to infer direct causality with any degree of confidence. Prospective studies are needed wherein patient-provider interactions can be experimentally manipulated and longitudinal compliance empirically assessed.

Information-Education: Effects on Patient Adherence It could be argued that the content of the information received by the patient from the provider is inherent in the patient-provider interaction. It is treated separately in this chapter for two reasons. The first reason follows from the observation that patients frequently acquire information and knowledge regarding their disease from sources other than the health care provider. Friends, family members, lay publications, and the mass media in general are all viable, if not entirely accurate, sources of health information for the patient (Masur, 1979). Second, due to tremendous time demands, many providers have resorted to what might be called noninteractive educational approaches. Professionally prepared pamphlets, books, films, video and audio tapes, etc., are often used by the busy clinician as time and cost efficient ways to educate the patient; these strategies often require little or no patient-provider interaction. Even though it is more appropriately considered a sociodemographic variable, let us briefly consider the question of whether the patient's formal educational level is in any way related to compliance. As was mentioned earlier, Haynes (1976a), after reviewing 30 separate compliance studies in which educational level was assessed, found that only 8 studies (36%) showed any positive association between the patients formal educational level and subsequent compliance. Twenty-two studies (64%) found no association between educational level and adherence. Similarly, a number of studies have failed to demonstrate any clear association between patient intelligence and subsequent compliance (Finnerty, Mattie, & Finnerty, 1973; Hare & Wilcox, 1967; Lund, Jorgenson, & Kuhl, 1964; Wilcox, Gillan, & Hare, 1965; Winokur, Czaczkes, & Kaplan de-Nour, 1973). Although the profoundly retarded child or adult would undoubtedly be unable to adhere to anything but the simplest of regimens without close supervision, the fact remains that for the most part no relationship has been established between estimated or measured intelligence and compliance. Practitioners might look askance at these results since many clinicians intuitively endorse the position that the brighter the patient the better compliance. As our discussion continues we shall see that, even with respect to the patient's knowledge and understanding of the disease in question, there is almost no support for this position.

Although it is clear that patients must know what recommendations have been made before they can begin to appropriately adhere to the provider's instructions (Hulka, Cassel, Kupper, & Burdette, 1976; Linkewich, Catalano, & Flack, 1974), it has not been conclusively established that patients' knowledge about their illness or their understanding about the rationale for the treatment regimen enhances compliance (Haynes, 1976a; Kasl, 1975; Marston, 1970; Matthews & Hingson, 1977).

Although some studies have demonstrated a positive relationship between adherence and the patients' understanding of the disease and/or therapy (Elling, Whittemore, & Green, 1960; Latiolais & Berry, 1969; Marsh & Perlman, 1972; Watkins, Williams, Martin, Hogan, & Anderson, 1967), many other investigations have failed to demonstrate any correspondence between knowledge and compliance (Bergman & Werner, 1963; Evans, Rozelle, Lasater, Dembroski, & Allen, 1970; Gordis *et al.*, 1969; Malahy, 1966; Suchman, 1967; Vincent, 1971; Weintraub *et al.*, 1973). Haynes (1976a) also concluded that those studies demonstrating no relationship between knowledge and compliance were more methodologically sound than were those which had suggested such a relationship. In fact one study found a significant *negative* relationship between knowledge of the name of the prescribed medication and compliance (McKercher & Rucker, 1977).

Furthermore, those studies which have attempted to improve compliance by providing more information about the illness have often failed to do so (Billie, 1975; Sackett, Haynes, Gibson, Taylor, Roberts, & Johnson, 1977; Tagliacozzo, Luskin, Lashof, & Ima, 1974). Haynes (1976a) and Stone (1979) both have noted that these results are at variance with conventional wisdom and common sense by which most clinicians have generally assumed that improved compliance would automatically result from increasing patients' formal knowledge about their illnesses.

These results must be viewed with caution since patients' perceptions of their illnesses (in terms of perceived susceptibility, severity, etc.) do have important implications for compliance. Thus, although formal knowledge of the disease may not relate to compliance, the interpretation and subjective evaluation of the formal knowledge obtained may influence adherence. Two further points warrant consideration. First, *knowledge* of the illness is not a unitary, easily quantified dimension and there are many discrepancies between investigators in how this factor is defined and measured. Using an example cited earlier (Case #1), it may be of limited value, in terms of improving compliance, for a mother to know the pathogenesis of otitis media. However, it may be of paramount importance for her to understand that the remission of the child's overt symptoms does not mark the end of the child's infection. Thus, *knowledge of etiology* might be a poor predictor of subsequent compliance whereas *understanding the disease's course* might very well prompt continued compliance. Therefore, further research may need to elaborate upon the content of the knowledge base against which compliance is compared.

Additionally, one should not use improved compliance as the sole criterion against which patient education is based, or for which patient education is used. Patients as active agents in their own care must be considered and patient education as a prerequisite for a health care model of mutual participation (Szasz & Hollender, 1956) is, in this author's view, absolutely essential. A more detailed analysis of various patient-provider contractual systems has been provided by Stone (1979).

The studies reviewed in this section suggest that patients' formal knowledge regarding their illnesses does not significantly correlate with, predict, or guarantee improved compliance. These results have important implications for health care delivery; however, one must use caution in interpreting these results since knowledge of the illness is not a unitary concept nor has it been operationally defined or measured with any degree of consistency. It is also argued that the worth of patient education should not be gauged by its compliance effect alone and that educating patients is a sine qua non for a patient-provider interaction system which values mutual participation.

Behavioral and Environmental Factors Kasl (1975) has suggested that poor adherence to treatment regimens may be due to a number of variables operating in the patient's social environment. This analysis is essentially consistent with the traditional behavioral viewpoint (Gentry, 1977) that a specific behavior (compliance) is primarily a function of the environmental events which preceed it (antecedents), and those which follows it (consequences). Zifferblatt (1975) has further speculated that a careful functional analysis of compliance can delineate those specific environmental "cues" (both internal and external) which might prompt the patient to take action. The latency and specificity of the consequences that accrue from this action are also included in his analysis. Thus, the patient who is experiencing a particular set of disturbing symptoms (specific proprioceptive cues) who self-administers a treatment (e.g., antacid for upset stomach) may get fairly rapid relief (negative reinforcement, i.e., termination of an aversive stimulus contingent upon behavior) and therefore will be more likely to repeat the same behavior in the future. However, the patient who remains asymptomatic (e.g., a hypertensive) who has no clearly established environmental or proprioceptive cues to "trigger" medication taking behavior, and who receives no reinforcing consequences for such behavior is much less likely to comply. Zifferblatt also notes that the "salience" or degree to which the antecedents and consequences are significant and meaningful to the patient is important, as well as their compatibility, or the degree to which these events can be readily accommodated in the patient's life.

Antecedent cues which are highly salient, compatible, provide a short latency between the cue and triggered behavior, and are explicit to the behavior in question, all contribute to improved results. It should be noted, however, that Zifferblatt provides only anecdotal support for his behavioral analysis position.

Two earlier analogue studies lend limited support to behavioral techniques to improve compliance. Azrin & Powell (1969) developed a portable operant apparatus based upon the techniques of response priming and escape reinforcement. At the time a pill was to be taken, the small pill box apparatus automatically sounded a tone. When a knob was turned to terminate the tone the pill box delivered a pill into the experimental subject's hand. The apparatus was studied using a medically inert pill with six normal subjects. Each subject acting as her own control was also exposed to other "devices," one a simple pill container to be used in conjunction with the subject's wristwatch and the second an alarm timer set to give a fixed duration 3-sec signal. Each subject used each of the three devices for 4 days. The sequence of administering each device was counterbalanced for each subject. Inert pills were to be taken every one-half hour between 8:45 a.m. and 4:15 p.m. Self-report and independent recordings of participating observers demonstrated that each subject missed significantly fewer pills while using the experimental dispenser. The mean percentage of pills missed was 3% for the experimental dispenser, 11% for the alarm apparatus, and 16% for the simple container. Although the authors concluded that their results provide support for the use of such an apparatus, they fail to mention the artificiality of taking inert pills 16 times per day! The claimed utility and practicality of such an apparatus awaits further clinical study.

Although the use of behavioral techniques in the treatment of an assortment of physical disorders has begun to gain wide acceptance (Masur, 1977), the behavioral analysis and treatment of noncompliance is still in its infancy (Dunbar & Stunkard, 1979; Gentry, 1977). A recent analogue study has attempted to extend the use of response cost and other behavioral approaches to outpatient drug compliance (Epstein & Masek, 1978), token economy systems have been effectively utilized to enhance the dietary compliance of renal dialysis patients (Barnes, 1976; Magrab & Papadopoulou, 1977), and contingency management techniques have been successfully employed to improve adherence to a complex medical regimen (Dapcich-Miura & Hovell, 1979). Contingency contracting (DeRisi & Butz, 1975) also has been used to help patients learn more about their disease and to improve compliance with follow-up outpatient visits.

By employing response cost, response priming, contingency contracting, and more elaborate token economy systems the clinician might well be able to affect improvements in adherence. However, as the next section demonstrates, the patient's belief system and cognitive strategies also play an important role in compliance. A more comprehensive approach to compliance including cognitive-behavioral concepts and self-management techniques needs to be developed (Bandura, 1974; Foreyt & Rathjen, 1978; Mahoney & Arnkoff, 1978; Mahoney & Thoresen, 1974; Meichenbaum, 1977).

The Health Belief Model (HBM) A considerable number of compliance studies have been reviewed thus far. Almost without exception these investigations, in their descriptive and correlational analyses, have not evolved from, nor are they based upon, any well formulated conceptual theory regarding compliance behavior. It therefore is frequently difficult to compare and contrast results, and in the absence of a theoretical map by which to guide and direct research efforts, a fair amount of extraneous, redundant, and perhaps irrelevant data have emerged.

In marked contrast to such haphazard experimentation, the last two decades have witnessed the development of an elegant, albeit incomplete, social-psychological model which attempts to describe, explain, and predict the health actions of individuals. From a social-psychological perspective, behavior can in large part be predicted from an individual's expectations that a given action will produce an outcome which in turn is perceived as possessing a specific value. Drawing upon dynamic personality theory (Lewin, 1935), the initial formulation of such a value-expectancy model was developed by Rosenstock (1966) to explain preventive health behavior. Later, as we shall see, the model was expanded to describe and explain sick-role behaviors including compliance. Time and space do not permit an in-depth review of the Health Belief Model. Interested readers are strongly encouraged to peruse a number of excellent reviews (Becker & Maiman, 1975; Kasl & Cobb, 1966a, 1966b), especially the Health Education Monographs devoted to "The Health Belief Model and Personal Health Behavior" (Becker, 1974).

In its original form the Health Belief Model (HBM) contained the following elements (see Figure 23.1): (*a*) the individual's readiness to take action with respect to a particular health action; this subjective state is determined by both the perceived likelihood of susceptibility to the particular illness in question, and the individual's perception of the probable severity of the consequences of contracting the disease; (*b*) the individual's subjective appraisal of the advocated health behavior in terms of its feasibility, availability, and efficaciousness; this critical costs-benefits analysis involves the individual's weighing the health action's potential benefits in reducing susceptibility and/or severity against perceived physical, psychological, financial, and other costs or barriers involved in the proposed action; (*c*) cues to action which are inter-

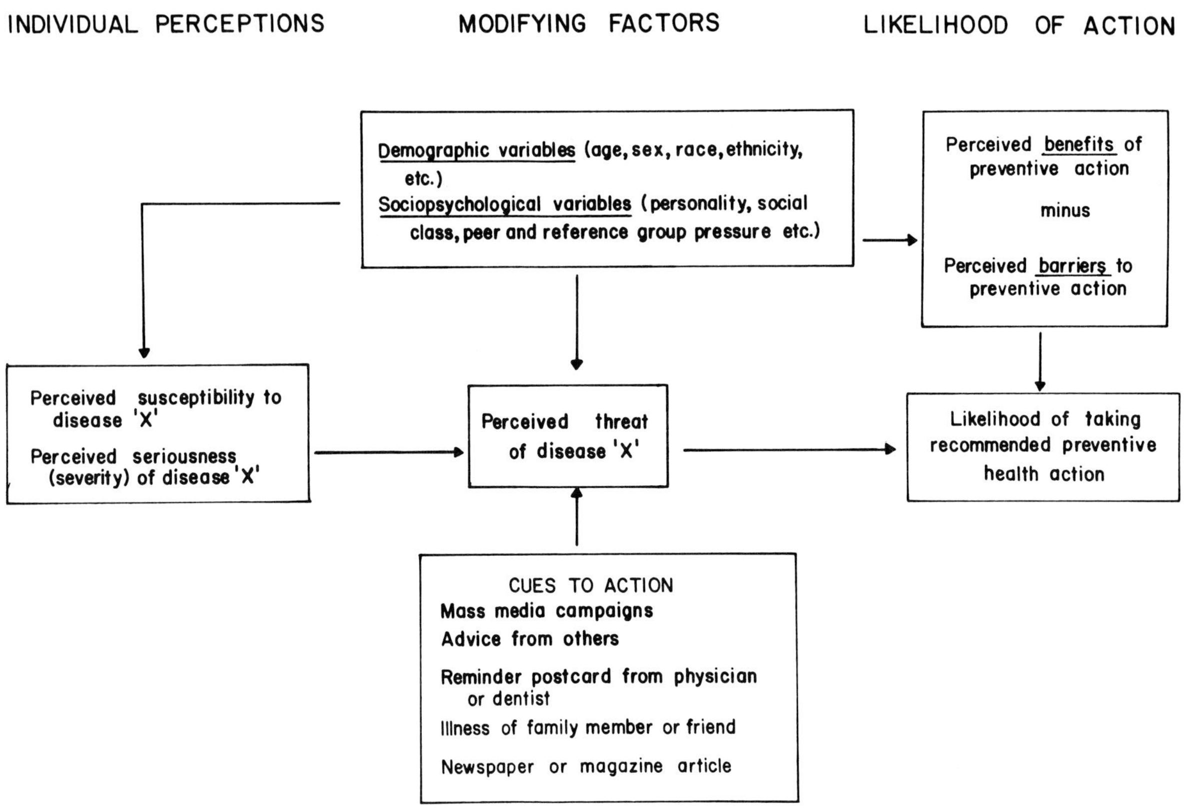

Figure 23.1. The original formulation of the Health Belief Model. (From "Sociobehavioral Determinants of Compliance with Health and Medical Care Recommendations" by M. H. Becker and L. A. Maiman, *Medical Care,* 1975, *13,* 10–14. Copyright © 1975. Reprinted with permission.)

nal stimuli (e.g., perceptions of bodily states) and/or external stimuli (e.g., mass media campaigns) which must occur to trigger the appropriate health behavior; and (*d*) various demographic, personality, structural and social factors which are viewed as modifying variables and as such are not considered as directly causal of specific health behaviors.

In their review and analysis of each of the model's components Becker and Maiman (1975) list six retrospective and four prospective studies of preventive health behaviors that have demonstrated positive correlations between relatively higher levels of perceived susceptibility and compliance. Individuals with higher levels of subjectively perceived vulnerability are more likely to obtain screenings for cervical (Kegeles, 1969), breast (Fink, Shapiro, & Roester, 1972) or other forms of cancer (Haefner & Kirscht, 1970); tuberculosis (Haefner & Kirscht, 1970; Hochbaum, 1958); heart disease (Haefner & Kirscht, 1970); Tay-Sachs disease (Kaback, Becker, & Ruth, 1974); and dental problems (Kegeles, 1963). As one might expect, persons who perceive themselves (or their dependents) as being susceptible to potentially avoidable illnesses are also more likely to engage in preventive health action such as obtaining immunizations (Leventhal, Hochbaum, & Rosenstock, 1960; Rosenstock, 1960; Rosenstock, Derryberry, & Carriger, 1959).

It was noted previously that no significant relationship exists between the medical severity of a disease and patient compliance. However, the HBM is not concerned with the "real" or medically evaluated seriousness of a disease but rather the patient's perceived appraisal of severity. Severity in this sense goes beyond the pathophysiology and potential physical complications of the illness to include the possible disruption of social patterns (e.g., loss of work, restricting activities, adverse economic consequences, stress on the family system). Heinzelmann (1962) found that the individual's assessment of the seriousness of rheumatic fever, in both an absolute sense and when compared against other diseases, was predictive of penicillin prophylaxis. Charney *et al.* (1967) concluded that mothers of children with streptococcal pharyngitis and otitis media were significantly more likely to continue the medication regimen if, at the outset, they perceive their child's illness to be severe. Becker *et al.* (1972, 1974) and Francis *et al.* (1969) have reported similar associations between perceived seriousness (organic severity and interference with activities) and compliance with both medication therapy and appointment keeping. The relationship between perceived severity and subsequent compliance is not a simple one, and may in fact be a "U" shaped curvilinear function (Hochbaum, 1958; Ley & Spelman, 1965). In any case perceived severity remains an essential element of this sociobehavioral model of compliance.

The likelihood of action element of the HBM is multidimensional in that it subsumes a variety of costs and benefits related to the health behavior in question as these are perceived by the individual. Elling *et al.* (1960) and Heinzelmann (1962) both demonstrated a significant positive correlation between the belief in the ability of pencillin to prevent the recurrence of rheumatic fever and adherence to the medication regimen. Becker *et al.* (1974) reported that "belief in efficacy of clinic medication" accurately predicted antibiotic use, and that "belief in doctors' ability to cure illness" was associated with keeping clinic appointments. Similarly, Donabedian and Rosenfeld (1964) found that patients who had "doubt about a recommended procedure" were more likely to disregard their physician's instructions. In terms of costs, if a treatment's safety is in question (Rosenstock *et al.*, 1959), if it is perceived with fear (e.g., anticipated pain; Kegeles, 1963), or if it is expensive (Alpert, 1964), patients are much less likely to comply. As discussed previously, the complexity, duration, and behavioral change required of a treatment protocol can all be considered potential "costs."

Becker (1974) has modified the HBM to incorporate more recent findings on health related behaviors (see Figure 23.2). The original model, based on a disease-avoidance orientation, did not adequately take into account positive health motivations and health behaviors. To address this deficiency the category health motivations was added to represent varying degrees of concern regarding health matters. Similarly, since the earlier model focused exclusively on an index condition,

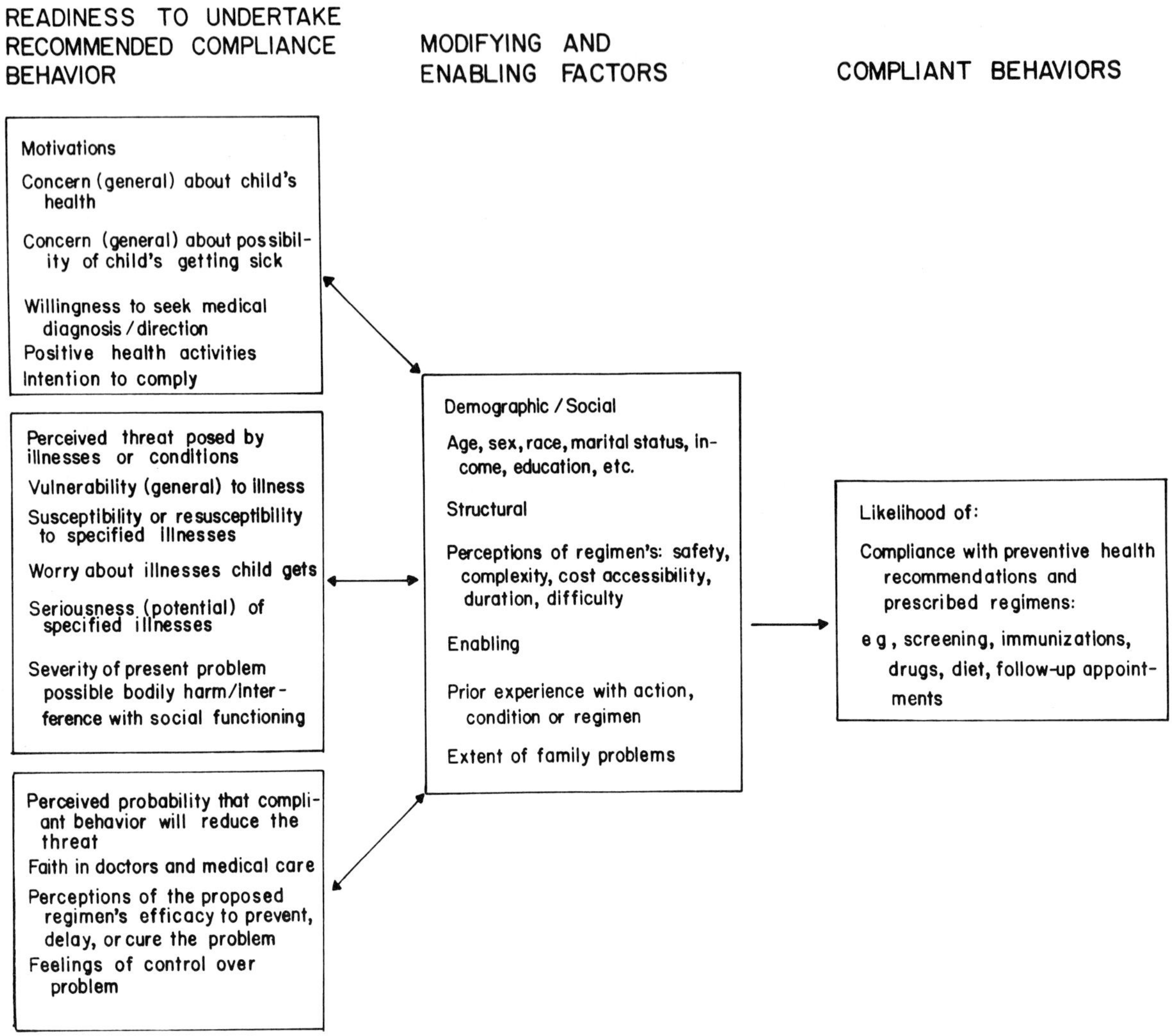

Figure 23.2. Hypothesized model for predicting and explaining mothers' compliance behaviors. (From "The Health Belief Model and Prediction of Dietary Compliance" by M. H. Becker, L. A. Maiman, J. P. Kirscht, D. P. Haefner, and R. H. Drachman, *Journal of Health and Social Behavior,* 1977, *18,* 348-366. Copyright © 1977. Reprinted with permission.)

more general measures of perceived vulnerability, overall confidence in health care providers, and general intention to comply were added. This last element is particularly relevant since one study has demonstrated that only 55% of interviewed patients stated that they even had any intention of complying with their physicians' directives (Davis, 1968b). It is unclear as to where the original cues to action component fits into this new schema or what the rationale might have been for its purposeful omission. More will be made of this point later, for "cueing" techniques form the basis of many of the behavioral strategies aimed at improving compliance.

In considering compliance behavior, Becker (1974) expanded the modifying and enabling factors to include the structural aspects of the treatment regimen (e.g., cost, duration, complexity, side effects, etc.) as well as the interaction elements of the patient-provider system (e.g., continuity, quality of dyadic relationship, etc.) Further, Becker and Maiman (1975) noted that interpretable and reliable relationships generally have been found to exist between compliance and severity, costs, and perception of susceptibility. This has been the case in a variety of circumstances and settings, and has involved differing health and medical care recommendations. Becker and Maiman also noted that

> Although no single effort has provided (or could provide) convincing confirmation of the HBM variables, most studies have produced internally consistent findings in the predicted direction, which taken together, yield relatively strong support for this conceptual model of compliance behavior [p. 17].

However, the HBM is not without its critics (Dunbar & Stunkard, 1979). It has been accurately noted that since most of the HBM studies are retrospective in design it is impossible to determine whether the health belief came before or after the health behavior. Correlational analyses do not support causal inferences, and the hypothesis that behavior is determined by a particular constellation of beliefs can only be adequately tested when the beliefs are known to have existed prior to the behavior that they are supposed to determine (Rosenstock, 1974). The decision to adhere or not adhere to a therapeutic regimen may in and of itself modify the patient's subsequent perception of the treatment through the mechanism of cognitive dissonance (Festinger, 1957). In this sense the mother who prematurely terminates her child's antibiotic therapy, if interviewed after the fact, may express the belief that the medication was only minimally effective. Without knowing her view regarding the medication prior to the initiation of therapy it would be erroneous to conclude that her belief caused her behavior when in fact cognitive dissonance theory would suggest that her behavior modified her belief. In fact, one study (Taylor, Sackett, & Haynes, 1978) indicated that beliefs were not predictive of compliance but that health beliefs expressed after treatment had begun were correlated with compliance levels.

Nevertheless, in a well controlled prospective experimental design (Becker, Maiman, Kirscht, Haefner, & Drachman, 1977), the HBM was evaluated in terms of its ability to predict and explain mothers' adherence to a diet prescribed for their obese children. The study also tested the efficacy of two levels of fear-arousing communication in improving compliance. Subjects ($N = 182$) were randomly assigned to one of three intervention groups: high fear, low fear, and control. Prior to any intervention a structured interview was conducted to gather sociodemographic characteristics, and to assess both general and obesity-specific attitudinal dimensions, health motivations, illness threat, perceived benefits of the diet, perceived barriers to compliance, and perceived control over health matters. Dependent measures included the child's weight over a two-month period and the mother's previous appointment-keeping behavior. Extensive statistical analyses that included multiple regression equations demonstrated significant correlations between each major dimension of the HBM and outcome measures.

To briefly summarize this section, the HBM, originally designed to explain preventive health behaviors has, after modification, demonstrated its usefulness in describing and explaining some illness behaviors including compliance. This social-psychological model places a heavy emphasis on cognitive factors as they relate to behavior. In this respect the model may be of tremendous heuristic value for a cognitive-behavioral approach to improving compliance. In its present form the model no longer incorporates a cues to action dimension which, in the opinion of this reviewer, needs to be reincorporated. Although the model has been criticized for its retrospective analysis, at least one study has demonstrated its prospective utility. It should be noted that the model as a theoretical construct cannot specify which elements are more amenable to change so as to optimize intervention strategies. Certainly some components are immutable givens (e.g., age, sex, race). However, it has yet to be empirically determined which elements or set of elements is the best intervention point (cf. Kirscht, 1974).

Finally, the HBM in both its original and modified form fails to include both the immediate and remote consequences that may result from engaging in the health behavior in question. Here is where a more traditional behavioral schema can be combined with the HBM, particularly when one considers ongoing behaviors such as continued compliance. (See Figure 23.3).

Figure 23.3 represents the present author's attempt to graft basic behavioral principles onto elements of the original and modified forms of the HBM. Readiness components consisting of general health motivations, the perceived value of the threatened illness, and the perceived probability that compliance will reduce threat compose the essential cognitive base from which adherence can develop. These components, along with the modifying and enabling factors, are essentially unchanged from Becker and Maiman's conceptualizations (see Figure 23.2). Using a behavioral analysis, however, those conditions (both internal and/or external) that immediately precede the compliance behavior are important antecedents which often serve as cues to action. These cues which had been identified in the original HBM are reintroduced here. Cues might be internally generated (e.g., feeling of physical discomfort) or they might be externally programmed (e.g., pill box buzzer). Finally, one needs to consider the direct and indirect consequences of engaging in the specific compliance behavior. Reinforcers vary in terms of their source and latency. Reinforcing events can be internal (e.g., pain relief) or external (e.g., social support), immediate (e.g., covert self-praise), or remote (e.g., decreased health costs). Thus, there

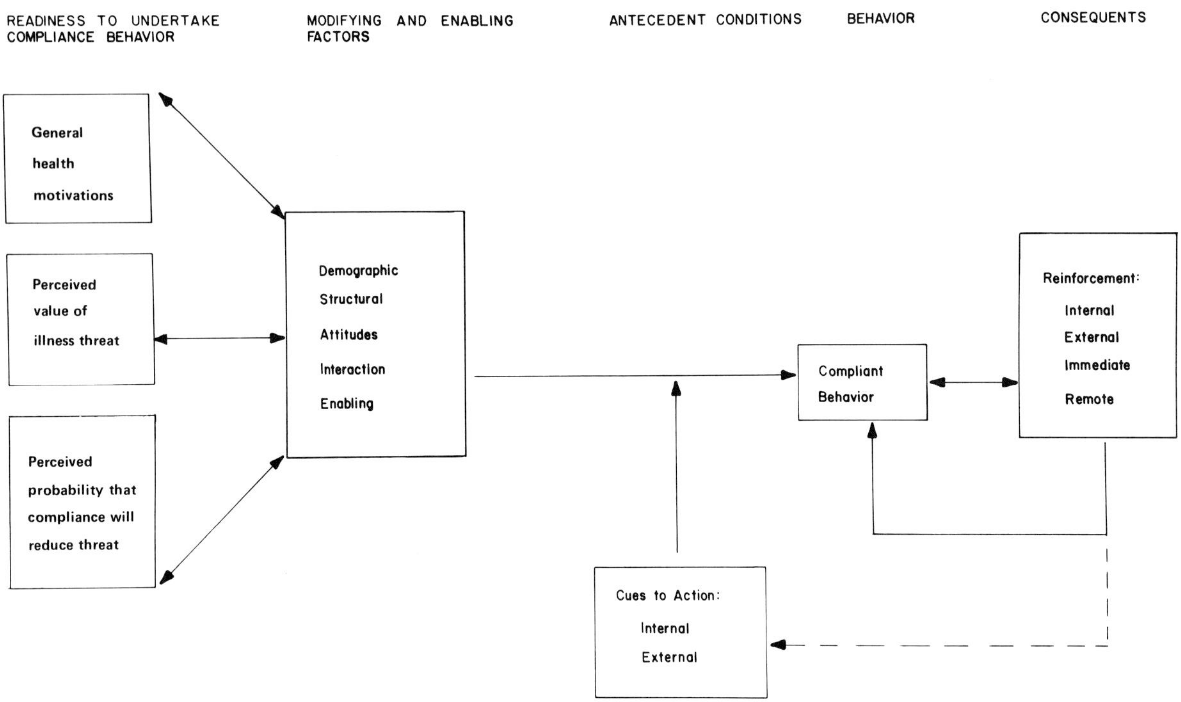

Figure 23.3. Proposed model of compliance grafting basic behavioral paradigm onto a modified form of the Health Belief Model.

are at least four possible combinations of reinforcing events (2 loci of reinforcement × 2 time dimensions). These reinforcers not only increase the future probability of compliance behavior but also increase the likelihood that the patient will continue to respond to the antecedent cues to action.

Improving Compliance

Thus far the problem of noncompliance has been explicated, the various ways in which it is operationally defined and studied have been delineated, and a review of those parameters that seem to influence compliance behavior has been presented. This final section briefly examines an assortment of techniques and strategies that have been employed to improve or enhance compliance. The curious reader may find it somewhat surprising, if not ironic, that there is apparently little correspondence between the intervention techniques outlined here and the descriptive studies previously reviewed. In large part this is probably due to clinicians' attempts to alter compliance behavior without formulating their interventions from any empirically based theoretical formulations.

Many studies have fruitlessly searched for a noncompliant personality or have spent their efforts attempting to correlate immutable demographic factors into predictive equations. Conversely, clinical researchers, hoping to formulate practical strategies to improve compliance, often have neglected the empirical data that have relevance for models of adherence.

Broadly speaking, intervention techniques consist of either (*a*) educating the patient; (*b*) tailoring the regimen; or (*c*) employing behavioral techniques. Very little prospective research has been done on manipulating the patient-provider interaction system or prospectively altering the patient's health belief system.

Educating the Patient

As was noted earlier, the patient's formal knowledge about the disease bears no relationship to subsequent compliance (Bergman & Werner, 1963; Donabedian & Rosenfeld, 1964; Evans *et al.*, 1970; Gordis *et al.*, 1969; Malahy, 1966; Suchman, 1967; Vincent, 1971; Weintraub, Au, & Lasagna, 1973). Haynes (1976b), in a review of educational strategies to improve compliance, concluded that, in terms of therapeutic outcome, educational approaches employed alone achieved a success rate of only 50%. The educational techniques he reviewed included brief health messages, individual patient instruction, counseling plus written instructions, programmed instructions, lecture-demonstration series, and emotional role playing. Neufeld (1976), however, in a methodological critique of patient education studies concluded that "patient education, when executed as a therapeutic maneuver specifically intended to improve compliance, has yet to be scientifically validated [p. 83]." The reader will recall, however, the earlier discussion regarding the patient-provider communications system, specifically with respect to the information that is processed in that dyadic interaction. Patients can never hope to adhere to regimens they do not even understand, and expert instructions in the conduct of the regimen will definitely improve compliance (Dickey, Mattar, & Chudzek, 1975; Linkewich *et al.*, 1974; McKenney *et al.*, 1973). Since many physicians are either unable or unwilling to take the time necessary to provide such educational prescriptions, other health care providers, including pharmacists (MacDonald, MacDonald, & Phoenix, 1977; Schneider & Cable, 1978), nurses (Romankiewicz, Gotz, Capelli, & Carlin, 1978; Steckel & Swain, 1977), physical therapists (Mayo, 1978), and physicians' assistants (Vidt, 1978), have become actively involved in patient education. The practicing clinician would be well advised to assess the patient's understanding of the treatment instructions before the consultation ends (Matthews & Hingson, 1977), and whenever possible supplement verbal instructions with a written protocol (Romankiewicz *et al.*, 1978). Neufeld (1976) has noted that one reason for the generally mediocre success of educational approaches per se may be that most of the cited studies "utilized educational maneuvers designed solely to achieve knowledge acquisition and ignored considerations of attitudes more closely linked to compliance behavior [p. 89]." Newer educational programs directed toward cognitive restructuring await application and review.

Tailoring the Regimen

The provider's negotiation of the treatment regimen or management plan with the patient has been posited as an effective way to improve compliance (Fink, 1976). Although one study has demonstrated the utility of such an approach (Haynes, Sackett, Gibson, Taylor, Hackett, Roberts & Johnson, 1976) it is difficult to control for the reactive effect of spending more time with the patient to tailor the treatment. A common sense approach argues for adapting the treatment insofar as possible to the patient's daily routine and using already established habit patterns (e.g., nighttime toothbrushing) as the context for the desired intervention (e.g., taking oral contraceptive). Other tailoring strategies include adjusting dosage schedules to fit eating habits (e.g., b.i.d. dose for patients who always skip breakfast); offering the therapy in the most palatable form (e.g., liquid medication for patients who find it difficult to swallow tablets); single injectable dosing; easy to read and open containers; simplifying treatment by reducing dosages to smallest number possible and so forth.

A useful but grossly underutilized tailoring system involves packaging medications in a form that can be more easily remembered and used by the patient (Atkinson, Gibson, & Andrew, 1978; MacDonald *et al.,* 1977; Schneider & Cable, 1978). Oral contraceptives which have for years been packaged in reminder dose packs might well serve as the model for the dispensing of other medications. Even a short-term regimen (e.g., a 10-day course of b.i.d. oral antibiotics) might be improved if the medication were dispensed in a dated blister strip form clearly specifying the complete use of all of the pills dispensed. Unfortunately, drug companies may be reluctant to market their products in this format since such packaging usually cuts profit margins. Finally, it goes without saying that before successful tailoring can come about both the patient and the provider must be willing to provide each other with necessary information and feedback to develop a workable system.

Behavioral Techniques

A number of behavioral techniques have been employed to improve compliance. These include cueing, self-monitoring, token economies, and contingency management.

Cueing The provision of cues or discriminative stimuli which may act to trigger compliance behaviors has been attempted. Medication charts and calendars are good examples of behavioral cues to aid in compliance (Gabriel, Gagnon, & Bryan, 1977; Liberman, 1972; Schwartz, 1965). Azrin & Powell's (1969) response priming apparatus also involved a cueing component. With the advent of microcomputer chips the potential technological advances in devising medication monitors is phenomenal (Yee, Hahn, & Christiansen, 1974). Moulding (1979) has cogently argued for the more general use of medication monitors; he has speculated that by employing digital watch computer chip microelectronics, a programmable medication monitor could be developed not only to cue the patient but also to assist the potential researcher with data collection.

Simpler cueing strategies include telephone or postcard reminder for follow-up appointments and posting a reminder in a highly visible area to prompt medication usage. Larson, Olsen, Cole, and Shortell (1979) found that using a simple postcard reminder significantly increased influenza vaccination rates. This simple cueing strategy was both time and cost efficient and produced immunization rates significantly higher than those of a control group and national samples.

Self-Monitoring The use of self-monitoring is a well-established technique in dietary control not only for diagnostic purposes but also as a treatment tool (Dunbar & Stunkard, 1979). Although this technique has not yet found wide application in compliance research, some support is accumulating for its use (DeBerry, Jefferies, & Light, 1975; Dunbar, 1977; Moulding, 1961). Although self-monitoring may be of limited value in long-term treatments (e.g., hypertension), the present author has found it to be clinically useful with short courses of therapy. It may well be that the patient's improved adherence is actually due to the additional attention provided by the health professional and the implicit communication of genuine interest in seeing that the regimen is actually followed.

Contingency Contracting Utilizing negotiated contracts is another behavioral technique that has demonstrated some success in improving compliance. This process, by specifically delineating operationally defined goals (usually reached in a graduated sequence), fosters a reciprocal and more egalitarian relationship between the patient and provider and enables the patient to take an active part in the treatment process. Although patients often will not choose to contract around compliance issues (Steckel & Swain, 1977), contingency management techniques have been successfully employed to improve adherence to a complex postcoronary medical regimen (Dapcich-Miura & Hovell, 1979), to enhance the dietary compliance of children on hemodialysis (Magrab & Papadopoulou, 1977), to increase medical compliance with a juvenile diabetic (Lowe & Lutzker, 1979) and to control fluid overload with a hemodialysis patient (Barnes, 1976). Unfortunately, almost all of these reports are single case studies, therefore, the more widespread utilization of contingency contracting systems with large groups of patients awaits further study. Ziesat (1977-1978), using a group therapy format and employing an assortment of behavioral techniques (e.g., cueing, positive reinforcement), was able to demonstrate significant improvement in hypertension control.

Conclusions and Future Directions

This chapter has reviewed compliance in terms of its magnitude as a problem for the present health care system. The various ways compliance is defined, measured, and experimentally studied have been examined. The parameters thought to affect adherence have been explicated, as have an assortment of strategies to enhance compliance.

The literature indicates that it is fruitless to attempt to define a noncompliant personality. This line of research, having generally been unproductive, should be replaced by carefully controlled investigations aimed more directly at identifying high-risk noncompliers. While it is certainly true that every patient should be considered a potential noncomplier, it may be more cost effective in terms of intervention efforts to initially identify those patients who are the least likely to adhere, and to focus our intervention efforts on improving their compliance rates.

As a tool the medication monitor holds a great deal of promise for both clinical practice and clinical research. The technology is presently available for the development of sophisticated, relatively inexpensive, practical medication dispensers. A great deal more research needs to be done in this area. Similarly, novel medication packaging has yet to be fully exploited. Pharmaceutical companies which are far too willing to make unsubstantiated claims for improved compliance in detailing their product lines should be strongly encouraged to investigate the compliance effects of various forms of packaging.

Social scientists will be challenged by the prospect of improving compliance via interventions directed at altering the patient-provider interface. Research methodologies must now move beyond correlational analyses. Behavioral scientists representing various disciplines and theoretical persuasions must analyze the patient-provider interaction system with the goal of developing educational programs for health care providers to improve patient satisfaction and compliance.

As stated earlier, the behavioral treatment of noncompliance is still in its infancy. It is this author's hope that the recent "rediscovery of thought" best reflected in contemporary cognitive-behavioral approaches will provide an exciting forum for the development of new and powerful techniques to improve compliance. It is also the author's opinion that cognitive-behavioral theorists would do well to take into account the already established data on the Health Belief Model. Although this model has begun to delineate the sociopsychological context in which health decisions are made it still awaits the cognitive-behavioral researcher and/or clinician to fully test its clinical viability through carefully controlled intervention–outcome studies.

Similarly, educational strategies to improve adherence must now move beyond simply providing the patient with formal knowledge. Research based upon an understanding of the factors involved in persuasion, social influence, and social control must be directed at educational strategies to alter patients' values, expectancies, and belief systems. Finally, little work has been done to prospectively alter compliance rates by directly manipulating the patient–provider interaction system. All of these areas offer a rich agar for the growth of research efforts in social psychology and theories of cognitive-behavioral change.

Compliance as a multifaceted problem places enormous financial burdens on our present health care system and, despite intervention efforts, the burdens continue unabated. A problem of this magnitude requires a multidisciplinary effort to formulate solutions. Methodologically sound, empirically based research needs to be undertaken evaluating cost-efficient, practical intervention strategies. An interactionistic model taking into account the patient, the provider, and the social context of the health behavior must be developed. Medical psychology can and should become a major force in leading this research effort.

Acknowledgments

The author would like to express his thanks to Elizabeth Snyder for her untiring help in collecting the many references needed to write this chapter. Special thanks also go to Jane Stone and Linda Winberry who provided the necessary secretarial assistance, to Janie Clark for her help in the figure designs, and to Linda Vierling for her excellent editorial comments.

References

Alpert, J. J. Broken appointments. *Pediatrics,* 1964, *34,* 127–132.

Atkinson, L., Gibson, I., & Andrews, J. An investigation into the ability of elderly patients continuing to take prescribed drugs after discharge from hospital and recommendations concerning improving the situation. *Gerontology,* 1978, *24,* 225–234.

Azrin, N. H., & Powell, J. Behavioral engineering: The use of response priming to improve prescribed self-medication. *Journal of Applied Behavioral Analysis,* 1969, *2,* 39–42.

Bales, R. *Interaction process analysis.* Cambridge: Addison-Wesley, 1951.

Bandura, A. Self-reinforcement processes. In M. J. Mahoney & C. E. Thoresen (Eds.), *Self-Control: Power to the person.* Monterey, Ca.: Brooks/Cole, 1974.

Barnes, M. R. Token economy control of fluid overload in a patient receiving hemodialysis. *Journal of Behavior Therapy and Experimental Psychiatry,* 1976, *7,* 305–306.

Becker, M. H. (Ed.). The health belief model and personal health behavior. *Health Education Monographs,* 1974, *2,* 324–473.

Becker, M. H., Drachman, R. H., & Kirscht, J. P. Predicting mothers' compliance with pediatric medical regimens. *Journal of Pediatrics,* 1972, *81,* 843–854.

Becker, M. H., Drachman, R. H., & Kirscht, J. P. A new approach to explaining sick-role behavior in low income populations. *American Journal of Public Health,* 1974, *64,* 205–216.

Becker, M. H., & Maiman, L. A. Sociobehavioral determinants of compliance with health and medical care recommendations. *Medical Care,* 1975, *13,* 10–24.

Becker, M. H., Maiman, L. A., Kirscht, J. P., Haefner, D. P., & Drachman, R. H. The health belief model and prediction of dietary compliance. *Journal of Health and Social Behavior,* 1977, *18,* 348–366.

Bergman, A. B., & Werner, R. J. Failure of children to receive penicillin by mouth. *New England Journal of Medicine,* 1963, *268,* 1334–1338.

Bierenbaum, M. L., Fleischman, A. I., Raichelson, R. I., Hayton, T., & Watson, P. B. Ten year experience of modified-fat diets on younger men with coronary heart disease. *Lancet,* 1973, *1,* 1404–1407.

Bierenbaum, M. L., Green, D. P., Florin, A., Fleischman, A. I., & Caldwell, A. B. Modified-fat dietary management of the young male with coronary disease: A five year report. *Journal of the American Medical Association,* 1967, *202,* 59–63.

Billie, D. A. Patients' knowledge and compliance with post-hospitalization prescriptions as related to body image and teaching format. (Doctoral dissertation, University of Wisconsin, Madison, 1975). *Dissertation Abstracts International,* 1976, *36,* 6070B–6071B. (University Microfilms No. 76-6068, 205)

Blackwell, B. The drug defaulter. *Clinical Pharmacology and Therapeutics,* 1972, *13,* 841–848.

Blackwell, B. Patient compliance. *New England Journal of Medicine,* 1973, *289,* 249–253.

Boyd, J. R., Covington, T. R., Stanaszek, W. F., & Coussons, R. T. Drug-defaulting, II. Analysis of noncompliance patterns. *American Journal of Hospital Pharmacy,* 1974, *31,* 485-491.

Bradshaw, P. W., Ley, P., Kincey, J. A., & Bradshaw, J. Recall of medical advice: comprehensibility and specificity. *British Journal of Social and Clinical Psychology,* 1975, *14,* 55-62.

Caldwell, J. R., Cobb, S., Dowling, M. D., & de Jongh, D. The drop out problem in antihypertensive treatment. *Journal of Chronic Diseases,* 1970, *22,* 579-592.

Caron, H. S., & Roth, H. P. Patients' cooperation with a medical regimen. *Journal of the American Medical Association,* 1968, *203,* 922-926.

Charney, E. Patient-doctor communication: Implications for the clinician. *Pediatric Clinics of North America,* 1972, *19,* 263-279.

Charney, E., Bynum, R., Eldredge, D., Frank, D., MacWhinney, J. B., McNabb, N., Scheiner, A., Sumpter, E., & Iker, H. How well do patients take oral penicillin?: A collaborative study in private practice. *Pediatrics,* 1967, *40,* 188-195.

Christensen, D. B. Drug-taking compliance: A review and synthesis. *Health Services Research,* 1978, *13,* 171-187.

Colcher, I. S., & Bass, J. W. Penicillin treatment of streptococcal pharyngitis: A comparison of schedules and the role of specific counseling. *Journal of the American Medical Association,* 1972, *222,* 657-659.

Copi, I. M. *Introduction to logic.* New York: Macmillan, 1961.

Dapcich-Miura, E. D., & Hovell, M. D. Contingency management of adherence to a complex medical regimen in an elderly heart patient. *Behavior Therapy,* 1979, *10,* 193-201.

Davis, M. S. Variations in patients' compliance with doctors' orders: Analysis of congruence between survey responses and results of empirical investigations. *Journal of Medical Education,* 1966, *41,* 1037-1048.

Davis, M. S. Predicting non-compliant behavior. *Journal of Health and Social Behavior,* 1967, *8,* 265-271.

Davis, M. S. Variations in patients' compliance with doctors' advice: An empirical analysis of patterns of communication. *American Journal of Public Health,* 1968, *58,* 274-288. (a)

Davis, M. S. Physiologic, psychological, and demographic factors in patient compliance with doctors' orders. *Medical Care,* 1968, *6,* 115-122. (b)

DeBerry, P., Jefferies, L. P., & Light, M. R. Teaching cardiac patients to manage medications. *American Journal of Nursing,* 1975, *75,* 2191-2193.

DeRisi, W. J., & Butz, G. *Writing behavioral contracts: A case simulation practice manual.* Champaign, Ill.: Research Press, 1975.

Dickey, F. F., Mattar, M. E., & Chudzek, G. M. Pharmacist counseling increases drug regimen compliance. *Hospitals,* 1975, *49,* 85-88.

DiMatteo, M. R. A social psychological analysis of physician-patient rapport: Toward a science of the art of medicine. *Journal of Social Issues,* 1979, *35,* 12-33.

DiMatteo, M. R., & Friedman, H. S. (Eds.). Interpersonal relations in health care. *Journal of Social Issues,* 1979, *35,* 1-208.

Donabedian, A., & Rosenfeld, L. S. Follow-up study of chronically ill patients discharged from hospital. *Journal of Chronic Diseases,* 1964, *17,* 847-862.

Dunbar, J. M. Adherence to medication regimen: An intervention study with poor adherers. Unpublished dissertation. Stanford University, 1977.

Dunbar, J. M., & Stunkard, A. J. Adherence to diet and drug regimen. In R. Levy, B. Rifkind, B. Dennis, & N. Ernst (Eds.), *Nutrition, lipids, and coronary heart disease.* New York: Raven Press, 1979.

Ekehammar, B. Interactionism in personality from a historical perspective. *Psychological Bulletin,* 1974, *81,* 1026-1048.

Elling, R., Whittemore, R., & Green, M. Patient participation in a pediatric program. *Journal of Health and Human Behavior,* 1960, *1,* 183-189.

Endler, N. S., & Magnusson, D. Toward an interactional psychology of personality. *Psychological Bulletin,* 1976, *83,* 956-974.

Epstein, L. H., & Masek, B. J. Behavioral control of medicine compliance. *Journal of Applied Behavioral Analysis,* 1978, *11,* 1-9.

Evans, R. I., Rozelle, R. M., Lasater, T. M., Dembroski, T. M., & Allen, B. P. Fear arousal, persuasion, and actual versus implied behavioral change. *Journal of Personality and Social Psychology,* 1970, *16,* 220-227.

Feinstein, A. R. "Compliance bias" and the interpretation of therapeutic trials. In D. Sackett & R. Haynes (Eds.), *Compliance with therapeutic regimens.* Baltimore: Johns Hopkins University Press, 1976.

Feinstein, A. R., Spagnuolo, M., Jonas, S., Levitt, M., & Tursky, E. Discontinuation of antistreptococcal prophylaxis. *Journal of the American Medical Association,* 1966, *197,* 949-952.

Feinstein, A. R., Wood, H. F., Epstein, J. A., Taranta, A., Simpson, R., & Tursky, E. A controlled study of three methods of prophylaxis against streptococcal infection in a population of rheumatic children. II. Results of the first three years of the study, including methods for evaluating the maintenance of oral prophylaxis. *New England Journal of Medicine,* 1959, *260,* 697-702.

Festinger, L. *A theory of cognitive dissonance.* Evanston, Ill.: Row Peterson, 1957.

Fink, D. L. Tailoring the consensual regimen. In D. L. Sackett & R. B. Haynes (Eds.), *Compliance with therapeu-*

tic regimens. Baltimore: Johns Hopkins University Press, 1976.

Fink, R., Shapiro, S., & Roester, R. Impact of efforts to increase participation in repetitive screenings for early breast detection. *American Journal of Public Health,* 1972, *62,* 328-336.

Finnerty, F. A., Mattie, E. C., & Finnerty, F. A. Hypertension in the inner city. I. Analysis of clinic dropouts. *Circulation,* 1973, *47,* 73-75.

Foreyt, J. P., & Rathjen, D. P. *Cognitive behavior therapy.* New York: Plenum, 1978.

Fox, W. Problem of self-administration of drugs; with particular reference to pulmonary tuberculosis. *Tubercle,* 1958, *39,* 269-274.

Francis, V., Korsch, B. M., & Morris, M. J. Gaps in doctor-patient communications. *New England Journal of Medicine,* 1969, *280,* 535-540.

Freeman, B., Negrete, V., Davis, M., & Korsch, B. M. Gaps in doctor-patient communication: Doctor-patient interaction analysis. *Pediatric Research,* 1971, *5,* 298-311.

Friedman, H. S. Nonverbal communication between patients and medical practitioners. *Journal of Social Issues,* 1979, *35,* 82-99.

Friedman, H. S., & DiMatteo, M. R. Health care as an interpersonal process. *Journal of Social Issues,* 1979, *35,* 1-11.

Gabriel, M., Gagnon, J. P., & Bryan, C. K. Improved patient compliance through use of a daily drug chart. *American Journal of Public Health,* 1977, *67,* 968-969.

Gentry, W. D. Noncompliance to medical regimen. In R. B. Williams & W. D. Gentry (Eds.), *Behavioral approaches to medical treatment.* Cambridge, Ma.: Ballinger, 1977.

Gillum, R. F., & Barsky, A. J. Diagnosis and management of patient noncompliance. *Journal of the American Medical Association,* 1974, *228,* 1563-1567.

Goldsmith, C. H. The effect of differing compliance distributions on the planning and statistical analysis of therapeutic trials. In D. Sackett & R. Haynes (Eds.), *Compliance with therapeutic regimens.* Baltimore: Johns Hopkins University Press, 1976.

Gordis, L. Methodologic issues in the measurement of patient compliance. In D. L. Sackett & R. B. Haynes (Eds.), *Compliance with therapeutic regimens.* Baltimore: Johns Hopkins University Press, 1976.

Gordis, M. D., & Markowitz, M. Evaluation of the effectiveness of comprehensive and continuous pediatric care. *Pediatrics,* 1971, *48,* 766-776.

Gordis, L., Markowitz, M., & Lilienfeld, A. M. Why patients don't follow medical advice: A study of children on long-term antistreptococcal prophylaxis. *Journal of Pediatrics,* 1969, *75,* 957-968.

Greenwald, H. P., Becker, S. W., & Nevitt, M. C. Delay and noncompliance in cancer detection: A behavioral perspective for health planners. *Milbank Memorial Fund Quarterly,* 1978, *56,* 212-231.

Haefner, D. P., & Kirscht, J. P. Motivational and behavioral effects of modifying health beliefs. *Public Health Reports,* 1970, *85,* 478-484.

Hare, E. H., & Wilcox, D. R. Do psychiatric in-patients take their pills? *British Journal of Psychiatry,* 1967, *113,* 1435-1439.

Haynes, R. B. A critical review of the "determinants" of patient compliance with therapeutic regimens. In D. L. Sackett & R. B. Haynes (Eds.), *Compliance with therapeutic regimens.* Baltimore: Johns Hopkins University Press, 1976. (a)

Haynes, R. B. Strategies for improving compliance: A methodologic analysis and review. In D. L. Sackett & R. B. Haynes (Eds.), *Compliance with therapeutic regimens.* Baltimore: Johns Hopkins University Press, 1976. (b)

Haynes, R. B., Sackett, D. L., Gibson, E. S., Taylor, D. W., Hackett, B. C., Roberts, R. S., & Johnson, A. L. Improvement of medication compliance in uncontrolled hypertension. *Lancet,* 1976, *1,* 1265-1268.

Haynes, R. B., Sackett, D. L., Taylor, D. W., Roberts, R. S., & Johnson, A. L. Manipulation of the therapeutic regimen to improve compliance: Conceptions and misconceptions. *Clinical Pharmacology and Therapeutics,* 1977, *22,* 125-130.

Haynes, R. B., Taylor, D. W., & Sackett, D. L. *Compliance in Health Care.* Baltimore: Johns Hopkins University Press, 1979.

Heinzelmann, F. Determinants of prophylaxis behavior with respect to rheumatic fever. *Journal of Health and Human Behavior,* 1962, *3,* 73-81.

Hippocrates. [Volume II: On decorum and the physician] (W. H. S. Jones trans.). London: William Heinemann, Ltd, 1923.

Hochbaum, G. M. *Public participation in medical screening programs: A sociopsychological study.* (Public Health Services, Public Health Service Publication Number 572) Washington, D.C.: U. S. Government Printing Office, 1958.

Hogarty, G. E., & Goldberg, S. C. and the collaborative study group. Drug and sociotherapy in the aftercare of the schizophrenic patient. One-year relapse rates. *Archives of General Psychiatry,* 1973, *28,* 54-64.

Hulka, B. S., Cassel, J. C., Kupper, L. L., & Burdette, J. A. Communication, compliance, and concordance between physicians and patients with prescribed medications. *American Journal of Public Health,* 1976, *66,* 847-853.

Ireland, H. D. Outpatient chemotherapy for tuberculosis. *American Review of Respiratory Disease,* 1960, *82,* 378-383.

Jenkins, B. W. Are patients true to t.i.d. and q.i.d. doses? *General Practice,* 1954, *9,* 66-69.

Kaback, M. M., Becker, M. H., & Ruth, M. V. Sociological studies in human genetics: I. Compliance factors in a voluntary heterozygote screening program. *Birth Defects,* 1974, *10,* 145-163.

Kagan, N. I. Teaching interpersonal relations for the practice of medicine. *Lakartidningen,* 1974, *71,* 4758-4760.

Kasl, S. V. Issues in patient adherence to health care regimens. *Journal of Human Stress,* 1975, *1,* 5-17.

Kasl, S. V., & Cobb, S. Health behavior, illness behavior, and sick role behavior. I. Health and illness behavior. *Archives of Environmental Health,* 1966, *12,* 246-266. (a)

Kasl, S. V., & Cobb, S. Health behavior, illness behavior, and sick role behavior. 2. Sick role behavior. *Archives of Environmental Health,* 1966, *12,* 531-541. (b)

Kegeles, S. S. Why people seek dental care: A test of a conceptual formulation. *Journal of Health and Human Behavior,* 1963, *4,* 166-173.

Kegeles, S. S. A field experiment attempt to change beliefs and behavior of women in an urban ghetto. *Journal of Health and Social Behavior,* 1969, *10,* 115-124.

Kirscht, J. P. Research related to the modification of health beliefs. *Health Education Monographs,* 1974, *2,* 455-469.

Korsch, B. M., Fine, R. N., & Negrete, V. F. Noncompliance in children with renal transplants. *Pediatrics,* 1978, *61,* 872-876.

Korsch, B. M., Gozzi, E. K., & Francis, V. Gaps in doctor-patient communication. I. Doctor-patient interaction and patient satisfaction. *Pediatrics,* 1968, *42,* 855-871.

Korsch, B. M., & Negrete, V. F. Doctor-patient communication. *Scientific American,* 1972, *227,* 66-74.

Kriesberg, L., & Treiman, B. R. Socioeconomic status and utilization of dentists' services. *Journal of the American College of Dentists,* 1960, *27,* 147-165.

Larson, E. B., Olsen, E., Cole, W., & Shortell, S. The relationship of health beliefs and a postcard reminder to influenza vaccination. *Journal of Family Practice,* 1979, *8,* 1207-1211.

Latiolais, C. J., & Berry, C. C. Misuse of prescription medications by out-patients. *Drug Intelligence and Clinical Pharmacy,* 1969, *3,* 270-277.

Leventhal, H., Hochbaum, G., & Rosenstock, I. Epidemic impact on the general population in two cities. In, *The impact of Asian influenza on community life: A study in five cities.* United States Department of Health, Education and Welfare. (Public Health Service, Publication Number 766). Washington, D.C.: U.S. Government Printing Office, 1960.

Lewin, K. [*A dynamic theory of personality: Selected papers*] (D. K. Adams & K. E. Zener, trans.). New York: McGraw-Hill, 1935.

Ley, P. What the patient doesn't remember. *Medical Opinion and Review,* 1966, *1,* 69-73.

Ley, P. *Memory aspects of doctor-patient communication.* Unpublished doctoral dissertation, University of Liverpool, 1969.

Ley, P. Primacy, rated importance, and recall of medical information. *Journal of Health and Social Behavior,* 1972, *13,* 311-317.

Ley, P. Psychological studies of doctor-patient communication. In S. Rachman (Ed.), *Contributions to medical psychology.* New York: Pergamon Press, 1977.

Ley, P., Bradshaw, P. W., Eaves, D. E., & Walker, C. M. A method for increasing patient recall of information presented to them. *Psychological Medicine,* 1973, *3,* 217-220.

Ley, P., & Spelman, M. S. Communications in an outpatient setting. *British Journal of Social and Clinical Psychology,* 1965, *4,* 114-116.

Ley, P., & Spelman, M. S. *Communicating with the patient.* London: Staples Press, 1967.

Liberman, P. A guide to help patients keep track of their drugs. *American Journal of Hospital Pharmacy,* 1972, *29,* 507-509.

Linkewich, J. A., Catalano, R. B., & Flack, H. L. The effect of packaging and instruction on out-patient compliance with medication regimens. *Drug Intelligence and Clinical Pharmacy,* 1974, *8,* 10-15.

Lowe, K., & Lutzker, J. R. Increasing compliance to a medical regimen with a juvenile diabetic. *Behavior Therapy,* 1979, *10,* 57-64.

Lund, M., Jorgenson, R. S., & Kuhl, V. Serum diphenylhydantoin (Phenytoin) in ambulent patients with epilepsy. *Epilepsia,* 1964, *5,* 51-58.

MacDonald, E. T., MacDonald, J. B., & Phoenix, M. Improving drug compliance after hospital discharge. *British Medical Journal,* 1977, *2,* 618-621.

McClellan, T. A., & Cowan, G. Use of antipsychotic and antidepressant drugs by chronically ill patients. *American Journal of Psychiatry,* 1970, *126,* 113-115.

McGuire, G. P. Training medical students to obtain a history of the current problems. In A. E. Bennet (Ed.), *Communications in medicine.* London: Oxford University Press, 1976.

McKenny, J. M., Slining, J. M., Henderson, H. R., Devins, D., & Barr, M. The effect of clinical pharmacy services on patients with essential hypertension. *Circulation,* 1973, *48,* 1104-1111.

McKercher, P. L., & Rucker, T. D. Patient knowledge

and compliance with medication instruction. *Journal of the American Pharmaceutical Association*, 1977, *17*, 282-286, 291.

Maddock, R. K. Patient cooperation in taking medicines: A study involving isoniazid and aminosalicylic acid. *Journal of the American Medical Association*, 1967, *199*, 137-140.

Magrab, P., & Papadopoulou, Z. L. The effect of a token economy on dietary compliance for children on hemodialysis. *Journal of Applied Behavioral Analysis*, 1977, *10*, 573-578.

Mahoney, M. J., & Arnkoff, D. Cognitive and self-control therapies. In S. L. Garfield & A. E. Bergin (Eds.), *Handbook of psychotherapy and behavior change: An empirical analysis* (2nd ed.). New York: Wiley, 1978.

Mahoney, M. J., & Thoresen, C. E. *Self-control: Power to the person.* Monterey, Ca.: Brooks/Cole, 1974.

Malahy, B. The effect of instruction and labeling on the number of medication errors made by patients at home. *American Journal of Hospital Pharmacy*, 1966, *23*, 283-292.

Markowitz, M., & Gordis, L. A mail-in technique for detecting penicillin in urine: Application to the study of maintenance of prophylaxis in rheumatic fever patients. *Pediatrics*, 1968, *41*, 151-153.

Marsh, W. W., & Perlman, L. V. Understanding congestive heart failure and self-administration of digoxin. *Geriatrics*, 1972, *27*, 65-70.

Marston, W. V. Compliance with medical regimens: A review of the literature. *Nursing Research*, 1970, *19*, 312-323.

Masur, F. T. Assorted physical disorders. In R. B. Williams & W. D. Gentry (Eds.), *Behavioral approaches to medical treatment.* Cambridge, Ma.: Ballinger, 1977.

Masur, F. T. Resumption of sexual activity following myocardial infarction. *Sexuality and Disability*, 1979, *2*, 98-114.

Matthews, D., & Hingson, R. Improving patient compliance: A guide for physicians. *Medical Clinics of North America*, 1977, *16*, 879-889.

Mayo, N. E. Patient compliance: Practical implications for physical therapists. *Physical Therapy*, 1978, *58*, 1083-1090.

Mazzulo, J. M., Lasagna, L., & Griner, P. F. Variations in interpretation of prescription instructions. *Journal of the American Medical Association*, 1974, *227*, 929-931.

Meichenbaum, D. *Cognitive-behavior modification.* New York: Plenum, 1977.

Miettinen, M., Turpeinen, O., Karvonen, M. J., Elosuo, R., & Paavilainen, E. Effect of cholesterol-lowering diet on mortality from coronary heart-disease and other causes: A twelve year clinical trial in men and women. *Lancet*, 1972, *2*, 835-838.

Mitchell, J. H. Compliance with medical regimens: An annotated bibliography. *Health Education Monographs*, 1974, *2*, 75-87.

Moulding, T. Preliminary study of the pill calendar as a method of improving the self-administration of drugs. *American Review of Respiratory Disease*, 1961, *84*, 284-287.

Moulding, T. The medication monitor for studying the self-administration of oral contraceptives. *American Journal of Obstetrics and Gynecology*, 1971, *110*, 1143-1144.

Moulding, T. The unrealized potential of the medication monitor. *Clinical Pharmacology and Therapeutics*, 1979, *25*, 131-136.

Moulding, T., Onstad, G. D., & Sbarbaro, J. A. Supervision of outpatient drug therapy with the medication monitor. *Annals of Internal Medicine*, 1970, *73*, 559-564.

Mushlin, A. I., & Appel, F. A. Diagnosing potential noncompliance. *Archives of Internal Medicine*, 1977, *137*, 318-321.

Neufeld, V. R. Patient education: A critique. In D. L. Sackett & R. B. Haynes (Eds.), *Compliance with therapeutic regimens.* Baltimore: Johns Hopkins University Press, 1976.

Nugent, C. A., Ward, J., MacDiarmid, W. D., McCall, J. C., Baukol, J., & Tyler, F. H. Glucocorticoid toxicity—Single contrasted with divided daily doses of prednisolone. *Journal of Chronic Diseases*, 1965, *18*, 323-332.

Park, L. C., & Lipman, R. S. A comparison of patient dosage deviation reports with pill counts. *Psycholpharmocologie*, 1964, *6*, 299-302.

Paulson, S. M., Krause, S., & Iber, F. Development and evaluation of a compliance test for patients taking disulfiram. *Johns Hopkins Medical Journal*, 1977, *141*, 119-125.

Paxton, R., & Bernacca, G. Urinary nicotine concentration as a function of time since last cigarette: Implications for detecting faking in smoking clinics. *Behavior Therapy*, 1979, *10*, 523-528.

Preston, D. F., & Miller, F. L. The tuberculosis outpatient's defection from therapy. *American Journal of the Medical Sciences*, 1964, *247*, 21-25.

Rodin, J., & Janis, I. L. The social power of health-care practitioners as agents of change. *Journal of Social Issues*, 1979, *35*, 60-81.

Romankiewicz, J. A., Gotz, V., Capelli, A., & Carlin, H. S. To improve patient adherence to drug regimens: An interdiscipliary approach. *American Journal of Nursing,* 1978, *78,* 1216-1219.

Rosenstock, I. M. What research in motivation suggests for public health. *American Journal of Public Health,* 1960, *50,* 295-302.

Rosenstock, I. M. Why people use health services. *Milbank Memorial Fund Quarterly,* 1966, *44,* 94-127.

Rosenstock, I. M. The health belief model and preventive health behavior. *Health Education Monographs,* 1974, *2,* 354-386.

Rosenstock, I. M., Derryberry, M., & Carriger, B. K. Why people fail to seek poliomyelitis vaccination. *Public Health Reports,* 1959, *74,* 98-103.

Roth, H. P., & Berger, D. G. Studies on patient cooperation in ulcer treatment. I. Observation of actual as compared to prescribed antacid intake on a hospital ward. *Gastroenterology,* 1960, *38,* 630-633.

Roth, H. P., Caron, H. S., & Bartholomew, P. H. Measuring intake of a prescribed medication: A bottle count and a tracer technique compared. *Clinical Pharmacology and Therapeutics,* 1970, *11,* 228-237.

Sackett, D. L. The magnitude of compliance and noncompliance. In D. L. Sackett & R. B. Haynes (Eds.), *Compliance with therapeutic regimens.* Baltimore: Johns Hopkins University Press, 1976.

Sackett, D. L., & Haynes, R. B. *Compliance with therapeutic regimens.* Baltimore: Johns Hopkins University Press, 1976.

Sackett, D. L., Haynes, R. B., Gibson, E. S., Taylor, D. W., Roberts, R. S., & Johnson, A. L. Hypertension control, compliance and science. *American Heart Journal,* 1977, *94,* 666-667.

Sannella, J. J. Glycosylated hemoglobin: A new approach to diabetes control. *Journal of the Tennessee Medical Association,* 1978, *71,* 285-287.

Schneider, P., & Cable, G. Compliance clinic: An opportunity for an expanded role for pharmacists. *American Journal of Hospital Pharmacy,* 1978, *35,* 288-295.

Schwartz, D. The elderly patient and his medications. *Geriatrics,* 1965, *20,* 517-520.

Sheiner, L. B., Rosenberg, B., Marathe, V. V., & Peck, C. Differences in serum digoxin concentrations between outpatients and inpatients: An effect of compliance? *Clinical Pharmacology and Therapeutics,* 1974, *15,* 239-246.

Steckel, S. B., & Swain, M. A. Contracting with patients to improve compliance. *Hospitals,* 1977, *51,* 81-82.

Stimson, G. V. Obeying doctor's orders: A view from the other side. *Social Science and Medicine,* 1974, *8,* 97-104.

Stone, G. C. Patient compliance and the role of the expert. *Journal of Social Issues,* 1979, *35,* 34-59.

Suchman, E. A. Preventive health behavior: A model for research on community health campaigns. *Journal of Health and Social Behavior,* 1967, *8,* 197-209.

Svarstad, B. Physician-patient communication and patient conformity with medical advice. In D. Mechanic (Ed.), *The growth of bureaucratic medicine.* New York: Wiley, 1976.

Szasz, T. S., & Hollender, M. H. A contribution to the philosophy of medicine: The basic models of the doctor-patient relationship. *Archives of Internal Medicine,* 1956, *97,* 585-592.

Tagliacozzo, D. M., Luskin, D. B., Lashof, J. C., & Ima, K. Nurse intervention and patient behavior. *American Journal of Public Health,* 1974, *64,* 596-603.

Taylor, D. W., Sackett, D. L., & Haynes, R. B. Compliance with antihypertensive drugs. *Annals of the New York Academy of Science,* 1978, *304,* 390-403.

Turpeinen, O., Miettinen, M., Karvonen, M. J., Roine, P., Pekkarinen, M., Lehtosuo, E. J., & Alivirta, P. Dietary prevention of coronary heart disease: Long-term experiment. *American Journal of Clinical Nutrition,* 1968, *21,* 255-276.

Veterans' Administration Cooperative Study Group on Antihypertensive Agents: Effects of treatment on morbidity in hypertension. III. Influence of age, diastolic pressure, and prior cardiovascular disease: Further analysis of side effects. *Circulation,* 1972, *45,* 991-1004.

Vidt, D. G. The struggle for drug compliance in hypertension. *Cardiovascular Clinics,* 1978, *9,* 243-252.

Vincent, P. Factors influencing patient noncompliance: A theoretical approach. *Nursing Research,* 1971, *20,* 509-516.

Watkins, J. D., Williams, T. F., Martin, D. A., Hogan, M. D., & Anderson, E. A study of diabetic patients at home. *American Journal of Public Health,* 1967, *57,* 452-459.

Weinstein, M. C., & Stason, W. B. *Hypertension: A policy perspective.* Cambridge: Harvard University Press, 1976.

Weintraub, M., Au, W. Y. W., & Lasagna, L. Compliance as a determinant of serum digoxin concentration. *Journal of the American Medical Association,* 1973, *224,* 481-485.

Werner, A., & Schneider, J. M. Teaching medical students interactional skills. A research-based course in the doctor-patient relationship. *New England Journal of Medicine,* 1974, *290,* 1232-1237.

Wilcox, D. R., Gillan, R., & Hare, E. H. Do psychiatric out-patients take their drugs? *British Medical Journal,* 1965, *2,* 790-792.

Winokur, M. Z., Czaczkes, J. W., & Kaplan de-Nour, A. Intelligence and adjustment to chronic hemodialysis.

Journal of Psychosomatic Research, 1973, *17,* 29-34.

Yee, R. D., Hahn, P. M., & Christiansen, R. E. Medication monitor for ophthalmology. *American Journal of Ophthalmology,* 1974, *78,* 774-778.

Ziesat, H. A. Behavior modification in the treatment of hypertension. *International Journal of Psychiatry in Medicine,* 1977-1978, *8,* 257-265.

Zifferblatt, S. M. Increasing compliance through the applied analysis of behavior. *Preventive Medicine,* 1975, *4,* 173-182.

24 Professional Services Evaluation in a Medical Setting

THOMAS W. MILLER

The mid-1960s marked the beginning of a period of expanded activities for psychologists in medical settings. The traditional role of psychologists as diagnosticians and therapists for individual patients was broadened to include assessment of and intervention within the larger health care delivery system. As a result, many psychologists have been able to expand their skills in diagnosing and solving problems related to the provision of health care to patients. This new role in professional services evaluation reflects the mandate of the various accrediting agencies and health professions to seek quality assurance for patients. It has produced the need for continuing education of psychologists already established in medical settings as well as the development of new programs of training for those aspiring to enter the field of professional services evaluation.

The purpose of this chapter is to provide a history of the field of professional services evaluation and an overview of the basic components of a professional services evaluation system in a medical center. This overview examines research methods appropriate for the evaluation of health care programs, a peer review model for the evaluation of health service professionals' competencies, and the procedures necessary for the implementation of an evaluation program in a medical center.

Historical Perspective[1]

Public Law 92-603 enacted in October, 1972 established Professional Standards Review Organizations (PSRO) to determine the necessity, appropriateness, and quality of care provided to the beneficiaries of the major programs offered and authorized under the Social Security Act. The hospital review system under PSRO is based on three interrelated review mechanisms. These include (*a*) *concurrent review*, which encompasses admission, certification, and length of patient stay reviews; (*b*) health care *program evaluation* studies;

[1]The reader who is unfamiliar with the development of professional services evaluation may wish to refer to a glossary of terms used by the Joint Commission on Accreditation of Hospitals which appears in Appendix A.

Medical Psychology
Contributions to Behavioral Medicine

ISBN 0-12-565960-1

and (*c*) *process* and *retrospective* assessment of a tripartite model of health care involving the medical center administration, the health service professional, and the patient consumer. The ultimate goal of the PSRO program is to maximize the quality of services rendered to the consumer.

Related to the review mechanisms required by the PSRO are the Consolidated Standards of the Joint Commission on Accreditation of Hospitals (Joint Commission, 1979; JCAH). The JCAH states that the identification of problems in the delivery of health care shall be the responsibility of a quality assurance program. Quality assurance activities include program evaluation studies, peer review of professionals' competencies (i.e., granting of clinical privileges), and professional growth and development activities. The guiding JCAH principle, standard and components for quality assurance are summarized in Table 24.1.

Both the JCAH and the federally legislated PSROs interpret quality assurance as the removal of deficiencies in patient care which have been identified through program evaluation and patient care audits. Continuing education programs are endorsed as the preferred method of improving patient care. Thus, although one purpose of professional services evaluation is regulatory in the sense that governmental funding and JCAH accreditation are dependent upon meeting prescribed standards of care, evaluation is intended primarily to identify the strengths and weaknesses of health care programs and, when necessary, to raise the quality of care to an acceptable level. The requirements of health insurance and licensing boards serve a similar purpose. Such requirements provide protection to patients by excluding institutions from funding benefits if they do not comply with accreditation standards.

An essential question related to professional services evaluation is who should assume responsibility for the evaluation. Fortunately, the expertise possessed by psychologists regarding measurement, research design, and the provision of constructive feedback to individuals and groups are critical to quality assurance and professional services evaluation. There are, however, additional skills which the evaluator must employ.

Education for the Professional Evaluator

Formal training in professional services evaluation was first provided in various university graduate departments. Most training centers are now found within medical centers in the divisions of medical

Table 24.1. Principle, Standard, and Essential Components for the 1979 JCAH Accreditation Criteria

Principle	The hospital shall demonstrate a consistent endeavor to deliver patient care that is optimal within available resources and consistent with achievable goals. A major component in the application of this principle is the operation of a quality assurance program.
Standard	There shall be evidence of a well-defined, organized program designed to enhance patient care through the ongoing objective assessment of important aspects of patient care and the correction of identified problems.
Components	The essential components of a sound quality assurance program, in the aggregate, shall include: Identification of important or potential problems, or related concerns, in the care of patients. Objective assessment of the cause and scope of problems or concerns, including the determination of priorities for both investigating and resolving problems. Ordinarily, priorities shall be related to the degree of adverse impact on patient care that can be expected if the problems remain unresolved. Implementation, by appropriate individuals or through designated mechanisms, of decisions or actions that are designed to eliminate, insofar as possible, identified problems. Monitoring activities designed to assure that the desired result has been achieved and sustained. Documentation that reasonably substantiates the effectiveness of the overall program to enhance patient care and to assure sound clinical performance.

Note. From *Consolidated Standards* by the Joint Commission on Accreditation of Hospitals, 1979. Copyright © 1979 by the Joint Commission on Accreditation of Hospitals. Reprinted by permission.

planning and evaluation, health sciences and evaluation, or health and human services. Regardless of the title, all evaluation training programs attempt to provide skills necessary for planning, managing, evaluating, and intervening within health care programs. In addition, evaluation training programs attempt to promote interdisciplinary efforts among professional clinical staff in conjunction with community groups to assess and improve the health services available to the consumer (Fink & Kosecoff, 1978a, 1978b; Fitz-Gibbon & Morris, 1978; Franklin & Thrasher, 1976).[2] Coursework, therefore, tends to focus on (*a*) research design; (*b*) health service program design, management, and evaluation; (*c*) organizational structure and function; and (*d*) legal issues, public health law, and other related topics. Additionally, supervised field placements are often provided. The final training requirement is the completion of a research project in some important aspect of health services delivery and evaluation.

As already noted, knowledge of research design and methodology is essential to the well-trained professional services evaluator. The evaluator must also demonstrate a commitment to work with the health service administration, the staff, and consumers to improve communication, despite their sometimes conflicting objectives, in order to ensure the highest quality of health care services. Thus, evaluation training includes the development of the novice evaluator's talents in communicating with the persons who represent each of the evaluator's constituencies.

With training and experience, the professional services evaluator learns that in assessing the quality of health care, emphasis must be placed on three important aspects of the health service delivery system or *program*. The first aspect is the program's *structure*, which includes the psychological and physical environment (e.g., staff, facilities, and equipment). The structural aspects are usually evaluated by applying standards enumerated by various accrediting organizations, such as state licensing boards for staff, governmental health codes, and JCAH. The second aspect of the program that requires scrutiny is the *process* of service provision. The process is evaluated by determining the particular services provided by specific staff members to various patient populations. Also included in process evaluation is the frequency with which the particular services are provided. The third aspect of the program which requires evaluation is its *outcome*. Outcome is evaluated by assessing to what extent the process of service provision achieves the goals that have been established by the staff. If these goals are not being achieved, it is necessary to determine whether changes are required in the structure and/or process aspects of the program.

In addition to learning to examine the structure, process, and outcome of the program, the professional services evaluator must learn to determine the professional competencies of the staff. Albee and Kessler (1977) note that it is particularly important for the profession of psychology to develop its own mechanism of peer review of competencies rather than be led by the dictates of other professions. Thus, the remainder of this chapter examines in detail several models of program evaluation and one peer review model that may be used by the professional services evaluator.

Program Evaluation: Theory and Procedures

Definition

As noted earlier, a program is defined by the JCAH as an organized system of services designed to address the treatment needs of patients (i.e., a health service delivery system). A program evaluation, therefore, represents an attempt to determine the outcome of a program in achieving its stated objectives. An adequate assessment of program outcome involves an examination of the program's structure and process.

A program evaluation, further, does not end with the evaluation of outcome. That is, it is necessary to ensure that the results of a program evaluation are used effectively to improve the quality of patient care. The following section examines the

[2] The term staff will be used to denote professional clinical staff throughout the remainder of this chapter.

theoretical and practical issues of evaluation of a medical center program.

The Evaluator and the Quality Assurance Committee

The professional services evaluator must work as a member of an organized group of medical center personnel who are responsible for the systematic review of the center's programs. These personnel, sometimes referred to as the *quality assurance committee,* represent all of the health professionals within the medical center, both administrative and staff, and the patient population. The members of the quality assurance committee should have some understanding of the various evaluation research issues discussed in this chapter. It is highly desirable, however, for a psychologist who has received graduate training in research methodology and additional program evaluation training to chair the quality assurance committee in order for the benefits of such training to be maximally used in policy decisions within the medical center. Unfortunately, psychologists are not always permitted to chair the quality assurance committee.

The evaluator's role as chairperson or member of the quality assurance committee is to advise and aid the committee in performing the initial program evaluations within each service or unit of the medical center. It is the particular responsibility of the evaluator to organize and educate the staff in such a manner that they will eventually be able to assume the evaluation responsibilities for their own services. The evaluator, therefore, must perform a great deal of preevaluation planning within each service of the medical center to answer the questions of (*a*) what personnel of each service understand evaluation research; (*b*) what personnel are interested in evaluation activities; and (*c*) how amenable are these personnel to forming an evaluation team within their service? In order to answer these questions, the evaluator conducts interviews with all staff from each service of the medical center regarding their perception of the need for evaluation, their expertise in evaluation, and their perception of other staff members' levels of evaluation expertise. These interviews may represent a portion of the needs assessment phase of program evaluation that will be discussed on pages 477–478. The evaluator then may recommend training seminars to educate staff on evaluation procedures and their utility. Such seminars may include topics such as program planning and evaluation, and development of criteria with which to assess patient care problems. The preevaluation planning stage, therefore, serves as a means to gain information from staff and to provide them with an introduction to evaluation procedures that may be used later on their services. In this manner, the staff may be prepared to work closely with the quality assurance committee during the initial evaluation procedures and to gradually assume responsibility for their own evaluations in the future.

A major issue which confronts the evaluator concerns whether the evaluation should be performed on a *retrospective* (i.e., *patient care auditing*), *concurrent,* or *process* basis. Program evaluation generally has been retrospective in nature. That is, health care interventions have been assessed by determining whether the ensuing outcomes for patients have been consistent with the objectives (as defined by measurable criteria) noted by the administration, staff, and consumers. The JCAH recently has recommended that evaluators place less reliance on retrospective patient care audits and instead choose concurrent or process forms of evaluation (Affeldt, 1979). Concurrent evaluations involve the assessment of health care interventions with respect to specific objectives as the patients receive the prescribed interventions. Process evaluations are similar to concurrent evaluations but represent a somewhat more rigorous form of assessment. Process evaluations require examinations of the diagnostic, treatment planning, therapeutic, and/or follow-up phases of patient care using experimental or quasi-experimental procedures.

Regardless of its form, a program evaluation should be used not only to measure the performance of a health care program, but also to identify alternative practices and health care interventions to the program administrators, staff, and consumers. To this end the evaluator should provide feedback to the three constituencies to help refine and improve program objectives and the health care interventions designed to meet those objectives. The new objectives and interventions then may be studied in a *focus review* to determine if they have been successfully implemented. The JCAH currently recommends that, following initial evaluation, focus review of newly implemented changes in objectives and interventions should be maintained at all times (Affeldt, 1979). Figure 24.1 illustrates the review procedures recommended by the JCAH.

Program Evaluation Models

Another important issue which confronts the program evaluator is the choice of a particular program evaluation model. The present chapter thus far has examined program evaluation within the context of a *goal attainment* model. This model requires that the evaluator specify the particular organizational objective to be studied and determine if the intervention strategies employed to obtain the objective are successful. Most of the current evaluation studies, regardless of whether they are labeled as retrospective, concurrent, or process studies, are based upon a goal attainment model. A more complex approach to program evaluation which sometimes is used is the systems approach. The systems approach model makes the assumption that one cause of ineffectiveness in meeting program objectives may be an inappropriate allocation of resources (e.g., funds and equipment) within a program of health care service. The model therefore requires the evaluator to determine the most effective allocation of resources within a program and then to study the medical center's degree of success in achieving the optimal distribution of resources. As one might expect, a larger amount of valuable information is generated by the systems approach relative to the goal

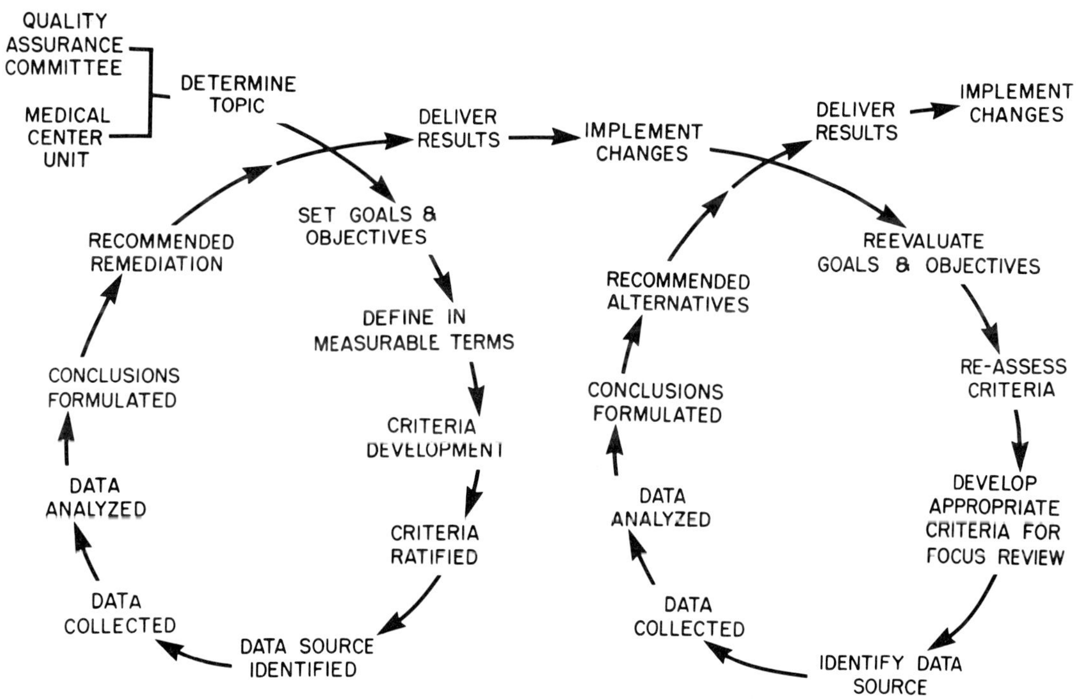

Figure 24.1 Dual cycle for program evaluation studies.

attainment model. However, the design of systems approach studies is more complex and expensive than that associated with goal attainment studies.

A highly innovative model recently has been introduced by Levine (Note 1) wherein a program may be examined in a courtroom-like setting. Testimony is elicited from witnesses in favor of the existing program and from those who wish to suggest alternatives to the program's objectives and interventions. Testimony is also elicited from evaluation experts who may offer empirical evidence that supports or opposes the positions of the other witnesses. The courtroom model is still in its formative stages; nonetheless, it holds promise as an evaluation model and as a group process model for aiding administrators, staff, and patients in understanding the intricacies of providing professional services within a medical center.

Before considering specific examples of program evaluation studies, attention should be directed toward the problem of research design in program evaluation. The sophistication of the research materials and procedures used in the 1980s ranges from openended interviews to very elaborately weighted questionnaire schemes, and from simple field studies to complex computer simulations. There is no consensus within the evaluation community as to the appropriateness of these various methodologies. The present discussion presents an overview of evaluation methodology; the interested reader will find more detailed discussions of research design in the sources cited below.

Research design is a critical issue for the program evaluator. Several discussions of program evaluation have concluded that rigorous experimental methodology, rather than quasi-experimental or nonexperimental procedures, should be used by the evaluator (Borgatta, 1966; Campbell & Stanley, 1963; Cook & Campbell, 1979; Freeman & Sherwood, 1965). For example, Cook and Campbell (1979) contend that randomized experiments that maximize internal validity should be conducted "when the cost of being wrong about a causal inference is high—e.g., when because of experimental results, an ineffective policy could be implemented widescale or an effective one reduced in scope [p. 385]." However, a number of recent papers have presented alternative, quasi-experimental designs for program evaluation (Attkisson, McIntyre, Hargreaves, Harris, & Ochberg, 1974; Caporaso & Roos, 1973; Guttentag, 1977; Guttentag, Kiresuk, Oglesby, & Cann, 1975; Patton, 1978; Wortman, 1975). In addition Schulberg, Sheldon, and Baker (1969) have contended that the design selection should be related to the degree of knowledge currently available about the program under study. That is, as knowledge about the program increases, a more rigorous research design should be employed.

The present author believes that both the experimental and quasi-experimental designs discussed in the references cited offer strategies appropriate for use in a medical setting. Experimental methods, however, are essential for studying the effects of intervention strategies administered to a patient sample. That is, the value of an experimental design is that it may provide evidence that an objective has or has not been met by the provision of a particular treatment to a sample of patients. The data produced by an experiment then can be used for the purpose of treatment planning for current and future patients.

It should be noted, however, that the design of experiments within a field setting such as a medical center service may break down and provide data that may be analyzed only by quasi-experimental procedures (cf. Abt, 1976; Cook & Campbell, 1979). For example, faulty randomization procedures used to select experimental and control subjects may produce subject groups that are not comparable to one another. An excellent discussion of the problems caused by faulty randomization procedures and potential solutions to these problems is presented by Cook and Campbell (1979, Chapter 8). Other factors contributing to the breakdown of experimental designs in the field setting include the use of survey questionnaires for which little or no reliability or validity data have been collected and failure to control for the nonspecific effects of medical interventions. The evaluation of medical center programs may also suffer from a lack of resources or time to conduct an adequate evaluation of all services or the exclusion of particular services from evaluation due to reasons of expedience (e.g., staff reluctance to participate in evaluation, intentional exclusion from evaluation of programs known to be unsuccessful). Efforts must be made to eliminate these potential confounding factors from evaluation studies using experimental designs.

Case Illustrations of Program Evaluation

The following discussion presents two examples of program evaluation research. Both studies were designed following an initial retrospective evaluation of all medical-surgical and psychiatric services at a 888-bed Veterans Administration Medical Center (VAMC) in Buffalo, New York. The initial evaluation required each medical center service to provide objectives for review regarding diagnosis, treatment, and follow-up interventions with its patients. The services were also responsible for providing criteria for assessing the degree to which each objective was met. The initial evaluation included a needs assessment. It is important to note that a needs assessment should be included in the first phase of any systematic internal review of an organization such as a medical center. A variety of techniques may be used for needs assessment. The most simple technique involves either a representative sampling or a full survey of the administration, staff, and patient population regarding their perceptions of current treatment needs within a particular hospital service. A frequency distribution of needs may be developed that will allow the evaluator to determine the relative importance of various needs to the administration, staff, and patients. A more complex assessment procedure may include consultation and openended interviews with administrators, staff, and patients regarding service functioning. The initial evaluation of the VAMC in Buffalo used the latter form of needs assessment.

The initial retrospective evaluation and needs assessment identified a number of problems that could be addressed only by additional surveys and experimental studies. The following two brief case illustrations represent a survey and a process study designed to produce possible solutions to the problems identified in the initial evaluation. It should be noted that although the illustrations represent studies completed on a psychiatric service, the techniques presented may be applied to any other medical center service.

Case Illustration A

PROBLEM The results of the retrospective evaluation and needs assessment in the ambulatory care (i.e., outpatient) unit identified patients with specific problems who were not receiving some services available to inpatients at the medical center. The unit's evaluation team was requested to assess the needs of ambulatory patients and provide data regarding patient demographics, the major forms of pathology exhibited by patients, and the course of treatment. Recommendations for program planning and intervention alternatives also were requested.

SOLUTION During a 3-month period, staff responsible for the care of outpatients were asked to complete a questionnaire regarding every patient seen for treatment. The patients were divided into three categories:

1. *Initial Contact,* which included patients seen for the first time during the course of the survey.
2. *Continued Treatment,* which included patients already registered in the ambulatory care unit at the beginning of the survey.
3. *Initial Contact at Termination,* which included first contact patients on whom questionnaires also were completed either at the completion of 3 months of treatment, or at the end of treatment, if this occurred in less than 3 months.

The survey instrument consisted of questions in the following groupings: (*a*) identifying data; (*b*) patient characteristics; (*c*) patient clinical condition; and (*d*) treatment characteristics. The results indicated that there was a bimodal distribution of patients according to age. Consequently, a more detailed investigation (that is currently in progress) of the illness and treatment characteristics of the two patient age groups was established. In addition, the survey results led to a proposal for the formation of hospital-based, mobile treatment teams that may provide periodic services to clusters of patients in distant areas who have difficulty in finding transportation to the medical center. If the mobile treatment teams are formed, their effectiveness in achieving their stated goals may be evaluated by a focus review.

Case Illustration B

PROBLEM During the retrospective evaluation and needs assessment, the inpatient unit nursing staff indicated that they did not perceive their interventions with the patients to be effective. It therefore was necessary to more fully assess staff and patient perceptions of ward environment and level of patient satisfaction.

SOLUTION A process study (Miller & Schlesinger, Note 2) investigated staff and patient perceptions of ward atmosphere under actual and ideal conditions (cf. Moos, 1974). It was found that the staff's perceptions of the quality of the health care provided to patients were very negative relative to those of patients. It was inferred that perceived inadequacies on the part of staff may have resulted from deficient training for their roles as primary counselors for patients. A counseling training program for nursing staff was implemented and evaluated using an experimental research design. The training program produced improved levels of staff self-esteem and reduced the discrepancy between staff's actual and ideal perceptions of ward atmosphere (Miller & Orsolits, 1978).

The Evaluation Report

A most important issue which confronts the program evaluator is the manner in which to present the results of an evaluation study. That is, the evaluator must report the results in such a manner that they will be accepted by the staff, administration, and consumer recipients and possibly serve as a catalyst for change in the program. Thus, similar to other research reports, the evaluation report should include a discussion of (*a*) the rationale for and goals of the program evaluation; (*b*) the parameters of the evaluation (i.e., demographic data regarding the subject sample, time sequence of the evaluation, description of the medical center service which provides the health care program); (*c*) the design and methodology including sampling and data analysis procedures; (*d*) the dependent measures including information regarding the reliability and validity of the measures and normative data; and (*e*) the results and recommendations for further study or implementing change in the health care program. In addition to this information, the report should also include a discussion of the potential value of carrying out the recommended research or change. Any recommended changes should be supported by a cost-benefit analysis of the services, personnel, and related variables associated with the current program relative to those projected for the revised program. A cost-benefit analysis may encourage the administration to pursue program changes despite the reluctance of the staff to adopt the recommendations of a program evaluator.

Additional Issues in Program Evaluation

Thus far the present chapter has examined several issues related to the procedural aspects of program evaluation within a medical setting. There are two issues, however, regarding the organization of evaluation activities within the medical center that require discussion. First, the evaluator must determine if all of the evaluation activity will be conducted by medical center personnel (i.e., quality assurance committee and service-based evaluation teams) or if external evaluators will be contracted to conduct a portion of the evaluation. The present author believes that external evaluators should periodically review the evaluation procedures of the medical center personnel; these external evaluators may be able to provide suggestions for alternate procedures or recommendations for program change. The evaluator must also decide whether or not the data and results of various program evaluations should be made available to interested persons external to the service evaluated and those administratively responsible for the service. This is a controversial question that has no absolute answer. That is, if the evaluator views program evaluation only as a source of empirical data and a measure of service accountability, nonconfidential evaluations are appropriate. If however, the evaluator additionally views program evaluation as a data source that may be used by administration in personnel decisions (e.g., salary), then confidential evaluations are appropriate.

Peer Review: Standards for the Health Care Professional

The concluding section of this chapter deals with the peer review of psychologists within a medical center. Federally mandated PSROs and JCAH quality assurance procedures require the establishment of peer review committees to assess the competencies of physician and nonphysician health care professionals. The following discussion presents a model for peer review of psychologists considered for use at the VAMC in Buffalo, New York that may be used to assess the competencies of psychologists (as well other professional groups) in any medical setting.

It should be noted that all professional psychologists, regardless of the setting in which they practice, are subject to evaluations of their competencies. For example, state licensure or certification laws require various forms of objective evidence concerning applicants' knowledge of the core areas of psychology. Somewhat more stringent review procedures have been established by the National Register of Health Service Providers in Psychology (1978). The examination required by the American Board of Professional Psychology, however, represents the most demanding evaluation of psychologists since it entails an oral examination and submission of various work samples in addition to evidence regarding education, postdoctoral experience, and reputation within the psychological community (cf. Albee & Kessler, 1977). Nonetheless, several critics have noted that these review procedures fail to adequately assess the psychologist's competence and effectiveness in the diagnosis and treatment of patients (Gross, 1978; Koocher, 1979; Steindorf, 1978; Terris, 1973).

The quality assurance procedures of JCAH accredited medical centers, however, provide a means by which psychologists may carefully examine the clinical practices of their peers and enhance the health care provided by the entire psychology staff. The peer review procedures for psychologists at the Buffalo VAMC are as follows:

1. Self-ratings in which each psychologist notes individual competence in each of several areas of health care provision by requesting a category of specified clinical privileges in each area as well as the general privileges accorded to all psychologists in the medical center (see Table 24.2).
2. Evaluation by a committee composed of the chief of the psychology service and two staff psychologists (appointed on a rotating basis for terms of 6 months) of each remaining psychologist's (*a*) educational credentials and licensing status (e.g., acceptance by the Council for the National Register for Health Service Providers in Psychology); (*b*) education and continuing education in areas for which specified privileges are requested; and (*c*) documentation of assessment, treatment, and follow-up of all patients as required by the quality assurance program of the medical center.

The review committee may approve the category of privileges requested by a psychologist in each area or approve a lower category of privileges and require a program of continuing education before the requested category of privileges is approved. If deficiences are found in the psychologist's activities associated with general privileges (e.g., deficiencies in patient assessment), the psychologist is responsible for demonstrating the resolution of the deficiencies or the planned resolution (e.g., participation in continuing education) to the review committee within 3 months.

These peer review procedures allows psychologists to better understand their competencies in various areas of clinical activity and the range of professional skill available within the psychology service. However, the success of these peer review procedures and that of any other form of peer review are dependent upon the staff's trust that their colleagues will perform their evaluations in a competent manner. Therefore, if peer review is to be accorded full credibility, the evaluators must be adequately trained in evaluation procedures and the staff must believe that the procedures used by

Table 24.2. Definition and Classification of Clinical Privileges Needed in Peer Review Privileges

General privileges	Those activities or procedures usually considered to be within the purview of the Service to which a psychologist is assigned and are automatically extended to the psychologist.
Specified privileges	Those activities and procedures which require specifically extended approval before they may be performed by psychologists of the service.
Classification of specified privileges	Four categories of clinical privileges may be granted. The category of privilege requested, if any, in each area should be specified.
Category A	Psychologists with these privileges are considered to be learning the basic skills and theory of the area and are to be supervised by a qualified psychologist.
Category B	Psychologists with these privileges are expected to request consultation from a qualified psychologist (or other professional) on a regular basis for purposes of improving clinical skills and theoretical knowledge, and when problematic situations arise in clinical practice. Psychologists should consider themselves within this category if: (*a*) they have had no previous supervised clinical experience in the area; (*b*) they have had no formal training in the area; or (*c*) they have not practiced the particular skills within the previous three years.
Category C	Psychologists with these privileges are expected to have had formal training and supervised clinical experience in the area (or the equivalent). In addition, they are familiar with the important theoretical foundations and issues of the area and have practiced the particular skills within the previous three years. Such psychologists may supervise other psychologists and hospital personnel at a lower level of formal education. They may act as consultants to others and are, in turn, expected to request consultation when problematic situations arise.
Category D	Psychologists with these privileges have the highest level of competence and expertise within a given area (i.e., a broad foundation in the appropriate theory and extensive clinical experience). They may supervise other psychologists and hospital personnel at an equal or higher level of formal education. They are qualified to act as consultants and should, in turn, request consultation from within or outside the hospital staff whenever needed.

their colleagues are acceptable to the community of professional evaluators. The former condition is relatively easy to satisfy by continuing education or inservice training; the latter condition, however, presents a serious problem since the evaluation literature presents no consensus regarding the acceptability of any model of peer review. Therefore, it appears crucial for professional evaluators to establish standards for the peer evaluation procedures used by medical center psychology services.

Summary

The purpose of professional services evaluation is to produce reliable and valid data needed to make decisions concerning medical center policies, health care programs, and staff competencies. Ideally, evaluation efforts should use the rigorous experimental methodologies and standards of scientific inquiry. There are, however, practical limitations associated with field setting research that at times cannot be avoided. Although the application of rigorous experimental designs in process studies may not always be feasible, it is necessary to generate the best possible data through accepted quasi-experimental or high quality survey procedures.

The present chapter noted several features of adequate program evaluation and peer review efforts. First, program evaluation studies should not be conducted solely on a retrospective basis; rather adequate program evaluation should include concurrent and process evaluation studies. Second, program evaluation studies, regardless of their form should address the question of whether or not a particular intervention strategy used with a particular patient sample effectively fulfills the objectives established by the staff. Third, when deficiencies in health care services are found, recommendations should be made regarding alternate intervention strategies or additional training experiences for staff that are supported by cost-benefit analysis of their implementation. If the recommendations are accepted, focus reviews of the effectiveness of the new interventions or training experiences should be conducted. Finally, the goal of the peer review procedures described in this chapter as well as other models of peer review are to enhance the quality of health care provided by the staff. However, in order for peer review to be accepted, it is necessary that the evaluators (e.g., the entire psychology staff) receive training in evaluation procedures and that the professional evaluation community reach some consensus regarding adequate peer review procedures for medical center personnel.

The present chapter examined the purpose and the procedural aspects of professional services evaluation within a medical setting. Medical psychologists are particularly well-suited because of their training to assume the role of professional services evaluators on medical quality assurance committees. Since demands for accountability of professional services will increase as the federal government increasingly becomes involved in health service delivery, the medical psychologist-evaluator should enjoy an expanding role in medical center decision making.

Acknowledgments

I would like to express my sincere appreciation to several distinguished colleagues for their support, editorial review and expertise in the development of this chapter. My gratitude is extended to S. J. Williamson, VAMC, St. Louis, Missouri; Stephen E. Schlesinger, VAMC, Hines Illinois; Nelson Ribble, Lily I. Lee and Phillip Meringola, VAMC Buffalo, New York. In addition, appreciation is extended to Chelle O'Connell and the Medical Library staff and to Robert C. Johnson and Ms. D. Potter of the Medical Media Production Service for their assistance.

Appendix: Glossary of Terms[3]

Audit, patient care. A retrospective review of the program's services with primary emphasis on the outcomes of patient care.

Clinical privileges. Authorization by the governing body to render patient care and treatment services in the program within defined limits, based upon an individual's professional qualifications, experience, competence, ability, and judgment.

Clinical staff. The personnel of the program who are directly involved in patient care and treatment services.

Community education services. The dissemination of information specifically aimed at increasing the awareness, receptivity, and sensitivity of the community to the disabilities treated by the program.

Concurrent reviews. The evaluation of specifically stated criteria at the same time the patient is receiving the treatment intervention prescribed. It is to be differentiated from *retrospective reviews* which are completed on specifically stated criteria after the patient has received the prescribed intervention.

Facility. The physical area (grounds, buildings, or portions thereof) where program functions take place that is under the direct administrative control of a program's chief executive officer.

Focus review. A microevaluation study in that it aims to assess a specific aspect of a larger program evaluation project to study a key element in greater depth and/or to determine if recommended changes from an earlier study have been made.

Patient. Term used for an individual who receives treatment services. Patient is synonymous

[3]From *Consolidated Standards for Psychiatric Facilities* by the Joint Commission on Accreditation of Hospitals, Copyright © 1979 by the Joint Commission on Accreditation of Hospitals. Reprinted by permission.

with client, resident, consumer, and recipient of treatment services.

Process evaluation. An ongoing study of the principle components of the health service delivery system. Thus, a process evaluation involves an evaluation of the diagnostic, therapeutic, treatment planning and/or follow-up phases of care through an experimental or quasi-experimental design.

Program. A general term for an organized system of services designed to address the treatment needs of patients. Program is synonymous with facility agency, unit, organization.

Program evaluation. The management component of a program which has as its objective the determination of the degree to which a program is meeting its stated goals and objectives.

Psychologist, qualified. An individual who has a doctoral degree in clinical psychology from a training program approved by the American Psychological Association; or who has been certified in the appropriate specialty by the American Board of Professional Psychology; or who has been licensed or certified by a state examining board; or who has been endorsed by the state psychological association through voluntary certification; or who is listed in the National Health Registry for Psychologists; or who has the documented equivalent in training and/or experience.

Reference Notes

1. Levine, M. *Program evaluation on trial.* Joint presentation of the Division of Community Psychiatry at State University of New York at Buffalo and Division 27 of the American Psychological Association; Buffalo, New York, State University of New York at Buffalo, November 1979.
2. Miller, T. W., & Schlesinger, S. E. *Staff and patients evaluate ward atmosphere and patient satisfaction.* Manuscript in preparation, 1980.

References

Abt, C. C. (Ed.). *The evaluation of social programs.* Beverly Hills: Sage, 1976.

Affeldt, J. E. Accreditation clinic: New quality assurance standards allow flexibility, innovation. *The Hospital Medical Staff,* 1979; *8* 7-10.

Albee, G. W., & Kessler, M. Evaluating individual deliverers: Private practice and professional standards review organizations. *Professional Psychology,* 1977, *8,* 502-515.

Attkinson, C. C., McIntyre, M. H., Hargreaves, W. A., Harris, M. R:, & Ochberg, F. M. A working model for mental health program evaluation. *American Journal of Orthopsychiatry,* 1974, *44,* 741-753.

Borgatta, E. Research problems in the evaluation of health service demonstrations. *Milbank Memorial Fund Quarterly,* 1966, *44,* 182-201.

Campbell, D. T., & Stanley, J. C. *Experimental and quasi-experimental designs for research.* Chicago: Rand McNally, 1963.

Caporaso, J. A., & Roos, L. L., Jr. (Eds.). *Quasi-experimental approaches.* Evanston, Ill.: Northwestern University Press, 1973.

Cook, T. D., & Campbell, D. T. *Quasi-experimentation.* New York: Rand McNally, 1979.

Fink, A., & Kosecoff, J. *An evaluation primer.* Washington, D.C.: Capitol Publications, 1978. (a)

Fink, A., & Kosecoff, J. *An evaluation primer workbook: Practical exercises for education.* Washington, D.C.: Capitol Publications, 1978. (b)

Fitz-Gibbon, C. T., & Morris, L. L. *Program evaluation kit* (8 vols.). Beverly Hills: Sage, 1978.

Franklin, J. L., & Thrasher, J. *An introduction to program evaluation.* New York: Wiley, 1976.

Freeman, H. E., & Sherwood, C. C. Research in large scale intervention programs. *Journal of Social Issues,* 1965, *21,* 11-28.

Gross, S. J. The myth of professional licensing. *American Psychologist,* 1978, *33,* 1009-1016.

Guttentag, M. (Ed.). *Evaluation studies review annual* (Vol. 2). Beverly Hills: Sage, 1977.

Guttentag, M., Kiresuk, T., Oglesby, M., & Cann, J. *The evaluation of training in mental health.* New York: Behavioral Publications, 1975.

Joint Commission on Accreditation of Hospitals. *Consolidated standards.* Chicago: JCAH, 1979.

Koocher, G. P. Credentialing in psychology: Close encounters with competence? *American Psychologist,* 1979, *34,* 696-702.

Miller, T. W., & Orsolits, M. B. A model for training nursing staff as primary counselors for psychiatry service. *Journal of Psychiatric Nursing,* 1978, *16,* 28-33.

Moos, R. H. *Evaluating treatment environments: A social ecological approach.* New York: Wiley, 1974.

National register of health service providers in psychology.

Washington, D.C.: Council for the National Register of Health Service Providers in Psychology, 1978.

Patton, M. Q. *Utilization-focused evaluation.* Beverly Hills: Sage, 1978.

Schulberg, H. C., Sheldon, A., & Baker, F. (Eds.). *Program evaluation in the health fields.* New York: Behavioral Publications, 1969.

Steindorf, D. R. Issues concerning the national licensing examination. *APA Monitor,* 1978.

Terris, L. D. The national licensing examination. *Professional Psychology,* 1973, *4,* 386–391.

Wortman, P. M. Evaluation research: A psychological perspective. *American Psychologist,* 1975, *30,* 562–575.

25

Methodological Issues in Medical Psychology and Behavioral Medicine Research

CHARLES K. PROKOP
LAURENCE A. BRADLEY

An examination of the contents of this volume clearly indicates that investigators in medical psychology and behavioral medicine have been extremely productive during the past 10 years. As in any area that is rapidly expanding, particularly in which interdisciplinary research is involved, there often is disagreement regarding what methodological procedures are most appropriate and useful. This chapter reviews what we believe to be the methodological issues of major importance to investigators of medical psychology and behavioral medicine. Examples of the issues described in this chapter are drawn primarily from the chronic pain literature, as this is our area of expertise; although examples from other research areas also are presented.

The fields of medical psychology and behavioral medicine are quite young; consequently, research efforts are sometimes unsophisticated and frequently exploratory. It is not our intent to unduly criticize other investigators; rather we wish to examine the assets and liabilities of important methodological procedures found in the literature. We also wish to note some procedures that have been considered appropriate for exploratory research but which now require refinement in order to more adequately validate early, suggestive findings. Refinement of our investigative procedures is of critical importance given that the research generated will often have direct implications on patient care and preventive efforts.

The chapter is divided into three sections. The first presents a sequential outline of the major methodological issues that investigators may consider during the formulation of a clinical outcome study in medical psychology or behavioral medicine. The second section reviews several statistical issues to which investigators of various phenomena in medical psychology and behavioral medicine often must attend. The final section contains suggestions for future research.

Methodological Issues

In a large number of treatment outcome studies, patients suffering a specific disorder (e.g., chronic pain, essential hypertension, or tension headaches) are randomly assigned to treatment and control

Medical Psychology
Contributions to Behavioral Medicine

ISBN 0-12-565960-1

groups. However, patients also may be differentiated from one another on the basis of some criterion (e.g., organic versus functional pain etiology, sensitizers versus repressors); the resultant groups then may be assessed on several personality or behavioral variables (Fordyce, Brena, Holcomb, DeLateur, & Loeser, 1978) or with regard to their response to specific treatments (Kendall & Watson, Chapter 12). Two issues that must be considered when differentiating patient groups according to some criterion are the reliability and validity of the criterion measure.

Reliability of Criterion Measures

There are very few reliable instruments or diagnostic criteria for the differentiation of patient groups within the literature in medical psychology and behavioral medicine.[1] Barth and Boll (Chapter 14), for example, noted the futility of attempts to use single instruments in order to infer various types of CNS dysfunction. In a similar fashion, we reviewed the poor psychometric characteristics of various scales designed to distinguish between organic and functional pain patients (Chapter 8). Investigators, therefore, sometimes have attempted to use physicians or other judges to distinguish between patients on the basis of diagnostic indicators or behavior. Reviews of the reliability of medical diagnoses (Feinstein, 1977; Koran, 1975) suggest that the uncritical use of such diagnoses as criteria may be inadvisable. Indeed, Fordyce *et al.* (1978) examined the reliability of physicians' judgments regarding the etiologies of chronic pain and found it to be no more than that expected by chance. The unreliability of medical diagnosis is due in part to the fact that some disorders, such as the many chronic pain syndromes, are actually subjective states that may be influenced by a wide variety of social, cultural, and psychological factors (Weisenberg, 1977).

In an attempt to reduce the unreliability inherent in the diagnosis of subjective states, some investigators have used observers' recordings of various patient behaviors. The reliability of behavioral ratings, however, is subject to risk due to the base rates of the behaviors in question. That is, most investigators who use behavioral ratings report interrater reliability in terms of a ratio between the number of rater agreements and the total number of rater observations. A very high or a very low base rate of the behavior will lead to a high percentage of interrater agreement; however, the level of agreement will probably be inflated due to chance factors. The reader is referred to Mitchell (1979) for a more detailed discussion of this problem.

In summary, we suggest that psychometric instruments be used to differentiate patients only if their test–retest and internal consistency coefficients of reliability equal or exceed .80. A reliability coefficient of .80 or greater also should be used as the standard for interdiagnostician judgments. When such coefficients are not attainable due to a lack of availability of reliable instruments or diagnostic procedures, the investigators should scrupulously report the obtained coefficients so the reader can assess the applicability of the findings to his or her research or clinical efforts and exercise caution in conclusions and inferences based on the data. Finally, investigators who use behavioral raters should not merely examine the level of agreement between raters; instead, they should determine interrater reliability according to the procedures noted by Mitchell (1979).

Validity of Criterion Measures

Cox, Chapman, and Black (1978) note that the degree of overlap between members of various patient groups typically has not been addressed in examinations of the validity of patient differentiation. For example, even if patients with chronic pain can be reliably classified, some patients labeled as "organic" may not have physiological damage and, more likely, some "functional" patients may have undetected physiological problems that introduce error into the results of validity or treatment studies. A similar difficulty exists in the generation of discriminant function weights for the classification of brain-damaged and neurologi-

[1]The Structured Interview described by Chesney, Eagleston, and Rosenman (Chapter 3) represents an important exception to the statement.

cally intact persons (Parsons & Prigatano, 1978). As demonstrated in the Fordyce *et al.* (1978) investigation, a large amount of overlap between patient groups will lead to a paucity of significant findings in validity and treatment studies. We recommend that investigators use extensive cross-validational procedures in order to ensure that their methods for differentiating patient groups are associated with minimal between group overlap.

Experimental Design and the Control of Placebo Effects

Given that patients may be randomly assigned to treatment groups or may be successfully differentiated from one another on some personality or behavioral dimension, the researcher must design an investigation that will allow attribution of significant patient change to the treatment intervention rather than to extraneous variables such as placebo effects. The need to control placebo effects in research investigations is discussed below. In addition, suggestions on the control of placebo effects are provided for investigators using group designs as well as for those who use single-subject designs.

Placebo Effects A placebo may be defined as "any therapy or component of therapy that is deliberately used for its nonspecific, psychological, or psychophysiological effect, but is without specific activity for the condition being treated [Shapiro & Morris, 1978, p. 371]." A placebo effect, therefore, may be considered as the "psychological or psychophysiological effect produced by placebos [Shapiro & Morris, 1978, p. 371]." Implicit within the above definitions are the assumptions that (*a*) placebo effects may be positive or negative; (*b*) placebo effects are not equivalent to behavioral changes due to "mere passage of time, repeated testing, or other 'spontaneous' influences occurring while on placebos [Jospe, 1978, p. xiv];" and (*c*) treatments considered to have specific, active therapeutic components also may contain placebo components.

A great deal of effort has been directed toward the development of procedures for controlling placebo effects in clinical outcome research (Evans, 1974; Jospe, 1978; Mahoney, 1978; Shapiro & Morris, 1978). Unfortunately, several authors in the present volume have documented repeated failures on the part of investigators to use adequate placebo controls in studies of the therapeutic efficacy of, or the specific mechanisms of change within various intervention strategies (Barth & Boll, Chapter 14; Burish, Chapter 21; Holmes, Chapter 22; Ziesat, Chapter 16). We agree with Jospe (1978) and Bootzin and Lick (1979) that the factors which mediate placebo effects are worthy of investigation and should not be considered only as nuisance variables; for example, we are particularly intrigued by recent, preliminary evidence that placebo analgesia for acute dental pain may be related to endorphin release (Levine, Gordon, & Fields, 1979). Nonetheless, unless investigators use adequate placebo control procedures in their outcome studies, they will be unable to ascertain the *construct validity* (Cook & Campbell, 1976; Kazdin, 1979) of their intervention strategies. In other words, if placebo controls are inadequate, investigators may be able to determine that their intervention strategies are associated with desirable changes in patient behavior, but they will be unable to assume that the theoretical constructs that purportedly underlie their strategies actually produce patient change.

Failure to control for placebo effects also may be associated with negative consequences for patients despite the fact that they may display or report positive behavior change. For example, Hendler, Derogotis, Avella, and Long (1977) provided EMG frontalis feedback to 13 patients with chronic pain of various etiologies with the assumption that a reduction in general tension and anxiety would reduce pain levels. Six patients reported at least some pain relief after a 1-month follow-up period. The lack of placebo controls, however, prevents one from assuming that the positive self-reports noted by Hendler *et al.* were due to the effects of EMG biofeedback training. Indeed, the fact that there is little data indicating that single-site, EMG biofeedback training very effectively reduces multidimensional stress responses (Burish, Chapter 21) suggests that the purchase of individual biofeedback machines by the six improved patients may have represented a financial outlay for a therapeutic aid that has not been definitively demonstrated to be more effective for general tension reduction than relaxation training.

The negative consequences that potentially may accrue to patients as a result of inadequate placebo controls may be more pervasive than financial loss alone. For example, Sternbach (1974) has documented the sense of helplessness experienced by chronic pain patients who view themselves as having to endure a lifetime of uncontrollable pain. Given that biofeedback and other pain control interventions discussed by Ziesat (Chapter 16) contain many of the same properties as do effective placebos (Lynn & Freedman, 1979), it may be that many pain control techniques will produce transient improvements similar to those produced by placebo therapy (Evans, 1974). Thus, if pain control treatments are not shown to produce lasting, specific effects, their application to chronic pain patients eventually may reinforce the sense of hopelessness experienced by many of those patients and discourage their attempts to successfully function in vocational, leisure, and social activities.

Control of Placebo Effects

Single-Subject Designs The majority of single-subject investigations assess the efficacy of a particular treatment intervention by examining patient behavior at various times during which the intervention either is (treatment period) or is not (baseline period) provided to the patient. If positive behavioral change occurs only during treatment periods and diminishes during baseline periods, the change may be confidently attributed to the intervention strategy rather than to extraneous variables. There are several potential methodological problems common to single-subject investigations of various designs such as incorrect applications of the intervention, failure to ascertain the reliability of observer-generated data, and spurious changes in patient behavior due to the conditions under which baseline and treatment periods are alternated (Kazdin, 1978). Nevertheless, even when methodological problems are avoided, it is sometimes difficult to determine if positive behavioral change actually is due to the specific therapeutic components of the intervention rather than to nonspecific agents. For example, Cairns and Pasino (1977) used a multiple baseline reversal design to determine whether verbal reinforcement and visual feedback were both necessary to increase activity levels among low back pain patients. It was found that verbal reinforcement alone was sufficient to produce significant increases relative to baseline levels in walking and bicycle riding. As noted by Sanders (1979), however, the placebo effects of increased social attention inherent in the verbal reinforcement procedure may have been the factor responsible for the observed changes in patient behavior.

There are two strategies available to the investigator who wishes to control for placebo effects in single-subject investigations. One alternative is to design complex investigations in which the relative efficacies of specific and placebo control interventions may be assessed for a single person (Kazdin, 1978). Because of the need to include controls for sequence effects, the design of these studies may become cumbersome if several interventions are compared. A more desirable alternative may be to assess the efficacy of an intervention found to be useful with single individuals in a group investigation that includes one or more placebo control treatments.

Group Designs Several methodological problems may produce threats to the internal validity of group outcome studies. These include difficulties associated with random assignment of subjects, operationalizing independent variables, and experimenter bias (Mahoney, 1978). Mahoney (1978) provides an excellent discussion of precautions an investigator should follow in order to avoid the threats to internal validity presented by these difficulties. In addition, he offers a very useful table of experimental designs that may be used to ensure the control of observable (Wilkins, 1979) nonspecific variables associated with the delivery of treatment to patients.[2] For example, the strongest design described by Mahoney (1978) is the placebo and control group investigation in

[2]Kazdin (1979) makes the important point that variables considered as nonspecific may vary across interventions.

which patients are assigned to two experimental and no-treatment control conditions as in a Solomon four-group design (Campbell & Stanley, 1963) and two additional conditions in which an intervention is provided that does not have a specific component but is equally credible to patients as the experimental intervention. While this design and similar, although somewhat weaker, designs using placebo controls may appear relatively easy to implement, the *manner* in which they are implemented determines their effectiveness in controlling for placebo effects. The following discussion regarding implementation of placebo control procedures is applicable both to controls used in group designs and those used in complex, single-subject designs described on page 488.

PLACEBO CONTROL PROCEDURES A placebo control intervention should have the same credibility and generate the same positive expectancies for improvement as an experimental intervention (Burish, Chapter 21). Thus, it is necessary to control the unobservable (Wilkins, 1979) nonspecific factors of various interventions that may be assessed only on the basis of patient response to expectancy of change and credibility measures (Borkovec, 1972; Borkovec & Nau, 1972). Unless patient expectancies and beliefs in treatment efficacy are similar across experimental and control interventions, it is impossible to attribute any positive effects that may be associated with an experimental intervention to its specific therapeutic components.[3] For example, a recent investigation (Turner, Heinrich, McCreary, & Dawson, Note 1) reported that patients who received a form of cognitive-behavioral therapy rated themselves as more able to tolerate their chronic pain and participate in normal activities than did patients who either received progressive relaxation training or no treatment. The failure to control for patient expectancies and intervention credibility, however, prevents one from confidently attributing the between-group differences to the provision of coping skills uniquely associated with cognitive behavioral training. It is strongly recommended that investigators assess the credibility of and patient expectancies associated with their experimental and placebo control interventions both in pilot studies and actual outcome investigations (Mahoney, 1978).[4]

In addition to equating experimental and placebo control interventions with respect to these variables, investigators should attempt to employ double-blind procedures in which the various interventions are provided with equal enthusiasm and competence (Burish, Chapter 21; Mahoney, 1978) in order to eliminate experimenter bias effects. It should be noted, however, that double-blind procedures often are quite difficult to implement in field settings. When it is impossible to retain the blindness of the personnel involved in the provision of interventions, it is advisable to use persons to obtain patient self-report and behavioral outcome data who are unaware of what constitute the experimental and control interventions and the investigation's hypotheses (Jospe, 1978). This procedure, recently used by Rybstein-Blinchik (1979), tends to reduce the potential effects of experimenter bias.

Spontaneous Recovery A phenomenon that is sometimes confused with the placebo effect is the spontaneous recovery from disorders displayed by some patients who do not receive *any* treatment. Spontaneous remissions usually are attributed to changes in physiological or environmental factors (Bergin & Lambert, 1978; Turk, Meichenbaum, & Berman, 1979). They may be observed, for example, in some chronic pain patients with vocational difficulties who find more satisfactory employment. In order to demonstrate that changes in patient behavior following an intervention are not due merely to spontaneous recovery, investigators using single-subject designs either must demonstrate that behavior during baseline periods is quite stable or use special designs or statistical procedures that allow one ro rule out the influence of spontaneous recovery (Kazdin, 1978). Inves-

[3]See Wilkins (1979) for a somewhat different view regarding control of patient expectancies.

[4]The use of a single-subject design may force an investigator to rely solely upon pilot patient ratings of expectancy and treatment credibility.

tigators using group designs must employ at least one no-treatment control group in order to rule out the confounding effect of spontaneous recovery. It should be noted, however, that ethical questions may arise when the issue of witholding treatment is considered. This may account, in part, for the paucity of well-controlled group studies of outcome in some areas such as the chronic pain literature.

Outcome Measurement

Once an investigator has decided upon the use of a particular experimental design for an outcome study, the issue of outcome measurement must be resolved. The measurement issue is quite complex; there are three major decisions that the investigator must make. These are (*a*) what dependent measures are appropriate; (*b*) how change is to be assessed; and (*c*) what is an appropriate time period for patient follow-up procedures.

Choice of Dependent Variables The dependent variables most often used in medical psychology and behavioral medicine research consist of (*a*) patient self-reports on psychometric instruments or various rating scales; (*b*) observational measures of patient behavior, global rating, and patient self-monitoring procedures; and (*c*) direct behavioral measures (e.g., automated recorders of patient uptime, physiological measurements). Patient self-reports are inadequate as the *sole* measures of outcome due to the psychometric deficiencies associated with a large number of paper-and-pencil instruments (e.g., poor reliability and validity data associated with the Illness Behavior Questionnaire) and rating scales (e.g., category scales used to assess pain intensity.) In addition, self-reports are vulnerable to impression management effects and demand characteristics.

Observer ratings or recordings of patient behavior often are used in addition to or as a substitute for patient self-reports. There are, however, two difficulties associated with the use of observational data. First, unless the observations are made on a covert basis, reactivity effects may influence the observed outcome. Second, as noted on page 486, the degree of interobserver agreement will be influenced by the base rates of the behaviors being observed and recorded.

In an effort to avoid these difficulties, some investigators have used judges' global patient ratings as outcome measures. Regardless of whether subjective variables such as patient pain intensity or improvement or more observable variables such as activity level or quality of family relations are used, it is necessary to ensure that the reliability coefficients of judges' ratings equal or exceed .80 if confidence is to be placed in the empirical findings. It should be noted, however, that even the most reliable global ratings may be contaminated by factors such as previous judgments on the same dimensions or the investigator's use of the ratings as either dichotomous or continuous variables (Jamison, Ferrer-Brechner, Brechner, & McCreary, 1976).

Another method used to collect data regarding patient behavior involves asking patients to monitor and record their own behavior through the use of diaries, mechanical counters, and other techniques. Mahoney and Arnkoff (1978) and others (Bradley, Prokop, Gentry, Van der Heide, & Prieto, Chapter 8; Glasgow & Bernstein, Chapter 19; Nelson, 1977), however, have expressed serious doubts concerning the reactivity effects and potential inaccuracies associated with self-monitored measures of behavior.[5] The reader is referred to Nelson (1977) for an excellent review of the use of self-monitoring in the assessment of behavior change.

The most direct method of assessing patient behavior is to record it by means of automated devices (Cairns & Pasino, 1977) or to count simple movement cycles of behavior (Fordyce, 1976). Some concern has been expressed in the present volume with regard to the reliability of movement cycle counts (Bradley *et al.*, Chapter 8). In addi-

[5]Glasgow and Bernstein (Chapter 19) note that measures of the level of carbon monoxide in expired breath have been used as an alternative to self-monitoring in the smoking literature. Carbon monoxide levels, however, may be affected by variables other than smoking.

tion, the use of both the automated recording and movement cycle strategies of measurement must be evaluated in terms of their clinical significance for the patient. For example, Agras and Jacob (1979) note that investigations of blood pressure biofeedback for the treatment of hypertension often use measures of systolic or diastolic pressure recorded during treatment sessions in order to assess treatment outcome. This practice is considered inadequate given that the crucial question from the patients' perspectives is whether or not they may reduce the risk of incurring cardiovascular disease by maintaining lowered levels of blood pressure in the natural environment. In a similar fashion, it may be argued that measuring the rate at which a chronic pain patient performs situps will be of little value unless an increase in situp behavior is also associated with a return to employment, increased enjoyment of social activities, and other indicators of improved functioning in the vocational, social, and family environments.

We believe that one cannot assume that patient change on a single dependent variable measured in the laboratory or clinic necessarily ensures change that is meaningful to the patient. Several authors in this volume (e.g., Chesney *et al.,* Chapter 3; Kendall & Watson, Chapter 12) have advocated the use of multiple dependent measures that assess several different behavioral or affective domains. As will be noted on pages 492–493, the use of multiple measures requires sophisticated data analysis procedures. Nonetheless, the credibility of medical psychology and behavioral medicine research will be diminished unless investigators demonstrate that their methods of intervention produce specific changes in important aspects of patient functioning. Thus, we advocate the use of multiple dependent measures that are of significance both to the investigator and to the patient's functioning in the natural environment (e.g., verbal descriptor scales of sensory, affective, and evaluative pain qualities, uptime recordings, analgesic intake, social activities, etc.). In addition, we advocate the use of follow-up investigations in order to determine whether the changes produced in patient functioning are lasting (p. 492). A treatment's success may be judged largely by the degree to which patient changes associated with the treatment are shown to be stable across time.[6]

The Assessment of Change

CHANGE SCORES AND ALTERNATIVES TO CHANGE SCORES A common procedure for measuring the results of an intervention involves the use of change scores for a single dependent variable whereby differences in pre- and posttreatment levels of a behavior or rating are compared for groups receiving various interventions. However, as Cronbach and Furby (1970) point out, posttreatment levels are dependent upon pretreatment levels; change scores thus may be less than optimum indicators of treatment response. Further, Mintz, Luborsky, and Christoph (1979) have raised questions regarding the reliability of change scores, and Melzack (1975) has pointed out that in some cases change scores may be impossible to compute.

These problems suggest that alternatives to the analysis of treatment outcome should be used whenever possible. Indeed, Cronbach and Furby (1970) state that "there appears to be no need to use measures of change as dependent variables and no virtue in using them [p. 78]" when examining gains following a treatment intervention. Instead, the final score of the subjects on the variable of interest is entirely suitable as a dependent variable. Parametric procedures comparing outcomes among groups of individuals whose pretreatment scores are equivalent may be used (Agras & Jacob, 1979) or the data may be analyzed using the initial level of the dependent variable as a covariate in an analysis of covariance (Cronbach & Furby, 1970). In the case where the correlation between the dependent variable and the covariate is low (i.e., less than .4) blocking may be the optimum method to control for the effect of the pretreatment level (Elashoff, 1969).

[6]The choice of dependent variables for evaluators of preventive and life-style programs is complicated by the fact that there currently are no adequate measures of quality of life. The reader is referred to Sechrest and Cohen (1979) for a detailed discussion of the problem.

Follow-up Investigations As noted on pages 487–488, placebo treatments may produce positive short-lived effects upon patient behavior. Thus, even if a treatment intervention is shown to produce immediate effects superior to those produced by a placebo control treatment, the intervention may be regarded only as a complex placebo if its effects are not maintained over time. Adequate outcome investigations, therefore, must include long-term follow-up periods in order to assess whether or not the behavioral changes displayed by patients are maintained in the natural environment. This is a particularly crucial issue in outcome studies of interventions for chronic pain given the tendency of some family members to reinforce pain behaviors displayed by patients (Fordyce, 1976).

It is rather easy to call for long-term follow-up of the effects of treatment interventions; however, it is difficult to specify what constitutes an *acceptable* follow-up period. We believe that a treatment cannot be adequately assessed unless the follow-up measures are identical to those gathered immediately after treatment (although additional measures also may be included at follow-up). For example, Fordyce and Steger (1979) note that the results of the 2–5-year follow-up studies performed at the University of Washington must be viewed with caution given that subjective questionnaire data were assessed during follow-up rather than behavioral data that could have been directly compared with measurements collected prior to and following treatment. We recommend, therefore, that follow-up periods be designed so that a maximum number of subjects will be available to generate data directly comparable to that produced during the outcome study.

Statistical Issues

The following section examines a variety of statistical issues which frequently confront the medical psychology or behavioral medicine researcher. Multivariate procedures and the issue of regression to the mean are discussed, as these are of primary importance when outcomes of intervention are being evaluated. Additionally, the need for complete reporting of a study's results is discussed, as this is necessary for the reader to place credence in the statistical analyses reported.

Multivariate Procedures

Multiple Outcome Measures As previously noted, the use of multiple outcome measures is becoming more frequently recommended. Although the use of such measures certainly enhances the credibility of a study with regard to its generalizability to a variety of settings, it also requires the researcher to give serious consideration to the possibility of a Type I error due to the larger number of significance tests which may be performed. In many studies, subjects have been examined on a large variety of variables (e.g., psychometric scales, physiological and/or behavioral parameters) and univariate statistics, such as t tests, have been computed for each of the variables. Not only does this practice raise the probability of a Type I error, but the intercorrelations frequently found between the variables in such a study even further complicate the issue. In order to deal with the increased risk of Type I error which such an approach entails, Cox and Chapman (1976) have suggested the use of multivariate statistical procedures such as multivariate analysis of variance. Additionally, Shaffer (1979) has outlined an approach to multivariate outcome data relying upon factor analysis and trend analysis. Such procedures not only reduce the risk of Type I error inherent in multiple univariate tests, but they also allow for an assessment of the intercorrelations between the variables.

Determination of Group Characteristics In addition to dealing with error rate problems, multivariate procedures also offer some advantages given the previously noted difficulties regarding the differentiation of patient groups. Rather than relying upon diagnostic criteria based upon ratings of preexisting medical characteristics, the researcher may employ multivariate techniques such as cluster analysis or discriminant function analysis to describe patient groups. For example, subgroups of patients derived in this manner (Bradley, Prokop, Margolis, & Gentry, 1978; Prokop, Bradley, Margolis, & Gentry, 1980) may be examined as to possible differential response to treatment interventions. Alternatively, treatment successes and failures might be retrospectively compared using such techniques, and variables which discriminate between the groups might then be more closely examined in a prospective manner using approaches suggested by Shaffer (1979).

Garside and Roth (1978) have presented some precautions regarding the use of multivariate statistics in the derivation of diagnostic classification systems. While Garside and Roth's suggestions may be unduly restrictive, their point with regard to the need for replication of categories derived in this manner is well-taken, whether replication is attempted through an additional study in the original setting or through studies using settings and populations different from those of the original study. Additionally, the use of multivariate procedures requires a ratio between subjects and dependent variables of at least 5:1 (Shaffer, 1979). For an example of the problems which may ensue if such cautions are not heeded, see the discussion of the Illness Behavior Questionnaire (Pilowsky & Spence, 1975) in chapter 8 of this volume.

Regression to the Mean

Regression effects are a particularly important source of error that must be controlled in outcome studies. As noted by Achenbach (1978), most behavioral variables are likely to change across time, such that persons with extremely high and low scores on a particular variable at one measurement period are likely to produce scores closer to the population mean for that variable upon subsequent measurements. Bond (1973, 1976), for example, presented data indicating that cancer patients with extremely high and extremely low scores on the neuroticism scale of the Eysenck Personality Inventory prior to cordotomy displayed scores that were closer to the population mean for neuroticism following surgery. Bond erroneously attributed these changes to "cessation of noxious stimuli along with an attendant reduction in activation of centers in the brain [1976, p. 315]." In actuality, these changes would be expected on the basis of regression alone. It is quite apparent, therefore, that if an experimental and control group used in an outcome study differ from one another on some dependent variable prior to the introduction of a treatment intervention, the results of the study may be attributed to regression effects rather than the intervention. Investigators must randomly assign patients to experimental and control groups and demonstrate that the groups do not differ from one another with regard to the outcome variables prior to treatment. If group differences do occur despite randomization or if random assignment is impossible, it is necessary to use analysis of covariance for the post-treatment comparisons (Cronbach & Furby, 1970). In a similar fashion, investigators using single-subject designs must not shift from baseline to treatment periods following the production of an extreme score on an outcome variable in order to rule out the confounding effects of regression (Kazdin, 1978).

Complete Presentation of Relevant Results

As previously noted with regard to multivariate procedures, it is important that results be replicable if confidence is to be placed in their stability. Additionally, a clear explication of the links between the data and the inferences drawn from that data is important if other professionals are to be capable of either replicating the study's results or evaluating the research and its applicability to their practice. For this to be possible, the data must be reported in sufficient detail so that the reader is able to reconstruct the essential features of the analysis. Additionally, all subjects involved in the initial stages of the analysis must be accounted for in the final outcome report. If data are not reported and reasons are not given for the lack of the data, the reader is unable to accurately assess the significance of the study's results. For example, Hendler, Viernstein, Gucer and Long (1979) failed to report the treatments provided to or outcome data for 180 of 315 patients subjected to a retrospective evaluation based on a screening test used in the diagnosis of back pain patients; treatment and outcome information was not provided regarding 18 of 32 patients involved in a prospective study using the same instrument. Their conclusion that the results "confirm(s) the test's value as a predictor of patients' response to surgical procedures [p. 805]" is thus difficult to evaluate. Relying upon data not included in the presentation of the results (e.g., Bond, 1973) also creates problems as to the reader's ability to integrate the study's results with other research findings. Replication becomes even more problematic, if not impossible, in the case of such incomplete reporting.

Conclusions and Suggestions for Further Research

As interest in the influence of behavioral and psychological factors on health and illness continues to grow, potential areas of research and clinical applications undoubtedly will correspondingly expand. Consequently, it will become even more important to carefully conduct research investigations so that the initial enthusiasm for medical psychology and behavioral medicine is not followed by rapid disillusionment as poorly validated techniques do not live up to expectations. Further research thus should be rigorously conducted and carefully evaluated in order to minimize the chances for such overenthusiasm followed by profound skepticism (Miller, 1979).

This chapter has reviewed a variety of methodological and statistical issues commonly encountered in medical psychology and behavioral medicine research. If future research is to enhance the credibility and applications of medical psychology and behavioral medicine techniques, it is essential that investigators attend to these issues. Of paramount importance is the need for investigators to utilize control groups and credible placebo interventions in the assessment of treatment outcome. The viability of the field may well depend upon the development of effective and lasting treatment interventions. Controlled studies incorporating placebo treatments are prerequisites to the development of such interventions.

Careful follow-up of patients is also essential to the thorough assessment of treatment programs, as is the appropriate analysis of multiple outcome measures that are meaningful to both investigators and patients. It is impossible to determine whether the effects of an intervention may be focused or general, short-lived or long-lasting, or generalizable across settings without follow-up investigation. For example, following participation in a comprehensive pain treatment program, various patient behaviors used to assess outcome (e.g., subjective pain estimates, up-time, medication use) may differentially change across the follow-up period. In addition, the outcome measures may correlate with additional follow-up measures (e.g., time involved in job-related activities, time spent in recreation activities, use of health care resources) in a variety of ways. Careful follow-up analyses also may aid in the identification of behaviors or treatment strategies that are unrelated to, or nonproductive with regard to, posttreatment adjustment. For medical psychology to make significant contributions to behavioral medicine, it will be necessary for psychologists to document independent information which may be integrated into a patient's overall treatment program. Important examples of medical psychology's potential contributions to behavioral medicine include (*a*) use of multivariate strategies to delineate subgroups among patient populations that might aid the matching of patients to optimal treatments and (*b*) efforts to reduce reliance upon constructs of questionable validity such as the organic versus functional etiology of pain.

A review of this and other chapters in the present volume indicates that the refinement of medical psychology and behavioral medicine research is crucial for the acceptance and application of the clinical procedures described by the volume's contributors. While rigorous research may reduce the enthusiasm for some of the procedures involved, such a reduction in enthusiasm for less effective procedures may add to the maturity of the field. Correspondingly, more exact specification of the relationships between patient, treatment, and outcome variables may increase enthusiasm for promising intervention strategies and thus add to the field's credibility and growth. It is only through vigorous research conducted in close cooperation with the experience of daily clinical practice that such growth and maturity may be attained.

Reference Note

1. Turner, J. A., Heinrich, R., McCreary, C. P., & Dawson, E. *Evaluation of two behavioral interventions for*

chronic back pain. Paper presented at the meeting of the American Pain Society, San Diego, September, 1979.

References

Achenbach, T. M. Psychopathology of childhood: Research problems and issues. *Journal of Consulting and Clinical Psychology,* 1978, *46,* 759-776.

Agras, S., & Jacob, R. Hypertension. In O. F. Pomerleau & J. P. Brady (Eds.), *Behavioral medicine: Theory and practice.* Baltimore: Williams & Wilkins, 1979.

Bergin, A. E., & Lambert, M. J. The evaluation of outcomes in psychotherapy. In S. L. Garfield & A. E. Bergin (Eds.), *Handbook of psychotherapy and behavior change: An empirical analysis* (2nd ed.). New York: Wiley, 1978.

Bond, M. R. Personality studies in patients with pain secondary to organic disease. *Journal of Psychosomatic Research,* 1973, *17,* 257-263.

Bond, M. R. Pain and personality in cancer patients. In J. J. Bonica & D. Albe-Fessard (Eds.), *Advances in pain research and therapy* (Vol. 1). New York: Raven Press, 1976.

Bootzin, R. R., & Lick, J. R. Expectancies in therapy research: Interpretive artifact or mediating mechanism? *Journal of Consulting and Clinical Psychology,* 1979, *47,* 852-855.

Borkovec, T. D. Effects of expectancy on the outcome of systematic desensitization and implosive treatments for analogue anxiety. *Behavior Therapy,* 1972, *3,* 29-40.

Borkovec, T. D., & Nau, S. D. Credibility of analogue therapy rationales. *Journal of Behavior Therapy and Experimental Psychiatry,* 1972, *3,* 257-260.

Bradley, L. A., Prokop, C. K., Margolis, R., & Gentry, W. D. Multivariate analyses of MMPI profiles of low back pain patients. *Journal of Behavioral Medicine,* 1978, *1,* 253-272.

Cairns, D., & Pasino, J. A. Comparison of verbal reinforcement and feedback in the operant treatment of disability due to chronic low back pain. *Behavior Therapy,* 1977, *8,* 621-630.

Campbell, D. T., & Stanley, J. C. *Experimental and quasi-experimental designs for research.* Chicago: Rand McNally, 1963.

Cook, T. D., & Campbell, D. T. The design and conduct of quasi-experiments and true experiments in field settings. In M. Dunnette (Ed.), *Handbook of industrial and organizational psychology.* Chicago: Rand McNally, 1976.

Cox, G. B., & Chapman, C. R. Multivariate analysis of pain data. In J. J. Bonica & D. Albe-Fessard (Eds.), *Advances in pain research and therapy* (Vol. 1). New York: Raven Press, 1976.

Cox, G. B., Chapman, C. R., & Black, R. G. The MMPI and chronic pain: The diagnosis of psychogenic pain. *Journal of Behavioral Medicine,* 1978, *1,* 437-443.

Cronbach, L. J., & Furby, L. How we should measure "change"—or should we? *Psychological Bulletin,* 1970, *74,* 68-80.

Elashoff, J. D. Analysis of covariance: A delicate instrument. *American Educational Research Journal,* 1969, *6,* 383-402.

Evans, F. J. The placebo response in pain reduction. In J. J. Bonica (Ed.), *Advances in neurology* (Vol. 4). New York: Raven Press, 1974.

Feinstein, A. R. A critical overview of diagnosis in psychiatry. In V. M. Raskoff, H. C. Stancer, & H. B. Kedward (Eds.), *Psychiatric diagnosis.* New York: Brunner/Mazel, 1977.

Fordyce, W. *Behavioral methods for chronic pain and illness.* St. Louis: C. V. Mosby, 1976.

Fordyce, W. E., & Steger, J. C. Chronic pain. In O. F. Pomerleau & J. P. Brady (Eds.), *Behavioral medicine: Theory and practice.* Baltimore: William and Wilkins, 1979.

Fordyce, W. E., Brena, S. F., Holcomb, R. J., DeLateur, B., & Loeser, J. D. Relationship of patient semantic pain descriptions to physician diagnostic judgments, activity level measures, and MMPI. *Pain,* 1978, *5,* 293-303.

Garside, R. F., & Roth, M. Multivariate statistical methods and problems of classification in psychiatry. *British Journal of Psychiatry,* 1978, *133,* 53-67.

Hendler, N., Derogatis, L., Avella, J., & Long, D. EMG biofeedback in patients with chronic pain. *Diseases of the Nervous System,* 1977, *38,* 505-514.

Hendler, N., Viernstein, M., Gucer, P., & Long, D. A preoperative screening test for chronic back pain patients. *Psychosomatics,* 1979, *20,* 801-808.

Jamison, K., Ferrer-Brechner, M. T., Brechner, V. L., & McCreary, C. P. Correlation of personality profile with pain syndrome. In J. J. Bonica & D. Albe-Fessard (Eds.), *Advances in pain research and therapy* (Vol. 1). New York: Raven Press, 1976.

Jospe, M. *The placebo effect in healing.* Lexington, Mass.: D. C. Heath, 1978.

Kazdin, A. E. Methological and interpretive problems of single-case experimental designs. *Journal of Consulting and Clinical Psychology,* 1978, *46,* 629-642.

Kazdin, A. E. Nonspecific treatment factors in psychotherapy outcome research. *Journal of Consulting and Clinical Psychology,* 1979, *47,* 846-851.

Koran, L. M. The reliability of clinical methods, data, and judgments: Part I. *New England Journal of Medicine,* 1975, *293,* 642-646.

Levine, J. D., Gordon, N. C., & Fields, H. L. The role of

endorphins in placebo analgesia. In J. J. Bonica, J. C. Liebeskind, & D. G. Albe-Fessard (Eds.), *Advances in pain research and therapy* (Vol. 3). New York: Raven Press, 1979.

Lynn, S. J., & Freedman, R. R. Transfer and evaluation of biofeedback treatment. In A. P. Goldstein & F. H. Kanfer (Eds.), *Maximizing treatment gains: Transfer enhancement in psychotherapy.* New York: Academic Press, 1979.

Mahoney, M. J. Experimental methods and outcome evaluation. *Journal of Consulting and Clinical Psychology,* 1978, *46,* 660-672.

Mahoney, M. J., & Arnkoff, D. B. Cognitive and self-control therapies. In S. L. Garfield & A. E. Bergin (Eds.), *Handbook of psychotherapy and behavior change* (2nd ed.). New York: Wiley, 1978.

Melzack, R. The McGill pain questionnaire: Major properties and scoring methods. *Pain,* 1975, *1,* 277-299.

Miller, N. E. Behavioral medicine: New opportunities but serious dangers. *Behavioral Medicine Update,* 1979, *1,* 5-7.

Mintz, J., Luborsky, L., & Christoph, P. Measuring the outcome of psychotherapy: Findings of the Penn Psychotherapy Project. *Journal of Consulting and Clinical Psychology,* 1979, *47,* 319-334.

Mitchell, S. K. Interobserver agreement, reliability, and generalizability of data collected in observational studies. *Psychological Bulletin,* 1979, *86,* 376-390.

Nelson, R. O. Self-monitoring: Procedures and methodological issues. In J. D. Cone & R. P. Hawkins (Eds.), *Behavioral assessment: New directions in clinical psychology.* New York: Brunner/Mazel, 1977.

Parsons, O. A., & Prigatano, G. P. Methodological considerations in clinical neuropsychological research. *Journal of Consulting and Clinical Psychology,* 1978, *46,* 608-619.

Pilowsky, I., & Spence, N. D. Patterns of illness behavior in patients with intractable pain. *Journal of Psychosomatic Research,* 1975, *19,* 279-287.

Prokop, C. K., Bradley, L. A., Margolis, R., & Gentry, W. D. Multivariate analyses of the MMPI profiles of patients with multiple pain complaints. *Journal of Personality Assessment,* 1980, *44* (3), 246-252.

Rybstein-Blinchik, E. Effects of different cognitive strategies on chronic pain experience. *Journal of Behavioral Medicine,* 1979, *2,* 93-101.

Sanders, S. H. Behavioral assessment and treatment of clinical pain: Appraisal of current status. In M. Hersen, R. M. Eisler, & P. M. Miller (Eds.), *Progress in behavior modification* (Vol. 8). New York: Academic Press, 1979.

Sechrest, L., & Cohen, R. Y. Evaluating outcomes in health care. In G. C. Stone, F. Cohen, & N. E. Adler (Eds.), *Health psychology: A handbook.* San Francisco: Jossey-Bass, 1979.

Shaffer, J. W. On the analysis of repeated measures over time in medical, pharmacological, and behavioral research. *Journal of Behavioral Medicine,* 1979, *2,* 221-238.

Shapiro, A. K., & Morris, L. A. The placebo effect in medical and psychological therapies. In S. L. Garfield & A. E. Bergin (Eds.), *Handbook of psychotherapy and behavior change* (2nd ed.). New York: Wiley, 1978.

Sternbach, R. A. *Pain patients: Traits and treatment.* New York: Academic Press, 1974.

Turk, D. C., Meichenbaum, D. H., & Berman, W. H. Application of biofeedback for the regulation of pain: A critical review. *Psychological Bulletin,* 1979, *86,* 1322-1338.

Weisenberg, M. Pain and pain control. *Psychological Bulletin,* 1977, *84,* 1008-1044.

Wilkins, W. Expectancies in therapy research: Discriminating among heterogeneous nonspecifics. *Journal of Consulting and Clinical Psychology,* 1979, *47,* 837-845.

26

Medical Psychology and Behavioral Medicine: Summary and Future Concerns

LAURENCE A. BRADLEY
CHARLES K. PROKOP
DAVID A. CLAYMAN

In the first chapter of this volume, it was noted that the unique contributions of medical psychology to behavioral medicine are the development and empirical evaluation of diagnostic, preventive, and treatment approaches for medical disorders. The purpose of this chapter is to summarize a number of important themes regarding assessment, treatment, and prevention presented by the contributors to the present volume and to discuss some issues that should be more fully addressed by medical psychologists and other workers in the behavioral medicine area.

Current Concerns

The Adequacy of Traditional Forms of Psychological Assessment

A major problem that was discussed by several chapter authors was that of the adequacy of some traditional clinical assessment approaches with medical patients. For example, Barofsky (Chapter 5) and Levy (Chapter 9) pointed out that various forms of cancer and chronic illness among geriatric patients often result in patient behaviors that may be regarded as pathological by traditional clinicians, but which actually represent attempts to cope with disease. A similar phenomenon was discussed by Barth and Boll (Chapter 14); they warned medical personnel that what may appear to be pathological denial on the part of brain-injured persons may actually represent the use of protective coping mechanisms. In short, the psychological assessment of individuals who suffer from chronic or life threatening diseases or neuropathological disorders compels psychologists to abandon some traditional assessment strategies that focus primarily on individual variables. Persons must be viewed within the context of the factors that impinge upon them as a consequence of their physical disorders (e.g., reduced cognitive abilities and self-sufficiency, impending loss of life) and to contexts within which they find themselves (e.g., home versus institution).

A second major concern of the authors of the assessment chapters was the inappropriate use of traditional psychometric instruments with medical

Medical Psychology
Contributions to Behavioral Medicine

ISBN 0-12-565960-1

patients. Bradley and his colleagues (Chapter 8) pointed out that the MMPI often has been used inappropriately in regard to both determining the etiologies of patients' chronic pain problems (e.g., functional or organic) and predicting pain patients' responses to treatment. Goldstein (Chapter 4) presented discouraging evidence regarding the power of traditional psychometric instruments to delineate a hypertensive personality profile. In addition, Levy (Chapter 9), Barofsky (Chapter 5) and Bradley *et al.* (Chapter 8) discussed their concerns regarding the fact that some instruments (e.g., MMPI, Halstead-Reitan Neuropsychological Battery) are being used to assess chronic pain, cancer, and geriatric patients despite the fact that little or no normative data have been produced by representative samples of those patient populations. Similarly, some short or modified forms of accepted assessment techniques such as the MMPI and the Structured Interview (cf. Chesney, Eagleston, & Rosenman, Chapter 3) have been produced and are available for use by practitioners of behavioral medicine despite the fact that evidence regarding their reliability and validity is scant or of poor quality.

The authors of the chapters devoted to assessment issues have presented two major, promising diagnostic approaches that may help resolve the problems noted above. First, Chesney *et al.* (Chapter 3), Sobell and Sobell (Chapter 7), and Boll, O'Leary, and Barth (Chapter 6) described methods of assessing behaviors that are directly related to coronary heart disease, alcohol problems, and central nervous system dysfunction. The use of these behavioral methods of assessment preclude the difficulty of attempting to infer intraperson constructs that may mediate people's behaviors on the basis of their responses to personality inventories. In addition, the model for the functional analysis of alcohol problems may be regarded as an exemplary method of assessment in that it incorporates evaluation of people's environments as well as their overt behaviors.

The second primary diagnostic approach involves the use of relatively traditional assessment instruments to delineate homogenous patient subgroups within heterogenous patient populations (i.e., patients with essential hypertension and chronic pain) that may show differential responses to various treatment modalities. The use of actuarial prediction techniques eventually may allow behavioral medicine practitioners to determine which treatment techniques (or treatment packages) may be most effectively administered to particular patients.

The Adequacy of Current Methods of Intervention

The authors of the chapters concerned with interventions for medical disorders consistently discussed several issues that require a great deal of further research. These were (*a*) the proper goal of interventions; (*b*) adherence to treatment regimens; (*c*) maintenance of intervention effects; and (*d*) cost effectiveness of interventions.

The Proper Goal of Intervention A large number of the authors noted that, while there are a variety of intervention techniques available to practitioners of behavioral medicine, there also is considerable confusion regarding what represents the proper goals of the interventions. For example, Glasgow and Bernstein (Chapter 19) and Nirenberg and his colleagues (Chapter 15) pointed out that the traditional treatment goal for smokers and alcoholics, respectively, has been abstinence. However, given that neither smoking behavior nor alcoholism represents a unitary phenomenon, there may well exist subsets of smokers and alcoholics for whom total abstinence is an unreasonable treatment goal. It may be that programs designed to teach people to control and maintain their smoking and drinking behaviors at reduced, moderate levels may be most appropriate for these persons.

A related question concerning the focus of intervention is whether one should attempt to alleviate the suffering experienced by patients or merely teach them to better cope with their medical problems. Ziesat's (Chapter 16) discussion of inpatient programs for chronic pain patients indicated that the major goal of these programs is to increase well behavior and reduce inappropriate pain behavior despite the fact that patients may continue to suffer pain. Thus, the major goal may be defined as teaching patients to cope with rather than to reduce their suffering.

A similar position was taken by Barth and Boll (Chapter 14), Alexander (Chapter 20), and Burish (Chapter 21). Barth and Boll stated that some neuropathologic conditions cannot be remediated and that the proper focus of treatment must often be the facilitation of adaptating to impaired functioning. Alexander provided very strong evidence for the position that behavioral change interventions are ineffective and inappropriate for the treatment of asthma. These interventions, however, are highly appropriate and may prove themselves to be effective for the treatment of the psychological sequelae of asthma. Finally, Burish emphasized that the use of EMG biofeedback for stress-related disorders should be considered as a palliative coping strategy that may help patients to better cope with stress reactions rather than as a technique with which patients may remove the causes of their subjectively experienced stress. Hence, EMG biofeedback may be inappropriate as the sole treatment for patients with stress-related disorders.

The use of intervention techniques for the purpose of facilitating patient coping also was addressed by Wellisch (Chapter 13) and Levy (Chapter 17). These authors discussed the goal of coping in the context of treating patients who face impending death from cancer and other diseases. The difficulties faced by these patients are compounded by the fact that medical technology sometimes may be used to prolong their lives and, coincidentally, their suffering. As noted by Levy (Chapter 17), there is growing concern and support within the medical community for fostering more open communication with dying patients and the omission of life-prolonging treatments. There remain, however, numerous ethical problems in dealing with patients with chronic or terminal illnesses. For example, how should health care professionals react toward family members who do not wish to accept the emotional burdens or expense of providing long-term care to parents, siblings, or spouses with chronic or terminal diseases? What assistance may be provided to families whose stability may be threatened by financial pressures stemming from attempts to meet the health care costs of an ill relative? May informed consent procedures for organ donation be devised such that prospective donor adults *and* children will be protected from coercive influences (Saks, 1978)?

Ethical issues are rarely addressed in the literature of behavioral medicine. Two of the present authors (Bradley and Prokop), however, are encouraged by the fact that the American Pain Society has made a commitment to present programs regarding ethical issues (i.e., management of pain in the hospice) at its annual meeting. It would be desirable for workers in other behavioral medicine areas to develop interest in presenting programs devoted to ethical issues at conventions within their respective specialty areas or at the meetings of the Society of Behavioral Medicine. Discussion among behavioral medicine professionals would seem to be a prerequisite for the development of a literature regarding ethical issues in behavioral/medical health care.

Finally, it should be noted that there are some disorders for which prevention, rather than treatment, may represent the optimal intervention strategy. For example, Glasgow and Bernstein (Chapter 19) and Coates and his colleagues (Chapter 11) suggested that it may be more efficient to provide preventive interventions to adolescents for problems such as smoking and obesity rather than attempt to change the smoking and eating behavior patterns of adults. Given that these two behavioral problems are associated with the development of the leading cause of death in this country, cardiovascular disease (cf. Coates *et al.* Chapter 11; Herd, Chapter 10), attempts to prevent their occurrence among young people should receive a great deal more attention from investigators. The attempts to provide preventive interventions to families and entire communities, described by Coates *et al.*, are particularly exciting research ventures.

It should be noted that preventive efforts in areas of health care other than those related to cardiovascular disease require further investigation. For example, Ziesat (Chapter 16) demonstrated that the efficacy of inpatient contingency management programs thus far has been shown to be moderate; indeed, Ziesat emphasized the need to develop and examine the effectiveness of relatively less expensive, outpatient programs for chronic pain. The present authors suggest that it also would be worthwhile to develop and examine the efficacy of programs that are designed to prevent persons who suffer acute physical injuries from developing chronic pain and its associated problems. Furthermore, the interventions for stressful medical procedures described by Kendall and Watson (Chapter 12) also may be considered to be preventive interventions in that they are provided in order to reduce adverse patient reactions to procedures such as endoscopy and cardiac catherization. The cognitive-behavioral interventions described by Kendall and Watson offer great promise in that the preferred coping strategies of individual patients are utilized and they allow for the incorporation of additional stress-reduction techniques (e.g., deep breathing) that may prove to be closely related to successful coping with specific procedures (e.g., endoscopy).

Adherence to Treatment Regimens Regardless of their foci, the interventions discussed in this volume will prove ineffective unless patients carefully adhere to their behavioral requirements. Masur's (Chapter 23) suggestions for increasing patient adherence may be incorporated by investigators and providers of every intervention technique discussed in this volume. Indeed, it is essential that all investigators and practitioners attempt to elicit maximum patient adherence; otherwise, investigators cannot provide the most powerful tests of their hypotheses and practitioners cannot provide optimal services to patients.

Maintenance of Treatment Gains An issue that was addressed in nearly every chapter concerning interventions for medical disorders was the need to demonstrate the long-term effectiveness of those interventions. With the exception of EMG biofeedback, which has been shown to produce reductions in EMG levels in target muscles that will generalize beyond the training situation (cf. Burish, Chapter 21), none of the behavioral interventions discussed in the present volume have been shown to *reliably* produce changes in patients' behavior that will be maintained in contexts outside of the treatment setting. It is quite clear that workers in various behavioral medicine areas must devote a great deal more attention to the problem of maintenance of treatment gains if the intervention approaches associated with behavioral medicine are to be given credence by medical and psychological practitioners and the governmental agencies that eventually may administer funds in national health programs. The present authors believe that medical psychologists may provide crucial contributions to behavioral medicine by using their expertise in experimental design to operationalize and evaluate maintenance-enhancing procedures. The suggestions provided by several authors in the present volume (Nirenberg *et al.*, Chapter 15; Ziesat, Chapter 16; Stuart *et al.*, Chapter 18) as well as those discussed in Goldstein and Kanfer's (1979) recent work may have a significant impact upon the field of behavioral medicine.

Cost Effectiveness The final issue that was consistently addressed by the contributors to this volume was the cost effectiveness of the various interventions available to behavioral medicine practitioners. For example, Kendall and Watson (Chapter 12) noted that the brevity and efficiency of a cognitive-behavioral intervention for cardiac catheterization patients (Kendall, Williams, Pechacek, Graham, Shisslak, & Herzoff, 1979) made it particularly attractive as a means for reducing the stress experienced by these patients. Another concern for cost effectiveness was found in the chapter by Burish (Chapter 21) regarding the use of EMG biofeedback for stress-related disorders. He concluded that the treatment effects produced with the relatively expensive biofeedback technology were no greater than those associated with procedures such as progressive muscle relaxation and thus discouraged the use of EMG biofeedback as a treatment modality for the reduction of stress. The present authors believe that an integral part of any research program regarding a treatment intervention is the comparison of the effectiveness of the treatment of interest to that of other relevant treatments that may cost either more or less than the treatment of interest. Doubts may be raised concerning the usefulness of an intervention if it is shown to produce effects that are no greater than those produced by less expensive treatments or less than those produced by somewhat more expensive treatments. The authors also believe that, eventually, concerns regarding cost effectiveness will begin to be expressed regarding various preventive strategies (e.g., is it more cost effective to intervene at the individual or the community level?). However, much more research regarding the efficacy of preventive efforts must be performed before it will be reasonable to compare various preventive strategies with one another.

Future Concerns for Medical Psychologists

The preceding chapters indicated that there are numerous empirical questions concerning assessment, preventive, and treatment approaches in the field of behavioral medicine that medical psychologists may address in the future. However, in order to provide useful research contributions, medical psychologists must become more familiar with physiological and medical concepts than they are at the present time (cf. Gentry & Matarazzo, Chapter 2). Some psychological concepts that have little value to behavioral medicine, such as the unitary concept of brain damage (Barth & Boll, Chapter 14) and the distinction between organic and functional etiologies of chronic pain (Bradley *et al.,* Chapter 8), may continue to be accepted by some psychologists in part because of lack of knowledge concerning the structure of the nervous system. In order for medical psychologists to ask increasingly meaningful research questions, they will have to increase their own sophistication in the areas of physiology and medicine. The present authors recommend, therefore, that doctoral level clinical training programs with medical psychology specialty tracks offer training in physiology in addition to that provided by the one general course provided by a large number of programs. Courses in behavioral pharmacology and medical terminology also would be useful. Medical psychologists who already are working in behavioral medicine may wish to increase their expertise in physiology and other areas of medicine either by means of formal courses or with the help of their medical colleagues.

Another task for both medical psychologists and other workers in the behavioral medicine area will be to present to the lay public a realistic view of the efficacy of behavioral medicine interventions. The public is becoming quite cognizant of behavioral medicine interventions (e.g., biofeedback, behavioral treatment for sexual dysfunction) as a result of publicity provided by newspapers and television. In addition, the official journal of Phi Kappa Phi, *National Forum,* devoted nearly an entire issue to behavioral medicine (Evans, 1980). It is most appropriate for workers in behavioral medicine to be quite cautious in their reports both to fellow professionals and to the media. Otherwise, publicity regarding behavioral medicine will only serve to increase public expectations and then produce public frustrations when those expectations cannot be met. For example, two of the present authors (Bradley and Prokop) often have had the difficult task of explaining to a disappointed chronic pain patient that endogenous-based analgesics are not available to the public or that several sessions of biofeedback treatment by no means guarantees that their pain will be alleviated.

Conclusion

The present volume has presented a comprehensive overview of research in the areas of assessment, treatment, and prevention of medical disorders. A very large literature across the various specialty areas in behavioral medicine has emerged in the past 10 years. Unfortunately, as documented by the contributors to this volume, the quality of the research literature shows great variability. The present authors hope that empirical investigations of more consistently high quality will appear during the next several years. In order for this to occur, investigators will have to seek additional educational experiences and develop more sophisticated methodological procedures. At the same time, workers in behavioral medicine will have to grapple with complex ethical issues regarding the impact of medical advances upon the quality of patients' lives. Thus, the challenges to medical psychology and behavioral medicine are great; equally great, however, is the opportunity to provide improved health care services to the public by means of interdisciplinary efforts. The contributors to this volume look forward to the challenges and potential rewards that lie ahead.

References

Evans, R. I. Focusing on behavioral medicine: Perspective from the guest editor. *National Forum*, 1980, *60*, 2.

Goldstein, A. P., & Kanfer, F. H. *Maximizing treatment gains: Transfer enhancement in psychotherapy*. New York: Academic Press, 1979.

Kendall, P. C., Williams, L., Pechacek, T. F., Graham, L. E., Shisslak, C., & Herzoff, N. Cognitive-behavioral and patient education interventions in cardiac catherization procedures: The Palo Alto medical psychology project. *Journal of Consulting and Clinical Psychology*, 1979, *47*, 49-58.

Saks, M. J. Social psychological contributions to a legislative subcommittee on organ and tissue transplants. *American Psychologist*, 1978, *33*, 680-690.

Author Index

Numbers in italics refer to the pages on which the complete references are cited.

A

C

I

J

K

M

O

P

S

Subject Index